THE OXFORD HANDBOOK OF

LAW AND ANTHROPOLOGY

THE OXFORD HANDBOOK OF

LAW AND ANTHROPOLOGY

Edited By

MARIE-CLAIRE FOBLETS, MARK GOODALE,

MARIA SAPIGNOLI, OLAF ZENKER

OXFORD

UNIVERSITY PRESS

OXFORD
UNIVERSITY PRESS

Great Clarendon Street, Oxford, OX2 6DP,
United Kingdom

Oxford University Press is a department of the University of Oxford.
It furthers the University's objective of excellence in research, scholarship,
and education by publishing worldwide. Oxford is a registered trade mark of
Oxford University Press in the UK and in certain other countries

First Edition published in 2022
Impression: 1

Published in the United States of America by Oxford University Press
198 Madison Avenue, New York, NY 10016, United States of America

British Library Cataloguing in Publication Data
Data available

Library of Congress Control Number: 2022902574

ISBN 978–0–19–884053–4

DOI: 10.1093/oxfordhb/9780198840534.001.0001

Printed and bound in the UK by
TJ Books Limited

Contents

Acknowledgements

THIS is a collective volume in the truest sense of the term. It has benefitted greatly from the input of all those who have been prepared to contribute to it, either by submitting an individual chapter or by serving as discussants or reviewers and who, by posing challenging and insightful questions and comments, indisputably left their mark on this collective endeavour. Without mentioning them by name here, we as editors wish to express our profound gratitude to them.

Special thanks go to Dr Brian Donahoe. We are confident that we speak for everyone involved in the volume when we say that it would have been impossible to carry out this long-term publication project without his continuous and very generous efforts, which included both his organizational and editorial skills and his invaluable intellectual guidance. His stewardship of the volume was an essential task that kept the many interrelated processes moving forward over the years. He was in communication with every single author and painstakingly followed the genesis of each chapter, from the very first version to the final proofs, without ever losing his patience or showing signs of discouragement. For a volume of this size, this is no minor achievement. Trained in legal anthropology himself, he offered input that touched not only on the form but, more importantly, on the content of some decisive arguments. Brian Donahoe's contribution to this publication is reflected not only in the individual chapters, but throughout the volume itself, which is imbued with his supportive spirit and valuable insights.

Sincere thanks also go to the entire team at Oxford University Press, especially Jamie Berezin, who commissioned the project, and Brianne Bellio, who worked very closely with us as she ushered the project through the various stages of production.

While we were working on this *Handbook*, we were saddened to learn that Sally Engle Merry (1944–2020) had passed away. Sally played an absolutely central role in different ways in the development of this volume. She lent her support from the outset to the formation of the Law & Anthropology Department, including by serving as a member of its Consultative Committee, where the idea of this *Handbook* was first discussed in 2014. Her last visit to Germany was in December 2018, when she kicked off the editorial conference for this volume as the first keynote discussant.

Sally was an invaluable and inexhaustible source of inspiration for a great many authors who contributed to this volume. She had a decisive impact on both their thinking and the kind of research they undertook. In her own unprecedented way, she was a very future-oriented thinker and prescient regarding a number of core themes that are addressed in this volume. She herself published pioneering work on many of those themes: legal pluralism, gender, human rights, translation and vernacularization, and law and quantitative indicators, to name but a few. She has left us orphans in many respects, but her legacy is so rich that it will most certainly remain with us for many years to come. This volume can be seen as a tribute to her, along with several others that have already been published in her honour.

All expenses associated with this project, including the conference held in Berlin in December 2018, were borne by the Law & Anthropology Department of the Max Planck Institute for Social Anthropology, Halle, Germany.

About the contributors

Katayoun Alidadi is Assistant Professor of Legal Studies at Bryant University in Smithfield, Rhode Island and Research Partner at the Max Planck Institute for Social Anthropology in Halle, Germany. Her research focuses on comparative law, human rights, employment law, and the intersections of law and religion. She is the author of *Religion, Equality and Employment in Europe: The Case for Reasonable Accommodation* (Hart, 2017) and co-editor of *A Test of Faith: Religious Diversity and Accommodation in the European Workplace* (Routledge, 2012), *Belief, Law and Politics. What Future for a Secular Europe?* (Routledge, 2014), and *Public Commissions on Cultural and Religious Diversity: Analysis, Reception and Challenges* (Routledge, 2018).

Frédéric Audren is Director of Research at the French National Centre for Scientific Research (CNRS) and Professor of Law at the Sciences Po Law School in Paris. His research is devoted to the history of legal knowledge in the nineteenth and twentieth centuries and to the history of social sciences. He was a founding member of the *Revue d'histoire des sciences humaines* and of *Clio@Thémis: Revue électronique européenne d'histoire du droit.*

Pratiksha Baxi is Associate Professor at the Centre for the Study of Law and Governance at Jawaharlal Nehru University. Her research engages with critical perspectives on medical jurisprudence, ethnographies of courts, sociology of violence, gender studies, politics of judicial reform, judicial iconography, courtroom architecture, and feminist legal theory in and beyond India. Her publications include *Public Secrets of Law: Rape Trials in India* (Oxford University Press, 2014).

Keebet von Benda-Beckmann is the former Co-Head of the Project Group 'Legal Pluralism' at the Max Planck Institute for Social Anthropology. With her late husband Franz von Benda-Beckmann, she conducted decades of anthropological research in the social working of law under conditions of legal pluralism in Indonesia. Among her many books is *Political and Legal Transformations of an Indonesian Polity: The Nagari from Colonisation to Decentralisation* (Cambridge University Press, 2013).

Katia Bianchini is a researcher in the Department of Law & Anthropology at the Max Planck Institute for Social Anthropology. She holds a Ph.D. in law from the University of York, UK. From 2015 to 2018, she was a research fellow at the Max Planck Institute for Ethnic and Religious Diversity in Göttingen. Before engaging in research, she practised immigration law in England and the United States for ten years. Her publications include the book *Protecting Stateless Persons: The Implementation of the Convention Relating to the Status of Stateless Persons across EU States* (Brill/Nijhoff, 2018).

Markus Böckenförde is Associate Professor and Chair of the Comparative Constitutional Law Programme at Central European University (CEU)'s Department of Legal Studies. Before joining CEU, he was the Founding Executive Director of the Centre for Global Cooperation Research at the University Duisburg-Essen (2012–2018). As head of the advisory team to the Policy Planning Staff at the German Ministry for Economic Cooperation and Development (Bonn–Berlin) in 2011–2012, he gained first-hand experience in political decision-making. From 2009 to 2011, he was Programme Officer and temporarily Acting Programme Manager for the Constitution Building Project at International IDEA, Stockholm, Sweden. Between 2001 and 2008, Böckenförde was the Head of Africa Projects and a Senior Research Fellow at the Max Planck Institute for Comparative Public Law and International Law (MPIL) in Heidelberg. In 2006–2007, he was seconded by the German Foreign Office to be the legal expert for the Assessment and Evaluation Commission (AEC) in Sudan, which was mandated to support and supervise the implementation of the Sudanese Comprehensive Peace Agreement.

Erica Bornstein is Professor of Anthropology at University of Wisconsin-Milwaukee. A political and legal anthropologist, her research interests include non-governmental organizations (NGOs), voluntary sector regulation, and humanitarianism. She is the author of two monographs: *The Spirit of Development: Protestant NGOs, Morality, and Economics in Zimbabwe* (Stanford, 2005) and *Disquieting Gifts: Humanitarianism in New Delhi* (Stanford, 2012), and, and is co-editor of *Forces of Compassion: Humanitarianism between Ethics and Politics* (School for Advanced Research Press, 2011). She is currently writing a book on the regulation of non-profits, philanthropy, and civil society in India.

Paul Burke has had a long career as both a lawyer and an anthropologist. In the legal phase of his career, he appeared as a lawyer for claimants in land claims in the Northern Territory, Australia. Since his conversion to anthropology, he has worked as an anthropologist on native title claims. His first book, *Law's Anthropology: From Ethnography to Expert Testimony in Native Title* (Australian National University Press, 2011), is a Bourdieu-inspired account of the interaction of law and anthropology in native title claims. His most recent work, *An Australian Indigenous Diaspora: Warlpiri Matriarchs and the Refashioning of Tradition* (Berghahn, 2018), is a detailed ethnographic account of the cultural implications of Indigenous migration away from traditional country. He is currently an honorary lecturer in the School of Archaeology and Anthropology at the Australian National University.

Jennifer Burrell is Associate Professor of Anthropology at the University at Albany SUNY, where she is also affiliated with the Department of Latin American, Caribbean, and US Latino Studies. She is the author of *Maya after War* (University of Texas Press, 2013) and co-editor (with Ellen Moodie) of *Central America in the New Millennium* (Berghahn, 2013). She has recently co-edited (with Ellen Moodie) two special collections, 'Beyond the Migrant Caravan' in *Cultural Anthropology* (2019) and 'Generations and Political Lives in Central America' in the *Journal of Latin American and Caribbean Anthropology* (2020).

Matthew Canfield is Assistant Professor of Law and Society & Law and Development in the Van Vollenhoven Institute at Leiden Law School. His research examines the law and governance of global food security, specifically focusing on how social movements are formulating new social justice claims and practices of mobilization in response to changing forms of food and agricultural regulation. He is the author of *Translating Food Sovereignty: Cultivating Justice in an Age of Transnational Governance* (Stanford, 2022), as well as articles in *Public Culture, Law & Society Review, Transnational Legal Theory*, and *Studies in Law, Politics, and Society*, among other journals.

Martin Chanock has degrees in history and law from the University of the Witwatersrand. His legal education was in both civil and common law and allowed him to escape the prisons of both traditions. After leaving South Africa in 1965, he took a Ph.D. in history from Cambridge, and went on to teach history at universities in East and West Africa, at the University of Sussex, and the University of Texas in Austin. In 1977, he joined the inter-disciplinary School of Legal Studies (later the School of Law) at La Trobe University in Melbourne, and accidentally stayed forever. He has published widely on legal history in colonial and postcolonial situations, including two books: *Law, Custom and Social Order* (Cambridge, 1985) and *The Making of South African Legal Culture* (Cambridge, 2001). He is currently working on a book on constitutional illusions in Africa. Another major area of engagement has been in questions of how and what to teach about law in universities.

Lynette J. Chua is Associate Professor at the Faculty of Law and Yale-NUS College, National University of Singapore. She is a law-and-society scholar with research interests in legal mobilization, legal consciousness, rights, and social movements. She is the author of *Mobilizing Gay Singapore: Rights and Resistance in an Authoritarian State* (Temple University Press, 2014) and *The Politics of Love in Myanmar: LGBT Mobilization and Human Rights as a Way of Life* (Stanford University Press, 2019).

Priscilla Claeys is Associate Professor in Food Sovereignty, Human Rights and Resilience at the Centre for Agroecology, Water and Resilience, Coventry University (UK). She received her Ph.D. in Political and Social Sciences from the University of Louvain (UCL) in 2013. From 2008 to 2014, she worked as a Special Advisor to Olivier De Schutter, the UN Special Rapporteur on the right to food. Her research areas include the right to food and food sovereignty, agrarian movements, global food governance, legal mobilization, and the creation of new human rights. She has published *Human Rights and the Food Sovereignty Movement: Reclaiming Control* (Routledge, 2015) and co-edited two books. Her research has notably featured in the *Journal of Peasant Studies, Sociology*, and *Globalizations*.

Kamari Maxine Clarke is Distinguished Professor of Transnational Justice and Socio-legal Studies at the University of Toronto. Trained in anthropology and law, she has spent her career exploring theoretical questions of culture and power, detailing the relationship between new transnational formations and contemporary problems. Her acclaimed book *Fictions of Justice: The International Criminal Court and the Challenge of Legal Pluralism* (Cambridge University Press, 2009) analyses how human rights conceptions are negotiated in global legal plural contexts, especially regarding international criminal law. Her most recent book, *Affective Justice: The International Criminal Court and the Pan-Africanist Pushback* (Duke University Press, 2019), is concerned with challenges over the legitimacy of the International Criminal Court in Africa.

Philipp Dann is Professor and Chair of Public and Comparative Law at Humboldt University Berlin. His research focuses on the encounter of the Global South and North in all registers of public law. He is Editor-in-Chief of the journal *World Comparative Law*. His recent publications include (with Jochen von Bernstorff) *The Battle for International Law in the Decolonization Era* (Oxford University Press, 2019), (with Michael Riegner and Maxim Bönnemann) *The Global South and Comparative Constitutional Law* (Oxford University Press, 2020) and (with Arun Thiruvengadam) *Democratic Constitutionalism in India and the EU* (Edward Elgar, 2021).

Eve Darian-Smith is Professor and Chair of Global Studies at the University of California, Irvine. Trained as a lawyer, historian, and anthropologist, she is interested in issues of postcolonialism, legal pluralism, global governance, human rights, authoritarianism, and socio-legal theory. She is a prize-winning author and has published widely, including eleven books and edited volumes and numerous articles in the fields of anthropology, global studies, history, and law and society. Darian-Smith serves on seven editorial boards and is an invited board member of *Contemporary Social Science: Journal of the Academy of Social Sciences* (UK).

Sara L. M. Davis is Senior Researcher leading the Digital Health and Rights Project at the Global Health Centre, Graduate Institute of International and Development Studies, Geneva. She is the author of *Song and Silence: Ethnic Revival on China's Southwest Borders* (Columbia University Press, 2005) and *The Uncounted: Politics of Data in Global Health* (Cambridge University Press, 2020). Davis was founding executive director of Asia Catalyst, Senior Human Rights Advisor at the Global Fund, and earned her Ph.D. at the University of Pennsylvania. She has worked as a consultant with the Joint United Nations Programme on HIV/AIDS (UNAIDS), the United Nations Development Programme (UNDP), and international civil society advocacy networks. Her current research focuses on digital technologies, artificial intelligence, health, and human rights.

Brian Donahoe is Senior Scientific Editor of the Law & Anthropology Department at the Max Planck Institute for Social Anthropology, Halle, Germany. He holds an M.A. in journalism and a Ph.D. in anthropology, both from Indiana University. He conducted long-term fieldwork among the hunting and reindeer-herding communities of the Saian Mountain region in southern Siberia (Tozhu, Tofa, Soiot, and Dukha), and has published on the politics of indigeneity in Russia. He is co-editor of two volumes (with Joachim Otto Habeck) *Reconstructing the House of Culture: Community, Self and the*

Makings of Culture in Russia and Beyond (Berghahn, 2011) and (with Julia Eckert, Zerrin Özlem Biner, and Christian Strümpell) *Law against the State: Ethnographic Forays into Law's Transformations* (Cambridge, 2012).

Baudouin Dupret studied law, Islamic sciences, and political sciences. He is Director of Research at the French National Centre for Scientific Research (CNRS). He is also guest lecturer at the University of Louvain (Belgium). He has published extensively in the fields of sociology and anthropology on law, legislation, and media, especially in the Middle East. He has (co-)edited numerous volumes, the most recent being (with Michael Lynch and Tim Berard) *Law at Work: Studies in Legal Ethnomethods* (Oxford, 2015) and (with Julie Colemans and Max Travers) *Legal Rules in Practice: In the Midst of Law's Life* (Routledge, 2020), and single-authored several books, including *Practices of Truth: An Ethnomethodological Inquiry into Arab Settings* (Benjamins, 2011), *Adjudication in Action: An Ethnomethodology of Law, Morality and Justice* (Routledge, 2011), *What Is the Sharia?* (Hurst, 2017), and *Positive Law from the Muslim World: Jurisprudence, History, Practices* (Cambridge, 2021).

Thomas Duve is Director at the Max Planck Institute for Legal History and Legal Theory, and Professor of Comparative Legal History at Goethe University (both in Frankfurt). He works principally on the legal history of the imperial spaces of the Iberian monarchies in the early modern period, especially the history of early modern canon law and moral theology, as well as the history of legal practices.

Julia Eckert is Professor of Political Anthropology at the University of Bern, Switzerland. Her research focuses on the transnationalization of legal norms, the anthropology of crime and punishment, changing notions of responsibility and liability, security, and citizenship. Her publications include *The Charisma of Direct Action* (Oxford University Press, 2003), *Law against the State: Ethnographic Forays into Law's Transformations* (Cambridge University Press, 2012), *The Bureaucratic Production of Difference: Ethos and Ethics in Migration Administrations* (transcript Verlag, 2020), and 'Legal Responsibility in an Entangled World' (*Journal of Legal Anthropology* 4 (2) 2020). She is also co-editor of the journal *Anthropological Theory*.

Didier Fassin is the Professor of Social Science at the Institute for Advanced Study in Princeton and holds a Direction of Studies at the École des Hautes Études en Sciences Sociales in Paris. Based on research conducted on three continents, his work focuses on political and moral issues in contemporary societies. A former Vice- President of Médecins Sans Frontières, he is currently the President of the French Medical Committee for Exiles. His books include Humanitarian Reason: A Moral History of the Present (University of California Press, 2011), Enforcing Order: Ethnography of Urban Policing (Polity, 2013), The Will to Punish (Oxford University Press, 2018), Life: A Critical User's Manual (Polity, 2018), and Death of a Traveller: A Counter Investigation (Polity, 2021).

Balázs Fekete is Associate Professor at the Eötvös Loránd University, Faculty of Law, Department of Law and Society, and Senior Research Fellow at the Centre for Social Sciences, Institute for Legal Studies, both in Budapest. His main areas of research include rights consciousness, legal alienation, and comparative legal studies methodology. His most recent book is *Paradigms in Modern Comparative Law. A History* (Hart, 2021).

Marie-Claire Foblets is Director of the Law and Anthropology Department at the Max Planck Institute for Social Anthropology and Honorary Professor of Law & Anthropology at Martin Luther University Halle-Wittenberg, both in Halle/Saale, Germany. Trained in law and anthropology, she taught law as well as social and cultural anthropology at the universities of Antwerp and Brussels and the Catholic University of Leuven, where she headed the Institute for Migration Law and Legal Anthropology, before joining the Max Planck Institute. She has also been a member of various networks of researchers focusing on the study of the application of Islamic law in Europe and on law and migration in Europe, paying particular attention to family law. Her numerous publications include *Family, Religion and Law: Cultural Encounters in Europe* (Ashgate, 2014).

Günter Frankenberg is Professor of Public Law, Comparative Law, and Jurisprudence (em.) at Goethe University Frankfurt am Main. His main areas of research include authoritarian regimes, comparative constitutionalism, transfer of laws and constitutions, security regimes and infection protection law. He is the author of *Political Technology and the Erosion of the Rule of Law* (Edward Elgar, 2014), *Comparative Law as Critique* (Edward Elgar, 2016), *Comparative Constitutional Studies—Between Magic and Deceit* (Edward Elgar, 2018), and *Authoritarianism—Constitutional Perspectives* (Edward Elgar, 2020).

Berihun A. Gebeye is a Humboldt Postdoctoral Research Fellow at the Max Planck Institute for Comparative Public Law and International Law. He was previously a postdoctoral research fellow at the University of Göttingen and has held visiting fellowships at Columbia Law School, the Centre for Socio-Legal Studies at the University of Oxford, and at the Max Planck Institute for the Study of Religious and Ethnic Diversity. He has taught comparative constitutional law and politics at the Central European University, the University of Yangon, and the University of Göttingen. He holds degrees in law, human rights, and comparative constitutional law, and has published extensively in these fields, with a particular focus on Africa. He is the author of *A Theory of African Constitutionalism* (Oxford University Press, 2021).

Mark Goodale holds a chair at the University of Lausanne, where he is Professor of Cultural and Social Anthropology and former Director of the Laboratory of Cultural and Social Anthropology (LACS). The founding Series Editor of Stanford Studies in Human Rights, he is either author, editor, or co-editor of fifteen volumes, including (co-ed. with Sally Engle Merry) *The Practice of Human Rights: Tracking Law Between the Global and the Local* (Cambridge University Press, 2007), *Surrendering to Utopia: An Anthropology of Human Rights* (Stanford University Press, 2009), (ed.) *Human Rights:*

An Anthropological Reader (Blackwell, 2010), (ed.) *Human Rights at the Crossroads* (Oxford University Press, 2013), *Anthropology and Law: A Critical Introduction* (NYU Press, 2017), and (ed.) *Letters to the Contrary: A Curated History of the UNESCO Human Rights Survey* (Stanford University Press, 2018). His most recent books are *A Revolution in Fragments: Traversing Scales of Justice, Ideology, and Practice in Bolivia* (Duke University Press, 2019) and *Reinventing Human Rights* (Stanford University Press, 2022).

Michele Graziadei is Professor of Comparative Law at the University of Torino and Collegio Carlo Alberto Fellow, Past President, European Law Faculties Association. He is the author of over a hundred publications on comparative law, civil law, legal history, and legal theory. His recent publications include (ed. with Lionel Smith) *Comparative Property Law: Global Perspectives* (Edward Elgar, 2018) and (ed. with Marie-Claire Foblets and Alison D. Renteln) *Personal Autonomy in Plural Societies* (Routledge, 2018).

Carol J. Greenhouse is the Arthur W. Marks '19 Professor of Anthropology Emeritus at Princeton University. She earned her A.B. and Ph.D. degrees from Harvard University. Her primary research interests lie in the ethnography of law, particularly in relation to federal power in the United States. Her books include *The Paradox of Relevance: Ethnography and Citizenship in the United States* (University of Pennsylvania Press, 2011), (ed.) *Ethnographies of Neoliberalism* (University of Pennsylvania Press, 2012), and (with Alfred C. Aman) *Transnational Law: Cases and Problems in an Interconnected World* (Carolina Academic Press, 2017). She is past president of the American Ethnological Society, the Association for Political and Legal Anthropology, and the Law & Society Association, and past editor of American Ethnologist. Her work on the ethnography of law has been recognized by the Law & Society Association and the Association for the Study of Law, Culture and Humanities. She is a member of the American Philosophical Society and the American Academy of Arts and Sciences.

Anne Griffiths is an Emeritus Professor of Anthropology of Law at Edinburgh University. Her research focuses on anthropology of law, comparative and family law, African law, gender, culture, and rights. Over the years she has held a number of research grants and affiliations, including a research fellowship on *Framing the Global* at Indiana University and a senior research fellowship at the International Research Centre on Work and the Human Lifecycle in Global History, Humboldt University, Berlin. She has worked with colleagues at the Max Planck Institute for Social Anthropology in Halle/Saale, Germany and has had visiting appointments at the International Institute for the Sociology of Law in Oñati, Spain, the University of Texas-Austin School of Law, the Southern and Eastern African Regional Centre for Women's Law (SEARCWL) at the University of Zimbabwe, and the University of Witwatersrand in South Africa.

Laetitia Guerlain is Professor of Legal History at the University of Bordeaux and a junior member of the Institut universitaire de France. She works on the history of legal thought and legal knowledge in the nineteenth and twentieth centuries, with a strong focus on the relationship between legal science and other human and social sciences, such as sociology and anthropology.

Armando Guevara Gil is a Peruvian legal anthropologist and historian. He holds a law degree (Pontificia Universidad Católica del Perú), an M.A. in cultural anthropology (University of Wisconsin-Madison), and a Ph.D. in law (University of Amsterdam). He specializes and publishes in the fields of legal pluralism, colonial and republican law in the Andes, water law, and Indigenous rights. He was a visiting professor at the University of Torino (2019) and a guest researcher at the Max Planck Institute for European Legal History (Frankfurt, 2019–2020). He is currently Director of Research at the Universidad para el Desarrollo Andino (UDEA, Huancavelica, Perú), a professor of law at the Universidad Peruana de Ciencias Aplicadas (UPC, Lima), an affiliated researcher at the Max Planck Institute for Legal History and Legal Theory (Frankfurt), and an associate researcher at the Instituto del Perú (USMP, Lima).

Dirk Hanschel is Professor of German, European and International Public Law at Martin Luther University Halle-Wittenberg, Germany. His research focuses on, among other topics, issues at the junction of environmental law and human rights from interdisciplinary perspectives, as well as comparative constitutional law. As a Fellow at the Max Planck Institute for Social Anthropology, he currently leads a research project entitled Environmental Rights in Cultural Context (ERCC). By conducting selected case studies, the ERCC project aims to examine the extent to which environmental rights as inscribed in constitutions provide valid norms in the local context in the face of environmental threats resulting from climate change, mining activities, large-scale infrastructure projects, etc. Another of his current research projects, funded by the German Research Foundation (DFG), focuses on the Indian National Green Tribunal's implementation of UN Sustainable Development Goal #6 (SDG 6) on clean water and sanitation.

Aytalina Ivanova is a Postdoctoral Researcher at the Arctic Centre of the University of Lapland (Finland) and Docent in Law at Northeastern Federal University, Yakutsk, Russia. She earned a Russian Ph.D. (*kandidat nauk*) in history with a thesis on Sakha statehood in the early twentieth century. Unusual for a Russian legal scholar, she describes herself as a fieldwork-based legal anthropologist with a focus on the lived experience of the law in the Russian North. She has worked and published on Indigenous peoples and extractive industries in the Russian North and on Russian Indigenous and Arctic legislation. She has worked at the Arctic University of Norway (Tromso) and the Centre for Northeast Asian Studies at Tohoku University (Japan).

Andrzej Jakubowski is affiliated with the UNESCO Chair in Cultural Property Law at the University of Opole. He also acts as Chair of the Committee on Participation in Global Cultural Heritage Governance of the International Law Association. He holds a Ph.D. in international law from the European University Institute in Florence and an M.A. in art history from the University of Warsaw. His publications include the monograph *State Succession in Cultural Property* (Oxford University Press, 2015) and the edited collection *Cultural Rights as Collective Rights: An International Law Perspective* (Brill, 2016). Jakubowski is currently co-editing, with Ana Filipa Vrdoljak and Alessandro Chechi, a commentary on the 1970 UNESCO and 1995 UNIDROIT conventions (under contract with Oxford University Press).

Rita Kesselring is Associate Professor of Urban Studies at the University of St Gallen, Switzerland. Her research focuses on inequality, solidarity, corporate practices, urban development, and memory in South Africa and Zambia. She is the author of *Bodies of Truth: Law, Memory, and Emancipation in Post-Apartheid South Africa* (Stanford University Press, 2017).

Dodom Kim is a Ph.D. candidate in anthropology at the University of Chicago. Her research explores how legal and technological infrastructures shape the shifting values of human labour and bodies at the intersection of migration and citizenship. Her current project focuses on documentation practices that mediate people's narratives of their social and legal mobility as state citizens in southern China. The provisional title of her forthcoming dissertation is 'Documenting Uncertainties: Legal Identity, Bureaucratic Promises, and Mobility in Southern China'.

Juliette Koning is Professor of Business in Society at the School of Business and Economics, Maastricht University, The Netherlands. She holds a Ph.D. in social anthropology from the University of Amsterdam. Recent research focuses on the privatization and organization of security. She recently co-edited a special issue for *Organization Studies* (2020) with Marianna Fotaki and Yochanan Altman titled *Spirituality, Symbolism and Storytelling in Twenty-First-Century Organizations*. Her latest edited volume (with Gweneal Njoto-Feillard) is *New Religiosities, Modern Capitalism and Moral Complexities in Southeast Asia* (Palgrave Macmillan, 2017). Juliette is also Associate Editor of *Human Relations*.

Felix-Anselm van Lier is a public law scholar focusing on constitution-making processes and, more recently, on public procurement. He is a Research and Policy Associate at the Government Outcomes Lab at the University of Oxford's Blavatnik School of Government, where he investigates how new approaches in social policy and outcomes-based commissioning can help to better organize the provision of public services. He was previously a Research Fellow in the Law & Anthropology Department of the Max Planck Institute for Social Anthropology, where he researched the role of technology in constitution-making. Lier studied law in Germany and Italy before completing an M.Sc. in Law and Anthropology at LSE and a D.Phil. in Socio-Legal Studies at the University of Oxford. Among other professional positions, he has worked as a consultant for the Bingham Centre for the Rule of Law, Democracy Reporting International, the Berghof Foundation, and Lawyers for Justice in Libya.

Sally Engle Merry (1944–2020) was Silver Professor of Anthropology at New York University, Co-Faculty Director of the Center for Human Rights and Global Justice at the New York University School of Law, and past President of the American Ethnological Society. Her many research topics over her career included conflict resolution and legal consciousness, law and colonialism, human rights and gender violence, and global technologies of quantification. Her later published volumes include *Colonizing Hawaiʻi* (Princeton University Press, 2000), *Human Rights and Gender Violence* (University of Chicago Press, 2006), (co-edited with Mark Goodale) *The Practice of Human Rights* (Cambridge University Press, 2007), and *Gender Violence: A Cultural Perspective* (Blackwell, 2009). Her final book, *The Seductions of Quantification: Measuring Human Rights, Gender Violence, and Sex Trafficking* (University of Chicago Press, 2016) examines indicators as a technology of knowledge used for human rights monitoring and global governance. She also co-edited three books on quantification, (with Kevin Davis, Angelina Fisher, and Benedict Kingsbury) *Governance by Indicators: Global Power through Quantification and Rankings* (Oxford University Press, 2012), (with Kevin Davis and Benedict Kingsbury) *The Quiet Power of Indicators* (Cambridge University Press, 2015) and (with Richard Rottenburg, Song-Joon Park, and Johanna Mugler) *A World of Indicators* (Cambridge University Press, 2015). She received the Hurst Prize for *Colonizing Hawaiʻi* in 2002, the Kalven Prize for scholarly contributions to sociolegal scholarship in 2007, the J. I. Staley Prize for *Human Rights and Gender Violence* in 2010, and the AAA Franz Boas Award for Exemplary Service to Anthropology in 2019.

Elizabeth Mertz is a Senior Research Professor at the American Bar Foundation, as well as John and Rylla Bosshard Professor Emerita at the University of Wisconsin Law School. She was Lichtstern Distinguished Research Scholar in Residence 2020–2021 at the Department of Anthropology, University of Chicago; Katherine and Martin Crane Fellow at Princeton University's Programme in Law and Public Affairs; Visiting Scholar at the Institute for Advanced Studies in Princeton, School of Social Science; and Visiting Professor in the Department of Anthropology, Princeton University. She has served as Editor of *Political and Legal Anthropology Review (PoLAR)*, as well as of *Law & Social Inquiry*. Her research focuses on the language of law, from the semiotics of legal training to the difficulties of cross-disciplinary translation as confronted by the New Legal Realist movement.

Ralf Michaels is Director at the Max Planck Institute for Comparative and International Private Law in Hamburg, Germany, Chair in Global Law at Queen Mary University in London, and Professor of Law at Hamburg University. Until 2019, he was the Arthur Larson Professor at Duke University School of Law. He is a widely published scholar of private international law, comparative law, and legal theory. His current research focuses on decolonial comparative law, regulatory conflicts, and theoretical foundations of private international law. He is a member of the Academia Europaea, the American Law Institute, and the Comparative Law Associations of the United States, Germany, and France.

Sindiso Mnisi Weeks is Associate Professor of Law and Society in the School for Global Inclusion and Social Development at the University of Massachusetts—Boston and Adjunct Associate Professor in the Department of Public Law at the University of Cape Town (UCT). She was previously a senior researcher in the Rural Women's Action Research Programme at UCT, combining research, advocacy, and policy work on women, property, governance, and participation under customary law and the South African Constitution. Mnisi Weeks received her D.Phil. in Law from the University of Oxford's Centre for Socio- Legal Studies as a Rhodes Scholar, and previously clerked for Dikgang Moseneke, then Deputy Chief Justice of the Constitutional Court of South Africa. She is the author of *Access to Justice and Human Security: Cultural Contradictions in Rural South Africa* (Routledge, 2018) and co- author of *African Customary Law in South Africa: Post- Apartheid and Living Law Perspectives* (OUPSA, 2015).

Dominik M. Müller is Professor of Cultural and Social Anthropology at Friedrich Alexander University Erlangen-Nuremberg (FAU), where he is also Speaker of the Elite Graduate Programme 'Standards of Decision-Making across Cultures'. He is also heading the DFG Emmy Noether Research Group 'The Bureaucratization of Islam and Its Socio-Legal Dimensions in Southeast Asia'. He is a cooperation partner with the Law & Anthropology Department at the Max Planck Institute for Social Anthropology, where he worked from 2016 until 2019, prior to his appointment at FAU.

Faris E. Nasrallah is a Solicitor of the Senior Courts of England and Wales. He earned his LLB (first class) from the School of Oriental and African Studies (SOAS) at the University of London and his LLM from the University of Cambridge. Nasrallah is specialized in international arbitration, having worked for leading US and international law firms in London and Dubai. He has represented clients in complex and high-value international arbitration proceedings and has extensive advocacy experience. He is currently leading a research project on the relationship between theory and practice in international arbitration at the Max Planck Institute for Social Anthropology in Halle, Germany, and in 2019 established the International Arbitration Working Group as part of the Max PlanckLaw Network. With experience as counsel, expert, and arbitrator, his international arbitration practice focuses on commercial, construction, energy, and telecommunications disputes, with specialist knowledge of Middle Eastern laws.

Ronald Niezen is Distinguished James McGill Professor in the Department of Anthropology and Associate Member of the Faculty of Law at McGill University. He has conducted research on an Islamic reform movement in West Africa, justice campaigns in Indigenous communities in Canada, and the international movement of Indigenous peoples in the United Nations. His books include *The Origins of Indigenism: Human Rights and the Politics of Difference* (University of California Press, 2003), *Truth and Indignation: Canada's Truth and Reconciliation Commission on Indian Residential Schools* (University of Toronto Press, 2017), (co-edited with Maria Sapignoli) *Palaces of Hope: The Anthropology of Global Organizations* (Cambridge University Press, 2017), and *#HumanRights: The Technologies and Politics of Justice Claims in Practice* (Stanford University Press, 2020).

Math Noortmann is Professor of Transnational Law and Non-State Actors at the Centre for Trust, Peace and Social Relations (CTPSR), Coventry University (UK). He has taught and researched at universities in the Netherlands, Singapore, Germany, and the United Kingdom. He holds a Ph.D. in International Law and an M.Sc. in Political

Science, combining the two disciplines in his transdisciplinary pursuit of knowledge and understanding of law and politics. He queries the links between security and order, on the one hand, and justice and human dignity on the other. More specifically, he investigates the roles of non-state actors in transnational security governance, in particular, the private security sector, non-governmental organizations, and intergovernmental organizations. He received research funding from ESRC/AHRC (PaCCS), Newton (Institutional Links), and ESRC (CREST).

Karine Peschard is Research Associate at the Albert Hirschman Centre on Democracy, Graduate Institute of International and Development Studies (Geneva). Trained as an anthropologist, her research interests centre on intellectual property rights, agrobiodiversity, legal activism, peasant rights, and seed sovereignty, with a focus on Brazil and India. Her work has appeared in the *Journal of Peasant Studies (JPS)*, the *Canadian Journal of Development Studies*, and the *Annual Review of Anthropology*, as well as in edited books. She is the co-editor of a Special Forum on Seed Activism (*Journal of Peasant Studies*, 2020), and the author of an ethnography of court challenges to intellectual property rights on biotech crops in Brazil and India (MIT Press, forthcoming 2022).

Fernanda Pirie is Professor of the Anthropology of Law at the Centre for Socio-Legal Studies at the University of Oxford. An anthropologist specializing in Tibetan societies, she has used her research into legal practices and legal codes to develop the anthropology of law. *The Anthropology of Law* (OUP, 2013) builds on themes and debates developed in the *Legalism* research group, which she convened with colleagues in anthropology and history (*Legalism*, 4 vols, Oxford University Press). As well as studying contemporary Tibetan societies, Pirie has written on the legal history of medieval Tibet (see www.tibetanlaw.org). Her latest book is a global history of law, *The Rule of Laws: A 4,000-Year Quest to Order the World* (Profile Books, Basic Books, 2021).

Alison Dundes Renteln is Professor of Political Science, Anthropology, Public Policy, and Law at the University of Southern California. She has a Ph.D. in Jurisprudence and Social Policy (Berkeley) and a JD (USC). A public law scholar, she studies international law, human rights, comparative legal systems, constitutional law, and legal and political theory. An expert on cultural rights, she served on the State Bar Commission on Access to Justice and the California Judicial Council Access and Fairness Advisory Committee. She also served as a member of the California Attorney General's Commission on Hate Crimes and was appointed in 2020 to the California State Advisory Committee to the US Commission on Civil Rights. She has taught judges and attorneys at meetings of the American Bar Association and the National Association of Woman Judges. She serves on the Board of Trustees for the Law and Society Association and the editorial board of *Law and Social Inquiry*. Her publications include *The Cultural Defense* (Oxford University Press, 2004), *Multicultural Jurisprudence* (Hart, 2009), *Cultural Law* (Cambridge University Press, 2010), *Images and Human Rights* (Cambridge Scholars,

2017); *Global Bioethics and Human Rights* (Rowman and Littlefield, 2020), and many articles.

Annelise Riles is Executive Director of the Roberta Buffett Institute for Global Affairs, Associate Provost for Global Affairs, and Professor of Law and Anthropology at Northwestern University. Based on legal and anthropological research in China, Japan, and the Pacific, her work focuses on the transnational dimensions of law, markets, and culture across the fields of private law, conflict of laws, financial regulation, and comparative legal studies. Her books include *The Network Inside Out* (University of Michigan Press, 2000), *Collateral Knowledge: Legal Reasoning in the Global Financial Markets* (University of Chicago Press, 2011) and *Financial Citizenship: Experts, Publics, and the Politics of Central Banking* (Cornell University Press, 2018). Annelise Riles was awarded the Certificate of Merit of the American Society of International Law, 2000–2001.

Maria Sapignoli is Assistant Professor of Social Anthropology in the Department of Philosophy Piero Martinetti (University of Milan). She is a cooperation partner of the Max Planck Institute for Social Anthropology, where she is also a member of the scientific committee accompanying the research cluster she contributed to setting up, entitled 'The Anthropology of AI in Policing and Justice'. Sapignoli has spent the past ten years conducting ethnographic fieldwork in southern Africa, as well as in several international organizations, including the United Nations, on topics of institutional reform, Indigenous and minority rights, social movements and advocacy and, ultimately, justice. Most recently, she has started a new project which engages, critically and collaboratively, with the legal and social challenges and opportunities presented by the use of artificial intelligence technologies and big data in society and in environmental governance. She is the author of *Hunting Justice: Displacement, Law, and Activism in the Kalahari* (Cambridge University Press, 2018), as well as numerous articles and book chapters. She is also co-editor (with Ronald Niezen) of *Palaces of Hope: The Anthropology of Global Organizations* (Cambridge University Press, 2017).

Katrin Seidel is Senior Research Fellow in the Law & Anthropology Department of the Max Planck Institute for Social Anthropology (Germany), a former postdoctoral fellow at Käte Hamburger Kolleg/Centre for Global Cooperation Research, and former Academic Coordinator of the Joint Network Rule of Law Support at Freie Universität Berlin, in collaboration with the German Federal Foreign Office. Based on her interdisciplinary background (law and African/Asian studies), her research is situated at the intersection of legal pluralism, heterogeneous statehood, and governance. Seidel's studies are concerned with the interdependent relationships between plural normative and judicial orders at different levels of regulation. Her research and *Habilitation* project focused on the local–global nexus of peace and constitution making in the (post-)conflict settings of South Sudan and Somaliland.

Rachel Sieder holds a Ph.D. in Politics from the University of London. She is Senior Research Professor at the Center for Research and Graduate Studies in Social

Anthropology (CIESAS) in Mexico City, where she teaches legal and political anthropology. She is also an associate senior researcher at the Chr. Michelsen Institute in Bergen, Norway. She has worked for the past three decades on Central America, and her research interests include human rights, Indigenous rights, social movements, Indigenous law, legal anthropology, the state, and violence. Her most recent books include (with María Teresa Sierra and Rosalva Aída Hernández) *Justicias Indígenas y Estado: Violencias Contemporáneas* (FLACSO/CIESAS, 2013), *Demanding Justice and Security: Indigenous Women and Legal Pluralities in Latin America* (Rutgers University Press, 2017), and (with Karina Ansolabehere and Tatiana Alfonso Sierra) *The Routledge Handbook of Law and Society* (Routledge, 2019).

Florian Stammler is Professor of Anthropology at the University of Lapland in Rovaniemi, Finland. He coordinates the European Union's northernmost anthropology research team and has led multiple Finnish and international Arctic research projects. Stammler has lived for years in the Russian Arctic, conducting fieldwork with reindeer herders, government officials, and representatives of extractive industries. He has published on Indigenous peoples and industrial development, the anthropology of extractivism, northern nomadic pastoralism, human–animal relations, oral history, and the anthropology of well-being. His publications include *Reindeer Nomads Meet the Market* (Lit-Verlag, 2005) and the edited volumes (with Hugh Beach) *People and Reindeer on the Move* (Berghahn, 2006), (with Hiroki Takakura) *Good to Eat—Good to Live With* (Centre for Northeast Asian Studies, 2010), (with Timo Koivurova, Else Grete Broderstad, Dorothée Cambou, and Dalee Dorough) *Routledge Handbook of Indigenous Peoples in the Arctic* (Routledge, 2020), and (with Reeta Toivanen) *Young People, Wellbeing and Sustainable Arctic Communities* (Routledge, 2021).

Elizabeth Steyn is Cassels Brock Fellow and Assistant Professor in Mining and Finance Law at Western University, Canada. She is also a faculty member of the Western Institute for Earth and Space Exploration. At Western Law, she heads the Mining, Finance and Sustainability Programme. She is a member of the Rocky Mountain Mineral Law Foundation (RMMLF), the Natural Resources Law Teachers Institute (NRTLI), the Canadian Institute of Mining (CIM), and the Prospectors and Developers Association of Canada (PDAC). At present, she is working on three main projects: the potential domestic liability of transnational extractive companies for abuses committed abroad by their foreign subsidiaries; regulatory gaps relating to deep-sea mining; and the development of an International Environmental Law (IEL) framework for space mining. The United Nations Environment Programme (UNEP) also recently appointed Steyn as Principal Investigator for the development of Guiding Principles for a Responsible and Sustainable Mining and Metals Sector to Achieve the Paris Agreement and Sustainable Development Goals in the Context of the Green Recovery.

Brian Thom is an Associate Professor in the Anthropology Department at the University of Victoria, where, in 2010, he founded the Ethnographic Mapping Lab (https://www.uvic.ca/socialsciences/ethnographicmapping/). He has worked for more than twenty-five years with Coast Salish communities in British Columbia on the recognition of Indigenous land rights and jurisdictions, attending to the cultural and political priorities of their engagements with the ongoing legacies of colonialism. From 1994–1997 and 2000–2010 he worked as researcher, senior advisor, and negotiator for several Coast Salish First Nations (Canada) engaged in treaty, land claims, and self-government negotiations, and currently collaborates with the Centre for Indigenous Conservation and Development Alternatives (https://cicada.world). His research focuses on issues of Indigenous territoriality, knowledge, and governance; revealing contemporary practices of Indigenous law; and clarifying the ontological imperatives behind Indigenous political strategies. Thom's publications 'The Paradox of Boundaries in Coast Salish Territories' (*Cultural Geographies*, 2009) and 'Reframing Indigenous Territories' (*American Indian Culture and Research Journal*, 2014) critically attend to state-reinforced discourses of overlapping claims; his ethnography 'Entanglements in Coast Salish Ancestral Territories' in (Françoise Dussart and Sylvie Poirier, eds) *Entangled Territorialities* (University of Toronto Press, 2017) examines political ontology in reconciling land rights.

Bertram Turner holds a Ph.D. in anthropology from the University of Munich and is Senior Researcher in the Department of Law & Anthropology at the Max Planck Institute for Social Anthropology in Halle, Germany. He has conducted extended field research in the Middle East and North Africa, Germany, and Canada, and has held university teaching positions in Munich, Leipzig, and Halle. He has published widely on the anthropology of law, science and technology, religion, conflict, development, and resource extraction. Among his more recent publications are a chapter on the anthropology of property in (Michele Graziadei, ed.) *Comparative Property Law: Global Perspectives*, (Edward Elgar, 2017) and a chapter (with Keebet von Benda-Beckmann) on the anthropological roots of global legal pluralism in (ed. Paul Schiff Berman) the *Oxford Handbook on Global Legal Pluralism* (Oxford University Press, 2020).

Melanie G. Wiber is an economic and legal anthropologist and Professor Emerita in the Department of Anthropology, University of New Brunswick. She has published several books and edited volumes on property rights, including *Politics, Property and Law in the Philippine Uplands* (Wilfred Laurier University Press, 1994), as well as a volume on gender in human evolution imagery. Her work includes analysis of the property aspects of irrigation rights, dairy quota and supply management, and of the Canadian fisheries. For the past twenty years, Wiber has conducted participatory, action-based research in the fisheries of the Canadian Maritime provinces. Most recently, this research has focused on local ecological knowledge, ecological threats such as marine debris and oil spills, and the impact of climate change on fishing communities.

Richard A. Wilson is Board of Trustees Professor of Law and Anthropology and Associate Dean of Faculty Development and Intellectual Life at the University of Connecticut School of Law. As author or editor of eleven books, he researches and writes about international human rights, social media and online hate speech, and post-conflict justice institutions such as truth and reconciliation commissions and international criminal tribunals. He edited *Human Rights, Culture and Context* (Pluto Press, 1997), the first edited book on the anthropology human rights, and authored an influential ethnographic study of the South African Truth and Reconciliation Commission, *The Politics of Truth and Reconciliation in South Africa* (Cambridge University Press, 2001). His most recent book is *Incitement on Trial: Prosecuting International Speech Crimes* (Cambridge University Press, 2017). He is a member of the Hate Crimes Advisory Council of the state of Connecticut and served as Chair of the State Advisory Committee to the US Commission on Civil Rights (2009–2014).

Olaf Zenker is Professor of Social Anthropology at Martin Luther University Halle-Wittenberg, Germany. Focusing on Southern Africa, Northern Ireland, and Germany, his research has dealt with politico-legal issues such as conflict and identity formations, plural normative orders, statehood, bureaucracy, the rule of law, modernity, inequality, and justice, as well as sociolinguistics and anthropological epistemologies. His recent publications include (co-edited with Gerhard Anders) *Transition and Justice: Negotiating the Terms of New Beginnings in Africa* (Wiley-Blackwell, 2015); (co-edited with Steffen Jensen) *South African Homelands as Frontiers: Apartheid's Loose Ends in the Postcolonial Era* (Routledge, 2017); and (co-edited with Markus Hoehne) *The State and the Paradox of Customary Law in Africa* (Routledge, 2018).

INTRODUCTION
Mapping the Field of Law and Anthropology

MARIE-CLAIRE FOBLETS, MARK GOODALE,
MARIA SAPIGNOLI, AND OLAF ZENKER

The *Oxford Handbook of Law and Anthropology* is a comprehensive collection of essays that provides an original and internationally framed conception of the field. The volume's structure and thematic framework are the result of a number of years of drafting, modification, and conference discussion that involved a wide range of colleagues, constructive critics, and volume contributors. The *Handbook* is closely associated with the innovative, interdisciplinary research programme of the Law & Anthropology Department at the Max Planck Institute for Social Anthropology in Halle, Germany. The Law & Anthropology Department is engaged in a number of long-term initiatives that aim to enlarge the boundaries of the field of law and anthropology, particularly through the collaboration between legal scholars, legal practitioners, and anthropologists. This *Handbook* counts among the activities that figure at the top of the list of such initiatives. It has its genesis in a meeting of the Department's Consultative Committee.[1] During discussions at the 2014 meeting, there was felt to be a need among those present for a reference work that would bring together a diverse spectrum of contributors, recognized experts in the topics under consideration, to lay out a new vision for the broad field of law and anthropology. Clearly, such an undertaking represents a major commitment of time and resources and, for a time, the idea remained merely conceptual. It was, however, taken up again, and the decision to pursue the project was made in 2016. The result is an expansive volume of essays on law and anthropology, each of which provides a survey of the current state of scholarly debate and an original argument about the future direction of research in this dynamic and interdisciplinary field.

The motivation behind this volume is to provide a space for critical thinking and writing about the relationship between law and anthropology. While a certain amount of historical background is necessary, the point of the *Handbook* is not to give a general overview of the development of legal anthropology as a sub-discipline of sociocultural anthropology—that has already been done thoroughly and well (see, e.g. Donovan 2007; Goodale 2017; Moore 2004; Pirie 2013; Rouland 1988). Rather, we wanted this *Handbook* to focus on current and projected future trends that point towards issues and/or observations to be pursued in the coming years. We believe that this is not only what is called for, but is also what will make the volume unique and valuable far into the future. We envisioned bringing together legal scholars and social and cultural anthropologists to explore the various ways in which the two disciplines, each with its own perception of topics of shared interest, can join forces to provide a richer, more sophisticated analysis of the issues under study.

To achieve this goal in a more concrete sense, we adopted a fourfold method that was, to a large extent, experimental. *First*, we strove to have roughly equal numbers of scholars from the two disciplines involved in order to achieve a disciplinary balance. *Second*, contributors were encouraged, if possible, to team up and produce co-authored chapters, with legal scholars and anthropologists working side by side. *Third*, we organized a review process in which contributors were assigned to produce written 'peer reviews' of other contributors' draft chapters. Here again, to the extent possible, one anthropologist and one legal scholar was assigned to each chapter. This had the added benefit of giving the reviewers the opportunity to gather insights from scholars from the other discipline, which served as preparation for the *fourth* step, the conference: all contributors were invited to a conference in Berlin (30 November–2 December 2018) with the aim of presenting preliminary chapters and facilitating the interaction between them. The conference served as another layer of peer review of sorts, with discussants commenting on groups of papers and drawing out common themes, and all participants having the opportunity to ask questions, challenge perspectives and underlying assumptions, and offer constructive feedback. Contributors, for their part, were encouraged to reflect on and incorporate the insights from the written reviews, from the discussants' observations, and from the open discussions during the conference when reworking their contributions.

We as editors know from our continuing interaction with contributors how demanding the entire exercise has been and how much invaluable effort and intellectual energy has gone into this process. As we look back on it now, with the benefit of hindsight and with the outcome—this *Oxford Handbook of Law and Anthropology*—in our hands, we realize what a rewarding and productive endeavour it has been. If this volume succeeds in establishing a scholarly benchmark at a moment in which the subject area is both growing and becoming more diffuse, then the lion's share of the credit and thanks goes to our contributors for rising to the challenge as authors, as reviewers, and as collaborators.

Structure of the Volume

The *Handbook* presents the discipline, with its emerging research interests and new developments, within a coherent collective narrative about how law and anthropology have related and should relate to each other as intersecting domains of inquiry that concern fundamental questions of dispute resolution, normative ordering, social organization, and legal, political, and social identity. The need for such an overarching project has become even more pressing as lawyers and anthropologists have, in our view, much to gain by working together more systematically within an ever-increasing number of key contemporary spheres, including immigration and asylum processes, international justice forums, debates over cultural heritage, and the writing of new national constitutions, among many others. The *Handbook* takes critical stock of these various points of intersection in order to both document the wide range of collaborative work that is currently being done in the field and, as important, to suggest new avenues for future research and practice. At the same time, the *Handbook* examines the ways in which theoretical and disciplinary conventions within law and anthropology, because of the very nature of the disciplines, lead to different forms of engagement with sociolegal processes. The chief objective of the *Handbook* is to establish a new framework for the field of law and anthropology that both identifies and conceptualizes its most promising areas of innovation and sociolegal relevance, while also acknowledging its points of tension, its open questions, and its areas for future development.

In developing this framework, the *Handbook* adopts an internal structure that organizes its forty-nine chapters into five thematic parts. Each of these parts is described below.

Part I: Global Perspectives on Law and Anthropology

The *Handbook* begins with fourteen chapters that collectively present a new introduction to the field of law and anthropology. The history of the field has been written many times, usually with a particular orientation that privileges a genealogy that is heavy on its colonial roots and later permutations through the emergence of the ethnography of law, legal realism, dispute resolution, and legal consciousness studies (Donovan 2007; Moore 2004). More recent histories of the field, while still keeping within this general framework, emphasize newer developments, such as the comparative approach to anthropology and law (Pirie 2013), the importance of anthropological studies of cosmopolitan legalities (Goodale 2017), and the impact of wider scholarly concerns with power, history, and language on the anthropology of law (Mertz and Goodale 2012; see also Starr and Collier 1989). Notable exceptions to this general Anglo-American line of analysis in the history of anthropology and law would include Norbert Rouland's (1988) introductory textbook, *L'anthropologie juridique*, from a Francophone perspective and Franz and Keebet von Benda-Beckmann's extensive studies of the emergence of a distinct Dutch tradition of anthropology and law (e.g. 2002). Although not as widely studied as the alternative framings of Rouland and the Benda-Beckmanns, important counter-narratives to the dominant Anglo-American introduction to anthropology and law can also be found in the German and Italian traditions, including Fikentscher (2009), Lampe (1970), Sacco (2007), Sack et al. (1991), and Scillitani (1980).

Nevertheless, Part I of the *Handbook* is intended to do much more than simply offer an alternative to the orthodox history of the field of law and anthropology. Instead, its chapters are meant to present a collective overview of the field that is thoroughly decentred and heterodox. Even though certain historical outlines remain relevant—for example, the different legacies of colonialism and empire-building and the tension between centre and periphery in the development of academic traditions—the vantage points in Part I offer readers significantly new ways through which to approach the multiple geographies, cultures, and ethical turns that constitute the field of anthropology and law from a global perspective.

Despite the breadth presented in Part I, it is worth underscoring several commonalities that emerge across the fourteen chapters. First, the chapters demonstrate the fact that the meanings of both 'law' and 'anthropology' are often articulated in different historical and cultural contexts in different ways. The meanings of law will vary by legal and political system, by disciplinary perspective, and by cultural and linguistic tradition. Much the same is true for anthropology, whose epistemological points of reference and institutional affiliations differ from country to country and across time. This also explains why the first part of the *Handbook* presents these multiple perspectives and meanings as a new approach to the history of the field, rather than attempting to condense them into yet another unified global history of law and anthropology.

Second, the chapters in Part I reveal the different ways in which the relationship between law and anthropology—in all of its global diversity—is nevertheless deeply imbricated in wider political processes and developments, from colonial rule, to legal mobilization by marginalized populations, to the use of law by states to consolidate political power and suppress dissent. In a sense, the chapters in Part I serve as evidence for the proposition that the relationship between law and anthropology is often forged in the crucible of political life.

And finally, Part I of the *Handbook* also provides diverse perspectives on the ways in which lawyers and anthropologists have taken a mutual interest in both the forms of knowledge and action to be found on one side or another and, even more important, in exploring forms of joint collaboration in legal and political processes. Indeed, the specific ways in which anthropological knowledge has been used in legal practice has become such an important part of the field that the *Handbook* devotes an entire part to these forms of appropriation (see Part III). Yet across Part I's chapters on law and anthropology from a global perspective, what is revealed are complicated legacies of interaction, interest, and sometimes misapprehension, in which law and anthropology are always differently situated in relation to state power, institutional prestige, and research outcomes.

Part II: Recurring Themes in Law and Anthropology

If the chapters in Part I of the *Handbook* offer a broad introduction to the field of law and anthropology that emphasizes diversity and heterodoxy, the chapters in Part II collectively identify—from within this global diversity—a number of themes that are likely to endure as key conceptual and interdisciplinary bases. These are topics that have become foundational for the field, domains of inquiry and professional practice that crystallize the distinct epistemological syntheses that emerge when legal phenomena are studied and analysed anthropologically. At the same time, it is important to view the chapters in Part II in relation to those in the *Handbook's* final Part V, which features topics of increasing importance for the field. Viewed retrospectively, it is likely that at least some of these 'current directions' for law and anthropology will mature into 'recurring themes'.

In considering the enduring themes for the field that are represented by the chapters in Part II, three more general observations can be made. First, anthropological studies of law and legal processes show the ways in which law serves to constitute various forms of identity: class, gender, ethnic, religious, and linguistic. This happens both in the more conventional ways that law defines or legally recognizes protected categories and through the more diffuse forms through which legal practice becomes a performative mechanism that validates identities and assures their public visibility. Second, the recurring themes in Part II of the *Handbook* also demonstrate the extent to which legal forms or 'logics' (Thompson 1977) impose limits to the ways in which the law can be mobilized for the social good. And third, the chapters in Part II provide further evidence of the importance of a dynamic that was recently described elsewhere (Goodale 2017): that an enduring characteristic of law, as documented by anthropologists, has been a dialectical movement between social agency through law on one side, and social regulation through law (often, but not always, by the state) on the other.

Part III: Anthropology in Law and Legal Practice

The chapters grouped in Part III can been seen as further building on this image of a dialectical movement. They offer critical reflection and discussion on the role of anthropologists who do consultancy work within the framework of legal practice, on the one hand, and, on the other, the constraints practising lawyers must consider when drawing on insights gained from anthropology. The illustrations draw from a variety of fields of law and cover a broad range of topics: environmental justice, the use of the cultural defence in court, the proliferation of alternative dispute resolution mechanisms, international criminal law and transitional justice, cultural heritage and its preservation, and family justice, including issues of private international law. Ethnographic baseline studies can undoubtedly improve our understanding of the sometimes highly complex and often difficult situations and settings in which individuals and/or communities are living, and may offer insights that cannot be gained in any other way. The more relevant issue at stake, however, is whether and under what conditions such understanding is transferrable to legal reasoning, properly speaking, without losing its very significance and integrity (Kandel 1992).

Debates revolving around applying anthropological knowledge to legal matters and in formal legal settings are certainly not new; in fact, they have accompanied the discipline from the outset (Singer 2008; Strathern and Stuart 2005; Warren 2008). In today's context, however, with the intensification of communication and exchange among and across communities and cultures worldwide, the significance of these issues has been heightened (Holden 2011; Ríos Vega et al. 2020). Who are the expert witnesses? Under what conditions are they working to be able to provide the information requested? How much control do they keep over the data and their analyses once they have submitted their reports or delivered their testimonies? There is no unanimity, certainly (and especially) not among anthropologists, when it comes to making ethnographic data available to those who apply the law in concrete cases (Baogang 2006; Brutti 2005; Daly 2004; Davis 2008; Dyck 1993; Morris and Bastin 2004; Sarat 2019, Zenker 2016). Their reservations are both principled (the ethical considerations of such a prospect) and methodological (the feasibility) in nature.

The six chapters contained in this part clearly do not and cannot provide a complete picture when it comes to assessing the role of anthropology and ethnographic accounts in contemporary legal practice. They do, however, offer a revealing sample of the problems this role raises for every anthropologist who engages in legal issues, as well as for legal practitioners who, in their search for just solutions to individual cases, are prepared to invest in the complex and often uncertain effort that drawing on ethnographic accounts and anthropological scholarship entails.

Two key issues emerge from the contributions. The first issue, undeniably, revolves around the need for rigorous professionalism in the provision and use of anthropological expertise. The emergent situation in which consultancy work places anthropologists today requires a sharpening of the understanding of specific professional matters—theoretical, ethical, and material—that accompany some forms of consultancy work. But to achieve that aim, a number of conditions must be met. There are many anthropologists who, unfortunately, after a number of experiences of providing their expertise, find themselves disappointed and disillusioned and have therefore decided that they will no longer lend themselves to such endeavours: facts were not accurately represented or not in their full complexity; elements of the analysis were left out; the translation of anthropological into legal concepts was flawed. These are but a few of the concerns anthropologists have expressed. In other cases, anthropologists wish they had been consulted at the appropriate moment so as to prevent misunderstandings in the resulting legal reasoning that could have easily been avoided.

For anthropological knowledge to be constructively and effectively applied in legal practice, and to better understand what is to be gained from applying insights that draw from anthropology for the purposes of legal practice (Menski 2011), the experiences of intensive collaboration between a practising lawyer and an anthropologist should be studied in more depth and published widely. Such experiences deserve to be highlighted also because they revolve—directly or indirectly—around the very question of how to achieve justice in concrete contexts. Such experiences, and the lessons learned from them, are thus highly relevant for the purposes of decision-making in an increasing number of very topical spheres: accommodation of diversity in plural societies, persecution of asylum seekers in the country of origin, land grabbing, native title claims, the interconnectedness of law and religion (including non-faith-based beliefs), and so forth.

The second recurring theme that runs through all six chapters is the role of human rights in legal practice. In reality, recourse to standards of protection as they are defined in international human rights instruments may not produce the expected effects if the concept of 'protection' is not sufficiently critically considered and assessed in the context of its very concrete application (Ibhawoh 2004; Pityana 2004; Ringelheim 2010; Takirambudde 2001). Each of the six chapters engages in its own way with a number of human-rights-related issues, explaining why the main legal mechanisms put into place for their effective protection do not necessarily produce the desired effect(s). Human rights, as protected by most existing international human rights treaties (with a few notable exceptions), are derived from specific historical circumstances that did not affect to the same extent all countries that, today, have formally subscribed to international human rights law. Ethnographic accounts show that reality, as lived by individuals and the groups they form, cannot simply be reduced to an issue of whether international human rights law is violated or not. Instead, through ethnographic observations, anthropology shows that, when it comes to dealing with concrete situations in daily legal practice, a certain degree of acceptance of pluralism within international human rights law is probably the more realistic and just way to go (Breau 2007; Goodale and Merry 2007; Hinz 2009; Turner et al. 2009).

In paying due attention to people's own representations and practices in the context of the situations they are in, including the historical circumstances, anthropological scholarship offers an unparalleled grasp of such situations. In doing so, anthropologists have contributed a great deal to the development of an ethnographically grounded understanding of the manifold ways in which international human rights standards are being taken up, translated, resisted, and transformed, and of the implications that engagement with several of these rights in particular can have, not only for the individuals and groups involved, but also for the broader society (Destrooper and Merry 2018). Detailed ethnographic work may help unravel the intricate dynamics at play between the generalizing normative orientation of international human rights law and the values and identities of people in local contexts. In legal practice, however, this work is, regrettably, more often than not ignored or, where it is not completely ignored, it is not effectively used or proves extremely difficult to put into practice. The lack of recourse to anthropological scholarship is not necessarily to be seen as a principled refusal or reluctance on the part of legal practitioners, but rather as a matter of fact that is linked to a clear lack of resources, appropriate training, and experience when it comes to interdisciplinary collaboration (Vetters and Foblets 2016).

Part IV: Anthropology at the Limits of Law

The chapters in Part IV reflect research that reveals in several ways the ultimate limits of law from both an anthropological and a legal perspective. This follows closely upon the chapters of Part III, which address key themes that emerge from 'law's anthropology' (Burke 2011) or the 'law's legal anthropology' (Niezen 2014), that is, forms of legal practice that intentionally borrow from anthropological methods or theories, as well as the various uses and misuses of legal anthropological knowledge, theories, and methods in law and legal practice.

The chapters in this section collectively constitute one of the key innovations of the volume: the recognition that law, broadly defined, has its limits as a mechanism for social change, economic redistribution, and the provision of justice after mass atrocities and protracted social conflict. This is an area of the anthropology of law that examines what can be understood as law's outer boundaries in the face of rapidly changing political, social, and economic conditions.

Taken together, the chapters in Part IV should not necessarily be seen as a critique of law itself, but rather as a recognition of law's limits when it comes to addressing the enduring dilemmas of inequality, social suffering, humanitarian interventions, citizen security, and so on. The section reveals both the pitfalls and the potentials of the law as a mechanism for engendering structural changes, economic redistribution, and the provision of justice.

The recourse to what John and Jean Comaroff refer to as 'lawfare'—the use of law as an instrument of political leverage or coercion—'becomes most readily visible when those who act in the name of the state conjure with legalities to act against some or all of its citizens' (Comaroff and Comaroff 2006: 30). Legal processes, however, should not only be narrowly treated as sources of domination and hegemony, but also, in some circumstances, as resources that are malleable, offering possibilities for negotiation with the potential for recognition and redistribution.

For instance, the concept of 'juridification' has been developed as a way to understand how different forms of identity—of individuals, collectivities, ethnicities, genders, and so on—can emerge, either through state law or against it (Eckert et al. 2012). State law sometimes changes to recognize individual and collective rights claims that are products of legal construction and the formalization of identities. At the same time, marginalized populations have found ways to use the law creatively, and even subversively, to alleviate inequalities that have been produced by state-directed forms of legal enforcement, legal regulation, and legal 'exclusion' (Goodale 2017). However, whenever law is mobilized in defence of collective rights, identity is transformed by legal conceptions of rights, tradition, and belonging.

The emphasis on legal victimization does not present the complete story of how law becomes part of the lives of those on the margins of a dominant society; above all, it does not tell the story of their uses of law, how it can be a rallying point for claims-making, for using the state's courts to call the state to account. Law, Kirsch argues, can in fact become 'a resource for promoting political and economic transformation' (Kirsch 2014: 87).

In this regard, Boaventura de Sousa Santos and César Rodríguez-Garavito (2005: 2) call for more attention to be given to an 'unprecedented effervescence of debate and experimentation in bottom-up legal reform and new international legal regimes'. In their view, a 'subaltern cosmopolitan legality' is upending the common assumption that those on the margins lack political and legal agency. These once-excluded actors are now the beneficiaries of 'new forms of global politics and legality' (Sousa Santos and Rodríguez-Garavito 2005: 9). Taking a 'bottom-up' perspective does not, of course, consistently reveal the success of counter-hegemonic projects or legal alternatives to hegemonic regimes. Sousa Santos and Rodríguez-Garavito do acknowledge the 'constant danger of cooptation and obliteration' (2005: 17), though in the context of a celebration of the overlooked possibilities for the resistance that persists and alternatives to oppression that continue to be put forward, despite opposition from the powerful (2005: 12). This approach to agency from 'below' was more justified, perhaps, in the context of the burgeoning cosmopolitanism that marked the turn of the twenty-first century. Now such optimism might have to be tempered due to the rise of numerous instances of authoritarian populism, the weakening of democratic institutions, and the implications these developments have for legal activism. Furthermore, agency from below is also being tamed by the growing reach of new digital technologies, along with legally sanctioned powers of surveillance, intrusions on privacy, and repression of dissent. Where there might be space for 'bottom-up' efforts towards truth-seeking and justice in this emerging techno-political ecosystem is an open question, yet to be fully addressed by critical scholarship at the nexus of law and anthropology.

In summary, some general observations can be made regarding the chapters in Part IV. The first step towards engaging with emerging legal realities is to closely consider both the limits and the potential of the law in changing circumstances. To this end, the chapters in this section stress the importance of ethnography and the need to move beyond the concepts and methodologies of law to consider the dynamic interaction between formal principles and informal (including resistant) practices. In order to make this distinction, it is often necessary to challenge the centrality of state law and consider plural legal realities with differing degrees of institutionalization. The authors in this section underline the importance of intensifying the dialogue between legal scholars and anthropologists, in part to understand how and in what contexts legal regulatory frameworks define, enable, and restrict individual, collective, and institutional agency. Their analyses are also animated by an interest in how law and norms are vernacularized and mobilized by individuals, groups, and institutions, sometimes through acts of dissent, to bring about social and economic change. Finally, the chapters in this section share a sense of the importance of exploring how law and politics are embedded in one another. This embeddedness goes beyond the structures of law to become more broadly socially constructive or constitutive. Subjectivities and collective identities can be generated by engagement with dominant norms and institutions.

Part V: Current Directions in Law and Anthropology

Against the backdrop of decentring and repositioning law and anthropology in heterodox global perspectives, revisiting key themes of enduring importance, charting the multiple ways in which the law and legal practice have engaged anthropological expertise, and having reflected anthropologically upon the potentials and pitfalls of the law to bring about social transformation in all its complexity, the final part of the *Handbook* takes the measure of topics in the field that are vital, yet still emergent or in the process of being profoundly transformed in light of contemporary developments. As such, the ten chapters offer a sample of important current directions in law and anthropology, with the potential to inspire colleagues and students as they contemplate future projects at the intersections of law and anthropology. We are convinced that some, if not all, of these featured concerns will, over time, develop into recurring themes of their own.

Despite the considerable topical breadth and diversity of theoretical, methodological, and disciplinary perspectives covered in these chapters, they are still united in addressing, one way or the other, crucial implications of our contemporary moment—a time when the Westphalian order of nation-states has been, and is being, profoundly challenged and transformed through multifarious and increasingly globalized processes. The dynamics unfolding around the shifting constellations of nation-states and their divergent legalities in the early twenty-first century comprise various dimensions, of which six are particularly important for the chapters assembled in this part.

First of all, anthropology has, for a long time, highlighted the de facto coexistence of, and complex interferences between, multiple normative orders, especially in colonial and postcolonial contexts. While legal pluralism in itself is thus hardly a recent phenomenon, the generation of norms and laws beyond the state has nevertheless massively increased in recent decades. The multiple actors involved in such norm creation and implementation—of which the state is often but one—include global legal institutions such as United Nations agencies and the World Bank, as well as partners from civil society and the private sector. In light of the massive expansion of laws and normative regulations no longer easily imaginable in terms that place the state at the centre, the state is challenged to reposition itself within a rapidly transforming new global order.

At the same time (and this leads to the second concern), it would be grossly misleading to assume the demise of the nation-state as some had optimistically presaged in the final years of the twentieth century under the impression of accelerating globalization, when a post-national world with explicit cosmopolitan inclinations seemed in much closer reach. By now, it has become abundantly clear that the state is here to stay, at least for the foreseeable future, and often reasserts itself with renewed legal and extra-legal force. This is particularly evident with regard to expanding regimes of surveillance and punishment, often with the help of new digital technologies (on which more below), through which states have attempted to reclaim their monopoly on legitimate violence.

Over the past decades, the need for renewed expressions of state sovereignty, securitization, and punitive reason has been couched in terms of criminal and terrorist threats, especially under conditions of vastly increased flows of migration across state borders, including multiple forms of displacement and refugee movements. To someone who is 'seeing like a state' (Scott 1998), such migrants and refugees often look as though they are disrupting the 'national order of things' (Malkki 1995). This highlights the third issue of crucial importance: the veritable explosion of identity politics over the past fifty years, which—partly juridified and legally restricted, partly unfolding their normativities beyond the law—have coexisted with, and increasingly challenged, *citizenship* as the master signifier of state-accorded rights and duties. Such accelerated politics of belonging have not only comprised, besides citizenship, contested autochthonies at shifting scales—including ethnic, national, diasporic, and Indigenous identities—but also non-territorial subjectivities, such as gender, sexuality, race, class, religion, and able-bodidness and their various intersections, as well as the normative demands that have been mobilized around them.

A fourth concern running through the chapters is a heightened awareness of the importance of, and consequent theoretical and empirical engagement with, the material semiotics of different legalities. Under the influence of science and technology studies (STS), anthropologists and legal scholars have started paying greater attention to specific materialities and their inscribed modalities of signification as they become instantiated in variable entanglements of laws, both on the books and in action. Taking seriously the differentially enabling constraints of form, this applies to crucial questions of legal technique, comprising legal reasoning and its fictions, as well as its modes of inscription, most notably in documents and filing systems (Hull 2012; Vismann 2008). The years of the new millennium have seen great transformations of legal or law-related technologies, from shifts towards indicators and other quantitative measures of evidence-based governance to a multiplication of new digital technologies increasingly using artificial intelligence, all of which profoundly shape the global order of domestic and international laws and its increasingly powerful normative others.

This emergent global order is not only one in which 'the state' is increasingly challenged by multiple normative dynamics from below, beyond, and across its Westphalian order. Moreover, it is not only an order characterized by an expansive juridification of politics within a globalized ideology of the rule of law. Rather, it is a world ever more haunted by a return of the political (if not the repressed) instantiating antiliberal forms of agency from an ultranationalist above and a right-populist below that, not too long ago, seemed all but overcome. In short, it is a postcolonial, postnational, and postdemocratic world of a highly ambivalent, normative super-diversity (Vertovec 2007), in which legal plurality once and for all has lost its innocence and no longer constitutes a self-evident value in and of itself. In light of this new legal, political, and moral complexity, a fifth concern animating the chapters consists in the challenge—for legal scholars, legal practitioners, and anthropologists alike—of how to navigate this ambiguous assemblage not only empirically and theoretically, but also normatively.

This leads to the sixth and last issue increasingly recognized as crucial for a deeper understanding of how justice is perceived, experienced, and remade—namely, the affectual grounding and embodied emotional responses mobilized in order to reinforce or oppose the legitimacy of entire normative orders, specific legal processes, or singular, norm-related events. Such 'affective justice' (Bens and Zenker 2017; Clarke 2019) draws our attention, again, to the materiality of the social life of the law, yet this time highlighting the bodily responses of those actors assembled by particular legalities. As ethnographic studies show, this embodiment of the law is not a neutral process; rather, the intersections of emotion, affect, and law vary profoundly depending on the place, culture, and time period in question, and deeply impact the ways in which the law is differentially experienced and practised.

Moreover, this focus on embodiment is also a powerful reflexive reminder of the embodied presence of the researchers themselves, as they empirically engage in their own specific sociolegal fields. It draws our attention to both the need to rethink and the potential of rethinking the actual *presence* of the law (comprising our own presence therein as scholars) as differentially embodied and positioned in particular moments and various longer *durées*, with regard to entangled dialectics of power and empowerment, and thus as sites of hope and despair and, ultimately, as a *problématique* through which legal practitioners, legal scholars, and anthropologists can reflexively learn from each other and productively join forces in expanding future legal anthropological research and practice.

By way of conclusion

There is a final thought we would like to share with our readers. Like any such project, this volume is ineluctably a product of its time. Thus, not only the distribution of topics across the various chapters, but also their organization and the choice of authors are the fruit of an effort that, in a different era, would produce a different work. From the outset, we sought to balance the structure of the *Handbook* as a whole in three ways: first, by inviting an even mix of well-recognized senior scholars and more junior scholars; second, by creating a good balance of legal scholars and anthropologists; and third, by highlighting and giving voice to scholars from different intellectual traditions, including traditions that are often overlooked simply because their work is not disseminated via the usual mainstream channels of scholarly knowledge. We feel we have succeeded in achieving the first two of these objectives but, due to circumstances beyond our control, only to a lesser degree in attaining the third.

While we have managed to assemble a multidimensional volume on law and anthropology, one that brings together a wide range of authors and perspectives, it nevertheless proved difficult in the end to achieve the kind of linguistic, regional, and thematic diversity that we had imagined from the outset. Although one of our objectives with the *Handbook* was to go well beyond the more conventional narratives of the field, which have been indelibly shaped by Euro-American institutions, histories, and languages, we nevertheless found it difficult to produce a volume that ultimately surpassed these narratives. In some cases, scholars from whom we had solicited chapters were prevented from contributing because of the very difficult working and living conditions they find themselves in. This explains, for example, why we have no contribution from—or addressing—the Middle East, which we recognize as a shortcoming of the volume as a whole.

Our hope is that future scholars and students will continue to address questions of diversity and representation in ways that reflect their own visions of law and anthropology, visions that will no doubt be nourished by their own experiences and points of view within the context of a dynamic and rapidly evolving interdisciplinary field.

Note

1. The Consultative Committee is a group of experienced scholars from outside the Department who act as a board of advisors in support of the Department's research agenda. The current list of members is available at <https://www.eth.mpg.de/3220891/consultative_committee>.

References

Baogang, H. 2006. 'Consultancy: A Different Gate to the Field'. In M. Heimer and S. Thogersen, eds. *Doing Fieldwork in China*, 168–87. Copenhagen: NIAS Press.

Benda-Beckmann, F. von and K. von Benda-Beckmann. 2002. 'Anthropology of Law and the Study of Folk Law in the Netherlands after 1950'. In H. Vermeulen and J. Kommers, eds. *Tales from Academia: History of Anthropology in the Netherlands, Part 2*, 695–731. Saarbrücken: Verlag für Entwicklungspolitik.

Bens, J. and O. Zenker, eds. 2017. *Gerechtigkeitsgefühle: zur affektiven und emotionalen Legitimität von Normen*. Bielefeld: Transcript.

Breau, S. C. 2007. 'Human Rights and Cultural Relativism: The False Dichotomy'. In J. Rehman and S. C. Breau, eds. *Religion, Human Rights and International Law: A Critical Examination of Islamic State Practices*, 137–65. Leiden/Boston: Martinus Nijhoff Publishers.

Brutti, L. 2005. 'Where Anthropologists Fear to Tread: Notes and Queries on Anthropology and Consultancy, Inspired by a Fieldwork Experience'. In P. J. Stewart and A. Strathern, eds. *Anthropology and Consultancy: Issues and Debates*, 106–23. New York/Oxford: Berghahn Books.

Burke, P. 2011. *Law's Anthropology: From Ethnography to Expert Testimony in Native Title*. Acton, ACT (Australia): ANU Press.

Clarke, K. M. 2019. *Affective Justice: The International Criminal Court and the Pan-Africanist Pushback*. Durham: Duke University Press.

Comaroff, J. and J. Comaroff, eds. 2006. *Law and Disorder in the Postcolony*. Chicago: University of Chicago Press.

Daly, R. 2004. 'Anthropological Consultancy and the Crisis of Globalization'. In B. Morris and R. Bastin, eds. *Expert Knowledge: First World Peoples, Consultancy and Anthropology*, 80–8. New York/London: Berghahn Books.

Davis, D.-A. 2008. 'Knowledge in the Service of a Vision: Politically Engaged Anthropology'. In V. Sanford and A. Angel-Ajani, eds. *Engaged Observer: Anthropology, Advocacy, and Activism*, 228–38. New Brunswick/London: Rutgers University Press.

Destrooper, T. and S. E. Merry, eds. 2018. *Human Rights Transformation in Practice*. Philadelphia: University of Pennsylvania Press.

Donovan, J. 2007. *Legal Anthropology*. Latham: Altamira Press.

Dyck, N. 1993. '"Telling It Like It Is": Some Dilemmas of Fourth World Ethnography and Advocacy'. In N. Dyck and J. B. Waldram, eds. *Anthropology, Public Policy, and Native Peoples in Canada*, 192–212. Montreal: McGill-Queen's University Press.

Eckert, J., B. Donahoe, C. Strümpell, and Z. Biner, eds. 2012. *Law against the State: Ethnographic Forays into Law's Transformations*. Cambridge: Cambridge University Press.

Fikentscher, W. 2009. *Law and Anthropology: Outlines, Issues, and Suggestions*. Munich: C. H. Beck.

Goodale, M. 2017. *Anthropology and Law: A Critical Introduction*. New York: NYU Press.

Goodale, M. and S. E. Merry, eds. 2007. *The Practice of Human Rights: Tracking Law between the Global and the Local*. Cambridge: Cambridge University Press.

Hinz, M. O. 2009. 'Human Rights between Universalism and Cultural Relativism? The Need for Anthropological Jurisprudence in the Globalising World'. In A. Bösl and J. Diescho, eds. *Human Rights in Africa: Legal Perspectives on their Protection and Promotion*, 3–32. Windhoek: Macmillan Education Namibia.

Holden, L., ed. 2011. *Cultural Expertise and Litigation: Pattern, Conflicts, Narratives*. Abingdon/New York: Routledge.

Hull, M. S. 2012. *Government of Paper: The Materiality of Bureaucracy in Urban Pakistan*. Berkeley: University of California Press.

Ibhawoh, B. 2004. 'Restraining Universalism: Africanist Perspectives on Cultural Relativism in the Human Rights Discourse'. In P. T. Zeleza and P. J. MCConnaughay, eds. *Human Rights, the Rule of Law, and Development in Africa*, 21–39. Philadelphia: University of Pennsylvania Press.

Kandel, R.F. 1992. *Double Vision: Anthropologists at Law*. Hoboken, N.J.: Wiley.

Kirsch, S. 2014. *Mining Capitalism: The Relationship between Corporations and their Critics*. Oakland: University of California Press.

Lampe, E.-J. 1970. *Legal Anthropology: A Structural Analysis of Man in Law*. Berlin: Duncker & Humblot.

Malkki, L. H. 1995. 'Refugess and Exile: From 'Refugee Studies' to the National Order of Things'. *Annual Review of Anthropology* 24: 495–523.

Menski, W. 2011. 'Life and Law: Advocacy and Expert Witnessing in the UK'. In L. Holden (ed.), *Cultural Expertise and Litigation: Pattern, Conflicts, Narratives*, 151–71. Abingdon/New York: Routledge.

Mertz, E. and M. Goodale. 2012. 'Comparative Anthropology of Law'. In D. S. Clark, ed. *Comparative Law and Society*, 77–91. Cheltenham: Edward Elgar.

Moore, S. F. 2004. *Law and Anthropology: A Reader*. Malden: Wiley.

Morris, B. and R. Bastin (eds). 2004. *Expert Knowledge: First World Peoples, Consultancy, and Anthropology*. Oxford: Berghahn.

Niezen, R. 2014. 'The Law's Legal Anthropology'. In M. Goodale, ed. *Human Rights at the Crossroads*, 185–97. Oxford: Oxford University Press.

Pirie, F. 2013. *The Anthropology of Law*. Oxford: Oxford University Press.

Pityana, N. B. 2004. 'Toward a Theory of Applied Cultural Relativism in Human Rights'. In P. T. Zeleza and P. J. McConnaughay, eds. *Human Rights, the Rule of Law, and Development in Africa*, 40–51. Philadelphia: University of Pennsylvania Press.

Ringelheim, J. 2010. 'Minority Rights in a Time of Multiculturalism: The Evolving Scope of the Framework Convention on the Protection of National Minorities'. *Human Rights Law Review* 10: 99–128.

Ríos Vega, L.E, I. Ruggiu, and I. Spigno (eds). 2020. *Justice and Culture: Theory and Practice Concerning the Use of Culture in the Courtroom.* Naples: Editoriale Scientifica.

Rouland, N. 1988. *L'anthropologie juridique.* Paris: PUF.

Sacco, R. 2007. *Antropologia Giuridica.* Bologna: il Mulino.

Sack, P., P. C. Wellman, and M. Yasaki. 1991. *Monismus oder Pluralisus der Rechtskulturen? Anthropologische und ethnologische Grundlagen traditioneller und moderner Rechtssysteme.* Berlin: Duncker & Humblot.

Sarat, A. (ed). 2019. *Cultural Expertise and Socio-legal Studies (Studies in Law, Politics and Society*, v. 78, special issue edited by L. Holden). Bingley, UK: Emerald Publishing Limited.

Scillitani, L. 1980. *Studi di antropologia giuridica.* Naples: Jovene, Napoli.

Scott, J. C. 1998. *Seeing Like a State: How Certain Schemes to Improve the Human Condition Have Failed.* New Haven: Yale University Press.

Singer, M. 2008. 'Applied Anthropology'. In H. Kuklick, ed. *A New History of Anthropology*, 326–40. Malden: Blackwell.

Sousa Santos, B. de and C. Rodriguez-Garavito. 2005. 'Law Politics, and the Subaltern in Counter-Hegemonic Globalization'. In B. de Sousa Santos and C. Rodriguez-Garavito, eds. *Law and Globalization from Below: Towards a Cosmopolitan Legality*, 1–26. Cambridge: Cambridge University Press.

Starr, J. and J. F. Collier, eds. 1989. *History and Power in the Study of the Law: New Directions in Legal Anthropology.* Ithaca: Cornell University Press.

Strathern, A. and P. Stuart. 2005. 'Introduction: Anthropology and Consultancy—Ethnographic Dilemmas and Opportunities'. In P. J. Stewart and A. Strathern, eds. *Anthropology and Consultancy: Issues and Debates*, 1–24. New York/Oxford: Berghahn Books.

Takirambudde, P. 2001. 'Building the Record for Human Rights Violations in Africa—the Functions of Monitoring, Investigation and Advocacy'. In D. Barnhizer, ed. *Effective Strategies for Protecting Human Rights: Prevention and Intervention, Trade and Education*, 11–19. Aldershot: Ashgate.

Thompson, E. P. 1977. *Whigs and Hunters: The Origins of the Black Act.* London: Penguin Books.

Turner, T., L. R. Graham, C. Fluehr-Lobban, and J. K. Cowan. 2009. 'Anthropology and Human Rights: Do Anthropologists Have an Ethical Obligation to Promote Human Rights? An Open Exchange'. In M. Goodale, ed. *Human Rights: An Anthropological Reader*, 198–205. Malden: Wiley-Blackwell.

Vertovec, S. 2007. 'Super-Diversity and Its Implications'. *Ethnic and Racial Studies* 30(6): 1024–54.

Vetters, L. and M.-C. Foblets. 2016. 'Culture all Around? Contextualising Anthropological Expertise in European Courtroom Settings'. *International Journal of Law in Context* 12(3): 272–92.

Vismann, C. 2008. *Files: Law and Media Technology.* Stanford: Stanford University Press.

Warren, K. B. 2008. 'Perils and Promises of Engaged Anthropology. Historical Transitions and Ethnographic Dilemmas'. In V. Sanford and A. Angel-Ajani, eds. *Engaged Observer: Anthropology, Advocacy, and Activism*, 213–27. New Brunswick/London: Rutgers University Press.

Zenker, O. 2016. 'Anthropology on Trial: Exploring the Laws of Anthropological Expertise'. *International Journal of Law in Context* 12(3): 293–311.

PART I

GLOBAL PERSPECTIVES ON LAW AND ANTHROPOLOGY

CHAPTER 1

SOCIAL CONTROL THROUGH LAW

Critical Afterlives

CAROL J. GREENHOUSE

INTRODUCTION

SOCIAL *control* became a term of art in the twentieth century, a phrase once used routinely by scholars from law and anthropology to refer to law's presumed effects on determining social norms and the values that shape everyday relationships. Today, given its implication of pervasive coercion, it has a jarring—perhaps even ugly—ring. Over the past century, its history of usage has been shaped by world events and corresponding debates over law's hegemony. The controlling practices of law (e.g. in contexts of policing, migration, labour, and various forms of social support) continue to be areas of active research engagement among anthropologists; however, social control is no longer their unifying theoretical rubric. The assumption that law is controlling as if by definition has given way to considerations of personal agency, resistance, political mobilization, and interlegality. But projects of social control through law are a fact of public policymaking, potentially affecting anyone in their personal autonomy, partnerships, or community status. If the term still has meaning today, it is as a reference to the creation of legal subjects for political purposes—i.e. subjects defined in ways that are integral to the means and ends of governing.

Even if the idea of law as social control is no longer part of anthropology's current theoretical repertoire, it is a principle of governance. In various ways, especially where the line between public and private interests fades, the relation between law and social control looms large. Questions of who is controlling whom through law, and to what ends, are perhaps even more pressing now than they were decades ago, given the extent to which state power has become concentrated in executive authority and institutions of supranational governance have accumulated powers and authorities of their own.

Anthropologists no longer accept the inevitability of top-down power without alternatives or response, but this does not mean that assertions of power and attempts to restrict opposition are any less important as social facts; rather, it means that social control through law is not a one-way street. Social control through law entails plural multilateral political projects.

Those multisided projects involve the play of interests, norms, and strategic alliances such as have been of longstanding concern to anthropologists. In this sense, the ethnography of law is well-suited to analysing the pervasively blurred boundaries we see today between public and private interests. As liberalization has aggrandized the private sector in recent decades, ethnographers' absorption in questions of agency and self-interest in everyday life has tended to conflate the controlling *purposes* of state law with the *functions* of law more broadly conceived (see Starr and Collier 1989: 5). In this sense, some renewed attention to social control through law as a politics of purpose offers a necessary and at least partial corrective, where evidence is available. It is law's functions (intended or unintended) that have been of primary interest to anthropologists, but this leaves to one side the ongoing role of state actors and others in setting up the conditions of private life, as well as the specific purposes those actors and their challengers bring to law before and after the fact. The purposes of such laws—as conceived, refused, or defended *before* the fact—are as important to anthropological understandings of law and society as are law's functions after the fact.

Where evidence can be found (in documents or by other methods), examining social control through law, approached as a politics of purpose, would add to scholars' understanding of the specificity of law's power in governing as well as in relation to the idea of governability—including law's availability to call governors to account (see Green 2013; Thomas and Clarke 2013). By *politics of purpose* in the context of social control projects, I refer to competing demands for law substantiated explicitly in a discourse of social evaluation that conjures identity as a legal object (e.g. cultural attributes, behavioural probabilities, social costs). Quite apart from the social effects of law after the fact, such ongoing political contests for control through law inform both democratic possibility and the legibility of experience.

The thesis of this chapter is that the idea *social control through law* still has life—not, as in the past, as a reference to generalized functions of law presumed to be its social effects, but as a reference to specific purposes of law integral to national governance in a transnational context. The organization of the rest of this chapter is in two main parts. The first part traces a twentieth-century history of ideas, focusing on anthropologists' early engagements with legal scholars in a context of their mutual awareness of and shared interests in rules, legal systems, and the pragmatic development of law in contexts of coloniality and modernization. Over the decades, while anthropologists' sense of the social life of law broadened, states' controlling practices most directly targeting individuals, communities, and populations *also* shifted significantly into the private sector under the banner of liberalization. In the second part, I focus on the United States in the 1980s and 1990s to suggest how the political project of liberalization—conceived there as a project of global modernization—involved particular projects of social control specifically targeting racial minorities and the urban poor.[1] This period precedes our own troubled times, but in the United States, I believe it is in that earlier era that key conditions of possibility were set for the current nativist populist resurgence—since it was then that liberalization, broadly conceived as disembedding social security from the state, achieved the status of common sense in both of the major political parties, breaking a social contract with the poor, especially the African American and Latinx urban poor.[2] Projects of social control are inseparable from the very meanings of state, nation, personhood, race, class, and gender as human relations—a source of instrumental inequality. In the conclusion, I suggest that in the current environment, in the United States and elsewhere, anthropologists and legal scholars have much to say to each other, given the stakes in resolving the ambiguities that make understanding what is public and what is private both difficult and urgent in these demanding new scenarios of social control.

Three decades ago, anthropologist Andrew Arno offered the insight that the production and maintenance of inequality is the fundamental question for the anthropology of law (Arno 1985: 40). His observation was prescient, as today that question is precisely the most urgent one inspiring ethnographic research and interdisciplinary collaboration between anthropology and law. Current events make inescapably clear (if indeed escape was ever possible before) the political and economic character of social control, especially where social regulation is accomplished through protocols of eligibility for public assistance or restrictions on movement. Promoting such antagonisms as rich and poor, owners and workers, migrants and natives, self-sufficiency and dependency as if they were the natural consequence of inherent differences is integral to the legitimation of political authority and its controlling effects through the legal process—an effect of what John and Jean Comaroff call 'lawfare' (Comaroff and Comaroff 2006: 22). A focus on the making of political subjects highlights a thread connecting domains of law, economy, politics, and religion (among others), yet without putting law everywhere and without conflating all norms as if essentially legal in character. Even legal norms are not only or wholly legal; a basic premise of social studies of law is that law does not govern alone.

Shifting Conversations between Anthropology and Law

A century ago, and for some decades subsequently, anthropologists and lawyers interested in the cultural aspects of law found common ground in their studies of particular types of legal projects in colonial settings, notably involving labour, land and other forms of property, governance, and rights (see Nader 1965: 3). Anthropology came to social control as a theoretical concern in the context of the legal administration of indigenous communities and settler interests in colonizing projects in Africa, the United States, and elsewhere. Those histories are well established (Anders 2015; Chanock 1985, also this volume; Simpson 2014; Starr and Collier 1989). In the early decades of the twentieth century, both disciplines focused on judges or other authorities such as chiefs, representing their judgments as applications of rules that, in turn, were presumed to reflect cultural norms. The idea of culture carried with it—at that time for both lawyers and anthropologists—a corporate implication (i.e. culture constituting the lifeways and systems of thought binding a discrete social unit together).

Lawyers' interest in the pragmatics of self-regulation broadened with globalization and became more instrumental in relation to policy debates over regulation (Shamir 2011). Lawyers interested in promoting alternative dispute resolution forums as a means of broadening access to law also borrowed extensively from anthropologists (Edwards 1986; Stone 2004; see also Nader 1980). Meanwhile, in contrast to these projects of scaling up, and drawn by their own understandings of globalization as cultural flows accessible locally, anthropologists scaled down to pursue questions of power, agency, and legal change as localized cultural practices (Starr and Collier 1989: 25). The new formulations of globalization as cultural 'scapes' (Appadurai 1990) also inspired new comparative and translocal projects, as key elements of localized authority could be found in the transnational circulation of particular forms of power and legal authority (Clarke 2009; Merry 1992).

Paradoxically, as legal anthropology, sociolegal studies, and law and society scholarship flourished, the exchanges between lawyers and anthropologists over issues of social control waned, leaving a rift that remains challenging today (Anders 2015: 412; Kesselring et al. 2017; Mertz 2008; Mertz, Mitchell, and Macaulay 2016; Riles 2011; Sapignoli 2017). It leaves relatively unexplored a conceptual divide between the local and the global, as well as between understandings of globalization as an emergent sphere of harmonization (more readily embraced by lawyers than by anthropologists) or as an intensification of difference (vice versa). It risks leaving unaddressed crucial questions of the disparate distribution of law's violence, as both means and ends of an international security strategy predicated on embodied forms of social control. In short, that zone between disciplines is precisely where social control issues now re-emerge as a shared concern for anthropologists and lawyers.

The ongoing relevance of colonial and settler histories to the development of anthropology as a discipline is well established. Less well remarked are the ongoing associations of social control with class and racial formations as neoliberalism has advanced globally as a political movement—currently visible in the diverse forms of neoliberal nationalism that have emerged under the banner of populism in Europe, Latin America, and the United States. In this context, new debates engaging anthropologists and lawyers have emerged, building on their earlier debates and collaborations over the cultural defence in the criminal law context, the limits of legal pluralism, and the legal rights of cultural minorities and women—to name just a few examples.[3]

Social control between anthropology and law

As a history of ideas, the century of anthropological scholarship *on* law is marked by a series of classic theoretical conversations between anthropology *and* law.[4] The genealogy of the field of legal anthropology points to this dual ancestry.[5] At least in the Anglophone world, in the first decades of the twentieth century, anthropologists turned to law so as to respond to the claims lawyers were making about 'primitive law'—cartoonish stereotypes well known to anthropologists from Malinowski's critique of them (Malinowski 1926: Chapter 1). Lawyers were interested in anthropology, meanwhile, specifically with regard to issues framed as questions of legal evolution, social control, and law enforcement outside the Western world (Moore 1969: 257). Those exchanges shaped anthropologists' early conversations with academic law, especially after Malinowski stimulated questions that were absorbing to both anthropologists and lawyers with regard to classifying and comparing legal systems, together with descriptions of their rules and sanctions (Moore 1969: 253, 260, 268).

To the extent that their searches for law originated in questions advanced by the legal profession, anthropologists for much of the twentieth century found law more or less by analogy, and therefore more or less everywhere.[6] Throughout most of the twentieth century, legal anthropology was in a sense the essence of sociocultural anthropology as a whole—crystallized around the normative aspects of social organization and an idea of culture as a system of shared beliefs.

The common purpose behind the earliest exchanges between lawyers and anthropologists around the turn of the last century was predicated on conceptual distinctions that neither anthropologists nor lawyers defend today, even if they leave their traces. These included key distinctions between simple and complex societies, primitive and modern law, and law and norms. Early anthropologists, like their law colleagues, maintained a view of so-called primitive society as homogeneous and primitive culture as conformist and inherently controlling. In scholars' imaginations, the default condition of social life was essentially one of order, normally self-regulated by the effects of social pressures ritually or regularly applied, if occasionally punctuated by acts of deviance or offence that constituted isolated disruptions calling for repair under the law. In retrospect, the category *law*, conceived in this way, is *post hoc*, as if self-evident and self-reinforcing in common attitudes and behaviours.

By mid-century, among anthropologists, these premises had slipped away (in some cases, because they were pushed), as they developed the concept of law ethnographically around other understandings of culture and society, as well as other questions, methods, and rationales—particularly as the discipline expanded beyond small-scale societies under colonial rule. By the 1960s, the premise that had portrayed social order and normative coherence as the default conditions of social life gave way to different expectations—now regarding conflict as a normal feature of social experience, and pluralism as normal to the social reality of law. As Moore phrases the matter retrospectively, 'No society is without law; *ergo*, there is no society outside the purview of the "legal anthropologist"' (Moore 1969: 252). Or, as Jane Collier states the premise, 'Legal processes are social processes. Law is not above and apart from society, but is an aspect of ongoing social life' (Collier 1975: 121). It was anthropologists' very concept of law that made their society-level descriptions possible in the first place, making localism into a legalism (see e.g. Brown 1952).

When the first syntheses of legal anthropology appeared in print around mid-century (Nader 1965; Moore 1969; Collier 1975), legal anthropology was not yet a recognized subfield, perhaps in part because its theoretical contributions to the discipline had not yet been articulated, remaining submerged within the very idea of society and culture as units of study and analysis, in Nader's original formulation (Nader 1965: 3). Indeed, in 1965, Nader formulated the state of the discipline in these very terms: 'Anthropologists are no longer attempting to prove the absence or presence of law in primitive societies by reference to any single definition of law. Rather the question has become: How is the law best conceived of *for research purposes?*' (Nader 1965: 6; my emphasis). She ascribes the search for legal universals among anthropologists to the influence of legal scholars (Nader 1965: 4–7)—even as anthropologists developed more context-sensitive comparative analyses across their ethnographic case studies.

Indeed, as her own critical readings also make plain (Nader 1965: 9–11), the assumption that the ethnography of law is an inherently comparative project is but a small step from the conviction that law presents a unified field procedurally, substantively, and theoretically. The specificity of law, then, was to be found elsewhere, and this led anthropologists to their concerns with conflict, disputes, and normative claims as articulated in law cases or other expressions of conflict (see Moore 1969: 271–82). The idea of ethnography as instantiating a universal paradigm of legal authority and normative judgment faded as ethnographic work accumulated. Today, legal anthropologists study diverse forms of agency, interest, discursivity, and power relations associated with the interlegalities of colonial and state law and indigenous custom, formal and informal law, demands for rights and recognition, and the substantive claims on legal authority arising from those situations. Jane Collier's observation from 1975 remains true today, that 'with the passage of time, anthropologists have become less concerned to identify the "legal" and more concerned with law as a social process' (Collier 1975: 139).

The ethnographic focus on *dispute settlement* as indicative of law meant that ethnographic description of settlement processes was prone to muddle the enunciation of norms with observations of behaviour in public. An advance on this approach came about when anthropologists began to consider more seriously the sources of conflict in social stratification, inequalities, indignities, and other sources of grievance—i.e. beyond instances of normative disrepair. As Collier observes, anthropologists at mid-century remained divided over whether conflict is an outcome of randomly distributed disregard for others' sensibilities or interests or—very much on the contrary—symptomatic of social cleavages concealed by the denials or occlusions apparent in the normative order (1975: 122).

The idea of law was subsumed into a blended focus on prescription, description, mobilization, and disposition (the terms are Collier's; see Collier 1975: 121). Disputing and dispute settlement formed the ethnographic domain most closely associated with the anthropology of law, lending legal anthropology an implicit identification with the perspectives of judges, plaintiffs, juries, and partisans. Looking ahead from the discipline as she saw it in the early 1960s, Laura Nader advocated for a more multistranded approach: 'If we are to develop a true ethnography of law the angle of vision of the ethnographer needs to be broadened in order to include descriptions that would explicate law as part of a many-threaded fabric. Furthermore we should look at both the latent and the manifest functions of the law' (Nader 1965: 17).

But even as the anthropology of law became more embedded in social processes and attuned to the social functions of law beyond dispute settlement, its preferred objects largely retained their implicit association with judgment and punishment, sustaining that association with a concept of culture defined by consensus and coercion (i.e. two infrastructures of social control). As she formulated the priorities of a future legal anthropology in 1965, Nader's first recommendation was that 'empirical studies of law should be set in the general context of social control (although of course not equated with social control)' (Nader 1965: 17). The emphasis on social control reflected the Malinowskian tradition—in his day, advancing the anthropology of law with the implication that 'law' can be understood as 'embrac[ing] all forms of social control' regardless of its institutional location or apparatus (Comaroff and Roberts 1981: 11; see also Hermitte 1970).

Legal anthropologists at mid-century noticed the intersection of their theories and methods with those of academic lawyers and colonial administrators (or their postcolonial successors), even as they parted company. Some lawyers who pursued descriptions of rules and their application did so in aid of their aspirations to a global jurisprudence (see e.g. Black 1965: ix, x; cf. Kingsbury, Krisch, and Stewart 2005: 16). In retrospect, it seems that lawyers' interest in 'preliterate societies' might have been a proxy for their more fundamental interest in debates within liberalism—over rights and regulation, for example, for individuals and corporations (cf. Moore 1969: 257–8). Today, to the extent that such proxies persist, it is perhaps especially in the realm of corporate form—corporations that are assumed to enjoy regulatory autonomy (and allowed by law to do so) to an extent formerly imagined for indigenous communities without law (or as we understand more fully today, with law under colonial rule).

For anthropologists, pursuing law ethnographically through discourse opened fresh ethnographic and comparative possibilities, as attention to the forms of agency inherent in (and performed as) language vastly expanded the ethnographic domains of interpretation and political relations (Arno 1985; Bernstein 2017; Mertz 1994; Richland 2018; Spears 2000). Relatedly, as Jane Collier emphasizes in her influential essay (1975), the ethnography of law was turning to agency ('choice making' in Collier's formulation), putting interpretation and the asymmetries of social relatedness on the same side of the processual coin.

Social control: from content to context

The ethnography of law in the 1970s and 1980s yielded a rich archive of localized studies of disputing, third-party interventions, and strategies of interpersonal contest. New debates over legal pluralism—a further conversation between lawyers and anthropologists—expanded the scope of legal anthropology from law and courts to other domains associated with the choreography of contests for social control (Benda-Beckmann 2002). The scholarship on legal pluralism also contributed significantly to blurring (yet without entirely erasing) the theoretical premises that had divided 'pre-industrial' societies from the 'modern West'—bringing into a shared conceptual space for the first time the interlegalities of former colonies and colonizers, formal and informal law, law and other forms of coercion and constraint (Demian 2015: 93; Benda-Beckmann 2002: 37).

Given world developments since the 1980s affecting the development of national states, transnational mobility, the relation of national states to global institutions, and the implications of these issues for citizens and communities (Sassen 1996), legal anthropology is well placed at the forefront of the discipline with respect to issues of power, agency, resistance, and change in these contexts. Anthropologists started bringing history and power into their ethnographic frames, connecting questions of meaning in time and place to political contests and their wider social contexts (Geertz 1983; Hirsch and Lazarus-Black 1986; Just 1992: 375; Moore 1986; Starr and Collier 1989). *Power* became a new keyword for anthropology at this time, adjoining questions of contest and hierarchy to problems of knowledge and meaning (Ortner 1995: 175; Just 1992: 375). In this milieu, social control was less useful as a theoretical rubric given its implicit one-sidedness. The localism of legal anthropology tended to keep national states outside the ethnographic frame; nonetheless, anthropologists contributed extensively to the study of state law from the vantage point of law's hegemony in private social relations (Comaroff and Comaroff 1991: 19, 27; Hirsch and Lazarus-Black 1986; see also Merry 2000 and Ortner 1995: esp. 184–6). Significantly, their focus on localized 'dynamics of hegemony and resistance' (Hirsch and Lazarus-Black 1986: 6) suspended what had long lingered as a methodological divide between ethnographies of the global South and the global North. Distinctions such as simple/complex, pre-industrial/industrial, and traditional/modern faded from anthropology as marginalized communities in North and South alike were targeted for 'structural adjustment' and 'liberalization' (Comaroff and Comaroff 2016). The economization of social control represented a significant shift in policy fields, one with direct bearing on the constitution of legal subjects and the politics of purpose as related to law. This brings us to the extended example from the United States, illustrating connections between social control through law as a project involving the creation of legal subjects for political purposes.

Social control: new means to old ends

At the time that structural adjustment and other liberalization reforms were being put in place in the 1980s in the name of economic development, policymaking was not yet the major ethnographic focus that it has since become (influential exceptions were Ferguson 1994 and Gupta 1998). Still, ethnography flourished in communities directly in the policy shadows. The social control motives of policymakers were both explicit and implicit. In the United States, in the late 1980s and 1990s, major legislative 'reforms' curtailed aid to the poor, migrants' rights, and other social resources—restructuring not only the social fields in which anthropologists were primarily engaged, but also the very meaning of *identity* in the discipline (Greenhouse 2011; Morgen and Maskovsky 2003; Rouse 1995). In this brief discussion, I refer to the Civil Rights Act of 1991 (on discrimination in employment practices), the Welfare Reform Act of 1996 (curtailing entitlements to federal relief for the poor), and criminal justice reform acts in 1984 and 1988 that established federal sentencing guidelines and expanded the criminalization of drug use.

Promoted politically throughout the 1980s and early 1990s on claims that welfare payments incentivize dependency and undermine marriage, the welfare reform campaign at the federal level targeted racial minorities—effectively (and falsely) blaming a 'culture' of dependency for the disparate rate of poverty in African American and Latinx communities, and as a rationale for terminating key federal social security supports. The language of the legislation that was ultimately passed in 1996 is race neutral, but as the extensive transcripts of congressional committee hearings attest, congressional proponents of the Welfare Reform Act of 1996 racialized welfare as a strategy for depoliticizing inequality—i.e. shifting the discourse of benefits to costs, and uncoupling race from class by pathologizing poverty among racial minorities (Greenhouse 2011). After extensive debate, the measure passed the Congress with bipartisan support. The federal welfare rolls were further cut by reducing the eligibility of immigrants.

The late 1980s were also a period of intense political investment in measures aimed at controlling crime. 'The culture of control' (Garland 2001) expanded criminalization and imposed heavy mandatory sentences, resulting in massive incarcerations disproportionately affecting young men of colour. Among its many effects, prison overcrowding became a pretext for federal contracts with private prisons, a controversial innovation advanced with the express purpose of reducing barriers to privatization of core governmental functions.[7] Federal prisons have long required inmates to work (under a combination of rehabilitative and revenue-generation rationales), but now, for the first time, the same legislation that filled the prisons included provision for inmate labour in the private sector, in areas where there was no appropriate local labour pool—a form of reverse outsourcing. The connections between criminalization, mass incarceration, privatization, and transnational labour markets are explicit in the debates in Congress and elsewhere related to these developments (Aman and Greenhouse 2014).

In the markedly pro-business climate of this period, Congress meanwhile faced rising demands for protection against discrimination on the basis of race and other criteria barred by legislation or court rulings—and, from business owners, demands for protection against anti-discrimination lawsuits. The U.S. Supreme Court had narrowed the grounds for a finding of race discrimination, and liberal members of Congress now sought to backstop that retreat. Their first effort, the Civil Rights Act of 1990, passed the Congress but was vetoed by President George H. W. Bush on the grounds that it might add excessively to employers' exposure to litigation; there were insufficient votes to overturn the veto. But the following year, a successor bill passed as the Civil Rights Act of 1991.[8] This version of the law shifted the burden of proof of discrimination from the employer to the disappointed employee, and it eliminated non-discrimination requirements for U.S. companies overseas under foreign management—two important accommodations to the demands for flexibilization and maximum circulation of capital that advanced liberalization at the expense of anti-discrimination rights enforcement (Greenhouse 2011).

These were new forms of exclusion, in the sense that they were accomplished through a politicization of a new discourse of equality—on the one hand restricting access to law where anti-discrimination could be reframed as special or community rights and, on the other hand, expanding it where a discourse of universal individual rights could prevail. A direct trade-off between civil rights and social security could thereby be submerged within a discursive reconfiguration of equality defined as a relation *apart* from race.

As the U.S. government deregulated industry and other market sectors in the 1980s and 1990s, it relied on theories of self-regulation predicated on social science notions of the corporate form as inherently self-governing (Sarfaty 2015; Shamir 2011). The importance of these developments for purposes of this chapter is the extent to which they relied on specific and explicit ideas of social control as both principles of governing and practices of governance. It is in this sense that liberalization and social control came to be interrelated through the creation of fiscal regimes predicated on the racialization of class: criminalized (and literally penalized) at the low end, and privileged at the high end. The implications of these differentials for anthropology were a source of controversy within the discipline.[9]

Social control: Law against itself

With the end of social control as legal anthropology's principal subject, it became instead its principal critical object. Since the 1990s, anthropology's critical resistance to economic globalization as a project of social control has drawn ethnographers into the study of legalisms and legal technique as ethnographic objects in themselves (Latour 2010; Pirie 2013; Riles 2011). This new scholarship has broadened the shared horizon with legal studies while also revealing differences of method and purpose.

As Mark Goodale (2017: 20) has observed, the geopolitical and legal ground under these disciplinary developments has been subject to significant shifts, and sociolegal studies disciplines have marked new paths for themselves, conscious of an increasingly globalized world. After the 1970s, the globalization of law became the dominant path of reform. The 'basic needs revolution' of the 1970s that had been central to the emergence of human rights as a scholarly and activist project became caught in a struggle between equality and sufficiency as competing core principles (Moyn 2018). As 'the dream of a welfare world achieved its highest visibility and was shattered as a neoliberal turn began instead' (Moyn 2018: 120), anthropologists remained with local welfare worlds and counter-globalization movements (e.g. Muehlebach 2012, esp. 53–100; see Aman and Greenhouse 2017: 255–68). In the context of this chapter, it is important to see this disciplinary distance as relatively recent, grounded as it is in contemporary formulations of regulation and social control that do not automatically or inevitably belong to either discipline (on disciplinary translation, see Mertz, Mitchell, and Macaulay 2016; on history, see Moyn 2018).

The legal infrastructures of global neoliberalism after the 1970s—structural adjustment, privatization, the authority of transnational and global non-state institutions, and corporate self-regulation—involved projects of social control that pushed new forms of regulation into locations and relations where anthropologists were already prepared to engage. Developing those infrastructures as matters of state law and policy, and normalizing them as if common sense, absorbed extensive political and material capital on the part of many actors—politicians, lobbyists, and other proponents. In marked contrast to the situation of the 1980s and 1990s, there is now a rich ethnographic literature on the techniques of neoliberal governance and their social effects (Davis 2015; Ferguson 2006; Ganti 2014; Greenhouse 2010; Hirsch 2012; Muehlebach 2012; Pfeiffer and Chapman 2010).

Conclusion

The modern context of concerns with law as social control involves broad sectors of contemporary government and governance. The examples cited in this chapter may be read as clear reminders of the multitudes around the world who live in the gaps between different ideas of *the public*, conceived of as an object of social engineering (see Cody 2011). The rich and the poor are subject to radically different conceptions of law—particularly where an ideology of control undergirds laws governing public expenditure. Housing, employability, pensions, and personal debt figure in such ideologies, clearly, as well as more intimate scenarios of personal liberty. The exclusion of third-party beneficiaries and other stakeholders from participation in setting the terms of contracts between states and private-sector providers marks another crucial zone of inequality (or outright non-recognition). Other current projects of control in the

United States explicitly target the mobility, social security, and access to law by politically disfavoured groups, especially immigrants. It seems social control begins where the social contract ends.

In the early exchanges between lawyers and anthropologists, social control was assumed to be inherent in a natural alignment between legal authority and social norms—the coercive element for the most part submerged within ritualized cultural practices, including incentivized action and, in the breach, punitive sanctions. Today, such an alignment is no longer assumed, even as it has become central to the political promotion and legal expression of liberalization and privatization transnationally. Anthropologists know too much about the diversity of interests and the sources and circuits of power outside of state institutions and their private-sector partners to accept without question the efficacy of deliberate projects of social engineering. Indeed, any stable binary distinction between top/down and bottom/up or insider/outsider is unsustainable as an empirical matter for these same reasons. Anthropologists today tend to approach law in terms of lateral, overlapping social fields of indeterminate scale, contingent on (among other things) networked lines of communication, responsibility, and accountability (Moore 1973; Richland 2013; Valverde 2014). Accordingly, lawyers and anthropologists may be surprised by the extent to which they work at the same scale—for example, in relation to the inner workings of domestic, international, and transnational legal institutions, as well as their impact on individuals and communities, or in relation to public-facing projects of law reform (see e.g. Jean-Klein and Riles 2008; Sarfaty 2015; Offit 2018).

As the connection between the first and second parts of this chapter underscores, privatization has imported a discourse of social control from state regulation into national and transnational private-sector arrangements, blending public and private interests in a complex politics of purpose. For workers, consumers, migrants, and other stakeholders excluded from participation in the regulations that affect their lives, though, the distinction between public and private wants and needs remains sharp-edged (see Larkin 2013). Migration also highlights the social distances between the purposes and functions of social control, as politically popular legal restrictions on migration persistently fail to address questions of the social integration, accommodation, or social security of migrants and natives alike (Coutin 2016). The strategic creation of legal subjects for political purposes also works towards inclusion, for example in humanitarian projects (see Ticktin 2014), human rights (see Goodale 2012: 468; Merry 2006), and campaigns of corporate accountability (see Fortun 2001; Sawyer 2004). These are just some examples of contemporary developments that make this a timely moment for scholars and practitioners in anthropology and law to renew their conversations about social control and the recursivity of power along the 'fault lines of survival' (Petryna and Follis 2015; see also Fitz-Henry 2018). The relevance of anthropology for law is well known as a resource for bringing human faces and voices to impersonal doctrinal debates; however, its relevance to issues of democratic reform is less widely appreciated (see Paley 2002).

Looking to the future, anthropology and law have much to say to each other with respect to broader issues of equality and equity, for example, in the domain of developing legal checks on governmental and corporate powers when these disproportionately affect particular communities negatively or seem to select others for privilege (whether citizens or non-citizens, majority or minority). The benefits of such exchanges also go the other way, enriching ethnography with a sense of interconnected problems, stakes, and agentive commitments within and across locations and jurisdictions. Lawyers and anthropologists can usefully share knowledge in the contractual realms of outsourcing or foreign direct investment to ensure that citizens' and workers' rights are protected as third-party beneficiaries (see Calvao 2016; Sarfaty 2015; Sawyer 2004). No list—no matter how extensive—could encompass all the possibilities. To be sure, the work of lawyers and anthropologists may not always be mutually assimilable, but convergence need not (and sometimes should not) be the goal. 'Unrequited engagements' between disciplines are productively informative in themselves, not impasses to be avoided (Brunson et al. 2018).

Examples abound, once social control, in its relation to the concept of law, is understood as a multisided and varied political relation *through* law, rather than a definition *of* law. The idea of social control through law is at the core of the Weberian implication of states as monopolizing legitimate violence, but that is not the end of the story.

Notes

1. I focus my examples on the United States since my longstanding ethnographic concerns have been with the means and ends of US federal power in everyday life.
2. The current context of this observation includes the refugee crisis in Europe and the travel bans, family separations, and other bars to immigration under the Trump administration—ongoing as this chapter is being written, as are court challenges brought by civil liberties and human rights advocates. In general, it is far from obvious how the idea of culture or the significance of cultural minority status will fare in law or among the public as the scope for investment in a perceived contradiction between democracy and diversity widens—making reflection both more urgent and more difficult (Foblets 2005: 81; 2014).
3. See Alidadi and Foblets 2016 (on legal rights of religious minorities), Sharafi 2008 (on cultural defence), and Benda-Beckmann and Turner 2019 (on legal pluralism and the state); also this volume.
4. I date the century from Barton's 1919 study of the Ifugao.
5. I use 'legal anthropology' and 'anthropology of law' interchangeably. This is not universal practice (see Kesserling et al. 2017).
6. For critical overviews, see Benda-Beckmann 2002 and Benda-Beckmann and Turner 2019.
7. Federal Prison Industries (FPI) took its modern form with the passage of the Anti-Drug Abuse Act of 1988 (P.L. 100-690) (100th Congress, 2nd session)—legislation that resulted in a massive rise in convictions and incarcerations in federal prisons.
8. Public Law 102-166; 102nd Congress.
9. E.g. on domination and resistance as ethnographic questions, compare Ortner (1995: 177, 190) and Comaroff and Comaroff (1991: 19, 27). See also Unger 2017.

References

Alidadi, K. and M-C. Foblets. 2016. 'European Supranational Courts and the Fundamental Right to Freedom of Religion or Belief: Convergence or Competition?'. *Oxford Journal of Law and Religion* 5(3): 532–40.

Aman, A. C., Jr. and C. J. Greenhouse 2017. *Transnational Law: Cases and Problems in an Interconnected World*. Durham, NC: Carolina Academic Press.

Aman, A. C., Jr. and C. J. Greenhouse. 2014. 'Prison Privatization and Inmate Labor in the Global Economy: Reframing the Debate over Private Prisons'. *Fordham Urban Law Journal* 42: 355–409.

Anders, G. 2015. 'Law at Its Limits: Interdisciplinarity between Law and Anthropology'. *Journal of Legal Pluralism* 47(3): 411–22.

Appadurai, A. 1990. 'Disjuncture and Difference in the Global Cultural Economy'. *Theory, Culture & Society* 7(2–3): 295–310.

Arno, A. 1985. 'Structural Communication and Control Communication: An Interactionist Perspective on Legal and Customary Procedures for Conflict Management'. *American Anthropologist* 87(1): 40–55.

Barton, R. F. 1919. 'Ifugao Law'. *University of California Publications in American Archaeology and Ethnology* 15(1): 1–186.

Benda-Beckmann, F. von. 2002. '"Who's Afraid of Legal Pluralism?"' *Journal of Legal Pluralism* 34(47): 37–82.

Benda-Beckmann, K. von and B. Turner. 2019. 'Legal Pluralism, Social Theory, and the State'. *Journal of Legal Pluralism and Unofficial Law*. (January). DOI: 10.1080/07329113.2018.1532674.

Bernstein, A. 2017. 'Bureaucratic Speech: Language Choice and Democratic Identity in the Taipei Bureaucracy'. *PoLAR: Political and Legal Anthropology Review* 40(1): 28–51.

Black, C., Jr. 1965. 'Foreword'. In M. Gluckman, *Ideas of Barotse Jurisprudence*, ix–xii. New Haven: Yale University Press.

Brown, P. 1952. 'Changes in Ojibwa Social Control'. *American Anthropologist* 54(1): 57–70.

Brunson, E. K., J. M. Mulligan, E. Andaya, M. Melo, and S. Sered. 2018. 'Public Anthropologies—Unrequited Engagement: Misadventures in Advocating for Medicaid Expansion'. *American Anthropologist* 120(3) (August) DOI: 10.1111/aman.13064.

Calvao, F. 2016. 'Unfree Labor'. *Annual Review of Anthropology* 45: 451–67.

Chanock, M. 1985. *Law, Custom, and Social Order: The Colonial Experience in Malawi and Zambia*. Cambridge: Cambridge University Press.

Clarke, K. 2009. *Fictions of Justice: The International Criminal Court and the Challenge of Legal Pluralism in Sub-Saharan Africa*. Cambridge: Cambridge University Press.

Cody, F. 2011. 'Publics and Politics'. *Annual Review of Anthropology* 40: 37–42.

Collier, J. 1975. 'Legal Processes'. *Annual Review of Anthropology* 4: 121–144.

Comaroff, J. 1991. *Of Revelation and Revolution, vol. 1: Christianity, Colonialism, and Consciousness in South Africa*. Chicago: University of Chicago Press.

Comaroff, J. and J. L. Comaroff. 2016 [2012]. *Theory from the South: Or, How Euro-America is Evolving Toward Africa*. Oxford: Routledge.

Comaroff, J. L. 2006. 'Law and Disorder in the Postcolony: An Introduction'. In J. and J. L. Comaroff, eds. *Law and Disorder in the Postcolony*, 1–56. Chicago: University of Chicago Press.

Comaroff, J. L. and S. Roberts. 1981. *Rules and Processes: The Cultural Logic of Dispute in an African Context*. Chicago: University of Chicago Press.

Coutin, S. B. 2016. *Exiled Home: Salvadoran Transnational Youth in the Aftermath of Violence*. Durham: Duke University Press.

Davis, E. 2015. '"We've Toiled Without End": Publicity, Crisis, and the Suicide "Epidemic" in Greece'. *Comparative Studies in Society and History* 57(4): 1007–36.

Demian, M. 2015. 'Dislocating Custom'. *PoLAR: Political and Legal Anthropology Review* 38(1): 91–107.

Edwards, H. T. 1986. 'Alternative Dispute Resolution: Panacea or Anathema?' *Harvard Law Review* 99(3): 668–84.

Ferguson, J. 1994. *The Anti-Politics Machine*. Minneapolis: University of Minnesota Press.

Ferguson, J. 2006. *Global Shadows: Africa in the Neoliberal World Order*. Durham, NC: Duke University Press.

Fitz-Henry, E. 2018. 'Challenging Corporate "Personhood": Energy Companies and the "Rights" of Non-humans'. *PoLAR: Political and Legal Anthropology Review* 41(S1) DOI: 10.1111/plar.12255.

Foblets, M-C. 2005. 'Anthropologie versus droits de l'homme: Une opposition qui trompe'. *La Revue Nouvelle* 3: 75–83.

Foblets, M-C. 2014. 'Preface: Family, Religion and Law in Europe: Embracing Diversity from the Perspective of "Cultural Encounters"'. In P. Shah with M-C. Foblets and M. Rohe, eds. *Family, Religion and Law: Cultural Encounters in Europe*, xi–xvi. London: Routledge.

Fortun, K. 2001. *Advocacy After Bhopal: Environmentalism, Disaster, New Global Orders*. Chicago: University of Chicago Press.

Ganti, T. 2014. 'Neoliberalism'. *Annual Review of Anthropology* 43: 89–104.

Garland, D. 2001. *The Culture of Control: Crime and Social Order in Contemporary Society*. Oxford: Oxford University Press.

Geertz, C. 1983. *Local Knowledge. Further Essays in Interpretive Anthropology*. New York: Basic Books.

Goodale, M. 2012. 'Human Rights'. In Fassin, D. (ed), *A Companion To Moral Anthropology*, 468–81. Malden, MA: Wiley-Blackwell.

Goodale, M. 2017. *Anthropology and Law: A Critical Introduction*. New York: New York University Press.

Green, S. 2013. 'Borders and the Relocation of Europe'. *Annual Review of Anthropology* 42: 345–61.

Greenhouse, C. J. 2011. *The Paradox of Relevance: Ethnography and Citizenship in the United States*. Philadelphia: University of Pennsylvania Press.

Greenhouse, C. J., ed. 2010. *Ethnographies of Neoliberalism*. Philadelphia: University of Pennsylvania Press.

Gupta, A. 1998. *Post-colonial Developments: Agriculture in the Making of Modern India*. Durham, NC: Duke University Press.

Hermitte, E. 1970. *Poder sobrenatural y control social: En un pueblo Maya contemporaneo*. Ediciones especiales 57. Mexico, DF: Instituto Indigena Interamericano.

Hirsch, E. 2012. 'Property and Persons: New Forms and Contests in the Era of Neoliberalism.' *Annual Review of Anthropology* 39: 347–60.

Hirsch, S. F. and M. Lazarus-Black. 1986. 'Introduction—Performance and Paradox: Exploring Law's Role in Hegemony and Resistance'. In M. Lazarus-Black and S. Hirsch, eds. *Contested States: Law, Hegemony and Resistance*, 1–34. Oxford: Routledge.

Jean-Klein, I. and A. Riles. 2008. 'Introducing Discipline: Anthropology and Human Rights Administrations: Expert Observation and Representation After the Fact'. *PoLAR: Political and Legal Anthropology Review* 28(2): 173–202.

Just, P. 1992. 'Review: History, Power, Ideology, and Culture: Current Directions in the Anthropology of Law'. *Law & Society Review* 26(2): 373–412.

Kesselring, R., E. Babül, M. Goodale, T. Kelly, R. Niezen, M. Sapignoli, and R. A. Wilson. 'The Future of Anthropology of Law. Emergent Conversation'. *PoLAR: Political and Legal Anthropology Review Online*, 10 February 2017, available at <https://polarjournal.org/2017/02/10/emergent-conversations-part-6/>.

Kingsbury, B., N. Krisch, and R. Stewart. 2005 'The Emergence of Global Administrative Law'. *Law and Contemporary Problems* 68(3–4): 15–61.

Larkin, B. 2013. 'The Politics and Poetics of Infrastructure'. *Annual Review of Anthropology* 42: 327–43.

Latour, B. 2010 [2002]. *The Law Factory: An Ethnography of the Conseil d'Etat*. Cambridge: Polity Press.

Malinowski, B. 1926. *Crime and Custom in Savage Society*. London: Routledge and Kegan Paul.

Merry, S. E. 1992. 'Anthropology, Law and Transnational Processes'. *Annual Review of Anthropology* 21: 357–79.

Merry, S. E. 2000. *Colonizing Hawai'i: The Cultural Power of Law*. Princeton: Princeton University Press.

Merry, S. E. 2006. 'Transnational Human Rights and Local Activism: Mapping the Middle'. *American Anthropologist* 108(1): 38–51.

Mertz, E. 1994. 'Legal Language: Pragmatics, Poetics, and Social Power'. *Annual Review of Anthropology* 23: 435–55.

Mertz, E. 2008. 'Introduction: Toward a Systematic Translation of Law and Social Science'. In E. Mertz, ed. *The Use of Social Science in Legal Decisions*, xiii–xxx. Aldershot: Ashgate.

Mertz, E., T. W. Mitchell, and S. Macaulay, eds. 2016. *The New Legal Realism, vol. 1: Translating Law-and-Society for Today's Legal Practice*. New York: Cambridge University Press.

Moore, S. F. 1969. 'Law and Anthropology'. *Biennial Review of Anthropology* 6: 252–300.

Moore, S. F. 1973. 'Law and Social Change: The Semi-Autonomous Social Field as an Appropriate Subject of Study'. *Law and Society Review* 7(4): 719–46 (summer).

Moore, S. F. 1986. *Social Facts and Fabrications: 'Customary' Law on Kilimanjaro, 1880–1980*. Cambridge: Cambridge University Press.

Morgen, S. and J. Maskovsky. 2003. 'The Anthropology of Welfare "Reform": New Perspectives on U.S. Urban Poverty in the Post-Welfare Era'. *Annual Review of Anthropology* 32: 315–38.

Moyn, S. 2018. *Not Enough: Human Rights in an Unequal World*. Cambridge, MA: Harvard University Press.

Muehlebach, A. 2012. *The Moral Neoliberal: Welfare and Citizenship in Italy*. Chicago: University of Chicago Press.

Nader, L. 1965. 'The Anthropological Study of Law'. *American Anthropologist* 67(6, 2): 3–32.

Nader, L., ed. 1980. *No Access to Law: Alternatives to the American Justice System*. New York: Academic Press.

Offit, A. C. 2018. 'The Jury is Out: An Ethnographic Study of Lay Participation in the Norwegian Legal System'. *PoLAR: Political and Legal Anthropology Review* 41(2) (December) DOI: 10.1111/plar.12268.

Ortner, S. 1995. 'Resistance and the Problem of Ethnographic Refusal'. *Comparative Studies in Society and History* 37(1): 173–92.
Paley, J. 2002. 'Toward an Anthropology of Democracy'. *Annual Review of Anthropology* 31: 469–96.
Petryna, A. and K. Follis. 2015. 'Risks of Citizenship and Fault Lines of Survival'. *Annual Review of Anthropology* 44: 401–17.
Pfeiffer, J. and R. Chapman. 2010. 'Anthropological Perspectives on Structural Adjustment and Public Health'. *Annual Review of Anthropology* 39: 149–65.
Pirie, F. 2013. *The Anthropology of Law*. Oxford: Oxford University Press.
Richland, J. B. 2013. 'Jurisdiction: Grounding Law in Language'. *Annual Review of Anthropology* 42: 209–26.
Richland, J. B. 2018. 'Jurisdictions of Significance: Narrating Time-Space in a Hopi-U.S. Tribal Consultation'. *American Ethnologist* 45(2): 268–380.
Riles, A. 2011. *Collateral Knowledge: Legal Reasoning in the Global Financial Markets*. Chicago: University of Chicago Press.
Rouse, R. 1995. 'Questions of Identity: Personhood and Collectivity in Transnational Migration to the United States'. *Critique of Anthropology* 15(4): 351–80.
Sapignoli, M. 2017. '"Bushmen" in the Law: Evidence and Identity in Botswana's High Court'. *PoLAR: Political and Legal Anthropology Review* 40(2): 210–25.
Sarfaty, G. 2015. 'Shining Light on Global Supply Chains'. *Harvard International Law Journal* 56: 419–63.
Sassen, S. 1996. *Losing Control? Sovereignty in an Age of Globalization*. New York: Columbia University Press.
Sawyer, S. 2004. *Crude Chronicles: Indigenous Politics, Multinational Oil, and Neoliberalism in Ecuador*. Durham: Duke University Press.
Shamir, R. 2011. 'Socially Responsible Private Regulation: World-Culture or World-Capitalism?' *Law & Society Review* 45(2): 313–36.
Sharafi, M. 2008. 'Justice in Many Rooms since Galanter: De-Romanticizing Legal Pluralism through the Cultural Defense'. *Law and Contemporary Problems* 71(2): 139–46.
Simpson, A. 2014. *Mohawk Interruptus: Political Life at the Borders of Settler States*. Durham, NC: Duke University Press.
Spears, A. K. 2000. 'Commentary—Contest Talk: Language, Ideology, and Social Control'. *Transforming Anthropology* 9(1) (January): 51–3.
Starr, J. and J. Collier. 1989. 'Introduction: Dialogues in Legal Anthropology'. In J. Starr and J. Collier, eds. *History and Power in the Study of Law: New Directions in Legal Anthropology*, 1–28. Ithaca: Cornell University Press.
Stone, K. V. W. 2004. 'Alternative Dispute Resolution'. In S. Katz, ed. *Encyclopedia of Legal History*. Oxford University Press. Available at <https://ssrn.com/abstract=631346>.
Thomas, D. A. and M. K. Clarke. 2013. 'Structures of Inequality, New Sovereignties, and Citizenship in a Neoliberal Era'. *Annual Review of Anthropology* 42: 305–25.
Ticktin, M. 2014. 'Transnational Humanitarianism'. *Annual Review of Anthropology* 43: 273–89.
Unger, S. 2017. 'In Dialogue—More Thoughts on Resistance and Refusal: A Conversation between Sherry Ortner and Andrew Shryock'. *Comparative Studies in Society and History* 59: 3 (July). Available at <http://cssh.lsa.umich.edu>.
Valverde, M. 2014. *Chronotopes of Law: Jurisprudence, Scale and Governance*. New York: Routledge.

CHAPTER 2

ANTHROPOLOGY, LAW, AND EMPIRE

Foundations in Context

MARTIN CHANOCK

[B]y and by anthropology will have the choice between being history and being nothing. Frederick Maitland quoted in Cairns 1931: 40

THE anthropology of law is a small sliver of anthropology. It is an even tinier sliver when considered as part of a far larger but necessary context, which is the great amassing of Western knowledge and misrepresentations of the non-Western world from the second half of the nineteenth century onwards. The confrontation with the Other, complicated by its being a relation between rulers and ruled, spawned bodies of knowledge and theorization about the nature of civilization, of savages, of progress, of morality, sexual and otherwise, and of government and social order. Amongst these, 'law' is important symbolically, but it is not really at the centre of the West's confrontation with the Other. Nevertheless, in abstracting law from these larger discourses, we need to be aware of its connections to them. The important issue is not to trace the precise nature of, and differences among, the band of 'forefathers', whose works were profoundly flawed, but to consider what questions they were really addressing. As with all scholarship, their apparent concerns with the minutiae of their field obscure the broader political and moral issues that lay behind their intellectual pursuits. Perhaps too much can be made of 'context', but no intellectual endeavour is embarked on by persons with heads empty of the major concerns surrounding their work.[1]

Though Maitland had in mind the speculative and evolutionist anthropology of early times, and of law that dominated the late nineteenth century, it is the argument of this chapter that his remark applies also to much of the later development of the separate discipline of the anthropology of law. This chapter addresses the 'antecedents' and early developments in the anthropology of law. Interest in the law of non-Western peoples burgeoned in the context of imperialism and colonialism. As the initial grand questions about what the development of law could show about the evolution of human society were cast off, the new focus became how best to govern those who were not just the subjects of research, but were also the subjects of empire. Evolutionist speculation about law and the development of human societies collapsed in the years after the First World War. Embarrassed by its racist origins, and later bemired in its functionalist phases, the new anthropology was reliant on the 'findings' of a very small cohort of researchers. It turned its back on much that would have been illuminating. The emerging discipline largely missed the major historical development of its times, which was, to use Polanyi's term only as shorthand, 'the great transformation' to market capitalism, which impacted on all legal concepts and behaviours—indigenous, imposed, and adopted. The chapter also considers, as a part of the development of legal anthropology, the analyses by colonial officials, who were key agents in understanding the laws of their subjects.

Forefathers may sometimes bequeath new and useful ways of understanding.[2] They are often touchstones whose sayings, understood or misunderstood, serve as starting points for roads which veer off into territories they had not envisaged. Towards the end of his life, the former British Prime Minister, Stanley Baldwin, 'was asked whether he had been influenced by any thinker or book. After a long pause he replied, "Sir Henry Maine". In his once celebrated book *Ancient Law* (1861), Baldwin continued, the eminent Victorian jurist showed that history was a process of progressive development in which societies governed by status were gradually replaced by ones based on contract. Then Baldwin paused again, seemingly puzzled, and asked: "Or was it the other way around?"' (Gray 2018). Baldwin's confusion is an excellent guide to the misunderstandings of anthropologists regarding 'law'. While de Montesquieu was the most distinguished predecessor in suggesting links between law and culture, Henry Maine may have been the most influential person, according to accounts of the early anthropology of law. He would not have seen himself as such. In 1876, he wrote to Lewis Henry Morgan, the pioneering American anthropologist, as follows:

> As you truly say, we have attacked the same subject from opposite sides. I understand you to have begun with observations of the customs of savages, whereas I began as a Professor of Jurisprudence. ... I am still apt to limit my enquiries to ancient institutions which I can more or less distinctly connect with modern ideas and ways of thought. (Letter from Henry Maine to Lewis Henry Morgan in 1876, quoted in Chanock 1983: 107)

Maine provided a clear evolutionist account of law. The study of law had to start with the most 'rudimentary' state. This turned out to be the all-powerful patriarch. Gradually, the father's empire was 'whittled away' (Stocking 1987: 123), and the determination of personal and proprietary rights moved from the domestic forum to public ones. Starting from '"a condition of society in which all the relations of persons are summed up in the relations of Family", one moved ... "towards a phase of social order in which all these relations arise from the free agreement of individuals"' (Maine 1861: 169, quoted in Stocking 1987: 123). George W. Stocking, Jr (1987: 178) writes of 'filling the void in cultural time with the data of contemporary savagery'. This was the way Maine understood the contemporary Indian world. As he wrote in *Village-Communities in the East and the West* (1871), the India of the present was 'the great repository of verifiable phenomena of ancient usage and ancient judicial thought' (Maine 1871: 22, quoted in Owen 1973: 22).

EVOLUTIONISM AND EMPIRE

Despite Maine's evolutionist framework, anthropology was later to develop as an explicitly non-evolutionist discipline. We should therefore be chary of finding the origins of the anthropology of law among the antiquarian evolutionists of the Victorian era. There are a number of reasons why this is fruitless. One is that the break between their form of evolutionism and functionalism and its successors means that the forms of enquiry, and of answers, changed completely. Ptolemy is not the forefather of Copernicus or Galileo, though all looked at the stars. From the nineteenth to the mid-twentieth century, the changes in basic understandings and paradigms regarding people who were the subject matter of anthropology were too great to form a developmental continuity in science. But this is not to deny that there was a significant overhang of evolutionist ideas when it came to attempts to write history, rather than anthropology. 'Conjectural history', made necessary by a combination of ignorance and the undeveloped state of historical research, remained full of evolutionist ideas. And, more significantly, colonial governors, and administrators, whose views frame a significant part of the history of legal anthropology, automatically and unthinkingly incorporated social evolutionism into their thoughts about their missions. For what else could justify what they were imposing on colonized peoples?

In the evolutionist frame (Owen 1973: 22), human progress was seen as a linear development from savagery to civilization. If there were similarities between the institutions of early Europe and contemporary peoples deemed to be primitive, it was legitimate to assume both that one could learn about Europe's past from present-day primitives and that one could understand primitives with reference to Europe's past. Importantly, there must also be moral evolution. This idea produced many accounts of the history of marriage. The basic assumption was that people had been unrestrainedly promiscuous in the beginning, but had moved towards restraint in steps towards the evolution of marriage in its monogamous form (Stocking 1987: 186–237). The moralizing framework of the early scholars was rejected by later representatives of mainstream anthropology. But sexual relations, marriage, and (hypocritically) the position of women, remained a key point of fascination, not only for anthropologists but also for missionaries and governments and their subjects.

Where, then, should one look for historical predecessors? It all depends on what narrative one thinks is important. The basic thesis of this chapter is that mainstream anthropologists of law, because of their functionalist orientation, misunderstood the nature of their subject—and the lives of their subjects. Few anthropologists knew much about law. In place of the knowledge they lacked, they relied on various reflections, some popular, some simplified versions of the dominant legal ideas of the day. Like many interested in the anthropology of law, they were puzzled, irritated, bemused, and occasionally contemptuous of the intellectual world of lawyers and jurists.[3] Law was not really a matter of major interest for most important anthropologists; and, even more so, anthropology did not interest lawyers. Philip Gulliver (1978: xiv, fn. 3) noted that, as late as 1970, the Association of Social Anthropologists turned down a request to devote a meeting to law and anthropology because it represented 'too small a minority interest'.

Nineteenth-century social evolutionism ranked human societies. This became especially important in the legal field where early Western law and contemporary non-Western law were considered to be alike. This kind of history was partly displaced in a developing legal anthropology by the functionalist phase, which conflated law with order, leaving no place for history. But the peoples being studied were being forcibly dragged into wrenching historical changes both to their systems of government and their economic life. Though no longer considered to be a part of an imagined social evolutionism, they were being submersed in an economy that was developing as a single world-wide story. The primary changes being lived through in the legal field included the individualization of the legal subject—a person whose actual individuality and social place were in the process of being homogenized, making him or her the bearer of the same rights and duties as others. Writing in 1938, Jomo Kenyatta, the future President of Kenya, who attended Bronislaw Malinowski's seminars at the London School of Economics, wrote that, among the Gikuyu (or Kikuyu), '[i]ndividualism and self-seeking were ruled out. ... The personal pronoun "I" was used very rarely' (Kenyatta 1938: 195). 'According to Gikuyu ways of thinking nobody is an isolated individual. ... [I]n Gikuyu language individualism is associated with black magic' (Kenyatta 1938: 309–10). But central to the rights and duties imposed under colonialism was the individualized legal subject who could own property, dispose of it, and enter into contracts which were not simply arrangements between individual persons, but which would be enforced by the institutions of a new state.

The importance of property was plain to Morgan. While British evolutionists dominated early English-language musings about primitive law and the nature of civilization, it may well be that Morgan has a better claim to be the 'forefather' of legal anthropology.[4] Morgan was an American lawyer and property speculator, and he was also an 'amateur' anthropologist. Unlike others of his time, he did detail ethnographic research among the Iroquois in New York State. While his focus was on the nature of government, I want here to draw attention to his interest in property, because he emphasized that it was of crucial importance. '[T]he property of savages was inconsiderable', he wrote.

> Their ideas concerning its value, its desirability and its inheritance were feeble. ... A passion for its possession had scarcely been formed in their minds, because the thing itself scarcely existed. It was left to the then distant period of civilization to develop

> into full vitality that 'greed of gain' (*studium lucri*), which is now such a commanding force in the human mind. (Morgan 1985 [1877]: 527)

Morgan thought that ownership in land had passed through evolutionary stages. First, land was held by tribes in common; then tribal land was divided among 'the gentes', each of which held their portion in common; and then allotments were made to individuals, 'which ... finally ripened into individual ownership in severalty' (Morgan 1985 [1877]: 541–2). With the growth of field agriculture and the several ownership of the surface of the earth,

> the new property career of mankind was inaugurated. ... A little reflection must convince any one of the powerful influence property would now begin to exercise upon the human mind, and of the great awakening of new elements of character it was calculated to produce. ... [T]he feeble impulse aroused in the savage mind had now become a tremendous passion in the splendid barbarian of the heroic age. ... Since the advent of civilization, the outgrowth of property has been so immense, its forms so diversified, its uses so expanding and its management so intelligent in the interests of its owners, that it has become, on the part of the people, an unmanageable power. The human mind stands bewildered in the presence of its own creation. (Morgan 1985 [1877]: 544, 551).

But we must emphasize that, as with all other forms of anthropological knowledge, Morgan's views were formed within a particular political context. The debates among early American anthropologists about Indian property rights were framed in terms of evolution from 'collective' to 'individual', but they took place in a context characterized by genocide, the seizure and rapid diminution of Indian lands, an aggressive policy of individualizing landholdings through the federal General Allotments Act of 1887, and the confiscation of lands not so allocated (Feit 1991: 112–13). The individual use of property was seen as a source of 'immense moral learning' (Feit 1991: 113) The U.S. federal government had clearly decided that Indian societies had not developed the idea of private property, because it could not possibly acknowledge the existence of this idea among Indians in the context of the white settlement of Western lands.

When Friedrich Engels wrote *The Origin of the Family, Private Property and the State* (1948 [1884]), he subtitled it *In the Light of the Researches of Lewis H Morgan.*[5] Engels thought of himself as a contributor to a line of literature which included Bachofen, McLennan, Tylor, and Lubbock; and he says explicitly that his book was based upon Morgan's *Ancient Society.* There is also a direct link between Morgan's work and Marx, who had planned to follow up on Morgan's ideas but who died before he could complete this project. Engels took up the task (Tooker 1985: xvi). Though its reputation has been crippled due to its subsequent role as a classic of the Marxist canon, Engels's book is significant among the works of the nineteenth-century forefathers of the anthropology of law. This is because it takes up and expands Morgan's brief account of the origins of property; and it relates this to the anthropological debates about the origins of marriage.

It is my contention that the individualization brought about by market relations and by the changes in the ideas relating to property is the main story of the period. This, therefore, could be where the most useful strand of legal anthropology could be said to begin. As Engels wrote, capitalist production transformed 'all things into commodities, it dissolved all ancient traditional relations, and for inherited customs and historical rights it substituted purchase and sale, by the "free contract"' (Engels 1948 [1884]: 78). Maine's 'status to contract', Engels claimed, 'insofar as it is correct, was contained long ago in the *Communist Manifesto*' (Engels 1948 [1884]: 78).

While Marx may have underlined his differences with Maine, both were evolutionists, and, in this context, both were concerned with the same questions. As Marx wrote, these questions included, especially, '[f]irst the tearing of individuality loose from the originally not despotic chains (as blockhead Maine understands it), but rather satisfying and agreeable bonds of the group, of primitive community—and therewith the one-sided elaboration of the individuality' (Marx in Krader 1972: 39). This was vital for the development of law. Both Bentham and Maine, from different political positions, were clear on the connections between law and individually-owned private property. Bentham was explicit: 'Property and law are born and must die together. Before the laws, there was no property: take away the laws, all property ceases' (Bentham, in Bowring 1843, vol. I: 309). Marx agreed: 'Civil law develops simultaneously with private property out of the disintegration of the natural community' (Marx and Engels 1970 [1846]: 80).

Along with the musings of the Victorian anthropologists about human development, we must consider the main legal issues of nineteenth-century England, which centred on how to fashion a legal regime for the Indian empire. Following on Thomas Babington Macaulay's period as first head of the Indian Law Commission in the 1830s, the project of codification became dominant. The major codes, The Penal Code and the civil and criminal procedural codes, were enacted in the 1860s. The project of codifying the civil law, including the law of contract, remained. Maine, it must be emphasized, was not simply academically concerned, but a powerful part of the imposition of British law on India. In his first speech to the Governor's Council in India, in his capacity as Law Member, he suggested that social progress was 'almost mysteriously dependent' on the 'completest freedom of contract' (Maine, quoted in Stocking 1987: 124). Maine's successor, James Fitzjames Stephen, completed the imposition of English codes of law upon India. This was, in his view, a 'moral conquest more striking, more durable and far more solid than the physical conquest which renders it possible'; for Stephen, English law was 'the sum and substance of what we have to teach ... [the] gospel of the English ... [a] compulsory gospel which admits to no dissent and no disobedience' (Stephen, quoted in Smith 1988: 134). In Alfred Lyall's view, once Hindus had 'been rescued by the English out of a chronic state of anarchy, insecurity, lawlessness and precarious exposure to the caprice of despots, they will surely introduce, at least, some ideas of our rule, organised purpose and moral law' (Lyall, quoted in Owen 1973: 229). English law was to be certain, uniform, enforced, and morally superior.

The anthropology of law of this period existed only because of imperialism and colonialism; and interest in it flourished in colonial contexts because colonial governments needed information about what might be the legal ideas and practices of their conquered subjects. While it does make some sense to distinguish between what one might call 'governmental' and 'academic' versions of the anthropology of law, it is necessary to keep their links visible. Governments collected a lot of knowledge to use, and much was collected for them by anthropologists working on the government payroll. A handful of determined persons, including Malinowski and A. R. Radcliffe-Brown, worked hard to make the enquiry into the law of savages a respectable academic discipline, equipped with theory. Others, like Isaac Schapera, Paul Bohannan, and E. E. Evans-Pritchard, spanned both government and academic enterprises. In the post-Second World War period, the Rhodes-Livingstone Institute in British Central Africa tried hard to straddle the gap between government and its own work, which was rapidly tending towards academic thought. Others, notably Charles Kingsley Meek, wrote his major works for government. To say that the anthropology of law existed in a colonial context and was entwined within it is not a criticism of the politics of the anthropologists, but simply a fact of their time in the world, their sources of funding, and their audience for a substantial part of their output.

Government, or state, anthropology, also resided in commissions on the law of the conquered, and in the judgments of those who purported to apply knowledge of this law to cases with which they were concerned. The most thoroughgoing of this type of legal colonialism of both power and knowledge was developed in South Africa from the mid-nineteenth century onwards (see Chanock 2001: 243–346). Governments wanted certain rules of law that courts could apply. This was not the main concern of academic anthropologists' enquiry, and indeed scepticism that such rules were discoverable ultimately prevailed, rendering their work more or less useless to government.[6] Much of what was 'known' about primitive law pre-dated systematic anthropological enquiry, though Maine's dicta crept in at a very early stage. As we have seen, the knowledge was all based simply on the notion of the profound difference between 'civilized' and 'savage', and also on the belief that primitive law resembled the early stages of the law of the civilized. The earliest of the books used in the African context was perhaps *A Compendium of Kafir Laws and Customs* (Maclean 1968 [1858]), collected following the annexations in the Eastern Cape. One contributor noted that the 'system of government' was destitute of 'fixed principles ... it affords no guarantee for the uniform administration of justice. – There is no "*letter* of the law"' (Dugmore, in Maclean 1968 [1858]: 32, 34). Kafir marriage, it was noted, had usage 'which is mentioned, without prohibition, in the Old Testament' (Dugmore, in Maclean 1968 [1858]: 55). It was convenient that 'the grand principle of Kafir Law is *collective responsibility*' (Warner, in Maclean 1968 [1858]: 60, emphasis in original), for this allowed governments to punish all for the wrongdoing of one, In 1880 the Cape government set up a commission to enquire into 'native laws and customs', and it reported in 1883. Evolution remained firmly entrenched. The commission found that African law was 'not unlike that which prevailed among our Saxon ancestors in the early days of civilisation' (see Chanock 2001: 253).

We must consider also, as antecedents of the academic anthropology of law, the studies done by Christian missionaries in the field. I take Henri Junod (1912) as an example, though there are of course others, notably Edwin W. Smith and Andrew Murray Dale (1920). Junod's study of the Thonga aimed, among other things, to be of practical help to missionaries and Native Commissioners. As early as 1912 he wrote that '[t]o govern savages, you must study them thoroughly' (Junod 1912: 8). He was aware that 'colossal changes' were taking place, affecting the life of his subjects (Junod 1912: 11); but his account of judicial cases began with the not unusual view that tribal life was governed by unchanging custom: 'Bantu possess a strong sense of justice. They believe in social order and in the observance of the laws ... [which] are universal and perfectly well known. The law is the custom, that which has always been done' (Junod 1912: 410). Bantu, because of their 'collectivist notions', consider relatives to be responsible for the debts of their own kin (Junod 1912: 410). In his general reflections, however, Junod put his finger on the crucial point: 'the era of individualism has set in. ... The proclamation during the French revolution of the "rights of man", which is looked upon as the greatest progress made by modern politics, is a direct result of this assertion of the value of the individual' (Junod 1912: 266). Writing before the academic anthropologists met Africa, Junod was perhaps better attuned than they would be to the larger processes at work.

There were very few independent professional anthropologists in inter-war Africa (see Hailey 1938: 40–59). Most were young. This cohort was seen by colonial governments as only justifiable if it provided them with knowledge useful to administration. But administration itself collected far more knowledge about African law. District officers generally spent a relatively longer time in their districts, and many were interested, in an intellectual way, in the people they ruled. Their knowledge is not usually counted as part of the inheritance of legal anthropology, but it ought to be. While I shall not discuss it in detail here, I have written about it elsewhere (Chanock 1985). I mention it now because it is a part of a larger point, which is that we should look 'inside' governments if we want to understand how the knowledge of the practices of colonized peoples developed. The Privy Council in London also thought of itself as an ultimate depository of anthropological expertise. In a series of notorious cases, it pronounced on African land rights (see Chanock 1991).

South African judges in the special courts which dealt with 'native law' also had few doubts about their own anthropological expertise. I have written about this elsewhere (Chanock 2001: 243–346), so now will simply offer a flavour of the framework within which they worked, which was a fusion of evolutionism and racism. The issues around which the debates turned were the nature of African marriage; the despotic powers of the chieftaincy; the position of women; the powers of family heads over the property of their extended 'households'; and the question of codification. In line with the Cape Commission's view that contemporary native law echoed early Western law, much credence was given over many years to a paper by the Reverend Kropf which found that bride wealth payments were not simply African barbarism, but that similar practices had existed among Orientals, Hebrews, Greeks, and 'early German monogamists' (Chanock 2001: 264). Judges invoked the Roman law regarding the powers of the *paterfamilias* over family members and family property as analogous to the 'native law' they would enforce. They found the doctrine of *patria potestas* particularly appealing. In a not atypical judgment about African law, Henry Maine was invoked and comparisons were made with the Roman Law Digest and Justinian's code.

Towards professional anthropology: functionalism and empire

In 1922 both Radcliffe-Brown and Malinowski published their first major works, and these marked the shift away from evolutionary approaches to functionalist approaches among a new cohort of academics. In the anthropology of law, the search for origins was set aside. We must ask, however, whether Malinowski's celebrated proclamation in *Crime and Custom in Savage Society*—that law was not a matter of 'codes, courts and constables'—was not largely incorrect and misleading (Malinowski 1926). Essentially, he drove the bus of what might have become a developing understanding of non-Western law towards a quicksand of studies of how disputes were settled. Under, usually, the umbrella of colonial powers, anthropologists tried to discover the secrets of the law of small scale non-literate peoples. The whole idea, however, of finding anything like the socially remote, vast written corpus of their own societies' law, was, in retrospect, absurd. Malinowski clearly saw this, and proclaimed it. But so much of the functionalists' account, as we shall see, derived from the colonial situation under whose aegis these ideas developed. The primary colonial question was how to maintain order among their subjects. It is not surprising, therefore, that a primary anthropological focus was on how order was maintained, and disputes settled, among people who were—though anthropologists often seemed oblivious of this—colonial *subjects*.

It is important to recognize that the new ethnographic method represented a profoundly different means of both studying and understanding social phenomena, one that insisted on the value in seeing these living phenomena from the inside out. This 'emic' epistemology also carried broader implications, particularly in an age in which the colonial anthropologist, notoriously on the veranda, had been accustomed to summoning informants for a round of 'hearsay note-taking' which Malinowski rejected. This earlier approach was flawed both scientifically and ethically. Malinowski's *Crime and Custom in Savage Society* (1926) became the foundation text of the new legal anthropology. It proclaimed that neither written law, nor institutions of enforcement were necessary. Their absence did not result in anarchy: '[L]aw and order pervade the tribal usages of primitive races, they govern all the humdrum course of daily existence as well as the leading acts of public life' (Malinowski 1926: 2). Law still consisted in 'rules' and 'binding obligations' (Malinowski 1926: e.g. 12, 22), though it was based on the principle of reciprocity rather than a sovereign authority: order without apparent coercion.[7]

While functionalism became dominant in British anthropology, there was some hesitation across the Atlantic. Huntington Cairns began his response to Malinowski with reference to Maine and to the German ethnologists Albert Hermann Post and Josef

Kohler, who had indicated at the birth of cultural anthropology that 'a profitable field of research for the law had been opened' (Cairns 1931: 32). However, he wrote, 'the field of enquiry which they uncovered soon ceased to attract the attention of either jurists or anthropologists' (Cairns 1931: 33). Now, in both law and anthropology, a functional attitude was developing, which no longer regarded law as a 'self-contained system of thought'; and 'definitions of law in terms of supreme authority have been abandoned' (Cairns 1931: 36). 'Anthropology has warned the jurist', he continued, 'that his conception of law is perhaps egocentric' (Cairns 1931: 39). But Cairns was unwilling to abandon history. He thought that the 'origins of customs and institutions are irretrievably lost' but that, with greater anthropological research, 'it may be possible to construct a scheme of social evolution which will be, if not history, at least the best possible substitute for history' (Cairns 1931: 40–1). But for Cairns, ultimately, it was a matter of immediate utility: 'When we turn from the historical and conceptual relation of law and anthropology to the problem of law and anthropology in action' the issue becomes 'the system of justice to be adopted by the dominating power in colonies populated by people of simpler culture. ... It is here that anthropology can render assistance to immediate and practical benefit' (Cairns 1931: 52–3).

In North America, the legal realism of Roscoe Pound and Karl Llewellyn, with its emphasis on how law 'really worked', influenced the singular study, *The Cheyenne Way* (Llewellyn and Hoebel 1941).[8] Based on reminiscence of the elderly, rather than Malinowskian fieldwork, and organized around the study of cases of conflict, it is considered to be the main influence on the domination of the case method in the anthropology of law that followed in America.

But we should focus, rather, on the anthropology of law's relationship with government, in the vein in which Cairns ended his review of Malinowski. Lord Hailey's monumental *African Survey* (1938) discussed at its start the nature of social anthropology and its uses for colonial governments. There could be no doubt, he wrote, as to the value of anthropological knowledge to governments, which had tended to rely on the expertise of their own administrative officers (Hailey 1938: 45). It could supply the government 'with the knowledge that must form the basis of administrative policy' (Hailey 1938: 48). Imperial administrators wanted help from anthropology in finding in local cultures the kinds of judicial authorities who could be associated with colonial governments in accordance with the policy of Indirect Rule. But relationships on the ground between anthropologists and administrators were often difficult and hostile, especially where different attitudes towards racial superiority, and disagreements over the interpretation of policy were involved.

For Hailey (and for most others who actually governed colonies), academic anthropology was at best a supplement to their own sources of knowledge. It is to the anthropologists working within or for colonial governments directly that we now turn. Perhaps the best example of a colonial legal anthropologist was Meek, who was employed as an anthropological officer by the government of Nigeria and who produced a number of books, the most important of which were *Law and Authority in a Nigerian Tribe* (1937) and *Land Law and Custom in the Colonies* (1946). *Law and Authority* was produced as a response to the rebellion in the South East of Nigeria in 1929. The rebellion was seen by the colonial authorities as a response to the Native courts, introduced in the South on the Indirect Rule model which had been applied in the North. But in the South East there had been no similar indigenous authorities on which to build the courts. Meek (1937: xii) noted that, apart from R. S. Rattray's *Ashanti Law and Constitution* (1929), there had been 'few English works which deal adequately with the subject of African government and law'. While 'our' idea of 'law' 'carries with it very definite implications of state authority, judges and magistrates, codes and courts, police and prisons' these had no counterpart in 'primitive' society' (Meek 1937: xiii). Malinowski had moved us towards 'a newer and truer conception of … primitive law, … removing a multitude of misconceptions, such as the assumption that the primitive individual is completely dominated by the group, or that "communism is in general existence in the domain of law"' (Meek 1937: xiii, paraphrasing without exact citation Durkheim 1893). Meek settled for a definition of law that included all modes regulating conduct. He accepted the colonial state's reasons for supporting his work:

> [I]n instituting anthropological inquiries in Iboland, the Government of Nigeria was not actuated by any academic or antiquarian interest, but by the purely practical motive of bettering the administration. This indeed has always been the Government's attitude towards anthropological research, namely, that it should serve as a handmaiden of administration. (Meek 1937: xv)

Meek (1937: 38) wrote that 'collective responsibility' was an 'important aspect of native law', which was still operative. In Ibo society, he continued, 'a man's conduct is largely conditioned by his status' (Meek 1937: 338). Persons were unequal, and 'the English principle of complete personal responsibility' was absent (Meek 1937: 338). However, this English conception was 'now being recognized in all Native Courts—an inevitable change for the better, but one which, unfortunately, goes hand in hand with the general loosening of the bonds of brotherhood' (Meek 1937: 339). In Ibo society, though, the ancestors still were 'a governing factor in the maintenance of law and order'; indeed, the 'whole system of magic and taboo served as a solid buttress on the law' (Meek 1937: 340). What would happen now that people were abandoning their old beliefs? 'With the breakdown of the magico-religious system law will become more and more secularized; and with the growth of individualism, consequent on … social inequality … [n]ew laws would be required' (Meek 1937: 326). Debt was a heavy burden. 'Normal' interest charged was compounded at 100 per cent. The principal heir inherited debt. To pay tax people might have to lose their land, or pawn a child, or even themselves. Like so many of his contemporaries in the colonial world, Meek was worried that 'a backward people' was 'liable to lose its stability, and indeed its soul' when confronted by a powerful modern state: 'Its political and social organisation is likely to break up, and what was before a well-ordered community, in which all members had a definite series of obligations to one another, may become nothing but a disorganized rabble of self-seeking individualists' (Meek 1937: 326).

It is important to try to imagine what the image of 'law' was in the minds of the anthropologists of this era. I have referred to the legal environment created by lawyers such as Bentham, Stephens, and John Austin,[9] for whom law was about sovereignty, rule, and rules: the application of power according to rules, which were backed up by sanctions. Without this, the alternative was anarchy, which was the state of savages. Some English writers after the First World War, who interested themselves in savages, replied that they were not anarchic, but bound by ancient customs, usually unwritten, which were backed up by superstitious beliefs (e.g. Hartland 1924). Anthropologists went into the field, I suggest, with all of this in mind, and discovered that it was not a correct picture. But the echoes remained. Their search for authority suggests an underlying notion of anarchy in its absence, even though it was partly driven by the colonial governments' need to find usable legal institutions among is primitive peoples. But both governments and anthropologists did learn that the 'new-caught sullen peoples' (Kipling 1899) were (mostly) rational—that they did not live in anarchy but were acquainted with rules, if not with Austin's implacable version of sovereignty.

Lucy Mair (1962: 19) later complained that '[f]loods of ink have been wasted' on the matter of defining law; nonetheless, she offered Radcliffe-Brown's definition of law as 'the application of direct or indirect penal sanctions, ... the settlement of disputes and the provision of just satisfaction for injuries' (Mair 1962: 19, quoting from Radcliffe-Brown 1940: xviii). Radcliffe Brown's concept was simple, based on the idea that 'every community has the same primary public policy—the control of violence'—and that this necessitated in 'each community ... the provision of some means for the adjudication of disputes' (Colson 1974: 14). The functionalist ambition was large: Radcliffe-Brown insisted that '[t]he system of laws of a particular society can only be fully understood if it is studied in relation to the social structure, and inversely the understanding of the social structure requires ... a systematic study of the legal institutions' (Radcliffe-Brown 1952: 199, quoted in Moore 1978: 62). Max Gluckman (1965b: 23) affirmed this ambition: 'The search for systematic interdependence of customs remains a hallmark of ... anthropology'.

In 1938, Godfrey Wilson, then director of the Rhodes-Livingstone Institute in Northern Rhodesia,[10] provided the following definition of law, which reveals the mindset of most contemporary anthropologists and which I shall take as an exemplar:

> [Law is] that normal or customary form of action in society which is kept in being by the inherent necessities of systematic cooperation among its members. ... A breach of law is a course of action which would ... if unchecked, make continued relationship between the lawbreakers and other members of their society wholly impossible; it threatens to dissolve society into anarchy... .
>
> If law is to be preserved it is necessary that the actions which sanction it should have an irresistible force. ... [I]n civilised areas of society ... legal sanctions must be applied by a central authority... .

> But in primitive society largely composed of personal acquaintances ... the facts of every dispute, every breach of law, are soon widely known. ... And so the typical method of legal procedure in a primitive society is for action to be taken against a lawbreaker by those more nearly concerned. ... [A]ny request which an individual may make to his kinsmen or neighbours for practical assistance ... any appeal to their opinion in a dispute is a legal procedure. (Wilson 1938: 22–3, fn. 3)

Wilson's definition was, however, just a model of something he had learned, not what he was currently observing. Nyakyusa society, he concluded, was no longer isolated and primitive, and legal procedure was becoming more and more an affair of the central territorial authorities. The colonial court apparatus, with its magistrates, district officers, and Native courts, was already in place when he was writing, and, substantially, his observations corresponded to something already past. 'Law versus anarchy' and law's relationship to sanction seemed to him to be of the essence in both primitive and civilized societies. There was also the crucial societal fact that in small groups the holding of land involved personal relationships, while in civilized societies impersonal relationships were key. It was possible, but not certain, that 'ever more effective integration with world society increases the new legal importance of impersonal relationships' (Wilson 1938: 30).[11]

Gluckman, an anthropologist of law whose work had a major impact on the development of the discipline, had a mission, which is entirely comprehensible given his liberal, white South African background. It was to show that 'African law contains the same fundamental conceptions as our law' (Gluckman 1955: 96). Even more basically, he wanted to show that Africans reasoned, that their judicial processes were 'controlled by logical reasoning' (Gluckman 1955: 24). It was sad, but necessary, to have had to say this. His painstaking analyses of disputes before the Lozi courts in Northern Rhodesia, influenced by *The Cheyenne Way*, purported to show how the judicial reasoning was dominated by the concept of the 'reasonable man' and was based on ideas comparable to Western equivalents (Gluckman 1955, 1965a).[12] But, given the historical importance of Gluckman's work, it is as well to look at his subjects through another lens. Local officials observed corruption and oppression rather than reason, reporting that 'justice has never been dealt with impartially by any Khotla'; 'cattle were impounded at will; cases were not heard for long periods; and starving litigants and witnesses were detained for long periods' (Chanock 1985: 114). In 1929 magistrates reported that laws were made without sufficient consideration; penalties and procedures were 'very severe and no attempt was made to make the punishment fit the crime'; evidence in matrimonial cases was 'often very weak'; and the general behaviour of the court was extortionate, presumably because 'the ruling caste', following the abolition of slavery, tribute labour, and tribute, was 'feeling the pinch very considerably' (magistrates' 1929 Annual Report, Sesheke sub-district, in Chanock 1985: 114).

Different worlds

This importance of British colonial Africa's prevailing image of law, empty of content, and focused on order, becomes plainer if we briefly shift our focus to the Dutch debates about the nature and future of *adat*, the customary law of their Indonesian colonies. The prominent Dutch jurist, Cornelis van Vollenhoven (1981 [1931]: 25), described how, in nineteenth-century debates in the Netherlands, it was the prevailing official view that Indonesians would be better off once their law was replaced by the 'pure and sound rules' of Roman law—which had 'stood up to the test of centuries'—and of Dutch law. While many Dutch lawyers thought that *adat* should be removed and replaced, van Vollenhoven argued that those arguing against *adat* had still not learned the lessons of Friedrich Carl von Savigny about law's dependence on time, place, and people. He was supported in this approach by the development of ethnological studies of *adat* in the late nineteenth century, but there was still very little interest among lawyers. However, outside of the narrow legal world, work was being done in the field of ethnological jurisprudence. Van Vollenhoven (1981 [1931]: 28–9) referred to the development of German scholarship and to Post's large collections of 'the colourful variety of customs and legal usages' but thought that they were without an 'inkling that law is an historical phenomenon with countless complexions'. Later, Post did develop 'a framework within and around which the legal history of less developed societies could be fitted', and Morgan had more clearly revealed the ethnological aim 'of showing that the evolution of law and custom are related to successive stages of human progress from savagery to civilisation' (van Vollenhoven 1981 [1931]: 29). A new legal history could enquire, van Vollenhoven wrote, into indigenous and foreign law which is still extant, and could, in conjunction with efforts to 'reconstruct the popular law of the misty past' of peoples such as the Egyptians and Greeks, 'discover the line of legal development in the past and present':

> It could then put forward another conception of law than the rationalistic interpretation of the code-minded lawyers the dominant majority of whom seek to ascribe everything to the conscious human will. (van Vollenhoven 1981 [1931]: 30)

What is of major importance here is that an excursion into this intellectual world takes us far from the developments that would dominate the structural functional classics of English social anthropology. While it overlaps slightly with the discarded conjectural history of law of the evolutionists, its primary interest was in actual legal history, not function—a history to which ethnological studies would contribute. Legal ethnology was the handmaiden to the development of history, not a field which could do without history and strike out on its own.

In 1931 Margaret Read, a talented anthropologist and a member of the cohort of students of Malinowski who dominated British anthropology, published *The Indian Peasant Uprooted: A Study of the Human Machine*, in which she perceived precisely what so many contemporary anthropologists had not. People were becoming 'human machines' in the new factories and mines. Read's study was based on the evidence of an official enquiry, not on fieldwork.[13] Most importantly she reminds us that Maine's 'contract' was not a sunny world of freedom of choice and personal autonomy, but a darker world in which people were tied into new subordinations, fictionally based on their choices. Her book covered all aspects of the industrial life in India from the standpoint of these new 'machines'. They were torn out of and cut off from their villages, living in squalor and hunger, and bound to their new 'contracts' by the legislation in British India, which made breach of a labour contract a criminal offence. Of necessity they 'are born, live and die under a curse. That curse is the curse of credit. Poverty, borrowing, debt, interest ... so the circle begins and continues' (Read 1931: 194). Debtors were liable to be imprisoned if they defaulted (see Meek's remarks on debt above). While this territory is far from the conventional concerns of anthropology and law, I think it vital, because it shows that attention could be paid to the new world that the subjects of legal anthropology were moving into. This new world offered to people the ability to enter into contracts to sell their labour, just as it offered to them a new ability to buy and sell goods, and, eventually, land. Read later went on to do fieldwork in central Africa, where in many parts a majority of young men were labour migrants, working in mines under harshly oppressive conditions with contracts to which they had not 'consented' in any meaningful sense (see Chanock 2001: 173–4). As Sally Falk Moore (1978: 59) later commented, Gluckman had to write about ideas and processes because only those aspects remained 'appreciably unchanged'. Although he was well aware of the new realities of the society he was writing about, he chose not to present them as having an impact on of his legal studies.[14] 'This was no self-contained *Gemeinschaft*', Moore (1978: 59) noted; rather, by 1941, nearly two-thirds of men were absent, working in the cash economy. A good deal of the early British anthropology of law is to be found in studies of central Africa, but these small-scale, closely focused studies did not offer an understanding of the new legal world in which their subjects participated. Read (1931: 253) cited a study from the Dutch East Indies which said that the 'change in the economic sphere produced a spiritual revolution. ... The basis of the former community was destroyed ... individualism increased'.

The introduction of 'capitalist enterprise' had led to the de-population of some areas by labour migration. But most anthropologists of the early to mid-twentieth century represented 'their' peoples as 'existing' separately from the harsh new regimes that ruled over them. Only in the latter part of the twentieth century did works which focused on changes begin to appear; but they had missed the early parts of the processes of economic and social transformation. An example of how this could have been be done sensitively was provided by Paul and Laura Bohannan. Their detailed analyses of Tiv markets before and after the widening circles of trade brought about by the colonial 'peace'—and most importantly the introduction of all-purpose money—suggest how the 'market has become pervasive: it is no longer merely an institution – it threatens to become a way of life' (Bohannan and Bohannan 1968: 240–8).

The narrative turns

Evolutionism, in the sense of a racial hierarchy, has gone from the anthropology of law. Malinowskian functionalism is no longer dominant. The dominance of the study of disputes and dispute resolution has waned. What of the missed opportunities? Moore, who had already published the classic study that relieved sociolegal studies from the idea that there must be a single dominant legal order enforced by violence (Moore 1978), later presented a 'time-oriented anthropology' in the pre-eminent monograph in the field (Moore 1986). Ignoring the colonial state in the study of the law of the colonized was nonsensical because, as she wrote, 'the practices of the state are inseparable from the operations of the nonstate' (Moore 1986: 330).

Above all, what was missing from the early anthropology was an understanding of law that departs from law as command or as obedience to rules—an understanding that order can be secured by means other than state command. Law is better understood primarily as a matter of ideas. Fernanda Pirie (2013) notes how, in the history of anthropology and law, anthropologists have avoided law itself. Law describes ideas about peoples' capacities and behaviours, and it reflects systems of thought which lie behind its distinctive categories such as 'property, ownership, contract, responsibility, guilt and personality' (Pirie 2013: 55). The task is 'how to understand law as a system of meaning, rather than letting it dissolve into dynamics of power and control' (Pirie 2013: 68). Law can be understood as an 'intellectual system', a 'realm of ideas', and 'ideals and aspirations' (Pirie 2013: 72, 93, 158). An anthropology of law needs to be a study of thought and ideas as much as a description of practices. In Pirie's conclusion, we have the final break with Malinowski: law should be 'defined by its form, rather than its functions' (Pirie 2013: 216).

The successors to Victorian anthropology did their work in a colonial world. Colonial rule was authoritarian and racist. Its basic premise was that its subjects were not 'ready' to govern themselves. It punished disaffection and rebellion extremely harshly. Criminal law in the colonies was punitive. It relied heavily on corporal punishment, and deportation and collective punishment were common measures. The offences most commonly punished by colonial courts were not common-law crimes but the failure to pay tax and breaches of labour contracts. Native courts punished breaches of the multifarious ordinances regarding methods of cultivation, use of vacant lands and forest, hunting, brewing, marriage, movement, and residence, thus drawing them into the apparatus of colonial control. The point here is that this entire apparatus of control and punishment was a part of the legal world in which Africans lived, but it was in the main not a part which interested anthropologists of law. The new legal world could make them feel bewildered and dismayed as they experienced the effects of the imposed changes. Levi Mumba has captured this feeling:

> Differing from the European a native East African is not an individual. He is a member of a body. … The European came with his individualism and thrust it on

> the native. ... I hate individualism because it has torn the son from the father, or one man from another. The native shook himself and found that all his relatives have not adhered to him. (see Chanock 1985: 134–5)

Colonial administrators ruled unabashedly, but that said, they also accumulated a great deal of important description and analysis of the people they ruled over. While not based on the 'ethnographic method', this body of literature is a far larger resource for understanding the conflicts and norms of colonial peoples than the small corpus of the anthropology of law. These officials ran the colonial courts, and as the primary judges in the colonial system they knew a great deal about local systems of law and dispute settlement and how they were changing. But their knowledge was treated with scorn and hostility by the new 'scientific' anthropologists, from Malinowski onwards (Clifford 1988: 26). Though often marred by historical fantasy and racial contempt, the writings of colonial administrators should be resurrected now as part of the early anthropological canon, even though it was not produced by scholars with theoretical ambitions. In and of itself, however, this would not be enough to remedy the limitations of the early anthropologists. For this we need a truly 'emic' understanding of the experiences of becoming individually responsible, freely contracting subjects, living along the rocky road between Maine's status and contract.

Notes

1. My focus is mainly, though not entirely, on the British empire and its lawyers, officials, and anthropologists.
2. There was a robust strand of evolutionist/racist theorizing about law in the works of, among others, Tylor, Lubbock, McLennan, Bachofen, and Westermarck.
3. The temptation to quote Claude Levi-Strauss's (1961: 57) comment is irresistible: 'Himself a subject for serious study, the jurist is, to me, like an animal trying to explain to a zoologist the workings of a magic lantern'.
4. See in general Kuper (1985).
5. The title of the German-language original is *Der Ursprung der Familie, des Privateigenthums und des Staats. Im Anschluss an Lewis H. Morgan's Forschungen* (1884).
6. But note the number of 'rule books', i.e. treatises on tribal law, written by anthropologists, e.g. Cory (1953); Holleman (1952); Rattray (1929); Schapera (1938).
7. For a full analysis see Conley and O'Barr (2002), who regard it as the foundational text of the anthropology of law. However, a colonial magistrate *was* present in the Trobriands. Hogbin (1934) followed with another island study emphasizing the mechanism of reciprocity as the key to law.
8. *The Cheyenne Way* is fully analysed, and its influence dissected, in Conley and O'Barr (2004).
9. Austin's *The Province of Jurisprudence Determined* (1832) was the canonical text in the English understanding of law.
10. The Institute was funded by the government of Northern Rhodesia and the British South Africa Company. Both donors became increasingly suspicious of its work.

11. Wilson was later to write *An Essay on the Economics of Detribalisation in Northern Rhodesia* (1941–42), the classic on economic change in the region, one which incurred the extreme displeasure of the colonial government; but these intimations are not present in his definition of law.
12. Gluckman, who did not finish his basic legal education, did not seem to have understood the main function of the idea of the 'reasonable man' in common law, which was to limit liability in cases of negligence.
13. The Royal Commission on Labour in India (Cmd. 3883, 1931).
14. As I have shown, the ability to earn money drastically changed the balance between young men and old, and it had a profound impact on marriage law (Chanock 1985).

References

Austin, J. 1832. *The Province of Jurisprudence Determined.* London: John Murray.

Bentham, J. 1843. 'Principles of the Civil Code'. In J. Bowring, ed. *The Works of Jeremy Bentham, vol. 1*, 297–364. Edinburgh: William Tait.

Bohannan P. and L. Bohannan. 1968. *Tiv Economy.* Evanston, IL: Northwestern University Press.

Cairns, H. 1931. 'Law and Anthropology'. *Columbia Law Review* 31(1): 32–55.

Chanock, M. 1983. 'Signposts or Tombstones? Reflections on Recent Works on the Anthropology of Law'. *Law in Context* (1): 106.

Chanock, M. 1985. *Law, Custom and Social Order: The Colonial Experience in Malawi and Zambia.* Cambridge: Cambridge University Press.

Chanock, M. 1991. 'Paradigms, Policies and Property: A Review of the Customary Law of Land Tenure'. In K. Mann and R. Roberts, eds. *Law in Colonial Africa*, 61–84. London: Heinemann.

Chanock, M. 2001. *The Making of South African Legal Culture 1902–1936: Fear, Favour and Prejudice.* Cambridge: Cambridge University Press.

Clifford, J. 1988. *The Predicament of Culture: Twentieth-Century Ethnography, Literature, and Art.* Cambridge, MA: Harvard University Press.

Colson, E. 1974. *Tradition and Contract.* Chicago: Aldine Publishing.

Conley, J. M. 2004. 'A Classic in Spite of Itself: *The Cheyenne Way* and the Case Method in Legal Anthropology'. *Law and Social Inquiry* 29(1): 179–217.

Conley, J. M. and W. M. O'Barr. 2002. 'Back to the Trobriands: The Enduring Influence of Malinowski's *Crime and Custom in Savage Society*'. *Law and Social Inquiry* 27(4): 847–74.

Cory, H 1953. *Sukuma Law and Custom.* Oxford: Oxford University Press.

Durkheim, Émile. 1893. *De la division du travail social.* Paris: Félix Alcan.

Engels, F. 1948 [1884]. *The Origin of the Family, Private Property and the State.* Moscow: Progress Publishers.

Feit, H. A. 1991. 'The Construction of Algonquian Hunting Territories: Private Property as Moral Lesson, Policy Advocacy, and Ethnographic Error'. In G. W. Stocking, Jr., ed. *Colonial Situations: Essays on the Contextualization of Ethnographic Knowledge*, 109–34. Madison: University of Wisconsin Press.

Gluckman, M. 1955. *The Judicial Process among the Barotse of Northern Rhodesia.* Manchester: Manchester University Press.

Gluckman, M. 1965a. *The Ideas in Barotse Jurisprudence.* New Haven: Yale University Press.

Gluckman, M. 1965b. *Politics, Law and Ritual in Tribal Society.* Oxford: Blackwell.

Goodale M. 2017. *Anthropology and Law: a Critical Introduction.* New York: NYU Press.

Gray, J. 2018. '*Circling the Square*'. Review of N. Ferguson, *The Square and the Tower: Networks and Power, from the Freemasons to Facebook*. In *The New York Review of Books* LXV(5): 29; citing *Portraits and Miniatures* by R. Jenkins. London: Macmillan, 1993.

Gulliver, P. H. 1978. Preface. In P. H. Gulliver, ed. *Cross Examinations: Essays in Memory of Max Gluckman*, xi–xvii. Leiden: E. J. Brill.

Hailey, W. M. 1938. *An African Survey: A Study of Problems arising in Africa South of the Sahara*. Oxford: Oxford University Press.

Hartland, E. S. 1924. *Primitive Law*. London: Methuen and Co.

Hogbin, H. I. 1934. *Law and Order in Polynesia: A Study in Primitive Legal Institutions*. London: Christophers.

Holleman, J. F. 1952. *Shona Customary Law: With Reference to Kinship, Marriage, the Family and the Estate*. London: Oxford University Press.

Junod, H. 1912. *The Life of a South African Tribe, vol. I. The Social Life*. Neuchatel: Imprimerie Attinger Frères.

Kenyatta, J. 1938. *Facing Mount Kenya: The Tribal Life of the Gikuyu*. London: Secker and Warburg.

Kipling, R. 1899. 'The White Man's Burden: The United States and the Philippine Islands'. *The Times*, 4 February 1899.

Krader, L. 1972. *The Ethnological Notebooks of Karl Marx*. Assen: Von Gorcum.

Kuper, A. 1985. 'Ancestors: Henry Maine and the Constitution of Primitive Society'. *History and Anthropology* 1(2): 265–86.

Levi-Strauss, C. 1961. *Tristes Tropiques*. New York: Athenaeum.

Llewellyn, K. N. and E. A. Hoebel. 1941. *The Cheyenne Way: Conflict and Case Law in Primitive Jurisprudence*. Norman: University of Oklahoma Press.

Maclean, J. 1968 [1858]. *A Compendium of Kafir Laws and Customs*. London: Frank Cass & Co.

Maine, H. 1861. *Ancient Law*. London: Charles Murray.

Maine, H. 1871. *Village-Communities in the East and West*. London: John Murray.

Mair, L. 1962. *Primitive Government*. Harmondsworth: Penguin Books.

Malinowski, B. 1926. *Crime and Custom in Savage Society*. London: Routledge and Kegan Paul.

Marx, K. and F. Engels. 1970. *The German Ideology*. London: Lawrence and Wishart.

Meek, C. K. 1937. *Law and Authority in a Nigerian Tribe*. London: Oxford University Press.

Moore, S. F. 1978. 'Archaic Law and Modern Times on the Zambesi'. In P. H. Gulliver, ed. *Cross-examinations: Essays in memory of Max Gluckman*, 53–77. Leiden: E. J. Brill.

Moore, S. F. 1978. *Law as Process: An Anthropological Approach*. London: Routledge and Kegan Paul.

Moore, S. F. 1986. *Social Facts and Fabrications: 'Customary' Law on Kilimanjaro, 1880–1980*. Cambridge: Cambridge University Press.

Morgan, L. H. 1985 [1877]. *Ancient Society*. With a Foreword by E. Tooker. Tucson: University of Arizona Press.

Owen, R. 1973. 'Anthropology and Imperial Administration: Sir Alfred Lyall and the Official Use of Theories of Social Change Developed in India after 1857'. In T. Asad, ed. *Anthropology and the Colonial Encounter*, 223–43. London: Ithaca Press.

Pirie, F. 2013. *The Anthropology of Law*. Oxford: Oxford University Press.

Radcliffe-Brown, A. R. 1940. 'Preface'. In M. Fortes and E. E. Evans-Pritchard, eds. *African Political Systems*, xi–xviii. London: Oxford University Press.

Radcliffe-Brown, A. R. 1952 [1940]. 'On Social Structure'. In *Structure and Function in Primitive Society*, 188–204. Glencoe, IL: The Free Press.

Rattray, R.S. 1929. *Ashanti Law and Constitution*. Oxford: Clarendon Press.

Read, M. 1931. *The Indian Peasant Uprooted: A Study of the Human Machine*. London: Longmans, Green and Co.

Schapera, I. 1938. *A Handbook of Tswana Law and Custom*. London: Oxford University Press.

Smith, E. W. and A. M. Dale. 1920. *The Ila Speaking Peoples of Northern Rhodesia, vol. I*. London: Macmillan & Co.

Smith, K. J. M. 1988. *James Fitzjames Stephen: Portrait of a Victorian Rationalist*. Cambridge: Cambridge University Press.

Stocking, G. W., Jr. 1987. *Victorian Anthropology*. New York: Macmillan.

Tooker, E. 1985. 'Forward'. In L. H. Morgan, *Ancient Society*, xv–xxviii. Tucson: University of Arizona Press.

Van Vollenhoven, C. 1981 [1931]. 'The Study of Adat Law'. In J. R. Holleman, ed. *Van Vollenhoven on Indonesian Adat Law*. Selections from *Het Adatrecht von Nederlandsch-Indië* (trans. J. F. Holleman, R. Kalis, and K. Maddock), 24–40. Dordrecht: Springer-Service & Business Media, B. V.

Wilson, G. 1938. *The Land Rights of Individuals among the Nyakyusa*. Livingstone: Rhodes-Livingstone Institute.

CHAPTER 3

SOUTH AFRICAN LEGAL CULTURE AND ITS DIS/EMPOWERMENT PARADOX

SINDISO MNISI WEEKS

INTRODUCTION

A quarter of a century since South Africa became a constitutional democracy, the country presents a striking paradox: it has what is arguably the most progressive constitution in the world (especially in that it recognizes economic and social rights as justiciable) while continuing to hold the dubious distinction of being the most unequal country in the world, according to the World Bank (2018). How might such a state of affairs have come to be, and what role can and should the law realistically play in addressing it?

The evidence of South Africa's limited transformation even subsequent to the adoption of its progressive Constitution can be found in a World Bank report released in March 2018, finding that the top 1 per cent of South Africans own 70.9 per cent of the country's wealth, while the bottom 60 per cent control only 7 per cent of the nation's assets (World Bank 2018). While some assets have been transferred to or acquired by a few elite members of the majority black population, the lion's share of assets remain under white ownership (Lehohla 2017).

The distinct tension between the promise of what the Constitution can deliver and what has actually been accomplished under it is well represented by the latest Statistics South Africa data on poverty in the country. Those data reflect that, as of 2015, 30.4 million individuals—or 55.5 per cent of the population—were living in poverty on ZAR 992 ($74) or less per person per month, from which they had to cover the costs of food, shelter, clothing, and transportation (Lehohla 2017). This represents an increase from the 27.3 million people, or 53.2 per cent, reflected in the last report, issued in 2011 (Lehohla 2017).

Of this number, 93 per cent of the total 30 million (55.5 per cent) of South Africans declared poor were black. Proportionately, 28.3 million (64.2 per cent of) 'African/Black' people, 2 million (41.3 per cent of) 'Coloured', and 79,460 (5.9 per cent of) 'Indian/Asian' South Africans live in poverty. The same Statistics South Africa report noted that 47,494 (1 per cent of) white people lived under the poverty line (Lehohla 2017). Women and children also experienced higher rates of poverty than men, though the degree of difference between men and women was noted to have diminished in the ten years prior (Lehohla 2017).

This chapter makes the argument that this alarming paradox of a very progressive rights regime co-existing with extreme inequality and persistent poverty can be at least partly understood in terms of a 'dis/empowerment paradox' (Sigauqwe 2018) endemic to South Africa's legal culture. What is referred to here as legal culture is the shared standards, beliefs, values, and attitudes that characterize the relevant legal system (Merry 2010; Rosen 2006). Such legal culture is maintained through education and traditional practice by members of the legal profession, which Bourdieu (1987) compositely referred to as 'habitus', and has its own politics based on language, economics, and culture. This legal culture is internally contested even as members of the profession protect it against outsiders who do not, as Bourdieu theorized, possess the technical expertise deemed necessary to enable one to make authoritative judgements of the social world based on the law that is valued in that space.

To be clear, the argument in this chapter is *not* that the contributions to South Africa's legal culture made by its judiciary are solely—or even predominantly—responsible for the 'dis/empowerment paradox' here asserted. The argument is rather that—at least part of—the explanation for this paradox can be found in the judicial participation in the formation and maintenance of the country's legal culture as grasped in terms of the continuities between the past and the present.

The chapter therefore takes a historical view of the formation and impact of this legal culture and the various levels and ways in which the dis/empowerment paradox argued for here has been, and continues to be, characteristic of South Africa's legal culture. In essence, this dis/empowerment paradox can be described in terms of the possibilities for liberty and justice, along with the tendencies towards repression and injustice, that are simultaneously presented by law (Ellmann 1992)—whether the legal system is wicked (Dyzenhaus 2010) or otherwise.

The chapter begins with an overview of the history of law, paying particular attention to the development of legal pluralism and the prevailing legal culture in South Africa. As such, this history demonstrates the growing and excessive importance of law and legal regulations in South African colonial history. It particularly highlights the ways in which state-imposed laws increasingly affected the majority black population in the bifurcated state through both direct and indirect rule, which led to the creation of official customary law (Mamdani 1996).

This discussion leads into reflections on South African legal culture (Chanock 2001; Meierhenrich 2008) under an apartheid regime that gave tremendous importance to 'the rule of law'—at least formally—when, in fact, what prevailed was rather rule *by* law (Abel 1995; Dyzenhaus 2010; Ellmann 1992). The apartheid constitution, and the concomitant conditions of parliamentary supremacy, also peculiarly created opportunities for a shift towards legal activism and cause-lawyering or public interest litigation to take place in the context of ever-shrinking legal possibilities for political protest (Abel 1995; Budlender et al. 2014; Ellmann 1992).

The discussion turns to the legal transformation that occurred with the shift to constitutional supremacy. This forms the background for a discussion of the legal advocacy work that accompanied and then followed the adoption of the Interim Constitution (1993) and Final Constitution (1996), especially by organizations including the Black Sash, Centre for Applied Legal Studies, Community Law Centre, Institute for Poverty, Land and Agrarian Studies, Law, Race and Gender Research Unit, Lawyers for Human Rights, Legal Resources Centre, National Women's Coalition, Rural Women's Movement, Section27, Socio-Economic Rights Institute, Treatment Action Campaign, Women's Legal Centre, as well as by actors within state departments such as Land Affairs.

The hope is that the historical arc helps legal, anthropological, and wider audiences not familiar with South Africa's specific circumstances to better understand the argument with which the chapter then concludes: namely, that the purported solution of 'transformative constitutionalism' itself presents both possibilities and pitfalls. As Karl Klare defines it, 'transformative constitutionalism' is

> a long term project of constitutional enactment, interpretation, and enforcement committed ... to transforming a country's political and social institutions and power relationships in a democratic, participatory, and egalitarian direction. Transformative constitutionalism connotes an enterprise of inducing large-scale social change through non-violent political processes grounded in law. (1998: 150)

In Klare's conception, 'the Constitution suggests not only the desirability, but the legal necessity, of a transformative conception of adjudicative process and method' (1998: 156)—that is, 'transformative adjudication'. Indeed, former Deputy Chief Justice Dikgang Moseneke argues that 'the judiciary is commanded to observe with unfailing fidelity the transformative mission of the Constitution' (2002: 319).

Of this mandate, Klare later observes that

> the broad values and transformative aspirations embraced by the Constitution are indeterminate with respect to their legal and institutional implications. They can only be given concrete application on the basis of a myriad of intermediate judgments and choices that reflect moral and political perspectives and sensibilities. (2011: 872)

Unfortunately, this chapter finds that the necessary 'intermediate judgments and choices' have been few and far between—at least, relative to the scale of socioeconomic transformation that is needed.

Essentially, the chapter argues that an understanding of South Africa that observes the contributions of the judiciary to shaping the country's legal culture over the course of history and into the present points to judicial complicity in restraining the full realization of freedom and justice under the law by under-utilizing law's potential for liberation.[1] This complicity of the judiciary has contributed to the dis/empowerment paradox expressed in the fact that the promised transformative constitutionalism in South Africa has not delivered nearly as much transformation as was hoped or expected, and very slowly at that (Roux 2009; cf. Klug 2016).

History of South African Law and Politics

A summary of the historical background of South African law readily makes evident that economics, politics, and law are almost inextricably entwined. Perhaps the most important observation to be made from the beginning is that the law in South Africa has been at the centre of a broader sociopolitical dispute between—at least—two people groups (black Africans and white European settlers) who have different sociolegal orders (indigenous law, Roman-Dutch and common law) that observe markedly distinct epistemologies and cultures.

Particularly under the guise of the 'rule of law', law has played a peculiar role in the formation and evolution of South Africa as a set of colonies, then a unified republic, and now a fledgling democracy; law is purportedly the primary contingency upon which the resolution of some significant socioeconomic and political questions hinges. This notable trait of the South African legal system and its distinguishing culture has attracted much scholarly consideration (Abel 1995; Chanock 2001; Dyzenhaus 2010; Ellmann 1992; Mamdani 1996; Meierhenrich 2008; Ngcukaitobi 2018)—with good reason. It therefore compels one to start this chapter from colonialism to the latter days of apartheid.

In terms of definitions, colonialism is taken here to have begun in 1652, when the Dutch first arrived at the Cape. The form of segregation that would ultimately crystallize into apartheid gradually entered between 1910, the year of unification of the four colonial provinces of the Cape and Natal (under British rule) and the Orange Free State and Transvaal (under Afrikaner control), and 1948. The latter was the year in which the National Party government was installed, which marked the official instatement of the policy of 'apartheid' or 'separate development'. While the transition to democracy took place over a four-year period of formal negotiations amidst civil unrest starting in 1990, the first democratic elections occurred in April 1994, and it is the latter that is therefore taken as the beginning of the democratic era.

On Colonialism

The history of South Africa from 1652 to 1994 tells a story of political struggle between the colonizers and colonized over resources, authority, and cultural legitimacy or validation thereof by the state. The colonizing state's means of acquiring resources attributable to the indigenous population was the assertion of power, implementation of authority by coercion, and propagation of stereotypes about cultural differences (Benton 2002; Chanock 2001; Lugard 1922; Mamdani 1996).

The enforcement of a foreign legal system—initially Roman-Dutch, then British—played a major role in securing the colonial state's domination (Delius 2008; Guy 1987; Peires 1981). Natural resources and labour, power and authority, and morality and culture were amongst the things battled for by both groups in the legal realm, both shaping the law and legitimizing colonial rule in ways that are detailed below (Mattei and Nader 2008). When the imposition of foreign law was found to be ineffective in subjecting and controlling the native population (and also more costly than desired), the colonial order evolved into one involving the manipulation of indigenous law (Chanock 2001; Lugard 1922; Mamdani 1996). Still, both the colonizing and indigenous groups used the law as a tool against each other and within their groups (Mann and Roberts 1991; Mattei and Nader 2008).

As argued by Martin Chanock (1991), the law was the sharpest tool used by the colonialist state to enforce its coercive power. He continues that an understanding of customary law cannot be divorced from one of the capitalist economy introduced by colonizers to the indigenous populations of Africa. This argument is reinforced by Ugo Mattei and Laura Nader (2008) in their argument that this 'imperial use of the rule of law' constructed, legalized, and legitimized what they refer to as 'plunder', pointing to the 'dark side' that can be the 'illegality' of the rule of law. Similar arguments are made by Richard Abel (1995), who highlights the official importance of 'the rule of law' as a key aspect of what David Dyzenhaus (2010) aptly describes as the apartheid regime's 'rule by law' (also see Ellmann 1989).

Of course, as many of these scholars stress, the colonizers were not singularly responsible for the oppression of those who were governed by law or solely responsible for the suppression of customary law's development under the distorting pressures imposed by state law. Rather, if only because elite members of the colonized population were rendered instruments against their own people, both colonial and customary agents were contributors to the relationship between the legal systems and the impact internally of colonialism on customary law.

Although the Dutch East India Company had only wanted it as a stop-over point when it came to the Cape, its need for commodities required that a thriving economy develop in the area. As a result, a Dutch population was established in the Cape, occupying territory that belonged to the Khoi people. Since much colonial policy was centred on economic expansion, in South Africa, where the focus of the economy would be on agriculture, land was the commodity in most demand (Mamdani 1996). Consequently, a great need arose amongst the settler population for the regulation (and 'creation') of property rights.

According to Lauren Benton (2002), the colonial government was careful to divide areas of property law into those with which it concerned itself and those which could be relinquished to non-state bodies, such as indigenous authorities, for administration. Hence, property disputes that were valuable to the government's welfare or analogous to colonial state interests were dealt with by colonial administrators and judges. Those disputes related to family, religion, and culture were relinquished to other authorities, including traditional ones, for settlement. Nonetheless, the characterization of interests changed readily as the colonial enterprise and state concerns expanded. Thus, inconsequential matters relating to marriage and succession could rapidly become vital to commercial issues such as labour, revenue collection, and the regulation of land markets, at which point their designation would change (Benton 2002).

Between the late 1800s and early 1900s, no unified model of native control was used in South Africa. Although 'direct rule' was the official policy, the de facto situation varied between regions, dependent on the authorities involved and the administrative resources and personnel available. Once it became apparent that colonial authorities needed a customized way to rule indigenous communities who subscribed to a unique kind of culture and normative order, a formalized system of dealing with the legally pluralistic society was developed.

The principle of indirect rule—whereby indigenous law was used as an efficient means of enforcing government policy—was initially informal during British colonial rule. Yet in 1846 (subsequent to the annexation of Natal in 1843), a British commission recommended

> aggregating the natives in separate locations and administering their day-to-day activities under a 'system of justice' that 'should conform as much to their own law as is compatible within the principle of ours.'
>
> (Mamdani 1996: 63, 115–16)

Thus, the already informally existent policy of 'indirect rule' was institutionalized in South Africa as part of the British authorities' system of 'native administration' in the late nineteenth century (Lugard 1922; Mamdani 1996; Mann and Roberts 1991). Under this policy, customary ways (particularly concerning authority and power) were moulded to be more conducive to the government's implementation of its policies of control over the African population.

In the early 1900s, in Nigeria, Frederick Lugard institutionalized the practice of indirect rule and is credited with this policy's spread throughout the British empire (Lugard 1922; Mamdani 1996; Mann and Roberts 1991). The policy was embodied by three specific institutional reforms: namely, the recognition of the traditional leaders (Native Administration), the establishment of Native Courts, and the inauguration of Native Treasuries into which indigenous leaders were required to collect taxes from their subjects.

> In the face of African resistance to direct intervention and in the interest of containing administrative costs, indirect rule retreated from aggressive legal and governmental reform … . The task of the British colonial administrator was now to reform indigenous administration from within indigenous institutions.
>
> (Lugard 1922: 211; Mann and Roberts 1991: 20)

This approach spread to many other British-administered territories.

Mamdani (1996) argues that the policy of indirect rule was adopted as a solution to 'the native question', which in settler colonies was: how would the immigrant minority rule the majority indigenous population? Indirect rule provided a way of fragmenting the overwhelming black populace into tribes (thus causing them to perceive themselves as small groups, rather than a dominant race). It also suppressed revolt by creating the impression of the communities' autonomy and independence. As Mamdani (1996) remarks, while the chiefs were autonomous, they were far from independent.

In essence, insufficient genuine interest in customary law, its import and development (even as a means of rule), made it progressively easier to alter it for the benefit of civil law and colonial society. The resource limitations that the state faced also contributed to it taking liberties with customary law. In light of this, the qualification made by Chanock (2001) and Mamdani (1996) regarding the reciprocal relationship of colonialism is fitting: although customary communities contributed to the subordination of their own law(s), their effectual involvement in shaping relations between their law and that of the state remained nominal. Their impact was always constrained by the colonial state's agenda and interests.

Unification: Colonialism Turned Into Apartheid

There was no bright line between colonialism and apartheid (Chanock 2001). As Mamdani summarizes: '[w]hat [General Jan] Smuts termed institutional segregation the Broederbond called apartheid' (1996: 6–7). The shift from British colonial rule (mostly felt in Natal and the Cape) to post-Union Afrikaner Nationalist Party rule officially occurred in 1948 when Smuts, who had served as prime minister of the Union of South Africa in 1919–24 and 1939–48, lost his political bid. However, this was a subtle and confused transition that really transpired over several decades referred to as the union period (1910–48).

Having had its problems, indirect rule was still found to be the most effective way of ruling the majority black population and was therefore retained as the official policy of the union and then apartheid governments. The ostensible reasons for its existence (namely minimal cost and effort, maximal control of labour and land resources, and the natives' lack of civilization) remained cogent. The philosophy also later proved consistent with the apartheid government's broader vision to see the native population pushed out into 'self-governing territories' so as to ensure 'separate development' (Mamdani 1996: 6–7, 89).

Two major 'developments', however, occurred during the union and then apartheid periods—both being segregationist regimes. The government attempted to reverse urbanization by forcibly relocating black people to tribal areas or, if they were required for labour purposes, to local townships and hostels (Mamdani 1996). Then also, in the midst of the systematic legislative structuring of the government's separatist policy, indirect rule was entrenched in a unified national statute (Church 2005).

Section 11 of the Native Administration Act 38 of 1927 provided that customary law would apply (in state courts) solely in the native courts established by the same legislation and would do so only if consistent with public policy and natural justice (Chanock 2001). The Act also deemed the Governor-General (later State President) Supreme Chief of all Indigenous People and assigned him arbitrary powers (Chanock 2001).

Though unification of the four provinces took place in 1910, for years thereafter the courts in each of the four former colonies followed their prior choice of law practices in native cases (Chanock 2001). In most of the provinces there had been some legislation or ordinance that regulated this, and thus the vague wording of section 11 was simply interpreted in accordance with its predecessor. Therefore, the courts in some colonies applied civil law and in others customary law, ultimately determined (in every region) on a case-by-case basis. This inconsistency was finally remedied by the Appellate Division of the Supreme Court in 1948. It held that no presumption was to exist in favour of applying either common or customary law but that courts should apply the law that was most applicable to the parties and the circumstances of the case.

Joan Church describes this decision as having resulted, in its application, in customary law's recognition 'only as a special and personal law that operated outside of but only as determined by the general law' (2005: 95). This was consistent with recent colonial practice. Consequently, although there was evidently a great lack of community self-determination, according to Thomas Bennett (concerned with the mid-1900s onwards), what became the mark of the system was a lack of individual autonomy. Whether civil or customary law was to apply was not left to the choice of individuals but was determined by race: culture became the basis for 'legal segregation' (Bennett and Peart 1991: vii).

Furthermore, some Africans took the opportunity to enrich themselves by taking the positions of authority offered by the state with the intended purpose of doing its bidding and benefiting from government favour. Those black traditional leaders who would not cooperate with the state often lost their birthright and were replaced by opportunists. Because of this, the system of traditional leadership became corrupted and lost its rooting in community legitimation, contributing further to the disintegration of strong community ties and distortion of culture (Luthuli 1962; Mamdani 1996; Mandela 1959; Mbeki 1964).

Youths and women (the most disadvantaged by the government's policy) increasingly moved out of the villages (Mann and Roberts 1991). The state had initially sought to assist women and, hence, they were sympathetically regarded by judges who thought it injudicious to force them into marriage; such a perception had been exploited by the women to avoid matches that did not please them. However, this was replaced by the state will to curtail their supposedly loose morals by subjecting them to greater spousal control (Chanock 2001; Mamdani 1996; McClendon 1995). This reform constituted part of the government's broader realization of the error of its interference with cultural ways, as it identified its interference as causing the dissipation of communal links and degradation of codes of conduct and control mechanisms that had been inherent therein (Mamdani 1996).

In the early twentieth century, the number of women who moved into the cities was alarming to all powerful groups (Chanock 2001). The escape of women and children from the realm of spousal and parental authority, respectively, left communities short on labourers and thus weakened their ability to propagate wealth, fecundity (and hence their means of perpetuating kinship ties), and sheer control (Bronstein 1998). In response, the community leaders created stricter rules to constrain the movement of these groups into urban areas. This was also consistent with government objectives to limit the influx of black people into the cities, which was causing overcrowding in urban townships and fuelling popular resistance movements (Chanock 2001; Mamdani 1996).

The indigenous forms of law were sure to be disrupted in the process of all of this turbulence. For instance, a civil law approach was applied to them, resulting in the indirect infiltration of civil law into customary law. One illustration of this is how attempts were made to imbue customary law with 'certainty' under the principle of 'legality' and the 'rule of law' by codifying it in precedent and statute. The KwaZulu Act on the Code of Zulu Law 16 of 1985 and the Natal Code of Zulu Law[2] each provide an example of this phenomenon.

Furthermore, concepts in customary law with no direct equivalents in civil law discourse were extended, reinterpreted, or created to suit the prevailing legal framework. Consequently, notions of personal property became more dominant and communal property less valued as a form of 'ownership', which itself was defined in ways that were more consistent with colonial law than customary law. The individual as an independent bearer of rights became more prominent while the family, kinship duties, and reciprocal responsibilities providing symbiotic social security came under criticism. Moreover, the application of customary law by judges was subject to the proviso that it not be 'repugnant to the principles of public policy or natural justice'. The 'public' taken into account was the white minority and the perceptions of 'nature' and 'justice' were Eurocentric.[3]

Furthermore, with unification, separate courts were established to hear customary disputes even as appeals went to the civil appeal courts. Meanwhile, the customary courts were staffed by colonial officials who were, in some instances, given the artificial status of being customary chiefs. In relation to this point, Chanock (2001) observes that matters of criminal law quickly became mostly reserved for the control of the state, chiefs' powers increasingly being given to magistrates. The expectation was that by this intervention, 'primitive' law would evolve and be subsumed under the formal regime.

By the mid-twentieth century, three forms of customary law had developed: official, academic, and living law. Official law comprised the customary law captured in precedent (and influenced by Roman-Dutch and English legal principles) and statute law. Academic law was constituted by the body of treatises on customary law, referred to by the courts when deciding disputes. These texts were overwhelmingly written by white scholars and colonial administrators. Due to an insufficiency of empirical research, the living law was left to speculation (Bennett and Peart 1991). The state and academic law had, supposedly, at some point, reflected indigenous law. However, they had now both been ossified by their application through the filter of the civil legal system and its processes, particularly the doctrine of *stare decisis* as well as the strict, formal methods of framing proceedings and presenting arguments.

Apartheid's Sunset and Democracy's Dawn

Chanock notes that under apartheid '[m]aintaining "law and order" was an overriding preoccupation' for the Nationalist government (Chanock 2001: 28). In 1985 a state of emergency was declared, followed by others in close succession in the four subsequent years. This was at a time when opportunities for resisting apartheid through law seemed all but closed—at least on paper. Indeed, as Steven Budlender, Gilbert Marcus, and Nick Ferreira (2014) report in their strategic evaluation of public interest litigation in South Africa, the 'mechanisms for public interest litigation' were extremely constrained in theory by the doctrine of near-complete parliamentary sovereignty, among other obvious limitations in an unjust legal system (2014: 8). However, as they continue to observe based on interviews with several long-time South African public interest lawyers, there were still opportunities for challenging the unjust body of laws in court.

Their characterization summarizes the assessment repeatedly made by scholars, among them Abel (1995), Dyzenhaus (2010), Stephen Ellmann (1992), Heinz Klug (2010), and Jens Meierhenrich (2008), namely that:

> Despite its flagrant violation of human rights, [the apartheid] government purported to hold the judiciary in the highest esteem and professed respect for the rule of law. This attitude, combined with government's attempts to use the law to entrench apartheid, ironically created opportunities for public interest lawyers to exploit gaps in the system.
>
> (Budlender et al. 2014: 8)

Consequently, public interest litigation was robust in South Africa during this time, under the institutionalized leadership of lawyers like Arthur Chaskalson, Geoffrey Budlender, George Bizos, and Wim Trengrove at the Legal Resources Centre and Edwin Cameron at the Centre for Applied Legal Studies at the University of the Witwatersrand, as well as independent advocates such as Ismail Mahomed, Dullah Omar, Dikgang Moseneke, and attorneys Griffiths and Victoria Mxenge, among many more. The support of the international community and foreign donors helped to challenge the foundations of apartheid and extend civil and political rights.

By the time the Interim Constitution was passed in 1993 and the Final Constitution in 1996, South Africa already had a lively public interest litigation sphere. It also had a dual legal system whereby customary law applied to most of the black population, while Roman-Dutch and common law applied to the white population (Mamdani 1996).

It is a truism that the values embodied in customary law sometimes differ from those represented in the Bill of Rights of South Africa, whether in essence or in the way in which they are understood. The Constitutional Court anticipated the confrontation between customary law and the Bill of Rights in the *Certification* judgment,[4] where it warned that such a tension ought not to destroy customary law or suppress its fluid nature. In the well-known death penalty case of *S v Makwanyane*,[5] the Court discussed the interaction of the Bill of Rights with customary law and its values in general. Sachs J gave the statement that 'we do not automatically invoke each and every aspect of traditional law as a source of values, just as we do not rely on all features of the common law' (383).

Since then, several developments have been introduced to customary law that some have argued run the risk of quashing it and its fluid nature in the way warned of in the *Certification* judgment (Mnisi Weeks 2015; Sibanda and Mosaka 2015). For instance, in *Bhe v Khayelitsha Magistrate*,[6] customary law was 'developed' by substituting a civil law statute that embodies the value of the nuclear family, drawn from the common law idea thereof, and making provision for polygynous marriages but not extended family outside of that. The Constitutional Court said that it was developing a temporary solution and government would pass a permanent solution. When government passed permanent legislation, it based it on the solution developed by the Court, thus perpetuating the imposition of a civil law solution under the guise of developing customary law.

Part of what skews courts towards imposing civil or common law frameworks of understanding onto customary law and the cultures of communities that observe it is that, according to section 1(c) of the South African Constitution, the state is founded on the value of the rule of law. Implicitly, laws must satisfy the principle of legality and, hence, be clear and specific, consistently applicable, foreseeable, and (easily) ascertainable.[7] Given that this principle is rooted in a positivistic understanding of law (Dyzenhaus 1992, 2010), it appears that the South African Constitution thereby ensconces a broadly positivistic approach to the making and enforcement of law. Part of the dis/empowerment paradox lies herein, as the positivistic notions inherent in legality do not naturally lend themselves to the faithful ascertainment, interpretation, and application of living law that the Constitutional Court presents as the primary preference.

Beyond customary law, in the period between 1994 and 2000, there was marked caution exercised by the Constitutional Court, which wanted to give the government the benefit of the doubt and room to fulfil its obligations under the new Constitution, especially in the realm of socioeconomic rights. An example of this was the case of *Soobramoney v Minister of Health, KwaZulu-Natal*,[8] where the Court interpreted the right to health care rather narrowly and excluded minimum core standards.

That said, significant victories were subsequently had, such as in the cases of *Government of the Republic of South Africa v Grootboom* and *Minister of Health v Treatment Action Campaign*.[9] Nonetheless, one of the things that the public interest litigation sphere has struggled to achieve is a sustained, profound, and equitable connection 'between [NGOs] that work on the ground with people experiencing socioeconomic rights deprivations, and litigation organisations' (Budlender et al. 2014: 9; also see Madlingozi 2014). This leads us back to the dis/empowerment paradox that I have suggested is the continuous mark of the South African legal system and its culture.

The Dis/empowerment Paradox Persists

So far, in this chapter, I have canvassed the foundations of the pluralistic South African legal system as it developed through colonialism, apartheid, and into the present democratic dispensation. I have posited that one area of continuity in the South African legal system and its culture is a dis/empowerment paradox. Under colonialism, indirect rule allowed some room for autonomous rule by traditional leaders and some opportunities for the exploitation of gaps in the law by vulnerable groups like women and youths who appealed to the sympathies of the courts.

Under apartheid, the 'rule by law' and its somewhat dependent relationship with the 'rule of law' allowed for some of the black population to appeal to the courts for reprieve from some of the injustices of the wicked legal system (Dyzenhaus 2010: 253; also see Moseneke 2016; Ngcukaitobi 2018). As Dyzenhaus explains:

> Of course, whether or not judges will use their jurisdiction to realize law's potential will depend, as Ellman [sic] clearly shows, on many of the variables that together make up a distinct legal culture. And, as he asserts, jurisprudence plays a distinctive role in legal culture. (1992: 249)

Dyzenhaus goes on to argue that Ellmann (1992) is restrained by an embrace of 'high positivism' from recognizing the full extent of the role played by jurisprudence in this scenario. Essentially, as Dyzenhaus argues, judges can create more or less 'legal space' for political activism and opposition by how they interpret the 'rule of law' and law's content in their legal culture (1992: 250). In this sense, Dyzenhaus argues in agreement with Ellmann that law—and the work of judges—is by no means apolitical.

This truthfully political exercise of its role by the judiciary is important to the possibilities that ordinary people can see in and through the law and, consequently, to the very 'legitimacy' of the law and the 'constitutional enterprise' (Davis 2006; Dyzenhaus 1992, 2010). Whereas, under colonialism and apartheid, the disempowerment dimension of South African legal culture was more self-evident than the empowerment dimension and scholars therefore worked hard to emphasize the agency of oppressed populations, under the democratic dispensation the positions are reversed. This chapter therefore concludes by confronting the question of the hidden disempowerments that can be found in the otherwise overtly very empowering legal framework that is created by the progressive Constitution and its rights protections.

It bears repeating that my argument is *not* that the courts are exclusively, or even primarily, responsible for the failures of the progressive rights regime under the Constitution to deliver equality and freedom (especially from the precarity and other perils of persistent poverty). The government under the African National Congress (ANC) should rightly get most of the blame for that. Rather, my argument is that, as under apartheid (which was an undeniably wicked legal system), the courts and their contribution to South African legal culture are worth examining for potential complicity and, hence, for possible ways in which they can be a bigger part of the solution going forward.

Conclusion

Post-apartheid, the public interest litigation sector has taken advantage of the potential offered by the perpetuated elements of the South African legal culture's supposed fidelity to the rule of law as well as the expanded opportunities created by the Bill of Rights under the progressive Constitution. Indeed, this sector has even taken to heart Dyzenhaus's conclusion that 'law's potential to vindicate individual rights' offers us the promise of a substantive debate about what should be the content of those rights (1992: 251). Much of the South African socioeconomic rights jurisprudence is an expression of this hope that

> South Africa might yet teach us that with the necessary elements of the right kind of legal culture in place, and with an appreciation of the importance of the role jurisprudence plays in legal culture, the law offers us more as a site of struggle than many would grant.
>
> (Dyzenhaus 1992: 251)

Here, Dyzenhaus is implicitly calling for 'lawfare'.

'Lawfare' is a term that was first used by John Carlson and Neville Yeomans (1975) to describe the blending of the strategies of 'law' and 'warfare' with the consequence that adversarial legal processes are used to replace alternative dispute resolution methods (such as negotiation and mediation). As Carlson and Yeomans summarize the effect, '[l]awfare replaces warfare and the duel is with words rather than swords' (1975: 2). The concept has been further developed by John and Jean Comaroff (2009) to situate it within the broader 'fetishism of law' into which 'lawfare' falls, whereby the legal sphere 'is objectified, ascribed a life-force of its own, and attributed the capacity to configure a world of relations in its own image' (2009: 33).

Embrace of 'lawfare' in South Africa, as in much of the world (Comaroff and Comaroff 2009), has led to mixed empirical results (Budlender et al. 2014). However, I primarily want to highlight the questionability of whether South Africa yet has 'the right kind of legal culture in place' (Dyzenhaus 1992: 251). A statement by Budlender, Marcus, and Ferreira clarifies the pertinence of the question I raise. As they write of apartheid:

> … (at least in theory) the mechanisms for public interest litigation were very limited. There was no Bill of Rights, almost complete parliamentary sovereignty, very

> strict prescription laws that favoured the state, and a judiciary which often followed the letter of the law even though it may have taken the view that the laws were unjust.
>
> (Budlender et al. 2014: 8)

The last clause is especially apt: the judiciary could have done more to alleviate the trauma and suffering endured by the majority (Gobodo-Madikizela 2008, 2016) under the extremely unjust legal system of apartheid.

The point here is that everything in the law has changed from what Budlender, Marcus, and Ferreira's interview subjects (2014) describe—except for the legal culture as expressed in and through the courts. During apartheid, the courts did not do more because of their 'high positivist' cultural interpretation of the rule of law. Today, the opportunities can be found under the Constitution and its Bill of Rights for the courts to broaden South Africa's legal culture and be more transformative in their approach and, consequently, the content of their decisions; yet, as many a scholar has argued, these opportunities are largely unclaimed (Davis and Klare 2010; Modiri 2012, 2015; Roux 2009; Sibanda 2013).

I therefore agree with scholars who have explained the constraints on transformative constitutionalism—as a phenomenon that centres on moral and political opportunities for achieving freedom and social justice presented by and within the law—in terms of the conservative legal culture of South African courts (Davis and Klare 2010; Klare 1998; cf. Klug 2016) and the inherent limits of liberal constitutionalism (Sibanda 2013; cf. Michelman 2011; Roux 2009). As Sanele Sibanda summarizes, 'adjudicators may, owing to the prevailing legal culture and/or their politics, interpret and enforce the Constitution in ways that subvert the progressive and egalitarian social and political vision of transformation' (Sibanda 2011: 489; see also Moseneke 2002: 315–16; Pieterse 2005: 164).

By making this argument, I do not mean to absolve the government of its blatant failures to deliver on its promises and duties to its electorate. Yet the skewed political economy and the lack of political will within the ANC-led democratic government also does not exonerate the courts and the South African legal culture they perpetuate from complicity when it comes to the failures of South Africa's Constitution to achieve the extent, or even kind, of transformation that was hoped.

Notes

1. As discussed below, law, in this chapter, is conceived of in a pluralistic sense; it should therefore not be taken to be co-extensive with Western law (i.e. South African law that finds its roots in Roman-Dutch and common law or the colonial encounter) but inclusive of customary law in both its official (institutionalized) form and living form (developed and practised by ordinary people).
2. Published in Proclamation R151 of 1987, Government Gazette No. 10966.
3. An interesting case to consider in this regard is *Ismail v Ismail* 1983 (1) SA 1006 (A). This concerned the 'potentially polygamous marriage' between a Muslim man and his wife. At

1024D–26C, Trengrove JA of the Supreme Court of Appeal (SCA) held that it would be *contra bonos mores* and the *jus publicum* to recognize such a marriage.

4. *Ex parte Chairperson of the Constitutional Assembly: In re Certification of the Constitution of the Republic of South Africa, 1996* 1996 (4) SA 744 (CC).
5. *S v Makwanyane* 1995 (3) SA 391 (CC).
6. *Bhe and Others v Khayelitsha Magistrate and Others* 2005 (1) SA 580 (CC).
7. *Pharmaceutical Manufacturers Association of SA and Another: In Re Ex Parte President of the Republic of South Africa and Others* 2000 (2) SA 674 (CC), 2000 (3) BCLR 241 at paras 17, 19–20, and 50; *Fedsure Life Assurance Ltd and Others v Greater Johannesburg Transitional Metropolitan Council and Others* 1999 (1) SA 374 (CC), 1998 (12) BCLR 1458 at para. 58.
8. *Soobramoney v Minister of Health, KwaZulu-Natal* 1998 (1) SA 765 (CC).
9. *Government of the Republic of South Africa and Others v Grootboom and Others* 2001 (1) SA 46 (CC); *Minister of Health and Others v Treatment Action Campaign and Others (No 2)* 2002 (5) SA 721 (CC).

References

Abel, R.L. 1995. *Politics by Other Means: Law in the Struggle against Apartheid, 1980-1994*. New York: Routledge.

Bennett, T. W. and N. S. Peart. 1991. *A Sourcebook of African Customary Law for Southern Africa*. Cape Town: Juta & Co.

Benton, L. A. 2002. *Law and Colonial Cultures: Legal Regimes in World History, 1400–1900*. Cambridge: Cambridge University Press.

Bourdieu, P. 1987. 'The Force of Law: Toward a Sociology of the Juridical Field'. *Hastings Law Journal* 38(5): 814–53.

Bronstein, V. 1998. 'Reconceptualizing the Customary Law Debate in South Africa'. *South African Journal on Human Rights* 14(3): 388–410.

Budlender, S., G. Marcus, and N. M. Ferreira. 2014. *Public Interest Litigation and Social Change in South Africa: Strategies, Tactics and Lessons*. Atlantic Philanthropies, available at <https://www.atlanticphilanthropies.org/wp-content/uploads/2015/12/Public-interest-litigation-and-social-change-in-South-Africa.pdf>.

Carlson, J. and N. Yeomans. 1975. 'Whither Goeth the Law—Humanity or Barbarity'. In M. Smith and D. Crossley, eds. *The Way Out: Radical Alternatives in Australia*. Melbourne: Landsdowne Press.

Chanock, M. 1991. 'Law, State and Culture: Thinking about Customary Law after Apartheid'. *Acta Juridica* 1991: 52–70.

Chanock, M. 2001. *The Making of South African Legal Culture, 1902–1936: Fear, Favour, and Prejudice*. Cambridge: Cambridge University Press.

Church, J. 2005. 'The Place of Indigenous Law in a Mixed Legal System and a Society in Transformation: A South African Experience'. *Australia & New Zealand Law & History E-Journal*: 94–106.

Comaroff, J. and J. L. Comaroff. 2009. 'Reflections on the Anthropology of Law, Governance and Sovereignty'. In F. von Benda-Beckmann, K. von Benda-Beckmann, and J. M. Eckert, eds. *Rules of Law and Laws of Ruling: On the Governance of Law*, 31–60. Farnham: Ashgate.

Davis, D. M. 2006. 'To Defer and Then When? Administrative Law and Constitutional Democracy: The Constitutional Context'. *Acta Juridica* 2006: 23–41.

Davis, D. M. and K. Klare. 2010. 'Transformative Constitutionalism and the Common and Customary Law'. *South African Journal on Human Rights* 26(3): 403–509.

Delius, P. 2008. 'Contested Terrain: Land Rights and Chiefly Power in Historical Perspective'. In A. Claassens and B. Cousins, eds. *Land, Power & Custom: Controversies Generated by South Africa's Communal Land Rights Act*, 211–37. Cape Town: UTC Press.

Dyzenhaus, D. 1992. 'Law's Potential'. *Canadian Journal of Law and Society* 7(2): 237–51.

Dyzenhaus, D. 2010. *Hard Cases in Wicked Legal Systems: Pathologies of Legality*. Oxford: Oxford University Press.

Ellmann, S. 1989. 'Legal Text and Lawyers' Culture in South Africa'. *New York University Review of Law & Social Change* 17: 387–418.

Ellmann, S. 1992. *In a Time of Trouble: Law and Liberty in South Africa's State of Emergency*. Oxford: Oxford University Press.

Gobodo-Madikizela, P. 2008. 'Transforming Trauma in the Aftermath of Gross Human Rights Abuses: Making Public Spaces Intimate Through the South African Truth and Reconciliation Commission'. In A. Nadler, T. Malloy, and J. D. Fisher, eds. *The Social Psychology of Intergroup Reconciliation*, 57–76. Oxford: Oxford University Press.

Gobodo-Madikizela, P. 2016. 'Interrupting Cycles of Repetition: Creating Spaces for Dialogue, Facing and Mourning the Past'. In P. Gobodo-Madikizela, ed. *Breaking Intergenerational Cycles of Repetition*, 113–34. Opladen: Barbara Budrich Publishers.

Guy, J. 1987. 'Analysing Pre-Capitalist Societies in Southern Africa'. *Journal of Southern African Studies* 14(1): 18–37.

Klare, K. E. 1998. 'Legal Culture and Transformative Constitutionalism'. *South African Journal on Human Rights* 14(1): 146–88.

Klare, K. E. 2011. 'Concluding Reflections: Legal Activism after Poverty Has Been Declared Unconstitutional'. *Stellenbosch Law Review* 22(3): 865–74.

Klug, H. 2010. *The Constitution of South Africa: A Contextual Analysis*. Oxford: Hart Publishing.

Klug, H. 2016. 'Challenging Constitutionalism in Post-Apartheid South Africa'. *Constitutional Studies* 2: 41–58.

Lehohla, P. 2017. *Poverty trends in South Africa: an examination of absolute poverty between 2006 and 2015*. Pretoria: Statistics South Africa, available at <https://www.statssa.gov.za/publications/Report-03-10-06/Report-03-10-062015.pdf>.

Lugard, F. J. D. 1922. *The Dual Mandate in British Tropical Africa*. Edinburgh: William Blackwood and Sons.

Luthuli, A. J. 1962. *Let My People Go: An Autobiography*. London: Collins.

Madlingozi, T. 2014. 'Post-Apartheid Social Movements and Legal Mobilisation'. In M. Langford, B. Cousins, J. Dugard, and T. Madlingozi, eds. *Socio-Economic Rights in South Africa*, 92–130. New York: Cambridge University Press.

Mamdani, M. 1996. *Citizen and Subject: Contemporary Africa and the Legacy of Late Colonialism*. Princeton: Princeton University Press.

Mandela, N. 1959. 'Verwoerd's Grim Plot by Nelson Mandela'. *South African History Online* (36), available at <https://www.sahistory.org.za/archive/verwoerds-grim-plot-nelson-mandela>.

Mann, K. and R. L. Roberts, eds. 1991. *Law in Colonial Africa*. Portsmouth, NH: Heinemann Educational Books.

Mattei, U. and L. Nader. 2008. *Plunder: When the Rule of Law Is Illegal*. Malden, MA: Blackwell Publishing.

Mbeki, G. 1964. *South Africa: The Peasants' Revolt*. Baltimore: Penguin Books.

McClendon, T. V. 1995. 'Tradition and Domestic Struggle in the Courtroom: Customary Law and the Control of Women in Segregation-Era Natal'. *The International Journal of African Historical Studies* 28(3): 527–61.

Meierhenrich, J. 2008. *The Legacies of Law: Long-Run Consequences of Legal Development in South Africa, 1650–2000*. Cambridge: Cambridge University Press.

Merry, S. E. 2010. 'What Is Legal Culture—An Anthropological Perspective'. *Journal of Comparative Law* 5(2): 40–58.

Michelman, F. I. 2011. 'Liberal Constitutionalism, Property Rights, and the Assault on Poverty'. *Stellenbosch Law Review* 22(3): 706–23.

Mnisi Weeks, S. 2015. 'Customary Succession and the Development of Customary Law: The Bhe Legacy'. In A. Price and M. Bishop, eds. *A Transformative Justice: Essays in Honour of Pius Langa*, 215–55. Cape Town: Juta.

Modiri, J. M. 2012. 'Towards a "(Post-)Apartheid" Critical Race Jurisprudence: "Divining Our Racial Themes"'. *Southern African Public Law* 27(1). UNISA Press: 232–58.

Modiri, J. M. 2015. 'Law's Poverty'. *Potchefstroom Electronic Law Journal/Potchefstroomse Elektroniese Regsblad* 18(2): 223–73.

Moseneke, D. 2002. 'Transformative Adjudication'. *South African Journal on Human Rights* 18(3): 309–19.

Moseneke, D. 2016. *My Own Liberator: A Memoir*. Johannesburg: Picador Africa.

Ngcukaitobi, T. 2018. *The Land Is Ours: South Africa's First Black Lawyers and the Birth of Constitutionalism*. Cape Town: Penguin Random House.

Peires, J. B. 1981. *The House of Phalo: A History of the Xhosa People in the Days of Their Independence*. Berkeley: University of California Press.

Pieterse, M. 2005. 'What Do We Mean When We Talk about Transformative Constitutionalism?'. *South African Public Law* 20(1): 155–66.

Rosen, L. 2006. *Law as Culture: An Invitation*. Princeton: Princeton University Press.

Roux, T. 2009. 'Transformative Constitutionalism and the Best Interpretation of the South African Constitution: Distinction without a Difference?'. *Stellenbosch Law Review* 20 (2): 258–85.

Sibanda, S. 2011. 'Not Purpose-Made! Transformative Constitutionalism, Post-Independence Constitutionalism and the Struggle to Eradicate Poverty'. *Stellenbosch Law Review* 22(3): 482–500.

Sibanda, S. 2013. 'Not Quite a Rejoinder: Some Thoughts and Reflections on Michelman's "Liberal Constitutionalism, Property Rights and the Assault on Poverty"'. *Stellenbosch Law Review* 24(2): 329–41.

Sibanda, S. and T. B. Mosaka. 2015. 'Bhe v Magistrate, Khayelitsha: A Cultural Conundrum, Fanonian Alienation and An Elusive Constitutional Oneness'. *Acta Juridica* 2015: 256–80.

Sigauqwe, G. 2018. 'Using Courts as a Resistance Tool: A Case Study of Makause Community Development Forum (Macodefo)'. *Master's Thesis*, University of the Witwatersrand.

World Bank. 2018. *Overcoming Poverty and Inequality in South Africa: An Assessment of Drivers, Constraints and Opportunities*. World Bank, available at <http://documents.worldbank.org/curated/en/530481521735906534/pdf/124521-REV-OUO-South-Africa-Poverty-and-Inequality-Assessment-Report-2018-FINAL-WEB.pdf>.

CHAPTER 4

THE ETHNOGRAPHIC GAZE ON STATE LAW IN INDIA

PRATIKSHA BAXI

Introduction

Recent courtroom ethnographies, which describe the fatiguing experiences of inhabiting courts, including both the stultifying quest for justice and the liberating encounters with the law, offer a powerful critique of the doctrinal view of law. This review essay does not offer an exhaustive catalogue of anthropological and sociological writings on law in India in the last two to three decades; rather it aims to illustrate how the ethnographic gaze constitutes state law in this body of work. This essay may be read as a supplement to the magisterial reviews of sociological and anthropological writings on law until the late 1970s by Veena Das (1974) and Upendra Baxi (1979), which map how law came to be constituted as a field of study in sociology and social anthropology in India.

It would be fair to say that legal anthropology and the sociology of law have remained nascent in India until recently (see Baxi 1986; Cohn 1965; Das 1974; Galanter 1989; Galanter and Krishnan 2002; Moog 2003). Legal anthropology and the sociology of law were not always institutionalized as sub-disciplines as in the West. Ethnographic work on law and disputes was organized under the category of political sociology, which is indicative of the disciplinary histories of sociology in postcolonial contexts in India. Even though there are many studies under the rubric of political sociology that have looked at dispute resolution in the realm of non-state law or at the intersection of state and non-state law (Cohn 1965; Srinivas 1962), these have not often been categorized under the framework of the literature that debates the contested meaning and claims attributed to 'legal pluralism'. Ethnographic or empirical works on the legal profession, for example, have formed a component of the study of political institutions and processes and of the sociology of professions (Kidder 1973). For instance, Robert Moog's (2003) important essay on lower courts figures in the section on political institutions in the *Oxford Companion to Sociology and Social Anthropology*.

It is now well known that the privileging of appellate law as a source for legal studies is constituted by a judicial hierarchy in which 'lower' courts are not seen as important sites in the making of legal doctrine. Marc Galanter (2014: 79) argues that 'the higher courts, that is the Supreme Court and the High Courts, with their extensive original jurisdiction, are not only the hierarchic controllers of the lower courts, but also their rivals for attention, prestige and power—a rivalry that manifests itself in reluctance to accord the lower courts a sphere of autonomy and initiative'. Further, the location of the ethnographic project in criminal courts or family courts offers a critique to the internal hierarchy among courts (Baxi 2014; Basu 2015; Berti and Bordia 2015; Berti et al. 2016).

With a few notable exceptions such as Robert M. Hayden (1984), Robert L. Kidder (1973), Perveez Mody (2002), and Sylvia Vatuk (2001, 2017), anthropological and sociological methods had not been used to study state law until recently (also see Baxi 1986; Das 2003). Moog argues that the existing studies have not looked at courts as institutions or as part of the judicial hierarchy; rather, 'they have tended to concentrate on actors outside the courts, considering the courts primarily as tangential factors affecting the lives of these people, or they have studied the functioning of particular groups located within the lower courts, but not courts as a whole' (Moog 2003: 1390).

It is also important to note here that the histories of official law reform do not intersect with sociological and anthropological research. It is surprising that mainstream discourse about law reform borrows models of law reform from the United States but does not refer to the work of Laura Nader (2002), who critiques the state's re-enforcement of harmony ideologies adopted by alternative dispute resolution. Nor does it refer to the work of Sally E. Merry (1990), who critically analyses the work of court-annexed systems of mediation in the United States. It seems that there is disengagement with the anthropology of law per se in the reform discourses, even when the models of judicial reform are influenced by reform agendas in the United States, the United Kingdom, or Australia. In other words, the works of legal anthropologists critiquing mainstream models of reform do not find circulation in mainstream legal debates in India, signalling how transnational circuits of legal elites insulate state law against critique. Even though the *access to justice* agenda remains concerned with problems in the administration of the law, such as judicial delay, there is no emphasis on studying courtroom talk or courtroom culture in the project of official law reform.

Locating ethnography in police stations, forensic laboratories, customary courts, or trial courts implies a rejection of the idea that appellate law exhausts state law. Emphasizing everyday processes of the law and providing accounts of subjection and resistance is important since it allows us to re-think the categories that are normalized in the doctrinal picture of law. Ethnographic descriptions of state and non-state law in different sites and temporalities do not merely rehearse Dean Roscoe Pound's well-known distinction between law in books and law in practice. Rather, these works offer a compelling account of how law is localized, often ceasing to bear resemblance to itself (P. Baxi 2014). The complex relationship between state and non-state law, sometimes conceptualized in terms of legal pluralism, makes it possible for state law, at times, to mimic non-state law and, at other times, to displace it. This suggests that justice (and its iconographic incarnation in the form of statutes or murals) is often a stranger to law, while residing in the same neighbourhood as the court building.

In South Asia, the social life of law finds compelling narration in ethnographic writings that 'descend into the ordinary' (Das 2006). These ethnographies of law grapple with the afterlife of colonial law in the post-colony on three registers. First, the ethnographic gaze on state law reminds us that the codification of constitutional law is based on the foundational violence of the Partition of India in 1947. Most mainstream histories of constitutional law in India are premised on forgetting how courts, prisons, asylums, the bar, and the bench were partitioned. The division of prisons on either side resulted in disease and death (Tanwar 2006). We do not know much about how courts and cases were partitioned, and the organized forgetting of the effect of Partition on courts and the legal profession marks official legal histories. For example, the 'Lahore High Court library' was divided 'in the ratio of 60 per cent to East Punjab and 40 per cent to West Punjab, while the furniture of the court was to be divided equally' (Tanwar 2006: 550). History and memory cast their shadows on the social life of constitutional law. This is illustrated by R. De's (2018) evocative account of how marginalized citizens shaped constitutional law in the early years of the Supreme Court in independent India.

Second, turning the ethnographic gaze on state law makes it possible to interrogate how the ethnographic present is constituted by the colonial legal categories in those sites of law that are not codified and governed by law reform. The customary practices of state law find explication in these works. The relationship between law, history, and memory have been revealed in explorations of colonial archives (Sarat and Kearns 2002). Sociological and anthropological work that traces the genealogy of ethnographic categories to colonial categories of law and governmentality has produced a fascinating terrain of conversation between anthropologists and historians (see Sharafi 2015).

Third, the ethnographic exploration of non-state law offers a powerful critique of how modern law itself came to be defined as characterized by codes, courts, and constables:

> [T]he conventional legal dualisms that many social scientists considered universally applicable in 19th- and early 20th-century anthropology were also simply too connected to the central governments, courts, codes and constables—leading them to implicitly claim that every culture must possess the same sorts of courts, codes and constables as modern culture. The way in which the legal dualisms were constructed made these modern legal attributes universal and thus, eo ipso, legitimate—and by correlation, any law that did not possess the same or at least very similar attributes was not recognised or only semi-recognised as Law. (Ledvinka 2016: 5)

The ethnographic writing reviewed in this essay invites attention to the everyday life of the law. Do courtroom ethnographies conceive of trials as a mere reflection of the social, or does law constitute forms of sociality? Is the material culture of law constitutive of forms of life that escape the image of law based on case law? How do paper-workers—notaries, clerks, and office workers—constitute legal subjectivity (Ghosh 2019)? Does court architecture narrate a story about the work of judicial hierarchy and access to justice? Multisited ethnographies of law reveal how an understanding of state law is contingent on far more factors than doctrinal accounts of law would have us believe. They raise questions about the neat distinction that is assumed to exist between state and non-state law; for the social life of customary law often absorbs forms of state law, mimicking state law, yet rejecting it.

This essay focuses on the anthropological quest to understand the world of law and justice in its everydayness. Although we cannot always discern an emphatic discussion among sociologists and anthropologists about how to turn the ethnographic gaze on human rights in India, the works reviewed in this essay may be read in relation to Goodale's (2006: 5) argument that the 'anthropology of human rights should be re-conceptualized in part by envisioning the object of inquiry to be a subset of a slightly larger set of normative processes, in which human rights are always embedded'. Ethnographic research also shapes the practice of human rights in newer ways.

This essay proceeds by locating the emergence of the sociology of law and legal anthropology in the context of the official histories of legal education in India to signal the forms of learning and unlearning at stake in turning the ethnographic gaze to the field of law. The catalogue of ethnography in courts, police stations, laboratories, and neighbourhoods that finds citation in this chapter explores how written and spoken law produce different logics posing the question of translation and legibility. Equally, the field of law—both state law and non-state law—is explored through unwritten law, court architecture, and medico-legal conventions.

The shifts

The official history of legal education in India represses what Upendra Baxi (2007: 8, emphasis in original) calls the history of 'law teaching as a form of *madness*'. Austin Sarat, Lawrence Douglas, and Martha Merrill Umphrey (2006: 1, emphasis in original) use the 'trope of "madness" to signal an unstable, disrupting, indeterminate, yet constitutive *relation* – the relation between that which is imagined *as law* and that which is withheld or masked *as something other than law* in order to produce that imagining'. The unwritten histories of legal education haunt its official histories. Baxi (2007) has argued that the official history of legal education begins by characterizing law colleges as chaotic pedagogical spaces, because law was taught by practising lawyers who defined law as expert knowledge in the service of governance. This telling of history emphasizes that law had not yet emerged as a 'discipline' that invited method, research, or exegesis. However, Baxi argues that this characterization of law teaching and of lawyers as teachers does not take into account the role of lawyers in challenging colonial rule:

> How is it that the relatively unencultured legal professional in India, ... in the colonial times, these pleaders and *vakils*, these half baked, forensic creatures, were actually able to torment the British Raj legalities? How may we ever understand the social fact that the 'premodern' and poorly educated lawyers in the Indian independence

> struggle achieved so much to transform the unBritish rule of law (to borrow a phrase from Dadabhai Naoroji) into what now parades as some paradoxes of postcolonial Indian law and jurisprudence? (Baxi 2007: 16)

However, even today, history is relegated to a separate syllabus in law schools. It is not part of the *core* course, say, on criminal law or commercial law; and, even today, members of the social science faculty continue to be paid less in law schools as compared to their law colleagues. The characterization of sociology or history in law schools as a 'non-law' course, as if the social or historical can be separated from the technique or the craft of law, is a symptom of what Baxi calls law teaching as madness. For such a separation represses that which 'must be disavowed or forgotten for law to be sustained' (Sarat, Douglas, and Umphrey 2006: 2).

This terse relationship between law, history, and memory is reflected in the scripting of the official history of the emergence of law as a discipline in India. Jayanth K. Krishnan (2004) traces the emergence of law as an academic discipline in the post-Independence era in a fascinating analysis of the archive containing the confidential memos of the Ford Foundation. Documents from the 1950s reveal the traffic of ideas between American legal scholars in Indian law schools, who were hired as consultants by Ford, and Indian scholars and lawyers who struggled to reform law teaching in India. Krishnan (2004) identifies three significant developments that are traced to these conversations with academic-consultants from the United States: the shift from having practising lawyers teach law to developing a class of legal academics; the transformation of the two-year law course into a three-year course; and the adoption of the case method, as in American law schools. On the one hand, these academic-consultants were careful not to colonize legal education in India by transplanting U.S. methods of teaching law. On the other hand, these histories of collaboration or cooperation, when read with the politics of funding, tended to stymie Indigenous approaches to law and law teaching.

The adoption of the case method was not successful, for not only did this presume the prevalence of case books that did not exist, it also assumed that the dominant pedagogical culture allowed students to ask questions of teachers who primarily lectured (U. Baxi cited in Krishnan 2004). This period was marked by the emergence of 'comparative law' and 'law and society' as a Ford-funded field of research, at a time when law academics in Delhi and elsewhere insisted law must be 'socially relevant' (U. Baxi cited in Krishnan 2004: 482).

The intimate entwining of U.S. and Indian histories of legal education was limited to an elite class of academic-consultants. This meant that the critical energies in the field of law, such as the emergence of critical legal studies, race theory, or feminist jurisprudence, were not the model that was offered for emulation. Rather than staging an exciting and possibly subversive conversation between theorists of postcolonial law and critical legal theory and feminist or black jurists, these perspectives remained outside the academic consultant-funder complex. In other words, the critical traditions in American law were constituted as 'the contaminations that constantly threaten to undermine law's authority and legitimacy' (Sarat, Douglas, and Umphrey 2006: 12).

In 1986, the first national law school was started in Bangalore—headed by the legal academic and entrepreneur Madhava Menon (Krishnan 2004). These law schools have since proliferated and claimed to usher in interdisciplinary approaches to law. While there have been exciting moments of interdisciplinarity, these have been inconsistent and irregular. Yet the hierarchization of legal knowledge into law and non-law treats social science or humanities as law *plus*—a minor *addition* to law. The division between law and non-law courses is predicated on the belief that the non-law is that world of knowledge upon which the technical or the expert acts. The non-law syllabus is set apart from the core technical law course as if the non-law makes sense of the realm of the excessive, subjective, external, and irrational. This may be contrasted to the depiction of the law as technical, expert, closed, or consistent. Whether or not sociologists believe that their task is to inculcate a sociological imagination rather than teach only sociology of law courses in law schools, the separation between legal theory and social theory, or the doctrinal and the everyday, remains institutionalized even in law schools that purport to be interdisciplinary. In turn, the charge against legal sociologists or legal anthropologists has been that they do not take the legal form or doctrine seriously. Yet ironically, the distance between legal practice and legal academia is also vast, so much so that a law student well versed in doctrine or constitutional law may feel totally alienated in the everyday world of litigants, notaries, and defects and cause lists, while an ethnographer or a litigant inhabiting a court may not find the idea that state law is devoid of legality or justice surprising.

Alongside these institutional histories, the shift to creatively craft ethnographies of law in recent years may be contextualized with reference to six different trends:

1. the emergence of conversations with other social science disciplines and, especially, with history, which use law as a distinct object of enquiry (Balachandran et al. 2018; De 2018; Kolsky 2010; Pierce and Rao 2006; Singha 1998);
2. the shift in public discourse such that courts of law become sites of intense public debate on law and society, regarding, for instance, the role of public interest litigation in shaping everyday life (Bhuwania 2016; Jaoul 2015; Tschalaer 2017; Vatuk 2017);
3. the impact of global discourses on access to justice and alternate dispute resolution, which create avenues for funding research on legal processes and dispute resolution (Kokal 2019; Parmar 2015; Solanki 2011);
4. the emergence of gender studies which privilege and challenge state law as a site of social change (Das 1996; Holden 2008; Kannabiran 2005; Menon 2007; Rao 1999; Saria 2019; Uberoi 1995, 1996);
5. legal events such as the mass torts following the Bhopal disaster or the aftermath of mass violence in Delhi (1984) or Gujarat (2002), which engender issues of testimony, reconciliation, and rehabilitation (Chatterjee 2016, 2017; Das 1995; Mehta 2002; Robinson 2005);
6. the concern with emergency or exception, whereby the implementation or suspension of state law is not reducible simply to bias or politics that law merely

manifests (Duschinski 2010; Duschinski and Ghosh 2017; Kikon 2009; Sayeed 2020; Sethi 2014; Sharma 2020; Suresh 2019; Tarlo 2003).

It should be emphasized that ethnographies of law were reinvigorated by the emergence of gender studies and the subsequent insistence on looking at how law is embedded in social processes (see Basu 2015; Baxi 2005; Mody 2002; Moore 1994; Rao 1999; Uberoi 1996; Vatuk 2017). For instance, the concerns of feminist scholarship and feminist jurisprudence have found resonance in sociological and anthropological writings on property, sexuality, violence and law in India (Chowdhry 2006; Das 1996; Mody 2002; Uberoi 1996; Vatuk 2001). In the United States and the United Kingdom, scholars have brought the concerns of feminist scholarship to legal anthropology and the sociology of law (Abu-Lughod 1990; Merry 1994, 2005), thereby shifting the focus from law-as-rule to law-as-process, and from written law to spoken law and law as a site where meaning is produced, interpreted, and conveyed in a field of force. These works have looked at what it means for women to be subjects of personal law, customary law, family law, and state law as overlapping fields of subjection (see Abu Lughod 1990). While some of these works have critiqued legal discourse by subjecting appellate judgments to textual analyses, others have moved towards using ethnographic methods to detail the everyday processes of law and custom.

In the last decade, several law graduates have turned to sociological and anthropological modes of research (Bhuwania 2016; Ghosh 2019; Kokal 2019; Suresh 2019). These scholars avoid the sceptical reception experienced by sociologists who do not have a law degree, and their work helps to show what it means for a lawyer, as an 'insider', to do fieldwork. Kalindi Kokal's (2019) ethnographic work on state law, disputes, and legal pluralism opens with scenes of unlearning doctrinal legal education. As she shows, it is not just that state law is one among many legal orders; often people do not know what state law is. '[L]aw school was clearly not a neutral ground', Kokal concludes. 'We were taught to survive in courts, police stations, and state institutions. Part of this also included learning how to capitalise on this knowledge and people's ignorance of it' (Kokal 2019: xiii). In other words, doing ethnographic work on state and/or non-state law also means unlearning legal pedagogy.

Ethnographers in Courts

While legal subjects may understand that the law's criteria of rights, obligations, and legality are different from those shared within the community, the space of the court also becomes an occasion to address issues of social control (Baxi 1986). Courts have historically been arenas of social control; nor are litigants passive consumers of law. Rather, litigants often use courts for sustaining honour and prestige in the community. More recently, scholars have critiqued the emphasis on court hearings merely as ritualized performances that reveal social structures or norms. For instance, Merry (1990) has argued that everyday lives of litigants in courts cannot be meaningfully understood only by thinking of the court hearing as a dramatic revelation of the norm. She borrows from studies on dispute resolution to argue that in lower courts, law acts on the consciousness of litigants, inflects their everyday life, and changes their perception about the case, as it unfolds over time. This viewpoint allows us to demonstrate the instability of the norm, while detailing the micro-techniques by which law's power is exercised (Baxi 2014).

Courtroom speech has found only inadequate ethnographic attention in India (see Berti and Bordia 2015; Baxi 2014). As Susan Philips (1998: 123) has argued, it is a mistake to think of judges as mere implementers of the law. The source of this misrepresentation, she argues, 'begins with the equation of law with written law'. Rather than thinking of judges as 'mere conduits of written law', their speech inside and outside of courtrooms remains central to the interpretation of law and judicial outcomes, for 'spoken law has a life of its own, logic and rationales of its own that are separate from and cannot be found in written law' (Philips 1998: 123).

Srimati Basu (2015: 59) explores 'questions of legibility and method in law by examining speech, expression, and translation of categories in courts'. Pooja Parmar (2015: 95–6) shows how 'the abstraction and decontextualization involved in the process of translating complex issues into a "legal problem" lead to a loss of critical meanings that limits the possibility of justice for those on whose behalf demands for justice are being made'. Mayur Suresh's (2019) ethnographic work on terror-trials in a court in Delhi departs from ethnographies that look at courts as reflections of social processes or courtrooms as sites where sociality is constituted. In his view, legal processes are not merely products or producers of social processes; rather, the ethnographic gaze on procedure and process describes how technicalities of law engender life itself (Suresh 2019; see also Sayeed 2020).

At the intersection of science and technology studies and the sociology of science (Thayyil 2015), the ethnographic method has been used to study the effects of policing and truth technologies (Lokaneeta 2020; see also Wahl 2017) and the social life of biometric identification (Sriraman 2018). It has also been used to document abject life in the aftermath of the Bhopal gas catastrophe. Ethnographers also follow 'non-human' petitioners such as gods and corporations, which are ascribed with juristic personality in state law. For example, Daniela Berti (2016) describes the meanings ascribed to the litigation filed by plaintiff deities, which is made possible by a legal fiction that recognizes juristic persons in state law.

Writing the Law

The shift from privileging doctrine to paying close attention to everyday practices of legal writing marks recent work on law in history and anthropology (De 2018). The world of notaries, stamp vendors, and typists had been relegated to the routine and boring bureaucratic functioning of the courts, devoid of any jurisprudential insights. Yet, as the recent work on bureaucracy and paper-workers shows, the legal file (Latour 2010; Riles 2006), the petition (Raman 2012), and stamp paper (Dhagamwar 1992; Holden 2008; Taneja 2017) are constitutive of sociality and legal subjectivity.

Bhavani Raman (2012: 2) describes the 'protocols of law' assembled by the British East India Company in the Madras Presidency. In what she calls the 'document raj', 'micro-practices of writing reordered the production of juridical truth and interlocked the rule of paper with a subtle but devastating discretionary authority' (Raman 2012: 3). Following Das (2004), Raman notes that documentary practices of the state are often illegible, creating the possibility of forgery or imitation, that is, of performing power mimetically. The writing of petitions and the certification of documents generated concerns about forgery or imitation, and the problem of authenticating documents led to crafting newer regimes of certification and taxation (see also Pati 2019).

Raman traces the complex histories of taxation and the embedding of stamp paper in colonial legality. Shrimoyee Nandini Ghosh (2019) constitutes stamp paper as an ethnographic object, arguing that 'law's own hierarchies of knowledge' are reproduced when stamp paper is treated as 'positive law', divorced from social, historical, or political context. The social life of stamp paper throws up complex questions of legitimacy, validity, legibility, and legality. Further, Ghosh argues that it is the oscillation of the stamp paper between 'contradictory fields of significations that structure law's sovereign and everyday life' that gives 'legality its living power'. In other words, it is not sufficient for anthropologists to look only at the performative dimensions of law or focus entirely on the material culture of law. Vasudha Dhagamwar (1992), Livia Holden (2008), and Ghosh (2019) show how sexuality, divorce, and marriage are negotiated through stamp paper documents that re-shape love and intimacy in surprising ways. Raman's (2012) rich archival description of the Company's textual habitus offers an important analysis of the history of the petition as a form of writing that acted to consolidate the Company's monopoly over violence.

The cultural life of petitions

The use of the stamp paper petition is not limited to courts of law. The centrality of petitions as appeals for justice finds powerful description in Aditya Malik's (2016) ethnographic work on the oral narratives about the local god of justice, *golu devta*, in the Central Himalayan region. Malik describes how devotees write petitions on stamp paper to appeal to this god of justice. These petitions are appeals for justice for all manners of things ranging from intimate stories to the desire to win court cases. Anand Vivek Taneja (2017) also writes about written petitions to *jinns* in Delhi. The idea that the stamp paper is a source of legal legitimacy, irrespective of whether or not it has evidentiary value, moves into the realm of divine justice by absorbing the legal form of the stamp paper as the effective technique of writing petitions to gods.

Legal files

Following Anneliese Riles (2006), some authors have argued that legal files or other aspects of the bureaucratic practices of the law, which are often thought to be outside the purview of law, society, and politics, are in fact constitutive of legal subjectivity in important ways (also see Hull 2012; Latour 2010; Mathur 2016; Vismann 2008). Creating and filing legal records is governed by rules determining how long such records must be stored and when or how material evidence, objects, or records are auctioned, destroyed, or used in courts or police stations. With the advent of digital technology, more and more legal records are scanned and stored digitally, changing the question of authenticity, editing, and certification. In his ethnography of terror trials, Suresh suggests that the file may be thought of as a hypertext:

> [T]he world is drawn to the file and enters it, causing the file to speak against itself. In the file several worlds are created: one world may counter another, a second world may contest reality. Each time the world enters the files, the file itself creates another world. Each point at which the world enters the file is itself a point of departure for other forks, a new fulcrum around which the file may be read. The file is not only an archive of the world, but produces several counter-archives. Files yield worlds that could not be foreseen, their meaning in a flux, like Borges' novel, producing several worlds, all at the same time. (Suresh 2016: 114)

Legal documents are now increasingly digitalized, and hyperlinks lead to a proliferation of other legal documents. The discourse that links digitization indexically with accountability and transparency ignores how technology gets folded into writing cultures of the police. Pooja Satyogi (2019), for example, describes how the police scan the first and last page of complaints in domestic violence and cruelty cases. This allows them to add middle pages to the complaint. The complaint is shaped by the interaction between police officers and the victim, for the former translate the narrative of violence as told over time into juridical categories (Satyogi 2019). Satyogi draws our attention to the writerly practices of the police, and makes a case for recognizing that police's interpretation of the law and its discretionary power is constitutive of whether or not an act of violence is recognized as such in law. Satyogi also argues that there is a need to recognize work of creativity in the way the police interpret and write complaints. In a similar vein, Katherine Biber (2018: 206) draws our attention to 'official secrecy' as 'bureaucratic creativity' and to redaction as one of the 'visual techniques of official secret keeping', i.e. techniques that 'display the art of administration, driven by the need to create new methods of destruction, obfuscation, and concealment'.

Suresh (2019) emphasizes the saturation of the procedure of the criminal legal trial with the visual, with broken links and grainy screens. As Desmond Manderson (2018: 13) points out, 'the *jouissance* of the legal system, assiduously denied in its legal texts, is revealed through visual materials'. Visuality, when it is exploited by the state, says more than it means (Manderson 2018: 13). Suresh (2019) points to the unintended consequences of introducing video-conferencing in terror-trials (on legal aesthetics, also see Sehdev 2017). On a different aesthetic register, Mani Shekhar Singh (2019) looks at how women artists reimagine the word and the world of law through a series of painting on matrimonial violence. Sonal Makhija (2019) goes beyond privileging the visual, to explore the different sensory registers that are manifest in everyday encounters with the law, as women litigants wait in courts for something to happen.

Unwritten law

The premise of ethnographic work on law is the idea that not all law is codified; rather, law is inscribed on bodies and buildings (Khorakiwala, 2017, 2018; Kumar 2017); or it is actualized in courtroom speech (Baxi 2014; Berti and Bordia 2015; Tschalaer 2017) or made manifest through legal emblems (Ghosh 2019); or it is inscribed by medico-legal conventions (Baxi 2014; Kolsky 2010).

While analyses of the doctrine remain important to understanding the nature of law, attention to everyday practices of the law takes the form of thick description of unwritten law, for example, the humiliation and violence inscribed on the bodies of those illegally detained by the police as terror suspects (Sethi 2014). State impunity has also emerged as a site of ethnographic enquiry in critical interrogations of encounter killings by the police (Duschinski 2010; Eckert 2005; Ibrahim 2013; Jauregui 2011). Torture in police custody is a lethal example of how law is inscribed on the incarcerated body (Lokaneeta 2020). Law inscribes itself on bodies through practices of policing in a number of routine ways, each of which poses a challenge to legal theory based only on doctrinal law (Jauregui 2016). There are more mundane examples. For example, contrary to the rule that prisoners cannot be handcuffed in courts, Jaoul records the 'frequent spectacle of individual prisoners being led through the lanes by policemen bound with thick rope' in the Lucknow court (2015: 177). Court compounds are marked by the presence of prison vans where people on trial wait for their hearing. At times they are moved to small and overcrowded lockups on the court premises. Prison ethnographies and diaries, however infrequent, provide the minutiae of the everyday life of incarceration.

Courts, custom, and legal pluralism

It would not be an exaggeration to note that most courtroom ethnographies refer to or evoke legal pluralism, even though some of these works may not necessarily engage with the key debates about this topic (Suresh 2019; Kokal 2019). Earlier work on courts (e.g. Galanter 1981; Cohn 1965) and later ones (e.g. Berti and Bordia 2015) trace the ways in which the social order or the community constitutes the lower courts. The overlapping and co-constitutive nature of lawyers' law and local law-ways shapes this body of work, signalling how law acts as a technique of social control. For example, Cohn (1965: 106) notes that M.N. Srinivas shows us how the written and spoken pleadings of a caste panchayat were inflected by the 'lawyer's culture': the plaint and rebuttal were written; there was reliance on written evidence; and the word 'damages' in legal English was used in the vernacular.[1] What, then, is the theory of power that frames work on legal pluralism?

Upendra Baxi (1985) offers a compelling critique of those theories of legal pluralism that ignore the work of disciplinary and sovereign power in constructing state and non-state law. Similarly, Julia Eckert's (2004: 33) essay on the courts run by the Shiv Sena, a Hindu Right group, links the question of legal pluralism to the 'competitive relations of various institutions of governance' in Mumbai. She makes the important argument that the 'laws generated in organizational practices become part of the operative legal order and are, through the interaction of these institutions, re-introduced into the practices of state agencies and thus enter, via practice rather than legislation, the state legal order' (Eckert 2004: 33). The practices adopted by the courts of the Shiv Sena are not 'outside' the state legal system. They are not in opposition to, independent of, or soon to be replaced or circumscribed by state law; rather, they are part of a regime of governance that also involves state institutions in a division of labour regarding control, allocation, and adjudication. In other words, 'the resulting situation of legal pluralism is a function of the power relations of a particular society at a particular point in time' (Eckert 2004: 55).

Panchayats and Policing

The overlap between police and panchayat is yet another site where the relationship between law and governance is explored. Bordia (2015) makes this point persuasively in reflecting on what she calls the 'panchayat-police' practice amongst the Bhil and the Girassia in Rajasthan. 'The ideas, terminology and languages that people in Rajasthan use to describe panchayat-police practices can also be traced to particular forms of statecraft that were found in former princely states' (Bordia 2015: 207). Bordia details the genealogy between colonial policing and panchayats after independence. Not only are police officers often present at the panchayat meetings, she notes, but the language of policing often frames the proceedings, as the tribal leaders cite relevant sections of the penal code. The foundational violence that underpins customary law is linked, then, to practices of policing and specific genealogies of statecraft.

The codes of caste have been subjected to 'thick description' in Indian sociology. Informal caste councils or caste panchayats that regulate sociality on the basis of caste codes have been an abiding object of sociological interest (see Hayden 1984; Headley 2015; Jaffe 2015). Headley (2015) talks about how non-state caste panchayats called *katta* panchayats are also held in police stations in south India. While state law represses recognition of the manifold conventions and customs of non-state law, it recognizes that non-state legal actors can displace its monopoly over the legitimate use of violence. State courts impose labels on the pathologies of non-state law by describing non-state adjudication as decisions of 'kangaroo courts'. The phrase 'kangaroo courts' serves to frame assertions of difference between state and non-state law and to emphasize the illegal use of violence by caste panchayats, especially in so-called honour killings.

The metaphor of 'kangaroo courts' circulated in global media reports of sexual violence after the brutal gang-rape of a twenty-three-year-old woman in a moving bus in Delhi in 2013, and it folded back into the legal discourse in India. The dictionary meaning of 'kangaroo court' is 'a judicial proceeding or trial which has a predetermined outcome or where the basic legal rights of a party are jumped over'.[2] In *R v O'Dea*, an Australian court characterized a kangaroo court as 'an un-authorised or irregular court conducted with disregard for or perversion of legal procedure'.[3] The Supreme Court of Nebraska described it as 'an irresponsible, unauthorized, or irregular tribunal, or one in which, although conducted under some authorization, the principles of law and justice are disregarded or perverted'.[4] The British High Court of Justice states that a kangaroo court is one where a disciplinary proceeding 'jumped from the accusation to the condemnation without pausing to find out what the accused person had to say about it' (*Clark v Chief Constable of Essex Police* 2006 EWHC 2290 (QB)). Similarly, with reference to the withholding of evidence by the police or prosecution in violation of principles of natural justice, the Rajasthan High Court has held that 'in case the relevant evidence in favour of the accused is not supplied, we would be creating "Kangaroo Courts" and weaving an illusion of justice. Such Courts and such illusions are an anathema to the judicial sense of fair play'.[5]

Calling attention to the fact that there is nothing honourable in so-called honour killings, Justices Markandey Katju and Gyan Sudha Misra note that 'often young couples who fall in love have to seek shelter in the police lines or protection homes, to avoid the wrath of kangaroo courts'.[6] State law here is upheld as modern, while non-state law is pictured as barbaric. The barbarism of the kangaroo courts then meets a jurispathic response (Cover 1995), which mandates such lethal forms of legal pluralism be put to death, so to speak. This othering of caste panchayats represses the barbaric violence of the practices of state law on which doctrinal law is built. The assumption that the law of caste speaks primarily through caste panchayats hides how caste colonizes state law. This split between state law and non-state law is made contingent when we consider how the police routinely criminalize love. Not only are consenting couples routinely incarcerated and charged with criminal offences, they also experience barbaric custodial violence (Baxi 2014; see also Chowdhry 2006; Mody 2002; Srinivasan 2020).

Concluding comments

Ethnographers of courts often write under the threat of being charged with contempt of the law. The chilling effect of the law on contempt on the publication of ethnographic work, as described by Hans Dembowski and Rüdiger Korff (2011), illustrates one of the manifold difficulties that ethnographers face in the field. However, at times research frames grounds for legal challenges (Sundar 2016). Social movements, communities, researchers, and lawyers write briefs to give life to constitutional law—for example, the petition filed in the Supreme Court of India by Nandini Sundar and others (see *Nandini Sundar and Ors. v State of Chhattisgarh* MANU/SC/0724/2011). Sociologists have made germinal contributions to law reform, although this contribution has been largely ignored—for instance N. D. Kamble's (1982) contribution to cataloguing and naming caste atrocities. Sociologists are occasionally, though rarely, cited in judgments. For example, the Supreme Court of India, in *Punit Rai v Dinesh Chaudhary*, approvingly cites Srinivas's *Caste in Modern India and other Essays* as follows:

> [A] sociologist would define caste as a hereditary, endogamous, usually localized group, having a traditional association with an occupation, and a particular position in the local hierarchy of castes. Relations between castes are governed, among other things by the concepts of pollution and purity, and generally, maximum commensality occurs within the caste. (Srinivas 1962: 3)[7]

In the field of education law, the court cited André Béteille (1983) to underscore his critique of formal conceptions of equality and his argument that those who enter the education system with social disabilities should be compensated.[8] The relevance of the sociology of law is sometimes recognized in the field of criminal law. For example, court ethnography by Baxi and Berti has been cited in recognition of the culture of compromise in criminal trials.[9] In other words, given the intimate relationship between law and social movements in India, it is not surprising that academics also find themselves in court as petitioners. Although rarely, judges may use sociological work in developing legal doctrine, even if such sociological work is not directly concerned with questions of law or equality.

Ethnographers today face the challenge of grappling with how cultures of constitutionalism are challenged by a majoritarian and authoritarian political regime that reconfigures law and society in new and disturbing ways. The relation between law, politics, and publicity has been marked by a significant shift, with the issue of the independence of the judiciary acquiring a dire significance. The constitutional meanings of secularism are hollowed out with the reconfiguration of citizenship laws. The relationship between law and violence shifts, with the rise of targeted violence against minorities and subjugated castes by mobs, and the virtual and mobile riot apparatus. Religious, caste, and gender discrimination expands, while the freedom of speech and expression languishes under the shadow of censorship and sedition law (see Singh 2018). This places a responsibility on policymakers to collect data with newer categories and to engage critically with the numerical narratives of the state (Bhat 2018). With the rise of majoritarian and authoritarian laws brought about through legislative change or through litigation and adjudication, sociology and anthropology of law are in a unique position to unpack the reconfiguration of state law that serves both to make state (and non-state law) illegible and to inscribe state law with impunity. It would not be far-fetched to surmise that the very relation between law, society, and violence is marked by a foundational shift today in India and elsewhere in the world.

Acknowledgements

I am deeply grateful to have worked with such generous editors, especially Professor Mark Goodale who encouraged me to finish this essay at a difficult time. I am also indebted to Karine Peschard, Brian Donahoe, and John Eidson for their meticulous editing and thoughtful comments. I would not have been able to write this essay without the insightful conversations with Deepak Mehta, Upendra Baxi, Mani Shekhar Singh, Jinee Lokaneeta, Mayur Suresh, Ghazala Jamil, Nupur Chowdhury, and P. Puneeth.

Notes

1. Moog (1991: 550) says that 'while there may well no longer be any truly "traditional" panchayats left which are unaffected by the formal legal system, there still are tribunals of a traditional type in many areas. Panchayats are councils historically consisting of five members, although that number is by no means sacrosanct. Village panchayats ordinarily are made up of respected men from the village, especially from the dominant caste if there is one in that village. In some villages, and within certain castes, there are also caste panchayats, comprised of members of one caste, which hear only intracaste disputes.' There are state-recognized panchayats and non-state panchayats such as caste panchayats or katta panchayats, to which reference is made in this chapter.
2. <http://www.duhaime.org/LegalDictionary/K/KangarooCourt.aspx>.
3. <http://www.duhaime.org/LegalDictionary/K/KangarooCourt.aspx>, with reference to *R v O'Dea* 72 FLR 436 (1983, Australia).
4. <http://www.duhaime.org/LegalDictionary/K/KangarooCourt.aspx>, with reference to, *Nebraska State Bar Association v Rhodes* 177 Neb 650 (1964).
5. *Dhananjay Kumar Singh v State of Rajasthan* 2006 Cr. L. J. 3873 at para. 28.
6. *Bhagwan Dass v State (NCT) of Delhi* MANU/SC/0568/2011 at pp. 6–7.
7. Quoted in *Punit Rai v Dinesh Chaudhary* MANU/SC/0608/2003 at para. 29.
8. *Kranth Sangram Parishath and Ors. v N. Janardhan Reddy and Ors.* 18.09.1992, MANU/AP/0272/1992 at para. 57.
9. See *Ramesh and Ors. v State of Haryana* MANU/SC/1517/2016.

References

Abu Lughod, L. 1990. 'Can there be Feminist Ethnography?' *Women and Performance: A Journal of Feminist Theory* 5(1): 7–27.

Balachandran, A., R. Pant, and Bhavani Raman, eds. 2018. *Iterations of Law: Legal Histories from India*. Delhi: Oxford University Press.

Basu, S. 2015. *The Trouble with Marriage: Feminists Confront Law and Violence in India*. New Delhi: Orient Blackswan.

Baxi, P. 2005. 'The Medicalisation of Consent and Falsity: The Figure of the Habitué in Indian Rape Law'. In K. Kannabiran, ed. *The Violence of Normal Times: Essays on Women's Lived Realities*, 266–311. New Dehli: Women Unlimited.

Baxi, P. 2014. *Public Secrets of Law: Rape Trials in India*. Delhi: Oxford University Press.

Baxi, U. 1979. 'Notes Towards a Socially Relevant Legal Education'. In *Towards a Socially Relevant Legal Education: A Consolidated Report of the University Grants Commission's Workshop on Modernization of Legal Education*. New Delhi: University Grants Commission.

Baxi, U. 1985. 'Discipline, Repression and Legal Pluralism'. In P. Sack and E. Minchin, eds. *Legal Pluralism Proceedings of the Canberra Law Workshop VII*, 51–61. Australia: Pink Panther, Law Department, ANU.

Baxi, U. 1986. *Towards a Sociology of Indian Law*. New Delhi: Satvahan Publications.

Baxi, U. 2007. 'Enculturing Law? Some Unphilosophic Remarks'. In M. John and S. Kakarala, eds. *Enculturing Law: New Agendas for Legal Pedagogy*, 2–21. New Delhi: Tulika Books.

Berti, D. 2016. 'Plaintiff Deities: Ritual Honours as Fundamental Rights in India'. In D. Berti, G. Tarabout, and R. Voix, eds. *Filing Religion: State, Hinduism, and Courts of Law*, 71–100. New Delhi: Oxford University Press.

Berti, D. and D. Bordia, eds. 2015. *Regimes of Legality: Ethnography of Criminal Cases in South Asia*. Delhi: Oxford University Press.

Berti, D., G. Tarabout, and R. Voix, eds. 2016. *Filing Religion: State, Hinduism, and Courts of Law*. New Delhi: Oxford University Press.

Béteille, A. 1983. *The Idea of Natural Inequality and Other Essays*. Delhi: Oxford University Press.

Bhat, M. Mohsin Alam. 2018. 'The Case for Collecting Hate Crimes Data in India'. *Law & Policy Brief* 4(9): 1–6.

Bhuwania, A. 2016. *Courting the People: Public Interest Litigation in Post-Emergency India*, New Delhi: Cambridge University Press.

Biber, K. 2018. 'The Art of Bureaucracy: Redacted Ready-mades'. In D. Manderson, ed. *Law and the Visual: Representations, Technologies, and Critique*, 286–309. Toronto: University of Toronto Press.

Bordia, D. 2015. 'Cultures of Policing: Panchayat-Police Practices and the Making of a Criminal Case'. In D. Berti and D. Bordia, eds. *Regimes of Legality: Ethnography of Criminal Cases in South Asia*, 202–26. Delhi: Oxford University Press.

Chatterjee, M. 2016. 'Against the Witness: Hindu Nationalism and the Law in India'. *Law, Culture and the Humanities* 15(1): 172–89.

Chatterjee, M. 2017. 'The Impunity Effect: Majoritarian Rule, Everyday Legality, and State Formation in India'. *American Ethnologist* 44(1): 118–30.

Chowdhry, P. 2006. *Contentious Marriages, Eloping Couples: Gender, Caste and Patriarchy in Northern India*. Delhi: Oxford University Press.

Cohn, B. S. 1965. 'Anthropological Notes on Disputes and Law in India'. In L. Nader, ed. *The Ethnography of Law*. Special issue of *American Anthropologist* 67(6), Part 2: 82–122.

Cover, R. 1995. 'Violence and the Word'. In M. Minow, M. Ryan, and A. Sarat, eds. *Narrative, Violence, and the Law: The Essays of Robert Cover*, 203–38. Ann Arbor, MI: University of Michigan Press.

Das, V. 1974. 'Sociology of Law'. In *ICSSR: A Survey of Research in Sociology and Social Anthropology*, Vol. 2. Bombay: Popular Prakashan.

Das, V. 1995. *Critical Events: An Anthropological Perspective on Contemporary India*. Delhi: Oxford University Press.

Das, V. 1996. 'Sexual Violence, Discursive Formations and the State'. *Economic and Political Weekly* XXXI (35, 36, & 37): 2411–23.
Das, V., ed. 2003. *The Oxford India Companion to Sociology and Social Anthropology*. New Delhi : Oxford University Press.
Das, V. 2004. 'The Signature of the State: The Paradox of Illegibility'. In V. Das and D. Poole, eds. *Anthropology at the Margins of the State*, 225–52. Santa Fe: School of American Research Press.
Das, V. 2006. *Life and Words: Violence and the Descent into the Ordinary*. New Delhi: Oxford University Press.
De, R. 2018. *A People's Constitution: The Everyday Life of Law in the Indian Republic*. Princeton: Princeton University Press.
Dembowski, H. and R. Korff. 2011. 'Stealth Censorship: How the Calcutta High Court is Suppressing a Sociological Book on Public Interest Litigation'. *Socio-Legal Review* 7: 71–86.
Dhagamwar, V. 1992. *Law, Power and Justice: The Protection of Personal Rights in the Indian Penal Code*. Delhi: Sage Publications.
Duschinski, H. 2010. 'Reproducing Regimes of Impunity: Fake Encounters and the Informalization of Violence in Kashmir Valley'. *Cultural Studies* 24(1): 110–32.
Duschinski, H. and S. N. Ghosh. 2017. 'Constituting the Occupation: Preventive Detention and Permanent Emergency in Kashmir'. *Journal of Legal Pluralism and Unofficial Law* 49(3): 314–37.
Eckert, J. 2004. 'Urban Governance and Emergent Forms of Legal Pluralism in Mumbai'. *The Journal of Legal Pluralism and Unofficial Law* 50: 29–60.
Eckert, J. 2005. 'Death and the Nation: State Killing in India.' In A. Sarat and C. Boulanger, eds. *The Cultural Lives of Capital Punishment: Comparative Perspectives*, 195–218. Stanford: Stanford University Press.
Galanter, M. 1981. 'Justice in Many Rooms: Courts, Private Ordering, and Indigenous Law'. *Journal of Legal Pluralism and Unofficial Law* 19: 1–47.
Galanter, M. 1989. *Law and Society in Modern India*. Delhi: Oxford University Press.
Galanter, M. 2014. 'Snakes and Ladders: *Suo Moto* Intervention and the Indian Judiciary'. *Florida International University Law Review* 10(1): 69–83.
Galanter, M. and J. Krishnan. 2002. 'Lok Adalats and Legal Rights in Modern India'. Paper presented at the First South Asian Regional Judicial Colloquium on Access to Justice, New Delhi, 1–3 November 2002.
Ghosh, S. N. 2019. '"Not Worth the Paper It's Written on": Stamp Paper Documents and the Life of Law in India'. *Contributions to Indian Sociology* 53(1): 19–45.
Goodale, M. 2006. 'Introduction to "Anthropology and Human Rights in a New Key"'. *American Anthropologist* 108(1): 1–8.
Hayden, R. M. 1984. 'A Note on Caste Panchayats and Government Courts in India: Different Kinds of Stages for Different Kinds of Performances'. *Journal of Legal Pluralism and Unofficial Law* 23: 43–52.
Headley, Z. E. 2015. '"The Devil's Court!" The Trial of "Katta Panchayat" in Tamil Nadu'. In D. Berti and D. Bordia, eds. *Regimes of Legality: Ethnography of Criminal Cases in South Asia*, 227–57. Delhi: Oxford University Press.
Holden, L. 2008. *Hindu Divorce: A Legal Anthropology*. Aldershot: Ashgate.
Hull, M. 2012. *Government of Paper: The Materiality of Bureaucracy in Urban Pakistan*. Berkeley: University of California Press.

Ibrahim, A. 2013. '"Who is a Bigger Terrorist than the Police?" Photography as a Politics of Encounter in Delhi's Batla House'. *South Asian Popular Culture* 11(2): 133–44.

Jaffe, J. A. 2015. *Ironies of Colonial Governance: Law, Custom and Justice in Colonial India*. Cambridge Studies in Law and Society. Cambridge: Cambridge University Press.

Jaoul, N. 2015. 'A Strong Law for the Weak: Dalit Activism in a District Court in Uttar Pradesh'. In D. Berti and D. Bordia, eds. *Regimes of Legality: Ethnography of Criminal Cases in South Asia*, 171–201. Delhi: Oxford University Press.

Jauregui, B. 2011. 'Law and Order: Police Encounter Killings and Routinized Political Violence.' In I. Clark-Decès, ed. *A Companion to the Anthropology of India*, 371–88. Chichester: Wiley-Blackwell.

Jauregui, B. 2016. *Provisional Authority: Police, Order and Security in India*. Delhi: Permanent Black.

Kamble, N. D. 1982. *The Scheduled Castes*. Delhi: Ashish Publishing House.

Kannabiran, K. 2005. *The Violence of Normal Times: Essays on Women's Lived Realities*. New Delhi: Women Unlimited & Kali for Women.

Khorakiwala, R. 2017. 'Judicial Iconography and Access to Justice in the Bombay High Court'. *South Asia Chronicle* 7: 351–74.

Khorakiwala, R. 2018. 'Legal Consciousness as Viewed through the Judicial Iconography of the Madras High Court.' *Asian Journal of Law and Society* 5(1): 111–33.

Kidder, R. L. 1973. 'Courts and Conflict in an Indian City: A Study in Legal Impact'. *Journal of Commonwealth Political Studies* 11(2): 121–39.

Kikon, D. 2009. 'The Predicament of Justice: Fifty Years of Armed Forces Special Powers Act in India'. *Contemporary South Asia* 17(3): 271–82.

Kokal, K. 2019. *State Law, Dispute Processing and Legal Pluralism: Unspoken Dialogues from Rural India*. London and New York: Routledge.

Kolsky, E. 2010. '"The Body Evidencing the Crime": Rape on Trial in Colonial India, 1860–1947'. *Gender & History* 22(1): 109–30.

Krishnan, J. K. 2004. 'Professor Kingsfield Goes to Delhi: American Academics, the Ford Foundation, and the Development of Legal Education in India'. *American Journal of Legal History* 46(4): 447–99.

Kumar, S. 2017. 'Interpreting the Scales of Justice: Architecture, Symbolism and Semiotics of the Supreme Court of India'. *International Journal for the Semiotics of Law—Revue internationale de Sémiotique juridique* 30(4): 637–75.

Latour, B. 2010. *The Making of Law: An Ethnography of the Conseil d'État*, trans. M. Brilman and A. Pottage. Cambridge: Polity Press.

Ledvinka, T. 2016. *Bronislaw Malinowski and the Anthropology of Law*. MUNI Law Working Paper No. 2016.01, available at <http://www.law.muni.cz/dokumenty/35744>.

Lokaneeta, J. 2020. *Truth Machines: Policing, Violence, and Scientific Interrogations in India*. Ann Arbor: University of Michigan Press.

Makhija, S. 2019. *'Nothing Happens Everyday': An Ethnographic Study of the Everyday in a Lower Court in Mumbai*. PhD Dissertation, Faculty of Law, University of Helsinki.

Malik, A. 2016. *Tales of Justice and Rituals of Divine Embodiment: Oral Narratives from the Central Himalayas*. New York: Oxford University Press.

Manderson, D., ed. 2018. *Law and the Visual: Representations, Technologies, and Critique*. Toronto: University of Toronto Press.

Mathur, N. 2016. *Paper Tiger: Law, Bureaucracy and the Developmental State in Himalayan India*. Cambridge: Cambridge University Press.

Mehta, D. 2002. 'Writing the Riot: Between the Historiography and Ethnography of Communal Violence in India'. In P. Chatterjee and A. Ghosh, eds. *History and the Present*, 149–74. Delhi: Permanent Black.
Menon, N. 2007. *Recovering Subversion: Feminist Politics beyond the Law*. Delhi: Permanent Black.
Merry, S. E. 1990. *Getting Justice and Getting Even: Legal Consciousness among Working-class Americans*. Chicago: Chicago University Press.
Merry, S. E. 1994. 'Courts as Performances: Domestic Violence Hearings in a Hawai'i Family Court'. In M. Lazarus-Black and S. F. Hirsch, eds. *Contested States: Law, Hegemony and Resistance*, 35–59. New York: Routledge.
Merry, S. E. 2005. *Human Rights and Gender Violence: Translating International Law into Local Justice*. Chicago: University of Chicago Press.
Mody, P. 2002. 'Love and the Law: Love-Marriage in Delhi'. *Modern Asia Studies* 36(1): 223–56.
Moog, R. S. 1991. 'Conflict and Compromise: The Politics of Lok Adalats in Varanasi District'. *Law and Society Review* 25(3): 545–69.
Moog, R. S. 2003. 'The Significance of Lower Courts in the Judicial Process'. In V. Das, ed. *The Oxford Companion to Sociology and Social Anthropology*, Vol. II, pp. 1389–412. New Delhi: Oxford University Press.
Moore, E. 1994. 'Law's Patriarchy in India'. In M. Lazarus-Black and S. F. Hirsch, eds. *Contested States: Law, Hegemony and Resistance*, 89–117. New York: Routledge.
Nader, L. 2002. *The Life of the Law: Anthropological Projects*. Berkeley: University of California Press.
Parmar, P. 2015. *Indigeneity and Legal Pluralism in India: Claims, Histories, Meanings*. Cambridge: Cambridge University Press.
Pati, S. 2019. 'The Productive Fuzziness of Land Documents: The State and Processes of Accumulation in Urban Villages of Delhi. *Contributions to Indian Sociology* 53(2): 249–71.
Philips, S. 1998. *Ideology in the Language of Judges: How Judges Practice Law, Politics, and Courtroom Control*. Oxford and New York: Oxford University Press.
Pierce, S. and A. Rao. 2006. *Discipline and the Other Body: Correction, Corporeality, Colonialism*. Durham, NC: Duke University Press.
Raman, B. 2012. *Document Raj: Writing and Scribes in Early Colonial South India*. Chicago: University of Chicago Press.
Rao, A. 1999. 'Understanding Sirasgaon: Notes Towards Conceptualising the Role of Law, Caste and Gender in a case of "Atrocity"'. In R. S. Rajan, ed. *Signposts: Gender Issues in Post-Independence India*, 204–47. Delhi: Kali for Women.
Riles, A. 2006. *Documents: Artifacts of Modern Knowledge*. Ann Arbor: University of Michigan Press.
Robinson, R. 2005. *Tremors of Violence: An Ethnographic Study of Muslim Survivors of Ethnic Strife in Mumbai*. Delhi: Sage Publications.
Sarat, A., L. Douglas, and M. M. Umphrey, eds. 2006. *Law's Madness*. Ann Arbor: University of Michigan Press.
Sarat, A. and T. R. Kearns. 2002. 'Writing History and Registering Memory in Legal Decisions and Legal Practices: An Introduction'. In A. Sarat and T. R. Kearns, eds. *History, Memory, and the Law*, 1–24. Ann Arbor: University of Michigan Press.
Saria, V. 2019. 'Begging for Change: Hijras, Law and Nationalism'. *Contributions to Indian Sociology* 53(1): 133–57.

Satyogi, P. 2019. 'Law, Police and "Domestic Cruelty": Assembling Written Complaints from Oral Narratives'. *Contributions to Indian Sociology* 53(1): 46–71.

Sayeed, M. 2020. 'All that Happened Inside the Happening: Fear, Law and Politics after the Police Encounter at Batla House, New Delhi'. *Contributions to Indian Sociology* 54(1): 51–75.

Sehdev, M. S. 2017. *Interim Artifacts of Law: Interruption and Absorption in Indian Domestic Violence Cases*. PhD Dissertation, Johns Hopkins University.

Sethi, M. 2014. *Kafkaland: Prejudice, Law, and Counterterrorism in India*. Gurgaon: Three Essays Collective.

Sharafi, M. 2015. 'South Asian Legal History'. *Annual Review of Law and Social Science* 11: 309–36.

Sharma, S. 2020. 'Labouring for Kashmir's Azadi: Ongoing Violence and Resistance in Maisuma, Srinagar'. *Contributions to Indian Sociology* 54(1): 27–50.

Singh, A. 2018. *Sedition in Liberal Democracies*. Delhi: Oxford University Press.

Singh, M. S. 2019. 'What Should Happen, but Has Not Yet Happened: Painterly Tales of Justice'. *Contributions to Indian Sociology* 53(1): 184–216.

Singha, R. 1998. *Despotism of Law: Crime and Justice in Early Colonial India*. Delhi: Oxford University Press.

Solanki, G. 2011. *Adjudication in Religious Family Laws: Cultural Accommodation, Legal Pluralism, and Gender Equality in India*. Cambridge: Cambridge University Press.

Srinivas, M. N. 1962. *Caste in Modern India and Other Essays*. Bombay, Calcutta, New Delhi, Madras, London, and New York: Asia Publishing House.

Srinivasan, R. 2020. *Courting Desire: Litigating for Love in North India*. New Brunswick: Rutgers University Press.

Sriraman, T. 2018. *In Pursuit of Proof: A History of Identification Documents in India*. New Delhi: Oxford University Press.

Sundar, N. 2016. *The Burning Forest: India's War in Bastar*. New Delhi: Juggernaut Press.

Suresh, M. 2016. 'The File as Hypertext: Documents, Files and the Many Worlds of the Paper State. In S. Motha and H. van Rijswijk, eds. *Law, Memory, Violence: Uncovering the Counter-Archive*, 97–115. Abingdon, New York: Routledge.

Suresh, M. 2019. 'The Social Life of Technicalities: "Terrorist" Lives in Delhi's Courts'. *Contributions to Indian Sociology* 53(1): 72–96.

Taneja, A. V. 2017. *Jinnealogy: Time, Islam, and Ecological Thought in the Medieval Ruins of Delhi*. Stanford: Stanford University Press.

Tanwar, R. 2006. *Reporting the Partition of Punjab 1947: Press, Public and Other Opinions*. New Delhi: Manohar Publishers.

Tarlo, E. 2003. *Unsettling Memories: Narratives of India's 'Emergency'*. Delhi: Permanent Black.

Thayyil, N. 2015. 'Claiming the Social: Beyond "Law as Technology"'. *Socio-Legal Review* 11(2): 1–21.

Tschalaer, M. H. 2017. *Muslim Women's Quest for Justice: Gender, Law and Activism in India*. New Delhi: Cambridge University Press.

Uberoi, P. 1995. 'When is a Marriage Not a Marriage? Sex, Sacrament and Contract in Hindu Marriage'. *Contributions to Indian Sociology* (N. S.) 129 (1 and 2): 321–45.

Uberoi, P., ed. 1996. *Social Reform, Sexuality and the State*. Delhi: Sage.

Vatuk, S. 2001. '"Where Will She Go? What Will She Do?" Paternalism towards Women in the Administration of Muslim Law in Contemporary India'. In G. J. Larson, ed. *Religion and Personal Law in Secular India: A Call to Judgment*, 226–50. Bloomington and Indianapolis, IN: Indiana University Press.

Vatuk, S. 2017. *Marriage and Its Discontents: Women, Islam and the Law in India*. New Delhi: Women Unlimited, an associate of Kali for Women.
Vismann, C. 2008. *Files: Law and Media Technology*, trans. G. Winthrop-Young. Stanford: Stanford University Press.
Wahl, R. 2017. *Just Violence: Torture and Human Rights in the Eyes of the Police*. Stanford: Stanford University Press.

CHAPTER 5

THE ANTHROPOLOGY OF INDIGENOUS AUSTRALIA AND NATIVE TITLE CLAIMS

PAUL BURKE

THIS chapter explores the interaction of law and anthropology through a national case study of the belated recognition of indigenous land rights in a settler society. It focuses on the role of anthropology in 1) contributing to a relevant archive for use in the claims process, 2) providing experts to facilitate the process, and 3) analysing the social effects of such processes. 'Native title' refers to the legal doctrine recognized by the Australian High Court in 1992 in the *Mabo* case that Indigenous rights to land could be recognized under the common law of Australia if the Indigenous people concerned had maintained their traditional connection to the land under their own traditional laws and customs, provided that their rights had not been extinguished by inconsistent government titles or public works. The Australian parliament ultimately accepted the court's decision and, in the Native Title Act 1993, provided a process for making claims and defined how native title related to the rest of the legal system. The Act created a hybrid legislative scheme combining common law rights and statutory rights. This approach, of facilitating the case-by-case adjudication of Indigenous claims to land within existing legal processes, can be compared to the Canadian comprehensive land claim settlement approach to non-treaty lands (see Thom, Chapter 6 of this Handbook, for an account of a Canadian Aboriginal group which had not reached a comprehensive settlement and was not covered by treaty rights). The Australian approach has some conceptual similarities to 'original' Indian title claims in the U.S. Indian Claims Commission, although the U.S. claims could not provide legal recognition of a continuing title, only monetary compensation (Rigsby 1997; Sutton 1985). A common thread here is settler societies belatedly insisting upon the proof of deep traditional continuity of a distinctive culture despite the ravages of colonization. This contrasts with the post-apartheid South African approach, which attempts to avoid a focus on indigeneity and limit land restitution to undoing the effects of racially discriminatory laws after 1913 (Walker 2008; Weeks and

Zenker, Chapters 3 and 44 of this Handbook, respectively). The Australian case study develops some themes which are relevant to all settler societies: the problematics of the anthropologist as expert witness, the interaction of subcultures (juridical and anthropological), and the juridification of indigenous lifeworlds. It also tries to understand why anthropologists have pursued the themes of juridification and legal pluralism without explicitly referring to them.

Australian National Context

All of Australia had been occupied for tens of thousands of years, making it one of the longest continuous indigenous civilizations, when the process of dispossession began with the first European settlement at Sydney Cove in 1788.[1] Although there were cultural variations among Indigenous groups (as demonstrated in Keen's (2004) study of seven different Australian Indigenous societies at the threshold of colonization), there were common features which tended to emphasize the relatively small-scale affiliation to a locale and to networks of kin. Large gatherings for ceremonies did take place and local groups were typically connected to neighbouring groups through shared mythology. In desert areas this mythology included segmented ownership of long-distance dreaming tracks or song lines recounting the creative exploits of ancestral beings over vast distances. The Indigenous hunting and gathering economy proceeded on a relatively small scale and social organization was relatively loose, there being no large-scale tribal organization as in the chiefdoms of Africa and no standing armies approaching the scale of the militaristic clubs of the plains Native Americans or the Maori warriors of New Zealand. Among Australian Indigenous people, punishment for the breach of laws was mostly a question of self-help and the mobilization of kin for relatively small-scale raids or revenge expeditions. This meant that, for the most part, the dispossession of Indigenous people happened in a piecemeal and localized fashion along an expanding frontier as white settlements spread from a few colonial towns in the eastern and southern coasts of Australia. This spread was often preceded by alien diseases and brutal violence, sometimes described by historians as the frontier wars (see e.g. Connor 2002).

This gradual colonization and localized resistance meant that at the time of the federation of the separate colonies into the Commonwealth of Australia in 1901, large areas of central and northern Australia remained largely under informal Indigenous control. Indeed, the historian Tim Rowse has recently described the overarching narrative of Indigenous/non-Indigenous relations in Australia since 1901 as the gradual and deliberate incorporation of the Indigenous North by the settler South. Initially this occurred via Christian missions and pastoral enterprises, then by successive legislative regimes of 'protection' (segregation and control), then assimilation, and then recognition (self-determination) (Rowse 2017). One strand of this statecraft story is the changing governmental understanding of who should be counted as an 'Aboriginal native' and the persistence of different imagined trajectories for 'full-blood' (protection and expected decline) and mixed-race descendants or 'half castes' (assimilation and ultimately equal civil rights). In the more liberal era of recognition from the 1970s onwards, official definitions eventually landed upon a threefold cumulative test: any degree of biological descent, plus self-identification, plus community acceptance. This definition encompassed Australian Indigenous people who suffered widely differing impacts over the course of colonization; who looked very different, in the old terminology incorporating both 'full-blood' and 'half caste'; with widely differing degrees of continuity and attenuation in the use of traditional languages and traditional high culture (rituals, song, dance, arts); and with differing degrees of social mobility within the broader society.

Thus, Rowse noted that when 'Southern' Indigenous people started asserting themselves in terms of the nationally applicable terminology of the time, 'Aboriginal' (rather than, say, 'part-Aboriginal'), their 'Aboriginal' identity referred to a tradition of struggle, resistance, and survival (2017: 351). It was often tinged with a sense of cultural loss vis-à-vis 'Northern' Indigenous people with their shorter contact history. The broad bifurcations of 'North' and 'South' may be a useful expository device, but Merlan's recent examination of the dynamics of Indigenous/non-Indigenous relationships over contact history demonstrates that, even in the 'North', identity and culture were made and remade in ongoing interaction with the settlers. Changes in different aspects of Indigenous culture occurred at different rates (Merlan 2018). Cultural variation within the Indigenous people of Australia presents one of the key underlying issues of the interaction of law and anthropology in the native title era—in particular, whether native title legal doctrine forces on anthropology an ahistorical separation of Indigenous and non-Indigenous social domains.

One of the effects of the broader definition of 'Aboriginal' in an era of the societal revaluation of distinctive cultures has been an increased identification as 'Aboriginal' in the nationwide census. Despite this, Indigenous people remain a small minority, estimated to be 669,881 people in 2011, which is 3 per cent of the total population of Australia. Within the total number of Indigenous people, about 6 per cent identified as Torres Strait Islanders. About a third of Indigenous people live in capital cities; only one quarter live in remote or very remote regions, and the remainder (about 44 per cent) live in regional towns and cities (other than capital cities).[2] Under a patchwork of national and state legislative schemes, Indigenous people have since the 1960s accumulated a variety of land titles, particularly in the Northern Territory under the federal Aboriginal Land Rights (Northern Territory) Act 1976 (see Figures 5.1 and 5.2).

Native title was thrust upon an unsuspecting Australian polity in the very belated decision of the High Court in *Mabo* in 1992.[3] In what could be considered as a courageous yet politically astute decision, the High Court recognized that native title rights could survive the assertion of British sovereignty as a burden on the Crown's radical title while also recognizing both the Crown's right to extinguish native title through inconsistent land grants and the possibility that native title may be lost by the Indigenous people if they lost their traditional connection to their land. The High Court defined the title as variable depending upon the nature of the traditional laws acknowledged and customs observed of the particular Indigenous group in question. Thus, native title

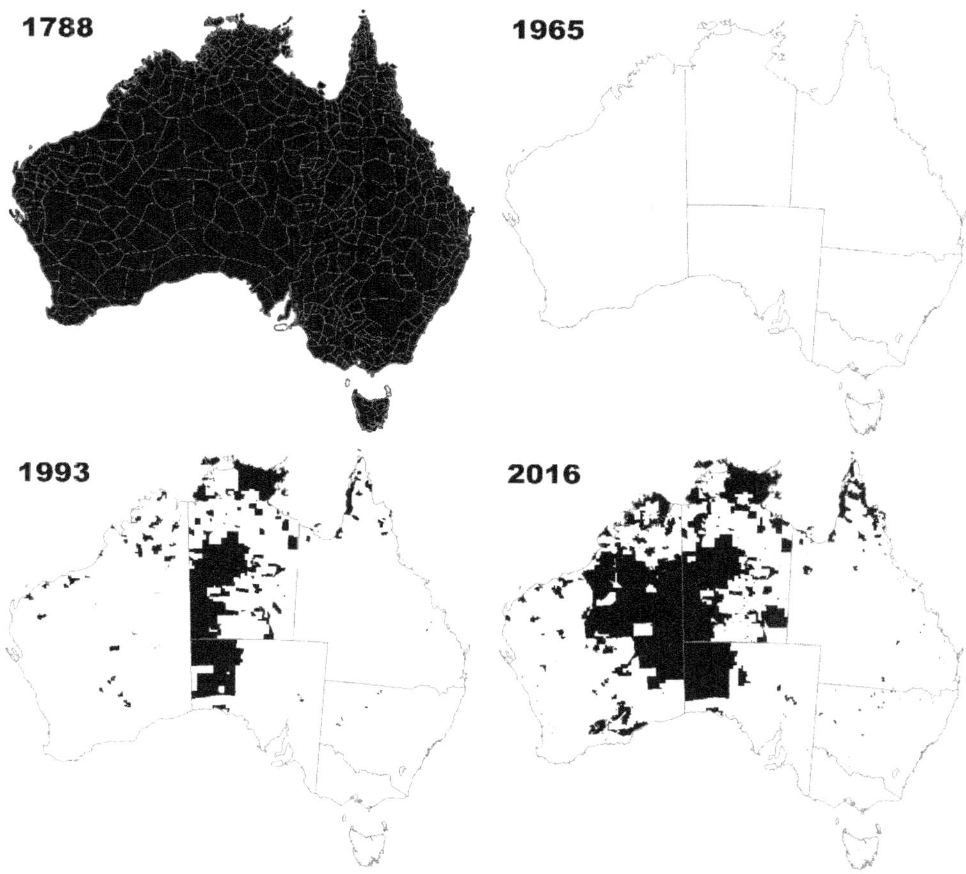

FIGURE 5.1 Indigenous dispossession and partial repossession of Australia[11]

was conceptualized as a variable bundle of rights which had to be ascertained in each case. This conceptualization has been variously criticized by Indigenous intellectuals as being too much influenced by anthropology[4] and in legal commentary as 'compromised jurisprudence' (Strelein 2009). Other elements of the conception of native title include: that it is a communal title; that some degree of change of traditional laws and customs is allowable, provided that the general nature of the traditional connection to the land has been maintained; but that once traditional laws fail to be acknowledged and traditional customs are no longer observed, native title ceases to exist and cannot be revived; and that the continuity of traditional connection involves the continuation of the normative system of the society out of which the traditional laws and customs arose. Following a period of intense political contestation, the Native Title Act 1993 was passed by the Australian parliament. When the High Court significantly enlarged the area subject to native title by recognizing co-existing, partial native title rights on pastoral leases in the *Wik* decision[5] in 1996, a conservative Liberal National Coalition government was in

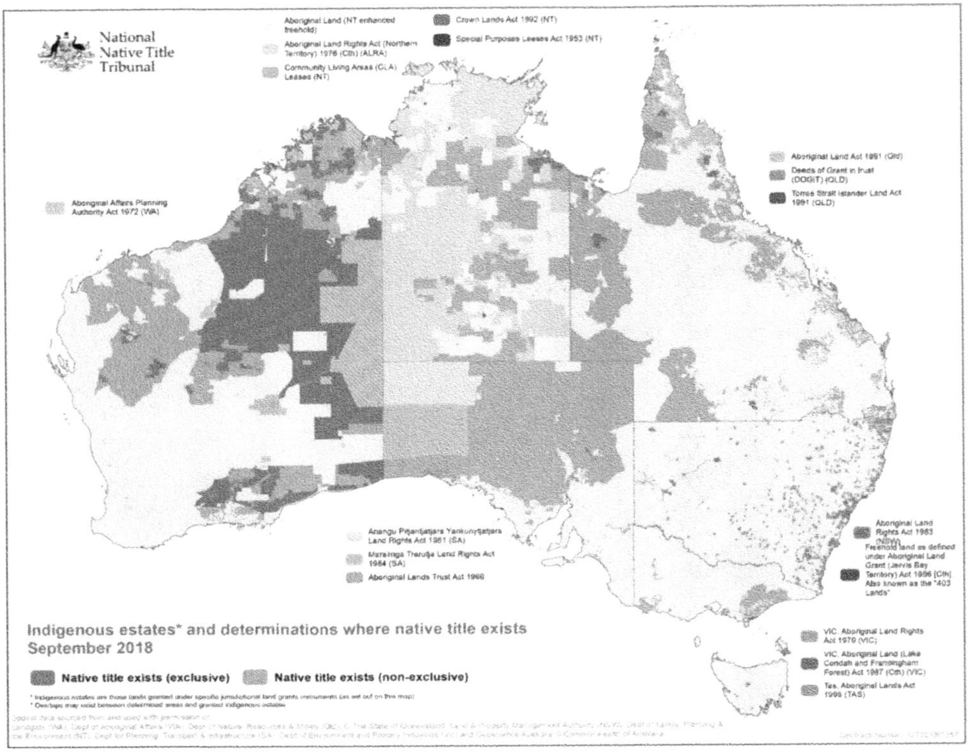

FIGURE 5.2 The Australian Indigenous estate (*reproduced with the kind permission of the National Native Title Tribunal*)

power. The legislation in response to the *Wik* decision, while accepting the possibility of co-existing rights on pastoral leases, sought to pre-empt subsequent court decisions about other leasehold tenures. Indigenous interests lost the battle against this potential pre-emptive extinguishment of native title on those other tenures, but the overall political effect of the *Wik* amendments was to signal bipartisan support for the rest of the native title system, which has endured up to the present.

State recognition: Its reasons, uses, and limits

Contestation about the appropriate anthropological framing of native title tends to contrast 1) the opportunity native title provides for the deployment of expert knowledge of traditional land tenure to assist Indigenous claims, with 2) native title as a 'total social fact' (Weiner 2003), which I take to mean analysing native title in the broad context of

Indigenous/non-Indigenous relations in the settler state. Some macro analyses situate native title and prior statutory land rights schemes in the statecraft of late liberalism and the international context of economic globalization. Peterson (1985) wondered whether the extraordinary gift of the Land Rights Act in the Northern Territory was really about securing an orderly process to facilitate the international market for minerals and whether the rights granted under that Act would be vulnerable if Indigenous social conditions did not improve as a result. Merlan saw in the definition of traditional owner in the Land Rights Act a state mimesis of tradition which had the unintended effect of regimenting the tradition (Merlan 1995, 1998: Chapter 5). In a similar way, Povinelli (2002), emphasizing the incommensurability of traditional relations to land and the liberal state, saw the limits of state recognition as pernicious and cunning. A similar attitude is taken by the structuralist historian Patrick Wolfe, who characterized schemes for the granting of land rights as state systems of 'repressive authenticity' (Wolfe 1999: 163–214). While all these critiques were developed in response to claims under the Land Rights Act, they could also be applied to native title.

While state-centric approaches have their uses in seeking a critical edge, they tend to underplay the extent to which native title and land rights schemes are the result of partially successful Indigenous struggles. Moreover, there are complementary levels of analysis which can make the most of anthropology's signature experience-near methodology. Rather than assuming a unified state, native title can also be analysed as the interaction of legal and academic subcultures. Another experience-near complement to the critique of statecraft is describing how the lifeworld of the participants changes as a result of involvement in the recognition process, what could be called the social effects of native title.

Analysing Anthropologists and Judges in the Claims Process

An important preliminary question is why expert anthropologists should be needed. Surely the Indigenous elders are the experts on their own traditions and can speak for themselves? This is widely acknowledged in native title jurisprudence, for example, in oft-repeated judicial formulations which characterize the evidence of the Indigenous witnesses as 'the primary evidence'. The exclusive prominence given to experts in the early days of the U.S. Indian Claims Commission (Rigsby 1997: 17) has never been contemplated in native title litigation in Australia. Yet lawyers invariably seek to supplement the evidence of the Indigenous witnesses with that of experts, probably for a host of pragmatic reasons. The experts can provide independent evidence of deep traditional continuity beyond the living memory of the Indigenous witnesses through the analysis of the ethno-historical record. If they are accepted as objective and unbiased, the experts can provide independent confirmation of the primary evidence to sceptical judges.

Moreover, because of the cultural distance between Indigenous lifeworlds and the world of legal proceedings, the odds are stacked against Indigenous witnesses performing at their best. There are also perennial problems of translating from one language and culture to another.

Much of the writing by anthropologists about native title has been focused on the immediate practical questions of how anthropologists might best be able to fulfil their roles as expert witnesses in native title claims and grapple with the requirements of the legal doctrine of native title (see Bauman 2010; Bauman and Macdonald 2011; Finlayson et al. 1999; Palmer 2011; Toussaint 2004; Sutton 2003; among others listed in Burke 2013). To ensure the appearance of expert independence in native title, anthropologists had to learn to be circumspect about avoiding involvement in the formulation of claims and avoiding giving practical assistance to legal counsel. Anthropologists also found themselves to be only one of many possible experts to be called as witnesses, including historians, linguists, and archaeologists (Henderson and Nash 2002; Lilley 2000; Paul and Gray 2003).

In my own attempt to supplement the professional discourse of the anthropologist as expert witness, I deployed Bourdieuian concepts to analyse expert testimony as the problematic interaction of two different social fields (anthropological and juridical), each with its own distinctive habitus (Burke 2011). The concepts of 'habitus' and 'social field' provided an antidote to what I sometimes detected as the contradictory tendencies of my fellow anthropologists to be apprehensive about law's mystique *and* to be overconfident about the likely reception of their testimony by judges. Anthropologists were quick to point out the differences between legal formulations of native title and ethnographic reality, but slow to deploy cultural analyses of the juridical field as a whole.

In my description of the social field of anthropology, I proposed a model of how 'scientific' capital could be accumulated by conducting long-term ethnographic fieldwork and writing it up in a way that makes a contribution to metropolitan theorizing (Burke 2011: 3–13). With the application of social competence to the possibilities of academic advancement, such 'scientific' capital could be converted to general academic capital, which could then be deployed in the witness box by being addressed as 'Doctor' or, better still, 'Professor'. The field of anthropology occupies an intermediate social standing among other disciplines, with medicine at the top and the humanities at the bottom, reflecting broader social stratification. The ability to project academic capital is also influenced by general perceptions of anthropology and anthropologists circulating in the public sphere. In Australia, the earlier positive reception of W. E. H. Stanner, anthropologist and public intellectual (Hinkson and Beckett 2008), must be weighed against images, such as those arising out of the Hindmarsh Island affair (however unfairly), of the naive anthropologist who accepts the existence of restricted traditional knowledge which may have been fabricated by Indigenous people for their own ends (Brunton 1996; Hemming 1996).

I argue that the juridical field, on the other hand, is inherently a creature of the constitutional state and modern law. There is an informal aspect of the social field which would include the judge's private thought processes, corridor discussions, conversations between lawyers and their clients, and the accumulation of knowledge of the idiosyncrasies of particular judges. At its core, though, is the following of explicit procedures for identifying law and facts and explicitly justifying decisions. The pervasive attitude of the acceptance of law as it is makes the juridical field relatively impervious to academic critique. In native title, for example, internal anthropological debates about the idea of legal pluralism (see e.g. Tamanaha 1993, 2000) have become irrelevant within the juridical field since the *Mabo* decision. Since then, at least for the trial judge, it became a question of finding those traditional laws and customs in the facts of a case, not whether this kind of legal pluralism is a feasible intellectual project. The sceptical critique of judicial rule-finding and fact-finding coming from American Realism emphasizes the relatively broad leeway in the interpretation of law at the appellate level and the possibility of triers of fact retrospectively shaping facts to their preferred outcome in the case. Such critiques need to be weighed against the constraints of the legal habitus which provide some predictability amid wide judicial discretion.

Arguably, part of the judicial habitus is scepticism that experts invariably act as advocates for the party calling them, although the degree of scepticism is likely to vary. While there are many examples of judicial scepticism of experts, for example the trial judge's decision in the Canadian case of *Delgamuukw*,[6] the United States probably represents the apogee of such scepticism, reflected in the leading case of *Daubert v Merrell Dow*.[7] The U.S. Supreme Court in that case required judges to perform a gatekeeping role, evaluating the reliability of scientific evidence using some factors that scientists might themselves use in evaluating their colleagues' work, such as testability (falsifiability), peer-review and publication, and the known or potential error rate. This was part of a wider campaign to keep so-called junk science out of the courtroom. Although not as particularized as the United States, the legislative framework in Australia also took scientific expertise as the paradigmatic case for all experts. I predicted that the ideal images of science deployed in U.S. jurisprudence might be matched in Australia by the deployment of ideal images of anthropological research involving long-term, total immersion fieldwork unrelated to any pending litigation. Indeed, such a judicial discourse disparaging anthropological 'research for litigation' did emerge.

Having outlined some of the features of the social field of anthropology and the juridical field, what can be anticipated about their interaction in a native title claim hearing? In *Law's Anthropology* (Burke 2011: 23–9), I invoked Luhmann's theory of law as an autopoietic system to suggest that, in the juridical field, law swallows anthropology (Luhmann 1985 [1972]: Chapter 2; Teubner 1988, 1993). The autonomous, self-reproducing system of law recognizes anthropology as part of its environment. When law interacts with anthropology, however, it is not in a dialogue, but an act of digestion in which law converts anthropology into what it needs for its own functioning. Thus, anthropological knowledge is converted into a legal fact which sits alongside other facts, which are then assembled by the judge into findings of fact, eventually reproducing law's unique binary code: native title/not native title.

The image of law swallowing anthropology does not exhaust the possible ways of characterizing the interaction of the two fields. From Bourdieu's 'The Force of Law'

(1987) comes the idea of the collusion of all the professionals involved in the resolution of a dispute. Using neutralizing language, they all collude to produce a misrecognition of the arbitrary and constructed nature of judicial pronouncements as autonomous and impartial. In a parallel way, the science-law literature is suggestive of the sharing of the burden of responsibility for difficult decisions between judge and expert. Thus, in costly findings against the interests of the state, judges might accentuate the independence, professionalism, and scientific nature of the expert anthropological testimony.

More fundamentally, Bourdieu's theorizing about habitus and social field envisaged mismatches, discordance, and misfiring of the habitus when unfamiliar social fields were encountered (Bourdieu 2000, 2004). It could be anticipated that the habitus inculcated in the field of anthropology would be subject to misfiring in the juridical field. In undertaking research for a native title claim, the anthropologist must reorientate towards a strange world where the mastery of the field of anthropology is discounted. Practical mastery of the seminar, the academic conference, the corridor discussion, departmental administration; or, alternatively, in the consultancy practice, the practical mastery of dealing with clients and helping them solve practical problems, all count for very little. What counts is the mastery of the rules of evidence in the legal doctrine of native title, and these are part of the professional repertoire of judges and lawyers. Thus, for example, the neophyte anthropological expert witness who is used to steadfastly defending opinions in an academic seminar has to learn to make reasonable concessions during cross-examination to avoid giving the impression of inflexibility and bias.

There are key indeterminate concepts in native title legal doctrine: what practices can be considered to be 'traditional laws and customs' relating to land; what is the relevant level of inclusiveness of the group having traditional ownership; what is the 'society' out of which the traditional laws and customs arose; and what degree of change of traditional laws and customs is allowable to conclude that traditional connection has been maintained? Identifying these indeterminacies enables a more penetrating analysis of the agency of anthropologist and judge in actual cases. I undertook a painstaking analysis of four such cases in *Law's Anthropology* (Burke 2011). I also proposed a general model of the task of the anthropologist: the deconstruction of the relevant anthropological archive and its reconstruction having regard to the Indigenous claimants' evidence and the requirements of the legal doctrine of native title. In a similar way, Mantziaris and Martin have identified the native title process as one of translation within a 'recognition space' between two separate systems (Mantziaris and Martin 2000). While these general characterizations would seem to be indisputable, differences remain among anthropologists about the extent to which the process of translation should be explicitly canvassed in an expert report and the extent to which legal formulations should be resisted in favour of anthropological concepts.

A typical anthropologist's report in native title would commence by characterizing the traditional laws and customs at the initial assertion of sovereignty. Legal doctrine allows inferences to be made about this earlier time period from the period of first European settlement, which is usually much later. Thus, native title reports tend to speak of the period of 'effective sovereignty' and characterize it by extracting relevant information from early memoirs and works by amateur ethnographers and later professional anthropologists. Although 'primitive law' was rarely investigated, 'local organization' and hence traditional land tenure was a significant ethnographic category. Indeed, the so-called local organization debate provides a useful resource for anthropologists trying to provide an account of the pre-contact traditional land tenure. That debate concerns the best way to generalize about Indigenous group relations to land and is typified by the critique, defence, and modification of Radcliffe-Brown's claim that the 'horde', with its patrilineal descent group at its core, was the basic unit of land utilization and ownership (Hiatt 1962; Radcliffe-Brown 1931; Stanner 1965; Sutton 2003: 38–53, 68–70, 98–110, 140–58). Subsequent research clarified that typically there are a multiplicity of traditional bases of rights to particular land and it is rarely as neat as a one-to-one relationship between the 'horde' and exclusive rights to its territory. Mantziaris and Martin referred to this as 'a layering of rights' (2000: 172–5). Local groups invariably exist within regional interconnections involving secondary rights to mother's father's country; limited rights to spouse's country; sharing of hunting grounds; visiting of neighbouring kin; regional initiation ceremonies; trade; far-flung connections through dreaming tracks; and the patchwork of identification between broad tracts of land and language varieties. Thus, the aim of the legal doctrine, to identify the grouping which holds the communal native title, applies pressure to simplify and approximate rather than explore regional complexities. Similar issues of deciding between local and regional groupings attend the question of identifying the relevant native title 'society' (Burke 2010; Glaskin and Dousett 2011; Palmer 2009; Redmond 2011). The delineation of traditional laws and customs relating to land is also complicated by how many aspects of traditional culture relate to land, including cosmology, religion, sacred rituals, and songs. Some aspects of tradition, such as believing land to be a sentient being and that there will be direct supernatural punishment for breaches of traditional law, are difficult to incorporate directly in modern law (the issue of incommensurability) (Langton 2010).

The anthropological archive on Indigenous Australia is rarely focused on processes of historical transformation of culture (cf. Keen 1999; Merlan 1998, 2018). However, some historical tendencies have been reported. One is the tendency for the significance of local clan estates to decline in favour of the significance of broad tracts of country associated with a language variety, in other words, the landowning group being known as a language group (Merlan 1981; Rumsey 1989, 1993). Another is the tendency towards the broadening of membership criteria for landowning groups, typically from strict patrilineal inheritance to cognatic systems (Sutton 2003: Chapter 8). The demonstration of traditional continuity also depends on identifying the circumstances for the passing on of traditions over the generations, including sometimes the unintended effect of the social segregation of Indigenous people and their concentration in large Indigenous camps on pastoral stations or missions.

The analysis of the cross-examination of anthropological witnesses and the judicial reception of their evidence benefits from Bourdieuian theorizing in three ways: 1) it alerts us to the possibility that the judicial reception of expert anthropological testimony may vary according to the academic capital of the expert involved; 2) it provides an explanation of the ease with which judges feel they can reorder the anthropological archive (anthropology's intermediate position within the social stratification of academic disciplines); and 3) it predicts the problems of anthropologists adjusting to the unfamiliar social field of judicial process.

Anthropology's intermediate position between the sciences and the humanities began to have its influence, somewhat unexpectedly, in the relative ease with which some judges took it upon themselves to disagree with the expert anthropologist appearing before them and prefer their own interpretation of the relative merits of contributions to that archive (Burke 2011: 240–1, 254–9). Typically, the judges involved preferred the views of older, well-known anthropologists whose work had, according to the anthropological experts in the case, been re-evaluated and superseded by subsequent research. This became known as the problem of the 'phantom experts': dead anthropologists raised back to life by judges in order to contradict the living expert appearing before them. This struggle over the 'ownership' of the anthropological archive was most dramatically played out in the *Jango* case.[8] In that case, the judge explicitly overturned the contemporary anthropological consensus about the flexibility of traditional land tenure among Western Desert groups, preferring his own reading of earlier contributions to the relevant anthropological archive which had emphasized patrilineal descent groups (see, among many others, Burke 2011: Chapter 8; Dousset and Glaskin 2007; Morton 2007; Sackett 2007; Sutton 2007).

The *Jango* case was also notable as the first appearance in Australia of a judge deploying ideal images of anthropological research to question the value of anthropological 'research for litigation' in areas where the anthropologist has not conducted long-term fieldwork prior to the native title claim. Using the American terminology, it could be seen as the emergence of a judicial discourse of 'junk anthropology'. Not all judges take this view, but it is still the case that anthropologists who are engaged to produce native title reports for groups with whom they have conducted long-term fieldwork prior to the native title era tend to have privileged influence with judges, as exemplified in the *Ngarinyn* and *Blue Mud Bay* claims.[9]

The social effects of native title

Beyond the immediate legal processes of a native title claim, anthropologists have also observed the unintended effects of participation in native title claims on the claimants, particularly the acceleration of the objectification of traditional culture, its regimenting effect, and the drawing of previously private matters into the purview of state legal processes (juridification). These observations provide a sometimes unwelcome contrast to the ideology embedded in the legal doctrine of native title which assumes that a native title determination merely recognizes what is already there, denying its own creative impact on Indigenous lifeworlds (see Smith and Morphy 2007 for a sophisticated overview of such transformative acts in the native title era). Merlan was the first to document how the definition of traditional owner in the Land Rights Act put pressure on her town-dwelling informants to conform to the ideal of a knowledgeable, authoritative, spiritual relationship to sacred sites even though they had moved away from their traditional country and knowledge about it was becoming attenuated (Merlan 1995, 1998: Chapter 5). Povinelli made a similar point about the long-term Indigenous migrants of Belyuen, who were not traditional owners, yet had developed spiritual connections to their new home which were not easily recognized under the Land Rights Act (Povinelli 1993, 2002). In the native title era, Glaskin traced in some detail how the lodging of a large native title claim in the northwest of Western Australia by the Bardi Jawi precipitated a reordering of relations within the group, which had a complicated history of involvement in diverse missionizing projects, exile in a nearby town, and return to traditional country encouraged by the outstation movement (Glaskin 2002, 2007). Their involvement in the claim necessitated an unprecedented level of cooperation, which was previously confined to ritual settings. There was also an unprecedented need to formalize membership of a representative working group to run the claim and to draft a constitution specifying the internal dimensions of this diverse group for the eventual native title corporation. Thus, ceremonial leaders (*madja-madja*), who had operated authoritatively outside European structures by directly asserting their traditional knowledge and skill and gaining acceptance from the rest of the community, were identified as a critical category in their new constitution.

Other anthropologists have noted how involvement in native title processes have increased opportunities for family disputation over the divergent views of traditional relations to land that in the past could be accommodated by different family traditions developing in isolation from one another (see the papers collected in Smith and Finlayson 1997). Eve Vincent has recently documented, in a fine-grained ethnography of a remote town in South Australia, how the advent of native title overturned long-established relations between two migrant Indigenous groups in the town (Vincent 2017). The consensus reached by the older generation of Indigenous people about the traditional responsibility for nearby land was fractured when the long historical view required in native title unexpectedly favoured one group over another as having the required continuous traditional connection to the land. Some influential Indigenous figures who were thus marginalized continued to assert their traditional care for their country but explicitly adopted an attitude of being 'against native title'. In my experience, such overturning of prior cooperation is endemic in Queensland, where protectionist era policies radically redistributed large sections of the Indigenous population away from their traditional country. This redistribution meant that their claims to their present location were based not on time immemorial tradition but a much shallower colonial history (the so-called historical people). This created long-standing divisions between those with traditional connections, who belatedly benefited from native title, and the 'historical people' who sometimes had a stronger local presence.

The social effects of native title could also include the intensification of tensions within anthropology in Australia over 'advocacy', variously understood, and the relative worth of applied anthropology. In the juridical field, advocacy for the client is seen as the province of legal representatives and as self-defeating in an expert witness because it undermines judicial expectations of objectivity. In the field of anthropology, 'advocacy' or 'engagement' (see Kirsch 2018), especially of the rights of minority indigenous peoples in the political sphere, has been seen as a more positive obligation on anthropologists. Although in theory individual action in these different social spheres can be separated in time and space, there is also potential for further tensions within the field of anthropology over accepting consultancy work from powerful state and corporate interests, which are not necessarily aligned with indigenous interests, and performing objectivity in the juridical field, which may not advance indigenous interests. In Canada, the debate about anthropologists in *Delgamuukw* exposed some of these tensions (see French 1996). In Australia, the tensions seem to be a little more subterranean, perhaps because many of the key figures in native title anthropology endorse professional independence and objectivity in the juridical field.

Sometimes the tensions within anthropology are expressed as explicit justifications of anthropologists working in native title against what is seen as a moralizing relegation to a lesser status within the discipline by those working exclusively in academia and non-applied research (Trigger 2011, 2012).

Future directions

For all the anthropological effort in native title over the last twenty-five years and research on the social effects of native title, it is still quite rare to find research linking the experience of the claims process with metropolitan theorizing in legal anthropology. One perennial problem is that, with a few exceptions,[10] anthropological reports in native title cases remain confidential and anthropologists remain under contractual obligations which limit their ability to comment in detail about their experience of the claims process. I suspect another reason is that there is no institutional base or tradition of legal anthropology in Australia.

While the regimenting effect of state mimesis of tradition (Merlan) and the limits of the liberal state recognition (Povinelli, Langton) have been identified, the link to legal pluralism, variously conceived, has not been explicitly made. Questions could be explored about whether the recognition of native title involves a weakening of non-state Indigenous law and its transformation into state law, along the same lines as Habermas's more general diagnosis of modernity as the systems colonization of the lifeworld. Following Tamanaha's (2000) suggestion for a non-essentialist version of legal pluralism, questions could be explored about the implications of the adoption of the word 'law' in native title by both Indigenous people and the state. Similarly, while aspects of juridification have been addressed in other terms (regimentation, objectification), another aspect of juridification has not been explicitly addressed, namely the depoliticization of political struggles (Teubner 1987: 9–10), also described as the juridification of protest (see Zenker 2012 for an example of its application to South African land restitution). Exploring this aspect of juridification would allow a link to be made between native title and continuing Indigenous struggles for constitutional recognition and a treaty.

The possibility of a judicial finding that native title has been extinguished because of loss of traditional connection sometimes tends to direct native title research towards the continuation of distinctive traditional laws and customs, and away from intercultural entanglements over the course of colonization. This understandable research tendency has been challenged in a number of ways: by asserting that tradition is always a process of reconstructing the past in the present (Merlan 2006); that some Indigenous groups now practise a secular version of Indigenous law without spiritual foundations (Macdonald 2011); and that some forms of Christian syncretism are not necessarily antithetical to continuing traditional connection to land (Trigger and Asche 2010). Further research could explore the limits of bringing together these divergent streams of pure and applied research.

Notes

1. 'Indigenous' is now the standard way to refer to the Aboriginal and Torres Strait Islander peoples of Australia, whereas in the past the word 'Aboriginal' was used to describe the indigenous people of continental Australia. Initially, 'Aboriginal' did not include people of mixed Aboriginal and non-Aboriginal descent, who were sometimes described as 'part-Aboriginal'. However, in the liberalization of the self-determination era, 'Aboriginal' was defined as comprising 1) any degree of biological descent, 2) self-identification as Aboriginal, and 3) acceptance by an Aboriginal community. Thus, the term 'part-Aboriginal' has been dispensed with. The word 'Indigenous', based on this more inclusive definition of 'Aboriginal', has now become firmly entrenched in government nomenclature and also vernacular usage, although of recent years the North American terminology of 'First Nations' is becoming more frequent. The capitalization of 'Indigenous' alerts the reader that this is a reference to the particular indigenous people of Australia rather than the global category of indigenous peoples.
2. Australian Bureau of Statistics (ABS) Estimates of Aboriginal and Torres Strait Islander Australians, June 2011, via ABS website (accessed 20 October 2018).
3. *Mabo v Queensland* [No. 2] (1992) 175 Commonwealth Law Reports 1.
4. Noel Pearson in *The Age* newspaper, 28 August 2002.
5. *Wik Peoples v Queensland* (1996) 187 Commonwealth Law Reports 1.
6. *Delgamuukw v British Columbia* (1991) 3 WWR 97.
7. *Daubert v Merrell Dow Pharmaceuticals Inc.* (1993) 509 U.S. 579 (United States Supreme Court).
8. *Jango v Northern Territory of Australia* (2006) 152 Federal Court Reports 150.
9. In relation to the *Ngarinyin* claim (*Neowarra v Western Australia* [2003] Federal Court of Australia 1402 (8 December 2003)), see paras 71–82 and 112–19. In relation to the *Blue Mud Bay* claim (*Gumana v Northern Territory of Australia* [2005] 141 Federal Court Reports 457), see paras 167–78.
10. The native title claim reports which have been published include Bagshaw's (2003) report from the *Karajarri* claim, Cane's (2002) report from the *Spinifex People* claim, and an edited version of Palmer's (2016) report in the single *Noongar* claim. Glaskin's *Crosscurrents: Law*

and Society in a Native Title Claim to Land and Sea (2017) is the only full-length treatment of a native title claim in which the author was an expert witness.

11. This map appears in Jon Altman and Francis Markham's 'Burgeoning Indigenous Land Ownership: Diverse Values and Strategic Potentialities' in Brennan et al. (2015). Reproduced with permission.

References

Bagshaw, G. C. 2003. *The Karajarri Claim: A Case Study in Native Title Anthropology, Oceania Monographs* 53. Sydney: Oceania Publications.

Bauman, T., ed. 2010. *Dilemmas in Applied Native Title Anthropology in Australia*. Canberra: Australian Institute for Aboriginal and Torres Strait Islander Studies (AIATSIS).

Bauman, T. and G. Macdonald, eds. 2011. *Unsettling Anthropology: The Demands of Native Title on Worn Concepts and Changing Lives*. Canberra: AIATSIS.

Bourdieu, P. 1987. 'The Force of Law: Towards a Sociology of the Juridical Field'. *The Hastings Law Journal* 38: 814–53.

Bourdieu, P. 2000. *Pascalian Meditations*. London: Polity Press.

Bourdieu, P. 2004. *Esquisse Pour Une Auto-Analyse*. Paris: Editions Raisons D'Agir.

Brennan, S., M. Davis, B. Edgeworth, and L. Terrill, eds. 2015. *Native Title from Mabo to Akiba: A Vehicle for Change and Empowerment?* Alexandria: Federation Press.

Brunton, R. 1996. 'The Hindmarsh Island Bridge and the Credibility of Australian Anthropology'. *Anthropology Today* 12(4): 2–7.

Burke, P. 2010. 'Overlapping Jural Publics: A Model for Dealing with the "Society" Question in Native Title'. In T. Bauman, ed. *Dilemmas in Applied Native Title Anthropology in Australia*, 55–71. Canberra: AIATSIS.

Burke, P. 2011. *Law's Anthropology: From Ethnography to Expert Testimony in Native Title*. Canberra: ANU E Press.

Burke, P. 2013. 'Anthropologist as Expert Witness in Native Title Hearings'. In I. Freckelton and H. Selby, eds. *Expert Evidence (Loose Leaf Service)*, 36.7051–36.7062. Sydney: Thomson Reuters.

Cane, S. 2002. *Pila Nguru: The Spinifex People*. Fremantle: Fremantle Arts Centre Press.

Connor, J. 2002. *The Australian Frontier Wars 1788–1838*. Sydney: University of New South Wales Press.

Dousset, L. and K. Glaskin. 2007. 'Western Desert and Native Title: How Models Become Myths'. *Anthropological Forum* 17(2): 127–48.

Finlayson, J. D., B. Rigsby, and H. J. Bek, eds. 1999. *Connections in Native Title: Genealogies, Kinship and Groups. CAEPR Research Monograph No. 13*. Canberra: Centre for Aboriginal Economic Policy Research.

French, R. R., ed. 1996. 'Forum: The Role of Anthropologists in Canadian Courts'. *Political and Legal Anthropology Review* 19(2): 39–84.

Glaskin, K. 2002. 'Claiming Country: A Case Study of Historical Legacy and Transition in the Native Title Context'. PhD, School of Archaeology and Anthropology, Australian National University, Canberra.

Glaskin, K. 2007. 'Outstation Incorporation as a Precursor to a Prescribed Body Corporate'. In J. F. Wiener and K. Glaskin, eds. *Contemporary Land Tenure and Registration in Australia and Papua and New Guinea: Anthropological Perspectives*, 199–221. Canberra: ANU E Press.

Glaskin, K. 2017. *Crosscurrents: Land and Society in a Native Title Claim to Land and Sea*. Perth: University of Western Australia Publishing.

Glaskin, K. and L. Dousett. 2011. 'Asymmetry of Recognition: Law, Society and Customary Land Tenure in Australia'. *Pacific Studies* 34(2/3): 142–56.

Hemming, S. J. 1996. 'Inventing Anthropology'. *Journal of Australian Studies* 48: 25–39.

Henderson, J. and D. Nash, eds. 2002. *Language in Native Title*. Canberra: Aboriginal Studies Press.

Hiatt, L. R. 1962. 'Local Organisation among the Australian Aborigines'. *Oceania* 32: 267–86.

Hinkson, M., and J. Beckett. 2008. *An Appreciation of Difference: Weh Stanner and Aboriginal Australia*. Canberra: Aboriginal Studies Press.

Keen, I. 1999. 'The Scientific Attitude in Applied Anthropology'. In S. Toussaint and J. Taylor, eds. *Applied Anthropology in Australasia*, 27–59. Perth: University of Western Australia Press.

Keen, I. 2004. *Aboriginal Economy and Society: Australia at the Threshold of Colonisation*. Oxford: Oxford University Press.

Kirsch, S. 2018. *Engaged Anthropology: Politics Beyond the Text*. Berkeley: University of California Press.

Langton, M. 2010. 'The Estate as Duration: "Being in Place" and Aboriginal Property Relations in the Areas of Cape York Peninsular in North Australia'. In L. Godden and M. Tehan, eds. *Comparative Perspectives on Communal Lands and Individual Ownership: Sustainable Futures*, 75–97. Oxon: Routledge-Cavendish.

Lilley, I., ed. 2000. *Native Title and the Transformation of Archaeology in the Postcolonial World, Oceania Monographs 50*. Sydney: University of Sydney.

Luhmann, N. 1985 [1972]. *A Sociological Theory of Law*. E. King and M. Albrow (trans), 2nd ed. London: Routledge & Kegan Paul.

Macdonald, G. 2011. 'The Secularisation of Riverine Law in South-East Australia'. *Anthropological Forum* 21(3): 307–28.

Mantziaris, C. and D. Martin. 2000. *Native Title Corporations: A Legal and Anthropological Analysis*. Sydney: The Federation Press.

Merlan, F. 1981. 'Land, Language and Social Identity in Aboriginal Australia'. *Mankind* 13 (2): 133–48.

Merlan, F. 1995. 'The Regimentation of Customary Practice: From Northern Territory Land Claims to Mabo'. *The Australian Journal of Anthropology* 6(1/2): 64–82.

Merlan, F. 1998. *Caging the Rainbow: Place, Politics, and Aborigines in a North Australian Town*. Honolulu: University of Hawai'i Press.

Merlan, F. 2006. 'Beyond Tradition'. *The Asia Pacific Journal of Anthropology* 7(1): 85–104.

Merlan, F. 2018. *Dynamics of Difference in Australia: Indigenous Past and Present in a Settler Country*. Philadelphia: University of Pennsylvania Press.

Morton, J. 2007. 'Sansom, Sutton and Sackville: Three Expert Anthropologists?' *Anthropological Forum* 17(1): 170–3.

Palmer, K. 2009. *Societies, Communities and Native Title*. In C. Ganesharajah, ed. *Land, Rights, Laws: Issues of Native Title. Volume 4, Issue Paper No. 1*. Canberra: Native Title Research Unit, AIATSIS.

Palmer, K. 2011. *Anthropologist as Expert in Native Title Cases in Australia*. Canberra: Native Title Research Unit, AIATSIS.

Palmer, K. 2016. *Noongar People, Noongar Land: The Resilience of Aboriginal Culture in the South West of Western Australia*. Canberra: Aboriginal Studies Press.

Paul, M. and G. Gray, eds. 2003. *Through the Smoky Mirror: History and Native Title*. Canberra: Aboriginal Studies Press.

Peterson, N. 1985. 'Capitalism, Culture and Land Rights: Aborigines and the State in the Northern Territory'. *Social Analysis* 18: 85–101.

Povinelli, E. A. 1993. '"Might Be Something": The Language of Indeterminacy in Australian Aboriginal Land Use'. *Man* 28(4): 679–704.

Povinelli, E. A. 2002. *The Cunning of Recognition: Indigenous Alterities and the Making of Australian Multiculturalism*. Durham: Duke University Press.

Radcliffe-Brown, A.R. 1931. *The Social Organisation of Australian Tribes, Oceania Monographs No. 1*. Sydney: University of Sydney.

Redmond, A. 2011. 'Identifying the Relevant Level of a Society in Australian Native Title Claims'. *Anthropological Forum* 21(3): 287–305.

Rigsby, B. 1997. 'Anthropologists, Indian Title and the Indian Claims Commission: The California and Great Basin Cases'. In D. E. Smith and J. Finlayson, *Fighting over Country: Anthropological Perspectives*, 15–45. Canberra: Centre for Aboriginal Economic Policy Research, Australian National University.

Rowse, T. 2017. *Indigenous and Other Australians since 1901*. Sydney: University of New South Wales Press.

Rumsey, A. 1989. 'Language Groups in Aboriginal Land Claims'. *Anthropological Forum* 6: 69–79.

Rumsey, A. 1993. 'Language and Territoriality in Aboriginal Australia'. In M. Walsh and C. Yallop, eds. *Language and Culture in Aboriginal Australia*, 191–206. Canberra: Aboriginal Studies Press.

Sackett, L. 2007. 'A Potential Pathway'. *Anthropological Forum* 17(1): 173–5.

Smith, B. R. and F. Morphy. 2007. 'The Social Effects of Native Title: Recognition, Translation, Co-Existence'. In B. R. Smith and F. Morphy, eds. *The Social Effects of Native Title: Recognition, Translation, Co-Existence*, 1–25. Canberra: Centre for Aboriginal Economic Policy Research, Australian National University.

Smith, D. E. and J. Finlayson, eds. 1997. *Fighting over Country: Anthropological Perspectives. CAEPR Research Monograph No. 12*. Canberra: Centre for Aboriginal Economic Policy Research.

Stanner, W. E. H. 1965. 'Aboriginal Territorial Organisation: Estate, Range, Domain and Regime'. *Oceania* 36: 1–26.

Strelein, L. 2009. *Compromised Jurisprudence: Native Title Cases since Mabo*. 2nd ed. Canberra: Aboriginal Studies Press.

Sutton, I., ed. 1985. *Irredeemable America: The Indians' Estate and Land Claims*. Albuquerque: University of New Mexico Press.

Sutton, P. 2003. *Native Title in Australia: An Ethnographic Perspective*. Cambridge: Cambridge University Press.

Sutton, P. 2007. 'Norms, Statistics and the Jango Case at Yulara'. *Anthropological Forum* 17(1): 175–92.

Tamanaha, B. Z. 1993. 'The Folly of the "Social Scientific" Concept of Legal Pluralism'. *Journal of Law and Society* 20(2): 192–217.

Tamanaha, B. Z. 2000. 'A Non-Essentialist Version of Legal Pluralism'. *Journal of Law and Society* 27(2): 296–321.

Teubner, G., ed. 1987. *Juridification of Social Spheres: A Comparative Analysis in the Areas of Labor, Corporate, Antitrust and Social Welfare Law*. Berlin: Walter de Gruyter.

Teubner, G. 1988. *Autopoietic Law: A New Approach to Law and Society*. Berlin: Walter de Gruyter.

Teubner, G. 1993. *Law as an Autopoietic System*. Oxford: Blackwell.

Toussaint, S., ed. 2004. *Crossing Boundaries: Cultural, Legal, Historical and Practice Issues in Native Title*. Melbourne: Melbourne University Press.

Trigger, D. 2011. 'Anthropology Pure and Profane: The Politics of Applied Anthropology in Aboriginal Australia'. *Anthropological Forum* 21(3): 233–55.

Trigger, D. 2012. 'Response to Comments on the Article Anthropology Pure and Profane: The Politics of Applied Research in Aboriginal Australia'. *Anthropological Forum* 22(1): 84–93.

Trigger, D. S. and W. Asche. 2010. 'Christianity, Cultural Change and the Negotiation of Rights in Land and Sea'. *The Australian Journal of Anthropology* 21(1): 90–109.

Vincent, E. 2017. *'Against Native Title': Conflict and Creativity in Outback Australia*. Canberra: Aboriginal Studies Press.

Walker, C. 2008. *Landmarked: Land Claims and Land Restitution in South Africa*. Athens, Ohio: Ohio University Press.

Weiner, J. F. 2003. 'The Law of the Land: A Review Article'. *The Australian Journal of Anthropology* 14: 97–110.

Wolfe, P. 1999. *Settler Colonialism and the Transformation of Anthropology: The Politics and Politics of an Ethnographic Event*. In P. Darby, M. Thornton, and P. Wolfe, eds. *Writing Past Colonialism Series*. London: Cassell.

Zenker, O. 2012. 'The Juridification of Political Protest and the Politicisation of Legalism in South African Land Restitution'. In J. Eckert, B. Donahoe, C. Strümpell, and Z. Ö. Biner, eds. *Law against the State: Ethnographic Forays into Law's Transformations*, 118–46. Cambridge: Cambridge University Press.

CHAPTER 6

ENCOUNTERING INDIGENOUS LAW IN CANADA

BRIAN THOM

DRAWING OUT INDIGENOUS LAW THROUGH ETHNOGRAPHY

THIS chapter reflects on the work happening at the intersection of anthropology and law in Canada, in particular with respect to the interlegalities (de Sousa Santos 2002) of Indigenous peoples' rights, title, governance, and Indigenous legal orders. In my view, we are at a moment of profound change and innovation in both Indigenous legal discourses and anthropology's engagement with them. Key in this moment of change is the effort to move beyond merely making sense of Indigenous law through the lens of recognition in terms of Western equivalents, and to understand in their own terms how Indigenous laws continue to address local moral and social priorities and practices, and their implications alongside state-ordered law. The chapter develops a brief ethnographic case-study involving several closely related Island Hul'q'umi'num' (Coast Salish) communities on the east coast of Vancouver Island (British Columbia) as they work to mobilize longstanding Indigenous principles and understandings of land tenure and harvest rights among themselves in a complex, state-regulated environment of shellfish harvesting. The purpose of the case-study is to highlight a path of anthropological engagement with contemporary Indigenous law, working both to appreciate the ways Indigenous and state legal orders are brought to life concurrently over time, and to reflect on the on-the-ground ways legal pluralism is experienced. The case also offers conceptual opportunities to transcend problematic state discourses of 'overlapping claims' and makes space for workable principles of co-existence through Indigenous legal sensibility.

In mainstream Canadian legal discourses, Indigenous legal traditions have come to be recognized as important and valid legal orders, a fundamental part of legal pluralism in Canada alongside legislation, common law, and civil code (Borrows 2005). The recent Truth and Reconciliation Commission (TRC) recognized the promise of Indigenous law 'to reveal treasured resources for decision making, regulation, and dispute resolution' (TRC 2015: 47). Canada has become a place where the work done by Indigenous communities, judges, legal scholars, and, indeed, anthropologists to grasp Indigenous legal principles and their application to contemporary, real-world problems has heightened relevance. Insights on Indigenous legal orders are highly sought after. In 2018 the University of Victoria launched a four-year *Juris Indigenarum Doctor* programme alongside the conventional *Juris Doctor* that qualifies graduates to practise Canadian law and Indigenous law (see Borrows 2019, especially Chapter 6). As Indigenous legal scholar Val Napolean stated, Indigenous law 'is integrally connected with how we imagine and manage ourselves both collectively and individually. … [It] is about building citizenship, responsibility and governance, challenging internal and external oppressions, safety and protection, lands and resources, and external political relations with other Indigenous peoples and the state' (Napoleon 2013: 34). While these have long been important conversations within communities (despite the imposition of colonial and state power and structures and the forcible marginalization of Indigenous peoples' autonomy and territory), in the resurgence of Indigenous legal traditions alongside state law in Canada, there is still rarely consensus on how issues of Indigenous jurisdiction, authority, procedure, and enforcement manifest in the society at large (see also ICHRP 2009: 95). As the legal community is turning its attention to matters of how Indigenous law can be incorporated more broadly into social, political, and economic life, it is a remarkable time and place to be an anthropologist engaged in dialogues on the principles and theories of Indigenous law (for some examples of significant Canadian anthropological work in this area, see Asch 2014; Feltes 2015; Fiske and Patrick 2000; Miller 2016: Part III; Mills 1994; Noble 2007, 2008; Reagan 2009).

One particularly important space for the emergence of Indigenous legal traditions has been in defining the legal foundations of Indigenous land title and territorial rights in Canada. Over the past twenty years, the resurgence of Indigenous law has come alongside findings from Canada's Supreme Court that recognize how Indigenous law is essential to reconciling the exercise of state sovereignty and the pre-existing social and legal orders of Indigenous peoples. This has been particularly true in the Supreme Court's characterization of Aboriginal title, a *sui generis* property right that is recognized and affirmed by the Canadian Constitution. Aboriginal title, wrote the Supreme Court, 'arises from the prior occupation of Canada by aboriginal peoples … [including] the physical fact of occupation, which derives from the common law principle that occupation is proof of possession in law, … [and because it] arises from possession before the assertion of British sovereignty. … What this suggests is a second source for aboriginal title—the relationship between common law and pre-existing systems of aboriginal law.'[1] Legal scholars have argued that this finding opened the door 'for Indigenous peoples to claim title on the basis of their own laws, as an alternative to occupation-based title' (McNeil 2009: 262).

The Gitksan peoples in the *Delgamuukw* case argued that judges must not only look at evidence of the physical occupation of the land in question—a common law test for title which has significant methodological burdens when extending the evidence to the time before the European assertion of sovereignty—but that Aboriginal title may in part be established by reference to 'the pattern of land holdings under aboriginal law'.[2] The Supreme Court Chief Justice incorporated this argument into the test for proof of Aboriginal title, saying that 'if, at the time of sovereignty, an aboriginal society had laws in relation to land, those laws would be relevant to establishing the occupation of lands which are the subject of a claim for aboriginal title. Relevant laws might include, but are not limited to, a land tenure system or laws governing land use'.[3] Indeed, in the *Delgamuukw* case, the courts had the thoughtful and engaged work of anthropologists Richard Daly (2005) and Antonia Mills (1994), along with the extensive oral histories and testimonies of elders and leaders from the plaintiff communities, which set out Indigenous principles of land tenure for the judge.

Despite the opening for the incorporation of Indigenous legal orders into defining landscapes of property and jurisdiction, much of the work by anthropologists in the years following *Delgamuukw* served to develop the ethnography of indigenous practice in terms that the state's political and legal apparatus would readily be able to make sense of. Much of this has been in the vein of land use and occupancy mapping, working to satisfy common law principles of land holding through, documenting map biographies, detailing itineraries of place names, and accumulating other forms of Indigenous knowledge in cartographic terms, which in turn highlights the incompatibility of industrial/extractive political-economic systems and indigenous ways of life (see e.g. Bryan and Wood 2015; Freeman 2011; McIlwraith and Cormier 2015/2016; Natcher 2001). Done well, these research approaches can admirably demonstrate past and present territorial land use and occupancy as familiar categories to common law systems of legal reasoning. Researchers, in collaboration with their Indigenous counterparts, produce maps that have become commonplace in state-led processes such as consultation over resource development, and help to address such questions as: To what extent were the lands proposed for this development used or occupied by your community? Where could the state better locate this industrial development to avoid conflict? However, this kind of approach tends to frame Indigenous land tenure as a kind of artefact or as pieces of evidence that 'can be tested for their veracity and accuracy as descriptions of past practices (or rejected as mythology) rather than themselves practices embedded within legal institutions' (Anker 2018: 30). This approach of site-by-site cartographic inscription leaves the literal and metaphorical 'white spaces' on maps of Indigenous territories and omits the ways that Indigenous peoples articulate their jurisdictions and arrangements around these places.

In the years since *Delgamuukw* brought this principle of dual perspectives of common law and Indigenous law as a founding principle for articulating Indigenous rights into the legal mainstream, the Supreme Court has further stressed the notion that Indigenous peoples' own perspectives need to be fully appreciated to incorporate Indigenous law as a foundation for Aboriginal title and rights.[4] In discussing this, Indigenous laws need not be seen merely as the equivalents of common law concepts; rather, as the Supreme Courts has suggested, they need to be taken on their own terms: 'This said, the court must be careful not to lose or distort the Aboriginal perspective by forcing ancestral practices into the square boxes of common law concepts, thus frustrating the goal of faithfully translating pre-sovereignty Aboriginal interests into equivalent modern legal rights'.[5]

In making the very first on-the-ground finding of Aboriginal title in Canada in 2014, the Supreme Court emphasized that the common law idea of 'possession' needs to be understood through the Indigenous peoples' 'laws, practices, size, technological ability and the character of the land'.[6] This approach widened the scope of recognition for Indigenous peoples' property rights and jurisdictions across a broad territory, going far beyond the state's characterization of Indigenous land title as the narrowly circumscribed footprints of villages, fishing spots, hunting trails, or the favoured salt licks of animals. This was a significant moment of recognition of Indigenous legal principles for the plaintiffs of the case, the Tsilhqot'in community, who have since worked to formalize laws, land use designations, and conservation objectives over its title lands. This work has further catalysed the efforts of other communities to carry out field research on Indigenous law.

One example of this can be seen in the efforts of the Tsleil-Waututh Nation (near metro Vancouver) to draw on extensive review of oral histories alongside ethnographic and archaeological research to frame the potential impact of oil pipelines and tankers in their territories (TWN 2016). In particular, this Coast Salish First Nation adopted a formal stewardship policy based on legal principles 'to protect, defend, and steward the water, land, air, and resources of our territory ... to provide the environmental cultural, spiritual, and economic foundation' for future generations (TWN 2016: 52). As sources of law for this stewardship policy, the Tsleil-Waututh Nation drew on *snuw'uyulh* ('the teachings', see also Morales 2016; TRC 2015: 70) of the Creator and core cultural values of reciprocal respect and caring for people, land, animals, ancestors, and supernatural beings in the world to provide the rationale and underpinning for their approach to rejecting the pipeline and tankers (TWN 2016). This framing, alongside more conventional mapping of land use and occupancy and analysis of risks for environmental impacts, is at the centre of an ongoing legal and political challenge to the state's efforts to build large-scale oil pipeline infrastructure in Tsleil-Waututh territories.[7] The Tsleil-Waututh Nation has gone well beyond demonstrating common law principles of 'possession' as a source of their own jurisdictions. Legal proceedings around this nationally important industrial development project continue to unfold in 2021; nevertheless, this very public articulation of Indigenous legal order as the nexus for political action has already gained a significant profile in Canada today.

While the potential of Indigenous legal order to reformulate legal reasoning is high, Indigenous legal scholar Al Hanna has observed that, to date, there have been only a 'few places where Indigenous laws function on their own vis-à-vis state law, and [there is] constant pressure to convert them into a western legal framework' (Hanna 2017: 159). Canadian courts have come to recognize the application of Indigenous law in matters of the internal governance of communities[8] and in a few cases around issues of marriage and adoption (see Grammond 2013: 375–6), but many judges still do not appear to be equipped to think with Indigenous law in formulating their legal reasoning (Hanna

2017: 144, 149; see also Borrows 2019: 22). Notable exceptions with respect to land and resources have included Judge Buller-Bennet's decision in the First Nation Court (a division of the Provincial Court of BC), where sentencing in a hunting case was made through 'an Indigenous legal process carried out in a contemporary setting according to indigenous laws' (Hanna 2017: 152).[9] I have also documented a series of cases on Vancouver Island in which trial judges made findings on hunting rights cases according to the legal principles articulated in court with respect to the appropriate manner to exercise harvesting rights in neighbouring First Nations' territories (Thom 2020).

The challenges of codifying principles of Indigenous legal orders in terms that are broadly recognizable are well understood, and have been experienced in Africa and elsewhere around the world (see e.g. Zenker and Hoehne 2018). Canadian legal scholars like John Borrows have grappled with this, trying not to distil Indigenous law into a fixed form, but rather revealing the way it works by reflecting on a broad range of encounters and experiences that inform and inspire legal reasoning. Borrows retells his community's oral traditions, with all their ambiguity and artistry, alongside explicitly dwelling on 'a grandparent's teachings, a law professor's reflections, an animal's behaviour, an engraved image, and a landscape's contours' (2010a: xiii). He insists that Indigenous law is best not represented through codification of ancient or 'traditional' practices, which freezes any understanding of Indigenous legal principles in time and place (Borrows 1998). Rather, through attending carefully to story, experience, and practice, Indigenous law can continue to be a 'living and dynamic force' (Borrows 2019: 15; see also Borrows 2010a: xiii). Val Napoleon and other Indigenous legal scholars have adapted a common law analysis framework, working through Indigenous stories and oral histories to draw out fundamental principles relating to social values and norms to inform legal reasoning (Friedland and Napoleon 2015; Napoleon 2015). These legal scholars call for attention to be paid to the everyday application and implementation of Indigenous legal principles in order to better grasp how they can be applied to the 'messy' lives of people (see Borrows, quoted in Napoleon and Friedland 2014: 1). It is about 'walking along with people who know what they're doing and us gathering possibilities ... for whatever we're doing' (Borrows quoted in Ball 2018). It is about 'a project that requires not just articulation and recognition, but also mindful, intentional acts of recovery and revitalization' (Friedland and Napoleon 2014). This approach from legal scholars sounds in many ways like a kind of reflexive ethnographic practice, a kind of work to which anthropologists can productively contribute.

But how might anthropology engage with this important, emerging dialogue? As an anthropologist working closely and in long-term relationships with Indigenous communities, I assert that it is possible to attend ethnographically to the ways people articulate and engage with Indigenous legal orders outside formal codification and outside the reasons for decisions provided after extensive, strategic, and expensive engagements in the courts. Anthropology allows us to ask such questions as: How are Indigenous legal principles enacted in everyday life? How do they shape local social and political relations and outcomes? What are the small ways in which Indigenous legal principles operate, not only within Indigenous communities, but at the intersection of Indigenous and state-ordered legal practice? These are substantive elements that, through ethnographically informed approaches, anthropology can contribute to the important objectives of contemporary Indigenous legal discourses.

Napoleon and Borrows both acknowledge that it is not only Indigenous peoples who can 'draw out' Indigenous law (a term coined by Borrows to reveal the storied process of engaging Indigenous law as a living and dynamic way of being and knowing; see Borrows 2010a). In attending to the principles, metaphors, contexts, and experiences these sources reveal, the goal is to make Indigenous law 'intelligible, accessible, legitimate, and applicable' (Napoleon 2015: 893; see also Borrows 2010b). Indeed, Napoleon has argued that 'we must develop an understanding of law across social boundaries so we can argue on an inter-societal basis' (Napoleon et al. 2013: 26). This has anthropological implications, as the core work of ethnography is also often to develop a sufficient understanding of cultural and social context to see across social boundaries, categories, and metaphors. I agree with Borrows's view that 'law is best understood and practised when we are not mesmerized by its generalized, abstract nature' and that 'law must be lived as well as theorized' (Borrows 2010a: 22). Ethnographic practice provides a critical window into the storied world in which Indigenous peoples' laws may be encountered and entangled. Through walking together and sensing the world, stories, and places, anthropologists come into conversation about the practice of legal principles in everyday life.

Below I provide a brief ethnography of encountering Indigenous legal orders through the contemporary landscape of shellfish harvesting in the Salish Sea, a beautiful archipelago of islands on the west coast of Canada near the cities of Victoria, Vancouver, Nanaimo, and Duncan. The Island Hul'q'umi'num' communities with which I most closely work (including Cowichan Tribes, Stz'uminus First Nation, Penelakut Tribe, Halalt First Nation, Lyackson First Nation) are Coast Salish peoples—about 7,800 individuals in total—whose territories are deeply rooted in this Island landscape. Island Hul'q'umi'num' peoples, like many other Indigenous peoples in British Columbia, have never signed a treaty with the British Crown or later Canada extinguishing or otherwise modifying their Indigenous title, rights, and governance (Egan 2012). In spite of this, colonial expansion starting in the mid-1800s has taken up much of their territories, most notably though the 'land grab' of 1884, which was carried out to facilitate settlement and economic exploitation of the east coast of Vancouver Island (Thom 2014). These politically independent communities (Thom 2010) have been engaged in various petitions, negotiations, and litigation for the recognition of their rights and title almost continuously since the 1860s, including since 1993 through the Canadian land claims negotiation process (Thom 2014). Today about half the population lives on-reserve—about 6,000 ha in total between these communities, a tiny fraction of the 334,000-hectare territory they claim—while the other half lives off-reserve, mostly in the nearby cities and suburban areas. These historical circumstances of territorial alienation have contributed to the stark economic disparity between Island Hul'q'umi'num' and neighbouring non-Indigenous peoples. Unemployment among the Island Hul'q'umi'num' community is very high (between

32 and 35 per cent), especially in comparison to the provincial rate of 8 per cent, and the 2011 median annual income $11,478 (CAD) on-reserve and $21,556 off-reserve was significantly lower than the provincial median of $28,573. In these economic contexts, harvesting local traditional foods and engaging in small-scale economic practices are critical for the well-being of families and households. They provide a vital context for encountering Indigenous legal orders.

Encountering Indigenous law at *Wuqw'wuw'qw'* ('Drifted Down Slowly'), Round Island

On a warm fall day in 2000, I piloted my small aluminium boat out of Ladysmith Harbour and went 14 km south to Round Island. Round Island (ca. 3 ha) is one of a number of tiny islands in the Chemainus River estuary, located just off the east coast of Vancouver Island (see Figure 6.1).[10] The concern I have with the largest possible impact stems from this footnote. This note correctly identifies the sources I used to draw the map in figure 6.1. But then the content of this footnote is reproduced under this figure, and recurs verbatim under each figure that follows. A better, more compact and space-saving approach would have been to acknowledge in this foot not that the source of base data used in all the figures is this public source, and then not have the "source" information spaciously detailed again and again below each figure. However, I suspect that this is an impossible change at this point, as it would change the pagination and layout, making my article more compact. If this is something OUP would like to do, however, I think it would be better than having "source" repeated over and over again with each figure.). Round Island is surrounded by several nearby Island Hul'q'umi'num' (Coast Salish) communities. It is a mere 160 m north-west of Halalt Island Indian Reserve (IR) 1 (Halalt First Nation), where the permanent winter village of Xulelthw was located prior to being resettled in the late nineteenth century. It is 1.25 km from the present-day Squaw-hay-one IR 11 community of the Stz'uminus First Nation, and 2.5 km from Tsussie IR 6, a reserve community of the Penelakut Tribe. Title to the island is registered as Crown land, with a 0.85 ha private moorage lease tenure on the north-east side of the island, though Aboriginal title has never been extinguished nor formally recognized by the state. Its close proximity to the ancestral communities and reserve lands of several First Nations and the fact that, through colonial omission, it was never designated as an Indian Reserve make Round Island a good place to think through how Indigenous legal orders around land tenure and resource use are intertwined and practised.

Round Island is one of the many ecologically rich locales in the Island Hul'q'umi'num' landscape. Four large archaeological sites encompass nearly the entire island (these sites have the official state designation DfRw-44, 45, 46, and 109; Eldridge 2016). Round

Island is a centre of longstanding intensive shellfish production; the culturally modified trees bear witness to a long history of human inhabitance; and it is a place where Island Hul'q'umi'num' peoples once interred their dead. The name for the Round Island in the Hul'q'umi'num' language is Wuqw'wuw'qw', which the late Lyackson elder Agnes Thorne said means 'drifted down slowly' (Rozen 1985: 122). Given the pulse of tidal and fresh waters over this shallow marine estuary, the place name evokes a sense of how the place is encountered as our small vessel navigates Round Island's landscape. At the beginning of time, the First Ancestors of the Island Hul'q'umi'num' communities fell from the sky with their knowledge, ceremonial prerogatives, and powers, landing at particular locales and establishing the original villages (Boas [1897] 2002: 140; Thom 2005). Swutun—'the growler'—came noisily down at Tl'elt'qt, another tiny island right beside Wuqw'wuw'qw', making the earth shake when he landed (Curtis 1913: 37; Jenness 1935: 12). He later took the now-famous hereditary name St'uts'un (Rozen 1985: 126), and through his own and his children's marriages came to be closely related to numerous auspicious property-owning founders of other original winter village communities (Thom 2005: 90).

Wuqw'wuw'qw' continues today to be a vital point for Island Hul'q'umi'num' fishers to access the flourishing (but often contaminated) shellfish and crab beds in the Chemainus

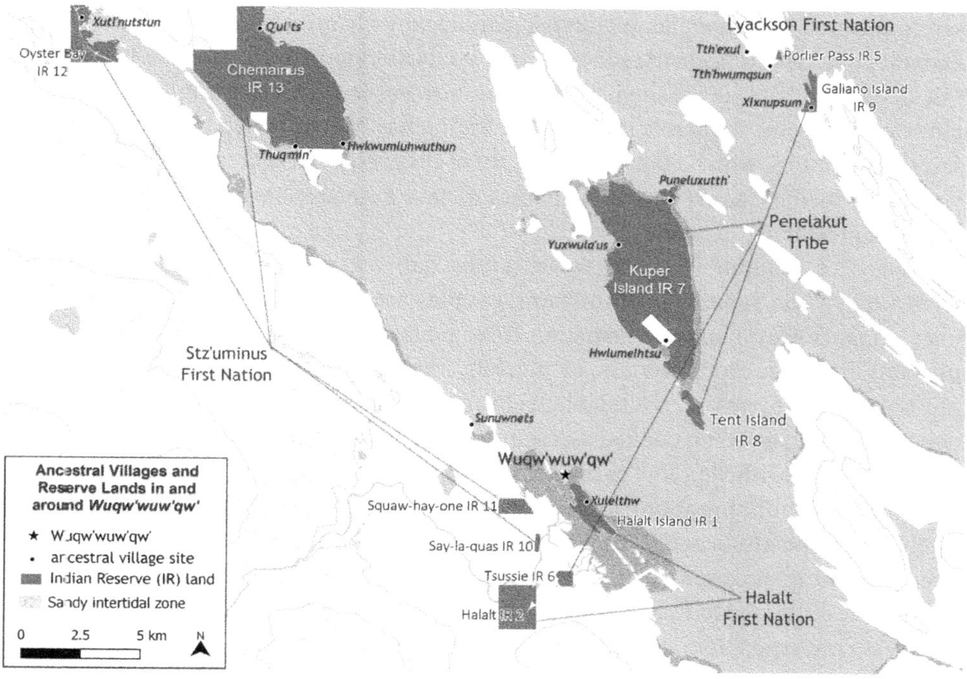

FIGURE 6.1. Round Island and nearby First Nations villages and Reserve lands

Source: Cartography by B Thom, assisted by J Baker. Cadastral and topographic data courtesy of BC Data Catalogue (http://catalogue.data.bc.ca), Open Government Licence—British Columbia (https://www2.gov.bc.ca/gov/content/data/open-data/open-government-licence-bc).

River estuary. The intertidal foreshore is easily accessible with even the smallest of boats, and during particularly during low tides a person could walk there in rubber boots. It is surrounded by commercial log booms, is in the direct line of agricultural and septic outflow from the Chemainus River valley, and is often swept up in the currents of toxins and effluent from the Crofton pulp and paper mill, located 3.5 km to the south-east. In spite of these contemporary physical challenges, Round Island's intertidal habitat and location have reinforced its place as a vital locale for ongoing harvesting practices.

The chief of the Penelakut Tribe, Suliisuluq (also known as Earl Jack), had asked my colleague, friend, and Indigenous researcher the late Joey Caro and me to look into Round Island, hoping to help some of his community members to harvest shellfish there. While his community members often harvested along the beaches fronting Penelakut Island (their main reserve about 4 km away across Stuart Channel), those beaches had faced some pressure recently. Given that Round Island is very close to another of their reserve communities at Tsussie on Vancouver Island, Chief Jack was considering how he might support shellfish harvesting there. Strictly speaking, under Canadian fisheries law, all of the wild shellfish stock in the intertidal beaches, including the shellfish in and around Round Island and the Chemainus River estuary, are a 'commons' resource. While recreational licences allow for relatively unrestricted domestic harvest for non-Indigenous harvesters throughout the region, Indigenous harvesters may dig clams for food and social and ceremonial purposes as long as there are no public health or safety closures. Commercial openings for Indigenous harvesters are provided through Federal government licensing schemes that establish opportunities for the landing and sale of defined volumes of shellfish taken on beaches in defined administrative areas.[11] However, the most profitable shellfish harvesting has been through provincially issued foreshore tenures, which effect an enclosure of these commons areas for intensive, privately run shellfish aquaculture companies to have exclusive harvest rights on many of the most productive beaches.

Because of pollution (faecal as well as industrial), a great many of the beaches in the territories of the Island Hul'q'umi'num' peoples are permanently closed to shellfish harvesting. However, in the Chemainus River estuary, the closure does not apply to manila and littleneck clams, oysters, or mussels. Manila and littlenecks tend not to easily bio-accumulate toxins, are found relatively high on the tide line, and are a highly desired delicacy, especially when cooked as 'steamers'. The abundance of a desirable shellfish in this area, along with very low barriers to accessing the foreshore around Round Island, had Chief Jack thinking about how he could help encourage his community members to safely and respectfully access this particular foreshore for an upcoming commercially licenced Aboriginal dig, as well as for their own food needs that winter.

So while under the federal fisheries system Round Island was considered 'open', Chief Jack was concerned about being faithful to the delicate protocols for shared resource harvesting with other First Nations. In this traditional territory of tightly knit, interrelated kin, he is a keen observer of Coast Salish legal principles, and is respectful of cultural tradition, protocol, and practice. He appreciates the teachings in stories of the First Ancestors, and respects how peoples' ancestral names and affiliations connect them to the property rights that flow through descent groups. This small island is very close (less than 0.5 km) to the ancestral village of the neighbouring Halalt First Nation on Willy's Island (Halalt IR 1). Where harvesters from Penelakut taking shellfish at beaches directly fronting the ancestral Halalt village would be inappropriate without being invited guests, harvesting close by on Round Island may not be unreasonable, given the close proximity of these neighbouring communities and the spirit of reciprocity between them. Indeed, reciprocity among closely related kin is a fundamental lesson often iterated in *snuw'uyulh*, ('the teachings'). The people I work with often refer to this reciprocity principle as *ts'its'uwatul'*—which has a literal sense of 'helping one another', but more than that, it evokes a strong moral grounding for social action, a basis in which to root one's best manners, thoughts, and intentions towards others—and others towards you. *Uy' ye' thut ch 'u' suw ts'its'uwatul' ch*, the proverb goes: 'Be kind, and you help each other' (Thom 2017: 156). *Ts'its'uwatul'* is a 'simple law', as one elder explained to me, but following it has significant implications in lived experience, including Coast Salish engagements with land tenure and resource management.

Chief Jack had spoken several times publicly, and with Joey and me more privately, about how he had ensured that Penelakut beaches were open for other neighbouring Island Hul'q'umi'num' community members to utilize when they were in need. Members of neighbouring First Nations had frequently come over to Penelakut Island by ferry and harvested during open harvesting times. His vision was that, in the spirit of *ts'its'uwatul'*—helping one another—Penelakut members, including those at Tsussie who live walking distance from the Chemainus Estuary, would be welcome to harvest shellfish at Round Island, supported and perhaps joined by neighbouring First Nations such as Halalt. Chief Jack wanted to extend this spirit of reciprocity, but also wanted to avoid 'stepping on anyone's toes' by violating some families' private areas or the territories of a neighbouring First Nation. In this, he was being mindful of another Coast Salish legal principle around land tenure. This principle, which I have taken up in detail elsewhere (Morales and Thom 2020; Thom 2005, 2009, 2014), recognizes that the productive resource locales in the Coast Salish world are generally owned by extended families or held in common by local residence groups. A place like Round Island, which is so close to the ancient village of Xulelthw—the founding community of the neighbouring Halalt First Nation—is also considered to be in Penelakut territory, though how to use this place was not exclusively up to Chief Jack to decide. While individual residents in one of the Penelakut Tribe's villages may be able to exercise their family's harvest rights at places like Round Island, in the present political context Chief Jack recognized Coast Salish land tenure principles, whereby such a decision must be made in concert with the leaders of his neighbouring First Nation communities. This is the way shared exclusive title and jurisdiction (to invoke the language of the Supreme Court in *Delgamuukw v British Columbia*) operates in a place like this.[12]

In looking into Round Island for Chief Jack, Joey and I spoke with the late Abner Thorne, a widely respected Elder from the Island Hul'q'umi'num' community. We asked him how he would navigate the interconnected territorial boundaries of each First Nation in a way that would help explain the rules of access to such a central place as Round Island. He told us that 'it has to be sorted out between the three groups [Halalt, Penelakut, and Stz'uminus, whose reserves and historic villages are close by, see Figure 6.1]. Their areas are so intertwined that it's too hard to separate them. They [the leaders of these communities] have to come to an agreement that they all co-exist within that area.... It's not only today that we have been interrelated. We've always been interrelated and the governments know that.'[13] Abner elaborated on the depth of these relations, connecting their shared histories through the First Ancestor stories. His implications were clear: while leaders like Chief Jack know very well they must respect the foundations of Coast Salish land tenure and live by the teachings of *ts'its'uwatul'*, the government's licencing and tenure schemes undermine those indigenous legal principles, creating challenges for everyone concerned.

Chief Jack decided to table an 'openness protocol' with other Island Hul'q'umi'num' communities. The protocol restated the well-known foundation of common ancestry and interconnectedness of Island Hul'q'umi'num' communities, and offered recognition of this as the basis for future resource sharing throughout the territory. His idea for a formal protocol soon became the focus of critical attention by other Island Hul'q'umi'num' leaders and community members. In discussing the protocol, they found that, regarding harvesting shellfish for food, social, and ceremonial purposes, there was little controversy. People are always willing to share where there is a need, when a family has to put food on the table. One leader responded, 'I think we can really move towards a document, a protocol document without getting stuck in all the DFO's [Department of Fisheries and Oceans] rules if we say, "We already have a set of rules." And I believe that what we're trying to generate here is a reflection of what the oral history said, a reflection of what our traditional protocols were. And yeah, there's a whole other set of rules and laws, but these ones are ours and that's where we work from.' This leader continued, 'I think if we're going to trump that [DFO] system somehow, it's going to be because we've got strong oral history that says our people harvested according to traditional knowledge in this whole area and then we respect that as *hwulmuhw mustimuhw* [Coast Salish peoples] because we're not going to get the same sort of respect from the Department of Fisheries and Oceans as we could give to each other' (fieldnotes, 2000). Chief Jack was encouraged. These views reinforced his idea that grounding territorial decision-making about resource harvesting in Indigenous land tenure and knowledge would be a powerful approach to actualizing Indigenous legal principles and moving forward in a good way.

However, more critical concerns about a formalized protocol were expressed from many other quarters. While digging for food was one thing, the protocol also connected to commercial harvesting and the ways it might interact with the terms of the licences for small-scale economic opportunities that the government issued to First Nations in the area. Some leaders were more cautious in their support. As one of them said about the protocol, 'I think that part of what we're doing here concerning... us trying to come up with a protocol that respects our traditional relationship [is good], but we are talking about it in the context of Area 17 [a DFO management area that extends through and beyond Island Hul'q'umi'num' and neighbouring First Nations territories; see Figure 6.2]

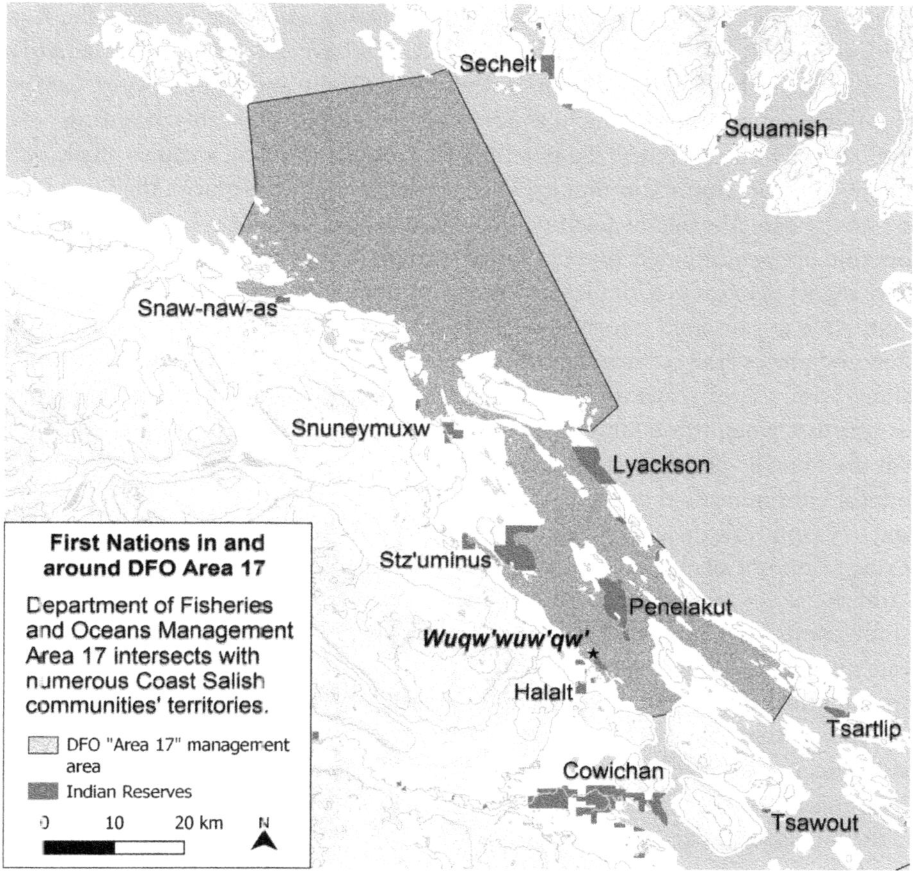

FIGURE 6.2. First Nations in and around the DFO management area 17.

Source: Cartography by B Thom, assisted by J Baker. Cadastral and topographic data courtesy of BC Data Catalogue (http://catalogue.data.bc.ca), Open Government Licence—British Columbia (https://www2.gov.bc.ca/gov/content/data/open-data/open-government-licence-bc).

and those are two different sides.' There are hazards, his words cautioned, in the concurrent exercise of state law and Indigenous law.

Initial concerns were expressed that formalizing protocols around resource access and territorial recognition—in other words, codifying these principles—would create unwanted and unwelcome complications for how Coast Salish principles of respectful reciprocity actually work on the ground. If areas such as DFO Area 17 are declared 'open' to members of other First Nations through a formalized agreement, it could very well undermine local mechanisms that allow families and local leadership to guard against over-harvesting at a particular beach, or change the expectation that reciprocity is a two-way street.

Where shellfish are concerned, there is always the apprehension that a given beach may have too many people harvesting on it, which puts too much pressure on the resource. This is particularly the case for more readily accessible beaches like Round Island, as most Island Hul'q'umi'num' people do not have the capital to buy and maintain small boats that could take them further afield (Thom and Fediuk 2009). Concerns about this are made more acute in the context of commercial-scale harvesting, which, if not carefully managed, has the potential to wipe out the local shellfish stock. At the time the Hul'q'umi'num' communities were considering the protocol, the DFO had issued about 250 Aboriginal Commercial Licences to harvesters looking to have an economic opportunity over a very limited number of low-tide events (about seven to twelve nights per year). With these licences, any uncontaminated and untenured beach within Area 17 was open to commercial digging. There are very few uncontaminated, untenured places easily accessible without a boat. The experience of several other First Nations within Area 17 whose beaches fronting reserve lands were accessible by car or foot was that when those kinds of permissions were granted, 250 people would show up at the same low tide, creating incredible pressure on the resource and diminishing the local community's economic opportunities through competition. The 'commons' licence system introduced by Canada potentially throws open Coast Salish lands, removing local control and undermining the Coast Salish legal principle of *ts'its'uwatul'*.

Additional concerns were expressed about keeping the spirit, power, and flexibility of Indigenous law and social orders. Some people feared that such a protocol could create unwanted, binding state law-based obligations between First Nations that might transcend these more relational connections and decision-making processes. A related concern was that formalizing such a protocol could formally transpose authority for making decisions regarding traditionally owned resources from families to the elected band councils that govern the affairs of First Nations on-reserve communities. While band councils are, quite pragmatically, the venue for many such decisions today, off-reserve fisheries are by and large not part of their formalized or codified jurisdiction in Island Hul'q'umi'num' communities.

Perhaps even more influential were views expressed by some Island Hul'q'umi'num' leaders that drawing out Indigenous law should not hinder the small but important economic opportunities that the commercial licences provide for their community members. These opportunities include exercising harvesting rights throughout and beyond the traditional territories of any particular First Nation (at the time, DFO Management Area E was the widest zone of commercial harvesting under these licences; see Figure 6.3). These communities face serious poverty, and small-scale commercial shellfish harvesting is a critical way for families to earn much-needed supplemental cash. If commercial licences provided openings in 'the commons', this argument goes, there should not be Indigenous law barriers to accessing those opportunities. As such these leaders were reluctant to exercise their concurrent Indigenous authority, saying, 'I don't want to restrict our people by saying you can only go on these *hwulmuhw* [First Nations] beaches or something, if they're really open. Any beach that's open according to DFO, they could go to.'[14] Another leader emphasized the individual rights of the licence holders: 'I think it is up to the individual licence holders to find out where they could go. I think it is not for us to decide where our Aboriginal Communal Licence persons can

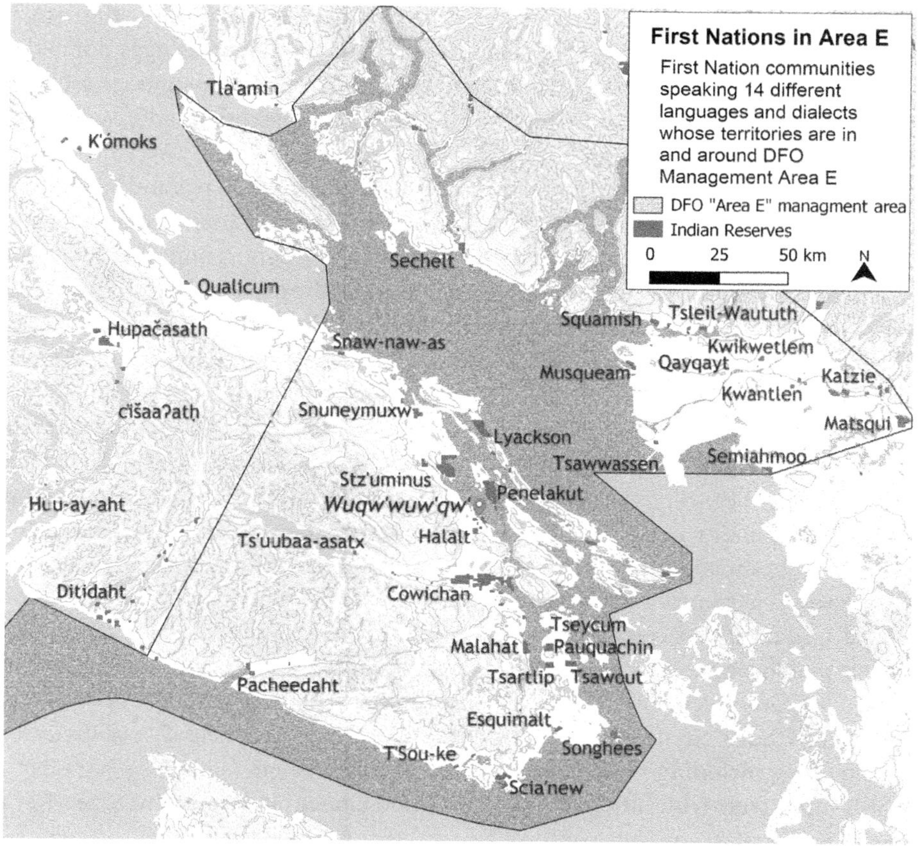

FIGURE 6.3. Map of the numerous First Nations whose territories and jurisdictions intersect with DFO Management Area E

Source: Cartography by B Thom, assisted by J Baker. Cadastral and topographic data courtesy of BC Data Catalogue (http://catalogue.data.bc.ca), Open Government Licence—British Columbia (https://www2.gov.bc.ca/gov/content/data/open-data/open-government-licence-bc).

go in. I don't think that would be Chief and Council decisions, telling people where they can go digging under their Area E opening. The responsibility is up to the individuals.'[15]

In the end, the protocol was considered for over a year by the leadership of Island Hul'q'umi'num' communities, but was never signed. Frustrated by the impass, one leader stated, 'We know that the Department of Fisheries and Oceans has got a whole different set of rules that's not consistent with what we believe in as Hul'q'umi'num' people. … Unless we start saying, "Here's what the real teaching is and here's what the real territory or the harvesting territory of our people is", we're still going to keep banging into a comment like, "You know, who cares about what Hul'q'umi'num' people have agreed on a protocol? I've got my DFO license and I'll go where that license says I can go".'[16] The implication is that jurisdictions that are exercised to implement the federal system for management of commercial shellfish harvesting undermine or operate at cross-purposes to Indigenous laws that would otherwise mitigate disagreements and conflicts between communities. These are exactly the kinds of challenges pointed out nearly fifteen years later by the TRC, which found that 'Aboriginal peoples must be recognized as possessing the responsibility, authority, and capability to address their disagreements by making laws within their communities' (TRC 2015: 51). What is the point of recognizing Indigenous law if state law simply undermines its logics and intents? New relationships are needed that respect Indigenous communities' attempts to recover and revitalize their legal principles, which in this case include at a minimum the principles of Indigenous land tenure, resource decision-making, and the expectation that Indigenous communities, families, and individuals will be able to realize the full benefits of the land.

Despite the fact that Chief Jack's protocol was not formally codified, Island Hul'q'umi'num' members and leadership have continued to respect the principles he articulated, particularly as they pertain to harvesting on beaches fronting (or near) Indian reserves. First Nations commercial licence holders, though free to dig anywhere within the area of their licence, in practice generally honour local prerogatives. For example, the following winter Cowichan Tribes harvesters stepped back from a commercial dig on Penelakut Island even though it was technically 'open', engaging on-the-ground with the Indigenous legal order being exercised by Penelakut Tribe. This was in spite of the fact that pollution closures, provincial foreshore leases, and challenges in accessing more remote locations had practically reduced the off-reserve areas where harvesters could go for commercial digs to a very limited number of places like Round Island and Nanoose Bay. Such circumstances create intense pressure on shellfish resources from multiple users, including non-Indigenous recreational fishers (some of whom harvest shellfish intensively with little regulation or enforcement, and no knowledge of or responsibility to Indigenous legal orders).

In the last twelve years, several First Nations have organized limited and highly regulated opportunities to harvest and depurate shellfish (i.e. flush toxins out of shellfish in freshwater vats) for commercial sale. In 2006 the Hul'q'umi'num' communities created a joint venture, Qum'ul Seafoods, which obtained a permit to commercially harvest about 11,000 kg of clams near Round Island (Hill 2006: 3). While there was initially great hope that the joint venture would be a commercial success, it faced many challenges. Taking up a different strategy, individual First Nations started to register exclusive shellfish tenures for beaches near their reserve lands (in many cases holding their noses at the act, as Elders had often pointed out the seeming injustice of having to ask the province for a tenure for their own lands). The Halalt First Nation and Halalt Shellfish Development Corporation registered three commercial shellfish aquaculture tenures for exclusive harvesting near Round Island, while Penelakut and Stz'uminus First Nations obtained similar tenures, mainly in areas fronting their reserves (see Figure 6.4). In many ways, these actions in the years following Chief Jack's call for a protocol have effected a hardening of borders and an enclosure of Indigenous inter-tidal lands, though the terms are carefully crafted with legal counsel to be without prejudice to Indigenous title and rights.

However, even an 'enclosure' like an aquaculture tenure does not fundamentally change or extinguish Island Hul'q'umi'num' law. In 2011, in a case over water rights in the

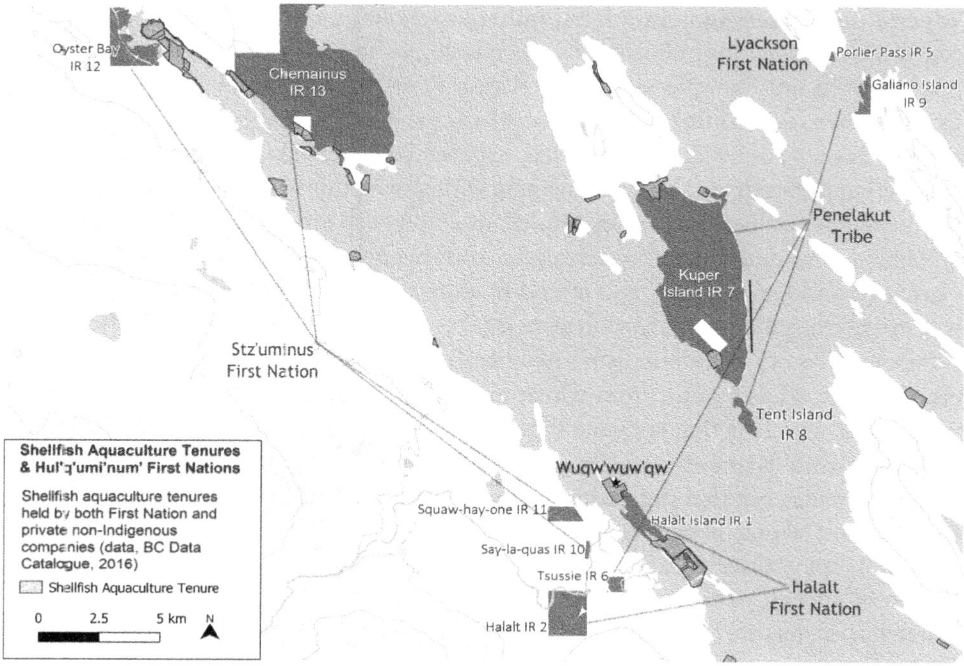

FIGURE 6.4. Shellfish aquaculture tenures held by Island Hul'q'umi'num' and non-Indigenous ventures

Source: Cartography by B Thom, assisted by J Baker. Cadastral and topographic data courtesy of BC Data Catalogue (http://catalogue.data.bc.ca), Open Government Licence—British Columbia (https://www2.gov.bc.ca/gov/content/data/open-data/open-government-licence-bc).

Chemainus River estuary, the BC Supreme Court recognized that the Halalt First Nation and their Island Hul'q'umi'num' neighbours (including Penelakut) had established the prima facie case for shared exclusive Aboriginal title in this area.[17] Rather than leveraging a 'protocol' to effect Indigenous land tenure, the focus of the Island Hul'q'umi'num' leadership has been to continue valuing the practice and the relationships that Indigenous legal orders are rooted in. Island Hul'q'umi'num' leadership use licences and tenures to continue to engage the world with Indigenous legal orders firmly in mind. On the ground, families continue to navigate their subsistence and livelihoods through acting on ancestral prerogatives and embodying *ts'its'uwatul'* in sharing opportunities and resolving disputes.

Anthropology and Indigenous Legal Orders

Anthropology is in a new position with respect to Indigenous law in Canada. Indigenous legal scholars and communities are not looking to anthropologists as 'experts' on Indigenous cultures, but rather as scholars and collaborators who are engaged with Indigenous philosophies and ontologies and are able to comment on these not as frozen museum pieces, but in relation to ordered social life in the present. As in this case-study, anthropologists bear witness to the legal orders of Indigenous peoples as they are lived and expressed, experienced, and entangled in mutual worlds (Dussart and Poirier 2017), while engaging with abstractions of Indigenous legal orders and principles of legal reasoning. Our ethnography can strive to embrace complexity, ambiguity, and multiplicity in narratives of Indigenous legal orders as they are both expressed and experienced, and attend to situated knowledge and practices. We can work to reveal entanglements with state legal orders, and to bring to our analysis questions of the forces of colonialism, neoliberalism, governance, and social order. Such ethnography offers a point from which to reflect on how these legal orders might be understood in terms that resonate with Indigenous values and norms and how legal reasoning unfolds in everyday life. The ethnographic view is, of course, always partial and incomplete, but this situatedness is something that Indigenous legal scholars like Borrows and Napoleon have embraced.

Ethnography raises important questions about the circumstances under which anthropologists can work with Indigenous legal traditions. We need to cautiously ask: What stories may we tell, and how can we situate ourselves within them? What details are important to include, and what is sidelined or silenced? How can we know that we have adequately interpreted local metaphors and concerns in our work of drawing out Indigenous law? Long-term collaborative ethnography can provide a basis for sharing in this work, as we walk the land together, listen to the stories, and become mutually entangled. It can provide a framework of accountability and ethical practice through committed attention to our shared worlds. Anthropologists working in this mode are not tasked with codifying Indigenous law from our partial and fallible positions, steeped in our own personal theoretical, political projects. In the spirit of all good anthropology, such work is offered with humility and often in the spirit of helping illuminate these difficult points of intersection—like 'looking into' clam beaches—in hopes of achieving some measure of social justice in our shared worlds.

Notes

1. Lamer CJ, *Delgamuukw v R* [1997] SCR para. 114.
2. Lamer CJ, *Delgamuukw* [1997] SCR para. 147.
3. Lamer CJ, *Delgamuukw* [1997] SCR para. 148.
4. I use the terms 'Aboriginal title' and 'Aboriginal rights' when referring specifically to the language of the Canadian Constitution and how Canadian courts have defined the nature and scope of these concepts. 'Indigenous' and 'Indigenous rights' are terms used by legal scholars in Canada in a more encompassing way, not only acknowledging these common law notions of Aboriginal title and rights, but also the rights that flow from Indigenous legal orders irrespective of the common law and from international Indigenous rights frameworks.

5. McLaughlan CJ in *Tsilhqot'in v R* [2014] SRC 257, SCC 44 (CanLII) para. 32.
6. McLaughlan CJ in *Tsilhqot'in v R* [2014] SRC paras 41, 49.
7. *Tsleil-Waututh Nation v Attorney General of Canada, et al.*, 2020 CanLII 17604 (SCC), <http://canlii.ca/t/j5pw2>; *Tsleil-Waututh Nation v Canada (Attorney General)* [2018] FCJ No 876 (QL).
8. See e.g. *Pastion v Dene Tha' First Nation*.
9. See also *R v Joseph Thomas* and *R v Christopher Brown*, 2015, First Nations Court, Duncan.
10. Cartography by B Thom, assisted by J Baker. Cadastral and topographic data courtesy of BC Data Catalogue (<http://catalogue.data.bc.ca>), Open Government Licence—British Columbia (<https://www2.gov.bc.ca/gov/content/data/open-data/open-government-licence-bc>).
11. 'Landing' refers to bringing in the harvest for measuring and weighing to ensure that it does not exceed the allowable quota or size regulation.
12. *Delgamuukw v British Columbia* [1997] 3 SCR 1010, 1997 CanLII 302 (SCC).
13. Interview with Abner Thone, November 2000.
14. Excerpt from fieldnotes, 2000.
15. Excerpt from fieldnotes, 2001.
16. Excerpt from fieldnotes, 2001.
17. *Halalt First Nation v British Columbia (Environment)* [2011] BCSC 945 (CanLII) paras 486–7.

References

Anker, K. 2018. 'Aboriginal Title and Alternative Cartographies'. *Erasmus Law Review*. 1(1): 14–30.<https://dx.doi.org/10.5553/ELR.000098>

Asch, M. 2014. *On Being Here to Stay: Treaties and Aboriginal Rights in Canada*. Toronto: University of Toronto Press.

Ball, D. 2018. 'Changemakers: John Borrows'. *Toronto Star*, 15 November 2018.

Boas, F. 2002. *Indian Myths and Legends from the North Pacific Coast of America: A Translation of Franz Boas' 1895 Edition of Indianische Sagen von der Nord-Pacifischen Kuste Amerikas*, ed. R. Bouchard and D. Kennedy, trans. D. Bertz. Vancouver: Talonbooks.

Borrows, J. 1998. 'Frozen Rights in Canada: Constitutional Interpretation and the Trickster' *American Indian Law Review* 22(1): 37–64.

Borrows, J. 2005. 'Indigenous Legal Traditions in Canada'. *Washington University Journal of Law and Policy*. 19: 167–223.

Borrows, J. 2010a. *Drawing out Law: A Spirit's Guide*. Toronto: University of Toronto Press.

Borrows, J. 2010b. *Canada's Indigenous Constitution*. Toronto: University of Toronto Press.

Borrows, J. 2019. *Law's Indigenous Ethics*. Toronto: University of Toronto Press.

Bryan, J. and D. Wood. 2015. *Weaponizing Maps: Indigenous Peoples and Counterinsurgency in the Americas*. New York: Guilford Press.

Curtis, E. 1913. *The North American Indian, Volume 9: Salishan Tribes of the Coast*. New York: Johnson Reprint Co.

Daly, R. 2005. *Our Box Was Full: An Ethnography for the Delgamuukw Plaintiffs*. Vancouver: UBC Press.

de Sousa Santos, B. 2002. *Towards a New Legal Common Sense: Law, Globalization, and Emancipation* (2nd ed.). Oxford: Butterworths.

Dussart, F. and S. Poirier, eds. 2017. *Entangled Territorialities: Negotiating Indigenous Lands in Australia and Canada*. Toronto: University of Toronto Press.

Egan, B. 2012. 'Sharing the Colonial Burden: Treaty-Making and Reconciliation in Hul'qumi'num Territory'. *The Canadian Geographer* 56(4): 1–21.

Eldridge, R. 2016. *Round Island. Permit 2016-0026: An Archaeological Inventory*. Unpublished Report on file at BC Archaeology Branch, Victoria. Victoria: Millennia Research Limited.

Feltes, E. 2015. 'Research as Guesthood: The Memorial to Sir Wilfrid Laurier and Resolving Indigenous–Settler Relations in British Columbia'. *Anthropologica* 57(2): 469–80.

Fiske, J. and B. Patrick. 2000. *Cis Dideen Kat (When the Plumes Rise): The Way of the Lake Babine Nation*. Vancouver: UBC Press.

Freeman, M. 2011. 'Looking Back—and Looking Ahead—35 Years after the Inuit Land Use and Occupancy Project'. *Canadian Geographer* 55(1): 20–31.

Friedland, H. and V. Napoleon 2015. 'Gathering the Threads: Developing a Methodology for Researching and Rebuilding Indigenous Legal Traditions'. *Lakehead Law Journal* 1(1): 16–44.

Grammond, S. 2013. *Terms of Coexistence: Indigenous Peoples and Canadian Law*, trans. J. Lazare. Toronto: Carswell.

Hanna, A. 2017. 'Spaces for Sharing: Searching for Indigenous Law on the Canadian Legal Landscape'. *UBC Law Review* 51(1): 105–59.

Hill, E. 2006. 'Treaty Group Ready to Make Foreshore Footprint'. *Ladysmith Chronicle*, 4 April 2006, p. 3.

International Council on Human Rights Policy. 2009. *When Legal Worlds Overlap: Human Rights, State and Non-State Law*. Geneva: ATAR Roto Press. Available at <http://ichrp.org/files/reports/50/135_report_en.pdf>

Jenness, D. 1935. *Coast Salish Mythology*. VII-G-9M, Box 39, F.1. Hull: Canadian Museum of Civilization.

McIlwraith, T. and R. Cormier. 2015/2016. 'Making Place for Space: Site-Specific Land Use and Occupancy Studies in the Context of the Supreme Court of Canada's Tsilhqot'in Decision'. *BC Studies* 188: 35–53.

McNeil, K. 2009. 'Judicial Treatment of Indigenous Land Rights in the Common Law World'. In B. Richardson, S. Imai, and K. McNeil, eds. *Indigenous Peoples and the Law: Comparative and Critical Perspectives*, 256–83. Oxford: Hart Publishing.

Miller, B. 2016. *The Contemporary Coast Salish: Essays by Bruce Granville Miller*. Edited by B Miller and D Stapp. Memoir 12, Journal of Northwest Anthropology, Richland, Wa.

Mills, A. 1994. *Eagle Down is our Law: Witsuwit'en Law, Feasts, and Land Claims*. Vancouver: UBC Press.

Morales, S. 2016. 'Stl'ulnup: Legal landscapes of the Hul'qumi'num Mustimuhw'. *Windsor Yearbook of Access to Justice* 33(1): 103–23. <https://doi.org/10.22329/wyaj.v33i1.4813>

Morales, S. and B. Thom. 2020. 'The Principle of Sharing and the Shadow of Canadian Property Law'. In A. Cameron, S Graben, and V. Napoleon eds. Creating Indigenous Property: power, rights, and relationships, 120–160. Toronto: University of Toronto Press. https://doi.org/10.3138/9781487532116-005.

Napoleon, V. 2013. 'Thinking about Indigenous Legal Orders'. In R. Provost and C. Sheppard, eds. *Dialogues on Human Rights and Legal Pluralism*, 229–45. Dordrecht: Springer.

Napoleon, V. 2015. 'Tsilhqot'in Law of Consent'. *UBC Law Review*. 48(3): 873–902.

Napoleon, V. and H. Friedland. 2014. 'Indigenous Legal Traditions: Roots to Renaissance'. In M. Dubber and T. Hörnle, eds. *Oxford Handbook of Criminal Law*, 225–247. Oxford: Oxford University Press. <http://dx.doi.org/10.1093/oxfordhb/9780199673599.013.0011>

Napoleon, V., J. Henshaw, K. Steacy, J. Johnston, and S. Roy. 2013. *Mikomosis and the Wetiko*. Victoria: University of Victoria Indigenous Law Research Clinic.

Natcher, D. 2001. 'Land Use Research and the Duty to Consult: A Misrepresentation of the Aboriginal Landscape'. *Land Use Policy* 18(2): 113–22.

Noble, B. 2007. 'Justice, Transaction, Translation: Blackfoot Tipi Transfers and WIPO's Search for the Facts of Traditional Knowledge Exchange'. *American Anthropologist* 109(2): 338–49.

Noble, B. 2008. 'Owning as Belonging/Owning as Property: The Crisis of Power and Respect in First Nations Heritage Transactions with Canada'. In C. Bell and V. Napoleon, eds. *First Nations Cultural Heritage and Law: Case Studies, Voices, and Perspectives*, 465–488. Vancouver: UBC Press.

Regan, P. 2009. 'An Apology Feast in Hazelton: Indian Residential Schools, Reconciliation, and Making Space for Indigenous Legal Traditions'. In Law Commission of Canada, ed. *Indigenous Legal Traditions*, 40–76. Vancouver: UBC Press.

Rozen, D. 1985. *Place-names of the Island Halkomelem Indian People*. MA thesis, Department of Anthropology and Sociology, University of British Columbia. Available at<http://hdl.handle.net/2429/25517>

Thom, B. 2005. *Coast Salish Senses of Place: Dwelling, Meaning, Power, Property and Territory in the Coast Salish World*. PhD dissertation. Department of Anthropology, McGill University. <https://escholarship.mcgill.ca/concern/theses/vm40xs07v>

Thom, B. 2009. 'The Paradox of Boundaries in Coast Salish Territories'. *Cultural Geographies*. 16(2): 179–205. <http://dx.doi.org/10.1177/1474474008101516>

Thom, B. 2010. 'The Anathema of Aggregation: Towards 21st Century Self-Government in the Coast Salish World'. *Anthropologica* 52(1): 33–48. <http://www.jstor.org/stable/29545993>

Thom, B. 2014. 'Reframing Indigenous Territories: Private Property, Human Rights and Overlapping Claims'. *American Indian Culture and Research Journal* 38(4): 3–28. <http://dx.doi.org/10.17953/aicr.38.4.6372163053512w6x>

Thom, B. 2017. 'Entanglements in Coast Salish Ancestral Territories'. In F. Dussart and S. Poirier, eds. *Entangled Territorialities: Indigenous Peoples from Canada and Australia in the 21st Century*, 140–62. Anthropological Horizons Series. Toronto: University of Toronto Press. <https://doi.org/10.3138/9781487513764-008>

Thom, B. 2020. 'Addressing the Challenge of Overlapping Claims in Implementing the Vancouver Island (Douglas) Treaties'. *Anthropologica* 62(2): 295–307. <https://doi.org/10.3138/anth-2020-0014>

Thom, B. and K. Fediuk. 2009. 'Coast Salish Food Security in the 21st Century', invited keynote address to the 6th Annual Anthropology Conference on Culture, Community, and Well-Being, Sustaining Food: Conference on Past and Present Food System, Kwantlen University College, Surrey, 20 March 2009. Available at <http://www.web.uvic.ca/~bthom1/Media/pdfs/abrights/ThomFediuk2009_foodsecurity.pdf>

TRC (Truth and Reconciliation Commission). 2015. *Canada's Residential Schools: The Final Report of the Truth and Reconciliation Commission of Canada, Volume 6: Reconciliation*. Montreal & Kingston: McGill-Queen's University Press.

TWN (Tsleil-Waututh Nation). 2016. *Assessment of the Trans Mountain Pipeline and Tanker Expansion Proposal*. North Vancouver: Tsleil-Waututh Nation Treaty, Lands and Resources Department. Available at <https://twnsacredtrust.ca/assessment-report-download/>

Zenker, O. and M. Hoehne. 2018. 'Processing the Paradox: When the State has to Deal with Customary Law'. In O. Zenker and M. V. Hoehne, eds. *The State and the Paradox of Customary Law in Africa*, 1–40. London: Routledge.

CHAPTER 7

RUSSIAN LEGAL ANTHROPOLOGY

From Empirical Ethnography to Applied Innovation

FLORIAN STAMMLER, AYTALINA IVANOVA, AND BRIAN DONAHOE

THIS chapter discusses the history of legal anthropology in Russia, which, since the fall of the Soviet Union, has developed along two separate but parallel branches—one practised by legal scholars, the other by anthropologists.[1] Drawing on contrasting case studies from two of the most thoroughly studied and widely publicized Indigenous groups of Siberia, the Nenets and the Sakha, we argue for bringing these two branches together in an interdisciplinary, historically informed, fieldwork-based legal anthropology. Such a joint endeavour, combining the strengths of the two disciplines, can help answer certain fundamental questions related to the various approaches to law encountered within Russia today, such as why some societies are more inclined towards juridification and eagerly embrace and engage in countrywide legislative processes, while others avoid drafting codified laws, preferring instead to focus on ad hoc, pragmatic action in the organization of their internal affairs. Doing so also has the potential to establish a unified, uniquely Russian legal anthropology as a discipline in its own right, with its own strong conceptual and methodological tradition founded in the highly detailed empirical work of ethnographers, historians, and legal scholars of the Russian Empire and the Soviet Union.

The historical development of 'legal anthropology' in Russia

The Study of Indigenous Legal Systems in Imperial Russia

Legal anthropology as a discipline in the Russian academe became institutionalized only after the fall of the Soviet Union. In a Russian social anthropology textbook (Dobren'kov and Kravchenko 2005), legal anthropology is considered a branch of the sociology of law, with a special focus on 'archaic' legal cultures in different regions of the world. However, the study of Indigenous legal systems, customary law, and the relation between the study of Russia's diverse societies and Russian state law has a much longer tradition. Travellers, administrators, missionaries, and military personnel wrote up their observations of the 'exotic' legal customs of the many diverse peoples within the Russian Empire, from the Caucasus through Central Asia to Siberia and the Far East. Empirical research on law, legal systems, customary law, normative orders, etc. was carried out as early as the eighteenth century, and a focus on 'custom' became a staple component of virtually any ethnographic work throughout this long history: 'Custom rapidly grew in importance, acquiring a separate value and gradually congealing into a "spirit of nations" (and eventually "culture"). . . . Stripped down to ethical and liturgical precepts collectively known as "law" (*zakon*), it usually came toward the end of Russian ethnographic accounts, after subsistence and before festivals' (Slezkine 1997: 33).

For nineteenth-century France and England, information gathered by anthropologists was used to facilitate administration of the peoples inhabiting their overseas colonies. In the Russian Empire, this was an important *internal* matter: the customs of its remote, non-Russian inhabitants sharing the same land mass needed to be mapped for these societies to be assigned a distinct legal status. Throughout the nineteenth century, the Department of Ethnography of the Russian Geographical Society organized the systematic study of the customs of all peoples in the empire with the goal of informing state policy. In 1867, the department issued systematic instructions on how these data were to be collected (Uvachan 2001: 2).[2]

The late nineteenth-century scholar Maksim Kovalevskii is considered the founder of legal anthropology as a discipline that is separate from the study of the history of law (Dobren'kov and Kravchenko 2005).[3] Kovalevskii, a legal scholar, engaged in extensive fieldwork in the Caucasus (Ignatieva 2006), and thus is more aligned with the idea of the legal anthropological method as it is understood in Western scholarship. A number of other pre-Soviet legal ethnographies also focused on the Caucasus, and a great deal of research was conducted on Central Asia.[4]

Later, during the revolutionary period in the early twentieth century, the normative systems of the Indigenous peoples of Siberia started attracting the attention of scholars. A number of detailed legal ethnographies (Bogoras 1904; Jochelson 1905; Riasanovsky [1938] 2017; Samokvasov 1908) can be classified as late pre-Soviet, early Soviet, or perhaps most accurately, as both.[5] These were in the tradition of classic ethnographies about one particular group. During Soviet times, these and other scholars became the 'state ethnographers', tasked with identifying and defining the peoples and cultures of the Soviet Union, providing authoritative information about them, and demarcating 'autonomous' areas for them (e.g. Anderson 2000). As such, these ethnographies were expected to contain information on the legal systems. Many of these descriptions remain important for the self-identification and cultural revitalization projects of these peoples to this day.

The Soviet Era

The sections on legal systems in the classic ethnographies of the early Soviet 'state ethnographers' were detailed descriptions of how conflicts were resolved, marriage rules implemented, family matters regulated, and so forth. In this section, we highlight the influence of three of these ethnographers in particular—Waldemar Bogoras (also Bogoraz), Lev Shternberg, and Sergei Shirokogoroff—as their work helps us to understand the success (or lack thereof) of the implementation of state law in those societies, and thus serves our argument for a new Russian legal anthropological research agenda.

The most detailed and well-known of these ethnographies is probably Bogoras's seminal volume *The Chukchee*, originally published in English in 1904, before the Russian Revolution, and in Russian in two volumes in 1934 and 1939. This was particularly important for the ruling regime because the Chukchi were the only people in the Russian Empire that were never fully integrated into the state and were, in Bogoras's words, 'beyond the Russian sphere of influence (Bogoraz 1934: 76). Therefore, Bogoras (1904: 34) emphasized that the Chukchi had the right to deal with their affairs according to their own custom, which mainly followed a generally egalitarian social organization in which even the clan (*rod*) did not figure as an organizational unit; the only relevant social unit was the family.[6] Through his detailed legal ethnography of one Indigenous group, Bogoras showed how difficult it was for the empire to reach out to the Chukchi because there was no leader to talk to, and because Russian law was as remote from the lives of Chukchi families as St Petersburg was from the Chukchi Peninsula. The Chukchi's reputation as an 'unsubdued' people within the Russian Empire and the need for the new Soviet regime to make an example of them would become one reason why Sovietization measures were imposed so much more thoroughly and forcefully among the Chukchi than among other Indigenous groups (Gray and Stammler 2002).[7]

Bogoras conducted his fieldwork in 1900–1901 in the framework of the Jesup North Pacific Expedition, organized by Franz Boas, which is the same research programme that employed Shternberg. For his part, Shternberg wrote an enthusiastic ethnography of the Gilyaks of Sakhalin Island, with a particular focus on the clan (*rod*), which he saw as fulfilling an important regulatory function in society in harmony with individual freedom and collective interests (1933: 418). Perhaps most remarkable is his detailed description of the *Khlai-Nivukhov*—an inter-clan council for conflict resolution.

Shternberg's ethnographic description of what he calls 'court trials' among the Gilyaks is exemplary in its detail and refinement.

Shirokogoroff's *Social Organization of the Northern Tungus* (1929), also published first in English after Shirokogoroff had emigrated to China, was a milestone in legal ethnography, with its persuasive demonstration that not only is it worthwhile to understand non-state legal systems, but also that a great deal can be learned from them about legal principles of broader relevance, and from there on to fundamental anthropological theories of cultures and ethnic groups in general. He identifies the institution of expert witnessing among the Tungus (Evenki) to help determine whether an act is criminal or not. Moreover, an important addition in his ethnography is the observation that if someone was possessed by a spirit and, as a result, committed a crime, that person would not be held guilty.[8] In its claim to broader theoretical relevance, Shirokogoroff's work has also received recent attention from international scholars (Alymov et al. 2018; Anderson and Arzyutov 2016), and can therefore be seen as having the broadest theoretical relevance in legal anthropology internationally of the three 'state ethnographers' discussed here.

The studies of Indigenous legal systems that came out in early Soviet times later came to be labelled under the general term *normativnoi etnografii* ('normative ethnography'). In Soviet times, they served as a basis for theoretical discussions within the framework of Marxism (Pershits 1979), where Indigenous legal systems were referred to as *obychnoe pravo* ('customary law'). 'Law' proper was believed to pertain only to societies with their own states; 'pre-class societies', therefore, were not highly developed enough to have 'law'.[9]

Post-Soviet 'Legal Anthropology'

After the fall of the Soviet Union, the Russian field opened up to foreign scholars, including legal scholars and anthropologists. Russian scholars likewise became more engaged in international academic conversations regarding legal pluralism and related concepts, although there seems to be relatively little connection to the classic anglophone trajectory of legal anthropology that runs from Morgan and Maine through Malinowski to Llewellyn and Hoebel, Bohannan, Gluckman, Moore, and Nader. Even more remarkable is that present-day Russian legal anthropological scholarship does not build as explicitly as one might expect on the rich tradition of its own nineteenth- and twentieth-century predecessors (e.g. Ladyzhenskii, Bogoras, Shternberg, Shirokogoroff). Rather, Russian legal anthropology takes as its principal inspiration and reference point the seminal volume *Anthropologie Juridique* by the French legal scholar Norbert Rouland (1988). Anatoly Kovler, a legal scholar and former judge in the European Court of Human Rights, got to know Rouland personally while he was living in Strasbourg. Kovler subsequently translated Rouland's textbook into Russian (Rouland 1999). The volume was edited by another key figure from legal studies, Vladik Nersesiants. Through this edition, the entire field of Russian legal anthropology is familiar with one part of the French tradition, which includes some anthropological classics such as Durkheim. The more or less exclusive awareness of Rouland, to the neglect of other French legal anthropologists such as Henry Lévy-Bruhl and Étienne Le Roy (not to mention other European or anglophone scholars),[10] gives this stream of French legal anthropology a somewhat disproportionate influence on Russian legal anthropology. Kovler followed up with his own textbook, the focus of which is on the principles of processes that he calls the 'juridization of human life', which he observes across 'all historical types of civilization' (Kovler 2002: 23).[11] With this emphasis on the legal—or jural—in every sphere of life, Kovler is in line with general tendencies in Western legal anthropological scholarship, focusing, for example, on the discussion revolving around juridification (see e.g. Sieder, this volume). From that point on, we see the development of the field running mostly along two parallel lines, one coming from legal studies, the other from anthropology. Although representatives of both claim to practise 'legal anthropology', in fact they are rather different in character and do not seem to engage much in common debates.

'Legal anthropology' within legal studies

The legal-studies-oriented scholarship in this field developed more within the theoretical realm of law. This is mainly represented by a number of dissertations in the past two decades. For example, the dissertation by Puchkov (2001) reviews earlier studies on law and society in order to move 'legal anthropology' within legal studies beyond the focus on traditional societies and to apply anthropological methods more to the analysis of contemporary state law. Puchkov introduces the main international currents of classic legal anthropological research, at least as far as they are presented in Rouland's (1999) work. On the Russian side, Puchkov links himself with the legal scholarly tradition started by the aforementioned Maksim Kovalevskii (Ignatieva 2006). However, his analysis completely ignores the classic legal ethnographies of the late imperial and early Soviet ethnographers, as well as the early post-Soviet legal anthropological publications from the 1990s.

Ignatieva's (2006) work is of interest for the history of the discipline, as she focuses on how Kovalevskii, a legal scholar who also became a parliamentarian, based his studies of the history of law in society on fieldwork. This shows that long-term ethnographic fieldwork *by legal scholars* was instrumental in the formation of legal anthropology as a discipline in Russia. Agrafonova's dissertation (2009) is a broader, but less detailed analysis of the history of legal anthropology within legal studies, categorizing it according to theoretical paradigms (much as Puchkov's 2001 study does): the evolutionary, functionalist, conflictological, and ethnocultural. She contributes to further terminological diversity, if not confusion, by identifying *iuridicheskaia etnologiia* ('juridical ethnology') as one of the directions in legal anthropology that focuses on 'ethnic legal cultures' and 'ethno-legal mentalities'.

While all these works aim to use 'legal anthropology' to contribute to a renewal of legal scholarship as a discipline, Shushkova (2017) presents legal anthropology's quest to refocus on customary law to understand how legal traditions of the Finno-Ugric people change over time. More anthropological (in the Western sense) than her other legal studies colleagues, but without referring to any of the seminal works of Western anthropology, she emphasizes that law is not to be defined in terms of stable (evolutionary) stages, but rather as dynamic processes.

'Legal anthropology' within post-Soviet anthropology

An emphasis on law in post-Soviet anthropology (*etnologiia*), on the other hand, was initially motivated by practical concerns of anthropologists who were involved in developing, and even writing, laws concerning ethnic minorities and Indigenous peoples of Russia. It started with a seminar series in 1995–1996 organized by Valery Tishkov and Natalya Novikova of the Institute of Ethnology and Anthropology, Russian Academy of Sciences (IEA-RAS).[12] The focus widened beyond the writing of laws by anthropologists, as participants discussed their common experiences and the value of law (both state and customary) and legal processes as a subject of anthropological research and cultural critique. The seminar series was followed up in short order by a four-day conference on legal anthropology in June 1996. Conference proceedings were published in 1997 under the title *Homo Juridicus* (Novikova and Osipov 1997). In 1997, the IEA-RAS hosted the annual meetings of the Commission on Legal Pluralism and Customary Law, which attracted prominent researchers from all over the world.

Legal anthropological scholarship within anthropology became increasingly formalized over the following twenty years with the Summer Schools in Legal Anthropology organized by Novikova of the IEA-RAS. In stark contrast to the late-Soviet evolutionary categorization of societies, these summer schools focused on the concept of 'legal pluralism' as it applies to the Russian Federation. This is indicative of the influence of some English language scholarship, most notably the work of Franz and Keebet von Benda-Beckmann, with whom Novikova had personal connections through their mutual involvement in a number of conferences. In fact, the Benda-Beckmanns participated as instructors in the 1999 Summer School, and some of their work has been published in Russian, which has made it accessible to Russian-language scholars (e.g. Benda-Beckmann 1999).

Novikova's work has been particularly influential in this field, focusing on the regulation of relations between Indigenous peoples and the advancing extractive industries in the Arctic (Novikova 2002, 2016). In her 2014 monograph (2014), Novikova enlarges the concept of customary law to include the legal behaviour of industrial companies in their encounter with Indigenous livelihoods. Corporate social responsibility policies and the adoption of best practices by extractive companies are also treated as customary law. The orientation of legal anthropology to the encounter of industry with Indigenous peoples has also opened up commercial opportunities for this expertise. Novikova and her colleagues have created an organization that conducts ethnological impact assessments (*ekspertiza*) with industry money (e.g. Vasil'kova et al. 2011).[13]

Ol'ga Murashko, in contrast, has made a point of avoiding working with the extractive industries. Her work in legal anthropology (Murashko 2006) has shifted towards fighting for Indigenous rights and highlighting the problematic behaviour of companies and the aspects of current legislation that violate international law (Murashko 2014). In this function, she has long worked with the Russian Association of Indigenous Peoples of the North (RAIPON) and its regional branches (Dallmann et al. 2011).

What characterizes all of these lines of post-Soviet legal anthropology *within anthropology* (as opposed to legal studies) is its applied orientation. One publication, 'Ethnographers Write Law' (*Etnografy pishut zakon*) (Sokolova et al. 1995), highlights both the problems and the potential of this orientation. At the request of Indigenous politicians, the authors drafted a framework law on Russia's Indigenous peoples, in which they suggested reorganizing Indigenous territoriality and self-governance. Some of these ideas would later become part of the 1999 law 'On Guarantees of the Rights of the Indigenous Peoples of the Russian Federation'. Interestingly, in a rare instance of explicit reference to their own legal anthropological predecessors, Sokolova et al. (1995: 75) note that Bogoras and colleagues had made similar suggestions in the 1920s that were never implemented. The authors highlight throughout the importance of flexibility in the law in order to accommodate the great cultural diversity in the country and the necessities of nomadic life, without, however, referring to similar statements from the nineteenth-century ethnographies (see fn. 2). On the other hand, they rightly note that after 300 years under Russian rule, people themselves seem to have internalized the more static legal language of the state. As applied anthropologists, the authors therefore ask where legal anthropology should position itself in this field: should it be more critical and theoretical, pointing out the problems and inconsistencies, or more applied, actively taking the side of Indigenous peoples?

This shows the clear division between the disciplines of law and anthropology when it comes to the meaning of 'legal anthropology' in Russia: it seems that the anthropologists continue to speak to themselves in analysing the functioning of cultures and societies and pushing legal anthropology in a more applied direction, while the legal scholars limit themselves to authors mentioned in Rouland's (1999) textbook and their own predecessors in their efforts to analyse the nature of law (in a more philosophical sense) and overcome the dogmatic and static nature of legal studies. In the following sections, we shall show the value for both sides of uniting these two currents.

Case studies from interdisciplinary research in law and society in the Russian North

In recent years, due to climate change and industrial development, there has been increased attention to the Arctic regions, both nationally in Russia and internationally. This has led to numerous policies, laws, and strategy documents by the Moscow authorities and associated transformations in the lives of the inhabitants of the Arctic.[14] Furthermore, changes in important Russia-wide federal legislation, such as the law 'On specially protected natural areas' (1995) and the Land Codex (1995, 2020), have had a particularly adverse impact on northern inhabitants, especially those who continue to pursue mobile forms of livelihood in the forest and the tundra. The Russian North remains, even in times of rather chilly relations between Russia and the West, an area of intense cooperation both industrially (e.g. the Sabetta Yamal LNG development) and politically (through the Arctic Council). For these reasons, a great deal of the work conducted by legal anthropologists in recent years has focused on establishing a solid legal foundation for measuring the impacts of such developments on traditional northern livelihoods and understanding how Russia's northern minorities are struggling to find a niche amid this rapid change (Murashko 2006; Vasil'kova et al. 2011).

In the following section, we briefly outline two case studies, based on the authors' regions of expertise in the Russian North, that combine anthropology and legal studies to explain our principal theoretical understanding of the interaction between state law and Indigenous peoples' historically formed regulative practices. What we call the 'full research lifecycle' integration of the two disciplines has the potential to overcome the colonial—or at least the paternalistic—attitude that still characterizes much of the legal anthropological scholarship, in which there is still an implicit, underlying assumption that the legal systems of Indigenous peoples are at a lower level on an evolutionary hierarchy of law. In terms of a decolonizing agenda, such an approach goes beyond the mere academic study of customary law, and even beyond the well-intentioned but ultimately status quo-maintaining attempts to provide for better governance of Indigenous peoples within the existing 'real' (meaning state-recognized and codified) law.

The Nenets of Yamal

The Yamal-Nenets Autonomous Region (YNAO, hereafter, Yamal) in West Siberian is Russia's natural gas powerhouse and home to its most vibrant group of full-time reindeer nomads, the Nenets (Stammler 2005). The co-existence of these two very different forms of land use—the natural gas industry and reindeer herding—has made the need to clarify the legal status and the rights to land and resources on and under its surface more urgent, especially since the break-up of the Soviet Union. Yet neither the Russian-dominated regional authorities nor the Nenets themselves have insisted on legalizing the terms and conditions of livelihood pluralism in this area. This is all the more remarkable because the Nenets are the most numerous of the officially recognized 'Indigenous Small-Numbered Peoples of the North', and account for fully half of the Indigenous population of the entire area defined as the Russian Arctic (Tishkov et al. 2016: 10, table 2). This is not a matter of general legislative lethargy (the regional parliament passed more than 100 regulatory acts per year between 2000 and 2015 under its Nenets speaker, Sergei Khariuchi, who was also the president of RAIPON for most of the post-Soviet period), it is just that none of these addressed land rights.[15] Based on fieldwork and document analysis, we argue that clarifying the land rights question is not in the interests of the industry-dominated authorities. But more relevant for our point here is that doing so would also run counter to the Nenets's own legal culture.

Nenets nomads historically had an egalitarian, acephalous form of social organization without permanent leadership and never had territorial boundary defence; rather, they relied on social boundary defence.[16] Leadership was recognized only in times of practical need (Golovnev 1997), when leaders would emerge through the force of their own actions, and then retreat to their normal herder status after the immediate need was over. Evladov's detailed ethnography from the early Soviet times (Evladov 1992) provides ample evidence of this. Nenets social organization revolves around two exogamous moieties (the Nenets use the Russian term *poloviny*—'halves'—to refer to this concept), consisting of a number of clans (Nen: *erkar*). However, these units are not of political relevance. Leadership was always spontaneous and personal. The Nenets word *erv* can be translated as 'master', meaning somebody who is able to get something done, but also the head of a nomadic camp. This is the relevant unit of decision-making. Another indicative word for a Nenets decision-maker is *serm'pertya*, meaning 'the one who conducts affairs' (Golovnev 2000: 129). He goes ahead of the rest when making seasonal migrations and decides on the route, the next camp site, the duration of the stay, the rotation of pastures, and other related business. This was also the job description of the *brigadir* ('team leader') in the Soviet *sovkhozy* (state enterprises). However, the position of *serm'pertya* has never implied any institutionalized privileges or status, and the *serm'pertya* can be replaced at any time if, in practice, it turns out that someone else can 'conduct the affairs' better in a given concrete situation. In such cases, the previous *serm'pertya* continue to be herders and fishers equal to all their neighbours.

We can thus state that the Nenets's internal set of rules is *situational* in nature. In this context, deviations from rules, and even from taboos regulating the gendered division of space and labour, access to and use of pastures, food sharing, and so forth, are acceptable, and even expected if the urgency of the situation requires it. The sedentary population also recognizes this set of informal guidelines *and the need to deviate from them*, a complex system that they refer to as *zakon tundry* ('the law of the tundra') (Stammler 2005: 83–90). The emphasis on flexibly 'getting on' in concrete situations rather than creating codified legal regimes shows the Nenets's strong orientation towards maintaining their nomadic lifestyle, with leadership and normative systems all subordinated to its successful execution.

The important point for the purposes of our argument is that Nenets nomads recognize their current institutionalized leadership mainly in settlements and in their relations to the Russian state, but not for governing their own practices on the land, where entitlements and access rights are based on knowing, flexibility, cooperation, and negotiation among equals (see Stammler 2005: Chapter 6). Over the course of the last century, sedentary administrators have tried numerous times to solidify the relationship of Nenets nomads to land and territory, coming up with a variety of concepts to describe how industry and nomads share the land. Such efforts included the division of land into herding and hunting grounds of the *sovkhozy*, various concepts of stewardship that were put into legal terms at the municipal level (*pozhiznennoe vladenie*), lands loosely registered to Indigenous reindeer enterprises or communities (*obshchiny*), and, most recently, servitude (*servitud*), the attempt to record the de facto occupation of land by private nomadic herding families without codified titles. However, these official Russian attempts to formalize land rights and status existed only on paper and have never had a significant impact on Nenets internal territorial governance (Stammler 2005: Chapter 7). Golovnev (2000: 130) notes accordingly that '[r]elationships between people ... depended on respect for norms and ethics rather than on legal claims over territory, kin, or property'.

This orientation of Nenets agency to applied concrete goals rather than to establishing stable legal regimes is also something that we observe in current regulatory practice in the Yamal area: for many years following the break-up of the Soviet Union, much of the Nenets's political activity was focused on executive programmes rather than on legislative acts. This was often done through lobbying to allocate budgetary resources to particular activities for the support of the Nenets. Without any corresponding legislation, nomadic schools have been implemented (Terekhina 2017), the impact of industry on the Nenets has been documented in several anthropological impact assessments (*etnologicheskaia expertiza*; see Martynova and Novikova 2011; Vasil'kova et al. 2011), and numerous ad hoc decisions have been implemented to facilitate the coexistence of different land users (for more details, see Ivanova and Stammler 2017). Rather than relying on institutionalized hierarchies or power structures and positions according to a legal system, such achievements depend exclusively on the personalities of the Indigenous persons involved, as Golovnev and colleagues' (2016) cross-cultural comparison in Siberia convincingly shows. The Nenets have thus become 'showcase' nomads of a sort. On the one hand, their spontaneity and unpredictability create headaches for industrial developers and administrators, who would find it much easier to deal with sedentary populations. On the other hand, these same institutions use the Nenets to polish their public relations images, emphasizing in speeches and events that Russia's large-scale, extractive industries do not necessarily destroy the diversity of cultures and lifestyles. One of the best examples of this is the showcasing of nomads as among the first to vote in Russian elections, most recently for the changed Russian constitution in 2020.

The Republic of Sakha (Yakutia)

The Republic of Sakha (Yakutia) (hereafter RSY) is another resource-rich region in the Russian North, best known throughout the world as the source of 90 per cent of Russia's diamonds and within Russia for having one of the most ambitious movements for the creation of an independent state (Sharafutdinova 2016; Tichotsky 2000; Young 2000). Interdisciplinary, fieldwork-based legal anthropological analysis helps us understand the specific historical trajectories of this process. The Sakha population is significantly larger than that of the Nenets. They have a history of larger-scale social organization in pre-Soviet times and a correspondingly different level of official recognition as non-Russian aliens (*inorodsy*) in Russian imperial times and as a *natsional'nost'* in Soviet times.[17] This was a more fruitful ground for centuries-long tendencies of juridification of politics (see Sieder, this volume), which reflects a greater sense of 'statehood' among the Sakha.

Following the break-up of the Soviet Union, the first act of the RSY political elite, which consists mainly of ethnic Sakha, was to declare land and subsurface resources the exclusive property of their own 'sovereign state'.[18] The main law of the RSY, the 1992 constitution, pre-dated the Russian constitution by one-and-a-half years and was the first of its kind. After Russia started recentralizing, the RSY was forced to rewrite more than half of this constitution, as its far-reaching rights of Sakha sovereignty were considered a threat to the integrity of the Russian Federation as a whole.[19] This process can be considered complete as of 17 June 2009, when the RSY parliament *Il Tumen* officially deleted the articles on sovereignty and RSY citizenship from its constitution.[20]

While similar processes have also occurred in other Russian republics, such as Tatarstan, Bashkortostan, Kalmykia, and Tyva, the RSY has earned a reputation as a trailblazer in legal activity, specifically in the field of regulating the encounter between industry and Indigenous livelihoods. In the absence of federal-level laws, the RSY adopted a number of regional-level laws for its territory, including laws on Indigenous tribal clan-communities (*rodoplemennye obshchiny*, 1992), nomadic housing (2004), nomadic schools (2008), ethnological impact assessment (*etnologicheskaia expertiza*, 2010), protection of Indigenous habitats, traditional life and economy of Indigenous peoples (2011), the nomadic family (2016), and protection of the permafrost (2018). Many of these laws have served as blueprints for similar laws at the federal level, often upon the initiative of Sakha activists. However, just as with its constitution, the RSY often had to change these laws to bring them in line with later-adopted federal legislation in Russia.

Our argument regarding the RSY follows the same lines as the previous example of Yamal: legal anthropological analysis combining evidence from older ethnographies and historiography with interdisciplinary fieldwork helps us explain the basis for differences in the present-day legal behaviour of particular societies. In the case of the Sakha, Seroshevskii's (1896) classic, late-nineteenth-century ethnography is the authoritative source, comparable to Bogoras (1904) for the Chukchi and Shirokogoroff (1929) for the Tungus.

Seroshevskii explains how the legally relevant unit of Sakha social organization is the clan and its council of elders, which makes all decisions. Clans were led by chiefs (*toiony*), whose leadership was institutionalized and could also extend to several clan groups. Adrian Borisov (2005) mentions that the idea of leadership across several clans among the Sakha dates back at least as far as the seventeenth century, when Russian colonization was just getting under way. Nevertheless, there were power struggles between clans, leading some *toiony* to see recognition by the encroaching Russian state as a welcome resource in their struggle to solidify their position. Borisov (2005: 24) calls this the quest for *edinonachal'e* (Russian: 'unified leadership'). He even mentions the names of specific *toiony* who were trying to get the Russian state to grant them court powers as well as tax collection rights. Local legal historian Vasilii Ivanov (2007: 40–1) mentions that, as early as 1680, Sakha leaders were granted the title of *kniaztsa* (Russian: 'ruler') by the tsars. This gave them administrative and police powers within their territories (*ulus*), five of which are mentioned in Borisov's chapter (2005: 23) as pre-Russian legal-administrative units.

This elaborate hierarchy also enabled the Sakha to organize resistance to Russian conquest in the seventeenth century, and later to resist Russian tax collectors. While it remains taboo to openly discuss armed conflicts between Russians and Sakha even historically, unofficial internet sources describe battles in 1642, 1675, 1682, and 1684 (Garmatnii 2017). Among the officially recognized scholarly sources, a work by Fedorov (1991: 42) acknowledges such armed conflicts, but states that the Sakha quickly succumbed to the superior firearms of the Russians and surrendered. Also relevant for our argument is the assessment that when the first Russians arrived, 'judging from the available data, Yakutia was on the verge of creating a single state, whose centralization was being realized through the great efforts of the *toion* Tygyn' (Garmatnii 2017).

Even after incorporation into the Russian Empire, the Sakha kept their own social organization, based on institutionalized clan administrations (Russian: *rodovoe pravlenie*; Sakha: *uuhunan oloron salaiyy*) that had their own institutional buildings (*suglan*) (see Seroshevskii 1896: 448). Decisions of broader relevance were made by inter-clan councils, where respected elders called *seseny* were instrumental in consolidating the will of the council into unanimous decisions. The highest institutionalized organ was the union council (Russian: *soyuznyi sovet*), a general assembly conducted in three circles: the inter-clan chiefs (*toiony* and *seseny*) in the inner circle; the clan chiefs (*toiony*) and warriors in the second; and the rest of the people in the third circle (Seroshevskii 1896: 453–4). Compared to the explicitly acephalous egalitarian society described for the Nenets, here we see clear hierarchies, institutionalized governance, and state-like structures even prior to Russian colonization.

The dream of complete independence became even stronger after colonization and the introduction of Russian imperial administration. For example, at the end of the eighteenth century, the Sakha stubbornly insisted on the introduction of something like a 'steppe Duma' (Seroshevskii 1896: 482), but this was shut down after only twelve years out of fear that it would grow into an organ of genuine self-governance and anti-tsarist opposition. Following that, the Sakha's tactics shifted from conflict to a form of diplomacy that highlights the paradoxical nature of Sakha's quest for statehood, whereby the Sakha had to ask the Russian Empire for the right to be independent from the Russian Empire (Ivanova and Stammler 2017: 216).[21] Sakha historians have meticulously documented the Sakha elite's diplomatic missions to the tsar requesting independence or, barring that, at least tax sovereignty, court power, and equal rights and freedoms.

Thus, the history of Sakha near-statehood became closely intertwined with the goal of gaining as much recognition as possible under Russian and Soviet central authorities. In the recent cycles of Russian–RSY relations, we see both of these tendencies expressed: the near-statehood came up again in a political movement in the 1920s (suppressed by the Bolsheviks), and in the 1990s with the declaration of the Sakha sovereign constitution of 1992. In the twenty-first century, we see the historical pattern of conciliation repeated, as the RSY reluctantly aligns its constitution and other legislation with those of the Russian Federation and tries to focus on those niches of legal agency that the federation leaves it.

What unites all of these tendencies is the attempt of the Sakha elite to solidify their status, practices, and mechanisms of governance through laws. Sakha legal activity beyond their own territory also supports our argument of the Sakha's tendency towards juridification. Since the break-up of the Soviet Union, the usual pattern has been for Sakha political activists to first adopt their own laws, after which they initiate similar legal initiatives for the entire Russian Federation. The most recent example is the July 2020 initiative of the Sakha parliament to introduce a Russian federal law on permafrost protection after RSY had adopted a similar regional law in 2018.[22]

While this faith in the power of law appears to be true for the Sakha elite and intelligentsia, our fieldwork with practitioners—both those engaged in animal husbandry and those engaged in the extraction of natural resources—reveals shortcomings in the implementation of these laws. On numerous occasions, we heard people mocking the obsession of the elite to make laws for everything, seeing in this a sort of over-juridification of life. As one field partner put it, 'They don't even leave the permafrost in peace anymore; even for that they invented a law!' The contradictory nature of the social life of law became especially apparent during Ivanova's fieldwork, as Indigenous forest dwellers continued to express faith that their legal land title would protect them from industrial encroachment, despite the overwhelming evidence of their own experience, which showed that extractive companies could occupy land regardless of land titles if they held a licence to extract.

The 'Full Research Lifecycle' Integration of Law and Anthropology

We have seen that contact with the Russian state since the seventeenth century has not led to the formation of a ruling elite or to juridification within Nenets society. While an Indigenous intelligentsia did develop among the Nenets and other Russian Indigenous minorities in Soviet times, some of whom have become active in the Russian state legal system, they do not dominate political life in the way the Sakha elite do. First, they are not very influential within their own region, and second, the tundra and taiga population does not recognize them as an elite within their own system. Such insights from long-term fieldwork show how, among the Nenets, tundra society remains basically egalitarian, while Russian notions of stratification hold more sway in the settlements. As one Nenets friend told Stammler, 'Russian law does not extend to the tundra—it ends at the outskirts of town.'[23] Regional regulations regarding the livelihoods of non-Russian inhabitants in Yamal are more explicitly geared towards practical implementation of programmes that affect settlements, such as government subsidies and education policy, and tend to focus less on legal principles than on the financial sources for solving problems.

The Sakha, in contrast, have displayed a proactive approach to the legal sphere from the outset, based on their pre-Russian history of almost having a state. Lawmakers appear to be more interested in establishing certain principles and being the first in Russia to have passed such laws. Juridification thus serves the ideological purposes and identity-making projects of the Sakha elite, even if the practical application for people's lives remains limited.

More interdisciplinary legal anthropological research would be required to establish how the Sakha case compares to other groups that also have internally stratified societies and which were granted the status of 'autonomous republics' in Soviet times, such as Buriats, Tyva, Komi, and Karelians. Such research would also be needed to establish whether other relatively acephalous, egalitarian societies also, like the Nenets, have a focus on 'getting things done', rather than on establishing legal regimes. We propose that a 'full research lifecycle' integration of legal scholarship and anthropology can reveal how the study of history, social organization, livelihood practices, Indigenous legal traditions, and relations to a ruling state help us understand how a given society engages with the legal sphere.

However, in order to achieve such interdisciplinary cooperation, the existing antagonism between anthropologists, on the one hand, and lawyers and legal scholars on the other, must be overcome. Because both the Sakha and Yamal-Nenets regions are dominated by economically important extractive industries, have Indigenous populations known to have successfully preserved their 'traditional' livelihoods, and are outspoken on the national stage, their contrasting approaches to the jural have attracted national—and even international—attention and have therefore served as a springboard for more general debates between anthropologists and legal scholars regarding the best way to approach Indigenous legal questions in Russia. In the absence of a formal law on ethnological impact assessment in Yamal, several ethnological expert reviews of gas industry projects were carried out by anthropologists in agreement with the industry and the regional branch of RAIPON (Murashko 2002; Vasil'kova et al. 2011). In Sakha, where there is a formal law on ethnological impact assessment, Indigenous lawyers, legal scholars, and politicians dominate the expert commission responsible for the approval of the impact assessments, most of which are carried out without the participation of anthropologists.

Clashes between these 'two camps' were witnessed by Ivanova and Stammler during several conferences.[24] The anthropologists were critical of the legal scholars responsible for the Sakha expert reviews for failing to consider anthropological concepts such as the subjectivity of expert reviews and the idea of law as a process, and for not inviting them to participate.[25] The legal scholars countered, accusing anthropologists of intervening in a field in which they do not have the necessary expertise, a charge they support by pointing to the imprecise language and ensuing difficulty of implementation of laws that anthropologists had been instrumental in writing.

We believe that this tension can be turned into a more creative, productive, and forward-looking approach that brings legal scholars and anthropologists together from the very beginning, starting with the conception of a research project and the identification of research objectives, questions, and methods. This would entail having them work together, side by side, conducting joint fieldwork and combining the expertise of both disciplines to study ethnographic material, legal documents, other specialist literature, and land-use practices, and then conducting joint analysis and writing. This is what we mean by the 'full research lifecycle' integration of law and anthropology.

Such interdisciplinarity does not presume that the anthropologist must acquire the expertise of a legal scholar or vice versa; if each brings his or her own expertise to bear, supplemented with a basic understanding of the other field, that should be sufficient to provide the necessary common ground. We argue that this integrative method will not only lead to novel insights, but that it could also lend credibility to the researchers in their fields, as they can turn to the respective colleague for specialist knowledge: the anthropologist can refer questions concerning specific laws to the legal scholar, while the legal scholar can rely on the anthropologist for social and cultural background in the society where the fieldwork takes place. The ways in which the legal scholar in the field discusses with reindeer herders, hunters, and fishermen the legal implications of particular livelihood strategies and land-use practices serves, in turn, as valuable data allowing the anthropologist to understand how people perceive state law through the prism of their own legal system. We suggest that this further enables us to study the relations between centrally planned federal legislation that is supposed to apply equally to all citizens, and the 'social life' of such laws on the ground. The input of legal scholars also allows anthropologists to better identify those niches left open by codified state law and the application of Indigenous legal concepts and practices to fill those niches, much as Bogoras (1904) described for the Chukchi back in 1904. This is the type of space for Indigenous self-regulation we currently find more in the North American contexts (Borrows 2010, 2017; Napoleon et al. 2015) than in Russia. Such joint, full research lifecycle cooperation opens the door to seeing Indigenous, state, and corporate legal systems as equal in what Borrows (2010) has called for Canada a 'multi-juridical legal culture'.

Of course, our approach raises the question of the degree to which remnants of Indigenous legal systems are still to be found, either in recent state legislation on Indigenous peoples or in the niches left open. This, too, is an empirical question. Using earlier anthropological evidence and combining it with current fieldwork, we can identify which aspects of a given Indigenous legal tradition (if any) become part of codified state legislation. For example, laws on ethnological impact assessment have turned out to be implemented chiefly as instruments for getting compensation to Indigenous communities (Burtseva et al. 2019; Gassiy and Potravny 2017) rather than for protecting the conditions necessary to continue certain 'traditional' livelihoods (Stammler and Ivanova 2016: 1237). Laws such as 'On territories of traditional nature use' stipulate land rights, borders, and territorial boundary defence, which was never part of the internal system of Indigenous territorial governance. Laws on animal husbandry, hunting, and fishing tend to be about stipulating allowable quotas and providing the basis for subsidy policies. Thus, even in cases where Indigenous peoples are involved in writing such laws, the texts do not necessarily reflect their own legal heritage, but are more geared towards integrating them into current state structures. Interdisciplinary legal anthropological research can highlight such differences.

Conclusion

This chapter has introduced the tradition of legal anthropology in Russia historically and at present, shown the diversity and compartmentalization of scholarly approaches that have been subsumed under the general term 'legal anthropology' in Russia, and sketched out an interdisciplinary approach that we are calling the 'full research lifecycle' integration of law and anthropology.

The long tradition of legal anthropological research in the late Russian Empire and early Soviet Union, from Bogoras to Shirokogoroff, Shternberg, Evladov, and Seroshevskii, to name but a few, provides a knowledge base of the Indigenous legal practices of the past. When read from both an anthropological and a legal perspective, these works help us understand differences in how representatives of different non-Russian groups in Russia relate to lawmaking on their territories today.

Legal anthropology in Russia has always had an applied orientation, from the early programmes of the Russian Geographical Society to systematically map Indigenous legal systems all the way to post-Soviet discussions about how best to legalize the coexistence of Indigenous livelihoods with the development of extractive industries. The direction and the aims have changed radically, but the emphasis on the applied dimension has remained constant throughout.

This applied, historically informed, full-research-lifecycle cooperation between legal scholars and anthropologists, including joint fieldwork, presents an opportunity for empirical research and new theoretical insights into the lived experience of legal pluralism in Russia, the world's largest state with nearly 200 recognized ethnic formations, each of which potentially has its own approach to, and vision of, the encounter between its legal system and that of the Russian state. Our comparison of legal activity in an egalitarian and a more stratified non-Russian society in Russia illustrates the potential of this approach to answer complex questions such as why some people focus on legislative action to take greater control over their own lives, juridifying every field of society, while others eschew codified law in favour of ad hoc pragmatic solutions and executive action. This puts us in a better position to identify and appropriately interpret the varied processes of legal pluralism in Russia today, where codified state law predominates, yet also leaves gaps that, if recognized and exploited, could constitute niches for continuing (or renewing) historically formed Indigenous legal practices. This, in turn, would allow for solutions better tailored to each specific situation, and could lead to the development of a home-grown, uniquely Russian legal anthropology based on the long tradition of rich empirical ethnography and a history of applied orientation.

Acknowledgements

Research for this chapter was funded in part by the Finnish Academy (grant 343064) and the Russian Science Foundation (grant 20-68-46043). The authors also wish to thank Jean-François Gaudreault-DesBiens and Julia Eckert for their insightful comments on earlier versions of this chapter.

Notes

1. What we shall refer to as 'legal anthropology' throughout this chapter is in the Russian-language literature variously and interchangeably referred to as *iuridicheskaia antropologiia*, *antropologiia prava*, or *normativnaia etnografiia*.
2. For more on this history of ethnography within the Russian Geographical Society, including the history of customary law collection, see their official website, available at <http://www.rgo.ru/ru/proekty/etnografiya/istoriya-etnografii-v-rgo/komissiya-po-sobiraniyu-narodnyh-yuridicheskih>.
3. On the influence of Kovalevskii on legal anthropology in Russia, see Bocharov (2013: 62–91).
4. See Leontovich (1882–1883); on Ladyzhenskii, see Abazov (2012); for references on Central Asia, see Martin (2001).
5. See Tiukhteneva (1997) for more references.
6. The general assumption in Russian/Soviet ethnology of the day at that time was that the *rod* (clan) was the principal organizational unit in all pre-state societies.
7. Another reason was Chukotka's proximity to the United States (Alaska), which further warranted special attention.
8. See Renteln (this volume) on the use of the 'cultural defence' in US courts today.
9. See Semenov (1997) for a summary of such theoretical considerations in the Soviet Union.
10. For more on the development of French legal anthropology, see Audren and Guerlain in this volume.
11. Unless otherwise noted, all translations from Russian into English are by the authors.
12. It was also in this year (1995–1996 academic year) that the first course in legal anthropology was taught in Russia, at the Institute of State and Law, Russian Academy of Sciences (see Kovler 1997; for a more complete history of the teaching of legal anthropology in Russia, see Novikova [forthcoming]).
13. See the website of Novikova's company at <https://www.facebook.com/ethnoconsul/>.
14. See e.g. the Russian Arctic Strategy, the draft law on the Russian Arctic Zone, the Marine Doctrine of Russia, and the Far Eastern Hectare Law. For further discussion of these initiatives, see Fondahl et al. (2019, 2020); Ivanova and Fondahl (2020); Stammler et al. (2020).
15. For a list of active laws in Yamal, see <https://zs.yanao.ru/documents/active/>.
16. For definitions of these concepts, see Casimir (1992).
17. *Natsional'nost'*, literally 'nationality', was the highest level on the Marxist–Leninist evolutionary scale of social and political development.
18. Article 5 of the Declaration of Sovereignty of Yakutia (*Deklaratsiia o gosudarstvennom suverenitete iakutii*), 27 September 1990, No. 226-XII.

19. Of the eighty-nine administrative units that remained within the post-Soviet Russian Federation at that time, only Tatarstan and Chechnya were considered more independent than the RSY.
20. See '19 Let Suvereniteta' (2009), *Lenta.ru* news agency, available at <https://lenta.ru/articles/2009/06/18/saha/>.
21. On the 'indigenous paradox', see Bens (2020).
22. See <https://www.1sn.ru/247086.html> and <https://rg.ru/2020/07/02/reg-dfo/v-iakutii-zadumalis-o-ispolzovanii-i-ohrane-vechnoj-merzloty.html>.
23. Personal conversation in Yar-Sale, 28 July 2020.
24. For example, 'The Study of the Problems of the Indigenous Small-Numbered Peoples of the North through the Prism of Legal and Social Anthropology', hosted by North-Eastern Federal University, Yakutsk, 23 January 2015, and 'Industrial Development in the Arctic: A Dialog between Business and Local Communities', hosted by the Arctic Frost Project and the International Arctic Science Committee (IASC), Moscow, 24–25 April 2018.
25. The responsible legal experts were more inclined to recruit experts from other fields such as economics, as they were more interested in a quick calculation of damages and compensation than assessments of the impacts on culture and livelihood.

References

Abazov, A. Kh. 2012. 'A. M. Ladyzhenskii: Osnavatel' Iuridicheskoi Antropologii Narodov Kavkaza'. *Etnograficheskoe Obozrenie* 2012 (1): 102–9.

Agrafonova, E. A. 2009. *Yuridicheskaya Antropologiya: Kontseptual'nyye Idei i Printsipy*. PhD dissertation, Faculty of Law, Institut Vnutrennykh Del Rossiiskoi Federatsii (Rostov on Don, Russia).

Alymov, S. S., D. G. Anderson, and D. V. Arzyutov. 2018. 'Life Histories of the Etnos Concept in Eurasia: An Introduction'. *Ab Imperio* 2018(1): 21–67.

Anderson, D. 2000. *Identity and* Ecology *in Arctic Siberia: The Number One Reindeer Brigade*. Oxford: Oxford University Press.

Anderson, D. G. and D. V. Arzyutov. 2016. 'The Construction of Soviet Ethnography and "The Peoples of Siberia"'. *History and Anthropology* 27(2): 183–209.

Benda-Beckman, K. von. 1999. 'Pravovoi pliuralizm'. In N. Novikova and V. Tishkov, eds. *Chelovek i pravo*, 8–23. Moscow: Strategiia.

Bens, J. 2020. *The Indigenous Paradox: Rights, Sovereignty, and Culture in the Americas*. Philadelphia: University of Pennsylvania Press.

Bocharov, V. V. 2013. *Antropologiia Prava*. St. Petersburg: University of Saint Petersburg Press.

Bogoras, W. G. 1904. *The Chukchee* (3 vols). New York: Jesup North Pacific Expedition Publications.

Bogoraz, V. G. 1934. *Chukchi*, vol. 1. Leningrad: Izdatel'stvo Instituta Narodov Severa.

Borisov, A. A. 2005. 'Etapy bor'by za samoupravleniye Yakutov v XVII—pervoi polovine XIX veka i politika tsarskogo pravitel'stva'. In V. N. Ivanov, A. A. Borisov, and I. A. Ammosov, eds. *Istoriya liberalizma v Yakutii*, 21–6. Yakutsk: Akademiia nauk Respubliki Sakha (Yakutiia).

Borrows, J. 2010. *Canada's Indigenous Constitution*. Toronto: University of Toronto Press.

Borrows, J. 2017. 'Indigenous Constitutionalism: Pre-existing Legal Genealogies in Canada'. In P. Oliver, P. Macklem, and N. Des Rosiers, eds. *The Oxford Handbook of the Canadian Constitution*, 13–43. Oxford: Oxford University Press.

Burtseva, E. I., I. Potravny, V. Gassiy, A. Sleptsov, and V. Velichenko. 2019. 'Issues of Estimating and Compensating for Losses to Indigenous Peoples in the Conditions of Industrial Development of the Arctic'. *Arctic: Ecology and Economy* 1(33): 34–49.

Casimir, M. 1992. 'The Determinants of Rights to Pasture: Territorial Organisation and Ecological Constraints'. In M. Casimir and A. Rao, eds. *Mobility and Territoriality: Social and Spatial Boundaries among Foragers, Fishers, Pastoralists and Peripatetics*, 153–203. Oxford/New York: Berg.

Dallmann, W. K., V. Peskov, O.A. Murashko, and E. Khmeleva. 2011. 'Reindeer Herders in the Timan-Pechora Oil Province of Northwest Russia: An Assessment of Interacting Environmental, Social, and Legal Challenges'. *Polar Geography* 34(4): 229–47.

Dobren'kov, V. I. and A. I. Kravchenko. 2005. *Sotsial'naia antropologiia*. Moscow: Infra-M.

Evladov, V. P. 1992. *Po tundram Yamala k Belomu Ostrovu. Ekspeditsiya na Krayniy Sever poluostrova Yamal v 1928–1929 gg.* Tyumen': Institut problem osvoenia Severa, Siberian Branch of the Russian Academy of Sciences.

Fedorov, M. M. 1991. *Istoriia pravovogo polozheniia narodov Vostochnoi Sibiri v sostave Rossii.* Irkutsk: Izdatel'stvo Irkutskogo universiteta.

Fondahl, G., V. Filippova, A. Savvinova, A. Ivanova, F. Stammler, and G. Hoogensen Gjørv. 2019. 'Niches of Agency: Managing State–Region Relations through Law in Russia'. *Space and Polity* 23(1): 49–66.

Fondahl, G., A. Espiritu, and A. Ivanova. 2020. 'Russia's Arctic Regions and Policies'. In K. Coates and C. Holroyd, eds. *The Palgrave Handbook of Arctic Policy and Politics*, 195–216. London/New York: Palgrave Macmillan.

Garmatnii, I. 2017. 'Kak Iakutiia borolas' za svobodu ot Moskovskogo tsarstva'. Blog on Pan Turkism. *Turan Today*.

Gassiy, V. and I. Potravny. 2017. 'The Assessment of the Socio-Economic Damage of the Indigenous Peoples Due to Industrial Development of Russian Arctic'. *Czech Polar Reports* 7(2): 257–70.

Golovnev, A. 2000. 'Wars and Chiefs among the Samoyeds and Ugrians of Western Siberia'. In P. Schweitzer, M. Biesele, and R. K. Hitchcock, eds. *Hunters and Gatherers in the Modern World: Conflict, Resistance, and Self-Determination*, 125–49. New York: Berghahn.

Golovnev, A. V. 1997. 'Indigenous Leadership in Northwestern Siberia: Traditional Patterns and Their Contemporary Manifestiations'. *Arctic Anthropology* 34(1): 149–66.

Golovnev, A. V., E. V. Perevalova, S. Y. Belorussova, and T. S. Kisser. 2016. 'Etnoproekt, ili personalizatsiia etnichnosti'. *Ural'skii Istoricheskii Vestnik* 53(4): 142–8.

Gray, P. and F. Stammler. 2002. 'Siberia Caught between Collapse and Continuity'. *Max Planck Research* 2002 3: 54–61.

Ignatieva, M. V. 2006. M. M. Kovalevskii kak antropolog prava. PhD dissertation (Law), Herzen Pedagogical University (St Petersburg).

Ivanov, V. N., ed. 2007. *Rossiia i Yakutiia: Skvoz' Prizmu Istorii*. Yakutsk: Akademiia nauk Respubliki Sakha (Yakutiia).

Ivanova, A. and G. Fondahl. 2020. 'Legal Reform, Governance, and Security in the Russian Arctic'. In G. Hoogensen Gjørv, M. Lanteigne, and H. Sam-Aggrey, eds. *Routledge Handbook of Arctic Security*, 295–307. London: Routledge.

Ivanova, A. and F. M. Stammler. 2017. 'Mnogoobrazie Upravliaiemosti Prirodnymi Resursami v Rossiiskoi Arktike'. *Sibirskie Istoricheskie Issledovaniia* 5(4): 210–25.

Jochelson, W. 1905. *The Koryak: Material Culture and Social Organization*. Leiden: Brill.

Kovler, A. I. 1997. 'Iuridicheskaia antropologiia kak uchebnaia distsiplina'. In N. I. Novikova and A. G. Osipov, eds. *Homo Juridicus*, 58–65. Moscow: Rossiiskaia Akademiia Nauk.

Kovler, A. I. 2002. *Antropologiia prava*. Moscow: Norma.

Leontovich, F. I. 1882–1883. *The* Adat *of the Caucasian Highlanders: Materials on the Customary Law of the Northern and Eastern Caucasus* (2 vols). Odessa: P.A. Zelenago.

Martin, V. 2001. *Law and Custom in the Steppe: The Kazakhs of the Middle Horde and Russian Colonialism in the Nineteenth Century*. London/New York: Routledge.

Martynova, E. P. and N. I. Novikova. 2011. *Tazovskie nentsy v usloviiakh neftegazovogo osvoeniia: Etnologicheskaia ekspertiza 2011 goda*. Moscow: IP A. G. Iakovlev.

Murashko, O. A. 2002. *Opyt Provedeniia Etnologicheskoi Ekspertizy. Otsenka Potentsial'nogo Vozdeistviia Programmy OAO 'Gasprom' Poiskovo-Razvedochnykh Rabot v Akvatoriakh Obskoi i Tazovskoi Gub Na Komponenty Ustoichivogo Razvitiia Etnicheskikh Grupp Malochislennykh Narodov Severa*. Moscow: Radunitsa (RAIPON).

Murashko, O. A. 2006. 'What Is the Ethnological Expertise in Russia?' *Sibirica* 5(2): 77–94.

Murashko, O. A. 2014. 'Budut li diskriminirovany v pravakh korennye malochislennye narody iuzhnykh raionov Kamchatskogo kraia?' Moscow: Centre for Support of the Indigenous Peoples of the North (Russia).

Napoleon, V., J. Borrows, and E. Snyder. 2015. 'Gendered Violence: Resources from Indigenous Legal Orders'. *UBC Law Review* 48(1): 593–654.

Novikova, N. I. 2002. 'Self Government of the Indigenous Minority Peoples of West Siberia: Analysis of Law and Practice'. In E. Kasten, ed. *People and the Land: Pathways to Reform in Post-Soviet Siberia*, 83–97. Berlin: Reimer.

Novikova, N. I. 2014. *Okhotniki i Neftianiki: Issledovanie po Iuridicheskoi Antropologii*. Moscow: Nauka.

Novikova, N. I. 2016. 'Who Is Responsible for the Russian Arctic? Co-Operation between Indigenous Peoples and Industrial Companies in the Context of Legal Pluralism'. *Energy Research & Social Science* 16: 98–110.

Novikova, N. I. (Forthcoming). 'Legal Anthropology as an Applied Scientific Discipline in Russia'. In M. C. Foblets, G. Woodman, and A. Bradney, eds. *The Trials and Triumphs of Teaching Legal Anthropology: The View from Europe*. London: Routledge.

Novikova, N. I. and A. G. Osipov, eds. 1997. *Homo Juridicus*. Moscow: Rossiiskaia Akademiia Nauk.

Pershits, A. I. 1979. 'Problemy Normativnoi Etnografii'. In *Issledovaniia po Obshchei Etnografii*, 201–40. Moscow: Nauka.

Puchkov, O. A. 2001. Iuridicheskaia antropologiia i razvitie nauki o gosudarstve i prave:Teoreticheskie osnovy. Doctoral dissertation, Ural State Legal Academy (Yekaterinburg).

Riasanovsky, V. A. 1938 [2017]. *Customary Law of the Nomadic Tribes of Siberia*. London: Routledge.

Rouland, N. 1988. *Anthropologie Juridique*. Paris: Les Presses universitaires de France.

Rouland, N. 1999. *Iuridicheskaia Antropologiia*. V.S. Nersesiants, ed.; A. Kovler, trans. Moscow: Norma.

Samokvasov, D. I. 1908. *Kurs istorii russkogo prava*. Third edition. Moscow: Tipografiia Moskovskogo Universiteta.

Semenov, I. I. 1997. 'Obychnoe Pravo v Doklassovom Obshchestve: Vozniknovenie, Sushchnost' i Evoliutsiia'. In I. I. Semenov, ed. *Obychnoe Pravo Narodov Sibiri*, 9–46. Moscow: Staryi Sad.

Seroshevskii, V. L. 1896. *Yakuty: opyt etnograficheskogo issledovaniia*. Moscow/St Petersburg: Rossiyskaia Politicheskaia Entsiklopediia [Znanie].

Sharafutdinova, G. 2016. 'Redistributing Sovereignty and Property under Putin: A View from Resource-Rich Republics of the Russian Federation'. In C. Ross, ed. *The Politics of Sub-National Authoritarianism in Russia*, 191–210. London: Routledge.

Shirokogoroff, S. M. 1929. *Social Organization of the Northern Tungus*. Shanghai: Commercial Press.

Shternberg, L. I. 1933. *Gilyaki, Orochi, Gol'dy, Negidal'tsy, Ainy*. Khabarovsk: Dal'giz.

Shushkova, J. 2017. 'Metodologiia Iuridicheskoi Antropologii'. *Sotsial'no-Politicheskie Nauki* 1: 165–70.

Slezkine, Yuri. 1997. 'Naturalists versus Nations: Eighteenth-Century Russian Scholars Confront Ethnic Diversity.' In Brower, David R. and Edward J. Lazzerini (eds). *Russia's Orient: Imperial Borderlands and Peoples*, 1700–1917. Bloomington: Indiana University Press, 27–57.

Sokolova, Z. P., N. I. Novikova, and N. V. Ssorin-Chaikov. 1995. 'Etnografy Pishut Zakon: Kontekst i Problemy'. *Etnograficheskoe Obozrenie* 1: 74–88.

Stammler, F. 2005. *Reindeer Nomads Meet the Market: Culture, Property and Globalisation at the End of the Land*. Münster: Lit.

Stammler, F. and A. Ivanova. 2016. 'Resources, Rights and Communities: Extractive Mega-Projects and Local People in the Russian Arctic'. *Europe-Asia Studies* 68(7): 1220–44.

Stammler, F., K. K. Hodgson, and A. Ivanova. 2020. 'Human Security, Extractive Industries, and Indigenous Communities in the Russian North'. In G. Hoogensen Gjørv, M. Lanteigne, and H. Sam-Aggrey, eds. *Routledge Handbook of Arctic Security*, 377–91. London: Routledge.

Terekhina, A. N. 2017. 'Kochevyye Shkoly: Ogranicheniia ili Vozmozhnosti?' *Etnograficheskoe Obozrenie* 2: 137–53.

Tichotsky, J. 2000. *Russia's Diamond Colony: The Republic of Sakha*. Amsterdam: Harwood.

Tishkov, V. A., O. P. Kolomiyets, E. P. Martynova, N. I. Novikova, E. Pivneva, and A. N. Terekhina. 2016. *Rossiyskaia Arktika: Korennye Narody i Promyshlennoe Osvoienie*. Moskow/St Petersburg: Institut Etnologii i Antropologii RAN.

Tiukhteneva, S. 1997. 'Istoriia izucheniia obychnogo prava altaitsev'. In N. I. Novikova and A. G. Osipov, eds. *Homo Juridicus*, 236–44. Moscow: Rossiiskaia Akademiia Nauk.

Uvachan, V. V. 2001. *Obychnoye Pravo Evenkov v XVII–Nachale XX v*. Moscow: Knizhnyi Dom 'Universitet'.

Vasil'kova, T. N., A. V. Yevay, Ye. P. Martynova, and N. I. Novikova. 2011. *Korennye Malochislennye Narody i Promyshlennoe Razvitie Arktiki: Etnologicheskii Monitoring v I͡Amalo-Nenet͡skom Avtonomnom Okruge*. Moscow: Shadrinskii Dom Pechati.

Young, J. F. 2000. 'The Republic of Sakha and Republic Building: The Neverendum of Federalisation in Russia'. In K. Matsuzato, ed. *Regions: A Prism to View the Slavic–Eurasian World. Towards a Discipline of Regionology*, 177–207. Sapporo: Slavic Research Center, Hokkaido University.

CHAPTER 8

INDIGENOUS PEOPLES, IDENTITY, AND FREE, PRIOR, AND INFORMED CONSULTATION IN LATIN AMERICA

ARMANDO GUEVARA GIL

IN this chapter, I explore the close relationship between law and anthropology in Latin America. Within the field of Indigenous peoples' rights, I focus on the social life of the right to free, prior, and informed consultation on state measures that might directly affect Indigenous peoples, as granted by the 1989 International Labour Organization Convention 169 on Indigenous and Tribal Peoples (ILO 169).[1] As Rachel Sieder (2016: 419) has noted, the 'promise of "prior consultation" became a lightning rod for indigenous mobilizations' against extractivism and developmentalism. It is also a 'key tool for protecting [Indigenous peoples'] rights' (Sierra 2014: 22[2]). I show how Indigenous peoples, subaltern communities, and their advocates work at the intersection of law and anthropology both to *broaden* the right to prior consultation and to *deepen* it so that it can be realized in a substantive way. These two movements characterize the regional evolution of the right to consultation and, in general, 'the emergence of new legal categories' (Goodale 2015: 13).

The first movement, broadening, refers to redefining the legal subjects eligible to claim enforcement of the right. The second movement, which I am calling 'deepening', means that a consultation process can only be considered substantive when the social groups involved give their consent to the measure or exert their *veto power* as expressions of their right to self-determination (Clavero 2015: 647; Herrera 2019: 211, 221). Thus, a tacit coalition of Indigenous and grassroots leaders, lawyers, anthropologists, judges, legislators, and diplomats is expanding the right to consultation beyond the original intent of the signatories of ILO 169 as a way to seek redress for the injustices Indigenous peoples and subaltern communities experience across Latin America.

Before dealing with each movement, in the next section I refer briefly to legal indigenism as an example of the intersection of law and anthropology in Latin America and to the importance of the anthropological gaze for analysing legal categories in their political and cultural context.

Legal indigenism and ILO 169

In Latin America, lawyers and anthropologists play a key role in debates over the *Indian question*. During the early years of the twentieth century, a continental cadre of *indigenistas* oscillated between the celebration of racial and cultural distinctiveness and calls for assimilationist policies. They were white and *mestizo* artists, intellectuals, lawyers, and anthropologists who spoke on behalf of Indigenous people (Giraudo and Lewis 2012: 3–4) and were usually hired by governments as experts on Indigenous affairs. Legal indigenism, essentially paternalistic, was developed as a particular field to promote Indigenous rights and inclusive administrative reforms (Ramos 2006: 207).

By the final third of the century, indigenism had become outdated. Indigenous peoples' empowerment as (trans)national political actors and the call to decolonize Latin American anthropology and state policies had changed domestic and international ethnopolitical landscapes completely.[3] Integration and assimilationist policies were rejected, and the right to self-determination became the cornerstone of Indigenous demands against nation-states.

Along the way, legal anthropological knowledge acquired ever greater importance. Indigenous political demands were framed as rights, and Indigenous peoples' struggles were ever more frequently included on the agenda of the international human rights movement because they could not find redress at the national level within the modern states in which they resided (Niezen 2003: 37; Sieder et al. 2019: 8). As law and culture are 'inextricably linked' and the term *Indigenous* is in itself a legal-anthropological construct, the question of Indigenous rights is 'not an issue for cultural experts only; it is a phenomenon deeply embedded in legal processes' (Bens 2020: 21). As such, it requires an interdisciplinary approach.

In this dialogue, ILO 169 acquires great relevance, particularly in its establishment of the right to hold free, prior, and informed consultations. Any interpretation of its reach, whether to strengthen state sovereignty or to assert Indigenous self-determination based on ethnic and cultural difference, occurs at the intersection of law and anthropology. Emancipatory or regulatory readings (Santos and Rodriguez 2005) dealing with international treaties, constitutional and human rights, laws, jurisprudence, Indigenous/local law, and socio-legal practice are particularly prone to the anthropological approach to law (Goodale 2008: 227; Hale 2020: 622).

Before focusing on the regional evolution of this right, three caveats are in order. First, out of 193 countries in the world, only 23 have ratified the convention.[4] Accordingly, only 15 per cent of Indigenous peoples live in countries that have ratified ILO 169 (ILO 2019: 52). Out of a total of approximately 475 million Indigenous peoples worldwide, only 11.5 per cent (55 million),[5] forming more than 826 'Indigenous groups' speaking 558 Indigenous languages, live in Latin America (Congressional Research Service 2020: 7–8; ILO 2019: 45, 53, 57).

What is remarkable is that fourteen out of twenty Latin American states have ratified ILO 169.[6] The ethnopolitical importance of the convention throughout the region is unquestionable (Sieder 2016: 416), as is its impact on Latin American legal anthropology (Sierra 2014). A decade ago, Goodale concluded that 'the anthropology of law in Latin America remains much too incipient [and] does not exist in any meaningful sense', although he recognized advances made by scholars, social and political activists, and Indigenous intellectuals (2008: 214, 218). Conversely, by 2014 it was considered an established field of enquiry, 'critical, applied, and committed [*comprometida*] to the Indigenous peoples' demands for justice and recognition' (Sierra 2014: 16, 19; see also Goodale 2008: 216; Hale 2006; Sieder et al. 2019: 1, 6). Here, the role of the Red Latinoamericana de Antropología Jurídica (RELAJU), a branch of the Commission on Legal Pluralism, cannot be overstated (Sieder et al. 2019: 6; Sierra 2014: 19).

Second, I am perfectly aware of the 'implementation gap' of the right to consultation (Economic and Social Council 2006; Leyva 2018; Urteaga 2018; Weitzner 2017; Wright and Tomaselli 2019). Governments drag their feet in enacting ILO 169, narrow its meaning and application, transform a fundamental right into an endless administrative procedure, blatantly cheat Indigenous communities, deny or falsify their existence, and even propose 'post-consultations' (Aparicio 2015; Bengoa 2017; Flemmer 2018; Guevara Gil and Cabanillas 2019; Hirsch 2019).[7] Unfortunately, as many lawyers and anthropologists are committed to promoting extractivism and reducing consultations to a neoliberal form of governance as are *comprometidos* to the cause of Indigenous peoples (Bustamante 2015; Goodale 2015; Guevara Gil and Verona 2018; Rodriguez 2011; Sieder et al. 2019: 9; Torres 2019).

Third, one can read the Indigenous appropriation and full implementation of consultations as the emergence of a 'subaltern cosmopolitan legality' (Santos and Rodriguez 2005). Or, as Sieder and Barrera (2017: 12) suggest, as a new intervention in the autonomy of Indigenous peoples that leads to the translation of 'radical ontological difference into administrative procedures', which threatens to impose (neo)colonial 'forms of power through the idiom of the law'. I share the first view.

Indigenous and subaltern communities have historically confronted hegemonic pressures using the political and legal resources at their disposal and building coalitions with activists and scholars to resist and recreate their societies. Framing and interpreting themselves through a hegemonic language surely transforms them: 'Indigenous identity is created, invented and forged with and against legal discourse' (Ariza 2018: 8; see also Bens 2020: 20–2). That is part of their trajectory within (neo)colonial and global contexts (Fernández 2016; Hale 2006: 111; Kaltmeier et al. 2012: 107; Poole 2018: 202).

Indeed, some communities try to keep the state at bay, assert their right to self-determination (Sieder 2013: 235), and refuse to engage in consultations to prevent any form of negotiation over their livelihood, autonomy, and ontological difference (Torres 2019: 101). But most of them negotiate, albeit on unequal footing, their incorporation into the political economy of recognition and resource allocation imposed by state or corporate projects (Flemmer and Schilling-Vacaflor 2015; Goodale 2015; Torres 2019).

Still, the subaltern translation and contestation of such canonical legal concepts as 'consultation' unleashes struggles to determine the meaning of rights (Flemmer 2018: 521, 524), to define '*who* is entitled to *what*' (Flemmer 2019: 107; Sierra 2014: 25), and even to redefine relations between humans and nature in terms of 'equality and justice' (Doran 2019: 203). Consultation processes show the progressive transformation of rights enshrined in international legal instruments, often going far beyond the will of states. Latin American Indigenous peoples are vernacularizing international human rights discourse and ILO 169 through their 'co-production of knowledge' and their fluid relations with academia, civil society, and a 'transregional epistemic' community (Sieder et al. 2019: 9). Regional legal anthropology contributes to this endeavour with its 'interdisciplinary critical reflection' and fruitful 'encounters' with Indigenous and subaltern leaders and intellectuals (Sierra 2014: 18, 25).

Broadening: The Multiplication of Legal Subjects

The enforcement of a special legal regime requires the identification of its subjects (Ariza 2018: 2; Lara-Largo 2019). ILO 169 uses the concept of ethnicity to identify and grant special rights to Indigenous and tribal peoples as a way of righting the wrongs of conquest and colonization.[8]

As Barth states, ethnicity is about 'the social organization of culture difference' (1969). Legal anthropological analyses are particularly productive because the persistence of ethnic groups and their interactions demand 'a systematic set of rules governing inter-ethnic social encounters'. Be it in anarchic, polycentric, or (neo)colonial social settings, ethnic boundaries are maintained by selecting diacritical features for inter-group differentiation and applying sanctions for transgressing them. In the case of polyethnic archaic or modern states, official policies and laws reinforce group ascriptions and stratification (Barth 1969: 16, 37, 14, 28).

In Latin America, ethnicity was born out of the asymmetrical incorporation of structurally differentiated groups into the broader socioeconomic and political orders (Comaroff 1992: 54) of the Iberian empires and their successors, the modern nation-states. In these contexts, the colonizers and the colonized, including descendants of people brought over from Africa, forged their ethnic identities through contacts and frictions that gave rise to the contrast *we/other(s)*, expressed in markers such as language, phenotypical attributes, cultural traits, territorial attachment, and religion. These differences epitomize the tension or ethnic conflict between the groups (Sieder and Barrera 2017: 8; Wade 2010).

After racialist and primordialist views fixated on gene pools, blood, or lineage as determining ethnic markers were discredited (Baumann 1999: 63–4; Wade 2010: 16), Latin American Indigenous peoples and subaltern ethnicities have been approached from two angles. The first stresses the cultural survivals and essential traits of Indigenous peoples as 'living museums' (Bengoa 2018: 223). Distinct features, presumably persisting 'since time immemorial', serve as benchmarks of authenticity, justifying claims to special rights (Ariza 2018: 11; Fernández 2016; 189; Poole 2016: 290; 2018: 231). Here, 'indigenous people's claims to ancestral rights are grounded in radical cultural difference' (Hale 2006: 105), portrayed as endogenously produced and pre-political (Costa 2016: 9). This approach leads to essentialism and strategic essentialism, deployed to ground political and legal struggles (Bens 2020: 198). The cost of this strategy is the likelihood of overlooking 'the real-life practices of ordinary people living in local communities' (Bocarejo 2011: 109; Sieder and Barrera 2017: 7) and 'ignor[ing] centuries of cultural and physical mixing' (Canessa 2016: 78; Duve 2018: 826, 835).

The second approach focuses on the historical processes of dispossession, marginalization, ethnocide, and genocide that Indigenous and subaltern peoples have confronted and endured as collective subjects. Resistance, adaptation, mimesis, and revival or recreation of their differentiated collectivities are the strategies developed to retain their distinctiveness, construct their identities, and demand the enforcement of ILO 169 and other targeted legislative acts (Bengoa 2018; Duve 2018; Field 1994; Poole 2018; Singh 2018; Wade 2010). Strategic essentialism also plays a role in putting forward a collective subjectivity to strengthen Indigenous and subaltern struggles for recognition (Kaltmeier et al. 2012: 105).

Both views are widely used by committed lawyers and social scientists to interpret the authoritative definitions of Indigenous and tribal peoples set forth in ILO 169 and to broaden the scope of the pro-Indigenous framework. According to Article 1 of the Convention, Indigenous peoples are the descendants of preconquest or precolonization populations that, 'irrespective of their legal status, retain some or all of their own social, economic, cultural and political institutions'. In this case, aboriginality, historical continuity, and distinctiveness are the main grounds for their rights (Duve 2018: 822). Tribal peoples, on the other hand, possess social, cultural, and economic conditions different from mainstream society and their status 'is regulated wholly or partially by their own customs or traditions or by special laws'. Here, difference, not ancestry, is the main source of their rights. A progressive and open clause consecrates self-identification 'as a fundamental criterion for determining the groups to which the provisions of this Convention apply' (Articles 1.1, 1.2).

As the UN Commission on Human Rights warned in 1996, these factors 'do not, and cannot, constitute an inclusive or comprehensive definition'. Subjugation, dispossession, and discrimination have been experienced differently, shaping different ethnic profiles. Descriptive fuzziness should not hinder the enjoyment of special rights and, according to the UN Rapporteur, states should conduct 'reasonable decision-making in practice' (Daes 1996: 22).

Against these warnings, the Peruvian government initially alleged that the right to consultation was reserved to a fraction of its Indigenous peoples (Flemmer 2019: 108; Poole 2016: 291–2). It tried to dictate 'the very "being" (or ontology) of indigenous communities' (Bustamante 2015: 193). In the state narrative, only the surviving, pristine, and aboriginal Amazonian communities deserve the right to be consulted; Andean peasant communities are too Westernized and do not retain enough autochthonous ethnic markers.[9] The reason for this distinction was geological. A cadre of high-ranking mining bureaucrats joined forces with pro-corporate lawyers and devious anthropologists to concoct arguments *against* recognizing the right to consultation, sacrificing their own professional ethics and the historical and anthropological knowledge of Andean societies at the altar of extractivism (Guevara Gil and Verona 2018; Poole 2016).

Despite the politics of denial, also translated into domestic normative standards that were more stringent than those of ILO 169,[10] Andean peasant communities managed, through intensive lobbying, to get themselves recognized as collectivities with the right to demand consultation. To match the 'criteria for identifying indigenous or original peoples',[11] they strategically essentialize their ethnicity, portraying themselves as pristine descendants of colonized Andean peoples. Unfortunately, the results are not promising. Consulted communities end up 'invited [to] spaces dominated by the state' (Flemmer and Schilling-Vacaflor 2015: 11) where government facilitators side with corporations to promote extractivism (Bustamante 2015; Goodale 2015; Guevara Gil and Cabanillas 2019). However, the trend is important, as it shows a change in the way peasant communities are engaging with the state, radicalizing or inventing their ethnic difference to invoke the clout of ILO 169.

Similarly, Peruvian peasant patrols (*rondas campesinas*) broaden the right to consultation by representing themselves as deserving of ILO 169 protections. Born out of the demands for local security, they soon developed into grassroots social and jurisdictional organizations recognized by state law but not on the grounds of a specific ethnicity.[12] Like Andean peasant communities, they demanded 'their rights as Peruvian citizens, and not as "cultural others"' (Oliart 2008: 291; Gundermann 2013: 95–6). Only in the past ten years, with the help of Peruvian legal scholars and the renowned Spanish jurist and historian Bartolomé Clavero, have they asserted the enduring existence of their Indigenous ethnicity and fashioned a myth of origin as 'heirs to the Caxamarcas, Coremarcas and Chachapoyas indigenous peoples'.[13] As such, they requested that they be allowed to participate in consultations to authorize a huge mining project (Clavero 2013) and approve climate change legislation.[14]

Parallel processes of ethnogenic reconstruction to claim Indigenous rights, including the right to consultation, are taking place in Colombia. In the Pacific region, more than twenty-five ethno-territorial organizations have emerged in less than a decade. Realizing that today, 'legally and politically, it is better to be an Indigenous person than a peasant ... many peasant communities are on the path of identity revival' (Ariza 2018: 8; de la Cadena 2008: 345), ethnogenesis (Sieder and Barrera 2017: 9; Sierra 2014: 22), or a sort of recursive ethnogenesis in dialogue with state agents, intellectuals, activists, and Indigenous leaders (Gundermann 2013). Despite the *acompañamiento* of activists, these processes have not challenged internal gender, class, or age hierarchies. Male elites monopolize political representation by exaggerating their indigeneity, yet women remain *more Indian* in daily life (de la Cadena 1991). The elderly and those who are monolingual are still 'formally and informally excluded from these participatory arenas' (Schilling-Vacaflor 2019: 84; see also Eichler 2019: 69; Schilling-Vacaflor and Eichler 2017: 1455).

Not always, however, do *mestizo* communities have to appeal to ancestral roots or radical difference to match the 'metrics that give both legal form and technical precision to ethnic identities' (Poole 2016: 289). In some consultations, Indigenous and non-Indigenous communities participate in the same process, regardless of the ILO 169 definitions. In 2012, the Peruvian environmental bureaucracy displayed unusual flexibility in establishing an Amazonian natural protected area. It extended consultation rights to *mestizo* communities who refuse to be categorized as Indigenous (*nativos*) (Desmet 2016: 146–7).

In post-multicultural identity politics (Kaltmeier et al. 2012: 110), access to consultation rights should not depend on authenticating indigeneity. Peasant movements (Tsing 2010: 51) and Indigenous peoples (Torres 2019: 86) are creating alternatives to avoid 'the straitjacket of rights' tied to particular identities and spaces (Hale 2011: 204; 2018; de la Cadena and Starn 2010: 13). The practice of *comunalidad* in Oaxaca, Mexico (Mendoza 2014), designed to integrate flows of migrants into hybrid communities, and the creation of a decolonized place and memory in Huarochiri, Peru (Salomon 2002) exemplify the efforts of peasant intellectuals to overcome essentialist identity politics and deploy the 'logic of shared difference' (Merlan 2010: 105) to claim access to the protections built into ILO 169 and similar bodies of law (Bens 2020: 167).

Applying this logic to interpret international and domestic law, Latin American non-Indigenous collectivities such as Roma and descendants of people who came from Africa have made significant progress. To achieve these accomplishments, courts, lawmakers, leaders, and activists have resorted to the anthropologically questionable category *tribal*. African colonial administrations and anthropologists coined it to understand and manage the precolonial inter-ethnic landscape. Thus, tribes were not discovered, but invented. Despite this predicament, the Inter-American Court of Human Rights (IACHR) applies Article 1.2 of ILO 169 to protect so-called tribal peoples. In *Saramaka People v. Suriname* (2007), the Court concluded that the plaintiff was a *tribal community* descended from African slaves (Bens 2020: 171), and that they therefore enjoyed the right to be 'effectively consulted, in accordance with their traditions and customs' and to 'give or withhold their free, informed and prior consent with regards [sic] to development or investment projects that may affect their territory'.[15]

Colombia has also classified people of African descent as tribal people. First, the Constitution prescribed the enactment of a law recognizing collective property and cultural identity rights for the 'Black communities' of the Pacific region.[16] In 1993, a law recognized them '*as an ethnic group*' enjoying consultation rights in environmental, educational, and social programmes.[17] These rights were exercised between hope and despair (Arboleda 2015). In 2001 and 2003, the Constitutional Court decided that Afro-Colombians deserve constitutional protection as *a tribal people*. In 2014, the Court expanded consultation rights, initially granted only to communities with collective land titles and to the *Raizales* of San Andres, to similar rural and urban organizations representing people of African descent (Ariza 2017; Clavero 2015: 602–3).[18]

In the normative realm, Ecuador has given equal collective rights to Indigenous and 'Afro-Ecuadorian people'.[19] The 2009 Bolivian Constitution recognizes 'Afro-Bolivian people' and grants them the same rights accorded to 'indigenous native and peasant nations and people' (Canessa 2016: 77).[20] Both participated in the consultation process that led to the 2011 Law of Jurisdictional Demarcation, with dubious results (Albó 2012: 246; Santos 2012: 36). Chile, traditionally reluctant to acknowledge its cultural diversity, enacted Law 21.151, recognizing that 'Chilean tribal people of African descent' are entitled 'to be consulted according to ILO 169'.[21]

On the ground, Indigenous and subaltern communities defy neat ethnic classificatory systems. Even the progressive criterion of 'self-identification as indigenous *or* tribal' (ILO 169, Article 1.2; italics added) is too restrictive. The *Raizales* communities of Colombia illustrate the shifting grounds of identity politics, ancestry, and authenticity for claiming special rights. Their leaders and activists assert a hybrid ethnicity as 'indigenous to the Archipelago, being descendants of the Africans, British puritans, and indigenous islanders and Caribbeans that first colonized our territory in the seventeenth century'.[22]

In Honduras, 'some Garifuna ... readily refer to themselves as negro and indígena', resorting to 'Afroindigeneity' as a comprehensive category for encompassing their historical experience (Anderson 2007: 386, 407; Hale 2018: 504). In 2015, the IACHR followed suit, describing them as 'a differentiated culture and ethnic group arising from a syncretism of indigenous and African peoples'. Abiding by the legal opinion of James Anaya, the Court ruled that 'the Garifuna people can be regarded as a tribal people' who deserved to be consulted before establishing a national park and a touristic resort in their territories.[23]

In Colombia, the Roma are also considered a tribal people. This was a bottom-up process led by local activists (Gamboa 2015), but it was disregarded by the ILO and the United Nations. In 1998, the General Directorate of Indigenous Affairs recognized that the Roma had a 'traditional social organization [that is] clearly tribal'. Until 2001, the Colombian Roma Organization (PRORROM) had never received a reply from the ILO Committee of Experts on the Application of Conventions and Recommendations (CEACR) as to whether they qualified as subjects of ILO 169. According to Michael Brown), the CEACR's foot-dragging can be blamed on 'the current obsession of anthropology with indigenous peoples' and autochthony (Brown 2010: 199). Yet, in 2010, the government issued regulations for protecting the Roma's rights, and a special law was passed (2011) granting them integral reparations and land restitution. Finally, in 2013, the Constitutional Court recognized that the 'Romaní or Gypsy people ... form a legal and factual reality as comprised in the definition of tribal people' of ILO 169 (Gamboa 2015: 142–55).[24]

Indigenous and subaltern peoples' quest for recognition and redistribution has clearly broadened the scope of the right to consultation. Their engagement with national and international laws, rulings, and regulations, along with their collaboration with 'solidary interlocutors—human rights lawyers, activist anthropologists, expert witnesses, and the like' (Hale 2020: 626, 622), has expanded the original criteria established by ILO 169, multiplying the legal subjects entitled to exercise the rights and protections it affords.

Deepening: from consultation to consent

The struggles over which subjects are eligible to claim and exercise the right to consultation run *pari passu* with struggles to upgrade it from a soft to a solid right. The aim is to overcome the procedural trap that reduces consultations to rituals of domination in which Indigenous peoples are heard but not listened to, let alone respected. 'If we cannot say no, does this make any sense at all?', questioned a Kakataibo from the Peruvian Amazon after taking part in a preordained process (Flemmer 2018: 533; see also Flemmer 2019: 114–15). Evo Morales, the first Indigenous Bolivian president, adamantly rejected any new perspectives or approaches regarding consultations. In 2011, he imposed the construction of an 'ecological road' that would cross the TIPNIS, an Indigenous territory and national park. Responding to grassroots mobilizations, he declared, 'They want the consultation to be binding. That's impossible: it's non-negotiable' (Canessa 2016: 91; see also Hirsch 2019).

These regressive trends are being challenged through 'autoconsultations' and demands to transform consultation into meaningful consent, movements that are being aided by 'activist scholarship' and 'legal accompaniment' (Hale 2020: 619, 623).

Auto-consultations are a continent-wide reaction to overt government and corporate aggression or outright disregard of Indigenous rights. States question their legal value, but they have proven to be instrumental in strengthening oppositional coalitions, even to the point of paralysing invasive projects. In Guatemala, 67 *consultas comunitarias* (2004–2012) deterred the avalanche of mining and hydroelectric schemes (Bustamante 2015: 190; Xiloj 2019: 246–8). Ecuadorian Indigenous communities also challenged the aggressive policies of president Rafael Correa (2007–2017) by appealing to auto-consultations (Urteaga 2018: 16). In Chile, the Mapuche Pact for Self-Determination calls for community-ruled consultations in its political agenda (Doran 2019: 216). In Brazil, the 'government has never held a meaningful consultation regarding development and construction projects in Indigenous lands' (Mello 2019: 228), forcing Amazonian peoples to handle their own consultation and consent protocols. In Patagonia, Argentina, communities potentially affected by a gold mining project rejected the formal channels of participation and formed a Self-Convened Neighbours Assembly (*Asamblea de Vecinos Autoconvocados*) comprising Mapuche communities. Their 2003 plebiscite paralysed the investment (Urkidi and Walter 2011: 691–2). Communities of African descent also try to 'self-regulate community-controlled processes of consultation, monitoring, and verification' (Sieder and Barrera 2017: 20). Even in extremely violent extractivist contexts, Colombian *resguardos* and communities of African descent enforce their consultation protocols under the slogan *Nosotros somos Estado* ('We are the State') (Weitzner 2017).

The shift from form to substance is making ILO 169's right to consultation more concrete and attainable. To be fair, according to the original definition of the right, the consultations were supposed to be conducted 'through appropriate procedures and ... through their representative institutions ... in good faith and in a form appropriate to the circumstances, *with the objective of achieving agreement or consent to the proposed measures*' (ILO 169, Articles 6.1.a, 6.2; italics added). These conditions should have been enough to guarantee its proper and significant exercise as an expression of the right to self-determination. But texts respond to subtexts and contexts.

First, the debates that gave birth to ILO 169 oscillated between granting full control to Indigenous peoples over their livelihoods and a merely participatory approach that downgraded their self-determination rights. The idea of seeking the consent of Indigenous peoples before approving official measures affecting them directly was 'met with strong resistance from many states and employers' organizations'. Hence, the convention 'adopted the weaker formulation of "consultation"' (Rodriguez 2011: 283).

Second, the 'procedural compromise between two substantively opposing relations' meant subordinating 'free, prior, and informed consultation to the priority of economic development' (Rodriguez 2011: 283–4). In fact, ILO 169 was never intended as an instrument to 'challenge the underlying political-economic structures' Indigenous peoples face in their home countries or the global economy (Goodale 2015: 5–6).

Still, the text is open to counterhegemonic readings because consent was incorporated, albeit as an exception. The relocation of Indigenous peoples can 'take place only with their free and informed consent' (Article 16.2). In 2007, the United Nations Declaration on the Rights of Indigenous Peoples (UNDRIP) expanded the requirement of consent to include cases involving the use and disposition of Indigenous peoples' cultural property, the use and occupation of their traditional territories, and projects affecting their territories and resources.[25] Predictably, it has become 'a point of reference in indigenous organizations' campaigns and attempts to generate national and international jurisprudence in Latin America' (Sieder 2016: 419).

As we have seen, in *Saramaka People v. Suriname* (2007), the IACHR ordered the state to 'obtain [the Saramakas'] free, prior, and informed consent' for 'large-scale development or investment projects' in their territories.[26] Prior to that, the Colombian Constitutional Court had also judged that consent was necessary for developing projects with sizable negative impacts on local communities (Bustamante 2015: 194). The transformative dialogue between the Inter-American human rights system and the Latin American constitutional courts favours the requirement of Indigenous peoples' consent regardless of the scale of the intervention (Herrera 2019).

This trend is responsive to the socio-legal mobilization involving public intellectuals, legal scholars, anthropologists, and Indigenous leaders and intellectuals who seek an emancipatory use of the law (Hale 2006; Sieder 2013, 2016: 419; Sieder et al. 2019: 5, 7, 9). Interestingly, in this undertaking, 'international law itself has been shaped by decades of indigenous peoples' organizing' (Goodale 2008: 220; Sieder and Barrera 2017: 9). As a consequence, the meaning of the acronym FPIC has changed, from free, prior, and informed *consultation*, used by critical scholars like Rodriguez (2011) ten years ago, to free, prior, and informed *consent*, as is widely—and perhaps even exclusively—employed today.[27]

Different United Nations organs are also active in making the meaning of consultation more substantive. For the Committee on the Elimination of Racial Discrimination (CERD 1997), Indigenous peoples should express their consent to decisions directly affecting their rights. Two years later, the UN Human Rights Committee concluded that Indigenous peoples have the right to self-determination regarding the use and disposition of their natural resources, and in 2008 the CERD recommended that states seek 'consent prior to granting licenses to private companies' interested in investing in Indigenous peoples' territories (Eichler 2019: 45). The Committee on Economic, Social and Cultural Rights has called for obtaining consent from 'indigenous peoples and nationalities' facing extractive projects (Eichler 2019: 46). Similarly, the Expert Mechanism on the Rights of Indigenous Peoples (EMRIP, 2012) identifies consent as necessary for developing schemes with 'major, significant or direct' impacts on the livelihoods of Indigenous peoples (Bustamante 2015: 188; Eichler 2019: 52).

The role of the UN Special Rapporteur on the situation of human rights and fundamental freedoms of Indigenous people (UNSR) has also been noteworthy. In 2003, Rodolfo Stavenhagen, the first Special Rapporteur, asserted that the right to self-determination comprised the right to consent and should be respected in large development and extractivist projects (Cantú 2019: 33; Eichler 2019: 53). In 2009, James Anaya questioned the idea of consent being equated with veto power, but conceded that a direct and significant impact of a project on the lands and livelihoods of Indigenous peoples 'establishes a strong presumption that the proposed measure should not go forward without indigenous peoples' consent' (in Eichler 2019: 54) obtained in fair consultations (Cantú 2019: 33). In 2012, he was clearer, considering 'indigenous consent ... presumptively a requirement' for undertaking extractive projects on Indigenous lands (in Eichler 2019: 55; see also Bustamante 2015: 188).

Finally, the Permanent Forum on Indigenous Issues (PFII), an advisory board to the UN Economic and Social Council that promotes the application of the 2007 UNDRIP, recommends that corporations 'must obtain free, prior and informed consent from the indigenous peoples' affected by their investments (in Eichler 2019: 59). Hence, given the fact that states should protect, promote, and guarantee fundamental rights such as the right to consultation, they could be held accountable for the wrongdoings of extractive industries if consultations are not properly conducted.

Corporations and multilateral banks have developed standards and codes of conduct to respect the rights of Indigenous peoples and other marginalized communities.

Communities and their legal advocates resort to such codes to launch their struggles. For example, in 2012 UNSR James Anaya invoked the *Guiding Principles on Business and Human Rights*, which were designed to implement the UN's 'Protect, Respect and Remedy' framework, to call for extending to corporations the duty of due diligence to ensure that Indigenous peoples' rights are not violated.[28] If states fail to implement substantial consultations, corporations have the 'duty to not contribute to these violations' (Eichler 2019: 57; see also Cantú 2019: 28–30).

Meanwhile, the 2005 World Bank Operational Policy/Bank Procedure 4.10 on Indigenous Peoples, updated in 2013, follows ILO 169 with regard to conducting appropriate consultations. Consultations should start early, 'since decision making among Indigenous Peoples may be an iterative process', and must 'pay special attention to women, youth, and the elderly' (World Bank 2013: 1). The Inter-American Development Bank (IDB) insists that its operations should 'be based on socioculturally appropriate processes of consultation ... with a view to reaching agreement or obtaining consent'. The IDB is eager to finance 'their [Indigenous and subaltern peoples'] own consultation processes' and advises investors to 'include preliminary consultations with potentially affected indigenous peoples' (IDB 2006: 6, 43, 8). As a way of building reflexivity into its practices, the IDB must periodically evaluate its multicultural policies 'through independent reviews that will include consultations with ... indigenous peoples', governments, corporations, and civil society (IDB 2006: 11, 40, 46).

Likewise, the powerful International Council on Metals and Mining (ICMM) adopts the language of consultation and consent. Beyond official permits, ICMM acknowledges 'that successful mining and metals projects require the support of a range of interested and affected parties'. Indigenous peoples should be 'fully informed about the project and its potential impacts and benefits' before providing their consent 'without coercion, intimidation or manipulation' (ICMM 2015: 28). However, consultations 'should neither confer veto rights to individuals or subgroups nor require unanimous support'. If extractivist projects face opposition and governments decide to go ahead, 'ICMM members will determine whether they ought to remain involved' (Herrera 2019: 214; ICMM 2015: 11, 29).

Thus, the requirement to seek a 'social license to operate' remains part and parcel of the neoliberal governance milieu (Rodriguez 2011). Nevertheless, it still improves the chances for meaningful negotiation, and even for oppositional movements to prevail. Ideally, it aims at reconciling Indigenous rights and interests with those of business and industry. In conflictive social settings, 'consent is a prerequisite and companies should expect to face indigenous community opposition when attempting to proceed' without their permission. Protests, shutdowns, and international campaigns negatively affect the value of the investment. Therefore, 'to have any meaning, social license requires consent' of all the 'vulnerable communities' impacted by development or extractivist projects (Morrison 2014: 77, 79; see Cantú 2019: 37–8). Since some corporations are economically larger than their host countries (Herrera 2019: 195), the social license to operate can also serve as a step towards balancing an asymmetrical relationship.

Final remarks

While all the efforts of Indigenous leaders, legal and political advocates, activist anthropologists, state officials, international human rights bodies, multilateral banks, and corporations are commendable, we have to remember, first, that Latin American is the most violent continent in the world, particularly dangerous for Indigenous, peasant, and environmental leaders and activists (Doran 2017: 198). Between 2014 and 2018, 536 such activists were murdered (Alcázar 2020: 27, table 1).[29] I am not claiming that the corporations are involved in these murders, but clearly Indigenous and subaltern leaders and communities are operating in dangerous 'minefields' (Rodriguez 2011: 264–5; Sieder 2016: 420), and are taking their lives in their hands when they try to defend their rights.

Moreover, globally 'nearly 64 percent of the world's extractive conflicts take place in the Latin American region'. This is part of a global trend whereby '50–80 percent of mineral expansion worldwide is planned on indigenous land' (Torres 2019: 4, 5). Second, guerrillas, paramilitaries, drug cartels, and illegal logging and mining organizations also operate on Indigenous territories or their surroundings, hindering the governance of natural resource extraction and endangering Indigenous peoples' livelihoods (Bustamante 2015: 189; Sieder 2013: 231–4). Third, most Latin American states have passed harsh laws to criminalize social protest and pressurize local communities into yielding to extractivist and developmental projects (Doran 2017; Sieder 2013; Sieder and Barrera 2017).

As a response to this dire context, Indigenous and subaltern communities challenge the hegemonic roots of ILO 169 and reinterpret it from a decolonizing point of view. Broadening the right to consultation and trying to deepen it by making it more substantial and efficacious are creative steps Indigenous and subaltern communities take towards seizing control over their livelihoods and futures. In this endeavour, they 'employ an anthropological [approach to law] as part of broader legal and political movements' (Goodale 2008: 215) that involves *comprometidos* (committed) legal scholars and social scientists. It might not be enough to question structural inequalities, but it surely empowers Indigenous and subaltern peoples in their daily local struggles.

Acknowledgements

This chapter is dedicated to André Hoekema (1940–2020), *un hombre bueno y sabio*, whose knowledge of and solidarity with Latin American Indigenous people was remarkable and inspiring. I wish to thank Marie-Claire Foblets for her unfailing support and sharp criticism, Brian Donahoe for his masterful and patient editorial work, and Aníbal Gálvez Rivas for his assistance in compiling the bibliography.

Notes

1. Articles 6.1, 6.2, 15.2, 17, 22, 27, and 28.
2. Here, and for all other Spanish-language sources, the translations into English are by the author of this chapter.
3. The First Declaration of Barbados (1971), issued by a group of critical anthropologists, was a triggering factor in this process (Hale 2006: 99; Málaga 2019).
4. See <https://www.ilo.org/dyn/normlex/en/f?p=NORMLEXPUB:11300:0::NO::P11300_INSTRUMENT_ID:312314>. See also Goodale (2015: 443).
5. These figures are, of course, questionable: as Kaltmeier et al. (2012: 106) note, 'cultural belonging or the experience of postcolonial wrongs [are] fundamentally incommensurable with the arithmetic of censusing'. In the Russian Republic of Bashkortistan, the population of Bashkirs (the titular nationality) dropped dramatically two times in forty years, as 'large numbers of those who once identified themselves as Bashkir reclassified themselves as Tatar' (Chandra 2012: 3, cited in Singh 2018: 13), while in Bolivia the population of those who self-identified as 'Indigenous' decreased from 66 per cent in 2001 to 40 per cent in 2012, at the height of Evo Morales's presidency (Barabas 2014: 16; Sieder 2016: 415, 420, fn. 5).
6. All have adopted the 2007 United Nations Declaration on the Rights of Indigenous Peoples (UNDRIP) (although Colombia only 'supports' it) and the 2016 American Declaration on the Rights of Indigenous Peoples (ADRIP) (Bens 2020: 10–13; Congressional Research Service 2020: 17–18, table 3).
7. In 2015, the Peruvian government entertained the possibility of conducting nonsensical 'post-consultations' to legitimate the mining concessions it had already granted illegally (Guevara Gil and Cabanillas 2019: 11).
8. Going back as far as the Iberian empires' conquests of the Caribbean and Latin America in the fifteenth and sixteenth centuries.
9. Nevertheless, the state had no qualms about portraying these peasant communities as exotic for the purposes of attracting international tourism (Guevara Gil and Cabanillas 2019: 4).
10. The 2011 Law on Prior Consultation and its 2012 by-law require that for Indigenous peoples to be recognized as such, they must have preserved their language, remain on their ancestral territory, and be directly descended from aboriginal peoples. The exclusionary purpose of these norms is clear, given the history of forced Spanish alphabetization, violent displacements, and *mestizaje* (Guevara Gil and Cabanillas 2019; Urteaga 2018).
11. Law 29785 of 2011, Article 7; see <https://sinia.minam.gob.pe/normas/ley-derecho-consulta-previa-pueblos-indigenas-originarios-reconocido>.
12. See Gitlitz (2013) and Starn (1999) on *rondas campesinas*.
13. See Clavero (2013) and <http://www.servindi.org/pdf/CUNARC_Conga11Mar2013.pdf>.
14. See <https://www.servindi.org/actualidad-noticias/30/01/2019/rondas-campesinas-solicitan-inclusion-en-procesos-de-consulta-previa>.
15. See IACHR, Judgment of 28 November 2007, p. 62, available at <http://www.corteidh.or.cr/docs/casos/articulos/seriec_172_ing.pdf>.
16. Colombia, Constitución Política 1991, provisional article 53, available at <https://pdba.georgetown.edu/Constitutions/Colombia/colombia91.pdf>.
17. Colombia, Law 70 (1993), Articles 1, 22, 38, 58, available at <https://www.mininterior.gov.co/la-institucion/normatividad/ley-70-de-1993-agosto-27-por-la-cual-se-desarro

lla-el-articulo-transitorio-55-de-la-constitucion-politica>. See also Lara-Largo (2019: 234–5).

18. See the 2014 case on participation in rural development planning, available at <https://www.corteconstitucional.gov.co/relatoria/2014/t-576-14.htm>; the 2001 decision on political participation and consultation, available at <https://www.corteconstitucional.gov.co/relatoria/2001/C-169-01.htm>; and the 2003 decision on consultation over natural resources, available at <https://www.corteconstitucional.gov.co/relatoria/2003/T-955-03.htm>.
19. See Ecuador's Constitución de la República (2008), Articles 56, 57.7, 58, available at <https://www.oas.org/juridico/pdfs/mesicic4_ecu_const.pdf>.
20. Bolivian Constitution, Articles 30.II.15 and 32.
21. Law 21.151, Articles 1.2, 5 (Chile, 2019), available at <https://ojalanews.fiu.edu/wp-content/uploads/sites/9/2019/11/ley-afrochilena.pdf>.
22. Declaración de Autodeterminación del pueblo indígena Raizal del Archipiélago de San Andrés, Providencia y Santa Catalina, 28-04-2002, available at <https://www.urosario.edu.co/jurisprudencia/catedra-viva-intercultural/Documentos/DeclaracionAutodeterminacionRaizal.pdf>.
23. IACHR, *Comunidad Garífuna Triunfo de la Cruz v. Honduras*, judgment of 8 October 2015, pp. 16, 18, available at <https://www.corteidh.or.cr/docs/casos/articulos/seriec_305_esp.pdf>. Also, *Comunidad Garífuna de Punta Piedra v. Honduras*, judgment of 8 October 2015, available at <https://www.corteidh.or.cr/docs/casos/articulos/seriec_304_esp.pdf>.
24. Judgment C-359, 26 June 2013, available at <https://www.corteconstitucional.gov.co/relatoria/2013/C-359-13.htm>.
25. See UNDRIP (2007), Articles 10, 11.2, 28, 29.2, and 32.2.
26. See IACHR, Judgment of 28 November 2007, p. 62, available at <http://www.corteidh.or.cr/docs/casos/articulos/seriec_172_ing.pdf>.
27. Tellingly, the 2.0 version of the acronym, explicitly noted by the authors as referring to 'consent' and not to 'consultation', appears 319 times in the 294-page volume edited by Wright and Tomaselli (2019).
28. See <http://unsr.jamesanaya.org/?p=774>.
29. See also <https://internationalfunders.org/security-briefs/defenders-of-indigenous-rights-in-latin-america-briefing-for-funders/>.

References

Albó, X. 2012. 'Justicia Indígena en la Bolivia Plurinacional'. In B. Santos and J. Exeni, eds. *Justicia Indígena, Plurinacionalidad e Interculturalidad en Bolivia*, 201–48. La Paz: Ediciones Abya-Yala, Fundación Rosa Luxemburg.

Alcazar, A. 2020. 'La Criminalización de la Protesta Social: un Estado de la Cuestión'. *Revista Rupturas* 10(1): 25–43.

Anderson, M. 2007. 'When Afro Becomes (Like) Indigenous: Garifuna and Afro-Indigenous Politics in Honduras'. *Journal of Latin American and Caribbean Anthropology* 12(2): 384–413.

Aparicio, M. 2015. 'Derechos y Pueblos Indígenas: Avances Objetivos, Debilidades Subjetivas'. *Revista De Antropología Social* 24: 127–47.

Arboleda, S. 2015. 'Muerte, Destierro y Simulacro Estatal: la Consulta Previa entre los Afro Colombianos'. In D. Duprat, ed. *Convenção n. 169 da OIT e os Estados Nacionais*, 325–44. Brasilia: ESMPU.

Ariza, L. 2018. 'Legal Indigeneity: Knowledge, Legal Discourse and the Construction of Indigenous Identity in Colombia'. *Identities: Global Studies in Culture and Power*, available at <https://doi.org/10.1080/1070289X.2018.1543484>.

Ariza, R. 2017. 'Descolonización de prácticas judiciales constitucionales en Bolivia–Colombia'. *Revista Direitto & Praxis* 8(4): 3004–36.

Barabas, A. 2014. 'Multiculturalismo, Pluralismo Cultural e Interculturalidad en el Contexto de América Latina: la Presencia de los Pueblos Originarios'. *Configurações. Revista de Sociología* 14: 11–24.

Barth, F. 1969. 'Introduction'. In F. Barth, ed. *Ethnic Groups and Boundaries. The Social Organization of Culture Difference*, 9–38. Boston: Little, Brown and Company.

Baumann, G. 1999. *The Multicultural Riddle. Rethinking National, Ethnic and Religious Identities*. Abingdon/New York: Routledge.

Bengoa, J. 2017. 'Potencialidades y Limitaciones del Derecho Internacional sobre (o de) los Pueblos Indígenas'. *Revista Antropologías del Sur* 4(7): 259–69.

Bengoa, J. 2018. 'El Crepúsculo de las Lanzas'. *Revista Antropologías del Sur* 5(9): 217–33.

Bens, J. 2020. *The Indigenous Paradox. Rights, Sovereignty, and Culture in the Americas*. Philadelphia: University of Pennsylvania Press.

Bocarejo, A. 2011. 'Dos Paradojas del Multiculturalismo Colombiano: la Espacialización de la Diferencia Indígena y su Aislamiento Político'. *Revistas Colombiana de Antropología* 47(2): 97–121.

Bolivia, 'Constitución Política del Estado'. 2009, available at <https://www.oas.org/dil/esp/Constitucion_Bolivia.pdf>.

Brown, M. 2010. 'Traiciones de la Soberanía'. In M. de la Cadena and O. Starn, eds. *Indigeneidades Contemporáneas: Cultura, Política y Globalización*, 191–217. Lima: IFEA–IEP.

Bustamante, G. 2015. 'The Right to Consultation and Free, Prior and Informed Consent in Latin America: The Governmentality of the Extraction of Natural Resources'. *Revue Québécoise de Droit International* H-S 1: 179–97.

Canessa, A. 2016. 'Paradoxes of Multiculturalism in Bolivia'. In D. Lehmann, ed. *The Crisis of Multiculturalism in Latin America*, 75–100. New York: Palgrave Macmillan.

Cantú, H. 2019. 'Towards a Global Framework on Business and Human Rights. Indigenous Peoples and Their Right to Consultation and Free, Prior and Informed Consent'. In C. Wright and A. Tomaselli, eds. *The Prior Consultation of Indigenous Peoples in Latin America. Inside the Implementation Gap*, 27–40. Abingdon/New York: Routledge.

CERD (Committe on the Elimination of Racial Discrimination). 1997. 'General Recommendation No. 23 on the Rights of Indigenous Peoples', A/52/18, annex V. Geneva: United Nations.

Chandra, K. 2012. 'Introduction'. In K. Chandra, ed. *Constructivist Theories of Ethnic Politics*, 1–49. Oxford: Oxford University Press.

Clavero, B. 2013. 'Amicus Curiae: Informe sobre Visita a Cajamarca a Propósito del Caso Conga. Presentado a Comisión Interamericana de Derechos Humanos', available at <http://www.derechoysociedad.org/IIDS/Publicaciones/Informe_Bartolome-Clavero-Rondas_de_Cajamarca.pdf>.

Clavero, B. 2015. 'Consulta Indígena: Colombia (y España) entre Derecho Constitucional y Derechos Humanos'. In D. Duprat, ed. *Convenção n. 169 da OIT e os Estados Nacionais*, 11–51. Brasilia: ESMPU.

Comaroff, J. 1992. 'Of Totemism and Ethnicity'. In J. and J. Comaroff, eds. *Ethnography and the Historical Imagination*, 49–67. Boulder: Westview Press.

Congressional Research Service. 2020. *Indigenous Peoples in Latin America: Statistical Information*. Washington, DC: Congressional Research Service.

Costa, S. 2016. 'Freezing Differences: Politics, Law, and the Invention of Cultural Diversity in Latin America'. *Revista Brasileira de Sociologia do Direito*, 3(2): 8–32.

Daes, I. 1996. Working Paper by the Chairperson-Rapporteur, Mrs Erica-Irene A. Daes, on the concept of 'indigenous people'. United Nations Commission on Human Rights, Sub-Commission on Prevention of Discrimination and Protection of Minorities. Working Group on Indigenous Populations. E/CN.4/Sub.2/AC.4/1996/2.

De la Cadena, M. 1991. '"Las Mujeres son más Indias": Etnicidad y Género en una Comunidad del Cusco'. Revista Andina 9(1): 7–29.

De la Cadena, M. 2008. 'Alternative Indigeneities: Conceptual Proposals'. *Latin American and Caribbean Ethnic Studies* 3(3): 341–9.

De la Cadena, M. and O. Starn. 2010. 'Introducción'. In M. de la Cadena and O. Starn, eds. *Indigeneidades Contemporáneas: Cultura, Política y Globalización*, 9–42. Lima: IFEA–IEP.

Desmet, Ellen. 2016. 'Identifying Rights-Holders in Natural Resource Regimes: A Critical Assessment of the Peruvian Protected Areas Legislation'. *Hague Journal on the Rule of Law* 8(1): 135–54.

Doran, M.-C. 2017. 'The Hidden Face of Violence in Latin America. Assessing the Criminalization of Protest in Comparative Perspective'. *Latin American Perspectives* 44(5): 183–206.

Doran, M.-C. 2019. 'Indigenous Peoples in Chile: Contesting Violence, Building New Meanings for Rights and Democracy'. In G. Blouin-Genest, M.-C. Doran, and S. Paquerot, eds. *Human Rights as Battlefields. Changing Practices and Contestations*, 199–223. New York: Palgrave Macmillan.

Duve, T. 2018. 'Indigenous Rights: Latin America'. In M. Dubber and C. Tomlins, eds. *The Oxford Handbook of Legal History*, 817–38. Oxford/New York: Oxford University Press.

Economic and Social Council. 2006. 'Human Rights and Indigenous Issues Report of the Special Rapporteur on the Situation of Human Rights and Fundamental Freedoms of Indigenous People, Mr. Rodolfo Stavenhagen'. UN Doc. E/CN.4/2006/78.

Eichler, J. 2019. *Reconciling Indigenous Peoples' Individual and Collective Rights. Participation, Prior Consultation and Self-Determination in Latin America*. Abingdon and New York: Routledge.

Fernández, A. 2016. 'Constitución y Aporías del Indigenismo Global: Cultura, Raza y Soberanía. Reflexiones a partir del Caso Mapuche'. *Revista de Antropología Iberoamericana* 11(2): 177–98.

Field, L. 1994. 'Who are the Indians? Reconceptualizing Indigenous Identity, Resistance, and the Role of Social Science in Latin America'. *Latin American Research Review* 29(3): 237–48.

Flemmer, R. 2018. 'Stuck in the Middle: Indigenous Interpreters and the Politics of Vernacularizing Prior Consultation in Peru'. *Journal of Latin American and Caribbean Anthropology* 23(3): 521–40.

Flemmer, R. 2019. 'Prior Consultation as a Door Opener. Frontier Negotiations, Grassroots Contestation, and New Recognition Politics in Peru'. In C. Wright and A. Tomaselli, eds. *The Prior Consultation of Indigenous Peoples in Latin America. Inside the Implementation Gap*, 106–18. Abingdon/New York: Routledge.

Flemmer, R. and A. Schilling-Vacaflor. 2015. 'Unfulfilled Promises of the Consultation Approach: The Limits to Effective Indigenous Participation in Bolivia's and Peru's Extractive Industries'. *Third World Quarterly* 37(1): 172–88.

Gamboa, J. 2015. 'La Travesía de los Rrom de Colombia por el OIT-169: Notas para un Balance Preliminar de los Caminos Recorridos y por Recorrer'. In D. Duprat, ed. *Convenção n. 169 da OIT e os Estados Nacionais*, 139–67. Brasilia: ESMPU.

Giraudo, L. and S. Lewis. 2012. 'Introduction: Pan-American Indigenismo (1940–1970). New Approaches to an Ongoing Debate'. *Latin American Perspectives* 39(5): 3–11.

Gitlitz, J. 2013. *Administrando Justicia al Margen del Estado. Las Rondas Campesinas de Cajamarca*. Lima: Instituto de Estudios Peruanos.

Goodale, M. 2008. 'Legalities and Illegalities'. In D. Poole, ed. *A Companion to Latin American Anthropology*, 214–29. Malden /Oxford: Blackwell Publishing.

Goodale, M. 2015. 'Dark Matter: Toward a Political Economy of Indigenous Rights and Aspirational Politics'. *Critique of Anthropology* 36(4): 439–57.

Guevara Gil, A. and C. Cabanillas. 2019. 'Mineralizing the Right to Prior Consultation: From Recognition to Disregard of Indigenous and Peasant Rights in Peru'. *Global Jurist*: 1–21, available at <https://www.academia.edu/40297063/Mineralizing_the_Right_to_Prior_Consultation_From_Recognition_to_Disregard_of_Indigenous_and_Peasant_Rights_in_Peru>.

Guevara Gil, A. and A. Verona. 2018. 'Si No Hay Sujeto, No Hay Derecho. La Negación de la Historicidad del Sujeto Indígena y la Consulta Previa en el Perú'. *Forum historiae iuris*, available at <https://forhistiur.de/2018-12-guevara-gil-verona-badajoz/>.

Gundermann, H. 2013. Procesos Étnicos y Cultura en los Pueblos Indígenas de Chile'. *Alpha* 36: 93–108.

Hale, C. 2006. 'Activist Research v. Cultural Critique: Indigenous Land Rights and the Contradictions of Politically Engaged Anthropology'. *Cultural Anthropology* 21(1): 96–120.

Hale, C. 2011. '*Resistencia para qué*? Territory, Autonomy, and Neoliberal Entanglements in the "Empty Spaces" of Central America'. *Economy and Society* 40(2): 184–210.

Hale, C. 2018. 'When I Hear the Word Culture … '. *Cultural Studies* 32(3): 497–509.

Hale, C. 2020. 'Using and Refusing the Law: Indigenous Struggles and Legal Strategies after Neoliberal Multiculturalism'. *American Anthropologist* 122(3): 618–31.

Herrera, J. 2019. 'Judicial Dialogue and Transformative Constitutionalism in Latin America: The Case of Indigenous Peoples and Afro-Descendants'. *Revista Derecho del Estado* 43: 191–233.

Hirsch, C. 2019. 'Between Resistance and Negotiation: Indigenous Organisations and the Bolivian State in the Case of the TIPNIS'. *Journal of Peasant Studies* 46(4): 811–30.

ICMM (International Council on Mining and Metals). 2015. *Good Practice Guide. Indigenous Peoples and Mining*. Second Edition. London: ICMM.

IDB (Inter-American Development Bank). 2006. 'Operational Policy on Indigenous Peoples and Strategy for Indigenous Development'. Washington, DC: IDB, available at <http://idbdocs.iadb.org/wsdocs/getdocument.aspx?docnum=2032081>.

ILO (International Labour Organization). 1989. 'International Labour Organization Convention 169 on Indigenous and Tribal Peoples', available at <https://www.ilo.org/dyn/normlex/en/f?p=NORMLEXPUB:12100:0::NO::P12100_ILO_CODE:C169>.

ILO. 2019. *Implementing the ILO Indigenous and Tribal Peoples Convention No. 169: Towards an Inclusive, Sustainable and Just Future*. Geneva: ILO.

Kaltmeier, O., J. Raab, and S. Thies. 2012. 'Multiculturalism and Beyond: The New Dynamics of Identity Politics in the Americas'. *Latin American and Caribbean Ethnic Studies* 7(2): 103–14.

Lara-Largo, S. 2019. 'The Use of Multicultural Legal Instruments in a Dispute between Afrodescendants and Indigenous Peoples: The Case of Guamal, Colombia'. *Latin American and Caribbean Ethnic Studies* 14(3): 234–52.

Leyva, A. 2018. *Consúltame de Verdad. Aproximación a un Balance sobre Consulta Previa en el Perú en los Sectores Minero e Hidrocarburífero*. Lima: OXFAM–CooperAcción.

Málaga, S. 2019. 'Lo Indígena en las Declaraciones de Barbados: Construcción Simbólica e Imaginario Político de Igualdad'. *Revista Latinoamericana de Estudios Educativos* XLIX(2): 35–58.

Mello, J. 2019. 'Lack of Consultation and Free, Prior and Informed Consent, and Threats to Indigenous Peoples' Rights in Brazil'. In C. Wright and A. Tomaselli, eds. *The Prior Consultation of Indigenous Peoples in Latin America. Inside the Implementation Gap*, 225–39. Abingdon/New York: Routledge.

Mendoza, R. 2014. 'Ser Indígena sin Etnicidad en la Sierra norte de Oaxaca, México: Nativos, Foráneos e Identidades Comunitarias'. *Antípoda* 19: 45–68.

Merlan, F. 2010. 'La Indigeneidad como Identidad Relacional: la Construcción de los Derechos sobre la Tierra en Australia'. In M. de la Cadena and O. Starn, eds. *Indigeneidades Contemporáneas: Cultura, Política y Globalización*, 141–68. Lima: IFEA-IEP.

Morrison, J. 2014. *The Social License. How to Keep Your Organization Legitimate*. Basingstoke/New York: Palgrave Macmillan.

Niezen, R. 2003. *The Origins of Indigenism. Human Rights and the Politics of Identity*. Berkeley, Los Angeles/London: University of California Press.

Oliart, P. 2008. 'Indigenous Women's Organizations and the Political Discourses of Indigenous Rights and Gender Equity in Peru'. *Latin American and Caribbean Ethnic Studies* 3(3): 291–308.

Poole, D. 2016. 'Mestizaje as Ethical Disposition: Indigenous Rights in the Neoliberal State'. *Latin American and Caribbean Ethnic Studies* 11(3): 287–304.

Poole, D. 2018. 'La Ley y la Posibilidad de la Diferencia: la Antropología Jurídica Peruana entre la Justicia y la Ley'. In C. I. Degregori, P. Sendón, and P. Sandoval, eds. *No hay País más Diverso. Compendio de Antropología Peruana II*, 200–46. Lima: Instituto de Estudios Peruanos.

Ramos, C. 2006. *Historia del Derecho Civil Peruano*. Tomo V, vol. 2. Lima: Pontificia Universidad Católica del Perú.

Rodríguez, C. 2011. 'Ethnicity.gov: Global Governance, Indigenous Peoples, and the Right to Prior Consultations in Social Minefields'. *Indiana Journal of Global Legal Studies* 18(1): 263–305.

Salomon, F. 2002. 'Unethnic Ethnohistory: On Peruvian Peasant Historiography and Ideas of Autochthony'. *Ethnohistory* 49(3): 475–506.

Santos, B. 2012. 'Cuando los Excluidos tienen Derecho: Justicia Indígena, Plurinacionalidad e Interculturalidad'. In B. Santos and J. Exeni, eds. *Justicia Indígena, Plurinacionalidad e Interculturalidad en Bolivia*, 11–48. La Paz: Ediciones Abya-Yala, Fundación Rosa Luxemburg.

Santos, B. and C. Rodriguez. 2005. 'Law, Politics, and the Subaltern in Counter-Hegemonic Globalization'. In B. Santos and C. Rodriguez, eds. *Law and Globalization from Below. Towards a Cosmopolitan Legality*, 1–26. New York: Cambridge University Press.

Schilling-Vacaflor, A. 2019. 'The Coupling of Prior Consultation and Environmental Impact Assessment in Bolivia. Corporate Appropriation and Knowledge Gaps'. In C. Wright and A. Tomaselli, eds. *The Prior Consultation of Indigenous Peoples in Latin America. Inside the Implementation Gap*, 77–90. Abingdon/New York: Routledge.

Schilling-Vacaflor, A. and J. Eichler. 2017. 'The Shady Side of Consultation and Compensation: "Divide-and-Rule" Tactics in Bolivia's Extraction Sector'. *Development and Change* 48(6): 1439–63.

Sieder, R. 2013. 'Subaltern Cosmopolitan Legalities and the Challenge of Engaged Ethnography'. *Universitas Humanística* 75: 221–49.

Sieder, R. 2016. 'Indigenous Peoples' Rights and the Law in Latin America'. In C. Lennox and D. Short, eds. *Handbook of Indigenous Peoples' Rights*, 414–23. Abingdon/New York: Routledge.

Sieder, R. and A. Barrera. 2017. 'Legalizing Indigenous Self-Determination. Autonomy and Buen Vivir in Latin America'. *Journal of Latin American and Caribbean Anthropology* 22(1): 9–26.

Sieder, R., K. Ansolabehere, and T. Alfonso. 2019. 'Law and Society in Latin America'. In R. Sieder, K. Ansolabehere, and T. Alfonso, eds. *Routledge Handbook of Law and Society in Latin America*, 1–21. Abingdon/New York.

Sierra, M. 2014. 'Antropología Jurídica en México y América Latina. Balance, Perspectivas Contemporáneas y Retos para la Investigación'. In C. Filho, H. Sivini, and C. Nogueira, eds. *Direito Socioambiental: Uma Questâo para América Latina*, 15–29. Curitiba: Letra da Lei.

Singh, P. 2018. 'Global Configurations of Indigenous Identities, Movements and Pathways'. *Thesis Eleven* 145(1): 10–27.

Starn, O. 1999. *Nightwatch. The Politics of Protest in the Andes*. Durham: Duke University Press.

Torres, M. 2019. *Natural Resources, Extraction and Indigenous Rights in Latin America. Exploring the Boundaries of Environmental and State Corporate Crime in Bolivia, Peru and Mexico*. Abingdon/New York: Routledge.

Tsing, A. 2010. 'Identidades Indígenas, Nuevas y Antiguas Voces Indígenas'. In M. de la Cadena and O. Starn, eds. *Indigeneidades Contemporáneas: Cultura, Política y Globalización*, 45–82. Lima: IFEA–IEP.

Urkidi, L. and M. Walter. 2011. 'Dimensions of Environmental Justice in Anti-Gold Movements in Latin America'. *Geoforum* 42: 683–95.

Urteaga, P. 2018. 'Implementation of the Right to Prior Consultation in the Andean Countries. A Comparative Perspective'. *Journal of Legal Pluralism and Unofficial Law* 50(1): 7–30.

Wade, P. 2010. *Race and Ethnicity in Latin America*. New York: Pluto Press.

Weitzner, V. 2017. 'Nosotros Somos Estado': Contested Legalities in Decisionmaking about Extractives Affecting Ancestral Territories in Colombia'. *Third World Quarterly* 38(5): 1198–214.

World Bank. 2013. 'Operational Manual. BP 4.10 Indigenous Peoples', July 2005, revised April 2013, available at <https://ppfdocuments.azureedge.net/1570.pdf>.

Wright, C. and A. Tomaselli. 2019. *The Prior Consultation of Indigenous Peoples in Latin America. Inside the Implementation Gap*. Abingdon/New York: Routledge.

Xiloj, L. 2019. 'Implementation of the Right to Prior Consultation of Indigenous Peoples in Guatemala'. In C. Wright and A. Tomaselli, eds. *The Prior Consultation of Indigenous Peoples in Latin America Inside the Implementation Gap*, 243–60. Abingdon/New York: Routledge.

CHAPTER 9

RULE OF LAW AND MEDIA IN THE MAKING OF LEGAL IDENTITY IN URBAN SOUTHERN CHINA

DODOM KIM

As the People's Republic of China expands its reach into all corners of the globe, intellectuals, activists, politicians, international media, non-governmental organizations, and various other international bodies have been keeping a close eye on the Chinese government's policies and reactions. Especially after the protest against Hong Kong's extradition bill broke out in the summer of 2019 and the introduction of a new national security law in the following year—a process that has been described as 'making Hong Kong China' (Davis 2020)—the rule of law in China has been subject to unprecedented critical scrutiny. Under present conditions in which suspicion of China is widespread among outside observers, what questions can we ask to gain a productive understanding of China's laws? With this high-stakes question in mind, this chapter turns to a group of tenants facing a large-scale urban redevelopment project—i.e. evictions and demolition—in the prosperous metropolis of Shenzhen, China. In tracing the online conversations of tenants making demands (*suqiu*), I examine how law-invoking communication and ideas about law circulate and shape aggrieved tenants' identities and fields of action.

A cultural reading of China's rule of law

Shortly after Wang was released from overnight detention at the police station, he sent out the following message to several chat groups on WeChat, the most popular messaging app in China:[1]

> WANG: I just left the Haijing police station. Last night, I lost my freedom, and I was cut off from the rest of the world. All my belongings were confiscated, and a pair of cold handcuffs was the only thing that accompanied me. We must all make demands (*suqiu*) reasonably (*heli*), legally (*hefa*), and rationally (*lixing*), and trust that the government will come up with a comprehensive measure. I still believe that the people's government serves the people. . . .
>
> A: @Wang You have been wronged (*weiqu*)! You have suffered!
>
> B: @Wang You have been wronged! You have suffered!
>
> C: @Wang You have been wronged! You have suffered!
>
> D: @Wang You have been wronged! You have suffered!
>
> E: According to the rules on 'Regulations on Use and Management of Police Implements and Arms by the People's Police': Against suspects who resist by means of violence, attempted escape, suicide, or self-injury, the People's Police may proceed to restrain the suspect by using implements with restraining features such as handcuffs or police ropes. Public security organs shall decide only on whether there is suspicion of crime or not, and before adjudication by the judicial body, the public security organ may take coercive measures.
>
> E: If there were no such activities, then the police are violating the law (*fanfa*) by using handcuffs.

This dialogue comes from a chat group with around 500 members, the maximum group-size as determined by the WeChat messenger system. The group consisted mostly of people who were closely monitoring pending evictions and the demolition of housing in the Haijing area, caused by a large-scale redevelopment project led by a private developer, Yinshan. Haijing is an urban village, famous for providing affordable housing for those earning a low income in Shenzhen, a city renowned for its booming IT technology industry, its physical proximity to Hong Kong, and its exceptionally high real estate prices.[2] The WeChat chat groups congregated online shortly after Haijing was hit by sudden waves of eviction notices. Rumours of impending redevelopment had been haunting Haijing for over a decade, but because they had been circulating for such a long time, hardly anyone suspected such a sudden move by the developer or the landlords. It was nothing short of a crisis, threatening tens of thousands of aggrieved tenants with the loss of housing, livelihood, and schools for their children.

Wang and many other tenants had been to the local police station for 'tea meetings' (*hecha*) or 'conversations' (*yuetan*), both colloquial terms for being summoned by the authorities, usually for matters that were politically sensitive but legally ambiguous. It was generally understood that, although no one had yet crossed the red line that would justify indictment or criminal charges, the tenants were being summoned because of actively expressing their dissatisfaction and seeking solutions via the widely censored WeChat messenger platform. No one was heading out onto the streets with banners or blocking roadways, as were people in Hong Kong[3]—only a dozen metro stops from Haijing. Rather, the tenants were merely visiting government offices, seeking contact with journalists, responding to media interview requests, and doing their best to publicize their grievances to a wider online world. Indeed, later in the evening, after Wang sent out his message, another person informed the chat group that Wang had been detained at the police station for an alleged attempt to visit the provincial-level Petition Bureau (*xinfangju*)[4] instead of the local district or the municipal-level bureaus. Some people reacted strongly to this piece of news, condemning the authorities as inhumane and accusing them of taking illegal actions. Although 'skipping a level' (*yueji*) is often considered to be politically sensitive and sometimes administratively problematic, it is not necessarily criminal. Wang's experience revealed the possibility that the police might cross the line into illegal—or at best legally ambiguous—territory in handling this eviction crisis.

As academic observers interested in China's law and culture, how are we to approach Wang's announcement of his faith in the government and the law immediately after he was 'wronged'? Was he threatened or coerced into making the announcement as a subject of a lawless state? Or had he been thoroughly brainwashed as a subject of an authoritarian state and its draconian laws? For even the most seasoned observers, it would be tempting to raise the question of Wang's sincerity.[5] However, much more will be gained in understanding law in contemporary China by attending to the structure of the question rather than answering it (see Mazzarella 2015).

In his article, 'Legal Orientalism' (2002), which traces Orientalist readings of Chinese law, Teemu Ruskola raises the following question: 'Is Chinese law really law?' On one level, this question addresses the analytical difficulty that is involved in translating local norms and practices for an audience with different implicit or explicit understandings, as highlighted in the Gluckman–Bohannan debate.[6] On another level, the question speaks to the rule-of-law/rule-of-men dichotomy that undergirds the study of the Chinese legal tradition by Western scholars (Ruskola 2003). Through this dichotomy, the West has come to understand not only the notion of law but also itself as the home of 'real' law. Plainly put, law and the rule of law serve to demarcate modern, liberal subjectivity, while they are considered to be underdeveloped or absent among 'nonmodern', 'illiberal' subjects.

The controversies in recent decades concerning the 'rule of law' in China are particularly illuminating. Ever since the Peoples' Republic of China (PRC), led by the Communist Party, adopted the rule of law (*fazhi*) as one of its main tenets, lively academic debates and political controversies have ensued both domestically and internationally. The international debates, in particular, centre around issues such as whether meaningful improvements have been made in the Chinese legal apparatus and legal consciousness, whether China is adopting a 'Western' version of democracy, and whether

China's version of the rule of law is indeed the rule of law and not something else (e.g. rule by law, rule of men, etc.).[7] Though they have given rise to many exciting observations and theories about law, these debates are also characterized by an almost unanimous hesitation to apply the label 'rule of law' to what China claims to be the rule of law. The hesitation—Is China's rule of law *really* the rule of law?—derives, largely, from the unquestionably positive connotations of the idea of the 'rule of law'. In liberal democracy, the rule of law is usually characterized by what it is not: it is not the rule of men, rule by law, nor is it non-liberal, non-democratic, authoritarian, or communist, for example (Mattei and Nader 2008; Tamanaha 2004: 1–6).[8] Hence, the claim of the government of the PRC and of the ruling Communist Party to be committed to the rule of law is bound to amplify anxieties over the definition of the very notion of the rule of law and to challenge the carefully constructed link between the rule of law and other concepts such as liberal democracy. Perhaps, the world's increasing fascination with China—especially with the terrifying dystopian future that it seems to project or, alternatively, with a return to the totalitarian past with a major technological upgrade[9]—is symptomatic of the potential loss of the rule of law and the existential consequences of the limited ability to imagine alternatives.

In this sense, the question 'Is China's rule of law really the rule of law' betrays an anxious hope. An affirmative answer would suggest that China might be moving in the 'right' direction. A negative answer would prove that China is ruled by something other than law, and that its law is not real law. Either way, what remains in full force is the assumption that there is a *real* law and a *real* rule of law that can be used as a yardstick for evaluation. The rule of law as a prescriptive norm is an ideological commitment, no less than the Chinese variant *fazhi* (rule of law), which also operates as an ideology (Erie 2007); and both remain as something inherently good and exempt from further work of definition or examination. As long as we are captivated by this ideological commitment, we are likely only to reinforce a pre-existing set of assumptions about law rather than learning something new. In other words, pursuing questions such as 'Is China's rule of law really the rule of law' or 'Is China's law really law'—the fundamental questions that arise when one reflects on Wang's message, quoted at the outset, wondering whether or not he may be sincere—are not necessarily very productive in gaining a better understanding of what law means and how it shapes people's lives in China.

What, then, are other ways to question law in China? Julie Y. Chu's call for attention to law's operative potential is instructive. In her article on infrastructural disrepair and disputes at a demolition zone in Fuzhou, China, she observes that distressed residents are attracted to law not because of its claimed function or instrumental logic but rather for its potential to 'lend itself to all sorts of unexpected tactics and effects' (Chu 2014: 362). She distances herself from prescriptive ideas of what law should be and, instead, directs attention to the structure of belief that upholds law's rule and shapes social lives. Moreover, this approach, which approximates what Paul W. Kahn (1999) calls the cultural study of law, enables her to move beyond law's formal spaces. In addition to observing law courts, she also examines sites at the 'margins' of legal practices, ranging widely from the degenerating built environment to the invisible substance of the atmosphere (Chu 2014: 365).

Opening up the scope of inquiry beyond the law's official spheres holds methodological significance, especially in places such as contemporary mainland China, where the conditions for social science research are far from ideal. Many scholars face considerable challenges in obtaining even basic statistical information, policy documents, and written legal decisions.[10] There are additional difficulties to surmount for anthropologists, since, in China, presenting oneself to local interlocutors can be taxing, and at times, problematic. Official spheres, such as government offices and law courts, can be exceptionally restrictive and even hostile to outsiders. In fact, many sites and communities remain inaccessible, unless the right connections, the correct documents, a nonproblematic social environment, and a number of other unforeseeable elements fall into place for the researcher.[11] This includes sites that are readily accessible in other countries, such as archives and court hearings. While these practical difficulties might be responsible for the dearth of anthropological work on China's law, they have also led anthropologists to innovate and explore peripheral and liminal sites. In examining marginal sites such as a legal mediation forum in a poor rural village of Southwest China (Pia 2016), and even seemingly extrajudicial sites such as dairy farms (Tracy 2016) and mosques (Erie 2016), scholars have generated productive conversations regarding the everyday workings and meaning-making of law in China, in which many assumptions about law's rule fall apart or are reinforced in unlikely ways.

The role of WeChat in Haijing's eviction crisis

The act of circulating another's utterances always creates interdiscursivities in that represented speech appeals to a supposed source while reconstituting the elements of the discourse at issue (Goodman et al. 2014; Irvine 1996; Nakassis 2012). When an utterance is repeated, it does not mean or do the exact same thing as the source utterance. Rather, many things are reconfigured, including but not limited to the context, the speaker, and the audience. In the remaining pages, I trace how Haijing tenants reproduce and circulate law-invoking expressions as they struggle with life-crises created by massive eviction. What notion of law emerges as people make public yet mundane sets of utterances on the WeChat messenger platform (see Richland 2013)? How do people in contemporary China 'voice' themselves as deserving citizens, given the ambiguity of legal boundaries? By following not only the content but also the participant structure and the production format that constitute the online and offline conversations of aggrieved Haijing tenants, I attempt to show how the circulation of messages and the mediating platform affect the emergent notion of 'law'.

I pay particular attention to messages sent over WeChat, a smartphone messenger app developed by the Shenzhen-based IT technology giant Tencent. Although WeChat is essentially a communication tool, it has turned into a platform that hosts more features than Facebook, Instagram, PayPal, and Uber put together. In contemporary China, WeChat is ubiquitous in everyday life. For example, one of my typical days in Shenzhen would look like this: paying for a breakfast bun from a street vendor through WeChat Pay; checking updates from friends, news media, or other independent writers through WeChat Moment and WeChat public account feeds; riding a metro or a bus by swiping a WeChat QR code; ordering a dish at a restaurant through WeChat (some restaurants do not even have hard copies of the menu); obtaining a new acquaintance's contacts (calling cards are thing of a past); calling a cab through WeChat; and having dinner or groceries delivered using mini-programs hosted by the WeChat platform. WeChat also hosts many other functions that are directly linked to government services, such as utility bill payments, ID verification services, residence registration with the police, making appointments in government offices, and tracking one's individual COVID-19 status through a QR code. It is not at all an exaggeration to say that, given the scope of its functions, WeChat is a central tool used by the residents of mainland China to manage many aspects of their everyday lives.

For the people of Haijing, WeChat chat groups played a pivotal role in sharing information and exploring options for action. While a 500-person group cannot fully cover everything going on in this especially dense and complicated neighbourhood, such groups were important in circulating information that is otherwise difficult to obtain, including real-time updates on the location of journalists visiting Haijing, incidents unreported by the mainstream media, as well as new policy announcements and quasi-legal advice. Furthermore, the information provided in these groups sometimes inspired a loose form of collective effort, such as people visiting government or developers' offices at a set time or upvoting online news about Haijing on popular news platforms.

Besides WeChat's wide usage in people's everyday lives, there are two other reasons why it was so prominent for Haijing tenants. On the one hand, WeChat has been the only viable platform collectively shared by the Haijing tenants, who were essentially strangers to one another. Unlike Haijing's 'original villager' landlords, who belong to one or more of the influential families in the area, and unlike those working for the developer, tenants tend to lack strong ties to one another or common organizational membership outside of their shared grievances. Although networks of limited scope predated the eviction crisis, categories such as parent-tenants or tenants without legal permanent residency in Shenzhen hardly ever materialized, given the diversity of the Haijing's tenant population in terms of regional affiliation, spoken dialects, age, income level, and duration of residence.

On the other hand, WeChat does not depart radically from the more 'traditional' role that the media play in China, insofar as it serves as the platform through which the mainstream media and government institutions continue to distribute public messaging, including legal knowledge and legal awareness campaigns. In the PRC, one of the traditional responsibilities of the media is to maintain communication between the Communist Party and society. As intermediaries, media outlets should help the Party's leadership to understand the mass public, while propagating the Party's guidance (*lingdao*) and educating the masses politically, morally, and aesthetically (Sun 2012; Bai 2014; Zhao 2000). Naturally, media coverage has operated as one of the most important channels for distributing legal news and information (see Gallagher 2006). The mainstream media, such as television and newspapers, continue to fulfil this traditional role by diversifying their outlets, including especially WeChat's public accounts and mini-programs.

Messages communicated via WeChat chat groups can be impersonal and public, although many of them have a personal and mundane character. However, both the size of the chat groups and the heavy censorship of the platform can compel participants to assume a form of public speech. Even those participants who were initially unaware of the censorship became more restrained after several active ones announced that they had received phone calls or 'invitations' from the authorities as a result of communication via WeChat. Furthermore, all interested parties—the tenants, the developer, the landlords, and even the authorities—recognized the volatility of the Haijing demolition issue and were obsessed with 'keeping stability' (*weiwen*), especially in light of the Hong Kong anti-extradition bill protest and the PRC's celebration of its seventieth anniversary.

Considering WeChat's strict censorship, it is extremely difficult, if not impossible and even futile, to evaluate messages without taking fully into account the anticipated and actual consequences of posting a WeChat message. Also, WeChat chat logs cannot be understood in isolation, but must be read alongside of events in social life off the platform and on the broader historical horizon. Therefore, I analyse these chat logs together with the data from eighteen months of fieldwork at Haijing, collected through interviews, participant observation, and media and policy research.

Haijing's parent-tenant chat groups

The WeChat messages on which I report in this chapter derive from groups that are believed to consist mostly of parent-tenants who have children attending elementary or middle schools in the Haijing area. In an effort to control the number of children enrolled, Shenzhen's already overcrowded schools select pupils based on a point system, effectively limiting their ability to choose, enter, or transfer schools freely. Even before the eviction crisis, many children in Haijing were already more vulnerable to the point system, due to their families' lack of legal permanent residency[12] and access to real estate in Shenzhen—two of the most important requirements in the point system. The sudden nature of the eviction exacerbated these families' difficulties by making it practically impossible for them to transfer their children to another school in Shenzhen, which would normally require at least a year of paperwork in advance. As a result, these families were faced with extremely difficult choices: either they had to quickly find a place to live in or near Haijing, just as this area was being slowly dismantled and becoming increasingly unaffordable; or they had to send their children back to their hometown for schooling, away from their parents working in the city. Many of them had only two months or so before the new school year began in September.

While some other Haijing WeChat chat groups enforced a much stricter policy of identity verification to prevent moles, these parent groups were quite loose in filtering members. Within the WeChat system's automatic cap at a maximum of 500 people per group, anyone could join as long as they obtained the group's QR code or a group member was willing to pull them in. Therefore, I believe the chat group membership was quite diverse, contrary to the initial claims of some participants. It was clear that some members did not even reside in the Haijing area and that the group included not just parents but also scholars and researchers (myself included), social activists, landlords, developer employees, journalists, college students, real estate agents, architects, and so on.

While it is difficult to gauge accurately the demographic profile of these groups, some informed guesses can be made based on the text and voice messages. For instance, the voice messages of group members exhibited various accents and varied levels of proficiency in standard Mandarin, indicating that they came from different parts of China. Also, their choice of words, sentence composition, and types of expression suggested that the group members had varied educational backgrounds. Despite these divergences, however, it is reasonable to assume that most of these tenant-parents lacked the financial, social, or political capital to resolve their issues on their own. As one tenant bitterly remarked in one of the group chats: 'Anyone who has the ability [to hire a lawyer and resolve the issue by himself or herself] would not have to rent a room here [in Haijing] (*Dajia sheiyou zhege nengli jiu buyong zai zheli zufangle*).'

Making demands that conform to law, reason, and rationality

When the first wave of eviction notices appeared on the doors and walls of low-rise apartment buildings in Haijing, many tenants quickly congregated in various WeChat groups to figure out what was going on. Some chat groups predated the eviction notification, while others were created when the news broke. Most of the notified tenants were given one to three months to move out, which was deemed to be an insufficient amount of time for families with school-aged children to resettle elsewhere. Unfortunately, many tenants had little to no leverage for further negotiations. Because the rental agreements of long-term tenants had expired long ago, many had been subject to the landlords' whims, which included repeated increases in rent and the arbitrary termination of leases. Witnessing neighbouring tenants' predicaments, even those who had not received eviction notices flocked to the chat groups, anxious about their own uncertain future. Soon enough, it became clear that some landlords, especially the so-called original villagers (*bendiren* or *cunmin*), had coordinated in advance to send out eviction notices on a set date. It also became an established fact that the private developer, Yinshan, was orchestrating the evictions discretely by providing the landlords with incentives for the quick removals of tenants. What remained unclear was the government's stance vis-à-vis the eviction process.

The desperate parent-tenants sought various means to secure educational opportunities for their children, without having to undergo family separation. Many possible actions were given consideration in these WeChat groups, which hinged more or less on seeking and shaping the government's responses. The participants would post media contacts that could be used to gain publicity, send out calls for visits to government offices, and draft a petition letter (*qingyuanshu*) with the tenants' signatures and thumbprints. Some even alluded to civil disobedience taking place in the vicinity, including strikes by delivery truck drivers in a nearby neighbourhood[13] and the anti-extradition law protest in Hong Kong. While some of these suggestions quickly gained the consent of parent-tenants and were swiftly put to action, other suggestions were met with either fervent discussion or awkward silence.

At the core of these desperate and contentious discussions lies the question of law and legality. It is by no means a coincidence that Wang, who is quoted at the beginning of this chapter, called for rational (*lixing*) demands (*suqiu*) that conform to law (*hefa*) and reason (*heli*).[14] Such expressions were repeatedly used by the group chat participants, Wang being one of the more vocal and consistent advocates of these principles. Other notable phrases that appeared in the group chat include 'defence of rights' (*weiquan*), 'a society ruled with law' (*fazhi shehui*)[15], and 'legal rights' (*hefa quanyi*). All of these terms invoke legality and the notion of legal rights, reflecting tenants' strategies in framing their grievances (see also Gallagher 2006; O'Brien and Li 2006). As one tenant keenly observed, the group chat participants 'fear[ed] wolves ahead and tigers behind, always worried about touching the edge of the law (*falüde bianxian*).'

When and how were these law-invoking expressions mobilized? On one hand, the participants used such expressions as a way of reminding each other of the group's cause, which, in effect, refined and crystalized the group's identity as law-abiding and selfless parents. For example, when a mother announced that she had been approached by men claiming to be government authorities, another parent in the group chat sent out the following message: 'We are all law-abiding citizens (*shoufa de gongmin*). What is there to fear?' This and similar messages demonstrate the parents' efforts to use legality as a justificatory language. One can observe similar efforts in the messages sent by those others who had attended one of the so-called tea drinking (*hecha*) sessions with the police,[16] who almost always wrote of the need to make reasonable, rational, and legal demands. While these messages caused an unsettling stir among the group chat participants, it is important to note that they were often accompanied by justificatory expressions that endorsed the parent-tenants' demands, rather than discouraging their efforts altogether.

On the other hand, such invocations of the law were used either to support or refute specific ideas for concrete action. In particular, they appeared prominently when discussions skirted around ideas deemed more extreme, such as hanging slogans in streets and on buildings, organizing rallies on government grounds, or blocking or marching up a busy boulevard. At times, invocations of the law served as calming reminders during heated debates. For example, one of the most emotionally charged conversations took place right after a local resident attempted suicide in broad daylight on Haijing's main street. It was rumoured that the man had received an eviction notice shortly after investing his family fortune to open a store. After viewing on WeChat a series of real-time videos and photos of the man standing on the edge of a rooftop, several devastated parents remarked bitterly that they should all follow suit and leap from the upper floors of buildings in Haijing, one by one, with their children. Nothing less would finally get the government's attention, they declared. Their expressions of frustration and despair evoked responses from others, who desperately called for rationality. Some even tried to curb the conversation by calling for more practical solutions along legal lines. However, these invocations of the law were not always helpful in calming the already agitated discussions, especially when some chat participants questioned the boundaries of law, asking which actions could be considered legal or illegal. Some of them even touched on the question of whether their actions must stay within the supposed legal boundaries.

Whether they serve to support specific actions or the group's more general cause, law-invoking expressions in WeChat groups reinforce the idea that there exists a widely accepted social consensus that demands must stay within the bounds of reason, rationality, and the law. Unsurprisingly, the underlying language and logic of WeChat messages align with the official discourse of the Chinese government. For example, in one of the meetings held in October 2014, during the Fourth Plenary Session of the 18th Central Committee of the Communist Party of China, when the rule of law became a central theme for the first time in the history of the PRC, Xi Jinping called on each government bureau to take greater responsibility in mobilizing various means to 'resolve the reasonable and legitimate demands of the masses' (*ba qunzhong heli hefa de liyi suqiu jiejue hao*).[17] A more vivid example of this alignment might be seen in the circulation of a comment by a Shenzhen municipal party committee official in Haijing's chat groups. Soon after the crisis broke out, some parents managed to corner an official in front of a municipal government building, who was known only by his surname. He was said to have expressed his admiration for how rational the parents were and how reasonable their demands were, and to have promised that the government would swiftly follow up on the issue. For a brief moment, the parents were elated, as they saw a rare glimmer of hope; and they circulated widely this confirmation that their demands were reasonable, rational, and legal. One mother even spoke out in the chat group, saying that 'as long as we have reasonable demands (*zhiyaoshi helide yaoqiu*), the city will resolve problems for the people (*laobaixing*)!' In sum, the law-invoking expression implied that only the government (and ironically, not necessarily the law) could fundamentally resolve the schooling issue, and that the resolutions would be granted only to those who make reasonable, rational, and legal demands.

Determining the Bounds of the Law

It was the chat group members' preoccupation with reason, rationality, and law that led them to identify themselves as concerned parents. At an early stage in the formation of these groups, members had implicitly agreed to focus on problems with children's schooling, ruling out consideration of other issues in their exchange of concerns and agendas for the time being. By focusing on schooling, group members were able effectively to frame themselves as selfless parents who were ready to give up everything to educate their children (sometimes dubbed 'the future of the motherland'). This approach was further strengthened by the sheer number of the children involved: the larger the number of children, the more the parents were able to represent their intentions as selfless and urgent. They reframed their legal and bureaucratic battle as a moral one, in which the contestants sought to ensure that their struggle was represented as being in conformity with legally ratified forms of reasoning. In China, where education is deemed to be an absolutely crucial way of giving children a better life, comments such as this one, made by one of the parents in the chat group, have a moral force that it is difficult for anyone to challenge: 'I don't understand law, but if the [eviction] matter affects my children's school education, I would go [take actions] even if I get imprisoned for it'.

By taking a relatively clear stance, which affected how they were identified as a group, the parents were somewhat successful in making their demand that the government intervene to resolve the schooling issue appear to conform to reason. Through this strategy, they have even managed to garner attention from the mainstream media, which is not an easy achievement in the Chinese media environment, the representatives of which tend to turn a blind eye to sensitive issues such as demolition and eviction. However, conforming to law was a different issue. Unlike rationality and reason,[18] which are generally assumed to be shared by all members of the society, legality appeared as a less accessible idea with unsettled and ambiguous boundaries (Erie 2012; O'Brien and Li 2006). Regardless of people condemning police actions (as 'E' does in the dialogue quoted above), the police continued the problematic practice of 'inviting' chat group members to the police station. Although many people called for lawful demands, relatively few were able to cite particular laws, legal documents, or policy documents in support of such demands. Some people occasionally forwarded legal case studies or policy documents to the chat group, but these did not help much in clarifying the legal ambiguity for the parent-tenants. Besides, most of the supplementary data in circulation were far from being authoritative or credible, being hearsay from other chat groups or second-hand materials from the web. Some of the materials that were forwarded through WeChat contained information that was difficult to unpack and verify, and some of it seemed to be contradictory. For example, there were conflicting accounts regarding the correct procedure for petitioning (*xinfang*), which is already notorious for the seemingly intentional ambiguity of its rules and regulations (see Minzner 2006). During his detention at the police station, Wang sent a message to multiple groups stating that petitioning at the Petition Bureau in Guangzhou, the capital city of Guangdong province, might be considered to be breaking the law (*shexian weifa*). It took at least five days for someone else to point out that petitioning at Guangzhou is, in fact, legal. The irony was that the latter person obtained this piece of information from another police officer when he himself was 'invited' to the police station for his WeChat activity.

In addition to the lack of reliable legal knowledge and advice, there was an overall shortage of hard data that the parent-tenants could cite to produce bureaucratically and legally more legible claims. During the crisis, several activists, artists, and intellectuals worked with parents and journalists to secure and produce more reliable data that they could use to publicize their concerns. They requested that the government release information, circulated several online surveys, and collected individual accounts from Haijing tenants. However, due to the difficulty of gathering information from dispersed sources, the sensitivity of the Haijing issue, and ever-strengthening censorship, they found it very challenging to obtain in a timely manner even a concrete figure of the number of tenants residing in the area, let alone the number of impacted pupils. In the end, many of the efforts to publicize the tenants' cause could rely only on informed guesswork, insufficient survey data, and figures circulating among the WeChat groups.

This lack of factual tokens of a bureaucratic and supposedly scientific type (Richland 2013: 220) carried potential legal consequences. For example, an artist was investigated for 'misguiding the public' (*wudao minzhong*) with works of art, which were intended to raise public awareness by visualizing various data that the artist himself had collected in collaboration with the tenants, researchers, and other activists. He was said to have been convicted for using the following phrase in one of his images: 'Schooling issue for 4,000[19] of Haijing's school children remains unresolved'. There were two different stories explaining why this slogan was problematic. One explanation was that the government had indeed made sufficient efforts and had already resolved the Haijing issue—and that, therefore, the slogan was incorrect. The second explanation was that the artist erred in his estimation that 4,000 school children were affected, when there were really only 3,615—a figure that Shenzhen's education bureau released only much later. Either way, the artist was suspected of committing the infamous crime of 'picking quarrels and provoking troubles' (*xunxin zishi*). This example shows how the act of producing evidence runs the danger of turning into another tug-of-war in working out the ambiguous boundaries of the law.

Clearly, Haijing tenants were drawn to law-invoking talk. Such talk was largely addressed to both the officials and the broader public that engage with the ambiguous space at the law's margins. Although constrained by a regime that does not permit the emergence of a 'public sphere' or 'civil society' in the Habermasian sense, this marginal domain can reinforce or threaten official ways (Erie 2016).[20] By taking advantage of the law's silence, the tenants were leveraging this shadow sphere to influence the official sphere. As the authorities sometimes transgressed the law's boundaries, the tenants deployed phrases such as 'law-abiding citizens', 'legal rights', and 'legal demands' to provide some justification for the expression of their concerns. By leveraging opinions in this less than official space, the tenants sought some degree of legal protection from the officials, who were likewise struggling to navigate the uncertain margins of the law without breaching the law outright.

Law and the unit of action

Despite all their invocations of the law, no parents ever took legal actions against the developer or the government regarding the schooling problem in Haijing, as far as I am aware. Why were they so hesitant to initiate legal action? During the crisis, some members of tenants' chat groups insisted on seeking legal advice. Eventually, one of the groups managed to invite at least two lawyers who specialized in demolition issues, while some activists privately consulted other lawyers to gain a better legal understanding of the situation. Despite the initial demand, many group chat members reacted sceptically to the lawyers, all of whom recommended hiring lawyers or initiating lawsuits. Among the tenants, there was a general concern over the cost of hiring a lawyer. Because of the sudden eviction, many tenants were out of both money and time. Unlike many other legal disputes that were taking place in Haijing—including conflicts over compensation, litigation over forced demolition, and lawsuits over alleged criminal offences of physical violence—the children's schooling issue was unique in that securing a timely solution was the highest priority. Many of those parents who had already received eviction notices were given less than two months to vacate their apartment. Finally, some people exhibited a strong distrust of legal professionals, claiming that they are inclined to side with the privileged and the powerful, for example, with big developers or the government.

Another fundamental problem for group members concerned what might be called the unit of action. Taking legal actions would require tenants either to select representatives or to resolve their cases individually. Whether or not to choose representatives had been one of the burning issues since the inception of the parent-tenant chat groups. People experienced a pressing need to come together in solidarity in order to gain popular support and to empower their actions. At the same time, they were reluctant to choose representatives or to organize collectively, because doing so would surely increase the chance of police intervention under the guise of 'keeping stability' (*weiwen*).

Torn between the need for solidarity and the legal risk that it posed, people eventually came up with the tactic of including the phrase 'voluntary' (*ziyuan zifa*) in their WeChat messages, thus emphasizing that their actions were individually motivated. By implying, in this way, that the messages were not a 'call for collective action', chat group members hoped to avoid being convicted for instigating others and being charged with 'picking quarrels and provoking troubles'. Similarly, chains of copied comments, such as 'You have been wronged! You have suffered!', as in the exchange of messages quoted at the outset of this article, were a way of expressing solidarity but in the form of personal opinion. Under such circumstances, initiating legal action would have forced an immediate choice between collective or individual action. Especially with the lawyers characterizing the tenants' eviction issues as matters of individual rental contracts, tenants in WeChat groups knew well that taking legal action would hurt the shaky position that they had managed to carve out by claiming the morally formidable identity of caring and concerned parents. In short, resorting to official legal means would have widened the differences between individuals at a time when people felt the greatest need for solidarity.

Law's violence

Overall, the parent-tenants managed to establish their group identity and their demands on moral grounds, yet their morally articulated identity did not hold up well when transposed into bureaucratic and legal language. This is probably why these parent-tenants resorted to petitions based on moral claims rather than legal processes requiring the presentation of factual evidence (Gallagher 2006: 796–9). Unfortunately, their petitions were met with replies from multiple levels of the Petition Bureau, which channelled the aggrieved individuals to other government offices and formal legal institutions, a procedure comparable to the frequent diversion of petitions to the judicial system in China (Minzner 2006; Gallagher 2006). Although tenants were hesitant to file lawsuits, their strategic attachment to the identity of the law-abiding citizen is quite remarkable. The struggle of the tenants, who were simultaneously hopeful because of and disillusioned by the law (see Lee 2007), demonstrates how 'law' might operate in Chinese society. Also, it reveals that the 'rule of law' is not merely an empty slogan and that it can significantly condition people's identities and behaviours.

However, 'law' in China is not an occasion for romanticization either. As this chapter was being written, the Haijing redevelopment case, including the problem of relocating school-aged children, was still an ongoing controversy; but very little had been done to resolve or mitigate the problems. As a result, many families had already left the Haijing area, some even abandoning the city of Shenzhen. Numerous families were torn apart, with parents working in the city, while their children attended schools in their hometown; and others continued to rove around Haijing in search for rooms that had not yet been signed off to the developer. With Haijing's streets growing quieter, the parent-tenant chat groups were gradually becoming silent as well.

Haijing's eviction crisis exposes the law's violent potential. The tenants' various law-invoking strategies were deeply constrained by the state's monopoly over legitimate violence. Moreover, legal misconduct and breaches were not the only problem that these tenants had with the law. Rather, at the margins of law, they were struggling with the law's total and violent force in shaping their identities and their field of possibilities—their choice between collective and individual action, the scope of their demands, and the timeline to which they were subject. This law's violence (Erie 2012: 38) finds expression not only in legal pronouncements or actions in courts or police stations, but also in unspoken potentialities and ambiguities at its edges.

Acknowledgements

I thank Julie Y. Chu, Janet Connor, Moodjalin Sudcharoen, Kelsey Robbins, and Perry Wong for raising critical questions to different renditions of this chapter's materials. I am especially grateful to Mark Goodale, one of the editors of this volume, who offered useful suggestions for this chapter and showed great patience and understanding when the eviction crisis overshadowed the writing process. I owe many thanks to Katherine Yost for refining the earlier drafts into a presentable document, and to John Eidson and Brian Donahoe for their very thoughtful comments and edits. I am solely responsible for any errors, mistakes, and vagueness of expression in this chapter. Part of this material is based upon dissertation research supported by the US National Science Foundation. Any opinions, findings, or conclusions expressed here are those of the author and do not necessarily reflect the views of the National Science Foundation.

Notes

1. All names, including place names below the municipal level, are pseudonyms.
2. An urban village (*chengzhongcun*) is an area where a traditional rural village has been incorporated into the city by rapid urbanization. It is usually distinguished from the rest of the city by its distinctive land usage rights, infrastructural design, and cheap rent.
3. Even though news about the Hong Kong protest was heavily censored in mainland China in the initial months of the protest, most of the people I met in Haijing were well aware of the news due to its proximity and the high amount of daily traffic to Hong Kong. Also, many villagers from Haijing and other villages in Shenzhen migrated to Hong Kong in the latter half of the twentieth century, and they have continued to maintain ties to their villages of origin.
4. The official translation of the bureau's name is Public Complaints and Proposals Administration (which was previously called the Letters and Calls Bureau). In this chapter, I use the term Petition Bureau to spare readers an additional acronym.
5. This kind of discourse is not unfamiliar in Chinese society. E.g. when the Chinese Communist Party began pushing its legal reform in the 1980s, it identified the 'rule of man' and 'lawlessness' as key issues to be overcome (Feng 2016: 46).
6. The Gluckman–Bohannan debate centres on the question of defining and explaining law. In *The Judicial Process among the Barotse of Northern Rhodesia* (1955), Max Gluckman distinguishes between a folk category of law and an analytical concept of law. In contrast, Paul Bohannan, in *Justice and Judgement among the Tiv* (1957), emphasizes the value of understanding the native conception of laws, problematizing the analytical concept of law as an imposition of Western legal categories. While the Gluckman–Bohannan debate is one of the most important debates in the history of the anthropology of law, it also touches upon the more fundamental issue of anthropology's knowledge practices (Erie 2016: 17–18). See Nader (1969) and Moore (1969, 2002) for a fuller account on how the debate unfolded. See also Goodale (2017, esp. 17–18, 33–4) on the debate's aftermaths, contributions, and implications in understanding the anthropology of law in the post-Cold War era.
7. Since the 1980s, the PRC has made various efforts to establish the rule of law, involving revisions of the constitution, institutional reforms, nation-wide legal awareness campaigns, and so on. Under Xi Jinping's rule, China even coined the term 'socialist rule of law system with Chinese characteristics' (*zhongguo tese shehuizhuyi fazhi tixi*) as the foundation of

all future legal reforms, and the rule of law (*fazhi*) has turned into one of the twelve 'Core Socialist Values' (*shehuizhuyi hexin jiazhiguan*) that can be seen all over the walls and streets of China as of 2019. While many scholars have commented on the improvement in the Chinese legal apparatus and legal consciousness, others have demonstrated that the rule of law under China's party-state government continues the Marxist-Leninist tradition that prioritizes the dictatorship of the proletariat guided by the Communist Party, under which law is only recognized by its functional value (Feng 2016; Partlett and Ip 2016; Peerenboom 2002). See Garrick and Bennet (2016) for a fuller discussion on the socialist rule of law under the Xi Jinping regime.

8. See also Newendorp 2011 and Ng 2009 on how the rule of law has been regarded as a symbol of freedom in Hong Kong, which distinguishes itself from mainland China.
9. Comparisons of the PRC's government with Nazi Germany have become increasingly popular, as witnessed in protests against the 2019 Hong Kong extradition bill and in controversies surrounding the Xinjiang Uyghur detention camps. Also, international media frequently refer to George Orwell's novel *1984* when discussing China's surveillance practices.
10. In terms of public data availability, some improvements have been observed in past years. As of 2019, some written judgments can be accessed via China Judgements Online (<http://wenshu.court.gov.cn/>), and some court proceedings can be viewed online via China Open Trial Web (<http://tingshen.court.gov.cn/>). In addition to an array of government websites and state media reports, the Peking University Center for Legal Information (<https://www.pkulaw.cn>) is a good source of legal documents, including laws, regulations, and judicial cases.
11. In fact, several scholars have written about their fortune or misfortune in conducting ethnographic research on China's law and legal practices. See e.g. the introductory chapters in Erie (2016), Steinmüller (2013), and Pils (2015).
12. The household registration system (also known as the *hukou* system) is characteristically socialist and remains to date the bulwark of China's population governance and documentation regime. This system binds every legitimate individual to a region and a unit, which are the bases for the distribution of economic, social, and political resources (Chan and Zhang 1999: 818–19). Chinese megalopolises such as Beijing, Shanghai, and Guangzhou restrict people from other places from obtaining a local household (permanent residence) in order to cap the size of urban population.
13. The strike was unreported by the mainstream Mainland Chinese media.
14. The literal translations for the Chinese words *hefa* (合法) and *heli* (合理) are 'conforming to law' and 'conforming to reason', respectively. Some chat participants used the word *heqing* (合情), which also can be translated as conforming to reason. See Wong (2009) for some discussion on the relationship between *qing*, *li*, and *fa*.
15. The transliterated term *fazhi* can denote two different words: 法治 and 法制. They are pronounced identically in Mandarin Chinese and have often been a source of confusion for non-native speakers. The terms are conventionally translated as 'rule of law' (法治) and 'rule by law' (法制), respectively, although the latter could also mean 'legal system'. The former term is included as one of the 'Socialist Core Values' (see footnote 7). Strangely, several participants used the latter term to speak of *fazhi* society. While it is unclear whether the word choice was intentional, the speakers were emphasizing how *fazhi* society is supposed to provide them with some sort of protection from e.g. greedy developers or corrupt officials. Considering the context as well as the negative connotation of the term 'rule by

law' especially when describing China, I have translated the expression *fazhi shehui* as a society ruled with law.

16. Through online and offline channels, I was able to confirm that some people really had paid visits to the local police station, some more than once.
17. PRC Government, 'Youxiao bawo he jiejue qunzhong de heli hefa suqiu' (Effectively grasp and resolve the reasonable and lawful demands of the mass) <http://www.gov.cn/xinwen/2016-05/02/content_5069745.htm> accessed 6 December 2019.
18. The notion 'reason' (*li* or *qingli*) carries strong ethical connotation: it can be understood only by considering human nature, the character of things, worldly wisdom, and the case at hand in relationship to the broader patterns of the sociohistorical environment. See Pia (2016: fn. 2) on the Chinese understanding of reason.
19. Arbitrary numbers have been provided in order to maximize anonymity.
20. Matthew S. Erie (2016) calls it *minjian*, a popular Chinese term that literally means 'between people' and often designates an unofficial or folk sphere.

References

Bai, Ruoyun. 2014. *Staging Corruption: Chinese Television and Politics*. Vancouver: University of British Columbia Press.

Chan, Kam Wing and Li Zhang. 1999. 'The Hukou System and Rural-Urban Migration in China: Processes and Changes'. *The China Quarterly* 160: 818–55.

Chu, J. Y. 2014. 'When Infrastructures Attack: The Workings of Disrepair in China'. *American Ethnologist* 41(2): 351–67.

Davis, M. C. 2020. *Making Hong Kong China: The Rollback of Human Rights and the Rule of Law*. Ann Arbor: Association for Asian Studies.

Erie, M. S. 2007. 'China's (Post-)Socialist Property Rights Regime: Assessing the Impact of the Property Law on Illegal Land Takings'. *Hong Kong Law Journal* 37(2): 919–50.

Erie, M. S. 2012. 'Property Rights, Legal Consciousness and the New Media in China: The Hard Case of the 'Toughest Nail-House in History'. *China Information* 26(1): 35–59.

Erie, M. S. 2016. *China and Islam: The Prophet, the Party, and Law*. New York: Cambridge University Press.

Feng, Chongyi. 2016. 'China's Socialist Rule of Law: A Critical Appraisal of the Relationship between the Communist Party and Comprehensive Law Reform'. In J. Garrick and Y. C. Bennett, eds. *China's Socialist Rule of Law Reforms Under Xi Jinping*, 45–58. New York: Routledge.

Gallagher, M. E. 2006. 'Mobilizing the Law in China: 'Informed Disenchantment' and the Development of Legal Consciousness'. *Law & Society* 40(4): 783–816.

Garrick, J. and Y. C. Bennett, eds. 2016. *China's Socialist Rule of Law Reforms Under Xi Jinping*. New York: Routledge.

Goodale, M. 2017. *Anthropology and Law: A Critical Introduction*. New York: New York University Press.

Goodman, J. E., M. Tomlinson, and J. B. Richland. 2014. 'Citational Practices: Knowledge, Personhood, and Subjectivity'. *Annual Review of Anthropology* 43: 449–63.

Irvine, J. T. 1996. 'Shadow Conversations: The Indeterminacy of Participant Roles'. In M. Silverstein and G. Urban, eds. *Natural Histories of Discourse*, 131–59. Chicago: The University of Chicago Press.

Kahn, P. W. 1999. *The Cultural Study of Law: Reconstructing Legal Scholarship*. Chicago: The University of Chicago Press.

Lee, Ching Kwan. 2007. *Against the Law: Labor Protests in China's Rustbelt and Sunbelt*. Berkeley: University of California Press.

Mattei, U. and L. Nader. 2008. *Plunder*. Malden, MA: Blackwell Publishing.

Mazzarella, W. 2015. 'Totalitarian Tears: Does the Crowd Really Mean It?'. *Cultural Anthropology* 30(1): 91–112.

Minzner, C. F. 2006. 'Xinfang: An Alternative to Formal Chinese Legal Institutions'. *Stanford Journal of International Law* 42(1): 103–80.

Moore, S. Falk. 1997 [1969]. 'Introduction'. In Laura Nader, ed. *Law in Culture and Society*, 337–48. Berkeley: University of California Press.

Moore, S. Falk. 2002. 'Certainties Undone: Fifty Turbulent Years of Legal Anthropology, 1949–1999'. *Journal of Royal Anthropological Institute* 7: 85–116.

Nader, L. 1997 [1969]. 'Introduction'. In Laura Nader, ed. *Law in Culture and Society*, 1–10. Berkeley: University of California Press.

Nakassis, C. V. 2012. 'Brand, Citationality, Performativity'. *American Anthropologist* 114(4): 624–38.

Newendorp, N. 2011. 'Contesting "Law and Order": Immigrants' Encounters with "Rule of Law" in Postcolonial Hong Kong'. *Political and Legal Anthropology Review* 34(1): 95–111.

Ng, Kwai Hang. 2009. *The Common Law in Two Voices: Language, Law, and the Postcolonial Dilemma in Hong Kong*. Stanford, CA: Stanford University Press.

O'Brien, K. J. and Lianjiang Li. 2006. *Rightful Resistance in Rural China*. Cambridge: Cambridge University Press.

Partlett, W. and E. C. Ip. 2016. 'Is Socialist Law Really Dead?' *New York University Journal of International Law and Politics* 48: 463–511.

Peerenboom, R. 2002. *China's Long March toward Rule of Law*. Cambridge: Cambridge University Press.

Pia, A. E. 2016. '"We Follow Reason, Not the Law": Disavowing the Law in Rural China'. *Political and Legal Anthropology Review* 39(2): 276–93.

Pils, E. 2015. *China's Human Rights Lawyers: Advocacy and Resistance*. New York: Routledge.

Richland, J. B. 2013. 'Jurisdiction: Grounding Law in Language'. *Annual Review of Anthropology* 42: 209–26.

Ruskola, T. 2002. 'Legal Orientalism'. *Michigan Law Review* 101(1): 179–234.

Ruskola, T. 2003. 'Law without Law, or is Chinese Law an Oxymoron'. *William & Mary Bill of Rights Journal* 11(2): 655–70.

Steinmüller, H. 2013. *Communities of Complicity: Everyday Ethics in Rural China*. New York: Berghahn.

Sun, Wanning. 2012. 'Localizing Chinese Media: A Geographical Turn in Media and Communication Research' In W. Sun and J. Chio, eds. *Mapping Media in China: Region, Province, Locality*, 13–27. New York: Routledge.

Tamanaha, B. Z. 2004. *On the Rule of Law: History, Politics, Theory*. New York: Cambridge University Press.

Tracy, M. 2016. 'Multimodality, Transparency, and Food Safety in China'. *Political and Legal Anthropology Review* 39 (S1): 34–53.

Wong, Kam C. 2009. 'Chinese Jurisprudence and Hong Kong Law'. *China Report* 45(3): 213–39.

Zhao, Yuezhi. 2000. 'Watchdogs on Party Leashes? Contexts and Implications of Investigative Journalism in Post-Deng China'. *Journalism Studies* 1(4): 577–97.

CHAPTER 10

ISLAM, LAW, AND THE STATE

DOMINIK M. MÜLLER

Introduction

ANTHROPOLOGICAL enquiries into the intersections between Islam, law, and the state investigate social practices in institutional constellations that are framed with reference to Islamic normativities and embedded in the discursive arenas of nation-states. Although the anthropology of Islam has produced a multitudinous body of literature, ethnographically grounded work that takes Islam, law, *and* the state as central analytical categories remains comparably limited. In acknowledgement of key interventions that have shaped the field but are *not* centrally concerned with law and state power, this chapter limits itself to a selection among the fewer works that are. I hasten to add that even this field is extensive and I cannot provide a comprehensive overview, neither regionally nor of the multifold approaches that have been taken.

My chapter will first introduce some historical background to the development of legal anthropological explorations of the intersections of Islam, law, and the state in the twentieth century, focusing particularly on secular (post)colonial reconfigurations of the sharia (*sharīʿah*) and the genres of Islamic courtroom ethnography and disputing in contexts of legal pluralism studies. I will then turn to more recent streams of enquiry to demonstrate how ethnographers have been following the ways in which various actors ascribe social meanings to sharia-framed normativities and Islamic law in domains that would not necessarily fall within secular categorizations of 'law' and 'legal' spheres. These new directions of scholarship, which address themes such as corporate sharia and Islam-related marketization, the politics of *halal*, and the societal workings of government-sponsored attempts to bureaucratize and state-ify Islam and Muslimness, among others, provide a wide range of possibilities for timely and important future sociolegal research.

Sharia law as secular distortion and postcolonial emancipation

Christiaan Snouck Hurgronje (1857–1936), a colonial anthropologist conducting research in the government's service in the Dutch East Indies and the Arab world, considered Islamic law a threat to colonial rule and an 'example of how religion can go wrong' (Bowen 1996: 12). He recommended Dutch authorities not to interfere in Islamic ethics, ritual, and beliefs—which he considered part of the sharia but separate from its politically relevant dimensions, following European secular distinctions—and to hinder any space for positivized Islamic law, except family law, or related aspirations. Except in private ritual spheres, he suggested that Muslim subjects should assimilate to ensure peaceful co-existence (Büskens 2016: 32) and that Muslim understandings of Islam should follow secular logics. In this, he saw no contradiction with a proclaimed 'centuries-old [Dutch] guarantee of complete religious liberty for our Mohammedans' (cited in ibid.). He viewed codified Islamic law and related reasoning (*fiqh*) as a long-standing intellectual art that had rarely ever been applied (except in matters of personal obligations, ritual, inheritance, property, and endowments), partly due to its inherent inapplicability (Hurgronje 1957; see Alatas 2018 for a detailed discussion). A modern Islam, in his understanding, should be separate from politics (Bowen 1996: 12)—though, as later generations of anthropologists would hold, any insistence on a 'de-political', 'secular Islam' is itself political and generates a political Islam of its own.

In the early postcolonial anthropology of Islam, predominantly Western and conducted by non-Muslim men, power relations, the state, positive law, and politics of Islamic legal reasoning still received much less attention than from the 1990s onwards, and especially in the post-9/11 era. This shift in scholarly interests coincided with the transnationally growing popularity of decidedly legalistic conceptions of the sharia (i.e. the all-encompassing source of Islamic normativity and ethics as 'the path to be followed' and reflected upon[1]) among Muslim actors and institutions. The 'fetishization' of law and legalism, which is not exclusive to Islam (see Comaroff and Comaroff 2006) but finds particular forms of expression therein, has deeply invaded contemporary Islamic discourse, just as many researchers of Islam increasingly exhibit narrowly legalistic obsessions with political Islam and the sharia. As this phenomenon has deep roots in colonial legacies (compare Büskens and Dupret 2011 on the 'invention of Islamic law' and Wood 2016), it is not new per se, but has intensified in unprecedented ways in recent years.

However, this scholarly obsession with sharia law has not always been so predominant. Clifford Geertz, for example, in documenting religious reformism in the country with the world's largest Muslim population, Indonesia, alongside social changes pushed forward by the politically oriented Islamic *santri* movement (for an early account, see Geertz 1957), showed little interest in 'how law might have featured in the respective trajectories of religious [and social] change' (Ramstedt 2015: 44; cf. Geertz's unrelated elaborations on Indic, Islamic, and Malayo-Polynesian law, Geertz 1983: 167–234). He also did not explore the *santri*'s legal and political reasoning about the sharia vis-à-vis Indonesia's wider postcolonial state-building, in which multifold claims to Islamic truth and (in)correct ways of being Muslim have always competed, with far-reaching consequences.

Talal Asad, some of whose most influential writings centrally build upon attacking positions he ascribes to Geertz (Asad 1983, 1986), addresses Islam vis-à-vis law and the state primarily to elucidate how Protestant-shaped European thinking about the category of religion, conceptual dichotomies such as secular/religious, ethics/law, morality/law (cf. Asad 2005: 17), religion/politics, and private/public, epistemologies of 'functional differentiation', and the notion of law as *positive* 'modernized law' (Asad 2005: 13) have led anthropologists to obscure Islam (on the 'positivization' of Islamic law, see also Dupret 2007). This logic implies that most contemporary 'Islamists' (a problematic category—see the nuanced debate in Martin and Barzegar 2010) who consider themselves opponents of secularism operate on inevitably secular grounds (an argument made e.g. by Mohamad 2010).

Various scholars have analysed the transformative power that the modern nation-state, colonial epistemic regimes, and the 'positivization of law' (Asad 2005: 19) have exerted on conceptions of the sharia and Islamic authority (Agrama 2015; Hallaq 2013; Messick 1996, 1998; Peters 2002). Scholarly narratives according to which contemporary claims to the sharia have turned it into a secularistic misrepresentation of a supposedly 'authentic' pre-colonial tradition (e.g. as 'Anglo-Muslim law') are forcefully argued but difficult to reconcile with the perspectives of Muslim actors who see their own 'positivistic' treatments of the sharia as part of their emancipatory quest for de-secularizing postcolonial normative orders. These actors do not consider approaching the sharia *as law* to be a form of secular corruption, but rather a way of realizing the 'path to be followed' *through law* (cf. Dupret 2007).

Another risk is to essentialize an idealized pre-colonial past and ascribe omnipotence to colonialism, resulting in a too neatly functioning catch-all explanation.

Muslim futurities currently articulated by mainstream Islamic institutions and movements across the world are not often concerned with deconstructing positivistic logics in Islamic legal reasoning. The project of de-colonizing scholarship on Islam *in this sense* remains popular mostly among university scholars based at American and European elite institutions, although some postcolonial Muslim voices, for example the intellectually avant-garde leadership of the Islamic Religious Council of Singapore (MUIS) and Muslim academics emphasizing the '[ethical] goals of the Sharia' (*maqasid as-Sharia*) in order to overcome narrow legalism, share related critiques. Undoubtedly, the 'secularization of the Sharia' (Mohamad 2010) and the 'positivization of [Islamic] ethics and of social knowledge' (Asad 2005: 19) have deeply structured contemporary Muslim discourses.

While some anthropologists, including Asad, have aimed to conceptualize Islam in and of itself and explain what Islam *is*, others have merely taken what particular Muslim actors say Islam is *for them* as their yardstick. The pitfalls of either position have been extensively discussed. They range from an (unintended) reification of dominant actors' exclusionary politics of orthodoxy, resulting in the excommunication of marginal groups and denial of their self-determination as Muslims (a critique against Asad's concept of a 'discursive tradition'), to neo-colonially belittling the discursive tradition's autonomy to include and exclude whatever or whomever it deems appropriate in light of its 'past, present and future' (Asad 1986: 14–15).

Asad and his disciples have, at least in North America, for decades dominated scholarly debates over what an 'anthropology of Islam' should (not) be. The Asadian stream, building upon his theoretical, historiographic, and textual work and extensive critiques of other anthropologists, has been ethnographically[2] put into practice and deepened by an entire generation of disciples inspired by him, who are now training their own disciples. However, their approaches have dealt with themes such as ethics, personhood, the body, self-cultivation, gender, preaching, missionary work (*da'wa*), media, minorities, and above all secularism rather than ethnographically centring on the state, Islamic legal politics and institutions (cf. Agrama 2012, 2015; Bernard-Maugiron 2003; Botiveau 1993; Messick 1996, 1998; Starrett 1998), or the nexus between the two. As Salomon (2016: 6), himself a former student of the late Saba Mahmood (one of Asad's most influential disciples), sums it up in a pathbreaking ethnography of the 'Islamic State' of Sudan, 'the state' has 'not been a particularly popular topic of enquiry' in the anthropology of Islam for a long time.

The following sections will present some ethnographically generated anthropological works that examine Islam, law, and the state in more classical fields such as dispute resolution and courtroom ethnography. In most cases it is either Islam and law, or Islam and the state, but to varying extents they also point to interconnections between all three.

Islamic courts and legal disputing

State institutions, including bureaucracies and courts, present an obvious choice to observe the social workings of Islam, law, and the state. The tradition of courtroom ethnography includes many contributions examining Islamic law in action.

Lawrence Rosen, a legal anthropologist trained by Clifford Geertz, had to change initial plans for fieldwork in Indonesia following a coup and anti-communist mass killings in 1965, and instead headed to North Africa, where he observed Islamic court proceedings in Morocco for many years, most prominently in the town of Sefrou, resulting in anthropological reflections on Islamic disputing (Rosen 1984). His essay collection, *The Justice of Islam: Comparative Perspectives in Islamic Law and Society* (2000), for example, demonstrates how social actors turn Islamic law from an abstract set of concepts into everyday practice. His observations complicate stereotypes about Islamic *Kadi-Justiz* (a term famously coined by Max Weber) enacted arbitrarily by an Islamic judge (*kadi/qāḍī*), as they demonstrate the rationalities of Islamic justice, which may be less arbitrary than certain situations in the American legal system.[3]

Islamic court proceedings, in Rosen's account (2000: 186), are 'socially oriented' and 'chaos-reducing' sites for producing 'morality and civility', with the meta-aim of achieving Islamic yet locally shaped conceptions of justice in the sense of a contextually informed balancing of social relationships and interests. This balancing, Rosen argues, strives for Islamic notions of justice as equivalence, rather than the ideals of equality and rights that dominate American law.[4] Another difference, he claims, is the extent to which relationships and social status inform the adjudication of judges, who carefully examine the disputing parties' social background in their decision-making process (though some readers would object that social status related to race, class, and gender heavily affects American prosecutorial decision-making as well; see, for example, Frohmann 1997).

Notwithstanding his emphasis on contextuality, Rosen derives generalizing arguments about Islamic justice, and at times he has been criticized for mistakenly transferring findings from a North African village to Islam and the Muslim world at large (Hussain 2001: 19). Other critiques contend that he extrapolates an essentialized, culturalized notion of Islam on the basis of 'very local' cases, based on a flawed 'assumption that what characterizes such societies is firstly their belonging to Islam' (Baudouin Dupret, personal communication 2018). However, Rosen does stress the impossibility of understanding Islamic law beyond contextuality (Rosen 2018). Obviously, such tension between extending local findings to much larger claims while simultaneously emphasizing micro-level contextuality reflects one of anthropology's inherent challenges. Notably, Rosen's empirical focus is not only limited to North Africa but also addresses the United States (Rosen 2000: 201ff.). Rosen (2000: 104) furthermore notes how, to some extent, women are sometimes empowered, rather than disadvantaged, in Islamic court settings. Rosen, himself of Jewish background, also ethnographically questions generalizations about Islamic law's assumedly discriminatory outlook towards non-Muslims while stressing its flexibility in action.

In the 1990s, Rosen's pioneering Islamic courtroom ethnography was supplemented by Ziba Mir-Hosseini's (1993) comparative study of divorce court proceedings in Iran and Morocco, with Iran being her primary focus. During fieldwork stays between 1985 and 1988, she attended trials and interviewed judges, lawyers, and the disputing parties. She examined applied Islamic law as a site where women's positions in Muslim-dominated societies are negotiated. While carving out a nuanced picture of Iranian divorce laws and their realization, her book argues that it is necessary to distinguish between (1) the theory and rhetoric of sharia and (2) sharia in practice, conditioned by a modern legal system. She is particularly attentive to how involved non-experts understand and mobilize this system. Mir-Hosseini distinguishes 'legal' from 'social' realities of divorce procedures. The latter, of primary concern, is the messy sphere where judges and litigants creatively refer to transcendental concepts in pursuit of worldly interests. Many women utilize regulations to enhance their position in the negotiation process, for example pertaining to *mahr* (dower) and *nafakah* (maintenance), faced by parallel male attempts to manipulate the court. Class-based positionality (differently patterned in Iran[5] than Morocco) affects women's abilities to use their negotiating tools, and some face threats of violence outside the courtroom. The possibility to release husbands from their costly *mahr* obligation in return for a divorce agreement (if no marriage contract exists that lifts their unilateral right to divorce) makes *mahr* 'a strong negotiating card' and may sometimes put women 'on the same footing as their husbands' (Mir-Hosseini 1998: 47). Mir-Hosseini's ethnography, like Rosen's, thus problematizes generalized notions of Islamic law and courts disadvantaging women, notwithstanding that the letter of the law stipulates an unequal status regarding divorce, inheritance, and polygamy.

A strong tradition of studying Islam's sociolegal workings exists in Southeast Asia. One widely explored field is the study of actors' manoeuvrings between co-existing normativities, or 'legal pluralism' (although the ending '-ity' would be more adequate, except where an ideology rather than a condition is denoted). Normative plurality can characterize any area of social life and acquires particular salience where disputes arise. In Indonesia, frames of state law, Islamic normativity, and customary norms/institutions (*adat*) offer disputing parties various tactical options. Keebet and Franz von Benda-Beckmann, who established the Legal Pluralism project at the Max Planck Institute for Social Anthropology (2000–12), have been pioneers in this field. In a much-cited article, Franz von Benda-Beckmann (2002: 69–70) distinguished five forms of flexibly with regard to co-existing normativities (though it remains fiercely disputed whether non-state normativities count as 'legal'/'law'): disputing and adjudicating actors might (1) argue within the boundaries of only one normative frame, (2) mobilize two normative orders against each other and portray them as incompatible (or, alternatively, as superior/inferior), (3) combine normativities while using them selectively (e.g. by arguing that each normative order covers different aspects and that elements of both can be applied simultaneously wherever appropriate), (4) claim that there is no difference, as both are 'the same' (despite being aware of differences), or (5) creatively transform or compound elements of coexisting normativities and create new hybrid forms. Numerous facets, including tempo-spatial dimensions (see Benda-Beckmann and Benda-Beckmann 2009), add complexity and have shaped a generation's thinking about legal anthropology (for a critique, see Pirie 2013: 41). In Anglo-American anthropology, John Bowen, who like the Benda-Beckmanns began his extensive research in Indonesia in the 1970s (Aceh/Sumatra, before extending his scope to Europe), has made important contributions, including his monograph *Islam, Law and Equality in Indonesia: An Anthropology of Public Reasoning* (2003). Bowen unsettles stereotypes of rigid Islamic law by demonstrating its diverse, contextual, and actor-driven character. He provides ethnographic insights into plural, often conflicting sources of, and claims to, normativity that Indonesian discourses and institutions accommodate, and explains their constructedness, justificatory usages, and contestation (within/between e.g. *adat*, matrilineal kinship, Islamic law, internationalist Islamic universalism, state law, the nation) vis-à-vis deep local histories, resulting in various options and potential pitfalls for disputing actors in marriage, inheritance, and cases relating to orphans. These actors also include judges, the reasoning and debates of whom have been one of Bowen's many foci. Despite having been primarily located in Sumatra's Gayo Highlands, Bowen's multifaceted work also elucidates how the Indonesian nation-state, whose discursive arena features prominent *fiqh* experts, is locally influential, among other sovereignties (at the local, national, and transnational level). Bowen (2003: 268) stresses the 'reasonableness' of Islamic justice and its practitioners who engage in 'public reasoning'. Another theme he addresses, although merely contextually, is the state-driven bureaucratization of Islam. This is more centrally explored in Michael Peletz's work in neighbouring Malaysia.

Peletz's accounts of Malaysian sharia courts present a highly original contribution. His monograph *Islamic Modern: Religious Courts and Cultural Politics in Malaysia* (2002) addresses a vertiginous range of topics, including an historical analysis of the diversity of Islamic (or Islamically infused) legal procedures and the flexible (non-)application of sharia norms in pre-colonial, colonial, and postcolonial Southeast Asia. He elucidates colonially rooted reconfigurations of Islamic legal practice caused by bureaucratization, centralization, and standardization, and departing from this genealogical frame, his monograph provides extensive ethnographic detail of 'modern' Islamic court proceedings in the late 1980s.

Peletz also discusses the rational consistency inherent to Islamic legal reasoning by taking the example of a sharia court in Rembau, which handled family law cases (gender, on which he is a leading authority, being among the book's themes). But Peletz's court ethnography also provided insights into wider changes in Malaysian society of the 1980s under the government of Mahathir Mohamad, with its centralized, top-down 'Islamization' policies. Former village-based religious elites who were more inclined to draw upon *adat* became marginalized and gradually replaced by representatives of a powerful stream of Islamic reformism that conquered the Islamic bureaucracy. The government's well-funded Islamization initiatives, enabled by economic growth and a new religiously oriented middle class, were heavily legalistic, implying the strengthening of sharia law vis-à-vis British-derived 'civil law'. Measures for 'Islamizing' the law were (and are) presented as a form of postcolonial emancipation and became manifested in the constantly expanding scope and enforcement of codified Islamic law. This coincided with politicized appeals to the global Islamic *ummah* (community) as a source of identification for the nation-state, resulting in the centralizing bureaucracy's defeat of earlier local forms of village-based social organization. Islamic courts turned into generative sites of micro-level state- and truth-making, and of attempted state intrusion into social citizenship.

These findings were already important and spoke to intersections between Islam, law, and the state in postcolonial worlds. Yet Peletz (2015) gave his work a most fascinating twist when he returned to 'his' sharia court in Rembau almost three decades later, producing a comparative ethnography he called a 'tale of two courts'. This 'same (but ultimately very different) court' had changed dramatically (Peletz 2015: 144). Before, the judge had conducted proceedings informally at his house next to the court, in an atmosphere that had little in common with the formal, hypermodern court of the 2010s. His concern had been reconciliation, balancing interests, and re-establishing order. But gone were the days of informal, compromise-oriented discussions in the judge's private chambers. The new court resembled—and mimetically outdid—civil courts, with which sharia courts compete over hegemony in the juridical field. Sharia courts now aimed to 'beat the other team at its own game' (Peletz 2015: 157), a shift mirroring the growing dominance of Islamic politics. Even more pervasively, cultural forms of globalized capitalism, marketization, and neoliberal governmentality have changed the sharia court's *appearance*, design, spatial arrangements, and the behaviour and speech of everybody involved.

Appropriating registers of business culture and bureaucratic standardization, the sharia court has formalized a 'Vision and Mission', codified a 'Client's Charter' announcing 'friendly, fair, timely and satisfactory service', and produced colourful public relations materials stressing that the International Organization for Standardization (ISO) is properly followed. Sharia judges and lawyers, who wore everyday Malay attire in the 1980s, now dress, speak, and behave like business elites. Court proceedings are obsessively regulated, including standards for how, where, and when the defendant/litigant in criminal or family law cases must stand or sit, a dress code, and rules when (not) to speak and at which sound level. 'Cathartic ... no-holds barred' expressions of emotions (ibid.: 147), familiar in divorce cases of the 1980s, are a thing of the past. And unlike when litigants and *kadis* interacted directly, lawyers have entered the scene, forming a new class of specialists with exclusive technical knowledge. Technological innovations (including a 'customer-friendly' 'e-sharia' portal) have made inroads, and models of auditing originating in Japan provide new languages for governing the Islamic judiciary and its subjects.

Marketization went along with a 'punitive turn': while the judge of the 1980s followed the tradition of giving informal advice (*nasihat*) and seeking negotiated compromise-oriented solutions, this shifted to formal correction, warning, and punishment. The Islamic principle of 'commanding the good and forbidding evil' remains upheld, but while the earlier court prioritized 'commanding the good', the new passionately 'forbids evil' and enforces rules. This goes along with increasing moral policing and expanding Islamic criminal law. Court officers now habitually stress their authority and legitimacy, in contrast to the earlier informal atmosphere, while civil and sharia court symbolisms have fused. Illustrating this shift, the sharia judge now also uses a gavel.

Malaysia's 'state projects of rationalization, discipline, surveillance and control' (ibid.: 147) conditioned these changes. They build upon earlier developments that Peletz had already identified in *Islamic Modern*, although the dramatic extent had been unforeseeable.

Peletz's example—more extensively presented in a new monograph published in 2020 (Peletz 2020)—demonstrates how comparative ethnographies can yield exceptional insights with broad implications. Some of the most original interventions occurred where anthropologists broadened their regional, historical, and thematic scopes and embraced anthropological comparison, as Peletz did within Malaysia and Bowen by moving from Indonesia to Europe (see Bowen's lateral comparison of two Sharia Councils in Britain, Bowen 2013, and his account of Islam in Indonesia vis-à-vis France, Bowen 2010).

Having exemplified some influential classical works and recent innovation in the well-established fields of studying Islam-related disputing, courtroom ethnography, and legal pluralism, I will now shift the focus to some newer areas in which anthropologists have begun in novel ways to enquire into Islam, law, and the state, the relevance of which extends to readerships beyond conventional legal anthropologists and other legal specialists. These approaches derive their strength from in-depth ethnographic endeavours to follow the sharia and Islam-related normative matters wherever social actors themselves render them meaningful, particularly in fields that Anglo-European secular categorical distinctions would not necessarily consider 'legal' spheres.

Corporate sharia, the state, and politics of *halal*

The rise of large-scale *halal* (permissible under Islamic law) markets, certifying practices, related technologies, and consumption have attracted anthropological and legal attention (Fischer 2011, 2015; Tayob 2016). Other *halal*-related rising themes include animal rights, slaughtering, and livestock trade (Bergeaud-Blackler 2007; Istasse 2016; Stilt 2018) as well as 'sharia-compliant' financial, service, and insurance markets (Maurer 2005: 136–53; Rudnyckyj 2014). Bergeaud-Blackler, an anthropologist studying transnational *halal* markets (Bergeaud-Blackler 2017; Bergeaud-Blackler et al. 2016), argues that the concept of *halal*, as it is currently normalized, is an 'invented tradition' brought about at the hands of globalized capitalism and its intersection with Islamist political networks.

Other work turns its ethnographic attention to companies as sites where religious truths and normatively (un)desirable ways of being Muslim are negotiated in new ways. In these 'non-state' settings, Islamic legal politics unfolds as well, and where resourceful and interventionist-oriented states like Malaysia or Singapore are at work, states exhibit a peculiar 'absent-presence' (Comaroff and Comaroff 2016: 23), to borrow a term which aptly characterizes many state-ified frameworks of contemporary Islamic marketization and governmentality. An insightful example is Patricia Sloane-White's (2017) monograph *Corporate Islam: Sharia and the Modern Workplace*.

Sloane-White, who after doing her earliest research with Hildred Geertz in the 1980s worked for nearly a decade on Wall Street before returning to anthropology and obtaining a PhD from Oxford, conducted fieldwork among Malay business elites between the 1990s and 2010s. While in the 1990s, the bureaucratization of Islam in Malaysia was firmly tied to racial affirmative action policies aiming to empower the majority population of ethnic Malays (Sloane-White 1998), *de jure* Muslims, a new scenario has unfolded since the 2000s: ethnic 'Malay Supremacy' has given way to 'Supremacy of Islam'. Parallel to government support for a state-regulated Islamic finance industry and *halal* markets, Malay business elites began remodelling corporate governance in 'sharia-ized' (Sloane White 2018: 6) terms: assuming the government had failed to establish a 'real' Islamic state, at least their companies could become 'small Islamic states' fully governed by sharia norms (Sloane-White 2018). CEOs reconceptualized themselves as 'caliphs', and workplace settings became fundamentally reorganized. While every Islamic financial institution now legally requires religious supervisory boards with certified sharia experts, many companies in other fields also voluntarily establish such boards and hire 'sharia consultants', who represent part of a vast new job market. Consultants, but also business leaders and state-employed Islamic bureaucrats, ideally now have 'Islamic' *and* 'secular' educational and professional credentials.

Yet exclusivist tendencies towards Muslims-only recruitment policies and the moral surveillance of employees' or job applicants' private lives coincide with an ethical turn. In conversion-like narratives, new employees in the process of organizational socialization relate how joining the company led them to properly understand the sharia for the first time. CEOs and their companies view themselves as responsible for 'commanding the good and forbidding the bad' (see above). Success through full sharia-compliance brings rewards (*pahala*) for their afterlives but also affects successful commercial performance in this world (not answering phone calls during prayer times, e.g., is assumed to be spiritually and financially beneficial). Such dual benefits are considered quantifiable.

Sloane-White analyses authoritarian state power, legalistic Islamism, and marketization as intertwined rather than separate or even opposed forces. Her extension of the study of Islamic law beyond the more 'classical' domains of courts, legislations, judges, disputing, or punishment—following 'the sharia' wherever actors and discourses render it meaningful instead of merely observing it where secular logics locate 'law' and 'religion'—is timely vis-à-vis the shifting realities of Muslim religiosities and the multiple interlocked sovereignties that aim to govern them. Her approach evades dichotomies between domination and the dominated, compliance and resistance, or hegemonies versus anti-hegemonical spheres. With this dialectical sensibility for more subtle nuances, her work stands in a line with other important recent interventions in the wider anthropology of Islam (e.g. Salomon 2016; Spadola 2014).

Bureaucratizing the Sharia: Islamic Law and State Power

Contemporary-oriented and ethnographic (as opposed to Asadian textual) work centring on Islam and law in the context of state power remains relatively scarce. An outstanding contribution is Matthew Erie's work on Islam in China, including his monograph, *China and Islam: The Prophet, the Party, and Law* (2016). It unpacks how state and non-state actors (including Hui Muslim clerics, educational actors, state representatives, and other Communist Party members) in the town Linxia ('China's Little Mecca') make Islam compatible with the Chinese 'Party-State'. Erie's ethnography unravels how Hui Muslims reconcile Islamically infused 'ideas of the good life' (2016: 4) vis-à-vis state power and a China-specific state-ification of Islam. Rather than simply being controlled and governed, many Hui Muslims not only conform but also hermeneutically contribute to the government's socialist vision of Muslims' nationalism. They do so in an environment of ever-growing suspicion accompanying the age of 'wars on terror', where 'Sharia law' has come to be viewed as a 'law of terror', 'incompatible with (but aiming to infiltrate) the law of the modern nation state' (Erie 2016: 5).

Hui Muslims are positioned differently from the draconically persecuted Uyghur Muslims. Though they remain 'second-class citizens' (Erie 2016: 11), Hui Muslims are framed as China's 'good Muslims' ('familiar strangers' ethnically close to the dominant Han Chinese population), who have valuably contributed to the Party-state, past and present. Although the People's Republic revolutionary establishment initially had devastating consequences on centuries-old Chinese Muslim structures, including property rights and legal practices, Hui Muslims gradually negotiated spaces for Muslimness in the Chinese state and society. These spaces, however, are limited and fragile, and exclude *explicit* Islamic legal practice.

After a phase of harsh repression in early post-revolution China, the government realized that its wish to administer the 'disenchantment of the world' and the ultimate disappearance of religion would not materialize. Rather than only controlling Islam, it chose to *actively shape* Islam's exegetical contents. Like elsewhere (Müller and Steiner 2018), albeit with locally unique meaning-production, state-sponsored Islamic institutions, a 'Bureau for Religious Affairs', educational structures, and a social class of state-funded Muslim bureaucrats and teachers were established. While they remained under surveillance and faced heavy government pressure to accept prescribed parameters of (im)permissible Muslim religiosity, Chinese Muslims also created new scopes of acting as a result of this state engagement.

One of the book's first ethnographic anecdotes, from a local mosque, concludes that 'not only did state law and therefore the police appear to have limits, the clerics also seemed to have considerable influence, because there was an entirely different type of law [as opposed to official law, D.M.] that operated in the mosque office' (Erie 2016: 4). Erie found that in this setting, as in China generally, 'to a greater degree than in US legal practice ... it was relationships that gave meanings to the law, and while actors operate within asymmetries of power, there are asymmetries within asymmetries' (ibid.). Actors invert power relations in the dutiful application of local rule. The ethnography's actors relationally engage with their limited spaces and establish common grounds and overlapping visions of 'the good' with the Party-state. At the same time, they make government doctrines of 'Chinese Islam' work for themselves in ways that have not been, and could not be, fully planned by the control-obsessed state. Sharia law and the People's Republic's secular nationalism and state law have entered alliances in which both sides exhibit pragmatism, flexibility, and adaptiveness, problematizing the reputation of immutable rigidness that is shared by the Chinese state and sharia law. To be sure, this is a balancing act, and drastic counter-examples could be given as well. Yet by and large, what Erie considers elements of 'Islamic law' in substance—while not being officially called as such—find themselves refashioned as an acknowledged minority's 'customs' and are informally at work in everyday life—sometimes openly, sometimes secretly. The 'Party-State, to some extent', even 'subjects itself to the rules of the Hui' (ibid.: 26). It occasionally portrays itself towards Hui audiences as an *Islamically* legitimate, just, and fair sovereign whose rule is compatible with Islamic principles. Thus, 'the Hui social field can also contain the state' (ibid.), which sounds counter-intuitive vis-à-vis Uighur concentration camps in which other Chinese Muslims undergo 'citizenship education'.

Although practised 'Islamic law'—in Erie's understanding, disputed by critics for whom only formalized law is 'law'—remains mostly confined to ritual spheres, and state law intends to sever 'religion from religious law' (ibid.: 4), Islamic authoritative figures retain some micro-level powers in mosques, religious bureaus, *madrasa*-schools, ethnic schools, and *jiaonpai*[6] 'teaching schools'. They acquire de facto political roles, which must not be called 'political', insofar as they serve as intermediaries between state authorities, Muslim populations, and the *jiaonpai* (ibid.: 133).

A category related to local understandings of Islamic law—strictly not to be called as such—is *minjan*, a term denoting 'unofficial' or 'non-state' forms of sociality, norms, and institutions 'between people', operating mostly below the state level. Depending on a specific case, the state may acknowledge, silently tolerate, or forbid its existence. In a 'pull-and-tug of *minjan* and the state', state policies 'mold' religions, including Islam, 'into belief systems that are culturally expressive and empathetically Chinese' (ibid.: 14). The everyday expression of 'popular law' (*minjianfa*), though it is not grounded in formal law, can still entail 'religious law' (ibid.) and offers sharia law an entry point to relegitimize itself through resignification as 'apolitical', 'non-legal', and 'not sharia'. *Fiqh* remains mostly an oral rather than a scriptural practice. However, the Hui also hybridize official and unofficial categories of state law and Islamic law: they 'moralize law' and view state law as 'ethics-like', blurring secular boundaries between morality, ethics, law, and a shariatic totality reframed as 'life rule' (*shenghuo guilü*). Sharia-infused practices are thus permissible only if they are not explicitly called as such, but instead as ethnic customs. Erie, who carefully moves back and forth between emic and etic terms, views this 'Sharia' nevertheless as 'law', although it 'is neither backed by courts nor produced by jurists' (ibid.: 26–7), and he acknowledges that his views are problematic from both secular and Islamic perspectives. The Chinese state, 'in its efforts to produce its own version of Islam, governs through Muslim authorities and Islamic law itself' and produces projections of 'legitimate Muslims' (ibid.: 25, 26). It positions itself as an arbiter of defining the boundaries between 'good' and 'bad' Islam, framed as 'orthodox' (=good) and 'heterodox' (=bad, banned), and has thus given Islamic revival in China its very own '"official" form' (ibid.: 12).[7]

Many of Erie's other writings should also be credited, including on *halal* food and Islamophobia ('Shari'a as taboo', Erie 2018a), clerics (*ahong*), the China Islamic Association, and on how the state has employed a shifting set of strategies to manipulate the sharia since 2001, analysed vis-à-vis the 'post-secular turn' (Erie 2015a). He has also examined Hui dispute resolution in and beyond state courts (Erie 2015b) and the 'afterlife' of a pre-Communist Muslim endowment (*waqf*) (Erie 2018b).

Erie's work on Islam, law, and the state in China addresses broadly relevant themes: Muslim social citizenship, national Islamic meaning-making, complex diffusions of state forms of classification into society, overlapping sovereignties, and the role of social actors (including state actors) in putting Islamic law to work in context. He neither overemphasizes state power (even in China!) nor stops at highlighting the 'limits' of law and state power in an allegedly post-national age. His actor-oriented approach situates state power and Islamic legal politics in everyday life, with a non-formalistic conception of 'Islamic law' that many readers (especially lawyers) will find puzzling or difficult to accept. His ethnography of pragmatic alliances between an anti-religious state and pro-state religious actors furthermore points to counter-intuitive dialectics of authoritarianism and its provision of scopes of acting that resemble other 'restrictive' settings.

In another key contribution to the field, Salomon (2016) underlines this process in reverse: by appropriating political Islamist language, initially not overly religious actors in the 'Islamic State' of Sudan created scopes of acting while internalizing, albeit only to a certain extent, the ruling symbolic order and embodying the 'Islamic State'. In the same vein, my own ethnographic work in Brunei (Müller 2018) demonstrates how outlawed traditional healers choose to participate in the bureaucratization of Islam by appropriating powerful state symbols and becoming state-certified, 'Sharia-compliant Islamic healers'. In this way, they legitimize their work within the state's parameters, which allows them to engage in otherwise unacceptable esoteric practices (such as Japanese water-crystal photography proving the powers of their prayers). Such settings, and the analytic insights they offer, are rarely understandable or even detectable by textual approaches to the anthropology of Islam, law, and the state. They point to the enduring necessity and gains of long-term ethnographic fieldwork, notwithstanding the challenges faced by some of anthropology's methodological conventions in dealing with sharia politics as it takes on new social and cultural forms. Sociolegally interested lawyers, in turn, can benefit from integrating ethnographic findings, either of their own making or drawn from the literature, in their analysis. Regrettably, the potential avenues for mutual learning and cooperation between both disciplines in the study of Islam, law, and the state are still very rarely explored.

Concluding remarks

While classical fields of enquiry into Islam, law, and the state such as courtroom ethnography, disputing, legal pluralism, debates about secularism or the 'positivization' of Islamic law, *fatwa*-making and -appropriation, or 'law vs. practice' studies are here to stay, various new themes have entered the scene, only some of which I have been able to exemplify here. Islam-related science and technology studies, bio-ethics, Islamic legal education, intersections of Islamic law, state power, magic and non-human actors (such as *jinn*), media, emotions/affect, materiality, aesthetics, and new technologies of Islamic legal decision-making all deserve to be brought into the discussion,[8] and even these by no means exhaust a rapidly growing field.

This chapter's main purpose has been to present a few selected examples and, with the illustration of some exemplary case-studies, sketch the trajectory of how anthropologists have broadened their empirical focus on spheres of 'Islamic law' and sharia-based normativity beyond what would count as 'law' and 'legal' according to secular distinctions. Instead, we are now following 'the sharia' wherever social actors and institutions render it meaningful, which is highly contextual and may change rapidly within one and the same setting, as in those studied by Peletz and Sloane-White. To understand such transformations, ethnography will remain an irreplaceable instrument of knowledge-production.

While theoretical reflections on secularity, secularism, and secularization, studies of ethics, personhood, and cultivation, and text-based analyses in the anthropology of Islam continue to have important and new things to say, it is my sense that there is still rather little deep *ethnographic* work on the nexus between Islam, law, and state power in contemporary societies, especially pertaining to the state component. While some anthropologists have convinced themselves since the 1990s that 'the state' has lost much of its relevance at the hands of other sovereignties, globalizing markets, and other transnational flows, in the Islamic field many (though obviously not all!) states and the diverse networks of actors, ideas, and institutions that constitute them remain resourceful, highly engaged forces whose activities sometimes have far-reaching societal consequences and about whom little solid ethnographic knowledge and theorizing exists. Rather than studying state power *or* the market, state power *or* transnational de-territorialization, Islamic law *or* ethics (or subject-formations, ontologies, or self-cultivation), or Islamic law *or* politics, the empirical realities of some settings—especially those with religiously more intrusive state forces—give scholars good reasons to reconcile such dichotomies in less mutually exclusive and more dialectical ways. By centring on the intersections between Islam, law, and the state, anthropology and ethnographically informed sociolegal studies could generate interventions in existing dominant knowledge regimes and public debates—interventions whose significance might extend to broad readerships beyond our own discipline(s).

Notes

1. For a conceptual introduction to the Sharia and its polysemous semantic properties, see Dupret 2018.
2. Asad's anthropology has long shifted from ethnography to sociohistorical grand narratives, related theoretical debates, and practices of critique. This 'textualism' has been criticized for 'rendering invisible how people practice their (discursive) traditions (of Islam) and the experience they have' as well as the 'practical articulations' and 'messy politics of traditional fieldwork encounters', while in Asadian textualist accounts, 'only literate elite Muslim writers and commentators are visible' (Hammoudi 2009: 26ff.).

3. E.g. Rosen (1989: 2) mentions an American judge having 'had a fight with his wife at breakfast', which might affect his decision-making in court.
4. See the table juxtaposing American common law and Islamic principles in Rosen 2000: 53; on problems of comparison and conflation between Islamic and 'Western' conceptions of justice, see Agrama 2015.
5. For another study of Islamic justice, sovereign power, and human rights in Iran, see Osanloo 2006.
6. Muslims in northwest China individually identify with a *jiaonpai*, an 'ideologically driven group' cultivating its own *Hanafi*-rooted interpretation of Islam, centred around certain mosques or Sufi tombs with their own educational 'schools'.
7. This terminology (following state categorizations of 'evil cults') should not be confused with (anthropologically outdated) understandings of 'orthodoxy' versus 'heterodoxy' as great versus little traditions of scriptural versus folk Islam.
8. See Bowen 2018 for an excellent overview.

References

Agrama, H. A. 2012. *Questioning Secularism: Islam, Sovereignty and the Rule of Law in Egypt*. Chicago: University of Chicago Press.

Agrama, H. A. 2015. 'Justice between Islamic Shari'a and Western Legal Tradition: Remarks on the Comparative Context'. In S. A. Turki, ed. *A Companion to the Anthropology of the Middle East*, 363–90. Hoboke: Wiley-Blackwell.

Alatas, I. F. 2018. 'Review Essay: On the State of the Shari'a'. *PoLAR: Political and Legal Anthropology Review*, 16 July 2018. https://polarjournal.org/2018/07/16/review-essay-on-the-state-of-the-sharia/

Asad, T. 1983. 'Anthropological Conceptions of Religion: Reflections on Geertz'. *Man* 18(2): 237–59.

Asad, T. 1986. *The Idea of an Anthropology of Islam*. Washington, DC: Georgetown University, Center for Contemporary Arab Studies.

Asad, T. 2005. 'Thinking About Law, Morality, and Religion in the Story of Egyptian Modernization'. *Journal of the Interdisciplinary Study of Monotheistic Religions* 1: 13–24.

Benda-Beckmann, F. v. 2002. 'Who's Afraid of Legal Pluralism?' *Journal of Legal Pluralism and Unofficial Law* 34(47): 37–82.

Benda-Beckmann, K. v. and F. v. Benda-Beckmann, eds. 2009. *Spatializing Law: An Anthropological Geography of Law in Society*. Farnham: Ashgate.

Bergeaud-Blackler, F. 2007. 'Religious Slaughter: A European Perspective'. *Journal of Ethnic and Migration Studies* 33(6): 965–80.

Bergeaud-Blackler, F. 2017. *Le marché halal ou l'invention d'une tradition*. Paris: Éditions du Seuil.

Bergeaud-Blackler, F., J. Lever, and J. Fischer, eds. 2016. *Halal Matters: Islam, Politics and Markets in Global Perspective*. London: Routledge.

Bernard-Maugiron, N. 2003. *Le politique à l'épreuve du judiciaire: La justice constitutionnelle en Égypte*. Bruxelles: Bruylant.

Botiveau, B. 1993. *Loi islamique et droit dans les sociétés arabes*. Paris: Karthala.

Bowen, J. R. 1996. 'Religion in the Proper Sense of the Word: Law and Civil Society in the Islamicist Discourse'. *Anthropology Today* 12(4): 12–4.

Bowen, J. R. 2003. *Islam, Law, and Equality in Indonesia: An Anthropology of Public Reasoning.* Cambridge: Cambridge University Press.

Bowen, J. R. 2010. 'Religious Discrimination and Religious Governance Across Secular and Islamic Countries: France and Indonesia as Limiting Cases'. *American Behavioral Scientist* 53: 1749–62.

Bowen, J. R. 2013. 'Sanctity and Shariah: Two Islamic Modes of Resolving Disputes in Today's England'. In F. von Benda-Beckmann, K. von Benda-Beckmann, M. Ramstedt, and B. Turner, eds. *Religion in Disputes: Pervasiveness of Religious Normativity in Disputing Processes*, 129–45. New York: Palgrave Macmillan.

Bowen, J. R. 2018. 'Anthropology and Islamic Law'. In A. Emmon and R. Ahmed, eds. *Oxford Handbook in Islamic Law.* Oxford: Oxford University Press.

Büskens, L. 2016. 'Christiaan Snouck Hurgronje, "Holy War" and Colonial Concerns'. In E.-J. Zürcher, ed. *Jihad and Islam in World War I: Studies on the Ottoman Jihad on the Centenary of Snouck Hurgronje's 'Holy War Made in Germany'*, 29–52. Leiden: Leiden University Press.

Büskens, L. and B. Dupret. 2011. 'The Invention of Islamic Law: A History of Western Studies of Islamic Normativity and Their Spread in the Orient'. In F. Pouillon and J.-C. Vatin, eds. *After Orientalism Critical Perspectives on Western Agency and Eastern Re-appropriations*, 31–47. Leiden: Brill.

Comaroff, J. and J. Comaroff, eds. 2006. *Law and Disorder in the Postcolony.* Chicago: University of Chicago Press.

Comaroff, J. and J. Comaroff. 2016. *The Truth about Crime: Sovereignty, Knowledge, Social Orders.* Chicago: University of Chicago Press.

Dupret, B. 2007. 'What Is Islamic law? A Praxiological Answer and an Egyptian Case Study'. *Theory, Culture and Society* 24(2): 79–100.

Dupret, B. 2018. *What is the Sharia?* London: Hurst.

Erie, M. 2015a. 'Defining Shari'a in China: State, Ahong, and the Post-Secular Turn'. *Cross-Currents: East Asian History and Culture Review* 12: 88–117.

Erie, M. 2015b. 'Muslim Mandarins in Chinese Courts: Dispute Resolution, Islamic Law, and the Secular State in Northwest China'. *Law & Social Inquiry* 40(4): 1001–30.

Erie, M. 2016. *China and Islam: The Prophet, the Party, and Law.* Cambridge: Cambridge University Press, 2016.

Erie, M. 2018a. 'Shari'a as Taboo of Modern Law: Halal Food, Islamophobia, and China'. *Journal of Law and Religion* 33(3): 390–420.

Erie, M. 2018b. 'The Traveling Waqf: Property, Religion, and Mobility beyond China'. *Islamic Law and Society* (25): 1–2.

Fischer, J. 2011. *The Halal Frontier: Muslim Consumers in a Globalized Market.* New York: Palgrave Macmillan.

Fischer, J. 2015. *Islam, Standards, and Technoscience: In Global Halal Zones.* Abingdon: Routledge.

Frohmann, L. 1997. 'Convictability and Discordant Locales: Reproducing Race, Class, and Gender Ideologies in Prosecutorial Decisionmaking'. *Law & Society Review* 31(3): 531–66.

Geertz, C. 1957. 'Ritual and Social Change: A Javanese Example'. *American Anthropologist* 59(1): 32–54.

Geertz, C. 1983. *Local Knowledge: Further Essays in Interpretive Anthropology.* New York: Basic Books.

Hallaq, W.B. 2013. *The Impossible State: Islam, Politics, and Modernity's Moral Predicament.* New York: Columbia University Press.

Hammoudi, A. 2009. 'Textualism and Anthropology: On the Ethnographic Encounter, or an Experience in the Hajj'. In A. Hammoudi and J. Borneman, eds. *Being There: The Fieldwork Encounter and the Making of Truth*, 25–54. Berkeley: University of California Press.

Hurgronje, C. R. 1957. 'De la Nature u droit Musulman'. In G. H. Bousquet and J. Schacht, eds. *Selected Works of C. Snouck Hurgronje*, 259–62. Leiden: E.J. Brill.

Hussain, J. 2001. 'Book Review: The Justice of Islam by Lawrence Rosen'. *Melbourne University Law Review* 30: 865.

Istasse, M. 2016. 'Green Halal: How Does Halal Production Face Animal Suffering?' In F. Bergeaud-Blackler, J. Fischer, and J. Lever, eds. *Halal Matters*, 127–42. London: Routledge.

Martin, R. C. and A. Barzegar. 2010. *Islamism: Contested Perspectives on Political Islam*. Stanford: Stanford University Press.

Maurer, B. 2005. *Mutual Life, Limited: Islamic Banking, Alternative Currencies, Lateral Reasoning*. Princeton: Princeton University Press.

Messick, B. 1996. *The Calligraphic State: Textual Domination and History in a Muslim Society*. Berkeley: University of California Press.

Messick, B. 1998. 'Written Identities: Legal Subjects in an Islamic State'. *History of Religions* 38(1): 25–51.

Mir-Hosseini, Z. 1993. *Marriage on Trial: A Study of Islamic Family Law in Iran and Morocco*. London: I.B. Tauris.

Mir-Hosseini, Z. 1998. 'A Response to Shahla Haeri's Review of Marriage on Trial, A Study of Islamic Family Law in Iran and Morocco'. *International Journal of Middle East Studies* 30(3): 469–71.

Mohamad, M. 2010. 'The Ascendance of Bureaucratic Islam and the Secularization of the Shariah in Malaysia'. *Pacific Affairs* 83(3): 505–24.

Müller, D. 2018. 'Hybrid Pathways to Orthodoxy: Bureaucratised Exorcism, Scientisation and the Mainstreaming of Deviant-Declared Practices'. *Journal of Current Southeast Asian Affairs* 37(1): 141–83.

Müller, D. and K. Steiner. 2018. 'The Bureaucratisation of Islam in Southeast Asia: Transdisciplinary Perspectives'. *Journal of Current Southeast Asian Affairs* 37(1): 3–26.

Osanloo, A. 2006. 'The Measure of Mercy: Islamic Justice, Sovereign Power, and Human Rights in Iran'. *Cultural Anthropology* 21(4): 570–602.

Peletz, M. 2002. *Islamic Modern: Religious Courts and Cultural Politics in Malaysia*. Princeton: Princeton University Press.

Peletz, M. 2015. 'A Tale of Two Courts: Judicial Transformation and the Rise of a Corporate Islamic Governmentality in Malaysia'. *American Ethnologist* 42(1): 144–60.

Peletz, M. 2020. *Sharia Transformations: Cultural Politics and the Rebranding of an Islamic Judiciary*. Oakland: University of California Press.

Peters, R. 2002. 'From Jurists' Law to Statute Law or What Happens When the Shari`a Is Codified'. *Mediterranean Politics* 7(4): 82–95.

Pirie, F. 2013. *The Anthropology of Law*. Oxford: Oxford University Press.

Ramstedt, M. 2015. 'Anthropological Perspectives on Law and Religion'. In S. Ferrari, ed. *Routledge Handbook of Law and Religion*, 43–58. Abingdon: Routledge.

Rosen, L. 1984. *Bargaining for Reality: The Construction of Social Relations in a Muslim Community*. Chicago: University of Chicago Press.

Rosen, L. 1989. *The Anthropology of Justice: Law as Culture in Islamic Society*. Cambridge: Cambridge University Press.

Rosen, L. 2000. *The Justice of Islam: Comparative Perspectives in Islamic Law and Society*. Oxford: Oxford University Press.

Rosen, L. 2018. *Islam and the Rule of Justice: Image and Reality in Muslim Law and Culture*. Chicago: University of Chicago Press.

Rudnyckyj, D. 2014. 'Islamic Finance and the Afterlives of Development in Malaysia'. *Political and Legal Anthropology Review* 37(1): 69–88.

Salomon, N. 2016. *For Love of the Prophet: An Ethnography of Sudan's Islamic State*. Princeton: Princeton University Press.

Sloane-White, P. 1998. *Islam, Modernity and Entrepreneurship among the Malays*. London: Palgrave MacMillan.

Sloane-White, P. 2017. *Corporate Islam: Sharia and the Modern Workplace*. Cambridge: Cambridge University Press.

Sloane-White, P. 2018. 'Company Rules: Sharia and its Transgressions in the Malay-Muslim Corporate Workplace'. *Journal of Current Southeast Asian Affairs* 37(1): 89–116.

Spadola, E. 2014. *The Calls of Islam: Sufis, Islamists, and Mass Mediation in Urban Morocco*. Bloomington: Indiana University Press.

Starrett, G. 1998. *Putting Islam to Work: Education, Politics and Religious Transformation in Egypt*. Berkeley: University of California Press.

Stilt, K. 2018. 'Animals'. In A. Emon and R. Ahmed, eds. *The Oxford Handbook of Islamic Law*. Oxford: Oxford University Press.

Tayob, S. 2016. '"O You who Believe, Eat of the Tayyibāt (Pure and Wholesome Food) that We Have Provided You"—Producing Risk, Expertise and Certified Halal Consumption in South Africa'. *Journal of Religion in Africa* 46(1): 67–91.

Wood, L. 2016. *Islamic Legal Revival: Reception of European Law and Transformations in Islamic Legal Thought in Egypt, 1875–1952*. Oxford: Oxford University Press.

CHAPTER 11

LAW AND ANTHROPOLOGY IN THE NETHERLANDS

From Adat Law School to Anthropology of Law

KEEBET VON BENDA-BECKMANN

INTRODUCTION

On 2 October 1901, Cornelis van Vollenhoven held his inaugural lecture at the University of Leiden, where he had been appointed as a Professor in *adat* law of the Dutch Indies and constitutional and administrative law of the Dutch Indies, Surinam, and Curaçao'. He would become a core figure in what came to be known as the '*Adat* Law School' (*Adatrecht School*), which in the decades to follow would produce an unprecedented body of detailed studies of local legal orders in the Malay Archipelago, including Taiwan, the Philippines, Malacca, Indo-China, and Madagascar. The work of Van Vollenhoven is exceptional because he paired a keen academic interest in the comparative study of legal orders within the Archipelago with a passionate drive to have the injustices redressed that were imposed on the indigenous population of the Dutch Indies, on the basis of misconceptions of their legal orders. Some of his ideas preceded by decades conceptual work among English-speaking anthropologists of law. He argued for an analysis of local laws on a comparative basis, rejecting the use of concepts borrowed directly from Dutch law. Instead, he designed generic concepts more suitable to capture the characteristics of each of these laws.

This chapter presents, first, the *Adat* Law School of the early twentieth century and, second, postcolonial Dutch legal anthropology. The first part begins with a brief sketch of the precursors of the *Adat* Law School, then focuses on the work of Van Vollenhoven and his colleagues, showing how, in the last two decades of the colonial era, research on *adat* law became a legal science that was ever more conservative and shallow (K. von Benda-Beckmann 2002, 2011; K. von Benda-Beckmann and Strijbosch 1986; Burns 2007; Griffiths 1983, 1986; Henley and Davidson 2007; Holleman 1981; Strijbosch 1980, 1996; Trouwborst 2002; Van Rossum and Böcker 2009).[1] The second part describes the emerging Dutch anthropology of law after 1950, its institutional bases, and the main themes of Dutch research on the anthropology of law after 1950, emphasizing its increasing embeddedness in international debates.

Precursors

When in the late eighteenth century the Dutch Indies transformed from a mercantile to a capitalist economy based on resource extraction and a plantation economy, the colonial administration began to develop an interest in the social organization of indigenous communities. From the mid-nineteenth century onwards, several universities established academic positions in ethnology and 'Indology', the study of Indonesian cultures and languages, and developed curricula to prepare civil servants for their tasks in the Dutch Indies. This was also the time when Dutch ethnography emerged as a separate discipline. Civil servants, academics, and missionaries produced a remarkable number of ethnographic accounts, many of which dealt with matters of religion and religious law or custom and customary law.[2]

The professors in ethnology in the late nineteenth century had a background in the study of Semitic and Arabic languages and Islam, and they covered the study of cultures, geography, archaeology, and languages. Leiden professor G. A. Wilken was the first who explicitly considered ethnology as a separate discipline. Having served as a civil servant before turning to academia, he now began to engage with the social theories of the time, in particular evolutionism. In his work he devoted considerable attention to legal matters. Another important figure was Christiaan Snouck Hurgronje, a specialist in Islam and an important adviser to the colonial government, famous for his ethnography of Aceh. In contrast to Wilken's theoretical orientation, Snouck Hurgronje's ethnographic work was purely descriptive (Trouwborst 2002: 674–6). In his conception, Hinduism and Islam were foreign religions that had not replaced older 'heathen' spiritual and religious tenets that formed the basis of Indonesian cultures. His sharp distinction between Islam and the 'habits and customs', that is, *adat*, would become fundamental for Dutch colonial policies. The Arabic term *adat* had been in use in the literature of the Dutch Indies since Herman W. Muntinghe used it in 1817, but Snouck Hurgronje was the first to employ it as a generic term. He also argued that indigenous communities had their own native law that was part of *adat*, for which he coined the term *adatrecht* (*adat law*) (see K. von Benda-Beckmann 2002; J. F. Holleman 1981: li).

Van Vollenhoven and the Leiden *Adat* Law School

Van Vollenhoven built on the work of Wilken and Snouck Hurgronje, but the political landscape and attitudes towards law in the Dutch Indies were changing. In 1901, the same year that Van Vollenhoven took up his chair in Leiden, the Dutch government launched its 'ethical policy', the stated goal of which was to improve the living conditions of the indigenous population. The policy was a peculiar combination of humanitarianism and the wish to develop an educated indigenous middle class required for the expanding markets for capitalist enterprise (Ellen 1976: 313). As J. S. Furnivall (1944: 392) put it, it was 'capitalism dressed up like Christianity'. This tension gave rise to heated debates about the role of law in the Dutch East Indies during the first decades of the twentieth century, in which law professors from Leiden and Utrecht took radically different standpoints, especially on issues of land tenure (Otto 2009: 181). At the University of Utrecht, G. J. Nolst Trinité, Cassuto, and I. A. Nederburgh argued that *adat* land tenure, with its strong emphasis on communal rights, was an obstacle for economic development. In their view, economic development, including that of the indigenous population, was best served by a unified legal order and a land tenure system based on Dutch civil law that would replace *adat* land titles with individual rights to private ownership. This would allow the indigenous population 'to compete on equal terms by the same rules with everyone else' (Lev 1984: 150). By contrast, Van Vollenhoven and his colleagues in Leiden argued that indigenous populations and their institutions should be treated with respect, as promised in the treaties by which local populations were incorporated into the Dutch colonial empire. Besides, indigenous laws would offer the best chance to raise their welfare (see Burns 2007). This required a thorough understanding of the variable forms of *adat* and their land tenure systems—a task he took upon himself with zeal. At Van Vollenhoven's instigation, scholars, judges, and administrators produced a great number of studies of indigenous groups.

The Leiden-Utrecht debate is often understood as one between progressive (Utrecht) and conservative (Leiden) protagonists (Burns 2007; Henley and Davidson 2007). The Utrecht school considered itself progressive, because it aimed at establishing a modern unified legal order for the whole population to replace the outdated *adat* laws. Van Vollenhoven was considered conservative, because his preoccupation with *adat* logic suggested closed, unchanging communities, while in fact a rapidly developing economy and an expanding commercial sector generated mass migration and new labour relationships. It is true that Van Vollenhoven did not pay much attention to migration and labour relations, and that he may have overrated the capability of *adat* law to protect local communities against powerful outsiders (Sonius 1981: xxxvi–vix). Nevertheless, he did not consider them to be completely static, and he pointed out that mechanisms for change were inherent in *adat*—without, admittedly, offering many concrete examples of such change. In his criticism of the misrepresentations of land rights of indigenous communities, he was not conservative at all. This criticism was directed primarily at the infamous Domain Declarations, issued in the 1870s. Premised on the Dutch legal doctrine that made a fundamental distinction between public and private rights, it legitimated large-scale dispossession of 'waste land'. According to this doctrine, to which the Utrecht scholars adhered, the colonial government assumed all sovereign rights to territories upon incorporation into the colonial empire. While private rights to land similar to Dutch ownership and its legal derivatives would be protected, the sovereign held all public rights to land. This included uncultivated communal land and forests of local communities. On this land, the government could legitimately and at liberty grant concessions. *Adat*, according to this view, was mere custom, which the sovereign had the power and the right to disregard in the interest of the public good, such as economic development. It was with the legal, political, and economic implications of this doctrine that Van Vollenhoven and his colleagues took issue. They argued that *adat* was much more than mere custom; it contained law. They argued further that such indigenous laws were based on different legal categories that did not entail the Western legal distinction between public and private rights. These laws could not be set aside at the whim of the government but had to be recognized, in their own terms, and not jammed into the categories of Western law. Expropriation for the plantation economy of large tracts of land on which local communities held *adat* titles was therefore illegal. Many studies of land relations substantiated this in detail.

Van Vollenhoven was also interested in comparative work that required a conceptual framework that would do justice to a broad variety of legal systems. Indigenous communities had their own ways of living, called *adat*, which was highly pliable and changeable. In his opinion, it was possible to discern law from the broader set of practices and customs. Those rules to which sanctions were attached could be labelled as law, but, as they were also part of *adat*, an appropriate term would be '*adat law*' (*adatrecht*). In this, he followed Snouck Hurgronje. He insisted that sharp distinctions between *adat* law and *adat*, religion, morals, and customs were impossible to make. Most *adat* was oral, but some indigenous groups also had some written laws. He systematized the *adat* laws in nineteen law areas (*adatrechtskringen*), i.e. groupings of *adat* law systems that showed similar features—an approach widely used in anthropology and in German comparative law. Van Vollenhoven's major aim was to provide a comprehensive description (but not a codification) of each *adat* system and all *adat* law areas (see K. von Benda-Beckmann 2002: 697). An impressive body of detailed descriptions was collected in the *Adatrechtsbundels* (Vollenhoven 1911–49) and systematized in the *Pandecten van het Adatrecht* (Vollenhoven 1914–31). Dutch ethnologists, in particular J. P. B. de Josselin de Jong, adopted similar research methods, but they were critical of the notion of *adat* law and of the practical and political concerns of the *Adat* Law School (Trouwborst 2002: 686–7).

For this comparative work Van Vollenhoven also designed several new terms. Indigenous communities were '*adat* law communities' (*adatrechtsgemeenschap*), i.e. jural communities that could be based on territorial, kinship, or contract among their members, who lived according to their own flexible laws, regulations, and principles, subject to change, and sanctioned by their authorities.[3] The term resembles the concept of 'semi-autonomous social field' of Sally Falk Moore (1973). Like Moore, Van Vollenhoven insisted that external regulations were reinterpreted within the context of such communities. An *adat* law community held the 'right of avail' (*beschikkingsrecht*), common rights to grazing grounds, forests, and uncultivated land; but he did not consider the *adat* communities as ideal, homogeneous and conflict-free, as some have claimed (Henley and Davidson 2007). Many were internally stratified or differentiated into kin groups of different scale, and certain privatized rights to land were often acknowledged. Empirical studies offered insight in mechanisms of conflict prevention, 'preventive law care' (*preventieve rechtszorg*), and 'attested observance' (*gesteunde naleving*) that underscored the role of authoritative *adat* witnesses in important transactions (J. F. Holleman 1981: xxii, 222–4; F. von Benda-Beckmann and K. von Benda-Beckmann 2007: 699). The study of *adat* laws, thus, was for Van Vollenhoven an academic endeavour that also helped identify the injustices that occurred when the results of the studies were not taken seriously. In this respect he wanted to contribute to legal practice.

Under Barend ter Haar, one of the founding professors at the Law Faculty in Batavia in 1924, the *Adat* Law School took a more pronounced legal turn. While Van Vollenhoven was concerned primarily with revealing and understanding the character of *adat* law, Ter Haar wanted to help *adat* law to adjust to the exigencies of modern times. It should be subjected to a positive legal science (*positieve rechtswetenschap*), in order to aid colonial judges in deciding cases on the basis of principles that were distilled from previous decisions. Inspired by American ideas of legal realism, Ter Haar (1937: 5; 1948) developed his decision theory (*beslissingenleer*) as a method to analyse decisions within and outside of the context of disputes in order to discover the underlying legal principles. Descriptive accounts were made subservient to pragmatic legal reasoning and adaptation to changing social and economic circumstances. This induced scholars such as Furnivall and Raymond Kennedy to criticize the *Adat* Law School for having been instrumental in the colonial politics of *divide et impera* (Ellen 1976: 318; Sonius 1981: xxxvi).

A colleague of Ter Haar and a student of Van Vollenhoven, F. D. Holleman combined his work as a judge with anthropological research on Java and on Ambon. Like Van Vollenhoven, his primary aim was to describe and understand *adat* laws. In 1929 he took a professorship in ethnology (*volkenkunde*) and sociology in Batavia, and in 1934 he succeeded Van Vollenhoven in the chair in Leiden, but returned in 1939 to his country of birth, South Africa. F. D. Holleman was succeeded by V. E. Korn, another important *adat* scholar and the author of a monograph on Bali who, like his predecessor, continued the scholarly approach of Van Vollenhoven.

After Indonesia's independence, Ter Haar's approach would only remain influential among a small circle of Indonesian legal scholars aiming at an Indonesian legal system based on *adat* law, such as M. M. Djojodigoeno, Soepomo, and Mohammad Koesnoe. However, Indonesia opted for a unified legal system based on Dutch law with some lip service to *adat* law. *Adat* law relapsed into a marginal and ossified subject in legal education.

What made Van Vollenhoven exceptional was his combination of deep concern for the injustices perpetrated by the Dutch against the indigenous population and scholarly fascination for normative orders based on very different premises than those of Western law. He developed an academic line of inquiry that broke with the standard late nineteenth-century procedure of studying unwritten laws by means of questionnaires informed by purely Western legal categories that were sent out to administrators, missionaries, and travellers. Van Vollenhoven argued that legal systems should be understood in their own terms and categories. This discussion preceded by almost half a century a prominent debate on appropriate concepts between Paul Bohannan and Max Gluckman, who disagreed on the question whether normative orders should be described by using vernacular terms only. In the view of Van Vollenhoven, using Western legal concepts unreflectingly led to serious misconceptions with severe political and economic implications. His generic neologisms were designed to avoid falling into this trap. Notwithstanding the criticisms, he generated important insights in the social working of law and the interaction between legal systems. The following three sets of crucial insights, developed on the basis of detailed ethnographic accounts long before they were generated elsewhere, have been of lasting importance (see Benda-Beckmann and Benda-Beckmann 2002: 698–700):

1. *Adat* law scholars pointed to the dangers of trying to express indigenous legal concepts and institutions through Dutch legal concepts, and distinguished between 'folk *adat* law' (*adat volksrecht*) and 'lawyers' *adat* law' (*adatjuristenrecht*).2. Law was primarily important in conflict-neutral social practices, and researchers highlighted the role of preventive law care and authoritative witnesses.3. *Adat* decisions were taken by consensus and often contained not more than an indication of a principle, expressed in terms of the concrete issues and circumstances of the individual case.

Due to the language barrier, the work of Van Vollenhoven remained largely unknown outside the Netherlands. The most important publication by Ter Haar (1948) was translated into English by E. Adamson Hoebel in 1948, while major parts of Van Vollenhoven's work appeared in English only much later in a translation by J. F. Holleman (1981). While Van Vollenhoven's work had a lasting impact in the Netherlands, it became available for an English-speaking audience at a time when similar insights were emerging from research in Africa.

Repositioning the study of folk law after Indonesia's independence

Indonesia declared independence in 1945, sovereignty was transferred in 1949, and New Guinea was incorporated into Indonesia in 1962. Dutch academia began to reorient institutionally, regionally, and theoretically. Institutionally, the study of customary law was continued first in Leiden and Nijmegen, later also in Wageningen, Groningen, Rotterdam, and Amsterdam. Regionally, studies of folk law diversified to Africa, Latin America, and to the Netherlands (K. von Benda-Beckmann 2002). In 1963 J. F. Holleman, the son of F. D. Holleman, educated in Stellenbosch in anthropology and in Roman-Dutch law, accepted a new chair in sociology and cultural studies of Africa in Leiden where he also became the director of the African Studies Centre (ASC). In 1969 he was appointed to Van Vollenhoven's chair in the Faculty of Law. With his research on Zulu legal communities and on Shona law at the Rhodes Livingstone Institute, J. F. Holleman was eminently positioned to connect insights from the Dutch *Adat* Law School with debates among legal anthropologists working on Africa. His monograph on Shona customary law (J. F. Holleman 1952) was the first of the classical monographs on African customary law published at the Rhodes Livingstone Institute. Together with J. Keuning and H. W. J. Sonius, a Van Vollenhoven student who had also turned his attention to Africa, J. F. Holleman stimulated Dutch studies on African customary law. Most anthropologists at that time showed little interest in practical issues. In their view, the applied focus relegated the study of folk law to the legal domain (Büskens and Kommers 2002).

In 1949, the Documentation Center for Overseas Law was established to keep track of legal developments, including *adat* law, in the former colonies. In 1977 Franz von Benda-Beckmann, who had done research in Africa and Indonesia, became its director and under his leadership the documentation center mutated into the Netherlands Research Institute for Southeast Asia and the Caribbean (NORZOAC) with a pronounced anthropological signature. When Jan Michiel Otto took over in 1982, the institute's agenda was reoriented towards more strictly legal concerns, though much empirical work was anthropological in character. As the Van Vollenhoven Institute for Law, Governance and Society (VVI), it is a thriving centre for anthropological and sociolegal research of law in Sub-Saharan Africa, North Africa and the Middle East, and Asia. In particular, the section devoted to Indonesia, under Adriaan Bedner, draws inspiration from the work of Van Vollenhoven. Otto retired in 2018 and was succeeded by Janine Ubink, an expert on African legal pluralism.

A group of scholars in Nijmegen continued Van Vollenhoven's work, also echoing his concern for practical issues. Geert van den Steenhoven, trained as a lawyer in the Netherlands and as an anthropologist in Canada (Steenhoven 1962), accepted a personal chair in 'folk law and legal development' in 1972. Together with his Indonesian colleague, Mohammad Koesnoe, he initiated collaborative research by young lawyers and anthropologists on *adat* law in Bali and Lombok. With the intention of producing research results that were useful for Indonesian legal practitioners, the project sought to take a middle ground between a purely legal science and anthropology; but, for various reasons, little came of it (Strijbosch 1999). Fons Strijbosch, who had been a member of the project's team of researchers, succeeded Van den Steenhoven in 1991. When he took early retirement in 2000, the chair was discontinued and Nijmegen ceased to be a focal point for the study of law in the tradition of the *Adat* Law School.

In 1976, van den Steenhoven established the Dutch Folk Law Circle (*Volksrechtskring*), a group of scholars working on folk law in the context of legal pluralism and emphasizing the interplay of different types of law, including folk or customary law, religious law, domestic law of states, or newly created law (F. von Benda-Beckmann 2002; Griffiths 1986). The *Volksrechtskring* published a newsletter that later merged with the newsletter of the sociologists of law into the journal *Recht der Werkelijkheid*. This was a sign that the boundaries between the sociology of law, with its focus on the Netherlands, and the anthropology of law, with its focus on the global South, was no longer deemed relevant (F. von Benda-Beckmann 2008). In 1978, Van den Steenhoven, with the support of the *Volksrechtskring*, also took the initiative to found the *Commission on Folk Law and Legal Pluralism* as part of the International Union of Anthropological Ethnographic Sciences (IUAES). It developed into a vibrant forum for academics and practitioners interested in theoretical and empirical studies of law under conditions of legal plurality. Also, the journal *African Law Studies* became the *Journal of Legal Pluralism and Unofficial Law*, for which John Griffiths served as the editor-in-chief for many years.

By the 1980s, relations between the Netherlands and Indonesia had improved, and, under the Program of Legal Cooperation, collaborative research and research training programmes were initiated at Wageningen, Leiden, and Utrecht. The legal branch was located in Leiden and Utrecht. With his Indonesian counterpart, Professor Omas Ihromi, Franz von Benda-Beckmann was responsible for the legal anthropological part of the programme. The programme was abruptly aborted by President Suharto in 1992, when the Dutch Minister of Development Cooperation Pronk put Indonesia's Human Rights on the agenda. When many years later relationships could be re-established, the lead for legal cooperation was taken by the VVI.

Today, the anthropology of law is less institutionalized than it was two decades ago (Van Rossum and Böcker 2009). The main nodes are Wageningen, with its emphasis on natural resources, and the VVI in Leiden, which is engaged with legal development cooperation in Indonesia and a broad range of African and Near Eastern countries, with programmes for rule of law, legal certainty, human rights, and good governance.

From the Study of Folk Law to Legal Anthropology

Alongside the institutional reforms, Dutch anthropology of law underwent marked theoretical change from the 1970s onwards. The development towards a truly anthropological study of law and legal pluralism was stimulated most markedly under John Griffiths (1983) in Groningen, from 1978 to 2006, and under Franz von Benda-Beckmann (1989) in Wageningen, from 1982–2000.[4] At the VVI, under Jan Michiel Otto, the empirical study of law remained more closely related to legal and governance studies, though legal pluralism figures prominently in the research of many scholars there, notably the new directors Adriaan Bedner and Janine Ubink.

Today, Dutch legal anthropology can best be characterized as a sub-discipline with blurred boundaries. It includes scholars with very diverse backgrounds, ranging from anthropology and law, to sociology, religious and political sciences, development economics, agriculture, and water management. The overarching concern is to understand the social working of law, in particular under conditions of legal pluralism—a concept which Dutch legal anthropologists have helped to refine (F. von Benda-Beckmann 2002; Griffiths 1986). Most researchers employ actor-oriented approaches in their empirical studies. Apart from the theoretical work in the Netherlands, they follow developments in the international anthropology of law, drawing on the work of the Manchester School, and also of Sally Falk Moore, Laura Nader, Marc Galanter, Simon Roberts, John Comaroff, Jean Comaroff, and Boaventura de Souza Santos. Further influences include social theorists such as Anthony Giddens, Pierre Bourdieu, Michel Foucault, and Jean Baudrillard, legal theorists such as Ronald Dworkin and H. L. A. Hart, the political scientist Michael Lipsky, and, recently, Science and Technology Studies. Van Vollenhoven (but not Ter Haar) has been re-defined as a precursor of the modern anthropology of law.

Themes of Research

Dispute Management and Justice

Dispute management has been a main theme among Dutch legal anthropologists from the 1970s onwards (K. von Benda-Beckmann 1984; Van Rouveroy, van Nieuwaal, and Baerends 1975; Slaats and Portier 1986. See K. von Benda-Beckmann and Strijbosch 1986). Initially focusing on processes of traditional justice and courts of first instance in rural areas, studies of dispute management began to diversify in the last decade of the twentieth century. Pompe (2005) and Bedner (2000) investigated the Indonesian Supreme Court and administrative courts respectively. Today, topics of study include the Indonesian Human Rights Committee Komnas Ham, public prosecutors, ombudspersons as well as courts and extrajudicial dispute management in the Netherlands (see e.g. Simon Thomas 2016). More recently, dispute management by vigilante groups in Japan and in violence-ridden regions in Africa have been studied (Jacobs and Schuetze 2011b).[5] This research has generated many insights into how people, in their search for justice, navigate between legal orders with their different categories, logics, and attribution of power.

Governance—Authority—Access to Justice—Rule of Law

Legal anthropologists working on Africa have long studied the ambivalent position of chiefs, perched between state law and tradition. Van Rouveroy (1980; Van Rouveroy and Ray 1996) pointed to the multiple roles of chiefs, for example as heads of kin groups, judges and mediators, and state officials. At the VVI, Oomen (2005a, 2005b) and Ubink (2007, 2008, 2019) showed that neo-traditional chiefs in South Africa and Ghana have acquired unprecedented power by commodifying customs and rights. These chiefs claimed to act on the authority of customary law, but they were, in fact, no longer subject to the traditional checks and balances that served in the past to prevent unbridled self-enrichment. Providing a careful analysis of the legal basis of modern chieftaincy, they discuss to what extent it is an invention of tradition, and where continuity with the past might be found. Similar developments have been documented for Indonesia, especially after the fall of the Suharto regime in 1998, when policies of decentralization were introduced in the context of the Indonesian reforms. The problems seem to be most serious in particular social settings, for example in regions with mixed populations, in stratified societies where the new 'kings' claim to rule over a large population, and in resource-rich areas. These studies also documented the devastating impact of corruption on governance in general (see also Mooij 1998; Nuijten and Anders 2007).

A new, challenging, and particularly important line of inquiry concerns traditional governance—and the lack of it—in (post-)war regions and refugee camps. Such research is being conducted at the VVI by I. Griek and B. Braak, and in the Congo by Carolien Jacobs (2018). They show that, within the camps, there is a strong tendency to search for some kind of traditional authority.

Property Relations, Indigenous Rights, and Environmental Justice

There has been a sustained interest in property relations, especially to land, water, and forest. It is here that the conceptual discrepancies between state law and local laws have been shown to be particularly problematic (F. von Benda-Beckmann 1979; De Bruijn and Van Dijk 1995; Ibrahim 2017; Nuijten 2003; Nuijten and Lorenzo 2009; Slaats and Portier 1981). Interdisciplinary research on rights to water is carried out in Wageningen (see

Boelens et al. 2010; Pradhan et al. 2000; Roth 2003; Roth et al. 2005; Roth and Winnubst 2009; Spiertz 1992; for fisheries, see Bavinck 1998). Several researchers have paid specific attention to gendered property rights (Baerends 1998; K. von Benda-Beckmann et al. 1997). While most of these studies were carried out in regions with established communities, Griffiths set up legal anthropological research in Latin America with the aim of understanding how law is generated in the competitive use of forests in regions without well-established communities (Griffiths 2017).[6]

The global indigenous rights movement has spawned new studies of land claims and self-determination (Assies, van der Haar, and Hoekema 2000; Hoekema 2010). Indonesia offers particularly interesting examples for two reasons. One is that, in contrast to former white settlers' colonies, the question of indigeneity is not centred around the opposition of original peoples and white settlers. The other reason has to do with the *Adat* Law School legacy. In Indonesia, the indigenous rights movement became especially successful when it became part of a heavily contested *adat* revival after the fall of Suharto in 1998. Non-governmental organizations (NGOs) adopted the term 'indigenous communities', derived from international law, to call for the protection of rights of dispossessed minority groups, especially in forests and mining areas. Within Indonesia there is now confusion because the term '*masyarakat adat*', as the translation of the international term 'indigenous community', shows some resemblance with the concept of '*adat* law community' of Van Vollenhoven. Studies in various parts of Indonesia have shown the great variety of paradoxical ways in which the indigenous movement has adopted *adat*, and many scholars have pointed to its negative implications (Bakker 2009; F. von Benda-Beckmann K. von Benda-Beckmann 2013; Henley and Davidson 2007; Van der Muur 2019; Vel et al. 2012). *Adat* revival and the indigenous movement has also given renewed impetus to a critical assessment of registration of land rights and legal certainty, as propagated, for example, by Hernando de Soto (Bedner and Oomen 2018; F. von Benda-Beckmann 2003; Otto 2009).

Recently, researchers have taken up challenges to study environmental justice and the implementation of—or failure to implement—environmental law in plantation and mining industries (d'Hondt 2011; Vel and Simandjuntak 2014; De Vos et al. 2018). Most of these studies are closely related to the issues of indigenous rights and *adat* revival, and to problems related to the registration of land titles as well. Further studies from a legal anthropological perspective have been carried out on environmental issues in China, on mining in Latin America, and on energy transition and environmental justice.

Social Security, Food Security, and Migration

From the 1980s onwards, a strong strand in the anthropology of law has addressed local forms of social security under conditions of legal pluralism (see e.g. Benda-Beckmann et al. 1994; F. von Benda-Beckmann and K. von Benda-Beckmann 2007; Böcker 1992, 2004; Koning and Hüsken 2006). Research has shown that legal orders entail different notions of need and care, causing confusion among analysts about the ways in which social security is extended. Social security institutions designed in terms of one legal system are reinterpreted to fit local understandings. Reinterpretation of international programmes are also advanced by high civil servants in the global south who are looking for ways to fulfil their obligation to provide of social security (Anders 2005). Research on the material basis for social security, including land, water, and food, branches out into issues of property relations, management, and justice. It is not by chance that researchers working or having been educated at Wageningen, with its focus on agriculture, pay close attention to the material basis for social security. This is particularly clear from research on food security and the related issue of water security (e.g. Havinga 2018; Mooij 1998; Roth and Warner 2010).

In the Netherlands, as in other West European countries, social scientists and lawyers have produced a mass of literature on migration from very diverse perspectives. A few legal anthropologists look at the interplay of state law and the law that migrants brought with them. Most of these issues are closely related to family relations and social security. Over many decades, Anita Böcker studied Turkish migrants in the Netherlands and their connections to relatives in Turkey and in Germany. She is particularly interested in social security issues and the needs for care in old age (Böcker and Hunter 2017). Fons Strijbosch (1985, 1988) has investigated changes in ritual kinship and adoption, and Keebet von Benda-Beckmann has studied the emancipation of Moluccan women in the Netherlands. She discussed how needs of care and notions of obligation undergo unequal change in transnational legal spaces (K. von Benda-Beckmann 2015).

Religion and Family Law

Religion and religious law, especially Islamic law, are major themes in anthropological and legal studies at the VVI.[7] Empirical studies focus primarily on the frictions of family law in religious and state institutions (Van Eijk 2016; Van Huis 2015; Sonneveld and Lindbekk 2017; Van Rossum 2008). Léon Buskens (2003) discussed the rising political purchase of family law in Morocco. Mies Grijns and Hoko Horii (2018) conduct anthropological research on child marriages and adoption in Java. Carolien Jacobs and Christy Schütze (2011a) have pointed to the rising importance of witchcraft in dispute management in Africa.

Conclusions

The *Adat* Law School, and especially Van Vollenhoven, who was in many ways ahead of his time, laid a foundation for postcolonial Dutch legal anthropology. Today, only Dutch legal anthropologists working in Indonesia make explicit use of that work. Nevertheless, the legacy of Van Vollenhoven and the *Adat* Law School is still discernible in research on local law and legal pluralism and on the role of law not only in disputes but also in other social practices. Typically, those who have been influenced by or display affinities with this school have a sharp eye for different interpretations of legal concepts and for the importance of legal principles. They engage in international theoretical debates and employ actor-oriented approaches. Research is ethnographically based and sensitive to power differentials. It is generally informed by pressing social and political issues in a globalizing world, such as rights to land and other natural resources, environmental issues, the rule of law, human rights, and migration. At the VVI, the current focus on governance and the rule of law stands for a strong interest in legal practice and for engagement with the disciplines of law and anthropology. Wageningen is known for its interdisciplinary approach.

The anthropology of law in the Netherlands, as elsewhere, faces some urgent challenges. One would be to examine the impact of increasing securitization on social security, land claims, and displacement. A second challenge is to come to a better understanding of legal plurality in transnational legal spaces, be it in the field of migration, social security, or in transnational production chains, certification processes, and land claims. Perhaps the most difficult challenge would be to study how new local law and authority might emerge, given large-scale displacement, destruction of communities, dispossession, and forced migration in war or under war-like conditions. These challenges require designing appropriate multisited research methods, engagement with new anthropological theories, and collaborative research that bridges different disciplines.

Notes

1. I am grateful to Juliette Koning and Dominik Müller for their thoughtful comments on an earlier draft of this chapter.
2. Ellen (1976: 304) contrasts the colonial influence in Dutch anthropology with British anthropology with its roots in precolonial social and natural philosophy.
3. The concept of adat law community is currently a hot issue in indigenous rights politics in Indonesia.
4. From 2000–12, Franz and Keebet von Benda-Beckmann worked at the Max Planck Institute for Social Anthropology in Halle, Germany, where they set up the project group 'Legal Pluralism'. During this period, they stayed in close contact with Dutch legal anthropologists, remaining, arguably, part of the Dutch legal anthropological landscape.
5. See the section, 'Religion and family law' in this chapter.
6. See also Griffiths et al. 1998 for law generation in the field of euthanasia in the Netherlands.
7. Otto (2010) published a comprehensive comparative study of Islamic law in North Africa and the Near East.

References

Anders, G. 2005. *Civil Servants in Malawi: Cultural Dualism, Moonlighting and Corruption in the Shadow of Good Governance.* PhD dissertation. Erasmus University Rotterdam.

Assies, W. J., G. van der Haar, and A. J. Hoekema, eds. 2000. *The Challenge of Diversity: Indigenous Peoples and the Reform of the State in Latin America.* Amsterdam: Thela Publishers.

Baerends, E. A. 1998. 'Changing Kinship, Family and Gender Relations in Sub-Saharan Africa'. In C. Risseeuw and K. Ganesh, eds. *Negotiation and Social Space: A Gendered Analysis of Changing Kin and Security Networks in South Asia and Sub-Saharan Africa*. 47–86. Walnut Creek, London, New Delhi: Sage Altamira Press.

Bakker, L. 2009. *Who Owns the Land. Looking for Law and Power in Reformasi East Kalimantan*. Thesis. Faculty of Law, Radboud University Nijmegen.

Bavinck, M. 1998. *One Sea, Three Contenders: Legal Pluralism in the Inshore Fisheries of the Coromandel Coast, India*. Amsterdam: University of Amsterdam.

Bedner, A. 2000. *Administrative Courts in Indonesia: A Socio-Legal Study*. The Hague, London, Boston: Kluwer Law International.

Bedner, A. and B. Oomen, eds. 2018. *Real Legal Certainty and its Relevance: Essays in Honor of Jan Michiel Otto*. Leiden: Leiden University Press.

Benda-Beckmann, F. von 1979. *Property in Social Continuity: Continuity and Change in the Maintenance of Property Relationships through time in Minangkabau, West Sumatra*. The Hague: Martinus Nijhoff.

Benda-Beckmann, F. von. 1989. 'Scapegoat and Magic Charm: Law in Development Theory and Practice'. *Journal of Legal Pluralism* 28: 129–48.

Benda-Beckmann, F. von. 2003. 'Mysteries of Capital or Mystification of Legal Property?'. *Focaal-European Journal of Anthropology* 41: 187–91.

Benda-Beckmann, F. von. 2007. *Social Security between Past and Future: Ambonese Networks of Care and Support*. Münster: LIT Verlag.

Benda-Beckmann, F. von. 2008. 'Riding or Killing the Centaur? Reflections on the Identities of Legal Anthropology'. *International Journal of Law in Context* 4(2): 85–110.

Benda-Beckmann, F. von. 2011. 'Myths and Stereotypes about Adat Law. A Reassessment of Van Vollenhoven in the Light of Current Struggles over Adat Law in Indonesia'. *Bijdragen tot de Taal-, Land- en Volkenkunde* 167(2/3): 167–95.

Benda-Beckmann, F. von. 2013. *Political and Legal Transformations of an Indonesian Polity. The Nagari from Colonization to Decentralisation*. Cambridge: Cambridge University Press.

Benda-Beckmann, F. von. 2015. 'Social Security in Transnational Legal Space: Limitations and Opportunities'. In S. Köngeter and W. Smith (eds). *Transnational Agency and Migration. Actors, Movements and Social Support*. 245–61. London: Routledge.

Benda-Beckmann, F. von and K. von Benda-Beckmann. 2002. 'Anthropology of Law and the Study of Folk Law in The Netherlands after 1950'. In H. Vermeulen and J. Kommers, eds. *Tales from Academia. History of Anthropology in The Netherlands. Part 2*, 695–731. Saarbrücken: Verlag für Entwicklungspolitik Saarbrücken GmbH.

Benda-Beckmann, F. von, K. von Benda-Beckmann, and H. Marks, eds. 1994. 'Coping with Insecurity. An 'Underall' Perspective on Social Security in the Third World.' *Focaal* 1994(22/23).

Benda-Beckmann, K. von 1984. *The Broken Stairways to Consensus: Village Justice and State Courts in Minangkabau*. Dordrecht, Leiden, Cinnaminson: Foris Publications, KITLV Press.

Benda-Beckmann, K. von and F. Strijbosch (eds). 1986. *Anthropology of Law in the Netherlands. Essays on Legal Pluralism, vol. 116*. Dordrecht, Leiden: Foris Publications, KITLV Press.

Benda-Beckmann, K. von, Mirjam de Bruijn, Han van Dijk, Gertie Hesseling, Barbara van Koppen, and Lyda Res. 1997. 'Rights of Women to the Natural Resources Land and Water'. *Women and Development Working Paper No. 2*. The Hague: Ministry of Foreign Affairs, Development Cooperation Information Department.

Böcker, A. 1992. 'Social Security in Turkish Migrant Families in the Netherlands'. *Journal of Legal Pluralism* 32: 1–18.

Böcker, A. 2004. 'The Impact of Host-Society Institutions on Immigrant Integration: The Case of Turkish Immigrants in Germany and the Netherlands'. *Journal of Immigration, Asylum and Nationality Law* 18(4): 242–61.

Bocker, A. and A. Hunter. 2017. 'Legislating for Transnational Ageing: a Challenge to the Logics of the Welfare State'. *European Journal of Ageing* 14(4): 353–63.

Boelens, R., D. Getches, and A. Guevara-Gil, eds. 2010. *Out of the Mainstream: Water Rights, Politics and Identity*. London, Washington: Earthscan.

Bruijn, M.de and H. van Dijk. 1995. *Arid Ways, Cultural Understandings of Insecurity in Fulbe Society, Central Mali*. Amsterdam: Thela Publishers.

Burns, P. J. 2007. 'Custom, That is Before all Law'. In J. S. Davidson and D. Henley, eds. *The Revival of Tradition in Indonesian Politics. The Deployment of Adat from Colonialism to Indigenism*, 68–86. London and New York: Routledge.

Buskens, L. 2003. 'Recent Debates on Family Law Reform in Morocco: Islamic Law as Politics in an Emerging Public Sphere'. *Islamic Law and Society* 10(1): 70–131.

Buskens, L. and J. Kommers. 2002. 'The Delayed Reception of Colonial Studies about Adat Law and Islamic Law in Dutch Anthropology'. In H. Vermeulen and J. Kommers, eds. *Tales from Academia. History of Anthropology in the Netherlands*, 733–55. Nijmegen Studies in Development and Cultural Change. Saarbrücken: Verlag für Entwicklungspolitik Saarbrücken GmbH.

d'Hondt, L. 2011. 'Seeking Environmental Justice in North Maluku'. *Law, Social Justice and Global Development* 2010 (1).

Eijk, E.van. 2016. *Family Law in Syria: A Plurality of Laws, Norms, and Legal Practices*. London and New York: I. B. Taurus.

Ellen, R. F. 1976. 'The Development of Anthropology and Colonial Policy in the Netherlands: 1800–1960'. *Journal of the History of the Behavioral Sciences* 12(4): 303–24.

Furnivall, J. S. 1944. *Netherlands India: A Study of a Plural Economy*. Cambridge: Cambridge University Press.

Griffiths, J. 1983. 'Dutch Legal Anthropology'. *Nieuwsbrief voor Nederlandstalige Rechtssociologen, Rechtsanthropologen en Rechtspsychologen* 2: 132–240.

Griffiths, J. 1986. 'Recent Anthropology of Law in the Netherlands and its Historical Background'. In K. von Benda-Beckmann and F. Strijbosch, eds. *Anthropology of Law in the Netherlands*, 1166. Dordrecht/Berlin: Foris Publications/Walter de Gruyter.

Griffiths, J. 2017. 'What is Sociology of Law? (On Law, Rules, Social Control and Sociology)'. *The Journal of Legal Pluralism and Unofficial Law* 49(2): 93–142.

Griffiths, J., A. Bood, and H. Weyers. 1998. *Euthanasia and Law in the Netherlands*. Amsterdam: Amsterdam University Press.

Grijns, M. and H. Horii. 2018. 'Child Marriage in a Village in West Java (Indonesia): Compromises between Legal Obligations and Religious Concerns'. *Asian Journal of Law and Society* 5(2): 453–66.

Haar Bzn, B. 1937. *Het adatprivaatrecht van Nederlandsch-Indië in wetenschap, practijk en onderwijs*. Groningen, Batavia: Wolters' Uitgevers-Maatschappij N.V.

Haar Bzn, B. 1948. *Adat law in Indonesia* (trans. G. C. O. Haas, E. A. Hoebel, and A. A. Schiller). New York: International Secretariat Institute of Pacific relations.

Havinga, T. 2018. 'The Integration of Private Certification in Governmental Food Controls. A Survey on Public-Private Collaboration in Food Safety Governance'. *Nijmegen Sociology of Law Working Papers Series*, vol. 2018/1. Nijmegen: Radboud University.

Henley, D. and J. S. Davidson. 2007. 'Introduction: Radical Conservatism—the Protean Politics of Adat.' In J. S. Davidson and D. Henley, eds. *The Revival of Tradition in Indonesian Politics: The Deployment of Adat from Colonialism to Indigenism*, 1–49. London [u.a.]: Routledge.

Hoekema, A. J. 2010. 'Community Controlled Codification of Local Resource Tenure: An Effective Tool for Defending Local Rights?'. In R. Boelens, D. Getches, and A. Guevara-Gil, eds. *Out of the Mainstream: Water Rights, Politics and Identity*, 235–57. London: Earthscan.

Holleman, J. F. 1952. *Shona Customary Law: With Reference to Kinship, Marriage, the Family and the Estate*. Cape Town: Oxford University Press, Cumberlege.

Holleman, J. F., ed. 1981. *Van Vollenhoven on Indonesian Adat Law: Selections from het adatrecht van Nederlandsch-Indie. With an Introduction by H. W.J. Sonius, vol. 20*. The Hague: Martinus Nijhoff.

Huis, S. C. van. 2015. *Islamic Courts and Women's Divorce Rights in Indonesia: The Cases of Cianjur and Bulukumba*. Leiden: E.M. Meijers Instituut, Leiden University.

Ibrahim, S. 2017. 'Property Claims in Post-Gaddafi Libya: Political Debates and Justice Seeking in the Aftermath of Law 4/1978'. *Hague Journal on the Rule of Law* 9(1): 135–56.

Jacobs, C. 2018. 'Seeking Justice, Experiencing the State: Criminal Justice and Real Legal Uncertainty in the Democratic Republic of Congo'. *The Journal of Legal Pluralism and Unofficial Law* 50(3): 280–93.

Jacobs, C. and C. Schütze. 2011a. '"Justice with Our Own Hands": Lynching, Poverty, Witchcraft and the State in Mozambique'. In M. Berg and S. Wendt, eds. *Globalizing Lynching History: Vigilantism and Extralegal Punishment from an International Perspective*, 225–41. Basingstoke: Palgrave Macmillan.

Jacobs, C. 2011b. 'Violence against Violence. In Search of Security and Justice'. *Etnofoor State/Violence* 23(2): 17–36.

Koning, J. and F. Hüsken, eds. 2006. 'Ropewalking and Safety Nets: Local Ways of Managing Insecurities in Indonesia'. *Social Sciences in Asia, vol. 12*. Leiden, Boston: Brill.

Lev, D. S. 1984. 'Book Review. Van Vollenhoven on Indonesian Adat Law'. *Journal of Legal Pluralism* 22: 147–55.

Mooij, J. E. 1998. 'Food Policy and Politics: The Political Economy of the Public Distribution System in India'. *The Journal of Peasant Studies* 25(2): 77–101.

Moore, S. F. 1973. 'Law and Social Change: The Semi-Autonomous Social Field as an Appropriate Subject of Study'. *Law & Society Review* 7(4): 719–46.

Muur, W. E. van der. 2019. *Land Rights and the Forces of Adat in Democratizing Indonesia: Continuous Conflict between Plantations, Farmers and Forests in South Sulawesi*. Leiden: Faculty of Law, Leiden University.

Nuijten, M. 2003. *Power, Community and the State. The Political Anthropology of Organisation in Mexico*. London, Sterling, Virginia: Pluto Press.

Nuijten, M. and G. Anders, eds. 2007. *Corruption and the Secret of Law: A Legal Anthropological Perspective*. Aldershot: Ashgate.

Nuijten, M. and D. Lorenzo. 2009. 'Ritual and Rule in the Periphery: State Violence and Local Governance in a Peruvanian Comunidad'. In F. von Benda-Beckmann, K. von Benda-Beckmann, and J. Eckert, eds. *Rules of Law and Laws of Ruling. On the Governance of Law*, 101–23. Farnham and Burlington: Ashgate.

Oomen, B. 2005a. *Chiefs in South Africa: Law, Power and Culture in the Post-Apartheid Era.* Oxford: James Currey.

Oomen, B. 2005b. 'McTradition in the New South Africa: Commodified Custom and Rights Talk with the Bafokeng and the Bapedi'. In F. von Benda-Beckmann, K. von Benda-Beckmann, and A. Griffiths, eds. *Mobile People, Mobile Law. Expanding Legal Relations in a Contracting World*, 91–109. Aldershot and Burlington: Ashgate.

Otto, J. M. 2009. 'Rule of Law Promotion, Land Tenure and Poverty Alleviation: Questioning the Assumptions of Hernando de Soto'. *Hague Journal on the Rule of Law* Volume 1: 173–95.

Otto, J. M. 2010. *Sharia Incorporated. A Comparative Overview of the Legal Systems of Twelve Muslim Countries in Past and Present.* Leiden: Leiden University Press.

Pompe, S. 2005. *The Indonesian Supreme Court: A Study of Institutional Collapse.* Ithaca: Cornell Southeast Asia Program.

Pradhan, R., F. von Benda-Beckmann, and K. von Benda-Beckmann, eds. 2000. *Water, Land and Law: Changing Rights to Land and Water in Nepal.* Kathmandu, Wageningen, Rotterdam: FREEDEAL, WAU, EUR.

Rossum, W. M. van. 2008. 'Religious Courts Alongside Secular State Courts: The Case of the Turkish Alevis', available at <http://www.go.warwick.ac.uk/elj/lgd/2008_2/rossum>.

Rossum, W. M. van and A. Böcker. 2009. 'Death and Resurrection of Anthropology of Law: Introduction to the Special Issue'. *Recht der Werkelijkheid Special Issue Legal Anthropology in the Low Countries* 2009(3): 9–21.

Roth, D. 2003. *Ambition, Regulation and Reality: Complex Use of Land and Water Resources in Luwu, South Sulawesi, Indonesia.* PhD Dissertation, Wageningen University.

Roth, D., R. Boelens, and M. Zwarteveen, eds. 2005. *Liquid Relations. Contested Water Rights and Legal Complexity.* New Brunswick, New Jersey, London: Rutgers University Press.

Roth, D. and J. F. Warner. 2010. 'Food Security as Water Security: The Multi-Level Governance of Virtual Water'. In O. Hospes and I. Hadiprayitno, eds. *Governing Food Security: Law, Politics and the Right to Food*, 295–320. Wageningen: Wageningen Academic Publishers.

Roth, D. and M. Winnubst. 2009. 'Reconstructing the Polder: Negotiating Property Rights and "Blue" Functions for Land'. *International Journal of Agricultural Resources, Governance and Ecology* 8(1): 37–56.

Rouveroy van Nieuwaal, E. A. B. van. 1980. 'Chieftaincy in Northern Togo'. *Verfassung und Recht in Übersee* 13: 115–23.

Rouveroy van Nieuwaal, E. A. B. van and E. van Rouveroy van Nieuwaal. 1975. 'To Claim or Not to Claim: Changing Views about the Restitution of Marriage Prestations among the Anufóm of Northern Togo'. *African Law Studies* 12: 102–28.

Rouveroy van Nieuwaal, E. A. B. van and D. I. Ray, eds. 1996. 'The New Relevance of Traditional Authorities to Africa's Future'. *Journal of Legal Pluralism* 37/38 (special issue).

Simon Thomas, M. A. 2016. 'Theorizing Mediation: Lessons Learned from Legal Anthropology'. *Utrecht Law Review* 12(1): 50–60.

Slaats, H. M. C. and M. K. Portier. 1981. *Grondenrecht en zijn verwerkelijking in de Karo Batakse dorpssamenleving. Een beschrijvende studie* Band I en II. Nijmegen: Instituut voor Volksrecht.

Slaats, H. M. C. 1986. 'Legal Plurality and the Transformation of Normative Concepts in the Process of Litigation in Karo Batak Society'. In K. v. Benda Beckmann and F. Strijbosch, eds. *Anthropology of Law in the Netherlands*, 217–39. Dordrecht, Berlin: Foris, Walter de Gruyter.

Sonius, H. W. J. 1981. 'Introduction'. In J. F. Holleman, ed. *Van Vollenhoven on Indonesian Adat Law*. xxix–lxv. The Hague: Martinus Nijhoff.

Sonneveld, N. and M. Lindbekk, eds. 2017. *Women Judges in the Muslim World: A Comparative Study of Discourse and Practice*. Leiden: Brill.

Spiertz, H. L. J. 1992. 'Between Cannibalism and Pluralism: On the Construction of Legal Frameworks in Irrigation Management in Bali and Sri Lanka'. In F. v. Benda-Beckmann and M. v. d. Velde, eds. *Law as a Resource in Agrarian Struggles*, 89–109. Wageningen: Agricultural University Wageningen.

Steenhoven, G. van den. 1962. *Leadership and Law among the Eskimos of the Keewatin District, Northwest Territories*. Rijswijk: Uitgeverij Excelsior.

Strijbosch, F. 1980. *Juristen en de Studie van Volksrecht in Nederlands-Indië en Anglofoon Afrika*. Nijmegen: Instituut voor Volksrecht.

Strijbosch, F. 1985. 'The Concept of Pèla and its Social Significance in the Community of Moluccan Immigrants in the Netherlands'. *Journal of Legal Pluralism* 23: 177–208.

Strijbosch, F. 1988. 'Informal Social Security among Moluccan Immigrants in the Netherlands'. In F. v. Benda-Beckmann, K. v. Benda-Beckmann, E. Casiño, F. Hirtz, G. R. Woodman, and H. F. Zacher, eds. *Between Kinship and the State: Social Security and Law in Developing Countries*, 169–85. Dordrecht: Foris.

Strijbosch, F. 1996. 'De Rechtsantropologie in Nederland en België'. In J. Griffiths, ed. *De Sociale Werking van Recht: Een Kennismaking met de Rechtssociologie en Rechtsantropologie*. Third edition, 534–42. Nijmegen: Ars Aequi.

Strijbosch, F. 1999. 'In Memory of Geert van den Steenhoven'. *Journal of Legal Pluralism* 44: 1–14.

Trouwborst, A. A. 2002. 'Anthropology, the Study of Islam, and Adat law in the Netherlands and the Netherlands East Indies, 1920–1950'. In H. Vermeulen and J. Kommers, eds. *Tales from Academia. History of Anthropology in the Netherlands* Part 2, 673–94. Nijmegen Studies in Development and Cultural Change. Saarbrücken: Verlag für Entwicklungspolitik Saarbrücken GmbH.

Ubink, J. M. 2007. 'Tenure Security: Wishful Policy Thinking or Reality? A Case from Peri-Urban Ghana'. *Journal of African Law* 51(2): 215–48.

Ubink, J. M. 2008. *In the Land of the Chiefs. Customary Law, Land Conflicts, and the Role of the State in peri-urban Ghana*. Leiden: Leiden University Press.

Ubink, J. M. 2019. *Legal Pluralism, Capital and Democracy—Inaugural Lecture*. Leiden: Leiden University.

Vel, J. A. C., John F. McCarthy, and S. Afiff. 2012. 'Trajectories of Land Acquisition and Enclosure: Development Schemes, Virtual Land Grabs, and Green Acquisitions in Indonesia's Outer Islands'. *Journal of Peasant Studies* 39(2): 521–49.

Vel, J. A. C. and D. Simandjuntak, eds. 2014. *JARAK, the Short History of Jatropha Projects in Indonesia*. Leiden: IIAS.

Vollenhoven, C.van, ed. 1911–1949. *Adatrechtbundels*. 's-Gravenhage: Martinus Nijhoff.

Vollenhoven, C.van. 1914–1931. *Pandecten van het Adatrecht*. Amsterdam: Koninklijk Koloniaal Instituut.

Vos, R. de, M. Köhne, and D. Roth. 2018. '"We'll Turn your Water into Coca-Cola": The Atomizing Practices of Oil Palm Plantation Development in Indonesia'. *Journal of Agrarian Change* 18(2): 385–405.

Weyers, H. and K. von Benda-Beckmann. 2018. *In Memoriam John Griffiths. Recht der Werkelijkheid* 39(2): 6–17.

CHAPTER 12

LEGAL USES OF ANTHROPOLOGY IN FRANCE IN THE NINETEENTH AND TWENTIETH CENTURIES

FRÉDÉRIC AUDREN AND LAETITIA GUERLAIN

What does the history of the relationship between law and anthropology reveal? At first sight, the two disciplines appear to be organically linked, while also occasionally in conflict. After all, reflecting on normative phenomena, whether legal, moral, or religious, is at the heart of the discipline of anthropology itself.

Many seminal thinkers have tackled the question of the place that law should occupy in social life, including, in the nineteenth and twentieth centuries, Lewis Henry Morgan, Max Gluckman, Johann Jakob Bachofen, John Ferguson McLennan, Henry Sumner Maine, Émile Durkheim, Marcel Mauss, and Bronisław Malinowski. The list attests to a widely shared affirmation, namely, that the history of the relationship between law and anthropology is inextricably linked to the origins and development of social and cultural anthropology. For some, the starting point lies in the early theories of evolution, notably those concerning kinship systems. For others, that history begins with the Durkheimian concept of a social fact, and, in particular, that of forms of solidarity. Whatever the preferred paradigm, this social and cultural approach appears to be the precondition for an anthropological discourse on law. And yet, this position reduces anthropology to its most recent and academically endorsed definition, which simply ignores the multiplicity of viewpoints on the nexus of anthropology and law that have evolved over the past two centuries. Anthropology's own history seems truly to have been written by the victors and often leads to a narrative that gives value to legal pluralism, cultural diversity, and a relativization of the West.

Yet, the history of the relationship between law and anthropology cannot be reduced to that of social and cultural anthropology. The case of France is a good illustration of the manner in which practitioners of the two disciplines have engaged in dialogue, often far removed from this sociological and culturalist prism. In fact, the culturalist approach is one of the (most recent) paths taken by such discourse, albeit without being reduced to it. We should remember that in the field of anthropology, the Durkheimian approach to law has not had the success or development that had been presaged. By the twentieth century, competing paradigms such as Marxist anthropology and structuralism, to name but two, had consigned law to the history books. In legal circles, the strict division between academic disciplines, splitting law from the social sciences, and the positivist and legalistic culture of legal practitioners were partly responsible for isolating them from the achievements of the social sciences. Sociology and anthropology remained outside their preoccupations. However, these comments should not overshadow the efforts that were made to build an uninterrupted dialogue between legal and anthropological knowledge. Since the beginning of the nineteenth century, law has often found use for anthropology, albeit on the understanding that the diversity of definitions and approaches must be taken into consideration.[1] It should be recognized that, for the various actors involved, understanding law through the lens of anthropology meant drawing on history, philology, phrenology, natural sciences, and folklore, in addition to sociology and ethnology, to nurture legal thinking and engage in legal work.

The obscuring of this rich and complex history, of a plurality of knowledge that may sometimes appear outmoded or rejected is, in the French case, linked to a suppression of the past that the legal world is still struggling to confront. In the way they put anthropological knowledge into action, jurists cannot escape criticism for nationalism, racism, and colonialism. As such knowledge was highly dependent upon colonial power and the natural sciences, it was made to serve the domineering and expansionist legal policies of nineteenth- and twentieth-century France. In the wake of the totalitarian and colonial experiences of the Second World War, the promoters of a new, academically solid, and institutionalized 'legal anthropology' emerged in the 1960s. In 1963–1964, a new research centre, the *Laboratoire d'anthropologie juridique*, was established in Paris by Michel Alliot. The centre preferred to break all ties with previous attempts at linking law and anthropology, imagining instead the dialogue between the two as a new and fertile terrain through which to traverse. The invention of the term 'legal anthropology' (*anthropologie juridique*) led French jurists to consign the long history of relations between the two disciplines to the shadows. Drawing on recent insights from the history of knowledge (*histoire des savoirs*), our contribution returns to this forgotten history and offers an examination of the successive formulations and debates within France regarding the relationship between law and anthropology since the beginning of the nineteenth century.

In search of the origins of law: an anthropology of the French national legal identity (1804–1860)

From the promulgation of the Napoleonic Code in 1804 until the 1860s, French legal studies often intersected with the human and social sciences.[2] The shared intellectual path linking such disciplines converged around an emerging idea on the origins of law at the beginning of the nineteenth century. In many European countries, legal thinking experienced a period of unprecedented historicization. History and philology became the keys to any enquiry into the laws in force. Law and history joined forces to identify an essence of French law, although the results were often more imaginary than real.

The Crisis of the Interpretation and National Origins of Law

In the context of dissatisfaction with the priority accorded to the literal, or exegetical, method of textual interpretation, some French legal scholars turned their attention to history as a method for better understanding the relationship between law and social phenomena. In fact, for many authors from the 1820s and 1830s onwards, history became the scientific standard *par excellence* in the study of law. It authorized the search for a cultural substratum that anchored the rule of law within the social realm instead of making it the product of disembodied reason. In the opinions of this group of keen historian-jurists, including Athanase Jourdan (1791–1826), Eugène Lerminier (1803–1857), Henri Klimrath (1807–1837), and Édouard Laboulaye (1811–1883), *all* legal science *is* the history of law.

In the first half of the nineteenth century, the question of the material sources of law, especially those that were historical in nature, became all-important. It led jurists wanting to renew the methods of interpreting law to direct their thoughts towards researching the *origins of law*. This project, aimed at historicizing legal studies, in the period after the Congress of Vienna (1814–1815) and the emergence of European nation-states, was intricately linked to a major political problem, that of the search for a *national* legal identity (Audren and Halpérin 2013). Research and the publication of unedited historical documents, as well as the renewed attention that was being given to medieval customs, show clearly how this project of nationalization of the law had to proceed by way of a *return to the past*. Influenced by Savigny and the works of the German historical school, French jurists who wanted to write the legal history of the French nation had to walk in the footsteps of the historians, antiquarians, archaeologists, and philologists who, in the age of Romanticism, were writing their own national identities from scratch (Thiesse 2001; Venayre 2013).

Legitimization through appeal to the origins

It was historical research that lent intelligibility to the spirit of French law (Kelley 1984). This was, for example, the aim of the work on a geography of customs by Henri Klimrath, a Strasbourg jurist strongly influenced by German scientific thinking, who sought, in his *Studies on Customs* (1837), to prove the existence of a common French spirit beyond the diversity of medieval customs, which culminated in the Napoleonic Code of 1804. Klimrath's contribution constitutes a crucial threshold: behind the formality and abstraction of norms, the search for the earliest sources of French law was now underway—looking for the very essence of the law. There was a growing desire to shine a light on what 'lay beneath the norms' in order to find a socio-cultural substratum, of which those norms were but an external manifestation.[3] Following the first issue of the *Revue historique de droit français et étranger* in 1855, the ambitions of all legal history became fully anthropological. Indeed, the aim was nothing less than to reveal, beneath the law's surface, the deeper cultural characteristics and indigenous forms of social order. The law was no longer merely an expression of political or legislative will. It became a mark of *civilization*, to use the contemporaneous term, or a major cultural phenomenon.

The Story of Origins: A Legal Ethnogenesis of France

The ambitious objective to 'naturalize' the deeply anthropological national legal culture was driven by jurists importing the notion of 'race'. In the first half of the nineteenth century, race was seen less as a biological reality than as characteristics associated with different peoples. To bring the French legal conception up to date, it is therefore necessary to investigate the ethnogenesis of Gaul and, above all, of its people. The question of the Gallic origins of French law divided historiography and authors during the first half of the nineteenth century (Assier-Andrieu 2011: 214). This question may not be new, having first been addressed by liberal historians in the 1820s, notably by Amédée Thierry (1797–1873) in the *Histoire des Gaulois*, which was published in 1828 in three volumes (Reynaud-Paligot 2011; see also Lacoste 1982). The first jurist-historians dreamed up a special place for 'Gallic law' within the national spirit. They did so by mobilizing history and philology, which were the only two scholarly disciplines tackling the problem of national origins at a time when archaeology was still in its infancy and the racial question was little more than an afterthought. French legal historians, including Charles Giraud (1802–1881) and Firmin Laferrière (1798–1861), explicitly based their arguments on advances in historical science and Celtic philology that were underway at the time (Amédée Thierry, Lorenz Diefenbach, William-Frédéric Edwards, Wilhelm von Humboldt, Jean-Jacques Ampère, etc.). The 'Celtic fever' that emerged at the beginning of the nineteenth century also manifested itself in the number of legal practitioners and local scholars who joined the ranks of the *Académie Celtique* (1804–1814), the *Société des Antiquaires de France* (1816), the *Académie des Inscriptions et Belles-Lettres*, the *Académie des Sciences Morales et Politiques*, and the myriad local learned societies that flourished throughout the century. Such groups engaged in research into the ancient sources of French law, following in the wake of the historian-magistrate Armand Désiré de La Fontenelle de Vaudoré (1784–1847), who was the founder of the *Société des Antiquaires de l'Ouest* and the translator and editor of the customs of Charroux (1843).

The National in the Universal: Law, Poetry, and Legal Symbolism

The essence of French law, supposedly to be found within this primitive 'Gallic law', was considered to be revealed gradually through the work of these historian-jurists, notably in light of the lack of written sources relating to this protohistoric era. It was precisely in the attempt to resolve this thorny issue that some jurists showed undeniable methodological inventiveness, made possible by interacting with the human and social sciences. Following the path shown by Giambattista Vico[4] and Jacob Grimm, some legal historians, including Charles Giraud and Edouard Laboulaye, realized that symbols, myths, and even poetry could be considered a repository of the most important legal forms and are revelatory of a deeply buried cultural substratum. The (historical) science of law, therefore, needed to use such literary sources to continue to progress in the absence of written legal sources. In light of the difficulties facing the discipline, the first half of the nineteenth century saw the emergence of a new research area: the symbolism of law. This approach is enshrined in several texts, including the *Dissertation sur les cérémonies symboliques usitées dans l'ancienne jurisprudence française* (1828), written by the magistrate Arthur Beugnot (1797–1865), the *Origines du droit français cherchées dans les symboles et formules du droit universel* (1837) by the historian Jules Michelet (1798–1874) and the *Essai sur la symbolique du droit, précédé d'une introduction sur la poésie du droit primitif* (1847) by the lawyer Joseph-Pierre Chassan (1800–1871). Michelet's work is distinguished from that of Beugnot and Chassan by the dialogue that is created between national and universal origins of law, thus testifying to the epistemological potential of the symbolist method, which could 'transcend the principle to attest to the legal universality of humans' (Assier-Andrieu 2011: 231).

The National in the Indo- European: Law and Orientalism

This dialectic between universal and national origins of law found an outlet in many works of the day, which tried to reflect a delicate interconnectedness between the two. In the first half of the nineteenth century, many jurists believed that Roman, Greek, Celtic, and German law derived from common eastern roots, from Hindu law, in particular, and were embodied in the famous laws of Manou from the second century BCE. However, from the beginning of the nineteenth century, work after work of comparative grammar noted the troubling similarities between Sanskrit, the sacred language of India, and the majority of European language groups (Latin, Greek, Celtic, Gothic). Works of comparative philology hypothesized a migration of peoples to Europe from an Indian cradle (Demoule 2014: 66), and thus the ancient Indian culture became, from the point of view of these scholars, a privileged pathway towards a 'common European culture'. Historian-jurists, at the beginning of the nineteenth century, including Lafferière, Laboulaye, and Louis-Jean Koenigswarter (1814–1878) seemed, for the most part, to be won over to the cause of a common Indian legal heritage in Europe. Many had solid philological backgrounds, acquired through their exposure to the work on oriental philology conducted within the *Académie des Inscriptions et Belles-Lettres*, and if they were not themselves philologists, they drew upon the work of the most widely renowned India scholars (Eugène Burnouf, Abraham Hyacinthe Anquetil-Duperron, Auguste Loiseleur de Longchamp, and Albrecht Friedrich Weber) to support their assertions.

Mastering Legal Evolution: Ethnology as an Instrument of Legal Policy (1860–1950)

From the second half of the nineteenth century, political, economic, and societal transformation profoundly affected European law. As in other nations, the social question, the second Industrial Revolution, and the struggle to implement the rule of law undermined the French legal order. It was no longer a question of simply searching for the *original* intention of an omniscient legislator within these new challenges. It became imperative to adapt the law to the needs and expectations of a society in perpetual flux. The arrow of time was being reversed: no longer was the past the basis of the truth of the laws in force. Legal progress and the modernization of legal instruments became a major obsession in France, as society began to adopt the path towards a social republic. Without completely abandoning the historical approach, many jurists now preferred the emerging social sciences of sociology, economics, and ethnology, which offered, in their view, instruments conducive to better defining—and thus applying—legal policy.

Legal Evolutionism Debated: Primitive Law to the Rescue of Legal Studies?

At the beginning of the second half of the nineteenth century, French and European legal scholarship had a certain fascination with so-called 'primitive' or 'archaic' law. Contrary to received wisdom, legal scholars did not consider alien the 'anthropological turn', which saw the works of Bachofen, MacLennan, Morgan, and Maine become the main points of reference in the intellectual debates of the day. Again, one must understand exactly who the 'primitives' in this legal approach are. First, according to historian-jurists like Adhémar Esmein (1848–1913), Joseph Declareuil (1863–1938), and Rodolphe Dareste (1824–1911), they are the people of antiquity. In light of the work of British jurist Henry Sumner Maine (1822–1888), the author of the highly respected *Ancient Law* (1861), legal primitivism is deliberately confined to the Indo-European framework. For Maine, much as for his French epigones, the question of the origins and the development of law is closely linked to the interpretative preoccupations of the jurists of the day, eager to use history as an empirical method that can replace theoretical speculation. When French legal scholars claim they wish to do 'legal archaeology' or 'legal palaeontology' (the terms were created by the French translators of Maine), they are expressing a desire to push the boundaries of the history of law further and further in an attempt to return to the formative periods of ancient societies. Is this purely academic speculation? Not at all. On the contrary, this undertaking, designed, according to the remarks of the Celtic law specialist Arbois de Jubainville, to shed light on the 'primitive' social organization of the Indo-European race, allows for a more effective understanding of contemporary Western law.

Gradually and concurrently, 'primitive laws' came to designate the normative forms of non-Western peoples; that is to say, those foreign to the Roman tradition. However, once the so-called 'savages' burst the bounds of the ancient Indo-European framework, they became a recognized part of French and European legal thinking,[5] which was strongly influenced in the 1860s by the adoption of unilinear evolutionary theory in the humanities. The longstanding awareness of the evolution, or historicity, of legal forms gradually and almost exclusively took the form of the evolutionist approach, with its obligatory stages of legal development.[6] For many jurists, convinced of the superiority of Western bourgeois moral values and that their adoption is one of the benefits of colonization, absence of cultural relativism remained the norm. The 'primitives' were not '*others*': they merely represented a *delayed version of ourselves*. It was precisely this premise that allowed many European jurists of the second half of the nineteenth century to turn their attention towards 'primitive' peoples, now understood to include all 'savage' peoples and no longer limited to the peoples of classical antiquity, in order to understand Western legal rationality. Legal historians with proclivities for evolutionism, such as the Roman law expert Émile Jobbé-Duval (1851–1931), used collated ethnographic data as a means of reconstituting ancient laws. More generally, it is important to note the institutional investment on the part of the legal community in learned societies dedicated to furthering human knowledge, as well as the significant anthropological learning on the part of a segment of French legal scholarship. These jurists, like the professor of comparative legal history at the *Collège de France*, Jacques Flach (1846–1919), were well acquainted with the literature of their day in the areas of ethnography and folklore, which they discussed and used widely.[7] However, evolutionism was not welcomed unreservedly by French legal scholars, as is evident from the heated exchanges between law professors Édouard Lambert (1866–1947) and Charles Appleton (1846–1935) and the clash between the Berlin jurist Joseph Kohler (1849–1919) and the

French magistrate Gabriel Tarde (1843–1904). Contrary to a particularly stubborn historiographical cliché, the unilinear evolutionist postulate was subject to informed and lively debate.

Race and the Law: Jurists and Physical Anthropology

Thinking about legal evolution, however, does not mean merely bringing to light, by way of a study of 'primitive' peoples, the hidden origins of the jurists' own legal traditions. It also, and perhaps more than ever, means understanding and mastering the legal developments and trends within society. Furthermore, this approach claims to base a nation's legal policy upon social observation and scientific method. The appearance of the expression 'legal anthropology', circa 1890, notably in the writings of the anatomist Léonce Manouvrier, expresses precisely this wish to 'draw from the social sciences all that can be useful to progress (in the law)', and to attempt to apply anthropological findings to the legal field.[8] During this period, jurists seized upon works of physical anthropology, particularly those concerning race. In fact, race was gradually elevated to a privileged explanatory category in the history of peoples. Paul Broca's *Société d'anthropologie de Paris*, founded in 1859, helped institutionalize the science of race and the search for a 'natural history of man' (Blanckaert 2009). The results of a naturalist approach to anthropology were adopted by French and European learned elites, thoroughly imbued as they were with a veritable 'racial culture' (Reynaud-Paligot 2014: 116). Inheritance of individual and moral characteristics remained a widely shared belief among historians, philosophers, and jurists. It is in the field of crime that this causal link between the physical and the psyche, between moral sense and physical attributes, was most strongly emphasized. Physicians and jurists debated whether there was a 'criminal type' which, in the eyes of some, was the product of an atavism: the 'criminal man' failed to adapt to the social order and committed multiple transgressions. Criminal anthropology, following the work of Cesare Lombroso, unleashed passions throughout Europe, especially during the seven congresses on criminal anthropology that took place between 1885 and 1911. In France, this encounter between the medical and the legal worlds was supported by the creation of the *Archives d'anthropologie criminelle* in Lyon in 1886. Thus, the intense debates around this new field of knowledge were an opportunity to redefine the causes of crime and recidivism and the limits of criminal responsibility, and to re-evaluate the effectiveness of sentences (Mucchielli 1994). Biological and racial anthropology did not have the same impact on all branches of law, even if some jurists did not hesitate to subordinate the enjoyment of civil and political rights to racial considerations. For instance, Georges Vacher de Lapouge (1854–1936) was, from the beginning, the herald of a biological theory of inheritance law. Under the Vichy regime (1940–1944), racist and eugenicist theories of law were, unfortunately, promulgated and applied on an unprecedented and dramatic scale (e.g. in the laws that discriminated against Jews).

It is, not surprisingly, in the area of overseas affairs and the management of the French colonial empire that jurists mobilized physical anthropology in a visible manner. In the second half of the nineteenth century, the organization of justice in Indochina led the magistrates overseas to invoke the studies of orientalists of the *Ecole française d'Extrême-Orient* in their legal reasoning in order to try to classify the different populations of that territory and to define an 'Asian race' as distinct from the 'European race'. Similarly, in the mid-1920s and 1930s, references to physical anthropology and to the work of the *Ecole d'anthropologie de Paris* became more numerous in the legal assessment of miscegenation (the 'metis' question). Significantly, in the early 1920s, magistrates practising overseas made use of 'ethnic experts': taking on the role of anthropologists, they claimed to be able, based on rudimentary anthropological knowledge, to detect by a simple visual examination the ethnic origin or ethnic mix of individuals, and thereby to determine their citizenship or establish a relationship of descent (Falconieri 2011, 2019). However, this trend was not without resistance from a branch of French colonial doctrine that worried about the uncontrolled use of anthropological knowledge, even though they had no particular qualms about this way of shaping the colonial order and strengthening the bond of subjugation in the colonies. Legal circles in the Third Republic were, in general, more sensitive to the role of social context and environment in the development and application of the law than they were inclined to defend biological determinism and the physiological characterization of the human being.

Legal Ethnology: Between Comparative Legislation and Field Investigations

Colonialism led certain jurists to make use of anthropological knowledge and also contributed to the production of legal knowledge about indigenous peoples' rights and the forms of legal otherness. Alongside the work of magistrates such as Sautayra and Charbonneau on Muslim law (1873–1874) and Aristide Letourneux, with the help of General A. Hanoteau, on Kabyle customs (1872–1873), there were studies conducted by law professors, including Octave Larché on Algerian legislation and Arthur Girault on colonial law, as well as both private and official attempts at drafting customs, such as the customaries of French West Africa in the 1930s. All were guided by questions about the division of legal powers, as well as about the political expediency of respecting local specificities. Given the necessities of 'rational domination' and the good administration of justice, far from all works dealing with overseas law were driven by ethnological ambitions. Nevertheless, some undoubtedly contributed to the construction of an ethnological knowledge base pertaining to local laws. The famous investigation by Hanoteau and Letourneux, despite its limitations and widely evoked biases, constituted a very rich vein of material on the legal life in Kabylie. Their work was based on interviews with literate informants and members of the colonial administration, as well as on collecting *qawanin* (rules) promulgated by the village assemblies and the judgments handed down by such assemblies.

Such practical knowledge of indigenous laws and customs echoed the passion for comparative study that had taken hold among French legal circles from the beginning of the *Belle Époque*. The interest shown by the majority of French jurists in native laws and, concurrently, in the lessons drawn from ethnology, was motivated less by colonial reorganization than by classificatory and methodological concerns. The encyclopaedic ambition of comparative law, keen to unite and organize the totality of legal systems into a few 'families of law', could thus draw upon the African and Asian experiences (Pargendler 2012). Founded in 1869, the *Société de Legislation Comparée* occasionally opened itself up to the study of native customs. Significantly, the 1938 essays in honour of one of the founding figures of comparatism, Édouard Lambert (1866–1947), a law professor at the University of Lyon, devoted major sections to the *Histoire comparative du droit et ethnologie juridique* ('Comparative history of law and legal ethnology'). From this global approach to law, some hoped to learn lessons to improve French law, while others saw it as a means of defining law in such a way that it was truly common to humanity.[9] It is in this comparative and quasi-codifying perspective that Albert-Hermann Post published his *Grundriss der Ethnologische Jurisprudenz* (1894), a work whose impact on French legal history was, however, very modest.

Unlike in the United States and England, anthropology in France was, until the interwar period, dependent upon the colonial powers and less independent of the natural sciences. In the hands of jurists, anthropology revealed in an exemplary way its nature as a governmental science. This situation did not, however, prevent attempts to produce a properly ethnological knowledge of normative phenomena. The question was no longer simply to understand local law, but to fully grasp the specificity of other laws and normative orders (*juridicité*) that were irreducible to Roman formalism and a state framework. Efforts in favour of such 'legal ethnology', which focused more specifically on the questions and methods of social anthropology, found in the works of the Durkheimian school and the *L'Année sociologique* the tools to analyse legal traditions outside of the realm of Roman law. Some scholars believe that they allowed for the 'pre-legal' phase of social life to be taken seriously. According to the Durkheimian jurist Paul Huvelin, 'this means a period in which the law does not yet exist', one in which legal normativity was still confused with other social normativities, beginning with religion. This time of 'pre-law' was, according to the Durkheimian classicist Louis Gernet, a period in which 'the relations that we call legal were understood by another mode of thought than in the law proper' (Gernet, 1982: 12). While it may not be completely free of a certain evolutionism, this approach contributed to opening jurists' eyes to another manner of thinking about what constitutes law that was not overshadowed by state law. It is hardly surprising that several supporters of this anthropological approach to law, including Jacques Berque, Henri Lévy-Bruhl, and Michel Alliot, invoked the lessons of Gernet.

The promise of legal ethnology means not only distancing oneself as far as possible from state law, but also involves remaining closer to fieldwork. Prior to becoming a professor at the Faculty of Law of Paris, René Maunier (1887–1951) taught at the Faculty of Law of Algiers between 1920 and 1924. As a former student of Marcel Mauss, he led a vast, collective investigation in Algeria, using questionnaires, interviews, and the assistance of around forty French and Kabyle teachers, in addition to support given by research assistants and educated villagers. In an attempt to better understand the nature of the social bond in Kabylie, Maunier focused on domestic worship, ritual exchange of gifts (*taoussa*), and the role of women. Naturally, Maunier was not the only academic to engage in the field of ethnology. In the 1920s, the lawyer and doctor of laws, Mathéa Gaudry, led investigations into the conditions experienced by Berber women, based on her long periods of contact with the Algerian population. At around the same time, Georges Marcy, also a speaker of the Berber language and an accomplished linguist and jurist, undertook a study of the social organization and customs of the Berber people. From 1934, Jacques Berque, a scholar of Islam and a colonial administrator, took advantage of his privileged position to study North African contracts, notably the Beni-Meskine pastoral pacts. The list of such studies could easily be extended. It is, moreover, important to add an entire group of specialists whose work, at the intersection of orientalism, social anthropology, sociology of law, and history, engaged in ethnology to offer an updated view of non-Western practices and judicial institutions. Robert Lingat, a leading expert on Siamese law, is but one notable example. The 'ethnological moment' in the 1930s oscillates constantly between the analysis of social change, such as 'contact culture' and 'legal acculturation' in the colonies, and the rationalization of overseas domination.

With his personal experiences, intellectual ambition, and dynamism, René Maunier obtained a chair at the Faculty of Law of Paris in 1924, and founded a small working group, the *Working Room on Legal Ethnology*, which became official in 1929, upon its incorporation into the Institute of Comparative Law. Each year, this group hosted lectures that were published in the series *Études de sociologie et d'ethnologie juridiques* (more than thirty volumes appeared between 1930 and 1940). Legal ethnology began to institutionalize, benefitting from the efforts to recognize the importance of the social sciences in the education of jurists. Driven by his desire to form his own school, Maunier supervised many theses which, in his own words, were 'observations, not compilations' on North and sub-Saharan Africa, Madagascar, and the Far East. However, in his writings, he revealed himself to be increasingly sensitive to the question of the relations, or even conflicts, between legal systems (see Maunier 1932) and, more broadly, to the social aspects of the expansion of peoples (Maunier 1932–1942). The politician took precedence over the anthropologist: less concerned with ethnological descriptions, he became the architect of a colonial science that was quick to legitimize racial inequality and the domination of colonized peoples. At the same time, the study of the latter's customs stimulated Maunier's interest in the customs of colonizing nations, and particularly those of France. At the beginning of the 1930s, he participated in the development of research into folklore, meaning, in his opinion, popular customs, and he became the president of the *Société du Folklore Français et du Folklore Colonial*. In this role, he encouraged local collective investigations and strove to initiate projects that looked into 'legal folklore', which he introduced at the first International Congress of Folklore in 1937. As a focal point for regionalists and ruralists, who held a rather nostalgic view of France, 'legal folklore' enjoyed fleeting success before fading away under the authoritarian, xenophobic, and antisemitic Vichy regime.

Taking cultural diversity seriously: the invention of legal anthropology (post-1950s)

After the Second World War, legal ethnology quickly declined. Compromised by his ties to the Vichy regime, the most prominent promoter of the approach, René Maunier, was dismissed from his post and simply disappeared from academia. Systematically associated with the work of colonial domination, legal ethnology was definitively discredited in the 1950s and 1960s, under pressure from the decolonization movement and the increasing number of colonies proclaiming their independence. Supporting the essential development of the former colonies, jurists preferred to work on 'overseas law' or to specialize, for instance, in the study of African legal systems. Some professors and researchers coalesced around the legal scholar Michel Alliot (1924–2014) and the ethnologist Jean Poirier (1921–2009). In the 1950s, they aimed to re-establish legal ethnology on new foundations, wishing to break with the ethnocentrism and the Western-centredness of their predecessors. They promoted an approach based on cultural diversity, respectful of indigenous legal forms, and sought to inspire the institutionalization of the discipline within academia. To underline the distance between the old approach, compromised by its connections to the project of Western oppression, and this newer approach, which interacted with indigenous legal systems, the term 'legal anthropology' was reborn. Revived from the lexical graveyard almost half a century after Léonce Manouvrier, the expression was intended to convey the great ambitions of such a disciplinary renewal.[10] The teaching of legal anthropology had long been the preserve of the *École Nationale de la France d'Outre-Mer* (the former *École Coloniale*, or 'Colonial School'). Now, the field was recognized by the Paris Law Faculty and connected with the still-active Institute of Ethnology founded by Lévy-Bruhl, Mauss, and Rivet. Initially, this was a tentative process, starting with the creation of a 'Certificate of Overseas Law and Customs' (*certificat de droit et coutumes d'outre-mer*) in 1951. The incorporation of legal anthropology into the Faculty of Law curriculum became more permanent with the creation of the *Laboratoire d'anthropologie juridique de l'Université de Paris*, in 1963–1964,[11] under Alliot's encouragement.

This promotion of legal anthropology was accompanied by a radical redefinition of the scope and ambitions of the discipline. Due to the wars in Indochina and Algeria, which diverted the attention of jurists from Asia and the Maghreb towards sub-Saharan Africa, Senegal and Madagascar, which already had law faculties, became preferred sites of experimentation. The rich and original works of authors such as J. Berque, G. Marcy, and R. Lingat, which focused on Asia and North Africa, were no longer seen as essential reference works, nor were they viewed as legitimate models for anthropologists within law faculties. This geographical narrowing around sub-Saharan Africa was accompanied by a refocusing on legal instruments. Non-jurists were encouraged to abandon their studies of legal phenomena and make room for the 'professionals', who were, ostensibly, better armed to deal with such matters. For example, Jean Poirier, a professor in the humanities faculty who had played a decisive role in reviving ethno-legal studies in the 1950s, was pushed to the periphery of his discipline. As a result, the dialogue between law and social sciences faculties floundered; scholars of the former affirmed their hegemony over the field; and those of the latter, whether they identified with Marxist or structuralist approaches, tended to look upon legal matters with suspicion, deeming it superficial or secondary.

In general, legal anthropology focused its attention on customary phenomena, and some even described it as the 'science of customs'. Attached to the paradigm of legal pluralism, of which Africa would be an exemplary laboratory, and denouncing the excessive role accorded to the state in legal matters, the discipline drew on a vast number of studies (for instance, of land law) to highlight the complexity of legal systems (traditional law, customary law, local law, etc.). Despite its culturalist and relativist ambitions, from the 1950s to the 1970s this anthropology was not always immune to the temptation of an applied anthropology that participated in the legal modernization of decolonized countries and accompanied them in their endeavours to rationalize their norms and institutions. Equally, some ethno-jurists continued to produce a discourse that presented customs as a receptacle of the endangered 'primitive' African spirit. The legal anthropological dream, of a discipline purified of its colonial ghosts and of the romantic spectres of a popular spirit, had not yet been achieved. However, the promoters of such an anthropology worked tirelessly to write a disciplinary history worthy of their founding ambitions. Rejecting the discipline's past, they did not recognize any precursors. René Maunier, who had some claim to this title, was in fact *persona non grata*, and legal anthropologists were happy to designate Henry Lévy-Bruhl (1884–1964), professor of legal history at Paris and a key proponent of post-war Durkheimian theory, in Maunier's place as the inspiration, or even founder, of the discipline. Thus, French legal anthropology was born in the 1950s, unblemished by racist ramblings and imperial pretensions. It led, in the 1970s and 1980s, to the works of legal anthropologists such as Étienne Le Roy, Norbert Rouland, Raymond Verdier, and Louis Assier-Andrieu, the last two being well acquainted with American anthropological scholarship. However, such a historiographical rupture erased almost two centuries of history concerning the relationship between law and the social sciences—200 years during which jurists placed history, philology, physical anthropology, ethnology, and sociology at the service of an ever-greater elucidation of *homo juridicus*.

Acknowledgement

This article was translated from the French by David Foulk.

Notes

1. On the diversity of definitions and approaches, see Blanckaert (1989); Weber (2015).
2. The expression 'anthropology of identity' is freely borrowed from Bourguet (1984).
3. On this tendency, see Assier-Andrieu (2015).

4. On Vico's contribution to French legal history, see Gianturco (1977) and Navet (1987).
5. Regarding the English-speaking world, see Elliott (1985), Wilf (2009), and Tuori (2015); for Italy, see Negri (1983) and Motta (1986); and for Germany, Schott (1982).
6. For the history of thinking on legal evolution, see Stein (1980).
7. For more information on the anthropological culture of jurists in the nineteenth and twentieth centuries, see Guerlain (2015).
8. To the best of our knowledge, the expression 'legal anthropology' appeared for the first time in 1845 in a review by Jacques Rauter of a book by Stoeckhart in the *Revue de droit français et étranger*. This concept was then developed in Manouvrier's article 'De l'anthropologie criminelle considérée comme une branche de l'anthropologie juridique' (1889) and, as a prolonged reflection, in 'L'anthropologie et le droit' (1894). It can be also be found in a paper presented by the Belgian lawyer Paul Otlet to the *Société d'anthropologie de Bruxelles* (1894).
9. On the legal comparisons project, see Riles (2001).
10. On the institutionalization of legal anthropology in the 1950s, see Guerlain (forthcoming) and Chevreau et al. (2018).
11. On the direction of legal anthropology since 1960, see Rouland (1994).

References

Assier-Andrieu L. 2011. *L'autorité du passé. Essai anthropologique sur la Common Law*. Paris: Dalloz.

Assier-Andrieu, L. 2015. 'De l'idéologie à la culture: les géographies coutumières'. *Clio@Themis. Revue électronique d'histoire du droit* 9 [https://www.cliothemis.com/De-l-ideologie-a-la-culture-les].

Audren, F. and J.-L. Halpérin. 2013. *La culture juridique française. Entre mythes et réalités (XIXe–XXe siècles)*. Paris: CNRS éditions.

Blanckaert, C. 1989. 'L'anthropologie en France, le mot et l'histoire (XVIe–XIXe siècles)'. *Bulletins et Mémoires de la Société d'anthropologie de Paris*, new series, 1989: 13–43.

Blanckaert, C. 2009. *De la race à l'évolution. Paul Broca et l'anthropologie française (1850–1900)*. Paris: L'Harmattan.

Bourguet, M.-N. 1984. 'Des préfets aux champs. Une ethnographie administrative de la France en 1800'. In B. Rupp-Eisenreich, ed. *Histoires de l'anthropologie (XVIème–XIXème siècles)*, 259–72. Paris: Klincksieck.

Chevreau, E., F. Audren, and R. Verdier, eds. 2018. *Henri Lévy-Bruhl: juriste sociologue*. Paris: Mare & Martin.

Demoule, J.-P. 2014. *Mais où sont passés les Indo-Européens? Le mythe d'origine de l'Occident*. Paris: Seuil.

Elliott, E.-D. 1985. 'The Evolutionary Tradition in Jurisprudence'. *Faculty Scholarship Series*, paper 2194 [https://digitalcommons.law.yale.edu/fss_papers/5078/].

Falconieri, S. 2011. 'Les juristes d'outre-mer entre orientalisme et anthropologie. "Étrangers assimilés aux indigènes" et "métis" dans le façonnage de l'ordre colonial (XIXe–XXe siècles)'. *Clio@Themis. Revue électronique d'histoire du droit* 4 [https://www.cliothemis.com/Les-juristes-d-outre-mer-entre].

Falconieri, S. 2019. 'Droit colonial et anthropologie. Expertises ethniques, enquêtes et études raciales dans l'outre-mer français (fin du XIXe siècle–1946)'. *Clio@Themis. Revue électronique d'histoire du droit* 15 [https://publications-prairial.fr/cliothemis/index.php?id=627].

Gernet, L. 1982. *Droits et institutions en Grèce antique*. Paris: Flammarion.

Gianturco, E. 1977. 'Vico et les débuts de l'historiographie du droit français'. *Archives de philosophie* 40: 87–105.

Guerlain, L. 2015. 'Culture et usages des savoirs anthropologiques chez les juristes. De quelques apports de l'étude des recensions bibliographiques (XIXe–XXe siècles)'. *Revue d'histoire des facultés de droit, de la culture juridique, du monde des juristes et du livre juridique* 35: 233–77.

Guerlain, L. Forthcoming. 'Espace de la discipline vs. espace des savoirs. Dans la boîte noire des années 1950 de l'ethnologie juridique'. In C. Laurière, ed. *1950, aux sources de l'anthropologie française contemporaine. L'inventaire des possibles*, Carnet Bérose [online].

Kelley, D.-R. 1984. *Historians and the Law in Postrevolutionary France*. Princeton: Princeton University Press.

Klimrath, H. 1837. *Études sur les coutumes*. Paris: au bureau de la Revue de législation et de jurisprudence.

Lacoste, C. 1982. 'Les Gaulois d'Amédée Thierry'. In P. Viallaneix and J. Ehrard, eds. *Nos ancêtres les Gaulois*, 203–20. Clermont-Ferrand: Faculty of Humanities and Social Science.

La Fontenelle de Vaudoré, A. 1843. *Les coutumes de Charroux*. Poitiers: Imprimerie de Saurin frères.

Maunier, R. 1932. *Loi française et coutume indigène en Algérie*. Paris: Domat-Montchrestien.

Maunier, R. 1932–1942. *Sociologie coloniale*. Paris: Domat-Montchrestien.

Motta, R. 1986. *Teorie del diritto primitivo. Un'introduzione all'antropologia giuridica*. Milan: Materiali Universitari Scienze Politiche.

Mucchielli, L., ed. 1994. *Histoire de la criminologie française*. Paris: L'Harmattan.

Navet, G. 1987. *De l'usage de Vico en France. Le problème de la légitimité du droit civil*. Political Science thesis, University of Rennes.

Negri, A. 1983. *Il giurista dell'area romanista di fronte all'etnologia giuridica*. Milan: Giuffrè.

Pargendler, M. 2012. 'The Rise and Decline of Legal Families'. *American Journal of Comparative Law* 60(4): 1043–74.

Reynaud-Paligot, C. 2011. *De l'identité nationale. Science, race et politique en Europe et aux États-Unis, XIXe–XXe siècles*. Paris: PUF.

Reynaud-Paligot, C. 2014. 'Construction et circulation de la notion de "race" au cours du XIXe siècle'. In N. Bancel David and T. Dominic, eds. *L'invention de la race. Des représentations scientifiques aux exhibitions populaires*, 103–16. Paris: La Découverte.

Riles A., ed. 2001. *Rethinking the Masters of Comparative Law*. Oxford/Portland: Hart Publishing.

Rouland, R. 1994. *Legal Anthropology*. London: Athlone Press.

Schott, R. 1982. 'Main Trends in German Ethnological Jurisprudence and Legal Ethnology'. *Journal of Legal Pluralism* 37: 37–68.

Stein, P. 1980. *Legal Evolution*. Cambridge: Cambridge University Press.

Thiesse, A.-M. 2001. *La création des identités nationales. Europe, XVIIIe–XXe siècles*. Paris: Seuil.

Tuori, K. 2015. *Lawyers and Savages. Ancient History and Legal Realism in the Making of Legal Anthropology*. New York: Routledge.

Venayre, S. 2013. *Les origines de la France. Quand les historiens racontaient la Nation*. Paris: Seuil.

Weber, F. 2015. *Brève histoire de l'anthropologie*. Paris: Flammarion.

Wilf, S. 2009. 'The Invention of Legal Primitivism'. *Theoretical Inquiries in Law* 10(2): 451–76.

CHAPTER 13

LEGAL ETHNOLOGY AND LEGAL ANTHROPOLOGY IN HUNGARY

BALÁZS FEKETE

THIS chapter is about the history of legal ethnology and of legal anthropology in Hungary. This twofold subject matter may be surprising at first glance, as this volume is dedicated primarily to issues of law and anthropology. In Hungary, however, legal anthropology arrived at a fairly late date, and its connection to national traditions of scholarship was less obvious than was the case in various countries of the Western world. Modern Hungarian jurisprudence—like many other aspects of Hungarian cultural life—was influenced decisively by German ideas and the German way of legal thinking, beginning in the Habsburg era but especially during the nineteenth century and the interwar period. Thus, for Hungarian legal scholars, German scholarship has long represented a *beau idéal* and a point of reference, notwithstanding some rather fragmented initiatives to link Hungarian legal thinking more firmly to other European traditions, for instance to the English one.[1] Therefore, the very first moments in the birth of a scholarly attitude towards law as a sociocultural phenomenon, one embedded in a broader context, contrary to the usual rule-oriented and positivist approach to law, should be sought in parallel with the earliest ethnographical initiatives at the beginning of the twentieth century.

As one of the founding fathers of contemporary Hungarian legal anthropology, István H. Szilágyi (2009a), argues, a strict differentiation among legal anthropology, legal ethnology, and legal sociology is problematic. Since scholars in these fields all study regulation and self-regulation, as well as ways of settling disputes in societies, and as they all apply empirical methods, there are no proper epistemological grounds for their rigid separation. There are, admittedly, differences, which can be explained historically: legal ethnology and legal anthropology emerged within divergent cultural traditions, German and Anglo-American, respectively.[2] Nevertheless, their orientation and methodology display many commonalities as well (see Tárkány Szücs 1967; H. Szilágyi

2009a). Therefore, for Hungary, a common treatment of the history of legal ethnology and legal anthropology can be justified, historically, by the strong presence of German ideas and, epistemologically, by the closeness of these two disciplines.

This chapter focuses on the 'internal' story of both legal ethnology and legal anthropology in Hungary.[3] That is, it analyses the development of these disciplines in their own scholarly context, and it only reflects on 'external' historical or other circumstances when it is deemed to be an absolute necessity. An in-depth discussion of the historical and sociopolitical context is beyond the scope of the contribution. However, there are many excellent books that can help the reader to reconstruct the proper context (e.g. Cartledge 2011; Ormos and Király (eds). 2001; Kontler 1999).

This chapter is divided into two parts. The first part presents four phases in the development of Hungarian legal ethnology and legal anthropology over the course of more than a century: the birth of ethnographic interest in law around 1900; the emergence of a legislative programme out of the in-depth study of folk law at the end of the interwar period; the decline and rehabilitation of legal ethnology in the Socialist era; and the emergence of 'Western-style' legal anthropology beginning in the 1990s. The second part of the chapter provides an assessment of these developments from various perspectives in order to help the reader to comprehend this unusual development.

The History of Legal Ethnology and Legal Anthropology in Hungary

The Birth of Interest in the Ethnological Study of Law—Early Steps Before and After World War I

Although some Hungarian intellectuals had already steered public opinion towards the collection of 'old' Hungarian 'poems and songs' at the end of the eighteenth century (see Rát 1782: 33–4, cited in Voigt 1998: 41–2), a professional institutional framework for Hungarian ethnology was first established in the 1880s. Hugo Meltzl, a German professor at the University of Kolozsvár (Cluj), suggested the establishment of a professional academic society dedicated to the compilation and study of oral folk traditions all around the country in 1881. Meltzl's idea was inspired by the model of the English Folklore Society, founded in 1878. Finally, the *Magyar Néprajzi Társaság* (Hungarian Ethnographic Society) was founded in Budapest in 1889 with Pál Hunfalvy, professor of linguistics and history, as its first president.[4] Members of the Society declared as their main goal the scholarly study of the customs and traditions of all peoples living in the territory of Hungary, which was part of the Austro-Hungarian empire at that time. They also stressed the utility of a comparative perspective.

The first works of legal ethnology were published around 1900 by younger legal scholars, but their source of inspiration differed from that of general ethnology. First, these scholars were motivated by practical concerns, being intensively involved in ongoing efforts to modernize the Hungarian legal order. Therefore, their research programmes had obvious governmental support. Second, their research was not comprehensive in scope, compared to the ambitions of general ethnology, as they focused on narrow and somewhat technical legal issues. However, the works of Miklós Mattyasovszky (1904) and János Baross (1905) should be regarded as pioneering studies in this era, since their scholarly attitude, their view of law as a sociocultural phenomenon, and their methodology set them apart radically from the settled positivist canon of legal scholarship, which was focused predominantly on legal rules and provisions (see Szabadfalvi 2010, 2011).

Both Mattyasovszky and Baross wanted to make a contribution to the contemporary discussion regarding the reform of Hungarian inheritance law. What made their enterprise unique was their attitude towards unofficial folk law. Basically, their studies were aimed at getting to know the 'real' rules of inheritance law in the case of peasant lands, i.e. the rules that had a real impact on the everyday behaviour of people. Thus, they did not presuppose the supremacy of official or state law as a starting hypothesis; rather, they accepted the existence of diverging legal customs—'living law' in Eugen Ehrlich's (cf. 2017: 486–506) words—that had a strong capacity to govern the everyday relationships of the agrarian people. This meant that these 'real' rules had a much broader authority and a stronger impact on ordinary activities than state law could have had at that time. Even though they did not use the term legal pluralism, it can certainly be argued that they approached the law with a pluralist attitude.

This rather unusual attitude—regarding law as a social phenomenon—led these authors towards pioneering methodological decisions. Displaying the influence of German ethnology, both Baross and Mattyasovszky—the latter of whom had studied in Germany with governmental support in 1901—used questionnaire surveys (cf. Schott 1982: 444–7) in order to collect reliable information on how agrarian people settle their inheritance affairs in reality. Obviously, as individual scholars, they could not carry out extensive research covering the territory of the whole country on their own; rather, they relied on the assistance of various administrative organs. Mattyasovszky sent his questionnaire to local courts and public notaries, while Baross requested the help of village public notaries in filling out his questionnaire. Mattyasovszky's (1904: 287–8) questionnaire contained five broad sections that served not only to survey existing legal customs in the practice of inheritance law but also to discover explanatory variables such as nationality, religion, or the size of landholdings. In the end, Mattyasovszky's study was based on 642 questionnaires that were sent back by various local officials. In contrast, Baross (1905: 7–9) prepared a much more detailed questionnaire containing twenty-eight specific questions focused on ordinary situations and on the way in which people handled them in everyday practice. For instance, question no. 11 was about the attitude of fathers towards their sons when preparing a will: 'If one son, out of all children, gets all the lands owned by their father, is he the youngest one, the eldest one, or the most meritorious one?' (Baross 1905: 8; my translation). In addition, some of Baross's questions were dedicated to explanatory variables such as nationality or religion too. Almost

500 village notaries sent back the questionnaires to Baross, but, understandably, their quality varied to some extent.

In harmony with the strong official nationalization policies of the pre-World War I era, both Baross and Mattyasovszky regarded Hungary as a unitary national and legal area (cf. Péter 1998: 77), despite its obviously culturally heterogeneous character, given the presence of multiple ethnic groups. Nevertheless, they recognized that there were many, sometimes even locally divergent inheritance practices that were at variance with official state rule on many points. Thus, they called attention to the existence of a gap between the official legal provisions and the customary law of the agrarian population with respect to the inheritance of land within the family. While Baross's work was largely descriptive, including a multitude of tables with detailed data and explanations, Mattyasovszky adopted a critical stance in formulating his conclusions. For instance, he pointed out that these legal customs were overtly gender-biased, as they clearly disfavoured daughters. Moreover, he showed that local legal customs that were intended to stop the partition of farms into increasingly small units had the serious consequence of augmenting the emigration of agrarian people to foreign countries. Thus, Mattyasovszky's work also represents an early contribution to the social criticism of law.

The first general attempt to study legal customs in a more comprehensive scholarly framework was made by the historian and ethnographer Károly Tagányi. His aspirations differed radically from the largely practical attitude of Mattyasovszky and Baross, insofar as he drew on contemporary trends in legal ethnology. Tagányi's foremost aim was to broaden the scope of national legal scholarship, especially that of legal history, in order to discern the benefits to be drawn from a better understanding of 'the ancient Hungarian legal, social, and economic life' (Tagányi 1919). The sources of Tagányi's scholarly thinking can easily be identified, since his book discussing Hungarian legal customs with respect to family law and inheritance law contains very precise footnotes. Tagányi was clearly influenced by the oeuvre of Baltazar Bogišić, the 'founding father' of legal ethnology in the Balkan region (Tagányi 1919: 1, 10). In addition, Albert Hermann Post, Franz Bernhöft, Joseph Kohler, and other contributors to the German journal *Vergleichende Rechtswissenschaft* had a decisive impact on his thought (Tagányi 1919: 14, fn. 1). In short, Tagányi relied broadly on the intellectual mainstream of his day, especially on the evolutionary way of thinking about social development, which shaped his view of the utility of studying legal customs or folk law.

As for his research method, Tagányi advocated both the analysis of documents, with special regard for older and local documents, and the use of questionnaires. He also suggested the in-depth study of the questionnaires that had previously been used in other countries, for example, those used from 1862 to 1910 in Russia to collect folk law, which, in his view, could serve as inspiration and motivation for Hungarian research (Tagányi 1919: 17). Unfortunately, Tagányi was unable to complete the development of his questionnaire before his death in 1924, and, subsequently, his ideas on the preparation of a questionnaire for research on legal customs were not tested in the frame of any specific research programme.

Conceptually, Tagányi made a distinction between written customary laws and unwritten, 'living' legal folkways. The object of his study was the latter, i.e. the corpus of unwritten Hungarian legal folkways, conceived as the sum of various legal customs, legal ceremonies, and legal symbols passed on from one generation to the next (Tagányi 1919: 3). In his understanding, this unwritten folk law had been preserved and cultivated by the ordinary people, but it had largely disappeared from the thinking of the upper classes, due to the modernization of their life. Tagányi argued that these legal folkways cannot properly be interpreted in terms of contemporary ideas; rather, one must apply older legal concepts and principles to gain an appropriate reading of them. In addition, research on existing folk law may be helpful when studying the earliest phases of Hungarian history, for which there were almost no written sources (Tagányi 1919: 3).

In sum, Tagányi collected a formidable amount of foreign literature on legal ethnology and analysed it with special regard to the study of folk law as such, especially family law and inheritance law. Although he was prevented by his early death from completing his research agenda, his path-breaking and stimulating contributions were an important reference point for later generations of legal ethnographers.

Getting Closer to the 'People'—Expansion at the End of the Interwar Period

Following some sporadic efforts in the first two decades of the interwar period (Bognár 2016: 65–75), an extensive scholarly programme was launched to collect data pertaining to folk law at the beginning of 1939. This enterprise was coordinated by the *Országos Táj- és Népkutató Intézet* (National Institute for the Study of Land and People), led by István Győrffy, the well-known professor of ethnology. Within this Institute, a working group was established to start the study of folk law and legal folkways. This growing interest in unofficial legal phenomena was boosted intellectually by proponents of *népi mozgalom* or Hungarian populism, who advocated focusing intellectual inquiry on the Hungarian countryside, especially on the life of villagers, peasants, and farmers, which they viewed as part of a complex social and cultural phenomenon. Participants in this broad intellectual movement, who were predominantly young intellectuals with varying political backgrounds, wanted to narrow the cultural gap between the higher classes of the Hungarian society and the people of villages and small towns by studying and understanding the values of the latter. Thus, social criticism was an integral part of this influential intellectual movement as well (see Borbándi 1976).

In order to achieve a better understanding of everyday relations among 'the people', the working group at the National Institute for the Study of Land and People prepared a comprehensive questionnaire for fieldwork. This questionnaire, which contained ninety-five items, was partially inspired by the French *folklore juridique*. The scholars used René Maunier's *Introduction* (1938) when phrasing many parts of the questionnaire, but they also drew on Tagányi's earlier draft. The main topics that were covered by the questionnaire were (1) family and inheritance law, (2) property law, (3) contract law, and (4) criminal law (Bognár 2016: 90). In order to justify this work, one member of the working group, László Papp, argued that the collected data on folk law and legal customs could be used effectively for the renewal of the corpus of Hungarian private law. The inspiration coming from the settled customs of 'the people' would help make private legal provisions more Hungarian in 'character', contrary to the apparent foreign influences. Further, this would also help to make the entire legal order more just and social (see Papp 1939: 10–12).

In the second half of 1939, the Hungarian government decided to endorse the research programme of the working group of the National Institute for the Study of Land and People, in order to help resist the forced reception of foreign legal models and bring the law closer to 'the ancient and original' spirit of the Hungarian people (Bognár 2016: 93). Here, obviously, the political context of government support cannot be disregarded. In Hungary, the politics of the interwar period were dominated by a strong nationalist attitude in response to the shock of the Treaty of Trianon, which led to the loss of almost two thirds of the country's pre-World War I territory. The revision of the political consequences of the Treaty of Trianon became the overriding concern of the Hungarian political elite (cf. Péter 1998: 79). By 1939, with the expansion of the German Reich before and after the invasion of Poland, official support for research on Hungarian folk law may be seen as the government's attempt to help in defending Hungarian 'national existence' against the 'German imperialism'. The use of folk law—the 'treasures of peasant civilization', in the words of György Bónis (cited by Bognár 2016: 91)—in future legislation could contribute both to the identification of the Hungarian national character in legal terms and to the improvement of the various legal provisions of private law.

The enthusiastic support of the government for research on Hungarian folk law found expression in two letters, dated 22 July 1939 and 25 July 1940, in which the minister of justice asked the presidents of the country's local courts to provide effective help and support for the collection of data. Due to this strong administrative backing, ninety-five reports based on the previously drafted questionnaire were sent to the Ministry of Justice between 1939 and 1943. László Papp, lawyer and ethnographer, was given the assignment of preparing a summary of these reports, which were, admittedly, of rather mixed quality. While he completed this assignment, he never produced a scholarly publication based on the results of the survey (Bognár 2016: 96).

In addition to the research based on questionnaires, Hungarian legal ethnographers also started to include fieldwork in their methodological toolkit. After Northern Transylvania was ceded by Romania and became part of Hungary again in 1940, as a consequence of the Second Vienna Award arbitrated by Italy and Germany, György Bónis, an expert on Hungarian legal history of the medieval period and a newly appointed professor at *Ferenc József Tudományegyetem* (Franz Joseph University) in Kolozsvár (Cluj), organized a seminar for collecting legal folkways in the region. This seminar was attended by devoted law students—including Ernő Tárkány Szücs, later the leading personality of Hungarian legal ethnology[5]—who were sent to the thirty-five villages of Kalotaszeg, a small and ancient Hungarian area west of Kolozsvár, in order to map legal folkways and to learn how Hungarian and Romanian law interacted with each other. Having studied the history of the villages, the members of this team administered a questionnaire that had been adjusted to the specific conditions of the region. In their interviews with local inhabitants and community leaders, they focused on specific cases instead of abstract principles. As a general rule, fieldworkers interviewed forty to fifty individuals in each village, and they analysed some legal documents—wills, contracts, etc.—that they found in village archives (Bognár 2016: 100–1). Unfortunately, the collected primary material, which had been deposited in the university library in Kolozsvár, was destroyed at the end of World War II. Only the secondary reports prepared by the team members survived the end of the war. This model of fieldwork was used later, however, in some studies that were conducted in 1947 and 1948.

A Late Rehabilitation in the Socialist Era—The Oeuvre of Ernő Tárkány Szücs

Despite some promising research results under the direction of György Bónis between 1946 and 1948, Hungarian legal ethnology did not have much chance to develop as a distinct field of legal scholarship during the socialist era. The leaders of the newly emerging Soviet-backed communist 'popular democracy' strongly supported the comprehensive reorganization of the country's academic life according to Marxist-Leninist principles. In this context, some of the scholars who supported the communist regime started an intensive political campaign against the personalities whom they supposed to have had a strong political or intellectual attachment to the previous Horthy and Szálasi regimes.[6] In addition, the representatives of the new order regularly attacked some fields of study, accusing their proponents of negligence of the new and progressive principles of Marxism-Leninism. This was clearly an unfavourable atmosphere for most of those scholars of the interwar period who did not openly back the new regime.

Unsurprisingly, legal ethnology was on the list of regressive scholarly fields and was strongly criticized from a Marxist-Leninist perspective. This resulted, practically, in the banning of these studies for a long while. In 1961, Kálmán Kulcsár, a leading innovator in socialist legal sociology (see Fekete and H. Szilágyi 2017), provided a comprehensive Marxist-Leninist criticism of earlier legal ethnographic efforts. For a number of reasons, he found the entire tradition of legal ethnology incompatible with Marxist-Leninist principles. First, he noted that the movement behind research on 'folk law' was undeniably Hungarocentric, that is, it was nationalistic in character and biased. Second, he pointed out that the premises of legal ethnology did not match the Marxist understanding of society, insofar as it restricted the concept of 'the people' to the peasantry, thereby ignoring the peasantry's manifest social complexity. When carrying out their research programmes, Hungarian legal ethnographers never thought in terms of the opposition between the bourgeoisie and the working class, and so they neglected issues of oppression and class struggle. Lastly, Kulcsár argued that the scholars in this movement had diverging, even conflicting concepts of 'folk law' and 'legal customs', so that the conceptual basis of legal ethnology in Hungary was rather incoherent. In fact, Kulcsár

(1961) argued, no specific folk law ever existed; rather, the phenomena studied by the legal ethnologists were simply indications of general legal consciousness. Therefore, in Kulcsár's eyes, legal ethnology was an outdated approach with no relevance for the swiftly developing socialist studies of law, based on Marxist-Leninist principles and their conceptual corollaries.

The criticism of Kulcsár seemed to terminate the story of Hungarian legal ethnology once and for all, as it also represented the official academic position. However, Kulcsár's attitude towards legal ethnology softened in the second half of the 1970s (Bognár 2016: 131–3); and Tárkány Szücs—whose nascent academic career as legal ethnographer had been cut short in the late 1940s and who, subsequently, worked in the Ministry of Industry for decades as a legal officer—had the opportunity in 1975 to join the Institute of Ethnology in the Hungarian Academy of Sciences as a senior research fellow. This affiliation with the Academy of Science made it possible for Tárkány Szücs to carry out a unique research programme based on the earlier data of the Hungarian legal ethnologists and to prepare a synthesis of their findings.

The impressive *opus magnum* of Tárkány Szücs—*Magyar jogi népszokások* (Hungarian Legal Folkways)—was published in 1981. This almost 850-page work met with great success and brought recognition to its author: the Hungarian Academy of Sciences awarded a doctoral degree in history and ethnology to Tárkány Szücs for this work in 1983. What is more, the book's success also implied the rehabilitation of the entire movement of Hungarian legal ethnology. Ironically, after having opposed legal ethnology from a Marxist-Leninist perspective two decades earlier, Kulcsár, in his assessment of *Magyar jogi népszokások* during doctoral proceedings, praised this outstanding academic product passionately (Bognár 2016: 167–8).

The book by Tárkány Szücs (1981; second edition 2003) is composed of seven longer sections. The first and last sections are devoted to theoretical and conceptual issues, while the remaining five—the nearly 800-page backbone of the volume—contain the analysis of legal folkways or folk law. In these five substantive sections, Tárkány Szücs grouped the legal folkways mainly around private issues: II. Person, III. Marriage, IV. Family, V. Property, and VI. Control, Conflict, and Constraint (Tárkány Szücs 2003: 41). Insofar as this monumental enterprise was based not on contemporary fieldwork but on data collected decades earlier, it had historical rather than contemporary relevance. Tárkány Szücs's intention was to summarize and synthetize the results of research in the field of the Hungarian legal ethnology from 1700 to 1945 (Tárkány Szücs 2003: 19).

In the conceptual introduction to his book, Tárkány Szücs elaborates a sociological conception of folk law. He defines folk law as socially bounded patterns of behaviour having legal substance and followed by the majority of the members of a given autonomous community (Tárkány Szücs 2003: 22, 27–8). With the phrase 'legal substance', Tárkány Szücs implies that these patterns are or were related to subjective rights in broad terms and that their formulation corresponded, at least to a minimal degree, to legal conventions that were established, perhaps, centuries ago (Tárkány Szücs 2003: 27–8). Furthermore, Tárkány Szücs argued that folk law was economically and socially embedded and so could not be revived under the qualitatively different socioeconomic conditions of later periods, in contrast to successful efforts to revitalize some other folk traditions, for example, folk songs or folk tales (Tárkány Szücs 2003: 28). In short, folk law was rooted in the capacities of autonomous communities—mostly villages or small towns—to create and enforce their own customs in order to fill the numerous gaps in official state legislation.

Obviously, Tárkány Szücs noted, the study of folk law, understood as a collection of various and often divergent legal folkways, cannot be carried out using the conventional tools of legal scholarship, as these tools were developed for research and analysis of state law. Therefore, he suggested an in-depth study of both historical documents and existing oral folk traditions. Chief among the written sources were, in his eyes, official legal documents preserved in family or village archives, including collections that list the decisions of local or village judges, compilations of various 'village acts' regulating certain segments of life in a given village, and compilations of professional regulations, for instance, those of fishermen and hunters (Tárkány Szücs 2003: 24–6).

In Tárkány Szücs's approach, the concept of 'folkways' was embedded in the broader phenomenon of folk legal tradition. Obviously, folk legal tradition was a component of the general folk tradition. Folk legal tradition was always composed of the rules and processes that were generally considered fair and just by the people of previous ages (Tárkány Szücs 2003: 30). Specifically, folk legal tradition was characterized by three main features. First, it was comprehensive in scope, meaning that it offered rules for all possible situations of life, from the birth to the death of the individual person. Second, it was also strongly historical in character, as the rules and processes in which it consisted often had roots in earlier state or church law, which had meanwhile become outdated but which were still part of collective routines. Third, all folk legal traditions had an impressive capacity to adapt to changing circumstances, and this capability had ensured their survival for centuries (Tárkány Szücs 2003: 30–5).

Based on his analysis of the three main features of folk legal tradition, Tárkány Szücs prepared a detailed definition of legal folkways, which have the following five qualitative components. First, legal folkways always serve to influence human behaviour, that is, they have a strictly practical aim. Second, they are not created and enforced by the state, the church, or any other national body; but, third, they are established by larger or smaller autonomous communities, and they represent the public beliefs of the majority of people living in those communities. Fourth, their main function is the reconciliation of the different interests that emerge in those communities by permitting or prohibiting various kinds of action or inaction. Fifth, these legal folkways are always enforced by the traditional means of the communities, not by official acts. The scope of legal folkways varies from the smallest unit of the society—the family—to wider societal units such as those formed by the inhabitants of a village or small town. Thus, legal folkways that are broader, for example, national, in scope have never existed (Tárkány Szücs 2003: 41).

In his conclusion, Tárkány Szücs even reflects on a question that was, at that time, rather sensitive, politically: could legal folkways exist in socialist Hungary? Here, he presents an intriguing line of thought. His point of departure is the observation that the Hungarian legal reality had always been determined by the dichotomy of 'up and down'.

By this he meant to say that official state law had always had a strong impact on the higher social strata, while folk legal tradition had ruled the everyday life of everyone else. In addition, there had always been a need for legal folkways, since state law, despite the significant broadening of its scope in the last two centuries, seems to have been unable to provide comprehensive regulation for the various aspects of private life. Furthermore, the need for unofficial law was augmented by various deficiencies of legislation, judicial work, and legal education. In general, then, there had always been some room, however limited, for legal folkways in the myriad social interactions in Hungary, due both to the incapacity of state law to provide general regulation and to the constant transformation of social life.

In order to illustrate his argument regarding legal folkways in socialist Hungary, Tárkány Szücs mentioned some examples from everyday life in the early 1980s. For instance, representatives of various professions generally expected to receive tips for the provision of normal service; and administrators were increasingly willing to recognize block flats as private property, even if they were not officially entered into the land registry, as was prescribed by law. In sum, Tárkány Szücs regarded legal ethnology as a purely historical discipline, but he also made suggestions regarding its contemporary relevance, although in a rather timid way. In his words: 'Life goes on, people want to and will live, and for this they need such rules that follow life well' (Tárkány Szücs 2003: 830; my translation). Unfortunately, Tárkány Szücs died in 1984, soon after the publication of his *opus magnum*, so he had no opportunity to turn his scholarly attention to contemporary legal folkways.

The Formation of Legal Anthropology in the Early 1990s

The death of Ernő Tárkány Szücs meant the end not only of this scholar's magnificent contribution to legal ethnology but also of the whole tradition of research that he represented. No intellectual successors emerged in the following years, and the revived interest in his work and in that of his predecessors, beginning in the 2000s, has been predominantly historical and descriptive in character.[7] In short, in the *communis opinio doctorum*, the tradition of legal ethnology is regarded generally as an interesting episode in Hungarian legal history, but it has lost its scholarly relevance in the understanding of the contemporary relationship of law, regulation, and culture in Hungarian society.

Despite the stagnation of legal ethnology, sociocultural approaches to law did not disappear in the mid-1980s; rather, they continued to have limited relevance for Hungarian legal scholarship, which had been pervaded by the positivistic and logo-centric German style for centuries.[8] In the early 1990s, however, the impetus for the renewal of a sociocultural understanding of law came not from the ossified tradition of legal ethnology but from outside of the country. During the early years of the postsocialist transition, starting in 1989, some young legal scholars argued for the reception of the ideas of Western legal anthropology in Hungarian legal scholarship. This process was advocated and boosted by István H. Szilágyi and Sándor Loss, the founding fathers of the

Hungarian legal anthropology movement. H. Szilágyi argued passionately for the invention of Hungarian legal anthropology in his seminal article, 'Let Us Invent Hungarian Legal Anthropology' (2002a, 2002b), which must be regarded as a full-fledged scholarly programme for the establishment of a completely new discipline in Hungary.

As a starting point, H. Szilágyi discussed the relationship between the tradition of Hungarian legal ethnology and the newly-born Hungarian legal anthropology from a critical perspective. He argued that the Hungarian tradition of legal ethnology cannot be revitalized in the historical and intellectual context of Hungarian legal studies in the postsocialist era. As H. Szilágyi explained, the tradition of legal ethnology had already lost both its intellectual and public vitality following 1945, as the efforts of Tárkány Szücs, its only remaining representative in the Hungarian legal academy, were restricted to the compilation of previous findings and to their presentation abroad. Thus, there was an obvious need, H. Szilágyi (2002b: 187) insisted, for fresh intellectual impulses that might give rise to a new community of scholars taking a sociocultural approach to law.

H. Szilágyi found these new impulses in the Western literature on legal anthropology. From the very beginning of his academic carrier, he regularly spent time abroad, especially in Amsterdam, Paris, Toulouse, Groningen, and Aix-en-Provence. His overtly Western intellectual orientation was reflected in the way he defined legal anthropology for Hungarian lawyers and law students who had never heard about it before. Generally, H. Szilágyi based his approach on the contributions of John Griffiths (e.g. 1986) in the late 1980s. In his paper, he stated that 'legal anthropology is the study of the phenomena of social control in different legal cultures and different societies (or social groups), largely using comparative and micro-sociological methods' (H. Szilágyi 2002b: 187; see also Griffiths 1986: 18–23). Given this definition, H. Szilágyi aligned Hungarian legal anthropology clearly with the mainstream of Western European legal anthropology. Each of the succeeding steps in the process of institutionalization was made within this intellectual framework.

For practical purposes, H. Szilágyi made a number of suggestions for establishing a lively and well-functioning scholarly community devoted to the study of legal anthropology. For example, he advocated the 'intensive study of the history of legal anthropological thought', so that members of the Hungarian scholarly community could familiarize themselves with basic concepts and their evolution (H. Szilágyi 2002b: 194). H. Szilágyi's PhD thesis on the modern history of legal anthropology, which was published in 2000 and republished in 2005 under the title *A jogi antropológi főbb irányai* (The Main Directions of Legal Anthropology), may be viewed as his own contribution to this very important task.

Parallel to H. Szilágyi's conceptual efforts, other scholars began with legal anthropological fieldwork at the beginning of the 1990s. In the very first Hungarian publication in this field, Sándor Loss and Gábor Szabó (1996) analysed the role of godparents in four small Protestant villages in south-western Hungary. Chiefly, Loss and Szabó wanted to know why newborn children in Protestant villages have fifteen godparents or more, in contrast to the Catholic custom of limiting the number of godparents to one couple. This study was carried out using anthropological methods. The research team visited forty families in these four villages, and, besides using a questionnaire, they also conducted in-depth interviews on family history and on the existing customs of godparenting. When analysing the outcome of their fieldwork, Loss and Szabó (1996: 4–5) relied on the social-anthropological paradigm of functionalism and applied Baerends's (1994) understanding of reciprocity. They concluded that the custom of godparenting had lost its material substance—the claim to provide real help to the child—and that its actual function was merely symbolic, mostly on the occasion of important family events. No rational, interest-based answer could be given to the question of why this custom survived in these villages, despite having lost its real function. Only the communal faith in the value of tradition could properly explain it, Loss and Szabó (1996: 12) argued.

After the early efforts of Loss and Szabó, representatives of the emerging Hungarian legal anthropology turned their attention to a new target group and a corresponding set of topics: the Roma people and their relation to law as a modern and rational form of dispute settlement. Undeniably, these studies may be regarded as the most successful expressions of legal anthropology in Hungary. The legal anthropological study of the Hungarian Roma contributed effectively to the understanding of the 'otherness' of Roma people with respect to the law (H. Szilágyi 2002b: 196; H. Szilágyi and Loss 2002).

Loss and H. Szilágyi (2001) published an outstanding piece on the so-called 'Gypsy trial'. In essence, they tried to reveal the characteristics of trials in which either the applicants or the respondents were Roma. In 1998, with the help of students of law and anthropology, they carried out intensive fieldwork on criminal cases in courts, observing and recording the actions and interactions both of the Roma participants and of official actors such as judges, prosecutors, and advocates. The authors instructed the students to observe the trials and to prepare detailed notes on the events occurring at the front of the court, while blending in with the setting as much as possible. The research resulted in stunning conclusions: essentially, these 'gypsy trials' were—or are—nothing more than rites in an anthropological sense. That is, in these lawsuits, the courts did not fulfil the function ascribed to them by a constitution that was inspired by the principles of democracy and the rule of law; instead, they served the 'preservation of the mutual prejudices between the majority society and the Roma minority, thereby strengthening the discrimination of the Roma minority' (Loss and H. Szilágyi 2001: 100; translation by the author). Loss and H. Szilágyi argued that reform was necessary to transform these lawsuits from empty rites to real legal disputes, and they pointed out the necessity of a *de lege ferenda* reform focusing on the broadening of free legal assistance.

In addition to the study of the 'Gypsy trial', which uncovered the dysfunctionality of the courts with regard to Roma participants, Hungarian legal anthropologists have carried out other research projects that focus on the Roma community. In the second half of 2000, as H. Szilágyi (2003) reported, two anthropologists studied a homeless Roma family, whose members lived from the collection of metal and paper from household trash in a postindustrial city in north-eastern Hungary. Researchers employed the method of participant observation and relied, in part, on the concept of semi-autonomous social fields in order to analyse the relationship of this family to other normative orders and institutions. Their findings showed that this family was in a marginal situation, constantly shifting between two worlds: their traditional community, which they left for the 'city', and the majority society (H. Szilágyi 2003: 70). The authors concluded that the policemen, who had regular daily contact with family members, developed a rather nuanced view of them. For instance, an officer explained that he did not regard them as criminals, although they lived under unsanitary and generally unfavourable conditions; and he even got useful information from them pertaining to some local cases, for which he regularly gave them a small amount of money or some other useful object, such as a bicycle, as compensation. Thus, police officers were the representatives of the majority society with whom this deprived family had a relatively stable relationship (H. Szilágyi 2003: 71).

Lastly, it should be mentioned that Loss (2005) wrote a seminal study of the so-called *Romani Kris* (Gypsy law or Gypsy court). Until the publication of Loss's paper, members of the Hungarian academic community denied the contemporary existence of *Romani Kris*, which is the traditional way in *Oláh* Roma communities of settling conflicts by mediation, without the involvement any state agency. Loss did not want to accept this academic commonplace and decided to carry out fieldwork in the summer of 2001. Due to his remarkable sensitivity in doing participant observation, he was able to follow the everyday life of the *Mašari* Roma community in Békés county, in the south-eastern part of the country. Surprisingly, Loss could show that the unwritten, traditional *Romani Kris* still existed in this community and that it was used widely in settling conflicts related to market transactions (e.g. the purchase of horses) or to family affairs (e.g. the elopement of a bride) (Loss 2005). In effect, Loss demonstrated the existence of legal pluralism and revealed the limited impact of state law in a traditional Roma community.

In the 2000s, there were other factors as well that contributed to the creation of a scholarly community devoted to this new approach to law in society. Legal anthropology was integrated into the sociolegal studies curriculum of the Law School of the Pázmány Péter Catholic University, where H. Szilágyi had been teaching this discipline since its foundation. Loss also taught legal anthropology both in the Law School and in the Faculty of Humanities at the University of Miskolc. What is more, H. Szilágyi published both a course book in sociolegal studies that approached its subject from a predominantly legal anthropological perspective and an edited volume that contained classic and contemporary contributions to legal anthropology in Hungarian translation (H. Szilágyi 2000; H. Szilágyi, Cserne, and Fekete 2012). Thus, it can be said that the basics of legal anthropology have been accessible to Hungarian legal scholarship and law students since the 2000s.[9]

In conclusion, it may be argued that legal anthropology had a promising start in Hungarian legal scholarship, beginning in the early 2000s. All the prerequisites for the successful establishment of a new discipline had been fulfilled: the historical and conceptual work had begun; there was a lively discourse on the prospects of legal anthropology;[10] successful research projects had been carried out; and some law faculties were willing to integrate legal anthropology into their curriculum, at least to a degree. However, these hopes were dashed when Loss died in a car accident in 2004, as this unfortunate event paralysed the further development of the discipline. Due to the death of Loss, and for other professional reasons, H. Szilágyi stopped doing fieldwork in the mid-2000s, becoming increasingly involved in the formation of the Hungarian movement of 'law and literature' instead (H. Szilágyi 2012). As a result, Hungarian legal anthropology had lost its scholarly vitality by the late 2000s, and, since then, legal anthropology has been limited to a supplementary role in sociolegal studies at some law faculties. The energy and inspiration of a lively scholarly community and the dedication to fieldwork have disappeared.

Assessment

The Relevance of Foreign Reception

As is evident in the brief overview presented above, in Hungary, both legal ethnology and legal anthropology were shaped decisively by the reception of foreign works. To put it provocatively, one might say that, without foreign impetus, the birth of these disciplines would have been simply impossible. The most important factor in the intellectual history of modern Hungary has been the reception of German authors and ideas, but French and English ethnological and anthropological scholarship has been influential as well. The early proponents of legal ethnography were inspired mainly by the insights of German *Rechtsethnologie*, while during the interwar period the French *folklore juridique* too had a strong methodological impact. Beginning in 1989, English-language legal anthropology had a strong influence, and the translation of classic and contemporary pieces, published in H. Szilágyi's course book, strengthened this trend.

Despite the importance of foreign influences, however, the work of Hungarian scholars in these fields has not simply been limited to the recapitulation of Western European scholarship. The works of Tárkány Szücs, along with those of H. Szilágyi and Loss, may serve to illustrate the complexity of this issue. For instance, in 1981, Tárkány Szücs used Karl-S. Kramer's (1974) idea of the formation of legal folkways from various tensions among the individual, the community, and the administration as a starting point (Tárkány Szücs 2003: 37). However, he applied it to the realities of modern Hungarian legal and political development, and, in the end, he drafted a comprehensive theory on the nature of legal folkways in this specific national context. Similarly, legal anthropologists at the end of the 1990s applied the conceptual framework and the methodological toolkit of contemporary Western anthropology, for instance the concepts of the semi-autonomous social field or of legal rites (Loss and H. Szilágyi 2001). The result was, however, something that was nationally or regionally specific: the identification of the unique phenomenon of the 'Gypsy trial', in which the judiciary reproduces the marginalization of Roma people. Thus, the reception of foreign ideas has never replaced scholarly creativity; rather, it has helped Hungarian legal scholars with an interest in sociocultural phenomena to find a proper conceptual vocabulary and to connect their research to international standards.

The Critical Role of 'External' Factors

Our story also shows that neither legal ethnology nor legal anthropology has had a linear and organic development. On the contrary, their development has been characterized by various ruptures and discontinuities (Foucault 1969: 9–28). The first efforts to collect information about legal customs, particularly those concerning the law of inheritance, were interrupted by World War I and were not taken up again after its conclusion. The second wave of legal ethnology was boosted by the political claims of the late 1930s, trying to free, at least partially, Hungarian private law legislation from foreign, predominantly German, influence; yet the extensive primary materials that had been collected were destroyed in 1945. The new communist regime discredited legal ethnology, owing to its presumed nationalistic character; but, with the softening of the regime, beginning in the late 1960s, Tárkány Szücs was able to join the Institute of Ethnology within the Hungarian Academy of Sciences and to prepare his *opus magnum*, which was praised by the officials of the Academy. Legal anthropology got off to a promising start in the mid-1990s, but the death of Loss practically froze the possibility of an ongoing and organic disciplinary evolution.

The ruptures and discontinuities in the development of legal ethnology and legal anthropology in Hungary seem to confirm Tárkány Szücs's (2003: 13) insight that the study of folk law is largely dependent on place and subject matter. In Hungary, these disciplines never developed organically; rather they were influenced decisively by prevalent, often politically motivated research interests as well as historical circumstances (Bognár 2016: 30–1). Occasionally, a nationalistic agenda boosted these studies, resulting, for example, in the proliferation of field research at the end of the interwar period. However, political pressure was also capable of eliminating interest in ethnographical research, as was the case with Tárkány Szücs in the 1950s, the early years of the socialist era. Under favourable conditions, Hungarian legal scholars could produce works worthy of international attention: for example, those based on fieldwork in the villages of Kalotaszeg; Tárkány Szücs's impressive manual on Hungarian legal folkways; or the study of the attitudes of the Hungarian judiciary towards the Roma people.[11] Nonetheless, no scholar in these fields has ever had the opportunity to escape the given historical situation and its consequences.

Community Matters—Deficient Scholarly Communities

In his classic study, *The Structure of Scientific Revolutions* (1970), Thomas Kuhn directed our attention to the pre-eminent importance of scientific communities in the development of science in general. This insight also has relevance for the story of

Hungarian legal ethnology and legal anthropology. It is striking to realize how strongly the fate of these fields has been linked to individuals, rather than to the communities that they tried to establish. The only exception might be the seminar that formed around Professor Bónis in the 1940s. However that may be, the catastrophe of World War II and the subsequent emergence of the communist regime made the formation of a vibrant scholarly community, capable of providing a supportive and congenial environment for its members, more difficult. Beginning in the mid-1990s, the birth of legal anthropology in Hungary was spurred by the initiatives of H. Szilágyi and Loss, who invited law and anthropology students to participate in various fieldwork projects. Nevertheless, no second-generation legal anthropologists emerged in the following years to continue their work.

The main outcomes of Hungarian legal ethnology and legal anthropology have largely been the results of individual efforts, which, often, met not with the help and support of a community of legal scholars but with neglect or discouragement. Presumably, as long as this situation does not change, there will be little chance to reanimate either of these traditions.

Notes

1. Maine's *Ancient Law* (1861), a precursor to legal anthropology, was translated into Hungarian and published as early as 1875. Barna Horváth, an expert on legal theory and one of the founding fathers of Hungarian legal sociology, prepared a comprehensive manual on the history of English jurisprudence in order to promote the dissemination of English ideas about law, including the early anthropological approaches, in Hungarian legal scholarship (Horváth 1943).
2. An argument can also be made for the existence of a distinct Central-European tradition of legal ethnology. Ernő Tárkány Szücs (1967) discusses Hungarian, Albanian, Serbian, Croatian, Bulgarian, Polish, Czech, Slovakian, Romanian, and Latvian ethnological initiatives in his seminal article surveying legal ethnology in Europe.
3. I draw on Szabina Bognár's (2016) detailed history of legal ethnology in Hungary, though my perspective diverges from hers on some points.
4. For the recent activities of the society, see its homepage: <http://neprajzihirek.hu/>
5. The very first work by Tárkány Szücs, published in 1944 with the support of György Bónis in the series 'Legal History and Studies on Folk Law', presented the results of his fieldwork in Mártély, a village close to his home town, Hódmezővásárhely. Tárkány Szücs started the collection of data on folk law in this village while he was still in school.
6. See e.g. Szabó (1955), a work by the most influential legal academic of the socialist era which consists in a comprehensive Marxist-Leninist critique of the legal theory of the prewar and interwar periods and which represents an attempt to discredit the entire tradition of non-Marxist Hungarian legal theory.
7. This statement applies especially to the Tárkány Szücs Ernő Research Group for the Study of Cultural Legal History and Legal Ethnology, which was founded by three Hungarian law schools and is led by Janka Teodóra Nagy and Barna Mezei. For an example of their work, see Nagy (2018).
8. For an exception to this general rule, see the work of Csaba Varga (1983, 1988).

9. H. Szilágyi (2000) contains twenty chapters, including translations of papers by Sally Falk Moore, Bronislaw Malinowski, Edward Moffat Weyer, Isaac Schapera, Karl N. Llewellyn, Leopold Pospisil, Paul Bohannan, Philip Huge Gulliver, Jane F. Collier, Martin Chanock, Laura Nader, Franz von Benda-Beckmann, John Griffiths, Norbert Rouland, René Kuppe, Agnes T. M. Schreiner, and Peter A. Winn.
10. On the debate between H. Szilágyi and Mátyás Bódig regarding the 'methodological sensitivity' of legal anthropology, see H. Szilágyi (2002b: 195).
11. Excerpts from Tárkány Szücs (1981) were published in the journal *Droit et Cultures* (Tárkány Szücs 1997a, 1997b); and H. Szilágyi (2009b) published a synthesis of his research on Roma people in English.

References

Baerends, E. A. 1994. *The One-Legged Chicken in the Shadow of Indebtedness: Indebtedness and Social Relationships among the Anufom in Northern Togo*. Groningen: University of Groningen.

Baross, J. 1905. *Részleges jelentés az O.M.G.E. által a magyar parasztbirtokok öröklési módjaira vonatkozólag elrendelt adatgyűjtés eredményeiről*. Budapest: Uránia.

Bognár, S. 2016. *A népi jogélet kutatása Magyarországon*. Budapest: Magyar Néprajzi Társaság.

Borbándi, G. 1976. *Der ungarische Populismus*. Mainz: Hase & Koehler Verlag.

Cartledge, B. 2011. *The Will to Survive: A History of Hungary*. Oxford: Oxford University Press.

Ehrlich, E. 2017. *Fundamental Principles of the Sociology of Law*, trans. W. L. Moll. London and New York: Routledge.

Fekete, B. and I. H. Szilágyi. 2017. 'Knowledge and Opinion about Law (KOL) Research in Socialist Hungary'. *Acta Juridica Hungarica: Hungarian Journal of Legal Studies* 58(3): 326–58.

Foucault, M. 1969. *L'archéologie du savoir*. Paris: Gallimard.

Griffiths, J. 1986. 'Recent Anthropology of Law in the Netherlands and its Historical Background'. In K. von Benda-Beckmann, F. Strijbosch, and A. Strijbosch, eds. *Anthropology of Law in the Netherlands. Essays on Legal Pluralism*, 11–66. Dordrecht: Foris Publications.

H. Szilágyi, I. 2000. *A jogi antropológi főbb irányai. Történeti és elméleti vázlat*. Budapest: Osiris.

H. Szilágyi, I., ed. 2000. *Jog és antropológia*. Budapest: Osiris.

H. Szilágyi, I. 2002a. 'Találjuk ki a Magyar jogi antropológiát!' In *A jogi antropológia főbb irányai. Történeti és elméleti vázlat*, 84–94. Budapest: Osiris.

H. Szilágyi, I. 2002b. 'Let Us Invent Hungarian Legal Anthropology'. *Rechtstheorie* 33: 187–96.

H. Szilágyi, I. 2003. 'Romák közelről. A magyarországi romák antropológiai kutatása'. *Kontroll* 1: 56–73.

H. Szilágyi, I. 2005. *A jogi antropológia főbb irányai*. Budapest: Szent István Társulat.

H. Szilágyi, I. 2009a. 'Rokoni kapcsolatok. Jogi antropológia és jogi etnográfia'. In J. T. Nagy and B. Mezey, eds. *Jogi néprajz-jogi kultúrtörténet: tanulmányok a jogtudományok, a néprajztudományok és a történettudományok köréből*, 63–72. Budapest: ELTE Eötvös.

H. Szilágyi, I. 2009b. 'The Roma Way'. In A. Wagner and V. K. Bhatia, eds. *Diversity and Tolerance in Socio-Legal Contexts: Explorations in the Semiotics of Law*, 65–80. Aldershot: Ashgate.

H. Szilágyi, I. 2012. 'Law and Literature in Hungary. An Introduction'. *Acta Juridica Hungarica* 53(1): 1–6.

H. Szilágyi, I., P. Cserne, and B. Fekete, eds. 2012. *Társadalmi-jogi kutatások*. Budapest: Szent István Társulat.

H. Szilágyi, I. and S. Loss. 2002. 'Opening Scissors: The Legal Status of the Gypsy Minority in the Nowadays Hungary'. *Rechtstheorie* 33(2–4): 483–94.

Horváth, B. 1943. *Angol jogelmélet*. Budapest: Magyar Tudományos Akadémia.

Kontler, L. 1999. *Millennium in Central Europe: A History of Hungary*. Budapest: Atlantisz.

Kramer, K.-S. 1974. *Grundriss einer rechtlichen Volkskunde*. Göttingen: Verlag Otto Schwartz & Co.

Kuhn, T. S. 1970. *The Structure of Scientific Revolutions*. Second edition. Chicago: University of Chicago Press.

Kulcsár, K. 1961. 'Népi jog és nemzeti jog'. *MTA Állam- és jogtudományi Intézet Értesítője* 4: 153–93.

Loss, S. 2005. 'Romani Kris a dél-békési oláhcigányoknál'. In J. Szabadfalvi, ed. *Amabilissimus. A legszeretreméltóbbak egyike. Loss Sándor emlékkönyv*, 119–35. Debrecen: Debreceni Egyetem.

Loss, S. and G. Szabó. 1996. 'A szokásjog értelme és a hagyomány értéke: komaság és reciprocitás négy őrségi faluban'. *Acta Universitatis Szegediensis: Sectio politico-juridica* 50(8): 1–13.

Loss, S. and I. H. Szilágyi. 2001. 'A "cigány-per" '. *Beszélő* 6: 94–100.

Maine, H. S. 1861. *Ancient Law*. London: John Murray.

Maine, H. S. 1875. *A jog őskora*. Budapest: Akadémia.

Mattyasovszky, M. 1904. *Törzsöröklési jog és törzsöröklési szokás*. Budapest: Eggenberger.

Maunier, R. 1938. *Introduction au folklore juridique: definition, questionnaire, bibliographie*. Paris: Editions d'art et d'histoire.

Nagy, J. T. 2018. *A magyar jogi népélet kutatás (1939–1948) története és forrásai*. Szekszárd: PTE KPVK.

Ormos, M. and B. K. Király, eds. 2001. *Hungary: Governments and Politics, 1848–2000*. Highland Lakes, NJ: Atlantic Research and Publications.

Papp, L. 1939. 'Népi szemlélet: magyarabb, szociálisabb jog'. *Magyar Élet*, július, 10–12.

Péter, L. 1998. 'A magyar nacionalizmus'. In *Az Elbától keletre*. Budapest: Osiris.

Rát, M. 1782. 'Tudománybeli dolgok'. *Magyar Hírmondó* 3: 33–8.

Schott, R. 1982. 'Main Trends in German Ethnological Jurisprudence and Legal Ethnology'. *Journal of Lega: l Pluralism* 20: 37–68.

Szabadfalvi, J. 2010. 'The Beginnings of Hungarian Legal Philosophical Thinking'. *Archiv für Rechts- und Sozialphilosophie* 96(3): 337–47.

Szabadfalvi, J. 2011. 'From Original Sources—Neo-Kantian Legal Philosophical Thinking in Hungary'. *Acta Juridica Hungarica* 52(1): 73–81.

Szabó, I. 1955. *A burzsoá állam- és jogbölcselet Magyarországon*. Budapest: Akadémiai Kiadó.

Tagányi, K. 1919. *A hazai élő jogszokások gyűjtéséről. I. rész. A családjog és öröklési jog köréből*. Budapest: Néprajzi társaság.

Tárkány Szücs, E. 1944. *Mártély népi jogélete*. Kolozsvár: Kolozsvári Egyetem Jogtörténeti Szemináriuma.

Tárkány Szücs, E. 1967. 'Results and Tasks of Legal Ethnology in Europe'. *Ethnologia Europea* 1(3): 195–217. Reprinted in A. D. Renteln and A. Dundes, eds. 1994. *Folk Law: Essays in the Theory and Practice of Lex Non Scripta*, 161–86. New York: Garland.

Tárkány Szücs, E. 1981. *Magyar jogi népszokások*. Budapest: Gondolat Kiadó.

Tárkány Szücs, E. 1997a. 'Collecting Legal Folk Customs in Hungary'. *Droit et Cultures* 34: 188–204.

Tárkány Szücs, E. 1997b. 'Les coutumes juridiques populaires et les règles de succession de notre paysannerie'. *Droit et Cultures* 34: 169–85.
Tárkány Szücs, E. 2003. *Magyar jogi népszokások*. Second edition. Budapest: Akadémiai Kiadó.
Varga, Cs. 1983. 'From Legal Customs to Legal Folkways'. *Acta Juridica Academiae Scientiarum Hungaricae* 25(3–4): 454–9.
Varga, Cs. 1988. 'Anthropological Jurisprudence? Leopold Pospísil and the Comparative Study of Legal Cultures'. In *Law in East and West*, 265–85. Institute of Comparative Law, Waseda University. Tokyo: Waseda University Press.
Voigt, V., ed. 1998. *A magyar folklór*. Budapest: Osiris.

CHAPTER 14

THE ANTHROPOLOGY OF EUROPEAN LAW

MICHELE GRAZIADEI

INTRODUCTION

THIS chapter deals with European laws as an object of study from an anthropological perspective. The idea of an anthropology of law devoted to such an area is in itself problematic, however. The European region 'has a history of several anthropological approaches separated by different languages, political structures and intellectual traditions' (Barrera-González et al. 2017; Green 2012). To what extent there is a European legal order in Europe, as opposed to a multitude of national and local legal systems, is another major question, with no obvious answer. As a cultural entity, European law is a motley composition resulting from a multitude of sources. Nonetheless, in this respect, European law matches other fields covered by broad descriptors, such as 'Latin American law' or 'African law'. What counts as 'law' for such purposes is open to discussion as well, to be sure. Legal historians, comparative law scholars, and anthropologists have all highlighted this theme, while exploring modes of normativity in Europe across time and place. Much anthropology of law produced in Europe does not concern the European world, but other regions of the globe. Usually, this is considered to be revelatory of the additional difficulty of maintaining the distinction between 'self' and 'other', while pursuing an anthropological approach to law with respect to European societies. Nonetheless, of late, the erosion of the modernist 'us/them' divide has rendered similar distinctions 'no longer foundational or even relevant' to the subject; the challenge is thus to find 'alterity within' such a world (de Pina-Cabral 2015: 15). In the throes of meeting these and other challenges, research on the anthropology of law with respect to this region of the world has progressed substantially since the 1970s. This chapter presents a view of the subject and discusses its transformations from the particular perspective of an academic with a grounding in comparative law. An anthropologist's approach to the same topic could bring in different perspectives and illustrate other itineraries in considering European societies and the laws they live by. But, at some point, these various paths to the subject are bound to meet, hopefully in a productive way (Benda-Beckmann 2008).

This contribution is divided into three sections that explore how the anthropology of law developed and how it is practised with respect to Europe, with an introduction and a conclusion. The first section covers how nineteenth-century and early twentieth-century scholarship first approached the study of law and legal institutions from an anthropological point of view. Contemporary scholarship has distanced itself from these beginnings, but an illustration of the background is necessary to understand how anthropology evolved out of (and eventually abandoned) an older tradition.

The second section offers a presentation of the purposes and the tasks of the discipline in today's Europe. The fall of totalitarian regimes and the establishment of a single market brought about a new understanding of the purposes of law in Europe. Law and anthropology studies have thus explored a variety of themes linked to the transformations of European societies in the past decades. The third section considers how European institutions and norms (as opposed to national or local ones) have become an object of increased attention from the point of view of law and anthropology scholarship. The making of a common law for Europe opens up new fields of enquiry for the discipline as well. The conclusion highlights how the contributions coming from the field of law and anthropology, sparse as they are, have put on the research agenda crucial questions that mainstream legal studies do not address, and perhaps cannot address, except as a reflexive afterthought.

Our ancestors

The first beginnings of social and legal anthropological research as an academic subject are located in the nineteenth-century investigations of 'primitive law' (Kirkby 2018; Tuori 2015). Scholars who produced the first studies of what was then labelled as 'primitive law' were mostly jurists belonging to various European nations (Kuper 1988). The European past shows, however, at the beginning of the modern age, an earlier and persistent ethnographic interest in 'savages' that spanned several centuries, going back at least to the discovery of America (Ellingson 2001). The nineteenth century marks new beginnings when compared with previous epochs because the study of ethnology and socio-cultural anthropology was, for the first time, in the hands of professional researchers (Roldan and Vermeulen 1995). Anthropology in this age also responded to an evolutionary paradigm elaborated in the context of historical and philosophical theories of the constitution of society (Stein 1980). After the industrial revolution, this view contributed to propping up the European sense of overall superiority over other populations and human groups (Goody 1996). In the age of colonialism and imperialism, this sentiment of superiority was often racialized to confirm, by a 'scientific' theory, the irreconcilable distance between the peoples of Europe and their descendants and the other parts of mankind (Gould 1996). The same idea of hierarchy was present within the European polity as well (McMahon 2016). Similar ideas were not shared by all exponents of the scientific community, however. The works of Adolf Bastian (1826–1905) and E.B. Tylor (1832–1917), initiators of social and cultural anthropology, postulated the psychic unity of mankind. This different tradition is best reflected by the work of Franz Boas (1858–1942), who held that there was no inherent difference between the civilized and the 'primitive man' (Boas 1911).

In nineteenth-century Europe, what today would count as early or proto-anthropological research was not limited to evidence on 'the others' that the Europeans encountered in other parts of the world, through imperial expansion, colonial subjugation, missionary establishments, trading and exploration, etc., etc. (on this see the chapter by Chanock in this volume). Europe was itself a place to explore different forms of otherness, represented by popular culture and folk communities (Bendix and Hasan-Rokem 2012; Perla 2013; Storey 2009). Folk culture, an idealized alternative to the degraded life of the masses in the city, became the embodiment of the nature and character of a nation. Therefore, it was to be collected and treasured. This attitude reflected a transformation of the social life of the elites. In 1500, the upper classes despised common people but shared their culture; by 1800, 'their descendants had ceased to participate spontaneously in popular culture, but they were in the process of rediscovering it as something exotic and therefore interesting' (Burke 2009: 286). Among the jurists of this era, the German historical school supported this type of research with inquiries into folklore such as those conducted by Jacob Grimm (1785–1863) and Wilhelm Grimm (1786–1859). Their contributions represented a return to the nocturnal, the sacred, the original, and the preconscious (Bishop 2011). In England, Edward Tylor conceived of folklore not merely as the legacy of a more authentic way of life, but as the 'survival' of an earlier 'savage' culture. Taylor posited that, although all European societies show a division between 'the irrational beliefs and practices of the … peasantry' and 'the enlightened views of the educated classes', one could look at folklore as a reservoir of 'the fragments of an ancient, lower culture, the culture of primitive man' (Tylor 1891: 7). Primitive law, just like primitive culture, caught on as a cognitive category that could be applied to the early laws and customs of European peoples and to those of the extra-European worlds where the Europeans arrived. They were both approached through a culturalist framework in the works of Victorian jurist H.S. Maine (1822–1888), who worked on the making of British colonial policies in India (Mantena 2010; for the echo of his works among French jurists, see Guerlain 2015). At this juncture, we find the birth of Durkheim's sociology and the origins of anthropological investigations of social practices like the gift, which defied a purely utilitarian approach, lucidly elaborated by Marcel Mauss (Mallard 2019). These years are also the intellectual origins of the work of Lucien Levy-Bruhl, whose troublesome legacy has been recently re-evaluated (Nisio 2019; Szakolczai and Thomassen 2019).

Meanwhile, in the lands of the Austro-Hungarian empire, Eugen Ehrlich (1862–1922) had turned towards a more empirically grounded and theoretically sophisticated conception of popular law. Like the jurists of the German historical school, Ehrlich maintained that legislation created by the state was just one aspect of the law. But he went on to argue the more radical thesis that, beyond the official law, there is the living law made by the inner ordering of society and by the life patterns of groups and individuals, which 'dominates life itself even though it has not been posited in legal propositions' (Ehrlich 1936: 493). Mainstream legal scholarship in Europe did not receive Ehrlich's work well (although, in the United States, Roscoe Pound was an admirer of his work). Hans Kelsen (1881–1973), the great champion of legal positivism and formalism, sternly criticized Ehrlich's failure to maintain a clear distinction between facts and norms. Although not forgotten, Ehrlich was thus marginalized until the revival of interest in his legacy in more recent years (see e.g. Hertogh 2008; Rehbinder 1986; Teubner 1997). Ehrlich saw what many jurists failed to see: the records of the official sources of the law leave open a gap between the law resulting from these sources and the law people live by. Historians have documented this gulf on a great scale (see e.g. Gilissen 1982), even with respect to fields like property law (Grossi 1981), which were the bedrock foundation of the nineteenth-century legal order.

While Ehrlich was exploring the laws of his homeland, anthropologists like Malinowski worked at the foundations of an empirically grounded anthropology of law which rejected the previous evolutionary paradigm (Rosen 2012). The distance between these contributions, based on fieldwork conducted outside Europe, and the works of the historical school and its followers was huge. They marked a definitive turning point. I will just mention here the introductory pages of Malinowski's *Crime and Custom in Savage Society* (1926), with their scathing, damning review of previous scholarship, mostly attributable to lawyers such as Maine, Bachofen, Post, and Kohler. According to Malinowski, their works were handicapped by insufficient materials, useless amateur observations, and baseless assumptions (Malinowski 1926). This was why anthropology in general had so little to say about law as practised outside the West: what had been done until then was not credible, based as it was on the idea, or the myth, that the individual was completely dominated by the group. It took some time before this new, empirically informed approach began to be applied to European societies as well. This happened in more evident way in the period following the Second World War, in a process of transfer of knowledge that has not yet been fully explored (on the state of the art, see Anders 2015; Bens and Vetters 2018), which eventually led anthropology to confront, in a critical vein, the vexing fact of its systematic involvement in colonial regimes of domination.[1]

Law and anthropology in today's Europe

After the Second World War, with the passing of democratic constitutions and the creation of a new set of international and European institutions, Western European countries became more inclusive democracies, with the recognition of wide-ranging freedoms and social rights; this paved the way to an increasingly plural social life. In the eyes of many observers, the fall of the Berlin Wall in 1989, the reunification of Germany, and the enlargement of the European Union (EU) marked the culmination of liberal democracy in Europe. This process is now considered less univocal than it first appeared to be, as in some Member States it has engendered a good deal of resentment, discontent, and disappointment in recent years (see, with respect to Central and Eastern Europe, e.g. Krastev and Holmes 2019; Müller 2007; and more generally Azoulai 2020b).

What is the place of an anthropology of law in this context? The practice of anthropology of law 'at home' is a relatively young branch of the discipline (Conley and O'Barr 1993) with respect to contemporary European societies (Thelen et al. 2014). The European Association of Social Anthropologists (EASA), established in 1989, and the Society for the Anthropology of Europe, created as a section of the American Anthropological Association, foster these developments, while publication outlets such as the *Anthropological Journal of European Cultures*, or *Droit et Cultures*, and the newly established *Journal of Legal Anthropology*, as well as several specialized book series, showcase the increasing amount of research dedicated to Europe from the perspective of socio-cultural anthropology. Within the EASA, there is a subgroup (LawNET) that brings together former participants in the group on law and rights and participants in the more recent Network for Anthropology of International Governance. These initiatives are just a portion of what is done in the field because research on law and anthropology is carried on at several universities and in research centres all over Europe, whose mission is to cater to social and political anthropology as well. Furthermore, while the founding fathers of sociology did not build their expertise on fieldwork, much sociological research now sits on the fence dividing the two disciplines in methodological terms as well, such that this fence is increasingly perceived as artificial and difficult to maintain (Bens and Vetters 2018; Bourdieu 2005; Cotterell 2019; Demeulenaere 2012; Griffiths 2017; Riles 2019).

When it comes to law, anthropology has some difficulty in defining its object (see e.g. Anders 2015; Assier-Andrieu 2019; Comaroff 2018; Pirie 2019). This is a productive difficulty, however. Anthropology of law remains so relevant for social studies in general precisely because the narrow, positivist understanding of the law still prevailing in many legal environments in Europe—which, by the way, also has some trouble in defining what the law is—is rejected by anthropologists. It has been said that 'Euro-modernist law is, in all its inflections, a repertoire of naturalised cultural practices, one rarely concerned, save in spaces of exception, with what "others" do or think or say' (Comaroff 2018: 73). One of the main tasks of an anthropology of law is therefore to treat that construct 'as an ethnographic object, a polymorphous ensemble of signifying practices that require to be laid bare, to be analysed and theorised, all the better to understand its place in the contemporary Order of Things' (Comaroff 2018: 77). In pursuing this goal, anthropologists are not alone. In the field of comparative law, for example, Rodolfo Sacco's influential theory of legal formants and cryptotypes responds to the same call, and thus offers an empirical theory of normativity which allows for gaps, contradictions, and contestations in multilayered, dynamic approaches to comparative law (Sacco 1991 and, for his contribution to an anthropology of law, Sacco 2008). This is an emancipatory vision that paves the way to a critical knowledge of the law (see e.g. Muir-Watt 2000), which is a key, shared goal of current anthropological approaches to the law (e.g. Nafziger 2017). The very foundations of the Western legal tradition may be thus reconsidered from an anthropological perspective (see e.g. Munday and Pottage 2004). The broad field of law and society/socio-legal studies fosters the collaboration among empirically oriented disciplines, including anthropology, in the field of law more generally (see e.g. García-Villegas 2018; Hertogh 2018; Benda-Beckmann 2008). The stream of research exploring 'legal consciousness' is part of this trend (see e.g. Aidinlis 2019; Hertogh 2018). All these studies set aside the unruly, somewhat romantic notion of 'culture', which still features prominently in several European legal debates, mostly among legal academics (for criticism, see Cotterell 2019: 84; Dedek 2014; for a vindication of 'culturalism' see Legrand 2017). Anthropological research pushes to abandon all idealized and romantic versions of 'culture' in the field of law as well (for they have little explanatory power), in favour of a more empirically grounded analysis of cultural constructs, such as legal norms and practices as they play out in social life (von Benda-Beckmann and von Benda-Beckmann 2010; Pirie 2013). Under the lens of an anthropological study, conflicts and tensions among the players in the field come out, and the law is one of the weapons they have in their hands. Matters like consumer indebtedness and debt (Deville 2015; Hart and Hortiz 2014; Mikuš 2019); the way the family home is sold and purchased (Bourdieu 2005); how housing is provided (Alexander et al. 2018), denied (Brickell et al. 2017), or lived in precariously (e.g. Carr et al. 2018); how care is delivered to family members or others (Thelen 2015); how disasters and crimes are dealt with in the courtroom (Benadusi and Revet 2016; Besnier 2017); and how corruption is linked to a more general dialectic of order and disorder (Zerilli 2013), just to mention some recent studies, are hardly understood by simply consulting the statute book or the law reports. The law as a formal set of norms and institutions, and as a way to conceptualize social life, often lags behind the facts, as family law did for a good part of the twentieth century, or does not tell the full story of discretion exercised over citizens' behaviours (see e.g. Dubois 2014). The anthropological account of the languages of the law and of litigants in these contexts illuminate the biases that find expression in the law. As Conley and O'Barr (2005) put it, can the words of a lawyer who cross-examines a rape victim in the hopes of getting her to admit an interest in her attacker ever be considered just words?

Law and anthropology studies of such issues unveil the underlying power structures and the social practices that permeate the law. These studies investigate how those structures and practices are understood by those that take part in them, and how they are conceptualized within and outside the legal system. The distinction between the law in action and the law in the books, popularized by the legal realists, represents the proverbial tip of the iceberg in this respect. One should rather embrace conscious intentionalities and unconscious habits, ideologies, political designs, hopes about the future and desires, personal choice, and collective destiny, whether expressed through orality, conduct, or documentality or implicitly foreshadowed. In this respect, European law is less a special case than it was previously considered to be, although the learned laws in Europe have had a very visible presence since antiquity. On the other hand, life in many European societies is now marked by the creation of fleeting communities and transitory networks of relations, much more than in the past. Enduring social relationships capable of supporting the living law that Ehrlich described are a rarity nowadays in advanced economies.

Ethnographic research in Europe has traditionally investigated how the law of the state recognizes and governs ethnic minorities and their alternative forms of normativity. This line of research has focused in recent decades on the Roma (see e.g. Acton 2005; Nafstad 2019; Ruggiu 2016); the hatred and discrimination against this minority have led to recurring concerns over the respect of their human rights (Council of Europe 2012). In the legal camp, the study of ethnic minorities' rights has traditionally been mostly in the hands of international law scholarship. These rights were initially guaranteed by international treaties and conventions as a result of compromises among nations. From the late 1960s onwards, however, this began to change. A more pluralistic vision of society emerged, traditional social roles were challenged or underwent substantial change (e.g. with respect to family and gender issues), and the place of various cultural claims in the law became more visible with respect to minorities as well (see e.g. Poulter 1998). With the onset of globalization and public debates over multiculturalism, the notion of citizenship associated with the constitution of national states was challenged in various ways. As a result of migrations and increasing mobility, culturally homogenous nations made up of sedentary citizens were no longer to be found, not even in the imagery of the most fervent believers of the national idea (cf. Foblets et al. 2018b).[2] What identity meant for the purposes of minority protection changed in international law as well, with the proliferation of international conventions dedicated to cultural, religious, gender, and ethnic issues. Up to this period, the standard strategy of the liberal state in Europe was to proclaim the formal equality of all subjects, and then to assimilate them into a single form of national citizenship. A uniform notion of citizenship denied that particular identities could actually generate competing, particular legal regimes. The many overlapping communities in which people lived their everyday lives, and in which they discovered their particular identities, were reconfigured not as normative contexts but as brute, indeed mute, facts (MacDonald 2005). As mentioned above, by the late 1960s this approach gave way to the recognition that social life in a democracy brings in a richer understanding of pluralism, which is open to cultural and other differences, be they linked to religious faiths, ethnic affiliations, minority languages, or gender issues, etc.

The increased visibility of contentious social and cultural issues in the public sphere has resulted in a wave of new socio-legal and anthropological studies, often dedicated to settled minorities of migrant background. These have examined how religious beliefs, ethnic customs, personal laws, minority languages, etc. resulted in cultural and legal claims that confronted the legal systems at various levels, showing varying dimensions of pluralism across Europe (see e.g. Bowen 2007, 2016; Fournier 2016a, 2016b; Grillo 2015, 2017; Lapi 2018; Shah 2005; Shah et al. 2016; Simon et al. 2019; Walker 2016;

Wyvekens 2014). Meanwhile, public debates have marked a retreat from the stronger ideological tenets of multiculturalism, which has been criticized for fostering separatism and the self-segregation of migrants and their children (Levey 2018; Vertovec and Wessendorf 2010). The literature addressing these problems tackles some issues with large media coverage, like the ban of the Islamic veil in French public schools; the debates on the wearing of Sikh articles of faith at school or at the workplace; the prohibition of female genital mutilation (FGM), etc. Ultimately, how autonomy plays out in plural societies, where no single model of regulation or approach prevails, remains an open question (Foblets et al. 2018a). But quite apart from any 'cultural' issue, 'the world of migrants, refugees, and settled minorities is often multi-jurisdictional and trans-jurisdictional', and this by itself is a challenge for any law that is tied to a territory, like the laws of the European states and of the European institutions (Grillo 2015: 3; Sona 2014).

In this context, anthropologists have been called upon to provide professional expertise to public institutions, and especially to courts, confronted with unfamiliar norms, assumptions, practices, and conducts (Good 2008; Holden 2011; Ruggiu 2018). The difficulty of conveying expertise in this context is not to be underestimated, and the question of who has the power and authority to speak remains crucial for the outcome of each case. Anthropologists bringing their expertise to the court are not necessarily in a privileged position in this respect. The first European-wide survey of judicial practice shows that judges 'conceptualise "immigrant culture" in an operationalised manner closely related to their working environment, distinguishing between the different dimensions of culture as communication, culture as context, and culture as norms' (Vetters and Foblets 2016: 287).

The European level

Europe is, and shall remain for the foreseeable future, a world of worlds. There are huge variations of cultural and socio-economic conditions across Europe (Bréchon and Gonthier 2017; Crouch 2016). Even basic issues related to the administration of justice, such as judicial independence, show a lack of uniformity (Eurobarometer 2018). Still, Europeans share much in the field of law, as in other social and cultural spheres (see e.g. Grødeland and Miller 2015).

Beyond the national level, Europeans share common laws, established by European institutions. By pursuing European integration, and by securing a whole array of fundamental rights and values, these institutions have associated new meanings with the word 'community' and 'union' across the continent. The two key institutions in this respect are the Council of Europe and the EU. The European institutions that have their origins in the European Communities have evolved since their foundations in the late 1950s. In the same period, the law concerning the European Convention on Human Rights (ECHR) has changed as well, in substance and in geographical scope. Europe is thus an unstable object of anthropological interest. Furthermore, within the framework of the EU the construction of a transnational space remains fraught with difficulties. The incompleteness of this project 'play[s] out in a wide variety of spheres, from migration to the internal market, and from family law to fundamental rights in the European Union' (Foblets and Alidadi 2020). The transfer of sovereignty that this project requires is far from smooth. Brexit is a glaring example of how polarized public opinion can be about this transfer (Green et al. 2016; Knight 2017), and the current challenges to Europe also speak of a tendency to separate the local from the global, the nation from Europe. In this context, a mere insistence on shared values is a rather abstract way to respond to social needs and demands (Azoulai 2020a, 2020b).

Anthropologists have examined institutional steps towards a common European identity fostered by cultural policies and initiatives (Bellier and Wilson 2000; Galbraith 2015: 10 ff.). They have also taken an interest in the Eurocrats in Brussels as a group (Lewicki 2017). The larger question is, how does the European construction fare from the perspective of law and anthropology? EU law and the law of the ECHR do not live in a vacuum. They are neither self-contained nor self-sufficient: they have both drawn upon the intellectual resources provided by the states and legal cultures of Europe for their own purposes, as it has often been recognized by both institutions. To consider the European legal landscape is thus also to reflect on what emerges from the many legal orders and cultures that have found a common roof under the European treaties. The transnational dimensions of law in Europe historically go beyond the achievements of the European institutions. Europe has core common values rooted in the national legal cultures and in their rich, multifarious past, as well as in the ideals supporting democracy in Europe. All these elements can be presented, to an extent, as variations on common themes. These trajectories are mostly investigated by comparative law lawyers and EU lawyers, as well as legal historians and legal philosophers. Part of their task is also to critically address these themes (see e.g. Hansen and Jonsson 2014; Tuori 2020); law and anthropology approaches hardly cover them. Doctrinal legal scholarship still dominates much of the field, showing the full majesty of that quintessential feature—legalism (Pirie 2013; see also Latour 2010; cf. Arnull 2008; Micklitz 2018). One is left to wonder what conclusions would be reached by an ambitious, anthropologically informed study of the broad European landscape just evoked. Perhaps it could unveil a public secret, namely that the flip side of the coin is the intense competition of law firms on the market for legal services, as well as the coexistence, and indeed the promotion of, distinct legal styles in the Member States, with substantial variations both in the practice of law and in the notion of legality across Europe. The lack of a single language for the law in Europe complicates the rosy picture of a continent united under common laws. This empirical approach would also show how the Union has shaped a new model of citizenship, which depends upon the status of the individual as worker, having evolved as a consequence of the dynamic of market integration. This poses questions such as what kind of persona emerges in this context (Azoulai et al. 2016), and whether the notion of EU citizenship ultimately challenges the idea of equality under the law (Kochenov 2016).

The development of an anthropology of law in this new space is a pioneering venture and a real challenge, considering the incomplete nature of Europe as a political and legal entity. Some themes have nonetheless emerged as objects of an anthropological approach to the law in Europe.

Market integration in the Union brought about large-scale change concerning everyday consumption habits and production processes. European norms have reshaped the lives of local communities, firms, and individuals; for example, by establishing what is legal and what is illegal on the market (Aistara 2015; Davies 2015; Leitch 2003). The effects of this new form of governmentality have thus become the focus of anthropological research (Adler-Nissen 2016; Dunn 2004; Kim 2011).

The accession to the Union of Central and Eastern European countries has involved a massive and rapid transformation of the legal regimes of these countries. This has turned attention once more to that quintessential question; namely, what is the rule of law, and what is the legality that Europe promotes (Hertogh 2016)? The question is now being litigated at the level of the top courts in Europe, and has become a matter of concern for the future of Europe in the presence of authoritarian backsliding in Member States such as Hungary and Poland and the manifestation of anti-EU and xenophobic, nationalistic political discourses elsewhere, in countries such as France, Germany, and Italy. Similar forces have also played into the making of Brexit. It has thus become apparent that 'the very processes that generated cross-border influence also produced political groups and symbols aimed at reinforcing borders against, or channeling, that influence' (Verdery 1998: 294). Anthropological enquiries have thus cast light on how the notions of legality and the rule of law are to be approached in such a context, along with comparative political, sociological, and legal studies.[3] In considering this picture, one should keep in mind that for the Member States of Central and Eastern Europe, EU membership was wealth-enhancing but not wealth-equalizing (Epstein and Jacoby 2014). Within this picture, anthropologists have also engaged with the heavy consequences of the financial crisis of 2008 and its impact in context, especially in southern Europe, where that impact was most dramatic in terms of poverty and social exclusion (see e.g. Raudon and Shore 2018; Spyridakis 2016).

Turning towards a different object of enquiry covered by anthropological approaches to the law, much attention is currently being paid to how religious beliefs and religious manifestations play out in today's Europe, and to the way both public and private institutions deal with them. The stream of publications produced over the past decade or so on the related problems is impressive, and stands out as a major effort to bring to fruition the possibility of a dialogue between the two disciplines (Bottoni and Cristofori 2016; Shah et al. 2016). From this point of view, some reservations have been expressed about the capacity of human rights law to actually foster inclusion and the recognition of deep diversity linked to the expressions of minority religious beliefs (Alidadi and Foblets 2012).

The harmonizing efforts of European institutions are often confronted with legal issues that have a strong anthropological dimension, ranging from the contested use of genetically modified organisms (GMOs) in agriculture and, more generally, the way new technologies are introduced into society in the presence of unknown technological and social risks, to the variety of attitudes towards the regulation of industries involving a certain view of public morality, such as gaming and betting, to the way work is regulated in a transnational setting. Medical anthropology likewise intersects with the law in discussing issues such as patients' rights, informed consent, medically assisted reproduction, and end-of-life decisions in Europe.

While regulating emerging legal issues, Americanization has sometimes been presented as a dynamic affecting European laws and legal styles (Various Authors 2001). Although the EU pursues a distinct regulatory path in many matters, European institutions have also resorted to regulatory techniques that were first tested in the United States in order to mobilize European citizens in support of European policies (see e.g. Kelemen 2011). In any case, this is really just one aspect of a much wider story, which cannot be pursued here; namely, how Europe interacts with other parts of the world—a theme that has been at the centre of debates over globalization and its consequences.

Finally, law and anthropology in Europe join forces in considering the situation of migrants and asylum seekers. Bianchini's contribution in this handbook provides a full assessment of the state of the art with respect to the development of international refugee law. Here, one may simply note that the way law works across the many borders of Europe has raised troublesome and worrying questions that call for a less positivistic and more empirically informed analysis of the reality of migrations towards Europe. While the law provides for certain safeguards to asylum seekers, the lives of migrants reaching the European borders are in danger, and the applicable legal regime fully highlights the contradictions, indeterminacies, and tragic failures that, in this context, are associated with the operations of the state and its law (Dauvergne 2008). With respect to migrants, informal and formal practices come together as configurations of statecraft in ways that are all too familiar in the Global South (Agier et al. 2018; Andersson 2014; Comaroff 2018; Tuckett 2015).

Conclusion

This chapter has outlined some itineraries across the field of anthropology of law in Europe. To an outsider, both the richness of the experiences surveyed and their initially sparse appearance are noteworthy. An anthropology of the social facts inscribed in the normative universe of the law was scarce for the greater part of the twentieth century; that is, when it came to European societies as the object of enquiry. Until the last decades of the twentieth century, the anthropology of European law remained a niche subject. It was mostly practised at first in contexts marked by a certain degree of pluralism, or in areas undergoing quick, traumatic social change. In the meantime, a good number of studies have been dedicated to minorities, both old and new, to their treatment by the law of the state, and to their normative practices. These studies show to what extent and in which ways European societies and institutions recognize a plurality of values, beliefs, and lifestyles, or come short in this respect, when the law is at work. They also show how it can be that there are some who enjoy full citizenship, while others continue to fight for it. The principal contribution of the research examined in this chapter is to illuminate the dynamics of inclusion and exclusion operating through the sources of official law and the ways alternative, plural subjectivities play out in this arena, either individually or in collective form. When the subject is thought of in these broader terms, an anthropology of law with a focus on Europe still has huge potential because of the glaring lack of an empirical dimension in mainstream, doctrinal legal studies, which cover the law essentially for the benefit of the national judiciary and the national bar. Europe now shares a set of institutions and norms that were established in the aftermath of the Second World War as a guarantee against the risks of aggressive nationalism, authoritarian regimes, and the suppression of fundamental freedoms and rights. An anthropology of law that locates its fieldwork in the law and policies promulgated by European institutions is taking shape, showing what the moving target of European integration has meant in terms of building a new composite identity, putting pressure on the national and local levels of government, and devising new subjectivities. An anthropology of law for European societies has finally come of age. The studies mentioned in this piece are just a tiny fraction of a much larger, impressive corpus, which explores nearly all dimensions of the law as a social fact with respect to Europe. And yet, for those who take an interest in this fascinating story, it is tempting to conclude that there is still much unfinished business.

Notes

1. For a first, seminal contribution, see Lewis (1973); for similar reflections for the field of comparative law, see Corcodel (2019).
2. Increased mobility has also fostered inter-country adoptions: the number of EU citizens that have their origins elsewhere because they were adopted is by now significant. This practice, too, is located at the border between law and anthropology (see Leinaweaver et al. 2017).
3. For a general discussion, see Cheesman (2018); with specific regard to Central and Eastern Europe, see Mendelski (2016); Verdery (1998).

References

Acton, T. 2005. 'Conflict Resolution and Criminal Justice—Sorting out Trouble: Can Legislation Resolve Perennial Conflicts between Roma/Gypsies/Travellers and "National Majorities"?' *Journal of Legal Pluralism and Unofficial Law* 37(51): 29–49.
Adler-Nissen, R. 2016. 'Towards a Practice Turn in EU Studies: The Everyday of European Integration'. *Journal of Common Market Studies* 54(1): 87–103.
Agier, M. et al. 2018. *The Jungle: Calais's Camps and Migrants*. London: Polity.
Aidinlis, S. 2019. 'Defining the "Legal": Two Conceptions of Legal Consciousness and Legal Alienation in Administrative Justice Research'. *Journal of Social Welfare and Family Law* 41(4): 495–513.

Aistara, G. A. 2015. 'Good, Clean, Fair ... and Illegal: Paradoxes of Food Ethics in Post-Socialist Latvia'. *Journal of Baltic Studies* 46(3): 283–98.

Alexander, C., M. H. Bruun, and I. Koch. 2018. 'Political Economy Comes Home: On the Moral Economies of Housing'. *Critique of Anthropology* 38(2): 121–39.

Alidadi K. and M.-C. Foblets. 2012. 'Framing Multicultural Challenges in Freedom of Religion Terms: Limitations of Minimal Human Rights for Managing Religious Diversity in Europe'. *Netherlands Quarterly of Human Rights* 30(4): 388–416.

Anders, G. 2015. 'Law at Its Limits: Interdisciplinarity between Law and Anthropology'. *Journal of Legal Pluralism and Unofficial Law* 47(3): 411–22.

Andersson, R. 2014. *Illegality, Inc.: Clandestine Migration and the Business of Bordering Europe*. Oakland: University of California Press.

Arnull, A. 2008. 'The Americanization of EU Law Scholarship'. In A. Arnull, P. Eeckhout, and T. Tridimas, eds. *Continuity and Change in EU Law: Essays in Honour of Sir Francis Jacobs*, 415–31. Oxford: Oxford University Press.

Assier-Andrieu, L. A. 2019. 'Difficulté et nécessité de l'anthropologie du droit'. *Clio@Thémis* 15: 1–12.

Azoulai, L. 2020a. 'The Madness of Europe, Being Attached to It'. *German Law Journal* 21: 100–3.

Azoulai, L. 2020b. 'Droit de l'Union européenne et passions sociales'. *Confluence des—La revue*, available at <https://confluencedesdroits-larevue.com/>.

Azoulai, L., S. B. des Places, and E. Pataut, eds. 2016. *Constructing the Person in EU Law: Rights, Roles, Identities*. London: Bloomsbury Publishing.

Barrera-González, A., M. Heintz, and A. Horolets. 2017. *European Anthropologies*. New York: Berghahn Books.

Bellier, I. and T. M. Wilson, eds. 2000. *An Anthropology of the European Union: Building, Imagining and Experiencing the New Europe*. Oxford: Berghahn Books.

Benadusi, M. and S. Revet. 2016. 'Disaster Trials: A Step Forward'. *Archivio Antropologico Mediterraneo On Line* 18(2): 7–15, available at <http://www.archivioantropologicomediterraneo.it/?p=592>.

Benda-Beckmann, F. von. 2008. 'Riding or Killing the Centaur? Reflections on the Identities of Legal Anthropology'. *International Journal of Law in Context* 4: 85–110.

Benda-Beckmann, F. von and K. von Benda-Beckmann. 2010. 'Why Not Legal Culture'. *Journal of Comparative Law* 5: 104–17.

Bendix, R. and G. Hasan-Rokem, eds. 2012. *A Companion to Folklore*. Chichester: Wiley-Blackwell.

Bens, J. and J. Vetters. 2018. 'Ethnographic Legal Studies: Reconnecting Anthropological and Sociological Traditions'. *Journal of Legal Pluralism and Unofficial Law* 50(3): 239–54.

Besnier, C. 2017. *La vérité côté cour, une ethnologue aux assises*. Paris: La Découverte.

Bishop, P. 2011. *The Archaic: The Past in the Present*. London: Routledge.

Boas, F. 1911. *The Mind of Primitive Man*. London: The Macmillan Company.

Bottoni, R. and R. Cristofori, eds. 2016. *Religious Rules, State Law, and Normative Pluralism—A Comparative Overview*. Berlin: Springer.

Bourdieu, P. 2005. *The Social Structure of The Economy*. London: Polity.

Bowen, J. R. 2007. *Why the French Don't Like Headscarves: Islam, the State, and Public Space*. Princeton: Princeton University Press.

Bowen, J. R. 2016. *On British Islam: Religion, Law, and Everyday Practice in Shari'a Councils*. Princeton: Princeton University Press.

Bréchon, P. and F. Gonthier. 2017. *European Values. Trends and Divides over Thirty Years.* Amsterdam: Brill.

Brickell, K., M. Fernández Arrigoitia, and A. Vasudevan, eds. 2017. *Geographies of Forced Eviction.* London: Palgrave Macmillan.

Burke, P. 2009. *Popular Culture in Early Modern Europe.* Third edition. London: Routledge.

Carr, H., B. Edgeworth, and C. Hunter, eds. 2018. *Law and the Precarious Home: Socio Legal Perspectives on the Home in Insecure Times.* London: Bloomsbury Publishing.

Cheesman, N. 2018. 'Rule-of-Law Ethnography'. *Annual Review of Law and Social Science* 14(1): 167–84.

Comaroff, J. 2018. '"Does Anthropology Matter to Law?": Reflections, Inflections, Deflections'. *Journal of Legal Anthropology* 2(2): 72–8.

Conley, J. M. and W. M. O'Barr. 1993. 'Legal Anthropology Comes Home: A Brief History of the Ethnographic Study of Law'. *Loyola of Los Angeles Law Review* 27: 41–64.

Conley, J. M. and W. M. O'Barr. 2005. *Just Words: Law, Language, and Power.* Second edition. Chicago: University of Chicago Press.

Corcodel, V. 2019. *Modern Law and Otherness: The Dynamics of Inclusion and Exclusion in Comparative Legal Thought.* Cheltenham: Edward Elgar.

Cotterell, R. 2019. 'Comparative Law and Legal Culture'. In M. Reimann and R. Zimmermann, eds. *The Oxford Handbook of Comparative Law.* Second edition, 710–34. Oxford: Oxford University Press.

Council of Europe. 2012. *Human Rights of Roma and Travellers in Europe.* Strasbourg: Council of Europe Publishing.

Crouch, C. 2016. *Society and Social Change in 21st Century Europe.* London: Macmillan International Higher Education.

Dauvergne, C. 2008. *Making People Illegal: What Globalization Means for Migration Law.* Cambridge: Cambridge University Press.

Davies, G. T. 2015. 'Internal Market Adjudication and the Quality of Life in Europe'. *Columbia Journal of European Law* 21(2): 289–328.

Dedek, H. 2014. 'When Law Became Cultivated: "European Legal Culture" between Kultur and Civilization'. In G. Helleringer and K. Purnhagen, eds. *Towards a European Legal Culture,* 367–90. Munich: C. H. Beck; Portland: Hart; Baden-Baden: Nomos.

Demeulenaere, P. 2012. 'L'interprétation des terrains et le recours à des propositions théoriques'. *L'année sociologique* 62(1): 67–91.

Deville, J. 2015. *Lived Economies of Default: Consumer Credit, Debt Collection and the Capture of Affect.* Abingdon: Routledge.

Dubois, V. 2014. 'The State, Legal Rigor, and the Poor: The Daily Practice of Welfare Control'. *Social Analysis* 58(3): 38–55.

Dunn, E. C. 2004. *Privatizing Poland: Baby Food, Big Business, and the Remaking of Labor.* Ithaca: Cornell University Press.

Ehrlich, E. 1936 [1912]. *Fundamental Principles of the Sociology of Law.* New York: Russell and Russell Publishers.

Ellingson, T. 2001. *The Myth of the Noble Savage.* Berkeley: University of California Press.

Epstein, R. A. and W. Jacoby. 2014. 'Eastern Enlargement Ten Years On: Transcending the East–West Divide?' *Journal of Common Market Studies* 52(1): 1–16.

Eurobarometer. 2018. 'Flash Eurobarometer 461: Perceived Independence of the National Justice Systems in the EU among the General Public', available at <https://data.europa.eu/euodp/en/data/dataset/S2168_461_ENG>.

Foblets, M.-C. and K. Alidadi. 2020. 'Between Sovereignty and Transnationalism: The European Union as an Incomplete "Transnational Legal Space"'. In: C. J. Greenhouse and C. L. Davis, eds. *Landscapes of Law: Practicing Sovereignty in Transnational Terrain*, 216–49. Philadelphia: University of Pennsylvania.

Foblets, M.-C., M. Graziadei, and A. D. Renteln, eds. 2018a. *Personal Autonomy in Plural Societies: A Principle and Its Paradoxes*. London: Routledge.

Foblets, M.-C., L. Leboeuf, and Z. Yanasmayan. 2018b. 'Exclusion and Migration: By Whom, Where, When, and How?' Max Planck Institute for Social Anthropology Working Paper 190.

Fournier, P. 2016a. *Muslim Marriage in Western Courts: Lost in Transplantation*. London: Routledge.

Fournier, P. 2016b. 'Droit et cultures en sol français: récits de femmes juives et musulmanes à l'aube et au crépuscule du divorce'. *Anthropologie et sociétés* 40(2): 89–106.

Galbraith, M. H. 2015. *Being and Becoming European in Poland: European Integration and Self-Identity*. London/New York/Delhi: Anthem Press.

García-Villegas, M. 2018. *The Powers of Law: A Comparative Analysis of Sociopolitical Legal Studies*. Cambridge: Cambridge University Press.

Gilissen, J. 1982. *Typologie des sources du moyen âge occidental: La coutume*. Turnout: Brepols.

Good, A. 2008. 'Cultural Evidence in Courts of Law'. *Journal of the Royal Anthropological Institute* 14: S47–S60.

Goody, J. 1996. *The East in the West*. Cambridge: Cambridge University Press.

Gould, S. J. 1996. *The Mismeasurement of Man*. Third revised edition. New York: Norton and Company.

Green, S. 2012. 'Replacing Europe'. In R. Farndon et al., eds. *The SAGE Handbook of Social Anthropology*, 286–307. London: SAGE Publishing.

Green, S. et al. 2016. 'Brexit Referendum: First Reactions from Anthropology'. *Social Anthropology* 24(4): 478–502.

Griffiths. J. 2017. 'What is Sociology of Law? (On Law, Rules, Social Control and Sociology)'. *The Journal of Legal Pluralism and Unofficial Law* 49(2): 93–142.

Grillo, R. 2015. *Muslim Families, Politics and the Law: A Legal Industry in Multicultural Britain*. Farnham: Ashgate.

Grillo, R. 2017. 'Anthropologists Engaged with the Law (and Lawyers)'. *Antropologia Pubblica* 2(2): 3–24.

Grossi, P. 1981. *An Alternative to Private Property: Collective Property in the Juridical Consciousness of the Nineteenth Century*. Chicago: University of Chicago Press.

Grødeland, Å. B. and W. L. Miller. 2015. *European Legal Cultures in Transition*. Cambridge: Cambridge University Press.

Guerlain, L. 2015. 'Culture et usages des savoirs anthropologiques chez les juristes. De quelques apports de l'étude des recensions bibliographiques (XIXe-XXe siècles)'. *Revue d'histoire des facultés de droit, de la culture juridique, du monde des juristes et du livre juridique* 35: 233–77.

Hansen, P. and S. Jonsson. 2014. *Eurafrica: The Untold History of European Integration and Colonialism*. London: Bloomsbury Publishing.

Hart, K. and H. Ortiz. 2014. 'The Anthropology of Money and Finance: Between Ethnography and World History'. *Annual Review of Anthropology* 43: 465–82.

Hertogh, M., ed. 2008. *Living Law: Reconsidering Eugen Ehrlich*. London: Bloomsbury Publishing.

Hertogh, M. 2016. 'Your Rule of Law Is Not Mine: Rethinking Empirical Approaches to EU Rule of Law Promotion'. *Asia Europe Journal* 14(1): 43–59.

Hertogh, M. 2018. *Nobody's Law: Legal Consciousness and Legal Alienation in Everyday Life*. London: Palgrave MacMillan.

Holden, L., ed. 2011. *Cultural Expertise and Litigation: Patterns, Conflicts, Narratives*. London: Routledge.

Kelemen, R. D. 2011. *Eurolegalism: The Transformation of Law and Regulation in the European Union*. Boston: Harvard University Press.

Kim, D. J. 2011. 'Clutching the Ladder of Development: European Sugar Reform in Poland'. *Anthropological Journal of European Cultures* 20(1): 29–47.

Kirkby, C. 2018. 'Law Evolves: The Uses of Primitive Law in Anglo-American Concepts of Modern Law, 1861–1961'. *American Journal of Legal History* 58(4): 535–63.

Knight, D. M. 2017. 'Anxiety and Cosmopolitan Futures: Brexit and Scotland'. *American Ethnologist* 44(2): 237–42.

Kochenov, D. 2016. 'Neomedieval Permutations of Personhood'. In Azoulai, L., S. B. des Places, and E. Pataut, eds. *Constructing the Person in EU Law: Rights, Roles, Identities*, 133–58. London: Bloomsbury Publishing.

Krastev, I. and S. Holmes. 2019. *The Light that Failed: A Reckoning*. London: Penguin.

Kuper, A. 1988. *The Invention of Primitive Society: Transformations of an Illusion*. London: Routledge.

Lapi, C. 2018. 'Can Law "Sustain" Cultural Diversity? The Inheritance Laws of Indian Minority Communities and the Italian Legal System'. In K. Topidi, ed. *Normative Pluralism and Human Rights*, 207–18. London: Routledge.

Latour, B. 2010. *The Making of Law: An Ethnography of the Conseil d'État*. Cambridge: Polity.

Legrand,, P.. 2017. 'Jameses at Play: A Tractation on the Comparison of Laws'. *The American Journal of Comparative Law* 65 (suppl_1): 1–132.

Leinaweaver, J. B., D. Marre, and S. E. Frekko. 2017. '"Homework" and Transnational Adoption Screening in Spain: The Co-Production of Home and Family'. *Journal of the Royal Anthropological Institute* 23(3): 562–79.

Leitch A. 2003. 'Slow Food and the Politics of Pork Fat: Italian Food and European Identity'. *Ethnos* 68(4): 437–62.

Levey, G. B. 2018. 'Religion, Culture and Liberal Democracy: The Issue of Majority Cultural Precedence'. In S. Lefebvre and P. Brodeur, eds. *Public Commissions on Cultural and Religious Diversity*, 251–65. London: Routledge.

Lewicki, P. M. 2017. *EU-Space and the Euroclass: Modernity, Nationality and Lifestyle Among Eurocrats in Brussels*. Bielefeld: Transcript.

Lewis, D. 1973. 'Anthropology and Colonialism'. *Current Anthropology* 14(5): 581–602.

MacDonald, R. 2005. 'Legal Republicanism and Legal Pluralism: Two Takes on Identity and Diversity'. In M. Bussani and M. Graziadei, eds. *Human Diversity and the Law*, 43–70. Brussels: Bruylant.

Malinowski, B. 1926. *Crime and Custom in Savage Society*. London: Routledge and Kegan Paul.

Mallard, G. 2019. *Gift Exchange: The Transnational History of a Political Idea*. Cambridge: Cambridge University Press.

Mantena, K. 2010. *Alibis of Empire: Henry Maine and the Ends of Liberal Imperialism*. Princeton: Princeton University Press.

McMahon, R. 2016. *The Races of Europe Construction of National Identities in the Social Sciences, 1839–1939*. London: Palgrave McMillan.

Mendelski, M. 2016. 'Europeanization and the Rule of Law: Towards a Pathological Turn'. *Southeastern Europe* 40(3): 346–84.

Mikuš, M. 2019. 'Contesting Household Debt in Croatia: The Double Movement of Financialization and the Fetishism of Money in Eastern European Peripheries'. *Dialectical Anthropology* 43(3): 295–315.

Micklitz, H.-W. 2018. *The Politics of Justice in European Private Law*. Cambridge: Cambridge University Press.

Muir-Watt, H. 2000. 'La fonction subversive du droit comparé'. *Revue internationale de droit comparé* 52(3): 503–27.

Munday, M. and A. Pottage, eds. 2004. *Law, Anthropology, and the Constitution of the Social: Making Persons and Things*. Cambridge: Cambridge University Press.

Müller, B. 2007. *Disenchantment with Market Economics: East Germans and Western Capitalism*. New York/Oxford: Berghahn Books.

Nafstad, I. 2019. 'The Ideal Minority Victim—Roma in Swedish Criminal Courts'. *International Journal of Law, Crime and Justice* 58: 3–11.

Nafziger, J. A. (ed.). 2017. *Comparative Law and Anthropology*. Cheltenham: Edward Elgar.

Nisio, F. S. 2019. *Lucien Levy-Bruhl. Filosofia, scienze sociali, giustizia*. Milan: Giuffrè Francis Lefebvre.

Perla, L. 2013. 'Il contesto degli studi'. In G. L. Bravo, ed. *Prima etnografia d'Italia. Gli studi di folklore tra '800 e '900 nel quadro europeo*, 51–77. Milan: Franco Angeli.

de Pina-Cabral, J. 2015. 'Is There a European Anthropology?' Forum Rethinking Euro-Anthropology'. *Social Anthropology* 23(3): 15–6.

Pirie, F. 2013. *Anthropology of Law*. Oxford: Oxford University Press.

Pirie, F. 2019. 'Legalism: A Turn to History in the Anthropology of Law'. *Clio@Thémis* 15: 1–16.

Poulter, S. 1998. *Ethnicity, Law and Human Rights: The English Experience*. Oxford: Clarendon Press.

Raudon, S. and C. Shore. 2018. 'The Eurozone Crisis, Greece and European Integration: Anthropological Perspectives on Austerity in the EU'. *Anthropological Journal of European Cultures* 27(1): 64–83.

Rehbinder, M. 1986. *Die Begründung der Rechtssoziologie durch Eugen Ehrlich*. Berlin: Dunker and Humblot.

Riles, A. 2019. 'Comparative Law and Socio-Legal Studies'. In M. Reimann and R. Zimmermann, eds. *The Oxford Handbook of Comparative Law*. Second edition, 772–804. Oxford: Oxford University Press.

Roldan, A. A. and H. Vermeulen. 1995. *Fieldwork and Footnotes: Studies in the History of European Anthropology*. London: Routledge.

Rosen, L. 2012. 'Comparative Law and Anthropology'. In M. Bussani and U. Mattei, eds. *The Cambridge Companion to Comparative Law*, 73–87. Cambridge: Cambridge University Press.

Ruggiu, I. 2016. 'Is Begging a Roma Cultural Practice? Answers from the Italian Legal System and Anthropology'. *Romani Studies* 26(1): 31–62.

Ruggiu, I. 2018. *Culture and the Judiciary: The Anthropologist Judge*. London: Routledge.

Sacco, R. 1991. 'Legal Formants: A Dynamic Approach to Comparative Law'. *American Journal of Comparative Law* 37: 1–34, 343–400.

Sacco, R. 2008. *Anthropologie juridique: Apport à une macro-histoire du droit*. Paris: Dalloz.

Shah, P. 2005. *Legal Pluralism in Conflict: Coping with Cultural Diversity in Law*. London: Glass House.

Shah, P., M.-C. Foblets, and M. Rohe, eds. 2016. *Family, Religion and Law: Cultural Encounters in Europe*. London: Routledge.

Simon, C., B. Truffin, and A. Wyvekens. 2019. 'Between Norms, Facts, and Stereotypes: The Place of Culture and Ethnicity in Belgian and French Family Justice'. In A. Sarat, ed. *Cultural Expertise and Socio-Legal Studies*, 113–29. Bingley: Emerald Publishing.

Sona, F. 2014. 'Defending the Family Treasure Chest: Navigating Muslim Families and Secured Positivistic Islands of European Legal Systems'. In P. Shah, M.-C. Foblets, and M. Rohe, eds. *Family, Religion and Law: Cultural Encounters in Europe*, 115–41. Farnham: Ashgate.

Spyridakis, M. 2016. *The Liminal Worker: An Ethnography of Work, Unemployment and Precariousness in Contemporary Greece*. London: Routledge.

Stein, P. 1980. *Legal Evolution: The Story of an Idea*. Cambridge: Cambridge University Press.

Storey, J. 2009. *Inventing Popular Culture: From Folklore to Globalization*. London: John Wiley & Sons.

Szakolczai, A. and B. Thomassen. 2019. *From Anthropology to Social Theory*. Cambridge: Cambridge University Press.

Teubner, G. 1997. 'Global Bukowina: Legal Pluralism in the World-Society'. In G. Teubner, ed. *Global Law without a State*, 3–28. Brookfield: Dartmouth.

Thelen, T. 2015. 'Care as Social Organization: Creating, Maintaining and Dissolving Significant Relations'. *Anthropological Theory* 15(4): 497–515.

Thelen, T., L. Vetters, and K. von Benda-Beckmann. 2014. 'Stategraphy: Toward a Relational Anthropology of the State'. *Social Analysis* 58(3): 1–19.

Tuckett, A. 2015. *Rules, Paper, Status: Migrants and Precarious Bureaucracy in Contemporary Italy*. Stanford: Stanford University Press.

Tuori, K. 2015. *Lawyers and Savages: Ancient History and Legal Realism in the Making of Legal Anthropology*. Abingdon: Routledge.

Tuori, K. 2020. *Empire of Law: Nazi Germany, Exile Scholars and the Battle for the Future of Europe*. Cambridge: Cambridge University Press.

Tylor, E. B. 1891. *Primitive Culture: Researches into the Development of Mythology, Philosophy, Religion, Language, Art and Custom*, I. Third revised edition. London: Murray.

Various Authors. 2001. 'L'americanisation du droit', *Archives de philosophie du droit* 45: 1–400.

Verdery, K. 1998. 'Transnationalism, Nationalism, Citizenship, and Property: Eastern Europe since 1989'. *American Ethnologist* 25(2): 291–306.

Vertovec, S. and S. Wessendorf. 2010. *The Multiculturalism Backlash: European Discourses, Policies and Practices*. London: Palgrave.

Vetters, L. and M.-C. Foblets. 2016. 'Culture All Around? Contextualising Anthropological Expertise in European Courtroom Settings'. *International Journal of Law in Context* 12(3): 272–92.

Walker, T. 2016. *Shari'a Councils and Muslim Women in Britain: Rethinking the Role of Power and Authority*. Leiden/Boston: Brill.

Wyvekens, A. 2014. 'La justice et la "diversité Culturelle" "les yeux grand fermés"?' *Archives de politique criminelle* 1(36): 123–46.

Zerilli, F. 2013. 'Corruption and Anti-Corruption Local Discourses and International Practices in Post-Socialist Romania'. *Human Affairs* 23(2): 212–29.

PART II

RECURRING THEMES IN LAW AND ANTHROPOLOGY

CHAPTER 15

WITHIN AND BEYOND THE ANTHROPOLOGY OF LANGUAGE AND LAW

ELIZABETH MERTZ

INTRODUCTION

THE intersection of law and language has been well studied within legal anthropology, yielding a strong and vibrant body of theoretically sophisticated, empirically based research.[1] Although it speaks directly to questions that are important to legal scholars, this research—like much of anthropology—has yet to translate very effectively among legal academics. (Indeed, any imagined conversation between anthropology and legal scholarship in the United States remains largely just that—imagined—because academic law rarely seems to acknowledge, let alone draw on, anthropology in any meaningful way.) There is also language-focused research within legal scholarship, but it rarely looks to any ethnographically grounded linguistic studies from anthropology or related disciplines. The overall interdisciplinary field of language-and-law studies contains many distinct lines of scholarship, including work by legal and linguistic anthropologists, forensic linguists, legal philosophers, critical discourse scholars, sociolinguists, and others; for the most part, these lines do not communicate with one another (see Mertz and Rajah 2014). It is perhaps not surprising that the least contextually grounded scholarship on language remains most central in legal studies, for reasons to be discussed below. But the inability of legal anthropologists and scholars in the legal academy to translate between their fields is an intriguing puzzle, given some of the stated aims of both disciplines.

In this chapter, I approach this puzzle primarily by examining writings from the legal academy and from legal-linguistic anthropology, with a brief diversion into a transcript of scholars attempting to (verbally) communicate with each other across this disciplinary divide. The focus, then, is on *academic discourses* produced by law professors and by professors of anthropology. The chapter begins with a cursory review of the trajectory of anthropological research on language and law, noting its productive willingness to draw on diverse traditions to develop a holistic approach, but also its failure to translate in some key areas, including the legal academy. The chapter then turns to examine some recent anthropological scholarship on legal language that pushes the field towards a more integrative conversation with legal experts. The third part of the chapter summarizes work on language and law within the legal academy, demonstrating that, for some time, legal scholars have held onto an epistemological preference for approaches that limit law's ability to make use of large arenas within interdisciplinary research—including linguistic anthropological studies of law. In conclusion, the chapter reviews how our comparison of the two academic discourses (law and anthropology) raises fundamental questions about language, epistemology, and power in the process of interdisciplinary translations.

At the Crossroads of Legal and Linguistic Anthropology: Early Directions

Over the past several decades, linguistic anthropologists have made exciting strides in developing analytical tools that permit us to connect micro-level aspects of language use with wider social developments. This is of particular importance because it allows us to track the daily processes through which law works (or doesn't work), as well as the quotidian ways that the subjects of law negotiate in and around law.[2] We can analyse law as it actually operates, diluted and twisted through layers of institutional practices, lay and professional habitus, cultures, social structures, individual and collective agency, politics and economics, and more—all embedded in the flow of verbal and nonverbal communication by and through which we interact.[3]

In formulating this holistic approach to studying language, linguistic anthropologists have not only drawn on sociocultural anthropology but also incorporated forms of analysis that originated in other social science disciplines (see Ahearn 2011; Duranti 1997; Ottenheimer and Pine 2018). For example, these anthropologists have drawn on sociolinguistics, ethnomethodology and conversation analysis, discourse analysis, semiotics, textual analysis, linguistics, and other allied fields. They have even engaged with the field of philosophy, in the process casting serious doubt upon approaches emanating from ordinary language philosophy (which carries on at full steam nonetheless)—as well as upon other decontextualized kinds of language study, such as Chomskian universal grammar. The anthropological linguistic critique of these decontextualized approaches should be of importance to language studies within the legal academy because ordinary language approaches have had a major impact on legal theory. However, to the contrary, the critique emanating from anthropology has not been understood, or even heard, within mainstream legal scholarship.

This poses a puzzle: how is it that cutting-edge empirical research and critiques from linguistic anthropology have failed to translate within scholarly worlds to which they speak directly (even when citing the same founding scholars)? The examples abound, including work by linguistic anthropologists providing empirically based critiques of philosophical writings on 'pragmatics' (the contextual structuring of language), as well as crucial linguistic anthropological research on 'speech act theory', which could significantly improve the way legal scholars conceptualize and study legal language.[4] In this arena, as in others, anthropologists have led the way in pushing purveyors of supposedly universal claims to examine the diversity of language as it is actually used in practice—and to look outside of Anglo-American societies.

From early on, like the rest of anthropology, linguistic anthropology has situated itself firmly in knowledge practices that favour the observation of naturally occurring language within sociocultural contexts and across a variety of locations and times (Duranti 1997). Linguistic anthropologists have also maintained an open conversation with those in other disciplines who share that vantage, incorporating insights from sociolinguistics and from the subfield of sociology known as 'ethnomethodology' (closely related to 'conversation analysis', hereinafter 'CA'), which provides precise ways of mapping turn-taking and other aspects of real-time communication.[5] To augment analyses of naturally occurring speech, the standard methodological toolkit of linguistic anthropologists additionally includes structured and informal interviews, as well as community surveys that track language competencies (see, e.g. Briggs 2007; Gal 1979; Mertz 1989). Despite the continued insistence in some disciplines on analysing language 'in the abstract', empirically grounded research on human communication has spurred a growing movement to examine spoken language using social science methods such as observation, taping, and interviewing. This interest has also grown to include studies of the social practices surrounding written language, developing forms of textual analysis that pay attention to the creation and performance of texts in institutional and other social settings (see, e.g. Bauman and Briggs 1990; Briggs and Bauman 1992; Hanks 1989; Messick 1996; Richland 2008).[6] Linguistic anthropologists John Conley and William O'Barr explain the magnitude of this shift in their now-classic book *Just Words*: 'Until the 1960s, it was common for theories of the structure of language to be based on ideal, perfectly formed utterances, which typically existed only in the imaginations of linguists' (Conley and O'Barr 2005: 10).

In terms of research on legal language in particular, Conley and O'Barr's (1990) early work on language in small claims courts demonstrated the openness of the field to interdisciplinary syntheses, drawing not only on anthropology and linguistics but also on sociolinguistics, psychology, and on CA studies of linguistic interaction in courtrooms. The CA research was based on detailed examinations of how legal discourse structured witness examinations, openings, plea bargaining, and other aspects of institutionally shaped language patterning (Atkinson and Drew 1979; Maynard 1984). Using CA, anthropologists studying legal language analysed tacit 'rules' governing the ordering of verbal interactions, demonstrating how underneath apparently simple everyday exchanges lie many complicated, socially shared structures for coordinating the complex dance of communication. For example, linguistic anthropologists drew on CA to track how the ordering of legal talk varies from everyday talk in quiet but crucial ways. Thus, rules for courtroom communication that differ from the norms to which laypeople are accustomed can cause serious problems, especially for poorer litigants (see, e.g. Gruber 2014; Philips 1998).

Anthropological work on legal language also moved beyond the situational focus of CA research to look at the impact of wider sociocultural contexts.[7] Conley and O'Barr (1990) were interested in how repeat players in small claims court (e.g. landlords) used linguistic resources to gain advantages over the less powerful one-shot litigants for whom the courts were ostensibly created (e.g. tenants). Closely related work on legal discourse within anthropology pushed linguistic anthropologists to think about the impacts of social identities and economic divisions (Merry 1990; Greenhouse 1989). These lines of research uncovered the subtle effects of law upon cultural beliefs, both of them deeply entwined with power arrangements in a society—and all of these enacted in and through ongoing linguistic interactions, often in the contexts of institutional structures that are themselves continually expressed and recreated through language (see Richland (2013) for a helpful overview). For example, Susan Hirsch's (1998) early work tracked how micro-linguistic aspects of women's and men's speech in Kenyan courts enacted and channelled wider political and social changes surrounding gender roles. Justin Richland's (2008) study of linguistic exchanges in Hopi courts revealed a complicated power struggle in which indigenous experts contested the hidden usurpation of their control over the terms of law in their communities. Both Hirsch and Richland combined detailed attention to spoken exchanges in courts with analyses of legal and other texts that partially shaped the interactions in court (see also Philips 1998). A robust anthropological linguistic literature has continued to develop, demonstrating how the details of legal and political language play out in specific situations in interaction with wider institutional and sociocultural dynamics—often imbricated with struggles over power (see, e.g. Appadurai 2016; Deeb 2010; Duranti 1994; Hoëm 2015).[8]

A New Generation of Anthropologists on Language and Law

While these kinds of analyses have a long history in linguistic anthropology, recent years have seen a new generation of scholarship that is more willing to tackle the stubborn division that prevents much anthropological work from reaching a readership within law. To take just one small subset of examples, some of these younger legal-linguistic anthropologists have turned their attention to the U.S. criminal justice system, examining the language of criminal trials. In her research on the death penalty, Robin Conley (2016) spent twelve months observing four capital trials in the state of Texas, known for its high level of death sentences.[9] She employed detailed linguistic analyses of courtroom interactions and jurors' narratives to track the way jurors process their roles in making life-and-death decisions. Subtle but systematic aspects of language framing—from deixis to grammatical constructions of agency—provide 'the precise linguistic mechanisms by which the translation of legal rules into a juror's denial of responsibility for her sentencing decision is accomplished' (Conley 2016: 164). In a strikingly hopeful move, Conley includes two sections towards the end of her book that lay out implications for legal practice and advice for legal practitioners—an arguably controversial move within the wider norms of both the law-and-society and anthropological traditions.[10] She explains, for example, how linguistic exchanges during jury selection permit the seating of jurors who are least likely to adhere to the stated ideal of juror conduct in death penalty cases. Conley also demonstrates in detail how jury instructions similarly undermine the stated ideal. In her concluding discussion of 'humanizing law', she makes a case, writing very accessibly, for why the importation of anthropological understandings of language and linguistic ideologies could be helpful in mitigating the 'dehumanizing effects of legal practice' (2016: 206). Conley is a linguistic anthropologist whose training and research have permitted her to cross the divide between legal and anthropological approaches with fluency, in the process refusing to bow to norms on either side that might have discouraged this effort.

Taking this one step further, and now examining the prosecutorial side of U.S. criminal law, anthropologist and lawyer Anna Offit has joined a growing number of joint-degree anthropological researchers in her boundary-crossing work (Offit 2018, 2019).[11] Informed by her training both in law and in anthropology, she conducted fieldwork and interviews across multiple years with 113 Assistant U.S. Attorneys as they discussed and made decisions about jury selection in the criminal trials they were prosecuting (2019: 1084–8). One of her conclusions is that these prosecutors' metalinguistic calculations in preparing for trial often hinge on imagined jurors, whose imputed sensibilities guide the attorneys as they prepare and carry out their cases (2019: 1105–14). When reporting on her findings to a legal audience in a law review, Offit builds from her research to offer recommendations for legal professionals, stressing the importance of prosecutors' accountability to hypothetical jurors as a democratizing influence in the quest for justice through the legal system (2019: 1114–19). Her general recommendations are paired with very concrete suggestions about things such as circulating trial calendars and altering the language of jury instructions.[12]

On the one hand, a broadly anthropological vision often points in directions that are bleak, demonstrating why deep critique is unlikely to be heard, and why efforts to ameliorate the local effects of neoliberalism are as likely to make things worse as better. It can be tempting to retreat into a despair that negates engagement with—or attempted intervention in—the disciplines and institutions closer to power in society. Yet, I would argue that a willingness to work between the languages and worlds of anthropological and legal scholarship augurs well for future interdisciplinary work in an arena that has been notoriously resistant to the kinds of insights anthropology can offer. A perennial problem facing interdisciplinary exchange in this area has been the imperviousness of scholars on each side of the divide to the linguistic demands of the other field. This is even more problematic in light of power differentials that leave those trained in law with little incentive to incorporate any disciplinary perspective that might unsettle a fundamental epistemological habitus which is deeply situated in both their training and professional vision (Goodwin 1994)—and which is useful to them in many ways.[13] Unlike mainstream legal philosophical and doctrinal analyses of language, anthropological and other research demonstrates how legal language, though deemed to be a neutral servant of justice, in fact folds in many layers of inequality—both as it is formulated and, most importantly, as it hits the ground in courts, police encounters, everyday bureaucracies, and other venues.[14] Certainly, many recognize that the US legal system often fails in delivering justice, but the way that shared legal language serves as a deep mechanism in that failure is an important and often under-analysed part of the picture. One need only look at dominant approaches to language within legal theory to see this.

In a different key: Legal scholars on language

Scholars in jurisprudence and philosophy who are interested in law and language tend to look back to figures like Bentham (1782 [1970]), J. L. Austin (1962), and H. L. A. Hart (1994) as key progenitors of their field. Early on, Bentham famously insisted that legal philosophers should focus on the actual pronouncements and enactments—words—that constitute law as it is experienced by human actors. This contrasted with a more traditional focus within jurisprudence on ephemeral 'rights' and 'duties' understood as naturally or morally correct in the abstract. In this sense, Bentham tried to shift jurisprudence away from abstractions without 'real-world' foundations. In his formulation, legal pronouncements and enactments were undergirded by the power of a sovereign—the political leader who could use force to back up stated laws (see also Austin 1962). Legal statements and words only took on meaning to the degree that they were associated with 'sensible' (i.e. perceptible) substances, actions, etc. (see Endicott 2010). H. L. A. Hart (1994) picked up on Bentham's approach but with a more sophisticated understanding of language meaning. For Hart, legal language had meaning because it was a set of socially structured language practices to which people responded. Thus, words did not have to designate 'sensible' entities or activities in order for legal language to have power and meaning (see Schauer 2011; Weissbourd and Mertz 1985).

Along with many other scholars, Hart built heavily on J. L. Austin, whose famous *How to Do Things with Words* (1962) has been a key resource for philosophy and jurisprudence, on the one hand, and more empirically grounded research on language, on the other. Austin distinguished a number of functions that language fulfilled; *referring* to 'things' in the world was only one of those functions. Austin importantly highlighted another way that language works in communication: it can actually perform the actions it names—fittingly denominated the 'performative' function (as in 'I hereby marry you',

'I apologize').[15] Austin did not only have an important impact on Hart; his keen insights on language function were also very generative in the fields that study language empirically in social context (such as pragmatics, anthropological linguistics, sociolinguistics, and others). By contrast with legal philosophers and formal linguists (who have tended to limit their inquiries into language function to their own readings of legal texts, their own intuitions as speakers, and abstract analytical discussions), these empirical researchers study how speakers 'do things' with language in practice.[16]

We can see this ambivalent positioning of legal scholarship regarding the role of context for language in a fascinating exchange that occurred at a conference that brought together a group of (non-anthropological) linguists and legal philosophers (Washington University Law Quarterly (WULQ) 1995; for a fuller discussion, see Mertz 2016). The goal of the conference was to find out if linguistics could help legal scholars in their analyses of legal texts. Although members of both disciplinary groups expressed disappointment afterwards, characterizing the gathering as a failed attempt at interdisciplinary translation, in fact their interactions provided a wonderful linguistic microscope through which to view some of the fundamental challenges facing such translations. One of the key difficulties that these scholars faced was the fact that the linguists—who, for the most part, subscribed to a very abstract, Chomskian understanding of language—could not articulate an analysis of legal language that paid adequate attention to linguistic practices that are particular to law. In a discussion about how one would determine whether an ambulance was a 'vehicle' for purposes of interpreting a statute, the following exchange highlighted some of the difficulties in translation:

> BE [LAWYER]: How do you know [what the meaning of a particular word is]?
> JS [LINGUIST]: Because we speak the language.
> BE: What happened to all those conventions?
> GG [LINGUIST]: We try to discover the conventions.
> BB: Yes, I know you try to discover the conventions, but I am astounded at your technique for doing so. You ask yourself!
> JL [LINGUIST]: That's one way of asking —
> BB: It's a terrible way.
> GG: All right, we can ask each other. It makes no difference.
> BB: Yes it does. You are a sub-community that—you're consulting each other for conventions and then claiming that they are the conventions of the larger community.
> JS: This can be a problem. But we try to guard against it.
> BB: Can be a problem –! ... It's the central problem of communication that has been exemplified by the past day and a half.
>
> (WULQ 1995: 910–11)

While the linguists persisted in postulating universal static meanings, as opposed to meanings based in contexts and communities of discourse, the legal scholars insisted that legal language depended on a distinct community with its own conventions of interpretation. As they debated the potential range of the word *vehicle*, for example, the linguists insisted that under any interpretation based in standard English, an ambulance is a vehicle. For the lawyers, interpretation of the words in the statute was a more complicated matter, one which could not be resolved by using a 'dictionary definition' of the word *vehicle*. In an interesting twist, these experts in the interpretation of legal texts cared more about the linguistic context than did the Chomskian linguists.

And yet, turning back to an anthropological linguistic perspective, there was a tacit set of unexamined metalinguistic assumptions underlying the lawyers' interrogation of linguistics. They sought a certainty, a set of 'scientific' rules, that would help them determine the meanings of words and phrases in legal documents (Mertz 2016; Mootz 1995). James Boyd White described this phenomenon in his own study of legal language, showing that law turned to other disciplines primarily to colonize them—to grab 'findings' or 'methods' in order to plug them into pre-existing legal frames (White 1990). Those frames have already delimited the relevant linguistic contexts for the process of legal interpretation, shutting out much of the social and cultural context to which anthropologists would look in analysing the operation of legal language in practice. In the process, issues of power latent in neoliberal contexts for law are elided (Greenhouse 2011). What use, then, for the critical analytical lens afforded by linguistic anthropological studies of legal language?

If, to quote Mark Goodale, legal discourse is 'deeply and essentially heteroglot', then as he suggests, it has the capacity to carry not only the weight of hegemony but also contestations and subversions, irony and poetry, within its many layers (2017: 52). I have been concerned here largely with the register of academic legal language produced by professors, and at that, with a dominant strand within that register—the work of traditional legal scholarship on language. This is not unimportant: it is a space in which a hegemonic ideology of legal language is worked out, where power is repeatedly naturalized, and where injustice is normalized through linguistic analysis. It is also the place where we can discern the micro-level machinery through which everyday law operates—where ordinary people and trained legal professionals negotiate what law will mean in practice. Against that backdrop, the potential contributions of linguistic anthropological perspectives and their failure to translate are placed in sharp relief.

Linguistic Ideology in Spoken and Written Legal Language

In the largely failed attempt at interdisciplinary communication described above, we see the crucial role of metalinguistic assumptions and structures. Research in linguistic anthropology has increasingly stressed the particular importance of 'metapragmatics'—metalinguistic structuring that continually assesses the contextual meanings at work (Silverstein 1979, 1993). For example, two utterances of 'the same' phrase can have opposite meanings, depending on contextual features. In the present-day United

States, one could say, 'Oh shut up!' with a smile, and have this taken as a friendly comment. (Even this generalization depends on speech communities and norms.) If the same words are uttered angrily, interlocutors are likely to code the comment—at a metapragmatic level—as an attack. This is a very basic example of how our *ideas about language* shape our communications: in this case, they provide us with metalinguistic categories ('angry speech', 'deferential speech') that have profound connections with social relationships and wider cultural values. Metapragmatic conceptions (or 'linguistic ideologies') regarding 'proper' use of language in combination with socially held values about people and contexts shape our minute-by-minute comprehension of one another (Schieffelin et al. 1998).

This means that we are all at times limited by a fast-moving filter that shapes our responses to language along lines of culture and social structure. A woman may use assertive speech to fit a professional metapragmatic norm ('forceful speech is an important indicator of good lawyering') but then violate a gendered metapragmatic norm ('women who speak forcefully are bitchy'). Taking this kind of insight to interdisciplinary communication, we see that law has its own set of metapragmatic norms giving lawyers a sense of why people are talking, how people should talk, how to assess which utterances are authoritative, and more. These norms can make effective communication difficult even between legal academics and academics from different fields—because their goals for an interdisciplinary linguistic exchange can differ subtly but dramatically (Mertz 2016). At the same time, because legal metapragmatics place faith in the way legal process supposedly creates equal playing fields, lawyers and judges can be blind to the way social context continues to 'leak' into legal proceedings through language (see Gruber 2016; Matoesian 2016; Silverstein 2016). Conscious attention to the metapragmatic level of communication can help us understand where roadblocks and distortions are emerging—whether in academic exchanges among disciplines or in exchanges in courtrooms and law offices.

A thorough exploration of legal metapragmatics, even just in the United States, is beyond the scope of this article, so a brief overview will have to suffice. First, we know that from early legal training through many later contexts of law practice, lawyers learn to approach language as an instrument through which social effects are achieved (see Burns 1997; Mertz 2007; Philips 1988). They may adopt other approaches to language at other moments of their professional lives, but this core orientation—much like the background provided by grammar and speech norms within language communities—forms a broad touchstone for common understandings in the language community of trained lawyers, leading to epistemic narrowing along a number of dimensions. Probing phenomena without reaching some kind of actionable conclusion does not fit well with instrumental approaches to linguistic exchange. And within the core 'grammar' of law, shared orientations to textual and procedural layers of authority dictate what kinds of social details can be considered, while radically limiting how the search for 'facts' and 'truth' and 'justice' can proceed. The subtle metapragmatic understandings that undergird this approach to authority in legal texts—and in legal language generally—have dramatic but often invisible effects on what is important, as well on what can be known at all. Language itself becomes valuable to the extent that it accomplishes things. We see this in the frustrating exchanges between lawyers and linguists described above: the lawyers want to know what they can *do* with the linguists' insights. They value the intellectual exchange itself in these very particular, instrumentalist terms. All else is sifted out and discarded—much as law students are taught to do from the beginning of their training. The linguists, on the other hand, are satisfied with discussions whose goal is more centrally intellectual in nature—seeking clarity, working towards shared understandings and definitions, furthering knowledge for its own sake.[17]

Conclusion: Rethinking anthropology's audiences

And here we arrive at a fundamental problem in interdisciplinary translation—that all disciplines incorporate underlying metapragmatic regimentations that, absent conscious reflection, can stymie effective communication. This is more likely to occur when the underlying linguistic structures and assumptions of the disciplines in question have fundamental incompatibilities or conflicts. Lawyers steeped in instrumentalist approaches to language may not be willing—or even able—to hear from disciplines whose metapragmatic assumptions and knowledge practices shake their fundamental orientation.

Looking at the other side of this question, we can ask: if anthropological linguistics has developed sophisticated tools for studying legal language, why have those tools not been used to craft translations for legal audiences? With a growing younger generation of anthropologists entering the legal academy, the question is a timely one. In his recent review of law-and-language research, Justin Richland argues that linguistic approaches could bridge a growing division between interpretivist and empirical approaches to law because 'the kind of hermeneutic empiricism exemplified by the best legal language scholarship ... affords a way of analyzing law in both its microlinguistic details and its macrosociological effects' (2013: 211). And yet, anthropologists' aversion to the reductive extraction of knowledge from its context for instrumentalist purposes may continue to create roadblocks for them as well.

Recent years have seen a return to the perennial anthropological question of how to integrate our own field's division between 'academic' anthropology and 'engaged' (or 'applied', or 'action', or 'collaborative') anthropology (Clarke 2010; Low and Merry 2010). A recent collection of essays by anthropologists engaging with law in courts challenges us to ask how incompatibilities between anthropological tenets and the exigencies of law practice could be bridged through insights gained from applied anthropology (Bens 2016; Foblets 2016; Hoehne 2016; Zenker 2016). This chapter has investigated a general failure of translation between 'academic' anthropology and 'academic' law with regard to scholarship on legal language, albeit casting a hopeful glance at a new generation of scholars with new sets of skills—including experience in law practice. This raises an interesting question that can only be alluded to here. What if, in studying 'up' (studying and engaging with the elite legal academy), we conclude that this is an arena that is unlikely to budge in its views of law, language, and society, no matter how strong the empirical evidence or acute the analytic insights emanating from anthropology? Do we give up on this endeavour? *For* whom do we write, *to* whom do we write—and to what ends? Perhaps some of the best roads toward a better translation between anthropology and law come from the edges of both disciplines—from clinical law and/or applied anthropology.[18] Is there any way to push for attention to this 'edgy' wisdom in the centres of either disciplinary tradition?

There is no easy solution here. Lawyers deploy language to do things. Anthropologists have good reasons to resist instrumentalist reductions. And yet, if legal language, in all its power, falls short when translating the rich contexts where it actually takes effect, perhaps we should keep trying. Asking what those who wield the language of law *do* with it is just the beginning of any in-depth or accurate inquiry into law itself, whether in philosophizing or reforming or any other serious reflecting upon law. Linguistic anthropology affords a possible bridge to the world beyond, where the expressive and instrumental effects of legal language shape lives in ways that legal analysis cannot fully comprehend on its own. At the same time, anthropology has yet to use its own tools to analyse how to communicate in ways that could build that bridge. Perhaps a new generation with feet on both sides of this divide will help us to move the discussion forward.

Acknowledgements

I would like to thank Kamari Clarke, Baudouin Dupret, and Olaf Zenker for their very helpful comments and suggestions—as well as all of the organizers of, and participants in, the 2018 Max Planck Institute for Social Anthropology conference in Berlin for conversations that provided a wonderful foundation for this collaborative effort.

Notes

1. Within legal scholarship, there was actually an attempt to exclude qualitative research such as participant observation and interviewing from the label 'empirical'; while newer definitions of 'empirical' within the legal academy nominally include 'qualitative' research, there is still a strong push to characterize quantitative work as more 'scientific' (and therefore valid) than qualitative research (see generally Suchman and Mertz 2010). There has been a rise of interest in quantitative research within the U.S. legal academy, but it would have to increase very rapidly indeed to make any major impact on mainstream legal scholarship (see Diamond and Mueller (2010), who found little growth over time in the amount of original empirical research published in law reviews, which ranged from a high of 8.5% to a low of 3.3% in different groups of journals).

2. On quotidian processes, see Macaulay (2016); Silbey and Ewick (1998). Related anthropological work has examined gendered children's play (see, e.g. Goodwin 1990), how everyday speech encodes responsibility and evidence (see, e.g. Hill and Irvine 1993), and much more.
3. Matoesian and Gilbert (2018) add that we need to attend as well to material objects.
4. See, e.g. Mertz and Rajah (2014) on critiques of philosopher H.P. Grice's maxims and of decontextualized uses of speech act theory; also see Levinson (1983) for an alternative view of pragmatics.
5. Harvey Sacks built on work by ethnomethodologist Harold Garfinkel (1956) in developing this approach (Sacks 1972). Sacks also co-authored, with Emanuel Schegloff and Gail Jefferson, a groundbreaking article for scholars studying conversation and turn-taking (Sacks et al. 1974).
6. One vibrant example is the stream of research on literacy and education, much of which involved ethnographies of language in school settings. See, e.g. Collins (2011); Cook-Gumperz (2012).
7. Conversation analysts have taken issue with a focus on social power in many linguistic anthropological analyses, arguing instead that scholars should take each interaction simply on its own 'surface' terms (Travers 2006). Linguistic anthropologists have disagreed, on the grounds that ignoring wider social and cultural structures fails to account for significant aspects of these local exchanges—and that analyses of social power are precisely what can be missed (Conley 2006). This chapter leans more towards the anthropological perspective on that point—while also noting the important insights of conversation analysis, and the substantial areas of overlap. Even ethnomethodologists have critiqued CA research that focuses too much on recorded talk sequences without a more in-depth examination of the 'local, embodied production' of interactional meaning (Dupret et al. 2015: 12).
8. To keep within this volume's focus on anthropology, I do not review important, closely related work on legal language from other disciplines (but see, e.g. Berk-Seligson 2009; Matoesian 2001; Ng 2009; Trinch 2001).
9. In addition to participant observation in court, she interviewed jurors and other trial participants, and either audiotaped or obtained transcripts for all the trials. The sites of the trials ranged from rural locales to the capital city of Texas. Conley was also able to study the 'backstage' behind the trials through becoming embedded with the defence attorneys. This gave her access to strategy meetings, aspects of jury selection, discussions with defendants' family members and witnesses, and close-hand observation of the drafting of legal documents, such as jury instructions. Discussions outside of the courtroom with judges, attorneys, activists, and others, as well as observations and interviews in the prison, also added depth to her ethnography. The core data on which she relies, however, are transcripts and tapes of courtroom interactions and interviews with jurors. It is the jurors' language and perceptions with which her book is primarily concerned.
10. The longstanding suspicion of 'gap studies' in law-and-society, although now subject to some new critiques, has admonished that any attempt to simply put a bandage on the gaping wounds in neoliberal law risks shoring up an unjust system, rather than pushing for more thoroughgoing critical analyses of the entire system (Gould and Barclay 2012). Although some anthropologists have long engaged in action and applied anthropology, the 'normal science' work in our field tends rather to deliver very detailed studies of how neoliberalism in its many forms continues to triumph, in the process decimating ways of life and alternative values all over the world. It is little wonder that this strand of research tends towards the pessimistic, and to wax cynical about proposed reforms or efforts to

ameliorate very bad situations. However, there are signs of a younger generation in anthropology that has become restless with that bottom line.

11. There have been anthropologists with law degrees for some time, and some have worked specifically on the intersection of law and linguistic analysis (examples include John Conley, Baudouin Dupret, and Elizabeth Mertz). Some of their work speaks across the audience divide between anthropologists and lawyers, but it has yet to receive broader attention among legal academics studying the language of law. Scholars from other fields have done exemplary work at the intersection of practical law and technical linguistic analysis (see, e.g. Burns 2001; Eades 2008). I highlight here a new generation that is tackling that issue head-on, from the 'trenches', exemplifying the New Legal Realists' renewed effort at translation.
12. Looking beyond specifically linguistic anthropological work, there is a growing group of similar interdisciplinary 'translators' between anthropology and law. Like Offit, anthropologist Riaz Tejani has a law degree and has worked to bridge the discursive gap between anthropological and legal scholarship (and teaching). In addition to performing traditional fieldwork in France, he has conducted a multimethod study of a for-profit law school in the United States, and has introduced anthropological insights into traditional law review articles, as well as into law training from first-year to advanced courses (Tejani 2013, 2014, 2017). Anthropologist Deepa Das Acevedo, who is a law professor, has performed fieldwork in India, as well as conducting qualitative research on gig work regulation; she is equally fluent in the technical details of employment laws such as the Employment Retirement Income Security Act (ERISA) 1974 and the technical requirements of good anthropological research and writing (Das Acevedo 2018, 2020). Anya Bernstein and Annelise Riles, both on law faculties, have written to both law and anthropology audiences with different but equally compelling approaches to interdisciplinary translation (see, e.g. Bernstein 2017; Riles 1999, 2014). They are part of a growing group of scholars at this interdisciplinary crossroads.
13. Why anthropologists, who are arguably at the other end of the power divide, have been reluctant to work in meaningful ways at bridging this divide is a more complicated question, and one to which I can only gesture at this point. Certainly it would be realistic for anthropologists to fear that translating their work for legal readers might drain it of its core contribution (see discussions in Mertz et al. 2016).
14. See, e.g. Bernstein (2020); Burns (2001); Deeb (2010, 2013); Hull (2012).
15. Linguistic anthropologist Michael Silverstein has convincingly critiqued Austin on this point (Silverstein 1979: 210–14).
16. Legal philosophers studying language did use actual texts of written law in their analyses, so that they did, in one sense, examine naturally occurring textual language. Unfortunately, their work drew so much on the 'armchair linguistics' approach bequeathed to jurisprudence by philosophy that it tended to overlook the potential value of studying speech acts empirically as they occur in social interactions.
17. In fairness, the linguists in this particular set of exchanges also had an instrumental goal: to find ways that their professional expertise could be picked up by lawyers. This led to a power imbalance that was completely unexplored but also impactful (Mertz 2016).
18. I use oversimplified categories with clear boundaries for the sake of making the argument, but of course these genres are complicated and leak across those boundaries. Any individual scholar can write in multiple genres—applied, theoretical, doctrinal, empirical, interpretive, and more—sometimes simultaneously!

References

Ahearn, L. 2011. *Living Language: An Introduction to Linguistic Anthropology*. Malden: Wiley-Blackwell.

Appadurai, A. 2016. *Banking on Words: The Failure of Language in the Age of Derivative Finance*. Chicago: University of Chicago.

Atkinson, J. M. and P. Drew. 1979. *Order in Court: The Organization of Verbal Interaction in Judicial Settings*. Atlantic Highlands: Humanities Press.

Austin, J. L. 1962. *How to Do Things with Words*. Oxford: Clarendon Press.

Bauman, R. and C. Briggs. 1990. 'Poetics and Performance as Critical Perspectives on Language and Social Life'. *Annual Review of Anthropology* 19: 59–88.

Bens, J. 2016. 'Anthropology and Law: Historicising the Epistemological Divide'. *International Journal of Law in Context* 12: 235–52.

Bentham, J. 1782 [1970]. *Of Laws in General*. H. L. A. Hart, ed. London: Athlone Press.

Berk-Seligson, S. 2009. *Coerced Confessions: The Discourse of Bilingual Police Interrogations*. Berlin: Mouton De Gruyter.

Bernstein, A. 2017. 'Before Interpretation'. *University of Chicago Law Review* 84: 567–653.

Bernstein, A. 2020. 'Porous Bureaucracy: Legitimating the Administrative State in Taiwan'. *Law & Social Inquiry* 45: 28–51.

Briggs, C. 2007. 'Anthropology, Interviewing, and Communicability in Contemporary Society'. *Current Anthropology* 48: 551–80.

Briggs, C. and Bauman, R. 1992. 'Genre, Intertextuality, and Social Power'. *Journal of Linguistic Anthropology* 2: 131–72.

Burns, S. 1997. 'Practicing Law: A Study of Pedagogic Interchange in a Law School Classroom'. In M. Travers and J. Manzo, eds. *Law in Action: Ethnomethodological and Conversation Analytic Approaches to Law*, 265–87. Aldershot: Dartmouth.

Burns, S. 2001. '"Think Your Darkest Thoughts and Blacken Them": Judicial Mediation of Large Money Damage Disputes'. *Human Studies* 24: 227–49.

Clarke, K. 2010. 'Toward a Critically Engaged Ethnographic Practice'. *Current Anthropology* 51(S2): S301–S312.

Collins, J. 2011. 'Literacy as Social Reproduction and Social Transformation: The Challenge of Diasporic Communities in the Contemporary Period'. *International Journal of Educational Development* 31: 614–22.

Conley, J. 2006. 'Power Is as Power Does'. *Law & Social Inquiry* 31: 467–75.

Conley, J. and W. O'Barr. 1990. *Rules versus Relationships: The Ethnography of Legal Discourse*. Chicago: University of Chicago Press.

Conley, J. and W. O'Barr. 2005. *Just Words: Law, Language and Power*. Second edition. Chicago: University of Chicago Press.

Conley, R. 2016. *Confronting the Death Penalty: How Language Influences Jurors in Capital Cases*. Oxford: Oxford University Press.

Cook-Gumperz, J., ed. 2012. *The Social Construction of Literacy*. Cambridge: Cambridge University Press.

Das Acevedo, D. 2018. 'Unbundling Freedom in the Sharing Economy'. *Southern California Law Review* 91: 793–837.

Das Acevedo, D. 2020. 'Changing the Subject of Sati'. *Political and Legal Anthropology Review* 43: 37–53.

Deeb, H. 2010. 'Constructing Restructuring: Legal Narrative, Language Ideology, and the Financial Rehabilitation of Iraq'. *Law and Contemporary Problems* 73: 109–28.

Deeb, H. 2013. 'Boiling Down to the M-Word at the California Supreme Court'. *Journal of Linguistic Anthropology* 23: 41–64.

Diamond, S. and P. Mueller. 2010. 'Empirical Legal Scholarship in Law Reviews'. *Annual Review of Law and Social Science* 6: 581–99.

Dupret, B., M. Lynch, and T. Berard. 2015. 'Introduction: Law at Work'. In B. Dupret, M. Lynch, and T. Berard, eds. *Law at Work: Studies in Legal Ethnomethods*, 1–23. Oxford: Oxford University Press.

Duranti, A. 1994. *From Grammar to Politics: Linguistic Anthropology in a Western Samoan Village*. Berkeley: University of California Press.

Duranti, A. 1997. *Linguistic Anthropology*. Cambridge: Cambridge University Press.

Eades, D. 2008. *Courtroom Talk and Neocolonial Control*. Berlin: Mouton De Gruyter.

Endicott, T. 2010. 'Language-and-Law'. In E. Zalta, ed. *The Stanford Encyclopedia of Philosophy*, available at <http://plato.stanford.edu/archives/fall2010/entries/law-language/>.

Foblets, M.-C. 2016. 'Anthropological Expertise and Legal Practice: About False Dichotomies, the Difficulties of Handling Objectivity and Unique Opportunities for the Future of a Discipline'. *International Journal of Law in Context* 12: 231–4.

Gal, S. 1979. *Language Shift: Social Determinants of Linguistic Change in Bilingual Austria*. New York: Academic Press.

Garfinkel, H. 1956. 'Conditions of Successful Degradation Ceremonies'. *American Journal of Sociology* 61: 420–4.

Goodale, M. 2017. *Anthropology and Law: A Critical Introduction*. New York: New York University Press.

Goodwin, C. 1994. 'Professional Vision'. *American Anthropologist* 96(3): 606–33.

Goodwin, M. 1990. *He-Said-She-Said: Talk as Social Organization among Black Children*. Bloomington: Indiana University Press.

Gould, J. and S. Barclay. 2012. 'Mind the Gap: The Place of Gap Studies'. *Annual Review of Law and Social Science* 2: 187–210.

Greenhouse, C. 1989. *Praying for Justice*. Ithaca: Cornell University Press.

Greenhouse, C. 2011. *The Paradox of Relevance: Ethnography and Citizenship in the United States*. Philadelphia: University of Pennsylvania Press.

Gruber, C. 2014. *I'm Sorry for What I've Done: The Language of Courtroom Apologies*. Oxford: Oxford University Press.

Gruber, C. 2016. 'Translating Defendants' Apologies during Allocution at Sentencing'. In E. Mertz, W. Ford, and G. Matoesian, eds. *Translating the Social World for Law: Linguistic Tools for a New Legal Realism*, 29–54. Oxford: Oxford University Press.

Hanks, W. 1989. 'Text and Textuality'. *Annual Review of Anthropology* 18: 95–127.

Hart, H. L. A. 1994. *The Concept of Law*. Second edition. Oxford: Oxford University Press.

Hill, J. and J. Irvine, eds. 1993. *Responsibility and Evidence in Oral Discourse*. Cambridge: Cambridge University Press.

Hirsch, S. 1998. *Pronouncing and Persevering: Coast Kenyan Courts*. Chicago: University of Chicago Press.

Hoehne, M. 2016. 'The Strategic Use of Epistemological Positions in a Power-Laden Arena: Anthropological Expertise in Asylum Cases in the UK'. *International Journal of Law in Context* 12: 253–71.

Hoëm, I. 2015. *Languages of Governance in Conflict: Negotiating Democracy in Tokelau.* Amsterdam: John Benjamins.

Hull, M. 2012. *Government of Paper: The Materiality of Bureaucracy in Urban Pakistan.* Berkeley: University of California Press.

Levinson, S. 1983. *Pragmatics.* Cambridge: Cambridge University Press.

Low, S. and S. E. Merry. 2010. 'Engaged Anthropology: Diversity and Dilemmas'. *Current Anthropology* 51(S2): S203–S226.

Macaulay, S. 2016. 'A New Legal Realism: Elegant Models and the Messy Law in Action'. In E. Mertz, S. Macaulay, and T. Mitchell, eds. *The New Legal Realism, vol. I: Translating Law-and-Society for Today's Legal Practice*, 29–50. New York: Cambridge University Press.

Matoesian, G. 2001. *Law and the Language of Identity: Discourse in the William Kennedy Smith Rape Trial.* New York: Oxford University Press.

Matoesian, G. 2016. 'Translating Token Instances of "This" into Type Patterns of "That": The Discursive and Multimodal Translation of Evidence into Precedent'. In E. Mertz, W. Ford, and G. Matoesian, eds. *Translating the Social World for Law: Linguistic Tools for a New Legal Realism*, 55–84. Oxford: Oxford University Press.

Matoesian, G. and K. Gilbert. 2018. *Multimodal Conduct in the Law: Language, Gesture and Materiality in Legal Interaction.* Cambridge: Cambridge University Press.

Maynard, D. 1984. *Inside Plea Bargaining.* New York: Plenum Press.

Merry, S. E. 1990. *Getting Justice and Getting Even.* Chicago: University of Chicago Press.

Mertz, E. 1989. 'Sociolinguistic Creativity: Cape Breton Gaelic's Linguistic Tip'. In N. Dorian, ed. *Investigating Obsolescence: Studies in Language Contraction and Death*, 103–16. Cambridge: Cambridge University Press.

Mertz, E. 2007. *The Language of Law School: Learning to 'Think Like a Lawyer'.* Oxford: Oxford University Press.

Mertz, E. 2016. '"Can You Get There from Here?" Translating Law and Social Science'. In E. Mertz, W. Ford, and G. Matoesian, eds. *Translating the Social World for Law: Linguistic Tools for a New Legal Realism*, 237–60. Oxford: Oxford University Press.

Mertz, E. and J. Rajah. 2014. 'Language-and-Law Scholarship: An Interdisciplinary Conversation'. *Annual Review of Law and Social Science* 10: 169–83.

Mertz, E., W. Ford, and G. Matoesian, eds. 2016. *Translating the Social World for Law: Linguistic Tools for a New Legal Realism.* Oxford. Oxford University Press.

Messick, B. 1996. *The Calligraphic State: Textual Domination and History in a Muslim Society.* Berkeley: University of California Press.

Mootz, F. 1995. 'Desperately Seeking Science'. *Washington University Law Quarterly* 73(3): 1009–23.

Ng, K. 2009. *The Common Law in Two Voices: Language, Law, and the Postcolonial Predicament in Hong Kong.* Stanford: Stanford University Press.

Offit, A. 2018. 'The Jury Is Out: An Ethnographic Study of Lay Participation in the Norwegian Legal System'. *Political and Legal Anthropology Review* 4: 231–46.

Offit, A. 2019. 'Prosecuting in the Shadow of the Jury'. *Northwestern Law Review* 113: 1071–119.

Ottenheimer, H. J. and J. S. Pine. 2018. *The Anthropology of Language: An Introduction to Linguistic Anthropology.* Fourth edition. Boston: Cengage Publishing.

Philips, S. 1988. 'The Language Socialization of Lawyers: Acquiring the Cant'. In G. Spindler, ed. *Doing the Ethnography of Schooling: Educational Anthropology in Action*, 176–209. Prospect Heights: Waveland.

Philips, S. 1998. *Ideology in the Language of Judges: How Judges Practice Law, Politics and Courtroom Control*. New York: Oxford University Press.

Richland, J. 2008. *Arguing with Tradition: The Language of Law in Hopi Tribal Court*. Chicago: University of Chicago Press.

Richland, J. 2013. 'Juris-Diction: Grounding Law in Language'. *Annual Review of Anthropology* 42: 209–26.

Riles, A. 1999. 'Wigmore's Treasure Box: Comparative Law in the Era of Information'. *Harvard Journal of International Law* 30: 221–83.

Riles, A. 2014. 'Managing Regulatory Arbitrage'. *Cornell International Law Journal* 47: 63–119.

Sacks, H. 1972. 'An Initial Investigation of the Usability of Conversational Data for Doing Sociology'. In D. Sudnow, ed. *Studies in Social Interaction*, 280–93. New York: Free Press.

Sacks, H., E. Schegloff, and G. Jefferson. 1974. 'A Simplest Systematics for the Organisation of Turn-Taking for Conversation'. *Language* 50: 696–735.

Schauer, F. 2011. 'Positivism before Hart'. *Canadian Journal of Law and Jurisprudence* 24: 455–71.

Schieffelin, B., K. Woolard, and P. Kroskrity, eds. 1998. *Language Ideologies: Practice and Theory*. Oxford: Oxford University Press.

Silbey, S. and P. Ewick. 1998. *The Common Place of Law*. Chicago: University of Chicago Press.

Silverstein, M. 1979. 'Language Structure and Linguistic Ideology'. In P. Clyne, W. Hanks, and C. Hofbauer, eds. *The Elements: A Parasession on Linguistic Units and Levels*, 193–247. Chicago: Chicago Linguistic Society.

Silverstein, M. 1993. 'Metapragmatic Discourse and Metapragmatic Function'. In J. Lucy, ed. *Reflexive Language*, 33–58. Cambridge: Cambridge University Press.

Silverstein, M. 2016. 'Performative Risks in Risking Performance'. In E. Mertz, W. Ford, and G. Matoesian, eds. *Translating the Social World for Law: Linguistic Tools for a New Legal Realism*, 85–104. Oxford: Oxford University Press.

Suchman, M. and E. Mertz. 2010. 'Toward a New Legal Empiricism: Empirical Legal Studies and New Legal Realism'. *Annual Review of Law and Social Science* 6: 555–79.

Tejani, R. 2013. 'Little Black Boxes: Legal Anthropology and the Politics of Autonomy in Tort Law'. *University of New Hampshire Law Review* 11: 129–70.

Tejani, R. 2014. 'National Geographics: Toward a Federalism Function of American Tort Law'. *San Diego Law Review* 51: 81–152.

Tejani, R. 2017. *Law Mart: Justice, Access, and For-Profit Law Schools*. Palo Alto: Stanford University Press.

Travers, M. 2006. 'Understanding Talk in Legal Settings: What Law and Society Studies Can Learn from a Conversation Analyst'. *Law & Social Inquiry* 31: 447–65.

Trinch, S. 2001. 'The Advocate as Gatekeeper: The Limits of Politeness in Protective Order Interviews with Latina Survivors of Domestic Violence'. *Journal of Sociolinguistics* 5: 475–506.

Washington University Law Quarterly (WULQ). 1995. 'Symposium: What Is Meaning in a Legal Text?' *Washington University Law Quarterly* 73(3): 769–1313.

Weissbourd, B. and E. Mertz. 1985. 'Rule-Centrism versus Legal Creativity: The Skewing of Legal Ideology through Language'. *Law & Society Review* 19: 623–60.

White, J. B. 1990. *Justice as Translation*. Chicago: University of Chicago Press.

Zenker, O. 2016. 'Anthropology on Trial: Exploring the Laws of Anthropological Expertise'. *International Journal of Law in Context* 12: 293–311.

CHAPTER 16

LAW AS AN ENDURING CONCEPT

Space, Time, and Power

ANNE GRIFFITHS

OVER the ages law has been with us as an enduring concept. It has taken many forms, from *Justinian's Institutes* of the sixth century (*Justinian's Institutes* 1987) to the comparative evolutionary perspective of Sir Henry Maine's *Ancient Law* (1861) and contemporary analyses of what has been termed 'global law' (Walker 2014). Its power in regulating the social, economic, and political life of society is widely acknowledged (Benda-Beckmann, Benda-Beckmann, and Griffiths 2009a; Hellum et al. 2011), so much so that it has been labelled 'a key category of contemporary world-making' (Goodale 2017: 17). In highlighting the relationship between law and power, questions are raised about where law is located, how it is constituted, and what forms it takes. How law is perceived depends upon the models or paradigms that are applied to its recognition, which may vary according to the differing methodological and epistemological approaches that underpin them. These play a crucial role in formulating matters of jurisdiction and in creating and ascribing authority and legitimacy, which have an impact upon the success or failure of claims that people and institutions pursue in multiple arenas. Understanding the dimensions of law in terms of space and place—which underpin and ground these models—and of their historical and temporal contexts, is crucial to comprehending law's dimensions *beyond its own terms*, with all the rhetorical and ideological assertions that it promotes.[1]

THE WESTPHALIAN MODEL OF LAW AND SOVEREIGNTY

A highly influential model of law that has sought to extend its jurisdiction, in terms of its territorial reach (or spatial extension) and its claim to universality—on a global scale in a way 'that implies a form of claimed hegemony' (Fassin 2012: 105)—is associated with the Westphalian state. This model of law developed out of the Peace of Westphalia (1648), which ended the Thirty Years' War in Europe and created the notion of sovereignty. This provides that, within its territory, a state is sovereign—that it has exclusive jurisdiction and that other states may not intervene in its domestic affairs; and it embraces the concept that all states are equal. It is a model that is predicated upon a separation of power between the executive, legislative, and judicial branches of government. Under it, the state claims jurisdictional sovereignty within its borders and is governed by law derived from a rigorous exposition of doctrinal analysis (law-as-text) founded on a specific set of sources, institutions, and personnel that form the heart of an abstract, formalist, legal discourse. In short, legitimate authority is based on state-centred law. This type of law operates in a monopolistic fashion, excluding all legal claims that do not fit within its highly circumscribed paradigm.

Contrasting perspectives: anthropological approaches

The Westphalian model, which rose to prominence in the nineteenth and twentieth centuries, has been highly contested; but it is not my intention to go into details here, other than to briefly highlight the way in which anthropologists have challenged it.[2] They have engaged in a contextual approach to law, one that situates law within a broader social compass, exploring its relationship with other bodies, institutions, and agencies that construct social relations, including the specific, lived everyday experiences and perceptions of law that inform people's lives.[3] As Sally Falk Moore (1969: 253) has observed, 'whatever is special about the anthropologist's view lies in his tendency to see the legal system as part of a wider social milieu'. Such an approach, in contrast to a focus on state-centred, dominant legal discourse, opens up avenues for discussing what constitutes a legitimate perspective for legal inquiry. Clifford Geertz (1983: 170–1) has written that 'law and ethnography are crafts of place: they work by the light of local knowledge ... absorbed with the task of seeing broad principles in parochial facts'; but, as Randy F. Kandel (1992: 1) notes, lawyers and anthropologists may still be at odds with one another, due to 'differences in implicit paradigms of thought' under which they operate.

Through their engagement with law and their promotion of alternative perspectives on what it entails, anthropologists have made a major contribution to the study of law. They have done so by challenging Western notions of what constitutes a legal domain and by extending the concept of law beyond rule-based formulations to incorporate views of 'law as process'.[4] In adopting actor-oriented perspectives that interrogate who is 'inside' and 'outside' of law,[5] these approaches have highlighted the frontiers of legality[6] and given voice to those who are rendered invisible or excluded from the terrain of state law or are operating at its intersections.[7]

While legal anthropologists acknowledge the existence of the state and state law, they have never perceived these domains as having exclusive control over law but have viewed them as expressions of one kind of organization along with local ('tribal', village) political or religious organizations that generate their own laws. The significance of this perspective is that it does not limit discussion of law to the co-existence of state, international, and transnational law in a hierarchical top-down fashion, which has been the focus of many studies in legal and political science dealing with globalization.

Instead, legal anthropologists analyse how different forms of the transnationalization of law affect the sovereignty of nation-states and how they affect other legal orders within the state, for example, religious law and/or customary or traditional law, including the interrelationships between these orders within and across states (Benda-Beckmann, Benda-Beckmann, and Griffiths 2005, 2009a, 2009b; Hellum et al. 2011).

Methodology, Fieldwork, and Orientation

This more social-scientific approach to law, which allows for the recognition of legally plural spaces, has been achieved through a particular methodological approach to gathering empirical data. One of the hallmarks of this data collection has been the production of a large, diverse body of ethnographic work, based on immersion in the field and participant observation and involving what Geertz (1973: 3–30) has referred to as 'thick description'.[8] Thus, the anthropology of law has engaged with methods that allow for a different theoretical orientation towards law by approaching it not as a given, an end in itself, but from a variety of standpoints, while providing a clear analysis of the way in which particular questions about law are framed and answered. These include questions about (a) who the actors are who are engaging with law at any one moment in time, (b) the purposes for which law is being invoked, i.e. the context in which it arises, and (c) the sources on which legal claims to legitimacy and authority are based.

Contemporary Dilemmas: The Rise of Transnationalism

Such an approach to law is critical in today's world, where the increasing proliferation of international and transnational regulatory frameworks, norms, and legal rules has given rise to 'the epochal transformation we call globalization' (Sassen 2008: 2), reflected today in the transnationalization of personal, economic, communicative, and religious relations, and giving rise to conditions of legal flux (Benda-Beckmann, Benda-Beckmann, and Griffiths 2009a, 2009b; Hellum et al. 2011). Such processes, in which local, national, and international regulatory domains are enmeshed, reconfigure law both within the nation-state and beyond its boundaries, so that there is now a growing acceptance 'that there may be sources of law other than that of the nation state' (Benda-Beckmann, Benda-Beckmann, and Griffiths 2009a: 1).

While law has always been mobile, and while the globalization of law is not a new phenomenon (Benda-Beckmann, Benda-Beckmann, and Griffiths 2005), there is a recognition of a broader conception of governance that forms part of what M. Patrick Cottrell and David M. Trubek (2012: 362) have termed *global* space, referring to 'an evolving regulatory environment created by globalization and the increasing role international norms play in domestic settings'. This is a space that blurs the general divide between internal and external state sovereignty, with states increasingly pooling capacities in international organizations at the expense of their mutually exclusive and often divided internal sovereignty (Walker 2014: 13). Under these conditions, sovereignty is much less about 'territorial integrity', along the lines of a Westphalian state, and more about 'being recognized as a legitimate participant in the international system' (Cottrell and Trubek 2012: 374).

International intervention

In this contemporary moment, an area that calls for the application of anthropological or social-scientific skills of analysis is that of international intervention. As Lee Wilson and Laurens Bakker (2016: 290) observe, we now live in an 'age of security' that not only engages with 'violence meted upon people in the name of national and global security' but also encompasses 'efforts to secure individuals and communities from "fear" or "want" in the name of "human security"'. Thus, international intervention revolves around notions of security and insecurity, involving both military engagement and processes of peace-building, as well as the management of crisis relief for those who are in need but whose nation-states cannot or do not want to secure their survival. Examining interventions in this context reveals the hierarchies of power between states that intervene and states in which intervention occurs—hierarchies which undercut the egalitarian principles on which the Treaty of Westphalia was based.

War-Making

In examining the U.S. led intervention in Afghanistan, Michael D. Smith (2014: 143) highlights the 'central, instrumental, and political role that law continues to play'. In doing so, he does not take an approach to legal analysis that treats the plural forms of law that are at work here as distinct and bounded entities, as objects in themselves. Instead, he focuses on the interplay between U.S. and Afghan law 'in the dynamic and hybrid spatiolegal relations arising from a western-led intervention that is at once a combat operation, a development program, a state building exercise and a legal transformation' (Smith 2014: 145). By extending his gaze to cover four overlapping moments, 'invasion, occupation, pacification, and autonomization', Smith (2014: 144) reveals the actions of an assemblage of different actors connected to differing spheres of activity.[9] Here, intervention represents 'a condition of polylegality in which the transplantation or imposition of law produces spaces and places crosscut by multiple, overlapping legal orders' (Smith 2014: 144). What emerges, under these conditions of multiple assemblages, is the extent to which multidimensional peace-keeping missions 'are increasingly hybrid affairs that manifest novel linkages between, and even the fusing of, security and development programs, military and civil functions, public and private entities, state officials and private contractors' (Smith 2014: 151).

What this approach makes visible is the degree to which the law of war, or martial law, has extended its remit. The introduction of the novel doctrine of pre-emption in international law, for example, supplied the legal basis for the 2003 invasion of Iraq. This allowed for the traditional boundaries of state sovereignty to be set aside, ignoring the principle of territorial integrity that provides for states to be sovereign within their own borders. It also led to an expansion of powers under martial law, beyond occupation as a temporary condition, 'in order to shore up the status quo in a defeated state' (Smith 2014: 150). Intervention has become associated with 'a new model of multilateral occupation that is less preservative than transformative' (Smith 2014: 151) and that now includes the reconstruction and rebuilding of a state (Roberts 2006). This has created a set of partnerships (both formal and informal) among 'states, businesses and civil society' (Mascarenhas 2017: 3), as these actors seek to implement a neoliberal agenda. Thus, Smith (2014: 151) observes, 'transformation is generally calibrated in neo-liberal logics concerned with securing private property and entrenching contractarian market relations ... as the path to a reclaimed national sovereignty and economic prosperity'.

All this is made possible under a rubric of peace and security that purports to extend 'global values to all, regardless of race, religion or creed' in a world order where 'everyone is, in effect, a citizen' (Wilson and Bakker 2016: 290). This order is one that legitimates international interventions 'both to protect civilians on human rights or humanitarian grounds', involving 'the responsibility to protect' or 'to defend prophylactically against terrorist or other emergent threats' (Smith 2014: 150).

Peace-Building

This expanded remit for action on the basis of justice and security also embraces peace-building as a reconstructive exercise. Yet, as Jan Selby (2013: 80) observes, the liberal narrative upon which it proceeds 'is only sustained by the abstraction of peace-building from its broader war-ending contexts, which are not explicable solely in terms of liberalism'. In analysing contemporary peace interventions, Selby (2013: 81) notes that they 'are not normatively consistent, and are not essentially liberal' so that 'the myth of a liberal peace-building discourse ... is just that, a myth'.

Charity and Humanitarian Aid: The Relief of Poverty and Need

From another perspective, Michael Mascarenhas addresses related issues in his book, *New Humanitarianism and the Crisis of Charity* (2017). He documents how humanitarian 'aid' has been acquired and circulated through 'the unprecedented rise in non-governmental organizations (NGO's) and their interconnected response with donor (Northern) governments and the business sector' (Mascarenhas 2017: 3). In tracing the connections between these diverse interest groups through a grounded, empirical inquiry, he seeks to answer the question 'how is this assemblage of global actors transforming the politics (decisions over who get what and when, and under what conditions) and power-knowledge dynamics (notions of expertise, data and measurement) of humanitarian policy and practice?' (Mascarenhas 2017: 3).

What distinguishes this new form from classic humanitarianism 'is the way in which human rights issues and political and economic reform are now joined with humanitarian intervention' (Mascarenhas 2017: 6), as was indicated by the gathering of global citizens in New York 'to express their solidarity with the world's poor' (Mascarenhas 2017: 133). These connections entail recognizing the extent to which human needs are now tied to human rights considerations and wider political objectives—a process that 'creates deserving and undeserving victims' (Mascarenhas 2017: 7). This is because decisions about who will be the recipient of aid are based not on need alone but on 'decisions in which aid might be withheld or suspended because of broader political and/or economic objectives, or in which racial, ethnic, gender or religious identities might influence or even take precedence over human suffering' (Mascarenhas 2017: 7).

Mascarenhas's (2017: 140) methodological approach and his analysis of what is really at stake in the new humanitarianism is one that makes visible 'the exploitative and power relations in doing good'. In this way, he challenges the reader to go beyond viewing poverty and dispossession as an *objects in themselves* that can be found 'in the slums of Kolkata or the fields of Rwanda, a thing that can be quantified in some meaningful way, captured and then managed' (Mascarenhas 2017: 144). Instead, he seeks to deconstruct the production of poverty through examination of 'the thick and obscure sites' in which it is constructed, which are linked with political and economic systems as well as 'knowledge-making practices, and institutional networks associated with a global humanitarian assemblage' (Mascarenhas 2017: 9). This involves understanding 'the way in which finance capital, corporate philanthropy, social entrepreneurialism and business management principles' (Mascarenhas 2017: 138) have converged in the definition and handling of poverty and need, thus giving rise to 'deserving victims'.

Convergent theoretical and methodological analyses

These studies are the product of scholars from differing academic disciplines. Wilson and Bakker were trained as anthropologists, Smith was trained in law and is a practising lawyer with an interest in law and geography, and Selby and Mascarenhas have a training in sociology. Despite this, their analyses of humanitarian interventions display a common thread derived from anthropological and/or social-scientific perspectives that are grounded in contextual and empirical approaches. On this basis, they challenge concepts such as 'security' and 'justice', their underlying logics, and the effects that they have when they are imposed on subject populations.

Wilson and Bakker (2016: 293), in highlighting the complex networks through which security is defined and produced, argue for the need to 'treat security as a relational entity embracing the ontological instability of the term itself'. To make sense of 'global security assemblages' there is a need to 'ascertain the ways in which insecurity is constituted and security enacted in its wake, to define the complex dynamics of security systems and the broader fields of power in which they are embedded' (Wilson and Bakker 2016: 294). For Smith (2014: 148), this involves acquiring a more extensive understanding of what the law of war involves at this moment in time and in light of the post-Cold War environment—an understanding that is contextualized within a broader frame of reference encompassing 'the intimate connections between law and war, legality and violence, regulation and coercion'. In his analysis of peace-building, Selby (2013: 81) argues that this cannot be treated as 'some discrete realm' but must be taken together with the 'war-ending process in the round—including the negotiation, agreement and implementation of peace settlements, and projects of reconstruction, including cases where these are internationalized and others where they are not pursued at all'. This allows him—and us—to comprehend what is in effect 'the influence of non-liberal political strategies and ideologies' (2013: 81) that are at work in producing 'security'.

For Mascarenhas (2017: 9), following the connections between the global players engaged in the construction of the new humanitarianism is essential because it highlights the ways in which relief efforts, for example in the wake of the Haiti earthquake or the South Asian Tsunami, 'have created a way to penetrate the Global South and ignore existing laws, conventions and constraints'. He argues that, by reducing questions of inequality and dispossession 'to economic growth and poverty reduction', attention is diverted from questions about 'political and economic reform' (Mascarenhas 2017: 140).

In following the interconnections or relational aspects of the production of security, all these scholars highlight the need for empirical research. Thus, Wilson and Bakker (2016: 289, 291) draw attention to the need for 'empirically grounded studies' that will attend to 'the everyday practices of security arrangements in the contemporary world' in order to 'address the need for a more nuanced analysis of security as a decentered and distinctly contextualized practice'. From the perspective of peace-building, Selby (2013:

81) argues for a methodological shift from the established, familiar narratives associated with it, 'to contextualised studies that attend more fully to heterogeneity and inconsistency of contemporary war-endings and peace processes'.

Challenging predominant assumptions about law

By emphasizing the linkages between differing sets of actors involved in humanitarian intervention, the studies reviewed above undermine, in different ways, any form of analysis that is based on the Westphalian model of sovereignty or on the assumption that clear distinctions can be drawn between state and non-state actors. As Wilson and Bakker (2016: 291) observe, 'Western notions of a clear separation of powers … are not easily transferable or even appropriate in contexts in which multiple actors, state as well as others, provide justice and security'. They argue that there is a need to 'move beyond simple state non-state binaries in the analysis of complex networks of actors working in security spaces' (Wilson and Bakker 2016: 293). This is because, as Mascarenhas (2017: 139) notes, 'the overlapping and active participation of state, market and civil society in the implementation of new humanitarianism under neoliberal logics has all but made these traditional institutions of modernity indistinguishable from one another'.

Studies by Selby (2013), Smith (2014), Wilson and Bakker (2016), and Mascarenhas (2017), among others, challenge uncritical normative and global assumptions that are employed in addressing justice, security, and insecurity, and they question the validity of the forms of interventions that are conceived on the basis of such assumptions. Selby (2013: 81) urges readers to reject a framing of liberal peace-building discourse in terms of 'a global–local dualism', because this 'overlooks the continued significance of geopolitical, inter-state dynamics in structuring war-endings and peace processes'. More research along the lines he recommends is needed on these important but hitherto neglected issues. Smith (2014: 150) argues that it is necessary to take account of the geopolitical circumstance and the geolegalities of 'Western war making' that have framed processes of intervention. Typically, these serve to maintain international order in the name of stability, while rendering the internal sovereignty of 'weak states (usually but not always in the global South)' (Smith 2014: 150) conditional upon their ability to discharge and uphold the enforcement of rights within their jurisdiction. Under these terms, their failure to do so 'opens up the possibility of outside intervention to preserve regional and global order and stability' (Smith 2014: 150) in an unprecedented way. Thus, the notion of sovereignty takes on a double-edged aspect: it serves to uphold the territorial integrity of the state in question, but it also allows for intervention when external powers determine that there is a deficit of law and order. For Mascarenhas (2017: 140), unmasking this sphere of geopolitical, legal, and economic intervention is critical, because while 'the ideology of global citizens … is a humane one' it also underpins 'a necessary condition for an economic and political system that helps the few at the expense of the many'.

The theoretical and methodological approaches addressed in this section allow for a move away from a standpoint that treats groups of actors and social entities as reflections of an internally coherent and bounded set of domains that are geared to addressing pre-determined objects such as security, justice, or poverty.[10] Instead, they explore relations between actors and entities or domains. At the forefront are the interactive dynamics that are at work in mutually constituting, reconstituting, or reconfiguring such entities in an ongoing process. Comprehending the dimensions of what this entails offers a 'better perspective on the realities of security provision ... in which forms of legitimacy, authority, moral and legal accountability are ambiguous, overlapping and contested' (Wilson and Bakker 2016: 295). It paves the way for engaging more reflexively with 'the relevance of forms of sociality, cultural milieu and political context in the consideration of security as an object of analysis' (Wilson and Bakker 2016: 291).

The limits and potential of anthropological methods

Yet in opening up these avenues for investigation, another set of questions arises. Given the recognition of global assemblages, with their complex array of networks and actors, how is research in this area to be framed? Such questions 'range from how one delimits the "field" and its asymmetries, to what gets foregrounded in the study of assemblages in which the technical and the social meet, mingle and multiply' (Murphy and Maguire 2015: 168).

Given the iterative process that is involved in conducting fieldwork, which consists in an ongoing dialogue with research participants in shaping and reshaping the research and its findings, it is hard to delimit its remit in advance. Ethnographic writing is not simply writing up a report; rather, it creates what Marilyn Strathern (1999: 2) has termed a 'second field'. These two fields are, first, fieldwork proper and, second, reflective analysis in a field beyond 'the field'. Bringing together these two fields, observation and analysis, creates the 'ethnographic moment' (Strathern 1999: 6) that is so strongly associated with anthropology. This open-ended process is impossible to delimit in advance. Rather than being regarded as defective, however, the element of risk that it involves may open up new and unanticipated horizons for study. This is because it contains 'the possibility of learning something unexpected' (Moore 1994b: 365), giving 'license to curiosity and to following up paths that at the outset simply could not have got on the map' (Strathern 1999: 8). These conditions allow for an interpretive and reflexive anthropology 'where partiality and not universality' is the basis for knowledge claims (Haraway 1991: 195). Its insights do not lay claim to a monopoly over knowledge, to primacy over all other visions. Indeed, once one acknowledges positionality, that is, once one recognizes the ways in which anthropologists are 'situated in relation to the people they study' (Naryan 1997: 24), what emerges from the encounter is a form of knowledge that cannot lay claim to an objective authenticity but must always be viewed as 'positional, partial and constitutive of reality' (Callaway 1992: 33). What is key here, is to make explicit the basis upon which such knowledge was acquired, including the assumptions upon which the fieldwork was carried out, the methods that were employed, and the feedback from those engaged in the project.

Law and space

The studies presented in this chapter clearly highlight the need to engage with law beyond the confines of the nation-state. This is in order to accommodate a broader concept of governance and governmentality that stretches across boundaries and coordinates via 'common knowledge and technology' (Sand 2004: 46). What is at work here are multiple networks of relations that cross territorial boundaries. They involve multilevel arrangements that reflect a 'great diversity of circumstances', creating 'complex coordination issues' and displaying a more 'fluid and complex regulatory environment' (Cottrell and Trubek 2012: 361). Under these circumstances, it is necessary to spatialize law or to perceive of law as inhabiting multiple spaces.[11] Approaching law in terms of space, means focusing not only on a physical, territorial place, but also on a more intangible domain of social relations. For legal geographers, law is inscribed in both domains so that it is always 'worlded' (Braverman et al. 2014: 1). Thus, law and space cannot be treated as separate domains but are 'conjoined or co-constituted' (Braverman et al. 2014: 1). Once one acknowledges that law cannot be abstracted from social life but forms an integral part of it, this brings into focus the normative spaces of law that allow for differing life-worlds, giving rise to varied applications of law in a variety of everyday settings. The dynamics of space in this context make it clear that such spaces cannot be divorced from ideology or politics (Lefebvre 1991). For space cannot be viewed as 'a natural medium that stands outside of the way it is conceived' (Crang and Thrift 2000: 3).

The temporal power of space and global outreach

Nor can space be divorced from time. While human behaviour 'is located in and constructed in space' (Low and Lawrence-Zúñiga 2003: 1), its duration in time is what creates human experience. These dimensions are at work in the studies discussed in this chapter, which highlight the ways in which international and transnational institutions have promoted a neoliberal agenda for humanitarian intervention. This is one that underpins the United Nations' Sustainable Development Goals (SDGs; previously called the Millennium Development Goals), which are contained in the United Nations Agenda 2030 and which reflect a wide range of aspirations, including access to justice, good governance, transparency, accountability (SDG 16), and the eradication of poverty (SDG 1). The SDGs lay claim to a global reach, both territorially and conceptually. They entail a geographic perspective that is planetary in scope as well as 'the affirmation of a moral superiority' (Fassin 2012: 106) on which normative assertions about the world are based. The power of this vision is not to be underestimated, for, as Neil Walker (2014: 60) observes, 'the UN framework possesses and exercises a depth and scope of normative authority unprecedented in any self-styled planetary legal regime'.

Global institutions such as the United Nations and the World Bank carry enormous normative authority in dealing with inequality, intervention, and the disbursement of international aid. In their approach to these issues, they categorize states as in terms of 'developing countries—including African countries, least developed countries, ... and middle-income countries' (United Nations 2015: §68). They do this in order to identify and reduce inequality within and among countries (SDG 10). While few could disagree with the aspirations underlying the SDGs, what remains problematic is the foundation upon which their interpretive remit is based. For what is at work here, as Mascarenhas (2017: 9) observes in his discussion of humanitarianism, is the power 'to form boundaries around particular territories, peoples and ideas', as well as the 'ability to transgress geographic boundaries, translate meanings, and transform values' (2017: 9).

Programs such as the SDGs of the United Nations are implemented on the basis of a linear understanding of time and space involving an evolutionary perspective on progress that global powers adopt in adjudicating the performance of countries worldwide. This takes a linear form that is constructed through a 'continual juxtaposition of equivalent intervals' that are constantly moving forward (Greenhouse 1998: 1637). As a result, this model is framed in terms of a 'single principle of selection' (Greenhouse 1998: 1636) that denies any legitimacy to any other form of space, temporality, or law. This is because its hierarchical nature rejects any plurality of views that may exist simultaneously. Instead, it endorses one particular perspective that operates to the exclusion of all others. As a result, this model lays claim to a universality, a form of timelessness that Carol Greenhouse (1998: 1650) refers to as an 'all-time' perspective. This temporal construction, which applies to certain forms of Western law and policymaking, gives rise to what Peter Fitzpatrick (1992) has termed 'the mythology of modern law'. Through its presentation of self, this mythology lays claim to neutrality, supposedly rendering it 'capable of balancing competing interests and engaging in value-free discourse' (Greenhouse 1998: 1642). In reality, however, it represents a juridical or weak form of legal pluralism that characterizes a lawyer's view of law, operating within a highly regulated, hierarchical legal framework.

What is being applied in the context of development aid and intervention is a particular perspective that has come to have a global outreach in its deployment in countries across the world. This singular world vision requires application of a supposedly universal form of analysis to render judgements as to whether countries are 'developed' or 'developing'. It is based on statistics representing a form of 'audit culture' (Power 1997; Strathern 2000) that is transnational in scope. An example of this is the ranking of countries in terms of calculations of Gross Domestic Product (GDP), which is 'one of the most widely used and accepted indicators' of national standing (Merry 2011: 83). Along with the human development index and various measures evaluating the rule of law, these indicators are used as data to rank countries as 'developed or less developed' (Morten 2013: 10) with all the consequences that follow from this.

Outsourcing governance from states

The widespread use of various indicators in the context of development aid and intervention marks a transfer of power from the state to evaluating organizations whose audits engage in 'a wide range of programmes for accountability and control' (Power 1997: 7). The indicators they apply not only represent a 'technology of ... knowledge production but also [contribute to a form of] governance'. They are used to manufacture 'evidence-based policy' feeding into 'results based management' that operates worldwide (Merry 2011: 84).

Especially troubling is the way in which indicators and targets are used to create an impression of certainty and objectivity that creates 'a dangerously misleading air of accuracy where the resulting numbers are used to make critical decisions that allocate resources' (Morten 2013: xi). For these mechanisms 'create an aura of "objective" truth' that, according to Merry (2011: 84), conceals 'their political and theoretical origins and underlying theories of social change and activism'. Under the guise of objective criteria, the ideological dimensions that frame their representation and interpretation remain hidden from view.

As Richard Rottenburg (2009: xxvi–vii) observes, in an international and global context, 'these models and technologies acquire an agency of their own'. Yet what they actually represent is 'an assertion of power to produce knowledge and to define or shape the way the world is understood' (Davis et al. 2012: 8). In this way, the political sovereignty of states is bypassed in favour of those who make authoritative decisions about intervention in, and aid to, countries all over the globe.

Beyond a Linear Model of Space and Time

However, the linear model of space and time that underlies international development aid and intervention represents just *one* particular vision of world progress. The assessment in terms of the SDGs and policies for intervention is one that is framed on a very particular formulation of space and its links to temporality based on techniques that measure GDP and other factors. This is the type of 'measuring' referred to earlier by Mascarenhas (2017: 3) that should be managed and controlled. But, as Doreen Massey (2013) observes, while space 'represents that dimension of the world in which we live', it is one 'within which distinct trajectories co-exist'. This perspective, which embraces the simultaneity of space, is, however, negated when countries are ranked by international agencies. For by classifying a country as *developing*, the country is no longer viewed as being on par with *developed* countries. Even though a developing country exists at the same time in space as a developed country, it is assigned to a different temporal location as 'a country which is following our path to becoming a developed country like us' (Massey 2013). What this form of categorization does, through a linear trajectory of time, is to deny 'the simultaneity, the multiplicity of space' that would acknowledge the co-existence of such countries or states. For it effectively turns all these differences between countries into 'a single historical trajectory' (Massey 2013) that is formulated on an evolutionary premise of the kind promoted by Sir Henry Maine in his earlier scholarship.

The power to impose this negative aspect of governance with all its concomitant effects is based on a particular interpretation of time. This is one that is built on the concept of progressively ongoing intervals underpinning a single, evolutionary narrative operating as *the* only authentic, authoritative, and legitimate perspective to the exclusion of all others. As such, it represents an aspect of *the global* and globalization that is premised on the supposed moral superiority of developed countries and on a hegemonic discourse that relies 'on exclusion as much as inclusion' (Fassin 2012: 99). This has the result of 'turning space into time, turning geography into history'; it 'is a way of denying the possibility of something different' and of opening up 'politics to the possibility of alternatives' (Massey 2013).

This comes about when distinctive temporal logics associated with different legal systems, with their own perceptions of time and space, become negated. This is achieved through the affirmative power of linear time in its ability to 'balance competing interests' (Greenhouse 1998: 1642) and 'resolve tensions among priorities, loyalties, and accountabilities' (Greenhouse 1998: 1638). In this way, any other views that may be simultaneously in existence are rejected in favour of one particular approach that is sustained to the exclusion of all others.

If, however, the power of time that purportedly operates in this way can be challenged by confronting its claims to historical authenticity based on an assumed natural order of things, and if the one reconstruction of the past (or construction of the present) may be displaced, then there is the possibility of creating a disjunction, so that what Lund (2013: 30) has called 'the inevitability of history' may become 'unsettled'. This disruptive juncture is necessary because of the inadequacy of what B. de Sousa Santos (2005: 31) describes as 'the linear time presiding over the Western [neoliberal] logic of development—based on a linear conception of development, according to which different pasts converge in a single future'. This must be contested, because only then is it possible to acknowledge 'a pluralistic conception of time based on the idea that there are alternative development paths and that therefore different pasts underlie different presents and may lead to different futures' (Santos 2005: 31). This is crucial for dismantling the legal myth of a single global vision and promoting recognition of globalization 'as a heterogeneous and historical phenomenon ... that can always be challenged' (Fassin 2012: 99).

Concluding observations

Anthropological and social-scientific studies of law play an important role in capturing the reality of what is occurring on the ground and articulating the inequalities of power that give rise to hierarchies of privilege, control, marginalization, and exclusion. In doing so, they provide new insights into political and social processes through which transnational law is locally appropriated and implemented by different actors. They also provide an understanding of the modern dynamics of legal change, challenging assumptions about increasing homogeneity in law, with a keen eye for the historical processes that are affecting current legal changes. They reveal how the transnationalization of law appears to result in homogeneity, fragmentation, and ambiguity, creating space for negotiation for some while barring others from legitimate claims to law, development, aid, and justice.

What emerges from these accounts is an understanding of the relational aspect of power—an understanding that goes beyond a top-down, vertical axis, incorporating more horizontal and multidimensional aspects and embracing the hetero-normative scope of regulatory decision-making that forms part of a broader system of governance.[12] These accounts highlight what might otherwise remain hidden from view, rendered invisible under conventional legal discourse rooted in a Western intellectual tradition of the nation-state, namely the connections between differing regulatory bodies (both formal and informal, state and non-state) that give rise to the spaces in which power is instantiated.

Through fieldwork and empirical studies an understanding can be acquired as to 'how tightly or loosely the compound parts of the large-scale composites are glued together at this particular historical moment, and what the potential is for increasing coherence or for violent, explosive fragmentation' (Strathern 1999: 372). It provides an opportunity to observe 'current history in the process of being produced' (Moore 1994b: 362). For engaging in fieldwork requires the ethnographer to be 'witness to the active construction and challenging of relationships, meaning, categories, patterns, systems, orders ... and their transformation and undoing as well' (Moore 1994b: 362). Unlike other researchers, the ethnographer, as positioned subject, has a 'lived experience which enables or inhibits particular kinds of insight' (Hastrup 1992: 119) that can be harnessed to provide a more contextualized and complex understanding and analysis of law and the many legal spaces that it inhabits.

Acknowledgements

The author would like to thank Anita Schroven and Christoph Sperfeldt for their comments and notes that any inadequacies in the text are hers alone. She would also like to thank the University of Arizona at Tucson, where an appointment as a Scholar in Residence in the fall of 2018 enabled her to complete this work.

Notes

1. For a discussion of the importance of spatializing law and the insights that it provides, see Benda-Beckmann, Benda-Beckmann, and Griffiths (2009b).
2. For a detailed discussion of law and anthropology and the relationship between them see Goodale (2017).
3. See e.g. the work of Malinoswki (1926).
4. On the legal domain, see e.g. Llewellyn and Hoebel (1941); Gluckman (1955); Bohannan (1957); Pospisil (1958); Evans-Pritchard (1940); and on law as process, see Moore (1973, 1978); Nader and Yngvesson (1973); Roberts (1979); Comaroff and Roberts (1981).
5. Harris (1996); Collier and Starr (1989).
6. Santos (1995).
7. It also involves what Nader refers to as 'studying up in order to enhance anthropology's 'understanding of the processes whereby power and responsibility are exercised' (Nader 1969: 284).
8. While questions have been raised from a number of standpoints about claims to knowledge, representation, and meaning that are the outcome of this process—e.g. Clifford and Marcus (1986); Marcus and Fisher (1986); Yang (1996); Oloka-Onyango and Tamale (1995)—Moore (1994a: 80) has cautioned that it is a 'huge polemic leap from recognizing the existence of an important blind spot to arguing that there is a total incapacity to see'.
9. Smith (2014: 159) uses the term 'autonomization' to refer to 'efforts to build the governing capacity of Afghan state institutions and promote reconstruction and economic development'.
10. Fassin (2012: 95–6), a medical anthropologist engaged in exploring the phenomenon of 'global health', notes that 'the idea' of it has generally been taken for granted ... as if we all knew what it was'; and he makes it his task to 'challenge some of the untested assumptions we may have about it'.
11. For a discussion of how space, law, and land come together in Botswana, see Griffiths (2013, 2019).
12. For an account of how power is spatialized in this way, see Griffiths (2018).

References

Benda-Beckmann, F. von, K. von Benda-Beckmann, and A. Griffiths, eds. 2005. *Mobile People, Mobile Law, Expanding Legal Relations in a Contracting World.* Aldershot: Ashgate.

Benda-Beckmann, F. von, K. von Benda-Beckmann, and A. Griffiths, eds. 2009a. *The Power of Law in a Transnational World: Anthropological Enquiries.* New York and Oxford: Berghahn Books.

Benda-Beckmann, F. von, K. von Benda-Beckmann, and A. Griffiths, eds. 2009b. *Spatializing Law: An Anthropological Geography of Law in Society.* Surrey and Burlington, VT: Ashgate.

Bohannan, P. 1957. *Justice and Judgment among the Tiv.* London: Oxford University Press for the International African Institute.

Braverman, I., N. Blomley, D. Delaney, and A. S. Kedar. 2014. 'Introduction: Expanding the Spaces of Law'. In I. Braverman, N. Blomley, D. Delaney, and A. S. Kedar, eds. *The Expanding Spaces of Law: A Timely Legal Geography,* 1–29. Stanford: Stanford University Press.

Callaway, H. 1992. 'Ethnography and Experience: Gender Implications in Fieldwork and Texts'. In J. Okely and H. Calloway, eds. *Anthropology and Autobiography*, 29–48. London and New York: Routledge.

Clifford, J. and G. E. Marcus, eds. 1986. *Writing Culture: The Poetics and Politics of Ethnography.* Berkley and Los Angeles: University of California Press.

Collier J. and J. Starr, eds. 1989. *History and Power in the Study of Law: New Directions in Legal Anthropology.* Ithaca and London: Cornell University Press.

Comaroff, J. and S. A. Roberts. 1981. *Rules and Processes: The Cultural Logic of Dispute in an African Context.* Chicago: University of Chicago Press.

Cottrell, M. and D. M. Trubek. 2012. 'Law as Problem Solving: Standards, Networks, Experimentation and Deliberation in a Global Space'. *Transnational Law and Contemporary Problems* 21: 359–93.

Crang, M. and N. Thrift, eds. 2000. *Thinking Space: Critical Geographies.* London and New York: Routledge.

Davis, K., A. Fisher, B. Kingsbury, and S. E. Merry. 2012. *Governance by Indicators: Global Power through Quantification and Ranking.* Oxford and New York: Oxford University Press.

Evans-Pritchard, E. E. 1940. *The Nuer: A Description of the Modes of Livelihood and Political Institutions of a Nilotic People.* Oxford: Oxford University Press.

Fassin, D. 2012. 'That Obscure Object of Global Health'. In M. C. Inhorn and E. A. Wentzell, eds. *Medical Anthropology at the Intersections: Histories, Activisms and Futures*, 95–115. Durham, NC: Duke University Press.

Fitzpatrick, P. 1992. *The Mythology of Modern Law.* London and New York: Routledge.

Geertz, C. 1973. *The Interpretation of Cultures: Selected Essays.* New York: Basic Books.

Geertz, C. 1983. *Local Knowledge. Further Essays in Interpretive Anthropology.* New York: Basic Books.

Gluckman, M. 1955. *The Judicial Process among the Barotse of Northern Rhodesia (Zambia).* Manchester: Manchester University Press.

Goodale, M. 2017. *Anthropology and Law: A Critical Introduction.* New York: New York University Press.

Greenhouse, C. 1998. 'Just in Time: Temporality and the Cultural Legitimation of Law'. *The Yale Law Journal* 98(8): 1631–51.

Griffiths, A. M. O. 2013. 'Re-envisioning the Local: Spatiality, Land and Law in Botswana'. *International Journal of Law in Context* 9(2): 213–38.

Griffiths, A. M. O. 2018. 'Negotiating Space and Place in Relation to Land: A View from Kweneng Land Board, Botswana'. In C. Rautenbach, ed. *In the Shade of an African Baobab: Tom Bennett's Legacy*, 175–92. Cape Town: Juta.

Griffiths, A. M. O. 2019. *Transformations on the Ground: Space and the Power of Land in Botswana.* Indiana: Indiana University Press.

Haraway, D. J. 1991. *Simians, Cyborgs, and Women: The Reinvention of Nature.* New York: Routledge.

Harris, O., ed. 1996. *Inside and Outside Law: Anthropological Studies of Authority and Ambiguity.* London and New York: Routledge.

Hastrup, K. 1992. 'Writing Ethnography: State of the Art'. In J. Okely and H. Calloway, eds. *Anthropology and Autobiography*, 115–32. London and New York: Routledge.

Hellum, A., S. S. Ali, and A. M. O. Griffiths, eds. 2011. *From Transnational Relations to Transnational Laws: Northern European Laws at the Crossroads.* Farnham: Ashgate.

Justinian's Institutes. 1987. Translated and with an Introduction by P. Birks and G. McLeod; with the Latin Text of P. Krueger. London: Duckworth.

Kandel, R. F. 1992. 'How Lawyers and Anthropologists Think Differently'. In R. F. Kandel, ed. *Double Vision: Anthropologists at Law (Napa Bulletin 11)*, 1–5. Arlington, VA: American Anthropological Association.

Lefebvre, H. 1991. *The Production of Space* (trans. D. Nicholson-Smith). Oxford: Blackwell.

Llewellyn, K. N. and E. A. Hoebel. 1941. *The Cheyenne Way: Conflict and Case Law in Primitive Jurisprudence*. Norman, OK: University of Oklahoma Press.

Low, S. M. and D. Lawrence-Zúñiga. 2003. *Anthropology of Space and Place: Locating Culture*. Malden, MA: Blackwell Publishing.

Lund, C. 2013. 'The Past and Space: On Arguments in African Land Control'. *Africa* 83(10): 14–35.

Maine, H.S. 1861. *Ancient Law, Its Connections with the Early History of Society, and Its Relations to Modern Ideas*. London: John Murray.

Malinowski, B. 1926. *Crime and Custom in a Savage Society: An Anthropological Study of Savagery*. Oxford: Harcourt Brace.

Marcus, G. E. and M. J. Fisher. 1986. *Anthropology as Cultural Critique: An Experimental Moment in the Human Sciences*. Chicago: University of Chicago Press.

Mascarenhas, M. 2017. *New Humanitarianism and the Crisis of Charity: Good Intentions on the Road to Help*. Bloomington, IN: Indiana University Press.

Massey, D. 2013. Doreen Massey on Space. A Dialogue between Doreen Massey and Nigel Warburton on *Social Science Bites*, published 1 February 2013, available at <https://www.socialsciencespace.com/2013/02/podcastdoreen-massey-on-space/>.

Merry, S. E. 2011. 'Measuring the World: Indicators, Human Rights and Global Governance'. *Current Anthropology* 52(S3): S85–S95.

Moore. S. F. 1969. 'Law and Anthropology'. *Biennial Review of Anthropology* 6: 252–300.

Moore. S. F. 1973. 'Law and Social Change: The Semi-Autonomous Social Field as an Object of Study'. *Law & Society Review* 7(4): 719–46.

Moore. S. F. 1978. *Law as Process: An Anthropological Approach*. London: Routledge & Kegan Paul.

Moore. S. F. 1994a. *Anthropology and Africa: Changing Perspectives on a Changing Scene*. Charlottesville, VA and London: The University of Virginia Press.

Moore. S. F. 1994b. 'The Ethnography of the Present and the Analysis of Process'. In R. Borofsky, ed. *Assessing Cultural Anthropology*, 362–74. London and New York: McGraw-Hill.

Morten, J. 2013. *Poor Numbers: How We Are Misled by African Development Statistics and What to Do About It*. Ithaca and London: Cornell University Press.

Murphy, E. and M. Maguire. 2015. 'Speed, Time and Security: Anthropological Perspectives on Automated Border Control'. *Etnofoor* 27(2): 157–77.

Nader, L. 1969. 'Up the Anthropologist: Perspectives Gained from "Studying Up"'. In D. Hymes, ed. *Reinventing Anthropology*, 284–311. New York: Random House.

Nader, L. and B. Yngvesson. 1973. 'On Studying Ethnography of Law and its Consequences'. In J. J. Honigman, ed. *Handbook of Social and Cultural Anthropology*, 883–921. Chicago: Rand McNally.

Naryan, K. 1997. 'How Native is the "Native" Anthropologist?'. In L. Lamphere, H. Ragone, and P. Zavella, eds. *Situated Lives: Gender and Culture in Everyday Life*, 23–41. New York and London: Routledge.

Oloka-Onyango, J. and S. Tamale. 1995. '"The Personal is Political," or Why Women's Rights are Indeed Human Rights: An African Perspective on International Feminism'. *Human Rights Quarterly* 17(4): 692–731.

Pospisil, L. 1958. *Kapauka Papuans and Their Law* (Yale University Publication in Anthropology, No. 54). New Haven, CT: Yale University Press.

Power, M. 1997. *The Audit Society: Rituals of Verification.* Oxford and New York: Oxford University Press.

Roberts, A. 2006. 'Transformative Military Occupation: Applying the Laws of War and Human Rights'. *American Journal of International Law* 100: 580–622.

Roberts, S. A. 1979. *Order and Dispute: An Introduction to Legal Anthropology.* London: Penguin.

Rottenburg, R. 2009. *Far Fetched Facts: A Parable of Development Aid* (trans. A. Brown and T. Lampart). Cambridge, MA and London: MIT Press.

Sand, I. J. 2004. 'Polycontextuality as an Alternative to Constitutionalism'. In C. Joerges, I. J. Sand, and G. Teubner, eds. *Transnational Governance and Constitutionalism*, 41–66. Oxford and Portland: Hart Publishing.

Santos, B. de Sousa. 1995. *Toward a New Common Sense: Law, Science and Politics in the Paraadigmatic Transition.* London: Routledge.

Santos, B. de Sousa. 2005. 'Beyond Neoliberal Governance: the World Social Forum as Subaltern Cosmopolitan Politics and Legality'. In B. de Sousa Santos and C. Rodríguez-Garavito, eds. *Law and Globalization from Below*, 29–63. Cambridge and New York: Cambridge University Press.

Sassen, S. 2008. *Territory, Authority, Rights: From Medieval to Global Assemblages.* Princeton: Princeton University Press.

Selby, J. 2013. 'The Myth of Liberal Peace-building'. *Conflict, Security & Development* 13(1): 57–86.

Smith, M. D. 2014. 'States that Come and Go: Mapping the Geolegalities of the Afghanistan Intervention'. In I. Braverman, N. Blomley, D. Delaney, and A. S. Kedar, eds. *The Expanding Spaces of Law: A Timely Legal Geography*, 142–66. Stanford: Stanford University Press.

Strathern, M. 1999. *Substance and Effect: Anthropological Essays on Persons and Things.* London and New Brunswick, NJ: Athlone Press.

Strathern, M., ed. 2000. *Audit Cultures: Anthropological Studies in Accountability, Ethics and the Academy.* London and New York: Routledge.

United Nations. 2015. *Transforming our World: The 2030 Agenda for Sustainable Development.* United Nations. Available at <https://sustainabledevelopment.un.org/post2015/transformingourworld>.

Walker, N. 2014. *Intimations of Global Law.* Cambridge and New York: Cambridge University Press.

Wilson, L. and L. Bakker. 2016. 'Cutting off the King's Head: Security and Normative Order beyond the State'. *Conflict, Security & Development* 16(4): 289–300.

Yang, M. 1996. 'Tradition, Travelling Theory, Anthropology and the Discourse of Modernity in China'. In H. L. Moore, ed. *The Future of Anthropological Knowledge*, 92–114. London and New York: Routledge.

CHAPTER 17

LEGALISM

Rules, Categories, and Texts

FERNANDA PIRIE

WHAT is distinctive about law as a social form? Much excellent work in the field of legal anthropology has analysed what law does and how legal rules and processes are used and abused, particularly in the modern world. It is an expanding field of scholarship which includes a diversity of subjects and approaches. But what is it that holds these subjects together? What is the legal? Following notorious and inconclusive debates over the meaning of 'law', which have troubled legal theorists even more than anthropologists, many scholars have sensibly decided simply to ignore the question of definition. To study the procedures of a truth and reconciliation commission or a sharia court, we may not need to grapple with the issue of what law is, or the boundary between law and other forms of normative order. But as anthropologists, we should also take an interest in the nature of law as a social form. In this chapter I argue for a focus on legalism, that is the tendency to describe and order the word by reference to general rules and abstract categories. Although somewhat broader than the concept of law, it draws our attention to distinctive features of law and legal processes. It is an enduring phenomenon, one that marks out a category of social forms, which is susceptible to more precise definition than the polythetic concept of law.[1] This, in turns, allows for fruitful comparisons across both time and space.

Contemporary governments inevitably create elaborate systems of law. Property regimes, traffic, taxation, and welfare are all organized through systems of rules and regulations. The modern nation-state is barely conceivable without an apparatus of legislation, courts, and lawyers. But lawmaking is not just the preserve of bureaucratic governments. Over the course of human history, scholars, religious leaders, village councils, guilds, and trade associations have all made laws. Anthropologists, with their experience in ethnographic methods, are often reluctant to delve too far into history. But the empirical study of legalism can encompass historical as well as contemporary examples, enabling us to take a long historical perspective on the forms and social significance of law. There is a widespread tendency, such examples reveal, for people to make explicit the categories into which they feel that ordinary life must be fitted and to use generalizing rules to set out a vision for how it ought to be organized. This legalism marks out the development of law as a social form. More than the study of 'law on the books', the anthropological examination of legalism, I argue here, helps to explain the varied things that law is and does, in the contemporary world as much as in history. It opens the way for an anthropology *of* law.

The fetishism of law

In their 2006 paper, which ranges widely over activities and experiences in the 'postcolony', the Comaroffs note a contemporary 'fascination with the law' (2006: 20). A 'preoccupation with legalities' and with the legal subject, they say, is a salient dimension of postcolonial disorder. Quite ordinary people turn to laws, courts, and law-oriented non-governmental organizations to make claims for the recognition of their human rights, to seek redress for injuries and past wrongs, and to secure social recognition (2006: 25). Litigants make these and other claims in legal terms, they point out, where we might have expected political action in the form of protest or class struggle. There is a 'culture of legality'. Law is a weapon of the weak, they say, which the less powerful employ to make claims for resources, recognition, voice, integrity, and sovereignty (2006: 31). But, at the same time, 'lawfare' characterizes the activities of the powerful, those who employ legal instruments in acts of political coercion, in the deployment of violence, and in order to 'launder brute power in the wash of legality' (2006: 30–1). Law is also the vehicle by which oligarchs and dictators 'seize the sinews of the state'.

Exploring the 'culture of legality', the Comaroffs note the large number of new constitutions being made and revised in postcolonies, and the 'almost salvific belief' in their capacity to conjure up equitable, just, ethically founded, and pacific polities. Their promulgation often marks a 'new beginning', they say, and a radical break, at once symbolic and substantive, with the past (2006: 22–3). Since their piece was published, the events of the 'Arab Spring' have given rise to a slew of new constitutions in the Middle East, about which many of the same comments could be made. Asking what might explain this 'fetishization' of legalities, the Comaroffs note the growing heterodoxy of the twenty-first-century polity. Legal instruments offer a 'ready means of commensuration', they suggest, a repertoire of more or less standardized terms and practices which permit the negotiation of values, beliefs, ideals, and interests across 'otherwise impermeable lines of cleavage' (2006: 32). Constitutions embrace heterogeneity, employing the language of universal rights, while global legal regimes transect nation-states and their borders. Laws and legal language, that is, are useful means of bridging cultural and linguistic divides.

The Comaroffs, in this way, focus on the dynamics and experiences of the 'postcolony' and look to changes in the contemporary world order to explain the 'culture of legality'.[2] But the phenomena they note are not as recent, nor as unique, as their analysis—convincing though it is—would suggest. They are historical phenomena, which warrant extended consideration and deeper reflection. What is it about law and 'legalities', we can ask, that makes it both attractive and useful in these very different projects, as both a weapon of the weak and an instrument of 'lawfare'? What is it about laws and legal processes that enable them to do such very different things, and with such very different results? Historical examples serve to put these important phenomena in context and make clear the importance of legalism.

A seemingly bizarre 'fascination' with law is not a new phenomenon. William Miller (1990) makes similar remarks in his study of law in medieval Iceland. Analysing the extensive lawbook of the Icelanders, with its 700 densely written pages of detailed rules—recited by a Lawspeaker at regular intervals—along with the evidence of both real trials and the mock courts staged by farmhands, Miller asks what it is that explains their 'will to make law' (1990: 228). The Icelanders of the twelfth and thirteenth centuries seem to have been obsessed with rule articulation and categorization, he says. It is not a phenomenon for which he offers a ready explanation: some rules do seem to have regulated practice and promoted order, he suggests, but others seem more like a meditation upon rules, or simply the satisfaction of 'a juristic and aesthetic urge towards systematization and conceptual order' (1990: 228). When the laws were later written down, in the twelfth or thirteenth centuries, the Icelanders were probably aware of the growth of laws and legal instruments across the seas in northern Europe. Maybe they wanted to both feel and demonstrate that they were a people with a sophisticated civilization, marked by explicit rules and legal practices. But whatever motivated them to create their rules, the laws seem to have acquired an importance of their own, not dissimilar to the constitutions in which, as the Comaroffs note, people now place so much faith. And although there were no obvious means of enforcement, as Miller remarks, the laws might have served to confer legitimacy and positive value on certain types of behaviour, making the rules in some ways self-enforcing (1990: 229). Fascination with law is a historical phenomenon which calls for comparative exploration.

The Comaroffs' remarks also raise important questions about the nature of law. What is it that is being fetishized? The Icelanders had their lawbook and conducted court cases with some formality. The Comaroffs refer to 'Law', 'legalities', and 'the Law' to characterize the legal phenomena they describe. Although they leave the object of their interest (sensibly) undefined, this invites us to think more deeply about what it is that holds such an attraction to different people. What is it that can become a political tool and a manifestation of violence, in some contexts, while in others it offers a 'ready means of commensuration' or a 'weapon for the weak'? The Comaroffs' examples comprise written constitutions, the idea of the 'rule of law', claims to 'rights', the resort to litigation and the courts, the language of jurisprudence, and the use of legal instruments—whether as 'lawfare' or as means to deal with conflicts and to negotiate rights and claims. These are not matters of custom and practice. They are not unwritten rules and norms, often loosely glossed as 'customary' or 'traditional' law. These are examples of explicit law, formalized in legal instruments and judicial practices. It is law made evident, just as the Icelanders' laws were written down in a rule book, so that they could be recited, accurately, to the people. This is legalism.

Legal language

What, then, can anthropologists gain by the study of this legalism and what explains its widespread appeal? As the Comaroffs' examples make clear, law provides people with a means of making arguments and claims. It is a medium through which political battles are fought out.[3] Ordinary people turn to the law to formulate claims to human rights, for access to resources, to seek redress for injuries, and for social recognition (Goodale 2017: Chapter 4). Crucially, as the Comaroffs point out, framing arguments in legal terms allows people to deal with conflict across 'otherwise incommensurable axes of difference' (2006: 22). The same points have been made by Koskenniemi (2001, 2011) about international law. Its formalism, as he puts it, brings together political antagonists as they invoke contrasting understandings of rules and institutions. These provide a 'shared surface for debate', allowing them to disagree within a structure of assumed universality. International laws put questions of just distribution and entitlement on the agenda and offer a language of community standards against which acts of public officials may be assessed (2011: 266). The modern phenomena of transnational law can be loosely traced back to the set of practices and instruments that came to be known as the *lex mercatoria*. Medieval merchants would use standard forms of agreement and commercial instruments in order to deal with partners from other parts of the world who spoke mutually incomprehensible languages and lived very different lives. Trade has for centuries been conducted through the use of formal instruments and standard mechanisms for the resolution of disputes, which facilitate relations over long distances and amongst people who probably had no other social or political ties (Pirie 2013: 207–9). Law, in the form of legalistic practices, provided people with a means of negotiating across linguistic, national, and jurisdictional divides, even before the increase in social heterogeneity noted by the Comaroffs.

Laws provide standardized, because explicit, rules and categories through which such negotiations may be conducted. They also provide people with a language in which to articulate claims that may be heard and understood by the powerful. Presented as legal arguments, claims to resources and recognition are more likely to be taken seriously by those who inhabit very different worlds—whether as judges, politicians, or the officials who preside over international organizations with valuable resources at their fingertips. Articulating a claim in terms of 'human rights', or 'transitional justice', or 'victimhood'—the terms in which many legal instruments are now formulated—may not guarantee recognition, but it does mean the claim is more likely to be heard. In modern societies, established rules and categories have acquired traction, shaping the ways in which power-holders and opinion-formers think about the world around them and the issues to which they feel they must pay attention. To understand the power of the law as a means of making arguments and claims, we must understand the ways in which general rules and explicit categories are employed, that is, the power of legalism.

Explicitly formulated rules, principles, and categories, the stuff of legalism, stand apart from practice. They can be used to order the messy reality of everyday life. This is why they are attractive to governments seeking to manage diverse populations, raise taxes, and coordinate economic activities in ways that may or may not benefit their citizens. They may symbolize equivalence, but they may also make explicit the strata of an ordered hierarchy, in these ways supporting the interests of the powerful and justifying practices of exclusion. Legalism also makes possible the giving of authoritative judgments. In the 1960s, Lloyd Fallers (1969) set out to analyse the court processes of the Soga in what is now Uganda. The structures and processes of their courts had obviously been influenced by the colonial regime, with its legal system, but the Soga ran their own courts. The judges addressed family and other local issues, such as claims for the return of bride-price and the consequences of marital problems and divorce. The Soga did not use written rules or records but, as Fallers noticed, their processes were 'legalistic'. That is, they used particular categories to describe and argue about the meaning of events, and these categories indicated to the judges how a case should be decided (1969: 21). For example, a mistreated wife had remedies under Soga law, but she could not simply return to her natal home without exposing her father to a charge of 'harbouring', and the Soga judges had developed a clear set of ideas about what constituted 'harbouring'. This legalism, as Fallers puts it, entails that the values of human conduct are reduced to normative statements, which enable judges to decide authoritatively whether or not a particular rule—such as the rule against harbouring—has been violated (1969: 21). Many of the Soga litigants accordingly framed their arguments in legalistic terms, although they also resorted to what Faller calls 'moral holism' when it suited them better. The legal categories did not always suit their purposes or allow them to pursue the claims they wanted, and a holistic style of argument could appeal more readily to popular morality. But it could also lead to a welter of blame and counter-blame, with all the moral ambiguity that exists in situations of interpersonal conflict, as Fallers puts it (1969: 32). Legalistic reasoning was, at least in some circumstances, a way of cutting through this ambiguity.

As the Soga example makes clear, law differs from other forms of social interaction largely because of its generality. Legal theorist Frederick Schauer (1993: xi–xii) points out that laws extend over time, over persons, and over events; law has a special form of language, 'shorn of contextual embellishments'. In the context of judicial activity, decisions made according to laws are projected onto a larger and less-known future. As Dresch (2012: 15) says, legalistic thought makes explicit use of generalizing concepts, addressing the world through legal categories and rules that stand apart from the flux of events and personalities. This is what lifts legal claims beyond the particular context, projecting them onto a larger plane in which statements and principles—about justice, rights, equality, or gender—may have general recognition. This is why people turn to the law to formulate claims in terms that will be heard.

An excellent example of this is provided by Merry's (1990) study of litigants in the lower courts in the United States. Although the categories and remedies of the law did not always reflect their interests, she found that most claimants, having turned to the courts, tried to frame their problems in legalistic terms (1990: 100). Attempting to persuade court officials to take them seriously, they presented private problems concerning spouses, lovers, children, neighbours, and landlords by squeezing them into the legal categories of 'assault', 'harassment', 'breach of contract', 'truancy', and so on (1990: 13, 98). It was the lawyers and court officials who tried to dissuade them from pursuing a legal case, framing their complaints in more general and moral terms. The Comaroffs also talk of the Indian villagers who pore over rule books in order to challenge the legality of the actions of local officials, the language of jurisprudence heard in Amazonia or among Australian Aboriginals, and litigation over access to AIDS medication in the Global South (2006: 25–8). Goodale (2017) offers several more examples, including the Chinese villagers who appropriate the language of human rights to negotiate the terms of a development project (Flower 2009), and women's rights activists in Iran, who adapt the language of human rights to articulate their own moral concerns (Osanloo 2006). Much of the interest in these examples lies in the evident attraction of legalism. The analysis would be impoverished if we merely focused on the failure of the laws in question to capture the ways in which the indigenous Amazonians related to their environment, or how U.S. litigants had to squeeze their claims into unfamiliar legal categories, although these are also important and worth noting. Law provides a language to which all sorts of people turn in lieu of political action, and into which they readily transform their claims.

It is the constitutive power of legal language that also explains why 'self-imaginings' may be 'grounded in the jural', as the Comaroffs (2006: 26) put it. Jural categories are more likely to be recognized by the powerful. They entail rights and entitlements as well as duties. Laws define the difference between migrant and citizen, for example, with all the consequences that that entails. It should be no surprise that over time people adopt the categories with which the powerful shape the world around them and may well come to think of themselves in these terms, as rights-bearing 'citizens', or 'indigenous people', or 'victims', rather than primarily as members of a family, community, or network. Indeed, people may move between the two without apparent contradiction, as Leve (2007) notes of Buddhists in Nepal, who adopt the language of individual rights in strategic contexts. In recent years, the categories of 'victim' and 'slave' have come to acquire particular legal purchase, attracting recognition as meaningful statuses with jural, political, and material consequences. 'Modern slavery' has proved notoriously difficult to define, but it is now the subject of legislation in the United Kingdom, the Modern Slavery Act 2015, which gives rights and protections to the 'victims' of modern slavery while imposing obligations and penalties on those who should address their needs or who are deemed guilty of slavery offences. The passing of the U.K. Act was preceded by several years of agitation by activists and reformers, leading to debate amongst politicians on a global scale, during which the problem of 'slavery' acquired general recognition. Several international conventions resulted (Johnstone 2017: Chapter 2). Yet it was not inevitable that this concept should be chosen to refer to a broad category of practices, some of which might, in other contexts, have been referred to as 'trafficking' or 'labour exploitation'. A desire to address a set of related problems involved giving it a name, and gradually a category was constructed, in terms of which rights and duties could be defined and laws could be made. This is not so different from the use of legalistic categories by the Soga judges to define marital problems and determine their consequences. This legalism is what distinguishes legal from other types of language. It is a particular set of characteristics in which much of the power of law originates—for good or for bad, historically and in the contemporary world. It marks law out as a distinctive social form.

Law, power, and justice

It is the nature of legalism and the power of legal language that also explain why laws can be used to organize social relations and exercise control on the part of governments, dictators, and oligarchs. Law can formalize difference, status, hierarchy, and categories of exclusion but, as the Comaroffs point out, it is also a powerful means of legitimation. Legal instruments may be employed in 'lawfare' as means to subordinate, appropriate, coerce, or exclude, thereby harnessing 'the violence inherent in the law' (2006: 30). At the same time, at least 'a minimal architecture of legalities' is necessary to transform power into sovereign authority (2006: 35). It is easy to equate law, too simply, with power and violence, in the manner suggested by Benjamin's (1996: 248) declaration that 'law-making is power making' (cited in Comaroff 2006: 35) or Nader's (2005: 199) bold statement that 'law is a means of legitimizing the take'. These may be features of many laws in many contexts, but this is not all that law does. There is a difference between enacting and legitimating power, which we should not overlook. Laws and legalistic instruments are techniques. They are means of making certain ideas explicit, and ways of categorizing and ordering the world. Although often used by the powerful, they are not always grounded in violence.

This is why laws also have a habit of being turned back against the powerful by those who seek to resist their activities. The 'rule of law' may have acquired something of a tarnished image in the modern world, often seeming little more than a fiction invented by the powerful to legitimize their status or justify their interference in other parts of the world. But it is an idea with an ancient history, which recognizes the ability of laws to constrain power. In his analysis of the eighteenth-century 'Black Act', E. P. Thompson (1975) famously described how the new legislation enabled the English gentry to strengthen their purchase upon power, allowing them to prosecute those who encroached on their newly established landed estates. The law defined and consolidated their landholdings at the expense of the peasants who had formerly depended upon the use of common lands for their subsistence. It was an 'atrocious' piece of legislation. However, as Thompson also recognizes, it was inherent in the very nature of the medium that the gentry had used for their self-defence, that it could not be reserved for the exclusive use of their own class. The law, in all its forms and traditions, entailed principles of equity and universality which, as he puts it, had to be extended to all sorts and degrees of men (1975: 264). Tenants, serfs, and peasants could, on occasion, use the law in their own interests. Thompson ends his analysis with a discussion of the paradoxes of the law: it provides ideological and instrumental support for rulers, he says, but law and justice are ideal aspirations which must pretend to absolute validity if they are to exist at all. Even the 'atrocious' Black Act could not wholly undermine this ideology, and its legacy was the vision of an ideal, an aspiration towards the universal values of law (1975: 267).

We find a similar ambiguity about the role of law, or at least about the role of the law-maker, in some of the earliest surviving examples of written legal codes. Hammurabi, king of Babylon, was the most powerful ruler in Mesopotamia when he ordered that his laws be inscribed on a black basalt stone in 1754 BC, or thereabouts (Bryce 2016). In the prologue to his laws, Hammurabi describes himself as a king 'who venerates the gods, to make justice prevail in the land, to abolish the wicked and evil, and to prevent the strong from oppressing the weak'.[4] In a long epilogue, the king reiterates his intention to bring justice to his people through the writing of laws, and he directs that every future king should read and follow them: 'so that a man unjustly treated ... [may] read what is written on my stele and may understand my precious commands; that my stele may demonstrate his position, that he should realize his case, that his heart should be lightened'. In fact, the Babylonian empire crumbled under Hammurabi's successors, but his laws were preserved, copied, and recopied on stones placed prominently in public places, and they were used as examples by scribes learning their craft over several centuries (Roth 1995: 40; Wright 2009: 25). They even formed a model for some of the laws in the biblical book of Exodus, probably written down almost a millennium later (Wright 2009: Chapter 4). In reality, Hammurabi was a powerful, ruthless, and war-like king who sacked the cities of his rivals and enslaved their populations, but he regarded the law as an emblem of justice, capable of correcting wrongs done to his citizens and ensuring that truth and justice would prevail under later monarchs. This may have been a project to 'launder brute power in a wash of legitimacy', as the Comaroffs put it, but his claims to be upholding truth and justice could hardly have done the work of legitimation if they did not ring true among his people.

Many of Hammurabi's laws were quite pragmatic, dealing with the sorts of issues that must have arisen among Babylonian citizens in the course of farming activities, commercial arrangements, and family tangles, in a largely agricultural society enhanced by flourishing trade. Writing down rules about how such cases should be dealt with probably did provide useful resources to litigants, even though they are never referred to directly in surviving court records (Roth 1995: 5). By putting people and things into categories, which entailed consequences about status and social relations, Hammurabi's laws promised an ordered society. They made careful distinctions between classes of citizens, expressed in terms of the different compensation to which they were entitled after injuries. They stipulated the consequences of unions between citizens and slaves and what should happen to their children, and they set out the liabilities of negligent farmers and herdsmen. People were categorized in terms of class, gender, occupation, and family position, and the laws represented social relations accordingly. They provided order to Babylonian society by indicating how things ought to be and how people ought to behave. Some rules were highly pragmatic, as they are in the modern world, dealing with property, taxation, and commercial relations, but this is obviously not all that Hammurabi's laws did. They also promised justice. It must have seemed possible, at least in theory, that a citizen could quote one of the laws against a corrupt magistrate or powerful official to prevent exploitation and discrimination. Even the rules that confirmed the status of slaves in Babylonian society promised a form of fairness. They may have reinforced an abhorrent system, but they provided slaves with the possibility of manumission, rights to marry, and some protections for their children, all within a system that took the fact of slavery for granted. The laws provided the people of Babylon with a set of resources through which to make claims to rights and justice.

Laws and legal instruments are techniques, then. Their legalism makes explicit the ideas that can be used to categorize and order the world. In this way, they can be used for good and for bad, by the weak in the name of justice as much as by the strong in the pursuit of power and authority.

Rules and Categories: Particular and General

How, then, do laws and legalism emerge and what is distinctive about them as social phenomena? One of the puzzles of Hammurabi's laws is the particular nature of many of them. I have been talking of legalistic rules as those making general statements about categories of people and events, but some of Hammurabi's laws verge on the particular, almost reading like records of actual cases. A rather touching group of laws stipulates, for example, that a doctor who saves a man's life by using a bronze lancet should be rewarded: for the life of a freeman he should be given ten pieces of silver, for a dependent citizen five, and for a slave he should receive two pieces from the slave's master. But the rules only specify treatment using a bronze lancet. Why not other successful cures? In another section of the code there are several rules dealing with penalties and compensation due after an injury: if a shepherd negligently allows disease to spread in an enclosure, he is to make restitution to the owner of the livestock. However, the law continues, if the loss is caused by an epidemic or a lion, then the loss falls on the owner. But why only lions and not other predators? The laws are quite specific and may reflect decisions in real cases, but they seem to have been chosen because they demonstrate basic principles: unavoidable losses should be treated differently from negligent damage. As other scholars have noted, the rules seem incomplete and sometimes inconsistent (Bottéro 1992: 162; Roth 1995: 4), but many of them are making important distinctions, for example between the statuses of different citizens. We can read particular rules as expressing general principles. Elsewhere, I have analysed the very detailed rules made by Tibetan nomads in similar ways (Pirie 2010). The Tibetan rules on compensation seem unrealistically specific and, as I have noted, they are never cited in actual mediation processes. But they are still regarded as important because they set out and illustrate the application of the sorts of principles that underlie the Tibetans' practices of mediation.

This is evidently how law often emerges in practice, as a movement from the particular to the general. Cheyette (1970, 1978) discusses the development of law in twelfth- and thirteenth-century France, contrasting the changing forms of judicial process. Records from the early part of the period indicate solutions being reached by arbitration and compromise rather than adjudication. The object was overwhelmingly to secure agreement and satisfy honour: in order to broker a compromise, courts and mediators would take into account insults to status and invoke general principles rather than specific, universally applicable rules (1970: 291–5). Cases were resolved without recourse to impersonal rules of law. They were characterized by what Fallers calls 'moral holism'. Notions of law, ideals of behaviour, political rules, and social mores were expressed together as statements about particular people doing particular things (Cheyette 1978: 158–61). The emergence of written laws in thirteenth-century France, Cheyette continues, involved the development of more abstract and objectively definable categories: 'movables' and 'immovables', 'inheritance' and 'gift', 'tenant' and 'lord'. These are categorizing concepts akin to those with which the Soga conducted their more legalistic reasoning. As Cheyette found, the appeal to such concepts was accompanied by the development of rules with atemporal force, abstracted from the immediacy of daily life, from the 'obstinate opacity and multiple referents of individual lived experiences' (1970: 289; 1978: 170). Their atemporality led to what Cheyette calls the formulation of 'a consciously constructed system of verbalized rules' (1978: 163), that is, to legalistic means of thinking and disputing. 'Why did this change come about?' Cheyette asks (1970: 289). It cannot be assumed, as many historians have done, that a court whose decisions are more 'rational' is necessarily more attractive to the people; there is no reason to believe that individuals, any more than their rulers, prefer objective neutrality to partiality in their own favour. Reasons for this transformation must be found in historical circumstances, a mixture of political changes at both royal and local levels, and the establishment of a new court machinery, along with the persistence of Roman legal categories and forms.

Not all people at all times, that is, have turned to legalism as a means to address disputes, seek justice, or order their society. Some quite complex societies, such as those of the Shang and Zhou in ancient China, only began to inscribe laws on bronze objects centuries after they first developed means of writing (Liu 1998: Chapter 1). But when they do, certain patterns recur, as do many tensions. Almost inevitably, it seems, laws and legal processes produce injustice, as legal anthropologists have often documented. It is not only that they consolidate social inequalities, as they did in Babylon and eighteenth-century England. Even the most well-intentioned and carefully crafted laws can fail to produce justice in 'hard' or unusual cases.[5] As Schauer (1988: 447–8) puts it, the generality of the law means that its rules are inevitably both over- and under-inclusive. They capture or omit marginal cases to which the principle enshrined in the rule was never intended to apply. Or the effect of their application is to bring about outcomes that could never have been intended by the lawmakers. The doctrine of *terra nullius*, for example, which was applied with such devastating effect to deprive Indigenous people of their lands in Australia and North America, was devised in a context in which almost all land was subject to some sort of recognized tenure.

At the same time, legal categories can take on a life of their own. If a legal category can be used to make claims to protection, compensation, or status—as, for example, the categories of 'citizen', 'victim', and 'tenant'—it can also shape the ways in which social relations are described and understood, sometimes with problematic consequences. An interesting, and striking, example is offered by Niezen's (2013, 2016) analysis of Canada's Truth and Reconciliation Commission (TRC) on Indian residential schools. This was set up to examine the maltreatment and abuse suffered by many of the children of Indigenous people sent to boarding schools. Although not a judicial process, the Commission was established under legal instruments and collected testimonies from 'survivors' in relatively formal ways. As Niezen (2016: 920) notes, concepts such as 'survivor, 'cultural genocide', 'trauma', and 'healing' became reference points for much of the testimony and for the ways in which the schools were represented. As in forms of human rights discourse, the focus on 'victim experience' created a conception of victimhood which erased the nuances of individual experience, as he puts it. The concept of 'survivor' had become recognized in the narratives that surrounded the Holocaust and the Vietnam War and it became one of the 'axial concepts' for the Commission, along with the examples offered to participants for how to give their narratives (Niezen 2016: 923). This legalism constrained and shaped what was presented and what could be heard by the Commission and, indeed, the wider world. In these ways, the structures and power of the public inquiry influenced the testimony presented to it. Indeed, many of the participants and the survivor groups that represented them were themselves active in the adoption and promotion of these concepts.

The power of laws and legalistic concepts to frame debates and claims to justice should not be underestimated. The nomads of eastern Tibet preserve and refer to laws, probably formulated in the early twentieth century, which are largely impractical. As I have argued elsewhere (Pirie 2010), they represent an ordered world amidst the messy, and often violent, relations between their tribes. Dresch (2006) found similar dynamics in his analysis of historical tribal documents from the Yemen. This explains the puzzle of the many ancient sets of laws into which people must have poured considerable time and resources—like those of Hammurabi chiselled onto a great slab of black basalt—but which seem never to have been enforced. Laws provide a model for how the world can and should be, and ultimately for the ways in which people think of themselves and their status within it.

Legalism in Legal Anthropology

Legal anthropologists have recently explored the world of modern governments, postcolonial states, human rights, global governance, power, domination, resistance, transitional justice, legal pluralism, and complex normative orders.[6] But inspired by Fallers's work, several ethnographers have used the concept of legalism to analyse rules, categories, and legal processes in contemporary settings, often far removed from the influence of state courts and legal systems. In Algeria, for example, Scheele (2014) found that Kabyle villagers carefully create and preserve their own constitutions, with explicit rules and directions about all sorts of village affairs and their relations with outsiders. Meanwhile, farmers in the northern Sahara insist on using the categories of Islamic jurisprudence, although these make little sense in the context of their own property transactions (Scheele 2012). Legalistic rules and categories were prominent in both cases. As I have also described, nomads in Tibet refer to a set of laws, although they do not assist in the mediation of their disputes in any practical ways (Pirie 2010). The tendency towards legalism in the ethical practices of Muslims in the contemporary Middle East has been discussed by Clarke (2015). Legal formalism also caught the attention of Riles, in her study of global financial networks (2011). The form of new financial laws in Japan, she says, had symbolic as much as practical value.

Such disparate studies indicate, if nothing else, the enduring attraction of legalistic rules and categories to different people in different contexts. These include situations in which people turn their backs on the laws and courts of the state's legal system. These studies can be multiplied many times over if we turn to the work of social and legal historians. Often legal records give us insights into the thought and practices of historical times and places, and this is an area in which engagement between anthropologists, historians, classicists, orientalists, area-studies scholars, and others produces fruitful results (Dresch and Scheele 2015; Dresch and Skoda 2012; Kantor et al. 2017; Pirie and Scheele 2014). In this chapter, I have described some of the themes and debates that have emerged in this body of work in order to show how they can help anthropologists address recurrent issues, complementing more recent themes and approaches. Critically, they allow us to explore the nature of law itself.

Conclusion

Human societies are endlessly variable, as are their laws. Some have been the instruments of powerful rulers, enforced harshly on the weak and powerless, while others have been the work of religious scholars or learned jurists, more intellectual than practical pursuits. Some laws have been quite baroque in their intricacy, while others are intensely pragmatic, serving to standardize trading practices and allow conflict to be negotiated across cultural and linguistic divides. The appeal of law in the modern world is hardly diminishing. It is used by power-holders, oligarchs, and dictators, as well as those who would resist them and who turn to legal instruments to voice claims to rights, entitlement, and recognition. But a fascination with law and its appeal in such a vast array of contexts is not a new phenomenon. The 'fetishization' of law is just as striking in medieval Iceland as it is in the heterogeneous societies of the contemporary postcolony.

And people needed to deal with conflict and trade across cultural, linguistic, and religious divides long before the rise of the nation-state gave us the impression that laws should form a rational and complete system within a bounded territory.

General rules present us with principles that often seem to be rooted in some higher power or being. Sometimes this is simply the state and its judicial system, whose higher courts can often hold governments and their representatives to account. This is the 'rule of law' so readily invoked by the champions of modern democracy.[7] But in earlier times, laws might have been seen as rooted in ancient religious principles, such as the Indian Vedas or, in the case of both Christian canon law and the Islamic sharia, the word of God. Hammurabi invoked the Babylonian gods in the introduction to his laws, citing the approval of Shamash, god of justice. In the contemporary world, the principles of human rights and transitional justice are held up as universal, the foundation of laws that should constrain even the most powerful rulers. A combination of these factors must lie behind the symbolic power of constitutions, as noted by the Comaroffs, and our belief in their capacity to bring about just and peaceful societies. Once laws are formulated as general principles, they acquire a life of their own. They present us with the promise of order, invoking what is right and just and offering a language that has at least the potential to hold the powerful to account.

Legalism transforms the verbal representation of particular people, things, places, and events into a world of categories and relations between them. General rules, in this way, take on a life of their own, representing a higher source of authority, providing a language for argument and the promise of justice. In the same way, they can become a tool for the powerful, practical instruments for ordering society—not always for the better—and the means to invoke a higher source of legitimacy. These are enduring themes. Through the study of legalism, using detailed empirical case studies, both contemporary and historical, anthropologists can shed valuable light on the nature of law as a social form.

Notes

1. The English language concept of law, as I have argued elsewhere (Pirie 2013: 8–9), is a 'polythetic' category, meaning that it encompasses a class of forms amongst which there are 'family resemblances' rather than uniform features allowing for precise definition.
2. They note that in recent years, corporate capitalism has sought to create a less regulated environment, which means that neoliberal states outsource many conventional areas of government. This leads both to a rise in litigation, as people try to challenge and control devolved activities, and to the rise of mafias and gangs, which duplicate legal rituals and processes, mimicking the state and 'counterfeiting a culture of legality' (2006: 33–4).
3. Historically, there are many examples of political claims that have been fought out in juridical terms, such as those of the Italian city-states described by Lantschner (2014).
4. The quotes are based upon King (1915).
5. The English legal maxim that 'hard cases make bad law'—often misunderstood—recognizes that when a law, properly applied, will produce an unjust result, a common law judge is

naturally inclined to subtly change its effects, with potentially negative consequences for subsequent cases.

6. Goodale (2017) presents an excellent summary.
7. Oddly, this has rarely been studied explicitly by anthropologists, one notable example being Eckert et al. (2012).

References

Benjamin, W. 1978. 'Critique of Violence'. In M. Bullock and M.W. Jennings, eds. *Selected Writings, vol. I, 1913–1926*, 236–52. Cambridge: Harvard University Press.

Bottéro, J. 1992. *Mesopotamia: Writing, Reasoning, and the Gods*, trans. Z. Bahrani and M. Van De Mieroop. Chicago: Chicago University Press.

Bryce, T. 2016. *Babylonia: A Very Short Introduction*. Oxford: Oxford University Press.

Cheyette, F. 1970. 'Suum Cuique Tribuere'. *French Historical Studies* 6: 287–99.

Cheyette, F. 1978. 'The Invention of the State'. In B. K. Lackner and K. R. Philp, eds. *Essays on Medieval Civilization*, 143–78. Austin: University of Texas Press.

Clarke, M. 2015. 'Legalism and the Care of the Self: *Sharī'ah* Discourse in Contemporary Lebanon'. In P. Dresch and J. Scheele, eds. *Legalism: Rules and Categories*, 231–57. Oxford: Oxford University Press.

Comaroff, J. and J. Comaroff. 2006. 'Introduction'. In J. Comaroff and J. Comaroff, eds. *Law and Disorder in the Postcolony*, 1–56. Chicago: Chicago University Press.

Dresch, P. 2006. *The Rules of Barat: Tribal Documents from Yemen*. Sanaa: Centre français d'archéologie et des sciences sociales.

Dresch, P. and J. Scheele, eds. 2015. *Legalism: Rules and Categories*. Oxford: Oxford University Press.

Dresch, P. and H. Skoda. 2012. *Legalism: Anthropology and History*. Oxford: Oxford University Press.

Eckert, J., B. Donahoe, C. Strümpell, and Z.Ö. Biner, eds. 2012. *Law Against the State: Ethnographic Forays into Law's Transformations*. Cambridge: Cambridge University Press.

Fallers, L. 1969. *Law without Precedent: Legal Ideas in Action in the Courts of Colonial Busoga*. Chicago: Chicago University Press.

Flower, J. 2009. 'Ecological Engineering on the Sichuan Frontier: Socialism as Development Policy, Local Practice, and Contested Ideology'. *Social Anthropology* 17: 40–55.

Goodale, M. 2017. *Anthropology and Law: A Critical Introduction*. New York: New York University Press.

Johnstone, O. 2017. *The Role of the State in the Construction of 'Human Trafficking' in the UK*. DPhil thesis, University of Oxford.

King, L.W., trans. 1915. *Ancient History Sourcebook: The Code of Hammurabi*. Champaign: Project Gutenberg.

Koskenniemi, M. 2001. *The Gentle Civilizer of Nations: The Rise and Fall of International Law, 1870–1960*. Cambridge: Cambridge University Press.

Koskenniemi, M. 2011. 'What is International Law for?' In M. Koskenniemi, ed. *The Politics of International Law*. Oxford: Hart Publishing.

Lantschner, P. 2014. 'Justice Contested and Affirmed: Jurisdiction and Conflict in Late Medieval Italian Cities'. In F. Pirie and J. Scheele, eds. *Legalism: Community and Justice*, 77–96. Oxford: Oxford University Press.

Liu, Y. 1998. *Origins of Chinese Law: Penal and Administrative Law in its Early Development*. Hong Kong: Oxford University Press.

Merry, S. E. 1990. *Getting Justice and Getting Even: Legal Consciousness Among Working-Class Americans*. Chicago: Chicago University Press.

Miller, W. 1990. *Bloodtaking and Peacemaking: Feud, Law, and Society in Saga Iceland*. Chicago: Chicago University Press.

Nader, L. 2005. 'The Americanization of International Law'. In F. von Benda-Beckmann, K. von Benda-Beckmann, and A. Griffiths, eds. *Mobile People, Mobile Law*. Aldershot: Ashgate.

Niezen, Ronald. 2013. *Truth and Indignation: Canada's Truth and Reconciliation Commission on Indian Residential Schools*. Toronto: University of Toronto Press.

Niezen, Ronald. 2016, 'Templates and Exclusions: Victim Centrism in Canada's Truth and Reconciliation Commission on Indian Residential Schools'. *Journal of the Royal Anthropological Institute* 22: 920–38.

Osanloo, A. 2006. 'Islamico-Civil "Rights Talk": Islamic Justice, Sovereign Power, and Human Rights in Iran'. *American Ethnologist* 33: 191–209.

Pirie, F. 2010. 'Law Before Government: Ideology and Aspiration'. *Oxford Journal of Legal Studies* 30: 207–28.

Pirie, F. 2013. *The Anthropology of Law*. Oxford: Oxford University Press.

Pirie, F. and J. Scheele, eds. 2014. *Legalism: Community and Justice*. Oxford: Oxford University Press.

Roth, M. 1995. *Law Collections from Mesopotamia and Asia Minor*. Atlanta: Scholars Press.

Schauer, F. 1988. 'Formalism'. *The Yale Law Journal* 97: 509–48.

Schauer, F. 1993. *Law and Language*. Aldershot: Dartmouth.

Scheele, J. 2012. 'Rightful Measures: Irrigation, Land, and the Shari'ah in the Algerian Touat'. In P. Dresch and H. Skoda, eds. *Legalism: Anthropology and History*, 197–227. Oxford: Oxford University Press.

Scheele, J. 2014. 'Community as an Achievement: Kabyle Customary Law and Beyond'. In F. Pirie and J. Scheele, eds. *Legalism: Community and Justice*, 177–200. Oxford: Oxford University Press.

Thompson, E. P. 1975. *Whigs and Hunters: The Origin of the Black Act*. London: Allen Lane.

Wright, D. P. 2009. *Inventing God's Law: How the Covenant Code of the Bible Used and Revised the Laws of Hammurabi*. Oxford: Oxford University Press.

CHAPTER 18

LEGAL TRANSFER

GÜNTER FRANKENBERG

INTRODUCTION

LAWS[1] neither fall 'from heaven' as lawmakers' ingenious insights nor grow organically from the soil of local culture. While brilliant ideas and context are crucial for the construction of laws, they may be more adequately understood as products of the confluence of information—some local, some that has travelled from elsewhere. In the following, the focus will therefore be on how legal information travels—or as it is described here: how it is transferred. The concept of transfer is meant to make comparatists sensitive to the different ways legal items, such as rights and values, organizational provisions and doctrines, are converted into standardized information and over time become products or commodities on the global or regional markets where elites, politicians, social movements, and legal consultants shop for inspirational legal ideas, 'commanding' constitutional models, efficient bankruptcy regulations, progressive family laws, or mechanisms to cope with corruption already tested someplace else.

Legal transfer is understood here to operate as part of world-making. First, it will be shown how the information needed to design or revise laws is gleaned from foreign contexts, and how it arrives in a new setting not in its pristine form or design but *always already* processed intensely on the way. Second, whether selected with care or haphazardly borrowed, imported in good faith or imposed with brute force, the translation and application of legal information to a new environment invariably presupposes intense modification and adaptation, which is here referred to as 'bricolage' in order to accentuate the aspect of ad hoc tinkering, in contrast to planned, systematic legal engineering (see Lévi-Strauss 1966). Third, it will be shown below that transfer entails considerable hazards. Since the process of transfer is open-ended and unpredictable, the final result never simply brings forth the initial item but reproduces a fragment, cut-out, hybrid, modified copy, or 'pastiche' that imitates the norm, argument, or institution to be transferred. Transfer calls for an analysis that pays special attention to contexts and cultures, risks and side-effects. Fourth, while the process of decontextualization may be read as another globalization story, this narrative receives a critical twist if the focus is shifted to items that resist transfer and call for an answer to why and which kind of legal information remains context-bound.

From 'transplant' to transfer

The concept of 'legal transplant', introduced in 1974 by the legal historian Alan Watson from a basically functionalist perspective (Michaels 2006), has been adopted without much theoretical ado, especially by comparatists with a historical or economic mindset.[2] Yet a return to *The Spirit of the Laws* might curb the career of this surgical term, which hardly complies with Montesquieu's (and other comparatists') observation that '[laws] should be so specific to the people for whom they are made, that it is a great coincidence if those of one nation can suit another' (Montesquieu 1961: 295), or with any comparative style privileging the analysis of concrete cultural-social circumstances over abstract general concepts. Situating the 'transplant' in this field of diverse comparative approaches elucidates its functionalist pedigree and limits.

From a less traditional and more contextual perspective, '[t]he moving of a rule or a system of law from one country to another' (Watson 1974: 20) neither resembles an organ transplant nor captures with passable precision what happens when legal information travels. A transplanted kidney is removed from one body and relocated to another one, whereas a 'transplanted' civil code neither emigrates from one nor settles in a new 'body of norms'. It remains in its cultural setting and is only imitated, adapted, doubled, cloned elsewhere. Hence, 'transplant' is a limping metaphor which invites wonky associations and analogies. First, it obscures just *what* is transferred. Laws and systematics, doctrines and arguments, rights and values, institutions and programmes, degrees and curricula—virtually anything qualifies for travel. However, each item does not migrate *en bloc* qua organ but as text or knowledge, that is *information*. Second, 'transplant' conceals that legal information, when transcending borders between legal systems and interpretive communities, is not reduced to its basic structure (atom-like) but remains layered. It can be described as the layered interplay or narrative of propositions, structures, decisions, mentalities, experiences, case histories, and so forth (Frankenberg 2006; Grosswald Curran 1998; Samuel 2007), a good deal of which gets lost in translation or gets transformed in 'translation chains' (Rottenburg 2009). The fragmentary nature of 'transplants' and the very selectivity of the process are profoundly misrepresented by the organicist analogy. Third, the technical term 'transplant' is based on a doubly formalist reduction: law is reduced to rules and rules are brought down to their propositional content (Legrand 1997, 2001). This way, law is transformed from a cultural artefact to an ensemble of words stripped of most of their contextual connotations. Fourth, in comparative practice, 'transplant' favours the presumption of similarity and projects of convergence. The concept is flanked by a unitary theory of law that guides comparatists to overestimate the (desired) harmonizing effect of 'transplants' and therefore to overlook how even unifying law ends up in new divergences (Atar 2007). Thus, the transplant thesis misses a great deal of law's peculiar properties, that it is produced 'somewhere in particular' (Nagel 1989), and offers instead a fairly uniform and deficient model of how and why laws travel—or why they do not.[3] In short: 'Translations are more delicate than heart transplants' (Panikkar 1982: 75).

In contrast, 'legal transfer' alerts comparatists to a *problematic* phenomenon (Graziadei 2006) that may be 'extremely common' but is anything but 'socially easy' (Watson 1974: 7, 96). Moreover, it supports a more contextual approach that focuses on comparison as practice and a theory of law constituting it as a cultural artefact (Frankenberg 2016). By choosing this term, one dismisses the 'naturalism' of legal transplants as well as the solipsism of the notion of a 'nomadic character of rules' (Legrand 1997). Directing the attention on what happens when transfer happens at least implicitly favours the analysis of differences (Legrand 2001; Monateri 2000; Samuel 2007) rather than the search for similarities (Zweigert and Kötz 1998), and moves away from thinking in terms of congruence and convergence or looking for 'common cores' or 'universal' categories, theories, and histories of law.[4] Finally, transfer captures the *commodity structure* of the exported/imported legal information as a product that comes with standardization.

The grammar of legal transfer (I): Concepts and typologies

As regards laws' travels, a dazzling array of concepts[5] and a remarkable diversity of typologies (Graziadei 2006; Miller 2003; Morin and Gold 2014) coincide with a salient scarcity of explanatory theories. This deficit testifies to (a) the narrow focus on specific events, such as the introduction of company law in Vietnam, the Argentine law on hazardous waste, or the legal protection of investment in Brazil (Miller 2003); (b) a generally descriptive orientation, such as tracing historical paths of influence (Watson 1974) rather than venturesome explanatory ideas or the recognition of contingence; (c) reliance on what 'the author knows best', i.e. the 'settled knowledge' (Popper 1994: 156) covering the domestic terrain with all its 'dangerous incorrectness' (Haraway 1988)—knowledge shaped by experience, habit, familiarity, and lack of curiosity, which is not exposed to further critical and competent inquiry and therefore tilts towards ethnocentric depictions of the foreign as other (Ruskola 2013); (d) reliance on quantitative methods and a spatial lag model to analyse the diffusion and 'presence' of 108 constitutional rights after World War II (Goderis and Versteeg 2014); (e) a combination of all or some of the features discussed above.

Typologies follow—albeit with variations and often implicitly—Max Weber's method of carving out ideal-types (explicitly Miller 2003; Morin and Gold 2014). If one disregards the pitfalls of determining the motivations and intentions of recipients and donors, and suspends the vexing distinction between voluntary and non-voluntary transfers, the following ideal-types plausibly capture dominant patterns:

> *Imposition* characterizes the coerced import of foreign laws in imperialist settings like military occupation or under colonial regimes (Baxi 2001, 2003, 2005; Benton 2002). Japan's MacArthur Constitution (1947) figures as the standard example for direct or imperialist imposition. The rather more common 'indirect imposition' (Morin and Gold 2014: 782) relies on negative political, economic, or other sanctions to ascertain 'voluntary' compliance (Graziadei 2006). In the context of asymmetric international relationships, this ideal-type can barely be distinguished from *contractualization*, when governments bargain with one another about the application of legal rules. 'One state will typically promote its own legal rules as constituting the common standard governing a particular issue-area ... [and offer] compensation or side payments in another issue-area'
>
> (Morin and Gold 2014: 782).

In contrast to externally dictated transfers, *imitation* or *emulation* appears to follow the logic of functionalism that still dominates comparative law (Frankenberg 2016). When legal institutions are confronted with problems, they look for better solutions elsewhere, functionalists tend to argue. Whoever wants to encourage foreign investment might import well-reputed investment protection schemes (such as Vietnam in 1992 or South Africa in 2015; see Stoll et al. 2017). A country coping with a congested criminal justice system might find the US practice of plea bargaining worth adopting despite its evident flaws. Drawing lessons from other countries' experience (Rose 1991) may misfire, though, and does not always turn out to be cost-saving (Miller 2003). For instance, imported legal education projects in Brazil not only failed but actually consolidated the authoritarian regime because they lacked the corresponding liberal ideological frame and institutional basis (Trubek 1972: 47). The controversy over whether *prestige* motivates imitation (Graziadei 2006: 458; Sacco 1993: 148), at least in states undergoing political transformation (Miller 2003), or whether prestige is a largely empty category, need not be decided here. If not prestige, then certainly authority plays a significant role in legal transfer. The French *Code civil* or the German *Bürgerliches Gesetzbuch* were widely considered to be authoritative legal sources. Likewise, the nineteenth-century German professoriate and the elite law schools of the United States served as models for imitation.

Regulatory competition (Morin and Gold 2014) is defined by the adoption of foreign rules and institutions, degrees and expertise in order to improve the position of one's country or oneself in a competitive world. Regulatory regimes or items (notably degrees and expertise) may enhance reputational or instrumental gains, depending on whether they are meant to generate legitimacy (decorating an authoritarian regime with rule of law, like Sadat's Egypt in 1971), procure economic rent (attracting investment, as in Vietnam, see above), or provide social capital and positions of influence, for instance for graduates of foreign masters programmes (Dezalay and Garth 2002).

THE GRAMMAR OF LEGAL TRANSFER (II): MODALITIES AND PATHWAYS

In default of an established methodology, the export and import of legal information may be described in analogy to Edward Said's 'traveling theory' (Said 1983) or in terms of a commodity theory of law (Frankenberg 2013, 2018; Michaels 2013). Said discerns four stages that, if translated into the legal domain according to the rules of the grammar of comparative practice, illustrate the pathways, risks, and side-effects of legal transfer. One can indeed analytically distinguish four moments of the transfer process:[6] a point of origin, the complex decontextualization of legal information, the inclusion in (or rejection from) the global reservoir or market, and finally the thorny recontextualization at the receiving end that involves bricolage and yields a variety of outcomes. The phases or moments of transfer outlined here are not to be taken as a strict sequence of discrete steps but as turns in the many possible pathways for the export and import of laws and constitutions.[7] As a matter of fact, if a set of initial circumstances cannot be pinned down—not even analytically—or calls for extensive (comparative) research or a critique of misleading originalist assumptions, the sequence moving from decontextualization via globalization to recontextualization may have to be reversed.

Initial Circumstances of Transfer

Originalist assumptions should be prudently weakened, though, as the starting point may only 'seem like one'—there is almost invariably a *before*. It is preferable to deprivilege origin and argue it down to a 'set of initial circumstances' (Said 1983)[8] when and where legal transfer could plausibly have begun. The 1831 Belgian Constitution, though widely regarded as one of the leading and original constitutional documents of nineteenth-century Europe, supplies an ironic comment on originalism: the intensive transfer activity of its designers left only 5 per cent of the text that could be classified as 'original', i.e. not gleaned from other constitutions (Frankenberg 2018: 173–6). Similarly, the origins of the French *Déclaration* are shrouded by the plurality of genealogies (Gauchet 1989); incidentally, Korean constitutionalism also attests to the ambiguity of origin (Hahm 2001).

Decontextualization

For the most part, comparatists agree that transfer presupposes that legal items have to be isolated from the formative conditions of their production and processed in order to transcend borders and contexts.[9] In the absence of transfer rules prescribed by an authoritative grammar, *decontextualization* can be circumscribed metaphorically: the items have to be stripped, shock-frozen, and packaged for the transgression of time, space, and culture—or 'skeletonized' (Geertz 2000: 170–2). In terms of a commodity theory,[10] which takes its cues—not its epistemology—from Marxism, decontextualization implies the standardization of legal information as marketable items, a process that presupposes three overlapping analytical operations:

> *Reification* transforms 'live' and contested ideas into objects by divesting them of their historical background, sociocultural environment, and political-legal controversies. Cases travel without their 'case history', rules without their diverse interpretations, and institutions without the background story of their construction. Thus, the 'rights of Englishmen', once reified, migrated as traditional rights or rights reserved for nationals.[11] The German Federal Constitutional Court was reduced to its competencies and institutional structures and exported/imported as a model of judicial review.
>
> *Formalization* reduces norms to bare texts, which is to say to propositional statements bereft of the interpretive debates and epistemic conventions that bestow them with meaning. Likewise, institutions are scaled down to the statutory provisions supplying the propositional state of their organizational arrangement and functions. For example, the prohibition laid down in the 1947 Italian Constitution against 'reorganiz[ing] under any form whatsoever, the dissolved Fascist party' (Art. XII), once formalized, inspired bans on extremist organizations within aversive constitutional schemes elsewhere but did not suppress neofascist temptations in Italy.
>
> *Idealization* transforms the appearance of legal information from *is* to *ought*. Norms and doctrines are presented as actually meaning what they *ought* to mean. Institutions are displayed as operating efficiently according to the official plan. In this way, the idealized object is enshrouded by normativist, ideological, or mythical narratives, such as 'the government of laws and not of men'
>
> (Art. XXX Constitution of Massachusetts 1780).

The long-distance travels of 'We the People' perfectly illustrate the three aspects of how legal information is standardized. Once disconnected from the imaginary United Statesean We, reduced to the propositional content, and severed from its background assumptions, the formula serves globally as a founding myth that elites from Afghanistan to Zaire almost invariably fall back on to enhance their legitimacy as *pouvoir constituant*. Likewise, decontextualization has initiated the transfer of a variety of very diverse items of legal information, such as the systematics of the *Codex Justinianus*, the principle of proportionality, rights catalogues, the concept of 'good faith', curricula and degrees of legal education, courtroom etiquette, and the notion of 'cruel and unusual punishment'.

Globalization

Having been extracted from a specific (local) context, legal information may be transferred to the global space, where lawmakers select from a variety of maxims of design, concepts and arguments, institutional patterns, catalogues of rights, cluster of values, and more. In contrast to narratives of global law and normative visions of a law of humanity (Allott 2007: 63; Held 2004),[12] the global is conceptualized here as a space, turning the focus on the archival aspect (storage centre, arsenal, or showroom),[13] where decontextualized and marketable legal items are registered, stored, and displayed. In contrast, the concept of a global network (Michaels 2013) accentuates the exchange of ideas and services. As a global arsenal (or consciousness), 'legal IKEA' contains the results of myriads of transfers while remaining silent over items not included or rejected. Inclusion and exclusion depend on a threshold test. Once legal information has passed through the three-pronged process of decontextualization and turned into a standardized commodity, it attains the appearance of universal, global, or at least regional applicability ('appearance' meaning that a new coating provided by political technology and the ideology of expertise is grafted onto legal information), and receives from the community of drafters, advisers, engineers, and scholars the seal of quality reserved for the modern idiom and its shiny parts.

While commodified items may look harmless, they are anything but innocent. They may transport colonial baggage, political projects, hegemonic intentions, ethnocentric perspectives, economic imperatives, human tragedies, hopes, and disappointed expectations. A perfect exemplification of IKEA-style globalization is the ambitious Comparative Constitutions Project[14] established in collaboration with Google Ideas. It contains an enormous dataset ready to be downloaded anywhere and anytime. One might call it global bookkeeping of constitutional provisions, digitalized and decontextualized, but it is nevertheless very useful as a tool for further research and interpretation.

Merchants of transfer—political elites, legal consultants, non-governmental organizations (NGOs), scholars, the media, etc.—visit the global showroom (internet) and shop for a complete legal regime or code, or for smaller items, like a rationale for an insolvency law, a balancing test, or rules of plea bargaining. Standardization does not preclude the availability of a plurality of models. To deal with race-based discrimination, Bangladesh, India, Sri Lanka, Canada, and other countries have picked different samples on display in the global showroom: they range from equality doctrines to affirmative action to criminal sanctions for discrimination.

In one of the darker corners, autocrats can find varieties of authoritarian constitutions and emergency regimes (Alviar García and Frankenberg 2019; Frankenberg 2020; Ramraj and Thiruvengadam 2009). Unless suffering imposition, customers have the choice between finished products *prêt à porter* and disassembled parts to be reconnected later, or very abstract, inspiring ideas that require a high degree of constructive elaboration.

Once deposited on the shelves of the market, globalized legal items generally refer neither to their (original) production site nor to the production process. Decontextualized and globalized legal information hardly ever comes with sufficient, in-depth background information about the local prerequisites, socioeconomic forces, conflicts, etc. that infiltrate the application of laws and affect the operation of institutions. Globalized items usually do not mention that expertise and experts are needed to set institutions 'in motion' and to guide the application of norms. Unlike medication, they remain silent over risks and side-effects. Where contextual information is or could be available, it is rarely heeded, because legal consultants and reformers operate within fairly rigid time-limits and political constraints, not to mention the constraints set by cultural-legal ignorance and lack of institutional imagination. Customers come to the showroom with an engineer's mindset rather than the disposition of an anthropologist or culture-conscious legal critic.

Recontextualization: Risks and Side-Effects

Finally, at the end of the 'translation chain' (Rottenburg 2009), globalized items have to be *recontextualized*, i.e. *adapted* to a new (host) environment; one could also say turned into the native or ordinary language, i.e. 'vernacularized' (Merry 2009) in their new life-world. There, whatever is being transferred meets with 'conditions of acceptance or, as an inevitable part of acceptance, resistance' (Said 1983: 227). These conditions determine the 'grand hazard' (Montesquieu 1961) of any legal transfer: rejection or recontextualization within the new legal-cultural setting.

Recontextualization presupposes the unfreezing and unpacking of the received items. Thereafter, any imported information is subject to reinterpretation, redesign, and bricolage (Lévi-Strauss 1966).[15] The simple reassembling of the imported parts/information usually does not provide the desired results. A great deal of improvising and experimenting is required when the now fully (or partly) accommodated (or incorporated) idea has to be inserted in the new legal framework and then put to use under the new circumstances by the new epistemic community—courts, governmental agencies, legal scholars, social movements, legal consultants, and more. Thereby, any imported item undergoes a process of transformation 'by its new uses, its new position in a new time and place' (Said 1983: 227), especially because it does not come with a master plan for the efficient functioning of an institution or the smooth interpretation and application of norms and doctrines. Legal transfer is 'a craft of place', performed by craftspeople who reassemble the decontextualized information (Geertz 2000: 167).

The deficit of contextual information accounts for the considerable risks and side-effects. *Immunoreactions* that block the transfer and recontextualization completely are rare but not unheard of. They occur especially under three circumstances: First, the commodified item simply does not make sense in the new setting, because there is no method or expertise in place to decode its message for proper readjustment. Second, the transferred item meets with unrelenting political opposition. This happened, for instance, in 1920 to the plans to transfer the Swiss federal system to (former) Czechoslovakia, and to the export of the US model of legal education mentioned above. Third, immunoreactions are also likely to occur when the operative logic of the transferred items remains obscure or misunderstood and institutions do not even remotely work as expected. Thus, the imported abstract judicial review of laws did not work in postsocialist Russia.

Bad fit is a more common transfer result if the package contains information that cannot be adequately decoded or adapted. Similarly, transfer may qualify as a *missing link* problem if important information for putting a transferred item into practice is not available. Unlike immunoreactions, bad fits and missing links do not create unsurmountable problems but send the bricoleurs either back to the drawing board for institutional redesigning or normative tinkering, or else to the global showroom to shop for additional or different information to accommodate certain existing power constellations or cultural dispositions.

Recontextualization: Results

The open-ended process of de- and recontextualization[16] is likely to produce—not a genuine copy of the 'original' item but—a diversity of results, as is illustrated by the mutations of the 'We the People' formula or the variations of law-rule. At best, the end-product turns out to be a modified replica, a respectful or ironic imitation or pastiche of different styles or models.

It is characteristic of a *modified replica* that one of its elements is changed (or dropped altogether) or another one added while preserving the general sense and logic of the item, like 'We the representatives of the people of the Argentine nation'. The formula turns into a *hybrid* if the imagination of a democratic polity and the invocation of a collective (We)—both yet to be established—are blended with a concept from a different political tradition or context to form a novel type or inspire a new imagination. The post-Taliban Constitution (2004)—'In the name of Allah ... We the people of Afghanistan'—places the imaginary democratic We into an ethnically fragmented setting and combines it with a unifying religious conception. If not for the religious connotation, the notion of an Afghan people would not resonate on the ground.

In the framework of a constitutional monarchy (Cambodian Constitution 1993), assuming good faith on the part of the designers, We the People qualifies as a *naïve novelty* grafting the popular We-rule onto the monarchic I-rule, thus trying to tap the magic of democratic constitutionalism while preserving traditional monarchy. The bad faith interpretation would treat the Cambodian formula either as an ironic imitation or as a respectful pastiche, depending on the framers' mindset and motives.

Defying Transfer, Resisting Globalization

Any theory trying to explain how legal information is turned into a market product and transferred needs to be corrected as far as it suggests that globalization invariably streamlines any legal idea and practice. Comparative studies bring to the fore that not all legal information travels (Frankenberg 2018: 136–51). From a distance, these items appear odd[17] or strange; up close, they remain unfamiliar. At any rate, they defy standardization. Identifying and understanding them calls for a complex hermeneutic that avoids the pitfalls of ethnocentrism and Western hegemony (Frankenberg 2016: 77–112). In comparative practice, odd items have to be brought very close and kept very far away (Geertz 1973: 3–30). Their strangeness has to be deciphered—not domesticated. Unless treated as legal information that is inferior to the kind one is familiar with, i.e. othered[18] (Spivak 1988; Young 1990), these strange items, if submitted to scrutiny, betray the influence of local traditions and experiences and reflect social struggles, political anxieties, and visions.

Identifying 'Odd Details'

Items resisting commodification—odd details—pose riddles. By the same token, it is perilous to identify and analyse them. Rough, unpolished, strange, and withdrawn, they flunk the threshold test to globalization, as it were, because they deviate from global standards and run against what mainstream scholars regard as the orthodoxy and critics as the ideology of 'Western law'.[19] Three categories can be distinguished, albeit tentatively.

Historical idiosyncrasy

History may be an obstacle to marketability if legal information is perceived as being inextricable from the historical situation of its creation. In terms of history, oddity is basically synonymous with obsolete, passé, no longer useful. Its meaning or logic can only be decoded and fully understood within the historical context. For instance, during the revolutionary epoch, constitutional elites put a cap on rulers' stipends to curb *ancien régime*-style luxury and executive greed.[20] Meanwhile, the practice of monetary compensation of officeholders is regulated more discretely by statutory law.

Not only constitutions but also criminal codes and civil codes testify to quite different regulations that are today considered obsolete due to the passage of time. For example, that husbands were entitled to determine their wives' breastfeeding period (Prussian General Civil Code 1794) was very much indebted to the era of patriarchal prerogatives one would now consider out-of-date. Likewise, the differentiated ordinances regulating in great detail the periods and garments of mourning bear witness to a premodern regime of disciplinary mechanisms. 'Quite different' and 'obsolete' may mean, though, that certain practices are abolished, as for instance hideous forms of criminal punishment,[21] only to be replaced by sanctions that appear less drastic and cruel but still cause damage beyond compare, notably sensory deprivation and other practices of 'modern' torture.

Cultural specificity

Legal information is not likely to pass the threshold test for inclusion in the global reservoir if it is (or appears to be) too context-specific, i.e. so intensely bound to its cultural-epistemic environment that it would simply not make sense elsewhere. Disregarding the notorious 'crazy laws' of the states of the US,[22] such items are conspicuously overdetermined by the practices, mores, and idiosyncrasies of the community at the local production site. They encapsulate local knowledge (Geertz 2000), for instance as vernacular entitlements or prohibitions. If practised over time and considered 'law' by the community or relevant local actors, these norms may constitute customary law (Comaroff and Roberts 1981).

Cultural specificity seems to be a necessary condition of constitutional preambles as well as of criminal codes to the extent that they are meant to protect the collective identity. Rwanda's commemoration of the genocide is elevated from the standard accounts, similar to the Iraqi Constitution, which grafts a biblical story onto the commodified 'We the People': 'We are the people of the land between two rivers, the homeland of the apostles and prophets[,] ... pioneers of civilization .... Upon our land the first law made by man was passed' (Preamble of the Constitution of Iraq 2005). The cultural context is encoded in normative aspirations, notably those of constitutions and criminal law,[23] such as the principles of a 'harmonious society' (Arts. 8 and 9 Constitution of Bolivia), the concept of Gross National Happiness (GNH) (Art. 9 (2) Constitution of Bhutan), the obligation of government authorities in the Netherlands to promote saving and 'keep the country habitable' (Art. 21 Constitution of the Netherlands), or legal rules of ethical conduct, like the prohibition on slaughtering cows and calves in India.

Cultural specificity is a particularly treacherous label. Other than the fact that an item has *not yet* been exported or imitated elsewhere after bricolage, there are no reliable criteria to distinguish global(ized) items from legal information that resists the pull of global constitutionalism or globalization in general. The resistant items might travel in a specific region. Especially with regard to cultural strangeness, one is left with the *appearance* of deepened context-dependence, as regards India's epic constitution spanning almost 500 pages, by far surpassing even its lengthiest counterparts (in Myanmar, Brazil, and Papua New Guinea); or the sixty-year gestation period of the 1992 Saudi Basic Law, which directs attention to a specific local, political-religious constellation that is not likely to be reproduced elsewhere. At the intersection of history, politics, and culture, one could locate Haiti's paradoxical provision that 'All men are born, live and die there free and French' (Art. 3 Constitution of 1801).

Political deviance

Unlike historical obsolescence and cultural idiosyncrasies, *rejection* from the global constitution follows a political logic. The showroom remains closed for items that defy, provoke, or subvert the dominant ideology and practice of law-rule and thus the hegemony of the liberal paradigm. Political deviance resists the dynamic of globalist colonization. The revolutionary 1805 Constitution of Haiti challenged the liberal notion of 'colour-blindness' and turned against colonial racism: regardless of their skin colour, all 'Haytians shall hence forward be known only by the generic appellation of Blacks' (No. 14). Conversely, the Jim Crow laws carried forward the institution of slavery by requiring racial segregation in the southern states of the United States until 1965. The infamous 'separate but equal' doctrine justifying this practice[24] was shared by the apartheid regime of South Africa, but would be excluded from transfer today as a political (and historical) oddity. Rather forcefully, Bolivia asserted a 'deviant' political project: 'We have left the … neo-liberal State in the past. We take on the historic challenge of collectively constructing a Unified Social State of Pluri-National Communitarian Law' (Preamble, Constitution 2009). Few other countries, if any, would dare confront the hegemons with such audacity.

Political deviance/resistance has many faces. Apart from institutional designs, like Nigeria's 'peculiar', 'bizarre', or 'irregular' federal system (see Suberu and Diamond 2009), it shows particularly in attacks on the columns of Western constitutionalism: secularity, neutrality, formal equality, and private property. To begin with *secularity*: unless they feature concepts of the divine state or a state religion or church, modern constitutions stay away from the transcendent.[25] After revolutionary moments or in times of transition, political elites take recourse to prefabricated religious materials, however, to buffer and sanctify their mandate as *pouvoir constituent*. They invoke the presence of the Most Holy Trinity (Ireland 1937/2015) or Supreme Being (Haiti 1805), or better yet: the protection of Divine Providence (US Declaration of Independence 1776) or hope for 'the guiding hand of God' (Constitution of Papua New Guinea 1975). On a lighter note, the breeze of transcendence refreshes the traveller in Tonga: 'Since it appears to be the will of God that man should be free as He has made all men of one blood therefore shall the people of Tonga and all who sojourn or may sojourn in this Kingdom be free forever' (No. 1 Constitution of the Kingdom of Tonga 1875).

As long as law, law-rule, and constitutionalism are standardized within the liberal paradigm, socialist legality qualifies as a prototypical political deviant. Socialist institutions, doctrines and ideas as well as social rights are shelved, if at all, in a corner for commodities with production damages. Legal IKEA would hardly display the provision '[that] work is remunerated to its quality and quantity … [and that] the social economic system … has thus eliminated unemployment and the "dead season"' (Art. 45 Cuban Constitution 1976). Likewise, the limitation of daily work hours, a thirteenth salary, and the rules that wages have to be paid weekly and that workers should be granted rest (preferably on Sundays), as laid down in Brazil's 1988 social-democratic Constitution (Art. 7, sec. XV), run against the standard of reality-blindness set by liberal constitutionalism.

The Oddity of a Right to Bear Arms

Identifying odd details meets with the charge that, once again, it is the Global South that produces bizarre laws and needs to be civilized. An analysis of the Second Amendment of the US Constitution might clarify that oddity is also a Northern phenomenon. It is here where history, culture, and politics intersect: 'A well-regulated militia being necessary to the security of a free State, the right of the people to keep and bear arms shall not be infringed.' After allocating competences and installing checks and balances, the

US Constitution, or rather the Federalists, tried to placate the distrust that may befall people in a federal system with the Second Amendment. Who exactly the bearer of these rights should be, and what purpose the arms-bearing was and is meant to serve, has been contested ever since. A grammatical reading privileges the institution of a well-regulated (i.e. trained and disciplined) militia as the point of reference. Bearing arms has distinctly military connotations. Historically, the Second Amendment appears to draw from at least two very different traditions. The institutional guarantee of a militia and the accessory rights of militiamen can be traced back to the Assize of Arms of King Henry II (1181), ordering freemen to provide for arms and military gear. In the practice of the early settlers and the colonial charters, these rights mutated into a duty that all 'able-bodied men' owed to their community.[26] History also offers a reading of the Second Amendment as granting individual rights: the common law right to self-defence, dating back to the 1689 Bill of Rights. Hence, the 1776 Constitution of Pennsylvania looked in both directions and referred the right to bear arms to 'the defence of themselves and the state' (Art. XIII). The US Supreme Court first privileged the institutional reading in several rulings; only recently, with a slim majority in *District of Columbia v. Heller* (2008), has the individual right come to triumph.[27] The very peculiar American way of balancing the military and political power of the people, states, and the nation qualifies as a unique specimen—an odd detail—by virtue of its history and structure, its controversial interpretation, and mainly the myth of the US as a gunfighter nation.

This historical, cultural, and political oddity is not derogated by half a dozen other provisions that carry forward a basically nineteenth-century project: Liberia's Constitution of 1847 follows the communitarian line and defines collective defence as the subject of protection and purpose. In 1853, the right reappeared in the Argentine Constitution as the obligation 'to bear arms in defense of the fatherland and of this Constitution' (Part I, sec. 21). Statutory rules in Switzerland and Nicaragua correspond to this purpose. Article 10 Constitution of Mexico (1917) entitles citizens 'to have arms of any kind in their possession for their protection and legitimate defense, except such as are expressly forbidden by law, or which the nation may reserve for the exclusive use of the army, navy, or national guard', and specifies that 'they may not carry arms within inhabited places without complying with police regulations'. The 1976 Cuban Constitution guarantees the 'right to struggle through all means including armed struggle' (Art. 3(2)), but qualifies it as a right to resistance 'against anyone who tries to overthrow the political, social and economic order'. Article 38 of Guatemala's Constitution (1985) comes close to the individualist reading of the Second Amendment: 'The right to own weapons for personal use, not forbidden by law, in the person's home, is recognized .... The right to bear arms, regulated by the law, is recognized.' Today's Constitution of Haiti (1987) is instructive insofar as it grants every citizen 'the right to armed self-defense, within the bounds of [his] domicile, but has no right to bear arms without express well-founded authorization from the Chief of Police' (Art. 268-1). These provisions send forth several messages: first, in most cases the right to keep and *bear* arms (or the corresponding duty) serves a public purpose; second, as a means of self-defence it is limited to the home; third, the personal use of firearms is generally subject to legal regulation. No other constitution sports the right to bear arms *in public* as an individual fundamental right, thus the comparative view confirms the oddity of the Second Amendment.

Local, regional, global items of law

The analysis of legal transfer and of items resisting transfer is burdened with the difficulty of differentiating, with sufficient certainty, between marketable and non-marketable items, between hybrids complementing and modifying the modern idiom and information deviating from its standard varieties. Instead of overrating categories, the analysis of oddity may turn out to be the domain for clarifying the 'foreign' and how it is related to the own/familiar (Resnik 2015). Searching for odd details may liberate comparative studies from the straightjacket of unitary thinking, challenge the narrative of globalization, and instigate the 'insurrection of subjugated knowledges' (see Foucault 1980: 78–108), that is, of an autonomous kind of juridical knowledge production whose validity does not depend on the approval of the established regimes of thought.

Merchants of transfer

Legal transfer does not 'just happen'; it is promoted by agents and agencies. It is difficult both to specify what they do and to determine who they are. The merchants of transfer are recruited from the 'small worlds' of elites, advisors, committees and commissions, social movements, and NGOs with a legal agenda. They populate the expertise networks within and without academia, parliaments, courts, corporations, and the media in a world of struggle (Kennedy 2016). Their influence should not be overrated, because quite often they see their proposals rejected or revised as they go through recontextualization and bricolage—and because they sometimes get entangled in 'palace wars' (Dezalay and Garth 2002; Ginsburg 2017). Despite the process of commodification, an expert's advice, a 'checklist' or model provided by a consultant, or a draft law or constitution may bend the course of the legal reform, codification, or constitutional debate in a country and manipulate it for the benefit of a hegemon.[28]

The merchants of transfer who populate the transnational networks, tapping the global reservoir as well as contributing to its contents, may simultaneously profess to be 'originalists' and claim to disregard foreign laws and doctrines in their judicial practice. They are people who pursue projects alongside their work of making decisions, securing investment, mobilizing protest, or strategizing foreign policies. Whether operating top-down, bottom-up, or sideways, their legal ideas and arguments usually come as collateral moves, unless of course they are involved in an official capacity in deciding cases, controversies, or lawmaking disputes. Merchants of transfer are likely to regard themselves as experts, yet they are always bricoleurs, too. They may travel as frequent flyers and reside in palaces of global expertise, but in the end they have to 'work by the light of local knowledge' (Geertz 2000: 167).

Notes

1. 'Laws' is used here as a summary of the items amenable to transfer, like statutes, rules, doctrines, principles, arguments, cases, institutions, systematics, etc. I am indebted to Katrin Seidel, Felix-Anselm van Lier, and Marie-Claire Foblets for their thoughtful comments on a previous version.
2. E.g. Horwitz 2009; Mattei 1994; Miller 2003. For a differentiated view: Graziadei 2006; Grosswald Curran 1998; and Monateri 2000.
3. For a critique of the transplant thesis, see Legrand 1997. See also the contributions to Frankenberg 2013 and Frankenberg 2018: 111–55.
4. Even if 'legal transfer' may not put to rest the semantic variety or overcome the polarization of the discursive field. For a more explicit analysis and further references, see Frankenberg 2013; 2016; 2018: 111–91; see also Friedman and Saunders 2003.
5. To name only the most commonly used terms: influence, inspiration, reception, diffusion, migration, borrowing, exportation/importation, adoption, adaption, proliferation, translation, transposition, imposition, octroy, transplant(ation), and transfer.
6. Regardless of whether the material is taken from civil, criminal, or (as for instance in the following) constitutional law.
7. This also means that 'grammar' is not to be understood as a set of prescriptive, systematic rules.
8. This also applies to the constitutional novelties at the turn of the eighteenth century, many of which originated from the works of enlightenment philosophers. It could be argued, though, that the human right to asylum had its origin in the original version of Art. 16 (2) German Basic Law 1949.
9. 'The institutional structures and normative patterns generated in the formative experience of one nation become blueprints autonomous of the particular circumstances of their birth ... ' (Arjomand 1992).
10. For a different description of this process as 'vernacularization', see Merry 2009.
11. E.g. the (Virginia) Act of May 1776, quoted by Swindler (1976: 1083, 1091).
12. For global narratives, see Ackerman 1997; Peters 2009.
13. Depending on the theoretical perspective, it may also be referred to as a global reservoir, showroom, supermarket, or consciousness. See Frankenberg 2010.
14. See <https://www.constituteproject.org/content/about?lang=en/> accessed 17 December 2020.
15. Comprising a series of introductory, adaptive, modifying, improvisational moves that may be translated as 'tinkering' to convey its makeshift, do-it-yourself character. For a theoretically elaborated concept of bricolage as a method of 'wild thinking', see Lévi-Strauss 1966: 16–32.
16. Open-endedness and bricolage are hugely simplified by the transplant metaphor.
17. I refer to them as 'odd details' not to suggest any derogatory connotation, but to stress the fact that they disrupt the global narrative and are in that sense *quite different*.

18. Othering is defined here as a comparative practice in which, through discursive routines of theory and method, foreign laws are perceived and interpreted as inferior to hegemonic (Western) legal regimes.
19. Regarding the ideology or 'white mythology' of Western law, see David 1983: 'As Westerners, we have an ideal: a society is ruled, so far as is possible, solely by law. In French, we write the word "law" with a capital letter .... Our ideal is to have the law reign' (David 1983: 126).
20. French Constitution of the Consulate (1799), Title IV, nos. 39 and 43; Constitution of Haiti (1805) Art. 1 (20).
21. E.g. Ancient Rome: being sewn into a sack with animals and thrown off a cliff; China: death by 1,000 cuts (Ling Chi), banned in 1905; England: drawing and quartering, from 1352 on a statutory penalty for men accused of high treason, abolished in 1867. For more examples see Foucault 1995; Peters 1996; Waldron and Dayan 2007.
22. It is illegal in Alabama to drive blindfolded, in Colorado to keep a couch on the porch, in Delaware to sell dog or cat hair, in Kentucky (for women) to marry more than three times, in Oregon to go hunting in a cemetery, in South Dakota to sleep in a cheese factory, and in Oklahoma to wrestle a bear, to take just a few examples. See <https://graduate.olivet.edu/news-events/news/united-states-crazy-laws/> accessed 17 December 2020.
23. Today's Constitution of Thailand mandates that the 'standard of morality for persons holding political positions, government officials and State officials at all levels shall be in conformity with the established code of morality' (Art. 270).
24. *Plessy v. Ferguson* 163 U.S. 537 (1896).
25. An interesting mélange is provided by the Constitution of the People's Republic of Bangladesh (1972), which proclaims the 'high ideal of secularism' (Preamble and Arts. 8 (2) and 12) and professes to eliminate 'communalism' and 'abuse of religion' to privilege the (secular) state, while declaring Islam as state religion (Art. 2A).
26. See the 1780 Constitution of Massachusetts: 'The people have a right to keep and to bear arms for the common defence' (Art. XVII).
27. *District of Columbia v. Heller* 554 U.S. 570 (2008). Despite J. Stevens's rather well-founded dissent, this reasoning was later pursued undauntedly in *McDonald v. Chicago* 561 U.S. 742 (2010) and *Caetano v. Massachusetts* 577 U.S. 14-10078 (2016).
28. See the analysis of a paradigmatic adviser by Kumarasingham (2017).

References

Ackerman, B. 1997. 'The Rise of World Constitutionalism'. *Virginia Law Review* 83: 771–97.

Allott, P. P. 2007. 'The Emerging Universal Legal System'. In J. Nijman and A. Nollkaemper, eds. *New Perspectives on the Divide between National and International Law*, 63–83. Oxford: Oxford University Press.

Alviar García, H. and G. Frankenberg, eds. 2019. *Authoritarian Constitutionalism*. Cheltenham: Edward Elgar Publishing.

Arjomand, S. A. 1992. 'Constitutions and the Struggle for Political Order'. *European Journal of Sociology* 33: 39–82.

Atar, N. 2007. 'The Impossibility of a Grand Transplant Theory'. *Ankara Law Review* 4(2): 177–97.

Baxi, U. 2001. 'Postcolonial Legality'. In H. Schwartz and S. Ray, eds. *A Companion to Postcolonial Studies*, 540–55. Oxford: Blackwell.

Baxi, U. 2003. 'The Colonial Heritage'. In P. Legrand and R. Munday, eds. *Comparative Legal Studies: Traditions and Transitions*, 46–75. Cambridge: Cambridge University Press.

Baxi, U. 2005. 'Colonial Nature of the Indian Legal System'. In I. Deva, ed. *Sociology of Law*. Eighth edition, 41–83. New Delhi: Oxford University Press.

Benton, L. 2002. *Law and Colonial Cultures. Legal Regimes in World History*. Cambridge: Cambridge University Press.

Comaroff, J. and S. Roberts. 1981. *Rules and Processes. The Cultural Logic of Dispute in an African Context*. Chicago: Chicago University Press.

David, R. 1983. 'On the Concept of Western Law'. *Cincinnati Law Review* 52(1): 126–35.

Dezalay, Y. and B. G. Garth. 2002. *The Internationalization of Palace Wars: Lawyers, Economists, and the Contest to Transform Latin American States*. Chicago: Chicago University Press.

Foucault, M. 1980. *Power/Knowledge*. New York: Pantheon Books.

Foucault, M. 1995. *Discipline and Punish. The Birth of the Prison*. Second edition. New York: Vintage Books.

Frankenberg, G. 2006. 'Comparing Constitutions. Toward a Layered Narrative'. *International Journal of Constitutional Law* 4: 439–59.

Frankenberg, G. 2010. 'Constitutional Transfer: The IKEA Theory Revisited'. *International Journal of Constitutional Law* 8: 563–79.

Frankenberg, G., ed. 2013. *Order from Transfer. Comparative Constitutional Design and Legal Culture*. Cheltenham: Edward Elgar Publishing.

Frankenberg, G. 2016. *Comparative Law as Critique*. Cheltenham: Edward Elgar Publishing.

Frankenberg, G. 2018. *Comparative Constitutional Studies. Between Magic and Deceit*. Cheltenham: Edward Elgar Publishing.

Frankenberg, G. 2020. *Authoritarianism. Constitutional Perspectives*. Cheltenham: Edward Elgar Publishing.

Friedman, B. and C. Saunders, eds. 2003. Special issue of *International Journal of Constitutional Law* 1(2): 177–403.

Gauchet, M. 1989. *La révolution des droits de l'homme*. Paris: Gallimard.

Geertz, C. 1973. *The Interpretation of Cultures*. New York: Basic Books.

Geertz, C. 2000. *Local Knowledge. Further Essays in Interpretive Anthropology*. Third edition. New York: Basic Books.

Ginsburg, T. 2017. 'Constitutional Advice and Transnational Legal Order'. *Journal of International, Transnational, and Comparative Law* 2: 5–32.

Goderis, B. and M. Versteeg. 2014. 'The Diffusion of Constitution Rights'. *International Review of Law and Economics* 39: 1–19.

Graziadei, M. 2006. 'Comparative Law as the Study of Legal Transplants'. In M. Reimann and R. Zimmermann, eds. *The Oxford Handbook of Comparative Law*, 441–75. Oxford: Oxford University Press.

Grosswald Curran, V. 1998. 'Cultural Immersion, Difference and Categories in U.S. Comparative Law'. *American Journal of Comparative Law* 46: 43–92.

Hahm, C. 2001. 'Conceptualizing Korean Constitutionalism: Foreign Transplants or Indigenous Tradition?' *Journal of Korean Law* 1: 151–96.

Haraway, D. 1988. 'Situated Knowledges: The Science Question in Feminism and the Privilege of Partial Perspective'. *Feminist Studies* 14: 575–99.

Held, D. 2004. *The Global Covenant*. Cambridge: Polity.

Horwitz, M. 2009. 'Constitutional Transplants'. *Theoretical Inquiries in Law* 10 (2), available at <http://www7.tau.ac.il/ojs/index.php/til/article/view/720/679/> accessed 17 December 2020.

Kennedy, D. 2016. *A World of Struggle. How Power, Law, and Expertise Shape Global Political Economy*. Princeton: Princeton University Press.

Kumarasingham, H. 2017. 'A Transnational Actor on a Dramatic Stage—Sir Ivor Jennings and the Manipulation of Westminster Style Democracy: The Case of Pakistan'. *Journal of International, Transnational, and Comparative Law* 2: 55–84.

Legrand, P. 1997. 'The Impossibility of "Legal Transplants"'. *Maastricht Journal of European and Comparative Law* 4: 111–24.

Legrand, P. 2001. 'What "Legal Transplants"?' In D. Nelken and J. Feest, eds. *Adapting Legal Cultures*, 55–70. Oxford: Hart Publishing.

Lévi-Strauss, C. 1966. *The Savage Mind*. Chicago: University of Chicago Press.

Mattei, U. 1994. 'Efficiency in Legal Transplants: An Essay in Comparative Law and Economics'. *International Review of Law and Economics* 14: 3–19.

Merry, S. E. 2009. 'Legal Transplants and Cultural Translation: Making Human Rights in the Vernacular'. In M. Goodale, ed. *Human Rights: An Anthropological Reader*, 265–302. Hoboken: Wiley-Blackwell.

Michaels, R. 2006. 'The Functionalist Method of Comparative Law'. In M. Reimann and R. Zimmermann, eds. *The Oxford Handbook of Comparative Law*, 339–82. Oxford: Oxford University Press.

Michaels, R. 2013. '"One Size Can Fit All"—Some Heretical Thoughts on the Mass Production of Legal Transplants'. In G. Frankenberg, ed. *Order from Transfer. Comparative Constitutional Design and Legal Culture*, 56–78. Cheltenham: Edward Elgar Publishing.

Miller, J. 2003. 'A Typology of Legal Transplants: Using Sociology, Legal History and Argentine Examples to Explain the Transplant Process'. *American Journal of Comparative Law* 51: 839–85.

Monateri, P. G. 2000. 'Black Gaius: A Quest for the Multicultural Origins of the Western Legal Tradition'. *Hastings Law Journal* 51: 3–72.

Montesquieu, C.-L. de Secondat. 1961 [1748]. *The Spirit of the Laws*. Paris: Garnier Frères.

Morin, J.-F. and E. R. Gold. 2014. 'An Integrated Model of Legal Transplantation: The Diffusion of Intellectual Property Law in Developing Countries'. *International Studies Quarterly* 58: 781–92.

Nagel, T. 1989. *The View from Nowhere*. Oxford: Oxford University Press.

Panikkar, R. 1982. 'Is the Notion of Human Rights a Western Concept?' *Diogenes* 30: 75–102.

Peters, A. 2009. 'The Globalization of State Constitutions'. In J. E. Nijman and A. Nollkaemper, eds. *New Perspectives on the Divide between National and International Law*, 251–308. *Oxford University Press*.

Peters, E. 1996. *Torture*. Philadelphia: University of Pennsylvania Press.

Popper, K. 1994. *The Myth of the Framework*. London: Routledge.

Ramraj, V. V. and A. K. Thiruvengadam, eds. 2009. *Emergency Powers in Asia: Exploring the Limits of Legality*. Cambridge: Cambridge University Press.

Resnik, J. 2015. 'Constructing the "Foreign"—American Law's Relationship to Non-Domestic Sources'. In M. Andenas and D. Fairgrieve, eds. *Courts and Comparative Law*, 437–71. Oxford: Oxford University Press.

Rose, R. 1991. 'What is Lesson-drawing?' *Journal of Public Policy* 11: 3–30.

Rottenburg, R. 2009. *Far-Fetched Facts: A Parable of Development Aid.* Cambridge: Cambridge University Press.

Ruskola, T. 2013. *Legal Orientalism—China, the United States and Modern Law.* Cambridge: Harvard University Press.

Sacco, R. 1993. *Introduzione al Diritto Comparato.* Fifth edition. Torino: UTET.

Said, E. 1983. *The World, the Text, and the Critic.* New York: Vintage.

Samuel, G. 2007. 'Taking Methods Seriously'. *Journal of Comparative Law* 2: 94–119.

Spivak, G. C. 1988. 'Can the Subaltern Speak?' In C. Nelson and L. Grossberg, eds. *Marxism and the Interpretation of Culture*, 271–313. Urbana: University of Illinois Press.

Stoll, P.-T., T. P. Holterhus, and H. Gött. 2017. *Investitionsschutz und Verfassung.* Tübingen: Mohr Siebeck.

Suberu, R. T. and L. Diamond. 2009. 'Institutional Design, Ethnic Conflict Management, and Democracy in Nigeria'. In A. Reynolds, ed. *The Architecture of Democracy*, 400–46. Oxford: Oxford University Press.

Swindler, W. F. 1976. '"Rights of Englishmen" since 1776: Some Anglo-American Notes'. *University of Pennsylvania Law Review* 124: 1083–1103.

Trubek, D. 1972. 'Toward a Social Theory of Law: An Essay on the Study of Law and Development'. *Yale Law Journal* 82: 1–50.

Waldron, J. and C. Dayan. 2007. *The Story of Cruel and Unusual.* Cambridge: MIT Press.

Watson, A. 1974. *Legal Transplants: An Approach to Comparative Law.* Edinburgh: Scottish Academic Press.

Young, R. J. C. 1990. *White Mythologies: Writing History and the West.* Abingdon: Routledge.

Zweigert, K. and H. Kötz, 1998. *An Introduction to Comparative Law.* Third edition. Oxford: Clarendon Press.

CHAPTER 19

LEGAL TRADITIONS

THOMAS DUVE

INTRODUCTION

THE aim of this chapter is to offer some reflections on the concept of 'legal traditions' as it has been used in comparative law and legal history. For legal anthropologists, the various conceptions discussed provide an inroad into the debates in legal history about the meaning of traditions, including the use of history as a tool to construct identities and claim rights. In this context, H. P. Glenn's concept seems especially useful for an exchange between legal history and legal anthropology. Not only does it affirm the complex evolution of legal regimes often left unexamined in conventional understandings of law, it also offers a better understanding of how societies construct these legal regimes and can assist in deconstructing statements of identity.

In this chapter, 'legal tradition' is considered to refer to two phenomena: the fact that legal regimes are historical processes, shaped and constructed over long periods of time; and that history is used as a tool in the constructive process itself, as a way to give authority and identity to a particular legal regime or culture. As a result, the various understandings of the concept have become important in the formation of normative orders. Four different conceptions are surveyed, although Glenn's construction is considered in more detail. In light of recent appeals to tradition as a source of legal rights, a point on the political uses of the term is briefly discussed. Finally, in the concluding remarks, a possible cross-disciplinary research avenue within legal history and legal anthropology is contemplated.

LEGAL TRADITIONS

It is hard to imagine a normative order without any dependence on or reference to the past. The mere words used in any normative sentence necessarily contain an idea about normativity, about its binding force, about an authoritative sphere, which precedes the reference. Moreover, just like any cultural product, most legal regimes—i.e. institutions, norms, and practices of law—are the result of a continuous construction with a long history. In many cases, the normative orders of a society can be understood as the result of a diachronic process of cultural translation, of normative information being passed on through time, interpreted and adapted to changing circumstances. Wars, disasters, and cultural change can lead to the disappearance of norms, institutions, and practices. New rules might replace older ones. Encounters with other legal cultures, or 'legal transplants', can bring about change. However, the continuous process of adaptation through the reinterpretation of extant or invention of new normative information is rarely disruptive. This continuous adaptation provides both stability and change, resulting in contingent historical formations. If these historical formations have been shaped within a communicative context which provided for a certain degree of stability, often because the space in which the communication took place was considered to be more or less stable, later observers will identify the result as a 'legal tradition'.

However, if every normative order is historically contingent, normative information stemming from the past also fulfils another important function: often, it invests some parts of the mass of normative information in circulation with a higher degree of authority than others. At least since the early Middle Ages, ancient normativity, precisely because it stems from the past, was deemed to be of high authority (and this was the case not only in the so-called Western legal tradition). It seemed to store higher truths, or was simply seen as a privileged expression of a community's identity, and a special means of maintaining its cultural and social coherence. Thus, protecting a community's identity often meant, and in many cases still means, protecting its historical legal regime. In many cases, 'the appeal of tradition is a recurrent theme, even within modern law, along with the invocation of an ancestral law-giver. In such cases the authority of the law transcends that of any known or contemporary law-maker, and presents the author of legal texts as primarily an interpreter of the law, whose task it is to explain or renew an ancient tradition' (Pirie 2013: 106).

Both dimensions—the fact of the historicity of law and the reference to a special authority and normative force of law from the past—are often summarized under the generic term 'legal tradition'. This term has been used widely and variously, in general discourse on traditions and their importance for the formation of normative orders (see *Traditions* below), and more specifically in the writings of comparative law scholars and legal historians (see *'Legal tradition': A survey* below). In this context, one concept stands out and seems especially useful for (legal) anthropology: H. P. Glenn's use of the term 'legal tradition', developed to deconstruct essentialist notions of 'legal cultures' and 'legal traditions' (*Deconstructing 'legal traditions'*).[1]

However, the term '(legal) tradition' has not remained a mere scholarly concept. It has acquired prominence and normative value in the increasing debates about law's response to cultural diversity and in debates on human rights, not least with regard to the rights of Indigenous Peoples in national and international law. Advocates of legal pluralism and multicultural jurisdictions sometimes conceptualize the state as a mediator between different communities that demand recognition for their legal traditions. In some countries, policies of 'reasonable accommodation' between these legal traditions have already been implemented (on this topic, especially with regard to religion, see Alidadi 2017; Foblets et al. 2010). In international law, the ILO Convention 169 applies to tribal peoples whose status is regulated wholly or partially by their own customs or traditions or by special laws or regulations, and the UN Declaration on the Rights of Indigenous Peoples from 2007 equally draws on the term 'tradition'.[2] Moreover, as there is no consensus definition of Indigenous Peoples, legal traditions are an important element in defining them, even more so as Indigenous Peoples' self-definition and self-recognition often draw on tradition. In 2009, only two years after the UN Declaration on the Rights of Indigenous Peoples, the United Nations Human Rights Council passed the resolution 'Promoting Human Rights and Fundamental Freedoms through a Better Understanding of Traditional Values of Humankind' (UNHRC 2009), the first of a series of contested declarations about the value of tradition for human rights law. The resolutions have been seen both as a particularist, conservative reinterpretation of international human rights as well as a means of enhancing the acceptability of human rights and even fostering diversity (on this, with further references, see McCrudden 2015). As a result, in an astonishing confluence, legal pluralists as well as fundamentalists, transnationalists, and nationalists today can be seen to employ the term '(legal) tradition'. So, what does this term mean?[3]

Traditions

While 'tradition' has, at least since Max Weber, often carried a pejorative connotation, suggesting resilience against change and opposition to rationality and modernity,[4] this seems to have changed in the last decades. After a long period of de-traditionalization—at least in the Euro-Anglo-Saxon world—sociologists have begun to observe a 're-traditionalization' in which traditions are simultaneously being abandoned and rekindled. In politics, the appeal to 'tradition' is used as a means of maintaining social coherence in a globalizing world. Often, speaking about tradition is a nationalist or localist rejoinder to perceived external domination and cultural homogenization. In notable synchrony, local, national, and global regimes of memory are explicitly dedicated to tradition-building. They use traditions as a tool in a political discourse on memory which has emerged forcefully in the last decades. In cultural studies and the humanities, theoretical developments like post-structuralism, intertextuality, and praxeology have enriched debates about the weight of implicit understandings, about practices like the accretion of experiences, and about webs of references, all of which contain information stemming from the past, from tradition. For many religions, tradition is a constitutive element of increasing importance in our post-secular age. Religious laws, among other kinds, are interpreted with particular understandings of tradition.[5] As pluralism 'relativizes and thereby undermines many of the certainties by which human beings used to live', variants of neo-traditionalism flourish (Berger 2014: 9, 10). Modern means of communication might turn out to aid the expansion and reinforcement of traditions, just as they could be a deadly threat to them. They render adherence to traditions easier by increasing the accessibility of information, but they also facilitate the assembly of heterogeneous traditions, causing interference in cultural, social, and political systems. Social media thus catalyse, with their specific effects like echo-chambers, filter-bubbles, etc., both the importance as well as the fluidity and fragility of group formation and thus of living traditions (on these specific effects of social media on the formation of groups, see Sunstein 2017).

Legal scholarship is not immune to the increasing importance of tradition, and not only in the form of religious laws, as already mentioned. As part of the 'worlding' of the social sciences and the humanities, the reorientation of their content towards understanding the global in terms of the local (D'Haen 2016), there is a steady stream of books and handbook chapters that summarize the legal tradition of an area or present certain aspects of it. The 'Hindu' and 'Chinese legal tradition(s)', for instance, are sometimes reconstructed in a mode observers would call 'essentialist', in search of 'Hindu' and 'Chinese way(s)', just as Europeans have a long history of creating and affirming identities and drawing boundaries. The intensity of such othering practices has undulated, with noticeable peaks in the 1930s, '50s, and '80s, and since the latter half of the last century in terms of European legal integration as well as, recently, in times of crisis (Duve 2018a).

Notably, some of the most progressive social and legal theories have paved the way for a new appreciation of 'tradition'. Constructivist approaches in the social sciences and cultural studies have emphasized the importance and power of social discourse. The declining authority of formal law, the widespread idea that justifying law rationally is impossible, and critiques of systemic legal thought seem to lend 'tradition' a constitutive function. Performative legal theories and those advocating a postmodern shift from rational-legal authority to 'self-expression' draw on 'tradition'. Reflections on the emerging world order and models of global law see historical encounters between traditions as a source of discursive legitimation for these normative orders. There is much debate about a 'transnational concept of law', where different traditions might merge. More practically, the inadequacy of national legal systems in facing challenges of transnationalization has led some comparatists to suggest that we should complement our legal sources by admitting 'tradition' or 'legal heritage' (*Rechtsüberlieferung*) as a source of law (Bucher 2000). Finally, those who worry about a 'crisis' of our legal systems often propose evaluating previous forms of social organization by their laws, which is to say, evaluating traditions.

'Legal Tradition': A Survey

'Legal tradition' and similar expressions, like 'tradition of regulation', are used widely and variously in academia, mainly by legal scholars coming from the field of comparative law and legal history (for a didactic overview and a list of possible criteria, see Head

2011: 5ff.). Many, if not most, legal scholars draw on John Henry Merryman's *The Civil Law Tradition: An Introduction to the Legal Systems of Europe and Latin America*, which was first published in 1969. Unchanged for nearly half a century, 'legal tradition' is defined in the current third edition (2007, co-authored with Rogelio Pérez-Perdomo) as 'a set of deeply rooted, historically conditioned attitudes about the nature of law, about the role of law in the society and the polity, about the proper organization and operation of the legal system, and about the way law is or should be made, applied, studied, perfected, and taught'. In other words: legal traditions are understood as historical perceptions that underpin modern law. To know them seems important because 'the legal tradition relates the legal system to the culture of which it is a partial expression. It puts the legal system into cultural perspective' (Merryman 1969: 2; Merryman 1985: 2; Merryman and Pérez-Perdomo 2007: 2).

Diverging considerably from this, the term 'tradition of regulation' (*Regelungstradition*), proximate to 'legal tradition', appears predominantly in German-language scholarship and studies influenced by institutional history and the history of legal dogmatics. Here, however, it is not usually employed as a means to grasp the context of legal texts. On the contrary, it refers to the fact that legal discourse, as specialized knowledge, can display resilience and even limited autonomy, which renders a study of its diachronic evolution possible and necessary. 'Tradition' serves to explain the diachronic evolution of a legal institution, like the regulatory framework for electing bishops (Thier 2011) and the law of obligations (Zimmermann 1990). It connects different elements of historical regulation over a longer period and represents them as parts of a process of diachronic cultural reproduction. Many of these institutional histories in combination compose what has been called the 'Roman law tradition' or the 'civil law tradition' as a particular set of historical formations.

A distinct and influential meaning of 'legal tradition' was coined by Harold J. Berman in his *Law and Revolution: The Formation of the Western Legal Tradition*, published in 1983 (Berman 1983), one of the most influential historical accounts of Western legal history.[6] For Berman, it is a particular characteristic of the Western tradition that it is built on 'tradition': 'By "tradition" I mean this sense of continuity between past and future, the partnership, as Edmund Burke put it, of the generations, the looking backwards to our ancestors for inspiration in moving forward to our posterity' (Berman 2000: 740). 'Tradition' thus refers not only to the fact that we are all part of a historically connected sequence that conditions our attitudes; it denotes a habit, a conscious way of constructing society and its law through dialogue with the past, and according to Berman, it is specific to the West.

For reasons of brevity, these examples illustrating three important types will have to suffice. We find, in the case of Merryman and those he has inspired, an unspecific use of 'legal tradition' as a concept comprising a set of attitudes about law that need to be taken into account when analysing legal systems. Embedding individual legal systems in their proper contexts is held to be so important that it is possible—perhaps even necessary—to classify them as parts of a group. 'Tradition' is the common denominator of this embeddedness, which is sometimes referred to as 'legal culture', and it identifies common genealogy as the main criterion defining the group. This usage does not necessarily suggest that the past dominates the present, although genealogy imposes its own constraints on the law. Remember that, for Merryman, traditions are 'deeply rooted, historically conditioned attitudes'. In fact, this interpretation is less interested in history than in its effect on the present, and it comes very close to what others call 'legal culture', which can be grounded on very different theories about cultural evolution and the course of history (on the relation between legal history and comparative law, see Head 2011: 29f.; Zweigert and Kötz 1998: 7–8). The second take on the term differs from this (only seemingly, as should now be clear) 'straightforward approach'—as John Head called it in his book *Great Legal Traditions* (Head 2011: 5ff.)—and refers to the diachronic history of legal institutions. Here, we find a concept used for research in legal history that is primarily focused on institutions rather than contexts and that is more interested in the past as such, even though this kind of enquiry might be motivated by the need to understand current regulation as a contingent product of this evolution. Finally, the third approach links 'legal tradition' specifically to the Western legal tradition. According to Berman, its most prominent advocate, this Western tradition is characterized by a distinct and conscious use of the past to construct its legal system. One might call this a philosophical or, in light of Berman's late writings, even prophetical use of the term 'tradition' (Berman 2003).

A fourth understanding of 'legal tradition' stems from Canadian comparative law scholar H. P. Glenn. He famously authored *Legal Traditions of the World*, a book received enthusiastically by some and criticized harshly by others (Glenn 2014).[7] Glenn's understanding of legal tradition diverges from all those previously mentioned.[8] Glenn developed his reasoning mainly in response to the mainstream of comparative law, which drew on macro-concepts identified with a certain space, like legal families and legal cultures (Glenn 2006a). Merryman was one representative of the mainstream; Konrad Zweigert, Hein Kötz, and René David counted among the others. For Glenn, these concepts served a useful purpose 'in a time of radical legal nationalism' to remind jurists 'of forms of belonging which the state could not encompass, or avoid'. They were part of what he calls the 'taxonomic project' of Western comparative law (Glenn 2006a: 422–3). Global studies today would call it a 'container approach'. According to Glenn, the taxonomic project was formulated from the perspective of nation-states. It was political, ideological, fixated on national legislation, static, essentialist, and blind to all other modes of transversal normativity. It was based on an insufficient binary logic, and it used dysfunctional, rigid categories. It enshrined a positivist vision of one particular tradition, the Western, and was grounded on the assumption that the existence of states, with their systemic closure against other nation-state systems, was a natural fact or a 'reflection of underlying and definite truths' (Glenn 2010: 609). For Glenn, moreover, it failed as a project because it did not develop legal reasoning for today and tomorrow, a legal order for an interconnected world with accelerated communication and mobility, growing transnational law, and increasingly conflictual relations among adherents of different identities (Glenn has clearly outlined his vision of the comparative law discipline in Glenn 2006a, 2012). As we can see, Glenn harshly criticized the analytical tradition of his discipline, especially the essentialist versions of 'legal culture' and the underlying imperialist notions in academic vocabulary, with his own thoughts influenced by the philosophy of science and critical legal, postcolonial, and postmodern approaches. Not surprisingly, his critique reveals some of his own aims, as a closer look at his concept of 'legal traditions' shows.

Deconstructing 'Legal Traditions'

For Glenn, tradition is simply information, a 'loose conglomeration of data, organized around a basic theme or themes' (Glenn 2014: 16). Legal tradition, thus, is normative information. To become 'legal tradition', the normative information must have been 'captured' in a first transformative moment (Glenn 2014: 7).[9] Once captured, that information goes on to be selected and appropriated in a continuous and dynamic process. 'A living tradition thus functions by way of the continual reflexive process, through looping or feedback' (Glenn 2006a: 428). An example of this process is quite visible in common law systems. Here, the decisions laid down by a court judge must conform to the prescriptions of the current legal tradition. The decision-making process captures normative information in adherence to that tradition, but also serves to (re)instate the meaning of that tradition. That is to say, when these court decisions become precedent, they contribute to and form part of the legal tradition itself, and the judge must make his or her next decision in accordance with the now enhanced scope of that tradition. The same can be said for the different layers of normative knowledge produced by the Church, collected in collections of canons, reassembled according to the necessity of its time by bishops or canonists. Legal history can be seen as a continuous process of diachronic intertextuality. Because of this continuous feedback, any tradition 'bears within itself the seed of diversity or, more radically, change' (Glenn 2014: 30), resulting in a 'remarkable process of oscillation between stability and variation' (Glenn 2006a: 429). This process gains its dynamism through continuous, but ultimately unsuccessful, attempts to achieve 'closure'. The grandest and most successful closure in history is the modern Western state and its specific techniques of controlling the sources of law. For Glenn, the modern state is 'an informational node within a larger body of normative information, or more precisely, legal tradition' (Glenn 2006b: 468). However, the 'system of the state cannot tolerate the possibility of other systems within it; this is the nature of systemic thinking. The system necessarily controls the interacting elements which compose it' (Glenn 2014: 54–5). Notwithstanding the flourishing of such legal systems in much of the world throughout the nineteenth and twentieth centuries, Glenn is convinced that these attempts at closure are only 'rarely successful', because 'there is no regress stopper in the face of informational challenge, whether internal or external' (Glenn 2013: 707). In the long run, closure caps dynamism, and closed legal systems implode under the pressure of adaptation. This pressure is caused by their internal diversity, which results from the fact that, according to Glenn, all major legal traditions have been incorporating 'multiple internal and lateral traditions which are not consistent with each other and which may not even be consistent with the leading version of the major tradition' (Glenn 2014: 367). The accessibility of these divergent options and their 'persuasive authority' inevitably cause transformation.

The internal dynamics described by Glenn as 'looping', the selection and mutation, are further enhanced by the fact that every legal tradition interacts constantly with others (Glenn 2014: 33). Even the slightest contact with another tradition implies a variation in the information base of the initial tradition. As soon as different traditions come into contact, a process of accommodation starts. 'If something is known to be out there, it is already in here. The simple existence of information derived from another complex tradition thus blurs the distinction between the two traditions' (Glenn 2014: 374). While this alone is reason enough to suggest that no contact is without consequences, exchange and mutual adaptation are further facilitated by structural similarities that Glenn sees at work in all major legal traditions, like casuistry and a common tendency to produce interaction between local, particular, and common laws. 'In today's world there are therefore no pure identities of tradition' (Glenn 2014: 34). It is this critical and constructive perspective which renders Glenn's approach so important for legal anthropology, opening its eyes to the role of legal traditions as catalysts for continuously evolving, diverse bodies of normativity.

A concern with this constructivist perspective of tradition in the anthropological literature has become increasingly evident since the 1980s.[10] No comprehensive comment on its extensive treatment can be attempted here, but a cursory glance reveals a theoretical distinction between genuine, authentic, in some sense unconscious traditions on the one hand and 'invented' traditions on the other (these are claims to traditions consciously invoked for symbolic, political, or commercial agendas and with or without historical continuity).[11] This narrow understanding of the constructed nature of traditions, taxonomic in its own way, remains a point of enquiry in the anthropological literature, but seems not to have held fast—or at least constructivism seems generally to be taken for granted.[12] Legal anthropology in particular has rather focused, for example, on reviving a concept of culture that includes 'tradition' as a major property in order to counter the Eurocentrism implicit in categorizing societies as legal or non-legal (Assier-Andrieu 2019), or on analysing the way conceptions of tradition are shaped through legal discourse in the context of the courtroom (Richland 2008).

The usefulness of Glenn's concept for the exchange between legal history and legal anthropology, however, lies not only in the parallel understanding that legal traditions are never anywhere truly 'genuine' (and here we may enquire into the concept of 'tradition' itself as it has been historically formulated in anthropology, that is to say, into the tradition of tradition),[13] but also in the shared acknowledgement of the integration and coexistence of conflicting norms and identities. An appreciation of this diversity prevents a taxonomic view of traditions, but also complicates statements of identity. Thus, one area in which we can see its value for both disciplines is in the legal recognition of Indigenous rights (see on this Duve 2018b). Legal anthropological conceptions about tradition can influence legal claims concerning Indigenous rights. Because Glenn's concept is sensitive to the complexity, to the 'impurity' of these identities, it provides a meeting point from which legal historians and legal anthropologists can communicate and develop insights that better understand, not to say deconstruct, the way in which people and institutions assert their legal rights as well as (here touching on the broader research possibilities for both disciplines) how they shape their normative regimes.

Returns: 'Legal Tradition' As a Defining Part of a Group's Self-identification

In this context, it is interesting to observe that at the same time that legal theory, cultural studies, and social science have been deconstructing essentialist ideas about (legal) traditions and questioning the idea of 'purity', international law and political action have contributed to a new proliferation of notions of legal traditions, not least through the recognition of diversity and limited legal autonomy for Indigenous Peoples. Not all of these notions escape the danger of essentialism. Thus, the use of the terms 'tradition', 'traditional values', and 'legal tradition' is highly contested, as shown by the debate on the use of 'tradition' in the context of Indigenous Peoples' rights.[14]

An important step in this process was the International Labour Organization's adoption of Convention 169, 'Indigenous and Tribal Peoples Convention', in 1989 (ILO 1989: C169; for a more extensive discussion, see Duve 2018b). ILO 169 made history and (legal) traditions a central argument in claiming the status and the attendant legal privileges of being recognized as 'Indigenous People'. Namely, the Convention applies to 'tribal peoples in independent countries whose social, cultural and economic conditions distinguish them from other sections of the national community and whose status is regulated wholly or partially by their own customs or traditions or by special laws or regulations'; and to 'peoples in independent countries who are regarded as indigenous on account of their descent from the populations which inhabited the country ... at the time of conquest or colonisation or the establishment of present state boundaries and who, irrespective of their legal status, retain some or all of their own social, economic, cultural and political institutions'. Similarly, the UN General Assembly adopted the UN Declaration on the Rights of Indigenous Peoples in 2007 (UNGA 2007: A/RES/61/295), which elevated a group's self-identification, its traditions, and historical identity formation, to the level of a fundamental consideration in determining its status.

This UN Declaration is the culmination of a long process in which Indigenous Peoples' rights have gained recognition on an international level as well as on the level of many national constitutions (Anaya 2005; Bengoa 2007; for a good introduction to Indigenous Peoples in international law, see Tomaselli 2016: 31–59). The emergence of indigeneity as a global identity during the Cold War, along with new communications technologies and greater sensitivity to the value of biological and cultural diversity, has provided Indigenous Peoples with new opportunities to generate and respond to public attention (on the performance of indigeneity, see Graham and Penny 2014). The various forms of *indigenismos* (Tarica 2016) and (re-)indigenization processes, for example in Latin America, have their own histories, rooted even in earlier periods (see e.g. de la

Cadena 2003; Earle 2007). However, they are facets of a phenomenon that extends beyond national borders (on the US, see e.g. Wilkins 2013), one that is inseparably bound to a global trend of addressing past injustices and the underlying global regimes of memory (Clifford 2013; Rousso 2015), enabling Indigenous Peoples to live according to their legal traditions.

It is for this reason that more than a few observers are increasingly worried about a process of essentializing the identities, traditions, and practices of groups that have succeeded in establishing themselves as relevant actors, not least by reconstructing their own legal traditions. Since Indigenous Peoples are usually identified genealogically, the conservation of their social practices, customs, and traditions as well as their self-identification—as, for example, in ILO 169—bears a certain danger of 'freezing differences' (Costa 2012) in the sense of creating seemingly stable historical identities through law (Kuper 2003). Another reason for concern is that, in order to obtain recognition as Indigenous Peoples, cultural stereotypes and preferences often prevail that romanticize and exoticize their referents or perpetuate and privilege other cultural patterns (for a survey of this debate and its problems relating to Brazil, see Carneiro da Cunha and Almeida 2000). Thus, on the one hand, Indigenous Peoples run the risk of becoming trapped in their own constructed pasts without the opportunity to develop them productively. On the other hand, other groups demanding autonomy then run the risk of their demands being ignored or even of their protests being criminalized. Moreover, in cases where Indigenous Peoples' rights have been affirmed through the recognition of their distinct legal traditions, the actual desire to restore historical tradition was not always the driving force behind the process. Not infrequently, the result was a simple calculation as to how to grant more autonomy to groups that successfully asserted their claims in a political debate.

Concluding remarks

European and Western law have a long history of building their normative orders on normative information stemming from the past. With the writing of legal texts since late Antiquity and their appropriation and cultural translation in the Middle Ages, together with the development of regional and later national legal cultures, legal history has rightly been understood as a great diachronic process of intertextuality. Since the nineteenth century—the era of the formation of national legal systems and, at the same time, the era of the globalization of law and legal thought—there has been a tendency to understand and describe regional developments as legal traditions.

In the late nineteenth century, European and US-American authors began to emphasize the peculiarity of the European or Western legal tradition and to regard it as exemplary for the whole world. This understanding formed part of a civilizing mission. Based on a wide range of very different ideological motives, it seemed a question of time until the superior Christian, Western legal culture would prevail. Those peoples which still practised their 'Indigenous' laws were not even seen to have a 'legal tradition'; they simply had 'customs'. In a certain way, the modernization theories of the second half of the twentieth century were just another variation of this nineteenth-century civilizing mission, which was intimately connected to European colonialism. Drawing on the writings of Max Weber, one could fall back on a scientifically founded, clear distinction of a European or occidental legal culture. Even today, despite all the criticism of Weber's construction of the West as a clearly distinguishable cultural sphere, the ideas underlying his view are still foundational for the great narratives of a unique 'Western legal tradition' (see on this Duve 2018a).

This division of the world into clearly distinguishable legal traditions, which arose from the need for order and taxonomy and was shaped by certain implicit or explicit philosophical assumptions, has been increasingly criticized during the last decades. Since the 1970s—not least in the context of the work of the Commission on Legal Pluralism, founded in 1969—legal anthropologists have increasingly turned to non-state law and its relationship to state law (Moore 1973). Processes of decolonization made the pluralist texture of law more visible; the political and intellectual upheavals of these years gave strength to the analyses. It was in the 1980s that John Griffiths in his famous essay 'What is Legal Pluralism?' defined legal pluralism as 'the presence in the social field of more than one legal order' or as 'that state of affairs, for any social field, in which behaviour pursuant to more than one legal order occurs' (Griffiths 1986: 1, 2). Two years later, Sally Engle Merry's similarly much-quoted analysis followed (Merry 1988). Legal pluralism seemed nearly the standard case, and thus the idea of homogenous legal traditions came under pressure.

It was also in the 1970s that the first (legal) historical works that explicitly spoke of 'legal pluralism' appeared on the European continent (see e.g. the contributions in Gilissen 1972). Since then, and more clearly since the 2000s, (legal) historians have been discovering legal pluralism almost everywhere—in the early modern Atlantic and Pacific, in the Ottoman Empire, in Asia, in Africa, in Europe. They find overlapping jurisdictions, unclear and deliberately open jurisdictional competences, and the resulting juridical practices wherever they look. These historical findings, as well as the postcolonial critique, the admission of non-legalistic and non-state-bound concepts of law, and more sensitive ideas about the evolution of law in cultural studies and legal theory, have led to a lively critique of the traditional idea of legal traditions as 'closed' concepts and opened up new perspectives. 'Legal traditions' are now increasingly understood as a product of a long-standing diachronic process of communication—isolated from the chaotic mass of historical normativity by later observers, but by no means pure and clearly delimited from each other. They say more about those who construct them than about the historical path-dependencies, which are much more complex evolutionary processes.

Interestingly, efforts to take diversity into account in international law, especially with regard to the rights of Indigenous Peoples, together with some societal developments mentioned at the beginning of this text, have led to a certain revitalization of essentialist notions of legal traditions. In view of this, it should be the permanent task of legal historians to point out the complexity of the evolution of law, the manifold processes of exchange, and thus also the constructed character of 'legal traditions'. These insights, this acknowledgement of diversity, mark a point from which legal historians and legal anthropologists can open common research avenues, tracing how not only legal traditions, but the social processes and identities co-constituted by those legal traditions, are shaped.

NOTES

1. Recently in legal anthropology, Glenn has been praised precisely for not perpetuating a Western, taxonomic approach to categorizing Indigenous societies, see Assier-Andrieu 2019: 6.
2. For an overview of the definition of Indigenous Peoples as communities 'having a historical continuity with pre-invasion and pre-colonial societies' (Commission on Human Rights, Sub-Commission on Prevention of Discrimination and Protection of Minorities, 1983), and of the application of ILO 169 (1989) to 'tribal peoples … whose status is regulated wholly or partially by their own custom or traditions' and to 'peoples … who are regarded as indigenous on account of their descent from the populations which inhabited the country', along with further criteria developed during the preparation of the UN Declaration, see Allen and Xanthaki 2011; Tomaselli 2016: 32–9.
3. The following parts on 'traditions' and 'legal tradition' draw on Duve 2018c.
4. For a good summary of the history of the concept, see the entry in *Geschichtliche Grundbegriffe*, Wiedenhofer 1990; and Steenblock 1998. For a general overview from the perspective of constitutional law, see Leisner 2013. On tradition from an anthropological perspective, see Bauman 2015.
5. In the case of the *Codex Iuris Canonici*, the *traditio canonica* is even included in the codification itself. See canon 6 § 2; and Pree 1995.
6. The first book was followed by a second entitled *Law and Revolution, II. The Impact of the Protestant Reformations on the Western Legal Tradition* (Berman 2003). On the significance of Berman, see the contributions in Duve 2013.
7. In 2006, the *Journal of Comparative Law* dedicated a special issue to debating this book under the title 'A Fresh Start for Comparative Legal Studies? A Collective Review of Patrick Glenn's *Legal Traditions of the World*, Second Edition'. For an account of the criticism and further review, see Foster 2006; Glenn answered this criticism in Glenn 2007; a rejoinder to Glenn appeared in Halpin 2007. On Glenn's work, see also Hasegawa 2016; Husa 2015: 223ff.; Kischel 2015: 158ff.
8. On Glenn's vision of Berman, see Glenn 2010. On his vision of the concept of legal culture, see Van Hoecke 2006.
9. 'A present past is one which has been captured, in a way which allows present use and present, further, transmission' (Glenn 2014: 7).
10. This and the following paragraph were written by Alexandra Woods.
11. See Handler and Linnekin 1984; Hobsbawm and Ranger 1983; Linnekin 1983. For an overview of the literature inspired by this distinction, see Briggs 1996; Turner 1997.
12. Understanding tradition as historically constructed, as a process more broadly, was indeed never dependent on the distinction. Jean Pouillon writes in 1971 e.g. that the typical expression 'We do this because our grandfathers did the same thing' reflects 'the

consciousness of the group of [the tradition's] structured character', but this is 'not to imply that recognising a tradition is the same as inventing it' (Pouillon 1971: 78). For tradition as a process, see Bauman 2015; Gailey 1989; Shanklin 1981.

13. For an example of this, see Lambek 2011.
14. On the similarly interesting debate on 'traditional values' in international human rights law, see McCrudden 2015.

References

Alidadi, K. 2017. *Religion, Equality and Employment in Europe. The Case for Reasonable Accommodation*. Oxford: Hart Publishing.

Allen, S. and A. Xanthaki. 2011. *Reflections on the UN Declaration on the Rights of Indigenous Peoples*. Oxford: Hart Publishing.

Anaya, J. S. 2005. *Los pueblos indígenas en el derecho internacional*. Madrid: Editorial Trotta.

Assier-Andrieu, L. 2019. 'Difficulté et nécessité de l'anthropologie du droit'. In F. Audren and L. Guerlain, eds. *Droit et anthropologie. Archéologie d'un savoir et enjeux contemporains*, available at <https://www.cliothemis.com/IMG/pdf/ASSIER_ANDRIEU-2.pdf> accessed 19 December 2020.

Bauman, R. 2015. 'Tradition, Anthropology of'. In J. D. Wright, ed. *International Encyclopedia of the Social & Behavioral Sciences*, 503–7. Amsterdam/Oxford/ Waltham: Elsevier.

Bengoa, J. 2007. *La emergencia indígena en América Latina*. México: Fondo de Cultura Económica.

Berger, P. L. 2014. *The Many Altars of Modernity. Toward a Paradigm for Religion in a Pluralist Age*. Berlin/Boston: De Gruyter.

Berman, H. J. 1983. *Law and Revolution. The Formation of the Western Legal Tradition*. Cambridge: Harvard University Press.

Berman, H. J. 2000. 'The Western Legal Tradition in a Millennial Perspective: Past and Future'. *Louisiana Law Review* 60(3): 739–63.

Berman, H. J. 2003. *Law and Revolution. The Impact of the Protestant Reformations on the Western Legal Tradition*. Cambridge: Harvard University Press.

Briggs, C. L. 1996. 'The Politics of Discursive Authority in Research on the "Invention of Tradition"'. *Cultural Anthropology* 11: 435–69.

Bucher, E. 2000. 'Rechtsüberliefung und heutiges Recht'. *Zeitschrift für Europäisches Privatrecht* 8(75): 394–543.

de la Cadena, M. 2003. *Indigenous Mestizos: The Politics of Race and Culture in Cuzco, Peru, 1919–1991*. Durham: Duke University Press.

Carneiro da Cunha, M. and M. W. B. de Almeida. 2000. 'Indigenous People, Traditional People, and Conservation in the Amazon'. *Daedalus* 129 (2): 315–38.

Clifford, J. 2013. *Returns: Becoming Indigenous in the Twenty-First Century*. Boston: Harvard University Press.

Costa, S. 2012. 'Freezing Differences: Politics, Law, and the Invention of Cultural Diversity in Latin America'. In A. Mascareño and K. Araujo, eds. *Legitimization in World Society*, 139–56. Farnham: Ashgate Publishing Limited.

D'Haen, T. 2016. 'Worlding the Social Sciences and Humanities'. *European Review* 24(2): 186–99.

Duve, T. 2013. 'Law and Revolution—Revisited'. *Rechtsgeschichte—Legal History* 21: 156–9.

Duve, T. 2018a. 'Global Legal History: Setting Europe in Perspective'. In H. Pihlajamäki, M. D. Dubber, and M. Godfrey, eds. *The Oxford Handbook of European Legal History*, 115–39. Oxford, New York: Oxford University Press.

Duve, T. 2018b. 'Indigenous Rights. Latin America'. In M. D. Dubber and C. Tomlins, eds. *The Oxford Handbook of Legal History*, 817–37. Oxford: Oxford University Press.

Duve, T. 2018c. 'Legal Traditions. A Dialogue between Comparative Law and Comparative Legal History'. *Comparative Legal History* 6(1): 15–33.

Earle, R. 2007. *The Return of the Native: Indians and Myth-Making in Spanish America, 1810–1930*. Durham/London: Duke University Press.

Foblets, M.-C., J.-F. Gaudreault-Desbiens, and A. Dundes Renteln, eds. 2010. *Cultural Diversity and the Law. State Responses from Around the World*. Brussels/Québec: Bruylant and Éditions Yvon Blais.

Foster, N. H. D., ed. 2006. 'A Fresh Start for Comparative Legal Studies? A Collective Review of Patrick Glenn's *Legal Traditions of the World*'. Second edition. *Journal of Comparative Law* 1(1): 100–99.

Gailey, A. 1989. 'The Nature of Tradition'. *Folklore* 100(2): 143–61.

Gilissen, J. 1972. *Le pluralisme juridique*. Brussels: Éditions de l'Université de Bruxelles.

Glenn, H. P. 2006a. 'Comparative Legal Families and Comparative Legal Traditions'. In M. Reimann and R. Zimmermann, eds. *The Oxford Handbook of Comparative Law*, 421–40. Oxford: Oxford University Press.

Glenn, H. P. 2006b. 'Transnational Common Laws'. *Fordham International Law Journal* 29(3): 457–71.

Glenn, H. P. 2007. 'Legal Traditions and *Legal Traditions*'. *Journal of Comparative Law* 2(1): 69–87.

Glenn, H. P. 2010. 'A Western Legal Tradition?' *Supreme Court Law Review* 49: 601–18.

Glenn, H. P. 2012. 'The Aims of Comparative Law'. In J. Smits, ed. *Elgar Encyclopedia of Comparative Law*, 65–74. Cheltenham/Northampton, MA: Edward Elgar.

Glenn, H. P. 2013. 'The State as Legal Tradition'. *Cambridge Journal of International & Comparative Law* 2(4): 704–14.

Glenn, H. P. 2014. *Legal Traditions of the World. Sustainable Diversity in Law*. Oxford/New York: Oxford University Press.

Graham, L. R. and H. G. Penny. 2014. *Performing Indigeneity. Global Histories and Contemporary Experiences*. Lincoln: University of Nebraska Press.

Griffiths, J. 1986. 'What Is Legal Pluralism?' *The Journal of Legal Pluralism and Unofficial Law* 18(24): 1–55.

Halpin, A. 2007. 'A Rejoinder to Glenn'. *Journal of Comparative Law* 2(1): 88–93.

Handler, R. and J. Linnekin. 1984. 'Tradition, Genuine or Spurious'. *Journal of American Folklore* 97(385): 273–90.

Hasegawa, K. 2016. 'A Glance at the Dynamics of "Confluence" in a Legal System—Notes on H. Patrick Glenn's Insights Concerning *Legal Traditions of the World*'. *Transnational Legal Theory* 7(1): 1–8.

Head, J. W. 2011. *Great Legal Traditions. Civil Law, Common Law, and Chinese Law in Historical and Operational Perspective*. Durham: Carolina Academic Press.

Hobsbawm, E. J. and T. O. Ranger. 1983. *The Invention of Tradition*. Cambridge: Cambridge University Press.

Van Hoecke, M. 2006. 'Legal Cultures, Legal Traditions and Comparative Law'. *Netherlands Journal of Legal Philosophy* 35(3): 331–4.

Husa, J. 2015. *A New Introduction to Comparative Law*. Oxford/Portland: Hart Publishing.

ILO 1989. *Convention Concerning Indigenous and Tribal Peoples in Independent Countries*, available at <https://www.ilo.org/dyn/normlex/en/f?p=NORMLEXPUB:12100:0::NO:12100:P12100_INSTRUMENT_ID:312314:NO> accessed 19 December 2020.

Kischel, U. 2015. *Rechtsvergleichung*. Munich: C.H. Beck.

Kuper, A. 2003. 'The Return of the Native'. *Current Anthropology* 44(3): 389–402.

Lambek, M. 2011. 'Anthropology's Ontological Anxiety and the Concept of Tradition'. *Anthropologica* 53(2): 317–22.

Leisner, W. 2013. *Tradition und Verfassungsrecht zwischen Fortschrittshemmung und Überzeugungskraft. Vergangenheit als Zukunft?* Berlin: Duncker & Humblot.

Linnekin, J. 1983. 'Defining Traditions: Variations on the Hawaiian Identity'. *American Ethnologist* 10(2): 241–52.

McCrudden, C. 2015. 'Human Rights and Traditional Values'. In U. Baxi, C. McCrudden, and A. Paliwala, eds. *Law's Ethical, Global and Theoretical Contexts. Essays in Honour of William Twining*, 38–72. Cambridge: Cambridge University Press.

Merry, S. E. 1988. 'Legal Pluralism'. *Law and Society Review* 22(5): 869–96.

Merryman, J. H. 1969. *The Civil Law Tradition. An Introduction to the Legal Systems of Western Europe and Latin America*. Stanford: Stanford University Press.

Merryman, J. H. 1985. *The Civil Law Tradition. An Introduction to the Legal Systems of Western Europe and Latin America*. Stanford: Stanford University Press.

Merryman, J. H. and R. Pérez-Perdomo. 2007. *The Civil Law Tradition. An Introduction to the Legal Systems of Western Europe and Latin America*. Stanford: Stanford University Press.

Moore, S. F. 1973. 'Law and Social Change: The Semi-Autonomous Social Field as an Appropriate Subject of Study'. *Law & Society Review* 7(4): 719–46.

Pirie, F. 2013. *The Anthropology of Law*. Oxford/New York: Oxford University Press.

Pouillon, J. 1971. 'Traditions in French Anthropology'. *Social Research* 38(1): 73–92.

Pree, H. 1995. 'Traditio Canonica: La norma de interpretación del c. 6 & 2 del CIC'. *Ius canonicum* 35(70): 423–46.

Richland, J. B. 2008. 'Sovereign Time, Storied Moments: The Temporalities of Law, Tradition, and Ethnography in Hopi Tribal Court'. *Political and Legal Anthropology Review* 31(1): 8–27.

Rousso, H. 2015. 'Hacia una globalización de la memoria'. *Nuevo Mundo Mundos Nuevos*, available at <https://doi.org/10.4000/nuevomundo.68429> accessed 22 January 2021.

Shanklin, E. 1981. 'Two Meanings and Uses of Tradition'. *Journal of Anthropological Research* 37(1): 71–89.

Steenblock, V. 1998. 'Tradition'. In K. Gründer and J. Ritter, eds. *Historisches Wörterbuch der Philosophie, Vol. 10: St-T*, 1315–29. Darmstadt: Wissenschaftliche Buchgesellschaft.

Sunstein, C. R. 2017. *#Republic. Divided Democracy in the Age of Social Media*. Princeton: Princeton University Press.

Tarica, E. 2016. 'Indigenismo'. In W. H. Beezley, ed. *Oxford Research Encyclopedia of Latin American History*. Oxford: Oxford University Press, available at <https://doi.org/10.1093/acrefore/9780199366439.013.68> accessed 19 December 2020.

Thier, A. 2011. *Hierarchie und Autonomie. Regelungstraditionen der Bischofsbestellung in der Geschichte des kirchlichen Wahlrechts bis 1140*. Frankfurt am Main: Klostermann.

Tomaselli, A. 2016. *Indigenous Peoples and Their Right to Political Participation. International Law Standards and Their Application in Latin America*. Baden-Baden: Nomos.

Turner, J. 1997. 'Continuity and Constraint: Reconstructing the Concept of Tradition from a Pacific Perspective'. *The Contemporary Pacific* 9(2): 345–81.

UNGA 2007. 'United Nations Declaration on the Rights of Indigenous Peoples', available at <https://undocs.org/A/RES/61/295> accessed 19 December 2020.

UNHRC 2009. 'Promoting Human Rights and Fundamental Freedoms Through a Better Understanding of Traditional Values of Humankind', available at <http://undocs.org/A/HRC/RES/12/21> accessed 19 December 2020.

Wiedenhofer, S. 1990. 'Tradition, Traditionalismus'. In O. Brunner, W. Conze, and R. Koselleck, eds. *Geschichtliche Grundbegriffe. Historisches Lexikon zur politisch-sozialen Sprache in Deutschland, Vol. 6*, 607–50. Stuttgart: Klett-Cotta.

Wilkins, D. E. 2013. *Hollow Justice. A History of Indigenous Claims in the United States*. New Haven: Yale University Press.

Zimmermann, R. 1990. *The Law of Obligations. Roman Foundations of the Civilian Tradition*. Cape Town: Juta.

Zweigert, K. and H. Kötz. 1998. *An Introduction to Comparative Law*. Oxford/New York: Oxford University Press.

CHAPTER 20

THE CONCEPT OF POSITIVE LAW AND ITS RELATIONSHIP TO RELIGION AND MORALITY

BAUDOUIN DUPRET

My contention is that the extension of the concept of law beyond what is ordinarily understood as law in the present-day context is, at best, useless and, at worst, misleading. Producing an intelligible jurisprudence of the concept of law means keeping it within the reasonable boundaries of what is meant by both lay and professional people when practising 'the' law. Remarkably enough, the same people do not confuse the many normative systems surrounding them and do not equate the legal order with, for example, moral or religious normativities. It does not mean that these many normativities do not influence each other. On the contrary, they actively do so but in ways that maintain their specificities.

This chapter aims to develop a socio-historical jurisprudence of law, as distinct from other normativities. It entails a threefold analysis: conceptual, historical, and praxiological. Following the ground broken by analytical philosopher Ludwig Wittgenstein, conceptual analysis engages in the exposition of the grammar through which concepts acquire their signification and are meaningfully used. In a manner inspired by philosopher of science Ian Hacking and by historian Reinhart Koselleck, historical analysis emphasizes the description of the birth, development, and use of concepts. Drawing on the work of sociologist Harold Garfinkel, praxiological analysis describes the practical methods used by people to make sense of their environment, to produce their local order, and to act accordingly. The three approaches converge in their insistence on adopting the endogenous/indigenous perspective towards legal life and its production.

Penumbral cases: religion and morality in their relationships to law

The concepts of law, religion, and morality should be understood from the vantage point of legal positivism, from which they originate, and not as universal categories which could be applied to any type of normativity. Considered as ordinary categories, they are particularly apt to describe the working of modern legal systems, while proving inept when addressing other contexts and normative settings.

The distinction between law and morality, including religious morality,[1] may be considered one of the basic principles on which modern legal theory was built. For example, John Austin argued that positive law is distinguished from other normative systems in that it is founded on a command issued by a factually legitimate authority that is endowed with the power to sanction (Austin 1832 [1954]). The same Austin made a distinction between 'law properly so called', metaphorical laws (e.g. the laws of nature), and laws by analogy (laws that proceed from an opinion generally shared by a human group). Under 'laws properly so called', however, one can find 'the laws established by God for His human creatures', as well as laws made by men for other men. In both cases, there is a conjunction of the two criteria for the definition of a law: the existence of a command and a sanction. What distinguishes the different categories of 'laws properly so called' is the third criterion: effective authority, which can only be satisfied through the intervention of a human agent. In other words, intentionality, coupled with the effective force of execution, makes up, according to Austin, positive law (Jackson 1996).

Although he challenged Austin's theory of command, Herbert Hart (1961) sought to maintain a moderate positivist understanding of law. He therefore defined legal positivism as an expression of the thesis according to which it is not at all necessarily true that rules of law reflect or satisfy certain moral exigencies, although in reality they have often done so (Hart 1961: 224). What is at stake, therefore, is the need to demonstrate that no necessary relation exists between law and morality. Legal and moral obligations might indeed share certain characteristics, but they remain distinctive forms of social control (Hart 1961: 232) due to the importance of obligation (no moral rule can be considered unimportant), the inaccessibility of moral rules to deliberate changes, the necessarily intentional character of moral errors, and the form of moral pressure that invites respect for the rules due to their importance and shared nature (Hart 1961: 203–21). According to Hart, in order to be legally valid, a rule of law does not necessarily have to conform to moral standards but to the formal criteria of a system of primary rules (i.e. duty-imposing rules) and secondary rules (i.e. power-conferring rules), even though some of these rules violate the specific morals of a society or trespass what one might consider to be authentic morals (Hart 1961: 250).

This positivist conception can be considered as a global phenomenon, which was acculturated to settings peripheral to the original core of positive law. Egyptian legal doctrine asserts, for instance, that there is a distinction between law and morality. For example, Hassan Gemei (a.k.a. Hasan Jamiʿi) aligns himself with Austin's theory of command with regard to the definition of law. Gemei sees law as a set of rules governing the behaviour of individuals in society, which people must obey, lest they expose themselves to sanctions imposed by a competent authority (Gemei 1997: 6). According to Gemei, legal rules are not the only ones aiming to regulate and stabilize relations among members of any given society. They act in concert with other rules, such as those of courtesy, customs, traditions, and religious rules. As for moral rules, they are principles and teachings that the majority of the members of society consider as constraining behavioural rules that aim to realize elevated ideals (Gemei 1997: 15). Moral rules share a number of characteristics with legal rules: they change according to time and place; they tend towards organizing society; they have a constraining nature associated with sanctions. However, they differ from legal rules in three domains. First, with regard to their field of application: 'Whereas morality includes personal and social manners, law addresses the relationship between the person and the others from the perspective of the ostensible aspect of behaviour without taking into consideration the intentions non-associated with physical action' (Gemei 1997: 16). They also differ with regard to the type of sanction imposed: 'Whereas the penalty of violating morality rules is a mere moral penalty ranging from remorse to denunciation and disdain, the penalty for violating legal rules is physical incarceration, imprisonment, hard labour, etc.' (Gemei 1997: 17). They also differ in respect to their objectives: according to Gemei, while moral rules seek to attain perfection in man, legal rules seek to realize stability and order within society (Gemei 1997: 17). Finally, they appear in different forms: legal rules, Gemei asserts, generally appear in a clear and specific form, while moral rules are not so clear because they are linked to internal feelings, which may vary from one person to another (Gemei 1997: 17). As to religious rules, they have a close relation to legal rules, but their field of action is far wider and violating them is punished in the afterlife (Gemei 1997: 18). Gemei insists that there is no difference between religious and legal rules, for such a difference 'cannot be recognized from the perspective of Islamic sharia'[2] (Gemei 1997: 18), in the sense that Islam is a total faith that encompasses law. This means that the field of application of sharia is wider than that of law: Islamic sharia, he notes, is the source of legislation from which legal rules must be derived in Islamic states (Gemei 1997: 27):

> Islamic Shari'ah was ordained as a divine law to govern the conduct of the Islamic society, formulate the thought of the Moslems, and regulate the human relations. Revealed by Allah, Shari'ah guides the society to the highest ideals and seeks to achieve wisdom for which God has created man on earth.
>
> (Gemei 1997: 28)

This modern distinction between law, religion, and morality should not be taken as a universal truth. On the contrary, this type of discourse regarding the relations between law, religion, and morality is totally contingent. It is the direct heir of the process of legal positivization and of the building of law as an autonomous order. Doing the anthropology of law today therefore means studying positive law as a concept that has its own historical ontology and practical translation.

THE CONCEPTUAL ANALYSIS OF LAW

'We should probably acknowledge the arbitrary element in language more than we do; for that would encourage us to invent new sounds for our new names, instead of taking an old sound and thus creating a new ambiguity' (Robinson 1956: 138). This sounds very much like Wittgenstein's prudential remark regarding the necessity to clear the mist surrounding our conceptual usages. Concepts are abstractions of features characterizing something which can be expressed with different words and in different languages. Of course, what seems relatively easy when the thing referred to is a material object becomes more problematic when this object of reference is, by definition, a social construct. If one considers that the word 'law' is a concept, the question is thus to know the features that are common to the many words referring to this abstraction.

The question 'what is law?' per se is devoid of relevance. There are only words and expressions sharing family resemblances across languages, cultures, institutions, activities, and contexts. As a consequence, there is no universal definition of law that should be looked for independent of its context of expression; one may only achieve descriptions of the surface and deep grammars of the language games surrounding words closely or loosely associated with what we mean by 'law' in English (or *droit* in French, or *qanun* in Arabic, etc.). However, when describing the grammar of such language games, we proceed with a paradigm from which to extend the analysis beyond its 'core of certainty' (Hart 1961). Although law is not an empirical but a conceptual reality, its core of certainty is contingent and not universal. The core of certainty of law is made of the empirical object of which positivist legal theories were the description. In other words, the concept of law corresponds to what legal theorists designated as positive law, as distinct from natural or religious law, or any other type of law, at the time of what one might call the 'positivist turn'. Other instances can share some features with this core of certainty—these are what Hart calls penumbral cases (i.e. instances having some resemblance to the paradigm), but this is only a resemblance and its relationship with the core is metaphorical. This is not to say that such theories are correct or complete, but that, despite their possible flaws, they constitute generalizations and abstractions from one specific and contingent object working as their paradigm.

Pace Montesquieu, law in the natural sciences does not belong to the same game as law in ... law. One must therefore identify the language games within which the word is used in order to discern its criteria of intelligibility and the concept of which it is an expression. However, every language game always relates to a core of certainty, in respect of which it is contextual and perspectival: it is 'relative to the purposes specific to those people and sensitive to circumstances from which it cannot be abstracted (without detaching it from what constitutes its identity)' (Hutchinson et al. 2008: 75–9).

Accordingly, it is clear that everything normative cannot be called legal, as it would run against the meaning constitutive of the core object of the concept of law—and this holds true if there are many concepts. Calling all forms of ordering by the name 'law' creates an analytical mist. Using a word which has some common-sense meaning to perform an analytical task that runs contrary to this meaning generates an ambiguity, especially when this alleged concept either does not carry anything which makes it distinct from other, less connoted words (like 'norm') or surreptitiously carries the distinctive characteristics of what it is supposed to be contrary to. For instance, claiming that *dharma* is law (Davis 2012; Geertz 1983) presupposes the existence of a concept of law including all cultural forms of normativity. On the contrary, taking the criterion of the union of primary and secondary rules (Hart 1961) excludes from the conceptual spectrum a series of configurations called, for example, infra-law, primitive law, proto-law, social, ethical, deontological norms, etc. It would exclude *dharma* because of the very composite nature of primary rules and absence of secondary ones. Both claims are conceptual. The grammatical inquiry into the many uses of the word *dharma* can tell us whether there is any heuristic value in speaking of *dharma* in terms of law. Heuristic concepts share two qualities: the capacity to precisely identify what they are the concept of; their affordance to a grammatical inquiry. It is conspicuously difficult to identify the object of the over-inclusive concept of law, not to speak of describing it. With Hart's positivist theory, and despite its many flaws and approximations, we have a clear object whose description it is possible to carry out.

An inquiry into normative concepts is thus both grammatical and context-dependent. The case of 'Islamic law' is illuminating in that respect, since it perfectly illustrates how a normative corpus was characterized in terms of 'law' at a specific historical time. It is a truism to say that 'Islamic law' is a concept belonging to a taxonomy. It is more striking, and sometimes irritating in the current context, to acknowledge that this concept is the product of a specific scholarly enterprise that aimed to better understand, control, and reframe the phenomenon of normativity in Muslim societies. Normativity existed prior to the attention Orientalist sciences gave it; Islamic law did not (Buskens and Dupret 2015).

Historical ontologies of a contingent concept

Law is not an empirical reality that must be discovered; it is a concept that was intended, at a specific point in history, to express the idea of a contingent normative order. In that respect, its study must be both historical and praxiological. In other words, it cannot be severed from the context of its uses and the practices of its accomplishment.

The coming into being of concepts is thoroughly historical. 'Historical ontology' is how I call the description of both the concept itself and its history. Concepts are historical objects that do not exist until they are created. For instance, in the past, before the concept of homosexuality was formed, there could be sexual acts between two people of the same sex, but there was no specific kind of person categorically called a 'homosexual' (Davidson 2001; Hacking 2002: 82). Historically and etymologically speaking, most of the many words used to express the contemporary concept of law have existed for a long time. However, as we observed in the first section, they were not used with their current meanings. To take but one example, between the meaning of the word *constitutio* in Medieval canon law and the current notion of national constitution, there is what Michel Foucault (1961) called, when writing about madness, a 'great divide'; that is, a radical and often incommensurable discursive gap.

Discourse on 'modern law', 'positive law', or 'law' *tout court* was made possible through the emergence of a conceptual space articulated by a style of reasoning (Davidson 2001: xii). This is not the place to explore the complex history of the concept and of the discourse in which it is embedded. It is enough to say that the concept evolved, spread, and transformed itself. It progressively referred to something like a homogenous, autonomous, autopoietic normative system. In this process, it was associated with values, which were themselves changing, but it always remained attached to an idea of the state, the rule of law, and the control of the population. Describing the ontological history of concepts allows us to understand how we think and why we seem compelled to think in certain ways (Hacking 2002: 71). It can be done *à la* Foucault, with snapshots taken on either side of the Great Divide, showing the transformation of one tradition into another, or it can be done in a synchronic way, with snapshots taken from two concurrent repertoires addressing a seemingly identical concept. In both cases, the discourse must be analysed within the circumstances and conditions under which the sentences comprising it have 'archeologically' acquired their truth value and can therefore be uttered (Hacking 2002: 79).

Ontological analysis can be conducted hypothetically. Through his fable about King Rex, Hart suggests a 'genetic-analytic' (Hacker 1977: 11) approach to the birth of law understood as a legal system. Although conceptual and not anthropological, this hypothetical story is anthropologically illuminating: 'We are asked to envisage a purely notional situation in order to perceive what crucial features characterize our own complex situation' (Hacker 1977: 11). The fable goes as follows (Hart 1961). There is a population living on a territory governed for years by an absolute monarch, Rex. He controls his people through general orders coupled with threats to do or to abstain from doing certain things. His people generally obey him, based on their personal relationship with Rex. After a happy reign, Rex dies, leaving an heir who starts giving general orders. The simple fact that his father was generally obeyed does not guarantee Rex II to be habitually obeyed. If orders are laws only when habitually followed, one must wait a certain time before knowing whether Rex II is in fact legislating. In other words, there is a legal discontinuity between the reigns of Rex I and Rex II. However, a pre-legal system has been born if one observes a continuity of the power to legislate through rules facilitating the transition from one lawmaker to another. Such is the case if Rex II has a title to succeed his father. This title gives him the right to legislate after his father's death, and his first orders can be considered laws, notwithstanding the eventual obedience of his subjects. It is not the habit of obedience that transforms orders into laws but the issuance of these orders on the basis of secondary rules that recognize Rex II's orders as valid; that is, as conforming to the rules of the same system that give him the right to succeed, and thus to legislate. The fable does not end here. Other secondary rules must be added in order to produce a fully fledged legal system. Hart calls them rules of adjudication and rules of change. Rules of recognition constitute remedies to the problem of uncertainty affecting the authority entitled to issue primary rules. Rules of change respond to the problem created by the static character of primary rules whose issuance is not governed by superior norms. Rules of adjudication are functional responses to the inefficiency of mere social pressure. Together, primary rules creating obligations and secondary rules (of recognition, change, and adjudication) organizing the power to issue primary rules are the elements necessary to the constitution of a fully fledged legal system. In this sense, Hart's conception can be considered genetic. It does not mean, however, that it is normative, in the sense that it does not imply that a legal system is per se a moral good (Gardner 2013).

This conception of law as the union of primary and secondary rules is contingent upon the specific legal systems scholars like Hart were aiming to describe. It was widely applauded, discussed, and criticized for its formal flaws, as well as for its ethnocentric or evolutionary stance. However, despite its inconsistencies, it can be safely taken as a valuable attempt at describing a legal historical paradigm. In that sense, Hart's concept of law is what is meant today by the word 'law'. It corresponds to the contemporary state of conceptualization obtained by the word if we are to describe its historical ontology.

Rex's story can be told in a purely anthropological manner, as demonstrated by Testart (2012) in his analysis of the evolution of societies in prehistorical times. It can also be told in a historical way. This is somehow what Jean-Louis Halpérin (2014) attempted in his collection on legal revolutions. Making a distinction between ordinary changes, which take place within a system, and revolutionary changes, which imply the substitution of an ancient order with a new one, Halpérin observes 'the possibility of "fits and starts" in legal history, contrary to the classical evolutionist schemes that insist on elements of continuity'. Going further, he states that these breaks are 'complete upheavals of the structure of legal systems based on secondary rules' (2014: xi). They can take two forms: either the passage from a pre-legal system, made of primary rules only, to a fully fledged legal order, made of the combination of both primary and secondary rules; or the substitution of a new system for an old one. Addressing the specific issue of codification, Halpérin stresses the revolutionary character of legal systematization. This can be contrasted with Roman law, which lacked the static and dynamic hierarchy of norms regarded by Kelsen as characteristic of both state and state law (Kelsen 1945; Troper 1994: 194).[3] The legal break Europe went through at the turn of the nineteenth century was the outcome of dynamics of 'legal systematization', which used inter alia the technique of codification frequently associated (from the end of the eighteenth century) with an idea of planning oriented to the construction of a new legal order (Halpérin 2014: 35), an idea rather different from earlier compilations. Not surprisingly, Max Weber saw, in the great codes of the nineteenth century, and especially in the French Civil Code of 1804, the paradigmatic example of formal rationalization (Halpérin 2014: 37; Weber 1978).

Legal positivism, nation-state building, and codification were an extraordinary success story. The nineteenth and twentieth centuries witnessed the transplantation (Watson 1993) of the Napoleonic code template at a global level. One can identify many reasons for this phenomenon: the unifying capacities of codes, their flexibility and adaptability, their symbolic force as 'talismans of modernity' (Halpérin 2014: 49). Both codes and systematized case laws were major tools supporting national projects. In Muslim societies, to take only one example, the conception of local norms largely followed the global movement. In this process, it was left to scholars to decide whether a norm was qualified to be elevated to the status of 'law'. When ratified at a political level, these scholarly opinions became the new law of colonial and even indigenous administrators. There are many reasons for this conceptually ethnocentric legal positivism; for example, the fact that colonial administrators were often trained in law and that a majority of scholars combined oriental and legal studies. This orientalist, positivist conception perpetuated itself and remains in place; it was reproduced, from generation to generation, in the West as well as in the East. It became natural to speak of Islamic normativity in terms of law. While using the expression 'invention of Islamic law' is often perceived as an attack against Islam, suggesting that this law is man-made and not divinely inspired, the question is not the divine nature of 'Islamic law', but that speaking of Islamic normativity in terms of law is, first, contingent on a specific time and place and, second, deeply influential on the understanding one has of that normativity.

Praxiological Ethnography: The Concept of Law in Context and in Action

I conceive of my task as the description of the actual uses of the concept of law. Drawing on its historical ontology, I have identified the period of its birth, some of its contingent, fundamental elements, and the ways in which it became autonomous from other normative repertoires, such as religion and morality. This paves the way for a contemporary inquiry into the ways professionals and laypeople refer to law in the ordinary accomplishment of their lives and tasks. This is what I call 'legal ethnomethods' (Dupret et al. 2015), which are the ordinary methods used in order to 'be legal' (Garfinkel 1974: 16) in the performance of 'law properly so called' (Austin 1832 [1954]). These ethnomethods concern the practice of the law understood not as an equivalent to any kind of normativity but as this very specific thing, which appeared together with the emergence of the nation state, which was made the object of the science of law, and which positivist theories attempted to describe.

Let us use examples extracted from studies into Egyptian lawmaking and application in order to sketch the lines of such a praxiological inquiry into legal ethnomethods and their relationships with religion and morality, or perhaps, in this case, religious morality (Dupret and Ferrié 2015). First, one must note that law is practised with both technical and mundane languages. Take the example of divorce trials in Egypt, for which a reconciliation committee is required by the statutory divorce law. If the committee in a given case states that the wife has faced 'humiliation, slander, insult and a blow to her honour from the husband', the praxiological attitude involves analysing these statements in their ordinary sense, whilst noting that they are reformulated by a specific institution (the reconciliation committee) within the context of a judicial proceeding (reconciliation in a divorce trial) and for practical purposes (coming to a decision).

Second, one must emphasize the importance of context; for example, institutional. Context means the constraints towards which people actually orient themselves in the course of their activities (Dupret and Ferrié 2008). In describing what parliamentarians do, for example within the Egyptian People's Assembly, we must show how a declaration such as 'the law proposal in its current format is contrary to the sharia ... [and] must be modified in order to comply with jurists' unanimous opinion' manifests the desire of the MP concerned not only to produce an utterance which has a meaning understandable by his colleagues (the non-compliance of the law proposal with 'Islamic law') but also, and especially, to act as an MP committed to the adequate accomplishment of his work (voting for a law proposal that complies with the Constitution).

Third, the grammar of interactions unfolds according to the various contexts in which interactions are embedded. The constraints exerted by such contexts are to be described not as a static element of interaction but as a reflexive and fluctuating framework that actors permanently reassess and in relation to which they constantly realign themselves. When the Speaker of the People's Assembly declares that 'the modification proposed by the government is in conformity with prevailing Maliki doctrine[4] in the Kingdom of Morocco as well as in several other Arab countries and is in line with the suggestions of MPs', he is manifesting and updating the institutional context in which he moves. In this sense, his intervention is contextualizing (it makes the context of this affirmation available) and contextualized (it situates the intervention retrospectively—what is done in other countries and what the MPs have suggested—and prospectively—it inscribes this intervention in the extended perspective of the parliament's passing of a law).

Fourth, legal procedures belong to the constraints exerted by the context. The legal sequence follows certain stages which, although formalized, nevertheless respond to a series of empirically observable accomplishments which are also explicitly produced by the participants. The production of a procedurally correct law is one of the priorities towards which practitioners tend. These procedural constraints do not correspond to a set of abstract rules drawn from an external, historical, and overhanging legal system but to the routine and bureaucratic dimension of the activities of those engaged in legal practice. When the reconciliation committee writes that 'the Honourable Court has designated us to arbitrate in case number [x] of the year 2000', it is producing procedural correctness in addressing judicial bodies, which subsequently will consider its report, more than it is describing the procedural rule that it followed.

Fifth, the participants in the judicial activity also orient themselves to what we might call sets of relevancies. The idea of relevance refers to the operation which relates a practice to the categories within which it must be embedded in order for it to take on its full sense, claim its validity, and produce its effects. Relevancies take on very different aspects according to the activity within which people are engaged. In the Egyptian parliamentary context, we can discern, for example, national, constitutional, and Islamic relevancies, which, in some way, constitute what Goffman calls the 'footing' that those involved will adopt to support their speech turn. The Islamic relevance often predominates in MPs' talk, but it is also important for them to recognize democratic relevance as the parliamentary order principle. This is demonstrated in the following extract which combines reference to an Islamic relevance (the discussion of the project before an Islamic body), a legal relevance (the procedure of adopting the law), and a democratic relevance (respecting the principle of a majority vote):

> The discussion of this proposed law at the Academy of Islamic Research lasted three months to allow members to express their opinions; we voted with the majority of the voices and that is quite normal; it is the opinion of the majority and this opinion engages all its members. (From unpublished parliamentary debates, cited in Dupret and Ferrié 2008)

In the judicial context, relevance has more to do with legal characterization (i.e. matching selected facts with the text of the law), as in the following extract, in which the reconciliation committee observes 'the impossibility of coexistence and marital life between them', characterizing in this respect relations between the spouses according to the legal category available and opening the way to the subsequent inferences of the judge.

Sixth, legal activities are instructed; that is, they are oriented to a norm of reference (Livingston 1995). By instructed action, I mean an action whose normative reference is immanent to the particularities of the site and the actions that are appropriate to it. Sometimes, the normative reference even transcends the site and the action itself, in the sense that it is not stipulated in a corpus (which may be tacit) of specific instructions. In sum, language games are referring in complex ways to demonstrably textual sources or to supposedly shared moral values (Livingston 1995). Thus, an individual within the parliament can carry out an action which is both instructed by a procedural rule and inspired by a religious relevance:

> The text submitted to us complies with the provisions of the Islamic sharia. [Nevertheless,] further to the request of MPs, the government proposes a modification to Article 20 so as to give the tribunal the right to call before it ... two arbiters in order to attempt to reconcile the spouses in case of *khul'*.[5] (From unpublished parliamentary debates, cited in Dupret and Ferrié 2008)

In the judicial situation, the instructed nature of the action is demonstrated by an orientation to procedural correctness and legal relevance, whilst the possibility for it to be inspired can only appear in a superfluous manner (like the notation 'in the name of God the Clement and Merciful' at the top of the written ruling, which is not legally required) or when judicial standards such as public order or good morals are referred to.

Law, religion, and morality: A pragmatic socio-historical jurisprudence

Under the denomination of 'pragmatic history', Simona Cerutti calls for the development of an approach that accounts for the practical attitude of members of society towards the many social institutions, reasons, logics, and norms that they actively help to craft (Cerutti 2008). Contesting Carlo Ginzburg's interpretive attitude, which uses biographical trajectories to provide for the reconstruction of complex cosmogonies, she advocates the search for non-anachronistic, indigenously relevant, and practical categories. Speaking of law, she insists that legal cultures constitute resources that are locally mobilized for all practical purposes. More specifically, legal documents incorporate the reasons why they were written; they are oriented to the goals of their production. In that sense, the analysis does not consist of the correction of the actors' versions of facts or of the disclosure to the actors of a reality of which they are not aware; it consists of the reconstruction of their capacity to make their own actions comprehensible, acceptable, and legitimate. Regarding the law, it means exploring legal cultures in their contextual, situated, local uses, including the reciprocal relationships between formal norms and social practices.

What Cerutti calls pragmatic history can be easily extended to contemporary contexts. I advocate a pragmatic socio-historical jurisprudence that concentrates on the concept of law and its 'glocal' translations. Combining analytic, grammatical, and praxiological approaches with legal theory, history, and ethnography, I seek to bypass at least two dichotomies opposing lawyers' law in the books and anthropologists' law in action, on the one hand, and positivist and realist socio-legal theories, on the other. I also seek to dilute the conundrum of the definition of law through, first, a conceptual analysis; second, its re-specification as the theoretical conceptualization of a contingent object: the positive legal system of the nation state; and third, the close description of the practices associated with the enactment of the concept. Within the frame so defined, speaking of law, religion, and morality as separate entities whose relationships must be investigated is closely associated with the positivization process that posited these repertoires as distinct, though comparable, entities. As a consequence, it is meaningful to speak of them in such terms if we confine ourselves to the specific context of their theoretical distinction, whereas using the same categories to speak of times and societies that did not conceive of the issue of normativity in such terms borders on absurdity. There is no way to properly understand how legal, religious, and moral repertoires interact in contexts where these very categories do not make sense. However, the case is completely different when societies claim the (total or partial) autonomy of their legal system from that of religion or morality.

Notes

1. Religion and morality should be analytically distinct, even though they can sometimes intersect.
2. The term 'sharia' is a polysemous concept that can refer in Islam to the divine teaching, Islamic law, Islamic ethics, or even an Islamic 'virtuous abstraction' (Berger 2013; see Dupret 2018).
3. Troper adds, 'One pays a huge price for this definition, as one cannot anymore speak of feudal law nor even of Roman law, at least during the Republican era, but it offers two advantages:—It allows [one] to understand the law and thus the state as a specific form of political power ...;—[I]t can contribute to the explanation of theories regarding the state, [that is, the] influence the historical emergence of this specific system exerted on the formation of concepts and theories' (1994: 195).
4. Islam's majority doctrine, Sunnism, is divided into four schools of jurisprudence: Malikism, Hanafism, Shafi'ism, and Hanbalism. In Morocco, Malikism is the official doctrinal school of the state.
5. *Khul'* is a specific form of repudiation in which the husband grants his wife a divorce in exchange of her renunciation of all the material benefits she has gained from her marriage with him (gifts, alimonies, dowry). In Egypt, Law No. 1 of the year 2000 transformed it into a divorce initiated by the wife, without her husband or the judge having any capacity to oppose it, providing she renounces the same material benefits.

References

Austin J. 1832 [1954]. *The Province of Jurisprudence Determined*. H. L. A. Hart, ed. London: Weidenfeld and Nicolson.

Berger, M. S. 2013. 'Introduction'. In M. S. Berger, ed. *Applying Shari'a in the West: Facts, Fears and the Future of Islamic Rules on Family Relations in the West*, 7–22. Leiden: Leiden University Press.

Buskens, L. and B. Dupret. 2015. 'The Invention of Islamic Law: A History of Western Studies of Islamic Normativity and Their Spread in the Orient'. In F. Pouillon and J. C. Vatin, eds. *After Orientalism: Critical Perspectives on Western Agency and Eastern Re-Appropriations*, 31–47. Leiden: Brill.

Cerutti, S. 2008. 'Histoire pragmatique, ou de la rencontre entre histoire sociale et histoire culturelle'. *Tracés* 15: 147–68.

Davidson, A. I. 2001. *The Emergence of Sexuality: Historical Epistemology and the Formation of Concepts*. Cambridge: Harvard University Press.

Davis, D. R. 2012. 'Centres of Law: Duties, Rights, and Jurisdictional Pluralism in Medieval India'. In P. Dresch and H. Skoda, eds. *Legalism: Anthropology and History*, 85–113. Oxford: Oxford University Press.

Dupret, B. 2018. *What Is the Sharia?* London: Hurst.

Dupret, B. and J. N. Ferrié. 2008. *Délibérer sous la coupole: L'activité parlementaire dans les régimes autoritaires*. Beyrouth: Presses de l'IFPO.

Dupret, B. and J. N. Ferrié. 2015. 'The Practical Grammar of Law and Its Relation to Time'. In B. Dupret, M. Lynch, and T. Berard, eds. *Law at Work. Studies in Legal Ethnomethods*, 27–48. Oxford: Oxford University Press.

Dupret, B., M. Lynch, and T. Berard. 2015. *Law at Work. Studies in Legal Ethnomethods*. Oxford: Oxford University Press.

Foucault, M. 1961. *Histoire de la folie*. Paris: Gallimard.

Gardner, J. 2013. 'Why Law Might Emerge: Hart's Problematic Fable'. In L. Duarte d'Almeida, J. Edwards, and A. Dolcetti, eds. *Reading Hart's The Concept of Law*, 81–96. London: Hart Publishing.

Garfinkel, H. 1974. 'The Origins of the Term "Ethnomethodology"'. In R. Turner, ed. *Ethnomethodology*, 15–18. Harmondsworth: Penguin.

Geertz, C. 1983. *Local Knowledge: Further Essays in Interpretive Anthropology*. New York: Basic Books.

Gemei, H. 1997. *Introduction to Law: Theory of Law, Theory of Right*. Cairo: Cairo University.

Hacker, P.M.S. 1977. 'Introduction'. In P. M. S. Hacker and J. Raz, eds. *Law, Morality, and Society: Essays in Honour of H. L. A. Hart*, 1–25. Oxford: Oxford University Press.

Hacking, I. 2002. *Historical Ontology*. Cambridge: Harvard University Press.

Halpérin, J. L. 2014. *Five Legal Revolutions since the 17th Century: An Analysis of a Global Legal History*. Dordrecht: Springer.

Hart, H. L. A. 1961. *The Concept of Law*. Oxford: Oxford University Press.

Hutchinson, P., R. Read, and W. Sharrock. 2008. *There is No Such Thing as Social Science: In Defence of Peter Winch*. London: Routledge.

Jackson, B. S. 1996. *Making Sense in Jurisprudence*. Liverpool: Deborah Charles Publications.

Kelsen, H. 1945. *General Theory of Law and State*. New York: Russell & Russell.

Livingston, E. 1995. *An Anthropology of Reading*. Bloomington/Indianapolis: Indiana University Press.

Robinson, R. 1956. 'A Criticism of Plato's Cratylus'. *Philosophical Review* 65(3): 324–41.

Testart, A. 2012. *Avant l'histoire: L'évolution des sociétés, de Lascaux à Carnac*. Paris: Gallimard.

Troper, M. 1994. *Pour une théorie juridique de l'Etat*. Paris: PUF.

Watson, A. 1993. *Legal Transplants: An Approach to Comparative Law*. Athens: University of Georgia Press.

Weber, M. 1978. *Economy and Society*. Berkeley: University of California Press.

CHAPTER 21

PROPERTY REGIMES

MATTHEW CANFIELD

INTRODUCTION

PROPERTY regimes refer to the political, legal, and economic systems through which societies order their relationships between people with respect to valued things. Although societies construct property arrangements in different ways, property is a social institution of all collective life—a system of appropriation, value allocation, and distribution of power and control. Property is thus a connective thread between all economic, political, and legal orderings. Anthropologists' insistence on studying the total social relations involved in property regimes distinguishes anthropology from other disciplines. Whereas legal theory has been uniquely concerned with ownership and private property as a system for allocating scarce goods and resources, anthropologists have investigated how property is constructed and shaped by everyday practice, illuminating how the distinctions between law and practice mutually constitute power relations.

Today, changes in the organization of the global economy are producing proliferating property claims to immaterial objects of knowledge such as data and debt. The *dematerialization* of property through informational and financial capitalism is occurring at a time when industrial modes of carbon-dependent accumulation are facing ecological limits brought on by climate change. However, technologies of informationalization and financialization are also *rematerializing* property regimes by constructing new calculative devices and global markets for increasingly limited natural resources. How these emerging regimes shape social relations between people, the distribution of social entitlements, and the boundaries between persons and things offers an important field of ethnographic inquiry.

In this chapter, I review how anthropologists have attended to aporias of property theory by ethnographically analysing conflicts and transformations between property regimes and what these insights suggest about emerging forms and regimes of property. In recent years, several excellent overviews of the anthropology of property have been written (see Hann 1998; Verdery and Humphrey 2004; Strang and Busse 2011;

Busse 2012; Turner 2017). The broad scope of property's impact on social life means that property is a central category for anthropologists and lawyers across a broad range of subfields. Therefore, in this essay, I focus on anthropological insights into three continuing processes of property regime transformation: decolonization, privatization, and enclosure, as well as emerging processes of de- and rematerialization.

The 'nature' of property

Legal and anthropological scholarship has been entangled in an ongoing dialogue about the nature and practice of property since the earliest anthropological studies. Henry Sumner Maine and Louis Henry Morgan both pointed to property as a defining feature in the evolution of human organization. In the nineteenth century, both authors offered teleological accounts of human development that were defined by the transition from open-access regimes of property inherent in 'savage' society to the apex—'civilization'—characterized by private property. These early anthropological accounts, which were constructed in order to furnish evidence for a natural progression to Western civilization, offered legal scholars justification for the expansion of private property regimes. Yet although the common law was premised on the mutual dependence of individual private property (*dominium*) and monarchical sovereignty (*imperium*) (Koskenniemi 2017), even the common law's most fervent defenders were wracked by what Carol Rose (1998) describes as 'ownership anxiety'. This anxiety reflected a long debate within Western philosophy over the relative virtues of collective and individual property.

Liberal theorists attempted to solve the friction between nature and private property by drawing on an imagined political anthropology that necessitated viewing private property as a natural right that enabled peaceful prosperity and state sovereignty. This theory was informed by a historical context of nation-state formation, capitalist development, and colonial expansion (Macpherson 2011). Bhandar (2018) points out that questions about law in the colonies had a constitutive effect on Western legality (see also Hussain 2009). Locke's labour theory of property—in which rights to ownership stemmed from the application of one's human labour to transform and improve land—was not only based a theory of the 'possessive individual', but also on particular forms of cultivation. These theories, in turn, were developed to racialize indigenous subjects. As Bhandar explains, assumptions about private property were 'articulated through the attribution of value to the lives of those defined as having the capacity, will and technology to appropriate, which in turn was contingent on prevailing concepts of race and racial difference' (2018: 4). The mutual constitution of property and personhood, race and privilege, based on an imagined state of nature remains an enduring legacy of dominant private property regimes (Harris 1993).

Moreover, often overlooked is the way that property distinguished nature from society. Neil Smith (2008) points out that the labour theory of value that turned nature into property constituted a contradictory ideology in which nature was constructed as external to humankind. The same logics used to subordinate indigenous inhabitants and women were premised on a belief in the virtue of dominating nature. This ideology distinguishing nature from culture, however, is now being reassessed as climate change compels political and legal theorists to reassess how dominant ideologies of property have produced environmental, racial, and gendered subordination (Chakrabarty 2009).

Since Malinowski ([1922] 2002), anthropologists have turned away from evolutionary accounts of property and cultural development, focusing instead on relativizing and denaturalizing liberal legalism's singular focus on private property. This absence of 'ownership anxiety' and the relativist epistemology of anthropology marks a major point of departure between anthropological and legal scholarship on property. For anthropologists, property is an analytical concept that refers to 'the many ways in which rights and obligations, privileges, and restrictions govern the dealings of humans with regard to resources and objects of value' (Turner 2017: 26). Riles (2004) suggests that the difference between legal and anthropological approaches to property lies in different relationships to means and ends. Whereas for anthropologists, property is a means for understanding social and political relations, for jurists, property is a means to produce order, reduce conflict, and allocate scarce resources. For Wiber (2015), therefore, property serves as a 'boundary object' that enables interdisciplinary dialogue.

Ethnographic approaches to property regimes

Property regimes are typically categorized through one of four ideal types: open access, common property, state property, and private property.[1] As the Benda-Beckmanns and Wiber point out, however, property regimes 'cannot be easily captured in one-dimensional political, economic or legal models' (2009: 2); they are multi-faceted and multi-functional. Anthropologists thus analyse property regimes empirically.

Turner (2017) describes three different approaches to conceptualizing property regimes—the 'triangle' of property's components, the 'bundle of rights' metaphor, and the four 'layers' of property's institutionalization. The first analyses property regimes by investigating the three elements of property regimes: actors, valuables, and rights and obligations. Anthropologists have problematized each category (Verdery and Humphrey 2004). For example, property theorists usually assume a direct relationship between persons and things, but anthropologists have pointed to the way in which property actually creates particular types of persons and 'individuals'. Marilyn Strathern (1988) famously argued that Papua New Guinea's Mt. Hageners are not individuals, but 'dividuals'—unstable subjects that are constituted through their relations with others in a social context. Through her account, Strathern illuminated how the bounded individual is in fact a culturally contingent artefact of the liberal paradigm of property. Anthropologists have also sought to unsettle the distinction between subjects and objects inherent in the valuables, instead showing how constituting objects is a process of boundary construction and negotiation (Hirsch 2010; Blomley 2016). A key thread of this research has come from feminist approaches which have challenged the assumption of women as objects of property and men as owners, and research that attends only to the role of men in exchange (Weiner 1976; Hirschon 1984). More recently, some scholars have turned to queer theory and relations to analyse the way in which the subject–object relation is subverted (Davies 1999). Anthropologists have also problematized the concept of 'ownership', demonstrating that exclusivity almost never entails complete dominion, but is part of an ongoing process of social communication, claiming, and symbolic action (Strang and Busse 2011).

While the 'triangle' metaphor is useful for disassembling the components of property, the metaphor of property as a 'bundle of rights' remains the dominant approach in legal scholarship. First articulated by Maine (1864), this bundle metaphor imagines property as a series of rights and obligations that includes, among other relations, the rights to possess, transfer, and access property (see Honoré 1961). Identifying the 'sticks' of the bundle is becoming increasingly complex, especially with the rise of informational capitalism and financialization, as I describe below. Nevertheless, the bundle metaphor is helpful in breaking down that multiplex rights, relations, and obligations constituted through any property regime.

Finally, Benda-Beckmann, Benda-Beckmann, and Wiber (2009) suggest a third approach—that property regimes can be analysed by attending to the four layers of social organization in which they are constructed and practised: the ideologies of property, their political institutionalization, the social relations through which property is claimed and transferred, and the practices where the first three layers intersect. The layers approach points analysts' attention to the sources and actors from which particular ideologies of property emanate. Today, these are increasingly transnational. While property was at the centre of the colonial legal endeavour, property claims were reconfigured through new forms of global legality beginning in the 1950s. Anghie (2007) documents how, after decolonization, former colonial powers articulated new ideologies of law that naturalized Anglo forms of contract law in order to secure private property rights to natural resources in their former colonies. The emergence of 'transnational law' secured property rights beyond sovereign authority and blurred the distinctions between international public law and private law to produce a new form of global governance by contract (Cutler and Dietz 2017). The export of U.S. legal models continued with the rise of neoliberalism in the 1970s and 1980s. Most recently, the Agreement on Trade-Related Aspects of International Property Rights (TRIPs), which was signed in 1994 and incorporated into the World Trade Organization (WTO), vastly expanded the private property protections to immaterial goods and resources. TRIPs and neoliberal globalization have not created a single global regime of property rights, but rather have generated resistance and friction, producing novel local property arrangements (Turner and Wiber 2009). The emergence of transnational law and regulation of property has significantly expanded global legal pluralism, requiring that attention be paid not only to the layers of property, but also to the different sociopolitical scales at which ideologies of property and the political institutionalization of property rights occur.

Finally, an increasingly important concern for anthropologists is the property relations in which they are embedded vis-à-vis their interlocutors. Archaeologists once thought of themselves as cataloguers and collectors of a universal heritage of humankind, but they have become increasingly accountable to the communities within which they work. The Native American Grave Protection and Repatriation Act in the United States (NAGPRA) (1990) transformed archaeological practices by giving Native Americans property rights in their cultural patrimony and grave goods (Ferguson 1996). Similarly, sociocultural anthropologists may now find themselves in encounters with interlocutors who themselves are suspicious of the 'intellectual trespass' historically and contemporaneously perpetrated by anthropological appropriation of indigenous knowledge. This concern over 'cultural appropriation' has become an increasingly important discussion between anthropologists and their interlocutors (Simpson 2007; Brown 2009; Berson 2010).

Property regime transformation: constructing persons and state power

Property regimes have been at the centre of efforts to promote social transformation. Yet whether proposed from the top-down or bottom-up, those who endeavour to reform property regimes have consistently encountered challenges. Ethnographic studies reveal how these transformations become entrenched within collective social relations that often persist in the face of reform. Scholarship on property regimes has focused on three enduring contexts: decolonization, privatization, and enclosure.

Colonial and Postcolonial Property Regimes

The first context in which anthropologists and lawyers were concerned with property regimes was in the colonial era. Colonial powers dealt with indigenous property regimes in one of three ways (Klug 1995)—through direct conquest, negating indigenous rights via the doctrine of *terra nullius*, or establishing indirect rule by recognizing 'customary law'. Each approach has generated enduring conflicts. In settler colonial regimes that sought to extinguish indigenous rights through negation or conquest, for example, anthropologists have shown how legal processes of land restitution often reproduce the liberal logics of settler colonialism by providing a grammar of rights that requires indigenous and Aboriginal peoples to articulate a static collective identity that reifies the dominance of the state through the guise of late liberal 'multicultural' society (Clifford 1988; Povinelli 2002). In other cases, such as South Africa, which have undertaken land restitution processes as part of a broader political project of transitional justice, conflicts over property have raised critical intra-communal conflicts over the legitimacy of law (Zenker 2014).

In places where a colonial variant of 'customary law' was imposed—particularly in Africa—the social relations of property imposed through colonial and postcolonial law continue to produce conflict over land, authority, and belonging (Chanock 1991). In the 1980s, international finance institutions required many poor states to engage in structural adjustment and land titling programmes as a condition for assistance with loan repayments. Yet as Sara Berry (2017: 109) notes, these were 'superimposed on rather than replacing customary and colonial land laws and practices', thereby producing a messy set of conflicting relations and law. Recently these tensions have once again been ignited as transnational corporations and foreign states engage in a new 'scramble for Africa' through land and resource grabs, which I describe below. States have often facilitated these land grabs by claiming authority over land under customary tenure, thereby entrenching their own power and producing further domestic conflict (Peters 2013).

Socialist Property Regimes and Neoliberal Privatization

In contrast to liberal-capitalist regimes of private property, socialist regimes of property aspired to abolish bourgeois property (Marx and Engels 1978). Marx elaborated how capitalism gave birth to the commodity form through a law of value that subordinated relational processes of production and social values to the value of market exchange. Pashukanis (1987) further developed Marx's theories to describe how private property and the commodity form produced the individual rights-bearing subject. Transforming property regimes was thus part of a larger effort to develop socialist personhood (Şerban 2018).

Following Marx's prognosis, the Soviet Union sought to create a socialist property regime, starting first with the nationalization of all land and assets and social ownership of productive assets. Yet neither the Soviet Union nor its satellites ever completely abolished private property. Rather, as Verdery (2003) details, property was embedded within a system of administrative rights that reflected the hierarchies of value inherent in socialist ideology. With the fall of socialism and the ascendance of the neoliberalism, anthropologists and legal scholars investigated the process of privatization. Both Hann (1993) and Verdery (2003) describe how the imposition of private property regimes may have given small-scale producers formal title, but failed to provide 'effective ownership', because those who owned land did not have the means of production or markets to profit from it. Both authors point to the fact that the hierarchies inherent in socialist property regimes continued to persist, leading to new forms of inequality that economists failed to estimate.

Neoliberal institutions continue to insist on private property regimes by funding projects for land titling and market-based agrarian reform (Lahiff et al. 2007). Ethnographic studies, however, indicate that the insistence that private property stimulates investment oversimplifies property regimes. As Woodhouse notes, 'customary tenures acts neither as an obstacle to investment ... nor as an inalienable safety net for the poor' (2003: 547). The movement for market-based agrarian reform is being contested by a growing set of transnational agrarian movements calling for popular land reform that supports rural workers and small-scale food producers. Supporters of these movements argue that the emphasis on private property 'ignores need in favour of the demands of rule and order' (Rosset et al. 2006: 3). Furthermore, anthropologists point out that indigenous peoples may also have different visions of property and sovereignty. Verran (1998) suggests that Aboriginal communities have radically different epistemological systems of knowing and acknowledging land title. More recent work in Latin America has emphasized an alternative set of relations between peoples and land inherent in some indigenous cosmovisions (De la Cadena 2015).

Enclosures and Common Property Regimes

Since the development of modern capitalism, the enclosure of common property regimes has served to remove small-scale producers' means of subsistence, thereby engendering greater reliance on the cash economy (Thompson 1977)—a process that Harvey refers to as 'accumulation by dispossession' (Harvey 2003). The push to provision of land through private property regimes has been supported by a throng of neoclassical and neoliberal economists, who argue that communal arrangements are inefficient. Most famously, Hardin's (1968) 'tragedy of the commons' thesis suggested that communal property leads to resource depletion because it fails to provide an incentive to invest and conserve resources. Since then, scholars such as Elinor Ostrom have sought to distinguish commons from open-access property regimes. In order to be sustainably managed, Ostrom (1999) argued, commons require boundaries and exclusions regarding who has access. Anthropologists have contributed this work by analysing the communal norms by which common property regimes are constituted and how they distribute power relations. In her research on oceans and fisheries, Mansfield (2004) suggests that the renewed focus on the commons has paradoxically facilitated neoliberal enclosures by reconstituting commons as an approach compatible with property rights to enable environmental conservation.

Today, questions about how to handle collective action problems related to 'the global commons'—the atmosphere, oceans, outer space, and other common-pool resources—have paradoxically generated new regimes of private property rights through tradable environmental allowances. These state-managed processes deploy market-based processes for the allocation and conservation of common resource stocks, such as carbon emissions credits, sulphur dioxide allowances, and future catch allowances in fisheries (Rose 1999). In response, scholars have sought to describe how capitalist enclosures through private property may be resisted through 'value practices' that engage in a constant process of 'commoning' (Angelis 2006).

Dematerializing property

For much of history, land has served as the historical paragon of property. While some English theorists distinguished 'real' and 'personal property' (corresponding to the civil law distinction between 'movable' and 'immovable' property), property, with a few exceptions, referred to relations with regard to physical objects. While Lowie (1928) described a variety of forms of what he called 'incorporeal property' within non-capitalist societies, these forms of property usually involved more relational rights and were anathema to the exclusionary paradigm of private property. However, over the past several decades, incorporeal or immaterial forms of property have become the primary site of accumulation in contemporary capitalism.

The dematerialization of property is a product of the reorganization of global capitalism. In the 1970s, inter-capitalist competition led to a global economic crisis that generated three transformations. First, as a result of the economic crisis, the United States unilaterally delinked the dollar from the gold standard, thereby dissolving the Bretton Woods system by which global capitalism had been organized. In doing so, the United States removed the 'pretense in this framework of any "real" relationship between property and money' (Hardt and Negri 2017: 198). The floating currencies that resulted from the end of the Bretton Woods system led to increasing financialization beginning in the 1980s. Second, after the crisis, states and multinational corporations sought out new forms of accumulation. While financialization was one product of the shift to post-Fordism, so too was the expansion of intellectual property rights to new cultural practices and biological materials. The expansion of these rights also spurred new claims to autonomy and sovereignty through the language of 'cultural property'. Finally, new information and communication technologies, which both enabled the crisis and have since developed at a rapid pace, have transformed global production and payment systems, facilitating new claims to property that transform relations between persons.

Intellectual Property Rights

Intellectual property rights (IPR) comprise a family of rights that include copyrights and patents, as well as newer forms such as trademarks, trade secrecy, rights of publicity, cybersquatting, and database rights. For much of history, ideas and information were understood to be freely in the public domain. Early forms of IPRs emerged in Europe with the development of capitalism in the fifteenth century. The rationale for these rights was to incentivize creators or authors to make public their inventions by offering rights of exclusive ownership for a limited time period (May and Sell 2006). Beginning in the nineteenth century, however, IPRs began to expand. This proved to be problematic for the dominant liberal paradigm of property because information has typically been understood as a good within the public domain. As Boyle notes, proponents of IPR had to provide a 'convincing explanation as to why a person who recombines informational material from the public sphere is not merely engaging in the private appropriation of public wealth' (Boyle 2009: 50).

In seeking to square the contradictions of IPRs with liberal ideologies of property, proponents of IPRs have relied on claims to the creativity and uniqueness of the individual author. The 'author-function' recognizes the individual as a proprietor of knowledge who is thus entitled to rents. As Boyle notes, it provides a 'moral and philosophical justification for fencing in the commons' (2009: 56). The modernist Euro-American ideology regarding the author, however, is alien to many societies. Fred Myers, for example, points out the incommensurability of Aboriginal ideas of authorship with the Western understanding of art and culture (Myers 2002). Myers suggests that intellectual property operates as a system of what Latour (1993) describes as 'purification' that serves to rearticulate objects within dominant regimes of value. Strathern (1999) stresses the role of IPRs in creating scarcity by making knowledge transactable, valuable, and commodifiable.

The expansion of IPRs has been critical to new forms of accumulation and has generated new sites of resistance. One area in which IPRs have played a particularly important role in post-Fordist capitalism is in the expansion of trademarks—symbols, icons, names, or other signifiers that point to a product's manufacturer or origin. In an era when brands increasingly sought to merge corporate and personal forms of value, Rosemary Coombe describes how trademarks have become key commodified forms through which cultural authority is enacted and contested. She argues that they now operate as 'a central locus for the control and dissemination of those signifying forms with which identities and difference are made and remade' (1998: 29). Another area in which IPRs have expanded is in the domain of plant and human genetic resources. As Brush (1993) notes, biological information is among the most prized information that social groups possess. In the late twentieth century, the United States began to give monopoly rights to biological knowledge to developers of biotechnology. The expansion of ownership rights over plant genetic resources as well as human genetic resources has generated considerable political and regulatory conflict (Pollack and Shaffer 2009; Jasanoff 2011). Transnational agrarian movements have emerged to contest corporate power over seeds (Kinchy 2012), motivating new articulations of social identity and belonging (Fitting 2010). Communities around the world have also resisted the growth of bioprospecting for pharmaceuticals (Hayden 2003), culminating in new transnational agreements such as the Convention on Biological Diversity's Nagoya Protocol on access and benefit sharing. Nevertheless, scholars have warned that the expansion of IPRs serves as an 'intellectual land-grab' (Boyle 2008) and that agreements like TRIPs put the 'common heritage of humanity' up for grabs (Aoki 1998). Drahos and Braithwaite (2007) warn that the ceaseless expansion of IPRs could lead to a new age of 'information feudalism'.

Cultural Property

In response to the expansion of IPRs, claims to cultural property have become a new resource for social groups struggling for political recognition, autonomy, and communal control (Anderson and Geismar 2017). Claims to cultural property draw on the framework established through IPRs, but entail a significant reconfiguration of international property law in the context of decolonization and late modernity (Coombe 2009). Indigenous communities, for example, draw on cultural property to articulate claims to protect their cultural heritage and material resources. Observers have suggested that claims to cultural property are inherently contradictory—that they reify culture as a static set of practices that can be 'owned' (Mezey 2007). However, anthropologists have shown how these arguments also miss the point—indigenous activists appropriate the dominant terms of intellectual and cultural property to construct new arrangements of exchange and entitlement (Geismar 2013). Geismar argues that copyright and intellectual property are sites of mediation between neoliberal legality and grassroots agency. Yet like all claims to property, the translation of practices into property is a process that is both constituted by and constitutive of power relations.

Property in Big Data and Digital Infrastructures

The rapid growth of new information and communication technologies is transforming economic activity, making it ever more virtual, networked, and reflexive. Castells (2009: 77) uses the term 'informational capitalism' to describe a global shift in which economic 'productivity and competitiveness of units or agents in this economy (be it firms, regions, or nations) fundamentally depend on their capacity to generate, process, and apply efficiently knowledge-based information'. While intellectual and cultural property reflect the rise of the information economy, new technologies have significantly expanded the kinds of information available to be mined, appropriated, and accumulated. As digital infrastructures and data become increasingly valued, they have emerged at the centre of debates over contemporary property regimes.

The data infrastructures of the networked economy that emerged in information and communication technologies represented an early frontier of property rights. The development of the personal computer in the 1980s was accompanied by promises of a techno-utopian future that would vastly expand the public domain. Yet rather than being a global commons, individuals and corporations have acted aggressively to enclose access to codes and data by securing rights to exclusions through secrecy and patenting (Lessig 2005). This move to enclose data infrastructures has generated resistance from a cadre of hackers and programmers who have created a variety of quasi-legal forms in an effort to promote open-access property regimes. For example, Kelty (2008) and Coleman (2013) analyse how the Free and Open Source Software movement (FOSS) protested the copyright of code by creating new kinds of licences that seek to maintain code as an open-access regime. While the FOSS movement has, to some extent, been successful in seeking to open up the data infrastructures to common property regimes, digital technology corporations have also expanded the field of intellectual property, creating new layers of rights of the control, use, and transfer of information. The rise of licensing agreements such as the End User License Agreements (EULA) and Digital

Rights Management (DRM) have allowed producers, platforms, and other intermediaries to maintain control over digital things by limiting consumers' ability to transfer or resell those objects. The growth of EULA and DRM led Perzanowski and Schultz (2016) to question whether digital life is leading to 'the end of ownership'. DRM not only curtails the property rights of consumers, it also allows copyright holders to collect extensive information and data on consumers' usage.

The collection, extraction, and commodification of data has thus emerged as one of the newest key factors of production in 'information capitalism'. Just as land, labour, and money were commodified with the emergence of capitalism, information and data have become new commodities subject to property claims in the informational age (Cohen 2017). Today, '"big data"' are constituted by capturing small data from individuals' computer-mediated actions and utterances in their pursuit of effective life' (Zuboff 2015: 79). They are collected from activities over the Internet, from a growing 'intelligent infrastructure' for objects and bodies, from corporate and government databases, and other sources of surveillance. The collection and control of these data are in turn driving corporate consolidation in everything from social media to farm machinery (Fraser 2019).

Control over data enables significant economic and social control, raising challenging questions about property rights. One way this has been approached is through increasing attention to infrastructure as a sociotechnical form that constitutes relations between public and private (Larkin 2013; Kitchin 2014). Paying attention to the materiality of 'big data'—where and how they are stored and accessed—provides another way of thinking about property and data (Hogan and Shepherd 2015). Others have focused on personal data as a form of personal and private property (Cohen 2012). As big data become increasingly integral to emerging strategies of accumulation, much of the debate about property hinges on what kind of 'thing' a datum is and the relations aggregated data entail. How we frame the problem of big data, whether through the framework of *individual* privacy or through a collective regulatory framework of 'surveillance capitalism', shapes the way in which property regimes will be constructed and designed (Dean 2016). With the approval and enactment into force of the European Union's General Data Protection Regulation (GDPR), however, private property regimes are emerging, once more, as the dominant framework for claiming control and possession of data.

Another sphere in which informational capitalism is constituting new valuables and relations between persons is through blockchain, smart contracts, and other payment systems (Nelms et al. 2018). Blockchain is a digital ledger technology for recording data and sharing it across a network of participants (Natarajan et al. 2017). By employing cryptographic methods to securely record data, it is being hailed as a way of sharing data about transactions as well as facilitating payment through new cryptocurrencies that have a range of applications, from land titling to recording IPRs. Proponents of blockchain suggest that it will revolutionize payment systems and property registries by making information securely available to the public. By loosening payment systems from their regulatory contexts, requiring secure identities across platforms, and creating a lasting ledger of exchanges, digital ledger technologies have the possibility of vastly expanding the kinds of persons and valuables that can be involved in exchange.

Financializaton of property

Financialization is a process that has been driven by a search for new forms of accumulation in an age of increased competition and declining profits from production. It is facilitated by new information and communication technologies as well as by law. Through new financial instruments such as derivatives and securities, financialization enables speculative capitalization based on risk (Lee and LiPuma 2004). Not only have non-financial firms and banks become increasingly reliant on financial products, but so too have individuals across the globe to secure their basic needs (Martin 2002).

Ethnographic accounts document the changing forms of property in an age of financialization in two ways. First, anthropologists have examined how property relations have become reconstituted among the brokers, traders, banking officials, and other actors involved in the repackaging of assets and risk. Maurer examines how the practices of securities clearance and settlement in high-frequency trading—a process in which the property interests in a set of securities are transferred from one person to another—has reconstituted 'the subject of property not as the bearer of rights but as a risk profile subject to the disciplinary practice of insurance' (1999: 366). He suggests that changing definitions of property reconstitute personhood through new forms of governmentality that are deeply connected to the changes in the corporate form. Similarly, Annelise Riles describes how practices of collateral within the transnational derivatives market have redefined collateral from physical property or assets to a 'kind of temporally delineated commons, or anti-commons depending on the specific rules of the transaction' through new legal technologies of private governance (Riles 2011: 165). By rendering the highly technical and dematerialized definitions of property visible, anthropologists have sought to illuminate the political nature of these processes.

Second, anthropologists have investigated the ways in which financialization's extension of credit and debt are reshaping social relations in everyday life (Peebles 2010). While relations of credit and debt are by no means new, the ability to repay debt based on personal credit in an era of financialization has been tied to changing understandings of moral personhood (Graeber 2011). However, widespread debt and default have also engendered attempts by debtors to form counter-publics to construct shared identities around resistance to such predatory logics (Stout 2016), as well as to form new common property regimes by purchasing debt through debtors' unions (Appel 2015).

Rematerializations: the nature of property reconsidered

The dematerialization of property through informational capitalism and financialization is occurring at a time when existing forms of capitalism are facing ecological limits. Climate change is transforming the conditions through which humans meet their basic needs. It is also posing limits to fossil-fuel based forms of production and consumption on which capitalist expansion over the past two centuries has been based. In 2007–08, the world faced overlapping food, fuel, and financial crises, prompting a transformation in how productive resources are valued.

One effect of the overlapping crises of over-accumulation within neoliberalism has been a rush for productive land by a variety of global actors across the North and South. Activists described the surge in land acquisition after the 2007–08 global food crisis as the 'global land grab'. Though this framing emphasized the scope of such processes, Peluso and Lund point out that 'there is no one grand land grab, but a series of changing contexts, emergent processes and forces, and contestations that are producing new conditions and facilitating shifts in both de jure and de facto land control' (2011: 669). What is clear is that a new set of global actors are buying up large tracts of land to produce food, agrofuels, and for financial speculation, but the property relations are highly varied (Borras et al. 2012); how these property relations dispossess, dislocate, or shape social relations with previous inhabitants of land is an empirical question that anthropologists are well positioned to examine.

Land is not the only resource that is now being 'grabbed'. Fairhead, Leach, and Scoones (2012) describe the phenomena of 'green grabbing'—which is extending ownership and control over other productive resources, particularly through new calculative devices such as 'payment for ecosystem services' (PES), which calculates, commodifies, and marketizes conservation. PES is based on a 'global environmental-economic paradigm' that 'reduces organisms and ecosystems to their allegedly fungible components, and assigns monetary prices, calculated with reference to actual or hypothetical markets, to those components. The result is a panplanetary metric for valuing and prioritizing natural resources and managing their international exchange' (McAfee 1999: 134). Scholars suggest that the turn to green grabbing represents a new phase of capitalism that is restructuring the relationship between nature and society.

Today, climate change poses an existential threat to human and animal life. By framing environmental challenges as a threat to the 'global commons'—the atmosphere, oceans, and polar ice—efforts to ameliorate climate change have turned to reshaping property regimes. One important result has been the commodification of carbon through schemes such as the EU Emissions Trading System and the Clean Development Mechanism, which seek to promote market-based processes of trading allowances for carbon emissions. Similarly, the Reducing Emissions from Deforestation and Forest Degradation (REDD) initiative creates a market-based process to purchase carbon offsets to prevent deforestation and forest degradation. The process of abstracting, objectifying, and commodifying carbon requires complicated calculative devices that are a product of law (Dehm 2019). These new initiatives are part of a broader approach to managing commons through tradable environmental allowances. Through this process of commodification, rights to emit carbon are being enclosed through emerging private property regimes. Whitington thus suggests that 'carbon is at the centre of a contemporary assemblage that is imaginative, materialist, heavily quantified, and oriented toward the technical modification of human affairs' (2016: 47).

The legal construction of new objects of value and property through the global climate regime has important implications for everyday social relations. Ethnographic studies of conservation initiatives in the Brazilian Amazon—a region which is critical for the mitigation of climate change—describe the emergence of new forms of 'speculative accumulation' in which colonists 'adopt the tools of environmental governance to the work of making and preserving illicit property claims' (Campbell 2015: 193). Campbell points out how climate change and environmental discourse are reconfiguring the value of different places, thereby shifting the ways in which property relations are organized and claimed. Similarly, as once valued coastal properties become increasingly dangerous as a result of both rising sea levels and increasingly extreme storms, they also engender reconsiderations about what is private and what is public. On one hand, legal scholars suggest that the Anthropocene requires new approaches to property that are less oriented around rigid ideals of ownership (Biber 2017; Sprankling 2017). On the other hand, however, if the Anthropocene is taken as a larger challenge to the externalization of nature that is constituted through capitalist property regimes, it may lead to re-evaluations of the relations between human and non-humans, the property rights of non-humans, and thus about the boundaries and hierarchies constituted between persons and things in dominant property regimes (Braverman 2018).

Conclusions

Anthropological and legal scholarship remain engaged in a dynamic dialogue about the organization and practice of property regimes. Transformations and reform of property, whether in the name of efficiency or equality, have consistently generated friction. Anthropology thus enables greater understanding of the productive role of this friction in generating relations between persons and things. Today, changes in the organization of global capitalism as well as new information technologies are the newest sources of friction, as they dematerialize some forms of property while rematerializing others. Data, debt, and carbon are rightfully prompting a new wave of 'ownership anxiety' and challenging the liberal legal models on which the distinction between public and private is based. Furthermore, the scale and scope of these new property regimes are generating new counter-publics through which common property regimes are being claimed and organized. By ethnographically observing and analysing emergent property regimes, anthropological scholarship is poised to illuminate whether they deepen global inequality or can, in fact, ameliorate it.

Note

1. In addition, Heller (1998) describes a fifth—the 'anticommons'—a property regime in which multiple owners hold effective rights of exclusion.

References

Anderson, J. and H. Geismar. 2017. *The Routledge Companion to Cultural Property*. London: Routledge.

Anghie, A. 2007. *Imperialism, Sovereignty and the Making of International Law*. Cambridge: Cambridge University Press.

Aoki, K. 1998. 'Neocolonialism, Anticommons Property, and Biopiracy in the (Not-so-Brave) New World Order of International Intellectual Property Protection'. *Indiana Journal of Global Legal Studies* 6(1): 11–58.

Appel, H. 2015. 'The Idea Life of Money and Poststructural Realism'. *HAU: Journal of Ethnographic Theory* 5(2): 427–33.

Benda-Beckmann, F. von, K. von Benda-Beckmann, and M. Wiber. 2009. *Changing Properties of Property*. New York and Oxford: Berghahn Books.

Berry, S. 2017. 'Struggles over Land and Authority in Africa'. *African Studies Review* 60(3): 105–25.

Berson, J. 2010. 'Intellectual Property and Cultural Appropriation'. *Reviews in Anthropology* 39(3): 201–28.

Bhandar, B. 2018. *Colonial Lives of Property: Law, Land, and Racial Regimes of Ownership*. Durham, NC: Duke University Press.

Biber, E. 2017. 'Law in the Anthropocene Epoch'. *Georgetown Law Journal* 106: 1–68.

Blomley, N. 2016. 'The Boundaries of Property: Complexity, Relationality, and Spatiality'. *Law & Society Review* 50(1): 224–55.

Borras, S. Jr., J. Franco, and C. Wang. 2012. 'Competing Political Tendencies in Global Governance of Land Grabbing'. TNI Agrarian Justice Program. Transnational Institute.

Boyle, J. 2008. *The Public Domain: Enclosing the Commons of the Mind*. New Haven, CN: Yale University Presss.

Boyle, J. 2009. *Shamans, Software, and Spleens: Law and the Construction of the Information Society*. Cambridge, MA: Harvard University Press.

Braverman, I. 2018. 'Law's Underdog: A Call for More-than-Human Legalities'. *Annual Review of Law and Social Science* 14(1): 127–44.

Brown, M. F. 2009. *Who Owns Native Culture?* Cambridge, MA: Harvard University Press.

Brush, S. B. 1993. 'Indigenous Knowledge of Biological Resources and Intellectual Property Rights: The Role of Anthropology'. *American Anthropologist* 95(3): 653–71.

Busse, M. 2012. 'Property'. In J. G. Carrier, ed. *A Handbook of Economic Anthropology*, 111–27. Cheltenham: Edward Elgar Publishing.

Campbell, J. M. 2015. *Conjuring Property: Speculation and Environmental Futures in the Brazilian Amazon*. Seattle: University of Washington Press.

Castells, M. 2009. *The Rise of the Network Society: The Information Age: Economy, Society, and Culture, vol. I*. Second edition with a new Preface. Hoboken, NJ: Wiley-Blackwell.

Chakrabarty, D. 2009. 'The Climate of History: Four Theses'. *Critical Inquiry* 35(2): 197–222.

Chanock, M. 1991. 'A Peculiar Sharpness: An Essay on Property in the History of Customary Law in Colonial Africa'. *The Journal of African History* 32(1): 65–88.

Clifford, J. 1988. *The Predicament of Culture: Twentieth-Century Ethnography, Literature, and Art*. Cambridge, MA: Harvard University Press.

Cohen, J. E. 2012. *Configuring the Networked Self: Law, Code, and the Play of Everyday Practice*. New Haven, CN: Yale University Press.

Cohen, J. E. 2017. 'Property and the Construction of the Information Economy: A Neo-Polanyian Ontology'. SSRN Scholarly Paper ID 2991271. Rochester, NY: Social Science Research Network. https://papers.ssrn.com/abstract=2991271.

Coleman, E. G. 2013. *Coding Freedom: The Ethics and Aesthetics of Hacking*. Princeton, NJ: Princeton University Press.

Coombe, R. J. 1998. *The Cultural Life of Intellectual Properties: Authorship, Appropriation, and the Law*. Durham: Duke University Press.

Coombe, R. J. 2009. 'The Expanding Purview of Cultural Properties and their Politics'. *Annual Review of Law and Social Sciences* 5(1): 393–412.

Cutler, A. C. and T. Dietz. 2017. *The Politics of Private Transnational Governance by Contract*. London: Routledge.

Davies, M. 1999. 'Queer Property, Queer Persons: Self-Ownership and Beyond'. *Social & Legal Studies* 8: 327–52.

De Angelis, M. 2006. *The Beginning of History: Value Struggles and Global Capital*. London: Pluto Press.

De la Cadena, M. 2015. *Earth Beings: Ecologies of Practice across Andean Worlds*. Durham, NC: Duke University Press.

Dean, J. 2016. 'Big Data: Accumulation and Enclosure'. *Theory & Event* 19(3).

Dehm, J. 2019. 'One Tonne of Carbon Dioxide Equivalent (1TCT2E)'. In J. Hohman and D. Joyce, eds. *International Law's Objects*, 305–18. Oxford: Oxford University Press.

Drahos, P. and J. Braithwaite. 2007. *Information Feudalism: Who Owns the Knowledge Economy?* New York: The New Press.

Fairhead, J., M. Leach, and I. Scoones. 2012. 'Green Grabbing: A New Appropriation of Nature?' *The Journal of Peasant Studies* 39(2): 237–61.

Ferguson, T. J. 1996. 'Native Americans and the Practice of Archaeology'. *Annual Review of Anthropology* 25(1): 63–79.

Fitting, E. 2010. *The Struggle for Maize: Campesinos, Workers, and Transgenic Corn in the Mexican Countryside*. Durham, NC: Duke University Press.

Fraser, A. 2019. 'Land Grab/Data Grab: Precision Agriculture and Its New Horizons'. *The Journal of Peasant Studies* 46(5): 893–912.

Geismar, H. 2013. *Treasured Possessions: Indigenous Interventions into Cultural and Intellectual Property*. Durham, NC: Duke University Press.

Graeber, D. 2011. *Debt: The First 5,000 Years*. London: Melville House.

Hann, C. M. 1993. 'From Production to Property: Decollectivization and the Family-Land Relationship in Contemporary Hungary'. *Man* 28(2): 299–320.

Hann, C. M. 1998. *Property Relations: Renewing the Anthropological Tradition*. Cambridge, MA: Cambridge University Press.

Hardin, G. 1968. 'The Tragedy of the Commons'. *Science* 162 (3859): 1243–8.

Hardt, M. and A. Negri. 2017. *Assembly*. Oxford: Oxford University Press.

Harris, C. I. 1993. 'Whiteness as Property'. *Harvard Law Review* 106(8): 1707–91.

Harvey, D. 2003. *The New Imperialism*. Oxford: Oxford University Press.

Hayden, C. 2003. *When Nature Goes Public: The Making and Unmaking of Bioprospecting in Mexico*. Princeton, NJ: Princeton University Press.

Heller, M. A. 1998. 'The Tragedy of the Anticommons: Property in the Transition from Marx to Markets'. *Harvard Law Review* 111(3): 621–88.

Hirsch, E. 2010. 'Property and Persons: New Forms and Contests in the Era of Neoliberalism'. *Annual Review of Anthropology* 39: 347–60.

Hirschon, R. 1984. *Women and Property—Women as Property*. London: Croom Helm.
Hogan, M. and T. Shepherd. 2015. 'Information Ownership and Materiality in an Age of Big Data Surveillance'. *Journal of Information Policy* 5: 6–31.
Honoré, A. M. 1961. 'Ownership'. In A. G. Guest, ed. *Oxford Essays in Jurisprudence*, 107–47. Oxford: Oxford University Press.
Hussain, N. 2009. *The Jurisprudence of Emergency: Colonialism and the Rule of Law*. Ann Arbor: University of Michigan Press.
Jasanoff, S. 2011. *Designs on Nature: Science and Democracy in Europe and the United States*. Princeton, NJ: Princeton University Press.
Kelty, C. M. 2008. *Two Bits: The Cultural Significance of Free Software*. Durham: Duke University Press Books.
Kinchy, A. J. 2012. *Seeds, Science, and Struggle: The Global Politics of Transgenic Crops*. Cambridge, MA: MIT Press.
Kitchin, R. 2014. *The Data Revolution: Big Data, Open Data, Data Infrastructures and Their Consequences*. Thousand Oaks, CA: SAGE.
Klug, H. 1995. 'Defining the Property Rights of Others'. *The Journal of Legal Pluralism and Unofficial Law* 27(35): 119–48.
Koskenniemi, M. 2017. 'Sovereignty, Property and Empire: Early Modern English Contexts'. *Theoretical Inquiries in Law* 18(2): 355–89.
Lahiff, E., S. M. Borras, and C. Kay. 2007. 'Market-Led Agrarian Reform: Policies, Performance and Prospects'. *Third World Quarterly* 28(8): 1417–36.
Larkin, B. 2013. 'The Politics and Poetics of Infrastructure'. *Annual Review of Anthropology* 42(1): 327–43.
Latour, B. 1993. *We Have Never Been Modern*. Cambridge, MA: Harvard University Press.
Lee, B. and E. LiPuma. 2004. *Financial Derivatives and the Globalization of Risk*. Durham, NC: Duke University Press.
Lessig, L. 2005. *Free Culture: The Nature and Future of Creativity*. Reprint edition. New York: Penguin Books.
Lowie, R. H. 1928. 'Incorporeal Property in Primitive Society'. *The Yale Law Journal* 37(5): 551–63.
Macpherson, C. B. 2011. *The Political Theory of Possessive Individualism: Hobbes to Locke*. Reprint. New York: Oxford University Press, USA.
Maine, H. S. 1864. *Ancient Law: Its Connection with the Early History of Society, and Its Relation to Modern Ideas*. London: John Murray.
Malinowski, B. [1922] 2002. *Argonauts of the Western Pacific: An Account of Native Enterprise and Adventure in the Archipelagoes of Melanesian New Guinea*. London: Routledge.
Mansfield, B. 2004. 'Neoliberalism in the Oceans: "Rationalization," Property Rights, and the Commons Question'. *Geoforum* 35(3): 313–26.
Martin, R. 2002. *Financialization of Daily Life*. Philadelphia: Temple University Press.
Marx, K. and F. Engels. 1978. *The Marx-Engels Reader*. Edited by Robert C. Tucker. New York: W. W. Norton & Company.
Maurer, B. 1999. 'Forget Locke?: From Proprietor to Risk-Bearer in New Logics of Finance'. *Public Culture* 11(2): 365–85.
May, C. and S. K. Sell. 2006. *Intellectual Property Rights: A Critical History*. Boulder, CO: Lynne Rienner Publishers.
McAfee, K. 1999. 'Selling Nature to Save It? Biodiversity and Green Developmentalism'. *Environment and Planning D: Society and Space* 17(2): 133–54.

Mezey, N. 2007. 'The Paradoxes of Cultural Property Essay'. *Columbia Law Review* 107: 2004–46.
Myers, F. R. 2002. *Painting Culture: The Making of an Aboriginal High Art*. Durham, NC: Duke University Press.
Natarajan, H., S. Krause, and H. Gradstein. 2017. *Distributed Ledger Technology and Blockchain*. Washington, DC: World Bank.
Nelms, T. C., B. Maurer, L. Swartz, and S. Mainwaring. 2018. 'Social Payments: Innovation, Trust, Bitcoin, and the Sharing Economy'. *Theory, Culture & Society* 35(3): 13–33.
Ostrom, E. 1999. 'Coping with Tragedies of the Commons'. *Annual Review of Political Science* 2(1): 493–535.
Pashukanis, E. 1987. *Law and Marxism: A General Theory*. Revised edition. London: Pluto Press.
Peebles, G. 2010. 'The Anthropology of Credit and Debt'. *Annual Review of Anthropology* 39(1): 225–40.
Peluso, N. L. and C. Lund. 2011. 'New Frontiers of Land Control: Introduction'. *The Journal of Peasant Studies* 38(4): 667–81.
Perzanowski, A. and J. Schultz. 2016. *The End of Ownership: Personal Property in the Digital Economy*. Cambridge, MA: MIT Press.
Peters, P. E. 2013. 'Conflicts over Land and Threats to Customary Tenure in Africa'. *African Affairs* 112(449): 543–62.
Pollack, M. A. and G. C. Shaffer. 2009. *When Cooperation Fails: The International Law and Politics of Genetically Modified Foods*. Oxford: Oxford University Press.
Povinelli, E. A. 2002. *The Cunning of Recognition: Indigenous Alterities and the Making of Australian Multiculturalism*. Durham, NC: Duke University Press.
Riles, A. 2004. 'Property as Legal Knowledge: Means and Ends'. *The Journal of the Royal Anthropological Institute* 10(4): 775–95.
Riles, A. 2011. *Collateral Knowledge: Legal Reasoning in the Global Financial Markets*. Chicago: University of Chicago Press.
Rose, C. M. 1998. 'Canons of Property Talk, or, Blackstone's Anxiety'. *The Yale Law Journal* 108(3): 601–32.
Rose, C. M. 1999. 'Expanding the Choices for the Global Commons: Comparing Newfangled Tradable Allowance Schemes to Old-Fashioned Common Property Regimes'. *Duke Environmental Law & Policy Forum* 10: 45–72.
Rosset, P., R. Patel, and M.l Courville. 2006. *Promised Land: Competing Visions of Agrarian Reform*. Oakland, CA: Food First Books.
Şerban, M. 2018. 'Regime Change and Property Rights Consciousness in Postcommunist Romania'. *Law & Social Inquiry* 43(3): 732–63.
Simpson, A. 2007. 'On the Logic of Discernment'. Edited by E. M. Garroutte and M. Brown. *American Quarterly* 59(2): 479–91.
Smith, N. 2008. *Uneven Development: Nature, Capital, and the Production of Space*. Athens: University of Georgia Press.
Sprankling, J. G. 2017. 'Property Law for the Anthroposcene Era'. *Arizona Law Review* 59: 737–72.
Stout, N. 2016. '#Indebted: Disciplining the Moral Valence of Mortgage Debt Online'. *Cultural Anthropology* 31(1): 82–106.
Strang, V. and M. Busse. 2011. *Ownership and Appropriation*. Oxford: Berg.
Strathern, M. 1988. *The Gender of the Gift: Problems With Women and Problems With Society in Melanesia*. Berkeley, CA: University of California Press.

Strathern, M. 1999. *Property, Substance, and Effect: Anthropological Essays on Persons and Things*. London: Athlone Press.

Thompson, E. P. 1977. *Whigs and Hunters: The Origin of the Black Act*. Harmondsworth: Penguin.

Turner, B. 2017. 'The Anthropology of Property'. In *Comparative Property Law: Global Perspectives*, 26–50. Cheltenham: Edward Elgar.

Turner, B. and M. G. Wiber. 2009. 'Paradoxical Conjunctions: Rural Property and Access to Rural Resources in a Transnational Environment'. *Anthropologica* 51(1): 3–14.

Verdery, K. 2003. *The Vanishing Hectare: Property and Value in Postsocialist Transylvania*. Ithaca, NY: Cornell University Press.

Verdery, K. and C. Humphrey. 2004. *Property in Question: Value Transformation in the Global Economy*. London: Bloomsbury Academic.

Verran, H. 1998. 'Re-Imagining Land Ownership in Australia'. *Postcolonial Studies* 1(2): 237–54.

Weiner, A. B. 1976. *Women of Value, Men of Renown: New Perspectives in Trobriand Exchange*. First edition. Austin, TX: University of Texas.

Whitington, J. 2016. 'Carbon as a Metric of the Human'. *PoLAR: Political and Legal Anthropology Review* 39(1): 46–63.

Wiber, M. G. 2015. 'Property as Boundary Object: Normative versus Analytical Meanings'. *The Journal of Legal Pluralism and Unofficial Law* 47(3): 438–55.

Woodhouse, P. 2003. 'African Enclosures: A Default Mode of Development'. *World Development* 31(10): 1705–20.

Zenker, O. 2014. 'New Law against an Old State: Land Restitution as a Transition to Justice in Post-Apartheid South Africa?' *Development and Change* 45(3): 502–23.

Zuboff, S. 2015. 'Big Other: Surveillance Capitalism and the Prospects of an Information Civilization'. *Journal of Information Technology* 30(1): 75–89.

CHAPTER 22

LAW & DEVELOPMENT

MARKUS BÖCKENFÖRDE AND
BERIHUN A. GEBEYE

INTRODUCTION

ORIGINALLY, 'law & development' (L&D) was used in reference to the Law and Development Movement, an initiative of U.S. academics and development experts in the 1960s. It was aimed at enabling economic growth by promoting legal and institutional reforms in Latin America and newly independent countries around the globe (Baderin 2011: 11; Messick 1999). According to the conventional narrative in L&D studies, this movement was at the core of the first out of three periods (referred to as 'moments') in which 'law and development doctrine ... crystalized into an orthodoxy that is relatively comprehensive and widely accepted' (Trubek and Santos 2006: 2). Against this background, Trubek's definition of L&D as 'organized efforts to transform legal systems in developing countries to foster economic, political and social development and to the academic projects stimulated by these efforts' (Trubek 2012: 1) may be deemed adequate.

Today, the label 'L&D' is an umbrella term used to describe the relationship between law and development as it is broadly conceived by various disciplines and actors. It has been the subject of inquiry for an increasing number of scholars, including economists, political scientists, lawyers, and social anthropologists. Their distinct discipline-specific understandings of 'law' and 'development' have resulted in different perspectives and discourses on L&D. The proliferation of goals and topics under the L&D label has led to its further fragmentation, since 'ever more activities are being categorized as belonging to the field of law and development even though they actually have different meanings for different stakeholders' (van Rooij and Nicholson 2013: 300). To a certain extent, it is fair to say that the scope of L&D 'depends ultimately on how scholars auto-define their work' (Lizarazo-Rodriguez 2017: 763). In addition, as L&D is not an academic end in itself but predominately driven by ideas of practical application, these multidisciplinary scholarships influence the design and practice of law and development policy.

Furthermore, evidence drawn from development practice, as well as the interest of development agencies, in turn, impact scholarly inquiries into L&D. Hence, the interactions between scholars and practitioners make law and development an even more dynamic subject of inquiry. It is at once a field or discipline, an approach or way of thinking, a phenomenon to be observed, or a 'funding' device to be deployed in development practice.

Opinions on the expansion of the L&D field differ greatly. At one end of the spectrum, it is seen as an obstacle to a coherent conceptualization of the field (Trubek 2012: 8). At the other end, it is taken as different approaches from different disciplines, which have gradually converged to serve as a basis for interconnected research (Lizarazo-Rodriguez 2017: 892). This perspective finds expression in debates within 'legal pluralism and development', where legal and social-anthropological understandings meet (Tamanaha et al. 2012).

This contribution starts with a broad sketch of development and law in the context of L&D, before analysing the different ways in which they interact. The three 'moments' are then introduced to help readers appreciate the narrowness of L&D's original framing and the bias of its trajectory. In conclusion, it recommends reconceptualizing parts of the L&D discourse by introducing the 'planetary boundaries' as the new yardstick for sustainable development, which is to be framed by law.

Development in L&D

The modern development discourse gained momentum in the aftermath of the Second World War and at the dawn of the Cold War. Defined by his containment policy, U.S. President Truman countered the world's economic decline with a two-pronged strategy: while Europe benefited from the European Recovery Program, 'so that the free people of that continent can resume their rightful place in the forefront of civilization', other parts of the world enjoyed his Point Four Program 'for making the benefits of our scientific advances and industrial progress available for the improvement and growth of underdeveloped areas [whose] economic life is primitive and stagnant'.[1] It is worth noting that in 1950, the per capita gross domestic products (GDPs) of Argentina, Chile, Uruguay, and Venezuela were higher than the corresponding figures for Greece, Italy, Portugal, and Spain (Lizarazo-Rodriguez 2017: 765).

Though the countries addressed were *all* recipients of U.S. support (Faundez 2017: 502), the wording and structure of Truman's inauguration speech bifurcated countries into two groups: the group of 'developed' countries, which required 'recovery'; and the group of 'underdeveloped' countries in need of 'development'. It hinted at the relative inferiority and inadequacy of a certain group of countries that needed to evolve into something else (Esteva 1992), thereby reviving, albeit implicitly, the colonial-era rhetoric of a civilizing mission (Dann 2019b): development is thought of in evolutionary terms and the developed world represents the ideal state, development's ultimate goal.

As poverty became the defining characteristic of underdevelopment in the 1950s, development was determined primarily by a country's economic growth, the yardstick for which was a country's GDP per capita. Modernization theory seemed to provide the definitive model for progress: all countries must pass a series of successive stages of economic growth (Rostow 1960), with the developed world acting as a standard template (Tamanaha 1995: 471). According to this theory, once developing countries achieve economic development, a spill-over effect is that many of their social, political, and cultural 'problems' also transform and modernize, enabling them to join the ranks of developed countries.

With decolonialization in full swing and growing frustration about the lack of economic growth in many countries of the developing world, the appeal of modernization theory had also decreased. It was contrasted with dependency theory, which argued that these countries were excluded from the different stages of development because the history and structure of the global economic relations had kept them in a state of dependency even after the end of colonialization. According to dependency theory, colonialism's exploitative logics remained largely intact, with 'a Western core and a developing periphery, whereby the wealth of the former is based upon keeping the latter in a state of permanent dependency and underdevelopment' (Tamanaha 1995: 477). To achieve development, according to the theory, a radical restructuring of economic world order was required. But despite dependency theory's fundamental opposition to modernization theory, its followers continued to understand development in economic terms (Dann 2014: 24).

Though already advocated for by the United Nations Educational, Scientific and Cultural Organization (UNESCO) in the 1960s,[2] it took another thirty years until the precursor to a more holistic conception of development would emerge in the form of the 'human development approach'.

The initial narrow understanding of development as a solely economic phenomenon changed with the 'Basic Needs' approach in the first half of the 1970s. This approach included physical, mental, and social aspects as elements of development, suggesting that poverty should be dealt with by focusing more directly on food, clothing, shelter, education, and employment. It was complemented by environmental considerations in the context of growth, development, and ensuring future generations' access to the basic means of sustenance. Environmental considerations would give birth to the concept of sustainable development, which would find expression in the Report of the World Commission on Environment and Development (UN 1988). Both extensions to the narrow development discourse were guided by political sensibilities in the West (i.e. Bretton Woods Institutions, Club of Rome) and 'highlights the extent to which policies are designed and imposed separate and apart from the communities they purport to serve' (Gordon and Sylvester 2004: 23). Over the years, they found their way onto the agenda of relevant institutions and projects, most visibly in the form of the Human Development Index (HDI). Originally conceived by Mahbub Ul Haq and rooted in Sen's work on human capabilities, the United Nations Development Program (UNDP) created the HDI in 1990. It was based on three key factors: longevity, knowledge, and standard of living. These factors, in turn, are measured using quantifiable variables, which allow for periodic comparisons between countries and their level of development. In further recognition of Amartya Sen's claim that '[d]evelopment requires the removal of major sources of unfreedom: poverty as well as tyranny, poor economic opportunity as well as systematic social deprivation, neglect of public facilities as well as intolerance or overactivity of repressive states' (Sen 1999: 3–4), other principles such as democratic (good) governance, justice, and gender equality figured prominently in the development thinking.

Some of those became part of the eight Millennium Development Goals (MDG) that were adopted by UN member states in 2000 and represented yet another effort aimed at a more comprehensive measurement of development. The binary of development providers *versus* development recipients still animated the discourse.

With the adoption of the Sustainable Development Goals (SDGs) by world leaders at the 2015 United Nations Summit on Sustainable Development, the understanding of development was partially reconsidered, since the development agenda now included all nations, 'developing' and 'developed' alike. Development was now understood as an ongoing movement towards a defined objective regardless of a country's economic condition or its status as 'developed' or 'developing'. Within this framework, development is no longer solely the agenda of the Global South, but is seen as a global agenda to sustain and promote prosperity, while protecting the planet.

Law in L&D

Two aspects of law have had a considerable impact on the L&D discourse: the nature and essence of law; and the genesis and advancement of public international law.

What is Law?

As early as Plato's *Minos*, questions such as the different forms of law (customary law, state law, natural law), their mutual relationships, and the preferred form of law were sources of great debate. Today, the same debates continue unabated.

Some scholars have attempted, albeit in vain, to synthesize these differing views into a singular and consistent understanding of the law (Berman 1958: 20), while others have chosen to highlight one of those focal points as the overriding determinant of the law. The three different aspects are also given varying levels of prominence in different academic disciplines.

Conventional legal scholarship and, to a larger extent, legal positivism have focused on law's formal and state-centred dimension: the state is the exclusive proprietor of laws that are made and enforced by state institutions, such as state legislature, state courts, and law enforcement agencies. Here, law is primarily the law codified in statutes, written in books, and applied by courts.

Legal anthropologists, in contrast, approach the nature of law from a different angle. In their conception, law's essence is not its institutionalized form, but rather its function and effect on the social order. Law forms a social order by guiding the behaviour of humans in a society. It differs from other social phenomena (such as etiquettes, fashions, and manners) as it consists of 'oughts' (shall clauses) that are either perceived as binding by the group members (Fikentscher 2009: 132) or sanctioned 'by a definite social machinery of binding force, based ... upon mutual dependence, and realized in the equivalent arrangement of reciprocal services' (Malinowski 1926: 55). In general, this functionalist approach[3] to law is broader than the legal positivist approach, as it extends beyond formal state law and institutions. Having said that, it may also have a limiting factor: in many societies, some codified laws remain dormant, as they are antithetical to social and cultural norms. Being too far out of step with cultural norms creates challenges not only for laws to be accepted and followed by citizens, but also for state institutions to find judges and functionaries who will consistently uphold the state law over traditional or majoritarian values. (Belton 2005: 15).

The extent to which the two concepts of law overlap depends on the historical context. As making and changing laws are rather easy for those with political power, changing social norms and traditional values is typically a long and difficult process; it is obvious that within an L&D discourse, the different perspectives on law yield different results (Barrett and Gaus 2018: 204; Bicchieri 2017).

What is International Law?

The basic elements of public international law are European in origin. Its doctrines and principles are rooted in European history and experience (Anghie 2006: 740). Indeed, it was initially grounded in natural law, and was followed in the nineteenth century by the understanding that sovereign states as actors had to consent to international law. The consent was given either explicitly by treaties to which states were bound as parties or implicitly by customary international law (Tamanaha 2017: 156) or as a gap-filler by general principles of law. In order to qualify as an actor under public international law, a territorial entity had to be categorized as, among other qualities, 'civilized'. Colonies did not fall under this category. But even entities that were no longer colonized were still required to attain a level of civilization as a precondition for being recognized as an actor (Matz 2005: 62) within public international law, since they were 'not yet able to stand by themselves under the strenuous conditions of the modern world'.[4] It is therefore little wonder that out of the fifty-one states negotiating the UN Charter in 1945, only eleven came from Africa or Asia. Shortly after, the international landscape changed dramatically due to the birth of dozens of new states amidst decolonialization. The number of UN member states increased from the original fifty-one to seventy-six in 1955. It then rose to 110 by 1962, the large majority of which were 'developing' countries (Gilman 2015).

As noted by Abi Saab, this growth triggered the 'transformation of very large parts of the globe, mostly in Africa and Asia, from objects to subjects of international law'

(Abi-Saab 1962: 97) and changed the composition of the international community significantly. Along with most of Latin America, they formed the 'Third World', a very accurate term coined by Sauvy, which was inspired by Emmanuel-Joseph Sieyès's notion of the third estate in France before the 1789 Revolution (Pahuja 2011: 261): 'For finally, this Third World, ignored, exploited and despised like the Third State, also wants to be something' (Sauvy 1952: 14). Public international law came into being at a time when Third World states were either not involved or non-existent. Since they were absent from negotiations when relevant agreements were being drafted and were not involved in the formation of international customary law, these states were born into a body of international obligations that reflected the approaches of another epoch, as well as the interests of predominately industrialized states.

Following drastic structural changes in the international community, a debate emerged on the reconceptualization of the tenets of international law. Many Third World scholars representing the first generation of Third World Approaches to International Law (TWAIL) made two partly overlapping claims. First, they argued that the existing body of law shall not automatically apply to new countries based on the basic rule that a state cannot be bound by international rules unless it has agreed to be (Anghie 2006: 748). New states would have the right to 'pick and choose' which rules of the established international system corresponded to their needs and which they deemed acceptable (Brunner 2019). More visionary, they also argued for a general clean slate through the creation of a new international (economic) legal order that accommodated the concerns and interests of all members of the new international community in a concerted manner (Koskenniemi 2019: 14).

While the previous turn in international law shifted the focus from natural law to the individual state's sovereignty, the new turn was partly meant to substitute the doctrinal requirement of individual, sovereign consent with that of lawmaking founded in democratic theory and global solidarity. Based on the new institutional architecture of the UN system, resolutions of the General Assembly of the United Nations (UNGA), the most representative organ, would become a source of international law,[5] or at least count as a kind of state practice necessary for forming new customary international law (Gordon and Sylvester 2004: 35). The idea of turning international law into an instrument of global justice also appealed to parts of the French legal academy and led to the formation of 'droit international du development' as a field (Koskenniemi 2019: 44).

Both efforts turned out to be Sisyphean, countered by Western states with contradictory lines of reasoning. The first one was refuted with the argument that by becoming an independent and sovereign state based on the established (customary) rules of the international system, they have implicitly been afforded statehood. The latter demand was declined by insisting that the voluntary basis of international law is fundamentally incompatible with the idea of being outvoted by a majority of states. Initiatives to adjust the international legal order by treaty law were mostly hampered by the First World through 'formal ways of non-ratification, reservations, and uncounted interpretative declarations and official statements' (von Bernstorff and Dann 2019: 15). This situation pre-determined the course of international law and development.

On the relationship between law and development in the L&D discourse

Overview

There are different views on the role of law in a society and, more specifically, the impact of law in the process of social and economic reform (Gessner 2001: 8492–6). For some, law is an element of society, and as such, a reflection of the underlying and constantly changing structure of a society (Gessner 2001: 8492). For others, law is a mere tool for steering society in any possible direction (Gessner 2001: 8492).

In the L&D discourse, law is predominately understood from the latter perspective. It is regarded as a viable instrument to influence, or even engender, change. Inspired by Max Weber's work on economy and society (Weber 1978), a specific type of law was privileged in this discourse. Weber attributes the rise of capitalism in Europe to the legitimate authority of statutory law and state bureaucracy. According to him, unlike European laws, non-European laws require an external legitimizer (e.g. customs, traditions, charismatic leaders), and thus lack the 'rationality' necessary for economic growth and capitalism (Trubek 1972: 12). Although an increasing number of scholars acknowledge the need for a broader definition of law and a more context-sensitive approach that includes local ownership and bottom-up dynamics, the inherent logic of the discourse remains the same: the idea of directing behaviour and development through law (referred to as 'Law *in* Development'). Law in Development comes in different forms. It largely refers to laws that initiate, facilitate, frame, or promote the course of development at both the national and international levels. It also includes the various administrative laws and regulations of a multifaceted regime of development finance and international development assistance: the relevant operational rules of international, supranational, national, and private institutions; agreements between these institutions and the recipient (or partner) states organizing the transfer of funds and the exchange of knowledge to programmatic national development law; and international soft law setting a normative framework within which actors and institutions (co)operate (Dann 2019b: 541). From the perspective of former European colonial powers, this type of international development law also marked the passage from 'internal' colonial law to international regulations on cooperation and aid (Lizarazo-Rodriguez 2017: 815).

The emergence of a broader understanding of development that was not limited to economic growth also expanded the relationship between law and development. Law reforms were no longer exclusively seen as an instrument of development, but were also regarded as an objective of development itself (referred to as 'Law *as* Development'). Primarily under the rubric of 'Rule of Law', legal reforms and foreign assistance are justified as being part of development, whether or not they can be tied directly to economic growth. In this context, law is not only a means to an end but also the end itself.

Law in Development at the National Level

Various macroeconomic theories about industrialization, economic growth, and their relationship with law as an instrument of development were discussed and applied in developing countries after the Second World War. Some theories are based on the concept of a 'strong' state using law to shape policies either through an import substitution approach, an export-oriented trade and growth strategy, or a socialist central planning (command economy) with very different regulatory frameworks. Others relied on the 'weak' state: law was no longer understood as an instrument of state policy but as 'the foundation for market relations and as a limit on the state' (Trubek and Santos 2006: 2). In between these two extremes lies the concept of the regulatory state.

From the 1950s to the 1970s, the concept of the strong state that fosters development was widely applied. Many developing states introduced import substitution policies in response to the economic situation after the Second World War. By creating the capacity to locally produce goods that would otherwise have had to be imported, countries aimed to diversify their economies and to reduce economic leakages (Adewale 2017: 141). The instruments of such a strategy comprised a combination of protective policies such as quota restrictions, tariffs, exchange controls, and overvalued exchange rates (Ahmad 1978: 356). A number of East Asian countries—chief among them South Korea and Taiwan—shifted to export-led growth in the mid-1960s by supporting manufacturing industries and introducing export-led policies, that is, legislation on export subsidies, credit subsidies, tax exemptions, and relying on undervalued exchange rates (Lee 2017: 461). The exception to the strong state concept could be found in the Soviet republics and the satellite states of Central and Eastern Europe. Here, however, the states are scarcely distinguishable from the communist or socialist parties. Following the nationalization of private businesses and properties, law served as an instrument to implement party policy and plans for the national economy. This was achieved by means of establishing collectives controlled by the party and a framework for realizing long-term development goals, among other ways. A more competitive version of this model emerged in China, where the so-called Beijing Consensus symbolizes 'one of the greatest economic transitions in human history' (Chen 2017: 2). It rejects the universal model of development and defines a nation's development in terms of innovation, dynamic policy toolkit, and self-determination (Ramo 2004: 11–12). Within these broader frameworks, informal institutions (e.g. personal connections, business networks, trust, and mediation) and formal institutions (e.g. political decentralization and competitive local governments) contribute to China's economic growth (Siems 2014: 344). In the context ... of the Communist Party's policies, law has been used for developmental ends, especially after 1978. In this respect, legislative regulation of various aspects of the labour market (e.g. mobility, remuneration, social services, workers' rights), capital (e.g. interest rates, exchange rates, credit allocation), land (e.g. confiscation, land-taking), and the environment has attracted investment (Xu 2012: 10–11). The Communist Party's performance-based promotion system and local government infrastructure have resulted in local government and party officials competing for investment and economic development (Xu 2012: 10–11). While this competition among local governments may have led to a race to the bottom, it has also contributed to massive economic development in the country.

Neoliberal *laissez-faire* strategies advocating for a weak state gained momentum in two waves: (a) during the 1980s, primarily in countries that had previously adhered to the import substitution approach; and (b) during the 1990s, in a number of 'Second World' countries after the collapse of the Soviet Union. The premise of such strategies is that the 'magic of the marketplace' will guide resource allocation and stimulate economic development. Tax reforms, trade liberalization, privatization of state enterprises, and legal protection for property rights were some of the strategies utilized to revitalize growth and development. The concept of the regulatory state was a response to the negative experiences of the weak state. In light of imperfections in the economy, as well as market failures, there is an imperative need for market regulation. However, the state refrains from involvement in this process (Lizarazo-Rodriguez 2017: 778).

Law in Development at the International Level

The fate of international law in the context of development can be adequately examined by looking at initiatives that would have allowed the majority of new states not only to gain formal political independence, but also—together with other Third World countries—economic stability in order to avoid other forms of dependency (Dann 2019a: 279).

Despite many normative efforts by developing countries to promote development in an international order since the 1950s and the fact that a plethora of institutions were established to reconfigure the development paradigm (Dann 2013: 284), the 'battle for international [hard] *law*' was mostly lost at both the institutional and substantive level (Koskenniemi 2019, emphasis added). First and foremost, pronouncements of the UN General Assembly, even when formulated in terms of obligations and rights, have not yet been acknowledged as a source of public international law (Schachter 1976: 3). Therefore relevant declarations, resolutions, and charters addressing pertinent issues such as the treatment of alien property in the context of state succession (UNGA Resolution 3281, adopted in 1974), the granting of trade preferences to developing countries (UNGA Resolution 3201, adopted in 1974), permanent sovereignty over natural resources (UNGA Resolution 1803, adopted in 1963), and the right to development (UNGA Resolution 41/128, adopted in 1986) were classified as non-binding soft law or *'pré-droit'* (Schachter 1976: 4). Hardly any of them further developed into customary international law or became part of a binding agreement.[6] Furthermore, most of the other development-related concerns accommodated in binding agreements had been worded in a non-mandatory form. An illustrative example of this approach was the decades-long process of adding 'exceptions' for developing countries (e.g. the 'Generalized System of Preferences' (GSP), the Enabling clause) into the relevant international trade agreements (e.g. the World Trade Organization's (WTO's) GATT 1947 and GATT 1994.[7] Although these adjustments became part of legally binding agreements, and thereby part of international law, the actual provisions did not go beyond legally non-binding measures. They merely enabled developed countries to give developing countries preferential treatment without violating the core legal principles of GATT. Said adjustments were a set of best-endeavour undertakings but did not affect the voluntary character of giving preferential treatment. Developing countries did not have a legal right to be granted such treatment, nor could they seek legal recourse upon its withdrawal (Fritz 2005: 14). Legally more substantiated preferential clauses were introduced under the new WTO regime, granting developing countries longer transition periods for implementing WTO regulations.

Furthermore, next to the general concern about the extent to which new states should be bound by the norms of international law (see above), some of these norms have been creatively reinterpreted in a way that is favourable to Western states but at the expense of former colonies. Probably the most striking example is the debate about the doctrine of 'acquired rights' and how its original meaning was imaginatively reconfigurated. By equating colonial concession holders operating under the umbrella of colonial authority with private foreign investors, acquired rights became 'the principal rationale for the protection of concessionary interests during decolonialization' (Craven 2019; Lalive 1965). This alone rendered particularly relevant two other debates: whether national or international law should regulate standards of expropriation and which requirements had to be observed (Brunner 2019: 129; Gordon and Sylvester 2004: 32).

In the area of development finance, governance structures were set up that would in turn cement Western dominance. The struggle for adequately institutionalizing the financing of economic development in Third World countries led to the creation of the International Development Association (IDA) in 1960 within the framework of the World Bank, at the expense of the Special United Nations Fund for Economic Development (SUNFED), which was initiated by ECOSOC (the Economic and Social Council) in 1952 and operated as a special agency under the auspices of the UN.[8] The difference between the two lay in their respective power structures: at the World Bank, the weight of a member state's vote reflected its financial contribution, whereas at the UN, a more egalitarian principle (one state: one vote) was in force. As a result, the IDA allowed for the political and developmental interests of a few Western states to be placed at the centre of its agenda (Dann 2019a: 284). What was originally thought to offer not only financial support, but also political autonomy was turned into a Western dominance in development finance, culminating in contentious, and often neoliberal, macroeconomic reforms as a conditionality for financial support in the 1980s (Dann 2019b: 554).

In sum, what is today referred to as 'International Development Law' (Mahiou 2013: 2) is in actuality a mosaic of institutional rules—which rarely favour developing countries—that coexist with predominately non-binding norms and commitments that are not considered to be 'hard law' in the conventional understanding of public international law. It requires, therefore, a certain boldness to claim that 'development has played a constitutive role in the international legal order' (Rittich 2016: 827), a statement that lacks factual support.

Granted, the issue of development has dominated discourses and debates in public international law, while relevant institutions have also been set up. But this hardly changed the legal order in favour of development. One of the few possible exceptions in this regard were 'common but differentiated responsibilities', which have made a legally relevant impact, predominately in the field of international environmental law, by ascribing different obligations to industrialized and developing countries with regard to the protection and sustainable use of the environment (Pauw et al. 2014). There is a clear shift in logic here: instead of focusing primarily on the proactive promotion of economic growth, sustainable resource management is brought into the limelight by acknowledging planetary boundaries.

Law as Development and Rule of Law Promotion

In Amartya Sen's reconceptualization of development as freedom, law is no longer merely a means to an end, but also an end in itself. Law can become an objective of development by constituting and manifesting basic individual freedoms. Law as a value in and of itself has been promoted as 'thick' rule of law (RoL). This stands in contrast to 'thin' RoL, which relies on formal procedures that ensure the functioning of a legal system, while remaining open with respect to the law's content (occasionally referred to as 'rule by law'). The 'thick' version requires the inclusion of additional ends; for example, human rights, democratic rights, and social rights (Belton 2005: 14–15; Carothers 2009: 54; Prado and Trebilcock 2014: 50). In short, the broader understanding of development has coincided with a more expansive definition of RoL. Predominately based on the 'thick' RoL concept, a multi-billion-dollar 'RoL industry' was set up after the end of the Cold War and the beginning of the era of 'economic transformation' and 'democratization' in Second and Third World countries. Today, RoL functions like a multipurpose tool in development circles. But despite this growing popularity, results have mostly been disappointing. RoL as an end of development came with value-driven contents equating to a concept of justice (Trubek 2006) that was often unfamiliar to the end-users of the respective legal system. The law at the core of RoL promotion towards justice was embedded in state law, while state institutions were tasked with achieving and maintaining justice (Janse 2013: 183). The neglect of cultural barriers, differing values, individuals' understanding of 'justice' (Channell 2005), and ignorance of the ubiquitous phenomena of legal pluralism—seen mostly as a 'problem' rather than an indispensable resource (Sage and Woolcock 2012: 3)—have contributed to the limited impact of many L&D activities. As Koskenniemi explains:

> [O]fficial Western values are raised to the level of 'universality', while non-Western values are relegated to the realm of exotic cultures. Behind the attempt to set up a

> hierarchy between 'human rights' and 'cultural values' lies an inability to conceive of human rights in 'cultural' terms and cultural practices as regimes of human rights.
>
> (Koskenniemi 1997: 582)

Afghanistan is often referred to as a paradigmatic case of the international community's failed efforts to rebuild a state in a post-conflict scenario and in line with a RoL blueprint for democracy, women rights, etc. (Eddy 2009; Stromseth et al. 2006). Similar constitution-building projects in conflict and post-conflict states have been unable to institutionalize constitutional democracy and respect for human rights, thereby doing little to realize these development goals.

Driven by these experiences, some voices have demanded a conceptual and methodological departure from traditional legal scholarship (Tan 2019: 294) towards the recognition of the hybridity of normative orders and shifting focus towards end-users, as well as their perceptions of laws and norms. 'Access to justice' would no longer be limited to state law and state institutions and would also include access to informal or traditional justice (Tamanaha 2011). Here, L&D is understood as a form of 'legal development' that recognizes—alongside formal state law based on legal transplants—norms rooted in society and regulates much of individuals' lives and the broader community as laws (Tamanaha 2011: 14). Furthermore, it often suggests taking this customary law as a basis for incrementally inducing social change. Yet, such a complementary bottom-up approach, which may foster an 'interlegality' between state law and non-state law (de Sousa Santos 2002: 473), is only hesitantly accepted by many RoL promoters, since it either (at least temporarily) acknowledges 'inhuman' customs as law or, more generally, turns into an extreme form of contextualism that risks reducing law and development studies 'to at best 150 country studies' (Trebilcock 2016: 335).

The orthodoxies of L&D

While the previous paragraphs aimed to paint a more comprehensive picture of L&D, chronologically speaking, the unfolding of L&D may be split into three distinct periods, or *moments,* during which 'law and development doctrine has crystallized into an orthodoxy that is relatively comprehensive and widely accepted' (Trubek and Santos 2006: 2). These three moments have a number of common characteristics. For instance, they all mirror Western development paradigms inspired by the United States (Ohnesorge 2007: 223).[9] They also make common assumptions about the role of law in the respective economic theories and practices (Tan 2019: 291). Tied to a narrow understanding of L&D and focusing on self-defined epochal junctures, other relevant dynamics are neglected in this trajectory (L&D between colonizers and colonies in the process of decolonialization and its aftermath; L&D in North-East Asia; L&D in public international law). While the first two moments are entangled in Cold

War dynamics, the third moment emerged in the 1990s, following a drastic change in global politics.

The beginning of the first L&D moment coincides with President Kennedy's strategy to end European colonialization but without newly independent countries adopting socialistic or communist systems (Lizarazo-Rodriguez 2017: 772). The doctrine informing the first moment was that the development of developing countries required a strong state that would transform the economy and society using modern—in particular American—laws. Building on modernization theory, the first moment posited that developing countries would get a 'jumpstart' by adopting American laws without having to go through the different stages of economic development (Rostow 1960). Like Weber, the underlying premise of the first moment is that the laws and legal cultures of developing countries are responsible for their underdevelopment; therefore, to remove the obstacles to development, these countries must adopt 'modern' laws and change their legal culture.

Based on these normative assumptions, it was believed that the diffusion of American legal education, as well as the archetypal American lawyer, judge, and law enforcement officer, were necessary conditions for development in these countries (Snyder 1982). Accordingly, the United States Agency for International Development (USAID), the Ford Foundation, the Rockefeller Foundation, and the Peace Corps spent millions of dollars to reform legal education in Latin America and Africa (Snyder 1982: 377–8). 'Legal missionaries' were sent to the field in Africa, Asia, and Latin America (Snyder 1982), and many lawyers in developing countries were trained in US law schools. However, neither the diffusion of legal education nor legal transplants brought the promised modernization and development in Latin America, Africa, and Asia. After a decade of mainly bilateral investment, funding decreased considerably in the early 1970s and even those within the law and development community would declare such programmes to be 'ethnocentric and naïve' (Trubek and Galanter 1974).

The second moment of L&D began in the mid-1980s. It emerged within a neoliberal political environment nurtured by national agendas in the United States and the United Kingdom ('Reagonomics' and 'Thatcherism'). The state was no longer the solution to a country's development challenges but rather its problem. Underdevelopment was considered to be the outcome of poor resource allocation due to incorrect pricing policies and state intervention (Trebilcock 2016: 334). Economic liberalization, market deregulation, and privatization were seen as the solution. The role of law in this neoliberal paradigm was twofold. It had to create a framework that facilitated transaction among private actors, but it also had to restrain excessive state intervention (Trubek 2016: 312). Clear and predictable rules (i.e. enforceable property rights and rules-based contract law) were promoted to ensure the operation of the private economy, while independent and effective courts were also promoted to uphold and protect these rules (Ohnesorge 2007: 247). In contrast to the first moment, the second moment was not driven by bilateral arrangements but dominated and managed by the World Bank and the International Monetary Fund. In order to get loans, as well as financial and technical aid, from the two Bretton Wood institutions, countries wrecked by the debt crisis had to accept and implement Structural Reform Programs (SAPs), more commonly known as the Washington Consensus, which epitomized the second moment of L&D practice and established a neoliberal and 'thin' concept of RoL that focused on characteristics such as transparency, predictability, stability, and enforceability of the legal system (Daniels and Trebilcock 2008). Within this framework, the SAPs required countries enact policies that controlled inflation, reduced governments' budget deficit and spending, lifted import and export restrictions, removed subsidies, devaluated currencies, and privatized with the goal of institutionalizing a free market system (Mohan et al. 2000). Although not developed for post-socialist transformation in the 1990s, the ideas of the Washington Consensus heavily influenced the path of reform in some of the affected countries. But, like the state in the first moment, the market in the second moment failed to deliver development promises. It became evident that markets could not create the conditions required for their own success and that unrestricted markets were often inefficient in their own way (Trubek and Santos 2006: 6).

The third moment of L&D has been in motion since the end of the Cold War and was in part a response to the failure of neoliberalism. Something between the 'strong' and 'weak' state, the 'regulatory' state was necessary to correct market failures (Vandenhole 2019). Beyond that, the third moment was formed by the RoL paradigm in its different facets. While the second moment regarded law as purely instrumental and relied on the procedural or 'thin' concept of RoL for achieving economic growth, the third moment added a 'thick' version emerging from a confluence of various dynamics. A more comprehensive development approach gained momentum, which was exemplified by the UNDP's focus on human development and Sen's identification of basic rights as an advancement of human capabilities (Sen 1999). In the meantime, the transformation of post-socialist states from planned to market economies went beyond mere reform, and was coupled to the promotion of liberal democratic reform (Rittich 2016: 833). Constitution-making in post-conflict scenarios was aimed at building states capable of accommodating religious and ethnic diversity, while curbing the spread of terrorism as a pre-condition for human development. For all these different dynamics, RoL was seen as the answer: procedural RoL continued to serve as an instrument of market reform, while substantive RoL served as an instrument of liberal democratic reform and respect for human rights in a rebuilt state. As Carothers noted, '[o]ne cannot get through a foreign policy debate these days without someone proposing the rule of law as a solution to the world's troubles' (Carothers 1998). And for Dave Trubek, one of the founding scholars of L&D, RoL became the new name for L&D (Trubek 2006: 80; 2016: 312).

Despite the historical specificities of each moment, they share one common characteristic: the enduring belief that transplanting formal laws in developing countries contributes to their development and then the later admission that top-down approaches had not been very successful.

Insights from socio-legal and anthropological research offer explanations for similar failures in all three moments (Stromseth et al. 2006; Vandenhole 2019). They have not considered the possibility of 'law of various kinds, with different foundations of legitimacy, validity, power and authority, and with different degree of institutionalisation and formalisation that can coexist in the same social space, often at different scales' (Benda-Beckmann and Benda-Beckmann 2014: 34). Only recently have they gained more attention in various initiatives under the term 'Legal Pluralism and Development' (Sage and Woolcock 2012).

Concluding remarks

Past and present L&D dynamics have been shaped by changes in the prevalence of different concepts of development. In the future, the role of new perspectives on L&D should not be limited to building on current concepts of development but ought to contribute more actively in forming them. The understanding of development has long been framed as the process of moving from an underdeveloped to a fully developed stage, suggesting that there is not only a point of departure but also a rather static and mature endpoint that is to be achieved. Seen in this light, development was a certain phase in a country's biography, during which it would shed the status of being underdeveloped and transform into a fully developed country.[10]

Yet, being 'developed' is not, and never was, meant to be a static status similar to plants or animals that grow to the point of maturity and then remain at an equilibrium (Hickel 2019: 14). As evinced by the UN Human Development Index (HDI), developed countries also undergo further progress in terms of economic growth and human development. Increasingly, there is a commitment to dismantle the binary (developed *versus* developing) logic of development. To a certain extent, this is also reflected in the SDGs that require all countries to define targets and to achieve 'development' goals. Following this path, one may wonder: what distinguishes normal political processes from 'development' in L&D, since 'states routinely use law to promote economic growth and social transformation, and "legal development" is a normal feature of every society'? (Rittich 2016: 829). Dann suggests the reduction of inequalities between states, classes, and individuals as the core of development (Dann 2019b: 544). In light of this broad definition, L&D discourses may also include increasing inequalities within one state, which is a global phenomenon and not limited to the Global North–South divide. One main protagonist of this idea, Yong-Shik Lee, advances this idea further by suggesting an increase in the utility of the L&D approach by applying it to the United States, its economic disparity, and growing income inequality (Lee 2019).

Promoting development agendas in industrialized countries to reduce inequality may also preoccupy the L&D discourse in the future. Economic growth and human development are costly. Warnings about planetary boundaries dates back to the early 1970s, when the Club of Rome published its report on *The Limits of Growth*. Recent studies have been able to offer more detailed data that frame the planetary boundaries in global (Steffen et al. 2015)[11] and national (O'Neill et al. 2018) terms based on a country's environmental footprint. Sustainable (social) development in each country must therefore take place within its individual biophysical boundaries. The additional marker of inequality here is the disproportionate exploitation of the planet's limited resources to promote growth. Although there are different ways to reduce a country's biophysical footprint, for many industrialized countries, 'degrowth' in economy has become an unavoidable part of sustainable development (Hickel 2019: 30). This has radical implications for the current international development agenda, as the current SDGs still demand exponential global GDP growth. The future L&D discourse has to examine the role of law in achieving progress in a country without, however, transgressing its individual boundaries, which would run the risk of turning many industrialized countries into new 'developing' countries.

Notes

1. President Harry Truman's inaugural address, available at: <https://www.bartleby.com/124/pres53.html>.
2. 12C/Resolution 8.1(c), 1962; l5C/Resolution 8.2.3, 1968. See UNESCO (1971: 85).
3. As a subject of inquiry, this early-twentieth-century approach has been replaced by broader concepts of law, including law as culture and an interactive web of meaning that allows for a plurality of co-existing normative orders (see Moore 1973).
4. Article 22 of the Covenant.
5. On the debate over the legal status of UNGA resolutions, see notes 56 and 57 in von Bernstorff and Dann (2019: 15).
6. To a certain extent, the 'Right to Development' can be considered an exception, as it was included in Article 22 of the African Charter of Human and Peoples' Right (Organisation of African Unity (OAU) 1981)—which was adopted in 1981 and entered into force in 1986—and in Article 37 of the Arab Charter on Human Rights (Akram 2007)—which was adopted in 2004 and entered into force in 2008.
7. The General Agreement on Tariffs and Trade (GATT).
8. The prevalence of IDA over SUNFED resulted not only from strategic manoeuvring of Western states at the height of the Cold War, but also from a disintegration of the Third World.
9. Within the framework of the Cold War, the Soviet Union also had its own version of L&D and supported the spread of socialist legal institutions.
10. South Korea's membership in the Development Assistance Committee (DAC) in 2010 exemplifies this process.
11. The nine boundaries identified by the planetary boundaries framework are as follows: climate change, novel entities, stratospheric ozone depletion, atmospheric aerosol loading, ocean acidification, biogeochemical flows, freshwater use, land-system change, and biosphere integrity.

References

Abi-Saab, G. M. 1962. 'The Newly Independent States and the Rules of International Law: An Outline'. *Howard Law Journal* 8: 95–121.

Adewale, A. R. 2017. 'Import Substitution Industrialisation and Economic Growth—Evidence from the Group of BRICS Countries'. *Future Business Journal* 3(2): 138–58.

Ahmad, J. 1978. 'Import Substitution: A Survey of Policy Issues'. *The Developing Economies* 16(4): 355–72.
Akram, S. 2007. 'The Arab Charter on Human Rights 2004'. *Boston University International Law Journal* 24(2): 147–64.
Anghie, A. 2006. 'The Evolution of International Law: Colonial and Postcolonial Realities'. *Third World Quarterly* 27(5): 739–53.
Baderin, M. A. 2011. 'Law and Development in Africa: Towards a New Approach'. *NIALS Journal of Law and Development* 1(1): 1–48.
Barrett, J. and G. Gaus. 2018. 'Laws, Norms, and Public Justification: The Limits of Law as an Instrument of Reform'. In S. A. Langvatn, W. Sadurski, and M. Kumm, eds. *Public Reason and Courts*, 201–28. Cambridge: Cambridge University Press.
Belton, R. K. 2005. *Competing Definitions of the Rule of Law: Implications for Practitioners* (Rule of Law Series 55). Washington, DC: Carnegie Endowment for International Peace.
Benda-Beckmann, F. von and K. von Benda-Beckmann. 2014. 'Places That Come and Go: A Legal Anthropological Perspective on the Temporalities of Space in Plural Legal Orders'. In I. Braverman, N. Blomley, and D. Delaney, eds. *The Expanding Spaces of Law*, 30–52. Stanford: Stanford University Press.
Berman, H. J. 1958. *The Nature and Functions of Law: An Introduction for Students of the Arts and Sciences*. New York: Foundation Press.
Bernstorff, J. von and P. Dann. 2019. *The Battle for International Law: South–North Perspectives on the Decolonization Era*. Oxford: Oxford University Press.
Bicchieri, C. 2017. *Norms in the Wild: How to Diagnose, Measure, and Change Social Norms*,. Oxford: Oxford University Press.
Brunner, A. 2019. 'Acquired Rights and State Succession: The Rise and Fall of the Third World in the International Law Commission'. In J. von Bernstorff and P. Dann, eds. *The Battle for International Law: South–North Perspectives on the Decolonization Era*, 124–40. Oxford: Oxford University Press.
Carothers, T. 1998. 'The Rule of Law Revival'. *Foreign Affairs* 77(2): 95–106.
Carothers, T. 2009. 'Rule of Law Temptations'. *Fletcher Forum of World Affairs* 33(1): 49–61.
Channell, W. 2005. 'Lessons Not Learned: Problems with Western Aid for Law Reform in Post-Communist Countries'. *Carnegie Papers* (Rule of Law Series) 1(57): 1–24.
Chen, W. 2017. 'Introduction: Debating the Consensuses'. In W. Chen, ed. *The Beijing Consensus? How China Has Changed Western Ideas of Law and Economic Development*, 1–12. Cambridge: Cambridge University Press.
Craven, M. 2019. 'Colonial Fragments: Decolonization, Concessions, and Acquired Rights'. In J. von Bernstorff and P. Dann, eds. *The Battle for International Law: South–North Perspectives on the Decolonization Era*, 101–23. Oxford: Oxford University Press.
Daniels, R. J. and M. J. Trebilcock. 2008. *Rule of Law Reform and Development: Charting the Fragile Path of Progress*. Cheltenham: Edward Elgar.
Dann, P. 2013. *The Law of Development Cooperation: A Comparative Analysis of the World Bank, the EU and Germany* (Cambridge International Trade and Economic Law). Cambridge: Cambridge University Press.
Dann, P. 2014. 'Ideengeschichte von Recht Und Entwicklung'. In P. Dann, S. Kadelbach, and M. Kaltenborn, eds. *Entwicklung Und Recht*, 17–48. Baden-Baden: Nomos Verlagsgesellschaft mbH & Co. KG.
Dann, P. 2019a. 'The World Bank in the Battles of the "Decolonization Era"'. In P. Dann and J. von Bernstorff, eds. *The Battle for International Law: South–North Perspectives*, 278–93. Oxford: Oxford University Press.

Dann, P. 2019b. 'Institutional Law and Development Governance: An Introduction'. *Law and Development Review* 12(2): 537–60.

Eddy, J. 2009. 'Rule of Law in Afghanistan: The Intrusion of Reality'. *Journal of International Cooperation Studies* 17(2): 1–23.

Esteva, G. 1992. 'Development'. In W. Sachs, ed. *The Development Dictionary: A Guide to Knowledge as Power*, 6–26. London: Zed Books.

Faundez, J. 2017. 'Between Bandung and Doha—International Economic Law and Developing Countries'. In L. Eslava, M. Fakhri, and V. Nesiah, eds. *Bandung, Global History, and International Law: Critical Pasts and Pending Futures*, 498–514. Cambridge: Cambridge University Press.

Fikentscher, W. 2009. *Law and Anthropology: Outlines, Issues, Suggestions*. Munich: Beck.

Fritz, T. 2005. *Special and Differential Treatment of Developing Countries* (Heinrich Böll Foundation Global Issue Paper 18). Berlin: Heinrich Böll Foundation.

Gessner, V. 2001. 'Law as an Instrument of Social Change'. In N. J. Smelser and P. B. Baltes, eds. *International Encyclopedia of the Social & Behavioral Sciences*, vol. 12, 8492–6. Amsterdam: Elsevier.

Gilman, N. 2015. 'The New International Economic Order: A Reintroduction'. *Humanity: An International Journal of Human Rights, Humanitarianism, and Development* 6(1): 1–16.

Gordon, R. E. and J. H. Sylvester. 2004. 'Deconstructing Development'. *Wisconsin International Law Journal* 22: 1–93.

Hickel, J. 2019. 'Is It Possible to Achieve a Good Life for All within Planetary Boundaries?'. *Third World Quarterly* 40(1): 18–35.

Janse, R. 2013. 'A Turn to Legal Pluralism in the Rule of Law Promotion?'. *Erasmus Law Review* 6(3/4): 181–90.

Koskenniemi, M. 1997. 'Hierarchy in International Law: A Sketch'. *European Journal of International Law* 8(4): 566–82.

Koskenniemi, M. 2019. 'What Is Law Got to Do with It? Recollections and Impressions'. In J. von Bernstorff and P. Dann, eds. *The Battle for International Law: South-North Perspectives on the Decolonization Era*, 443–54. Oxford: Oxford University Press.

Lalive, P. A. 1965. 'The Doctrine of Acquired Rights'. In The Rights and Duties of Private Investors Abroad, 145–200. Albany: Matthew Bender & Co.

Lee, Y.-S. 2017. 'General Theory of Law and Development'. *Cornell International Law Journal* 50(3): 415–71.

Lee, Y.-S. 2019. *Law and Development: Theory and Practice*. Abingdon: Routledge.

Lizarazo-Rodriguez, L. 2017. 'Mapping Law and Development'. *Indonesian Journal of International & Comparative Law* 4: 761–895.

Mahiou, A. 2013. 'Development, International Law Of'. In Max Planck Encyclopedia of Public International Law. Oxford: Oxford University Press, https://opil.ouplaw.com/view/10.1093/law:epil/9780199231690/law-9780199231690-e1428?rskey=hF4RWe&result=1&prd=MPIL.

Malinowski, B. 1926. *Crime and Custom in Savage Society*. New York: Harcourt.

Matz, N. 2005. 'Civilization and the Mandate System under the League of Nations as Origin of Trusteeship'. *Max Planck Yearbook of United Nations Law Online* 9(1): 47–95.

Messick, R. E. 1999. 'Judicial Reform and Economic Development: A Survey of the Issues'. *The World Bank Research Observer* 14(1): 117–36.

Mohan, G., A. B. Zack-Williams, E. Brown, and B. Milward. 2000. *Structural Adjustment: Theory, Practice and Impacts*. London: Routledge.

Moore, S. F. 1973. 'Law and Social Change: The Semi-Autonomous Social Field as an Appropriate Subject of Study'. *Law & Society Review* 7(4): 719–46.

Ohnesorge, J. K. M. 2007. 'Developing Development Theory: Law and Development Orthodoxies and the Northeast Asian Experience'. *University of Pennsylvania Journal of International Economic Law* 28: 219–308.

O'Neill, D. W., A. L. Fanning, W. F. Lamb, and J. K. Steinberger. 2018. 'A Good Life for All within Planetary Boundaries'. *Nature Sustainability* 1(2): 88–95.

Organisation of African Unity (OAU). 1981. 'African Charter on Human and Peoples' Rights'. *African Union*, available at <https://au.int/sites/default/files/treaties/36390-treaty-0011_-_african_charter_on_human_and_peoples_rights_e.pdf>.

Pahuja, S. 2011. *Decolonising International Law: Development, Economic Growth and the Politics of Universality*. Cambridge: Cambridge University Press.

Pauw, P., S. Bauer, C. Richerzhagen, C. Brandi, and H. Schmole. 2014. *Different Perspectives on Differentiated Responsibilities: A State-of-the-Art Review of the Notion of Common but Differentiated Responsibilities in International Negotiations*. Bonn: Deutsches Institut für Entwicklungspolitik.

Prado, M. M. and M. J. Trebilcock. 2014. *Advanced Introduction to Law and Development*. Cheltenham: Edward Elgar.

Ramo, J. C. 2004. *The Beijing Consensus*. London: Foreign Policy Centre.

Rittich, K. 2016. 'Theorizing International Law and Development'. In A. Orford, F. Hoffmann, and M. Clark, eds. *The Oxford Handbook of the Theory of International Law*, 821–43. Oxford: Oxford University Press.

Rooij, B. van and P. Nicholson. 2013. 'Inflationary Trends in Law and Development'. *Duke Journal of Comparative and International Law* 24: 297–348.

Rostow, W. W. 1960. *The Stages of Economic Growth: A Non-Communist Manifesto*. Cambridge: Cambridge University Press.

Sage, C. and M. Woolcock. 2012. 'Introduction—Legal Pluralism and Development Policy'. In B.Z. Tamanaha, C. Sage, and M. Woolcock, eds. *Legal Pluralism and Development: Scholars and Practitioners in Dialogue*, 1–18. Cambridge: Cambridge University Press.

Sauvy, A. 1952. 'Trois Mondes, Une Planète'. *L'Observateur* 118: 14.

Schachter, O. 1976. 'The Evolving International Law of Development'. *Columbia Journal of Transnational Law* 15: 1–16.

Sen, A. K. 1999. *Development as Freedom*. Oxford: Oxford University Press.

Siems, M. 2014. *Comparative Law*. Cambridge: Cambridge University Press.

Snyder, F. G. 1982. 'The Failure of Law and Development'. *Wisconsin Law Review* 1982: 373–96.

Sousa Santos, B. de. 2002. *Toward a New Legal Common Sense: Law, Globalization, and Emancipation*. Second edition. London: Butterworths.

Steffen, W., K. Richardson, J. Rockström, S. E. Cornell, I. Fetzer, E. M. Bennett, R. Biggs, S. R. Carpenter, W. de Vries, C. A. de Wit, C. Folke, D. Gerten, J. Heinke, G. M. Mace, L. M. Persson, V. Ramanathan, B. Reyers, and S. Sörlin. 2015. 'Planetary Boundaries: Guiding Human Development on a Changing Planet'. *Science* 347(6223). American Association for the Advancement of Science: 1259855.

Stromseth, J., D. Wippman, and R. Brooks. 2006. *Can Might Make Rights? Building the Rule of Law after Military Interventions*. Cambridge: Cambridge University Press.

Tamanaha, B. Z. 1995. 'The Lessons of Law-and-Development Studies'. *American Journal of International Law* 89(2): 470–86.

Tamanaha, B. Z. 2011. 'The Rule of Law and Legal Pluralism in Development'. *Hague Journal on the Rule of Law* 3(1): 1–17.

Tamanaha, B. Z. 2017. *A Realistic Theory of Law*. Cambridge: Cambridge University Press.

Tamanaha, B. Z., C. Sage, and M. Woolcock, eds. 2012. *Legal Pluralism and Development: Scholars and Practitioners in Dialogue*. Cambridge: Cambridge University Press.

Tan, C. 2019. 'Beyond the "Moments" of Law and Development: Critical Reflections on Law and Development Scholarship in a Globalized Economy'. *Law and Development Review* 12(2): 285–321.

Trebilcock, M. J. 2016. 'Between Universalism and Relativism: Reflections on the Evolution of Law and Development Studies'. *University of Toronto Law Journal* 66(3): 330–52.

Trubek, D. M. 1972. 'Toward a Social Theory of Law: An Essay on the Study of Law and Development'. *The Yale Law Journal* 82(1): 1–50.

Trubek, D. M. 2006. 'The "Rule of Law" in Development Assistance: Past, Present, and Future'. In D.M. Trubek and A. Santos, eds. *The New Law and Economic Development: A Critical Appraisal*, 74–94. Cambridge: Cambridge University Press.

Trubek, D. M. 2012. 'Law and Development 50 Years On'. *University of Wisconsin Legal Studies Research Paper* 1212: 1–11.

Trubek, D. M. 2016. 'Law and Development: Forty Years after "Scholars in Self-Estrangement"'. *University of Toronto Law Journal* 66(3): 301–29.

Trubek, D. M. and M. Galanter. 1974. 'Scholars in Self-Estrangement: Some Reflections on the Crisis in Law and Development Studies in the United States'. *Wisconsin Law Review* 1974: 1062–102.

Trubek, D. M. and A. Santos. 2006. 'Introduction: The Third Moment in Law and Development Theory and the Emergence of a New Critical Practice'. In A. Santos and D. M. Trubek, eds. *The New Law and Economic Development: A Critical Appraisal*, 1–18. Cambridge: Cambridge University Press.

UN (United Nations). 1988. 'Report of the World Commission on Environment and Development'. In Resolutions and Decisions Adopted by the General Assembly during Its 42nd Session, vol. 1, 154–6. New York: UN.

UNESCO. 1971. *Records of the General Conference, 16th Session, Paris, 12 October to 14 November 1970: Resolutions*, vol. 1. Paris: UNESCO, available at <https://unesdoc.unesco.org/ark:/48223/pf0000114046>.

Vandenhole, W. 2019. 'Towards a Fourth Moment in Law and Development?'. *Law and Development Review* 12(2): 265–83.

Weber, M. 1978. *Economy and Society: An Outline of Interpretive Sociology*. Berkeley: University of California Press.

Xu, G. 2012. 'Law and China's Economic Growth: A Macroeconomic Perspective'. *The Dovenschmidt Quarterly* 1(1): 3–15.

CHAPTER 23

RIGHTS AND SOCIAL INCLUSION

MARK GOODALE

Introduction: Contexts and Questions

In early 1947, UNESCO conducted a survey based on a questionnaire that asked respondents to reflect on the potential meanings of human rights. Responses to the survey were then analysed in a report that was sent to the UN Commission on Human Rights, which would soon draft the Universal Declaration of Human Rights (UDHR), adopted by the UN General Assembly on 10 December 1948. The survey was sent to an impressive list of leading writers, political figures, theologians, academics, labour activists, and social leaders, including Lewis Mumford, Pierre Teilhard de Chardin, Aldous Huxley, Benedetto Croce, Jawaharlal Nehru, Alfred Weber (brother of Max), T. S. Eliot, W. H. Auden, and Mahatma Gandhi. Although the extent of the survey was not exactly global in reach, it did manage to solicit responses from different cultural, political, and religious perspectives on the question of human rights (see Goodale 2018).

Two anthropologists responded to the UNESCO human rights survey: A. P. Elkin, professor at the University of Sydney and a dominant presence in mid-century Australian anthropology; and Melville Herskovits, an American anthropologist who had helped to establish African and African-American studies in the United States as a former student of Franz Boas and one of the leading proponents of the Boasian principle of cultural relativism. Elkin's response, entitled 'The Rights of Primitive Peoples', has largely been forgotten, although it retains value in the way it attempts to reconcile the concept of human rights with notions of justice and social regulation among Australia's Aboriginal populations.

But Herskovits's response, which he called a 'Statement on Rights', became famous/infamous decades later, when it was taken up within swirling debates over human rights during the early post-Cold War period (Engle 2001; Goodale 2009; Messer 1993; Nagengast and Turner 1997; Renteln 1988). This is because Herskovits's 'Statement on

Human Rights', though written in a personal capacity, was published in the December 1947 *American Anthropologist* with a note attached that seemed to imply that it was an official statement from the American Anthropological Association, then (as now) the largest association of professional anthropologists in the world. What made this supposedly official anthropological response to the UNESCO human rights survey so notable was the fact that it fundamentally rejected the validity of a potential universal declaration of human rights.

The 'Statement on Human Rights' offers several reasons for which anthropological research could not lend support to the concept of universal human rights, but two are most relevant for the purposes of this chapter. First, the Statement emphasized the fact that anthropological studies of justice, conflict resolution, law, and social life more generally revealed a palette of cultural diversity that could not be condensed into general universal principles. As it explains:

> Over the past fifty years, the many ways in which man resolves the problem of subsistence, of social living, of political regulation of group life, of reaching accord with the Universe and satisfying his aesthetic drives has been widely documented by the researches of anthropologists among peoples living in all parts of the world. All peoples do achieve these ends. No two of them, however, do so in exactly the same way, and some of them employ means that differ, often strikingly, from one another. (1947: 540)

And second, the Statement opposed the UN's efforts to make a declaration of human rights the basis for 'freedom, justice and peace in the world', as the UDHR's Preamble would later put it, on political grounds. The concern was that the doctrine of human rights, supported by the leading nation-states at the centre of the new UN, would inevitably become an instrument of power regardless of original intentions. As the Statement put it, in striking and even alarmist terms, human rights would eventually be 'employed to implement economic exploitation and ... deny the right to control their own affairs to millions of people over the world, where the expansion of Europe and America has not [already] meant the literal extermination of whole populations' (1947: 540).

Although anthropologists were involved in various forms of research and public action during the decades of the Cold War that touched on issues of justice, social change, and anti-colonialism, most notably the initiative to achieve scientific consensus on the question of race (also coincidently spearheaded by UNESCO), the subject of rights—especially human rights—was marginal to anthropological concerns. If anthropological research is in part a reflection of what social, political, and legal dynamics are important in any one historical period, then the absence of anthropological concern with rights until about the late 1980s should be read as evidence for the marginalization of rights more generally during the Cold War in relation to other geopolitical, ideological, and political economic currents (Moyn 2010).

However, with the end of the Cold War, the mid-twentieth-century rights project, which had remained, in a certain sense, latent for over forty years, was unleashed onto a global landscape in the midst of pervasive transition. The period of the 1990s was a time of rapid expansion and transformation of the rights project through political change (Wilson 2001), legal innovation (Hirschl 2004), the redefinition of social movements (Allen 2013), and the rearticulation of Cold War international development into a rights idiom (Englund 2006). In particular, what began in 1948 as a specifically 'human rights' project evolved into more differentiated normative categories—which nevertheless retained key aspects of human rights doctrine—including women's rights and Indigenous Peoples' rights.

This period of liminal expansion and optimism regarding rights categories and their transformative possibilities reached a peak just before the geopolitical and ideological shocks set in motion by the attacks of 11 September 2001. Indeed, just a year before, Kofi Annan, Secretary-General of the UN, could confidently proclaim that the world had entered what he described as 'the Age of Human Rights' (Annan 2000). From the mid-2000s to the present, the Age of Human Rights has given way to a quite different world order, one characterized by exploding global inequality (Piketty 2014), the rise of far-right nationalism, including neo-fascism (Holmes 2000; Shoshan 2016), the fracture of supranational bodies like the European Union (Green et al. 2016), and of course the retreat of the United States from global prominence after the election of Donald Trump (Gusterson 2017) and the emergence of what might be described as a politics of surreal populism.

Anthropological research played an important role in tracing the ethnographic contours of the rise and transformation of rights in the post-Cold War period. This chapter can only survey some of the most important currents in the anthropology of rights as an enduring context for the wider field of anthropology and law. In particular, for reasons of space, it is not possible to examine otherwise relevant topics, including the anthropology of rights in national legal systems, or the anthropology of rights categories that did not undergo the same level of transformation during the Age of Human Rights, such as property rights. Instead, the chapter focuses on four specific areas of anthropological research.

First, the chapter examines key developments in the anthropology of *human rights*, which served as a methodological and conceptual anchor for the post-Cold War anthropology of rights more generally. As will be seen, the anthropological study of human rights practices in different cultural, legal, and political contexts added a novel perspective on the broader understanding of human rights as law, discourse, and politics. Next, the chapter will take stock of central threads in the anthropological study of *gender rights*, which includes here both women's rights and, more recently, LGBT rights. The question of the relationship between human rights as a category of universal norms and gender rights has often been a contested one, so much so that it was necessary for Hillary Rodham Clinton (who was ironically then the anachronistically titled 'First Lady of the United States') to have to declare in 1995 at the UN Fourth World Conference on Women in Beijing that 'women's rights are human rights'. Although women's rights eventually became firmly established as a category of human rights—particularly through the Convention on the Elimination of All

Forms of Discrimination Against Women (CEDAW) and the work of the convention's monitoring institutions (see Merry 2006)—the same cannot be said of LGBT rights. Nevertheless, anthropologists have conducted innovative research on the fraught status of LGBT rights, which embody many of the contemporary challenges of human rights more generally in a historical period that bears few markers of post-Cold War liminality and optimism (see Goodale 2013).

The chapter then turns to another category of rights with which anthropologists have been closely associated, both as researchers and as engaged scholars: *Indigenous Peoples' rights*. Indeed, when the American Anthropological Association eventually repudiated the 1947 Statement on Human Rights through the adoption—this time, based on a membership-wide referendum—in 1999 of its ambitiously entitled 'Declaration on Anthropology and Human Rights', it was largely the culmination of over a decade of political activism by anthropologists working with indigenous populations, as defined under the 1989 International Labour Organization (ILO) 169 framework. For example, a leading figure in the push to replace the 1947 Statement with a very different disciplinary response to human rights was Terence Turner, who had conducted research with and advocated for the Kayapo people of the Brazilian Amazon for decades. In a 1997 special issue of the *Journal of Anthropological Research*, several of the anthropologists who played a leading role in the adoption of the 1999 Declaration published articles that argued for what they hoped would be a sea-change in anthropology's relationship with human rights. In his contribution, Turner (1997) drew from his long-term engagement with the Kayapo in arguing that anthropologists had an ethical obligation to use their research as part of what he called an 'emancipatory cultural politics'. This disciplinary call to arms soon found expression in the 1999 Declaration, which proposes a human right to the 'capacity for culture' and makes human rights activism—through anthropological research—a professional obligation.

Next, the chapter surveys anthropological research that has revealed the importance of what might be called non-liberal categories of rights, that is, rights that are not based, historically or conceptually, in the development of liberal rights within the Western philosophical and political tradition. As anthropological studies have shown, the deeper awareness of categories such as relational and biocentric rights has taken shape precisely against—and often as a critique of—international human and Indigenous Peoples' rights activism, which influences (though unevenly and with increasingly less force) domestic law and politics. Anthropological research on non-liberal rights has become more and more relevant as critiques of human rights from within the centres of Global Northern power (e.g. Hopgood 2013; Moyn 2018; Posner 2014) have led to questions about the possibility for radical alternatives to the current human rights system (Goodale 2018; Santos 2014).

The chapter concludes by looking to the future: how will the anthropology of rights evolve in the coming years, both in preserving certain core concerns and in moving in new directions? Regardless of these developments, the anthropology of rights will likely continue to be shaped by two underlying orientations, both of which were central from the beginning, that is, in Herskovits's 1947 Statement on Human Rights, which, as we have seen, came to be taken—quite unjustifiably—as the semi-official anthropological position on human rights for decades.

First, the anthropology of rights has emphasized the multiplicity of human normativity, including rights practices. This focus on normative diversity has led to productive insights into the ways in which tensions are created between universalist rights categories and what might be described as actually existing rights practices. And second, despite the hyperbolic language, Herskovits's 1947 Statement presciently imagined the ways in which international rights institutions and modes of activism would become instruments of global power. This focus on power—whether as grassroots social resistance or as top-down humanitarian virtue or as intermediating norm brokerage—has marked off the anthropology of rights as a unique vantage point from which to understand some of the most consequential developments in law and society, especially over the last thirty years (see Goodale 2017).

Human rights

Anthropological research on human rights has focused on human rights practices in ways that are distinct from how the practice of human rights is understood by disciplines such as political theory and international law, in which 'practice' refers principally to forms of human rights implementation undertaken by national or international political and legal institutions. In these other disciplines, a basic distinction is drawn between 'practice-dependent' and 'practice-independent' approaches, the latter referring largely to the work of philosophers and legal theorists who examine basic questions such as the difference between moral and legal obligations or the meaning of human dignity as conceptual problems that can be explored in the abstract (see McCrudden 2016).

The anthropology of human rights, by contrast, has developed quite a different understanding of human rights practices, one that is much more capacious and embedded in sociolegal life. In the introduction to a volume I co-edited with Sally Engle Merry, I defined this anthropological approach to human rights practice in the following way: 'all the many ways in which social actors ... talk about, advocate for, criticize, study, legally enact, [and] vernacularize ... the idea of human rights in its different forms' (Goodale 2007: 24). By 'social actors', I meant 'the different individuals, institutions, states, international agencies ... without privileging any one type of human rights actor: the peasant intellectual in Bolivia who agitates on behalf of *derechos humanos* is analytically equal to the executive director of Human Rights Watch'.

Based on this expansive methodological orientation, anthropologists have revealed a number of important dynamics at work in the post-Cold War lives of human rights. Here I focus on three of these. First, anthropologists have observed that the expansion of human rights took place within both existing and new networks, some of which intersected with global and regional assemblages of development and humanitarian aid. In this sense, scholars 'studied up' (Nader 1972) in order to examine the ways in which power flows shaped the emergence of a 'culture of human rights' (Cowan et al. 2001). For example, in a relatively early and innovative study, Annelise Riles (2000) conducted ethnographic research among Fijian activists and government officials both before and during the 1995 UN Fourth World Conference on Women in Beijing. As she found, human rights networks take on peculiar characteristics, including the fact that they are invested with a kind of moral authority in which the network becomes a 'good in itself' (2000: 173). The result is that the human rights network, which Riles learned to understand from the 'inside out', takes on a life of its own, marked by distinct discourse, histories, and the artefacts it produces.

Sally Engle Merry (2006), in her multisited ethnographic research on the global network established to monitor compliance with CEDAW, discovered yet other aspects of the human rights network. Most importantly, she focused on the ways in which human rights networks produce their own forms of knowledge through a process she describes as 'vernacularization', in which intermediating norm entrepreneurs act as translators between different levels, institutions, and social movements. As she showed, these circulations of human rights knowledge do not always follow expected directions. In particular, vernacularization never functions either as a top-down imposition by international human rights institutions or as 'local' cultural appropriation. Instead, human rights networks become sites of horizontal interconnection and contestation, a process of what might be called 'synchronic vernacularization' in which meaning is created through small-scale and often temporal relationships instead of through large-scale acts of social transformation.

Second, anthropologists have examined practices of human rights as a form of moral creativity in which human rights norms become a malleable resource within ongoing political and social struggles. Even more, research has revealed the extent to which creativity through the practice of human rights leads to unpredictable results. The creative appropriation of human rights norms sometimes leads to the kinds of potentially emancipatory social changes that are associated with human rights activism; on the other hand, however, human rights creativity can lead to much more ambiguous changes. For example, in her well-known ethnographic study of the Zapatista rebellion in Mexico, Shannon Speed (2008) conducted research among indigenous activists who were being counselled by foreign and national NGOs to frame their resistance to the Mexican state through human rights discourse. As she shows, peasant leaders organized themselves within *Juntas de Buen Gobierno*, or Good Governance Councils, in which the very idea of human rights itself was radically transformed into a local idiom based on cultural norms that emphasized collective action on behalf of the community. It was only in this way that 'human rights' became meaningful in practice for the Zapatista activists, even if what resulted bore little resemblance to orthodox human rights doctrine.

Yet in her study of human rights practices in nominally 'postconflict' Northern Ireland, Jennifer Curtis (2014) discovered another side to human rights creativity. As she found, both sides in the conflict appropriated the language of human rights in creative ways, yet as a form of what Curtis describes as 'war by other means'. In other words, the deployment of human rights accusations and rebuttals allowed the parties to the long-standing conflict to continue fighting in ways that ironically seemed to indicate compliance with international norms and 'peacebuilding'. In Curtis's analysis, recourse to human rights only perpetuated the conflict through forms of what might be described as strategic moral positioning.

And finally, the anthropology of human rights has innovatively examined the problematic role of the state within the practice of human rights. Much of the focus on the state has centred on a number of tensions created by a basic contradiction in the post-war human rights system: the fact that the 'universal'—that is, transnational—principle of human rights was made dependent upon what remained, even after the creation of the UN, a fundamentally Westphalian international political system based on the pre-eminence of state sovereignty. This meant that the implementation of human rights took place through deeply politicized processes of legal nationalization. The result was that the state, which was often the principal perpetrator of human rights violations against its own citizens, was also the entity responsible for protecting human rights through national laws and institutions, leading to a structural conflict of interest at the heart of the human rights system.

In his study of debates in the United Kingdom over the implementation of the 1984 UN Convention Against Torture, Tobias Kelly (2014) shows how the British government refused to prosecute its own soldiers for the crime of torture, since to do so would have been to admit that British citizens were capable of acts at the service of national interests that were contrary to a national self-image of 'civilized' conduct. However, when the British government finally did enforce the Convention, it was first used to convict an Afghan warlord in 2005 (in absentia) for crimes allegedly committed during the Afghan civil war of the 1990s under the doctrine of universal jurisdiction.

And in her study of human rights activism in Argentina in the late 1990s, Karen Faulk (2013) examines another problem with the relationship between state governance and human rights: the way the category of citizenship can become a mechanism for manipulation, the unequal distribution of social goods, and, ultimately, exclusion. Her research examined debates over social belonging in a context in which the Argentine state had come under intense criticism from international human rights activists and their national partners. As she argues, the Argentine state turned to national citizenship as a resource that could be given or withheld from people in a way that evoked Hannah Arendt's (1951) observations about the fragility of the 'right to have rights'. This intense nationalization of human rights, in Faulk's reading, created clear limitations to the use of transnational norms within domestic politics.

Gender rights

Another key domain of research within the more general anthropology of rights has focused on questions of gender. This work, despite its diversity and scope, can be divided into research that examines women's rights practices, especially anti-discrimination and anti-violence campaigns, and more recent research that has taken up the question of LBGT rights mobilization. In the first, anthropologists have explored the discursive and social ambiguities of the 'women's rights are human rights' movement, especially those that revolve around the enforcement and status of CEDAW. One important theme is the way in which the meaning of violation and vulnerability itself has shifted over time. Indeed, as Sally Engle Merry (2006) has argued, international women's rights law has played a key role in defining and shaping understandings of vulnerability. For example, although CEDAW does not mention violence against women as a specific form of 'discrimination', it was later added (through General Recommendation 19 to the treaty). Nevertheless, cultural practices and understandings continued to complicate efforts by the global women's rights movement to establish clear benchmarks against which 'gender violence' could be measured.

In her study of the implementation of a 2006 law against sexual violence in the Democratic Republic of Congo (DRC), Gaëlle Breton-Le Goff (2013) argues that human rights activism confronts what she describes as 'outer limits' in the campaign to improve the lives of women based on international norms and expectations. The 2006 law in the DRC was drafted with direct guidance by the American human rights NGO Global Rights, which worked closely with members of the Congolese parliament. Yet the law played almost no role in stemming the problem of sexual violence in the DRC, which had been plagued by an epidemic of rape associated with the country's long civil war. Apart from the sheer magnitude of the problem against the backdrop of state complicity, another important factor in Breton-Le Goff's ethnographic case study was the resistance of local village chiefs, who saw human rights as an extension of state law. In cases of sexual violence, Breton-Le Goff found, village leaders insisted that customary law be used as the mechanism of dispute resolution, making it even more difficult for the 2006 women's rights law to play any role at all in protecting women in regions most affected by sexual violence.

Yet in a different ethnographic context, Mindie Lazarus-Black (2001, see also 2007) found that the relationship between international women's rights law, national politics, and local practices created more ambiguous possibilities for women. Her case study also tracked the afterlives of a women's rights act, in this case in Trinidad and Tobago. As Lazarus-Black puts it, it is important to take stock of the symbolic importance of the legislation, which represented a

> radical legal development, a coup of social engineering sparked in large part by the efforts of a progressive women's movement in Trinidad that mobilized government attention and nongovernmental groups' intervention. For the first time, violent words and acts that formerly remained unspoken, invisible, and irrelevant to the project of the state became highly conspicuous and subject to immediate legal sanction. (2001: 388)

As her ethnography revealed, despite the fact that prosecutions under the women's rights act were uneven at best, even the process of making an unsuccessful claim changed women's lives by making public forms of violence that had historically remained hidden or denied.

Turning from women's rights to LGBT rights, anthropological research has examined a much different global landscape, one on which LGBT activism confronts a lack of consensus at the international level and often deadly resistance at the national and local level. The result is that LGBT rights mobilization often takes place through subtle and even hidden forms of social action. For example, Monika Baer (2010) conducted research among Polish LGBT activists at a university during a period in the country's history in which state institutions were grappling with socialist-era and post-socialist approaches to sexual regulation. As she argues, student activists adopted what she calls a strategy of invisible visibility, in which their status as LGBT people is formally hidden but otherwise revealed through activities such as publishing, conferences, and other avenues for informal militancy. Her research shows, among other things, that LGBT rights are often defended well beyond the boundaries of law.

And in a more recent study, Lynette Chua (2019) conducted extremely difficult ethnographic research among Myanmar's largely clandestine LGBT community. Nevertheless, as Chua discovered, it was precisely because of the unprecedented social and political context that Burmese LGBT activists were able to form a close working bond, based on solidarity and what she describes as an emergent culture of activism, to shape broader social understandings of their particular vulnerabilities. Although it was not able to harness state law on its behalf, the Burmese LGBT community managed to forge new forms of subjectivity around the concept of what she calls 'human rights as a way of life'. The changes produced by these new practices took place well below the level of political or social transformation. Their effects were felt, instead, at what might be called the affective dimension of human rights practice.

Indigenous Peoples' rights

Although the international Indigenous Peoples' rights regime could be said to have begun with the promulgation of International Labour Organization Convention 107 in 1957, formally titled the 'Convention concerning the Protection and Integration of Indigenous and Other Tribal and Semi-Tribal Populations in Independent Countries', the current system took shape with the ILO's follow-on convention, 169, which was the product of decades of debate and activism regarding the limitations and defects of Convention 107 (Anaya 1996). In particular, ILO 169 was supposed to eliminate the assimilationist approach of 107 and create a framework in which indigenous and tribal peoples could achieve a measure of autonomy and cultural valorization within nation-states in which they were typically a marginalized minority population.

At the same time, as the ILO 169 regime was emerging through country-level ratifications and discussions, an accompanying discourse of Indigenous Peoples' rights was also taking root in different parts of the world. Ronald Niezen (2003) has described the discursive dimensions of Indigenous Peoples' rights as 'indigenism', that is, the creation of a specific category of collective identity through law. In Niezen's analysis, the category of indigenous is unique in relation to other categories of collective identity, such as 'ethnic group'. As he explains,

> A proud Serbian might refer to him- or herself as a Serb, not as an 'ethnic Serb' or an 'ethnic person'. The term 'indigenous', however, has been taken a step further. It is not only a legal category and an analytical concept but also an expression of identity, a badge worn with pride, revealing something significant and personal about its wearer's collective attachments.
>
> (Niezen 2003: 3)

Nevertheless, as anthropological research revealed, the expansion of indigenism after 1989 created a number of unintended consequences, including those linked to the fact that 'indigenous' is 'both a fragile legal concept and the indefinite, unachievable sum of the historical and personal experiences of those ... who share ... the notion that they have all been oppressed in similar ways for similar motives by similar state and corporate entities' (Niezen 2003: 4). In particular, as Niezen's research showed, Indigenous Peoples' rights were suffused with imperatives of what he calls 'third-party representation' (2003: 11), organizations and individuals who rushed to work on behalf of Indigenous Peoples as a form of transnational activism. These forms of representation were often based around Orientalist conceptions of the 'inherently ecological Indian' (11) or other ideal indigenous categories, reductions that bore little resemblance to the complex realities of 'indigenous' lives.

In her long-term ethnographic research among the Maasai in Tanzania, Dorothy Hodgson (2002) focused on another aspect of Indigenous Peoples' rights mobilization. As she argues, the coming of indigenism to Tanzania often had the effect of exacerbating local political conflicts rather than providing a new framework for unified social and political resistance. This was particularly the result of the fact that Indigenous Peoples' rights were framed against a much longer colonial and postcolonial history in Tanzania, in which various dominating regimes had played a long game of divide and conquer among the region's tribal populations, including the Maasai. In addition, the Maasai, as pastoralists, were engaged in almost constant struggles over resources and land with other 'indigenous' populations that practised farming and other modes of production. The result was that Indigenous Peoples' rights activism fit awkwardly into existing cultural and political categories. As she explains,

> Despite attempts to foster unity, promote common political agendas (such as the protection of land rights), and coordinate their activities through innumerable meetings and workshops and the creation of at least two 'umbrella' coordinating groups, the indigenous peoples' rights movement in Maasai areas has continued to splinter into even more groups and to become fractured by sometimes quite hostile

> disagreements over priorities, competition over resources, and tensions over membership and representation. (2002: 1087)

Yet in her ethnographic research on fishing rights conflicts between the Cucapá of northern Mexico and the Mexican state, Shaylih Muehlmann (2009) reveals another dynamic at work in the anthropology of Indigenous Peoples' rights. As one of the first countries to ratify ILO 169, the Mexican state had long promoted itself as a leading sponsor of Indigenous Peoples' rights for a 'pluricultural' country in which roughly 22 per cent of the population identified as indigenous. Mexico's ratification of ILO 169 led to a series of legal protections in Mexican state law that gave officially recognized indigenous populations the right to demand resources and public investment. But it was precisely because of this extensive legal framework that the Mexican state found ways to wield the category of indigenous as a tool of state power.

In particular, the Cucapá were denied access to the Colorado River for fishing because their leaders were not able to demonstrate certain markers of indigeneity as defined by state law, including non-Spanish language use and the use of traditional clothing. During her research, Muehlmann observed a lawyer for the Cucapá become increasingly frustrated with his clients' inability to enact indigeneity in ways that would help their claims. As she explains, '[the lawyer] told the group that they had to speak their indigenous language if they wanted their government to take them seriously "as Indians." "How is the government even supposed to know you're Indians?" he concluded, pointing to one of the women. "You dress and speak like Mexicans!"' (2009: 468).

Anthropological research on Indigenous Peoples' rights thus reveals a mixed record. On the one hand, as Stuart Kirsch's (2012) research in Papua New Guinea has demonstrated, Indigenous People have in certain circumstances been able to find ways to mobilize law 'against the state' in order to protect resources and advance political claims. This takes place even against a backdrop of transnational corporate influence, in which Indigenous Peoples' rights can also serve as a mechanism for appropriation and capital accumulation (Goodale 2016; see also Sapignoli 2018). But on the other hand, as we have seen, the anthropology of Indigenous Peoples' rights has shown the ways in which the increasing importance of 'indigenism' in global politics, especially in certain key regions like Latin America, created new forms of social and political exclusion in an era of land-grabbing, resource depletion, and protracted ethnic conflict.

Relational, Biocentric, and Other Non-Liberal Rights

A final category to be surveyed in the wider anthropology of rights concerns what might be thought of as non-liberal rights, that is, rights systems that are not derived—juridically, politically, or historically—from the Western legal and political tradition. In this sense, even though Indigenous Peoples' rights are meant to protect traditional lifeways against the abuses of state and corporate actors, among others, they do so through a legal regime that is fundamentally embedded in an international legal and political system of treaties, monitoring bodies, and regional courts. Nevertheless, despite the profound changes to both international and national law that took place in the post-Cold War period, alternative rights systems continued to co-exist at the same time, sometimes well outside the boundaries of state institutions and surveillance. For the purposes of this chapter, two of these alternative rights frameworks are most striking.

First, particularly in Latin America, legal and social activists have promoted rights doctrines that Johannes Waldmüller (2018) has characterized as 'biocentric', meaning rights that do not repose in the first instance with humans, but rather with nature, the global ecological system, or what is known in Quechua as Pachamama, or Mother Earth (see also Gudynas 2014; Oviedo 2014). In at least two countries, Ecuador and Bolivia, the 'rights of nature' were codified in radical new national constitutions, which were presented as evidence of a 'postneoliberal' legal and political order that offered an innovative response to enduring conflicts such as neo-colonial resource exploitation, cultural discrimination, and environmental degradation (Bebbington and Bebbington 2011; Goodale 2019).

Yet as Waldmüller's ethnographic research revealed, the national effort in Ecuador to put into practice a 'strong eco-social, biocentric, or socionatural' rights regime confronted a number of obstacles, the most important of which was the tension between the social policy of implementing biocentric rights and the broader demands by the international human rights system to monitor rights compliance through indicators that were 'anthropocentric', or human-centred. To the extent to which Ecuador wanted to have influence within the international human rights system or through the UN OHCHR, it was obligated to focus on compliance with existing human rights treaties. Even more, although Ecuador worked through the Human Rights Council to push for a new human rights instrument that would regulate transnational corporations, domestically the state worked to restrict social protest in vulnerable areas by indigenous populations because these protests were seen as a threat to the state's reputation as a guardian of the country's biodiversity. The situation is much the same in Bolivia, where the government of Evo Morales has made *vivir bien*, or living well, the ideological basis for the state's post-neoliberal development policies, while at the same time pursuing national economic strategies that have at times required the exploitation of protected bioreserves or the industrialization of non-renewable resources such as natural gas and lithium (Goodale 2019; McNeish 2013).

And second, anthropologists have examined the ways in which rights can be understood not to repose in nature, but in social networks. In his study of rights regimes and legal practice in Papua New Guinea, Joel Robbins (2009) found that people did not conceive of themselves as rights-bearers in the liberal sense; instead, as Robbins argues, people understood rights to be embedded in complex webs of relationships. As he explains, the association between 'natural rights' and society is precisely the opposite in Papua New Guinea to how it is conceived within the Western liberal tradition. Natural rights inhere in relationships rather than in people; people, by contrast, are fluid and social entities that only take shape by enacting the various relationships of which they are constituted. As Robbins puts it, 'people understand themselves to be made out of the relationships of kinship, marriage, and nurture that produced them' (2009: 175).

Famously, people in Papua New Guinea enact these natural 'rights in relationships' through regular gift giving, even when this means the exchange of everyday items that everyone already has access to; as Robbins explains, 'people are constantly living off their relationships even though there is no material need for them to do so' (176). In fact, the reason for them to do so is to realize, create, and maintain a social system of rights that expresses the most important values through a relational praxis that comes as close as possible to embodying what Robbins describes as 'their notions of justice' (177).

Conclusion: Future directions

To conclude, this chapter has surveyed some of the more important currents in the anthropological study of rights, including research on human rights, gender rights, Indigenous Peoples' rights, and, finally, alternative rights systems based on biocentric or relationalist principles. In general, anthropological research responded to key developments in the post-Cold War rights revolution, a period that culminated with the 'Age of Human Rights' (Annan 2000), an era that then waned throughout the 2000s in the face of geopolitical challenges, exploding global inequality, and the continuing erosion of the post-war liberal project. Compared with anthropological research on the global diffusion of rights discourse and international institutions during the liminal period of the 1990s and early 2000s, scholars have been less adept at recognizing the profound more recent transformations in the status of rights against the background of what Samuel Moyn (2018) has described as the 'neoliberal maelstrom'. Without having to speculate about professional intentions, it is reasonable to assume that at least some of the epistemological lag among anthropologists of rights is due to the fact that commitments to 'engaged anthropology', many of which have—at least since the late 1990s—revolved around rights activism, have made it more difficult to concentrate ethnographic attention on the range of what might be construed as contemporary counter-human rights movements, from the continuing neoliberalization of the global political economy to the pervasiveness of cultural and religious populism.

Nevertheless, casting an eye towards future directions, there are at least three avenues that should draw the attention of anthropologists of rights. First, scholars will be interested in the ways in which the 'endtimes' (Hopgood 2013) of human rights give way to a more diverse global normative landscape, one in which rights will continue to play a role in politics, social resistance, and moral discourse, but a much more restrained one. What will human rights mean for people when their unquestioned universality gives way to a more plural, contingent framing? Second, in light of the dominance of neoliberal political economy, which Moyn has called the 'truly ambitious and successful moral program of our time' (Moyn 2018: xii), anthropologists will want to play close attention to the ways in which even much more limited accounts of human and collective rights can serve as a buffer against the worst abuses, even as they can also, at the same time, legitimate them through processes of juridification (Goodale 2016). And third, as nationalism and cultural identitarianism continue to (re-)emerge as political and ideological ordering logics from Washington, DC, to Budapest to Delhi, anthropologists should remember that rights frameworks are not inherently progressive, as Robert Hayden's (1992, 1996) ethnographic research in the early former Yugoslavia revealed. In showing how 'constitutional nationalism' could be based on rights doctrines that were ethnically and religiously exclusionary, Hayden's research underscores the fact that rights are normative tools whose ultimate impact depends fundamentally on political context, ideological history, and social meaning.

References

American Anthropological Association. 1947. 'Statement on Human Rights'. *American Anthropologist* 49(4): 539–43.

Allen, L. 2013. *The Rise and Fall of Human Rights: Cynicism and Politics in Occupied Palestine*. Stanford: Stanford University Press.

Anaya, S. J. 1996. *Indigenous Peoples in International Law*. New York: Oxford University Press.

Annan, K. A. 2000. 'The Age of Human Rights'. *Project Syndicate*, available at <http://www.project-syndicate.org/commentary/the-age-of-human-rights?barrier=true>.

Arendt, H. 1951. *The Origins of Totalitarianism*. New York: Harcourt, Brace and Co.

Baer, M. 2010. 'L'invisible visible'. *Ethnologie francaise* 40(2): 245–55.

Bebbington, A. and D. H. Bebbington. 2011. 'An Andean Avatar: Post-Neoliberal and Neoliberal Strategies for Securing the Unobtainable'. *New Political Economy* 16(1): 131–45.

Breton-Le Goff, G. 2013. 'Aux confins du doit positif: socio-anthropologie de la production normative non gouvernementale en république démocratique du Congo'. *Anthropologie et Sociétés* 37(1): 75–95.

Chua, L. J. 2018. *The Politics of Love in Myanmar: LGBT Mobilization and Human Rights as a Way of Life*. Stanford: Stanford University Press.

Cowan, J. K., M.-B. Dembour and R. Wilson, eds. 2001. *Culture and Rights: Anthropological Perspectives*. Cambridge: Cambridge University Press.

Curtis, J. 2014. *Human Rights as War by Other Means: Peace Politics in Northern Ireland*. Philadelphia: University of Pennsylvania Press.

Engle, K. 2001. 'From Skepticism to Embrace: Human Rights and the American Anthropological Association from 1947–1999'. *Human Rights Quarterly* 23: 536–59.

Englund, H. 2006. *Prisoners of Freedom: Human Rights and the African Poor*. Berkeley: University of California Press.

Faulk, K. 2013. 'Solidarity and Accountability: Rethinking Citizenship and Human Rights'. In M. Goodale, ed. *Human Rights at the Crossroads*, 98–108. Oxford: Oxford University Press.

Goodale, M. 2007. 'Introduction: Locating Rights, Envisioning Law Between the Global and the Local'. In M. Goodale and S. E. Merry, eds. *The Practice of Human Rights: Tracking Law between the Global and the Local*, 1–38. New York: Cambridge University Press.

Goodale, M. 2009. *Surrendering to Utopia: An Anthropology of Human Rights*. Stanford: Stanford University Press.

Goodale, M., ed. 2013. *Human Rights at the Crossroads*. Oxford: Oxford University Press.

Goodale, M. 2016. 'Dark Matter: Toward a Political Economy of Indigenous Rights and Aspirational Politics'. *Critique of Anthropology* 36(4): 439–57.

Goodale, M. 2017. *Anthropology and Law: A Critical Introduction*. New York: New York University Press.

Goodale, M., ed. 2018. *Letters to the Contrary: A Curated History of the UNESCO Human Rights Survey*. Stanford: Stanford University Press.

Goodale, M. 2019. *A Revolution in Fragments: Traversing Scales of Justice, Ideology, and Practice in Bolivia*. Durham: Duke University Press.

Green, S. F., C. Gregory, M. Reeves, J. K. Cowan, O. Demetriou, I. Koch, M. Carrithers, R. Andersson, A. Gingrich, S. Macdonald, S. C. Acksoz, T. H. Eriksen, C. Shore, D. R. Holmes, M. Herzfeld, M. Strathern, C. B. Jensen, K. Martin, D. Dalakoglou, G. Poulimenakos, S. Jansen, C. Brkovic, T. M. Wilson, N. Besnier, D. Guiness, M. Hann, P. Ballinger, and D. Dzenovska. 2016. 'Brexit Referendum: First Reactions from Anthropology'. *Social Anthropology* 24(4): 478–502.

Gudynas, E. 2014. 'Buen vivir: Sobre secuestros, domesticaciones, rescates y alternativas'. In A. Oviedo, ed. *Bifurcación del buen vivir y el sumak kawsay*, 23–45. Quito: Ediciones Yachay.

Gusterson, H. 2017. 'From Brexit to Trump: Anthropology and the Rise of Nationalist Populism'. *American Ethnologist* 44(2): 209–14.

Hayden, R.M. 1992. 'Constitutional Nationalism in the Formerly Yugoslav Republics'. *Slavic Review* 51(4): 654–73.

Hayden, R. M. 1996. 'Imagined Communities and Real Victims: Self-Determination and Ethnic Cleansing in Yugoslavia'. *American Ethnologist* 23(4): 783–801.

Hirschl, R. 2004. *Towards Juristocracy: The Origins and Consequences of the New Constitutionalism*. Cambridge, MA: Harvard University Press.

Hodgson, D. L. 2002. 'Precarious Alliances: The Cultural Politics and Structural Predicaments of the Indigenous Rights Movement in Tanzania'. *American Anthropologist* 104(4): 1086–97.

Holmes, D. R. 2000. *Integral Europe: Fast-Capitalism, Multiculturalism, Neofascism*. Princeton: Princeton University Press.

Hopgood, S. 2013. *The Endtimes of Human Rights*. Ithaca: Cornell University Press.

Kelly, T. 2014. 'Prosecuting Human Rights Violations'. In M. Goodale, ed. *Human Rights at the Crossroads*, 86–97. Oxford: Oxford University Press.

Kirsch, S. 2012. 'Juridification of Indigenous Politics'. In J. Eckert, B. Donahoe, C. Strümpell, and Z. Ö. Biner, eds. *Law against the State: Ethnographic Forays into Law's Transformations*, 23–43. Cambridge: Cambridge University Press.

Lazarus-Black, M. 2001. 'Law and the Pragmatics of Inclusion: Governing Domestic Violence in Trinidad and Tobago'. *American Ethnologist* 28(2): 388–416.

Lazarus-Black, M. 2007. *Everyday Harm: Domestic Violence, Court Rites, and Cultures of Reconciliation*. Urbana: University of Illinois Press.

McCrudden, C. 2016. 'Human Rights: Law, Politics, Philosophy'. Paper presented at the conference *Theorizing the Practice of Human Rights* (6–9 October), University of Michigan Law School, Ann Arbor, Michigan.

McNeish, J.-A. 2013. 'Extraction, Protest and Indigeneity in Bolivia: The TIPNIS Effect'. *Latin American and Caribbean Ethnic Studies* 8(2): 221–42.

Merry, S. E. 2006. *Human Rights and Gender Violence: Translating International Law into Local Justice*. Chicago: University of Chicago Press.

Messer, E. 1993. 'Anthropology and Human Rights'. *Annual Review of Anthropology* 22: 221–49.

Moyn, S. 2010. *The Last Utopia: Human Rights in History*. Cambridge, MA: Belknap Press of Harvard University Press.

Moyn, S. 2018. *Not Enough: Human Rights in an Unequal World*. Cambridge, MA: Belknap Press of Harvard University Press.

Muehlmann, S. 2009. 'How Do Real Indians Fish? Neoliberal Multiculturalism and Contested Indigeneities in the Colorado Delta'. *American Anthropologist* 111(4): 468–79.

Nader, L. 1972. 'Up the Anthropologist—Perspectives Gained from Studying Up'. In D. H. Hymes, ed. *Reinventing Anthropology*, 284–311. New York: Pantheon Books.

Nagengast, C. and T. Turner. 1997. 'Introduction: Universal Human Rights versus Cultural Relativity'. *Journal of Anthropological Research* 53(3): 269–72.

Niezen, R. 2003. *The Origins of Indigenism: Human Rights and the Politics of Identity*. Berkeley: University of California Press.

Oviedo, A., ed. 2014. *Bifurcación del buen vivir y el sumak kawsay*. Quito: Ediciones Yachay.

Piketty, T. 2014. *Capital in the Twenty-First Century*. Cambridge, MA: Belknap Press of Harvard University Press.

Posner, E. A. 2014. *The Twilight of Human Rights Law*. Oxford: Oxford University Press.

Renteln, A. D. 1988. 'Relativism and the Search for Human Rights'. *American Anthropologist* 90(1): 56–72.

Riles, A. 2000. *The Network Inside Out*. Ann Arbor: University of Michigan Press.

Robbins, J. 2009. 'Recognition, Reciprocity, and Justice: Melanesian Reflections on the Rights of Relationships'. In K. M. Clarke and M. Goodale, eds. *Mirrors of Justice: Law and Power in the Post-Cold War Era*, 171–90. Cambridge: Cambridge University Press.

Santos, B. D. S. 2014. *Epistemologies of the South: Justice Against Epistemicide*. London: Routledge.

Sapignoli, M. 2018. *Hunting Justice: Displacement, Law, and Activism in the Kalahari*. Cambridge: Cambridge University Press.

Shoshan, N. 2016. *The Management of Hate: Nation, Affect, and the Governance of Right-Wing Extremism in Germany*. Princeton: Princeton University Press.

Speed, S. 2008. *Rights in Rebellion: Indigenous Struggle and Human Rights in Chiapas*. Stanford: Stanford University Press.

Turner, T. 1997. 'Human Rights, Human Difference: Anthropology's Contribution to an Emancipatory Cultural Politics'. *Journal of Anthropological Research* 53(3): 273–91.

Waldmüller, J. 2018. 'Lost Through Translation: Political Dialectics of Ecosocial and Collective Rights in Ecuador'. In T. Destrooper and S. E. Merry, eds. *Human Rights Transformation in Practice*, 101–27. Philadelphia: University of Pennsylvania Press.

Wilson, R. 2001. *The Politics of Truth and Reconciliation in South Africa: Legitimizing the Post-Apartheid State*. Cambridge: Cambridge University Press.

CHAPTER 24

HUMAN RIGHTS ACTIVISM, SEXUALITY, AND GENDER

LYNETTE J. CHUA

INTRODUCTION

AT a conference where I was giving a talk about my research on a social movement in Myanmar—a self-described lesbian, gay, bisexual, and transgender (LGBT)[1] rights movement—an audience member asked, 'How can you say that LGBT identities are positive when some scholars have identified them as harmful and threatening to local populations?' A second audience member asked, 'What is your take on the global–local divide on human rights?'

These questions reflect the recurring theme of globalization in two areas of anthropological research, one on non-normative sexualities and genders and the other on human rights. Researchers in these two subfields—queer anthropology[2] and the anthropology of human rights—have investigated the seemingly unstoppable flows of ideas, people, and resources across national and other socially constructed borders. As anthropologists weigh in on concerns about the potentially hegemonic power of globalization and its effects on inequality, they reveal deep-seated anxieties that lie beneath those concerns—about selfhood and authenticity; about who we are, should be, and can become.

In this chapter, I consider a type of anthropological research that brings together queer anthropology and the anthropology of human rights to analyse the intersection of human rights and social justice activism for people with non-normative sexualities and genders. In a time characterized by a 'double movement of globalization' (Stychin 2004: 953)—the globalization of human rights as a marker of progress and of same-sex sexualities as identities, especially LGBT—anthropology has yet to explore this intersection extensively. Anthropologists who study non-normative sexualities and genders have illuminated the context-dependent, plural practices of sexuality and gender. However, they usually do not explicate the processes and patterns that arise out of interactions with human rights, much less study research subjects who participate in collective action. Meanwhile, anthropologists of human rights have discovered the assorted, sometimes surprising, interpretations and uses of human rights as well as mined their culturally constructed and unstable meanings. Yet, even those who study human rights activism around issues of gender have mostly focused on cisgender, heterosexual women and not on mobilization around non-normative genders or sexualities. By developing research on human rights activism, sexuality, and gender, the field of anthropology could further influence theories of social movements and collective action in the broader social sciences.

To pursue such an anthropological enquiry, I show how an ethnographic approach grounded in love, agency, and humanity can be used effectively. The approach focuses not merely on the interpretation, adaptation, and circulation of the substantive meanings of human rights and LGBT identities by and among a group of people. It also analyses the emotions and interpersonal relations that give rise to and emerge from those processes and treats them as inherent to the practices of human rights and LGBT identities. Taking this approach, scholars would pay attention to the emotions of people who engage with the two discourses as well as their relationships within the group and with others in their lives. These scholars would trace and theorize the patterns, if any, that link subjectivities—constituted by emotions and social relationships—to the making of a community and to political action that aims to change law and politics by collectively mobilizing human rights. Additionally, and critically, they would conduct ethnography with compassion for the agency and empirical realities of their research subjects.

Queer anthropology and LGBT identities

Despite slow and difficult beginnings, queer anthropology has helped us understand that sexualities are cultural constructions, showed us diverse practices of sexuality and gender, and reminded us that we have yet to fully comprehend the relationship between the two concepts themselves.[3] These three insights are highly relevant to my discussion on conducting anthropological research at the intersection of human rights activism, sexuality, and gender. In particular, they are salient to the concerns with globalization—namely, the interactions and experiences of (usually) non-Western populations with LGBT identities.

The first insight that sexualities are culturally constructed owes a great intellectual debt to other academic disciplines (Davis and Whitten 1987; Vance 2005). For example, sociologist Mary McIntosh in 1968 examined homosexuality as a 'social role', rather than a condition, which varies across societies. In what is probably the earliest constructionist account of the subject (Risman and Schwartz 1988; Vance 2005), McIntosh argued that homosexuals were labelled 'deviants', a role that served as a means of social control.[4] Building on McIntosh, the historian Jeffrey Weeks (1977) differentiated between homosexual behaviour, which can be found anywhere, and homosexual identity, which is specific to a society. Although constructionist approaches vary in their emphases, they share in common a rejection of universal definitions of sexuality. Rather, their point of departure is that the social significance and meaning of physically sexual acts vary depending on the cultural and historical periods in which they occur (Vance 2005). In other words, sexualities are constituted by sexual relations; in turn, sexual relations are embedded in the context in which the participants of those relations construct and find meaning (Blackwood 2002).

The cultural constructionist point that sexual identities are inconsistent across time and context is related to the second insight: there are myriad ways of doing sexuality and gender, and these practices are accorded different value and significance by different societies. Even before constructionist approaches flourished, anthropologists such as Ruth Benedict (1935, 1939) demonstrated that non-normative sexualities and genders were not necessarily abnormal or deviant (Weston 1993).[5] Later anthropological studies outside Euro-American societies thickly contextualized all kinds of sexual practices (Bacchetta 2002). These findings undercut the moral legitimacy of anti-homosexual bias and perversion models used to explain sexual variation (Rubin 2002), as well as disrupted colonial discourses about civilization and progress (Bacchetta 2002). Moreover, as anthropologists conducted research in more and more places, they consistently showed that sexualities (and genders—more on the relationship between the two below) are localized, reaffirming constructionist views that their meanings and definitions change and can be changed across and within contexts (Boellstorff 2007).[6]

The instability of sexualities as identities and the expansion of research into increasingly diverse places have enriched the third anthropological insight into the relationship between gender and sexuality, keeping it an open and live issue (Boellstorff 2007). From early anthropological accounts of non-normative sexualities, such as Benedict's work cited above, up to the 1970s, gender and sexuality usually meant the same thing (Jacobs and Roberts 1989).[7] Starting with feminist scholars, however, anthropologists began to treat the two as distinct but intertwined constructions (Vance 2005). From the 1970s onwards, as a contemporary gay and lesbian movement in the United States emerged, anthropologists and other social scientists eventually de-gendered homosexuality and solidified 'gay' and 'transgender' into separate realms of human experience (Valentine 2002). This separation became an important political and theoretical innovation (Rubin 1984) that allowed anthropologists to probe the complex dynamics between sexual and gender subjectivities, including social hierarchies, politics, and cultural meanings (Valentine 2002).[8] Notably, researchers who conduct ethnography in non-Western societies have frequently learned that the local subjectivities of sexuality and gender could be one and the same (e.g. Blackwood 2010; Boellstorff 2005; Chua 2019; Garcia 2009; Gilbert 2016; Sinnott 2004), and thus would appear to be at odds with LGBT discourses that they noticed were also in circulation in those places.

All three insights—on cultural construction, plural sexual and gender practices, and the intriguing relationship between sexuality and gender—come together in the debates about LGBT identities as a globalizing force. One big question is whether LGBT identities could push away older or traditional subjectivities. Scholars like Altman (1999) believe that LGBT identities could indeed displace earlier constructs, but take the positive view that the phenomenon could bring new opportunities to local activists. Other scholars, such as Puar (2002) and Massad (2002), criticize the incursion of LGBT identities as a form of Western imperialism, marginalizing local subjectivities for being premodern and unliberated and excluding people who do not or cannot adopt LGBT identities from gaining access to privileges and resources.

By contrast, anthropologists use extensive ethnographic research to show that the effects of globalization on non-normative sexualities and genders are neither foregone conclusions nor fates that necessarily have to be mourned.[9] They offer perspectives that resonate with the three insights above and emphasize the fluidity of agency. Because sexualities and genders are diverse and ever-shifting in their meanings and practices, so-called traditional and LGBT sexualities and genders alike are all malleable, capable of being challenged and transformed through social interactions and relations (Boellstorff 2005; Chua 2019). People actively reinterpret and adapt LGBT identities to fit their contexts (e.g. Blackwood 2005; Boellstorff 2005; Phua 2010; Wright 2000), such that global and local discourses about sexualities and genders thoroughly infiltrate each other (Blackwood 2005, citing Grewal and Kaplan 1994). As a result, the outcome is often a further diversification of subjectivities instead of an erasure of the old(er) and (more) traditional.

Another debate on globalization to which LGBT identities are commonly linked is that of human rights. Yet anthropologists who study non-normative sexualities and genders do not usually concentrate on the intersection of the two, especially where collective action is involved (Bacchetta 2002).[10] Save for a few exceptions, to which I will refer later, ethnographic studies that contain accounts of lesbian and gay movements in their research contexts do not devote much analysis to these movements' human rights practices (e.g. Blackwood 2005, 2010; Boellstorff 2005; Gilbert 2016; Sinnott 2004).

Perhaps the neglect has in part to do with the line that queer anthropologists tend to draw between activists and non-activists—roughly those who embrace 'Western' politics and those who do not or cannot—marking off the former as insufficiently representative of everyday struggles (Dave 2011). The line has endured, even though contemporary anthropologists do not necessarily insist that people who adopt and adapt LGBT identities are inauthentic. In the final section of this chapter, where I discuss the pursuit of an anthropology of human rights activism, sexuality, and gender, I explain why this line is blurry. To get to that point, let me next discuss the anthropological study of human rights, where activists take centre stage.

Anthropology of Human Rights and LGBT Activism

The anthropology of human rights has come a long way since the early part of the twentieth century, when anthropologists were largely unconcerned with this subject.[11]

One of the most exciting developments in this area of research is the ethnographic turn (Goodale 2006) towards studying human rights as cultural processes in and of themselves (Cowan et al. 2001; Cowan 2006). Like queer anthropology, human rights ethnography offers insights germane to the anthropological inquiry into human rights activism, sexuality, and gender—namely, the understandings that human rights are culturally constructed processes, possess plural meanings, and bear paradoxical effects.

According to human rights ethnography, human rights are social facts whose meanings shift with social interactions. This is because human rights, to use the language from the previous section, are constituted by social processes and relations. Their meanings emerge from the social lives of human rights (Wilson 2006), as people practise human rights—make sense of and use human rights—amid collective action or in other contexts to describe grievances, allocate blame, and make claims. Therefore, their meanings are often the result of mixing globally produced ideas and practices of human rights with familiar norms, images, symbols, and narratives (Chua 2019; Levitt and Merry 2009; Selby 2018).

Consequently, human rights ethnography often reveals tensions associated with human rights as a globalizing force. When human rights are 'translated' (Merry 2006), differences appear between human rights as defined in international documents and the home-grown versions (Cowan et al. 2001; Wilson 1997). Sometimes, the differences demonstrate the tension between challenging the status quo and gaining acceptance (Levitt and Merry 2009); that is, if human rights are adapted too much to suit a local context, it might diminish their capacity to alter social structures or norms that perpetuated the grievances in the first place. Other times, the differences highlight the tension between the purported universality of human rights and domestic conditions (Levitt and Merry 2009). Related to these tensions is the concern that choosing human rights as the redress for grievances reinforces unequal distribution of power, as transnational or national activists, compared to grassroots organizers, are often the ones with the status and resources to press forward their visions for human rights (Merry 2006). Another concern is that human rights could displace alternative discourses about social justice, some of which could be more indigenous to the community in question (Merry 2006).

Such tensions expose the paradoxically constraining and enabling nature of human rights (Cheng 2011; Chua 2019; Cowan 2006). Because human rights practices are culturally constructed, open, and multiple (Goodale 2007a, 2009), the tensions are always going to be mediated by the different actors involved and the meanings that they make out of adapting and circulating human rights. Human rights are neither innately good nor bad, powerful nor weak. Researchers often uncover co-existing, contradictory results of human rights mobilization. For example, although human rights activism did not improve their political conditions, Palestinian activists still managed to use human rights as an outlet to express Palestinian identity and to feel that they are doing something to speak out against oppression (Allen 2013). Put differently, the nature and impact of human rights are empirically open questions that might yield conflicting answers, depending on how people use human rights and how they experience this practice.

From the discussion thus far, we can see how human rights ethnography speaks to the concerns about human rights as a globalizing force. Ethnographic research on the practices of queer activists who engage not only with human rights but also with the now-conjoined discourse of LGBT (Kollman and Waites 2009) has great potential to advance this area of study. To date, however, such ethnographic studies are few and far between. Thoreson's study of the construction and institutionalization of LGBT rights by a transnational non-governmental organization (NGO) (Thoreson 2014), his analysis of the local adaptation of LGBT politics in the Philippines (2012), and my work on Myanmar's LGBT rights movement (Chua 2019) are some of these examples.

By and large, researchers whose studies focus on sexual and gender justice usually presume that their subjects are cisgender heterosexual women.[12] The queer anthropological studies cited in the preceding section concentrate on research subjects who are non-activists. Some writings, such as Babb (2003), do consider the collective action aspect, but they tend not to contain analyses of human rights as cultural practices. Thoreson (2012) pointed out that the growing literature on LGBT activism frequently fails to include an ethnographic investigation of how people in the Global South draw from the globalizing discourse of LGBT. To extrapolate from Thoreson's observations, human rights ethnography frequently misses the interactions between human rights activism and non-normative sexual and gender subjectivities.

Towards an Anthropological Inquiry into Human Rights Activism, Sexuality, and Gender

The anthropological study of human rights activism, sexuality, and gender builds on the insights of queer anthropology and human rights ethnography and remedies the areas where they remain inadequate. Whereas queer anthropology has been quite inattentive to human rights, human rights ethnography lacks studies on non-normative sexualities and genders. Bringing the two subfields together, anthropological study can identify the interwoven layers of power and resistance at work at the intersection of activism and sexuality and gender. At this intersection, scholars can analyse how people who fight for social justice engage with human rights and LGBT identities to mount resistance, resist those two discourses themselves, or otherwise respond to them. In the rest of this section, I elaborate on an ethnographic approach that could be used effectively for this kind of anthropological research.

Ethnography Grounded in Love, Agency, and Humanity

From 2012 to 2017, I conducted fieldwork to understand how a self-described LGBT movement emerged in Myanmar, how this group of self-described LGBT activists practised human rights, and what sort of implications their practice produced.[13] While I certainly learned from other human rights ethnographers to examine the human rights practice of Myanmar's LGBT activists as cultural processes, I came to develop my own approach, with its own distinctive theoretical orientation. My approach gets its name in part from the fact that it was developed from research about activists who are concerned with a fundamental aspect of our humanity, love—be it romantic passion, physical love, or other desires and affections. But it also gets its name from several characteristics that I will explain in turn.

The most essential characteristic is the centrality of emotions and interpersonal relationships. The further along I was with my fieldwork and the more I tried to theorize about what I was hearing and seeing, I realized that emotions and social relationships were core to these activists' human rights practice. Even though ethnographic studies of human rights give in-depth analyses of how activists adapt the substantive meanings of human rights to fit local contexts and how they circulate and implement those adaptations, these analyses usually do not elucidate the significance of emotions and relationships to a similar degree. Unlike these studies, I focused not only on the substantive meanings of human rights but also on the role of emotions and interpersonal relationships. After analysing my data and reading broadly across the social sciences, I conceptualized the relationship between human rights processes and emotions and interpersonal relationships to be a mutually constitutive one. Social actors involved in these processes bring human rights together with the norms, beliefs, distribution of power, and hierarchy in their society. Emotions and relationships reshape the actors, altering the processes as they continuously play out. Therefore, emotions and relationships do not merely serve instrumental purposes for activists, as conduits or strategies to be deployed. They embody *all* aspects of practising human rights, including meaning making, circulation, implementation, and the production of outcomes.

Following my approach, the interpretations of substantive meanings of human rights become fused with emotions. In one of the most pivotal interviews with the movement's founder, when I asked what he would say to sceptics who thought human rights were foreign to him and his compatriots, he replied, 'Our people know human rights from their suffering. The human rights concept comes from their lives. It comes from their real life, real suffering' (Chua 2019: 68).

What this interviewee means is that he and his compatriots understand human rights by feeling what it is like to live in their absence. For this interviewee, his fellow activists, and their followers, human rights represent the dignity of which they have been deprived, causing them to feel the emotions of suffering. Thus, to know human rights is to feel them. Such a fusion between cognition and emotions has its basis in anthropology as well as other disciplines in the social sciences, humanities, and biological sciences.

Increasingly, scholars across these disciplines are acknowledging that feeling is just as important as thinking, and that emotions are no longer separable from cognition along the lines of 'rational' vs. 'irrational' (Chua 2019).

The second characteristic of my approach is that it shows how personal and grassroots dimensions of change are interrelated and have the potential to build up to formal institutional outcomes, and how this interrelatedness emerges through processes that make and are made by emotions and relationships. In the case of Myanmar's LGBT movement, their human rights practice transformed the selfhood of queer Burmese, who together created a community as LGBT activists bound to one another by their distinctive emotional ties. This collective, an LGBT activist community, then takes political action by making claims for LGBT rights in their country. By comparison, the broader literature on human rights movements usually neglects to explain the social processes through which personal changes to activists or movement participants influence another outcome, much less analyse the critical involvement of emotions and social ties.

Taking my own approach, I thus made the connections between the personal, the collective, and political action in human rights practice by analysing emotions and interpersonal relationships. I started with my finding that selfhood is constituted by social relationships, which resonates with writings in anthropology about the relational construction of the self, contrary to the 'Western' conception of a bounded and distinctive whole (Rosaldo 1980; Geertz 1984; Strathern 1988; Strathern 2004). When movement leaders and newcomers practised their version of human rights, some of them undergo a transformation of selfhood. By feeling and knowing human rights, they changed how they felt about themselves—from feeling pain, self-hate, and fear to feeling worthy and hopeful, desiring to fight for a better future together. They became LGBT activists as they found belonging in a community bound by their emotional fealty to human rights and affective ties to one another. On the contrary, those who dropped out of the movement and stopped calling themselves LGBT activists did so because they felt less connected to the movement community or more attracted to other communities. For those who stayed, such transformations of selfhood also altered the manner in which they conducted their relationships with parents, siblings, friends, lovers, and others, changes which, in turn, further modified or reinforced their transformed sense of self.

By foregrounding emotions and relationships in my analyses of human rights practice and tracing the patterns in which emotions and relationships connected the self, the group, and their political actions, I was able to specify the theoretical links between human rights practice and collective mobilization. This is the third distinctive characteristic of my approach. It differs from other studies of human rights ethnography, which seldom theorize about how the acts of interpretation, adaptation, and circulation of human rights actually lead to collective action.[14] That is why, to me, the line between activists and non-activists is never clear. Activists emerge from non-activists, and activists sometimes go back to being non-activists again as they experience and partake in the processes of human rights practice over time.

These three key characteristics of my ethnographic approach make clear why it is presented both in terms of agency and love (in the sense of the range of emotions from love to its complete opposite). Driven by emotions and relationships, the activists in my study exercised their agency to create and sustain a human rights practice in their unique way. This emphasis on agency takes us to questions about power and resistance, especially with regard to the nature and impact of two globalizing discourses, human rights and LGBT identities.

Consistent with other human rights ethnography that analyses human rights practice culturally, I started from the point that the meanings given by Burmese LGBT activists to human rights are contingent and constructed—with the additional complication of analysing emotions and interpersonal relationships integral to these processes.[15] I watched and listened to my research subjects as they felt their way (Jasper 2014) through human rights, relating them to their living conditions, their relationships, their aspirations, as well as the norms and hierarchies in their society. I discovered that, to these activists, human rights contain three essential meanings: dignity, responsibility (of the rights-bearer), and social belonging. Although they drew from international human rights documents for the concept of dignity, they infused it with local notions that stress the importance of social belonging to dignity: to be accepted, to feel that one belongs in one's family or larger community, is to have dignity. And to earn this dignity, the rights-bearer has the responsibility to take action by participating in collective action.

I also discovered that these meaning-making processes are as much about human rights as they are about LGBT identities. When asked for their view on the local words for queer subjectivities, the activists usually drew from personal experiences to explain that those terms are humiliating and derogatory.[16] Conversely, they described LGBT identities as showing respect for their selfhood. One interviewee said that 'the feeling' of the two sets of words is different (Chua 2019: 91). As part of their interpretation and adaptation of human rights, these activists associated LGBT identities with the meaning of dignity embodied in human rights. In addition, because LGBT activists belong to a community that is bound by and through a certain human rights practice, the term LGBT signals a sense of belonging, which is another important meaning of human rights for them.

Hence, intricately tied to LGBT identities, the three meanings of human rights generate connotative power (Goodale 2007b) that renders human rights a collective good to be collectively achieved. The meanings index a social and collective self rather than project visions of individuated, automated persons, as feared by human rights critics. Scholars across disciplines argue that human rights need to have cultural legitimacy in order to work and do good (Merry 2006, citing Ignatieff 2001). In my study, human rights have cultural legitimacy not only because they are put in dialogue with local conceptions of dignity (Santos 2015), but also because they make emotional and relational sense to people's experiences and aspirations.

Relatedly, LGBT identities need not be seen as jeopardizing more traditional or older queer subjectivities. Queer anthropologists have already noted one reason, which is that local populations adapt and add LGBT identities to, rather than replace, their vocabulary of queer subjectivities. In Myanmar's LGBT rights movement, leaders do not enforce LGBT identities according to definitions in international parlance. Nor do their fellow activists or followers strictly adhere to such definitions. Instead, they produce their own understandings of LGBT meshed with local sensibilities of doing sexuality and gender.

The other reason, which highlights my ethnographic approach, is that LGBT identities for this movement connote a sense of dignity as well as belonging for the activists themselves. Indeed, it is possible that even after being locally redefined, the scope of LGBT identities does not encompass all non-normative sexualities and genders (Katyal 2002; Manalansan 1995, 2002) in a given society. But these activists know that. Or at least I did not presume that they were ignorant or negligent, without asking and trying to understand their perspectives.

One activist in my study said candidly that they were all different and that the use of the LGBT terminology was merely for 'political concern' (Chua 2019: 93). Their labels of LGBT and their LGBT activist community are not so much about expressing an essential truth about who they are; they are rather 'necessary fictions' (Weeks 1995, 1996). As I found from the emotional and relational connections between selfhood and community, LGBT identities and their LGBT activist communities provide comfort, support, and a force for political opposition based on a shared set of values (Weeks 1995, 1996), in this case, human rights practice.

But, of course, no human rights practice is perfect. Like many other human rights ethnographers before me, I also noticed cracks and weaknesses in my research subjects' practice of human rights. I cannot go into detail here, but it suffices to say that their practice contains unequal dynamics that are not uncommon for LGBT movements (e.g. Bacchetta 2002; Babb 2003; Chua 2016). Their practice also provokes frequently raised concerns about the mainstreaming effects of rights (Vaid 1995), which can end up drawing disciplining distinctions between 'good' and 'bad' queers (Moran 2004).

Nevertheless, human rights ethnographers often find that the problems with human rights practice co-exist with culturally legitimate meanings and other effects that activists have found to be helpful or positive. This is the case with Myanmar's LGBT rights movement as well. Confronted with the paradoxes of human rights' enabling and constraining nature (Cowan 2006), I interpreted the movement's human rights practice as having a meaningful impact while being far from dominant, co-existing with much more entrenched modes of knowing, feeling, and interacting that have long been shaped by social norms and hierarchy in their society.

I realized that these activists embrace human rights, bound by their community's fealty to human rights and to each other—*when* they are immersed in that community.[17] But they inhabit multiple social worlds, including older queer communities, and thus multiple identities. One identity is no less authentic than the other. In line with what anthropologists, including queer anthropologists, have already pointed out, people have the agency to strategically navigate multiple worlds and deploy corresponding identities, even when the relations may be unequal and hierarchical (Keeler 2017).

With such a response to the paradoxes of human rights, my approach recognizes fluid agencies within and across individuals by showing love—as in compassion—for research subjects as they are situated in their empirical realities. People who develop an emotional attachment to human rights are usually compelled by their local conditions to seek solutions to their suffering. LGBT activists in Myanmar, and I suspect elsewhere, are aggrieved and motivated by the plight of marginalized populations and unfair conditions in their society.

As ethnographers, we have to be careful about romanticizing or valorizing home-grown same-sex sexualities (Blackwood 2005). Communities built around older sexual or gender subjectivities may seem appealing for being local or traditional. But we also know from the wider field of anthropology that all communities have their own normative orders and modes of organizing social relations, which can be oppressive to some groups. All these communities and their discourses possess their own internal logics and disciplining effects. All are culturally constructed, capable of being empowering as much as constraining.

To show compassion for the agency of those who practise human rights is to try to understand how and why a group of activists chooses the discourse of human rights (and LGBT identities). Seen in this light, the ethnographer may have another response to the concern that seeking rights-based solutions could result in mainstreaming. Where human rights and LGBT identities had seemed foreign but were adapted and used to question deeply rooted beliefs and social hierarchies, perhaps there is cause for the ethnographer to wonder if such a discourse could possibly be groundbreaking instead (Chua 2014, 2019).

Therefore, the final meaning of my ethnographic approach refers to showing compassion for the human condition by committing to the empirically subjective with love. This commitment does not require ignoring the failings of research subjects or effusively singing their praises. The humans we study—just like us—have their biases, loyalties, strengths, and weaknesses. Committing to the empirically subjective with love is to embrace ethnographic thickness (Ortner 1995), and thus to commit to telling the paradoxes of human rights in all its jumbles and contradictions, including the emotions and relationships that nourish the lives of people whom the ethnographer has the privilege and fortune to meet.

Conclusion

Inherent in the scepticism about globalization is an assumption that there is a much more original (read: authentic) personhood to be protected or rescued from the onslaught of Western sensibilities that accompany human rights or the identity discourses affiliated with them. This is a bias that actually betrays the observer's assumption of a hermetically sealed self. Take Myanmar and its inhabitants, for instance. Like many other societies, Myanmar is ridden with fissures, contestations, and layers upon layers of history. What was once foreign, with the sands of time, fickleness of memory, and annals of the victorious, could one day become synonymous with the place and its people. Buddhism, so closely identified with Myanmar as we know it today, was once an outsider. It post-dated animistic worship, and in some instances eventually incorporated and subsumed such primordial practices. Moreover, for Myanmar's people who believe in the karmic cycle of birth and rebirth and the transmigration of the soul, they would have had many lives before this one. Each life would have been shaped by the ones before.

Putting aside the spiritual and returning to the secular, the idea that there is an authentic self, true to one's individual origins, is a rather peculiar notion that resonates very little in many parts of the world (Keeler 2016, citing Ewing 1990). In line with anthropological studies on Myanmar and other Southeast Asian societies, multiple selves co-exist, to be summoned and deployed according to place, time, and people. All of these selves would have been made and remade by social forces before outside ideas about rights and identities reached their shores. Whether to the people who embody them or to us, scholars and observers, the task of discerning the real self may not be as simple as it seems.

Anxieties about the authentic self were embedded in the two questions raised by audience members at the conference described at the start of this chapter. To the first question, I said I learned from my fieldwork that these activists responded to LGBT identities positively. I reminded the audience that these activists were resisting the local norms and hierarchies that they believed had shaped the difficult conditions for people with non-normative sexualities and genders in their society, and that they felt the local words for queer subjectivities had contributed to those conditions. In addition, I said, it would be ironic to dismiss their agency simply because they were trying to make use of something foreign to change locally inflicted hardships.

Scholars in queer anthropology and the anthropology of human rights have introduced us to complex and diverse social worlds, explained the ever-changing nature of selfhood, ideas, and practices in those worlds, and examined the social interactions, hierarchies, and relations that shape them. At the intersection of human rights activism, sexuality, and gender, we can broaden the influence of anthropological research to illuminate our understandings of collective action and dynamics of resistance and social change. Furthermore, we could extend the ethnographic approach that I have described to other areas of human rights ethnography. The empirical details of each case would be different, of course. After all, emotions are culturally specific (Rosaldo 1984). However, the attention to emotions and interpersonal relationships, whichever ones they are and whatever they mean, would travel well.

Most of all, as I said in response to the second question at the conference, it is important to move past binaries of the global–local that mirror those of the powerful–powerless, North–South, East–West, and so on. I did not start with such an aim, but my ethnographic approach—developed in the course of fieldwork—eventually led to that point. Once I allowed compassion for agency into my analyses, I could find no intellectual justification for assigning binary categories to the phenomena that I had observed. I found that I could avoid doing so by turning my ethnography towards the most personal aspects of our lives, our selfhood and intimacies. While this approach should not and cannot offer straightforward answers to our concerns about globalization, it does enable anthropology to do what it has always done at its best: show us the rich and messy emotions and relationships that weave together the web of humanity.

Notes

1. Even though the acronym 'LGBT' has been expanded to include other subjectivities, such as queer, questioning, intersex, ally, asexual and beyond (LGBTQIA+), I use 'LGBT' throughout this chapter to maintain consistency with the first mention here, which refers to this specific movement that I studied in Myanmar.
2. Naming this area of research is always difficult, and I use 'queer anthropology' as a 'parsimonious terminological handle' (Boellstorff 2007: 18).
3. On the development of queer anthropology, see Boellstorff (2007); Davis and Whitten (1987); Hekma (2000); Jacobs and Roberts (1989); Kennedy (2002); Lyons and Lyons (2004); Valentine (2002); Vance (2005); Weston (1993).
4. Contemporary scholars often neglect the early works of sociologists, historians, anthropologists, and other social scientists, crediting almost exclusively theorists such as Michel Foucault and Judith Butler for the development of constructionism (Rubin 2002; Vance 2005).
5. However, in these early works by Benedict, homosexuality was considered a matter of individual drive (Weston 1993) and conflated with being gender transgressive.
6. Queer anthropology used to be dominated by studies about cisgender gay men (Babb 2003; Bacchetta 2002), especially those who were white and middle- to upper-class. The range of studies has diversified, though studies on transgender issues and female same-sex sexualities are still lacking (Boellstorff 2007).
7. Note, however, that Mead (1935) appears to distinguish biological sex from gender roles and is probably the first social scientist to use ethnography to develop a distinction between the two (Visweswaran 1997).
8. For empirical or historical accounts in the American context, see examples such as Chauncey (1994) and Newton (1993). For non-American contexts, see works such as Boellstorff (2005); Blackwood (2010); Garcia (2009); Gilbert (2016); Chua (2019); Sinnott (2004).
9. For related criticisms in anthropology, see examples such as Babb (2003); Bacchetta (2002); Manalansan (1995).
10. Although the study of non-normative sexualities and genders was also initially marginalized in sociology, it has forged ahead of anthropology to document social movements and LGBT rights activism (Gamson and Moon 2004; Ghaziani et al. 2016).
11. For discussions about anthropology's different periods of challenges and developments in the field of human rights, see Messer (1993) and Goodale (2006).
12. Note, however, that in studies on women's rights activism such as Rajaram and Zararia (2009), the researchers might include groups that work on same-sex sexualities.
13. My fieldwork included interviews, observations, and analysis of videos, photographs, and printed materials produced by activists. In my book (Chua 2019), I employed 'queer' as a

broad reference to non-normative sexualities and genders in places where I was not specifically referring to the movement.

14. Studies about the 'translation' of human rights into the vernacular recognize the affinity of vernacularization to collective action framing in social movements research (Levitt and Merry 2009; Merry 2006), but they do not elaborate on the processes that lead from human rights translation to collective action.
15. Burmese scholars such as Keeler (2017) and Prasse-Freeman (2015) doubt that any rights discourse would make sense to Burmese people, because their society is traditionally hierarchal, with power and benefits flowing from a given status. The difference between their views and mine is that they start with the notion that rights embody a certain set of ideas that serve as the yardstick against which Burmese understandings are measured.
16. Some interviewees regarded certain local words as neutral, and even those who said that local terms are derogatory use them for self-identification depending on the context in which they are situated. On this issue, see my point later in this section on inhabiting and moving between multiple social worlds.
17. Also see n. 16.

References

Allen, L. 2013. *The Rise and Fall of Human Rights: Cynicism and Politics in Occupied Palestine*. Stanford: Stanford University Press.

Altman, D. 1999. 'The Internationalization of Gay and Lesbian'. In D. Epstein and J. T. Sears, eds. *A Dangerous Knowing: Sexuality, Pedagogy and Popular Culture*, 135–52. London: Cassell.

Babb, F. E. 2003. 'Out in Nicaragua: Local and Transnational Desires after the Revolution'. *Cultural Anthropology* 18(3): 304–28.

Bacchetta, P. 2002. 'Rescaling Transnational "Queerdom": Lesbian and "Lesbian" Identitary-Positionalities in Delhi in the 1980s'. *Antipode* 34(5): 947–73.

Benedict, R. 1935. *Patterns of Culture*. London: Routledge & Kegan Paul.

Benedict, R. 1939. 'Sex in Primitive Society'. *American Journal of Orthopsychiatry* 9(3): 570–3.

Blackwood, E. 2002. 'Reading Sexualities across Cultures: Anthropology and Theories of Sexuality'. In E. Lewin and W. L. Leap, eds. *Out in Theory: The Emergence of Lesbian and Gay Anthropology*, 69–92. Urbana: University of Illinois Press.

Blackwood, E. 2005. 'Transnational Sexualities in One Place: Indonesian Readings'. *Gender & Society* 19(2): 221–42.

Blackwood, E. 2010. *Falling into the Lesbi World: Desire and Difference in Indonesia*. Honolulu: University of Hawaii Press.

Boellstorff, T. 2005. *The Gay Archipelago: Sexuality and Nation in Indonesia*. Princeton: Princeton University Press.

Boellstorff, T. 2007. 'Queer Studies in the House of Anthropology'. *Annual Review of Anthropology* 36(1): 17–35.

Cheng, S. 2011. 'The Paradox of Vernacularization: Women's Human Rights and the Gendering of Nationhood'. *Anthropological Quarterly* 84(2): 475–505.

Chua, L. J. 2014. *Mobilizing Gay Singapore: Rights and Resistance in an Authoritarian State*. Philadelphia: Temple University Press.

Chua, L. J. 2016. 'Negotiating Social Norms and Relations in the Micromobilization of Human Rights: The Case of Burmese Lesbian Activism'. *Law & Social Inquiry* 41(3): 643–69.

Chua, L. J. 2019. *The Politics of Love in Myanmar: LGBT Mobilization and Human Rights as a Way of Life*. Stanford: Stanford University Press.
Cowan, J. K. 2006. 'Culture and Rights after Culture and Rights'. *American Anthropologist* 108(1): 9–24.
Cowan, J. K., M.-B. Dembour, and R. A. Wilson. 2001. 'Introduction'. In J. K. Cowan, M.-B. Dembour, and R. A. Wilson, eds. *Culture and Rights: Anthropological Perspectives*, 1–26. Cambridge: Cambridge University Press.
Dave, N. N. 2011. 'Indian and Lesbian and What Came Next: Affect, Commensuration, and Queer Emergences'. *American Ethnologist* 38(4): 650–65.
Davis, D. L. and R. G. Whitten. 1987. 'The Cross-Cultural Study of Human Sexuality'. *Annual Review of Anthropology* 16(1): 69–98.
Ewing, K. P. 1990. 'The Illusion of Wholeness: Culture, Self and the Experience of Inconsistency'. *Ethos* 18(3): 251–78.
Gamson, J. and D. Moon. 2004. 'The Sociology of Sexualities: Queer and Beyond'. *Annual Review of Sociology* 30: 47–64.
Garcia, J. N. C. 2009. *Philippine Gay Culture: Binabae to Bakla, Silahis to MSM*. Hong Kong: Hong Kong University Press.
Geertz, C. 1984. '"From the Native's Point of View": On the Nature of Anthropological Understanding'. In R. A. Shweder and R. A. LeVine, eds. *Culture Theory: Essays on Mind, Self and Emotion*, 123–36. Cambridge: Cambridge University Press.
George, C. 1994. *Gay New York: Gender, Urban Culture, and the Making of the Gay Male World, 1890–1940*. New York: Basic Books.
Ghaziani, A., V. Taylor, and A. Stone. 2016. 'Cycles of Sameness and Difference in LGBT Social Movements'. *Annual Review of Sociology* 42(1): 165–83.
Gilbert, D. F. 2016. *Everyday Transgender Belonging in Transitioning Yangon*. PhD Thesis. Australian National University.
Goodale, M. 2006. 'Introduction to "Anthropology and Human Rights in a New Key"'. *American Anthropologist* 108(1): 1–8.
Goodale, M. 2007a. 'Introduction: Locating Rights, Envisioning Law Between the Global and the Local'. In M. Goodale and S. E. Merry, eds. *The Practice of Human Rights: Tracking Law between the Global and the Local*, 1–38. New York: Cambridge University Press.
Goodale, M. 2007b. 'The Power of Right(s): Tracking Empires of Law and New Modes of Social Resistance in Bolivia (and Elsewhere)'. In M. Goodale and S. E. Merry, eds. *The Practice of Human Rights: Tracking Law Between the Global and the Local*, 130–62. Cambridge: Cambridge University Press.
Goodale, M. 2009. *Surrendering to Utopia: An Anthropology of Human Rights*. Stanford: Stanford University Press.
Grewal, I. and C. Kaplan, eds. 1994. *Scattered Hegemonies: Postmodernity and Transnational Feminist Practices*. Minneapolis: University of Minnesota Press.
Hekma, G. 2000. 'Queering Anthropology'. In *Lesbian and Gay Studies: An Introductory, Interdisciplinary Approach*, 81–97. London: SAGE Publications Ltd.
Ignatieff, M. 2001. *Human Rights as Politics and Idolatry*. Princeton: Princeton University Press.
Jacobs, S.-E. and C. Roberts. 1989. 'Sex, Sexuality, Gender, and Gender Variance'. In S. Morgen, ed. *Gender and Anthropology: Critical Reviews for Research and Teaching*, 438–62. Washington, DC: American Anthropological Association.
Jasper, J. M. 2014. *Protest: A Cultural Introduction to Social Movements*. Hoboken: John Wiley & Sons.

Katyal, S. 2002. 'Exporting Identity'. *Yale Journal of Law & Feminism* 14(1): 97–176.

Keeler, W. 2016. 'Shifting Transversals: Trans Women's Move from Spirit Mediumship to Beauty Work in Mandalay'. *Ethnos* 81(5): 792–820.

Keeler, W. 2017. *The Traffic in Hierarchy: Masculinity and Its Others in Buddhist Burma*. Hawaii: University of Hawaii Press.

Kennedy, E. L. 2002. '"These Natives Can Speak for Themselves": The Development of Gay and Lesbian Community Studies in Anthropology'. In E. Lewin and W. Leap, eds. *Out in Theory: The Emergence of Lesbian and Gay Anthropology*, 93–109. Urbana: University of Illinois Press.

Kollman, K. and M. Waites. 2009. 'The Global Politics of Lesbian, Gay, Bisexual and Transgender Human Rights: An Introduction'. *Contemporary Politics* 15(1): 1–17.

Levitt, P. and S. Merry. 2009. 'Vernacularization on the Ground: Local Uses of Global Women's Rights in Peru, China, India and the United States'. *Global Networks* 9(4): 441–61.

Lyons, A. P. and H. Lyons. 2004. *Irregular Connections: A History of Anthropology and Sexuality*. Lincoln: University of Nebraska Press.

Manalansan, M. F. 1995. 'In the Shadows of Stonewall: Examining Gay Transnational Politics and the Diasporic Dilemma'. *GLQ: A Journal of Lesbian and Gay Studies* 2(4): 425–38.

Manalansan, M. F. 2002. 'A Queer Itinerary: Deviant Excursions into Modernities'. In E. Lewin and W. Leap, eds. *Out in Theory: The Emergence of Lesbian and Gay Anthropology*, 246–63. Urbana: University of Illinois Press.

Massad, J. A. 2002. 'Re-Orienting Desire: The Gay International and the Arab World'. *Public Culture* 14(2): 361–85.

Mead, M. 1935. *Sex and Temperament*. New York: Routledge and Kegan Paul.

Merry, S. E. 2006. *Human Rights and Gender Violence: Translating International Law into Local Justice*. Chicago: University of Chicago Press.

Messer, E. 1993. 'Anthropology and Human Rights'. *Annual Review of Anthropology* 22: 221–49.

Moran, L. J. 2004. 'Sexuality in Law and Society Scholarship'. In A. Sarat, ed. *The Blackwell Companion to Law and Society*, 487–505. Oxford: Blackwell Publishing Ltd.

Newton, E. 1993. *Cherry Grove, Fire Island: Sixty Years in America's First Gay and Lesbian Town*. Durham: Duke University Press.

Ortner, S. B. 1995. 'Resistance and the Problem of Ethnographic Refusal'. *Comparative Studies in Society and History* 37(1): 173–93.

Phua, V. C. 2010. 'Shifting Sexual Boundaries: Comparing Gay-Identified and Non-Gay-Identified Men Who Have Sex with Men in Brazil and in the USA'. *Sexualities* 13(5): 583–98.

Prasse-Freeman, E. 2015. 'Conceptions of Justice and the Rule of Law'. In D. I. Steinberg, ed. *Myanmar: The Dynamics of an Evolving Polity*, 89–114. Boulder: Lynne Rienner Publishers.

Puar, J. K. 2002. 'Circuits of Queer Mobility: Tourism, Travel, and Globalization'. *GLQ: A Journal of Lesbian and Gay Studies* 8(1): 101–37.

Rajaram, N. and V. Zararia. 2009. 'Translating Women's Human Rights in a Globalizing World: The Spiral Process in Reducing Gender Injustice in Baroda, India'. *Global Networks* 9(4): 462–84.

Risman, B. and P. Schwartz. 1988. 'Sociological Research on Male and Female Homosexuality'. *Annual Review of Sociology* 14(1): 125–47.

Rosaldo, M. Z. 1980. *Knowledge and Passion: Ilongot Notions of Self and Social Life*. Cambridge: Cambridge University Press.

Rosaldo, M. Z. 1984. 'Toward an Anthropology of Self and Feeling'. In R. A. Shweder and R. A. LeVine, eds. *Culture Theory: Essays on Mind, Self and Emotion*, 137–57. Cambridge: Cambridge University Press.

Rubin, G. S. 1984. 'Thinking Sex: Notes for a Radical Theory of the Politics of Sexuality'. In C. S. Vance, ed. *Pleasure and Danger: Exploring Female Sexuality*, 267–319. London: Routledge & K. Paul.

Rubin, G. S. 2002. 'Studying Sexual Subcultures: Excavating the Ethnography of Gay Communities in Urban North America'. In E. Lewin and W. Leap, eds. *Out in Theory: The Emergence of Lesbian and Gay Anthropology*, 17–68. Urbana: University of Illinois Press.

Santos, B. D. S. 2015. *If God Were a Human Rights Activist*. Redwood City: Stanford University Press.

Selby, D. 2018. *Human Rights in Thailand*. Philadelphia: University of Pennsylvania Press.

Sinnott, M. 2004. *Toms and Dees: Transgender Identity and Female Same-Sex Relationships in Thailand*. Honolulu: University of Hawaii Press.

Strathern, M. 1988. *The Gender of the Gift: Problems with Women and Problems with Society in Melanesia*. Berkeley: University of California Press.

Strathern, M. 2004. 'Losing (out on) Intellectual Resources'. In A. Pottage and M. Mundy, eds. *Law, Anthropology, and the Constitution of the Social: Making Persons and Things*, 201–33. Cambridge: Cambridge University Press.

Stychin, C. F. 2004. 'Same-Sex Sexualities and the Globalization of Human Rights Discourse'. *McGill Law Journal* 49: 951–68.

Thoreson, R. R. 2012. 'Realizing Rights in Manila: Brokers and the Mediation of Sexual Politics in the Philippines'. *GLQ: A Journal of Lesbian and Gay Studies* 18(4): 529–63.

Thoreson, R. R. 2014. *Transnational LGBT Activism: Working for Sexual Rights Worldwide*. Minneapolis: University of Minnesota Press.

Vaid, U. 1995. *Virtual Equality: The Mainstreaming of Gay and Lesbian Liberation*. New York: Anchor Books.

Valentine, D. 2002. 'We're "Not about Gender": The Uses of "Transgender"'. In E. Lewin, W. Leap, and W. L. Leap, eds. *Out in Theory: The Emergence of Lesbian and Gay Anthropology*, 222–45. Urbana: University of Illinois Press.

Vance, C. 2005. 'Anthropology Rediscovers Sexuality: A Theoretical Comment'. In J. Robertson, ed. *Same-Sex Cultures and Sexualities: An Anthropological Reader*, 15–32. Malden: Blackwell Publishing.

Visweswaran, K. 1997. 'Histories of Feminist Ethnography'. *Annual Review of Anthropology* 26(1): 591–621.

Weeks, J. 1977. *Coming Out: Homosexual Politics in Britain from the Nineteenth Century to the Present*. London: Quartet Books.

Weeks, J. 1995. 'Necessary Fictions: Sexual Identities and the Politics of Diversity'. In J. Weeks, ed. *Invented Moralities: Sexual Values in an Age of Uncertainty*, 82–101. New York: Columbia University Press.

Weeks, J. 1996. 'The Idea of a Sexual Community'. *Soundings* 2: 71–84.

Weston, K. 1993. 'Lesbian/Gay Studies in the House of Anthropology'. *Annual Review of Anthropology* 22(1): 339–67.

Wilson, R. A., ed. 1997. 'Human Rights, Culture and Context: An Introduction'. In *Human Rights, Culture and Context: Anthropological Perspectives*, 1–27. London: Pluto Press.

Wilson, R. A. 2006. 'Afterword to "Anthropology and Human Rights in a New Key": The Social Life of Human Rights'. *American Anthropologist* 108(1): 77–83.

Wright, T. 2000. 'Gay Organizations, NGOs, and the Globalization of Sexual Identity: The Case of Bolivia'. *Journal of Latin American Anthropology* 5(2): 89–111.

PART III

ANTHROPOLOGY IN LAW AND LEGAL PRACTICE

CHAPTER 25

THE CULTURAL DEFENCE

ALISON DUNDES RENTELN

Introduction

THE cultural defence is a controversial strategy attorneys sometimes use to persuade authorities to consider important contextual information regarding the cultural background of litigants. This analytic essay offers an overview of the strategy, explains the different categories of legal disputes in which cultural evidence is necessary, discusses famous cases in which the cultural defence has been invoked, addresses epistemological debates about what constitutes 'culture', and finally identifies fields of law in which cultural defences are likely to be raised in the future.

The cultural defence is important because, without cultural context, there is a great risk of the miscarriage of justice. To ensure that individuals from minority communities and Indigenous groups are treated fairly, anthropologists and other social scientists perform an indispensable public service by providing the cultural context of acts to be examined by jurists.

The cultural defence may, at times, conjure up notions of culpability and crime. In actuality, however, it legitimizes cultural reasoning in a wide variety of situations. It authorizes courts and other institutions to consider specific cultural factors relevant to dispute settlement. Although legal practitioners may be inclined to use the term narrowly (i.e. applying it exclusively to the criminal law), the notion also refers to efforts to obtain exemptions from general statutes, as well as attempts to win larger damage awards in civil litigation.

The existence of an officially recognized cultural defence would mean that courts must treat cultural evidence as admissible. Judges are not permitted to exclude it as 'irrelevant', as they have been prone to do in many jurisdictions. If formally established, the cultural defence will open the door to the consideration of cultural factors without guaranteeing that these would necessarily affect the final disposition of a given case (Renteln 2004).

Although the formal adoption of the cultural defence as policy is yet to occur, attorneys often introduce cultural evidence for consideration by the court. This is more prevalent in cases involving migrants with deeply rooted traditions, arriving from abroad. A cultural defence is also needed when Indigenous people are prevented from following their time-honoured traditions, particularly on their own lands.[1]

The trend toward greater awareness of cultural imperatives has led conferences on judicial education to focus on appropriate ways to assess anthropological testimony, as well as other types of evidence related to these traditions. Developments in Italy (Ruggiu 2019), Israel (Tomer-Fishman 2010: 496), and the Netherlands (Kelsall 2009; Renteln 2011) show that twenty-first-century judges and government officials require more specialized knowledge about specific customs to handle cultural conflicts.

As a consequence, scholars and jurists are increasingly compelled to reconsider the monocultural paradigm (Renteln 2010). No longer will it suffice to refer to the proverb 'When in Rome, do as the Romans do' to settle the question. Conflicts in existing jurisprudence illustrate the limitations of such a response.

In the case of immigrants, for instance, ignorance of the law may result in the miscarriage of justice. Although due process requires that individuals receive fair notice about the requirements of the law to ensure that their behaviour conforms to the law, in practice, the newly arrived often have no inkling that their conduct violates the laws of the new country.

Even when migrants *do* receive lenient legal treatment for an initial offence, they are expected to assimilate once judges warn them that their culturally motivated actions conflict with the law. In reality, even when migrants wish to assimilate, it is challenging to shed customs central to their way of life, to alter their folkways, and to break with the past.

Anthropologists have the ability to serve as cultural brokers between migrants and powerful elites who control state institutions in host countries. Their expertise influences decision-making in ways that may have long-term consequences for this vulnerable group.

The role of anthropology in dispute settlement

Through ethnographic investigation, anthropologists can identify crucial aspects of a community's way of life, while providing insights into different ways of understanding social existence.

Culture has remained a central concept in anthropology (Woo 2004). It was in the twentieth century that anthropologists, led by the physicist-turned-social-scientist Franz Boas, developed the egalitarian theory of cultural relativism (Hatch 1983; Washburn 1987) to combat the racist theories of the nineteenth century. Despite the tendency in scholarship to misinterpret the theory as prescriptive (e.g. Howard 1993), it is more properly understood as descriptive (Renteln 1988). The presumption in scholarly circles used to be that the recognition of cultural differences required the acceptance of all value systems; this is an unfortunate consequence of early relativists assuming that the value of tolerance was itself part of the theory, rather than a value favoured by the anthropologists themselves. As Robert Redfield astutely notes, acknowledging the existence of multiple value systems does not commit one to embracing them: 'we could just as well hate them all' (Redfield 1962: 146–7). Separating relativism from the value of tolerance leaves us with the question of why this theory has generated so much controversy (see also Geertz 1984). Rather than a theory that promotes 'tolerance', cultural relativism calls attention to ethnocentrism and enculturation, the impulse to judge others based on the standards of one's own society and reacting to phenomena according to one's cultural background (Shweder 1991).

In law, the usual commitment to the monocultural paradigm tends to reinforce ethnocentric judgments. The cultural defence is beneficial because it highlights the existence of different world views and encourages individuals to reconsider their preconceived ideas about what constitutes acceptable conduct. Some cultural defence cases involve a cognitive difference, while others involve a behavioural dysfunction. Situating folkways in a cultural context has significant implications for practitioners in courts and other official institutions. Indeed, the idea of cultural relativism underlies the entire Law and Society Movement (Friedman 1986), which promotes the view that jurists should study not only the 'law on the books' but also the 'law in action in particular contexts.'

To help courts avoid cultural biases, anthropologists and other social scientists sometimes play the role of cultural experts to elucidate the meaning of particular traditions and the 'living law' (Kandel 1992; Rosen 1977). Their deep knowledge of the specific customs enables them to guide courts in their assessments. Without anthropological expertise, judges may have difficulty grasping the meaning of litigants' actions.

One of the challenges before experts is having their credentials formally recognized. Even when regarded as sufficiently authoritative to present testimony, they may face intense questioning and objections as to the relevance or admissibility of the cultural evidence.

The information provided by the anthropologist often calls into question the notion of 'objective' reasonableness. In light of the differing notions of reasonableness worldwide, anthropologist can show how problematic it is to apply 'Western' legal standards to culturally motivated actions of individuals from other places.[2]

Although cultural anthropology is a well-respected branch within anthropology, some scholars challenge the utility of the concept of culture itself. They argue against those who describe a 'culture' or 'national identity' on the grounds that these descriptions are simplistic or reductionist. To these academics, culture is a 'contested' notion that risks 'othering' people who are part of the community but also identify with subnational groups. Moreover, the critics contend that discussing a certain 'culture' as a monolith risks obscuring important differences among subgroups.

Another important critique is the idea that traditions are often a reflection of patriarchy.[3] Other prominent anthropologists have championed the study of culture as an empirical phenomenon (see e.g. Shweder 2001; Trouillot 2002). This line of argument against culture fails to acknowledge that some customs are benign, while others are objectionable. Sometimes, a cultural defence should be rejected because it results in irreparable harm (e.g. violence against women). Even though individuals should have the right to explain what motivated their actions, if the custom involves irreparable harm, the court should not mitigate the sentence (and legislatures should not grant exemptions). In practice, however, the cultural defence is often invoked in cases that do not involve violence against women or misogyny. In some contexts, women even benefit from invoking cultural rights (Veazey 2015). Indeed, cultural defences have been employed by women in famous cases (Renteln 2004).[4]

Although many commentators criticize the cultural defence because they believe it puts 'culture [in its entirety] on trial', in actuality, most cases involve a specific custom that can be documented. This legitimate concern highlights the need for a more nuanced analysis of cultural traditions.

Types of cultural defences

Culture figures into legal arguments in at least three areas: criminal law, exemptions, and civil litigation. In criminal law proceedings, cultural factors may influence decisions such as whether to arrest an individual, what charge to use, the verdict of guilt or innocence, and the sentencing. While jurists are more willing to allow cultural considerations to influence charging and sentencing, they tend not to accept cultural arguments during the guilt phase of a trial.[5]

Sentencing guidelines usually allow for mitigating factors, which may include culture, to be considered. But guidelines may also prohibit the consideration of national origin, as is the case in the United States. Here, the issue is whether this prohibition precludes the consideration of ethnicity or culture.

When legal practitioners wish to invoke cultural defences, they try to incorporate specific beliefs into particular criminal defences. When a defendant seeks to raise an insanity defence, anthropologists and transcultural psychiatrists may be asked to submit affidavits documenting the degree to which cultural factors influenced the individual's state of mind. The *Merck Manual* has an appendix that includes culture-bound syndromes, demonstrating that the medical community has acknowledged the importance of culture in diagnoses (Diamond 1978; Parzen 2003).

People v. Wu illustrates how culture and insanity may be combined in a criminal case. In a major U.S. homicide case, Helen Wu killed her son after learning that her son's father had maltreated him and had abandoned her.[6] She was in a fugue state and attempted to commit parent–child suicide. Four experts, including an anthropologist, provided reports for the court's consideration, thereby helping to persuade the California Court of

Appeal to remand the case. Ultimately, the California Supreme Court declined to review the case and depublished the decision.

As the lower appellate court had suggested a jury instruction indicating how to weigh the cultural evidence, it is likely that the Supreme Court was unwilling to allow possible use of the defence. Criticisms of this case include the fact that the son's right was ignored, that the characterization of Helen Wu reinforced stereotypes, and that culture and mental health were conflated in offensive ways. This case also shows that women can indeed benefit from invoking the cultural defence.

Attorneys may present cultural evidence via existing criminal defences. In these circumstances, the defences may be related to elements of the offence (Renteln 1993). One such defence is mistake of fact, which can result in exoneration, if successful. The underlying logic here is that if the facts were as a reasonable person would believe them to be, the act would not have been a crime and the defendant should be excused; however, the act must be 'objectively' reasonable. In a much-discussed case involving 'marriage by capture' in the Hmong community, the defendant attempted to use the mistake-of-fact defence (Evans-Pritchard and Renteln 1994). When a young Hmong man carried off a young Hmong woman from a college campus, students observed that she protested the abduction.[7] Since the man and woman were dating (and exchanging gifts) and customary law required that she prove her virtue by objecting to the 'marriage by capture', he claimed he had thought she was consenting. His attempt to use the mistake-of-fact defence was doomed to failure, however, because a jury in California would surely not have considered this mistake to be 'reasonable'. This requirement of objective reasonableness makes the mistake-of-fact defence difficult for minorities to employ.

There is a vast jurisprudence involving defendants who kill based on their belief in witchcraft. Here, one key question is whether courts should entertain cultural defences based on sincere belief in supernatural forces as a version of the mistake-of-fact defence (see e.g. Carstens 2009). This has been litigated in Africa and North America.

Sometimes, when defence counsel wish to introduce cultural evidence, the concern is that doing so may violate equal protection. In Portugal, for instance, courts have dealt with cases in which it has been argued that, since Roma girls marry at a younger age, Roma men charged with sexual acts should benefit from a cultural defence. Although the judges overseeing the cases have not considered the testimony of cultural experts, scholars have pre-emptively contended that accepting cultural arguments would undermine the rights of minors (Lopes et al. 2019: 63–5), thereby violating their right to equal protection. Jurisprudence in Italy and Spain reflects the same concern with the protection of Roma children (Ruggiu 2019; Truffin and Arjona 2009).

In other cases, the legal issue is proving 'specific intent'. Prosecution for sexually abusing a child requires proving *mens rea* and *actus reus*, while also demonstrating that the adult's conduct was for the purpose of sexual gratification. Hence, the motive or specific intent is one of the elements of the offence. Although startling to those unfamiliar with cultures that permit touching children in the genital area, anthropologists can explain to courts that the action is not necessarily sexual in nature. In the *Krasniqi* case, for instance, anthropologist Barbara Halpern played a critical role in the criminal prosecution of an Albanian Muslim father. Prior to being acquitted of the criminal charges, his parental rights to his daughter and son had been terminated in family court, where he and his wife were tried as unfit parents. The subsequent acquittal in criminal court had no effect on the family court's prior decision.

In another case involving 'touching', *State of Maine v. Kargar* (1996),[8] a father who had kissed the penis of his son was acquitted, based on a *de minimis* statute. The Italian Court of Cassation, in 2018, decided a similar case involving a child questionably touched by his father.[9]

Substantive cultural defences may also be based on constitutional principles. Some cultural defence cases involve the use of illicit substances where due process is allegedly ignored.[10] For example, the mild stimulant *khat* (or *qat*) is legal and widely used in countries such as Ethiopia, Kenya, Somalia, and Yemen, yet it is treated in the West as a controlled substance comparable to heroin (see e.g. Anderson et al. 2007; Travis 2013). Law enforcement officers have targeted those in possession of *khat* (AP 2014), sometimes much to their surprise. In such cases, a key question is whether defendants received fair notice as required by the due process principle. In *State v. Gurreh*, a conviction for sale and possession of *khat* was affirmed when the appellate court rejected the argument that the defendant had not received adequate notice.[11]

Inspired by its interpretation of religious freedom, the U.S. Supreme Court ruled, in *Gonzales v. O Centro Espirita Beneficente Uniao do Vegetal et al.* (2006),[12] that the federal government could not seize a *hoasca* tea shipment from Brazil. This confiscation by federal law enforcement officers, the Supreme Court found, had violated the right to free exercise of religion that had been re-established by the Religious Freedom Restoration Act (RFRA). The government, the Court held, had not demonstrated a compelling state interest to justify the seizure. In this remarkable decision, the Court rejected the common argument that only legislatures should vindicate cultural rights by creating exceptions.

A Canadian Supreme Court case, *Jack and Charlie v. The Queen* (1985),[13] illustrates the difficulty of raising a cultural defence through a religious freedom defence. Two members of the Coast Salish Indian people were charged with violating a provincial wildlife act by hunting and killing a deer out of season. The reason for the hunt was the need to burn deer meat as part of a religious ceremony. An anthropologist explained to the court the cultural significance of the practice among all Coast Salish people and how failure to burn deer meat could result in some form of divine retribution.

The Canadian Supreme Court dismissed the appeal on two grounds: first, because '[t]he prohibition of hunting deer out of season ... does not raise a question of religious freedom or aboriginal religion', since the meat-burning, and not the hunt itself, was part of the religious ceremony. The Court ruled that the Indians could have frozen some meat in advance for the purposes of the meat-burning ceremony. Second, the Court objected to the idea that a defendant's motive for violating the law should influence the determination of their culpability. This case shows how courts can reinterpret religious freedom so as to substantially narrow its scope. It also suggests that some courts remain opposed to the idea that motive is relevant to the assessment of blameworthiness.

The Canadian Supreme Court rejected another cultural claim brought before it under the Charter in *Ktnuxa v. British Columbia* (2017).[14] Here, the question was whether the proposed development of a ski resort would violate the religious freedom of this First Nation people by driving the grizzly bear spirit, known as Qat'muk, from their land. Rejecting the argument, the Court held that this would be an improper interpretation of Section 2 of the Charter and that the minister had made the decision to allow the development after having undertaken reasonable consultation.

In other cases, the constitutional principle at stake is equal protection. In provocation cases, defendants may claim that a verbal insult or gesture provoked them to commit violent acts. Insults in another culture, however, may not be understood by jurors from the mainstream culture. Although the average person from the minority culture may behave similarly to the defendant, courts continue to adhere to the fiction of objective reasonableness (i.e. that there is such a thing as the objective reasonable person), leading them to reject culture-based defences and to exclude cultural evidence as irrelevant.

A constitutional argument can be made that failure to consider this contextual information violates equal protection. An illustrative case in point is *Trujillo-Garcia v. Rowland* (2005).[15] A game of poker between Eduardo Trujillo-Garcia and Jose Padilla resulted in the latter losing $140 to the former. Four days later, Padilla returned to demand his money back. Upon hearing Padilla utter the words '*Chinga tu madre*' ('Go and f--- your mother'), Trujillo-Garcia reacted to this challenge to his honour by grabbing a gun and shooting Padilla dead. He later argued that the phrase had been so offensive that it provoked him to commit an act of violence. Those who do not speak Spanish have difficulty comprehending the seriousness of the insult. The phrase is considered as 'fighting words' and conjures up images of the mother (associated with the Virgin Mary) being violated. It has an obscene, as well as a blasphemous, connotation. Trujillo-Garcia was initially convicted of second-degree murder and received a sentence of fifteen years to life. On appeal in state court, he argued that the failure of the trial court to assess reasonableness by considering the words in their cultural context constituted unconstitutional discrimination, based on national origin and ethnic characteristics.[16] The specific argument was that a person's reaction to a particular insult depends upon his or her cultural upbringing.

At least two issues had to be decided. The first was whether words constitute adequate provocation. The second was whether to substitute the average reasonable Mexican for the average reasonable person to satisfy the 'objective' prong of the provocation test. With respect to the first argument, Californian law allows verbal provocation as adequate. The second argument (i.e. that the failure of the trial court to apply a culturally specific reasonable person test constituted a violation of equal protection) was more difficult to make: 'Equal protection requires that similarly provocative insults be similarly treated, without regard to their ethnic origin or cultural derivation. If certain insults are sufficiently offensive in American culture to mitigate murder to manslaughter ... then insults that are equally offensive in another culture should be treated as equally mitigating.'[17]

The district court rejected the defendant's habeas petition, noting that, regardless of whether his cultural background had been taken into account, his provocation defence would have been rendered 'inadequate'. The court emphasized that it refused to authorize use of a culturally specific reasonable person test. While noting that the equal treatment argument was 'not without merit', Judge Patel declined to elaborate because, according to her, Trujillo-Garcia 'did not respond as an ordinary, reasonable Mexican male would have responded to the same phrase'.[18] The U.S. Court of Appeals for the Ninth Circuit affirmed, concluding that even if the failure to consider the cultural background was erroneous, it was harmless because it did not 'substantially or injuriously' affect the outcome of the trial.

Unfortunately, the judges did not appreciate the offensiveness of the insult because they assumed that the average Mexican would not have been provoked. In order to persuade judges and juries, defence counsel must argue that the proper standard is the average person from the defendant's culture. If a jury instruction focuses on a person in the circumstances of the defendant, this might allow for contextual analysis.[19] This type of framework is crucial if such a defence is to succeed.

Some provocation cases involve 'honour' killings, whereby male relatives kill young women who have 'dishonoured' their families. In the Australian case of *R v. Dincer* (1983), a Muslim father of Turkish origin stabbed his sixteen-year-old daughter because he saw her sexual relationship with a man out of wedlock as unacceptable.[20] The father sought to raise the provocation defence, but the question was whether the jury could use the ordinary person test with the attributes of the accused. Because the father had gone to the man's house to confront the daughter, the prosecution argued that the provocation had been 'self-induced', but the court rejected this line of reasoning without argument.

One can point to similar examples of provocations in other pluralistic societies that may prompt attorneys to try to incorporate cultural information in the defence, albeit with varying degrees of effectiveness. For instance, cultural arguments have been introduced, without influencing judicial decisions, in Italy and New Zealand.[21] Using a culturally specific definition of a reasonable person as part of the provocation defence has also been documented in various jurisdictions, including Israel (Ben-David 2011) and South Africa (Dumin 2006; Seidman 1965).

In capital cases, defence attorneys may hire litigation experts to obtain evidence for mitigation during the sentencing phase of a trial, though not necessarily cultural information (Winkelman 1996). In countries with the death penalty (e.g. United States and China), this function is all the more consequential for those convicted of capital crimes, such as murder. In the United States, the lawyer's failure to provide effective assistance of counsel may also give rise to the constitutional argument that he or she is in violation of the Sixth Amendment.

Another U.S. case in which an anthropologist was consulted about mitigating circumstances is *Siripongs v. Calderon*.[22] Jay Siripongs was a former Buddhist monk accused of committing a murder in an Orange County convenience store. Although he admitted he was present during the commission of the crime, he denied that he had ever pulled the trigger. But he also refused to name the accomplice who *did* pull the trigger, even though naming him could have saved him from execution. Herbert Philips, a professor of anthropology at the University of California, Berkeley, who specialized in Thailand, wrote a detailed statement on why 'snitching' was unacceptable in Thai culture and explained the meaning of Siripong's demeanour during sentencing; the absence of emotion did not signify a lack of remorse. Although ultimately unsuccessful in avoiding execution, the case shows how the provision of cultural context by social scientists could play a significant role in allowing a condemned person to avoid the death penalty.

Some scholars focus on explaining why some cultural defences in criminal law succeed and others fail.[23] For instance, when the characterization of the minority community serves the interest of the dominant culture, the court tends to be more receptive to the argument.

Exemptions

When individuals from an ethnic minority wish to seek permission from the dominant culture to follow a tradition, they may have to request an exemption from a general statute. Despite the preference for legislatures, which represent the will of the majority, to make exceptions, in some instances, it is the judges who carve out exemptions. Among the more common illustrations of statutory exemptions are those for religious minorities seeking to wear symbols as required by their faith (on Sikhs donning the *kirpan*, see e.g. Juss 2013).

Those seeking to slaughter animals in accordance with religious laws may also request exemptions. This includes kosher or *glatt* meat for the Orthodox Jewish community and *halal* meat for Muslins (Shadid and van Koningsveld 1992).[24] Other cultural communities, such as Asian-Americans, have also sought exemptions from food safety laws for Peking duck and Korean moon cakes.

Civil litigation

In tort cases, plaintiffs may try to bring in cultural evidence to demonstrate how they were traumatized by the defendant's negligent behaviour (Black 2009; Renteln 2009a). In such cases, the gist of the argument is that some individuals will more likely be adversely affected by misconduct because of their cultural or religious background. For instance, in the English case *Bakhtiari v. The Zoological Society of London*, a court considered cultural factors when deciding on the appropriate size of the damage awarded to an Iranian girl whose three fingers were bitten off by a chimpanzee while visiting the zoo. The court increased her reward because of the stigma that she could purportedly experience in her community.[25]

There is also litigation dealing with airplane crashes resulting in the death of a son that would have provided for his parents in their old age had he survived the crash. A case in point is *In re Air Crash Near Nantucket Isl.* (2006).[26] Here, Egyptian-born Sami Makary had already begun to provide financial support to his parents prior to the crash that ended his life. Although it may be deemed sexist to assume that only the son would take care of his parents' needs, and not a daughter, the court did appear to take the family's cultural background into account and provided a somewhat larger damage award than would otherwise have been the case (Marzulli 2006).

In sexual harassment lawsuits, some defendants argue that their persistence during dating would have been considered appropriate in their countries of origin. Courts have thus far rejected such attempts to introduce cultural and religious factors. The Me Too movement may well lead to more such cases and generate more culturally based defences.

In civil litigation, the defendant may also attempt to use cultural background as a basis for avoiding damage payments. This was the case in *MacKinnon v. Kwong Wah Restaurant.* Two women filed lawsuits alleging that they had endured sexual harassment while working as waitresses at the Kwong Wah Chinese restaurant. The plaintiffs were dissatisfied with an award of $2,500 each for compensatory damages and claimed the district court had erred in declining to award them punitive damages. Here, the defendants had ostensibly referred to cultural and linguistic barriers in order to evade punitive damages.[27] Evidently, the women could not persuade the lower court that the defendants' misconduct met the standard for paying these damages. Despite the court's position that there was 'no question that Defendants' repeated sexual harassment was offensive' and 'might be strong evidence of malice or, at least, reckless indifference to Plaintiffs' rights', it held, however, 'that the behaviour of at least some Defendants was influenced by language, cultural, and educational barriers'. It concluded that the defendants had not acted 'with malice or reckless indifference' to the plaintiffs' rights.[28]

The plaintiffs attacked the logic underlying the trial court's decision, saying that 'the ethnic background' was 'not an excuse negating malice or reckless indifference'. The Court of Appeals held, however, that cultural background was 'not irrelevant in evaluating the appropriateness of punitive damages' and could, at times, 'likely have an impact on his consciousness of wrongdoing'. Despite affirming the relevance of cultural background, the appeals court ruled that the lower court's 'only explicit reason for denying punitive damages was the cultural, ethnic, and educational background of the defendants, and this is not the dispositive factor'. The lower court, it ruled, had failed to 'point to any evidence in the record to support its assumption that the defendants were not acting with reckless indifference to the plaintiffs' rights' and the 'primary reliance on cultural and educational background' had been 'tenuous and appears unsupported'.[29]

The appellate court remanded to the district court to clarify the basis of its decision to deny punitive damages. Although it left the door open to a cultural argument justifying a denial of punitive damages, the explanation would have had to be sufficiently elaborated, which was not the case here.[30]

Sometimes, the question is whether the custom is presented as a plausible version of the tradition. To determine this, courts may employ a cultural defence test to adjudicate matters in criminal and civil litigation proceedings (Renteln 2004: 207). It involves three questions which should ensure appropriate use of cultural imperatives:

1. Is the litigant a member of the ethnic group?
2. Does the group have such a tradition?
3. Was the litigant influenced by the tradition when he or she acted?

Even if all three requirements are met, legal systems may decide that the custom should be prohibited based on normative principles. If it involves irreparable harm, such as with 'honour' killings, even if the way in which the tradition is presented is consistent with the standards of the relevant cultural community, courts should reject it.

It may not be possible for judges to answer the above questions. They may lack sufficient information if attorneys neglect to introduce cultural evidence to elucidate the custom relevant to the case at hand. In civil law countries, judges may appoint experts to assist them in gathering relevant knowledge.

Adopting this practice would be beneficial for common law judges as well. In common law systems, although judges are usually limited to the facts in the record, they may still take judicial notice of facts that are part of common knowledge, depending on the rules of evidence in their jurisdiction. This may permit judges in some circumstances to reconsider a lower court's misinterpretation of a cultural tradition.

Future directions

In the future, we are likely to see attempts to extend cultural defence arguments to a wider array of institutions as a result of a trend towards greater migration and a heightened consciousness of rights. Furthermore, greater awareness of the potential use of cultural factors leads attorneys to refer to them in a wider range of contexts. One reason for this increased awareness is that training programmes for judges and attorneys often include cultural difference and anti-bias courses.

Military justice has distinct institutions, rules of evidence, and other procedures. Insofar as soldiers come from different cultural backgrounds, it is probable that their conduct may at times require contextual information. For instance, when a member of the U.S. Armed Forces used excessive force when disciplining a child, his judge advocate-general (JAG) attorney at the court martial sought to raise a cultural defence.[31] The question of whether ethnic and religious minorities in the military may wear religious garb, particularly headgear, has already arisen in several countries. The range of issues is not limited to attire. Sometimes, grooming policies are at stake. Similarly, military personnel may argue that they should be entitled to use substances in accordance with their religions. In other situations, defence counsels may argue that the reactions of victims from other countries should be explained by cultural experts.[32]

Given the mass incarceration of prisoners in the United States, it is unfortunately likely that the number of cases involving cultural and religious factors will increase dramatically. Already, inmates have litigated questions such as access to foodstuffs consistent with their respective religious laws. In *Holt v. Hobbs* (2015), for instance, the U.S. Supreme Court invalidated a correctional policy requiring that beards be cut when this was in violation of the inmate's religious beliefs.[33] Where statutes and human rights standards apply, inmates in diverse jurisdictions may try to advance arguments based on cultural rights and religious freedom (see e.g. Becci and Roy 2015; Higgins 2018; Renteln 2011).

Educational institutions also struggle with questions of due process in various contexts. For instance, universities may be asked to allow spiritual leaders to perform religious ceremonies in rooms just before examinations take place in them. Sometimes students ask that universities be required to accommodate requests for single-sex residence halls or floors. There is a question about whether universities should alter building entrances to accommodate Orthodox Jewish students during *Shabbat*. Professors react with surprise when international students who cite sources differently contend that this is acceptable citation practice in their countries of origin. There is also the matter of gift-giving: should instructors accept gifts from students right before taking an exam or requesting a recommendation letter?

Social workers evaluating the placement of children are also confronted with the question of whether cultural factors should influence their decisions. A debate has raged about the extent to which race and culture should affect these determinations and whether transcultural assignments are consistent with the 'best interests of the child' standard (Foley et al. 2011; Simon 2015).

We can also expect to see more civil litigation concerning improper conduct in the workplace. To date, cultural issues related to sexual harassment lawsuits have been mostly ignored. As discussed earlier, anthropologists may be called upon to describe courting or dating customs in particular regions.

The treatment of the dead is another understudied area of jurisprudence; for example, disputes about unauthorized autopsies, religiously segregated cemeteries, and malpractice by mortuaries (Renteln 2001).

Scholars of global bioethics have investigated cultural issues in the field of medicine. Some controversies relate to female genital cutting. To deter migrant families from continuing a tradition widely condemned as 'prejudicial to the health of children', countries have enacted penal laws criminalizing such practices. Although well intentioned, these policies have had the unfortunate effect of driving the practice underground. Families may take their daughters out of the country to be 'circumcised' in their countries of origin. Upon their return, they may be subject to body searches by customs officers, adding insult to injury.

There have also been challenges to national female genital mutilation (FGM) laws based on constitutional doctrines. For instance, in November 2018 a U.S. federal judge struck down the Female Genital Prohibition Act. In contrast, European courts have witnessed successful prosecution of those who cut girls, while parents receive suspended sentences and probation (Bellucci 2018). It is probable that more cases will go forward as international bodies, including the European Parliament, condemn this practice as a form of violence against women.

Laws that criminalize cutting also affect adult women seeking hymenoplasties to avoid honour-related violence. Although difficult to document, scholarship reveals that adult women seek reconstructive surgery to avoid having their husbands and wider families learn that they are not virgins (Renteln 2018). As general statutes sometimes ban cutting in the genital area altogether, surgeons may be legitimately concerned that they could be prosecuted for performing reconstructive surgeries such as episiotomies and hymenoplasties. Indeed, in 2014, one U.K. physician faced prosecution under national law, even though the prosecutor later dropped the case in response to public outcry.

Similarly, European countries have sometimes treated male circumcision as child abuse. As this operation is considered necessary by some Jewish and Muslim families, this has led to significant cultural conflicts in Germany and Italy (Foblets 2016; Levey 2013; Ruggiu 2019: 82–4).

Future research will have to focus on the question of whether the state can intervene to protect children from surgeries that their parents and cultural communities deem necessary. The ambiguity of international human rights law renders this matter problematic. Article 30 of the Convention on the Rights of the Child guarantees the right to culture for children of ethnic minorities and Indigenous peoples, while Article 24(3) forbids customs 'prejudicial to the health of children'. Failure to resolve such rights conflicts may jeopardize the well-being of children. Treating questions of 'health' independently from cultural considerations is misleading. Research on the cultural defence will likely focus on how procedures are deemed medically necessary or elective. As biomedical innovation makes more surgical intervention possible, further cultural objections to treatment may emerge and the tension between cosmopolitan and traditional medicine will be at the centre of disputes.

Another body of law which is likely to experience tremendous growth is economic crime. Limited research has been conducted on white-collar crimes (Carberry and Gordon 1996). Although there is widespread awareness that gift-giving differs across cultures (Mauss 1967), this phenomenon has received relatively little attention. The literature on domestic laws (e.g. the U.S. Foreign Corrupt Practices Act) and treaties is based on the premise that universal ethical standards exist. A case in point is the use of fortune-telling by some Roma as a means of subsistence, which is sometimes treated by local ordinances as a form of fraud.

How cultural defences affect anthropologists

Much ink has been spilled over ascertaining the 'authenticity' of particular customs. For example, the debate on whether begging is a cultural tradition of the Roma (Ruggiu 2019: 80) was central to a 2007 decision of Italy's Supreme Court of Cassation. This is where anthropologists, as well as other social scientists and leaders of ethnic communities, play a critical role, namely verifying cultural claims.

One major difficulty faced by jurists is identifying scholars who have the appropriate cultural expertise. To date, no comprehensive database or list has been established for the purpose of certifying the competence of cultural experts to guide courts and other institutions, which has created a serious risk of judges receiving inaccurate information about minority groups. This, in turn, may result in the erosion of support for use of the cultural defence.

When experts testify about ethnic and religious minorities, it is possible that those members of the community who are familiar with their cultural traditions may take offence, since they may not appreciate hearing experts explaining their traditions to them. The unfortunate reality is that courts may be more likely to accept the testimony of 'experts' with advanced degrees than leaders of ethnic groups. Therefore, to prevail in court, members of ethnic groups may feel compelled to rely on the testimony of cultural experts. Another challenge associated with having leaders of ethnic groups testify is that some traditions are not allowed to be shared or may be embarrassing. For example, disclosing the location of sacred sites or discussing certain sexual relationships may be proscribed. Hence, leaders and court interpreters may even deny the existence of certain customs.

Another significant concern is the impact of testifying in court on anthropologists themselves. Some worry that participating as experts in disputes may undermine their professional role as social scientists. If an anthropologist is viewed as 'partisan', it may affect his or her 'credibility' (Freckelton and Selby 2009: 147–53, 1098–109). Scholars have written reflexively about the toll presenting cultural evidence may take. An anthropologist who provided evidence in a provocation case worried about his role when the cultural defence was rejected (Caughey 2009).

Furthermore, many writers find 'authenticity' to be a vexing question (Lindholm 2008). They debate whether traditions are 'invented' and disagree about the length of time a custom should have existed in order to be categorized as 'authentic' (Levey 2015; Linnekin 1991). This is an elusive quest likely never to be resolved (Bendix 1997). If members of a group regard a custom as important for the maintenance of group identity, then outsiders cannot easily question its existence. Whether governments should regulate it is a separate matter.

Anthropologists may have misgivings about involvement in cases when they object to the cultural practices at stake. At times, explaining the cultural context in a case may run counter to the personal convictions of the anthropologist (see e.g. Wikan 2002). While some contend that repugnant or offensive cultural traditions should be rejected, their influence over human behaviour cannot be denied. The practice of rejecting certain traditions begs another question: what should be deemed unacceptable? Despite the challenges involved in drawing a line, traditions that cause irreparable harm should not be condoned. Cognizant of the power of cultural imperatives, experts recognize that other factors should also be considered. For instance, the right to culture, guaranteed in human rights law, must be balanced against other competing human rights enshrined in international law; for example, the rights of women and children.

When a custom of an ethnic minority group or Indigenous people conflicts with the majority's law, it is unlikely that it will be permitted. This could partly be a consequence of cultural hegemony: the judges are usually elites from the dominant ethnic group. It may also be the ideology of the monocultural paradigm, which promotes conformism.

When confronted with attitudinal barriers and fear of the other, anthropologists need to prepare to combat these prejudices. Some take the view that teaching judges to appreciate cultural differences requires either cultural immersion or putting them in the shoes of migrants.

If jurists consider what might happen to 'Westerners' who travel abroad, that may bring the point home. Sometimes those from Anglo-American traditions are astonished to find that kissing in public is considered obscene elsewhere (see e.g. Renteln 2009b). Yet if cultural defences are unacceptable in the West, Americans and Australians caught with drugs in non-Western countries where possession of drugs may result in a death sentence can hardly expect leniency.

Conclusion

Judges might be more inclined to allow cultural evidence if states sanctioned the consideration of culture in their official evidence codes. Some (e.g. Tomer-Fishman: 2010), argue that it is not the lack of authorization but rather an attitudinal barrier that prevents judges from letting culture in the courtroom. If this view is correct, then judicial education will be crucial to opening the minds of jurists to the relevance of anthropological evidence. Anthropologists will have a critical role to play in this consciousness-raising endeavour, and it would be ideal if they could have more frequent interactions with the decision-makers. Collaboration between experts and judges will pave the way to more nuanced interpretations of cultural traditions.

Notes

1. On the use of cultural defences by Indigenous peoples, see, e.g. Kanter (1995), Kozin (2011), and Miller (1998).

2. For the debate between Gluckman and Bohannan on the 'reasonable person' standard, see Nader (1969).
3. On the differing positions taken on the concept of culture and the degree to which it supports gender inequality, see, e.g. Abu-Lughod (1996) and Brumann (1999).
4. *People v Dong Lu Chen*, No. 8707774, NY Sup. Ct 2 December (1988); *People v Kimura*, Defense Sentencing Report and Statement in Mitigation; and Application for Probation, No. A-091133 (LA Super. Ct 1985); *Nguyen v State*, 505 S.E.2d 846, 234 Ga. App. 185 (Ct App. 1998); *Nguyen v. State*, 520 S.E.2d 907, 271 Ga. 475 (1999).
5. For arguments in support of giving consideration to culture, see, e.g. Donovan and Garth (2007); Ruggiu (2019).
6. *People v. Wu*, 286 Cal. Rptr. 868 (1991), *reh'g denied*, 1992 Cal. LEXIS 310 (opinion ordered unpublished).
7. In countries such as Botswana, some worry that cultural defences might be misused in attempts to justify abductions for the purposes of 'marriage' (Bennett 2010).
8. *State v. Kargar*, 679 A.2d 81, 1996 Me. 162 (1996).
9. Court of Cassation, 2 July 2018, n. 29613.
10. For discussion of cases involving Rastafarians prosecuted for possession of marijuana required for religious purposes, see Poulter (1998: 356–62).
11. *State v. Gurreh*, 60 Conn. App. 166, 758 A.2d 877 (App. Ct 2000).
12. *Gonzales v. O Centro Espírita Beneficente União do Vegetal*, 546 US 418, 126 S. Ct 1211, 163 L. Ed. 2d 1017 (2006).
13. *Jack and Charlie v. The Queen* [1985] 2 SCR 332.
14. *Ktunaxa Nation v. British Columbia* (Forests, Lands and Natural Resource Operations), 2017 Supreme Court of Canada 54, [2017] 2 SCR 386.
15. *Trujillo-Garcia v. Rowland*, 1992 US Dist LEXIS 6199, 28 April 1992; *Trujillo-Garcia v. Rowland*, 9 F.3d 1553 (Court of Appeals 1993).
16. See also Appellant's Supplemental Brief, *People v. Trujillo-Garcia*, Court of Appeal, California, First Appellate District, Division One, No. A038099 (hereinafter *Trujillo-Garcia* Brief). The Equal Protection argument was based on the 14th Amendment and the California Constitution, Article 1, Section 7.
17. *Trujillo-Garcia* Brief, at 13.
18. *Trujillo-Garcia v. Rowland*, 1992 US Dist. LEXIS 6199, 28 April 1992.
19. See *California Standard Jury Instructions* (Criminal), CALJIC No. 8.42 (6th ed. 1996).
20. *R v. Dincer* [1983] 1 VR 460.
21. Ruggiu discusses two cases in which courts consider cultural arguments introduced via provocation (Ruggiu 2019: 95–6).
22. *Siripongs v. Calderon*, 133 F.3d 732 (9th Cir. 1998).
23. On the role of power differential and 'cultural convergence', see Tomer-Fishman (2010) and Lee (2007), respectively.
24. See, e.g. *Cha'are Shalom Ve Tsedek v. France*, Merits, App. No. 27417/95, ECHR 2000-VII, IHRL 2966 (ECHR 2000), 27 June 2000, European Court of Human Rights [ECHR]; Grand Chamber [ECHR].
25. See *Bakhtiari v. The Zoological Society of London* [1991] Queen's Bench Division LEXIS 2432, also discussed in Poulter (1998). Poulter notes the sexist nature of the decision (Poulter 1998: 64). On cultural relativity as it relates to disability, see Renteln (2003).
26. *In re Air Crash Near Nantucket Isl., Oct. 31*, 462 F. Supp. 2d 360 (EDNY 2006).
27. *McKinnon v. Kwong Wah Restaurant*, 83 F.3d 498 (1st Cir. 1996).

28. Ibid., 508.
29. Ibid., 509.
30. Although the court here is somewhat receptive to cultural arguments, in a criminal sexual harassment case, a Korean immigrant man was convicted of criminal contempt (2nd degree) and aggravated harassment, despite an attempt to raise a cultural defence (Judge Richter 1995: 25). In a sexual harassment case, the jury considered the plaintiff's cultural background when computing her compensatory emotional distress damages; see *Luu v. Seagate Technology, Inc.*, Civil No. 99-220 (JRT/FLN) (D. Minn. 5 July, 2001).
31. Personal email communication on 20 July 2017 with Rodrigo M. Maruco, Capt., USAF Area Defense Counsel, located at 1398 Menoher Drive, Joint Base Andrews, Maryland 20762.
32. See, e.g. *US v. Owens*, 1998 CCA LEXIS 349 (US Air Force Court of Criminal Appeals 1998).
33. *Holt v. Hobbs*, 135 S. Ct 853, 190 L. Ed. 2d 747, 83 U.S.L.W. 4065 (2015).

References

Abu-Lughod, L. 1996. 'Writing against Culture'. In R. G. Fox, ed. *Recapturing Anthropology: Working in the Present*, 137–62. Santa Fe, NM: School of American Research Press.

Anderson, D., S. Beckerleg, D. Hailu, and A. Klein. 2007. *The Khat Controversy: Stimulating the Debate on Drugs*. New York: Berg.

AP. 2014. '17 Arrested in International Khat Drug Ring'. *ABC7 New York*, available at <https://abc7ny.com/khat-drugs-drug-bust/145137/>.

Becci, I. and O. Roy, eds. 2015. *Religious Diversity in European Prisons: Challenges and Implications for Rehabilitation*. Cham: Springer International Publishing.

Bellucci, L. 2018. 'Shaping Notions of Personal Autonomy in Plural Societies: Addressing Female Genital Cutting in France and the European Regulatory Framework's Approach to This Custom'. In M.-C. Foblets, M. Graziadei, and A. D. Renteln, eds. *Personal Autonomy in Plural Societies: A Principle and Its Paradoxes*, 192–205. Abingdon: Routledge.

Ben-David, G. 2011. 'The Integration of Cultural Arguments in the Provocation Doctrine in Rulings of the Israeli Supreme Court'. *Creighton International and Comparative Law Journal* 2: 1–29.

Bendix, R. 1997. *In Search of Authenticity: The Formation of Folklore Studies*. Madison, WI: University of Wisconsin Press.

Bennett, T. W. 2010. 'The Cultural Defence and the Custom of Thwala in South African Law'. *University of Botswana Law Journal* 10: 3–26.

Black, V. 2009. 'Cultural Thin Skulls'. *University of New Brunswick Law Journal* 60: 186–207.

Brumann, C. 1999. 'Writing for Culture: Why a Successful Concept Should Not Be Discarded'. *Current Anthropology* 40(S1). The University of Chicago Press: S1–S27.

Carberry, C. M. and H. K. Gordon. 1996. 'Anatomy of an Acquittal: The Cultural Use of Cash'. *Money Laundering Law Report* 6(9): 1.

Carstens, P. A. 2009. 'The Cultural Defence in Criminal Law: South African Perspectives'. In A.D. Renteln and M.-C. Foblets, eds. *Multicultural Jurisprudence: Comparative Perspectives on the Cultural Defense*, 175–96. Oxford: Hart Publishing.

Caughey, J. L. 2009. 'The Anthropologist as Expert Witness: The Case of a Murder in Maine'. In M.-C. Foblets and A. D. Renteln, eds. *Multicultural Jurisprudence: Comparative Perspectives on the Cultural Defense*, 321–34. Oxford: Hart Publishing.

Diamond, B. L. 1978. 'Social and Cultural Factors as a Diminished Capacity Defense in Criminal Law'. *Journal of the American Academy of Psychiatry and the Law Online* 6(2): 195–208.

Donovan, J. M. and J. S. Garth. 2007. 'Delimiting the Culture Defense'. *Quinnipiac Law Review* 26: 109–46.

Dumin, J. 2006. 'Superstition-Based Injustice in Africa and the United States: The Use of Provocation as a Defense for Killing Witches and Homosexuals'. *Wisconsin Women's Law Journal* 21: 145–73.

Evans-Pritchard, D. and A. D. Renteln. 1994. 'The Interpretation and Distortion of Culture: A Hmong Marriage by Capture Case in Fresno, California'. *Southern California Interdisciplinary Law Journal* 4: 1–48.

Foblets, M.-C. 2016. 'The Body as Identity Marker: Circumcision of Boys Caught between Contrasting Views on the Best Interests of the Child'. In M. Jänterä-Jareborg, ed. *The Child's Interests in Conflict: The Intersections between Society, Family, Faith and Culture*, 125–62. Cambridge: Intersentia.

Foley, R., K. Glancy, K. Menzano, and L. Shermeta. 2011. 'The Role of Culture in Foster Care Placements: A Comparative Study of South African and United States' Systems'. *Children's Legal Rights Journal* 31(1): 1–22.

Freckelton, I. R. and H. Selby. 2009. *Expert Evidence: Law, Practice, Procedure and Advocacy*. Sydney: Thomson Reuters (Prous Science).

Friedman, L. M. 1986. 'The Law and Society Movement'. *Stanford Law Review* 38(3): 763–80.

Geertz, C. 1984. 'Distinguished Lecture: Anti Anti-Relativism'. *American Anthropologist* 86(2): 263–78.

Hatch, E. 1983. *Culture and Morality: The Relativity of Values in Anthropology*. New York: Columbia University Press.

Higgins, N. 2018. *Cultural Defences at the International Criminal Court*. Abingdon: Routledge.

Howard, R. E. 1993. 'Cultural Absolutism and the Nostalgia for Community'. *Human Rights Quarterly* 15(2): 315–38.

Judge Richter. 1995. 'Sociologist's Testimony on Culture Is Precluded in Harassment Case: People v. Jaechoel Yi'. *New York Law Journal*.

Juss, S. S. 2013. 'Kirpans, Law, and Religious Symbols in Schools'. *Journal of Church and State* 55(4): 758–95.

Kandel, R. F. 1992. 'A Legal Field Guide for Expert Anthropologists'. In R. F. Kandel, ed. *Double Vision: Anthropologists at Law*, 53–76. Washington, DC: American Anthropological Association.

Kanter, A. M. 1995. 'The Yenaldlooshi in Court and the Killing of a Witch: The Case for an Indian Cultural Defense'. *Southern California Interdisciplinary Law Journal* 4: 411–54.

Kelsall, T. 2009. *Culture under Cross-Examination: International Justice and the Special Court for Sierra Leone*. Cambridge: Cambridge University Press.

Kozin, A. V. 2011. 'Native American Identity and the Limits of Cultural Defence'. *Law and Critique* 22(1): 39–57.

Lee, C. 2007. 'Cultural Convergence: Interest Convergence Theory Meets the Cultural Defense'. *Arizona Law Review* 49: 911–59.

Levey, G. B. 2013. 'Thinking about Infant Male Circumcision after the Cologne Court Decision'. *Global Discourse* 3(2): 326–31.

Levey, G. B., ed. 2015. *Authenticity, Autonomy and Multiculturalism*. New York: Routledge.

Lindholm, C. 2008. *Culture and Authenticity*. Malden: Blackwell Publishers.

Linnekin, J. 1991. 'Cultural Invention and the Dilemma of Authenticity'. *American Anthropologist* 93(2): 446–9.

Lopes, J. T., A. C. Leão, and L. Ferro. 2019. 'Assessing Cultural Expertise in Portugal: Challenges and Opportunities'. In A. Sarat, ed. *Studies in Law, Politics and Society*, vol. 78, 57–74. Bingley, UK: Emerald Publishing Limited.

Marzulli, J. 2006. 'Air Crash Victim's Kin Win $3.6M Award'. *New York Daily News*, 8 December 2006.

Mauss, M. 1967. *The Gift: Forms and Functions of Exchange in Archaic Societies*. Ian Cunnison, trans. New York: Norton.

Miller, B. G. 1998. 'Culture as Cultural Defense: An American Indian Sacred Site in Court'. *American Indian Quarterly* 22(1/2): 83–97.

Nader, L., ed. 1969. *Law in Culture and Society*. Berkeley: University of California Press.

Parzen, M. D. 2003. 'Toward a Culture-Bound Syndrome-Based Insanity Defense?'. *Culture, Medicine and Psychiatry* 27(2): 131–55.

Poulter, S. M. 1998. *Ethnicity, Law, and Human Rights: The English Experience*. Oxford: Oxford University Press.

Redfield, R. 1962. *The Primitive World and Its Transformations*. Ithaca: Cornell University Press.

Renteln, A. D. 1988. 'Relativism and the Search for Human Rights'. *American Anthropologist* 90(1): 56–72.

Renteln, A. D. 1993. 'A Justification of the Cultural Defense as Partial Excuse'. *Southern California Review of Law and Women's Studies* 2: 437–526.

Renteln, A. D. 2001. 'The Rights of the Dead: Autopsies and Corpses Mismanagement in Multicultural Societies'. *The South Atlantic Quarterly* 100(4): 1005–27.

Renteln, A. D. 2003. 'Cross-Cultural Perceptions of Disability: Policy Implications of Divergent Views'. In S. S. Herr, H. H. Koh, and L. O. Gostin, eds. *The Human Rights of Persons with Intellectual Disabilities: Different But Equal*, 59–82. Oxford: Oxford University Press.

Renteln, A. D. 2004. *The Cultural Defense*. New York: Oxford University Press.

Renteln, A. D. 2009a. 'The Influence of Culture on the Determination of Damages: How Cultural Relativism Affects the Analysis of Trauma'. In R. Grillo, R. Ballard, A. Ferrari, A. J. Hoekema, M. Maussen, and P. Shah, eds. *Legal Practice and Cultural Diversity*, 199–218. Farnham: Ashgate.

Renteln, A. D. 2009b. 'Cross-Cultural Justice and the Logic of Reciprocity: When Westerners Run Afoul of the Law in Other Countries'. *Judicature* 92: 238–42.

Renteln, A. D. 2010. 'The Cultural Defense: Challenging the Monocultural Paradigm'. In M.-C. Foblets, J.-F. Gaudreault-Desbiens, and A. D. Renteln, eds. *Cultural Diversity and the Law: State Responses from Around the World*, 791–817. Brussels: Bruylant.

Renteln, A. D. 2011. 'Cultural Defenses in International Criminal Tribunals: A Preliminary Consideration of the Issues'. *Southwestern Journal of International Law* 18: 267–85.

Renteln, A. D. 2018. 'The Human Rights Dimensions of Virginity Restoration Surgery'. In M.-C. Foblets, M. Graziadei, and A. D. Renteln, eds. *Personal Autonomy in Plural Societies: A Principle and Its Paradoxes*, 206–19. Abingdon: Routledge.

Rosen, L. 1977. 'The Anthropologist as Expert Witness'. *American Anthropologist* 79(3): 555–78.

Ruggiu, I. 2019. *Culture and the Judiciary: The Anthropologist Judge*. Jeremy Daw (trans.). Abingdon: Routledge.

Seidman, R. B. 1965. 'Witch Murder and *Mens Rea*: A Problem of Society under Radical Social Change'. *Modern Law Review* 28: 46–61.

Shadid, W. A. and P. S. van Koningsveld. 1992. 'Legal Adjustments for Religious Minorities: The Case of the Ritual Slaughtering of Animals'. In W. A. Shadid and P. S. van Koningsveld, eds. *Islam in Dutch Society: Current Developments and Future Prospects*, 2–25. Kampen: Kok Pharos Publishing House.

Shweder, R. A. 1991. *Thinking Through Cultures: Expeditions in Cultural Psychology*. Cambridge: Harvard University Press.

Shweder, R. A. 2001. 'Culture: Contemporary Views'. In N. J. Smelser and P. B. Baltes, eds. *International Encyclopedia of the Social & Behavioral Sciences*, vol. 5, 3151–8. Amsterdam: Elsevier.

Simon, C. 2015. 'The "Best Interests of the Child" in a Multicultural Context: A Case Study'. *Journal of Legal Pluralism and Unofficial Law* 47(2): 175–89.

Tomer-Fishman, T. 2010. '"Cultural Defense," "Cultural Offense," or No Culture at All?: An Empirical Examination of Israeli Judicial Decisions in Cultural Conflict Criminal Cases and of the Factors Affecting Them'. *Journal of Criminal Law and Criminology* 100(2): 475–522.

Travis, A. 2013. 'Theresa May Ignores Experts and Bans Use of Qat'. *The Guardian*, 3 July 2013.

Trouillot, M.-R. 2002. 'Adieu, Culture: A New Duty Arises'. In R. G. Fox and B. J. King, eds. *Anthropology beyond Culture*, 37–60. Oxford: Berg.

Truffin, B. and C. Arjona. 2009. 'The Cultural Defence in Spain'. In M.-C. Foblets, A. D. Renteln, and Alison Dundes, eds. *Multicultural Jurisprudence: Comparative Perspectives on the Cultural Defense*, 85–120. Oxford: Hart Publishing.

Veazey, L. L. 2015. *A Woman's Right to Culture: Toward Gendered Cultural Rights*. New Orleans: Quid Pro Books.

Washburn, W. E. 1987. 'Cultural Relativism, Human Rights, and the AAA'. *American Anthropologist* 89(4): 939–43.

Wikan, U. 2002. *Generous Betrayal: Politics of Culture in the New Europe*. Chicago: University of Chicago Press.

Winkelman, M. 1996. 'Cultural Factors in Criminal Defense Proceedings'. *Human Organization* 55(2): 154–9.

Woo, D. 2004. 'Cultural "Anomalies" and Cultural Defenses: Towards an Integrated Theory of Homicide and Suicide'. *International Journal of the Sociology of Law* 32(4): 279–302.

CHAPTER 26

CULTURAL RIGHTS AND CULTURAL HERITAGE AS A GLOBAL CONCERN

ANDRZEJ JAKUBOWSKI

INTRODUCTION

LAW and legal scholarship interact with culture and cultural heritage in numerous distinct ways. This interaction, which has been fostered and driven by the cultural turn in sociolegal analysis over the past four decades, also demonstrates the profound impact of anthropology on legal theory and practice in this period.

This impact can be perceived in two major dimensions. The first regards the role of law as both the product of culture and one of its driving forces (Mautner 2011). This explains the extensive anthropological research on law as a part of culture (Rosen 2006) and the rise of anthropological interest in legal pluralism, multiculturalism, and the role of law in transnational, transitional, and international processes (e.g. Cowan et al. 2001; Goodale 2017: 69–88; Merry 1992). Hence, a significant body of anthropological and sociolegal scholarship has engaged with the relation between culture and power dynamics within a society and/or between distinct societies, which in turn has contributed to the evolving fields of legal anthropology and comparative law analysis (see e.g. Nafziger 2017; Pospisil 1978). In these fields, the meaning of culture and heritage are couched in terms of legal traditions and sociopolitical practices as well as their axiological foundations and institutional designs.

The second major dimension of the impact of anthropology on law regards the more practical function of the law in regulating the cultural aspects of human existence in both its individual and collective forms. From a legal perspective, the notions of culture and cultural heritage have traditionally been applied within heterogeneous, methodologically differentiated areas of regulation and enforcement mechanisms. The nature of this application usually reflects pre-existing legal cultures and their regulatory models.

However, in recent decades, the concepts of cultural heritage and cultural rights have become much more prominent in the global arena. This trend is generally associated with a post-Cold War revival of the belief in human rights law and its gradual culturalization and anthropologization (Lenzerini 2014; Vrdoljak 2013). Furthermore, these forms of legal practice have greatly benefited from the rapid development of cultural and heritage studies, which—owing to the influence of cultural anthropology—focus on the relationship between people, identity, and ways of constructing and using heritage (Brumann 2014; Logan et al. 2016; Winter 2013).

In fact, since the 1960s, both legal and anthropological approaches to heritage have greatly expanded so as to gradually accommodate the demands of multiculturalism in Western societies (Brumann 2015: 414). This process has been part of a larger 'heritage boom' (Harrison 2013: 68–94) within various disciplines of the social sciences and humanities, which has been greatly affected by novel uses of the past, including its commodification (e.g. through the development of mass tourism). It has also involved an expansion of the idea of cultural heritage beyond literary and artistic sources to include a variety of cultural manifestations, such as television dramas, industrial heritage, cartoons, etc. This all-encompassing notion of heritage—reflecting, in a way, the ideas of Clifford Geertz's symbolic anthropology (Geertz 1973: 89)—goes beyond institutionalized and recognized cultural manifestations (of the past) to include a selection of other elements that are important for people and shape their present and future expectations (Lowenthal 1985, 1998). The rise of cultural heritage and cultural rights concerns in the global arena has also stemmed from an increased awareness of the holistic value of cultural and heritage considerations in constructing societal relations and supporting geopolitical frameworks of peace, security, and international cooperation. The value of culture and cultural heritage for individual and collective identities has thus been recognized as a key component of social development, including the empowerment of formerly marginalized groups and communities.

Considering the two major dimensions of the impact of anthropology on legal thought and practice in the realm of cultural rights and cultural heritage, this chapter focuses on the latter one, i.e. legal mechanisms of cultural governance at the global level. Hence, it looks at the mainstreaming of cultural heritage and cultural rights by analysing the normative and operational activity of the international community through its institutions and instruments of governance. It argues that the impact of anthropology on the global regime of cultural rights and cultural heritage consists in the employment of anthropological knowledge in the practical operationalization of culture in international law and policy. Accordingly, it looks at the nature and consequences of this employment in relation to two core aspects: the rhetorical and conceptual evolution of the notion of cultural heritage in international law, and the rise of cultural rights as collective rights. The chapter concludes with an evaluation of the current legal avenues for addressing global challenges in the domains of cultural heritage and cultural rights, which points to the pressing need for more efficient modalities of global solidarity.

Legal conceptualization of cultural heritage: from monuments to living cultures

It does not come as a surprise that legal regulation in cultural matters is generally a product of the West, with its traditional top-down models of shaping and administrating the spheres of art and culture. These developed in nineteenth-century Europe in parallel to the rise of the scientific disciplines of archaeology, museology, ethnography, and cultural anthropology. On the one hand, the traditional European legal approach to culture and cultural heritage primarily referred to freedom of conscience, belief, and expression (including the protection of the moral and material interests resulting from any scientific, literary, or artistic production). On the other hand, it concerned the protection, conservation, and management of the past: the value of the spiritual, artistic, and historical patrimony of the nation was officially recognized and institutionalized (Riegl 1903). Moreover, legal regulation reflected the evolutionism of early cultural anthropology, which created a hierarchy of cultures according to ascending levels of civilization. Indeed, local cultures, folklore, and Indigenous cultures—or more broadly speaking, 'primitive' cultures—were not considered worthy of legal protection, a pattern underlying and reflecting colonial policies of cultural appropriation and misuse.

While the legal conceptualization of cultural heritage as a global concern came into being much later, at the peak of decolonization in the 1960s, the recognition of cultural heritage as essential to the creation of human identity was by no means subsidiary or novel to international law and legal scholarship in the nineteenth century. Indeed, the contemporary development of international law was coupled with important regulatory interventions with respect to national cultures and cultural entitlements. The arrangements adopted in the international practice of that period are sometimes described as stemming from the axiological foundation of the '"sacred" link between people, place and cultural heritage' (Vrdoljak 2006: 77). Since then, the issues of cultural integrity and cultural sovereignty have been crucial in constructing the concept of statehood and state identity. Unsurprisingly, the international legal regulation of cultural aspects of social life has long been subject to core state interests, with a focus on counteracting the threats to cultural assets posed by destruction and theft both in time of war, during colonial rule, or in peacetime (trafficking and illicit excavations).

Notably, the international lawmaking process in the domain of material culture, initiated under the auspices of the League of Nations (LoN) in the 1920s and continued after the Second World War through UNESCO, was characterized by a certain degree of compromise and interplay between lawyers and experts from other disciplines: primarily European or European-trained art historians, museologists, archaeologists, and conservation architects. Consequently, the reasoning behind legislative solutions of the day straddled theoretical considerations of the aesthetic and historical values of heritage (which were universal, static, and 'objective' in nature) and practical legal mechanisms for their protection. Public, formal pronouncements on cultural heritage could be seen as a result of this compromise: a sociolegal construct reflecting both contemporary political and social interests and embodying modern-day conceptualizations of the past.

It is also true that cultural heritage has long found a place in the conceptual frameworks of both anthropology and law. While the former has always operated with a broader concept of culture (not restricted to publicly recognized things), the latter traditionally refers to material things (monuments, artworks, sites, antiquities, relicts, etc.) through the lens of property law and administrative law. Indeed, the legal approach to material culture is well evidenced by the names of academic sub-disciplines—'cultural property law' or 'art and law'—still employed in university programmes and related textbooks today. However, with the heritage boom, the legal conceptualization of culture became subject to a wide critique of the use of the term 'cultural property' in reference to protected material elements of heritage. The use of this term was described as 'inadequate and inappropriate for the range of matters covered by the concept of the "cultural heritage"', which had been 'recognized and universally used by historians, archaeologists, anthropologists and other researchers of human life both past and present' (Prott and O'Keefe 1992: 319). It was argued that 'property' would imply a commodification of cultural aspects of human life, whereas many of these aspects should not be perceived as ordinary goods (Blake 2000: 65–6; see also Francioni 2007). Moreover, the term 'property' was seen to reinforce the view that culture is static or that cultural values 'can be captured and frozen' (Handler 2003: 363; Lixinski 2019: 52–65; Smith 2006: 101).

This conceptual shift owed a lot to the World Heritage Convention.[1] Indeed, this treaty changed the paradigm of legal thinking with regard to culture, giving flesh to the idea that it is in the general interest of humankind to protect outstanding examples of natural and cultural heritage (communal legacies of the natural environment and the creations of human beings). The World Heritage Convention marked an important development within UNESCO, consisting in the wide employment of ethnological and anthropological knowledge and expertise in the legal operationalization of cultural heritage. The actions of the World Heritage Committee and its advisory bodies were crucial in fostering this change. The original understanding of outstanding universal value—the prerequisite for international protection under this legal regime—experienced a profound re-interpretation. It is to be recalled that many parts of the Global South were not initially considered to possess cultural heritage of universal importance. The shift began during the early work on a 'global study' that focused on creating a fixed inventory of all the cultural property of universal significance. This resulted in the 'Global Strategy for a Representative, Balanced and Credible World Heritage List' (UNESCO 1994), which employed an inclusive understanding of heritage (Lévi-Strauss 2000). This document, adopted by the World Heritage Committee in 1994, was not only meant to encourage a wide range of nominations from diverse cultures and regions of the world but also to open the door to nominations that went beyond 'monumental' heritage and to consider sites whose (potential) outstanding universal value could be seen in terms of their broad social and anthropological contexts through time. These inclusive goals were further developed in ICOMOS's Nara Document of Authenticity, which stated that '[c]ultural heritage diversity exists in time and space, and demands respect for other cultures and all aspects of their belief systems' (ICOMOS 1994: paragraph 6).

The nature of this fundamental conceptual shift has been subject of much examination in anthropological scholarship (see e.g. Bortolotto 2007: 40; Labadi 2013: 37–46). It has been analysed in terms of the 'anthropologization' and 'indigenization' of the World Heritage system, i.e. reflecting the impact of anthropology, geography, industrial archaeology, and sociology more than that of art history or conservation architecture (Gfeller 2015: 377–80). While UNESCO had been engaged with anthropological expertise since the early 1950s, most notably with Claude Lévi-Straus and his works on race, ethnocentrism, and culture (Lévi-Straus 1952), the final shape of the 'Global Strategy' was also influenced by the French school of anthropology (represented by Isac Chiva) and by the development of Indigenous studies (Gfeller 2015: 372–7). In this regard, the anthropological shift consisted in altering the existing model of identifying and protecting heritage, which was enshrined in the World Heritage Convention and reflected the viewpoint of the Global North and its boundaries (Australia, Norway, Japan, Canada), to better accommodate the Global South. Yet representatives of the Global South, the intended beneficiaries of this change, did not really contribute to this process (see Brumann 2018).

Based on the experience of the World Heritage Convention and its opening to the intangible elements of culture—as evidenced in a series of revisions to the 'Operational Guidelines' of this international legal instrument (see Labadi 2013: 31–54)—as well as the gradual advancement of Indigenous rights and peoples' rights, a second important movement in international law got underway in the late 1980s which addressed the realm of intangible heritage, or more broadly the safeguarding of living cultures. This movement, fostered by the anthropological shift in UNESCO, concerned the protection of traditional culture and folklore[2] and led to the establishment of an international legal regime for the protection of the living manifestations of culture, as embodied in the Convention for the Safeguarding of the Intangible Cultural Heritage (ICH Convention)[3] and the Convention on the Protection and Promotion of the Diversity of Cultural Expressions (CPPDCE).[4] These two UNESCO treaties promote and enshrine a very broad, inclusive, and dynamic notion of cultural heritage. Article 2(1) of the ICH Convention, which defines intangible heritage, refers to 'the practices, representations, expressions, knowledge, skills—as well as the instruments, objects, artefacts and cultural spaces associated therewith—that communities, groups and, in some cases, individuals recognize as part of their cultural heritage'. In turn, the CPPDCE promotes the societal value of the diversity and variety of living cultures around the world. It recognizes that 'cultural diversity forms a common heritage of humanity and should be cherished and preserved for the benefit of all' (Preamble, 2nd recital). In this fashion, the diversity of living cultures are portrayed as a common, global good that must be protected against threats stemming from the globalization of trade and industry.

In light of these developments, it seems that by 2005, an inclusive, holistic understanding of cultural heritage was widely acknowledged by international law and its scholarship. In fact, cultural heritage in all its diversity is today perceived as a global concern and a common interest of the international community. However, cultural heritage, even broadly understood, still takes the form of a resource to be protected and promoted within a given context or for certain purposes, or due to its formally recognized values (see Gillman 2010). In other words, for the law, cultural heritage continues to be a fixed abstract construct, not easily adaptable or modifiable according to the actual needs and expectations of its diverse stakeholders. These also comprise the right to alter, forget, or even destroy one's heritage. Thus, 'the challenge facing international law in this field is to try to satisfy as many of the legitimate interests in heritage as possible, while at the same time operating within a system primarily established by and for sovereign and equal States' (Blake 2015: 21–2).

The right to culture and cultural heritage in its collective dimension

Indeed, the dominant, Eurocentric approach in international law has long perceived states (or their plurality) as the primary cultural actors and cultural heritage stakeholders. The advancement and protection of the universal values of culture and cultural heritage, fostered by UNESCO as early as 1954 in its Convention for the Protection of Cultural Property in the Event of Armed Conflict[5] and substantiated in the World Heritage Convention, lacked virtually any connection to human rights in its first stages. In fact, international cultural heritage law and international human rights law initially developed separately from one another. This is evidenced by the detachment of cultural issues from the post-Second World War international legal regime for human rights. Although the 1948 Universal Declaration of Human Rights (UDHR)[6] and the International Covenant of Economic, Social and Cultural Rights (ICESR)[7] recognized the existence of cultural rights, they did not explicitly refer to any human rights guarantees in relation to cultural heritage. Moreover, the failure of international law to broaden the notion of 'genocide' beyond its biological dimension to include culture has long undermined the entire legal debate on cultural rights and resulted in the absence of a cultural element in the major international human rights treaties. Even the ICESCR, though it includes cultural rights in the title, does not make clear which human rights protections apply to cultural matters. It only contains one direct reference to culture, under Article 15(1)(a): 'the right to take part in cultural life'. Moreover, for a long time the rights protected under this treaty were not directly justiciable. This has only been the case since 2013, when the Committee on Economic, Social and Rights (CESCR), a monitory body of this treaty, began to consider complaints from individuals based on the 2008 Optional Protocol to the ICESCR.[8] The absence of cultural references also characterizes regional human rights regimes, such as the American Convention on Human Rights (ACHR)[9] and the European Convention of Human Rights and Fundamental

Freedoms (ECHR).[10] In this way, normative guarantees of culture-related human rights tend to be seen as mere political commitments or policy guidelines rather than truly substantive rights (see e.g. Meyer-Bisch 1993; Symonides 1998).

The major difficulty in addressing cultural rights as human rights stems from the very essence of culture and cultural heritage and their collective dimension. While fixed rights and freedoms originating from European legal traditions (freedom of creation, freedom of speech, right to benefit from the fruits of one's creativity) are considered individual in nature, the larger concept of cultural life involves collective enjoyment and participation. Hence, on a theoretical level, cultural rights are sometimes perceived as endorsing the uniqueness or exclusivity of particular groups and communities, which stands in contrast to the universal character of human rights, rooted in the notions of shared humanity and human dignity (Francioni 2008: 3). This juxtaposition of cultural rights and universal human rights has always generated tensions between institutionalized universal human rights and culture-oriented social studies. In fact, the idea of universal, indivisible human rights has been widely criticized by anthropologists since the inception of the post-Second World War system of international human rights law. Many argue that it represents an essentially Eurocentric or cosmopolitan point of view and overlooks cultural differences between societies (see e.g. Goodale 2017: 235; Herskovits 1947; Messer 1993: 224; Preis 1996: 288).

Another difficulty concerns the very existence of collective rights, collective standing, and self-determination for collectivities other than states in international law. Considering the crisis of the LoN system of minority protection, international law virtually excluded collective rights or non-state interests after the Second World War. Moreover, the collective dimension (group and minority rights) was detached from the international human rights regime, which was driven by a liberal, individualistic approach. As a result, it has often been claimed that collective rights in general, and particularly collective cultural rights, cannot be 'truly' accepted as human rights since their recognition and enforcement might to some extent hinder or relativize the enjoyment of fundamental rights and freedoms held by every human being individually (see e.g. Boggs 2004: 193–9; Jovanović 2016). In fact, in the vast UN treaty *instrumentarium*, the International Covenant on Civil and Political Rights (ICCPR)[11] alone addresses minority rights. It enshrines an anthropological notion of culture, according to which culture provides the members of ethnic, religious, or linguistic minorities with values and meanings by which they build their identity (see Capotorti 1979: paragraphs 195–210). Accordingly, the Covenant states that they 'shall not be denied the right, in community with the other members of their group, to enjoy their own culture, to profess and practise their own religion, or to use their own language' (Article 27). However, under the Optional Protocol to the ICCPR,[12] the monitoring body of this treaty (the Human Rights Committee) does not have the competence to hear collective complaints.

Notwithstanding these theoretical and procedural obstacles, the multiholder conceptualization of rights concerning culture and cultural heritage began to evolve in the 1960s. This was driven by the main wave of decolonization and by simultaneous social and political forces in Western Europe and North America that pushed for the inclusion of groups that had previously been marginalized or disadvantaged due to their race, ethnicity, economic status, or gender. This shift towards the collective dimension of culture took place in the form of theoretical endeavours and regulatory developments in certain national legal systems. In fact, the importance of cultural considerations for dealing with social injustices was widely addressed in the broader research on cultural liberalism, multiculturalism, and group rights (Jones 2016). Demands for the protection of culture translated into special representation rights for minorities within already functioning legislative institutions, poly-ethnic group rights to ensure the preservation of cultural practices, and powers of self-government for 'national minorities' (Kymlicka 1989, 1995), as well as more general recognition and respect for ethno-cultural differences (Taylor 1994). On the global level, this shift was articulated early on in the International Convention on the Elimination of All Forms of Racial Discrimination,[13] which enshrined the principle of non-discrimination in relation to the enjoyment of various culture-oriented rights.

The process of empowering collective cultural actors and pluralistic visions of culture was also driven by anthropologists, whose non-legal knowledge became instrumental in the legal operationalization of culture and cultural heritage, as mentioned above in relation to the 'Global Strategy'. The first larger area of this collective approach concerned Indigenous Peoples. The Indigenous and Tribal Populations Convention No. 107,[14] adopted within the framework of the International Labour Organisation in 1957, aimed to provide a standard framework for addressing the economic issues that many of these groups faced. The authors took for granted that such groups would gradually disappear by integrating into the societies in which they lived. However, the revised Convention No. 169[15] of 1989 adopted a different approach, which was driven by 'respect for the cultures and ways of life of Indigenous and tribal peoples, placing emphasis on their right to a continued existence and to development according to their own priorities' (Joona 2012: 201; see also Kuper 2003). This approach owed much to anthropological expertise and its fieldwork, which demonstrated that 'traditional' cultures can be fluid and subject to change according to peoples' needs, not petrified in their pre-colonial state (see e.g. Clifford 1988). In this regard, Convention No. 169 acknowledged the collective rights of Indigenous Peoples to preserve and develop their cultural identity according to their own cultural needs and processes.

Parallel to these efforts, the move to empower Indigenous Peoples continued within the various frameworks of the UN. In particular, the work of the UN Working Group on Indigenous Populations, established in 1982, involved the participation of Indigenous representatives, who were often supported by anthropologists. In fact, so-called engaged anthropology played an important role in shaping the legal operationalization of Indigenous rights in relation to their environment, land rights, culture, and political sovereignty at the national, regional, and UN legislative and policy levels (Kirsch 2018). In this regard, the 1993 Draft UN Declaration on the Rights of Indigenous Peoples[16] recognized the collective dimension of cultural rights for Indigenous Peoples, including their right to recover elements of their cultural heritage that were 'taken without their free and informed consent or in violation of their laws, traditions and customs' (Article

18). Since the 1990s, a number of states with sizeable communities of Indigenous Peoples have introduced special legislative and technical measures to accommodate these principles, including the recognition of Indigenous claims for the redress of cultural harm experienced in the past (Bell and Paterson 2009; Vrdoljak 2008).

This Indigenous turn has also involved anthropological evidence and expertise in domestic and international court proceedings (see e.g. Cassell 2009; Hausler 2012). Importantly, the value of culture and cultural heritage has gradually been addressed by the evolutionary approach of the Inter-American Court of Human Rights (IACtHR), irrespective of the absence of explicit guarantees under the ACHR. In particular, the IACtHR has interpreted the right to property under Article 21 of the ACHR to include certain cultural rights of Indigenous Peoples and local traditional communities, especially in relation to their land and cultural identity (see Hausler 2016). In this regard, expert testimony has played a very important role before this court. Indeed, in cases involving Indigenous Peoples, anthropologists and historians have often provided evidence that influenced the IACtHR's factual findings and final rulings (see Kirsch 2018: 180–222; MacKay 2018).

The influence of anthropological studies and engaged anthropology is clearly evidenced in the 2007 UN Declaration on the Rights of Indigenous Peoples (UNDRIP),[17] which was the fruit of difficult negotiations between governments and Indigenous Peoples' representatives, who were supported by anthropological and other cultural experts. The negotiations lasted for over twenty years prior to the adoption of the Declaration. It codified a novel conceptualization of the right to self-determination and established a universal framework of minimum standards for the survival, dignity, well-being, and rights of Indigenous Peoples. The UNDRIP states, inter alia, that Indigenous Peoples have 'the right to practice and revitalize their cultural traditions and customs', including 'the right to maintain, protect and develop the past, present and future manifestations of their cultures, such as archaeological and historical sites, artefacts, designs, ceremonies, technologies and visual and performing arts and literature' (Article 11(1)). The UNDRIP also imposes upon states a positive commitment to 'take effective measures to recognize and protect the exercise of these rights' (Article 31(2)) and to 'provide redress through effective mechanisms' of their cultural claims arising from past injustices (Article 11(2)).

Another area of the development of collective rights linked to the anthropological and heritage turn is that of peoples' rights, which fits under the label of 'third-generation human rights' (Vašák 1984). Although international law does not define 'peoples', this term is generally understood to describe pluralities of individuals that are considered and/or self-identify as wholes. In this regard, the right to self-determination is fundamental for the construction of peoples' rights, as enshrined in the ICCPR and ICESCR. This legal concept, which took form during the era of decolonization, entails the right of every people to freely decide on its sovereignty and choose its international status. In the 1970s and 1980s, with the encouragement of newly independent states and socialist states, it was extended to cover the rights to development and peace. Moreover, on the level of international human rights law, the concept of peoples' rights also came to embody certain collective cultural rights. Accordingly, the African Charter on Human and Peoples' Rights (ACHPR)[18] contains several cultural rights and provides for collective rights, including the right to cultural development and cultural identity (Article 22). This collective dimension is articulated to a degree unmatched by other binding international human rights law instruments, a fact which stems from the specificity of many African societies and their customary laws and collective cultural practices (see Shyllon 2016). Accordingly, the ACHPR ties cultural rights and cultural identity to cultural heritage, accommodating ideas that had driven earlier regional instruments, in particular the Cultural Charter for Africa,[19] a product of the Pan-African movement and its anti-colonial political, cultural, and anthropological facets (Viljoen 2007: 157–62). Among other things, cultural self-determination and the right to cultural development in the African postcolonial era have been associated with the claim to recover dispersed or looted cultural heritage as a means of regaining the memory, identity, and dignity of peoples (see M'Bow 1979; Sarr and Savoy 2018: 39–41).

The cultural shift of the 1990s, mentioned in relation to the activity of UNESCO, and the rise of peoples' and Indigenous rights also played out on the level of minority rights. This took place in the context of a profound transformation of international law caused by the end of the Cold War, which was accompanied by shocking instances of international crime against ethnic and religious minorities and their heritage in Rwanda and former Yugoslavia. Although work within the UN on the legal status of minorities started much earlier (see Capotorti 1979), it was not until 1992 that the UN General Assembly adopted its Declaration on the Rights of Persons Belonging to National or Ethnic, Religious and Linguistic Minorities.[20] Alongside the work on the UN level, legislative activity in this field was also undertaken under the auspices of the Council of Europe (CoE) and resulted in the Framework Convention for the Protection of National Minorities.[21] While both UN and CoE instruments refer to 'culture' as one of the fundamental spheres of minority protection, the latter explicitly obliges its state parties to undertake 'to preserve the essential elements of their identity, namely their religion, language, traditions and cultural heritage' (Article 5(1)), though it does not provide for the justiciability of such cultural minority rights. Moreover, the adoption of this treaty has obstructed the work on an additional cultural protocol to the ECHR, which would extend the competences of the European Court of Human Rights (ECtHR) into the field of cultural rights. Nonetheless, through a dynamic interpretation of various provisions of the ECHR, the ECtHR has recognized a catalogue of substantive rights in relation to culture (European Court of Human Rights 2017).

Recent decades have witnessed an expansion of states' positive obligations with respect to the human rights of minorities[22] as well as strides in the conceptual development of cultural rights in general. The latter aspect has been characterized by an interdisciplinary debate whose results are articulated in the Fribourg Declaration on Cultural Rights.[23] This doctrinal document, deeply rooted in the anthropological conceptualization of culture as a process (Merry 2001: 39), fosters broadly encompassing notions of culture(s) and heritage(s) (Articles 2–3), including their collective and communal dimensions. Similar considerations are explicitly substantiated in General Comment No.

21 on Article 15(a) of the ICESCR,[24] which not only recognizes the individual and collective aspects of the right to participate in cultural life (including the enjoyment of and access to cultural heritage) but also addresses culture both as a process and as an aggregation of the tangible and intangible ways that 'individuals, groups of individuals and communities express their humanity and the meaning they give to their existence, and build their world view representing their encounter with the external forces affecting their lives' (paragraph 13) (see Chow 2018: 105–7). Moreover, the ICESR clarifies states' obligations to realize the right to take part in cultural life: these should not only consist in the enactment of appropriate legislation but also involve the introduction of effective mechanisms for individual and group decision-making, with special attention paid to vulnerable groups (women, children, older persons, persons with disabilities, minorities, migrants, Indigenous Peoples, and persons living in poverty) (paragraphs 25–39). Such an inclusive, holistic approach is perhaps best visible in the text of the CoE's Faro Convention,[25] which addresses the questions of why and for whom heritage is transmitted. It adopts an essentially anthropological concept of cultural heritage (Article 2), emphasizing its continuous evolution in 'all aspects of the environment resulting from the interaction between people and places through time'. It also defines 'heritage community' as a group that identifies itself with a given heritage and wishes 'to sustain and transmit [it] to future generations'. In this regard, the full realization of the right to access to cultural heritage, which entails effective forms of public participation in heritage governance, lies in the rights-based approach fostered by this treaty.

Global governance of cultural heritage and participation

For at least two decades, the convergence between cultural rights and cultural heritage has been considered crucial for economic development, the realization of all human rights, and peaceful societal relations on a global scale. In this regard, it is worth noting the finding of the International Criminal Court (ICC) in the recent *Al Mahdi* case,[26] which concerned deliberate attacks on internationally protected cultural sites in Timbuktu. The ICC found that such attacks directly affected the entire regional community, violating its religious rights, damaging its collective identity, and constituting an affront to the values of humanity as a whole. Indeed, the importance of cultural heritage is clearly visible in the international struggle against terrorism and fundamentalism, and is gradually being addressed in the global agenda for sustainable development. However, for the global governance of cultural heritage to be effective, it must coordinate between the diverse legal instruments and rules (regime coordination) and various domestic and international actors involved in securing the protection of cultural heritage (Vadi 2012: 118–23). In this regard, the effort to achieve normative and institutional coordination is evidenced by the expanding legislative activity of the UN Security Council in relation to cultural heritage as well as by the increasing convergence of policy goals in the field of cultural rights and cultural heritage among international organizations and institutions, including human rights monitoring bodies (see Jakubowski 2018).

Perhaps the most significant enhancement of the concept of cultural rights, including those attached to cultural heritage, is embodied in the UN special procedure in the field of cultural rights, adopted by the UN Human Rights Council (HRC).[27] Since 2009, both UN Special Rapporteurs—Farida Shaheed (2009–15), a sociologist, and Karima Bennoune (2015–2021), a human rights lawyer—have published a series of thematic reports that deal with various aspects of the operationalization of cultural rights in their individual and collective dimensions and offer recommendations on further implementing such rights. These works directly incorporate current anthropological conceptualizations of culture(s) and heritage(s), putting an emphasis on the participatory facets of governance in this domain. In particular, a 2011 report by Shaheed on access to cultural heritage[28] emphasized that under current international law, '[c]ultural heritage is important not only in itself, but also in relation to its human dimension, in particular its significance for individuals and communities and their identity and development processes' (paragraph 77). Moreover, '[t]he right of access to and enjoyment of cultural heritage forms part of international human rights law, finding its legal basis, in particular, in the right to take part in cultural life, the right of members of minorities to enjoy their own culture, and the right of indigenous peoples to self-determination and to maintain, control, protect and develop cultural heritage' (paragraph 78). This right includes, inter alia, 'the right to participate in the identification, interpretation and development of cultural heritage, as well as to the design and implementation of preservation/safeguard policies and programmes' (paragraph 79).

In fact, participatory, multilevel, and multistakeholder governance appears to be one of the major concerns of the current rights-based approach to culture and cultural heritage. This approach also applies to tensions between cultural rights, other human rights, and the legal operationalization of cultural heritage (Francioni and Lixinski 2017), as acknowledged in Article 2(1) of the ICH Convention, which states that 'consideration will be given solely to such intangible cultural heritage as is compatible with existing international human rights instruments, as well as with the requirements of mutual respect among communities, groups and individuals, and of sustainable development'. Although the effective participation of all stakeholders is required in a number of international law instruments concerning natural environment and cultural heritage, the necessary modalities of participation are still not well developed. This is particularly the case for community participation (Urbinati 2015), which is critical for implementing the regimes established by the World Heritage Convention and the ICH Convention. In this regard, it has been noted that '[t]he system of international heritage law does not work to favour communities; rather, it ostensibly focuses on heritage as an end in itself, and, in so doing, privileges expert rule, or the co-option of heritage process by basic state values such as sovereignty and territoriality' (Lixinski 2019: 252).

Indeed, the negative aspects of internationally formalized 'heritigization' have been subject to much research. This work has underlined both the power inequality that exists between decision-makers and local communities (see e.g. Logan 2007) and the way that these communities and their narratives are silenced by the authoritative discourse of cultural experts (Smith 2006). In the former regard, the practices of global governance bodies, particularly UNESCO treaty bodies, have been widely criticized as primarily serving political claims or expectations (see Meskell 2018), while communities' voices are barely heard. While these critics acknowledge that culture cannot be dissociated from power and politics, they stress that important 'cultural questions' always need to be asked and negotiated in the specific context in which international law is applied (Chow 2018: 258). Regarding the expertization of cultural heritage governance, a current debate also concerns the conceptual chaos that starts to enshroud the notion of culture once it is passed back and forth between anthropologists, lawyers, and other experts engaged in this field of global governance (Brumann 2018). Similarly, studies have pointed to the practical challenges of employing interdisciplinary methodologies when implementing UNESCO's legal instruments (Blake 2017: 139–52). At the same time, it appears that the vast scholarly production in the domain of cultural heritage is still mainly a product of the Global North, while other perspectives or voices continue to be underrepresented. This might have serious consequences for the operationalization of cultural heritage as a global concern, especially in light of the renewed rise of nationalism and extremism in various parts of the world. Therefore, in order to ensure the human right to participate in cultural life, the widely held principle of participatory governance should be translated into effective mechanisms and procedural requirements for maintaining a dialogue with the actual right-holders. Simultaneously, such novel mechanisms should fully embrace an open, deliberative approach to culture and heritage that can adapt to the constantly changing societal and environmental contexts in play.

Acknowledgements

The author wishes to acknowledge the support received from a scholarship of the Ministry of Culture and National Heritage (Poland) in preparing this chapter.

Notes

1. Convention Concerning the Protection of World Natural and Cultural Heritage (adopted on 16 November 1972, entered into force on 17 December 1975) 1037 UNTS 151.
2. See Recommendation on the Safeguarding of Traditional Culture and Folklore (adopted on 15 November 1989 by the General Conference of UNESCO at its 25th sesssion) <http://portal.unesco.org/en/ev.php-URL_ID=13141&URL_DO=DO_TOPIC&URL_SECTION=201.html> accessed 28 November 2021.
3. Convention for the Safeguarding of the Intangible Cultural Heritage (adopted 7 October 2003, entered into force 20 April 2006) 2368 UNTS 3.
4. Convention on the Protection and Promotion of the Diversity of Cultural Expressions (adopted 20 October 2005, entered into force 18 March 2007) 2440 UNTS 311.

5. Convention for the Protection of Cultural Property in the Event of Armed Conflict (adopted 14 May 1954, entered into force 7 August 1956) 249 UNTS 240, Preamble, 2nd and 3rd recitals.
6. Universal Declaration of Human Rights (adopted in Paris 10 December 1948) UNGA Res 217A(III), UN Doc A/810, 71.
7. International Covenant of Economic, Social and Cultural Rights (adopted 16 December 1966, entered into force 3 January 1976) 993 UNTS 3.
8. Optional Protocol to the ICESCR (opened for signature 10 December 2008, entered into force 5 May 2013) 2922 UNTS 27.
9. American Convention on Human Rights (opened for signature 22 November 1969, entered into force 18 July 1978) 1144 UNTS 123.
10. European Convention for the Protection of Human Rights and Fundamental Freedoms (signed 4 November 1950, entered into force 3 September 1953) 213 UNTS 221.
11. International Covenant on Civil and Political Rights (adopted 16 December 1966, entered into force 23 March 1976) 999 UNTS 171.
12. (First) Optional Protocol to the ICCPR (adopted 19 December 1966, entered into force 23 March 1976) 999 UNTS 302.
13. International Convention on the Elimination of All Forms of Racial Discrimination (adopted 21 December 1965, entered into force 4 January 1969) 660 UNTS 195.
14. Indigenous and Tribal Populations Convention (No. 107) (adopted 26 June 1957, entered into force 2 June 1959) 328 UNTS 247.
15. Convention Concerning Indigenous and Tribal Peoples in Independent Countries (No. 169) (adopted 27 June 1989, entered into force 5 September 1991) 1650 UNTS 383.
16. Draft UN Declaration on the Rights of Indigenous Peoples (23 August 1993) UN Doc E/CN.4/Sub.2/1993/29.
17. UN Declaration on the Rights of Indigenous Peoples (adopted 13 September 2007) UN Doc A/RES/61/295.
18. African Charter on Human and Peoples' Rights (adopted 27 June 1981, entered into force 21 October 1986) 1520 UNTS 217.
19. Cultural Charter for Africa (adopted 5 July 1976, entered into force 19 September 1990) <https://au.int/en/treaties/charter-african-cultural-renaissance> accessed 29 November 2021.
20. Declaration on the Rights of Persons Belonging to National or Ethnic, Religious and Linguistic Minorities (adopted 18 December 1992) UN Doc A/RES/47/135.
21. Framework Convention for the Protection of National Minorities (opened for signature 1 February 1995, entered into force 1 February 1998) 2151 UNTS 243.
22. HRC General Comment No. 23, Article 27 (Rights of Minorities), 8 April 1994, UN Doc CCPR/C/21/Rev.1/Add.5.
23. Fribourg Declaration on Cultural Rights (adopted 7 May 2007) <https://culturalrights.net/en/documentos.php?c=14&p=161> accessed 28 November 2021.
24. CESCR General Comment No. 21, Right of Everyone to Take Part in Cultural Life (Art 15, para 1(a) of the Covenant), 21 December 2009, UN Doc E/C.12/GC/21.
25. Framework Convention on the Value of Cultural Heritage for Society (opened for signature 27 October 2005, entered into force 1 June 2011) 2758 UNTS 21.
26. *Prosecutor v Al Faqi Al Mahdi* (Judgment and Sentence) [2016] ICC-01/12-01/15-171.
27. HRC Resolution 10/23 (adopted 26 March 2009) UN Doc A/HRC/RES/10/23.

28. 'Report of the independent expert in the field of cultural rights, Farida Shaheed' (21 March 2011) UN Doc A/HRC/17/38.

References

Bell, C. and R. Paterson, eds. 2009. *Protection of First Nations Cultural Heritage: Laws, Policy, and Reform*. Vancouver/Toronto: University of British Columbia Press.

Blake, J. 2000. 'On Defining the Cultural Heritage'. *International and Comparative Law Quarterly* 49(1): 61–85.

Blake, J. 2015. *International Cultural Heritage Law*. Oxford: Oxford University Press.

Blake, J. 2017. 'Anthropology in International Law: The Case of Safeguarding Intangible Cultural Heritage'. In J. A. R. Nafziger, ed. *Comparative Law and Anthropology*, 135–52. Cheltenham/Northampton: Edward Elgar.

Boggs, J. P. 2004. 'The Culture Concept as Theory, in Context'. *Current Anthropology* 45(2): 187–209.

Bortolotto, C. 2007. 'From Objects to Processes: UNESCO's "Intangible Cultural Heritage"'. *Journal of Museum Ethnography* 19: 21–33.

Brumann, C. 2014. 'Heritage Agnosticism: A Third Path for the Study of Cultural Heritage'. *Social Anthropology* 22(2): 73–88.

Brumann, C. 2015. 'Cultural Heritage'. In J. D. Wright, ed. *International Encyclopedia of the Social and Behavioral Sciences*, 414–19. Oxford: Elsevier.

Brumann, C. 2018. 'Anthropological Utopia, Closet Eurocentrism, and Culture Chaos in the UNESCO World Heritage Arena'. *Anthropological Quarterly* 91(4): 1203–34.

Capotorti, F. 1979. 'Study on the Rights of Persons Belonging to Ethnic, Religious and Linguistic Minorities'. New York: United Nations, UN Doc. E/CN.4/Sub.2/384/Rev.1.

Cassell, E. 2009. 'Anthropologists in the Canadian Courts'. In M. Freeman and D. Napier, eds. *Law and Anthropology*, 187–217. New York: Oxford University Press.

Chow, P. Y. S. 2018. *Cultural Rights in International Law and Discourse. Contemporary Challenges and Interdisciplinary Perspectives*. Boston/Leiden: Brill-Nijhoff.

Clifford, J. 1988. *The Predicament of Culture: Twentieth-Century Ethnography, Literature, and Art*. Cambridge, MA: Harvard University Press.

Cowan, J. K., M.-B. Dembour, and R. A. Wilson, eds. 2001. *Culture and Rights: Anthropological Perspectives*. Cambridge: Cambridge University Press.

European Court of Human Rights, Research Division. 2017. *Cultural Rights in the Case-Law of the European Court of Human Rights*. Strasbourg: Council of Europe/European Court of Human Rights.

Francioni, F. 2007. 'A Dynamic Evolution of Concept and Scope: From Cultural Property to Cultural Heritage'. In A. A. Yusuf, ed. *Standard-Setting in UNESCO, Normative Action in Education, Science and Culture*, 221–36. Leiden: Martinus Nijhoff and UNESCO Publishing.

Francioni, F. 2008. 'Culture, Heritage and Human Rights: An Introduction'. In F. Francioni and M. Scheinin, eds. *Cultural Human Rights*, 1–15. Boston/Leiden: Brill.

Francioni, F. and L. Lixinski. 2017. 'Opening the Toolbox of International Human Rights Law in the Safeguarding of Cultural Heritage'. In A. Durbach and L. Lixinski, eds. *Heritage, Culture and Rights: Challenging Legal Discourses*, 11–34. Oxford/Portland: Hart Publishing.

Geertz, C. 1973. *The Interpretation of Cultures*. New York: Basic Books.

Gfeller, A. E. 2015. 'Anthropologizing and Indigenizing Heritage: The Origins of the UNESCO Global Strategy for a Representative, Balanced and Credible World Heritage List'. *Journal of Social Archaeology* 15(3): 366–86.

Gillman, D. 2010. *The Idea of Cultural Heritage*, 2nd edn. New York: Cambridge University Press.

Goodale, M. 2017. *Anthropology and Law: A Critical Introduction*. New York: New York University Press.

Handler, R. 2003. 'Cultural Property and Culture Theory'. *Journal of Social Archaeology* 3(3): 353–65.

Harrison, R. 2013. *Heritage: Critical Approaches*. London/New York: Routledge.

Hausler, K. 2012. 'Indigenous Perspectives in the Courtroom'. *International Journal of Human Rights* 16(1): 51–72.

Hausler, K. 2016. 'Collective Cultural Rights in the Inter-American Human Rights System'. In A. Jakubowski, ed. *Cultural Rights as Collective Rights: An International Law Perspective*, 222–51. Leiden/Boston: Brill.

Herskovits, E. M. 1947. 'Statement on Human Rights'. *American Anthropologist* 49: 539–43.

ICOMOS. 1994. Nara Document on Authenticity, 1–6 November 1994. UNESCO Doc. WHC-94/CONF.003/INF.008.

Jakubowski, A. 2018. 'Resolution 2347: Mainstreaming the Protection of Cultural Heritage at the Global Level'. *Questions of International Law*. 31 March 2018. <http://www.qil-qdi.org/resolution-2347-mainstreaming-protection-cultural-heritage-global-level>

Jones, P. 2016. 'Group Rights'. In E. N. Zalta, ed. *The Stanford Encyclopedia of Philosophy*. <https://plato.stanford.edu/archives/sum2016/entries/rights-group>

Joona, T. 2012. *ILO Convention No. 169 in a Nordic Context with Comparative Analysis: An Interdisciplinary Approach*. Rovaniemi: University of Lapland.

Jovanović, M. 2016. 'Cultural Rights as Collective Rights'. In A. Jakubowski, ed. *Cultural Rights as Collective Rights: An International Law Perspective*, 15–35. Boston/Leiden: Brill.

Kirsch, S. 2018. *Engaged Anthropology: Politics Beyond the Text*. Oakland: University of California Press.

Kuper, A. 2003. 'The Return of the Native'. *Current Anthropology* 44(3): 389–402.

Kymlicka, W. 1989. *Liberalism, Community, and Culture*. New York: Oxford University Press.

Kymlicka, W. 1995. *Multicultural Citizenship: A Liberal Theory of Minority Rights*. New York: Oxford University Press.

Labadi, S. 2013. *UNESCO, Cultural Heritage and Outstanding Universal Value: Value-based Analysis of the World Heritage and Intangible Cultural Heritage Conventions*. Lanham: Rowman & Littlefield.

Lenzerini, F. 2014. *The Culturalization of Human Rights Law*. Oxford: Oxford University Press.

Lévi-Straus, C. 1952. *Race and History*. Paris: UNESCO Publishing.

Lévi-Strauss, L. 2000. 'Diversité, universalité et representativité dans la list du patrimoine mondial'. In F. Francioni, A. Del Vecchio, and P. De Caterini, eds. *Protezione internazionale del patrimonio culturale: interessi nazionali e difesa del patrimonio comune della cultura: atti del Convegno, Roma, 8–9 maggio 1998*, 21–33. Milano: Giuffré.

Lixinski, L. 2019. *International Heritage Law for Communities. Exclusion and Re-Imagination*. Oxford: Oxford University Press.

Logan, W. 2007. 'Closing Pandora's Box: Human Rights Conundrums in Cultural Heritage Protection'. In H. Silverman and D. Fairchild Ruggles, eds. *Cultural Heritage and Human Rights*, 33–52. New York/Berlin: Springer.

Logan, W., U. Kockel, and M. Nic Craith. 2016. 'The New Heritage Studies: Origins and Evolution, Problems and Prospects'. In W. Logan, U. Kockel, and M. Nic Craith, eds. *A Companion to Heritage Studies*, 1–25. Chichester: Wiley Blackwell.

Lowenthal, D. 1985. *The Past is a Foreign Country*. Cambridge: Cambridge University Press.

Lowenthal, D. 1998. *The Heritage Crusade and the Spoils of History*. Cambridge: Cambridge University Press.

M'Bow, A.-M. 1979. 'A Plea for the Return of an Irreplaceable Cultural Heritage to Those Who Created It, 7 June 1978'. *Museum* 31(1): 58.

MacKay, F. 2018. 'The Case of the *Kaliña and Lokono Peoples v. Suriname* and the UN Declaration on the Rights of Indigenous Peoples: Convergence, Divergence and Mutual Reinforcement'. *Erasmus Law Review* 11(1): 31–42.

Mautner, M. 2011. 'Three Approaches to Law and Culture'. *Cornell Law Review* 96(4): 839–68.

Merry, S. E. 1992. 'Anthropology, Law, and Transnational Processes'. *Annual Review of Anthropology* 21: 357–79.

Merry, S. E. 2001. 'Changing Rights, Changing Culture'. In J. K. Cowan, M.-B. Dembour, and R. A. Wilson, eds. *Culture and Rights: Anthropological Perspectives*, 31–55. Cambridge: Cambridge University Press.

Meskell, L. 2018. *Future in Ruins. UNESCO, World Heritage, and the Dream of Peace*. New York: Oxford University Press.

Messer, E. 1993. 'Anthropology and Human Rights'. *Annual Review of Anthropology* 22: 221–49.

Meyer-Bisch, P., ed. 1993. *Les droits culturels, une catégorie sous-développée de droits de l'homme. Actes du VIIIe colloque interdisciplinaire sur le droits de l'homme*. Fribourg: Editions Universitaires Fribourg Suisse.

Nafziger, J. A., ed. 2017. *Comparative Law and Anthropology*. Cheltenham/Northampton: Edward Elgar.

Pospisil, L. J. 1978. *The Ethnology of Law*, 2nd edn. Menlo Park (CA): Cummings Publishing Co.

Preis, A.-B.S. 1996. 'Human Rights as Cultural Practice: An Anthropological Critique'. *Human Rights Quarterly* 18(2): 286–315.

Prott, L. V. and P. J. O'Keefe. 1992. '"Cultural Heritage" or "Cultural Property"?' *International Journal of Cultural Property* 1(2): 307–20.

Riegl, A. 1903. *Der Moderne Denkmalkultus: Sein Wesen Und Seine Entstehung*. Wien/Leipzig: Braumüller Verlag.

Rosen, L. 2006. *Law as Culture: An Invitation*. Princeton: Princeton University Press.

Sarr, F. and B. Savoy. 2018. 'The Restitution of African Cultural Heritage. Toward A New Relational Ethics'. November 2018. <http://restitutionreport2018.com/sarr_savoy_en.pdf>

Shyllon, F. 2016. 'Collective Cultural Rights as Human Rights Simpliciter: the African and African Charter Example'. In A. Jakubowski, ed. *Cultural Rights as Collective Rights: An International Law Perspective*, 204–21. Boston/Leiden: Brill.

Smith, L. 2006. *Uses of Heritage*. Abingdon: Routledge.

Symonides, J. 1998. 'Cultural Rights: A Neglected Category of Human Rights'. *International Social Science Journal* 50(158): 559–72.

Taylor, C. 1994. 'The Politics of Recognition'. In A. Gutmann, ed. *Multiculturalism: Examining the Politics of Recognition*, 25–74. Princeton: Princeton University Press.

UNESCO. 1994. Expert Meeting on the 'Global Strategy' and Thematic Studies for a Representative World Heritage List, 20–22 June 1994. UNESCO Doc. WHC-94/CONF.003/INF.6.

Urbinati, S. 2015. 'The Community Participation in International Law'. In N. Adell, R.F. Bendix, C. Bortolotto, and M. Tauschek, eds. *Between Imagined Communities and Communities of Practice: Participation, Territory and the Making of Heritage*, 123–40. Göttingen: Universitätsverlag Göttingen.

Vadi, V. 2012. 'Cultural Wealth of Nations in International Law'. *Tulane Journal of International and Comparative Law* 21(1): 87–133.

Vašák, K. 1984. 'Pour une troisième génération des droits de l'homme'. In C. Swinarski, ed. *Études et Essais sur le Droit International Humanitaire et sur les Principes de la Croix Rouge en l'Honneur de Jean Pictet*, 837–45. The Hague: Nijhoff.

Viljoen, F. 2007. *International Human Rights Law in Africa*. Oxford: Oxford University Press.

Vrdoljak, A. F. 2006. *International Law, Museums and the Return of Cultural Objects*. Cambridge: Cambridge University Press.

Vrdoljak, A. F. 2008. 'Reparations for Cultural Loss'. In F. Lenzerini, ed. *Reparations for Indigenous Peoples: International and Comparative Perspectives*, 197–288. Oxford: Oxford University Press.

Vrdoljak, A. F., ed. 2013. *The Cultural Dimension of Human Rights*. Oxford: Oxford University Press.

Winter, T. 2013. 'Clarifying the Critical in Critical Heritage Studies'. *International Journal of Heritage Studies* 19(6): 532–45.

CHAPTER 27

ALTERNATIVE DISPUTE RESOLUTION

FARIS E. NASRALLAH

ALTERNATIVE Dispute Resolution (ADR) is an umbrella term to describe an array of social and institutional methods for resolving disputes. These methods offer individual and collective disputants a panoply of forum shopping options, each taking place in different intrinsic, inherited, and constructed cultural contexts. While not immediately apparent to lawyers or anthropologists, different ADR methods in fact constitute the principal global tools utilized to resolve most international and interstate disputes concerning matters of investment, commerce, and industry. To grasp the magnitude of this necessarily requires both lawyers and anthropologists to break the barriers of habitual thinking about the nature and extent of their disciplinary and interdisciplinary work.

So vast are the offshoots of these different ADR methods as branches of the ADR tree,[1] it is arguably most accurate to apophatically describe ADR by alluding to what it is not; namely the referral or submission to dispute resolution processes in national court systems.[2] Yet, in a phenomenon which underscores the pervasive adoption of ADR methods, national court systems themselves increasingly incorporate ADR-style processes within the scope of their respective mandates, either through pre-action protocols,[3] settlement chambers,[4] or by directly adopting standing arbitration, mediation, and conciliation provisions for certain types of disputes.[5] Beyond bearing the fruits of prospective institutional efficiency, and offering a gateway to a monopoly over justice, ADR processes permeate almost every aspect of our social interactions, both as normative structures that inform ideal behaviour and, where contraventions arise, as forums for navigating disputes from cradle to grave.

Newcomers to interdisciplinary law and anthropology dialogue will observe that the voluminous literature proliferated on the uptake and possible profligacy of ADR methods tends to focus on societies outside the citadels of dominant frameworks of reference.[6] Such ADR systems, often underpinned by 'customary laws' and 'customary practices', can be easily misunderstood as being governed by an entirely separate set of epistemological norms than those applicable to ADR processes conducted within established legal centres and officiated by dominant legal cultures.[7] This chapter suggests that a more holistic view of law and anthropology, through the prism of ADR, can reveal shared tendencies among states, societies, organizations, and individuals alike to seek to resolve disputes on their own terms and in forums that derive their authority from shared normative understandings.

To illustrate certain adaptations of these shared ADR norms, this chapter utilizes ADR as an interface for considering three spheres of law and anthropology relations: (i) the conceptual boundaries between law and anthropology; (ii) convergences between theory and practice; and (iii) understanding emerging social and legal practices. A number of research recommendations are included within each section. In line with the broad chapter title, this contribution seeks to capture, in some small part, the pervasiveness and prevalence of what are ostensibly innumerable micro-legal systems operating globally at every level of social organization, and crucially in the interstices between them.

ADR and the Conceptual Boundaries between Law and Anthropology

The boundaries between law and anthropology have yielded considerable conceptual enquiries, 'from those of the nineteenth-century protolegal anthropologists like Henry Maine, Lewis Morgan, Johann Jakob Bachofen, and John McLennan' (Goodale 2017: 5), through to works on the sociology of law (Ehrlich 1936 [1912]), sharp critiques on the nature of anthropologists' work (Nader 1972), the inherent limits of law (Allott 1980), and contemporary comparative law enquiries (Menski 2006). ADR processes have been central to these enquiries, providing indispensable interfaces for elaborating the contours of law and anthropology respectively, as well as their intrinsic combination.

Sally Falk Moore's work on the relationship between state and non-state law through ADR processes, resulting in her ground-breaking contribution that law itself constituted a 'semi-autonomous social field' (Moore 1973), was followed by lesser known but equally valuable contributions on the utility of ADR for exploring the relationship between indigenous and received law (Chiba 1989),[8] and the theory of legal pluralism (Chiba 1989, 1993).[9] Amidst the continued relevance of ADR processes to both fields of study, the respective attentions of law and anthropology have since pivoted or been directed into the practice of human rights and international law, the former focusing on the emergence of transnational legal and moral forms (Berman 2012; Goldman 2007), and the latter on the role of transnational norms in shaping social practices (Goodale 2006; Merry 2006).

More than twenty-five years after the establishment of the 'ADR movement' in the United States (US) in 1976,[10] resulting in a dramatic surge of ADR in the private domain in the US,[11] Laura Nader delivered a scathing reproach against the movement, stating, 'ADR is not a universally desired improvement, but is often coercive and serving as a mechanism of pacification' (Nader 2002: 37). According to Nader, 'the force and ideological nature of the movement' presented institutional gaps such as the absence of published judgments, thereby preventing common law-style legal development,[12] which had consequently been dodderingly accepted or overlooked by lawyers and legal elites (Nader 2002: 46).[13]

Readers should avoid confusing this critique with an assumption that ADR techniques comprise a symmetrical and codified menu of forum shopping options, each being susceptible to procedural overlords and predictable outcomes. Notwithstanding the possible profligacy of institutionalized ADR processes in the US, the ongoing arbitration practices convened by sharia tribunals, rabbinical courts, and Christian panels within the US justice systems (Broyde 2017) continue to challenge notions about ubiquitous state legal hegemony while also raising questions about arbitrability,[14] applicable law,[15] and enforcement of awards in religiously administered US arbitrations (Bambach 2009).

The US aside, ADR processes, in both spiritual and substantive forms, become interfaces for the active relationships between law and society, law and culture (Cotterrell 1997, 2006; Felstiner et al. 1980; Nelken 2006, 2009, 2014; Provost 2017; Rosen 2006), and law and religion (Ferrari and Cristofori 2010; Sandberg 2015), thereby posing forceful conceptual questions about the nature of law and anthropology respectively, as well as the boundaries between them. A note must be made here on the conceptual impact of different linguistic and cultural terminology regarding the identification and procedural references inherent to varying ADR techniques in different social, national, transnational, and institutional contexts. Lawyers and anthropologists may find similar definitions of their disciplinary ADR terminology in different cultural settings, although ready-made equivalent terms for 'law', 'rules', 'order', and 'anthropology' can diverge significantly or indeed be absent altogether.[16]

Implicit in the design of any research work using ADR processes is a need to locate and appraise the conceptual impact that such processes might have on the principles underlying the research. Having selected their ADR technique and geographic and social contexts of choice, researchers may wish to consider the extent to which ADR processes can inform the underlying theories of law and anthropology, questions over the monopoly over justice and access to it, as well as the position of ADR in inter-jurisdictional conflicts (Nasrallah 2018b) and economic inequalities between states, societies, and individuals. Of further conceptual relevance is the potential for disputants to utilize ADR forums as relative safe spaces outside the guise of official legal forums, which in turn can accentuate identity markers as well as avoid different layers of institutional hierarchy.

For anthropologists entering the world of 'law', the very concept may seem beholden to irretractable battles for primacy (Dworkin 1986; Hart 1961), which are accentuated by certain ADR processes, although seldom subject to deeper enquiry.[17] For lawyers entering the world of anthropology, the discipline might appear to be existentially preoccupied (Comaroff 2010) with persistently proving its relevance (Ingold 2018; Moore 2001). The discipline of anthropology, perhaps trapped in a constant state of becoming, fears going out of fashion, while the concept of law tends to bask in officialdom, reaffirming its perennial in-vogue status. The interface of ADR can offer participants in the law and anthropology dialogue conceptual vantage points beyond disciplinary boundary disputes, commanding a genuine need for in-depth assessment and intimate knowledge gathering of social-legal-normative behaviours that inform and construct ADR processes in different cultural contexts.

ADR and Convergences between Theory and Practice

It has long been argued that systematized legal development takes place in so-called hard cases (Dworkin 1975; Hart 1961), in formal court room settings.[18] Notwithstanding the difficulties of obtaining reported decisions in different ADR fora, ADR processes and outcomes can equally provide fertile ground for understanding legal and social developments. As such, ADR processes compel us to consider not only the identity and context of the ADR technique and social actors involved, but also the technical practice issues at play during and after the lifespan of the proceedings. These practice issues include, but are not limited to, the capacity and nature of the disputing parties and decision-makers, the procedural and substantive issues in dispute, whether any decisions rendered are final and binding, the scope and procedure for any appeals, how parties might enforce those decisions, as well as their real-life consequences.

Insofar as this is the case, and given that ADR processes and practices persist almost irrespective of theoretical debates, ADR naturally becomes an interface for understanding the relationship between theory and practice. Some anthropologists remain wary of interacting with lawyers and judges or developing any sort of anthro-praxis, preferring instead to 'adopt a position of critical distance from the professional practice of both law and anthropology' (Burke 2011: 2). Perhaps understandably, this general aversion would appear to be a consequence of anthropology's dark colonial past, which in turn spawned internal guilt among anthropologists as well as a distrust among those subjected to or the subjects of their work (Dirks 2004; Lewis 1973). There are, however, suggestions that preparing future anthropologists for consultancy work can evolve the commonly held notion that anthropology is a purely theoretical discipline (Foblets 2015).

At the turn of the twenty-first century, it was observed that 'In the 1960s, the possibility of anthropologists regularly teaching in law school would have been anathema, but since the 1960s there has been enormous change and a blurring of disciplines' (Nader 2002: 38). This observation hinted at changes in systemic attitudes towards exchanges between lawyers and anthropologists, at least in North American educational institutions. Outside of the classroom, convergences between law and anthropology practice have been hastened by the incorporation of ADR processes into national legal systems,[19] the development of new legal service industries to accommodate ADR processes,[20] and a corresponding professionalization of anthropology practice, both in the types of research being funded and conducted (Kloos 2019; Sloane-White 2017) and in the application of cultural and other expertise in different dispute settings (Holden 2011, 2019, 2020).[21]

By way of concrete examples of the theory-practice interface, when considering community justice theories and indigenous forms of dispute resolution, researchers may turn to the *Gacaca* courts in Rwanda, a contemporary use of traditional ADR practices as a method for seeking peace and reconciliation following the Rwandan genocide outside the jurisdiction of the Rwandan criminal courts, national courts of other states, or the UN-mandated International Criminal Tribunal for Rwanda (Hankel 2019; Sullo 2018; Wielenga and Harris 2011). For those concerned with the conceptual utility of law and dispute settlement processes as pre-emptive alternatives to war, researchers might assess the value of the phrase 'arbitrating for peace' (Franke et al. 2016), and more broadly the use of arbitration in territorial and boundary disputes between states (Copeland 1999).[22] Similarly, those interested in conflict management and resolution theories can shed light on the growing institutionalization of different methods of international conflict management through ADR processes of negotiation, mediation, and what are sometimes referenced loosely as 'legal approaches' (Greig et al. 2019).

In this respect, as well as being invoked to ameliorate or avoid conflicts, ADR processes can become interfaces for measuring the applicability of different theoretical postulations and their capacity to inform new debates about the practical application of law and anthropology. By way of example, in the field of international arbitration, there are noticeable gaps between representations of practice from those within the international arbitration community (Gaillard 2015) and from those surveying the community from the outside (Dezalay and Garth 1996, 2002). As international arbitration becomes the leading global ADR technique for resolving commercial, trade, and investment disputes, its relationships with and within different national legal orders can become increasingly strained unless managed correctly. Arbitrations as pop-up transnational legal transplants of sorts can potentially provoke a variety of legal culture clashes with far-reaching consequences, revealing as much about the unstated norms deployed by different actors in daily arbitration practice as they do about the construction of narratives around the profession. Due to both educational and professional divergences, the gaps between these narratives are often underscored by a lack of awareness among legal academics and practitioners to consult the vast sociolegal and legal anthropology literature on ADR. Conversely, anthropologists remain largely reticent of practitioner guides and black-letter law resources on ADR (Association for International Arbitration 2009a, 2009b; Ingen Housz 2011).

Researchers drawing on the law and anthropology combination to study ADR processes might consider how their findings will reflect in points of theory within both disciplines. It is preferable that such considerations are borne in mind prior to or at the outset of any participant observation or other fieldwork method. Collecting data from ADR processes can be cumbersome and time-consuming, often resulting in limited access to certain documents or disputants which provide only part of the broader issues at play. Researchers may have to navigate various data collection limitations, regarding confidentiality (Poorooye and Feehily 2017; Rogers 2006), hierarchical or institutional oversight (Ward 2007), business or social secrecy (Dore 2006), the involvement of legal or other representatives in the proceedings and their own professional or social duties and interests, potential fragility and frictions between the disputing parties, questions over the authority of the ADR setting and its decision-makers (Tupman 1989), the technical issues in dispute, and the language of the parties and the proceedings (Harpole 2016).

While there is a growing body of ethnographic literature on the conduct and practices within courtroom settings (French 2009; Latour 2009; Lynch 1997; Scheffer 2010), there is scope for further ethnographic work in the boardrooms, business centres, and hospitality facilities where most hearings are conducted in more formal ADR processes.[23] To this end, researchers should not be deterred by the above-mentioned potential limitations, and should consider whether it is possible, practical, or desirable to collect data through inside access and observational participation in meetings, hearings, and other engagements surrounding a particular ADR process. Perhaps closer attention to these methodological and research design issues is needed to unlock future debates about the relationship between theory and practice through the interface of ADR.

ADR and Understanding Emerging Social and Legal Practices

By focusing on ADR processes in different cultural contexts, researchers can capture and understand emerging social and legal practices. When viewed through the law and anthropology combination, such ADR processes can draw out facets of normative social and legal behaviour. Taking ADR as an interface for capturing these trends, it is possible to explore the continuity and re-emergence of ancient forms of dispute settlement, dispute avoidance strategies, and religious dispute governance, the impact of transnational, globalized, and online ADR practices, as well as the role of state law in managing such movements. By reference to certain examples, it is suggested that new or reconstituted ADR processes and practices have an in-built capacity to guide and inform research on the emerging social and legal practices of individual and collective disputants. The following ADR examples are purposefully drawn from a vast canvas of historical, regional, religious, and cultural settings, and intend to offer users of this handbook multiple windows through which to consider the different applications of ADR, as well as their prevalence and pervasiveness. It is perhaps this apparent ubiquity that calls into question the accuracy of the term 'alternative' when situating ADR processes.

Whereas the development of most civilizations was coupled with the espousal or acquisition of different laws and procedures for dispute settlement, contemporary ADR practices can be used to assess the re-emergence or re-constitution of these ancient and historical methods. For example, it has been suggested that contemporary Indian societies continue to rely on classical Hindu law concepts such as *daṇḍa* (punishment), *vyavahāra* (dispute resolution), and *sadācāra* (good behaviour), which require disputants and those administering dispute processes to remain 'in constant consideration of situational relativity' (Menski 2003: 31–2). In these situations, 'the deeper purpose of disputation and settling disputes, as processes of ascertaining *dharma*, is to protect macrocosmic and microcosmic order, not just to decide disputes' (Menski 2003: 549–50).[24]

In the Arab world, a number of ancient Arab customary law concepts and processes continue to shape social and institutional interactions and dispute settlement throughout the modern Middle East. *Tahkeem* (arbitration) is an ancient Arab customary law technique deriving from the Arabic word for judgment or *hukum*, and is rooted as a concept in pre-Islamic Arab societies. Arbitration was adopted through the passage of Christianity and Islam, the Prophet himself sitting as an arbitrator (Hallaq 2005: 24), in various Arab empires and enlightenments as well as in the periods of Ottoman and European imperialism in the Middle East, retaining etymological continuity throughout. This is equally reflected in the Talmudic legal tradition, where arbitration is afforded pride of place in Jewish law (Steinberg 2000), and continued recourse to which is most poignantly underscored in contemporary arbitration and mediation services offered by various Beth Din institutions.[25]

Whether in the form of dedicated civil procedure code provisions or stand-alone legislation, arbitration resiliently takes its place within the dispute resolution tapestry of modern Middle Eastern states and Arab societies in personal, private, and public law disputes (El-Aḥdab and El-Aḥdab 2011; Najjar 2018). As dispute resolution practitioners working in the Middle East know all too well, facets of Arab customary law often invade the landscape of modern arbitration practice, whereby the desire to retain ostensible or substantive compliance with sharia principles can influence party engagement and cooperation as well as national court enforcement of arbitral awards and other settlement decisions.

Sulh (the act of resolving conflict, creating peace and reconciliation) is a pre-Islamic method of resolving disputes outside the guise of formal state processes, which continues to exist in various forms across the Middle East.[26] In contemporary Arab societies the concept of *sulh* is most commonly used as an informal dispute resolution mechanism for resolving family, village, or sectarian disputes outside the reach of state authorities. The technique of *sulh* is typically administered by a *mokhtar* (in Arabic literally meaning the 'chosen one'), denoting a local or village representative seeking authority from within their community to preserve social harmony and community relations and to resolve disputes invariably arising from breaches of personal or family honour (Nasrallah 2011: 201).

Tawseet (mediation), which has a different framework of reference in traditional and modern Arab customary law, continues to be applied in contemporary disputes, either as an escalation towards arbitration or as a self-sufficient process in its own right.[27] The coalescing norms and virtues inherent in these Arab customary law concepts and processes continues to inform not only contemporary ADR practices, but also approaches to diplomacy and international relations throughout the region. It is worth noting that similarly prevalent and resilient forms of ancient ADR in other customary and institutional law settings have become areas of interest for comparative law (Menski 2006) and commercial law enquiries (Kidane 2012).

With respect to dispute avoidance, ADR practices and processes can shed light on existing and emerging strategies deployed by individuals, communities, corporations, and states in order to avert the actual or perceived hostilities or inequities of formal dispute resolution settings. As Werner Menski (2003: 560) lucidly summarizes:

> Postmodern states everywhere in South Asia now realize that they cannot perform the various large-scale functions they claimed to exercise. The modern state manifestly took on too much, and now has to admit this. The resulting gap points to a need to engage in private and public postmodern re-education about the value of self-controlled ordering. While the state continues to offer a formal hierarchical framework for dispute settlement and adversarial claims, the deeper message of India's postmodern state law seems to be that it does not want to be used. Contemporary postmodern Hindu law operates, then, on the basis of a reworked symbiosis of central state law and local legal orders, within an overarching higher order.

At micro or interstate levels, dispute avoidance strategies through recourse to ADR can be useful for considering the interstices between unofficial law systems and national legal orders. Taking for example Chinese communities in the UK, where social exclusion (Chau and Yu 2001) collided with expected assimilation to 'English core values' (Poulter 1986), a particular cultural practice of formal dispute avoidance has occurred, notwithstanding a Chinese minority presence in the UK for over 150 years (May 1978). Whereas it is known that UK Chinese community organizations 'offer social, cultural, educational and mediation services in conversation with state public services' (Kwan et al. 2007: 528), due to a lack of resources, it has been suggested that such organizations 'might eventually turn from being what they are at present, "weak" organizations, into "silent" ones. The result is simply the further exclusion and misunderstanding of the UK Chinese people' (Kwan et al. 2007: 529). These active ADR processes and interactions evidently raise questions over the reach of official law systems, and how certain communities navigate their relationship with state power, that would appear to offer ripe raw materials for law and anthropology research.

Regarding religious ADR practices, academic attention has focused on minority religious communities and personal law systems, both in the European context with emphasis on Islamic ADR practices (Bano 2012; Cesari 2014; Sona 2016, 2018), but also with respect to Christian minority ADR practices in the Middle East (Elsässer 2019; Engelcke 2018) and South Asia (Chaterjee 2010). Religious ADR practices might also be assessed for their role in establishing internal authorities and systems of hierarchical power, which can have the capacity to construct and ringfence minority identities and communities (Keshavjee 2013). As such, there remains scope for up-to-date appraisals of religious ADR practices among majority religious communities in Europe[28] and North America (Canon Law Society of America 1969; Fitzgerald and Fitzgerald 1993; King et al. 1997). Perhaps of interest for future law and anthropology research are the influences of religiously inspired indigenous and inherited ADR practices on state systems and micro-jurisdictions across the vast hybrid legal expanses of different regions in Africa, which continue to be characterized by loose references to the entire continent (Nolan-Haley 2015).

With a view to ADR-related social trends, dominant voices have been heard in internationalized 'access to justice' aspirations, partly as a result of the ADR movement established in the US, but also in respect of broader social developments towards open government and increased transparency (Bianchi and Peters 2013). Conversely, the pervasive uptake of ADR processes invites further study into trends of increased litigiousness in different social, religious, and commercial contexts, even in legal cultures where participation in formal court proceedings is generally frowned upon or associated with dishonour or loss of face (Ginsburg and Hoetker 2006). When recognized ADR practitioners scoff at the fact that 'The only clubs missing in arbitration are those reflecting social class divides. The Proletarian Arbitration League has yet to be created' (Gaillard 2015: 9), the very mention of that fact appears to lay down the gauntlet for such enquiries. Whether in respect of contractual defaults or other breaches relating to the global financial crisis or Covid-19 pandemic, the default assumption can hardly be that national court systems will readily accept or be capable of solely undertaking the heavy lifting of voluminous caseloads arising from such disputes.

Concerning the role of the state in ADR practices and processes, obvious conceptual questions emerge on monopolies over justice and the limits of state law. Absent express national policies towards ADR practices as a whole, a large number of states invariably opt to encourage the development of independent ADR micro-systems for specific industries and communities, that seek judicial assistance in procedural and enforcement matters, if and when required.[29] Alternatively, trends towards the institutionalization and judicialization of ADR practices have been recognized, whereby ADR processes are increasingly influenced by or brought under the direct guise of national court systems (Trakman and Montgomery 2017).[30] To reaffirm the applicability of official state law, national legal systems ordinarily seek to regulate ADR practices, sometimes asymmetrically between different communities or types of disputes (Pearl and Menski 1998: 68–73). The regulatory powers of the state can relate to existential matters of state control, but equally to pressing financial or capacity concerns reflected in economic measures to streamline efficient and cost-effective dispute management.

Necessarily, states are also concerned with avoiding or punishing corruption in ADR practices, as well as the deployment of guerrilla tactics by parties in different local and international ADR forums (Wilske and Horvath 2013). To this end, there remains the constant threat of abuse and manipulation of traditional customary forms of ADR[31] as well as their institutionalized contemporary adaptations (Reisman and Skinner 2014). In respect of non-commercial disputes, state harnessing of indigenous forms of ADR appears to be a more intuitive process, distinct from the issues faced by states seeking or requested to officiate or recognize non-indigenous ADR practices. For example, considerable attention has been paid to the social, cultural, and institutional consequences of officially regulating sharia councils in Britain (Al-Astewani 2019; Bano 2012), which remains an open question. By way of contrast, in Iraq, Iraqi Law No. 13 of 2011, the Law of Mokhtars,[32] readily codifies the role of *mokhtars*,[33] the criteria for their candidacy and requirement for state licensing,[34] the term of their appointments,[35] their capacity to serve in certain disputes,[36] entitlement to remuneration,[37] and duties towards state agencies and confidentiality (Nasrallah 2011: 201–2).[38]

At a global legal level, ADR processes offer canvasses for assessing transnational social and legal practices and the internationalization of certain types of disputes and resolution techniques. Whether in respect of 'hybrid legal systems as legal laboratories' (Nasrallah and Blanke 2020), or legal transplants and implants, ADR processes and practices can shine light on emerging transnational communities comprising disputants, professional practitioners, and other stakeholders, as well as the norms and behaviours that these communities create and adhere to in culture-specific environments. Regarding less permanent importations of special tribunals, panels, and committees, including those under the auspices of international organizations, conventions, and treaties, constitutional law questions also arise about the jurisdictional efficacy of such forums and their compliance with national or religiously informed public order requirements.

The emergence of online dispute resolution (ODR), which has already been adopted into national court systems (Abdel Wahab et al. 2012), and at the European level in respect of online retail disputes,[39] has consequences for both governing bodies and disputing parties, which largely remain unexplored. ODR processes offer a window for the law and anthropology combination to assess these developments, particularly in a post Covid-19 world, where transnational face-to-face meetings have been suspended indefinitely and largely replaced by online interactions. Whereas certain ADR communities have moved faster than others in response to these developments,[40] developing new and existing ODR procedural rules and practices for convening meetings, hearings, and the taking of witness evidence fulfils only part of the mandate awaiting a brave new world (Piers and Aschauer 2018).

Conclusion

This chapter has endeavoured to offer insight into the prevalence and pervasiveness of ADR processes and practices both past and present. Using ADR as an interface for reconceptualizing interdisciplinary boundaries, appraising the relationship between theory and practice, and understanding emerging social and legal practices, it is suggested that ADR processes present fertile ground for novel conceptual and empirical research in law and anthropology, as well as in their combination. Focusing on the correlative questions that these interfaces raise, is it also suggested that lawyers, anthropologists, and those in between can utilize a cross-section of global ADR fora as canvasses for mapping the shared proclamations and proclivities of individuals, communities, corporations, and states in different dispute scenarios. Crucially, insofar as these shared norms are self-evident or capable of being revealed, they indicate that there is immense scope and value in combining both fields of study.

That there remains no universally agreed definition of law underscores its amorphous nature and is arguably the reason for its ubiquity. The concept of law is able to permeate fluidly between different social and institutional interactions, reasserting itself at different points in time, whether in the form of defined principles, authoritative decision-making capacities, or institutions. When appropriately contextualized, ADR processes invite assessments of the changing faces of law, its flexible nature, and the consequences of its permeations at different stages of state-administered or state-sanctioned dispute processes. With a more nascent institutional history, the discipline of anthropology more readily accepts what it can and cannot achieve or claim to achieve. This has not stopped the discipline from evolving to incorporate different types of professional expertise, which are increasingly applied in various dispute settings. Insofar as anthropologists lean towards engaging with that which is rare and exceptional over that which is commonplace, they are perhaps best placed to chart the existence of ADR processes that fall outside of state control entirely. Unconventional, non-institutionalized ADR practices and processes will most likely remain alluring for anthropologists pursuing the law and anthropology combination.

This chapter has alluded to the fact that cultures, societies, and legal systems invariably employ elements of ADR processes, whether administered socially or institutionally, in accordance with religious or other normative principles, in the context of family disputes, commercial disputes, or in disputes between states. This leaves researchers interested in ADR processes with an incredibly wide gambit of options. Perhaps daunting at first, this apparent innumerability can be refined through recourse to relationships between theory and practice, which are actualized by different ADR processes. This should encourage researchers in both disciplines, as well as those pursuing a combination, to undertake novel, technical, and conceptually challenging work on local, transnational, institutionalized, and informal ADR processes, including those closest to home.

Notes

1. The concept of the 'dispute tree' was recently deployed as a contemporary sociolegal revaluation of the 'dispute pyramid' metaphor devised by the Civil Litigation Research Project in the 1980s to broadly describe dispute resolution processes (see Albiston et al. 2014: 105–31).
2. Roberts and Palmer (2005: 44) define the contemporary ADR movement as follows: 'A general aversion to state-based formal justice, or religious, political, ethnic or territorial forces, or a felt need to refurbish courts and other agencies of formal justice are perhaps the most common contexts—sometimes enclaves—within which ideologies and practices of informal justice have most readily taken hold.'

3. Such pre-action protocols were introduced in England and Wales following the fundamental review of the civil justice system undertaken by Lord Woolf between 1994 and 1996, which resulted in the publication of the *Access to Justice, Interim Report* in 1995 and *Access to Justice, Final Report* in 1996 (Woolf 1995, 1996). For a contemporaneous review of what are commonly referred to as the 'Woolf reforms', see Zuckerman 1996. For a more recent appraisal of the Woolf reforms in the broader context of civil justice, see Genn 2010.
4. See e.g. Dubai in the United Arab Emirates, which established a Centre for Amicable Settlement of Disputes (the 'Dubai Courts CASD') in 2009, pursuant to Dubai Law No. 16 of 2009. Aimed at encouraging early settlement of disputes without resorting to formal litigation in the Dubai Courts, the Dubai Courts CASD became operational in 2011 and is one of a number of special tribunals established within the court system of Dubai. By way of further example, special tribunals were established pursuant to Dubai Law No. 26 of 2007, to resolve disputes between landlords and tenants; Dubai Decree No. 56 of 2009, for the settlement of cheque disputes relating to real estate transactions; and Dubai Decree No. 26 of 2013, which established the 'Rent Disputes Settlement Centre' to hear rent disputes.
5. Uniquely among other Middle Eastern jurisdictions, Bahrain has integrated arbitration into the standing judicial infrastructure of the state. Pursuant to Bahraini Decree No. 30 of 2009, on the Bahrain Chamber for Economic, Financial and Investment Dispute Resolution (amended by Legislative Decree No. 65 of 2014) ('Bahraini Decree No. 30 of 2009'), the Bahrain Ministry of Justice entered into a partnership with the American Arbitration Association, creating the Bahrain Chamber for Dispute Resolution-American Arbitration Association (BCDR-AAA). Under Art. 9 of Bahraini Decree No. 30 of 2009, the Court of the BCDR has primary jurisdiction over the Bahraini Courts to hear disputes brought by or against financial institutions licensed by the Central Bank of Bahrain or of an international commercial nature, where the claim value exceeds 500,000 Bahraini Dinars (about $1.3 million). In Germany, pursuant to a joint initiative of the German National Anti-Doping Agency and the German Arbitration Institute, the German Court of Arbitration for Sport was established on 1 January 2008 as an independent arbitration court for sports-related matters, with arbitration proceedings taking place on the basis of specific DIS Sports Arbitration Rules, see <https://www.disarb.org/en/tools-for-dis-proceedings/dis-rules> accessed 7 February 2021.
6. See e.g. Bohannan 1957, 1997; Chanock 1985; Gluckman 1955, 1997; and the locations chosen in Benda-Beckmann 1981 and Nader and Todd 1978. More recently and in the same vein, see Anying and Gausset 2017 on Northern Uganda. The well-trodden 'rural village', 'closed community' methods for anthropological fieldwork hardly need adumbrating.
7. For an assessment of the relationship and power differentials between 'Western' and 'non-Western' approaches to law, see Haldar 2008 and Ruskola 2013. When the disciplines of law and anthropology are combined to address normative systems in dominant legal cultures, these often focus on formal court systems and institutional dispute resolution arenas (see e.g. Latour 2009, and more recently Niezen and Sapignoli 2017).
8. For Masaji Chiba, the interconnected attributes of law were best described as (i) 'official law', defined as 'the legal system authorized by the legitimate authority of a country' (Chiba 1986: 319); (ii) 'unofficial law' as 'the legal system which is not officially authorized by the official authorities, but authorized in practice by the general consensus of a certain circle of people', and which has 'a distinct influence upon the effectiveness of official law' (Chiba 1986: 336); and (iii) 'legal postulates', which Chiba distinguished from legal rules,

as 'the system of values and ideals specifically relevant to both official and unofficial law in founding and orienting the latter' (Chiba 1986: 351).

9. Masaji Chiba developed an integrated model of law consisting of three dichotomies: 'official v. unofficial law', 'legal postulates v. legal rules', and 'indigenous v. transplanted law' (Chiba 1993).
10. The ADR movement is generally considered to have been founded following the National Conference on the Causes of Popular Dissatisfaction with the Administration of Justice, convened in St. Paul, Minnesota, in 1976, often referred to as the 'Pound Conference' (see Stone 2004 and Nader 2002).
11. According to Katherine Stone, 92,000 arbitration requests were filed with the American Arbitration Association in 1998 alone (Stone 2004 provides further statistics on the uptake of ADR in the US). Whereas such ADR processes ordinarily apply to trade, civil, and commercial disputes, the US Supreme Court has confirmed its extension to include recourse to arbitration in consumer disputes (see *AT&T Mobility LLC v. Concepcion Et Ux*, United States Supreme Court Case No. 09–893, decided on 27 April 2011).
12. On the increasing proliferation and value of published court decisions relating to arbitration in the United Arab Emirates, see Nasrallah 2018a.
13. This in part seems to have influenced Laura Nader's subsequent writing on the 'Americanization of international law' and US-led transnational legal processes, which she regarded as tools of hegemonic cultural and economic domination (see Mattei and Nader 2008). See also Roberts and Palmer (2005: 43–78), who recognized that the contemporary ADR movement faced 'stiff and sometimes fierce resistance', and explained the main strands of this criticism.
14. By way of example, the Beth Din of America based in New York 'serves the North American Jewish community as a forum for the adjudication of commercial, communal and matrimonial conflicts', see <http://bethdin.org/wp-content/uploads/2015/07/ArbBrochure.pdf> accessed 2 February 2021.
15. The Sharia Board of America offers arbitration in family matters as well as dispute resolution services 'related to business partnerships and various other issues posing challenges to the community', such disputes to be 'resolved and arbitrated in the light of the Qur'an & Sunnah', see <https://shariahboard.org/darulqadha> accessed 2 February 2021.
16. References to ADR processes and forum shopping options in established legal centres tend to be confined to an institutionalized cartography including arbitration, mediation, conciliation, adjudication, and med-arb (see e.g. Stone 2004, 2009). On the different aspects of translation in anthropology, see Montgomery 2000; Rubel and Rosman 2003; and Tymoczo and Gentzler 2002.
17. It is notable that even Thomas Hobbes, one of the foremost historical proponents of the sovereignty of law, was sufficiently moved by the prevalence of arbitration practice to repeatedly mention arbitrators as the proprietors of 'another justice' (Hobbes 1651: 92–6).
18. Ronald Dworkin defined 'hard cases' broadly as 'those cases in which the result is not clearly dictated by statute or precedent' (Dworkin 1975: 1057), and which as a result relied on the positivist theory of adjudication, that judges use their discretion to decide hard cases. According to Dworkin, the theory of adjudication, a far from morally perfected process, failed to resolve the dilemma of judicial decision-making and was susceptible to political and social influences as well as the process of judicial selection (Dworkin 1975). Attention should be paid not to conflate such references to 'judicial adjudication' with procedural forms of 'ADR adjudication', as is adopted in international tribunals (Jacob

2012) and increasingly in construction industry disputes (see e.g. Hibberd and Newman 1999). On the practice of rule-following and the adaption of rules in decision-making, see McDowell 1981 and Twining and Miers 2010.

19. For an example from the jurisdiction of England and Wales, and in accordance with the Arbitration Act 1996, see the *Practice Guidance: Arbitration in the Family Court*, issued by Sir James Munby, President of the Family Division on 23 November 2015, available at <https://www.judiciary.uk/publications/practice-guidance-arbitration-in-the-family-court/> accessed 2 February 2021.
20. See the Chartered Institute of Arbitrators, a not-for-profit charitable organization that operates through a global network of forty-one branches and which offers education, training, professional qualifications, and practitioner guidance resources on arbitration, with members from a broad range of occupational and academic backgrounds and disciplines (see <https://www.ciarb.org> accessed 2 February 2021). More recent examples of the burgeoning ADR services sector include the Family Law Arbitration Financial Scheme, launched by the Institute of Family Law Arbitrators in 2012 to provide arbitration for financial and property disputes in the family law context (see <http://ifla.org.uk/> accessed 2 February 2021), and the Centre for Effective Dispute Resolution, a London-based mediation and ADR body, founded as a non-profit organization in 1990 to promote mediation and ADR through accredited training courses offered to individual practitioners, law firms, and banks (see <https://www.cedr.com/> accessed 2 February 2021).
21. For a broader assessment of the anthropologist as an expert witness, see Foblets and Renteln 2009; Renteln 2004; and Vetters and Foblets 2016. To capture the historical trajectory of such mandates, see also Geertz 1973 and Rosen 1977. By way of example of this practice in the UK, social anthropology scholar-practitioners Anthony Good and Tobias Kelly each attested to having acted as a country expert in over 500 and 150 asylum and immigration appeals respectively as part of a 'best practice guide' drafted for experts (Good and Kelly 2013).
22. Notable examples include the *Rann of Kutch Arbitration*, concerning the dispute between India and Pakistan over the Rann of Kutch Indo-Pakistan Western Boundary; the Award rendered on 19 February 1968 (United Nations Report of International Arbitral Awards, XVII: 1–576); the *Taba Arbitration*, concerning the location of boundary markers in Taba between Egypt and Israel; the Award rendered on 29 September 1988 (United Nations Report of International Arbitral Awards, Vol. XX, 1–118); and a host of territorial boundary disputes concerning the international boundaries within the Arabian peninsula, involving Bahrain, Iran, Iraq, Jordan, Kuwait, Oman, Qatar, Syria, Saudi Arabia, the United Arab Emirates, and Yemen, and which are commonly referenced as the *Arabian Boundary Disputes*. A repository of documents relating to the *Arabian Boundary Disputes* has been published in a twenty-volume set comprising 18,000 pages (Schofield 1992).
23. For further reference on conducting qualitative research and the use of ethnography as a tool in legal research, see Griffiths 2005 and Travers 2001.
24. According to Werner Menski, it follows that '*vyavahāra* cannot properly just be read as 'civil law'. It is first of all a tool of dharma, a technique to bring about order and balance with minimal interference from outside agents, such as judges and the state. The concept of *vyavahāra* may look secular to an outside observer. But from an insider's perspective, it is not only religious, in the broad sense in which everything in the Hindu cosmic vision could be said to have a religious dimension ..., but is at the same time also social, legal, and everything else that may be relevant in any specific scenario of dispute settlement. A

diversity-focused, postmodern interpretation of this ancient concept confirms therefore that, long before the current postmodern age, ancient Hindus were able to handle plurality and interdisciplinarity in a way that reflects the integrated and central nature of dharma as self-controlled ordering rather than technical "law". Rather than being treated as skilfully constructed manuals for ancient litigators, texts like the *Nāradasmṛti* should therefore be read as expressions of concern for the protection of this dharmic self-controlled order' (Menski 2003: 549–50).

25. Notably, the London Beth Din offers arbitration services for commercial disputes, stating that 'the decision (Award) given by the Beth Din has the full force of an Arbitration Award and, if necessary, may be enforced by the civil courts. The arbitration process taking place at the Beth Din is known as a Din Torah. Arbitrations take place within the framework of the Arbitration Act 1996 and therefore conform to procedural aspects of English arbitration law' (see <https://www.theus.org.uk/article/arbitration-dinei-torah> accessed 3 February 2021). The English family law courts have gone as far as recognizing an arbitral award delivered by a New York Beth Din, thereby considering interactions between Jewish, US, and English law (see *Re AI and MT* [2013] EWHC 100 (Fam)).
26. It has been suggested that arbitration itself is an integral part of *Sulh*, which consequently represents an umbrella term for ADR in Arab customary law (Keshavjee 2013: 66–9).
27. See e.g. the Mediation Rules adopted by the Emirates Maritime Arbitration Centre, itself established in accordance with Dubai Decree No. 14 of 2016.
28. For references, see various contributions published in the *Ecclesiastical Law Journal* since 1987.
29. This form of equidistance is prevalent in the approach of most national legal systems towards the practice of local and international commercial arbitration, by reference to the United Nations Convention on the Recognition and Enforcement of Foreign Arbitral Awards signed in New York on 10 June 1958, and the UNCITRAL Model Law adopted by the United Nations Commission on International Trade Law on 21 June 1985, and amended most recently in 2006.
30. This has been particularly apparent in the global trend towards establishing international commercial courts as a way of importing the perceived efficiency and expertise of ADR processes into national court systems. See e.g. the establishment of the Dubai International Financial Centre Courts in 2004, Civil and Commercial Court of the Qatar Financial Center, Qatar International Court in 2009, Abu Dhabi Global Market Court in 2013, Singapore International Commercial Court in 2015, China International Commercial Court in 2018, Netherlands Commercial Court in 2019, and Frankfurt Chamber for International Commercial Disputes in 2019.
31. In Palestine, the indigenous ADR technique of *sulh*, historically reserved for Palestinian Jews, Muslims, Christians, Druze, and Bedouins (Cook and Jabbour 1993: 17), found itself subjected to abuse and manipulation by individual and institutional agents of settler colonialism after 1948. In a particular case involving the murder of Ahmed Qablawi in 1954 by a settler in the village of Saffourieh in Galilee, the settlers' use of *sulh* against the will of Qablawi's family as a method of avoiding criminal trial and punishment, despite applications for state involvement, has been described as 'forgiveness offered under extreme duress' (Hoffman 2009: 243).
32. Issued on 18 July 2011 by the Presidential Council of Iraq.
33. Defined in a legal context as a 'local or village representative, often an elder or wise male, whose place among other Mokhtars in a given region or locality, is to preserve social

harmony, develop community relations and arbitrate on matters including but not limited to personal disputes, escalations of local violence and matters concerning individual or family honour' (Nasrallah 2011: 201).

34. Articles 3 and 4 of Iraqi Law No. 13 of 2011, the Law of Mokhtars.
35. Article 5 of Iraqi Law No. 13 of 2011, the Law of Mokhtars.
36. Articles 6 and 7 of Iraqi Law No. 13 of 2011, the Law of Mokhtars.
37. Article 9 of Iraqi Law No. 13 of 2011, the Law of Mokhtars.
38. Article 10 of Iraqi Law No. 13 of 2011, the Law of Mokhtars.
39. See the European ODR platform provided by the European Commission for the resolution of consumer complaints and disputes over goods or services purchased via online stores, retailers, and traders in the European Union (EU), Iceland, Liechtenstein, and Norway, pursuant to Regulation No 524/2013 of the European Parliament and of the Council, dated 21 May 2013.
40. See e.g. the draft 'Protocol for Online Case Management in International Arbitration', prepared by the Working Group on LegalTechAdoption in International Arbitration, and circulated in July 2020, available at <https://protocol.techinarbitration.com/p/1> accessed 4 February 2021.

References

Abdel Wahab, M., E. Katsh, and D. Rainey, eds. 2012. *Online Dispute Resolution: Theory and Practice. A Treatise on Technology and Dispute Resolution*. The Hague: Eleven International Publishing.

Al-Astewani, A. 2019. 'The Legal Framework for Regulating Shariah Councils in the UK: A Potential Model for Ireland?' In K. O'Sullivan, ed. *Minority Religions under Irish Law*, 193–216. Leiden: Brill.

Albiston, C. R., L. B. Edelman, and J. Milligan. 2014. 'The Dispute Tree and the Legal Forest'. *Annual Review of Law and Social Science* 10: 105–31.

Allott, A. 1980. *The Limits of Law*. London: Butterworths.

Anying, I. W. and Gausset, Q. 2017. 'Gender and Forum Shopping in Land Conflict Resolution in Northern Uganda'. *The Journal of Legal Pluralism and Unofficial Law* 49(3): 353–72.

Association for International Arbitration, ed. 2009a. *Chinese Arbitration: A Selection of Pitfalls*. Antwerpen: Maklu.

Association for International Arbitration. 2009b. *Alternative Dispute Resolution in the Energy Sector*. Antwerpen: Maklu.

Bambach, L. A. 2009. 'The Enforceability of Arbitration Decisions Made by Muslim Religious Tribunals: Examining the Beth Din Precedent'. *Journal of Law and Religion* 25(2): 379–414.

Bano, S. 2012. *Muslim Women and Shari'ah Councils: Transcending the Boundaries of Community and Law*. London: Palgrave Macmillan.

Benda-Beckmann, K. von. 1981. 'Forum Shopping and Shopping Forums: Dispute Processing in a Minangkabau Village in West Sumatra'. *The Journal of Legal Pluralism and Unofficial Law* 13(19): 117–59.

Berman, P. S. 2012. *Global Legal Pluralism: A Jurisprudence of Law Beyond Borders*. Cambridge: Cambridge University Press.

Bianchi, A. and A. Peters, eds. 2013. *Transparency in International Law*. Cambridge: Cambridge University Press.

Bohannan, P. 1957. *Justice and Judgment Among the Tiv of Nigeria*. London: Oxford University Press.
Bohannan, P. 1997. 'Ethnography and Comparison in Legal Anthropology'. In L. Nader, ed. *Law in Culture and Society*, 401–18. Berkeley: University of California Press.
Broyde M. J. 2017. *Sharia Tribunals, Rabbinical Courts, and Christian Panels: Religious Arbitration in America and the West*. Oxford: Oxford University Press.
Burke, P. 2011. *Law's Anthropology: From Ethnography to Expert Testimony in Native Title*. Canberra: ANU E Press.
Canon Law Society of America. 1969. 'Due Process in Canon Law'. *The Catholic Lawyer* 15(4): 278–307 (*Report of the Ad Hoc Committee on Due Process to the Canon Law Society of America*, 21 October 1969, Cleveland, Ohio).
Cesari, J., ed. 2014. *The Oxford Handbook of European Islam*. Oxford: Oxford University Press.
Chanock, M. 1985. *Law, Custom, and Social Order: The Colonial Experience in Malawi and Zambia*. Cambridge: Cambridge University Press.
Chaterjee, N. 2010. 'Religious Change, Social Conflict and Legal Competition: The Emergence of Christian Personal Law in Colonial India'. *Modern Asian Studies* 44(6): 1147–95.
Chau, C. M. and W. K. Yu. 2001. 'Social Exclusion of Chinese People in Britain'. *Critical Social Policy* 21(1): 103–25.
Chiba, M. 1986. *Asian Indigenous Law: In Interaction with Received Law*. London/New York: Routledge and Kegan Paul.
Chiba, M. 1989. *Legal Pluralism: Toward a General Theory through Japanese Legal Culture*. Tokyo: Tokai University Press.
Chiba, M. 1993. 'Legal Pluralism in Sri Lankan Society: Toward a General Theory of Non-Western Law'. *Journal of Legal Pluralism and Unofficial Law* 33: 197–212.
Comaroff, J. 2010. 'The End of Anthropology, Again: On the Future of an In/Discipline'. *American Anthropologist* 112(4): 524–38.
Cook, T. C., Jr. and E. J. Jabbour, eds. 1993. *Sulha. Palestinian Traditional Peacemaking Processes*. Israel: House of Hope.
Copeland, C. S. 1999. 'The Use of Arbitration to Settle Territorial Disputes'. *Fordham Law Review* 67(6): 3073–3108.
Cotterrell, R. 1997. 'The Concept of Legal Culture'. In D. Nelken, ed. *Comparing Legal Cultures*, 13–31 Aldershot: Dartmouth.
Cotterrell, R. 2006. 'Law in Culture'. In R. Cotterrell, ed. *Law, Culture and Society: Legal Ideas in the Mirror of Social Theory*, 97–108. Aldershot: Ashgate.
Dezalay, Y. and B. G. Garth. 1996. *Dealing in Virtue. International Commercial Arbitration and the Construction of a Transnational Legal Order*. Chicago: University of Chicago Press.
Dezalay, Y. and B. G. Garth. 2002. *The Internationalization of Palace Wars: Lawyers, Economists and the Contest to Transform Latin American States*. Chicago: University of Chicago Press.
Dirks, N. B. 2004. 'Edward Said and Anthropology'. *Journal of Palestine Studies* 33(3): 38–54.
Dore, L. K. 2006. 'Public Courts versus Private Justice: It's Time to Let Some Sun Shine in on Alternative Dispute Resolution'. *Chicago-Kent Law Review* 81(2): 463–520.
Dworkin, R. 1975. 'Hard Cases'. *Harvard Law Review* 88(6): 1057–1109.
Dworkin, R. 1986. *Law's Empire*. Cambridge, MA: The Belknap Press of Harvard University Press.
Ehrlich, E. 1936 [1912]. *Fundamental Principles of the Sociology of Law*. Cambridge: Harvard University Press.

El-Aḥdab, A. E. and J. El-Ahdab. 2011. *Arbitration with the Arab Countries. Third Revised and Expanded Edition*. Alphen aan den Rijn: Wolters Kluwer Law & Business.
Elsässer, S. 2019. 'The Coptic Divorce Struggle in Contemporary Egypt'. *Social Compass* 66(3): 333–51.
Engelcke, D. 2018. 'Adjudicating Christian Family Law in Jordan: Legal Borrowing Across Religious Lines?' Paper delivered as part of the conference 'Law, Islam and Anthropology' at the Max Planck Institute for Social Anthropology, 9–10 November.
Fitzgerald, J. M. and M. L. Fitzgerald. 1993. 'Mediation: A Systemic Alternative to Litigation for Resolution of Church Employment Disputes'. *St. Thomas Law Review* 5: 507–22.
Felstiner, W., R. Abel, and A. Sara. 1980/1981. 'The Emergence and Transformation of Disputes: Naming, Blaming, Claiming'. *Law & Society Review* 15(3/4): 631–54.
Ferrari, S. and R. Cristofori, eds. 2010. *Law and Religion in the 21st Century: Relations between States and Religious Communities*. Farnham: Ashgate.
Foblets, M. 2015. 'Preparing Future Anthropologists for Consultancy Work'. *Social Anthropology* 23(4): 492–509.
Foblets, M. and A. D. Renteln, eds. 2009. *Multicultural Jurisprudence: Comparative Perspectives on the Cultural Defense*. Oxford: Hart Publishing.
Franke, U., A. Magnusson, and J. Dahlquist. 2016. *Arbitrating for Peace: How Arbitration Made a Difference*. Alphen aan den Rijn: Kluwer Law International.
French, R. 2009. 'Ethnography in Ordinary Case Law'. In M. Freeman and D. Napier, eds. *Law and Anthropology: Current Legal Issues, Vol. 12*, 126–42. Oxford: Oxford University Press.
Gaillard, E. 2015. 'Sociology of International Arbitration'. *Arbitration International* 31: 1–17.
Geertz, C. 1973. *The Interpretation of Cultures*. New York: Basic Books Inc.
Genn, H. 2010. *The Hamlyn Lectures 2008: Judging Civil Justice*. Cambridge: Cambridge University Press.
Ginsburg, T. and G. Hoetker. 2006. 'The Unreluctant Litigant? An Empirical Analysis of Japan's Turn to Litigation'. *The Journal of Legal Studies* 35(1): 31–59.
Gluckman, M. 1955. *The Judicial Process among the Barotse of Northern Rhodesia*. Manchester: Manchester University Press.
Gluckman, M. 1997. 'Concepts in the Comparative Study of Tribal Law'. In L. Nader, ed. *Law in Culture and Society*, 349–73. Berkeley: University of California Press.
Goldman, D. B. 2007. *Globalisation and the Western Legal Tradition: Recurring Patterns of Law and Authority*. Cambridge: Cambridge University Press.
Good, A. and T. Kelly. 2013. *Expert Country Evidence in Asylum and Immigration Cases in the United Kingdom: Best Practice Guide*. Edinburgh: The University of Edinburgh.
Goodale, M. 2006. 'Toward a Critical Anthropology of Human Rights'. *Current Anthropology* 47 (3): 485–511.
Goodale, M. 2017. *Anthropology and Law: A Critical Introduction*. New York: New York University Press.
Greig, J. M., A. P. Owsiak, and P. F. Diehl. 2019. *International Conflict Management*. Cambridge/Medford: Polity Press.
Griffiths, A. 2005. 'Using Ethnography as a Tool in Legal Research: An Anthropological Perspective'. In R. Banakar and M. Travers, eds. *Theory and Methods in Socio-Legal Research*, 113–31. Oxford: Hart Publishing.
Haldar, P. 2008. *Law, Orientalism and Postcolonialism: The Jurisdiction of the Lotus-Eaters (Discourses of Law)*. First edition. Abingdon and New York: Routledge-Cavendish.

Hallaq, W. B. 2005. *The Origins and Evolution of Islamic Law*. Cambridge: Cambridge University Press.

Hankel, G. 2019. 'Gacaca Courts'. *Max Planck Encyclopedia of Public International Law, Oxford Public International Law* (available online at: <https://opil.ouplaw.com/view/10.1093/law:epil/9780199231690/law-9780199231690-e1667>).

Harpole, S. 2016. 'Language in Arbitration Procedure: A Practical Approach for International Commercial Arbitration'. *Contemporary Asia Arbitration Journal* 9(2): 273–300.

Hart, H. L. A. 1961. *The Concept of Law*. Oxford: Oxford University Press.

Hibberd, P. and P. Newman. 1999. *ADR and Adjudication in Construction Disputes*. Oxford/Sussex: Wiley-Blackwell.

Hobbes, T. 1651. *Leviathan or the Matter, Forme, & Power of a Common-wealth Ecclesiasticall and Civill*. Andrew Crooke: St. Pauls Church-yard.

Hoffman, A. 2009. *My Happiness Bears No Relation to Happiness: A Poet's Life in the Palestinian Century*. New Haven: Yale University Press.

Holden, L., ed. 2011. *Cultural Expertise and Litigation*. Abingdon: Routledge.

Holden, L., ed. 2019. *Cultural Expertise and Socio-Legal Studies. Special Issue in Studies of Law, Politics, and Society*. Bingley: Emerald Insight.

Holden, L. 2020. 'Cultural Expertise and Law: An Historical Overview'. *Law and History Review* 38: 1–18.

Ingen-Housz, A., ed. 2011. *ADR in Business: Practice and Issues Across Countries and Cultures*. Alphen aan den Rijn: Kluwer Law International.

Ingold, T. 2018. *Anthropology: Why It Matters*. Cambridge/Medford: Polity Press.

Jacob, M. 2012. 'Precedents: Lawmaking through International Adjudication'. In A. von Bogdandy and I. Venzke, eds. *International Judicial Lawmaking. Beiträge zum ausländischen öffentlichen Recht und Völkerrecht (Veröffentlichungen des Max-Planck-Instituts für ausländisches öffentliches Recht und Völkerrecht)*, vol. 236, 35–68. Berlin/Heidelberg: Springer.

Keshavjee, M. M. 2013. *Islam, Sharia and Alternative Dispute Resolution: Mechanisms for Legal Redress in the Muslim Community*. London/New York: I.B. Tauris & Co. Ltd.

Kidane, W. 2012. *China-Africa Dispute Settlement: The Law, Economics and Culture of International Arbitration*. Alphen aan den Rijn: Kluwer Law International.

King, H. T., Jr. and M. A. Le Forestier. 1997. 'Papal Arbitration: How the Early Roman Catholic Church Influenced Modern Dispute Resolution'. *Dispute Resolution Journal* (Summer): 74–81.

Kloos, D. 2019. 'Experts beyond Discourse: Women, Islamic Authority, and the Performance of Professionalism in Malaysia'. *American Ethnologist* 46(2): 162–75.

Kwan, C., B. Cole, and G. Bowpitt. 2007. 'Beyond Silent Organizations: A Reflection of the UK Chinese People and Their Community Organizations'. *Critical Social Policy* 27(4): 509–33.

Latour, B. 2009. *The Making of Law: An Ethnography of the Conseil d'Etat*. Cambridge/Malden: Polity Press.

Lewis, D. 1973. 'Anthropology and Colonialism'. *Current Anthropology* 14(5): 581–602.

Lynch, M. 1997. 'Preliminary Notes on Judges' Work: The Judge as a Constituent of Courtroom Hearings'. In M. Travers and J. Manzo, eds. *Law in Action Ethnomethodological and Conversation Analytic Approaches to Law*, 99–130. Aldershot: Dartmouth Publishing Co.

Mattei, U. L. and L. Nader. 2008. *Plunder: When the Rule of Law is Illegal*. Malden, MA: Blackwell.

May, J. P. 1978. 'The Chinese in Britain 1860–1914'. In C. Holmes, ed. *Immigrants and Minorities in British Society*, 111–24. London: Allen and Unwin.

McDowell, J. 1981. 'Non-Cognitivism and Rule-Following'. In S. Holtzman and C. M. Leich, eds. *Wittgenstein: To Follow a Rule*, 141–62. London/Boston: Routledge and Kegan Paul.

Menski, W. 2003. *Hindu Law: Beyond Tradition and Modernity*. Oxford: Oxford University Press.

Menski, W. 2006. *Comparative Law in a Global Context: The Legal Systems of Asia and Africa*. Second edition. Cambridge: Cambridge University Press.

Merry, S. E. 2006. *Human Rights and Gender Violence: Translating International Law into Local Justice*. Chicago: Chicago University Press.

Moore, S. F. 1973. 'Law and Social Change: The Semi-Autonomous Social Field as an Appropriate Subject of Study'. *Law & Society Review* 7(4): 719–46.

Moore, S. F. 2001. 'Certainties Undone: Fifty Turbulent Years of Legal Anthropology, 1949–1999'. *The Journal of the Royal Anthropological Institute* 7(1): 95–116.

Montgomery, S. L. 2000. *Science in Translation: Movements of Knowledge through Cultures and Time*. Chicago: University of Chicago Press.

Nader, L. 1972. 'Up the Anthropologist: Perspectives Gained from Studying Up'. Washington, D.C.: ERIC Clearinghouse.

Nader, L. 2002. 'A Wide-Angle on Dispute Management'. *Willamette Journal of International Law & Dispute Resolution* 10(1): 37–46.

Nader, L. and F. T. Harry, eds. 1978. *The Disputing Process: Law in Ten Societies*. New York: Columbia University Press.

Najjar, N. 2018. *Arbitration and International Trade in the Arab Countries*. Leiden: Brill Nijhoff.

Nasrallah, F. 2011. 'Country Survey: Iraq'. *Yearbook of Islamic and Middle Eastern Law* 16: 197–207.

Nasrallah, F. 2018a. 'Book Review: Hassan Arab, Lara Hammoud, Graham Lovett (ed.), Summaries of UAE Court Decisions on Arbitration 2012–2016 Including DIFC Court Decisions (Second Edition), ICC: ICC Services Publication, 2017, 180 p.' *Yearbook of Islamic and Middle Eastern Law* 19: 479–81.

Nasrallah, F. 2018b. 'Article 257 of the UAE Penal Code: Inter-jurisdictional Conflict and the Battleground of Arbitration'. *Yearbook of Islamic and Middle Eastern Law* 19: 334–50.

Nasrallah, F. and G. Blanke. 2020. 'Reflections on the Future of Arbitration in Dubai and the Middle East?' *Transnational Dispute Management* 17(4): 1–14.

Nelken, D. 2006. 'Rethinking Legal Culture'. In M. Freeman, ed. *Law and Sociology*, 200–24. Oxford: Oxford University Press.

Nelken, D. 2009. 'Blinding Insights? The Limits of a Reflexive Sociology of Law'. In D. Nelken, ed. *Beyond Law in Context: Developing a Sociological Understanding of Law (Collected Essays in Law)*, 235–54. Burlington: Ashgate.

Nelken, D. 2014. 'Legal Sociology and the Sociology of Norms'. In S. P. Donlan and H. L. Urscheler, eds. *Concepts of Law. Comparative, Jurisprudential, and Social Science Perspectives*, 137–51. Farnham: Ashgate.

Niezen, R. and M. Sapignoli, eds. 2017. *Palaces of Hope: The Anthropology of Global Organisations*. Cambridge: Cambridge University Press.

Nolan-Haley, J. 2015. 'Mediation and Access to Justice in Africa: Perspectives from Ghana'. *Harvard Negotiation Law Review* 25: 59–106.

Roberts, S. and M. Palmer. 2005. *Dispute Processes: ADR and the Primary Forms of Decision-making*. Cambridge: Cambridge University Press.

Pearl, D. and M. Menski. 1998. *Muslim Family Law*. Third Edition. London: Sweet & Maxwell.

Piers, M. and C. Aschauer, eds. 2018. *Arbitration in the Digital Age: The Brave New World of Arbitration*. Cambridge: Cambridge University Press.

Poorooye, A. and R. Feehily. 2017. 'Confidentiality and Transparency in International Commercial Arbitration: Finding the Right Balance'. *Harvard Negotiation Law Review* 22 (Spring): 275–322.

Poulter, S. 1986. *English Law and Ethnic Minority Customs*. London: Butterworths.

Provost, R., ed. 2017. *Culture in the Domains of Law*. Cambridge: Cambridge University Press.

Reisman, M. W. and C. Skinner. 2014. *Fraudulent Evidence Before Public International Tribunals: The Dirty Stories of International Law*. Cambridge: Cambridge University Press.

Renteln, A. D. 2004. *The Cultural Defense*. Oxford/New York: Oxford University Press.

Rogers, C. A. 2006. 'Transparency in International Commercial Arbitration'. *University of Kansas Law Review* 54: 1301–37.

Rosen, L. 1977. 'The Anthropologist as Expert Witness'. *American Anthropologist* 79: 555–78.

Rosen, L. 2006. *Law as Culture: An Invitation*. Princeton: Princeton University Press.

Rubel, P. G. and A. Rosman. 2003. *Translating Cultures: Perspectives on Translation and Anthropology*. Oxford and New York: Berg.

Ruskola, T. 2013. *Legal Orientalism: China, the United States, and Modern Law*. Cambridge: Harvard University Press.

Sandberg, R., ed. 2015. *Religion and Legal Pluralism*. Farnham: Ashgate.

Scheffer, T. 2010. *Adversarial Case-Making. An Ethnography of English Crown Court Procedure*. Leiden: Brill.

Schofield, R. 1992. *Near & Middle East Titles: Arabian Boundary Disputes*. 20 Volumes. Cambridge University Press.

Sloane-White, P. 2017. '"Ethnography by Appointment": Studying Muslims in Corporate and Bureaucratic Settings'. Paper delivered as part of the conference: 'Conceptualizing the Bureaucratization of Islam and its Socio-Legal Dimensions in Southeast Asia: Anthropological and Transdisciplinary Perspectives' at the Max Planck Institute for Social Anthropology, 7 September.

Sona, Federica. 2016. 'Islām as Legal (Dis-)Empowerment: The Dynamic Interplay between Italian Legal Provisions and Sharīʿah-compliant Norms'. In K. Topidi and L. Fielder, eds. *Religion as Empowerment: Global Legal Perspectives*. First edition. ICLARS Series on Law and Religion, 21–51. London/New York: Routledge.

Sona, Federica. 2018. 'Gli Sharīʿah Councils nel Regno Unito: il ruolo del giudice islamico nell'adattamento interculturale del diritto familiare'. In I. Zuanazzi and M. C. Ruscazio, eds. *Le relazioni familiari nel diritto interculturale*. First edition. (E-Reprint: *Nuovi Studi di Diritto ecclesiastico e canonico* 16), 387–411. Tricase: Libellula Edizioni.

Steinberg, G. M. 2000. 'Conflict Prevention and Mediation in the Jewish Tradition'. *Jewish Political Studies Review* 12: 3–4.

Stone, K. 2004. 'Alternative Dispute Resolution: Encyclopaedia of Legal History'. University of California, Los Angeles School of Law Public Law & Legal Theory Research Paper Series, Research Paper No. 04-30, 1–6.

Stone, K. 2009. 'Alternative Dispute Resolution'. In S. N. Katz, ed. *The Oxford International Encyclopedia of Legal History*, Vol. 1: 128–32.

Sullo, F. 2018. *Beyond Genocide: Transitional Justice and Gacaca Courts in Rwanda—The Search for Truth, Justice and Reconciliation*. Heidelberg/New York/Dordrecht/ London: Springer.

Trakman, L. and H. Montgomery. 2017. 'The "Judicialization" of International Commercial Arbitration: Pitfall or Virtue?' *Leiden Journal of International Law* 30: 405–34.

Travers, M. 2001. *Qualitative Research through Case Studies.* Los Angeles: SAGE Publications.
Tupman, M. W. 1989. 'Challenge and Disqualification of Arbitrators in International Commercial Arbitration'. *The International and Comparative Law Quarterly* 38(1): 26–52.
Twining, W. and D. Miers. 2010. *How to Do Things with Rules.* Fifth Edition. Cambridge: Cambridge University Press.
Tymoczo, M. and E. Gentzler. 2002. *Translation and Power.* Amherst: University of Massachusetts Press.
Vetters, L. and M. Foblets. 2016. 'Culture All Around? Contextualising Anthropological Expertise in European Courtroom Settings'. *International Journal of Law in Context* 12(3): 272–92.
Ward, E. 2007. 'Mandatory Court-Annexed Alternative Dispute Resolution in the United States Federal Courts: Panacea or Pandemic?' *St Johns Law Review* 81: 77–97.
Wielenga, C. and G. Harris. 2011. 'Building Peace and Security after Genocide: The Contribution of the Gacaca Courts of Rwanda'. *African Security Review* 20(1): 15–25.
Wilske, S. and G. J. Horvath. 2013. *Guerrilla Tactics in International Arbitration.* Alphen aan den Rijn: Kluwer Law International.
Woolf, L. 1995. *Access to Justice: Interim Report to the Lord Chancellor on the Civil Justice System in England and Wales.* Lord Chancellor's Department.
Woolf, L. 1996. *Access to Justice: Final Report to the Lord Chancellor on the Civil Justice System in England and Wales.* HMSO.
Zuckerman, A. A. S. 1996. 'Lord Woolf's Access to Justice: Plus ça Change ... '. *The Modern Law Review* 59(6): 773–96.

CHAPTER 28

JUSTICE AFTER ATROCITY

RICHARD A. WILSON

INTRODUCTION

WHEN an era of armed conflict and/or authoritarian rule ends, many societies face the predicament of how to address past atrocities in settings where the main offenders retain substantial economic, political, and military power. Post-conflict societies are characterized by vigorous contestation over the meaning of justice as they consider whether and how to hold perpetrators accountable, provide remedy to survivors, and promote peaceful co-existence. A new and exciting field of anthropology has analysed the social and cultural consequences of mass violence and provided critical insights into how governments and citizens engage with local, national, and international transitional justice institutions.

Over the course of the 1990s, 'transitional justice' came to refer to a wide array of institutional mechanisms for addressing the legacy of mass crimes (Borneman 1997). Influential truth commissions emerged in Latin America as a response to amnesty laws that extinguished criminal liability for perpetrators and heightened the need for a reliable account of past crimes. Truth and reconciliation commissions, oriented to truth-finding and mediating between opposing parties, also vary in their constitutions and mandates. Some are coordinated and funded by the United Nations (e.g. in East Timor), whereas others are sponsored by a national government (e.g. South Africa) or a civil society actor such as the Catholic Church (e.g. Guatemala). Additionally, local community courts or mediation mechanisms can constitute the main sites for pursuing reintegration of offenders and intra-communal reconciliation (e.g. *gacaca* in Rwanda).

Criminal prosecutions of alleged human rights offenders have been pursued at international criminal tribunals (e.g. the International Criminal Court), in national criminal courts (e.g. the trial of former president José Efraín Rios Montt in Guatemala), and in 'hybrid' tribunals that combine national and international law and personnel (e.g. the Special Court for Sierra Leone).[1] Each transitional justice institution possesses a different capacity, internal structure, and (often contradictory) set of objectives that includes, *inter alia*, accountability for perpetrators, the reconciliation of survivors and offenders, financial and symbolic reparations, public memorialization of mass crimes, the recognition of past harms (including apologies), and amnesty for perpetrators.

This dizzying array of institutions has been studied by anthropologists and others under the rubric of 'transitional justice' or 'post-conflict justice', but neither term is entirely adequate. When is a society no longer 'transitional'? Can a society be considered 'post-conflict' when the full-scale war has ended but violence is still endemic in society? Each term suffers from conceptual frailties but became generally accepted as referring to a range of specific institutional measures to deal with a legacy of mass human rights violations.

Even though there is wide variation in narratives and institutions of justice, anthropological studies have tended to cohere around the following principal questions: How have post-conflict regimes sought to reconcile opposing parties and restore the social fabric through local-level community justice structures? What narratives do governments espouse to explain the conflict and to propel their nation-building projects? How have ordinary citizens co-opted mediation mechanisms to reconstruct moral and social orders? Why are some parties held to account and others not, and how does this reflect global asymmetries of power and domination?

In a field saturated with political scientists and legal scholars, anthropologists have emphasized the structural inequalities that shape transitional justice outcomes and focused on the interactions between transitional justice institutions and local communities and on the usually hidden norms and practices motivating courts and commissions. The official account of all justice institutions—their self-image—is one of doctrine and rules, the rule of law (understood as consistent, fair, and predictable application of the rules), equality before the law (where all actors are equal in formal status), and parity between national and global institutions. Anthropologists have contextualized these international legal norms and procedures, and examined how global human rights are vernacularized and rendered in a local idiom (Merry 1997, 2006). Transitional justice institutions operate alongside local social and cultural mechanisms of adjudication and mediation, a fact that is often ignored by policymakers. Far from being neutral and universal in their application, the 'social life of rights' (Wilson 2006) embeds human rights laws and discourses in status hierarchies, gender relations, religious affiliations, and wider relations of power that span the globe and that both replicate and, occasionally, challenge historical relations of domination and colonialism.

Global asymmetries in the power to judge

Anthropological accounts of transitional justice settings have identified complex power dynamics among international actors, nation-state officials, and representatives of local communities, all of whom contest the meaning and direction of 'justice' in a post-conflict setting (Anders and Zenker 2015). Drawing on an older tradition of legal pluralism, anthropologists are generally critical of what they see as the imposition of transitional justice mechanisms and normative principles such as reconciliation on affected communities.[2] National and international elites struggle to engage with local community structures of adjudication, mediation, and, sometimes, punishment; only rarely are the conceptions of justice and material remedy that are meaningful to local actors affirmed and implemented by the institutions of international courts or national truth and reconciliation commissions.

This disjuncture between a national or international project and the aims and objectives of community organizations and survivors' groups was apparent in one of the first ethnographies of a transitional justice institution, Richard Ashby Wilson's (2001) *The Politics of Truth and Reconciliation in South Africa*. After the end of apartheid, President Nelson Mandela and Truth and Reconciliation Commission (TRC) Chair Desmond Tutu led a programme of national reconciliation to 'heal the wounds of the past'. The South African TRC garnered international acclaim for bringing the voices of ordinary South Africans into the public space, for promoting an expansive idea of national reconciliation and restorative justice, and for adjudicating more than 7,000 applications for amnesty for human rights violations.

However, there was little in the way of practical follow-up in the lives of survivors, and many reported that they felt abandoned. Survivors received little or no mental health treatment after traumatic public testimony. Many waited years for paltry sums recompensing them for the crimes they suffered at the hands of state agents. Meanwhile, in return for limited public testimony, members of the security police—for example, Dirk Coetzee and Jack Cronje—were granted generous retirement packages and amnesty for crimes such as torture.

Truth Commissioners made exalted claims about reconciling survivors and perpetrators in a spirit of *ubuntu* ('humanity'), but their understanding of the term operated at a high level of abstraction that was often disconnected from specific requests by survivors for accountability for offenders, pensions, and medical treatment (Wilson 2001: 9–13). The TRC failed utterly to engage with the approximately 400 community justice institutions operating in South Africa, which at that time were doing the practical work of mediating political disputes and negotiating the return of alleged perpetrators (such as African policemen) to their communities. Wilson documented how, in African townships surrounding Johannesburg, the TRC held public hearings and then moved on, abjuring the day-to-day task of forging a truce between local armed groups associated with the Inkatha Freedom Party and the African National Congress. The disjuncture between the national agenda and community mediation institutions represented, in many ways, a lost opportunity to foster actual co-existence. For the new political elite, the primary function of the South African TRC was nation-building and extending state administrative capacity and control into urban African settings that the apartheid state had neglected.

Subsequent ethnographies of international organizations identified similar asymmetrical relationships between violence-torn communities and global justice organizations.

For Kamari Clarke (2009, 2019), international justice institutions embody a neocolonial legalism that advances a new form of imperial sovereignty and global governance. On the basis of empirical study in Africa and at diplomatic conferences in The Hague and New York City, Clarke (2009) offers a deeply critical account of international law on the grounds that it is insensitive to local religious difference and closely aligned with neoliberal markets and the agendas of donor governments. International tribunals conduct theatrical displays of accountability without adequately addressing the underlying structural causes of conflict in Africa, a phenomenon Clarke (2009: 98) calls 'the spectrality of justice'. This approach is consistent with Samuel Moyn's (2018: 177, 192) critique of human rights as an international language of justice that arose contemporaneously with neoliberalism in the mid-1970s, sharing a common moral framework built around the individual, and obscuring structural factors that cause mass human rights violations in the first place.

One conclusion of Clarke's research is that the move to establish international rule of law itself engenders oppositional political movements in Africa, some of which take the form of Islamic radicalism, as in Nigeria. Whether or not international justice institutions are the main trigger for anti-Western movements in Africa, Clarke was prescient about the wave of opposition from African governments to international justice efforts. These tensions reached a crescendo when the International Criminal Court (ICC) indicted sitting head-of-state President Omar Hassan Ahmad al-Bashir of Sudan in 2006, precipitating a profoundly negative response from the African Union. The crisis of confidence between the ICC and African states deepened further after the Kenyan elections of 2007 and the indictment of President Uhuru Kenyatta and Deputy President William Ruto (both acquitted in 2016) for instigating ethnic violence.

For over a decade, the ICC has been criticized by anthropologists and other scholars for its disproportionate focus on Africa, the glacial pace of its cases, the impoverished nature of prosecution evidence, and its inability to engage meaningfully with the political realities of the societies it operates in. Clarke's research charts the African Union's resistance to the extradition of sitting African presidents and lends support to the kinds of justice alternatives that Africans are actively pursuing through state and regional mechanisms such as the special court in Senegal that successfully convicted Chadian former president Hissene Habré. Crucially, Clarke's (2019) research develops a theoretical frame that highlights 'structures of emotion' and 'the narrativization of feeling', a highly constructive approach to the affective dimensions of justice that helps us to understand the sense of grievance in Africa motivated by colonialism and extant global hierarchies.

Given anthropologists' critiques of the disconnectedness of transitional justice institutions, to what degree have national or international institutions meaningfully engaged with local community structures in addressing the violations of the past? Scholars initially applauded the *gacaca* courts that adjudicated tens of thousands of cases of alleged perpetrators of the 1994 genocide against Tutsis. Ethnographers have provided a more accurate and complex picture of local justice in the aftermath of genocide. In *Remediation in Rwanda*, Kristin Conner Doughty's (2016) ethnography encompasses three settings of law: genocide courts (*gacaca*), mediation committees (*comite y'abunzi*), and a legal aid clinic pursuing law-based mediation.

Doughty documents the top-down nature of these three legal institutions, as well as the ways in which average rural Rwandans experience mediation. Drawing on Laura Nader's classic critique of 'harmony ideology', and echoing Clarke's and Moyn's critique, she shows how alternative dispute resolution (ADR) suppresses discussion of the structural factors that underlie social conflict, representing instead 'government through community'. These legal forms are neither neutral nor benign but represent a technique of governance associated with the expansion of other forms of social control practised by an increasingly authoritarian Rwandan state. As in Wilson's earlier account of the South African TRC, transitional justice institutions in Rwanda are co-opted into the nation-building and state-building projects of a post-conflict regime.

The 'community' in community justice is a fragile political and social construction, and government intervention at the local level may be subversive rather than generative. As anthropologists often point out, the notion of community can also obscure internal tensions. Doughty's ethnography closely documents the often-overlooked gender aspect of *gacaca*. In mediation settings, women are often silenced and pressured to conform to gender roles and expectations about the acceptable behaviour of women, wives, and daughters.[3]

Doughty challenges the widely-held view of international donors that *gacaca* courts are an authentic expression of local African justice. Along with Lars Waldorf (2009), Doughty destabilizes cultural readings of genocide courts by documenting the Rwandan government's record of internal suppression of expression through local community-level legal institutions. At the same time, ordinary Rwandans routinely resist the extension of state power and bend justice mechanisms to reshape the moral order in which they live. *Remediation in Rwanda* prompts us to take a more cautious approach to transitional justice institutions, and to see how international efforts (e.g. by the World Bank) to build 'rule of law' in post-conflict societies can be prone to political manipulation by successor regimes.

The anthropological critique of transitional justice institutions is accurate, but there are a number of possible rejoinders that merit our consideration. Human rights is a global language of justice and accountability for mass atrocities that is instantiated in popular legal consciousness as well as international legal doctrine and institutions. Social movements around the world frequently espouse the language of international human rights, justice, and accountability, and they are not excessively concerned with whether justice is delivered by local, national, or international institutions. Additionally, survivors often demand official apologies and recognition of harms, symbolic and material reparations for grievous injuries, and an intentional commitment to non-recurrence. Here I would note the presence and indeed the prominence of many individuals from the global South in transitional justice institutions. For example, the chief prosecutor of the ICC at the time of writing is an African lawyer from the Gambia, and the majority of judges who sat in judgment of Kaing Guek Eav ('Comrade Duch') were Cambodians. All share (more or less) the same conception of justice as due process and accountability for internationally recognized crimes. Anthropological critiques of the asymmetries of power in global relations explain why alleged war criminals George W. Bush and Vladimir Putin enjoy impunity, while so-called 'small fry' like Jean Kambanda (Prime Minister of Rwanda), Slobodan Milošević (President of Yugoslavia), and Charles Taylor (President of Liberia) are charged, arrested, and tried by international judicial bodies. The legitimacy of the international transitional justice project demands that leaders of powerful countries who have planned, directed, or otherwise participated in massive human rights violations also be held to account. At the same time, it is worth recalling that Kambanda, Milošević, and Taylor were not small fry to hundreds of thousands of their victims, over whom they held the power of life and death. The main beneficiaries of the dismantling of international justice institutions are not the survivors, but the powerful who stand to face trial for their mass crimes. They, of course, prefer impunity.

Social movements and new forms of sociality

The interactions between international institutions and local actors in the area of justice are seldom harmonious. Rosalind Shaw, Lars Waldorf, and Pierre Hazan (2010) have sought to bridge the chasm between the norms of international institutions and the priorities of survivors. They decry the bifurcation of the population into 'survivors' and 'perpetrators' by transitional justice institutions. Echoing Elizabeth F. Drexler's (2009) study of East Timor, they note that customary legal institutions have often played a prominent role in reintegrating combatants who may be both survivors and perpetrators. We could envisage additional measures to localizing justice. Transitional justice institutions need to devolve some accountability procedures and increase local investigative and prosecutorial capacity, rather than stage an empty display of justice and depart with minimal effect on the institutions of the nation-state or local community. Transitional justice institutions might build a stronger domestic constituency for accountability and lend capacity to social movements combatting impunity and corruption. When a local constituency already exists, as it did in Argentina, El Salvador, Guatemala, and Peru, international organizations can empower local actors rather than overpower and displace them. Finally, international justice needs to be more closely conjoined with social and economic justice, which is among the predominant daily concerns of the majority of the population in communities affected by mass violence.[4]

Yet anthropology's emphasis on legal and macro-political outcomes is only part of the story. Recent ethnographic studies have revealed how new forms of sociality emerge when survivors actively participate in the legal process, flawed as it is. Rita Kesselring's (2017) inventive monograph on South Africa, *Bodies of Truth: Law, Memory and Emancipation in Post-Apartheid South Africa*, makes a compelling case for the transformative potential of shared sociality forged by survivors as they seek reparations from U.S. multinational corporations that benefitted financially from apartheid. Kesselring worked closely with the Khulumani Support Group, a national survivors' organization that has over a hundred thousand members. Inspired by the successful legal campaign of Holocaust survivors, Khulumani sought financial redress in the U.S. and South African courts.

The Khulumani Support Group signed on as plaintiffs in a lawsuit against multinational corporations in the Eastern District Court of New York under the Alien Tort Statute, alleging that the corporations had aided and abetted violations of international human rights law including extrajudicial killings and torture between 1960 and 1994. From 1980 onwards, this statute had permitted foreign citizens in hundreds of civil suits to seek remedies in U.S. courts for human-rights violations committed outside the United States. *Bodies of Truth* charts the trajectory of Khulumani's case as it moved glacially through the courts, making surprising progress against the headwinds of antipathy of the U.S. and South African governments. Ultimately, the plaintiffs' case was reversed in 2013 as the result of the U.S. Supreme Court's decision in *Kiobel v. Royal Dutch Petroleum*, which denied non-citizens relief for violations that occurred outside the United States.

Disappointing as this legal defeat was for Khulumani members, Kesselring maintains that the terminal legal outcome is less important than the experience of the survivors in a legal campaign that engendered, over the course of its duration, a sense of solidarity and a set of aspirations formerly obstructed by the regular South African political process and the TRC. Kesselring reiterates the time-honoured anthropological observation regarding the constitutive power of law and the way in which political subjectivities are reshaped as actors engage in a trial process. In its emphasis on the embodiment of suffering and how 'the body is both the condition for and the limit to the formation of a social or political collective' (Kesselring 2017: 11), *Bodies of Truth* details the bodily states of survivors as they communicate their suffering in theatrical performances and public testimonials. Survivors involved in these forms of social recognition inevitably connect to dominant discourses of survivorhood and, in so doing, transform survivorhood into a politically oriented and active subjectivity. This allows Khulumani members to transcend their own individual experiences of suffering and see it as part of a political narrative of the (ongoing) liberation struggle. Shifts in the subjectivities of survivors result not from resounding legal victory, but from a collective solidarity of a quotidian kind that includes mutual aid associations, commemorative events, neighbourhood childcare, and other everyday forms of sharing and cooperation.

Anthropologists have been critical of the hierarchies embedded in transitional justice institutions. Truth commissions and mediation processes may be co-opted by states seeking to build nations and extend their coercive and normative capacity in local communities. International criminal courts may impose an alien version of justice in ways that interfere with and disrupt the national political process, including a national peace process. Litigation against companies for complicity in crimes against humanity may raise survivors' expectations, only to dash them when states refuse to recognize universal jurisdiction. Yet even when legal recourse is not successful, new forms of emancipatory political agency may still emerge. Thus, the official outcome of legal actions may matter less than the new forms of sociality and emancipatory bodily *habitus* that they engender.

Law's epistemological prison/prism

Anthropological studies of transitional justice have been inspired both by developments in legal anthropology[5] and the theoretical current of 'new legal realism' that has emerged in the interdisciplinary field of 'law and society'.[6] New legal realism posits that law is an inherently untidy human enterprise and that judicial outcomes result less from abstract doctrine than from contestation among legal actors, each with their own set of assumptions and interests, within a framework of shifting procedures, conventions, and practices.

A central aim of anthropological research is to lay bare the assumptions and strategies of legal actors, to understand the process that led to legal decisions, and, in the case of transitional justice, to show how these transitory institutions forge novel truths about the mass crimes they adjudicate.[7] In this theoretical model, process matters as much as product. This is not to deny that legal doctrine has a binding effect; and without formal reasoning and predictability, there can be no claim to rule of law.[8] Yet transitional justice institutions could benefit from a strong dose of legal realism and from a moment of pause and reflection on the narrow scope of fact-finding in a truth commission or criminal courtroom.

Transitional justice institutions, like all legal bodies, are established on the basis of a distinctive system of knowledge guided by its own (rather peculiar) principles for comprehending human behaviour. Legal ways of knowing are unique, as seen in their predilection for official documents over other forms of evidence and witnessing. Not only are documents preferred as sources, but there exists a hierarchy of documents in which primary texts are accorded more probative value than secondary sources, and official documents are given more weight than unofficial ones. By construing documents as the basis for objective knowledge, actors in transitional justice institutions overlook the degree to which documents are also created by individuals and therefore are just as artificial, 'subjective', and contingent as other forms of evidence.

At times, then, it seems as if courts and commissions of inquiry operate within a hermetically sealed textual universe of tightly controlled documentary evidence. These observations substantiate recent research by law and society scholars such as Austin Sarat, Lawrence Douglas, and Martha Merrill Umphrey (2007), and anthropologists such as Bruno Latour (2004), who note that, even though law may officially endorse the scientific method, its ways of knowing diverge widely from science and epistemological realism. Contrasting scientific and legal ways of knowing, Latour claims that there is no 'truth' to law in a scientific sense, since law only establishes truth through its own legal rhetoric and textual exegesis:

> The strange thing about legal objectivity is that it quite literally is *object-less*, and is sustained entirely by the production of a mental state, a bodily *hexis*, but is still quite unable to resign its faculty of judgment by appealing to incontrovertible facts. (Latour 2004: 107, emphasis in original)

Compared with science, legal epistemology is, for Latour (2004: 109), 'a mode of unfettered arbitrariness'. He describes only one aspect of fact-finding, and focuses on only one branch of law—administrative law—which is quite far removed from the evidential earthiness of, say, criminal law. This could be why he overstates law's reliance on documents and neglects other, non-documentary forms of evidence (for instance, the oral testimonies of survivors and witnesses).

Law's conceptions of causality and determination also diverge from those of science, social science, or history, confirming studies in national court settings by legal anthropologists such as Anthony Good (2008: 30–1). Ascertaining the causal connection between two acts or events is a richly regulated area of law, in which various levels of causation are isolated and accorded distinct weight. Courts and commissions seek linear connections that establish which acts caused which others, and they seek a particular kind of knowledge about the subjective intentions of actors committing the said acts, with a view to assigning criminal responsibility (read, blame). 'For lawyers', as Good (2008: 30) remarks, 'an event's cause is inseparable from allocation of responsibility for it'.

Clearly, anthropology's and law's distinctive epistemological dispositions stem from the different ways in which they use the knowledge they produce—an observation that would seem to confirm J. L. Austin's maxim that the meaning is the use. History and anthropology are less concerned with causality and responsibility, and when they do posit a link between events, their assertions often acknowledge a greater level of uncertainty. The greatest disparity of all, however, lies in how ethnographic research embraces multiple layers of causality, apprehending connections between events in a systemic and holistic manner. Transitional justice institutions, in their reports or court decisions, are more likely to radically pare down context to isolate the events and acts. While this may be necessary to arrive at a clear-cut determination, legal decontextualization comes at a price, namely, the full recognition of how any single human act is embedded in an intricate matrix of jointly sufficient causal relations.

Wilson (2001, 2011, 2017) has examined the truth-finding mechanisms of two different types of transitional justice institutions—truth commissions and international tribunals—finding similarities and differences between them. The official view in both truth commissions and courts is realist: there are independent facts out there in the world to be collected. It is scientific in that the methods of science are the preferred method for collecting such facts, and it is positivist in that evidence should meet the Popperian criteria of being objective, testable, and falsifiable. Wilson (2001) is critical of the South African TRC's commitment to positivism, and in particular how the statistical system it used to analyse more than 25,000 survivor statements drove the process of gathering survivors' narratives of apartheid era violations. The interview questionnaire, which started as an unstructured, open-ended enquiry, ended as a checklist of violations that radically excluded the narrative voice and subjectivity of ordinary South Africans. Similarly, Marie-Bénédicte Dembour (2004) has observed how judges in international courts, such as the International Criminal Tribunal for Rwanda, have been remarkably insensitive to women's narratives of rape during armed conflict and genocide. Narrative and experience, it seems, are largely incompatible with the overriding impulse to judge on the basis of objective evidence.

At the same time, there are good reasons to qualify the anthropological critique of positivist approaches to fact-finding in transitional justice institutions: things are a little more complicated than a simple story of law's exclusion of subjectivity and social knowledge. By calling on survivors to testify publicly about mass atrocities, both truth commissions and international courts have brought the ordinary voices and experiences of survivors into the public space in a way that is unprecedented in the societies concerned. They have provided a stage on which survivors' stories are told with dramatic effect to illustrate, in compelling and ordinary speech, the horrors of armed conflict or apartheid. The public display of *vox populi* has greater impact and intensity than the dry reports of truth commissions or final court judgments. Additionally, Wilson's (2005, 2016) research demonstrates that international justice institutions have exhibited an openness to wide-ranging historical debates in the courtroom about the origins and causes of conflict, in large part because prosecutors and defence attorneys seek to achieve concretely legal objectives (such as proving genocidal intentionality) by referencing prior atrocities. Furthermore, when anthropologists and historians appear as expert witnesses in criminal trials, their testimony has a measurably greater impact on the final judgments than engineers, medical experts, police, and military experts (Wilson 2016: 733). These findings indicate that narratives are embraced by transitional justice institutions in certain settings, and they offer an intriguing counterpoint to the conventional anthropological account of exclusion and marginalization by powerful institutions.

It is worth noting the unpredictability and contingency of newly established justice institutions. Transitional justice institutions are novel legal creations that have only appeared in the last thirty years; therefore, they require a special analysis that does not simply recapitulate the time-honoured truisms of the anthropology of law. Nigel Eltringham (2011) analyses how the international courtroom is characterized by improvisation and theatricality. International law is a kind of juridical Esperanto, part Anglo-American common law and part continental civil law, that is quite unlike any national legal system. This sows uncertainty for both prosecuting and defence attorneys with respect to the criminal doctrine, trial procedures, and the evidence necessary. As a result, Eltringham (2011: 207) observes, attorneys have to improvise: '[T]he enactment of international criminal law is a daily process of challenging habitual practice, revealing discordant assumptions, negotiating novelty, and developing new configurations.'

The broader legal literature homogenizes international justice institutions, treating their legal doctrine and procedure as predictable and unproblematic. This is the classic pitfall of an unreflective legal formalism. Anthropologists of international legal institutions overcome the oversimplification of international legal doctrine by closely documenting the beliefs and practices of cosmopolitan legal actors, who themselves have their own diverse set of interests and backgrounds. Moreover, the spaces of international justice, including Arusha, The Hague, and Freetown, can also be seen as 'the local' and as sites of quotidian practice.

One area of knowledge where transitional justice institutions have proved profoundly inadequate is in their understanding of the societal and cultural aspects of political violence. Race, ethnicity, class, gender, and sexuality all seem to be irrelevant or mystifying to attorneys adjudicating mass human rights violations. This is apparent in Eltringham's (2004) *Accounting for Horror: Post-Genocide Debates in Rwanda*, which critiques how the International Criminal Tribunal for Rwanda ignored the salience of race, which was the *génocidaires'* primary motivation and stated justification for carrying out the genocide. According to Eltringham, in failing to deal with how Tutsi were targeted on the basis of the perception of an indelible, racial distinction, the Tribunal missed the opportunity to confront the completely fabricated and ideational nature of the genocidal mindset.

Eltringham's (2004: 31–3) counter-proposal is that the Rwanda Tribunal should have adopted a subjective view of race. Specifically, it should have focused on the perpetrators' perception of race. Perpetrators' intent is, after all, the primary consideration when proving *mens rea* (criminal intentionality) in a court of law. If the Tribunal were to focus primarily upon the perpetrators' intent to destroy a protected group, then it really does not matter if the group in question is an objective, fact-based group or not, so long as the idea of group identification is firmly established in the mind of perpetrators and they demonstrate an intent to destroy a group in whole or in part, through their words and deeds. It is the act of stigmatization that matters, not the permanent fixity of the object of stigmatization.

Ultimately, transitional justice institutions are compelled to make a list of prohibited acts that fall within their jurisdiction and to define these acts in a way that is consistent with international law and universal standards; they must then apply abstract legal conceptualizations to the concrete and messy cases that come before them. Herein lies the rub, remarks Toby Kelly (2012) in his monograph, *This Side of Silence: Human Rights, Torture and the Recognition of Cruelty*, which analyses the rise of torture as one of the dominant legal and moral categories of our time. In his account of the prosecutions of Afghan citizens and British soldiers in the United Kingdom's courts for acts they allegedly committed in Afghanistan and Iraq, Kelly observes how, far from being a fixed and stable category, the meaning and use of the term 'torture' has undergone profound changes over time. He expertly charts how it has been shaped by recent developments in international law and medicine, media representations of the body and suffering, and the shifting fortunes of human rights since 1945.

In Kelly's account, courts applying English law experience profound difficulties in reconciling the absolutist definition of torture in international law with the specificities of actual cases, and then in determining beyond a reasonable doubt whether torture occurred. Torture is framed in an airtight and bounded way in statutes and case law, but categorical certainty becomes a liability when it confronts the specifics of each actual case. As Kelly (2012: 169) notes: 'Torture is so hard to acknowledge, not because survivors find it hard to express what has happened to them, but because we find it so difficult to say, hear and name what is in front of us. ... [I]n practice, legal processes create a set of requirements for recognition that very few people can meet.' These issues are not just a matter of framing and epistemology, however, and Kelly (2012: 120) recognizes the global asymmetries of power and punishment. He observes how English criminal law operates with a 'structural prejudice' by comparing the successful conviction of an Afghan citizen with the unsuccessful court-martial of the British soldiers charged with maltreating and murdering detainees in Iraq, acts that the British army have only belatedly admitted to.

Intimate and Performative Ethnographies of Justice

In recent years, a few anthropological studies of transitional justice have taken a reflexive turn and examined questions of accountability, reconciliation, and remedy through the lens of the authors' own families and their personal reactions to a set of legal proceedings. These experimental ethnographies defy chronological narrative and conventional social science theorization, transcending the usual genre of anthropological writing about law.

In her self-described 'intimate ethnography', *How to Accept German Reparations*, Slyomovics (2014) recounts a highly personal story of her Jewish family's suffering in German-occupied Europe and of her grandmother's quest for reparations. In 1944, the author's mother, Vera, and grandmother, Gizella Hollander, were deported from Hungary to the Auschwitz extermination camp. There, they were examined by the notorious 'Angel of Death', Dr Josef Mengele, and dispatched to serve as slave labourers at the Płaszów camp in Poland, the setting of the Hollywood film *Schindler's List*. After a time, they were sent to work in a Junkers munitions factory in Markkleeberg, part of a group of 7.6 million foreign forced labourers in Germany. In April 1945, as the German war machine collapsed, the slave labourers of the Markkleeberg Camp were sent on a 'death march', from which Vera and Gizella escaped.

The narrative tension is driven by a five-decade dispute between the author's mother and grandmother over whether to accept German reparations as Holocaust survivors. Whereas Slyomovics's grandmother, Gizella Hollander, chose to litigate in a relentless campaign for restitution from the German state, her mother Vera rejected compensation for her concentration camp imprisonment and chose instead to narrate her suffering in synagogues and high schools. Gizella Hollander began gathering the necessary documentation to support her legal claims immediately after she gained her freedom. Only two weeks after liberation, Gizella marched up to the German overseer of the slave battalion in Markkleeberg and requested a 'work certification' that would prove that she had been detained as a slave labourer. She then embarked upon a fifty-year campaign for financial reparations from the German government. On the basis of the opposing standpoints of her mother and grandmother, Slyomovics sensitively evaluates the various German restitution mechanisms and reparations protocols established after the war, as the German state and private companies paid more than $60 billion to Holocaust survivors and forced labourers from the Nazi era, as part of a programme of *Wiedergutmachung* (literally, 'making good again').

Reparations are, of course, not a straightforward matter and are freighted with moral dilemmas. Restitution in the form of a return to the situation *ex ante* is impossible in most instances. For some survivors, accepting 'blood money' betrays the memory of the dead. Survivors can be re-traumatized by the bureaucratic reparations process with its deadlines, application forms, and standards of evidentiary corroboration of claims. There is also something Kafkaesque about survivors having to prove to the country that brazenly committed the mass crimes that it indeed did commit those crimes, in conformity with the country's bureaucratic requirements. On the other hand, indemnification measures constitute an official recognition of wrongs and authorize important truths by careful documenting what happened to whom. They also provide financial remedy, even if limited and symbolic. Finally, granting reparations can facilitate democratization in the German case by compelling Germans to listen to and respect the voices of survivors.

Germany's programme of indemnifying European Jews has served as the template for all other restitution programmes since, but the political project that Slyomovics identifies is broader than the Holocaust, and demands for reparations now come from those enslaved and exploited during centuries of European colonialism. Slyomovics asks why there has been no large-scale programme of reparations for the crimes committed during European colonial domination that only ended in the 1960s. Slyomovics examines the differential treatment of Algerian Jews and Muslims by the post-war states of Germany and France, drawing on the historical connections between Nazism and colonialism. Slyomovics offers a unique anthropological perspective on the pressing global demands for a legal remedy for the Holocaust and colonial-era criminality. Its person-centred ethnography is propelled by a deep-seated sense of justice and fairness and conveyed in a personal voice characterized by openness, honesty, and empathy. Slyomovics shows how to transcend the usual literary restrictions of the academic genre and write a beautiful book about a traumatic subject.

A. L. Hinton's (2016) experimental ethnography *Man or Monster? The Trial of a Khmer Rouge Torturer* narrates the criminal trial at the Extraordinary Chambers in the Courts of Cambodia (ECCC) of Kaing Guek Eav (a.k.a. Duch), a central figure in the killing fields of the 1970s. Hinton interrogates the entire enterprise of pursuing accountability for those who perpetrated some of the most widespread and systematic human rights violations in the twentieth century, and he explores the limits of both law and literature to comprehend mass atrocities. Hinton finds the Manichean dualism posed in the title of his book to be simultaneously inadequate, haunting, and generative; and he illustrates how all accounts of one individual's role in past crimes are partial and incomplete or, in his words, 'redacted'.[9]

Man or Monster? is a 'performative ethnography' that is episodic, polyphonic, experimental, and includes poetry, the dreams of the ethnographer, and other literary techniques. For Hinton (2016: 241), the international criminal trial of Duch is less an attempt to determine accountability and challenge impunity than a 'performance of a liberal order', a quasi-religious quest for the grounds of redemption of the accused so that he might be returned to the fold of humanity. Law, according to Hinton, is quite unsuited to this latter task, given its epistemological framing of events and its winner-takes-all search for truth that leads to the attribution of guilt.

Hinton poses the questions, What explains the Cambodian genocide? Was Duch a man, or a monster? A zealous and ruthless revolutionary or the soft-spoken former mathematics teacher who quoted French romantic poetry in his trial? Hinton (2016: 82) embraces neither option and instead reaches for the long-standing 'perpetrator-in-all-of-us' interpretation that, 'under tragic circumstances, anyone can end up like Duch'. For Hinton, the Cambodian genocide cannot be grasped by the politically inclined explanations advanced thus far, such as the mass indoctrination of the population by a small Maoist clique led by Pol Pot, or by the violence of decolonization and its aftermath. Instead, Hinton (2016: 35) identifies the origins of the genocide in 'the banality of everyday thought'. By this, he means the quotidian social categories through which persons simplify, frame, and ultimately erase others. In short, 'social cognition' (although Hinton does not use this term) furnishes the causal mechanism for mass murder. To understand the S-21 prison of the Khmer Rouge, we need to look no further than ourselves and our inherent tendency to categorize people into groups and to obey authority.

Conclusions

Anthropology has a surfeit of intellectual treasures to offer the field of post-conflict justice, a policy arena premised on its transformative social purpose as well as its legal function. If it were both possible and sufficient to simply punish the guilty and exonerate the innocent in national criminal trials, there would be no need for transitional justice institutions at all. There would be no UN-sponsored truth commissions and international criminal tribunals staffed by international personnel. There would be no amnesties, no national memorials, and no apologies or programmes of reparations and reconciliation. These novel mechanisms aspire to more than simply the correct enactment of legal accountability, understood as retributive justice according to the black letter of the law. They aspire, in various ways, to transform the societies and cultures in which they operate—to render them more peaceful and less divided, more aware of the harms that were committed in the name of a misguided ideological project, and more willing to listen to the voices of the marginalized and dispossessed.

And yet commissions and courts possess little or no self-reflexive function to reliably evaluate their own work. They are projects of social engineering that often lack the necessary tools of measurement needed to understand their own social effects. Sometimes they even announce their results before they have started their work, as the South African TRC did when it brandished its motto 'Reconciliation Through Truth' on banners at public hearings. What is remarkable, especially given the mixed results identified by anthropologists and other scholars, is how transitional justice has captured the imagination of the international community and become the official policy of the UN Security Council for post-conflict societies.[10]

While philosophers marvel at the conceptual novelty of a secular notion of reconciliation and redemption, political scientists measure public attitudes towards democracy, and international scholars attend public hearings to hear survivors testify, so far it is mostly anthropologists who have spent long periods of time in the communities torn by political violence and interviewed scores of survivors and offenders to gauge the long-term impact of truth, reparations, prosecutions, and national efforts to reconcile. And it is anthropologists who interrogate the categories and procedures of law and find them to be highly mutable and contingent, as well as susceptible to being co-opted by elites advocating the same formations of global and local inequality that fuelled the violence in the first place.

Drawing on anthropological perspectives, we see the role of transitional justice in the long arc of a person's life or in the internal mediation efforts of a community, and we comprehend more fully what is happening alongside and outside the formal institutions of justice. In the long run, these socially embedded forms of mediation, memorial, reparation, and, at times, retribution, may be more important than transitional justice institutions in establishing co-existence and new forms of sociality that transcend the era of violence. Where transitional justice institutions can meaningfully connect with these quotidian forms of post-trauma sociality and facilitate new expressions of political agency, they will become something more than merely elite performances of justice.

Notes

1. On the Montt trial, see García (2019).
2. On reconciliation in Uganda in the context of conflict and investigations of the International Criminal Court, see Finnstrom (2010).
3. Doughty thus reinforces Ross's (2003) findings on South Africa and Theidon's (2013) on Peru.
4. See Theidon (2010) on the depoliticizing effects of the Peruvian Truth and Reconciliation Commission.
5. See Dembour and Kelly (2007) and Niezen and Sapignoli (2017) on the anthropology of international legal institutions.

6. On 'new legal realism', see Klug and Merry (2016).
7. See Sarat et al. (2007).
8. See Thompson (1991) on how the idea of the rule of law facilitated the growth of the labour movement and universal suffrage in the nineteenth century.
9. In legal parlance, to redact is to censor, erase, or excise.
10. See United Nations Security Council (2004).

References

Anders, G. and O. Zenker. 2015. *Transition and Justice: Negotiating the Terms of New Beginnings in Africa*. Malden: Wiley Blackwell.

Borneman, J. 1997. *Settling Accounts: Violence, Justice and Accountability in Postsocialist Europe*. Princeton: Princeton University Press.

Clarke, K. 2009. *Fictions of Justice: The International Criminal Court and the Challenge of Legal Pluralism in Sub-Saharan Africa*. New York: Cambridge University Press.

Clarke, K. 2019. *Affective Justice: The International Criminal Court and the Pan-Africanist Pushback*. Durham: Duke University Press.

Dembour, M. B. and E. Haslam. 2004. 'Silencing Hearings? Victim-Witnesses at War Crimes Trials'. *European Journal of International Law* 15(1): 151–177.

Dembour, M. B. and T. Kelly. 2007 *Paths to International Justice: Social and Legal Perspectives*. Cambridge: Cambridge University Press.

Doughty, K. C. 2016. *Remediation in Rwanda: Grassroots Legal Forums*. Philadelphia: University of Pennsylvania Press.

Drexler, E. 2009. 'Addressing the Legacies of Mass Violence and Genocide in East Timor and Indonesia'. In A. L. Hinton and K. O'Neill, eds. *Genocide: Truth, Memory and Representation*, 219–46. Durham: Duke University Press.

Eltringham, N. 2004. *Accounting for Horror: post-genocide debates in Rwanda*. London: Pluto Press.

Eltringham, N. 2011. 'Judging the "Crime of Crimes:" Continuity and Improvisation at the International Criminal Tribunal for Rwanda'. In A. L. Hinton, ed. *Transitional Justice*, 206–26. New Brunswick: Rutgers University Press.

Eltringham, N. 2013. '"Illuminating the Broader Context": Anthropological and Historical Knowledge at the International Criminal Tribunal for Rwanda'. *Journal of the Royal Anthropological Institute* 19(2): 338–55.

Finnstrom, S. 2010. 'Reconciliation Grown Bitter? War, Retribution, and Ritual Action in Northern Uganda'. In R. Shaw, L. Waldorf, and P. Hazan, eds. *Localizing Transitional Justice: Interventions and Priorities after Mass Violence*, 135–56. Stanford: Stanford University Press.

García, M. L. 2019. 'Translated Justice? The Ixil Maya and the 2013 Trial of José Efraín Ríos Montt for Genocide in Guatemala'. *American Anthropologist* 121(2): 311–24.

Good, A. 2008. 'Cultural Evidence in Courts of Law'. *Journal of the Royal Anthropological Institute*. Special Issue: *The Objects of Evidence* 14(s1): 47–60.

Hinton, A. L. 2016. *Man or Monster? The Trial of a Khmer Rouge Torturer*. Durham and London: Duke University Press.

Kelly, T. 2012. *This Side of Silence: Human Rights, Torture and the Recognition of Cruelty*. Philadelphia: University of Pennsylvania Press.

Kesselring, R. 2017. *Bodies of Truth: Law, Memory and Emancipation in Post-Apartheid South Africa*. Stanford: Stanford University Press.

Klug, H. and S. E. Merry. 2016. *The New Legal Realism. Studying Law Globally*. Cambridge: Cambridge University Press.

Latour, B. 2004. 'Scientific Objects and Legal Objectivity'. In A. Pottage and M. Mundy, eds. *Law, Anthropology and the Constitution of the Social: Making Persons and Things*, 73–114. Cambridge: Cambridge University Press.

Merry, S. E. 1997. 'Legal Pluralism and Transnational Culture'. In R. A. Wilson, ed. *Human Rights, Culture and Context: Anthropological Perspectives*, 28–48. London: Pluto Press.

Merry, S. E. 2006. *Human Rights and Gender Violence: Translating International Law into Local Justice*. Chicago: University of Chicago Press.

Moyn, S. 2018. *Not Enough: Human Rights in an Unequal World*, Cambridge: Harvard University Press.

Niezen, R. and M. Sapignoli, eds. 2017. *Palaces of Hope: The Anthropology of the United Nations*. Cambridge: Cambridge University Press.

Ross, F. 2003. *Bearing Witness: Women and the South African Truth and Reconciliation Commission*. London: Pluto Press.

Sarat, A., L. Douglas, and M. M. Umphrey. 2007. *How Law Knows*. Stanford: Stanford University Press.

Shaw, R., L. Waldorf, and P. Hazan. 2010. *Localizing Transitional Justice: Interventions and Priorities after Mass Violence*. Stanford: Stanford University Press.

Slyomovics, S. 2014. *How to Accept German Reparations*. Philadelphia: University of Pennsylvania Press.

Theidon, K. 2010. 'Histories of Innocence: Postwar Stories in Peru'. In R. Shaw, L. Waldorf, and P. Hazan, eds. *Localizing Transitional Justice: Interventions and Priorities after Mass Violence*, 92–110. Stanford: Stanford University Press.

Theidon, K. 2013. *Intimate Enemies: Violence and Reconciliation in Peru*. Philadelphia: University of Pennsylvania Press.

Thompson, E. P. 1991. 'Custom, Law and Common Right' and 'The Moral Economy of the English Crowd in the Eighteenth Century' in E. P. Thompson, *Customs in Common*, 97–258. London: Penguin Books.

United Nations Security Council. 2004. *The Rule of Law and Transitional Justice in Conflict and Post-Conflict Societies. Report of the Secretary General*. S/2004/616. <http://www.un.org/Docs/sc/sgrep04.html>.

Waldorf, L. 2009. 'Remnants and Remains: Narratives of Suffering in Post-Genocide Rwanda's *Gacaca* Courts'. In Richard A. Wilson and Richard D. Brown, eds. *Humanitarianism and Suffering: The Mobilization of Empathy*, 285–305. Cambridge: Cambridge University Press.

Wilson, R. A. 2001. *The Politics of Truth and Reconciliation in South Africa: Legitimizing the Post-Apartheid State*, Cambridge: Cambridge University Press.

Wilson, R. A. 2005. 'Judging History: The Historical Record of the International Criminal Tribunal for the Former Yugoslavia'. *Human Rights Quarterly* 27: 908–42.

Wilson, R. A. 2006. 'The Social Life of Rights'. *American Anthropologist* 108(1): 77–83.

Wilson, R. A. 2011. *Writing History in International Criminal Trials*. Cambridge: Cambridge University Press.

Wilson, R. A. 2016. 'Expert Evidence on Trial: Social Researchers in the International Criminal Courtroom'. *American Ethnologist* 43(4): 730–44, November.

Wilson, R. A. 2017. *Incitement on Trial: Prosecuting International Speech Crimes*. Cambridge: Cambridge University Press.

CHAPTER 29

KINSHIP THROUGH THE TWOFOLD PRISM OF LAW AND ANTHROPOLOGY

MARIE-CLAIRE FOBLETS

INTRODUCTION

THE vast field of study covering kinship and kinship structures has long been of great interest to anthropologists in their attempts to understand the functioning of social relationships in and across human societies. The analysis I develop here takes as its starting point the suggestion that legal scholars, lawyers, judges, and legislators would have much to gain by being more knowledgeable about findings and insights, that draw on anthropological studies of kinship, and I will attempt to demonstrate why.

In anthropology, the study of kinship focuses on the rules and principles by which humans are organized into social groups, typologies, and/or roles by means of family relations and the terminologies assigned to them.[1] Ethnographic accounts of kinship, which address topics such as alliances, the organization of descent, sexuality, and sexual prohibitions, reveal not only the great diversity of rules that govern these relations; they also show how, in some communities, kin-based relationships continue to play a central role in maintaining and regulating the social structure of the group. Some more accurate knowledge about this role may well prove to be useful in the search for justice in individual cases where kinship logics are at the heart of the (legal) issue at hand. This will be the argument underlying the following analysis.

The chapter is divided into three parts: in the *first part*, I provide a few signposts in the field of kinship anthropology and summarize a number of key questions that have preoccupied scholars writing on kinship, drawing on ethnographic accounts of the specificities of the most diverse kinship systems across the globe (see Bodenhorn 2013; Fox 1967; Héran 2009; Lévi-Strauss 1949 [1971]; McConvell et al. 2013).

In the *second part*, I identify certain lessons that can be drawn from these studies. I see *two* such fundamental lessons, each of which, in my view, remains useful for identifying changes that, in the contemporary era, are affecting the role and place of kinship in the organization of social relationships. The first lesson has to do with the profoundly social and cultural nature of kinship. Anthropology shows, via countless illustrations taken from ethnography, that the way in which the roles of individuals are understood in the transmission of life and in how identities, including the sexual dimension differs substantially depending on social, economic, and historical contexts. The second lesson is that one should not be too quick to conclude that the newest trends and tendencies we see in the organization and perception of kinship today are unprecedented, whether in the area of cutting-edge reproductive technologies that confound the concept of parentage, alternative partnership arrangements, including the multiplication of sexual partners, or extreme permissiveness with regard to sexual matters, to name only the examples to which I will return below. Ethnographic accounts collected from around the globe show that these tendencies are not as new as one might think.

Finally, in the *third part*, I draw on a quotation from Maurice Godelier that appears on the back cover of his *Métamorphoses de la parenté* (2004):

> [T]he enormous upheaval that Western societies are undergoing is unprecedented; what we have been seeing for the past 30 years does not herald the disappearance or the death throes of kinship, but rather its remarkable metamorphosis—one that, paradoxically, is bringing us closer to the "traditional" societies studied by ethnologists'[2]

This observation by a French anthropologist who spent several decades studying kinship (see e.g. Godelier 1982, 2004; Godelier and Strathern 1991) reflects a position that I will take a closer look at below. Can one postulate that anthropology, with some of its foundational work in the study of kin-based social relations and their role in different types of societies, is still well placed today to help one understand the metamorphoses to which Godelier refers and the prominent role he continues to attribute to ethnographic data on human kinship in his comparative anthropological analysis of patterns of human reproduction and intergenerational continuity in contemporary societies?

Godelier expresses a fair amount of optimism about the future of kinship studies in anthropology. The transformations ('metamorphoses', as Godelier calls them) move in different directions: in some cases, towards an ever greater individualization of kinship practices, and in other cases towards attributing greater weight to the rules inherited from the past in the areas of kinship, sexuality, and relations between the sexes, and to maintaining kin-based relationships as a way to cope with the 'threat' of individualization. In both scenarios, Godelier sees more continuity with the past than disruption. This opens up a broad field that remains to be assessed in its full complexity, by both anthropologists and lawyers. Based on the knowledge gained in kinship studies in anthropology, what can one say about the different forms of kin-based relationships currently in place in different parts of the world and how they impact those involved? Do these relationships have any status under state law, and if so, on what insights and/or concerns do the regulations related to that status draw?

Anthropology and Kinship Systems

One of the founding fathers of the anthropological study of kinship systems was Lewis Henry Morgan, who, in 1871, published his impressive volume *Systems of Consanguinity and Affinity of the Human Family*. He was followed, to mention but a few names here, by William Halse Rivers, Alfred Kroeber, A. R. Radcliffe-Brown, E. E, Evans-Pritchard, Meyer Fortes, G. P. Murdock, Claude Lévi-Strauss, Floyd Lounsbury, Louis Dumont (see especially 1998), and Rodney Needham, all of whom continue to occupy a significant place in the history of the study of kinship.

Their achievement, unprecedented in their time, was to map the different systems of kinship they found and to show in greater detail how each follows its own intrinsic logic, which was often very different from those of European and Euro-American kinship systems of the time. In retrospect, one may say that Morgan was the first researcher in anthropology who made the effort to gather the widest possible range of empirical information about kinship practices in societies from the four corners of the earth (Trautmann 2008). Morgan introduced some major distinctions that have significantly impacted future generations of scholars in their attempt to better understand the diversity of meanings of kinship terms, a topic on which he focused much of his attention.[3] During the past century, several generations of students in anthropology have been trained in the comparative study of some of the major principles governing the organization of the bonds of descent and alliance among individuals and groups. Studies published in this area have confirmed time and again the importance of kinship ties for the functioning of some societies in particular. Anthropologists have spoken in this regard of 'kinship societies'.[4] From about 1930 to 1960, structural functionalism was the dominant theoretical school in British social anthropology. It was originally formulated in opposition to evolutionism. The structural functionalists developed a focused interest in kinship and lineage, which they saw as a key to understanding how social networks function in the societies they studied.[5]

Anthropologists who have taken an interest in the study of kinship systems have identified, from the outset, a set of fundamental questions that remain to this day unresolved or without conclusive answers. Among these questions, the one that has probably seen more ink spilled than any other is the prohibition against incest. Incest prohibition takes different forms, depending on the context and the society concerned, but, as a general principle, it is universal.[6] Another major question is male domination, an issue that has been addressed by many authors, in particular since the 1970s, a period that saw enormous growth in interest in the position of women in the societies studied by anthropologists. The concept of male domination and the degree to which it is universal remain matters of vivid debate: what are its origins and what explains its endurance over time?[7] A third major question is the specific place of kinship terminologies and their evolution. These terminologies are a rich resource, as mentioned above, and notwithstanding the fact that they are often difficult to map out, experience has shown that they are useful for the study of how kinship systems function, even though it is not always clear why some terminologies have survived, while others are abandoned or undergo a transformation that may not necessarily be consistent with the role maintained, recovered, or lost by a particular kinship system. Interest in these major questions waxes and wanes, however, from one period to the next. Today no one seeks any longer to deduce from the formal analysis of kinship terminology the structure, and thus also the normative logic at play, among members of the group or society that uses it, as to do so is now regarded as reductionist.

The space allotted to the topic in this volume will not, of course, suffice to summarize, even in its bare essentials, the knowledge acquired over almost two centuries of anthropological research on kinship. So, I focus here on only two observations, both deeply rooted in those studies, that will serve to underpin the hypothesis I put forward in the third part of this chapter, namely, the hypothesis of *continuity* that Godelier refers in the passage quoted above, and how that continuity can inform law when it comes to regulating present-day forms of consanguinity and affinity.

The *first* of these observations is that anthropological studies, to their great merit, have demonstrated, by means of ample and diverse ethnographic documentation, the deeply social nature of kinship relations. What does kinship reveal about the organization of social relationships in human societies? Reduced to the essentials, kinship and the various ties that it creates (or prohibits) and that are binding on those who are defined as members by the system, mark the distinction between sexual unions that are socially sanctioned and those that are forbidden; kinship hence defines acceptable conjugal unions and the social arrangements for rearing the children born of those unions (Goody 1976). At the heart of kinship, as studied in anthropology, is the newborn or unborn child, who is given a social and sexual identity. The child finds itself surrounded by a family—large or small, more or less stable—made up of lines of filiation formed by alliances which provide it with a normative framework. Filiation and alliance (consanguinity and affinity, to use Morgan's terms) constitute the two major axes along which, broadly speaking, all kinship relations are situated. These, in turn, serve as the reference point for the nomenclature of kinship.

From a strictly biological perspective, it may make perfectly good sense to follow the vertical and horizontal axes of kinship, tracing filiation as far back into the past as possible or projecting it forward into the future. But in practice, this is not how kin-based relationships work. Human societies make choices, and ethnographic accounts demonstrate that there are numerous ways to give meaning to kinship and to determine its legal consequences. Over the centuries, anthropologists have identified several hundred distinct kinship systems, which can be grouped into a few main types (McConvell et al. 2013). The value of studying these kinship systems and the differences among them is that comparison makes it clear that societies follow their own reasoning, and the social (and legal) consequences they attribute to similar (biological) ties may diverge greatly.

The *second* observation is closely linked to the first: kinship anthropology reveals that groups or communities often use the rules that govern kinship relations for their own purposes and to maintain the existing social order, both internally, among the members of the group, and in their relations with the outside world. Being the eldest in a phratry,[8] for example, may confer exclusive rights, such as being the sole heir to all the land and buildings on the estate, but in return, this exclusive right is often accompanied by an obligation to support and/or care for one's parents and/or siblings. These rules constitute a binding regime of behaviour for a community or society that applies to all individuals involved, situating them in relationship to one another within a shared normative framework that creates a form of interdependence among the individuals and groups within the framework. Practices such as the payment of *mahr* to the bride, the *iddah* in Islamic law,[9] and widow inheritance, for example, all draw on, as well as create, a form of interdependence that biological ties alone cannot explain. This interdependence is inscribed within a (normative) system that invests some kinship relations with greater societal significance than others. The precise content of such interdependence varies from one system to the next, and brings with it a set of requirements and prohibitions that, to a large extent, shape the relationships among individuals and groups in a society. Empirical observations gleaned by anthropologists from their fieldwork show that these systems are often also political and economic ones that put the regulation of kin-based relationships at the service of their own reproduction.[10]

Most anthropologists today no longer subscribe to the functionalist thesis that pre-state societies were based mainly on kinship ties ('kin-based societies').[11] It takes more than that to build a society. However, the study of the underlying logic of the various ways in which human societies use kinship in their internal organization, and to distinguish themselves from other groups, has yielded a kind of knowledge that remains eminently valuable; this is its enduring merit. Such findings are indeed still useful today, in a world undergoing profound transformation, for understanding certain principles that govern individual behaviour and that sometimes keep in place inherited structures of interdependence among individuals and groups that, at first glance, may seem ill suited to the realities of life in contemporary society. Certain older, surviving forms of kinship ties are not necessarily to be regarded as relics of the past, and there is more to be gained by trying to apprehend them in their full complexity than from disparaging them. This is true not only from a strictly academic perspective, but also in a more practical sense, in light of the need of legal practitioners tasked with the search for justice in concrete cases to comprehend the logics at play. For example, early-age marriages and simultaneous marital relationships (i.e. polygamy) among immigrant communities are but two illustrations of persistent kinship practices that challenge European legal systems today.[12] An anthropological approach investigates why a given group or community would want to maintain certain kin-based practices and institutions, and can thereby show that prohibiting, or even criminalizing, such practices without sufficiently taking into account what they mean for the people concerned risks doing great injustice; it takes away the protection that such practices offer without providing an equivalent alternative.

Kinship in the Organization of Human Societies: Knowledge of Lasting Significance

Not only has interest in kinship in anthropology fluctuated over time, but it is also probably no exaggeration to posit that kinship as a field of disciplinary expertise is no longer in fashion among anthropologists itself. In fact, the relevance of kinship to a proper understanding of the design and regulation of social relationships is itself in dispute. This decline in interest can be attributed to a number of factors. On the one hand, changes that have been in process in many countries have led to the state and its institutions taking over many of the functions of solidarity, support, and interdependence that kin-based mechanisms traditionally fulfilled (Goody 2000; Lefebvre-Teillard 2003; Sabian and Teuscher 2007).[13] Kinship ties, which may have played a crucial role in the social and political organization of society in other periods, are now seen as much less significant. At least, that is the expectation. Another reason that no doubt has played a role in the decline of kinship studies is the desire on the part of anthropologists to distance themselves very clearly from the evolutionary paradigm that, for many decades, dominated the discipline, as well as from the ethnocentric conceptual framework that, directly or indirectly, took as its primary point of reference the Western model of kinship organization (Tucker 2014).

The turn away from kinship anthropology in its traditional meaning is now so widespread that it has disappeared from the curricula of many university programmes or, if maintained, it has been relegated to the rank of an optional field of study. This does not mean, however, that questions concerning the functioning of kinship systems within contemporary society have disappeared entirely from the agenda of research conducted in anthropology; it is just that they are no longer studied in the same way. Kinship as a subject matter of scientific enquiry has given way to questions related to new social conventions that accompany the formation of a person's identity (see e.g. Burke et al. 2003). This approach assigns greater value to identity-forming factors *outside* the family context, such as ethnic affiliation, minority status, upward social mobility, the role of world views and beliefs, the appearance of e-communities, and so on, and places the emphasis on individual agency, whether real or fictitious. Alternatively, kinship is studied as a mechanism for maintaining certain forms of loyalty, solidarity, and support that coexist alongside other mechanisms, particularly in circumstances where these other mechanisms have proven less effective, less protective, or inaccessible. I will return to this in the third part of this chapter. Generally speaking, it could be said that anthropologists apprehend kinship differently today, and where the topic still holds their interest, it appears to be much more difficult to study, given the profound, and at times contradictory, movements that have called into question the notion that kinship ties and the ways in which they are institutionalized could possibly allow one to also apprehend the deeper social organization of a group or community.

Nevertheless, I see two main insights gained from the study of kinship systems in anthropology that have lost nothing of their relevance and topicality. The *first*, already mentioned, is the inter demonstration, via numerous detailed ethnographic accounts, that kinship, because it is a social convention, makes it possible to ensure a certain degree of solidarity among the individuals who make up a group and, if necessary, to establish authority over or inter dependence among them. In the context of contemporary societies, in particular in welfare societies, the expectation is that the weight and power of kinship ties has decreased considerably as other conventions have appeared that replace the traditional kin-based logic (see e.g. Azzopardi and Grech 2012; Griffiths et al. 2017; Hoffmann and Larsson 2013; Tan 2015; Toğuşlu et al. 2014). Yet, their accounts offer a more nuanced picture, showing, by means of empirical observations, the continued importance of kinship ties as social *conventions*, their role in the normative framework to which a considerable number of individuals still belong to this day; and, more generally, their profound impact on the everyday reality of those involved (e.g. Benteler 2015; Thelen and Alber 2018).

Beyond the essentially conventional nature of kinship relations, there is another insight of enduring relevance to be gained from the study of kinship systems in anthropology, namely, the observation that what may, at first glance, appear to be new and unprecedented ways of organizing and expressing kinship ties are in fact not so new. While the frequency of their occurrence may be without precedent, many of these forms of organizing and structuring kinships ties have always existed (Godelier 2007). Studies of kinship systems in anthropology show that, despite the ever-greater diversification of family structures that we see today, it would be a mistake to consider this unique to the present time: diversity is nothing new (Porqueres 2009). Whether one thinks here of the role of co-fathers or co-mothers in same-sex partnerships, multi-parenting, surrogacy, or the multiplicity of partners and permissiveness in sexual matters, to give but a few examples, these practices have all been amply documented in earlier anthropological studies of kinship. At the risk of presenting an overly truncated and simplified list of illustrations (each of which merits more nuanced discussion in its own right), I limit myself here to the four situations I have already mentioned: blended families, same-sex unions, the role of fathers, and the alleged sexual permissiveness of contemporary Western societies.

The first example has to do with blended families, that is to say, families where at least one of the children is from a previous union (Martial 1998). These can be simple in form, including children from a single phratry, or they may be complex, combining children from different unions. Where dissolution of a union with children is legally permitted (Mazzurana 2018), the result is that new households are very often formed on a more or less permanent basis, with the arrival or departure of children from previous unions.

Moreover, with the growing mobility of people in today's world, the composition of families is also changing, and blended households as a result of international migration are ever more frequent (Bryceson 2019; Ducu et al. 2018; Tiilikainen et al. 2020). While longitudinal data do indicate a real decrease in the rate of marriage in many countries around the world (particularly in 'Western' societies), accompanied by a rapid rise in informal unions that are generally less stable and therefore lead to a steady rise in blended families, anthropological studies show that such families have always existed and are well documented in the ethnographic literature (see e.g. Inhorn 2018). Blended households generally adhere to the same sexual prohibitions, whether hetero- or homosexual, that apply to other households, which seems to suggest that the new blended families remain an integral part of the kinship system.

What is true of blended families is also true of other forms of organization and structuring of kinship ties. Same-sex unions, for example, may at first glance appear to be a distinguishing feature of liberal democracies, where the combination of the principles of self-determination and non-discrimination (Brems et al. 2020; Leckey 2015; Roy 2015) have opened the way to diversification (see e.g. Boele-Woelki and Fuchs 2017; Gallo 2014; Théry 2013). From the perspective of comparative ethnography, however, we can see that homosexual relations in some cases replace and in other cases complement heterosexual relations (Robertson 2005). Homosexuality is problematized, generally speaking, when it is perceived as a threat to the social order of a group or society; but as a form of sexuality, it has not been universally treated as a source of conflict, exclusion, or rivalry. In some cases, homosexuality is tolerated as long as it is confined to the private realm.

When it comes to the role of fathers, and in particular the cooperation between men and women in child-rearing, anthropological studies indicate that—despite appearances—men have very often collaborated, more or less closely, with women and supported them in bringing up the children they have brought into the world, even if they were not always designated as occupying the role of the 'father'. In his early twentieth-century ethnographic study of sexual behaviour on the Trobiand Islands, Malinowski (1927) noted that fatherhood was recognized as a social and nurturing role. Though local population was unaware of the physiological need for a male in siring a child, they regarded him as *socially* indispensable.

Finally, there is sexual permissiveness, allegedly characteristic of contemporary liberal societies. Anthropological studies have shown that societies differ as to the margin of liberty they allow to their members—both men and women—regarding sexual activity, but that permissiveness is in no way new or exclusive to the present era. Generally speaking, permissiveness ends where it threatens the functioning of institutions such as marriage and other political, religious, and economic formations.

In sum, all four illustrations are evidence that the regulation of sexuality and the control of fertility can take multiple, at times surprisingly lenient forms in different societies' approaches to their reproduction. This multiplicity, which is specific to human societies and has been so carefully studied in anthropology, should make more confident those who are reluctant to accommodate *in law* this multiplicity.

Kinship in decline? A field of research that retains its topicality

As I have mentioned, kinship as the classic subject of study by anthropologists has lost much of its appeal by virtue of the fact that, within the discipline today, it is no longer regarded as a sufficiently encompassing explanatory factor for social organization. This is not to say, however, that the relationship between kinship and belonging has completely lost its meaning. One can see the enduring value of keeping a finger on the pulse of kinship studies in anthropology in two specific contexts, both of which are related to legal practice and the need to accommodate, in law specific types of kin-based social relationships and their consequences for the individuals involved. The first context I will consider very briefly here is that of the unprecedented and very impressive scientific advances in the area of medically assisted reproductive technology (ART). The second context is that of the various situations in which people have more to gain from the protection they receive from a kinship system—whether or not based on consent—than from any other regime or mechanism of support.

Scientific Advances in Assisted Reproductive Technology

Assisted reproductive technology (ART) is undoubtedly a new reality in the history of humanity that brings with it substantial changes in the way of thinking of descendt and kin-based identity (Edwards 1999). With ART and the many possibilities it now opens up (*in vitro* fertilization, gamete or embryo donation, surrogate motherhood, etc.), the 'natural order' of things has been shaken up, and what was once considered inconceivable has, in no time, become within reach. This raises enormous questions of a philosophical, ethical, and religious nature (e.g. Clarke 2009) regarding, for example, the problem of eugenics ('designer babies') that challenge the legitimacy of the results of certain practices.

But more to the point for the purposes of this chapter are the legal challenges that come with recourse to ART, as it brings into play new actors and redistributes the contributions they make to the process of conceiving a child (e.g. Edwards 2009; Feuillet-Liger et al. 2014; Melhuus 2012). Recourse to ART comes into play for a variety of reasons—same-sex parenthood, persons who choose to have a child without a partner, medical complications, etc.—and with these technologies new configurations emerge that call for a new concept of family. The traditional concept of the family unit, made up of a male–female couple who take legal responsibility for their progeny, no longer constitutes the only frame of reference. Kinship issues arise ever more frequently when there is a desire to conceive a child, and new family configurations are built around that desire (Delaisi de Parseval 2008). ART offers 'made-to-measure' avenues—whether for the creation of an embryo through gamete, sperm, or egg donation, or for gestation, such as surrogacy arrangements—that must take into consideration the specificities of each individual situation, as well as the broader family context. These configurations have a number of repercussions regarding what constitutes a family and how to distribute the roles among its members; in practice, they may bear the seeds of conflicts of interest that can be extremely difficult to resolve in legal terms (Baumle 2015). Until recently, procreation and filiation, the two fundamental processes of kinship, had been the exclusive domain of the same set of players—a father, a mother, and their children. With ART, a new division of labour has emerged, and with it new roles: that of the ovum, the gestational womb, and, of course, the fertilizing sperm. This gives rise to fundamental dislocations: Who is/are the father(s)? Who is/are the mother(s) (e.g. Ross 2016)?

These 'dislocations' of fatherhood and motherhood today increasingly preoccupy legal scholars, who disagree among themselves about the priorities to be set. For some, laws and the solutions they propose must uphold the existing family model: man, woman, child (see Meulders-Klein 1999). For others, a retrograde approach is no longer warranted; instead, solutions must urgently be found that, while preventing abusive instrumentalization of the reproductive capacities of the human body,[14] safeguard new ways of being parents and children and grant them legal protection (Cooper 2017; Golombok 2015). According to the latter scholars, societies need to accept differences, abandon older, reassuring models, and give precedence to policies that embrace new concepts of family and procreation that are both more realistic and fairer, provided they are not discriminatory. Such acceptance necessarily has to involve their recognition in law (Boele-Woelki and Martiny 2019).

Anthropologists, for their part, have also begun to take an interest in the new contours of kinship (e.g. Naef 2017). Different to legal scholars, their concern is not to redefine the concept of 'family'. As mentioned above, kinship anthropology traditionally focused on the study of social ties organized around consanguinity and affinity, sexuality, and/or sexual prohibitions. The knowledge accumulated in anthropology, which draws on this approach to kin-based relationships, shows that by keeping in place the major axes along which sexuality and human reproduction are still regulated today in many legal systems (the familiar triad of father, mother, and child, religious representations that take a dim view of scientific advances in the field of ART, and the inertia of certain legislators, who appear hesitant to confer legal status on emerging models, such as that of surrogate mothers), precious time is lost. Anthropological studies show that a child can have a balanced upbringing in any family model, to cite just one recurring ethnographic observation.[15] Why not take this as a starting point at a time when an increasing number of legal systems around the world are repositioning themselves with regard to protecting new concepts of family and procreation? Several systems have started doing so, grounded in reasoning that takes ever more seriously the interests of the child as a legal subject, and drawing from this prioritization the need to grant formal legal protection to new forms of kin-based relations (Delaisi de Parseval 2008).

A Lasting Role for Traditional Kinship Systems?

The second context that shows the importance of not overlooking kin-based relationships is the numerous situations where kinship ensures a form of support or even refuge, a 'shield' so to speak, that provides more reliable protection than any other available mechanism against the risks of increased vulnerability caused by globalization, political, ethnic, or religious marginalization, or even persecution. In some instances, recourse to kin-based logics of mutual support and interdependence may serve as a means for a person to cope with demanding living conditions. Ethnographic accounts abound in illustrations that show how, more or less worldwide, kinship still serves as a shared bulwark against the risks associated with rampant globalization of the economy and with the absence of alternative mechanisms for assisting those who are rendered particularly vulnerable by these social and economic transformations. The bonds of kinship, whether by consanguinity, affinity, or ties to a shared, geographically rooted group to which one belongs, continue to play an important—and even a necessary—role by virtue of the obligations that they entail to share, to care, and to provide hospitality and mutual aid (see e.g. Alber and Drotbohm 2015; Geen 2013; Gelsthorpe et al. 2020; Haldis and Frances 2005; Harding et al. 2017). In one case, it might be the payment of a relatively large dowry that makes it possible to fulfil such an obligation (Nielsen and Mehdi 2011); in another case, the expectation is that members of the kin group who have 'succeeded' in a financial sense will look after their relatives—near or far—and allow them to stay with them for shorter or longer periods (McLean 2018). The logic of kinship can also help preserve a collective identity over a long period, notably in diaspora situations, where endogamous marriages are particularly valued (Çitlak et al. 2017; Grillo 2015; Shaw and Raz 2015).

Today, individual human rights are enshrined in law in most countries. The mainstream legal literature on human rights makes the case that (individual) human rights ought to benefit all. In reality, however, such an approach is misleading. Ethnographic studies explain in detail the numerous obstacles that may arise in the course of advancing this particular concept of human rights. One such obstacle is the fact that the notion of individual human rights, as protected by most existing international human rights treaties (with a few notable exceptions), is derived from specific historical circumstances that have not affected all human societies to the same extent or in the same way. As a result, their supposed universality is highly questionable. Kinship studies in anthropology show that reality, as lived by individuals and the groups they form, cannot simply be reduced to an issue of whether international human rights law is violated or not. Instead, through ethnographic observation, anthropologists explore the degree to which the acceptance of pluralism within international human rights law can serve as a way to deal with diversity, both within and across societies.

When applied to any of the situations mentioned above—be it the payment of a considerable dowry, the persistence of early-age marriages, or the practice of endogamous marriage in the context of international migration that offers possibilities for family reunification and therefore considerable improvement in the material living conditions for a large circle of relatives, the application of international human rights standards will more often than not lead to the conclusion that such practices cannot be granted recognition under state law because they do not meet the requirements of respect for individual self-determination and non-discrimination. In Europe, case law offers ample illustrations of such rulings, where a family judge, a juvenile court, a prosecutor, or any other state administration in charge of granting permission to enter the territory of the country (in the case of family reunification, for example) refers to the principles of individual self-determination and non-discrimination to conclude that the relationship in question cannot be granted recognition in law (Cole and C. Groes-Green 2016; Gaucher 2018; Groes-Green and Fernandez 2018). The result is what are known in the literature as 'limping' situations: they lack recognition in at least one of the domestic jurisdictions to which the situation is connected, either through habitual residence or citizenship. Limping situations put the individuals involved in a difficult legal position: their kinship-based practices may be perfectly legal in the country of origin (Hacker 2017; Rutten et al. 2019), but are denied legal effect in the country of residence because they are deemed to violate human rights standards. In response, over the past three to four decades, new kinship-based practices have been emerging that—regardless of whether they meet the classical standards of respect for human rights—nevertheless do allow relatives to continue mutually supporting each other, across borders of countries and jurisdictions. In their own way, these practices reflect the profoundly social nature of kinship (Evergeti and Zontini 2006; Kohlhagen 2013; Singh 2014). In a globalized world, kinship thus continues to play a role, enabling groups to put the logic of kinship at the service of their own needs and interests (Baldassar and Marla 2014; Carter and Duncan 2018; Decimo and Gribaldo 2017; Hromadzic and Palmberger 2018; Kilkey and Palenga-Möllenbeck 2016).

Conclusion

For well nigh two centuries, anthropologists have been gathering a wide range of data on the different types of kinship systems found throughout the world. Although things have changed significantly since the days when they saw in kinship the primary system through which to understand the functioning of entire societies, the study of kinship has not lost its relevance.

For their part, legal scholars today are searching for ways to regulate ever more complex situations created by the advance and implementation of scientific knowledge in the field of human reproduction. They also wonder why, in so many communities today, the logic of kinship continues to prevail *over* the principles of individual self-determination and non-discrimination.

While anthropology does not have a conclusive answer to the latter question, by emphasizing the primarily social function of kinship, ethnographic findings amply demonstrate that human societies have, throughout history and in all circumstances, proven to be particularly creative in addressing issues of reproduction and membership. Following Godelier's hypothesis, there is every good reason to believe that the study of kinship will *remain* a discipline that is essential to a good understanding of the functioning of contemporary societies, in spite of the fact that it is far more complex and dynamic today than in the heyday of the anthropology of kinship. Ethnographic baseline studies of kinship logics and the role they played (and are still playing) in a number of contexts can undoubtedly improve our understanding of the difficult situations and settings in which individuals and/or communities are living, and may offer insights that cannot be gained in any other way. These insights are an invaluable reminder of the crucial role that kinship continues to play in the organization of social relationships the world over. A better understanding of this role would most probably make it possible, in law, to adopt a less critical and more confident attitude towards certain forms of kinship organization and to ensure that they receive the recognition and protection they need to be able to play their role fully, not in contradiction to the law, but in complementarity with it.

Acknowledgements

I wish to express my gratitude here to Alice Margaria and Ralf Michaels for the time and effort they took to review the first version of this chapter. Their insightful comments and targeted questions have proven extremely helpful.

Notes

1. 'Kin-based relationships are traditionally defined as ties based on blood and marriage. They include lineal generational bonds (children, parents, grandparents, and great-grandparents), collateral bonds (siblings, cousins, nieces and nephews, and aunts and uncles)', and affinal ties (i.e. through marriage) (Dykstra 2009: 1). In his study *Kinship and Marriage*, Robin Fox (1967: 30) defines the study of kinship in anthropology as 'the study of what man does with these basic facts of life—mating, gestation, parenthood, socialization, siblingship, etc.' To him, human societies are 'working with the same raw material as exists in the animal world, but can conceptualize and categorize it to serve social ends'.
2. The quotation has been translated from the original French by the author.
3. After Morgan, G. P. Murdock conducted a large-scale comparative study of some 250 societies, which he used to identify major types of kinship terminology systems. For example, he distinguished between parallel and cross cousins, which are categories of great significance in governing marriage alliances in certain societies (Murdock 1949).
4. Morgan's work is now criticized for its evolutionist overtones and assumptions. He recognized that European kinship systems, with their focus on monogamy and the nuclear

family, represented but a fraction of the kinship models in existence, but he nevertheless presented them as the most rational and highly evolved models of family life.

5. For a selection of readings by kinship scholars, see Goody 1971.
6. Prohibitions against incest can be explained, generally speaking, by the principle of exogamy in kinship groups, but empirical studies have shown that it can take different forms (see especially Barry 2008).
7. An intensely discussed work in this regard that was 'rediscovered' in the 1970s by feminist scholars is J. J. Bachofen's *Das Mutterrecht* (1861 [1948]). Bachofen posited that motherhood was the principal source of all human society, morality, and religion, becoming an inspiration to feminist 'matriarchal studies' of the 1970s. See also Moore (1999, 2012), di Leonardo (1991), Cornwall (1994).
8. A phratry is a descent group composed of two or more clans, each of whose apical ancestors descend from a common ancestor.
9. In Islam, *iddah* or *iddat* ('period of waiting') is the period of time a woman must wait following a divorce or the death of her husband before she may marry another man.
10. In that sense, see Rouland (1988); for a concrete illustration, see de Heusch (2012).
11. Schneider's (1984) famous critique of this approach is widely regarded as having inspired a critical reassessment of how kinship patterns had been analysed in earlier ethnographic works. In doing so, he cautioned the next generation of anthropologists against ascribing too much analytical weight and explanatory power to kinship (see e.g. Feinberg 2001).
12. On early-age marriages, see Yassari and Michaels (2021); on simultaneous marital relationships, see Bourdelois (1993).
13. As the renowned French jurist and legal anthropologist Norbert Rouland put it, 'When man entered into what we call History, not only did he invent the family, but he endowed kinship structures with forms of such refinement and complexity that "civilized" societies had almost nothing to add, but on the contrary impoverished them in so far as they transferred to the state the functions formerly fulfilled by the family' (Rouland 1988: 181; translated from the French by the author).
14. For illustrations of such abuses, see Pande (2014); Robertson (2010); Twine (2011).
15. This is not to imply that kinship societies could therefore also serve as models for family configurations that are the result of scientific advances in the broad domain of ART. Some anthropologists, however, have not hesitated to take that step. See Delaisi de Parseval (1983); Godelier (2004).

References

Alber, E. and H. Drotbohm, eds. 2015. *Anthropological Perspectives on Care: Work, Kinship and the Life-course*. New York: Palgrave Macmillan.

Azzopardi, A. and S. Grech, eds. 2012. *Inclusive Communities: A Critical Reader*. Rotterdam: Sense Publishers.

Bachofen, J. J. 1861 [1948]. *Das Mutterrecht*. Reprinted in H. Fuchs and K. Meuli, eds. *Johann Jakob Bachofens gesammelte Werke, Band 3*. Basel: Schwabe.

Baldassar, L. and L. Marla, eds. 2014. *Transnational Families, Migration, and the Circulation of Care: Understanding Mobility and Absence in Family Life*. New York: Routledge.

Barry, L. 2008. *La parenté*. Paris: Gallimard.

Baumle, A. K. 2015. *Legalizing LGBT Families. How the Law Shapes Parenthood.* New York: New York University Press.

Benteler, M., ed. 2015. *Perspektiven auf Verwandtschaft: Soziale Beziehungen in Europa und Asien. Perspectives on Kinship—Social Relations in Europe and Asia.* Berlin: Weißensee Verlag.

Bodenhorn, B. 2013. 'The Anthropology of Kinship: The Kinship of Anthropology'. In J. Carrier and D. B. Gewertz, eds. *The Handbook of Sociocultural Anthropology*, 137–55. London: Bloomsbury.

Boele-Woelki, K. and A. Fuchs, eds. 2017. *Same-Sex Relationships and Beyond: Gender Matters in the EU.* Cambridge/Antwerp/Portland: Intersentia.

Boele-Woelki, K. and D. Martiny, eds. 2019. *Plurality and Diversity of Family Relations in Europe.* Cambridge: Intersentia.

Bourdelois, B. 1993. *Mariage polygamique et droit positif français.* Paris: GLN Joly.

Brems, E., P. Cannoot, and T. Moonen, eds. 2020. *Protecting Trans Rights in the Age of Gender Self-Determination.* Cambridge: Intersentia.

Bryceson, D. F. 2019. 'Transnational Families in Global Migration: Navigating Economic Development and Life Cycle across Blurred and Brittle Borders'. *Journal of Ethnic and Migration Studies* 45(16): 3042–64.

Burke, P. J., T. J. Owens, R. T. Serpe, and P. A. Thoits, eds. 2003. *Advances in Identity Theory and Research.* Boston: Springer.

Carter, J. and S. Duncan, eds. 2018. *Reinventing Couples: Tradition, Agency and Bricolage.* London: Palgrave Macmillan.

Çitlak, B., S. Kurtenbach, M. Lueneburg, and M. Zlatkova, eds. 2017. *The New Diversity of Family Life in Europe: Mobile Ethnic Groups and Flexible Boundaries.* Wiesbaden: Springer.

Clarke, M. 2009. *Islam and New Kinship: Reproductive Technology and the Shariah in Lebanon.* New York: Berghahn Books.

Cole, J. and C. Groes-Green, eds. 2016. *Affective Circuits: African Migrations to Europe and the Pursuit of Social Regeneration*, Chicago /London: University of Chicago Press.

Cooper, M. 2017. *Family Values: Between Neoliberalism and the New Social Conservatism.* New York: Zone Books.

Cornwall, A., ed. 1994. *Dislocating Masculinity, Gender Power and Anthropology.* London: Routledge.

Decimo, F. and A. Gribaldo, eds. 2017. *Boundaries Within: Nation, Kinship and Identity among Migrants and Minorities.* Cham: Springer.

de Heusch, L. 2012. 'Parenté et pouvoir en Afrique centrale'. In P. Descola, ed. *Claude Lévi-Strauss, un parcours dans le siècle*, 93–109. Paris: Odile Jacob.

Delaisi de Parseval, G. 1983. *L'Enfant à tout prix.* Paris: Seuil.

Delaisi de Parseval, G. 2008. *Famille à tout prix.* Paris: Seuil.

Di Leonardo, M., ed. 1991. *Gender at the Crossroads of Knowledge: Feminist Anthropology in the Postmodern Era.* Berkeley: University of California Press.

Ducu, V., M. Nedelcu, and A. Telegdi-Csetri, eds. 2018. *Childhood and Parenting in Transnational Settings.* Cham: Springer.

Dumont, L. 1998. *An Introduction to Two Theories of Social Anthropology: Descent Groups and Marriage Alliance* R. Parkin, ed. and trans. New York: Berghahn Books.

Dykstra, P.A. 2009. 'Kin relationships'. In H.T. Reis and S. Sprecher, eds. *Encyclopedia of Human Relationships*, 951-954. Thousand Oaks, CA: Sage.

Edwards, J. 1999. *Technologies of Procreation: Kinship in the Age of Assisted Conception.* London: Routledge.

Edwards, J., ed. 2009. *European Kinship in the Age of Biotechnology*. New York: Berghahn Books.
Evergeti, V. and E. Zontini. 2006. 'Introduction: Some Critical Reflections on Social Capital, Migration and Transnational Families'. *Ethnic and Racial Studies* 29(6): 1025–39.
Feinberg, R. 2001. 'Introduction: Schneider's Cultural Analysis of Kinship and Its Implications for Anthropological Relativism'. In R. Feinberg and M. Ottenheimer, eds. *The Cultural Analysis of Kinship*, 1–31. Urbana: University of Illinois Press.
Feuillet-Liger, B., T. Callus, and K. Orfali, eds. 2014. *Reproductive Technology and Changing Perceptions of Parenthood around the World*. Brussels: Bruylant.
Fox, R. 1967. *Kinship and Marriage: An Anthropological Perspective*. Cambridge: Cambridge University Press.
Gallo, D. 2014. *Same Sex Couples before National, Supranational and International Jurisdictions*. Berlin/Heidelberg: Springer.
Gaucher, M. 2018. *A Family Matter: Citizenship, Conjugal Relationships, and Canadian Immigration Policy*. Vancouver/Toronto: UBC Press.
Geen, R. 2013. *Kinship Care: Making the Most of a Valuable Resource*. Washington, DC: Urban Institute Press.
Gelsthorpe, L., P. Mody, and B. Sloan, eds. 2020. *Spaces of Care*. Oxford: Hart Publishing.
Godelier, M. 1982. *La production des Grands Hommes. Pouvoir et domination masculine chez les Baruya de Nouvelle-Guinée*. Paris: Fayard.
Godelier, M. 2004. *Métamorphoses de la parenté*. Paris: Fayard.
Godelier, M. 2007. *Au fondement des sociétés humaines. Ce que nous apprend l'anthropologie*. Paris: Albin Michel.
Godelier, M. and M. Strathern. 1991. *Big Men, Great Men. Personifications of Power in Melanesia*. Cambridge: Cambridge University Press.
Golombok, S. 2015. *Modern Families: Parents and Children in New Family Forms*. Cambridge: Cambridge University Press.
Goody, J., ed. 1971. *Kinship: Selected Readings*. Harmondsworth, UK: Penguin.
Goody, J. 1976. *Production and Reproduction: A Comparative Study of the Domestic Domain*. Cambridge: Cambridge University Press.
Goody, J. 2000. *The European Family. An Historico-Anthropological Essay*. Oxford: Blackwell.
Griffiths, A., S. Mustasaari, and A. Mäki-Petäjä-Leinonen, eds. 2017. *Subjectivity, Citizenship and Belonging in Law: Identities and Intersections*. Abingdon: Routledge.
Grillo, R. 2015. *Muslim Families, Politics and the Law: A Legal Industry in Multicultural Britain*. Farnham: Ashgate.
Groes-Green, C. and N. T. Fernandez, eds. 2018. *Intimate Mobilities: Sexual Economies, Marriage and Migration in a Disparate World*. New York/Oxford: Berghahn Books.
Hacker, D. 2017. *Legalized Families in the Era of Bordered Globalization*. Cambridge: Cambridge University Press.
Haldis, H. and P. Frances, eds. 2005. *Generations, Kinship and Care: Gendered Provisions of Social Security in Central Eastern Europe*. Bergen: University of Bergen.
Harding R., R. Fletcher, and C. Beasley, eds. 2017. *ReValuing Care in Theory, Law and Policy: Cycles and Connections*. London/New York: Routledge.
Héran, F. 2009. *Figures de la parenté: une histoire critique de la raison structurale*. Paris: PUF.
Hoffmann, T. and G. Larsson, eds. 2013. *Muslims and the New Information and Communication Technologies: Notes from an Emerging and Infinite Field*. Dordrecht: Springer.
Hromadžić, A. and M. Palmberger, eds. 2018. *Care across Distance: Ethnographic Explorations of Aging and Migration*. New York/Oxford: Berghahn Books.

Inhorn, M. 2018. 'Fertility, Demography and Masculinity in Arab Families'. In: J. Suad, ed. *Arab Family Studies: Critical Reviews*, 449–66. Syracuse: University Press.

Kilkey, M. and E. Palenga-Möllenbeck, eds. 2016. *Family Life in an Age of Migration and Mobility: Global Perspectives through a Life Course*. London: Palgrave Macmillan.

Kohlhagen, D. 2013. *Diasporas africaines et mondes du droit. Une anthropologie juridique d'une migration entre Douala et Berlin*. Doctoral thesis, Paris I-Sorbonne.

Leckey, R., ed. 2015. *After Legal Equality: Family, Sex, Kinship*. Abingdon/New York: Routledge.

Lefebvre-Teillard, A. 2003. 'Famille'. In D. Alland and S. Rials, eds. *Dictionnaire de la culture juridique*, 698–701. Paris: Quadrige/PUF.

Lévi-Strauss, C. 1949 [1971]. *Les structures élémentaires de la parenté*. Paris: PUF.

Malinowski, B. *Sex and Repression in Savage Society*. 1927. London: Kegan Paul.

Martial, A. 1998. 'Partages et fraternité dans les familles recomposées'. In A. Fine, ed. *Adoptions: Ethnologie des parentés choisies*, 205–44. Paris: Éditions de la Maison des sciences de l'homme.

Mazzurana, T., ed. 2018. *Über die Rechtfertigung der Scheidung: Wandel und Kontinuität von Ehescheidungsdiskursen*. Wiesbaden: Springer.

McConvell, P., I. Keen, and R. Hendery, eds. 2013. *Kinship Systems: Change and Reconstruction*. Salt Lake City: University of Utah Press.

McLean, E. K. 2018. 'The Application of Kafala in the West'. In N. Hosen, ed. *Research Handbook on Islamic Law and Society*, 48–76. Cheltenham: Edward Elgar.

Melhuus, M. 2012. *Problems of Conception: Issues of Law, Biotechnology, Individuals and Kinship*. New York: Berghahn Books.

Meulders-Klein, M.-T. 1999. *La personne, la famille, le droit. 1968–1998: Trois décennies de mutations en Occident*. Paris/Brussels: L.G.D.J./Bruylant.

Moore, H. L. 1999. 'Whatever Happened to Women and Men? Gender and Other Crises in Anthropology'. In H. L. Moore, ed. *Anthropological Theory Today*, 151–71. Cambridge: Polity Press.

Moore, H. L. 2012. 'Anthropology and Gender Studies'. In R. Fardon, O. Harris, T. H. J. Marchand, M. Nuttall, C. Shore, V. Strang, and R. A. Wilson, eds. *The Sage Handbook of Social Anthropology*, 307–24. London: SAGE Publications.

Murdock, G. P. 1949. *Social Structure*. New York: Macmillan.

Naef, S. 2017. *Kinship, Law and Religion: An Anthropological Study of Assisted Reproductive Technologies in Iran*. Tübingen: Narr Francke Attempto Verlag.

Nielsen, J. and R. Mehdi, eds. 2011. *Embedding Mahr in the European Legal* System. Copenhagen: DJØF Publishing.

Pande, A. 2014. *Wombs in Labor: Transnational Commercial Surrogacy in India*. New York: Columbia University Press.

Porqueres, E. G., ed. 2009. *Défis contemporains de la* parenté. Paris: EHESS.

Robertson, J., 2005. *Same-Sex Cultures and Sexualities: An Anthropological Reader*. Malden: Blackwell Publishing.

Robertson, J. A. 2010. 'Commerce and Regulation in the Assisted Reproductive Industry'. In M. Goodwin, ed. *Baby Markets*, 191–207. Cambridge: Cambridge University Press.

Ross, R., ed. 2016. *Interrogating Motherhood*. Athabasca: Athabasca University Press

Rouland, N. 1988. *Anthropologie juridique*. Paris: PUF.

Roy, A., ed. 2015. *Pour un droit de la famille adapté aux nouvelles réalités conjugales et familiales*. Montreal: Themis.

Rutten, S., B. Deogratias, and P. Kruiniger, eds. 2019. *Marital Captivity: Divorce, Religion and Human Rights*. The Hague: Eleven International Publishing.

Sabean, D. W. and S. Teuscher, eds. 2007. *Kinship in Europe: Approaches to Long-Term Development (1300–1900)*. New York: Berghahn Books.

Schneider, D. M. 1984. *A Critique of the Study of Kinship*. Ann Arbor: University of Michigan Press.

Shaw, A. and A. E. Raz, eds. 2015. *Cousin Marriages: Between Tradition, Generic Risk and Cultural Change*. New York Berghahn Books.

Singh, S. 2014. 'Boomerang Remittances and the Circulation of Care: A Study of Indian Transnational Families in Australia'. In L. Baldassar and L. Merla, eds. *Transnational Families, Migration and the Circulation of Care: Understanding Mobility and Absence in Family Life*, 220–34. New York: Routledge.

Tan, L. 2015. *Metropolitan Identities and the Twentieth-Century Decolonization*. New York: Palgrave Macmillan.

Thelen, T. and E. Alber, eds. 2018. *Reconnecting State and Kinship*. Philadelphia: University of Pennsylviania Press.

Théry I., ed. 2013. *Mariage de même sexe et filiation*. Paris: EHESS.

Tiilikainen, M. M. Al-Sharmani, and S. Mustasaari, eds. 2020. *Wellbeing and Transnational Muslim Families: Marriage, Law and Gender*. London, New York: Routledge.

Toğuşlu, E., J. Leman, and İ. Mesut Sezgin, eds. 2014. *New Multicultural Identities in Europe*. Leuven: Leuven University Press.

Trautmann, T. R. 2008. *Lewis Henry Morgan and the Invention of Kinship*. Lincoln: University of Nebraska Press.

Tucker, W. 2014. *Marriage and Civilization: How Monogamy Made Us Human*. Washington, DC: Regnery Publishing.

Twine, F. W. 2011. *Outsourcing the Womb: Race, Class, and the Gestational Surrogacy in a Global Market*. New York: Routledge.

Yassari, N. and R. Michaels, eds. 2021. *Die Frühehe im Recht—Praxis, Rechtsvergleich, Kollisionsrecht, höherrangiges Recht*. Tübingen: Mohr Siebeck.

CHAPTER 30

ENVIRONMENTAL JUSTICE

DIRK HANSCHEL AND ELIZABETH STEYN

> For the Oceti Sakowin ['Great Sioux Nation'], Mni Sose, the Missouri River, is one such nonhuman relative who is alive, and who is also of the Mni Oyate, the Water Nation. Nothing owns her, and therefore she cannot be sold or alienated like a piece of property. (How do you sell a relative?) And protecting one's relatives is part of enacting kinship and being a good relative, or Wotakuye, including from the threat of contamination by pipeline leak—in other words, death. This would also spell death for the Oceti Sakowin and its nonhuman relations. In this way, the rallying cry of Mni Wicone—'water is life'—is also an affirmation that water is alive.
>
> Nick Estes, *Our History is Our Future* (2019)

Introduction

Two points bear making before delving into this chapter. First, the concept of 'environmental justice' covers a potentially vast terrain, ranging from current environmental challenges relating to climate change (climate justice, climate refugees), to developmental needs (involving the extractive industries and large-scale infrastructure projects), to concerns over particularly vulnerable communities (poor, racialized, Indigenous, etc.). This chapter strives to provide some structure to an otherwise nebulous notion.[1]

Second, while the chapter—as, indeed, the book of which it forms a part—results from an exchange between jurists and anthropologists, its authors are trained international and comparative jurists with a penchant for anthropology, Indigenous legal traditions, and interdisciplinary studies. We do not claim to speak for anthropology or Indigenous communities, nor to represent the spectrum of anthropological or Indigenous thought in the field of environmental justice. Rather, we aim to report what we have witnessed in our perambulations of the environmental justice domain. In other words, this chapter flows from a conversation about transcending the limits of the law. It is framed in a particular context, namely the evolving quest to attain environmental justice by means that transverse the boundaries of any single discipline.

We believe that a distinctly interdisciplinary approach that merges legal and anthropological perspectives advances scholarship in this field. It enables us to capture multiple perspectives and instances of environmental (in)justice in particular contexts. It also delineates a plurality of notions and norms that determines the relationship between human beings and their environment—ranging from international and domestic state law to competing notions at the local level.[2]

THE MEANING AND ORIGINS OF 'ENVIRONMENTAL JUSTICE'

'Environmental justice' is a polyvalent term with multiple potential foci, depending on the vantage points and the disciplinary backgrounds involved. In the context of the *social movement* for environmental and economic justice, it refers to environmental fairness and the equitable distribution of environmental benefits and burdens (Ali 2003; Anglin 2017). In *social science literature*, it denotes an interdisciplinary body of literature that includes theories of the environment and justice (Whyte 2018), environmental laws and their implications (Percival et al. 2014), environmental policy and planning (Checker 2005; Kuyek 2019), governance for development and sustainability (Newell 2008), environmental anthropology (Kopnina and Shoreman-Ouimet 2017), political ecology (Hetherington 2019; Pellow 2018), and political economy (Bell 2014). In its *legal sense*, environmental justice straddles various fields ranging from civil rights law (Bullard 1990) to constitutional law (Jaria i Manzano 2014), Indigenous law (Cutfeet 2019; Estes 2019), environmental law (Aseron et al. 2015), property law, land use laws (Carruthers 2008), labour law (Smith et al. 2006), and international law (Ako 2014; Martin et al. 2015). Within this array of related disciplines, we employ a combined approach of law and anthropology that reflects upon work previously undertaken, while also intending to break new ground.

Two Primary Senses of 'Environmental Justice'

For the purposes of the discussion in this chapter, we distinguish two primary senses in which the concept is used: the original meaning of obtaining justice for those who have suffered *injustice due to environmental abuses* and the more recently crystalized notion of *justice for the environment*. In both instances, there are further distinctions to be made: calls for justice in the first sense identify specific human victims who are often particularly vulnerable, be they an impacted community living downstream from a toxic facility (Bell 2014) or a displaced Indigenous, racialized, or impoverished community (Newell 2008; Whyte 2018). In the second sense, the (potential) victim is the environment itself (Jaria i Manzano 2014; Estes 2019; Estes and Dhillon 2019).

Differing world views can be distinguished at the basis of these conflicting visions of 'environmental justice'. To some extent, these can be condensed to the difference between the anthropocentric Western world view that, reduced to its essence, puts human beings at the centre of a world with natural resources available for exploitation (Newell 2008), and more holistic Indigenous-(influenced) world views in terms of which humankind forms part of nature as a unit preconditioned on the maintenance of balance and harmony (Cutfeet 2019; Estes 2019; Jaria i Manzano 2014). Established traditions of legal thinking are very diverse, and they fluctuate, oscillate, and influence each other. In addition, concepts of environmental justice cannot be fully understood without taking into consideration contexts of colonialism and post-colonialism (Gonzalez 2015). Recognizing that there is far more nuance in environmental justice debates and discourses than we can hope to address here, we nevertheless believe that the basic distinctions employed here remain suitable to inform the analysis that follows.

The Emergence of the Environmental Justice Movement in the United States

The classic environmental justice concept emerged in the early 1980s in the United States at the intersection of environmental hazards and racial injustice and as a counterpart to mainstream environmentalism (Bullard 1994; Gauna 1995). Poor rural areas and people of colour were affected by issues such as toxic waste sites, chemical plants, industrial agriculture that contaminated their drinking water, accident-prone oil refineries on their doorsteps, and the like (Gauna 2002b). This led to the coining of the term 'environmental racism' (Gauna 2012).

The crisis that sparked the movement was a 1982 siting controversy in Warren County, North Carolina that related to a hazardous waste landfill site (Eady 2007). In 1987, the United Church of Christ Commission for Racial Justice released an influential national study, *Toxic Wastes and Race in the United States* (cited in Carruthers 2008). This was followed by the First National People of Color Environmental Leadership Summit in Washington, DC in 1991 (Gauna 2002b). Thus was created a movement that in its classical formulation grapples primarily with the fact that environmental risks are disproportionately borne by low-income communities and communities of colour (Outka 2017).

Religious and civil rights leaders stepped up to the plate and launched a moral call for intervention (Gauna 1995), which eventually gave rise to a governmental response in the form of Environmental Protection Agency (EPA) mobilization in 1994 with the promulgation of Executive Order 12989, which directed all federal agencies to take environmental justice objectives into account insofar as it was practical and legally permissible to do so.[3] The twentieth anniversary of Executive Order 12989 was marked by the publication of *Plan EJ 2014: Legal Tools*,[4] a document identifying a number of substantive and procedural provisions under existing statutes that could be mobilized in the advancement of environmental justice goals. In a nutshell, it meant that multiple preoccupations of the environmental justice movement were addressed in a manner that enabled disproportionately affected communities to bring meaningful challenges to developments that impacted their health and quality of life—pollution (air, water, noise, odour, and light), noxious land uses (hazardous waste facilities, chemical plants, lead smelters, industrial plants), disproportionate exposure to contamination (lands, aquifers, contaminated fish caught from unsafe bodies of water, inordinately high exposure to pesticides by farm workers and children), and lead (from smelters and paint in old housing stock).

Geographical and Ontological Expansions of the Environmental Justice Discourse

While the U.S. version of 'environmental justice' remains ineluctably entwined with its civil rights activist roots, most frequently framed in paradigms informed by discrimination on the basis of poverty and/or race (Checker 2005), the environmental justice discourse has since found fertile ground in the work of scholars, activists, and policymakers globally. An important angle that emerged here relates to the global distribution of developmental risk, in the sense that the Global South is largely left to pay the price (whether in terms of climate change, toxic waste, or extreme weather) for production and development undertaken by the industrial North (Newell 2008). Thus, Carruthers (2008) has done important work in the context of Latin America and the Caribbean. In contradistinction to the United States, with its hazardous siting inequities, he argues, people in Latin American countries experience environmental injustice as a universal issue and not a class-based one. He identifies structural differences, including the widespread distribution of industrial hazards throughout metropolitan areas; the relatively restricted capacity for democratic political participation and protest; and the weaker efficacy of Latin American legal institutions in practice. Ako (2014) has underscored the problems posed by these factors in the Nigerian context, notably in the context of the Ogoni people's struggle to obtain reparations for the dispossession of their natural resources in favour of oil giant Shell.

Important questions have been raised about the links between neoliberal economics and environmental injustice and the appropriateness of developed-world climate change strategies for the Global South (Carruthers 2008; Rolston 2017). Thus, arguments are made that the industrialized countries of the West have had a long period during which to develop their (social and physical) infrastructure, whereas the developing countries, who now see rapid industrialization, do not have the same levels of infrastructure in place (Bell 2014). This has had the consequence that where only the most vulnerable segments of society were traditionally subject to environmental justice concerns in North

America, it has become a much more universal phenomenon in developing countries, where mobile capital can potentially exploit the less substantial barriers posed by the environmental laws in place and/or the lack of local enforcement capacity or governmental appetite for enforcement (Newell 2008).

Criticisms are levied against the introduction of neoliberal policies, such as the privatization of state institutions (Bell 2014), and the deregulation of state utilities, such as water resource management and electricity provision on the recommendation of institutions, including the World Bank and other multilateral development banks (Shiva 2013).

In addition, calls for 'energy justice' and 'climate justice' (Roosvall and Tegelberg 2018) increasingly form part of the environmental justice landscape, against the background of the movement away from fossil fuels and towards low-carbon energy resources (Outka 2017). These have been recently articulated in a whole wave of climate lawsuits that has likely not even peaked (Setzer and Vanhala 2019). In its modern iteration, there is therefore a distinctive interlinkage between climate change, energy, and environmental justice (Outka 2017).

Litigating Environmental Justice

The subsequent analysis focuses explicitly on prominent cases of litigation that provide a better idea of what environmental justice has to do with the solution of very concrete conflicts.

The classic legal environmental justice concept has travelled both horizontally and vertically, in that it has been adopted and applied in many jurisdictions around the world and has, in parallel, entered the realm of international law—all of which has brought about important conceptual variations and modifications.

Environmental justice litigation in a wider sense of the word[5] can be characterized by four different dimensions displaying an increasing degree of internationalization. The first dimension is purely domestic, in the sense that domestic environmental injustice is litigated in domestic courts applying domestic law. The second concerns domestic litigation of environmental injustice that is of a transboundary nature and/or established on the basis of international standards. The third pertains to international litigation based on violations of international law, but resulting from domestic environmental injustice, whereas the fourth addresses cross-border and/or transborder environmental injustice.[6]

First Dimension: Domestic Litigation in Domestic Courts

In its classic form, first-dimension environmental justice litigation stems from U.S. civil rights litigation under Title VI of the Civil Rights Act of 1964. The unequal treatment meted out to African American and Latin American communities raises civil rights concerns (Foster 2004; Osofsky 2005; Purdy 2018). For instance, planning and licencing decisions that unduly burden minorities or communities living in poverty may constitute race discrimination under the U.S. Constitution (Purdy 2018). The same applies where the environmental burden is more or less equally distributed across the city or community, but where unequal measures of protection, compensation, or alleviation are taken. Often cases concern not simply the inaction of the relevant authorities but conscious decisions to shift costs to communities that are less powerful and less able to defend themselves (Leal 1994). Underlying that, there might be racist or other unacceptable motives (Foster 2004).

For instance, in the United States and in Canada, water quality standards do not provide sufficient protection for Indigenous and other vulnerable communities who are dependent on subsistence fishing because they assume much lower rates of average daily fish consumption than is the case for residents of some such communities (Gauna 2002a). The environmental justice movement has acted against that imbalance and sought to tackle the inherent injustice through the courts. A good example is provided by the Flint, Michigan water quality standards issue. In January 2017, the Environmental Protection Agency (EPA) Office of Civil Rights found that 'the preponderance of evidence supports a finding of discriminatory treatment of African Americans by [the Michigan Department of Environmental Quality] in the public participation process' when issuing a permit to the Flint power plant in 1994 (Outka 2017: 803).

Since the debut of environmental justice litigation in the United States, cases have proliferated worldwide at the domestic level. A good illustration of environmental justice in this evolving context is provided by the conflicts in the global extractive sector. Conflicts between the extractive sector and civil society organizations combine multi-dimensional environmental and social impacts, ranging from deforestation to loss of biodiversity, displacement of peoples, groundwater contamination, and elevated water consumption rates (Aydin et al. 2017; Outka 2017).[7]

Given the sheer scale of domestic environmental justice litigation that has since emerged globally (Boyd 2012), we simply highlight one marked achievement: the establishment of domestic environmental courts and tribunals in many countries around the world (Amirante 2012; Pring and Pring 2016). A good example of this is the National Green Tribunal (NGT) in India (Gill 2010), which was specifically set up in 2010 to deal with environmental cases that may require a multidisciplinary perspective.[8]

Second Dimension: Domestic Litigation with an International Dimension

Striking environmental injustice can also be found at the international level where, for instance, very poor people in developing countries are extremely vulnerable to environmental harms resulting from emissions that have a global impact. Such injustice may be subjected to domestic litigation. Probably the most striking example of this is climate change and the environmental justice litigation that has revolved around it, which has come to be known as climate justice (Robinson 2018; Schlosberg and Collins 2014). While climate change has been mainly caused by the industrialized nations, developing nations are often hit harder by the consequences and find it more difficult to adapt to them. Courts can sometimes help to redress aspects of this imbalance at the domestic level. International law provides many substantive norms on environmental justice that can inform such domestic judicial decision-making.

One striking example of domestic claims against the state is the *Urgenda* case, in which a group of individuals argued successfully before Dutch courts up to the Supreme Court that the Netherlands was not doing enough to effectively combat climate change (De Graaf and Jans 2015; Nollkaemper and Burgers 2020). The Supreme Court reasoned that the Netherlands indeed had an obligation to live up to promises made in the climate treaties which are underpinned by the rights to life and respect for private and family life in the European Convention on Human Rights (ECHR).[9]

This case has triggered a wave of lawsuits in other countries and a rich academic debate (Backes and Van der Veen 2020; Nollkaemper and Burgers 2020). One question in that debate is how far courts can go in demanding specific governmental action without overstepping their competencies and violating the principle of separation of powers. The more climate change compromises people's ability to live their lives, the bigger the ensuing fundamental rights issue will become. It will be interesting to see how the German Constitutional Court deals with the pending constitutional complaints that roughly follow this line of the argument.[10]

A prominent pending case (relying on private law) involves a claim before German civil courts filed by a Peruvian citizen, Mr Lliuya, against the German energy company RWE (Frank et al. 2019; Hanschel 2018). The claimant demands that RWE make a contribution proportional to its share of global carbon emissions to help cover expenses incurred for protecting his house in the Peruvian Andes against flooding risks pursuant to the rising water levels in a nearby lake caused by a melting glacier in the vicinity.[11]

These cases and many others[12] show that there is now a second wave of environmental justice litigation that still employs the domestic courts (as the state offers the rule of law and effective enforcement) but with the intention of remedying injustices that have either occurred at the international level or that result from the violation of international norms. It offers a perfect example of Georges Scelle's notion of *dédoublement fonctionel*, in terms of which national law must provide the remedies that international law does not (Cassese 1990; Scelle 1956).

This has a number of effects. First, it means that there is a substantial degree of forum shopping and strategic case selection worldwide. One issue that deserves further research from a law and anthropology perspective is how precisely such strategic litigation may affect local community structures in the short term and in the longer run.[13] Second, it means that the injustice that triggers litigation is different in nature from the first wave of environmental justice cases. Whereas the classic cases often dealt with decisions of municipalities or other local or regional authorities, globalized environmental justice litigation would typically entail an aspect of distributional injustice. Courts are likely to be very cautious in deciding what precedents they are about to establish in an arena that is both local and global (Dellinger 2018; Fitzmaurice 2017).

Third Dimension: International Litigation Resulting from Domestic Environmental Injustice

The third dimension of environmental justice litigation concerns cases where domestic environmental injustice is tackled by international courts or quasi-judicial forums applying international law. Fully fledged courts are rather rare at this level, in particular courts that have the specific competence to decide cases in the field of environmental justice (Bodansky 2017; Lehmen 2018). In the absence of an international environmental court, other judicial institutions have dealt with specific aspects of environmental justice, each within their particular area of competence (e.g. Hassan 2017).

One prominent example is the European Court of Human Rights (ECtHR). While there is no right to environmental protection in the ECHR, the Court has started to subsume local environmental harm under existing guarantees. In the *López Ostra* case,[14] the applicant relied on her rights to physical integrity (Art. 3 ECHR) and to family life (Art. 8 ECHR), arguing that the Kingdom of Spain had violated her rights by not taking measures against emissions arising from a local waste treatment plant. Similar arguments have been made relating to a tannery or an airport.[15]

Situations of environmental injustice have also been reported to the UN Committee on Civil and Political Rights (CCPR), as well as the UN Committee on Economic, Social and Cultural Rights (CESCR) (Boyle 2011; Shelton 2002). These international human rights bodies react to state (and parallel non-governmental organization (NGO)) reports and to individual complaints regarding domestic human rights violations, which may correspond to environmental injustice. One example is the requirement posited by the CESCR to consult with local communities and to conduct human rights impact assessments relating to, *inter alia*, the right to water before erecting large-scale hydroelectric dams, as exemplified in the concluding observations regarding Ethiopia.[16] A recent case of the CCPR was concerned with poisoning resulting from agrochemicals.[17]

International environmental justice jurisprudence has been particularly dynamic in Latin America. A prominent case decided in the regional Inter-American human rights system was *Awas Tingni v. Nicaragua*, which concerned the state's alleged failure to protect ancestral communal land. The Inter-American Court of Human Rights (IACtHR) held that the Indigenous community's property must be protected against intrusions by the government.[18] More recent findings by the IACtHR concerned Columbia and Argentina. In the advisory opinion on Columbia, the Court derived a right to a healthy environment as such and in its own right from the Convention, and not only because it provides benefits for human beings.[19] By this wording of the opinion and by referring to Arts 1 and 2 of the International Union for Conservation of Nature (IUCN)

World Declaration on the Environmental Rule of Law, the Court goes a long way towards recognizing nature as an independent rights holder. In the 2020 decision on the case *Indigenous Communities of the Lhaka Honhat (Our Land) Association v. Argentina*, the Court found, among other infringements, violations with regard to the right to a 'healthy environment', which was the first such finding 'in a contentious case'.[20]

A pertinent, well-known example from Africa is the *Ogoni* case before the African Commission on Human and Peoples' Rights (ACHPR). It was an early case, decided in 2001, but it is still frequently referred to today. The landmark decision concerned a violation of human rights under the Banjul Charter due to the involvement of the Nigerian government in oil development activities by a foreign company in the Niger delta, leading to suffering of the local Ogoni population. The Commission found that the 'Nigerian Government ha[d] given the green light to private actors, and the oil companies in particular, to devastatingly affect the well-being of the Ogonis'. It was decided that, '[g]iven the wide spread violations perpetrated by the Government of Nigeria and by private actors (be it following its clear blessing or not), the most fundamental of all human rights, the right to life ha[d] been violated'.[21]

Another relevant development here has been the 2016 announcement by the International Criminal Court (ICC) that it would henceforth include among its case selection criteria crimes whose impact results in 'the increased vulnerability of communities, the degree of terror instilled, or the social, economic, and environmental damage inflicted on affected communities' (ICC 2016: para. 41). The Court would particularly consider crimes encompassing environmental destruction, illegal natural resource exploitation, and illegal land dispossession. (ICC 2016: para 7). Commentators have pointed out the ICC's capacity to hold liable non-state actors such as company directors (but not legal persons such as transnational companies; see Lehmen and Advocacia 2017).

Fourth Dimension: International Litigation Resulting from Cross-border or Transnational Environmental Injustice

The fourth dimension of environmental justice litigation is an international arena in which not only the injustice but also the litigation occurs at the international level, the starting point being international arbitration to solve bilateral conflicts resulting from cross-border emissions. The classic example is the 1941 *Trail Smelter Arbitration*. This dispute between the United States and Canada arose from a factory on Canadian soil that emitted toxic fumes across the border to the United States, resulting in substantial damage. The arbitral award expressed the now famous 'no transboundary harm' principle.[22] Another well-known older case is *Lac Lanoux* in 1957, which related to a dispute between France and Spain regarding the use of river water (Epiney 2006).[23]

Other international forums to decide more recent environmental justice cases have included the International Court of Justice (ICJ), the World Trade Organization (WTO) panels, and the Permanent Court of Arbitration.[24] For instance, the ICJ heard the *Pulp Mills* case between Argentina and Uruguay, which dealt with a pulp mill near the mouth of the Uruguay River that had caused substantial cross-border pollution in Argentina (Bodansky 2017; Vernet 2010).[25] The Court held that environmental impact assessment duties 'may now be considered a requirement under general international law ... where there is a risk that the proposed industrial activity may have a significant adverse impact in a transboundary context, in particular, on a shared resource'.[26] It furthermore stated that the parties had to 'promote the equitable utilization of the river, while protecting its environment'.[27]

Another very recent example of climate litigation is the *Teitiota* case, in which a Kiribati citizen and his family asked to be granted asylum in New Zealand as climate refugees who had suffered from the rising sea level on their island. The Supreme Court denied the claim.[28] The case was then taken to the UN Committee on Civil and Political Rights, which decided that there was no violation of the right to life in the specific circumstances but recognized that 'given that the risk of an entire country becoming submerged under water is such an extreme risk, the conditions of life in such a country may become incompatible with the right to life with dignity before the risk is realized'.[29] This illustrates how cases regarding environmental justice may move from the domestic to the international arena.

Expanding environmental justice

Slippages and Shifts

The vernacularization of the phrase 'environmental justice' in the age of climate crisis comprises both ontological and geographical slippages and shifts. By 'slippages', we mean that it is sometimes employed by actors opposed to, for instance, large-scale infrastructure development or extractive projects as a kind of slogan removed from core ontological content (Ali 2003); by 'shifts', we allude to the fact that its core ontological content is not static but is determined through the alchemy of factors such as time, space, and disciplinary focus.

In this section, we pay attention to a more holistic phenomenon: the fact that Indigenous traditions have long held a notion akin to 'environmental justice' as part of their cultures and world views in a manner that contrasts sharply with neoliberal Western notions of resource exploitation for profit (Estes 2019; Tola 2019).[30] Legal recognition has recently been afforded to such pre-existing holistic Indigenous conceptions of nature as *Pachamama* and an Indigenous way of living in harmony with nature (*buen vivir/suma qamaña/sumaq kawsay/Wotakuye/kawsak sacha*). This way of employing 'environmental justice' has thus taken the form of an ontological shift from an anthropocentric to a holistic or ecocentric notion of environmental justice.[31] Some see the latter shift as being accompanied by post-humanist thought, a need to move beyond the nature/culture divide and to account for the nonhuman other, while caveats are also sounded that it should not take place at the expense of resolving the 'quintessentially human problems of marginalization, exclusion, and injustice' (Zeiderman 2019).

Partial State Recognition of Indigenous World Views

Pachamama refers to the Andean notion of 'capricious earthly forces embodied in rocks, rivers and mountains', in other words, an 'unpredictable, even terrifying entity' that needs to be treated with the requisite respect (Tola 2019). Translating it as 'Mother Earth' has been criticized not only for being simplistic and lacking in nuance, but, more grievously, for portraying nature as a weak female in need of rescue (Tola 2019). Tola charges that this has not prevented environmentalists of all stripes from appropriating the term. That recalls '*Mni wiconi*: Water is life!', the rallying cry of the Dakota Access Pipeline opposition movement (#NoDAPL), an Indigenous resistance movement that was widely embraced by environmental groups under the aegis of environmental justice (Estes and Dhillon 2019). Lakota scholar Nick Estes, while crediting the supporting role of allies in opposing the pipeline, notes that, to the Lakota, water is not merely life-giving, but alive—it 'is animated and has agency' (Estes 2019).

A similar flattening of meaning has occurred in two plurinational states of Latin America, Ecuador and Bolivia, where *Pachamama* has become the subject of legal rights. In this context, Spanish constitutionalist Jaria i Manzano (2014) has argued that the Ecuadorian provision constitutes a misguided attempt to fuse Western notions of rights with Indigenous holistic content through the central role afforded to the Quechua notion of *sumaq kawsay*, which features prominently in the 2008 Constitution. It is misguided, argues Jaria i Manzano, because in seeking to afford rights protection to nature through a legal structure that is inherently foreign to Ecuadorian Indigenous traditions, which consider nature to be a limitless entity, nature effectively becomes limited in accordance with those very rights. As proof, he points to the fact that the Constitution prohibits the extraction of non-renewable resources from protected areas and simultaneously provides a mechanism whereby the president can lift the prohibition. This, he explains, is predicated on the fact that it is a socially transformative constitution that tries to balance the protection of (human) interests as represented by the exploitation of finite natural resources against the protection of nature.

In other words, there is substantial cultural mistranslation between constitutionalists and Indigenous peoples when it comes to the interpretation and impacts of the Ecuadorian Constitution—one that would require more than the embedding of a Quechua phrase in the text to resolve.[32] Acselrad (2008) has demonstrated the same incommensurability of values at work in the Brazilian context, arguing that 'an efficiency revolution is evoked [by neoconservatives] to save the planet by putting a price on what has no price'.

Rights of Nature

New Zealand's *Whanganui River Claims Settlement Act, 2017* affords an innovative form of hybrid juristic personality to a river (Steyn 2021). At the heart of the legal structure created by the Act lies *Te Awa Tupua*—the Whanganui River—as a juristic person with a hybrid nature, recognized as both a living entity and a corporate one (Steyn 2018).

There have been other instances where rivers were treated as living entities, such as a recent Ecuadorian judgment that required a provincial government to remedy damage to the Vilcabamba River on the basis of the previously mentioned constitutional provision recognizing *Pachamama* as a living being (Boyd 2017; Salmond 2014).[33] Similarly, in the Australian state of Victoria, the *Yarra River Protection Act* of 2017 reflects Indigenous conceptions of the river by means of a preamble that acknowledges the river as being alive, having a heart and spirit, and forming part of their Dreaming (O'Bryan 2019).

There are other examples where nature, or natural entities, have been endowed with legal personality. The classic example here is Christopher Stone's famous article on whether trees should have standing (Stone 1972). In 2010, the city of Pittsburgh, Pennsylvania extended legal personality to nature. The state legislature attempted to override this in 2012, but in 2015 the Pennsylvania Supreme Court declared the overriding legislation unconstitutional (Collins and Esterling 2019). The Te Urewera National Park in New Zealand was vested with legal personality by the *Te Urewera Act, 2014*. In 2016, the Constitutional Court of Colombia declared the Atrato River to be a legal person (Macpherson and Ospina 2015), and the Supreme Court granted rights to the Amazon River (Villavicencio Calzadilla 2019). Advisory Opinion OC-23/17 by the IACtHR discussed earlier has clear ecocentric dimensions. In India, the High Court of Uttarakhand recognized the rights to protection of two rivers and their glaciers (Badrinarayana 2017; Houck 2018; Selkälä and Rajavuori 2017).

Conclusion

In the epigraph at the beginning of this chapter, Estes (2019) makes the point that protection of nature's rights is essential for our own continued existence. The relationship between human and non-human is thus symbiotic, not dualistic (Strang 2017). This means that the anthropocentric and ecocentric senses of environmental justice explored in this chapter need not be mutually exclusive but could, in fact, serve to reinforce each other (Descola 2014)—much like Strang (2017) argues in respect of the nature/culture debate in anthropology.

This chapter has shown that there are many facets and manifestations of environmental justice—a concept that sits at the junction of legal doctrine and anthropological realities. Law favours constancy and consistency in the interests of legal certainty; anthropology emphasizes nuanced perspective and values the regard of the other. Both disciplines therefore have a role to play when grappling with the notion of environmental justice.

This collaboration functions on multiple levels. One is that ethnographic work allows for the capturing of examples of environmental injustice, which, in turn, opens up the possibility of studying legal responses to it. This can tell us something about the nature and application of the law. It can also assist us in shining the light of examination on the fabric of the law—on the adequacy of its responses when there are incommensurable values at stake or on instances of cultural mistranslation. In the words of anthropologist James Clifford (2013: 48), 'Cultural translation is always uneven, always betrayed.'

This means that environmental justice is a moving target. On the one hand, it is space- and context-dependent; on the other, it is constantly adapting to new realities. An increasing tendency towards juridification can be observed. One can thus justifiably claim that litigation has become an important aspect of the environmental justice movement (Todd 2020). But anthropological insight serves to caution us that the multitude of environmental justice notions, conflicting interests and rights, and underlying power relations render it unrealistic to expect that courts will ever be able to achieve a perfect equilibrium that accommodates all interests appropriately. Many people—often the most vulnerable—cannot access courts. The real litmus test for environmental justice usually arises where competing rights, needs, and interests are at stake, whether they be of economic, social, cultural, or other origin. Finally, we should not forget that environmental justice can be negotiated completely outside of state law, on the basis of local norms that may or may not be in accordance with state law.

When environmental justice involves rights of nature, jurists find themselves operating at the limits of the law. The law favours certainty and detailed precision. Thus, extending rights to nature begs the question of who can invoke them in the event of a legal dispute. As Descola (2013: 81) has pointed out, 'One does not have to be a great seer to predict that the relationship between humans and nature will, in all probability, be the most important question of the present century.' Clearly, this requires putting into more concrete terms what that relationship entails. Again, law and anthropology have a lot to offer in this regard. As topics such as climate change and loss of biodiversity show, the human–nature relationship is, indeed, among the most pressing issues of our time. Environmental justice is therefore likely to gain even more importance in the coming decades, and further interdisciplinary research will be required to understand what that justice may entail in very concrete and context-specific circumstances.

The concept of the rights of nature offers a particularly striking example of legal analysis that depends on anthropological insight. This chapter has striven to show that law also benefits from anthropology in a much more general way, from the conceptualization of environmental justice to understanding its various facets and variations—most particularly, when it comes to understanding the specific and concrete contexts of injustice that the concept seeks to address.

Notes

1. For very recent, rather comprehensive overviews by way of textbooks, see Coolsaet (2020) and Villa et al. (2020).
2. For a related project on environmental rights, see Hanschel (2019), available at <https://www.eth.mpg.de/ERCC_outline>. More generally, on multidisciplinary approaches to environmental justice, see Nesmith et al. (2021).
3. Executive Order 12989, Environmental Justice Strategy, EPA/200-R-95-00 (1995).
4. Environmental Protection Agency Plan EJ 2014, September 2011.
5. This may include more informal ways of norm-based conflict resolution by judicial or quasi-judicial means such as arbitration, dispute settlement through tribunals, etc. For an overview of strategic environmental litigation see, for instance, the worldwide activities of Client Earth, available at <https://www.clientearth.org/>.
6. This distinction serves to display how environmental justice has expanded in terms of arena and law. One should keep in mind, however, that these dimensions sometimes overlap in light of multi-level issues and legal norms. Other categorizations (e.g. with regard to climate litigation) may distinguish between private and public law, or primary claims for action or omission from secondary claims for compensation, or choose other models of distinction (see e.g. Cournil (2020); Hanschel (2018).
7. Extractive sector conflicts form a significant portion of global environmental justice struggles: thus, of the 1,200 international ecological distribution conflicts that were recorded over a 4-year period up to October 2014, close to 30% were classified as mining conflicts. Of these, 39% related to precious metals, 36% to base metals, 19% to energy-related materials, and 7% to construction-related materials. Rural and semi-urban areas accounted for nearly 85% of conflicts (Aydin et al. 2017: 4).
8. For details, see <https://greentribunal.gov.in/about-us>.
9. *The State of the Netherlands v. Stichting Urgenda*, Supreme Court of the Netherlands, civil division, No. 19/00135, 20 December 2019 [*Urgenda* case].
10. See *Klimaklagen*, available at <http://www.germanwatch.org/sites/germanwatch.org/files/Constitutional%20Complaint_EN.pdf>; <https://klimaklage.com/>; for a complaint at the EU level, see <https://peoplesclimatecase.caneurope.org/>.
11. The so-called *Huaraz case*, a claim by Saúl Ananías Luciano Lliuya against RWE AG, 23 November 2015. The claimant lost in the first instance (District Court Essen), but has entered the evidentiary stage in the second instance at the Higher Regional Court in Hamm, which has been hailed as a great success by Germanwatch. It is conceivable that this case might ultimately reach the German Federal Constitutional Court. For details, see <https://germanwatch.org/en/huaraz>.
12. For an overview, see Sabin Centre for Climate Change Law Databases, available at <http://climatecasechart.com/>.
13. For such a research agenda, see Hanschel (2019).
14. *López Ostra v. Spain*, ECtHR, merits and just satisfaction, App. No. 16798/90, A/303-C, [1994] ECtHR 46, (1995) 20 EHRR 277, IHRL 3079 (ECtHR 1994), 9 December 1994.
15. For an overview of cases, see <https://www.echr.coe.int/documents/fs_environment_eng.pdf>.
16. See UN CESCR in Ethiopia, E/C.12/ETH/CO/1-3, 31 May 2012, para. 24: 'The Committee recommends that the State party continue to identify and address the adverse social and environmental impact of the Gibe III dam. The Committee also urges the State party to

initiate, prior to construction of hydro-electric projects, comprehensive impact assessments as well as extensive consultations with affected communities, involving genuine opportunities to present views and influence decision-making.'

17. UN International Covenant on Civil and Political Rights, Human Rights Committee, Views adopted by the Committee under article 5 (4) of the Optional Protocol, C/126/D/2751/2016, 20 September 2019.
18. *The Mayagna (SUMO) Awas Tingni Community v. Nicaragua* (Merits, Reparations and Costs) IACtHR Series C No. 79, 31 August 2001 [*Awas Tingni*], para. 153.
19. Inter-American Court of Human Rights, Advisory Opinion OC-23/17 on the Environment and Human Rights (15 November 2017), para. 62. For the World Declaration on the Environmental Rule of Law, see <https://www.iucn.org/sites/dev/files/content/documents/english_world_declaration_on_the_environmental_rule_of_law_final.pdf>.
20. *Indigenous Communities of the Lhaka Honhat (Our Land) Association v Argentina*, IACtHR, Judgment of 6 February 2020, available at <https://www.corteidh.or.cr/docs/casos/articulos/resumen_400_ing.pdf>.
21. On the decision *Social and Economic Rights Action Centre (SERAC) v. Nigeria* (2001), AHLHR 60 (ACHPR 2001) [*Ogoni* case], see <https://www.achpr.org/public/Document/file/English/achpr30_155_96_eng.pdf>. See also Coomans (2003).
22. *Trail Smelter* (*United States v. Canada*), RIAA, 16 April 1938 and 11 March 1941, Vol. III, pp. 1905–82 [*Trail Smelter Arbitration*]: p. 1965: '... under the principles of international law, as well as of the law of the United States, no State has the right to use or permit the use of its territory in such a manner as to cause injury by fumes in or to the territory of another or the properties or persons therein, when the case is of serious consequence and the injury is established by clear and convincing evidence'.
23. *Lac Lanoux Arbitration*, Arbitral Tribunal, *France v Spain* 12 R.I.A.A. 281, Judgment of 16 November 1957 [*Lac Lanoux Arbitration*], p. 315: '... l'Etat d'amont a, d'après les règles de la bonne foi, l'obligation de prendre en considération les différents intérêts en présence, de chercher à leur donner toutes les satisfactions compatibles avec la poursuite de ses propres intérêts et de montrer qu'il a, à ce sujet, un souci réel de concilier les intérêts de l'autre riverain avec les siens propres'.
24. On the connection of trade and environment generally, see <http://www.wto.org/english/tratop_e/envir_e/envt_intro_e.htm>. On environmental disputes before the PCA, with reference to pertinent case law, see <https://pca-cpa.org/en/services/arbitration-services/environmental-dispute-resolution/>.
25. *Pulp Mills on the River Uruguay (Argentina v Uruguay)*, Judgment, 2010 ICJ Rep 14, 20 April 2010 [*Pulp Mills*].
26. *Pulp Mills*, para. 204.
27. *Pulp Mills*, para. 266.
28. *Ioane Teitiota v The Chief Executive of the Ministry of Business, Innovation and Employment*, Supreme Court of New Zealand. NZSC 107. Judgment of 20 July 2015 (*Teitiota* case); see <http://www.refworld.org/cases,NZL_SC,55c8675d4.html>.
29. *Ioane Teitiota v New Zealand*. United Nations, International Covenant on Civil and Political Rights, No. 2728/2016, 23 September 2020.
30. McGregor et al. (2020: 35) even suggest using the 'distinct formulation of Indigenous environmental justice (IEJ)'. See also Jarrat-Snider and Nielsen (2020).
31. Note that the shift to a more ecocentric approach that provides for rights of nature is not limited to Indigenous world views only. Moreover, not all rulings that concern Indigenous

peoples necessarily endorse an ecocentric approach. However, Indigenous world views have arguably been quite influential in clearing the way for state recognition of environmental justice notions in the ecocentric sense.

32. Broad Indigenous participation in the drafting of the Constitution ensured that Quechuan concepts such as *sumaq kawsay* were captured in the text (Scofield 2017).
33. Provincial Court of Justice of Loja, Sentence No. 11121-2011-0010, 30 March 2011; see <https://elaw.org/system/files/ec.wheeler.loja_.pdf>.

References

Acselrad, H. 2008. 'Grassroots Reframing of Environmental Struggles in Brazil'. In D. V. Carruthers, ed. *Environmental Justice in Latin America*, 75–97. Cambridge: MIT Press.

Ako, R. 2014. 'Environmental Justice in Nigeria's Oil Industry: Recognizing and Embracing Contemporary Legal Developments'. In R. V. Percival, J. Lin, and W. Piermattei, eds. *Global Environmental Law at a Crossroads*, 160–92. Cheltenham: Edward Elgar.

Ali, A. H. 2003. *Mining, the Environment, and Indigenous Development Conflicts*. Tucson: The University of Arizona Press.

Amirante, D. 2012. 'Environmental Courts in Comparative Perspective: Preliminary Reflections on the National Green Tribunal of India'. *Pace Environmental Law Review* 29: 441–68.

Anglin, M. K. 2017. 'Challenging the Conventional Wisdom—Breast Cancer and Environmental Health'. In H. Kopnina and E. Shoreman-Ouimet, eds. *Routledge Handbook of Environmental Anthropology*, 370–83. London: Routledge.

Aseron, J., J. Williams, and N. Greymorning. 2015. 'Inclusive Practices, Innovative Collaboration, Governance and Recognising Cultural Capital: Environmental Law through a Cultural Lens'. In P. Martin, S.Z. Bigdeli, T. Daya-Winterbottom, and W. du Plessis, A. Kennedy, eds. *The Search for Environmental Justice*, 333–55. Cheltenham: Edward Elgar.

Aydin, C. I., B. Ozkaynak, B. Rodríguez-Labajos, and T. Yenilmez. 2017. 'Network Effects in Environmental Justice Struggles: An Investigation of Conflicts between Mining Companies and Civil Society Organizations from a Network Perspective'. *PLoS ONE* 12(7): 1–20.

Backes, C. W. and G. A. Van der Veen. 2020. 'Urgenda: The Final Judgment of the Dutch Supreme Court'. *Journal for European Environmental & Planning Law* 17: 307–21.

Badrinarayana, D. 2017. 'The "Right" Right to Environmental Protection: What We Can Discern from the American and Indian Constitutional Experience'. *Brook Journal of International Law* 43(1): 75–129.

Bell, K. 2014. *Achieving Environmental Justice*. Bristol: Policy Press.

Bodansky, D. 2017. 'The Role of the International Court of Justice in Addressing Climate Change: Some Preliminary Reflections'. *Arizona State Law Journal* 49: 1–24.

Boyd, D. R. 2012. *The Environmental Rights Revolution—A Global Study of Constitutions, Human Rights, and the Environment*. Vancouver/Toronto: UBC Press.

Boyd, D. R. 2017. *The Rights of Nature—A Legal Revolution That Could Save the World*. Toronto: ECW-Press.

Boyle, A. 2011. 'Human Rights and International Environmental Law: Some Current Problems', available at <https://www.eui.eu/Documents/DepartmentsCentres/Law/ResearchTeaching/WorkingGroups/08-03-HumanRights.pdf>.

Bullard, R. D. 1990. *Dumping in Dixie: Race, Class and Environmental Quality.* Boulder: Westview.

Bullard, R. D., ed. 1994. *Unequal Protection: Environmental Justice and Communities of Color.* San Francisco: Sierra Club Books.

Carruthers, D. V. 2008. 'Popular Environmentalism and Social Justice in Latin America'. In D. V. Carruthers, ed. *Environmental Justice in Latin America.* 1–19. Cambridge, London: MIT Press.

Cassese, A. 1990. 'Remarks on Scelle's Theory of "Role-Splitting" (*dédoublement fonctionel*) in International Law'. *European Journal of International Law* 1: 210–31.

Checker, M. 2005. *Polluted Promises.* New York: New York University Press.

Collins, T. and S. Esterling. 2019. 'Fluid Personality: Indigenous Rights and the *Te Awa Tupua (Whanganui River Claims Settlement) Act 2017* in Aotearoa New Zealand'. *Melbourne Journal of International Law* 20: 197–220.

Coolsaet, B., ed. 2020. *Environmental Justice—Key Issues.* London: Routledge.

Coomans, F. 2003. 'The Ogoni Case before the African Commission on Human and Peoples' Rights'. *The International and Comparative Law Quarterly* 52(3): 749–60.

Cournil, C. 2020. 'Les Grandes Affaires Climatiques, Confluence des Droits'. Aix-en-Provence, available at <https://dice.univ-amu.fr/sites/dice.univ-amu.fr/files/public/cdd10_-_les_grandes_affaires_climatiques_2.pdf>.

Cutfeet, J. 2019. 'Foreword'. In J. Kuyek, ed. *Unearthing Justice: How to Protect Your Community from the Mining Industry*, xii–xv. Toronto: Between the Lines.

De Graaf, K. J. and J. H. Jans. 2015. 'The Urgenda Decision: Netherlands Liable for Role in Causing Dangerous Global Climate Change'. *Journal of Environmental Law* 27(3): 517–27.

Dellinger, M. 2018. 'See You in Court: Around the World in Eight Climate Change Lawsuits'. *W&M Environmental Law and Policy Review* 42: 525–51.

Descola, P. 2013. *The Ecology of Others.* Chicago: Prickly Paradigm Press.

Descola, P. 2014. *Beyond Nature and Culture.* Chicago: University of Chicago Press.

Eady, V. 2007. 'Warren County and the Birth of a Movement: The Troubled Marriage between Environmentalism and Civil Rights'. Golden Gate University Environmental Law Journal 1: 41–52.

Epiney, A. 2006. 'Lac Lanoux Arbitration'. In *Max Planck Encyclopedia of Public International Law*, available at: https://opil.ouplaw.com/view/10.1093/law:epil/9780199231690/law-9780199231690-e154.

Estes, N. 2019. *Our History is the Future.* London: Verso.

Estes, N. and J. Dhillon. 2019. 'The Black Snake, #NoDAPL, and the Rise of a People's Movement'. In N. Estes and J. Dhillon, eds. *Standing with Standing Rock.* Minneapolis: University of Minnesota Press.

Fitzmaurice, M. 2017. 'Legitimacy of International Environmental Law. The Sovereign States Overwhelmed by Obligations: Responsibility to React to Problems beyond National Jurisdiction?' *ZaöRV* 77: 339–70.

Foster, S. R. 2004. 'The Challenge of Environmental Justice'. *Rutgers Journal of Law & Urban Policy* 1: 1–12.

Frank, W., C. Bals, and J. Grimm. 2019. 'The Case of Huaraz: First Climate Lawsuit on Loss and Damage Against an Energy Company before German Courts'. In R. Mechler, L. M. Bouwer, T. Schinko, S. Surminski, and J. Linnerooth-Bayer, eds. *Loss and Damage from Climate Change*, 475–82. Cham: Springer Nature Switzerland.

Gauna, E. 1995. 'Federal Environmental Citizen Provisions: Obstacles and Incentives on the Road to Environmental Justice'. *Ecology Law Quarterly* 22(1): 1–87.

Gauna, E. 2002a. 'Farmworkers as an Environmental Justice Issue: Similarities and Differences'. *Environs* 25(2): 67–75.

Gauna, E. 2002b. 'An Essay on Environmental Justice: The Past, the Present, and Back to the Future'. *Natural Resources Journal* 42: 701–22.

Gauna, E. 2012. 'Environmental Law, Civil Rights and Sustainability: Three Frameworks for Environmental Justice'. *Journal of Environmental & Sustainability Law* 19(1): 34–59.

Gill, G. N. 2010. 'A Green Tribunal for India'. *Journal of Environmental Law*: 461–74.

Gonzalez, C. 2015. 'Environmental Justice, Human Rights, and the Global South'. *Santa Clara Journal of International Law* 13: 151–95.

Hanschel, D. 2018. 'Climate Change and the Individual'. In Schmidt-Kessel, ed. *German National Reports on the 20th International Congress of Comparative Law*, 635–58. Tübingen: Moor Siebeck.

Hanschel, D. 2019. *Environmental Rights in Cultural Context (ERCC) 2019–2023. A Conceptual Outline*. Halle/Saale: Max Planck Institute for Social Anthropology.

Hassan, M. A. 2017. 'The Right to a Clean and Healthy Environment as a Tool for Seeking Redress for Damages Caused by Environmental Pollution in Nigeria, with Particular Reference to the Niger Delta Region: A Case Study of *Jonah Gbemre vs. SPDC* (2005) AHLR 151 (NgHC 2005)'. *Journal of the Mooting Society University of Lagos* 3: 1–26.

Hetherington, K., ed. 2019. *Infrastructure, Environment, and Life in the Anthropocene*. Durham: Duke University Press.

Houck, O. A. 2018. 'Noah's Second Voyage: The Rights of Nature as Law'. *Tulane Environmental Law Journal* 31: 1–50.

ICC. 2016. 'Policy Paper on Case Selection and Prioritisation' (15 September 2016). International Criminal Court, Office of the Prosecutor, available at <https://www.icc-cpi.int/itemsDocuments/20160915_OTP-Policy_Case-Selection_Eng.pdf>.

James Clifford, 2013. *Returns: Becoming Indigenous in the Twenty-First Century*. Harvard University Press.

Jaria i Manzano, J. 2014. 'The Rights of Nature in Ecuador: An Opportunity to Reflect on Society, Law and Environment'. In R. V. Percival, J. Lin, and W. Piermattei, eds. *Global Environmental Law at a Crossroads*, 48–62. Cheltenham: Edward Elgar.

Jarrat-Snider, K. and M. Nielsen, eds. 2020. *Indigenous Environmental Justice*. Tucson: University of Arizona Press.

Kopnina, H. and E. Shoreman-Ouimet. 2017. 'An Introduction to Environmental Anthropology'. In H. Kopnina and E. Shoreman-Ouimet, eds. *Routledge Handbook of Environmental Anthropology*, 3–9. London: Routledge.

Kuyek, J. 2019. *Unearthing Justice: How to Protect Your Community from the Mining Industry*. Toronto: Between the Lines.

Leal, F. 1994. 'Environmental Justice'. *Chicano-Latino Law Review* 14: 37–43.

Lehmen, A. and J. Advocacia. 2017. 'ICC to Focus on Environmental Crimes: A Landmark Move for International Environmental Law', 21 March 2017, available at <https://www.expertguides.com/articles/icc-to-focus-on-environmental-crimes-a-landmark-move-for-international-environmental-law/arljgbwe>.

Lehmen, A. 2018. 'International Environmental Court'. In *Max Planck Encyclopedia of Public International Law*, available at <https://www.academia.edu/40296385/International_Environmental_Court>.

Macpherson, E. and F. C. Ospina. 2015. 'The Pluralism of River Rights in Aotearoa, New Zealand and Colombia'. 25(6): 283–93.

Martin, P., S. Z. Bigdeli, T. Daya-Winterbottom, W. du Plessis, and A. Kennedy. 2015. *The Search for Environmental Justice*. Cheltenham: Edward Elgar.

McGregor, D., S. Whitaker, and M. Sritharan. 2020. 'Indigenous Environmental Justice and Sustainability'. *Current Opinion in Environmental Sustainability* 43: 35–40.

Nesmith, A. A., C. L. Schmitz, Y. Machado-Escudero, S. Billiot, R. A. Forbes, M. C. F. Powers, N. Buckhoy, and L. A. Lawrence. 2021. *The Intersection of Environmental Justice, Climate Change, Community, and the Ecology of Life*. Cham: Springer.

Newell, P. 2008. 'Contesting Trade Politics in the Americas: The Politics of Environmental Justice'. In D. V. Carruthers, ed. *Environmental Justice in Latin America*, 49–73. Cambridge/ London: MIT Press.

Nollkaemper, A. and L. Burgers. 2020. 'A New Classic of Climate Change Litigation: The Dutch Supreme Court Decision in the Urgenda Case'. *EJIL:Talk!*, available at: https://hdl.handle.net/11245.1/1e2f9a2e-77f7-4a2b-8ba9-1168ea3e91f8.

O'Bryan, K. 2019. 'The Changing Face of River Management in Victoria: The Yarra River Protection (Wilip-gin Birrarung murron) Act 2017 (Vic)'. *Water International* 44(6–7): 769–85.

Osofsky, H. M. 2005. 'Learning from Environmental Justice: A New Model for International Environmental Rights'. *Stanford Environmental Law Journal* 24: 71–131.

Outka, U. 2017. 'Fairness in the Low-Carbon Shift: Learning from Environmental Justice'. *Brooklyn Law Review* 82(2): 789–824.

Pellow, D. N. 2018. *What is Critical Environmental Justice?* Cambridge: Polity Press.

Percival, R. V., J. Lin, and W. Piermattei, eds. 2014. *Global Environmental Law at a Crossroads*. Cheltenham: Edward Elgar.

Pring, G. and C. Pring. 2016. 'Environmental Courts and Tribunals. A Guide for Policy Makers'. Nairobi: UN Environment, available at <https://wedocs.unep.org/bitstream/handle/20.500.11822/10001/environmental-courts-tribunals.pdf?sequence=1&isAllowed=y>.

Purdy, J. 2018. 'The Long Environmental Justice Movement'. *Ecology Law Quarterly* 44: 809–64.

Robinson, M. 2018. *Climate Justice: Hope, Resilience, and the Fight for a Sustainable Future*. London: Bloomsbury.

Rolston, H., III. 2017. 'Environmental Ethics and Environmental Anthropology'. In H. Kopnina and E. Shoreman-Ouimet, eds. *Routledge Handbook of Environmental Anthropology*, 276–87. London: Routledge.

Roosvall, A. and M. Tegelberg. 2018. *Media and Transnational Climate Justice: Indigenous Activism and Climate Politics*. New York: Peter Lang.

Salmond, A. 2014. 'Tears of Rangi: Water, Power, and People in New Zealand'. *Journal of Ethnographic Theory* 4(3): 285–309.

Scelle, G. 1956. 'La phénoméne juridique de déboublement fonctionnel'. In W. Schätzel and H.-J. Schlochauer, eds. *Festschrift für Hans Wehberg zu seinem 70. Geburtstag*, 324–42. Frankfurt am Main: Vittorio Klostermann.

Schlosberg, D. and L. B. Collins. 2014. 'From Environmental to Climate Justice: Climate Change and the Discourse of Environmental Justice'. *WIREs Climate Change* 5: 359–74.

Scofield, K. B. 2017. Indigenous Rights and Constitutional Change in *Ecuador*. PhD dissertation, Indiana University, Bloomington, IN, available at <https://pqdtopen.proquest.com/doc/1883607590.html?FMT=AI>.

Selkälä, T. and M. Rajavuori. 2017. 'Traditions, Myths, and Utopias of Personhood: An Introduction'. *German Law Journal* 18(5): 1017–68.

Setzer, J. and L. C. Vanhala. 2019. 'Climate Change Litigation: A Review of Research on Courts and Litigants in Climate Governance'. *WIREs Climate Change* 10(3): 1–19, available at: https://onlinelibrary.wiley.com/doi/full/10.1002/wcc.580.

Shelton, D. 2002. 'Human Rights and the Environment: Jurisprudence of Human Rights Bodies'. Background Paper No. 2, Joint UNEP–OHCHR Seminar on Human Rights and the Environment, 11–14 January 2002, Geneva.

Shiva, V. 2013. *Making Peace with the Earth*. London: Pluto Press.

Smith, T., D. A. Sonnenfeld, and D. N. Pellow, eds. 2006. *Challenging the Chip: Labor Rights and Environmental Justice in the Global Electronics Industry*. Philadelphia: Temple University Press.

Steyn, E. 2018. *At the Intersection of Tangible and Intangible: Constructing a Framework for the Protection of Indigenous Sacred Sites in the Pursuit of Natural Resource Development Projects*. LLD thesis, Faculty of Law, University of Montreal.

Steyn, E. 2021. 'Seeking Solutions in the Land of the Long White Cloud: The Whanganui River Settlement in Aotearoa New Zealand as Accommodative Measure'. In M. C. Foblets, K. Alidadi, and D. Müller, eds. *(Re)Designing Justice for Plural Societies: Accommodative Measures Put to the Test*. London: Routledge.

Stone, C. D. 1972. 'Should Trees Have Standing?—Toward Legal Rights for Natural Objects'. *Southern California Law Review* 45: 450–501.

Strang, V. 2017. 'Justice for All: Inconvenient Truths and Reconciliation in Human–Non-Human Relations'. In H. Kopina and E. Shoreman-Ouinet, eds. *Routledge Handbook of Environmental Anthropology*, 259–75. London/New York: Routledge.

Todd, J. 2020. 'A "Sense of Equity" in Environmental Justice Litigation'. *Harvard Environmental Law Review* 44: 169–233.

Tola, M. 2019. 'Pachamama'. In M. Schneider-Mayerson and B. R. Bellamy, eds. *An Ectopian Lexicon*, 194–203. Minneapolis: University of Minnesota Press.

Vernet, P. M. 2010. 'Pulp Mills on the River Uruguay (Argentina v Uruguay)'. In *Max Planck Encyclopedia of Public International Law*, available at: https://opil.ouplaw.com/view/10.1093/law:epil/9780199231690/law-9780199231690-e1983.

Villa, C., N. Ahmad, R. Bratspies, R. Lin, C. Rechtschaffen, E. Gauna, and C. O'Neill. 2020. *Environmental Justice. Law, Policy, & Regulation*. Third edition. Durham: Carolina Academic Press.

Villavicencio Calzadilla, P. 2019. 'A Paradigm Shift in Courts' View on Nature: The Artaro River and Amazon Basin Cases in Colombia'. *Law, Environment and Development Journal* 15(1): 49–59.

Whyte, K. 2018. 'Settler Colonialism, Ecology, and Environmental Injustice'. *Environment and Society: Advances in Research* 9: 125–44.

Zeiderman, A. 2019. 'Low Tide—Submerged Humanism in a Columbian Port'. In K. Hetherington, ed. *Infrastructure, Environment, and Life in the Anthropocene*, 171–92. Durham: Duke University Press.

PART IV

ANTHROPOLOGY AT THE LIMITS OF LAW

CHAPTER 31

CONSTITUTION-MAKING

FELIX-ANSELM VAN LIER AND KATRIN SEIDEL

Introduction

Over the last three decades, constitution making has witnessed an explosion of academic research from a variety of disciplines, including law, political science, history, and more recently international relations. Much research in the field of constitution making remains normative in its outlook. Recently, quantitative empirical studies have emerged which have significantly enhanced our understanding of constitution making. However, as such research focuses more on text than on context, many of the intricacies of law's interaction with society have been overlooked.

This chapter explores what anthropology can bring to the field of constitution making. It starts by highlighting how the multifaceted nature of constitution making complicates the task to define it, and proposes a broad definition which encompasses the context of such processes. It then sketches key themes in contemporary research on and practice of constitution making and provides a brief overview of the central criticism of contemporary constitution-making practice. After a discussion of the strengths and shortcomings of both quantitative and qualitative empirical approaches to constitution making, the chapter provides a snapshot of some recent anthropological scholarship in the field. Rather than attempting to give a complete overview of state of the field, the chapter carves out central tenets of this scholarship and concludes by outlining some avenues for further research.

Defining constitution making

Constitution making is generally viewed as either the process of creating a constitutional order where there was none or replacing an existing one completely (David E. Landau and Lerner 2019). Today, constitutions are most commonly understood as formal texts that regulate 'the allocation of functions, powers and duties among the various agencies and offices of government, and define the relationship between these and the public', although there are examples of unwritten constitutions (Negretto 2017). Constitutions are binding on all state institutions and claim superiority over ordinary legislation. The 'higher' or 'supreme status' of constitutional law is often derived from the claim that constitutions are the outcome of 'the people's' constituent power, and is further cemented by the high legal hurdles that tend to be imposed for constitutional change.

Partly due to its special higher-law status, the process that leads to a constitution's adoption is assumed to be systematically different to ordinary politics (Ackerman 1991). First, the substantive scope of constitution making is much broader than ordinary lawmaking, ranging from the allocation of powers among the branches of government to the provision of fundamental individual rights. Second, given that constitution making effectively concerns every citizen and institution of a country, the range of actors involved in a constitution-making process is potentially much wider. Thirdly, a constitution aspires to organize political power in a state for a long time to come, which further raises the stakes in this endeavour.

Constitution-making processes tend to occur in times of profound political and social change. They may be triggered as a response to an economic crisis, for reasons of political reform, by calls for a redefinition of political units or the formulation of a new constitutional identity, or by the creation of new states. While constitutions are historically associated with the emergence of the Western liberal state, they have become a 'near mandatory accoutrement of national sovereignty' and legitimate statehood (David E. Landau and Lerner 2019: 4). Constitutions can be employed as part of the democratic (re)construction of states, but they can also be a 'component of authoritarian regimes that seek to gain legitimacy by emulating the formalities of representative democracies' (Negretto 2017).

Constitution making, just like constitutions, is notoriously hard to define. The problem is arguably further complicated by the fact that in the vast majority of states today constitutions are already in place, which means that it may be difficult to distinguish between mere constitutional amendment or reform and constitutional replacement. Attempts have been made to draw a distinction between the two—for example, by examining the degree of substantive change in a constitutional text, the institution that adopts a new constitutional text, or the procedure that leads to constitutional change—but none offer conclusive definitional solutions. Landau and Lerner seek to solve the problem of defining constitution making by calling it so when the actors involved 'themselves say that is what they are doing' (David E. Landau and Lerner 2019: 2). This definition is broad enough to capture sociopolitical processes that may have triggered or influenced constitution-making processes. Its focus on actors in a process emphasizes the complex relationships between constitution making and social change and the wide range of actors that are often involved in constitution making today, which would elude narrower definitions of such processes. It also expands the temporal frame of constitution making by emphasizing that constitution making can be a drawn-out process which requires analysis both of what happens before the actual drafting process and after. Of course, such a broad definition risks being imprecise, but this is arguably necessary if one wants to reach a deep and contextual understanding of the subject matter.

The trajectory of scholarship on constitution making

While scholars have always contributed to the development of constitutional law by interpreting constitutional texts and conventions, elaborating on doctrine, and evaluating court decisions, the making of constitutions has for a long time received little attention (Ginsburg 2016). Questions concerning the making of constitutions have mostly been confined to theoretical considerations around the concept of constituent power, which articulates the principle that the modern state is built upon the people's political power. Yet what constituent power is exactly, how it is or should be expressed, and what its relationship is with other foundational concepts, most importantly sovereignty, have been and still are heavily disputed in the literature. In all its iterations, constituent power remains a *Grenzbegriff*—a boundary or limit concept—that is 'bound up with deeper disputes concerning the nature of legal, political, and constitutional ordering' (Loughlin 2014: 218). Overall, conceptions of constituent power tend to be normative evaluations of constitution-making practice; they are rarely, if ever, descriptive (Rubinelli 2020: 13).

Thus, historically, the theory rarely shed light on the actual reality of constitution making and was often detached from practice (Tushnet 2013: 1988). In fact, for most of the mid-nineteenth to mid-twentieth century, constitution making was not in the hands of 'the people', but tended to be a power wielded by the elites: constitution making was seen as an 'intimate and sovereign' (Horowitz 2002), 'pre-eminently political act' (Elazar 1985) which was largely withdrawn from academic—and indeed, popular—scrutiny. The empirical study of constitution making was regarded as a 'fruitless endeavour' (Breslin 2009: 2), and thus remained a niche field of academic research.

This gradually changed with globalization and the rapid increase in the scale and scope of transnational linkages. Constitution making further expanded with the new possibilities that arose from the disintegration of the Soviet Union and the end of the bipolar system of global politics. The beginning of the 1990s heralded the beginning of an 'era of constitution making' (Hart 2003: 2), as Eastern and Central European countries transitioned to constitutional democracies (Partlett 2019), followed by constitutional transformations in Africa (Abbiate et al. 2017) and Latin America (Albert et al. 2019). As constitution making began to be part of wider international peace-making and state-building activities, they came into the 'forcefield of global political and legal interests' (David E. Landau and Lerner 2019: 7).

This increased constitution-making activity was embedded in broader processes of the globalization of law, associated with a global spread of trade laws, human rights, and accompanying institutions. Heightened constitution-making activity mirrored a broader global trend of the 'apotheosis of law as the mechanism par excellence of social and political transformation' (Goodale 2017: 200). The global proliferation of constitution making sparked new research, particularly in the field of comparative constitutional law and constitutional design, and also brought into focus the actual process of constitution making. Since then, research on constitution making has exploded across different academic disciplines, predominantly in law, political science, history, and more recently international relations (Lerner and Lupovici 2019).

Themes in contemporary constitution making

The expansion of constitution-making processes around the world created new waves of study. Comparative constitutional law, in particular, flourished in the 1990s, arguably fuelled by the contemporaneity of many constitution-making efforts and 'new efforts to theorize and analyse institutional design' (Ginsburg 2012: 4).

Process Design

Much of the literature in constitution making has focused on questions of process design. For example, modern scholarship has examined the role that different types of constitution-making bodies can play in constitution making (David E. Landau and Lerner 2019: 4); how electoral laws should be designed to promote broad inclusiveness (Ellis 2018); the value of special electoral rules, such as quotas for women and minorities (Gilbert 2013; Williams 2009); and different design choices for public participation as a means to enhance the legitimacy and endurance of a new constitutional order (Samuels 2006). More recently, there is growing interest in more direct forms of public participation in constitution making, for example via randomly selected assemblies or the use of digital tools (Suteu 2015).

Much research in contemporary constitution making stems from studies in conflict and post-conflict constitution making and constitution making in divided societies, where wholesale constitutional replacements are more common than in established democracies. In such contexts, constitution-making processes are seen as a way to channel potentially violent political conflict through the allocation, accountability, and exercise of power, and to support the development of a sense of political community. In post-conflict scenarios and deeply divided societies, however, constitution making poses particular challenges, as state institutions are weak or non-existent and there is often no unitary vision for a state. These challenges have given rise to a variety of procedural design theories which are concerned with how constitution making can contribute to democracy building (see e.g. Arato 2015; Bell and Zulueta-Fülscher 2016).

International Dimensions of Constitution Making

One key aspect of contemporary constitution making, particularly in post-conflict scenarios, is the increasingly thick network of transnational actors who offer support and advice in such processes. While, in practice, direct or indirect international involvement has always been an important aspect of constitution making (Negretto 2017), international involvement today is more frequent, more professionalized and institutionalized, and more systematic (Saunders 2012). A plethora of international and transnational actors are now regularly part of constitution-making efforts, including intergovernmental agencies (Sripati 2013), international non-governmental organizations (NGOs) (Beijerman 2018), international experts (Aucoin 2004), academics and research centres (Rosenfeld and Sajó 2012: 6), and private enterprises and 'global pro bono law firms' (Daase 2014).

While international law does not contain specific provisions concerning the way in which a constitution should be drafted, international actors regularly invoke international law or soft law standards when providing 'technical assistance' and establishing procedural rules for writing legitimate constitutions (Hart 2010). Overall, however, there is only a slender formal legal basis in international law relating to constitutional processes, and most standards are gradually developed through international practice. Nevertheless, the heightened presence of international law, both soft and hard, may be an indication of the need to grasp the legitimacy that characterizes international involvement in constitution making (Goss 2015: 17).

Critique and Limits of Contemporary Constitution Making

Scholars have examined the implications of this development and other trends, both in terms of the theory and the practice of constitution making. One line of research, for example, grapples with the normative conflict 'between legitimate external intervention on the one hand and constitutional autochthony, grounded in sovereign equality, on the other hand' (Arato 2015). Dann and Al-Ali, for example, coined the term 'international pouvoir constituant' to underline that by moulding constitutional processes into universal standards and principles, international actors effectively become part of 'the people' who draft a constitution (Al-Ali and Dann 2006).

Scholars have started to examine the consequences of the global proliferation of norms and the juridification or formalization of constitutional processes for the practice of constitution making. Yeh and Chang note a shift in constitution-making practice, as previously constitutions were the 'end-result, a codified document of social and political consensus', and it was 'not the vocation of law or a constitution to stabilise social order and to form political consensus' (Yeh and Chang 2006: 1822). Some criticize this shift as a form of 'legocentrism' (Frankenberg 2006) which leads to a 'displacement of politics' whereby constitution making becomes a domain of expert knowledge and technical expertise, leaving little room for the accommodation of local political contexts (Kendall 2015). Other scholars criticize the use of constitution making in state-building for its idealized Weberian, thus legal-rational underpinnings, noting that the existence of a modern territorial state with its constitutive elements—such as a collective identity, agreed territory, and monopoly of power—is not a universal given and not always present (Lemay-Hébert 2013). These studies echo more sweeping critiques which see the trend towards the formalization of political processes and constitutional standard-setting as part of a long-standing tradition of 'legalised hegemony' through which the 'western' hemisphere seeks to establish its concept of the state around the world (Tully 2008).

Yet others have underlined the limits of international norms and external support in constitution making. Some emphasize that there are differences in the degree of international involvement, ranging from the 'relatively unusual case of constitutional imposition to proffering comparative constitutional knowledge or advice' (Saunders 2019). Others note that even where there is strong external involvement, such advice may be ineffective or counterproductive, as advisers tend to be insufficiently immersed in local constitutional culture or recommend reforms without sufficient consideration of whether they are suitable (Tushnet 2008). Similarly, scholars also question the practical relevance of international frameworks or 'global constitutionalism' vis-à-vis the context-dependent manner in which many constitutions are made (Saunders 2019). Indeed, scholars have shown how the influence of global international norms is nuanced by different regional trends and traditions in constitution making, for example in Europe (Thornhill 2019), the Middle East (Brown 2019), Asia (Guruswamy 2019), or Africa (Venter 2019).

Many of the issues raised point to gaps in our empirical knowledge about constitution making. For example, although there is emerging research on why and how constitutional norms are being diffused (Goderis and Versteeg 2014), the issues of how standards for constitution *making* move globally or regionally, how they are implemented in practice, and what their effects are remain understudied. Calls for more empirical scholarship are fuelled in view of the limited or ambiguous success that constitution-making efforts often have, particularly in war-torn or -prone countries. Thus, scholars have started questioning the relationship between constitutions and social change (Klug 2019).

EMPIRICAL APPROACHES TO CONSTITUTION MAKING

Much of the recent work in this field is comparative in nature, addressing particular aspects of constitution making to enhance our theoretical, institutional, and procedural understanding of such processes. Often this literature is normative in character and geared towards constructing 'general theories' of constitutional law and constitution making (Jackson 2012). While many studies do entail empirical elements, they tend to only selectively engage with case studies to illustrate and compare particular aspects of a constitution-making process vis-à-vis the theoretical stances taken. Thus, there often remains doubt 'whether [these assumptions] are empirically justified' (Law 2010: 381).

Admittedly, both qualitative and quantitative empirical analyses of constitution making struggle with the fact that such processes are rare events and that it is difficult to empirically capture a multifaceted and ill-defined phenomenon. Nevertheless, more recently, empirical analyses on constitution making have been thriving, 'newly energised' by the recent growth and expansion of the field (Ginsburg and Dixon 2011: 6). As disciplinary approaches to constitution making have been diversifying, so have the empirical vantage points. At the broadest level, one can distinguish between quantitative and qualitative empirical approaches to constitution making, although the distinction can be blurred when different methodological tools are combined. The choice of methodology necessarily comes with a trade-off between 'depth and breadth' (Meuwese and Versteeg 2012) and has an impact on the type of questions that can be addressed.

Quantitative Approaches

Over the last ten years or so, quantitative empirical analyses have been booming. This is partly because of the emergence of large databases of constitutional and other related legal or quasi-legal texts (see e.g. Comparative Constitutions Project 2016). Although they need not be, many quantitative analyses are large-n comparisons (i.e. looking for patterns in a large number of cases) and/or use statistical methods either to describe developments and identify similarities and differences across different constitution-making processes or to make causal claims about the effectiveness of procedural rules or institutional choices in particular cases. For example, scholars have examined factors that impact constitutional durability (Elkins et al. 2009), the relationship between participation and democracy promotion (Saati 2015), the impact of public participation on constitutional texts (Hudson 2018), and the way in which constitutional ideas are diffused (Goderis and Versteeg 2014).

Such research has significantly enhanced our understanding of theoretical, institutional, and procedural aspects of such processes; it has highlighted general trends in constitutional law, illustrated the effects of globalization on constitution making, and helped to assess the impact of constitutional design choices. Quantitative studies have tested articulated or unarticulated assumptions of constitution-making theory and produced new insights, giving rise to new research questions. Partly, new research questions also stem from the limitations of quantitative empirical analysis. Its two key challenges are data inadequacy and causal complexity, which are caused by the often limited amount of data available for analysis and the fact that constitution making's complexity makes such processes hard to quantify (Law 2010: 387). Causal inferences, even correlations, are notoriously difficult to identify and require researchers to 'think long and hard about alternative stories ... and competing explanations' (Meuwese and Versteeg 2012: 255). These problems also complicate comparative analyses, as each process is individually shaped by its politics, history, culture, religion, and geography (Hirschl 2014).

Quantitative research necessarily focuses on text rather than context, which 'inevitably means that we shall miss out on some of the intricacies of law's interaction with society' (Meuwese and Versteeg 2012: 239). For example, there is still a lack of detailed insights into the practice of the 'making' of constitutions, that is, how normative principles and standards are actually understood and used by different actors, and why they use them. Who are the actors in constitution making, why do they engage in it, and what formal and informal means of engagement do they use? When, how, and why can constitution making support peaceful transformations in conflict-ridden countries? These empirical gaps may have serious consequences for constitution-making practice. Quantitative knowledge alone, Sally Engle Merry warns, may lead to 'oversimplification, homogenization, and the neglect of the surrounding social structure' if it is not connected to more qualitative forms of knowledge (Merry 2016: 2). She also raises concerns about purely quantitative insights crossing into policymaking, when the 'drawbacks and complexities recognised by the researchers, such as limited data, the use of proxies, and the uncertainty of flawed or missing data', are stripped away (Merry 2016: 5).

Qualitative Approaches

Qualitative researchers may fill such empirical gaps and help to enhance quantitative knowledge by providing the 'alternative stories' and 'competing explanations' needed to help explain, disprove, or enrich the patterns and causal relationships found. Qualitative analyses are by their nature narrower in scope, but they apply a broader understanding of constitution making. Rather than focusing on text, qualitative research is interested in the way in which actors understand norms and processes and thus tends to see constitution making as a phenomenon that is embedded in social practices.

While much qualitative work on constitution making has been done in the form of case studies (see e.g. Miller and Aucoin 2010), the distinctive feat of anthropological knowledge-production is the deep and long-term-immersion of a researcher in a particular context (Parker-Jenkins 2018). Anthropologists seek to generate 'intimate understandings of local practice and social relations' of setting(s) relevant to the object of study, which helps to accrue grounded knowledge by connecting disparate units of data to an analytical whole (Stepputat and Larsen 2015: 6). This can lead to insights about the range of actors who engage in legal processes and why they engage, but also about how 'groups of people talk about law [and] what they do with law' in different contexts and situations (Tamanaha 2001: 155)—thereby fostering an understanding not so much about what law *ought* to do as about what law *is*.

As anthropology relies on direct human encounters, its methods do not seem instantly amenable to the study of large-scale phenomena such as the 'state' or, indeed, constitution making. But anthropologists constantly reinterpret and adjust methodologies and theoretical questions, balancing the need to remain ethnographically coherent against the desire for a scope that is expansive enough to problematize global developments and the growing 'legalization of social, political, and economic life' (Goodale 2017: 4). By applying methodologies such as multisited fieldwork, following networks, and tracing people and commodities, both offline and online, anthropologists have demonstrated how qualitative anthropological inquiry can still produce meaningful insights into the workings and interrelations of (trans)national, regional, national, and local legal orders, institutions, and practices (Carter 2005; Niezen and Sapignoli 2017).

Of course, an ethnographic approach, along with its practical challenges such as accessing people and institutions, is always interpretative and cannot claim to encompass all aspects of a complex and multilayered processes. Still, due to its focus on experience-based inquiry, ethnography generates empirical data which would be overlooked by purely quantitative analyses and would otherwise not enter into scholarly thinking. Considering that 'constitutional change is a multidimensional and cultural phenomenon ... it would be a mistake to rely only on quantitative approaches' for an understanding of such processes (Husa 2020).

Anthropological approaches to constitution making

While case study approaches to constitution making have been common, longitudinal, ethnographic approaches to constitution making have only recently started emerging. In a seminal paper from 2004, Kim Lane Scheppele advocates the approach of a 'constitutional ethnography' (Scheppele 2004: 401). Rather than relegating context to a background assumption, a constitutional ethnography looks 'deeply into particular cases' to illuminate 'complex interrelationships among political, legal, historical, social, economic, and cultural elements' (Scheppele 2004: 390). Such an approach, she argues, allows us to better understand the intricacies of a particular constitutional system (Scheppele 2004).

'Thick descriptions' (Geertz 1973) of constitutional orders nuance our understanding of 'the mechanisms through which governance is accomplished [and] the strategies through which governance is attempted, experienced, resisted and revised', which may, in turn, inform both theory and practice (Scheppele 2004: 395). A constitutional order may be perceived as following traditional patterns 'from a distance', but a closer look could reveal significant differences. An ethnographic approach strives to understand complex relationships in one setting which may also enable a researcher to see how far other settings can be understood in similar terms (Frankenberg 2018: 90).

Scheppele's approach is instructive for the study of constitution making. Recent work has started exploring more deeply the practice of constitution making, looking at why a host of new actors engage in constitution making and how they employ formal and informal strategies to promote their interests. Much of this work builds on anthropological studies that examine globalized and transnationalized legal processes, which question the universal aspirations and assumptions of law by focusing on the sociopolitical and socioeconomic contexts in which these norms are used (Merry 1992; Wilson 2001). Similarly, anthropological scholarship in constitution making has examined the often contradictory and ambiguous processes which emanate from the intersection of international normative regimes and their implementation at the local level.

Actors, Norms, and Processes

For example, scholars have looked into how and why a multiplicity of actors make use of law to achieve particular goals and, vice versa, how their forms of action have been shaped by the concepts of law, rules, and processes. De Silva de Alwis et al. describe how local women used the Tunisian constitution-making process as a vehicle for addressing deep-seated gender inequalities and how their strategic use of international legal instruments, such as CEDAW, led to the adoption of constitutional guarantees on gender rights (De Silva de Alwis et al. 2017). Omar Hammady finds similar patterns in post-conflict Libya, where civil society groups representing women, minorities, and youth regularly supported their claims by reference to international norms (Hammady 2018). Indigenous People, too, increasingly use 'the vocabulary of rights to position themselves in the national constitution-making process' (Thornhill 2018: 328).

Such detailed examinations illustrate how the multiplication of constitution-making agency seems to be intrinsically connected with the proliferation of human rights. Human rights appear to serve as a mechanism through which 'different actors across society can acquire constitution-making and constitution-reinforcing authority' (Thornhill 2018: 434). The notion of human rights is often attractive to local activists because of its universalized, principled, and abstracted claims to equality and dignity. As Fernanda Pirie explains, it is the 'universalizing language of rights' that allows them to challenge and resist state power by portraying these rights as 'lying beyond the particular context of the individual's social and political environment' (Pirie 2013: 214).

But legal anthropologists also explore the more ambiguous role of the global proliferation of norms. Sari Wastell, for example, highlights the ambivalences that the concept of rights brought to the surface during the constitution-making process in Swaziland. This ambivalence was produced by the fact that, although many supported the adoption of a new constitution, many Swazi citizens interpreted the implementation of human rights through the constitution as being opposed to Swazi custom: while human rights focus on one's individual humanness, Swazi custom emphasizes responsibilities to community and social relations more generally—a key element of what makes the 'Swazi nation' what it is (Wastell 2007). Thus, at its core, the implementation of a human rights regime via a constitution would essentially reject the 'structure of Swaziness, and thus the essence of the Swazi nation itself' (Goodale 2009: 34).

In other cases, local power holders may strategically employ international norms to consolidate political power. Mark Goodale shows how in Bolivia, the Morales administration symbolically mobilized and strategically appropriated the indigenous rights movement to point at the specificity and indigenous twist of the Bolivian 'revolution' (see Goodale 2019). Katrin Seidel examines the unintended side-effects of the promotion of international rule of law standards in South Sudan's constitution-making and state-building processes, showing how this effectively reduced the possibility of accommodating South Sudan's fragmented society into a unitary constitutional vision of the state. Here, powerful local political actors successfully appropriated international standards for their own political gain, thereby excluding various groups from the constitution-making process (Seidel 2018, 2020).

Similar ambiguities can be found in the procedural question of public participation. Joanne Wallis's analysis of constitution making in Bougainville and Timor Leste makes a claim about the importance of public participation for the creation of effective constitutions and stable post-conflict environments, but also underlines the importance of the right conditions for meaningful participation (Wallis 2014). Indeed, other analyses show that high public participation guarantees neither the democratization of a country nor the overall success of a constitution-making process. For example, the Icelandic constitution-making process—arguably the most participatory process yet—ultimately failed because political actors were largely excluded from the process (Meuwese and Gylfason 2017). These studies support what Christina Murray finds in her first-hand account of the Kenyan process: constitution making requires a balance between the expectations raised through public participation and the necessity of elite agreement (Murray 2018). More broadly, such qualitative work emphasizes the great variety of approaches there are to public participation in constitution making and its uncertain dynamics.

Constitution Making, State Formation, and Democratization

Detailed insights into how different actors engage in constitution making through law also allow for insights into the broader question of what role constitution making can play for state formation and democratization. In his analysis of the Libyan constitution-making process, Felix-Anselm van Lier shows how—in the absence of an institutionally organized and politically united community—the constitution-making process became a battleground for competing worldviews and interests as different actors used formal and informal political pressure to entrench their partisan policy preferences in the constitutional framework. His research indicates that when societal conflict is high and the political landscape deeply divided, constitution making risks exacerbating political tension rather than solving conflicts through a redistribution of power or resources or the elaboration of a unitary vision for a state (van Lier 2020). Research on other conflict-prone states, such as South Sudan, supports these claims by underlining the challenges of negotiating constitutional settlement 'within the normative frames of international actors, even if these frames and the mode of statehood are still under negotiation' (Seidel 2020; Seidel and Sureau 2015).

This work primarily challenges the paradigm of constitution making as a peace-making and state-building tool in post-conflict environments, but other work substantiates the risk of constitution making more generally. As Felix Petersen and Zeynep Yanaşmayan found in their analysis of the failure of the Turkish process in 2013, constitution making can exacerbate long-standing political, cultural, and religious divides; the ruling AKP hijacked the procedures, thereby preventing broad-based consensus building and fuelling the country's democratic backsliding (Petersen and Yanaşmayan 2020). As other authors have noted, due to the long-term importance attributed to constitutions, constitution making is often 'a high-stakes game that can undermine political stability and derail democratization' (Lerner 2011: 1).

Then again, Judith Bayer, for example, demonstrated how various episodes of constitutional change in Kyrgyzstan produced a form of 'constitutional faith' among Kyrgyz citizens. She shows how changing a constitution came to be perceived as a 'practice of hope' in the aftermath of large-scale political conflicts, and that the idea of constitution making was above 'dirty politics and beyond the corrupting reach of presidents, politicians and bureaucrats' (Beyer 2015: 340). Such anthropological work empirically substantiates the symbolic and aspirational appeal of the law (Ackerman 1997; Comaroff and Comaroff 2006), and perhaps illustrates an aspect of what legal theorists call 'constitutional identity' (Jacobsohn 2010).

Anthropology and Constitution-Making Theory

Anthropological research nuances and complicates more normative accounts of constitution making. It emphasizes the multilayered interactive processes of interpretation and the negotiation of frames of references and meanings that form the basis of constitution making. For example, by observing how different actors use norms, scholars provide new explanations for how constitutional norms, be they trans- or international, are diffused, but perhaps also how local and global dimensions interdependently constitute each other. This also allows for new insights into how contemporary constitutional texts emerge and bring to life theories on their 'intermestic' (Cope 2013) or 'hybrid' nature, whereby countries in transition will often draw on a 'collage of [international] constitutional mechanisms and principles [to] produce hybrid solutions tailored to local imperatives' (Klug 2003: 128).

The studies confirm the observation of the formalization of political processes or the 'judicialization of mega politics' (Hirschl 2008). But they also show that the effect of the juridification or formalization of constitution making does not necessarily depoliticize constitution making or transform it into a realm that is exclusive to experts. Inter- and transnational norms and practices do not remain apolitical, abstract, and rational constructs—on the contrary, they 'stand in a definite and active relationship (often a field of conflict) to social norms' in a given context (Thompson 1975). Similar to what anthropologists have found in their analysis of law elsewhere, procedural norms in constitution making can be used as a 'mechanism through which new categories of political action, new discourses of resistance, and new modes of institutional development have been forged'. At the same time, it can also 'restrict or channel action in particular ways, and set limits on the extent to which real innovation is possible within movements for social, economic, and political change' (Goodale 2017: 117). Put differently, these studies illustrate how norms that shape the process of constitution making, just as law does more generally, can work as a tool both for inclusion and exclusion, and how it both enables and constrains power (Goodale 2017: 117).

The role of norms during constitution making is particularly complicated, however, when such processes unfold in circumstances where the status of the state as the bearer of the monopoly of the legitimate use of force or state sovereignty more generally is unstable and disputed. Here, the anthropological notion of legal pluralism, for example, may sensitize scholars to the 'possibility of law of various kinds, with different foundations of legitimacy, validity, power and authority, and with different degrees of institutionalisation and formalisation [to] coexist in the same social space' (Von Benda-Beckmann 2014: 34). The challenge for scholars engaging in qualitative research, then, is to understand how the multiplicity of legal orders, institutions, and practices, be they (trans)national, regional, national, or local, are intertwined and co-exist (Moore 2001). Such insights may lead to a more nuanced understanding of 'constituent power', perhaps one which would need to be disassociated from the concept of sovereignty and territorial conceptions of the state.

Further research avenues and conclusion

If anything, this eclectic snapshot of anthropological research on constitution making suggests that the practice of establishing viable constitutional regimes is 'more complicated than previously thought' (Goodale and Merry 2007: 4) and that constitution making is a 'messy business' (Brown 2008). Anthropological research underlines the importance of the particular context of constitution making and challenges the often implicit assumption that constitution making is solely the product of rational design.

But anthropological research on constitution making should strive to offer more than merely observing complexity. As of now, many anthropological insights into constitution making are side products of ethnographic analyses of related phenomena. There is yet no 'anthropology of constitution making' which systematically addresses constitution making's distinct frames of references, governance tools, institutions, and actors. For example, more should be done to understand the nature different types of norms and to identify and differentiate specific practices attached to them; to analyse meaning-making processes and translation chains of legal rules, institutions, and procedures from one normative order to another; to investigate the modes of operation of constitution-making bodies, for example, constituent assemblies or randomly selected assemblies; to illustrate the 'epistemic community of international actors' and their relationship with national actors; to trace the sociopolitical events triggering constitution making; or to capture the impact of new technologies on constitution making.

Focusing on particular aspects of constitution making would not only allow anthropologists to better identify the phenomena of their study but also enable them to translate their findings into other contexts. Whilst being mindful of the limitations of any 'comparative ethnography' (Simmons and Smith 2019), focusing on and isolating particular aspects of constitution making could inform deliberate 'thick comparisons' of different processes (Niewöhner and Scheffer 2010). Thick comparisons could bring to the surface dynamics that would be overlooked if only studied in one particular context and support theory formation that could be translated across different cases. Finally, such a comparative approach would make ethnographic research more accessible to scholars who approach constitution making through different methodological lenses, and foster much-needed collaboration among different disciplines. After all, constitution making is a 'multidimensional phenomenon' and an intrinsically interdisciplinary field. To reach a richer understanding of such processes, different methodological approaches need to be combined. Constitution making needs more social science rather than less.

References

Abbiate, T., M. Böckenförde, and V. Federico, eds. 2017. *Public Participation in African Constitutionalism*. First edition. London: Routledge.

Ackerman, B. A. 1991. *We the People*. Cambridge, MA: Belknap Press of Harvard University Press.

Ackerman, B. A. 1997. 'The Rise of World Constitutionalism'. *Virginia Law Review* 83(4): 771–97.

Al-Ali, Z. and P. Dann. 2006. 'The Internationalized Pouvoir Constituant—Constitution-Making Under External Influence in Iraq, Sudan and East Timor'. *Max Planck Yearbook of United Nations Law Online* 10(1): 423–63.

Albert, R., C. B. Pulido, and J. Z. Benvindo, eds. 2019. *Constitutional Change and Transformation in Latin America*. Oxford: Hart Publishing.

Arato, A. 2015. 'International Role in State-Making in Ukraine: The Promise of a Two-Stage Constituent Process'. *German Law Journal* 16(3): 691–712.

Aucoin, L. 2004. 'The Role of International Experts in Constitution-Making: Myth and Reality'. *Georgetown Journal of International Affairs* 5(1): 89–95.

Beijerman, M. 2018. 'Conceptual Confusions in Debating the Role of NGOs for the Democratic Legitimacy of International Law'. *Transnational Legal Theory* 9(2): 147–73.

Bell, C. and K. Zulueta-Fülscher. 2016. *Sequencing Peace Agreements and Constitutions in the Political Settlement Process*. Stockholm: International Institute for Democracy and Electoral Assistance.

Beyer, J. 2015. 'Constitutional Faith Law and Hope in Revolutionary Kyrgyzstan'. *Ethnos* 80(3): 320–45.

Breslin, B. 2009. *From Words to Worlds: Exploring Constitutional Functionality*. Baltimore: Johns Hopkins University Press.

Brown, N. J. 2008. 'Reason, Interest, Rationality, and Passion in Constitution Drafting'. *Perspectives on Politics* 6(4): 675–89.

Brown, N. J. 2019. 'The Unsurprising but Distinctive Nature of Constitution Writing in the Arab World'. In D. Landau and H. Lerner, eds. *Comparative Constitution Making*, 447–62. Cheltenham: Edward Elgar Publishing Limited.

Carter, D. 2005. 'Living in Virtual Communities: An Ethnography of Human Relationships in Cyberspace'. *Information, Communication & Society* 8(2). Routledge: 148–67.

Comaroff, J. and J. L. Comaroff, eds. 2006. *Law and Disorder in the Postcolony*. Chicago: University of Chicago Press.

Comparative Constitutions Project. 2016. 'Download CCP Data'. *Comparative Constitutions Project*, available at http://comparativeconstitutionsproject.org/download-data/.

Cope, K. L. 2013. 'The Intermestic Constitution: Lessons from the World's Newest Nation'. *Virginia Journal of International Law* 53: 667–70.

Daase, C. 2014. 'Making the Client's Peace: "Privatizing" Peace? Global Law Firms Offering Pro Bono Services in Post-Conflict Settings'. *Indiana Journal of Global Legal Studies* 21(2): 423–52.

Elazar, D. J. 1985. 'Constitution-Making: The Pre-Eminently Political Act'. In K. G. Banting and R. Simeon, eds. *The Politics of Constitutional Change in Industrial Nations: Redesigning the State*, 232–48. London: Palgrave Macmillan UK.

Elkins, Z., T. Ginsburg, and J. Melton. 2009. *The Endurance of National Constitutions*. Cambridge: Cambridge University Press.

Ellis, A. 2018. *Electoral system design in the context of constitution-building*. International IDEA Discussion Paper 4/2018. Stockholm: International IDEA.

Frankenberg, G. 2006. 'Comparing Constitutions: Ideas, Ideals, and Ideology—Toward a Layered Narrative'. *International Journal of Constitutional Law* 4(3). Oxford Academic: 439–59.

Frankenberg, G. 2018. *Comparative Constitutional Studies: Between Magic and Deceit*. Cheltenham: Edward Elgar Publishing.

Geertz, C. 1973. *The Interpretation of Cultures: Selected Essays*. New York: Basic Books.

Gilbert, J. 2013. 'Constitutionalism, Ethnicity and Minority Rights in Africa: A Legal Appraisal from the Great Lakes Region'. *International Journal of Constitutional Law* 11(2): 414–37.

Ginsburg, T., ed. 2012. *Comparative Constitutional Design*. New York: Cambridge University Press.

Ginsburg, T. 2016. 'How to Study Constitution-Making: Hirschl, Elster, and the Seventh Inning Problem'. *Boston University Law Review* 96: 1347.

Ginsburg, T. and R. Dixon, eds. 2011. *Comparative Constitutional Law*. Cheltenham: Edward Elgar Publishing Limited.

Goderis, B. and M. Versteeg. 2014. 'The Diffusion of Constitutional Rights'. *International Review of Law and Economics* 39(C): 1–19.

Goodale, M. 2009. 'Introduction: Human Rights and Anthropology'. In M. Goodale, ed. *Human Rights: An Anthropological Reader*, 1–20. Oxford: Blackwell.

Goodale, M. 2017. *Anthropology and Law: A Critical Introduction*. New York: New York University Press.

Goodale, M. 2019. *A Revolution in Fragments: Traversing Scales of Justice, Ideology, and Practice in Bolivia*. Durham: Duke University Press.

Goodale, M. and S. Merry. 2007. *The Practice of Human Rights: Tracking Law between the Global and the Local*. Cambridge: Cambridge University Press.

Goss, C. 2015. *The Nature of Interim Constitutions: A Comparative Analysis*. PhD thesis, University of Oxford.

Guruswamy, M. 2019. 'Constitution Crafting in South Asia: Lessons on Accommodation and Alienation'. In D. Landau and H. Lerner, eds. *Comparative Constitution Making*, 463–87. Cheltenham: Edward Elgar Publishing Limited.

Hammady, O. 2018. 'Public Participation in African Constitutionalism'. In T. Abbiate, M. Böckenförde, and V. Federico, eds. *Public Participation in African Constitutionalism*, 159–76. Abingdon: Routledge.

Hart, V. 2003. *Democratic Constitution Making*. Washington, DC: United States Institute of Peace.

Hart, V. 2010. 'Constitution Making and the Right to Take Part in Public Affairs'. In L. Miller and L. Aucoin, eds. *Framing the State in Times of Transition: Case Studies in Constitution Making*, 20–56. Washington, DC: United States Institute of Peace Press.

Hirschl, R. 2008. 'The Judicialization of Mega-Politics and the Rise of Political Courts'. *Annual Review of Political Science* 11(1): 93–118.

Hirschl, R. 2014. *Comparative Matters: The Renaissance of Comparative Constitutional Law*. Oxford: Oxford University Press.

Horowitz, D. L. 2002. 'Constitutional Design: Proposals Versus Processes'. In A. Reynolds, ed. *The Architecture of Democracy: Constitutional Design, Conflict Management, and Democracy*, 15–36. Oxford: Oxford University Press.

Hudson, A. 2018. 'When Does Public Participation Make a Difference? Evidence from Iceland's Crowdsourced Constitution'. *Policy & Internet* 10(2): 185–217.

Husa, J. 2020. 'Comparative Methodology and Constitutional Change'. In X. Kontiades and A. Photiadou, eds. *Routledge Handbook of Comparative Constitutional Change*, 25–44. Abingdon: Routledge.

Jackson, V. C. 2012. 'Comparative Constitutional Law: Methodologies'. In M. Rosenfeld and A. Sajó, eds. *The Oxford Handbook of Comparative Constitutional Law*, 54–74. Oxford: Oxford University Press.

Jacobsohn, G. J. 2010. *Constitutional Identity*. Cambridge, MA: Harvard University Press.

Kendall, S. 2015. '"Constitutional Technicity": Displacing Politics through Expert Knowledge'. *Law, Culture and the Humanities* 11(3): 363–77.

Klug, H. 2003. 'Postcolonial Collages: Distributions of Power and Constitutional Models: With Special Reference to South Africa'. *International Sociology* 18(1): 114–31.

Klug, H. 2019. 'Constitution Making and Social Transformation'. In D. E. Landau and H. Lerner, eds. *Comparative Constitution Making*, 47–68. Cheltenham: Edward Elgar Publishing Limited.

Landau, D. E. and H. Lerner, eds. 2019. *Comparative Constitution Making*. Cheltenham: Edward Elgar Publishing Limited.

Law, D. S. 2010. 'Constitutions'. In P. Cane and H. Kritzer, eds. *The Oxford Handbook of Empirical Legal Research*, 376–98. Oxford: Oxford University Press.

Lemay-Hébert, N. 2013. 'Rethinking Weberian Approaches to Statebuilding'. In D. Chandler and T. D. Sisk, eds. *Routledge Handbook of International Statebuilding*, 3–14. Abingdon: Routledge.

Lerner, H. 2011. *Making Constitutions in Deeply Divided Societies*. Cambridge: Cambridge University Press.

Lerner, H. and A. Lupovici. 2019. 'Constitution-Making and International Relations Theories'. *International Studies Perspectives* 20(4): 412–34.

Lier, F.-A. van. 2020. 'The Libyan Constitution-Making Process: A Tool for State-Building in a Divided Socio-Normative Space?'. In K. Seidel and H. Elliesie, eds. *Normative Spaces and Legal Dynamics in Africa*, 76–92. First edition. London: Routledge.

Loughlin, M. 2014. 'The Concept of Constituent Power'. *European Journal of Political Theory* 13(2): 218–37.

Merry, S. E. 1992. 'Anthropology, Law, and Transnational Processes'. *Annual Review of Anthropology* 21(1): 357–77.

Merry, S. E. 2016. *The Seductions of Quantification: Measuring Human Rights, Gender Violence, and Sex Trafficking*. Chicago: The University of Chicago Press.

Meuwese, A. and T. Gylfason. 2017. 'Digital Tools and the Derailment of Iceland's New Constitution'. In C. Prins, C. Cuijpers, P. Lindseth, and M. Rosina, eds. *Digital Democracy in a Globalized World*, 249–73. Cheltenham: Edward Elgar Publishing.

Meuwese, A. and M. Versteeg. 2012. 'Quantitative Methods for Comparative Constitutional Law'. In J. Bomhoff and M. Adams, eds. *Practice and Theory in Comparative Law*, 230–57. Cambridge: Cambridge University Press.

Miller, L. and L. Aucoin, eds. 2010. *Framing the State in Times of Transition: Case Studies in Constitution Making*. Washington, DC: United States Institute of Peace Press.

Moore, S. F. 2001. 'Certainties Undone: Fifty Turbulent Years of Legal Anthropology, 1949–1999'. *Journal of the Royal Anthropological Institute* 7(1): 95–116.

Murray, C. 2018. 'Political Elites and the People: Kenya's Decade Long Constitution-Making Process'. Available at SSRN: https://ssrn.com/abstract=3147154 or http://dx.doi.org/10.2139/ssrn.3147154.

Negretto, G. L. 2017. 'Constitution-Making in Comparative Perspective'. *Oxford Research Encyclopedia of Politics*, vol. 1. Oxford: Oxford University Press.

Niewöhner, J. and T. Scheffer. 2010. 'Introduction Thickening Comparison: On the Multiple Facets of Comparability'. In J. Niewöhner and T. Scheffer, eds. *Thick Comparison: Reviving the Ethnographic Aspiration*, 1–15. Leiden: Brill.

Niezen, R. and M. Sapignoli, eds. 2017. *Palaces of Hope: The Anthropology of Global Organizations*. Cambridge: Cambridge University Press.

Parker-Jenkins, M. 2018. 'Problematising Ethnography and Case Study: Reflections on Using Ethnographic Techniques and Researcher Positioning'. *Ethnography and Education* 13(1): 18–33.

Partlett, W. 2019. 'Comparative Constitution Making'. In D. E. Landau and H. Lerner, eds. *Comparative Constitution Making*, 539–66. Cheltenham: Edward Elgar Publishing.

Petersen, F. and Z. Yanaşmayan, eds. 2020. *The Failure of Popular Constitution Making in Turkey: Regressing Towards Constitutional Autocracy*. Cambridge: Cambridge University Press.

Pirie, F. 2013. *The Anthropology of Law*. Oxford: Oxford University Press.

Rosenfeld, M. and A. Sajó, eds. 2012. *The Oxford Handbook of Comparative Constitutional Law*. First edition. Oxford: Oxford University Press.

Rubinelli, L. 2020. *Constituent Power: A History*. Cambridge: Cambridge University Press.

Saati, A. 2015. *The Participation Myth: Outcomes of Participatory Constitution Building Processes on Democracy*. PhD thesis, Statsvetenskapliga institutionen, Umeå universitet.

Samuels, K. 2006. 'Post-Conflict Peace-Building and Constitution-Making'. *Chicago Journal of International Law* 6(2): 663–82.

Saunders, C. 2012. 'Constitution-Making in the 21st Century'. *International Review of Law* 2012(1): 4.

Saunders, C. 2019. 'International Involvement in Constitution Making'. In D. Landau and H. Lerner, eds. *Comparative Constitution Making*, 69–89. Cheltenham: Edward Elgar Publishing Limited.

Scheppele, K. L. 2004. 'Constitutional Ethnography: An Introduction'. *Law & Society Review* 38(3): 389–406.

Seidel, K. 2018. 'The Promotion of the Rule of Law in Translation'. In T. Berger and A. Esguerra, eds. *World Politics in Translation: Power, Relationality and Difference in Global Cooperation*, 76–92. London: Routledge.

Seidel, K. 2020. *Internationalised Constitution-Making as a Tool for Negotiating Statehood and Rule of Law: South Sudan's and Somaliland's Constitutional Genesis in the Context of Plural Legal (Dis-)Ordering. Habilitation*, Martin Luther University of Halle-Wittenberg.

Seidel, K. and T. Sureau. 2015. 'Introduction: Peace and Constitution Making in Emerging South Sudan on and beyond the Negotiation Tables'. *Journal of Eastern African Studies* 9(4): 612–33.

De Silva de Alwis, R., A. Mnasri, and E. Ward. 2017. 'Women and the Making of the Tunisian Constitution'. *Berkeley Journal of International Law* 35(1): 90–149.

Simmons, E. S. and N. R. Smith. 2019. 'The Case for Comparative Ethnography'. *Comparative Politics* 51(3): 341–59.

Sripati, V. 2013. 'United Nations Constitutional Assistance in Statebuilding'. In D. Chandler and T. D. Sisk, eds. *Routledge Handbook of International Statebuilding*, 143–55. London: Routledge.

Stepputat, F. and J. Larsen. 2015. *Global Political Ethnography: A Methodological Approach to Study in Global Policy Regimes*. Copenhagen: Danish Institute for International Studies.

Suteu, S. 2015. 'Constitutional Conventions in the Digital Era: Lessons from Iceland and Ireland'. *Boston College International and Comparative Law Review* 38(2): 251–76.

Tamanaha, B. Z. 2001. *A General Jurisprudence of Law and Society*. Oxford: Oxford University Press.

Thompson, E. P. 1975. *Whigs and Hunters: The Origin of the Black Act*. New York: Pantheon Books.

Thornhill, C. J. 2018. *The Sociology of Law and the Global Transformation of Democracy*. Cambridge: Cambridge University Press.

Thornhill, C. J. 2019. 'Constitution Making and Constitutionalism in Europe'. In D. Landau and H. Lerner, eds. *Comparative Constitution Making*, 427–45. Cheltenham: Edward Elgar Publishing Limited.

Tully, J. 2008. 'The Imperialism of Modern Constitutional Democracy'. In M. Loughlin and N. Walker, eds. *The Paradox of Constitutionalism: Constituent Power and Constitutional Form*, 315–38. Oxford: Oxford University Press.

Tushnet, M. V. 2008. 'Some Skepticism About Normative Constitutional Advice'. *William & Mary Law Review* 49(4): 1473.

Tushnet, M. V. 2013. 'Constitution-Making: An Introduction'. *Texas Law Review* 91: 1983–2013.

Venter, F. 2019. 'Voluntary Infusion of Constitutionalism in Anglophone African Constitutions'. In D. Landau and H. Lerner, eds. *Comparative Constitution Making*, 510–38. Cheltenham: Edward Elgar Publishing Limited.

Von Benda-Beckmann, K. 2014. 'Trust and the Temporalities of Law'. *The Journal of Legal Pluralism and Unofficial Law* 46(1): 1–17.

Wallis, J. 2014. *Constitution Making during State Building*. New York: Cambridge University Press.

Wastell, S. 2007. 'Being Swazi, Being Human: Custom, Constitutionalism and Human Rights in an African Polity'. In M. Goodale and S. E. Merry, eds. *The Practice of Human Rights: Tracking Law between the Global and the Local*, 320–41. Cambridge: Cambridge University Press.

Williams, S. H., ed. 2009. *Constituting Equality: Gender Equality and Comparative Constitutional Law*. Cambridge: Cambridge University Press.

Wilson, R. A. 2001. *The Politics of Truth and Reconciliation in South Africa: Legitimizing the Post-Apartheid State*. Cambridge: Cambridge University Press.

Yeh, J. and W. C. Chang. 2006. 'From Origin to Delta: Changing Landscape of Modern Constitutionalism'. *bepress Legal Series*. Working Paper 1815.

CHAPTER 32

VIGILANTISM AND SECURITY-MAKING

JENNIFER BURRELL

VIGILANTISM, THE STATE, AND THE DESIRE FOR SECURITY

SECURITY-MAKING and vigilantism challenge notions of the formality of law and of penality. They call for acknowledging ambiguity while probing its contours, for thinking creatively about power and authority. A sustained investigation of boundaries and zones of contestation raised by these topics has pointed to the blurred lines between legal and illegal, state and non-state, legitimate and illegitimate, and what is moral (Thomas and Galemba 2013). As a result, vigilantism and the making of security have prompted rich debate on the nature of legal pluralism and normative forms of law, as well as their relation to popular judicial forms such as community policing and security forces, mediation, and local tribunals. They are closely intertwined with cultural forms, too, through domains of customary law, religion, witchcraft, generation, politics, and gender. This chapter captures some of the movement among and between these realms, ethnographically and at the intersection of debates from anthropology, law, and other disciplines, revealing the social, political, and ethical ideas, registers, and concealed forces at work and at stake in the domain of justice.

Vigilantism and security-making have a symbiotic relationship with the state, enabling us to see variability in who holds power, produces state effects (Trouillot 2001), and maintains order. Vigilantism points to specific 'watershed moments' in the state's existence (Pratten 2010: 118; Super 2017), as well as to quotidian flows of power. It connects us to conflicted histories and to hopes and visions for the future. At a moment when the state is changing rapidly in character and complexity (Comaroff and Comaroff 2006; Mbembe 2001), it nevertheless remains a form of power able to impose categories and representations (Bourdieu 1984; Corrigan and Sayer 1985; Navaro-Yashin 2007) and to engage in the fundamental re-orderings of personhood and sociality that normalize and legitimize political rule (Nugent 2010; Stoler 2002; Trouillot 2003). These productive capacities have contributed to a growing milieu of state-like actors, producers of state-effects, and crusaders for justice, producing a statehood composed of hybrids of indigenous, national, and international forms of law. They are capable of radically reconfiguring the relationship between state and citizens. For many of these actors, security (and the actions that are carried out in its name) allows legal fictions about where power is located, and how it functions, to flourish; and security aesthetics come to shape our everyday worlds (Clarke 2009; Ghertner et al. 2020; Jusionyte and Goldstein 2016; Maguire et al. 2014).

Many places in the world now turn to vigilantes or 'outsourced' security committees and community policing to maintain order. In post-war, post-conflict, and post-socialist states and consolidating democracies, in dense urban settings, in the seats of power in the world's most developed nations, as well as frontiers on the margins of centralized control, these groups provide security, localized forms of justice, and political promotion. Scholars have viewed them across a range of perspectives. For some, these groups seek to emulate the state in form and practice, taking power at times of perceived state weakness or crises of legitimacy (Buur 2005; Super 2017). Others see vigilantes as emerging from legal pluralism, multicentred power figurations, and political action from above or below (Chabal and Daloz 1999; Grätz 2011; Sieder 2002). Debates from a variety of disciplines have encouraged scholars to wonder about the utility of the concept 'vigilante', suggesting that the use of existing definitions pushes us to conflate 'what is with what ought to be in terms of understanding the state' (Buur and Jensen 2004: 140). But a well-rooted and multidisciplinary ethnography of the state and forms of vigilantism and security-making (Burrell 2013b; Buur and Jensen 2004; Englund 2006; Gupta 2012; Hansen and Stepputat 2005; Kloppe-Santamaria 2020; Sieder 2011; Super 2017; Weston 2011) demonstrates how people identify power, seek to control it, consent to it, or are subordinate to it. Taken together, the literature on vigilantism is particularly important for disaggregating and periodizing distinct emergences, capturing different faces of the state, and identifying stakes and goals of local security-making projects.

Vigilantes fashion subjectivities and different kinds of legibility for themselves, usually embedded in cultural and historical particularities. Case studies from around the world direct our attention to the distinctive ways in which they do so: as economically marginalized Aymara peasants in Cochabamba (Goldstein 2003); marginalized citizens in poor black townships in South Africa (Super 2017); Hindus in Bombay slums (Sen 2008); child vigilantes in urban Hyderabad (Sen 2018); Annang Muslim villagers in south-eastern Nigeria (Pratten 2008); engaged political actors in twentieth-century Mexico (Kloppe-Santamaria 2020); or the leftist *ronderos* of rural Peru, whose grassroots social movement grew into a system of peasant justice (Starn 1999). Embedded within these characterizations are usually the very means through which groups legitimize their connections (or opposition) to the state and their 'fitness' for security-making (Buur 2008; Gordon 2007). The desperately poor Aymara residents of a marginalized neighbourhood in Cochabamba insisted that their poverty was key to understanding their vigilantism; local police ignored their pleas for assistance in defending their meagre supplies, and 'human rights' did not attend to their concerns of survival from one day to the next. Instead, the thief who stole their last bit of cooking oil enjoyed the benefits of a powerful legal system when, at the end of their options, they attempted to lynch him.

In what follows, I discuss interpretive dilemmas and analytical debates, using an ethnographic case study from Guatemala to demonstrate some of the on-the-ground complexities of vigilantism and security. The chapter ends with reflections on a series of emergent forms of legal action in which insights derived from studies of vigilantes, security, and the law are utilized.

Bricolage, Legal Pluralism, and Ethnography

Postcolonial states are often discussed in terms of their legal pluralism: places where transnational, national, and local regimes of law compete for supremacy in areas of uneven and contested sovereignty. Vigilantism and security-making are areas where productive debates have raised prescient questions for socio-legal research and practice, among them: does legal pluralism represent an obstacle or an opportunity for rule of law, especially in the context of fragile democracies or transitional states (Kyed 2011)? This section explores legal pluralism in the light of vigilantism and security-making.

Vigilantes devote substantial effort to discursively justifying or legitimizing their projects in terms of both law and culture. Socio-legal scholars that have studied these tropes point to their inclusivity: they frequently contain diverse elements of whatever legal discourses circulate in wider contexts. Drawing upon the Lévi-Straussian concept of bricolage (1966), Daniel Goldstein argues that the marginalized indigenous Cochabambans he worked with in Bolivia are 'legal bricoleurs', creatively combining and recombining what's available to them in their efforts to create security (2012: 30). Guatemala offers another particularly exemplary case to explore these processes. There, indigenous, customary, religious, national, and international laws circulate and are acknowledged in an ambiguous landscape of contested sovereignties (Sieder 2011). Making and contesting security involves a selective embrace of a variety of powerful discourses in a post-conflict context—human rights; neoliberal capitalist imperatives; Mayan ways of being, aesthetics, and senses of personhood; and even Marxism, adapted by both ex-guerrillas and their supporters, as well as conservative members of security patrols. Among multilayered logics are the privatization of security, the economic marginalization of young people (Burrell et al. 2020), moral panics, and the use of violent exclusions to establish and concretize notions of community. Economically, recent experiences of accumulation by dispossession inflame ever-present generational conflict to new heights of violence.

While legal pluralism provides a framework for acknowledging the multiplicity of law and the competing domains that contribute to lawmaking, ethnographic research shows us how the assumption of unified singular systems may be analytically perilous (Goodale 2017). A brief ethnography of vigilantism and security-making in northwestern Guatemala illustrates a series of domains where people move in and out of plural normative legal systems, selectively acknowledging and contesting their claims. In this terrain, customary law is not always rooted in the kind of custom we assume, human rights may not be experienced as compassionate, and unexpected alliances form, while others dissolve.

Living vigilantism, tracing power

Over the course of two post-war decades researching in one municipality in the western highlands of Guatemala, I observed the steady rise of vigilante justice from a series of ad hoc groups of men to a political force that dominated municipal government for a dozen years. In 1998, I saw a lynching. It happened on a crowded market day when the mayor incited a crowd to go after his arch-enemy, a migrant returned from the United States and an alleged gang member.[1] The young man was physically attacked and dragged along the street until members of a local cooperative pulled him to safety in their building. An angry mob looked for kerosene to burn the wooden structure but were stopped by UN peacekeeping forces sent from the nearest city. They evacuated the young man in heavily guarded trucks under cover of night and connected him to national and international human rights groups (Burrell 2010, 2013a). In 2003, this young man was shot eight times in the back and killed by the national civil police during the annual *fiesta*. The mayor of the town asked the police to leave because he could not guarantee their safety during the unruly celebrations. The military stepped in to keep order.

In 2001, in this same town, a Japanese tourist, suspected of stealing children, was lynched and burned to death with his Guatemalan guide. Fuelled by rumours that members of a large Satanic group were robbing children to sacrifice, and targeting crowded markets in the area, people reacted to the cries of a woman terrified by a stranger reaching out to play with her child. Community members cooperated in the state's investigation of the incident and three individuals were jailed, including the young mother. The court acquitted the defendants, concluding that there wasn't sufficient proof or testimony at a fragile point in the consolidation of post-war democracy to establish that they had incited the mob to commit the lynching (Burrell 2013a, 2013b).

By 2004, 'voluntary' forced-service security committees, formed in the early 2000s, consolidated political power, were voted into the municipal government, and gradually began to control the civic realm.[2] They securitized everyday activities (neighbourly and family conflicts, domestic disputes and violence, land issues), and carried out public and punitive punishments—dunking in the fountain, lashings, and indiscriminate incarceration, often for long periods of time. *Seguridad* (security in Spanish), as they were called, cut off connections to the municipal water supply for non-compliance with their edicts, imposed a curfew, and forbid the sale of alcohol in the town. They held municipal political power for twelve years and by then were deeply intertwined with local culture. By 2014, the first mayor to follow their reign was able to claim: 'here the local citizenry has a lot of authority. And, we have the backing of the law.' This was a deliberate strategy to separate himself from the legal 'mistakes' of the past,[3] while still acknowledging the widespread communal support *Seguridad* enjoyed. This mayor also operated in a national context in which the now-defunct International Commission against Impunity in Guatemala (CICIG)[4] was experiencing unprecedented success in systematically addressing corruption and dismantling long-entrenched power structures.

More recently, my research on municipal governance revealed vigilantes' profoundly ambivalent yet beneficent relationship to the state; one in which state intentions are viewed benevolently but recognized to be unwieldy, careless, and not always reliable. Patience was required. Eventually, the state would probably/hopefully/maybe come through—with jobs, tax money, services. In the meantime, people made do across all sectors; the municipality carried on and picked up the slack (Burrell and El Kotni 2019).[5]

I have traced this very brief history of citizen security and vigilante justice in one town in relation to the 'watershed moments' of state-making and in terms of the complexities of how people imagine, create, and act on their conceptions of law and order over time. The state is, at one moment, a formal legal entity investigating and prosecuting a lynching, and, at other points, a decentralized and outsourcing one, standing back from local concerns and abuses of authority. It is capable of force, and worthy of villagers' beneficence and patience. The United Nations and its peacekeeping forces are also present, as are the CICIG and regional authorities, who create state effects, seeking to censure and reign in the worst abuses of *Seguridad*, while simultaneously supporting and educating the young people they once targeted.

A MULTIPLICITY OF LAW

People have different kinds of encounters with law, the state, and security-making. They draw upon culture, local materials, and practices and relationships on the ground to achieve security in insecure environments. The abbreviated ethnographic account above elides the post-civil war context of Guatemala; the ferocious divisions that divided towns, families, and individuals; the long-term processes of paramilitarization, legally dissolved at the signing of the Peace Accords as thousands of men relinquished their weapons, but firmly rooted in local repertoires; and the harsh economic realities of the post-war years. It does so to expose some of the immediate logics and ambiguities of vigilantism and citizen security in one particular place, while acknowledging the violence that is part of these processes. The police, for example, ultimately shot and killed a young man who had long been a thorn in the side of the municipality. Once they did so, however, they were asked to leave, as the municipality could not guarantee their safety. Instead, the military, formerly feared and maligned, stepped in to preside over the *fiesta* celebration. Here, the roles of police and military were mutable in ways that were previously unthinkable, and municipal authorities acted to protect the national civil police, charged with safekeeping following the end of armed conflict.

Following the lynching of a Japanese tourist, contrary to the popular portrayal of mob violence as having protected individuals who incited or participated in the crime, community members used the presence of state investigators to right wrongs of the past, to attempt to purchase land cheaply, to settle conflicts with one another by naming names and pointing to particular people (Burrell 2013b). The unusual presence of the legal and punitive state became an opportunity to address other kinds of conflicts. Finally, *Seguridad* became the mediator of civic life—fulfilling multiple, often contradictory roles: acting as justice of the peace for crimes committed under its aegis, settling land disputes and personal conflicts, and ignoring numerous regional, national, and international censures for abuses of power and human rights, as well as illegal acts. As townspeople later said, 'they extended their boundaries a little too far'.

The vigilantes that I first researched in the mid-2000s saw themselves as combating gang members who were infiltrating their community, setting a bad example for youth. This was an agenda to which regional, state, and even international groups were highly sympathetic. The 'gang members' the vigilantes targeted were returned young migrant men who had spent years in the United States. They challenged traditional authority structures that included no mechanisms for them to take part in local governance. Human rights delegations, as well as regional and national authorities, were informed by the vigilantes and committees of their supporters, 'Don't tell us how to discipline our youth.'

While *Seguridad* may have occupied what Lund (2006: 686) refers to as a 'twilight space' between legality and illegality in some normative senses, for people in the municipality, they were law, albeit one form among many. Soon, the state followed in this vision. After years of legal censure and attempts to reign in their power, responding to their success with gang control, the Guatemalan government endeavoured to incorporate the security committees through regulation, rendering their power officially normative (*Prensa Libre*, 12 March 2007). Many municipalities registered their groups, but *Seguridad* in Todos Santos resisted. They were, after all, already elected to municipal power. These official regulatory steps on the part of the state segued in later years into the transnational security model of community policing widely adopted in Guatemala (Hochmuller 2017).

Ethnographic research reveals the multiple ways in which pluralities of law exist in relation to vigilantes, as culturally constructed historical processes and the sites of political contestation (Comaroff and Comaroff 2006; Merry 1991). In Todos Santos, Sharp (2014: 35) writes of the forms and understandings that interpolated into everyday knowledge: the existential sovereignty enjoyed by Mayan communities for centuries;[6] the law of Guatemala, which protected the economic interests of the elite and upheld impunity; the transnational regimes of law, including human rights, imposed during the negotiation of peace accords; and Guatemala's role as a place of cheap labour for transnational capital, necessitating wage-labour migration.

The movement of people nationally, regionally, and transnationally brought them into contact with, or rendered them unable to access, legal systems. For example, young Mayan migrants to the United States, in the first post-war decade in Guatemala, came of age amidst substantial human rights education and support. They were acutely aware of how many of these rights shifted or disappeared once they crossed the US–Mexico border and became unauthorized migrants (Burrell 2010). Some pursued asylum cases in the United States or obtained U.S. citizenship in other ways, and when they returned to Guatemala, experienced realms of repression based on age and custom, tied to notions of chronological service to the community throughout a lifetime. This movement in and out of different legal regimes contributed to clashes, particularly over rights versus obligations and expectations (Ekern 2008), in which the moral was invoked by parties on all sides of conflicts. In this terrain of bricolage between discursive framing and the availability of different legal domains, individuals selectively chose from multiple forms of normative law to structure and make competing claims, often against one another.

Vigilantism, Culture, and the State

Seguridad, perhaps more insidiously, also became deeply imbricated in local culture. Because all men, and sometimes women, were required to serve in these groups, many people were complicit in their actions. But as their scope and span became more integrated, they refigured such things as intergenerational relations, civic participation, and access to resources. Claiming that these actions were modelled on ancestral methods of mediation, and keeping order, vigilantes connected to 'customary law'. In tone and action, however, they were more comparable to the paramilitary civil patrols imposed by the Guatemalan Army during the last decade of the civil war. Techniques, forms of leadership, and even the same leaders transferred from one configuration to another, and as their hold on the community deepened, the practices and effects of long-term militarization became evident. Forms of penality and clandestinity, the disciplining of youth, integrating spectacle into everyday life, and introducing threats for which the 'potentiality of security' (Jusionyte and Goldstein 2016) were part of the playbook. Public dunking in the fountain in the main square and imprisonment in 'clandestine' jails accessible for public viewing were consistent with the observation that it is 'beyond the reach of the legal and political that security's effective theater of operations is constituted' (Agamben 2005; Masco 2014: 3).

As these examples show, vigilantism and security are complex iterations of desire: to aid the state or to act state-like, and to exist counter to aspects of the state; to fully embrace citizenship, and at the same time to be aware of standing outside strictly regulated forms of state governance; to be part of the law, and to exist outside of some of its normative formalities; to connect to forms from the past, although perhaps to a different past than might be claimed or assumed. Vigilantes are acutely aware of power, and step into its vacuums. They provide the services—often security—that the state ought to make available to its citizens, but they do so based on their own sense of the law, ignoring censures and other mandates meant to regulate their control. They act effectively because they embrace local culture and practices. They seek authority in terms of world views, histories, and generational and gendered arrangements that are already in place. In this way, they present a knowable face of power, one that people can see and engage with, as opposed to the opaque and mercurial state.

Vigilante justice and security-making are about the nature of the state, of the production of state effects, and a sense of potentially knowable power, what Super (2017) refers to as the 'uneven trajectory of penal change and how statehood is practiced by a combination of state and non-state actors'. When the state encourages citizens to take responsibility for their own crime prevention (implicitly or explicitly), the boundaries between legality and illegality are shifted. It is in these margins, where power functions unexpectedly, that the ambiguities of liberal theory and the 'singular nature of the rule of law' become evident (Super 2017; Valverde 2008). Local-level understandings, then, become central in identifying how people understand power to operate and how they seek to control, dispute, or consent to it. In other words, how is governance carried out? This incorporates a sense of political and economic domination via the state and market, as well as the myriad forms in which people organize themselves, seek to exert control over each other, and devise strategies for achieving their goals (Gordon 2007: 359).

Among the responses to state attempts to censure, regulate, or otherwise control vigilante actions are a series of appeals to communal norms and morals. Vigilantes 'view themselves as the defenders, indeed the embodiment of the moral, virtuous community', write Buur and Jensen (2004: 146; Sharp 2014: 23). Their authority, however, is tenuous; the community they purportedly speak for may not agree, nor are they necessarily able to voice dissent. In Guatemala, many experienced the years of *Seguridad*'s rule as fearful, militaristic, and opaque, similar to how they experienced the hottest years of Guatemala's long civil war and its paramilitarized aftermath. Individuals and groups were never sure what logics pertained, how the various parts of what they individually experienced or saw were related to the bigger picture, pointing to the inherent ephemeral quality of vigilante rule and the ever-fragile Gramscian consensus that underlies vigilante power. Despite these ambiguities, however, there was consensus that *Seguridad* was one form of law, together with others, to which they could turn.

This history calls for subtle adjustments to Kyed's (2011) earlier query about legal pluralism, allowing us to see how it can be both an obstacle *and* an opportunity for rule of law in fragile democracies and transitional states. Vigilantism allows us to see the possibilities of multiple forms of law and how people understand them, and to inquire historically about the engagement and stability of these forms. It allows us to see how and why people move across, and even around, competing legal ideas and the kinds of claims they make with them. These observations allow for an expansion of the ideas of law and its rule that we bring to statecraft and transitional periods, opening up the possibility for an expanded incorporation of what exists on the ground, switching ambiguities to productive tensions.

Notes towards Emergent Forms and Future Action

Insights derived from the grey areas and inherent ambiguities of security and vigilantism are contributing to wide-ranging interventions in policy and practice. Below, I review several of these, pointing to the substantive orientations that they engage.

International Development and Legal Pluralism

One of the interesting fields of practice recently is international development interventions in situations of legal pluralism in order to support justice and security reform (Kyed 2011; Swenson 2018). Legal pluralism, in this iteration, becomes a 'policy field' in which donor agencies increasingly recognize the importance of 'non-state', 'informal', and 'customary' institutions and norms concerning the delivery of justice and security (Kyed 2011: 2).[7] Kyed notes that this represents a fundamental departure from the focus on formal state institutions and legal centrism (Kyed 2011: 2). While there is much to critique in the actual practice of recognizing legal pluralities and there is the ever-present threat of slipping into an already-present state bureaucratic logic, this represents a potentially powerful terrain.[8] However, as Swenson argues, 'it is not enough to merely recognize that legal pluralism exists; scholars and policymakers must understand how legal pluralism actually functions' (2018: 442). In the best case, it can be based on an understanding of justice and law that is always implicated in social and political relations and informed by culturally differentiated concepts and hierarchies of value (Lubkemann et al. 2011). Much of this work rethinks 'the state' to include more empirically grounded work, and privileges sets of relationships and wider political orders in which states are situated, moving away from dichotomous perspectives of state and non-state. Overviews of this work suggest that the most promising approaches are culturally grounded and engage non-state networks of authority and legitimacy in order to advance judicial state-building processes. As Swenson emphasizes, the rules that matter most may not stem from the state at all. Custom, tradition, religion, family lineage, generation, 'powers not sanctioned by law (such as those of criminal enterprises or powerful commercial interests), and a host of other sources may have equal or even greater influence than state law' (Swenson 2018: 441). Ethnographic methods and holistic socio-legal attention to social and political worlds clearly have a large role to play in this endeavour.

The notion of hybridity, while by no means new in socio-legal literature (see Goodale 2017; Merry 1988), has shifted from a pooling together of distinct sources to a coming-into-being of a new political order, with new institutional arrangements. This perspective acknowledges that justice and security institutions shift, overlap, and transform each other. Actors themselves cross boundaries that may be in effect at a given time, for example from state to traditional. Hybrid acts, then, also form part of individuals' efforts to consolidate power and constitute authority and coexist in productive tension with boundary-making (Kyed 2017).

Intersectionality, Gender, and Sexuality in Understanding Violence and Security Governance

Gender, sexuality, and intersectional frameworks are rising legal vectors for understanding how violence, including that perpetrated by vigilantism and security-making, figures in practices of in/justice (Amar 2013; Hernandez Castillo 2016; Sierra 2017; Stephen 2019). Intersectionality, coined by Kimberlé Crenshaw (1991), is a socio-legal critique originally developed to address US courts' ignorance of discrimination against black women. It specifically addressed gaps in legal and institutional frameworks to acknowledge and attend to the interplay of multiple layers of oppression. While there is debate about the transference of intersectionality to global legal contexts (Schiek 2018), the acknowledgment of how social categories intersect and contribute to the construction of specific contexts of violence has gradually entered into wider use in the law and as part of political movements and policymaking. These positionalities 'shape the lives of men and women as well as their ascribed social roles, experiences and life prospects' (Sieder and Barrera Vivero 2017: 637). Through this lens, the rippling effects of vigilantism, frequently predicated on extreme modes of masculinity and often encapsulated in forms of violence deeply embedded in patriarchal power, are more clearly visible. Controlling bodies, particularly women's bodies, through actual sexual violence and ongoing threats of sexual violence is one way to demonstrate influence, and even domination, of territories and peoples (Hernandez Castillo 2016: 13; Stephen 2019: 230).

Once the importance of intersectionality is acknowledged, the various domains that contribute to individual harm in contexts of security-making can be more closely analysed. The politics of sexuality, according to Amar (2013), has been central to a contemporary articulation of human security governance that systematically denaturalizes and re-politicizes people, who then need 'saving' by the state. In this framing, bodies that have been raced, classed, and gendered in particular ways may be classified, through a configuration called 'para-humanization', as sources of 'radical insecurity'. This classification permits the state and state-like actors to 'rescue' and 'protect' through various enforcement measures, regardless of the wishes of individuals (Amar 2013: 12). These insights have informed both critiques and new articulations of transnational justice and peacemaking efforts, which often have their basis in masculine and singular notions of law, order, and justice (Velásquez 2018). Collectively, these frameworks allow for a more nuanced accounting of the roles that gender, sexuality, class, race, ethnicity, and generation play in the specific iterations of violence, domination, and control and the multiple domains of life that can be affected by them. The judicial powers that may be accorded to vigilante groups, such as the aforementioned security committees in Guatemala, result in multiple legal orders that are not perceived as separate entities but as 'different legal spaces superimposed, interpenetrated, and mixed' in the minds and actions of women seeking gendered justice, creating spaces of inter-legality (see Barrera Vivero 2016; Sousa Santos 1987: 297–8). These insights are gaining traction in legal domains, such as immigration courts that hear asylum cases (Stephen 2019; Torres 2019), specialized feminicide and gender violence courts (Beck 2021), and transitional and intersectional justice (Butti and McGonigle Leyh 2019; Center for Intersectional Justice 2020).

Cybersecurity and Vigilantism

Vigilantism is 'transmuting' into cyber-forms like hacktivism, scam baiting, crowdsourcing, and citizen-led interventions (Coleman 2014; Silva 2018), creating new frontiers for debating law, legal pluralism, and vigilantism. Often associated with retaliation and/or collective efforts (Smallridge et al. 2016), vigilantes in this sphere are geographically dispersed but united by connectivity and the opportunities of the digital world, often under a common umbrella and a social movement (Coleman 2014; Silva 2018). They are highly skilled individuals who use technical expertise in computer science and engineering (Fazzini 2019). Although these efforts may encompass social media, they are more likely to take place behind the scenes, producing a public-facing result. Frequently, they are anonymous and/or crowdsourced, consistent with the observation that paranoid concealment and creative camouflage are the *modi operandi* of contemporary security regimes (Jusionyte 2015).[9]

The interface of cybersecurity vigilantism with the law is complex and developing, traversing various domains of existing law, including data security and cybercrime. An additional complexity is that the very production of security, as Jusionyte and Goldstein (2016) make clear, is contingent on *invisibility*—and most cyber vigilantes remain under the radar. The activities of cyber vigilantes, according to Silva (2018), have thus far fallen outside the concern of regulation and are largely governed by criminal law applicable to non-vigilantism. However, given the skill sets that these actors possess and the considerable support that they enjoy in global social movements that aims to protect rights and democracy, their inclusion in advancing cybersecurity could 'help to illuminate the grey zone where active citizenship in cybersecurity is currently trapped' (Silva 2018: 34).

Concluding Thoughts

Vigilantism and security-making ask that we both acknowledge the importance of legal pluralism and its lived and often contradictory experiences, and that we recognize its limits. They insist that we acknowledge statehood as a process engaged in by state and non-state actors, and that we rethink the contours of the contemporary state and the role of law within it. In imagining how anthropologists, lawyers, and legal scholars might think through these issues collaboratively and productively, vigilantism offers the insight that legal pluralism can only take us so far, and that ethnography is crucial to understanding how people engage, often simultaneously, various domains of law, and how those domains themselves are also objects for scrutiny and investigation. Bringing these insights to policymaking across various fields, vigilantism asks us to think about violence and to examine the roles and receptions of security-making and their integration into legal domains.

Acknowledgements

An earlier version of this chapter was presented at a workshop convened by the editors of this *Handbook* in Berlin in December 2018. I thank Carol Greenhouse, Juliette Konig, Maria Sapignoli, and Olaf Zenker for careful reading and suggestions. Their comments and guidance were crucial for rethinking this chapter.

Notes

1. In this case, a returned migrant who refused to abide by traditional forms of generational power structures. See Burrell (2013a) for more detail.
2. These groups were similar in form to the paramilitary patrols (PACS) instituted by the Guatemalan Army from 1983 to 1994.
3. In our interviews, he was careful to demonstrate both knowledge of the law and his compliance with it. He closed the jail in the main square, where so many had been held in a carnivalesque atmosphere, sometimes for days, and replaced it with a small holding cell behind the municipal offices. He noted that individuals could only be held there legally for six hours before they were transferred to the police. He also replaced the fountain, where so many had been dunked in the past decade, with a new ornamental one, refiguring a public space that was closely associated with the iron fist (*mano dura*) rule of his predecessors.
4. The CICIG, a hybrid independent entity, is an unprecedented experiment in international cooperation. Since 2007, it has supported domestic state institutions in their efforts to uncover and prosecute so-called parallel powers and clandestine groups that have infiltrated these organizations. It has also paved the way for the first-ever prosecution of genocide in a national court. These, as well as other achievements and successes, have wildly exceeded the hopes and expectations invested in the CICIG at its inception (Open Society Justice Initiative 2016). It was shut down by President Jimmy Morales in 2019, after it began an investigation of his family members.
5. In 2016, for example, state funds—the 10% of taxes returned to municipalities—had not been distributed to municipalities. As a result, there were no supplies in schools or health clinics. Teachers printed copies of textbooks and asked students to share. Nurses and doctors showed me plasters, gauze, and alcohol they had stashed away in locked cabinets for extreme emergencies. All were hopeful, however, that funds would be restored once the

CICIG had addressed various national institutions and the state had dealt with its corruption issues.

6. Excluded from legal systems, Mayan communities established parallel systems of justice to address local conflicts and other issues (Watanabe 1992).
7. Albrecht and Kyed estimate that 80–90% of disputes in the developing world are handled outside of the state justice system (2010: 1; Swenson 2018: 438).
8. While it is not dedicated to informal or customary justice, Guatemala's CICIG could be seen as one of the 'hybrid institutions' arising from such projects. It is worthy of discussing in this context, as it works with, supports, and helps to rebuild national legal institutions that have been shot through with corruption.
9. Some examples include Bellingcat (available at <https://www.bellingcat.com>), a crowdsourced site on online investigation, and Anonymous, explored by Gabriella Coleman in her 2014 book.

References

Agamben, G. 2005. *State of Exception*. Chicago: University of Chicago Press.

Albrecht, P. and H. Kyed. 2010. *Justice and Security: When the State Isn't the Main Provider*. Copenhagen: Danish Institute for International Studies Policy Brief.

Amar, P. 2013. *The Security Archipelago: Human-Security States, Sexuality Politics, and the End of Neoliberalism*. Durham: Duke University Press.

Barrera Vivero, A. 2016. *Violence against Women in Legally Plural Settings*. New York: Routledge.

Beck, E. 2021. 'The Uneven Impacts of Violence against Women Reforms in Guatemala Intersecting Inequalities and the Patchwork State'. *Latin American Research Review* 56(1): 20–35.

Bourdieu, P. 1984. *Distinction*. Cambridge: Harvard University Press.

Burrell, J. 2010. 'In and Out of Rights: Security, Migration and Human Rights Talk in Postwar Guatemala'. *Journal of Latin American and Caribbean Anthropology* 15(1): 90–115.

Burrell, J. 2013a. *Maya After War*. Austin: University of Texas Press.

Burrell, J. 2013b. '(After) Lynching'. In D. Nelson and C. McAllister, eds. *Aftermath: War by Other Means in Post-Genocide Guatemala*, 213–40. Durham: Duke University Press.

Burrell, J. and M. El Kotni. 2019. 'Corruption, Waiting, Exhaustion'. *Fieldsights*, available at <https://culanth.org/fieldsights/corruption-waiting-exhaustion>.

Burrell, J., M. El Kotni, and R. Fernando Calmo. 2020. 'The Anti/Corruption Continuum: Generation, Politics and Grassroots Anti-Corruption Mobilization in Guatemala'. *Journal of Latin American and Caribbean Studies* 25(4): 610–30.

Butti, E. and B. McGonigle Leyh. 2019. 'Intersectionality and Transformative Reparations: The Case of Colombian Marginal Youths'. *International Criminal Law Review* 19(5): 753–82.

Buur, L. 2005. 'The Sovereign Outsourced: Local Justice and Violence in Port Elizabeth'. In T. B. Hansen and F. Stepputat, eds. *Sovereign Bodies: Citizens, Migrants and States in the Postcolonial World*, 192–217. Princeton /Oxford: Princeton University Press.

Buur, L. 2008 'Fluctuating Personhood: Vigilantism and Citizenship in Port Elizabeth's Townships'. In D. Pratten and A. Sen, eds. *Global Vigilantes*, 127–50. New York: Columbia University Press.

Buur, L. and S. Jensen. 2004. 'Introduction: Vigilantism and the Policing of Everyday Life in South Africa'. *African Studies* 63(2): 139–52.

Center for Intersectional Justice. 2020. 'Intersectionality at a Glance in Europe', available at <https://www.intersectionaljustice.org/img/2020.4.14_cij-factsheet-intersectionality-at-a-glance-in-europe_du2r4w.pdf>.

Chabal, P. and J.-P. Daloz. 1999. *Africa Works: Disorder as a Political Instrument*. Oxford: James Currey.

Clarke, K. 2009. *Fictions of Justice*. Cambridge: Cambridge University Press.

Coleman, G. 2014. *Hacker, Hoaxer, Whistleblower, Spy: The Many Faces of Anonymous*. New York: Verso.

Comaroff, J. and J. Comaroff. 2006. *Law and Disorder in the Postcolony*. Chicago, IL: University of Chicago Press.

Corrigan, P. and D. Sayer. 1985. *The Great Arch*. Oxford/New York: Basil Blackwell.

Crenshaw, K. 1991. 'Mapping the Margins: Intersectionality, Identity Politics and Violence Against Women'. *Stanford Law Review* 43(6): 1241–99.

Ekern, S. 2008. 'Are Human Rights Destroying the Natural Balance of All Things? The Difficult Encounter Between International Law and Community Law in Mayan Guatemala.' In P. Pitarch, S. Speed and X. Leyca Solano, eds. *Human Rights in the Maya Region* 123–144. Durham: Duke University Press.

Englund, H. 2006. *Prisoners of Freedom*. Berkeley: University of California Press.

Fazzini, K. 2019. 'Why Some of the World's Top Cybersecurity Hackers Are Being Paid Millions to Use Their Powers for Good'. *CNBC*, available at <https://www.cnbc.com/2019/05/17/cybersecurity-hackers-are-paid-millions-to-use-their-powers-for-good.html>.

Ghertner, D. A., H. McFann, and D. M. Goldstein, eds. 2020. *Futureproof*. Durham: Duke University Press.

Goldstein, D. 2003. '"In Our Own Hands": Lynching, Justice, and the Law in Bolivia'. *American Ethnologist* 30(1): 22–43.

Goldstein, D. 2012. *Outlawed: Between Security and Rights in a Bolivian City*. Durham: Duke University Press.

Goodale, M. 2017. *Anthropology and Law: A Critical Introduction*. New York: New York University Press.

Gordon, R. 2007. 'Popular Justice'. In D. Nugent and J. Vincent, eds. *Companion to the Anthropology of Politics*, 349–66. Malden: Blackwell Publishing.

Grätz, T. 2011. 'Vigilantism in Africa: Benin and Beyond'. In M. Berg and S. Wendt, eds. *Globalizing Lynching History*, 207–23. New York: Palgrave Macmillan.

Gupta. A. 2012. *Red Tape*. Durham: Duke University Press.

Hansen, T. B. and F. Stepputat, eds. 2005. *Sovereign Bodies: Citizens, Migrants and States in the Postcolonial World*. Princeton/Oxford: Princeton University Press

Hernandez Castillo, A. 2016. *Multiple Injustices: Indigenous Women Law and Political Struggle in Latin America*. Tucson: University of Arizona Press.

Hochmuller, M. 2017. The Struggle over Security in Post-War Guatemala. PhD dissertation, Free University Berlin.

Jusionyte, I. 2015. *Savage Frontier*. Berkeley: University of California Press.

Jusionyte, I. and D. Goldstein. 2016. 'In/visible—In/secure'. *Journal of Global and Historical Anthropology* 75: 3–13.

Kloppe-Santamaria, G. 2020. *In the Vortex of Violence: Lynching, Extralegal Justice and the State in Postrevolutionary Mexico*. Berkeley: University of California Press.

Kyed, H. M. 2011. 'Introduction to the Special Issue: Legal Pluralism and International Development Interventions'. *Journal of Legal Pluralism and Unofficial Law* 43(63): 1–23.

Kyed, H. M. 2017. 'Hybridity and Boundary-Making: Exploring the Politics of Hybridization'. *Third World Thematics* 2(4): 464–80.

Lévi-Strauss, C. 1966. *The Savage Mind*. Chicago: University of Chicago Press.

Lubkemann, S., D. Isser and P. Chapman. 2011. 'Neither State nor Custom, Just Naked Power'. *Journal of Legal Pluralism* 63:73–110.

Lund, C. 2006. 'Twilight Institutions: Public Authority and Local Politics in Africa'. *Development and Change* 37: 685–705.

Maguire, M., C. Frois, and N. Zurawski. 2014. *The Anthropology of Security*. London: Pluto Press.

Masco, J. 2014. *The Theater of Operations*. Durham: Duke University Press.

Mbembe, A. 2001. *On the Postcolony*. Berkeley: University of California Press.

Merry, S. 1988. 'Legal Pluralism'. *Law and Society Review* 22: 869–96.

Merry, S. 1991. 'Law and Colonialism'. *Law and Society Review* 25(4): 889–922.

Navaro-Yashin, Y. 2007. 'Make-Believe Papers, Legal Forms and the Counterfeit: Affective Interactions between Documents and People in Britain and Cyprus'. *Anthropological Theory* 7(1): 79–98.

Nugent, D. 2010. 'States, Secrecy and Subversives: ARPA and Political Fantasy in Mid-20th-Century Peru'. *American Ethnologist* 27(4): 681–702.

Open Society Justice Initiative. 2016. 'Against the Odds: CICIG in Guatemala'. Open Society Institute, available at <https://www.refworld.org/docid/5799f4814.html>.

Pratten, D. 2008. 'Introduction: The Politics of Protection: Perspectives on Vigilantism in Nigeria'. *Africa* 78(1): 1–15.

Pratten, D. 2010. 'Bodies of Power: Narratives of Selfhood & Security in Nigeria'. In T. Kirsch and T. Grätz, eds. *Domesticating Vigilantism in Africa*, 118–38. Woodbridge: James Currey.

Schiek, D. 2018. 'On Uses, Mis-Uses, and Non-Uses of Intersectionality before the Court of Justice (EU)'. *International Journal of Discrimination and the Law* 18(2–3): 82–103.

Sen, A. 2008. 'Everyday and Extraordinary Violence: Right-Wing Women and Raw Justice in the Bombay Slums'. In D. Pratten and A. Sen, eds. *Global Vigilantes: Perspectives on Violence and Justice*, 69–92. New York: Columbia University Press.

Sen, A. 2018. 'Security and Purity: Female Surveillance, Child Vigilantism, and the Moral Policing of Deviant Women in Two Radicalized Indian Slums'. *Current Anthropology* 59(5): 549–71.

Sharp, E. 2014. Vigilante: Violence and Security in Postwar Guatemala. PhD dissertation, University of California, Los Angeles.

Sieder, R. 2002. 'Introduction'. In R. Sieder, ed. *Multiculturalism in Latin America*, 1–23. London: Palgrave.

Sieder, R. 2011. 'Contested Sovereignties: Indigenous Law, Violence and State Effects in Postwar Guatemala'. *Critique of Anthropology* 31(3): 161–84.

Sieder, R. and A. Barrera Vivero. 2017. 'Legalizing Indigenous Self-Determination: Autonomy and *bune vivir* in Latin America'. *Journal of Latin American and Caribbean Anthropology* 22 (1): 9–26.

Sierra, M. T. 2017. 'Indigenous Autonomies and Gender Justice: Women Dispute Security and Rights in Guerrero, Mexico'. In R. Sieder, ed. *Demanding Justice and Security: Indigenous Women and Legal Pluralities in Latin America*, 97–120. New Brunswick: Rutgers University Press.

Silva, K. K. e. 2018. 'Vigilantism and Cooperative Criminal Justice: Is There a Place for Cybersecurity Vigilantes in Cybercrime Fighting?' *International Review of Law, Computers and Technology* 32(1): 21–36.

Smallridge, J., P. Wagner, and J. Crowl. 2016. 'Understanding Cyber Vigilantism'. *Journal of Theoretical and Philosophical Criminality* 8(1): 57–70.

Sousa Santos, B. de. 1987. 'Law, A Map of Misreading: Toward a Postmodern Conception of Law'. *Journal of Law and Society* 114(3): 279–302.

Starn, O. 1999. *Nightwatch*. Durham: Duke University Press.

Stephen, L. 2019. 'Fleeing Rural Violence: Mam Women Seeking Gendered Justice in Guatemala and the U.S.'. *The Journal of Peasant Studies* 46(2): 229–57.

Stoler, A. 2002. *Carnal Knowledge and Imperial Power*. Berkeley: University of California Press.

Swenson, G. 2018. 'Legal Pluralism in Theory and Practice'. *International Studies Review* 20(3): 438–62.

Super, G. 2017. 'What's in a Name and Why It Matters: A Historical Analysis of the Relationship between State Authority, Vigilantism and Penal Power in South Africa'. *Theoretical Criminology* 21(4): 512–31.

Thomas, K. and R. B. Galemba. 2013. 'Illegal Anthropology: An Introduction'. *PoLAR: Political and Legal Anthropology Review* 36(2): 211–14.

Torres, M. G. 2019. 'Gender-Based Violence and the Plight of Guatemalan Refugees'. *Fieldsights*, accessible at <https://culanth.org/fieldsights/gender-based-violence-and-the-plight-of-guatemalan-refugees>.

Trouillot, M.-R. 2001. 'The Anthropology of the State in the Age of Globalization'. *Current Anthropology* 42(1): 125–38.

Trouillot, M.-R. 2003. *Global Transformations*. New York: Palgrave MacMillan.

Valverde, M. 2008. 'Analyzing the Governance of Security: Jurisdiction and Scale'. *Behemoth: A Journal on Civilisation* 1: 3–15.

Velásquez, E. 2018. 'Gendering Intergenerational Peacemaking in Post-Accords El Salvador'. Paper given at the Latin American Studies Association annual meeting, Barcelona, 23–26 May.

Watanabe, J. M. 1992. *Maya Saints and Souls in a Changing World*. Austin: University of Texas Press.

Weston, G. 2011. *Guatemalan Vigilantism and the Global (Re)Production of Collective Violence: A Tale of Two Lynchings*. London: Routledge.

CHAPTER 33

THE NORMATIVE COMPLEXITY OF PRIVATE SECURITY

Beyond Legal Regulation and Stigmatization

MATH NOORTMANN AND JULIETTE KONING

INTRODUCTION

THIS chapter critically assesses the debate on the privatization of security through the lenses of (international) law, politics, organization studies, and anthropology/ethnography. We argue that the debate regarding the private security sector is biased and preoccupied with its legal regulation. This preoccupation is grounded in the understanding that the current (legal) regulation of the private security sector is inadequate. We will show that the debate discounts not only the conceptual and practical limitations that are inherent in the law but also the idea that, beyond law, there is an authoritative normative space that guides the sector. This authoritative space includes self-regulation, social and corporate responsibility, and sector ethics. In order to capture this normative complexity, we need to move beyond the concepts and methodologies of law to understand the dynamic interaction between principles and practices. The way forward, we propose, can be found in organizational anthropology.

The use of private agencies that offer military and/or security services dates back centuries (Noortmann 2011; Noortmann and Chapsos 2015). However, since the 1990s, private security has re-emerged, as is evident in the truly global proliferation of private security companies (Godfrey et al. 2014). It is a result of a new type of 'top down, or post-modern privatization [which] is purposively planned and implemented by governments' (Wulf 2008: 192). The private security industry, which currently has an estimated global market value of $180 billion and a workforce that outnumbers public police officers (Sorensen 2015; Provost 2017), has become the subject of a largely normative debate.

A number of reported incidents and political affairs involving so-called private military companies (PMCs), and the increased outsourcing of security in military conflicts in the 1990s and the first decade of the twenty-first century have led academics, activists, and journalists to investigate and criticize the private security sector as a whole. They call for more robust (inter)national accountability schemes, regulations, and supervisory mechanisms. The tone of this evolving, post-1990 narrative was set by general predispositions against privatization and/or more specific biases against the privatization of security. This has sparked societal and academic discourses that question and criticize both the limitations of the law, in terms of regulation and oversight, and the ethics of the private security sector.

The security discourse has come to recognize that security in our time and age is 'simply too important and too complex to be left to one group of specialists' (Wiliams 2008: 11) and requires a 'multidisciplinary analysis of how, why, when and by whom security is deployed, constructed, institutionalised and structured' (Bourbeau 2015: 2). However, the dominating tenor still reiterates legal regulation, and governmental oversight, and it echoes the stigmatization of the security sector. Legal scholarship has predominantly focused on legal accountability associated with contract and crime (Kelly 2012), while the social sciences, including anthropology, have mainly concentrated on 'security' and 'security spaces' (Maguire et al. 2014; Goldstein 2015; Samimian-Darash and Stalcup 2017). The relevant disciplines have thus largely failed to produce accounts that include the multiple voices of the industry and/or maintain a proper level of critical self-reflection. What is missing is an *interdisciplinary deepening* of the academic discourse by (structurally) researching the private security sector *from within*—which requires, as we will show below, both access to multiple stakeholders and a tolerant and unprejudiced mindset with respect to these stakeholders. The failure to take these measures, we contend, must be explained with reference not only to enduring sentiments and biases towards the privatization of security and private security companies, but also to disciplinary traditions of law and anthropology.

We illuminate in this chapter the normative complexity of the privatization of security by discussing: (1) the main limits and biases in the current discourse on the privatization of security, (2) the existence of an authoritative normative space beyond law, and (3) the role of organizational anthropology/ethnography in uncovering biases and stigmas that interfere with the assessment of the sector. The chapter also offers a glimpse of what this approach can reveal through examples and illustrations based on fieldwork undertaken by the authors in South Africa in 2016 and 2017.

The Current Debate: The Limits of Legal Regulation and Stigmatization

The current discourse on the privatization of security proliferated with the growing employment of private security companies in military conflict zones, especially in Iraq.

The post-modern governmental outsourcing of security in military conflicts reintroduced the stigmatized concept of mercenarism, which states had gradually abandoned in the second half of the nineteenth century (Percy 2007: 94). In the post-1990 debate, 'mercenarism' became the notion around which the discussion revolved (Adams 1999; Brooks 2000; Avant 2012).

Perplexed by the activities of so-called private military and security companies (PMSCs), scholars started to address and critique general and specific issues of law such as accountability (Cullen 2000; Finer 2008), corporate criminal liability (Collins 2015), litigation (Ryngaert 2008), home state responsibility (Francioni 2009), and UN regulations (Gómez del Prado 2011). The corresponding debates differed from pre-1990 debates on private security in terms of the sheer numbers of contributions to them, but not necessarily in terms of approach (Hoover 1977; Mourning 1981). Unfortunately, the post-1990 discourse lacks a level of historical reflexivity (but see, Percy 2007).

Today's corporate, for-profit, private provider of security is a modern, not a post-modern phenomenon. It merely has stayed under the radar of public attention until the 1971 publication of the Rand Corporation Report on 'the private police industry' in the United States. The report, which was commissioned by the U.S. National Institute of Law Enforcement and Criminal Justice, explicitly aimed to 'describe the nature and extent of the private police industry ... *its problems, its present regulation and how the law impinges on it ... the costs, benefits and risks to society*' (Kakalik and Wildhorn 1971: iv; italics added). It resulted in a first serious critique of 'regulation and legal remedy':

> Licensing and regulation of private security businesses is at best minimal and inconsistent, and at worst completely absent. Sanctions are rarely invoked, Moreover, current tort, criminal and constitutional law has not been adequate—substantially or procedurally—to control certain problem areas involving private security activities, such as searches, arrests, use of firearms, and investigations, Finally, current law has not always provided adequate remedy for persons injured by actions of private security personnel.
>
> (Kakalik and Wildhorn 1971: viii)

In the United Kingdom, a similar 'general indifference' (George and Button 2000) existed with respect to an emerging private security industry. The sector did not face critical questions until 1979, when the U.K. Home Office issued a discussion paper on 'The Private Security Industry' (Wilkinson 2007) to be followed a full twelve years later by an (unpublished) 'Private Security Industry Background Paper' by the Home Office. In South Africa, which is widely considered to be the 'absolute champion' of private security (Diphoorn 2015: 9), PSCs started 'to emerge in the 1970s and 1980s in the mining sector and farming sector'.[1] According to Tessa Diphoorn (2015), the South African government facilitated this development as a means to free policing resources so that they could be used against the mounting political resistance.

In the 1970s and 1980s, academic publications on private security were notably limited and mainly informed by law (Bassiouni 1977; Draper 1978) and political science

(Lipman 1988). The post-1990 academic discourse demonstrates a similar preoccupation with law and politics, which in many respects resembles the mainstream discourse on the liability of multinational corporations (Kamminga and Zia-Zarifi 2000) and overlaps with general discourses on privatization (Boycko et al. 1996) and security studies (Williams 2008).

Today's dominant scholarly arguments push for more and/or improved regulation, based on a perceived lack of jurisdictional clarity and on concern for victim protection (Caparini 2008; Krahman 2008). Human rights are regularly brought into the debate, which recounts the absence or inadequacy of law, whether national or international (Francioni 2009; Baker and Pattison 2012; Karski 2018). The fixation with law and legal regulation, and the idea that the law's limitations can be overcome by more legal rules, is found not only among legal scholars. The traditional methodological differences between mainstream legal scholarship and social scientists are bridged by adopting similar normative approaches. Within scholarly circles there was, and in our opinion still is, little opposition to the politically correct view that the activities of private security companies must be legally curtailed and that their actions are questionable.

From a legal perspective, the limits of law are conceptually and practically given; but these are largely ignored in the private security debate. First of all, there is the indispensble conceptual distinction between public (criminal) law and private (contract) law, which reflects—as Tully (2007: 122) puts it—the conflict between 'public accountability and regulation of free enterprise'. The questions that have been raised by critical scholarship regarding that essential liberal distinction remain marginal (Cutler 2003; Norrie 2010), also with respect to its consequences for the freedom of contract and the prerogative of the state to enforce the law. Second, in practical terms the state's sovereign prerogative to legislate, adjudicate, and enforce both public law and private law may be limited. In order to mitigate some of the consequences of these limitations, states have adopted bilateral and multilateral agreements that regulate potential conflict of national private law(s) and such issues as criminal prosecution and extradition. Procedural guarantees of suspects, however, cannot be legally circumvented. Third, and equally relevant, are the practical limitations that states face in supervising and controlling the industry, due to a lack of resources and capacity.

These three different types of limitations are reflected in the criminal and tort proceedings against Blackwater Security Consulting and Blackwater employees, in the contractual dispute between Sandline International (a PMC) and Papua New Guinea, and in the pressing lack of inspectors that the South African Private Security Industry Regulation Authority (PSiRA) is facing. The criminal and tort proceedings against Blackwater and/or its employees are well discussed in the media and academic articles. The debates on the claims for immunity from prosecution and/or litigation, based on accepted doctrines, existing jurisprudence, standing legislation, and/or such orders as the infamous 'order 17', and the resulting verdicts, have received ample attention by journalists and researchers (Scahill 2007; Kelly 2012; Prince 2013). Less well-known is the case between Sandline and Papua New Guinea over an 'Agreement for the Provision of Military Assistance', amounting to US$36 million, which revolved largely around the determination of the applicable law (English, Australian, Queensland, Papua New Guinean, or international) in order to determine, in turn, whether the contract was valid or not (Dorney 1998).[2] The actual difference between the number of inspectors that the PSiRA can put in the field (approximately sixty) and the number of South African PSCs (some 9,000) and private security guards (around 2.5 million) shows the pressing practical problem for some states in supervising a booming industry (PSiRA 2018).

The conceptual and practical limits of the law hamper, in their own way, a better understanding of the privatization of security. At the same time, and closely related to these limits, there is an undertone of bias in the debates regarding the very existence of private security companies and the validity of outsourcing of security—which is considered to be a public good—to private entities. This part of the debate has generated a considerable amount of naming and shaming of private security and military companies as 'War PLC' (Armstrong 2008), 'corporate warriors' (Singer 2008), 'mercenaries' (Kwakwa 1990; Adams 1999), or 'dogs of war' (Joachim and Schneiker 2012; Sorensen 2015), which engage in 'twilight policing' (Diphoorn 2015). This 'image' problem is no longer restricted to the military side; it also affects private security organizations and has not contributed to a balanced debate on the roles and responsibilities of the private security sector. The painting of these organizations and their employees and owners as 'immoral' and 'ruthless' has created an '"anti-mercenary norm" [that] has become "institutionalised" across not only media outlets but also national and international governmental organizations and in wider public discourse' (Brewis and Godfrey 2018: 338). Albeit PMCs are especially subject to societal scrutiny, the sector as a whole has to deal with stigmatization.

Compared to debates on security in the fields of law, international relations, politics, and international studies, research on the private security sector from an organizational and/or anthropological perspective has been slow to catch up (Godfrey et al. 2014; Maguire, Frois, and Zurawski 2014). Since their engagement with this topic, however, neither field has really moved away from the stigmatization discourse. In organization studies, stigmatization of both the industry and its employees has resulted in an interesting debate on the impact of stigmatization on the identity of a sector and/or its employees. Drawing on Ervin Goffman's (1963) major work, *Stigma: Notes on the Management of Spoiled Identity*, an increasing body of research addresses how professions and workers in stigmatized settings manage such stigma and the 'dirty work' they are doing, including in the security sector (Vergne 2012; Higate 2012b; Hansen Löfstrand et al. 2016)

Tommy Jensen and Johann Sandstrom (2015: 128) define organizational stigma as 'stigma associated with a particular category of organizations (core stigma organizations) that is transferred to a group of people of single individuals (within or outside of the organization) who have to conceal, transform, or resist this stigma transfer in social encounters'. It is argued that morally stigmatized occupations (for instance, private security companies) tend to be regarded as 'dirtier' (i.e. more stigmatized) than physically or socially stigmatized occupations (such as working in a slaughter house) and that these morally stigmatized occupations will engage in very robust organization-level defensive tactics (Ashford and Kreiner 2014).

In research on organizational stigma, a lot of attention is given to coping with stigma and less with questioning the lingering tendency to stigmatize as such. Examples of mechanisms for coping with stigma include the construction of a professional identity by the private security firm contractors, which is achieved by minimizing the impact of their presence on the ground. For instance, keeping a low profile is seen as 'integral of good security practice' (Higate 2012a: 340). Other examples include the creation of a narrative highlighting the importance, necessity, and virtues of their work by security officers in Sweden and the United Kingdom (Hansen Löfstrand et al. 2016) and by private security guards in hospitals (Johnston and Hodge 2014). British contractors active in Iraq and Afghanistan have stressed 'just cause' and (military) professionalism (Brewis and Godfrey 2018), whereas others reverted to strategies of lessening disapproval of them by diversifying, as when arms firms also set up as elderly care home providers (Vergne 2012). Ashford and Kreiner (2014) observed the reframing, recalibrating, and refocusing of work as a defensive tactic in order to mitigate the stigma attached to 'dirty' work, the ultimate aim being to create positive meaning.

In short, the literature on organizational stigma in private security investigates the management of stigmatization. Attempts to move away from the stigma debate are hard to find; one example is the work by Jutta Joachim and Andrea Schneiker (2012), who argue that, due to an increase in civilian missions for private security firms, there is scope to reframe the stigmatized 'dirty' worker/'dogs of war' in private security as 'new humanitarians'. Based on the above, two points of critique have to be made: first, this line of research cannot rid itself of a conceptualization of private security organizations as stigmatized; and, second, there is hardly any attention devoted to private security at the micro-sociological level (Higate 2012a, 2012b; Joachim and Schneiker 2012).

To enhance research that considers the micro-sociological dimension of private security, anthropology would offer a very suitable lens. In the recently published edited volume, *The Anthropology of Security*, Mark Maguire, Catarina Frois, and Nils Zurawski (2014: 4) argue for a 'critical anthropology of security ... with historically informed anthropological perspectives on the politics of security, the key areas of policy and policing, and of course, experiences of security in different domains'. This is a much-needed addition to security studies, which are still dominated by the field of international relations and by state-ism. However, it is somewhat unfortunate that the authors do not take into consideration the experiences and stories of those active within the private security industry. Private security companies are virtually absent, save for comments, in the introduction to this volume, about the contract of G4S, a private security company, with the Lincolnshire Police Authority to 'built and staff many functions within a police station'—which the editors describe as '*disturbing portents* ... foretell[ing] a vision of the future already available elsewhere' (Maguire, Frois, and Zurawski 2014: 13; italics added). Here as well, we see unease with the private security sector. This is where organizational anthropology might have an important contribution to make. We return to this point following the next section.

Regulating private security beyond the law

There exists an immeasurable field of norms, standards, and procedures beyond the confinements of the law. Law, however defined, is but one normative, regulatory system among others that are *not* law. The difference between legal norms and non-legal norms is the constructed and cultivated authoritativeness of the former; legal norms are overall considered to be of a higher normative value than non-legal norms. In order to avoid that this doctrinal difference between law and non-law determines the outcome of specific normative debates, there is a tendency among legal scholars and anthropologists of law to define non-legal norms as law. This can be done in a variety of ways such as the upgrading of 'custom' to 'customary law' or conceptualizing 'transnational law' as a new legal system. Both exercises, in effect, secure the legal character of the debate by suggesting that the arguments can be located *within* the limits of law. While the construction of concepts such as 'customary law' and 'transnational law' is highly relevant for an engagement with law beyond 'black letter' national and international law, they create, in effect, a new plurality in law. Indeed, legal pluralism engages with the complexities of law that legal positivism seeks to avoid (Noortmann 2001), but that 'legal' approach equally fails to appreciate and engage with normative systems that are not law. Legal pluralism's conceptualizing characteristic is still the ultimate distinction between law and non-law (Merry 1988).

Any inter-subjective agreement on a definition of law that would be more inclusive of non-state *law* would still exclude regulations, procedures, and disciplinary mechanisms in the 'social field' that do assert authoritative normative value, but which are *not* law. Bringing all norms under the general heading of 'law' by simply labelling them as such prevents us from understanding the relevance of otherwise authoritative norms and their relationship with legal norms. Researchers on private security have to look beyond 'security practices that create a multiplicity of perhaps seemingly in-compatible versions of *law*', as Susan Bibler Coutin (2001: 502; italics added) asserts, and include relevant normative spaces beyond law. These normative spaces consist *inter alia* of collective voluntary self-regulation mechanisms that are initiated by branch organizations, published social corporate responsibility commitments of individual private security companies, and ethical standards that are held by individual private security contractors and by owners and staff-members of private security companies.

The idea that the private security sector is capable of meaningful self-regulation has triggered a contentious debate between civil society and activist scholarship, on one side, and corporations, on the other side. The *War on Want's* opinion that voluntary codes in the private security sector are 'a licence for abuse' and a tool 'to legitimise the industry and governments to sidestep proper controls' (War on Want 2013) is telling. Simon Chesterman and Chia Lehnardt (2007: 2) reflect scholarly concerns in stating the following:

> Acceptance of ... [the private security] market will largely depend on the reality and the perception of accountability mechanisms ... [A] central question is whether the normative framework and accountability structures adequately address the new environment.
>
> Most commentators agree that they do not.

Indeed, private codes and instruments of self-regulation in the private security sector have not met with much approval. In order to properly value normative development beyond the law, however, we must first of all accept that 'we may not like all the norms being articulated at any given moment, [but] it will do no good to ignore them or insist on their lack of authority' (Berman 2007: 329). This, we argue, is precisely what is happening with respect to the private security sector: ignoring or dismissing collective self-regulation, corporate social responsibility schemes, and individual ethics.

The private security sector has established a range of generic and specific national and international branch organizations, which have adopted a variety of standards and guidelines, as well as certification and oversight mechanisms. The International Code of Conduct Association (ICoCA), for example, monitors and assesses the compliance of its members with the International Code of Conduct for Private Security Providers (ICoC). To that extent the organization has established a complaints procedure. National security sector branch organizations such as the British Security Industry Association (BSIA) and also smaller more specific organizations such as the South African Intruder Detection Services Association (SAIDSA) also develop their own certification and training programmes. One of the research participants, who is a member of SAIDSA, stated that SAISDA membership is 'good for insurances and for standards and for marketing'.[3]

The perceived benefits of self-regulation in the private security sector indicate a relationship between standards and business. These private branch initiatives work next to and often in cooperation with semi-public or public/private branch organizations such as PSiRA and the U.K. Security Industry Authority (SIA). These 'authorities' are based on the 2001 Private Security Industry Regulation Act (South Africa) and the 2001 Private Security Industry Act (the United Kingdom) respectively. Both organizations perform similar licencing and supervision functions that are authorized by law, but they are also independent and linked to the sector, developing their own non-legal norms.

In addition to the development of specific branch standards, some of these organizations also participate in the development of more generic standards that can be adopted beyond the organization by national governments, international organizations, and non-governmental organizations (NGOs) such as the International Standard

Organization (ISO), which has issued such standards as the Management System for Private Security Operations (ISO 18788:2015) and Guidelines for Private Maritime Security Companies, pertaining to privately contracted armed security personnel on board of ships (ISO 28007-1:2015). On the ISO website, these standards are formulated, respectively, as follows:

> This international standard specifies requirements and provides guidance for organizations conducting or contracting security operations. It provides a business and risk management framework for the effective conduct of security operations. It is specifically applicable to any organization operating in circumstances where governance may be weak or rule of law undermined due to human or naturally caused events.[4]

'This part of ISO 28007 gives guidelines containing additional sector-specific recommendations, which companies (organizations) who comply with ISO 28000 can implement to demonstrate that they provide Privately Contracted Armed Security Personnel (PCASP) on board of ships.'[5]

These kinds of standard-setting activities support Lindsey Cameron's (2009: 115) conclusion that security companies 'cannot set international standards themselves when it comes to activities that are already regulated by ... law; rather, they may merely regulate in order to achieve a better compliance with existing standards. It is conceivable however, that they may set standards for matters that are not already governed by applicable law'. Her opinion that 'a will to self-regulate ... [is] laudable, but people handling weapons in situations of armed conflict clearly need to be bound by more than a voluntary code of conduct' (Cameron 2009: 138) can be met with a similar argument that 'people handling weapons in situations of armed conflict clearly need to be bound by more than a *legal* code of conduct'. Indeed, the legal regulation for the handling of weapons provides no guarantee that abuse will not happen. Anne Peters, Lucy Koechlin, and Till Förster (2009: 549) recognize the value of private standards in 'deploy[ing] an extremely strong compliance pull, which resembles "public" authority and enforceability'. Private security companies understand and work with the differences between legal rules, which, as one of our research participants expressed it, 'we have to comply with', and 'standards that are associated with professional "accreditations" and "good ethics"'.[6]

Apart from creating branch organizations that develop standards and guidelines, many private security organizations have also adopted social (corporate) responsibility schemes that include reference to such issues as sustainable development, human rights, and corruption (G4S 2016).[7] Christopher Kinsey (2008: 83) concludes that 'it seems that industry is aware of the concept and that it applies to them [but] that there appears to be a lack of understanding about exactly what it represents. And yet ... companies generally act in a socially responsible way'. According to Kinsey, this can be explained by 'competition and future markets' (Kinsey 2008: 83), which, as Anne van Aaken (2015) suggests, creates compliance incentives.

The relationship between corporate and branch ethics and individual/professional ethics, is considered to be a critical one (Soares 2003; Bénabou and Tirole 2010). There is a reflexive awareness within the sector that the potential negative reputation of the sector 'boils down to ethics. And very few guys can spell it these days.'[8]

At the corporate level, ethics are considered to reflect privately held norms of 'social responsibility', which inform individual positions but which are considered to lay outside a specific security 'function' or 'mandate'.[9] With the growing diversification in the sector comes a new dynamic of what Asa Kasher (2008) calls 'interface ethics'. Kasher (2008: 235) assumes that 'ethical problems emerge where actions are performed at one and the same time and one and the same place by members of two [different] organisations'. Assuming that the 'ethical problems of interface' are the result of 'simple exposure' ignores the development of ethical standards from cooperation between different organizations.

Interface ethics and resulting new interface norms are no longer confined to the interaction between public and private security providers. Increasingly, they are extended to interactions between different private security providers as well. Professional diversification in the sector comes with the introduction of new ethics and new norms. The traditional background of security personnel (former police officers and military personnel) is waning. In the new generation, executive officers, managers, and owners come into the sector with MBA degrees and add a new sense of business ethics to police and military ethics:

> New generations come up with new ideas, different backgrounds, education-wise ... [which] brings business forward[10] ... [but it is also] increasingly difficult to do business properly ... [I]n the old days you'd have a guarding company that would just do guards [but now] you can't sustain your business model just with guards or just with alarms or just with CCTV. It's impossible.[11]

Moving *into* the Private Security Sector

As stated by Robert M. Cover (1983: 4–5), 'no set of legal institutions or prescriptions exists apart from the narratives that locate it and give it meaning ... [I]n this normative world, law and narrative are inseparably related'. We have argued that a reconciliation of different norms in the privatization of security is seriously impeded by a combination of factors, including, especially, the dominant norms and notions of law and the biased questioning of private security sector ethics, as reflected in the stigmatization resulting from the naming, shaming, and blaming of the private security sector. This results in a normative debate that ignores the development and creation of norms beyond traditional legal instruments of accountability and regulation, as we have shown in the previous section.

There are a few approaches, such as critical security studies (Buzan et al. 1998) and the study of global security assemblages (Abrahamsen and Williams 2009; Higate 2017), that recognize the growing complexity and the multiple stakeholders engaged in today's security landscapes. In our view, however, these approaches have not yet been able to investigate the full complexity outlined above, as most studies focus on only a limited number of actors within the wider field. The way forward lies in an approach that investigates the private security sector from within and in its full complexity. Anthropology and ethnography, as the study of cultural and social life through close-up and context-sensitive research (Eriksen 2015), are very well placed to do so. However, as we have also shown, legal anthropology and social anthropology do have their limits, due either to a focus on regulation or to a general uneasiness with the 'field' as such.

Private security organizations are intriguing (and dominant) actors in the wider security landscape, but comprehensive research on these organizations and their relationship with other security actors in the sector is missing. The noted bias and stigma seem to prevent further understanding of the level and impact of their activities (Godfrey et al. 2014). This neglect begs the question of what these organizations (and their staff) are about. How did they get started and why, what drives them, how are they organized, what do they want to contribute to security, what is their take on regulation, and how do they make sense of their role within the wider security landscape? And of what does that landscape consist? These are the kind of questions we used in our research into the security sector in South Africa (with fieldwork in 2016 and 2017). By using an organizational anthropological lens and integrating our legal, anthropological, and organizational expertise in an attempt to 'go beyond' existing ideas and representations, we encouraged security actors to tell us 'their' story.

Paul Bate's (1997) core text 'Whatever Happened to Organizational Anthropology' is a good starting point to address the merits of this approach. From anthropology, the approach adopts fieldwork, a narrative style, and the premise that thought and behaviour can only be understood in the context in which they are situated. Since Bate's main work, organizational anthropology (or organizational ethnography) has attained an important position, in particular in the field of organization and management studies (more so than within anthropology). Its objects are the human networks of action we call organizations (Ciuk et al. 2018), which may be understood as 'systems of meaning and interpretation' (Schubert and Röhl 2019: 5). Organizational ethnographers are 'concerned with understanding how organization members go about their daily working lives and how they make sense of their workplaces' (Ciuk et al. 2018: 278).

Organizational ethnography strives to combine 'subjective experience and individual agency with a sensitivity to the broader social settings and the historical and institutional dynamics in which these are embedded' (Yanow et al. 2012: 335). This careful attention makes it possible to show how organizational actors go about and make sense of their daily lives, and it enables organizational ethnographers to shed light on hidden dimensions of organizational life (power and politics), to place actors in context, and to make polyphony audible. It asks the researcher to be open-minded, not to prejudge, and to study a particular organization on its 'own terms' (Burton et al. 2018: 11). In short, it offers the necessary 'mindset' to 'move into' the security sector and study the privatization of security and private security organizations in particular.

There is a dual meaning to 'moving *into*' as we use it here. There is of course the literal meaning of seeking access to the wide variety of stakeholders that make up the private security sector. These include private security companies—from small family firms to large international corporations with divergent expertise in maritime or landward security, surveillance, armed response, and/or specialized equipment installations—as well as regulatory bodies, local police, neighbourhood watches, campus security, municipality representatives; and receivers of security. To do justice to the complexity, we made contact with all of these and did not take refuge in engaging with only one of these core players. In most cases, our being there meant that we just knocked on doors or approached these stakeholders on the street if necessary. They were all very willing to talk to us. This is related to the other, more metaphorical and maybe more important meaning of 'moving into'.

The metaphorical 'moving into' implies a tolerant and open appreciation of the various stakeholders and their roles and work. Stakeholders in the security industry are very aware of the stigma, ethical questions, and demand for regulation that befalls their organizations and activities. In all cases, we made contact by asking them to 'tell us their story'; and they did, often in great detail and with historical momentum. Being partners in the conversation who were able to understand both the legal and regulatory issues as well as the organizational and cultural dynamics made us privy to engaging and sincere stories and narratives, as some of the statements made by research participants, quoted above (and below), indicate. It also led to invitations to come and visit their sites, surveillance rooms, and private homes, all of which added necessary contextualization to the stories.

South Africa is not a homogeneous society. Therefore, research into the South African private security sector faces an 'extra complexity', in the words of one research participant.[12] In addition, the South African security sector is immensely diverse:

> When you talk about private security, you're talking about a wide spectrum of services. You've got those who are providing security guards and those that are specializing in close protection, those that are providing dog handlers and the canine sector, and you also have locksmiths. You have those that are providing private intelligence, and so on and so forth.[13]

This contextual complexity and diversity alone make general comments on the regulation of 'the sector' and the ways in which the sector or private companies work particularly problematic. It also indicates that 'moving into' and 'going beyond' is of utmost importance in doing justice to what is 'actually' going on out there.

It is well known that South Africa grapples with substantial crime rates. In 2017, South Africa published a 'White Paper on Safety and Security', with the aim of promoting an integrated and holistic approach to safety and security, in support of its National Development Plan objective of 'Building Safer Communities'. This White Paper reaffirms that building safer communities is the collective responsibility of both the state and its citizens, and it emphasizes the need for an active citizenry, civil society, and private sector to contribute to the ongoing efforts of government to promote safety and to prevent crime and violence (South Africa White Paper on Safety and Security 2017). The 'moving into' created a wide range of connections, and while in the field we came into contact with such a security initiative. We were able to follow it and to conclude, on the basis of this example, that the 'cowboy-image' of private security companies is a one-sided view:

> So we've taken all the private security companies, the University, local law enforcement agencies that we have, and we've all combined them into one grouping, and they all work towards one major aim, and that is to be pro-active towards crime-prevention instead of re-active ... So all of them are working together in all the different areas, assisting one another sharing information. And yes, we've been very successful.[14]

The point to make is that focusing on stigma, accountability, and/or regulation is a far cry from what is actually taking place in the day-to-day 'realities' of the various actors involved in the security landscape. The following quotation attests to the fact that not all private security companies are building on fear to make money:

> What I realized was, very quickly ... there's a lot of people making an enormous amount of money out of people's misery rather than trying to fix problems. There's a complete disconnect here, and if people can sell you fences, gates, electric beams, and cameras, they will make a lot of money. They aren't necessarily fixing the problem of the person who's asked them to go and do that. My approach has been completely different: it's to teach people how to actually live their lives in a different way.... . If I teach people's mindsets, then I'm going to push away the idea that people are making phenomenal amounts of money from selling people stuff rather than teaching people how to live their lives in a safer way. That's where I go. That's what my business is all about.[15]

Academic research has not yet done a good enough job of tackling the more pertinent questions and offering a plurivocal 'insider's' view. Going beyond law and beyond anthropology, but combining their expertise in novel ways—a journey we have started on—is in our view a promising way forward.

Concluding remarks

In this chapter, we have argued that the current debate on the privatization of security and the private security sector displays a normative bias towards the sector that finds expression in a preoccupation with the legal regulation of private security companies and with the 'kind' of work they are engaged in. This bias has largely prevented researchers from looking beyond the law and exploring the private security sector from within, and it has led them to ignore regulatory alternatives and diversity within the sector. We have argued, first, that the law is conceptually and practically limited, which constrains effective public regulation; and, second, that a deeper, unbiased research engagement with the security sector reveals a plurality of actors and voices as well as the existence of norms and standards that can be authoritative and effective in their own right. We have shown that organizational anthropology, conducted at the crossroads of law, anthropology, and organizational studies, can uncover an ethical and normative diversity that is essential to a comprehensive understanding of the privatization of security and of private security organizations.

Notes

1. Interview with anonymous research participant, 31 March 2017, Western Cape region.
2. Agreement for the Provision of Military Assistance dated this 31 day of January 1997 between the Independent State of Papua New Guinea and Sandline International (<http://www.privatemilitary.de/pool_doc/documents_sandline-png.pdf> (accessed 7 November 2018).
3. Interview with anonymous research participant, 27 April 2017, Western Cape region.
4. See <https://www.iso.org/obp/ui/#iso:std:iso:18788:ed-1:v1:en> (accessed 27 March 2020).
5. See <https://www.iso.org/obp/ui/#iso:std:iso:28007:-1:ed-1:v1:en> (accessed 27March 2020).
6. Interview with anonymous research participant, 24 April 2017, Western Cape region.
7. See <https://www.adt.co.uk/corporate-social-responsibility> (accessed 27 March 2020).
8. Interview with anonymous research participant, 2 May 2017, Gauteng region.
9. Interview with anonymous research participant, 3 April 2017, Gauteng region.
10. Interview with anonymous research participant, 27 April 2017, Western Cape region.
11. Interview with anonymous research participant, 20 April 2017, Western Cape region.
12. Interview with anonymous research participant, 20 April 2017, Western Cape region.
13. Interview with anonymous research participant, 10 April 2017, Gauteng region.
14. Interview with anonymous research participant, 5 April 2017, Western Cape region.
15. Interview with anonymous research participant, 31 March 2016, Western Cape region.

References

Aaken van, A. 2015. 'Markets as Accountability Mechanisms in International Law'. In N. Gal-Or, C. Ryngaert, and M. Noortmann, eds. *Responsibilities of the Non-State Actor in Armed Conflict and the Market Place*. Leiden and Boston: Brill Nijhoff.

Abrahamsen, R. and M. C. Williams. 2009. 'Security Beyond the State: Global Security Assemblages in International Politics'. *International Political Sociology* 3(1): 1–17.

Adams, T. K. 1999. 'The New Mercenaries and the Privatization of Conflict'. *Parameters* 29: 103–16.

Armstrong, S. 2008. *War Plc: The Rise of the New Corporate Mercenary*. London: Faber and Faber.

Ashford, B. E. and G. E. Kreiner. 2014. 'Dirty Work and Dirtier Work: Difference in Countering Physical, Social, and Moral Stigma'. *Management and Organization* 10: 27.

Avant, D. 2012. 'Mercenaries'. In *The Wiley-Blackwell Encyclopedia of Globalization*. Hoboken, NJ: John Wiley & Sons.

Baker, D.-P. and J. Pattison. 2012. 'The Principled Case for Employing Private Military and Security Companies in Interventions for Human Rights Purposes'. *Journal of Applied Philosophy* 29: 1–18.

Bassiouni, M. C. 1977. *Citizen's Arrest: The Law of Arrest, Search, and Seizure for Private Citizens and Private Police*. Springfield, IL: Thomas.

Bate, P. 1997. 'Whatever Happened to Organizational Anthropology? A Review of the Field of Organizational Ethnography and Anthropological Studies'. *Human Relations* 50: 28.

Bénabou, R. and J. Tirole. 2010. 'Individual and Corporate Social Responsibility'. *Economica* 77: 1–19.

Berman, P. S. 2007. 'A Pluralist Approach to International Law'. *Yale Journal of International Law* 32: 301.

Bibler Coutin, S. 2001. 'Comment on Daniel Goldstein, An Anthropology of Security and Rights'. *Current Anthropology* 4.

Bourbeau, P. ed. 2015. *Security: Dialogue Across Disciplines*. Cambridge: Cambridge University Press.

Boycko, M., A. Shleifer, and R. W. Vishny. 1996. 'A Theory of Privatisation'. *The Economic Journal* 106: 309–19.

Brewis, J. and R. Godfrey. 2018. '"Never call me a mercenary": Identity Work, Stigma Management and the Private Security Contractor' *Organization* 25: 335–53.

Brooks, D. 2000. 'Messiahs or Mercenaries? The Future of International Private Military Services'. *International Peacekeeping* 7: 129–44.

Burton, N., J. Koning, and R. Muers. 2018. 'Organizational Ethnography and Religious Organizations: The Case of Quaker Decision-making'. *Journal of Management, Spirituality & Religion* 15: 349–67.

Buzan, B., O. Waever, and J. de Wilde. 1998. *Security: A New Framework for Analysis*. Boulder, CO: Lynne Rienner.

Cameron, L. 2009. 'New Standards for and by Private Military Companies?'. In A Peters, L. Koechlin, T. Förster, and G. Fenner Zinkernagel, eds., *Non-State Actors as Standard Setters*, 113–45. Cambridge and New York: Cambridge University Press.

Caparini, M. 2008. 'Regulating Private Military and Security Companies. The US Approach'. In A. Alexandra, D.-P. Baker, and M. Caparini, eds. *Private Military and Security Companies*, 171–88. London and New York: Routledge.

Chesterman, S. and C. Lehnardt. 2007. *From Mercenaries to Market: The Rise and Regulation of Private Military Companies*. Oxford and New York: Oxford University Press.

Ciuk, S., J. Koning, and M. Kostera. 2018. 'Organizational Ethnographies'. In C. Cassell, A. Cunliffe, and G. Grandy, eds. *The Sage Handbook of Qualitative Business and Management Research Methods*, 270–85. London: Sage.

Collins, P. 2015. 'International Corporate Criminal Liability for Private Military and Security Compagnies—A Possibility?' in N. Gal-Or, C. Ryngaert, and M. Noortmann, eds. *Responsibilities of the Non-State Actor in Armed Conflict and the Market Place*. Leiden and Boston: Brill Nijhoff.

Cover, R. M. 1983. 'Foreword: Nomos and Narrative'. *Harvard Law Review* 97: 4.

Cullen, P. 2000. 'Keeping the New Dog of War on a Tight Leash. Assessing Means of Accountability for Private Military Companies'. *Conflict Trends* 2000(1): 36–9.

Cutler, A. C. 2003. *Private Power and Global Authority: Transnational Merchant Law in the Global Political Economy*. Cambridge: Cambridge University Press.

Diphoorn, T. G. 2015. *Twilight Policing: Private Security and Violence in Urban South Africa*. Oakland: University of California Press.

Dorney, S. 1998. *The Sandline Affair: Politics and Mercenaries and the Bougainville Crisis*. Sydney: ABC Books.

Draper, H. 1978. *Private Police*. Sussex Atlantic Highlands, NJ: Harvester Press.

Eriksen, T. H. 2015. *Small Places, Large Issues: An Introduction to Social and Cultural Anthropology*. London: Pluto Press.

Finer, J. 2008. 'Holstering the Hired Guns: New Accountability Measures for Private Security Contractors'. *Yale Journal of International Law* 33: 259–513.

Francioni, F. 2009. 'The Responsibility of the PMSC's Home State for Human Rights Violations Arising from the Export of Private Military and Security Services'. *EUI Working Papers*.

G4S. 2016. 'Coporate Social Responsibility Report'. London: G4S plc.

George, B. and M. Button. 2000. *Private Security*. Leicester: Perpetuity Press.

Godfrey, R., J. Brewis, J. Grady, and C. Grocott. 2014. 'The Private Military Industry and Neoliberal Imperialism: Mapping the Terrain'. *Organization* 21: 106–25.

Goffman, E. 1963. *Stigma: Notes on the Management of Spoiled Identity*. New York: Simon and Schuster.

Goldstein, D. M. 2015. 'Anthropology/ies: Moving Beyond Disciplinary Approaches to Security'. In P. Bourbeau, ed. *Security: Dialogue Across Disciplines*, 45–61. Cambridge: Cambridge University Press.

Gómez del Prado, J. 2011. 'A United Nations Instrument to Regulate and Monitor Private Military and Security Contractors'. *Notre Dame Journal of International and Comparative Law* 1: 1.

Hansen Löfstrand, C., B. Loftus, and I. Loader. 2016. 'Doing "Dirty Work": Stigma and Esteem in the Private Security Industry'. *European Journal of Criminology* 13: 297–314.

Higate, P. 2012a. 'Drinking Vodka from the "Butt-Crack" Man: Masculinities and Patriarchy in the Privatized Military Security Company'. *International Feminist Journal of Politics* 14: 450–69.

Higate, P. 2012b. '"Cowboys and Professionals": The Politics of Identity Work in the Private and Military Security Company'. *Millenium* 40: 321–41.

Higate, P. 2017. 'Introduction'. In P. Higate and M. Utas, eds. *Private Security in Africa. From the Global Assemblage to the Everyday*, 1–14. London: Zed Books.

Hoover, M. J. 1977. 'The Laws of War and the Angolan Trial of Mercenaries: Death to the Dogs of War'. *Case Western Reserve Journal of International Law* 9: 323.

Jensen, T. and J. Sandström. 2015. 'Normal Deviants and Erving Goffman: Extending the Literature on Organizational Stigma'. *Nordic Journal of Working Life Studies* 5: 125–42.

Joachim, J. and A. Schneiker. 2012. 'New Humanitarians? Frame Appropriation Through Private Military and Security Companies'. *Millennium* 40: 365–88.

Johnston, M. S. and E. Hodge. 2014. '"Dirt, Death and Danger? I Don't Recall Any Adverse Reaction ... ": Masculinity and the Taint Management of Hospital Private Security Work'. *Gender, Work, Organization* 21: 546–58.

Kakalik, J. S. and S. Wildhorn. 1971. *Private Police in the United States: Findings and Recommendations*. Santa Monica: Rand.

Kamminga, M. T. and S. Zia-Zarifi, eds. 2000. *Liability of Multinational Corporations Under International Law*. The Hague: Kluwer Law International.

Karski, K. 2018. 'Draft Report on Human Rights Concerns in Private Military and Security Companies' Operations Affecting Third Countries'. Brussels: European Union.

Kasher, A. 2008. 'Interface Ethics: Military Forces and Private Military Companies'. In A. Alexandra, D.-P. Baker, and M. Caparini, eds. *Private Military and Security Companies: Ethnics, Policies and Civil-Military Relations*, 235–46. London and New York: Routledge.

Kelly, E. 2012. 'Holding Blackwater Accountable: Private Security Contractors and the Protections of Use Immunity'. *British International and Comparative Journal* 35: 14.

Kinsey, C. 2008. 'Private Security Companies and Corporate Social Responsibility'. In A. Alexandra, D.-P. Baker, and M. Caparini, eds. *Private Military and Security Companies: Ethics, Policies and Civil-Military Relations*, 70–86. London and New York: Routledge.

Krahman, E. 2008. 'The New Model Soldier and Civil-Military Relations'. In A. Alexandra, D.-P. Baker, and M. Caparini, eds. *Private Military and Security Companies: Ethics, Policies and Civil-Military Relations*, 247–64. London and New York: Routledge.

Kwakwa, E. 1990. 'The Current Status of Mercenaries in the Law of Armed Conflict'. *Hastings International & Comparative Law Review* 14: 67.

Lipman, I. A. 1988. *The Private Security Industry: Issues and Trends*. Newbury Park: Sage.

Maguire, M., C. Frois, and N. Zurawski. 2014. *The Anthropology of Security: Perspectives from the Frontline of Policing, Counter-terrorism and Border Control*. London: Pluto Press.

Merry, S. E. 1988. 'Legal Pluralism'. *Law & Society Review* 22: 869–96.

Mourning, P. W. 1981. 'Leashing the Dogs of War: Outlawing the Recruitment and Use of Mercenaries'. *Virginia Journal of International Law* 22: 589.

Noortmann, M. 2001. 'Non-State Actors in International Law'. In B. Arts, M. Noortmann, and B. Reinalda, eds. *Non-State Actors in International Relations*. Aldershot: Ashgate Publishing Company.

Noortmann, M. 2011. 'Auständische Gruppen und Private Militairunternehmen - Theoretische und practische Überlegungen zur Position bewaffneter nicht-staatliche Akteure im Humanitairen Völkerrecht'. In H.-J. Heintze and K. Ipsen, eds. *Heutige bewaffnete Konflikte als Herausforderungen and das humanitäre Völkerrecht*. Springer.

Noortmann, M. and I. Chapsos. 2015. 'Private Military and Security Companies: A transnational legal approach'. in A. von Arnauld, N. Matz-Lück, and K. Odendahl (eds), *100 Years Peace through Law: Past and Future* (Berlin: Dincker & Humbold).

Norrie, A. W. 2010. *Dialectic and difference: dialectical critical realism and the grounds of justice* (Routledge: London; New York).

Percy, S. V. 2007. *Mercenaries: the history of a norm in international relations* (Oxford University Press: Oxford; New York).

Peters, A., L. Koechlin, and T. Förster. 2009. 'Towards Non-state Actors as Effective, Legitimate and Accountable Standard Setters'. In A. Peters, L. Koechlin, T. Förster, and G. F. Zinkernagel, eds. *Non-State Actors as Standard Setters*, 492–562. Cambridge and New York: Cambridge University Press.

Prince, E. 2013. *Civilian Warriors: The Inside Story of Blackwater and the Unsung Heroes of the War on Terror*. New York: Portfolio/Penguin.

Provost, C. 2017. 'The Industry of Inequality: Why the World is Obsessed with Private Security'. *The Guardian*, 12 May 2017.

PSiRA 2018. Annual Performance Plan 2018/2019. <https://www.psira.co.za/psira/index.php>.

Ryngaert, C. 2008. 'Litigating Abuses Committed by Private Military Companies'. *European Journal of International Law* 19: 1035–53.

Samimian-Darash, L. and M. Stalcup. 2017. 'Anthropology of Security and Security in Anthropology: Cases of Counterterrorism in the United States'. *Anthropological Theory* 17: 60–87.

Scahill, J. 2007. *Blackwater: The Rise of the World's Most Powerful Mercenary Army*. New York: Nation Books.

Schubert, C. and T. Röhl. 2019. 'Ethnography and Organisations: Materiality and Change as Methodological Challenges'. *Qualitative Research* 19(2): 164–81.

Singer, P. W. 2008. *Corporate Warriors: The Rise of the Privatized Military Industry*. Ithaca: Cornell University Press.

Soares, C. 2003. 'Corporate Versus Individual Moral Responsibility'. *Journal of Business Ethics* 46: 143–50.

Sorensen, K. 2015. 'To Leash or Not to Leash the Dogs of War: The Politics of Law and Australia's Response to Mercenarism and Private Military and Security Companies'. *Adelaide Law Review* 36: 405.

South African White Paper on Safety and Security (2017) Civilian Secretariat for Police Service. Staatskoerant, 1 September 2017.

Tully, S. 2007. *Corporations and International Lawmaking*. Boston: Martinus Nijhoff Publishers.

Vergne, J.-P. 2012. 'Stigmatized Categories and Public Disapproval of Organizations: A Mixed-Methods Study of the Global Arms Industry, 1996–2007'. *Academy of Management Journal* 55: 1027–52.

War on Want. 2013. 'Charity Slams Conduct Code for Private Military and Security Companies'. <https://waronwant.org/media/charity-slams-conduct-code-private-military-and-security-companies>. 19 September 2013.

Williams, P. 2008. 'Security Studies: An Introduction'. In P. Williams, ed. *Security Studies: An Introduction*. New York: Routledge.

Wilkinson, P. 2007. *Homeland Security in the UK: Future Preparedness for Terrorist Attack Since 9/11*. New York: Routledge.

Wulf, H. 2008. 'Privatization of Security, International Interventions and the Democratic Control of Armed Forces'. In A. Alexandra, D.-P. Baker, and M. Caparini, eds. *Private Military and Security Companies: Ethics, Policies and Civil-Military Relations*, 191–202. London and New York: Routledge.

Yanow, D., S. Ybema, and M. van Hulst. 2012. 'Practising Organizational Ethnography'. In G. Symon and C. Cassell, eds. *Qualitative Organizational Research: Core Methods and Current Challenges*, 331–50. London: Sage.

CHAPTER 34

HUMANITARIAN INTERVENTIONS

ERICA BORNSTEIN

When considering the relationship between anthropology, law, and humanitarian intervention, one is confronted with problems of scale and scope. Is it a discussion of international agencies and institutions, citizen groups, or individuals? Is the *law* in question international humanitarian law or national, domestic law? Is the law a normative framework or a binding obligation involving sanctions and punishment? Social policies are only as good as the laws that support them and the enforcement of those laws. Some laws are strictly on the books with no bearing on humanitarian action, while others directly regulate intervention. International laws pressure states towards humanitarian responses, and international agencies and civil society groups utilize international law to articulate global justice directives (Merry 2006; Niezen and Sapignoli 2017).

The anthropology of law and humanitarian intervention is expansive by nature. It encompasses research on law and global institutions, human rights, public health, refugees, governance, security, state legitimacy, and judicial advocacy. Rather than a comprehensive approach, this essay is thematic, focusing on humanitarian actors, institutions, and the regulatory mechanisms that frame, govern, and define humanitarian practice in five overlapping areas: (1) bureaucratic and legal-regulatory processes; (2) affective economies of emergency response that harness moral sentiments and volunteer labour; (3) interventions in conflict and post-conflict settings involving international humanitarian law, 'humanitarian wars', and transitional justice programs; (4) rights-based judicial advocacy campaigns that use humanitarian logic to alter legal-regulatory frameworks; and (5) interventions residing at the limits of law, located outside of legal-regulatory frameworks altogether.

Emergencies in Context

Anthropologists can contribute a unique form of scholarship to critical studies of humanitarianism and law via the methodology of ethnography: long-term fieldwork with communities engaged in, and affected by, humanitarian events. Ethnographies are empirical, historically contextual case-studies that provide structural analyses gleaned from the daily, lived experiences of informant groups. Ethnographers research humanitarian intervention and its governance by analysing the practices of, and interactions between, providers and recipients of aid. Providers include international institutions such as the United Nations and non-governmental organizations (NGOs), civil servants, lawyers, and humanitarian advocates. Humanitarian intervention occurs in at least three interrelated legal registers: international humanitarian law (IHL), articulating international norms and conventions; national law governing citizens and domestic institutions; and local contexts where normative conventions direct social action. The relationship between these social-legal fields is key to understanding current tensions in humanitarian intervention, especially as studied by anthropologists. Though much humanitarian work may bleed across the borders of nations, transnational agencies require governmental permissions to provide services in national contexts. Governments occupy a pivotal role in humanitarian intervention: governments may be responsible for protecting citizens from disaster; governmental legitimacy is closely tied to aid provision; governments declare states of emergency; and governments may, at times, perpetrate crimes against humanity (Fassin and Vasquez 2005).

Anthropologists may align themselves with humanitarian agencies and even be employed by them, though most offer critical analysis. The field of critical humanitarian studies focuses on the dynamics and politics of aid (Benthall and Bellion-Jordan 2009; Bornstein and Redfield 2011; Fassin 2012; Fassin and Pandolfi 2010; Feldman and Ticktin 2010). In conflict and post-conflict settings, the anthropology of transnational justice has focused on truth and reconciliation commissions, hybrid courts, indigenous reconciliation strategies, and reparations. This body of scholarship approaches lawmaking as a humanitarian response to crimes against humanity, (Johnston and Slyomovics 2009; Wilson 2001). Recent work in the anthropology of humanitarianism focuses on how institutions and communities address post-war conflicts, structural adjustment programmes, and the failed promises of international development. Ethnographers analyse the lives of refugees in camps (Feldman 2018); immigrants and asylum seekers (Andersson 2014; Cabot 2014; Ticktin 2011); military humanitarianism (Fassin and Pandolfi 2010); the political economy of disaster relief (Schuller 2012); and medical humanitarianism (Redfield 2013). For anthropologists, regional understandings of context are imperative for analysing intervention. Anthropologists attend to social life—spending long periods of time with groups, learning the significance of what happens on the ground in the scope of experience. Through this intensely empirical, participatory approach, anthropologists analyse how humanitarian intervention is lived, deriving theoretical insights from observed behavioural patterns. Thus, while the term humanitarianism references legal fields and categories of social action, the contexts in which actors engage also define and shape anthropological analyses.

Colonial histories, global inequality, and geographical conditions make some regions of the world more prone to particular types of disasters such as earthquakes, tsunamis, and floods. Climate change is destabilizing entire regions of the world and instigating migratory flows. In South Africa, where the HIV crisis has been a target of humanitarian intervention, the history of apartheid framed official discourse, shaping governmental HIV-policy (Fassin 2007). In Burkina Faso and Cote d'Ivoire, local communities re-defined conceptions of self in relation to practices of HIV therapy, global activism, and conceptions of care (Nguyen 2010). In the United States, research on post-Katrina re-building underscored the privatization and outsourcing of social welfare (Adams 2013). In India, post-earthquake recovery became a nationalist, political, and developmental project (Bhattacharjee 2016; Simpson 2014). For Palestinians, their status of permanent refugee-ness has become a humanitarian condition that generates a demand for, and right to, aid (Feldman 2018). In Europe, refugee crises dominate ethnographies of hu-manitarianism. Anthropologists have researched the impact of a humanitarian clause in French law on asylum seekers, as they actually sought life-threatening illnesses in order to obtain legal papers (Ticktin 2011). The European 'illegality industry' of refugee entry and border governance is another topic of study (Andersson 2014; Fassin 2015). In Greece, anthropologists analyse asylum claims via legal forms and their afterlives, looking at pink cards and asylum interviews (Cabot 2014). In Russia, a compassion economy of faith-based NGOs addresses the need for social welfare neglected by the post-Soviet state (Caldwell 2017). In each of these settings, humanitarianism involves intergovernmental lawmaking bodies, state governments, NGOs, and citizen action groups. Anthropologists study legal institutions, advocates, and humanitarian profes-sionals and beneficiaries to analyse processes of formal legal jurisdiction as well as the limits of law in context.

INTERNATIONAL HUMANITARIAN LAW

Humanitarian intervention has come to mean many things, including: a type of force for peace and security; a form of military engagement, including war (Barnett 2011: 186–94; Fassin and Pandolfi 2010; Fassin and Vasquez 2005; Minear 2002); the right to relief (Barnett 2011: 192–4); and a condition, a form of political life (Feldman 2018). Humanitarianism often refers to the framework inspired by the International Committee of the Red Cross with its focus on neutrality, impartiality, and independ-ence, as well as international humanitarian law. Humanitarianism may justify military intervention in humanitarian wars to prevent humanitarian crises. It may be used by NGOs to articulate the need for development, human rights advocacy, peace building, and judicial stabilization.

Humanitarian intervention is political. During the Cold War, the United States and the Soviet Union used aid to maintain control over their former colonies. The fall of the Berlin Wall and the onslaught of civil wars in the 1990s shifted global justifications for humanitarian aid to security. As Washington, D.C. cut ties with its Third World cli-ents, internal conflicts produced regional insecurity and complex humanitarian emer-gencies involving multiple actors, institutions, and entire regions (Barnett 2011; Barnett and Weiss 2008:1–48; Davies 2012). Humanitarian interventions took the form of peacekeeping and peace-building. They included U.N.-facilitated military interventions with humanitarian objectives, motivated by increasing concern regarding failed states and accompanied by an expanding use of the term 'humanitarianism' by NGOs involved in promoting democracy, rebuilding judicial systems, and advancing law. Following the terrorist attacks of September 11, 2001, via the U.S.-led 'War on Terror', humanitarianism justified military occupation, as in Afghanistan and Iraq (Weiss 2013: 145).

A new form of international authority based on humanitarian principles emerged by the beginning of the twenty-first century. As Anne Orford (2011: 1) notes, 'The international authority to undertake executive action for protective ends was given a detailed normative articulation in the form of a 2001 report by the International Commission on Intervention and State Sovereignty ... entitled *The Responsibility to Protect*' (R2P). This report was a response to the NATO intervention into Kosovo in 1999, which was considered the first 'humanitarian war'. R2P policy argued that every state had a duty to protect its population; and if the state failed to do so the responsibility shifted to the international community. The policy, which was unanimously adopted by the U.N. General Assembly in 2005, was significant in its normative nature. It tasked the international community and the United Nations with the responsibility of maintaining order and protecting life in the decolonized world (Orford 2011).

Though the United Nations was authorized to preserve peace and security during decolonization in the 1960s, at the end of the Cold War and as the international executive authority of the United Nations expanded, some asked: Why should the United Nations govern in the decolonized world? R2P responded to the tension between international authority and state sovereignty; it provided the normative ground for an expansion of international executive action since decolonization. It was also an assertion that nation-states and the international community both had responsibilities to protect populations. It positioned responsibility, instead of control, as the essence of sovereignty: legitimate rule involves care for the welfare of citizens; and an inability to provide adequate care justified intervention by the international community (Kolb and Hyde 2008:16; Orford 2011). R2P was a departure from earlier approaches in that it tied legitimate, state sovereign authority to guaranteeing protection instead of control over territory. Failure to do so would result in humanitarian intervention by the international community. R2P did not impose legal duties on states. Instead, it functioned as a normative variety of international law, which conferred public powers and provided legal authority to international bodies for certain activities, including humanitarian intervention.

In general, international humanitarian law (IHL) determines when it is acceptable to wage war as well as how states must behave during war. *Jus in bello* (the law of war) is an important part of IHL, as it makes distinctions between civilians and combatants. Although it restricts the infliction of unnecessary suffering, IHL does not prohibit the use of violence and cannot protect all those affected by armed conflict. Historically, the term IHL comes from the Red Cross Movement and from the Hague Conventions of

1899 and 1907 that discussed 'methods of warfare conducted by belligerents' (Kolb and Hyde 2008: 17). It was the Geneva Conventions in 1949 that shifted focus to protect victims of war.

The International Committee of the Red Cross (ICRC) warrants mention due to its unique, hybrid status in the Law of Armed Conflict (LOAC). Founded in Geneva in 1863 as an association under Swiss private law, the ICRC is a formally recognized international actor in the Geneva Conventions and is entrusted with a humanitarian responsibility during armed conflict (Kolb and Hyde 2008: 114). The ICRC has treaty-based as well as non-treaty-based tasks. Its specific humanitarian rights and duties emanate from its role as a neutral and independent institution, and other organizations have followed this model to claim a 'humanitarian space' for their work. The ICRC's limits include proposing but not imposing political settlements. Though the ICRC has no army and no political mandate, and though belligerents are free to accept or reject its proposals, it still has a special status. As involved parties with protected status, INGOs such as the ICRC take on the humanitarian role of protecting persons in situations of armed conflict. The ICRC, unlike other INGOs, however, can undertake preventative action and can contribute to the development and interpretation of IHL (Kolb and Hyde 2008: 120). Thus, the ICRC, as an NGO with unique status, is integral to the production of the law of armed conflict as a living law, always in formation.

Categorically, international human rights law (IHRL) is a younger branch of public international law. While the Law of Armed Conflict is applicable during armed conflict, IHRL applies all the time, including during internal disturbances, tensions, riots, sporadic acts of violence, and in all cases of public emergency. IHRL fills the gaps where the law of armed conflict does not apply, thus assuring a humanitarian standard. In effect, the concept of humanitarian intervention in IHL has integrated the advocacy aspects of IHRL. NGOs implement IHL by providing humanitarian assistance to victims of armed conflicts, monitoring, reporting, and mobilizing public opinion concerning violations. This public role is sometimes perceived as threatening by states. While the United Nations is charged with monitoring the implementation of IHL, there is no single international entity that monitors armed conflicts and ensures compliance with it.

The robust era of interstate support for humanitarian intervention that emerged during the Cold War and thrived after its end may now be on the decline. If we consider the anthropology of humanitarianism as an attempt to deal with an increasing global awareness of suffering (Ticktin 2014), then we must also consider the growing criminalization of humanitarian efforts by states that are increasing legal restrictions and surveillance on civil society groups. This trend is evident in European states that seek to restrict refugee asylum claims; and the U.S. government that arrests humanitarian volunteers providing water to migrants from Central America and categorizes migrants as immigrants instead of refugees, skirting IHL protocols. At the time of writing, for example, one might ask if U.S. migration detention centres are refugee centres or migrant prisons? On the U.S. border, the humanitarian concerns of migrants are addressed in competing manners by the Department of Homeland Security and by civil society groups pressuring the state for a more humanitarian approach towards asylum seekers.

Regulatory processes

As much as national and international laws shape the limits of humanitarian intervention, intervention itself shapes legal fields. In the domain of international law, international institutions use the non-binding soft power of covenants to name and shame states into regulatory compliance, levying, for example, trade sanctions for breaching international standards (Davies 2012; Kolb and Hyde 2008; Minear 2002). National governments seek greater regulatory control of international agencies and NGOs, imposing legal-fiscal measures, such as laws regulating funding and the governance of charitable groups. Governments in Egypt, Ethiopia, Hungary, India, Kenya, Pakistan, Poland, Russia, Turkey, and Venezuela control the work of NGOs through anti-terrorism and anti-money laundering legislation (Huang 2013; ICNL 2017; Ismail and Kamat 2018; Salamon 2015; Sidel 2010). Increased regulation of NGOs can serve as a crackdown on resistance and dissent. NGOs are structurally ambivalent (Bernal and Grewal 2014; Bornstein and Sharma 2016; Ismail and Kamat 2018; Lewis and Schuller 2017). They are at once favoured partners of neoliberal states, and they also mobilize protest against state policies. In the aftermath of disasters lies an entire economy of humanitarian business (Weiss 2013), along with the potential for development and growth. Edward Simpson (2016) documents the case of Gujarat, India, where the earthquake led to an economic boom and facilitated political realignments. Jonathan Benthall (2017: 161) notes how the post 9/11 doctrine of 'asset substitution' guided the criminalization of certain charities, specifically Islamic ones.

Although humanitarian institutions may strive towards political neutrality as an ideal and a strategy (Redfield 2013), they must also abide by the laws in countries where they do their work. Transnational NGOs such as Oxfam, CARE, or World Vision work in nationally incorporated offices with national boards of directors required to follow national laws. In addition to depending on NGOs for humanitarian service provision, some governments sponsor national relief funds and agencies to address national disasters and emergencies. National laws, including those governing charity, have the potential to articulate who can legitimately provide humanitarian services. In the United States humanitarianism is state-supported through governmental agencies such as the Federal Emergency Management Agency (FEMA), which in turn outsources its work to nonprofit organizations and corporations. In the United States, the welfare reform initiatives of the mid 1990s integrated religious (almost exclusively Christian) organizations into state-funded welfare, whereas previously only nonreligious groups could be contracted by the government.[1] In post-Katrina intervention, private military corporations and religious groups were contracted to provide aid (Adams 2013).

In China, NGOs have been strongly regulated by the state though the state depends on their humanitarian work. Shu-min Huang (2013) paints a fascinating portrait of the Chinese context after the massive earthquake that hit western China's Sichuan province in 2008. This disaster inspired a new humanitarian movement in which over two hundred thousand Chinese volunteers provided assistance. The state had difficulty meeting needs at the local level, and NGOs helped the government meet emergent demands, creating a context in which the government paid particular attention to the formation and operation of 'civilian self-help organizations', as they competed for public space and legitimacy with the government. The government was hostile to NGOs, which embodied democracy via religion, transnationalism, and the charismatic nature of grassroots leadership, all of which had the potential to outshine the party-state bureaucracy. The love-hate relationship between the party-state and the many new NGOs created a type of legal limbo. International NGOs could not formally register because of the requirement that NGOs be under the wing of a government office. They were forced to operate in what Huang calls a legal 'gray area', under state control. Subsequently, in 2016 China implemented a Charity Law to regulate philanthropic, charitable, and nonprofit organizations.[2] In many national contexts where increasingly strict regulations have been put in place, international institutions are governed with greater oversight than domestic ones. In India, for example, civic groups that are not registered with the state fall outside of formal legal regulation (Bornstein 2012b). This can work to the advantage of NGOs, which may depend on the state's laissez-faire attitude in order to operate in this gray area (as in Caldwell 2017 on Russia); but it can also instigate a call for increased regulation, especially for organizations receiving international funds (Bornstein and Sharma 2016).

If laws governing humanitarian intervention are a type of bureaucratic power, with their regulatory purview manifest via international and national law, institutions such as NGOs navigate between these two legal contexts. Sometimes civil society groups operate at the margins of regulatory practices altogether, unregistered with the state and under the radar of governmental, legal reporting structures. The 'shape-shifting' for which NGOs are known (Bernal and Grewal 2014), inspires state initiatives to work with NGOs and/or to regulate them more strictly. Humanitarian intervention is a space of critique: the very need for humanitarian intervention may symbolically challenge governmental authority regarding its capacity to provide for citizens. Through humanitarian advocacy, NGOs challenge state policies directly, demanding intervention. Recently, scholars have traced an increasingly hostile and restrictive regulatory context for civil society groups globally. States have increased surveillance to address perceived threats to sovereignty posed by civil society groups, domestically and internationally, through the quick pace of technological communication. Social media platforms bring people together in a hurry after humanitarian disasters and also have the potential to expose the failure of state agencies regarding humanitarian intervention, shaming states into action. Recently, it has become apparent that technology itself can be weaponized to threaten state sovereignty. Another possible explanation for the criminalization of aid is the shift in legal-regulatory instruments towards an expanded audit culture, with heavy monitoring of civil society groups. If there has been a 'nonprofitization of the welfare state' (Salamon 2015), there has also been a criminalization of humanitarianism and a quest for states to stake claims on the legitimacy that providing aid confers on governmental bodies. Moreover, we see states partnering with corporations, bypassing civil society altogether, for example, in the case of post-Katrina rebuilding in the United States, and in a provision in India's corporate law that requires large companies to contribute a percentage of net income to state approved social welfare programs and/or disaster relief.

Bureaucracy, Affect, and Legitimacy

There is tension in humanitarian intervention between the regulatory functions of law and the affective dimensions of care, compassion, and the urgency to assist. The bureaucratic regulation of humanitarian intervention manifests itself in a particular type of authority, governed by rules and qualifications. Bureaucratic authority may be challenged by other forms, such as charismatic authority (Weber 1946: 196–243). State-based laws regarding humanitarian activity are inherently bureaucratic, restricting what can be done, including how humanitarian organizations may receive governmental permissions, access, and resources. As the humanitarian sector has grown into an industry, managed responses to crises have become increasingly rational and bureaucratic (Barnett 2012). In addition, the staunch professional stance of employees of humanitarian organizations may at times be considered an institutional ideal and a normative framework that protects staff from burnout and creates boundaries between their personal lives and the lives of those they attempt to assist (Redfield 2013). In the case of Médecins Sans Frontières, professionalism has entwined with secularism to become their motto for engagement. While professionalism confers advantages on humanitarian NGOs, their associational nature may also threaten the legitimacy, bureaucratic structure, and authority of national governments.

Humanitarian organizations are nimble. Officially, they are neither 'public' (state) nor 'private' (corporate), and they are less likely to be bogged down by bureaucratic directives. This may not be the case with large NGOs and government sponsored agencies—for example, the USAID in post-earthquake Haiti (Schuller 2012; see also Niezen and Sapignoli 2017). Humanitarian practitioners are professionals. They are lawyers, doctors, logistics experts, technology experts, and career administrators. The field is dominated by discussions of efficiency and effectiveness, though not of profit (recall that voluntarism is a key principle of the ICRC). It is considered unethical for institutions to reap profit from humanitarian engagement with suffering (Adams 2013; Schuller 2012). This does not prevent for-profit corporations from entering the sector, as demonstrated in the case of Katrina recovery. Some sites of humanitarian engagement, such as refugee camps and borders, require equipment. Given this technical aspect of humanitarian intervention, there may be less stigma attached to the profitability of the security industry, which overlaps with humanitarian and governmental concerns.

Affective economies emerge in this professionalizing context of increased audits, technocratic governance, and the corporatization of the humanitarian industry. Certain categories of humanitarian concern have the potential to produce affective responses, mobilizing global attention and volunteer labour to particular crises. For example, Syrian refugees and the European refugee crisis have become international humanitarian issues, potentially challenging existing immigration policies. Anthropologists study how laws surrounding migration tighten during refugee crises (Fassin 2015), focusing on how refugees navigate asylum regulations (Cabot 2014; Ticktin 2011) and borders (Andersson 2014). Some populations, such as refugees, children, and orphans, inspire affective, humanitarian responses and are also highly regulated by law (Benthall 2011: 103–4; Bornstein 2012a; Fassin 2012:161–80). The desire to help may motivate humanitarian workers and volunteers to reconstruct societies after disasters, assisting survivors with the emotional work of living through disasters and coping with memories of death and loss (Adams 2013; Malkki 2015; Simpson 2014). In such cases, affect may involve embodied memory, which provides experiential frameworks for understanding the motivation for humanitarian work and the experiences of aid workers and recipients. In the case of South Africa, for example, the histories of colonialism and apartheid framed and informed efforts by doctors, nurses, and community-based health workers who became AIDS activists as they cared for the sick and dying in the HIV epidemic (Fassin 2007).

One may be inclined to separate the affective dimension of humanitarian intervention from the bureaucratic governance of regulation. Affect inspires donations and volunteer labour, not bureaucratic responses, though laws that encourage donations and voluntarism to humanitarian efforts such as tax breaks and subsidies can harness the affective realm. It is precisely because the affective realm lies beyond the purview of the state and fuels donations that states step in with a heavy hand to regulate the funding of some humanitarian activities. The emotional currency of affect in humanitarian intervention potentially challenges the legitimacy of bureaucratic forms of governance by eliciting financial contributions from diasporic populations and encouraging the involvement of governmental forces outside national boundaries. This can be seen as 'foreign interference' by the state and strictly regulated. If, as Fassin (2015) notes, care and punishment are two basic functions of the state, the state's benevolent capacity to care for its citizens in times of disaster and emergency is a marker of its civility and a hallmark of its legitimacy. As much as 'the state' may in practice be a disaggregated collection of competing agencies, the provision of aid can consolidate the state into a single entity in the social imagination of citizenry. Humanitarianism is a symbol of moral and social good in the bureaucratic realm of governance, and we see this in efforts by states to facilitate and regulate humanitarian activities through law. The opposite is also true: strong states may demonstrate their authority through bureaucratic means, for example by cracking down on civil society groups involved in humanitarian aid. The state in these cases seeks to become the sole provider of social good in order to iterate their legitimacy and authority. In sum, humanitarian intervention has the potential, simultaneously, to reify the state and to threaten its sovereignty through critique. As we shall see in the section below, the state also deploys military power, in the name of humanitarian intervention, to protect life.

Conflict and post-conflict settings

Humanitarian intervention may occur as an exception to law. Although states make national laws, and international institutions develop international treaties and covenants, humanitarian intervention becomes an international project when states cannot address local needs. Intervention may be triggered by military conflict or national disasters, both of which instantiate, following Giorgio Agamben, a 'state of emergency' (Fassin and Pandolfi 2010). Emergencies have distinct temporalities justifying the suspension of the rule of law. During states of emergency, political and moral reasoning conflates to make intervention simultaneously military and humanitarian, as exemplified by the phrase 'humanitarian war' (Fassin and Pandolfi et al. 2010). This paradigm, which dictates the right to intervene, depends on 'humanitarian reason'—the logic of moral obligation rather than political principles (Fassin and Pandolfi 2010: 12). The first instance of a 'humanitarian war' was the intervention in Kosovo by NATO forces in 1999; subsequent examples have included the 2003 invasion of Iraq and recent military deployments in Syria, fighting crimes against humanity. The logic of intervention has shifted from international law to humanitarian principles, culminating in R2P, the Responsibility to Protect.

A humanitarian state of exception is a paradigm for political engagement. In their analysis of the 1999 Venezuelan landslides, Didier Fassin and Paula Vasquez (2005) note how the natural disaster was used to increase presidential powers, which subsequently were never relinquished. To declare a state of emergency is a legal procedure, involving the suspension of national law. In the Venezuelan case the media harnessed moral sentiment, which produced compassion and spurred support of the government's declaration of a state of emergency. In turn, this gave the military extra-ordinary authority, which was later abused through violence, and the state of emergency became a permanent state of affairs. For a comparative case, one can turn to the effects of the Gujarat earthquake in India, where Hindu nationalist groups consolidated power, via humanitarian work and discourses of aid. This foothold later translated into political and electoral state power (Bhattacharjee 2016; Simpson 2014).

Anthropologists have explored the relationship between humanitarianism and governance in studies of 'humanitarian government' (Ticktin 2014), which fills governance vacuums produced by war. Humanitarian governance is a form of 'mobile sovereignty', where humanitarian institutions take on the role of the state as guarantors of the rule of law (Pandolfi 2003). Analyses of humanitarian governance address the European refugee crisis and the closing of national borders (Andersson 2014, 2015; Cabot 2012, 2013; Fassin 2011; Ticktin 2011). Anthropologists studying refugees situate their research in border zones, with asylum seekers in medical centres making claims upon the state and seeking legal citizenship (Andersson 2014, 2015; Cabot 2012, 2013; Ticktin 2014). Ethnographies of humanitarianism explore the worlds of street-level bureaucrats such as social workers, civil servants, lawyers, and even employees of private companies subcontracted by states for border security work. Legal anthropology intersects with medical anthropology to explore the concern for suffering in studies of nurses, psychologists, lawyers, bureaucrats, policy makers, and public health officials (Fassin 2007; Redfield 2013; Ticktin 2014). Additionally, anthropologists focus on the humanitarian efforts of lawyers, courts, and community-based justice and advocacy organizations. The strength of longer, sustained, qualitative analysis is that the research can be communicated in the form of narratives, usually in books, which aim to paint nuanced portraits of how laws and policies shape and are shaped by the professional lives of those directly engaged with humanitarian practice.

Anthropologists also study post-conflict reconciliation efforts via reparations, courts, trials, and what is called restorative justice. Some of the same actors and institutions that intervene in conflict settings to provide humanitarian aid and relief may also be involved in reconciliation and reconstruction—for example, in negotiating reparations (Johnston and Slyomovics 2009), in pursuing post-genocide justice in courts (Wilson 2017), and in seeking post-apartheid justice via truth and reconciliation commissions (Wilson 2001). In many of these instances, global organizations are the primary actors, though the interests of states often determine what global organizations are able to do (Niezen and Sapignoli 2017). Anthropologists situate their ethnographies inside these institutions, analysing global bodies such as the United Nations. This trend to study cultures of expertise includes the study of bureaucracy itself. UN experts intervene in the world, but they are also of the world, and they require knowledge about the world. Anthropologists may simultaneously inhabit the role of the expert (Wilson 2017), the 'witness' (regarding legal testimony, see Benthall 2017), and the critic (Fassin 2012).

Other sites of ethnographic inquiry are post-conflict courts and international ad hoc tribunals for crimes against humanity, such as those in the former Yugoslavia, which prosecute violations of international humanitarian law (Wilson 2017). These extra-constitutional, courts rely on national governments for access to 'sites, witnesses and documentary evidence' (Wilson 2017: 270). Anthropologists in such settings can focus on epistemological questions. Wilson, for instance, was concerned with 'how international law knows what it claims to know' regarding crimes against humanity. This research is discursive; it focuses on problems of causation in international speech acts that may have incited genocide and/or ethnic cleansing. In post-conflict settings where anthropologists analyse legal-moral processes of accusation, justice, and reconciliation, humanitarian intervention may take three forms: ethnographers may participate as witnesses and experts in court proceedings; they may desire redress for crimes against humanity; and they may seek to contribute to the critical, scholarly study of judicial venues for addressing humanitarian crimes. Notable recent works in this genre include Rita Kesselring's (2017) study of the political status of victimhood in the aftermath of South Africa's Truth and Reconciliation Commission. By studying legal avenues for redress and transitional justice mechanisms, she analysed how South African apartheid victims used law to move beyond victimhood. Law was a space of emancipation, reparation, and class action, and legal frameworks were used as a form of activism and advocacy, through which solidarity was found in victimhood. Richard Wilson (this volume), argues that, in truth commissions and reparation courts, one must pay attention to the affective drama of the process of oral testimony, for it is not only formal documents that are important in processes of transitional justice, but also the staging and creation of dramatic effect (also see Wilson 2001, 2017). Kristin Doughty (2014, 2015) has studied indigenous *gacaca* courts in post-genocide Rwanda, documenting what she calls the 'violence of social repair'. These state-mandated *gacaca* courts used reimagined indigenous conceptions of justice and redress for social repair after genocide. Following Laura Nader's early work in legal anthropology, Doughty argues that these forums functioned as a type of harmony ideology in which mediation became a governance technique. In this case, transitional justice was structured by the state through indigenous law, which then became a form of social regulation.

Law's limits

Humanitarian intervention, when framed as a form of advocacy, emphasizes the law itself. Humanitarianism has increasingly become a space of activism, whereby practitioners must understand legal logic in order to challenge it, to work around it, and to address legislative regulations as a space of humanitarian concern and intervention. Saida Hodzic's (2017) ethnography of NGOs seeking to end the practice of female genital cutting in Ghana, argues that such campaigns spawn entire institutional worlds, political projects, and laws. Other global rescue projects intersecting with legal reform include anti-human-trafficking campaigns (Agustin 2007; Brennan 2014). Judicial activism, as a form of humanitarian intervention, may engage with law by skirting the repressive potential of national governance bodies. This practice is evident in the production of 'humanitarian goods'. Peter Redfield (2012) explores the proliferation of welfare services outside of the state via the provision of nonprofit drugs and therapeutic food and via human waste disposal technologies produced by public/private partnerships and 'ethically oriented corporations'. Médecins Sans Frontières addressed the humanitarian concern of unequal access to medicines in not-for-profit economic sectors by advocating globally for populations unable to afford drugs and by fighting against barriers created by national drug protocols. Traditionally, it was the state that provided for the welfare of its citizens, but with the global rollback of the welfare state other institutions, such as nonprofits, NGOs, charitable organizations, and citizen action groups, have come to the rescue. This is particularly important in global humanitarian contexts where no single regulatory body or institution is tasked with managing humanitarian response. Through its 1999 Campaign for Access to Essential Medicine, MSF challenged trade law to produce new drugs for malaria and sleeping sickness, making them accessible as humanitarian goods by using the logic of humanitarian intervention. Through campaigns for humanitarian technologies, new philanthropically subsidized hybrid public/private humanitarian markets were produced. Humanitarian organizations can thus become agitators, instigators, and civic alternatives to state-led welfare service provision. This form of humanitarian intervention expands the limits of humanitarian intervention beyond the temporary Band-Aid efforts, which were ill-equipped to address structural inequalities and injustices.

Some forms of humanitarian intervention lie outside the formal purview of states and regulatory bodies, and beyond the interpretive framework of law. This alternative arena—called 'vernacular humanitarianism'[3] takes shape in local and indigenous responses to urgent need following contextually relevant social codes. Local residents and citizens, including doctors, lawyers, social workers, teachers, and neighbours, are frequently the first responders in humanitarian crises (Bornstein 2012a; Huang 2013; Schuller 2012; Simpson 2014). These efforts exist conterminously with the work of large-scale institutions, which may harness them (Adams 2013). Employing local staff is considered best practice for culturally appropriate intervention strategies to address the challenge of post-crisis trauma and to repair and rebuild after lives have been saved. Humanitarian crises are lived experiences, situated in contexts requiring nuanced understandings of gender relations, age cohorts, religious beliefs, and social divisions.

Whether or not secular forms of humanitarianism differs in practice from religious ones is an empirical question that anthropologists have also explored (Barnett and Stein 2012; Benthall 2017; Bornstein 2012a; Petersen 2011; on secular aid, see Redfield 2013). 'Religion' consists in a set of humanitarian institutions, such as churches and faith-based groups, as well as beliefs and practices. In humanitarian intervention, religion may be foundational for intervening institutions. Barnett and Stein (2012) argue that attention to faith-based humanitarianism increased after the Rwandan genocide of the mid-1990s when the secular humanitarian sector experienced a moral reckoning and questioned the moral conditions for, and value of, intervention. The realities of medically treating all persons in distress in conflict settings, even perpetrators of genocide, forced humanitarian institutions to contend with political limitations while affirming the humanitarian protection of life as a sacred act (Barnett and Stein 2012).

Anthropologists attend to faith-based motivations for humanitarian intervention (on Russia, see Caldwell 2017), analysing how religious ideas may motivate the impulse to give and to help (Bornstein 2012a: 23–57). As the parable of the Good Samaritan inspires Christians to assist others, the directive to give *zakat* is one of the five pillars of Islam that traditionally favours support for Muslims in local communities and now also structures donations to Muslim humanitarian organizations working across national boundaries (Benthall 2017). Muslim aid embodies the relationship of Islamic law to humanitarian activity (Benthall 2017; Petersen 2011). Some NGOs accept *zakat* and redistribute it for social welfare and humanitarian purposes, such as orphan care (on ideological variation in Muslim aid, see Petersen 2011). For states with Islamic law, *zakat* may become a humanitarian tax (Petersen 2011). In cases where the state is not able to provide care, nongovernmental humanitarian groups, often religious ones, step in to fill the gap, providing services of health care and human rights advocacy. In cases of national populations with Muslim majorities and Islamic law, humanitarian intervention by a Christian organization may constitute a challenge to religious law and even the state.

Malini Bhattacharjee (2016) outlines the historic and current role of the Rashtriya Swayamsevak Sangh (RSS), a Hindu-nationalist volunteer society, in disaster relief in India. Based on research in three villages in rural Kutch (Gujarat), she documents how RSS used its volunteers to respond to disaster relief after a major earthquake by providing aid and expanding its cadre. RSS offered a 'ready army' for rescue operations and enhanced its political strength as a nationalist, militarist, and humanitarian force. *Seva* (service) was a form of mobilization for the Hindu right. In tracking relief and mobilization following the 2001 earthquake, Bhattarjee notes how villagers contrasted the relief work of RSS with inefficient state machinery. Humanitarianism, if not state-directed, operates in the shadow of states. In the process, RSS strengthened contacts with beneficiaries, donors, diaspora communities, media, and civil society groups, positioning itself as a humanitarian actor and downplaying its image as a 'divisive communal agitator' (Bhattacharjee 2016: 96). As a result, existing communal divisions became further entrenched through what Malini Bhattacharjee (2016: 96) terms 'insidious aid'. In the process of providing aid, RSS both bypassed the state and complemented it, using public/private partnerships to blur distinctions between RSS and the state. In this instance, and perhaps in others as well, RSS downplayed religion and defined itself as a cultural and patriotic organization.

We must not limit the scope of our analysis to governmental and non-governmental agencies. For-profit groups also engage in humanitarian intervention, whether through corporate social responsibility programmes or as contractors (Weiss 2013). For example, following Hurricane Katrina, the Army Corps of Engineers subcontracted emergency relief services to private-sector companies: The Shaw Group, Bechtel, Halliburton, Blackwater, and others. Vincanne Adams (2013) documents how this initiative failed, as private sector agencies were not equipped to deal with the actualities of disaster relief, and faith-based groups and churches dominated hands-on rescue efforts by harnessing an affect-driven economy of volunteers. Though the majority of actors providing humanitarian services remain nonprofits, the United Nations High Commissioner for Refugees (UNHCR) released a report on 'the tsunami of unchecked privatisation' of public goods, which led systematically to the elimination of human rights protections.[4] The report states:

> Privatisation of social protection often leads to a focus on economic efficiency concerns that aim to minimise time spent per client, close cases earlier, generate fees wherever possible, and cater to those better-off, pushing those with less resources and more complex problems to the margins.

How this trend affects programmes of humanitarian intervention is a topic for future research.

The issues discussed in this chapter are constantly in the making. Rather than offering a sweeping conclusion, I pose a few suggestions for thinking about humanitarian intervention, anthropology, and law in the future. Increased dialogue between scholars of comparative law and anthropologists could generate collaborative scholarship on shared interests. More legal scholars could explore the local contexts of humanitarian intervention, for example, by asking how IHL and the Right to Protection (R2P) are navigated by international legal professionals. What are the social lives of law? How are laws interpreted, mobilized, and enforced? How are they challenged? More anthropologists could write about international institutions. Ethnographers tend to be context-based in their orientation. Anthropologists could focus their ethnographic lens on different legal fields, looking at how their practitioners speak to each other or come into conflict. For example, how do state regulations, institutions producing IHL, and NGOs exert pressure for legal reform? There could also be more of a focus on the role of citizen groups in relation to law, and how they affect processes of legal reform. There could be more cross-communication between the scholarship on international law and anthropology. This interdisciplinary scholarship requires translation, and an understanding of how legal experts, law professionals, and anthropologists represent law and humanitarianism, each with their own vocabulary, frames of reference, and disciplinary expertise. Scholars from the global South, where humanitarian interventions tend to happen, would enhance this conversation as would a focus on other dimensions of power in humanitarian provision (on race, see e.g. Benton 2016). The way forward in this scholarly field will require increased dialogue across disciplines and cultural contexts to comprehend both the stakes involved in saving lives through humanitarianism and the legal regulatory frameworks that define, enable, and restrict humanitarian interventions.

Acknowledgements

Thanks are due to OHLA reviewers, Didier Fassin, Rita Kesserling; editor Olaf Zenker, and colleagues Jonathan Benthall and Anu Sharma for helpful suggestions on earlier drafts.

Notes

1. See the 2000 Charitable Choice legislation, <https://aspe.hhs.gov/report/personal-responsibility-and-work-opportunity-reconciliation-act-1996> (accessed 30 April 2020). See also Bornstein 2007.
2. See <https://www.icnl.org/post/report/china-philanthropy-law> (accessed 30 April 2020).
3. See <http://allegralaboratory.net/vernacular-humanitarianisms/> (accessed 30 April 2020).
4. See <http://www.ohchr.org/EN/NewsEvents/Pages/DisplayNews.aspx?NewsID=23740&LangID=E&fbclid=IwAR1vjTo7iiKPq3ejy_31a_Qq5DBNKobEdI6_O627i5NMQecO5dVD5psKpWU> (accessed 30 April 2020).

References

Adams, V. 2013. *Markets of Sorrow, Labors of Faith: New Orleans in the Wake of Katrina*. Durham: Duke University Press.

Agustin, L. M. 2007. *Sex at the Margins: Migration, Labour Markets and the Rescue Industry*. London: Zed Books.

Andersson, R. 2014. 'Time and the Migrant Other: European Border Controls and the Temporal Economics of Illegality'. *American Anthropologist* 116(4): 795–809.

Andersson, R. 2015. 'Hardwiring the Frontier? The Politics of Security Technology in Europe's "Fight Against Illegal Migration"'. *Security Dialogue* 1–18.

Barnett, M. 2011. *Empire of Humanity: A History of Humanitarianism*. Ithaca, NY: Cornell University Press.

Barnett, M. 2012. 'Faith in the Machine? Humanitarianism in an Age of Bureaucratization'. In M. Barnett and J. G. Stein, eds. *Sacred Aid: Faith and Humanitarianism*, 188–210. Oxford: Oxford University Press.

Barnett, M. and J. Gross Stein, eds. 2012. *Sacred Aid: Faith and Humanitarianism*. Oxford: Oxford University Press.

Barnett, M. and T. G. Weiss. 2008. 'Humanitarianism: A Brief History of the Present'. In M. Barnett and T. G. Weiss, eds. *Humanitarianism in Question: Politics, Power, Ethics*, 1–48. Ithaca, NY: Cornell University Press.

Benthall, J. 2011. 'Islamic Humanitarianism in Adversarial Context'. In E. Bornstein and P. Redfield (eds.), *Forces of Compassion. Humanitarianism Between Ethics and Politics*, 99–122. Santa Fe: SAR Press.

Benthall, J. 2017. 'Experto Crede: A Legal and Political Conundrum'. In D. Fassin, ed. *If Truth Be Told: The Politics of Public Ethnography*, 160–83. Durham, NC: Duke University Press.

Benthall, J. and J. Bellion-Jourdan. 2009. *The Charitable Crescent: Politics of Aid in the Muslim World*. London: Tauris.

Benton, A. 2016. 'African Expatriates and Race in the Anthropology of Humanitarianism'. *Critical African Studies* 8(3): 266–77. September.

Bernal, V. and I. Grewal. 2014. 'The NGO Form: Feminist Struggles, States, and Neoliberalism'. In V. Bernal and I. Grewal, eds. *Theorizing NGOs: States, Feminisms, and Neoliberalism*, 1–18. Durham, NC: Duke University Press.

Bhattacharjee, M. 2016. '*Seva*, Hindutva, and the Politics of Post-Earthquake Relief and Reconstruction in Rural Kutch'. *Asian Ethnology* 75(1): 75–104.

Bornstein, E. 2007. 'Faith, Liberty and the Individual in Humanitarian Assistance'. In M. Feher, G. Krikorian, and Y. McKee, eds. *Nongovernmental Politics*, 658–68. New York: Zone Books.

Bornstein, E. 2012a. *Disquieting Gifts: Humanitarianism in New Delhi*. Palo Alto: Stanford University Press.

Bornstein, E. 2012b. 'Religious Giving Outside the Law in New Delhi'. In M. Barnett and J. G. Stein, eds. *Sacred Aid. Sacred Aid: Faith and Humanitarianism*, 140–65. Oxford: Oxford University Press.

Bornstein, E. and A. Sharma. 2016. 'The Righteous and the Rightful: The Technomoral Politics of NGOs, Social Movements, and the State in India'. *American Ethnologist* 43(1): 76–90.

Bornstein, E. and P. Redfield, eds. 2011. *Forces of Compassion: Humanitarianism Between Ethics and Politics*. Santa Fe: School for Advanced Research Press.

Brennan, D. 2014. *Life Interrupted: Trafficking into Forced Labor in the United States*. Durham, NC: Duke University Press.

Cabot, H. 2012. 'The Governance of Things: Documenting Limbo in the Greek Asylum Procedure'. *Political and Legal Anthropology Review* 35(1):11–29.

Cabot, H. 2013. 'The Social Aesthetics of Eligibility: NGO Aid and Indeterminacy in the Greek Asylum Process'. *American Ethnologist* 40(3): 452–66.

Cabot, H. 2014. *On the Doorstep of Europe: Asylum and Citizenship in Greece*. Philadelphia: University of Pennsylvania Press.

Caldwell, M. L. 2017. *Living Faithfully in an Unjust World: Compassionate Care in Russia.* Berkeley: University of California Press.

Davies, K. 2012. 'Continuity, Change and Contest: Meanings of "Humanitarian" from the "Religion of Humanity" to the Kosovo War'. HPG Working Paper, Overseas Development Institute, London. Open access online.

Doughty, K. 2014. '"Our Goal is Not to Punish but to Reconcile": Mediation in Postgenocide Rwanda'. *American Anthropologist* 116(4): 780–94.

Doughty, K. 2015. 'Law and the Architecture of Social Repair: Gacaca Days in Post-Genocide Rwanda'. *Journal of the Royal Anthropological Institute* (N.S.) 21: 419–37.

Fassin, D. 2007. *When Bodies Remember: Experiences and Politics of AIDS in South Africa.* Berkeley: University of California Press.

Fassin, D. 2011. 'Policing Borders, Producing Boundaries. The Governmentality of Immigration in Dark Times'. *Annual Review of Anthropology* 40: 213–26.

Fassin, D. 2012. *Humanitarian Reason: A Moral History of the Present.* Berkeley: University of California Press.

Fassin, D. 2015. 'Governing Precarity'. In *At the Heart of the State: The Moral World of Institutions*, 1–14. London: Pluto Press.

Fassin, D. and M. Pandolfi. 2010. 'Introduction: Military and Humanitarian Government in the Age of Intervention'. In D. Fassin and M. Pandolfi, eds. *Contemporary States of Emergency: The Politics of Military and Humanitarian Interventions*, 9–25. New York: Zone Books.

Fassin, D. and P. Vasquez. 2005. 'Humanitarian Exception as the Rule: The Political Theology of the 1999 Tragedia in Venezuela'. *American Ethnologist* 32(3): 389–405.

Feldman, I. 2018. *Life Lived in Relief: Humanitarian Predicaments and Palestinian Refugee Politics.* Berkeley: University of California Press.

Feldman, I. and M. Ticktin (eds). 2010. *In the Name of Humanity: The Government of Threat and Care.* Durham, NC: Duke University Press.

Hodzic, S. 2017. *The Twilight of Cutting: African Activism and Life After NGOs.* Berkeley: University of California Press.

Huang, S.-M. 2013. 'Building China's Nascent Civil Society: The Roles of Nongovernmental Organizations'. *American Anthropologist* 115(3): 499–501.

ICNL (International Center for Not-for-Profit Law. 2017. 'India Philanthropy Law Report'. <http://www.icnl.org/research/Philanthropy/India%20Philanthropy%20Law%20Report%20final%202018.pdf>.

Ismail, F. and S. Kamat. 2018. 'NGOs, Social Movements and the Neoliberal State: Incorporation, Reinvention, Critique'. *Critical Sociology* 44(4–5): 569–77.

Johnston, B. R. and S. Slyomovics, eds. 2009. *Waging War, Making Peace: Reparations and Human Rights.* Walnut Creek, CA: Left Coast Press.

Kesselring, R. 2017. *Bodies of Truth: Law, Memory, and Emancipation in Post-Apartheid South Africa.* Stanford: Stanford University Press.

Kolb, R. and R. Hyde. 2008. *An Introduction to the International Law of Armed Conflicts.* Oxford: Hart Publishing.

Lewis, D. and M. Schuller. 2017. 'Engagements with a Productively Unstable Category: Anthropologists and Nongovernmental Organizations'. *Current Anthropology* 58(5): 634–51.

Malkki, L. 2015. *The Need to Help: The Domestic Arts of International Humanitarianism.* Durham: Duke University Press.

Merry, S. E. 2006. *Human Rights and Gender Violence: Translating International Law into Local Justice.* Chicago: University of Chicago Press.

Minear, L. 2002. *The Humanitarian Enterprise: Dilemmas and Discoveries*. West Hartford, CN: Kumarian Press.

Nguyen, V.-K. 2010. *The Republic of Therapy: Triage and Sovereignty in West Africa's Time of AIDS*. Durham: Duke University Press.

Niezen, R. and M. Sapignoli, eds. 2017. *Palaces of Hope: The Anthropology of Global Organizations*. Cambridge: Cambridge University Press.

Orford, A. 2011. Introduction, 'Protection in the Shadow of Empire'. In *International Authority and the Responsibility to Protect*, 1–41. Cambridge: Cambridge University Press.

Pandolfi, M. 2003. 'Contract of Mutual (in)difference: Governance and the Humanitarian Apparatus in Contemporary Albania and Kosovo'. *Indiana Journal of Global Legal Studies* 10(1): 369–81.

Petersen, M. J. 2011. *For Humanity or for the Umma? Ideologies of Aid in Four Transnational Muslim NGOs*. PhD thesis. University of Copenhagen.

Redfield, P. 2012. 'Bioexpectations: Life Technologies as Humanitarian Goods'. *Public Culture* 24(1): 157–84.

Redfield, P. 2013. *Life in Crisis: The Ethical Journey of Doctors Without Borders*. Berkeley: University of California Press.

Salamon, L. M. 2015. 'Introduction: The Nonprofitization of the Welfare State'. *VOLUNTAS: International Journal of Voluntary and Nonprofit Organizations* 26(6): 2147–54.

Schuller, M. 2012. *Killing with Kindness: Haiti, International Aid and NGOs*. New Brunswick: Rutgers University Press.

Sidel, M. 2010. *Regulation of the Voluntary Sector: Freedom and Security in an Era of Uncertainty*. New York: Routledge.

Simpson, E. 2014. *The Political Biography of an Earthquake: Aftermath and Amnesia in Gujarat, India*. Oxford: Oxford University Press.

Simpson, E. 2016. 'Is Anthropology Legal? Earthquake, Blitzkrieg, and Ethical Futures'. *Focaal: European Journal of Social Anthropology* (74)1: 113–128.

Ticktin, M. 2011. *Casualties of Care: Immigration and the Politics of Humanitarianism in France*. Berkeley: University of California Press.

Ticktin, M. 2014. 'Transnational Humanitarianism'. *Annual Review of Anthropology* 43: 273–89.

Weber, M. 1946. *From Max Weber: Essays in Sociology* (trans. and ed. H. H. Gerth and C. Wright Mills). Oxford: Oxford University Press.

Weiss, T. 2013. *Humanitarian Business*. Cambridge: Polity Press.

Wilson, R. 2001. *The Politics of Truth and Reconciliation in South Africa: Legitimizing the Post-Apartheid State*. Cambridge: Cambridge University Press.

Wilson, R. 2017. 'Propaganda on Trial: Structural Fragility and the Epistemology of International Legal Institutions'. In R. Niezen and M. Sapignoli, eds. *Palaces of Hope: The Anthropology of Global Organizations*, 266–93. Cambridge: Cambridge University Press.

CHAPTER 35

INEQUALITY, VICTIMHOOD, AND REDRESS

RITA KESSELRING

INTRODUCTION

IN the most basic sociological definition, social inequality is a societal situation in which resources are distributed unevenly among a group of individuals. Such uneven distribution is rarely aleatory. It is linked to social categories identified in a society and in turn often reinforces them. Categories such as race, class, gender, sexual orientation, and disability are reproduced in practice by inequality, and they find their expression in inequality. Legal norms are an important instrument for sorting people into categories, and sociologists of law have shown how laws can help create, maintain, or reduce inequality (see e.g. Goffman 2014; Van Cleve 2016). Legal norms can be used to create or formalize differences in a society, but social groups can also use legal norms in their attempts to attenuate inequality.

In spite of its long tradition (Goodale 2017), the anthropology of law has not developed such a clear-cut body of scholarship on law and social inequality in the way sociology has. Bronislaw Malinowski's *Crime and Custom in Savage Society* ([1926] 2013) established the anthropology of law as an empirical study. Like Schapera's *Handbook of Tswana Law and Custom* ([1938]1994), the law in these classical texts is seen as something systematic and centred on a group. Subsequently, anthropologists working in colonial and postcolonial contexts started studying the multiplicity of legal situations in which state systems exist alongside other strong normative institutions that regulate social practices. This scholarship of 'legal pluralism' broke open the compartmentalized understanding of law (Benda-Beckmann 2002). In recent decades, the anthropology of law has internationalized and been revitalized by globalization studies, analysing transnational and international law and its appropriation in specific contexts, as well as groups' increased use of extraterritorial law to further rights at home. Its preoccupation has been with the mobilization of transnational identities, such as indigeneity, and transnational networks of solidarity and action (Goodale and Merry 2007; Griffiths, Benda-Beckmann, and Benda-Beckmann 2005; Meckled-García and Çali 2005; Wilson and Mitchell 2003). In the course of its history, however, the anthropology of law has, to a certain extent, neglected the study of law's effects on inequality in modern societies. Notable recent exceptions are studies that examine both the recourse to law and the everyday experiences of the claimants (see e.g. Sapignoli 2018 on the Central Kalahari case).

There are at least three ways in which law can effect structures of inequality. The first is through legislation. This includes the human rights framework and laws that are passed to change society either through repression or emancipation (e.g. Bowen 2010; Thompson 1977). Second, through case law (jurisdiction) and law enforcement (Fassin 2013). Legislation does not automatically result in its enforcement, and it is often at this level that a piece of legislation is rendered effective or ineffective. This category includes the vernacularization of human rights (Merry 2006) as well as the enactment of bureaucratic rules and the interpretation of law (Maine 1861) that allows for its modification. The third way in which law influences structures of inequality is through law's discursive forms and legal practices. The engagement with the law, both in court and beyond, has societal effects (Conley and O'Barr 1990; Merry 1990). While this third approach is my focus in this chapter, my extended case-study also bears aspects of the other two possibilities for law to shape structures of inequality.

In terms of legal discourse, most anthropologists attribute some force to the law. There is consensus that law is not merely the codification of norms that exist outside of law, but that it has constitutive power (Nader 2002). To explain this force, many today have adopted a Foucauldian approach, arguing that everyone who engages with the law is subjected to the legalization of his or her personhood. Some go so far as to say that law equals power, and as a dimension of all modern social relations, law is a basic axis in the constitution of social self and other (Biolsi 1995: 543–4).

As a result of this assumed all-encompassing quality of law, many anthropologists are sceptical of the law's potential to alleviate inequality. If the legal discourse is indeed so powerful, it is difficult to translate experiences of violence into a legal language (Hastrup 2003; Merry 2008) and to translate subjective and unspeakable experiences into the logic of legal evidence and knowledge (Das 1996; Fassin and D'Halluin 2005; Scarry 1985). Consequently, legalization becomes a threat. In their work, Jean and John Comaroff refer to situations dominated by the 'fetishism of the law' (2007: 141–6) and a 'culture of legality' (2007: 146) that seem 'to be infusing everyday life' (2007: 146) and have become a common feature of the postcolony. Scholars fear that law's dominance detracts from positive visions of what a society wants to become; the narrow vocabulary of the language of human rights, for instance, is negative in the sense that it only tells us what we do *not* want for the future (Wilson 2001).

The force of law

Despite these valid notes of caution, we cannot assume that changes in legal subjectivities automatically effect changes in lived subjectivities. This causal link between forms of action and forms of sociality needs to be critically examined. In other words, I do not think that ascribing an all-encompassing power to law is helpful or analytically correct. The question of how law can possibly assume its power remains open. All we can say for sure is that 'the law regulates identity, value, and belief in often contradictory ways' (Goodale 2017: 138).

My perspective on the law and its effects on sociability follows Bourdieu:

> Our thought categories contribute to the production of the world, but only within the limits of their correspondence with preexisting structures. Symbolic acts of naming achieve their power of creative utterance to the extent, and only to the extent, that they propose principles of vision and division objectively adapted to the preexisting divisions of which they are the products. (Bourdieu 1986: 839)

In order to understand the 'force of law' (Bourdieu 1986) on social inequality, we need to look at the lived reality of those people affected by it. It is in these lived realities that we can track changes that result from people's engagement with the law.

This contribution examines a case where victims turned to courts to seek redress for gross human rights violations, and how, in that pursuit, new forms of inequalities were produced. I focus on the so-called apartheid litigations that were filed by South Africans against multinational companies in U.S. federal courts in 2001, claiming their human rights had been violated by the defendant companies' aiding and abetting human rights violations at the hands of the security forces under the apartheid regime. The extraterritorial hearings stretched over sixteen years, and the outcome was disappointing for the plaintiffs (amounting to some 100,000 and potentially more individuals). During these years, they had successes and setbacks, and had to deal with their hopes and fears, the reactions from a variety of actors, and the necessity to maintain solidarity among themselves. My contribution is based on twenty-two months of ethnographic field research over ten years at both the provincial and national levels of Khulumani, a South African apartheid victims support group and a party in the apartheid litigations, and with individuals and groups of Khulumani members and their families in a number of townships on the outskirts of Cape Town, including Philippi, Langa, KTC, Crossroads, and Nyanga (Kesselring 2017).

My focus on redress and victimhood draws on long engagement in legal anthropological scholarship with conflict settlement following harm generated by violations of people's integrity. For instance, blood money—compensation for homicide or bodily injury—can be seen as an alternative to revenge and to right wrongs and as a means to settle disruption in a community (Ben Hounet 2017). Since the 1990s, most related anthropological research has focused on more collective and institutionalized forms of redressing past wrongs and transitioning into a new political era, such as criminal courts (Wilson 2011), truth commissions (Hayner 2001), land restitution (Zenker 2014), and localized courts (Clark 2010)—that is, a bundle of practices and institutions that have come to be known as 'transitional justice' mechanisms.

Against the backdrop of this literature, I examine processes where law offers the potential to alleviate inequalities that had been produced under apartheid through its laws and policies and the enforcement of them. I also, however, look at the backlash that results from taking recourse to the law. To claim redress, people have to position themselves as victims of crimes—a move which may deepen their victimhood socially and politically and thus further cement their unequal opportunities in society. The law has its limits when it comes to 'revaluing' life and balancing inequalities, as I will show, a fact that has societal rather than mere technical causes.

Apartheid Victims in Post-Apartheid South Africa

After the end of apartheid, South Africa decided against prosecuting the majority of apartheid-era crimes within the criminal justice system. Instead, it pursued other avenues of redress, most prominently the Truth and Reconciliation Commission (TRC) (Bell and Ntsebeza 2003; Chapman and Van der Merwe 2008; Ramphele 2009; Sarkin-Hughes 2004). Apart from the TRC, the South African state has put in place a number of redress mechanisms to level the structural inequalities produced by apartheid, from social grants to the Black Economic Empowerment policies, affirmative action, land reform, and land redistribution programmes. Most of these programmes do not directly address the injuries people experienced under apartheid rule; rather, they are forward looking, economically oriented, and operate on a primarily individual basis (Kesselring 2017: 23ff.). The majority of apartheid's victims were not directly involved in the truth commission process. The TRC gave 'victim' status to roughly 21,000 persons who had, directly or indirectly, suffered politically motivated, 'body-bound' (Ross 2002, 11) gross human rights violations. Through this limited list, the TRC's notion of victimhood has had an enormous impact, even on the majority of victims who were not on the list, contributing to a strong societal image of who an apartheid victim is and should be. This dominant discourse excludes many different experiences of victimhood. The commission attempted to develop a representative definition of victimhood, performatively collectivizing the suffering and pain of all survivors (see Cole 2009). It did so, however, by singling out individual victims, who could then speak for all victims and survivors. As a result of its individualistic approach, the commission also lost sight of structural violence (Feldman 2003; Mamdani 2002). Hence, injury ultimately remained individualized, a fact that the movement for redress and recognition first had to overcome.

Life for many apartheid victims twenty-five years after the first democratic elections in 1994 cannot be described as ordinary in comparison to their neighbours who had fewer degrading experiences. Many people still struggle to move beyond the past and participate in the so-called new South Africa. They go through frequent social ruptures and often have few resources, financial and otherwise, to protect themselves from tragedies in the family (crime, death, disability, unemployment). Ruptures are also initiated by the state. Under President Mbeki, the South African government adopted a liberal approach to development and quickly turned away from the past and the experiences of victims. Even those victims on the TRC's list had to wait for five years to receive the final reparations in 2003. The money was often not enough to repay the accumulated debt or to support a child's education. In a climate shaped by a public and private inability to confront the past (Ross 2002: 163; 2003: 172), victims were often unable to come forward during the mid-1990s. Many felt excluded from a process that promised transformation and healing, but did not publicly acknowledge their own injuries (such as rape and other forms of sexual violence).

From early on, victims expressed their discontent with the TRC process. The most important voice for victims' concerns has been the Khulumani Support Group (henceforth Khulumani). The legal interventions it took, together with allied organizations, individuals, and lawyers, changed the reconciliatory and non-retributive path South Africa had taken with the truth commission, and gave it a judicial turn. Khulumani was launched in 1995 and has grown into a national organization with provincial and local branches. Its more than 105,000 members are persons who survived forms of violence emanating from the apartheid security forces or its collaborators, including torture, detention without trial, sexual assault, abuse, and harassment; banning and banishment orders; deliberate withholding of medical attention, food, and water; the destruction of homes; and the mutilation of body parts. Members also include those whose family members were abducted, disappeared, or killed.

Only about 10 per cent of Khulumani's members were officially recognized as victims by the TRC (Madlingozi 2007: 120). The organization started as a self-help group with a focus on providing psychological and social support to victims (on its early history, see Wilson 2001). However, it soon began to focus on political change and made more articulate demands for reparations. The organization relies on voluntary staff, many of whom are victims themselves.

From the outset, Khulumani was based on the idea that victims should organize and speak for themselves. Adhering to its own vision, however, has never been easy due to the societal context and an inherent tension between victimhood and activism, and it became much more difficult as the organization grew and attained international fame. In spite of its broad base, Khulumani has not always developed very democratically. Professionalization and centralization of its structures have made its leadership lose touch with the membership, and power struggles within the organization have lingered for many years. Nevertheless, at the local level, people keep the organization going with little or no financial resources.

Legal challenges after the TRC

In spite of the reconciliatory focus of the TRC process, victims' struggles for recognition were from the start pursued in legal fora. A number of cases submitted in South Africa upheld the victims' right to be consulted in questions arising from apartheid crimes. While the rulings strengthened victims' rights, they also helped to cement the TRC's notion of victimhood.

At the international level, a different set of legal actions challenging the TRC's shortcomings garnered much more attention. In Alien Tort Statute (ATS) claims filed in U.S. courts (Henner 2009; Mattei 2003), victims demanded reparations for the injuries they had sustained at the hands of the security forces during apartheid. The ATS dates back to 1789[1] and gives foreign citizens the right to sue in a U.S. federal court over violations of international law, whether they arose in the United States or abroad. In 2001, legal proceedings were initiated against multinational companies. The original complaint, *Khulumani et al. v Barclays National Bank et al.*, led by U.S. attorney Michael Hausfeld and advised by South African attorney Charles Abrahams, sued twenty-three multinationals and banks in six different countries (Switzerland, Germany, France, the Netherlands, the United Kingdom, and the United States) and involved six different industries (arms and ammunition, oil, transportation, banking, computer technology, and mining). Khulumani and eighty-seven individuals alleged specific violations of international human rights law that corporate actions had made possible: extrajudicial killing, torture, detention, and cruel treatment (between 1960 and 1994). A few months before the Khulumani litigation was filed, the American personal injury lawyer Ed Fagan filed *Lungisile Ntsebeza et al. v Daimler Chrysler Corporation et al.* In 2002, the U.S. Judicial Panel on Multidistrict Litigation consolidated the different apartheid cases and had them heard by the Southern District Court of New York.[2]

Despite initial assurances by the cabinet of South Africa that the government neither supported nor opposed legal action in this matter, President Mbeki strongly condemned the legal actions in 2003, backed by Minister of Justice Penuell Maduna. The U.S. secretary of commerce described the litigations as an 'unhelpful development' (Friedman 2003), and the Bush administration, in a statement of interest by the Department of State, argued that the 'continued adjudication of the [apartheid litigations] risks potentially serious adverse consequences for significant interests of the United States' by threatening to be an 'irritant in U.S.-South African relations' and for international economic relations with other countries whose firms are defendants.

The 2004 Supreme Court ruling in *Sosa v Alvarez-Machain* upheld the right of foreigners to seek compensation under the Alien Tort Statute's provisions, but it also urged the federal courts to interpret the statute narrowly to avoid judicial interference in foreign affairs. As a result, later in 2004, Judge Sprizzo dismissed the apartheid litigations on the grounds that aiding and abetting international law violations was not a universally accepted standard of international law. Plaintiffs appealed to the Second Circuit

Court of Appeals, which, in 2007, reversed the lower court's dismissal. The defendant companies petitioned the U.S. Supreme Court for an order of certiorari, but the Court could not pass judgment for a lack of quorum,[3] which allowed the Appeals Court ruling to stand.

Seizing this opportunity, the plaintiffs' legal teams changed some crucial characteristics of the case. They reduced the number of defendants to eight and reformulated the claims into a class action suit with thirteen individuals standing for the classes. The amended cases were heard by Judge Shira Scheindlin in 2009. It was she who finally issued the first substantial ruling and allowed the claims to proceed. She ordered the exclusion of banks as defendants and removed Khulumani's standing as a plaintiff. The amended complaint was met with another appeal to dismiss by the companies. Importantly, a couple of months after Judge Scheindlin's decision, the South African government reversed its opposition to the case. This good news was tempered for the plaintiffs by a decision in another ATS case, *Kiobel and Others v Royal Dutch Petroleum Company and Others*, in which the Second Circuit Court of Appeals ruled in September 2010 that companies could not be held liable for violations of international human rights law. The Nigerian plaintiffs filed a petition of certiorari with the Supreme Court, which did not rule on corporate liability, but rather on the ATS as a whole. Its April 2013 ruling restricted the application of the ATS in cases alleging torts outside U.S. territory. This prompted Judge Scheindlin to exclude non-U.S. companies (leaving only IBM and Ford). The updated complaint was nevertheless dismissed on the grounds that the plaintiffs had not shown sufficient connection to the United States. Hopeful after a ruling in the ATS case *Mastafa v Chevron Corp.*, the South African plaintiffs submitted a brief to the court appealing the dismissal of the apartheid cases, but in October 2015, the court affirmed Scheindlin's order. A petition for a writ of certiorari filed with the U.S. Supreme Court was also unsuccessful.

Law and social inequality

How do law and inequality relate here? First, the plaintiffs hope that financial redress, as a legal remedy for the political injustice they experienced under the apartheid regime, will help them to fully participate in post-apartheid South Africa. Reparations are not seen as a total remedy, but as a step in the right direction and what should rightfully be given to all victims of apartheid. Second, to hear legal claims, the law needs defined groups. Plaintiffs have to single themselves out as a distinctive group; in other words, they must, in effect, declare, 'We are victims'. This legal process produces a social reality and the associated risk that the category hardens and becomes exclusionary. Finally, the law produces procedural side-effects. People are grouped in classes according to injuries suffered, and some qualify as members of these classes whereas others do not.

All three aspects—the search for justice and remedy, the delineation or redefinition of a new group, and the effects of the law's procedures—are part of the fabric of law. The law has the advantage of relying on procedures and it lends itself to consensus. Procedures, however, need to be translated into the realities of the case, and it is in these realities that procedures have social effects that create, maintain, or alleviate inequality. It is to this aspect that I now turn.

Lawyers: Intermediaries of Procedures and Universal Law

A statute like the Alien Tort Statute might be (or perhaps used to be) universal, but its effects are always very localized. For obvious reasons, universal applicability of a law does not automatically streamline its effects across social and political contexts.

A number of intermediaries work to bridge not only the gaps between the experience of victimhood and legal procedures, most prominently legal practitioners (but also NGOs and researchers), as well as between different contexts, such as U.S. jurisdiction and politics and South Africa's history of dealing with its apartheid legacy. In the example at hand, administrations have changed three times in the United States—from Clinton to Obama to Trump—and three times in South Africa—from Mbeki to Motlanthe to Zuma. Given that politics exerted such direct influence on the judicial process, the strategies around the lawsuits had to continuously adapt to changed political environments.

Indeed, for Charles Abrahams, legal adviser in the Khulumani case, partner at AbrahamsKiewitz and once active in the movement calling for the cancellation of unjust and odious debts, the lawsuits were always only part of a much broader political campaign (Abrahams 2019). He always warned people not to base the campaign for redress and an opening up of the victim question on legal action alone. 'It will weaken the campaign', he cautioned. 'The lawsuit is very narrowly framed. There is lots to be campaigned for beyond the lawsuit.'

Equally, for Dumisa Ntsebeza, former TRC commissioner, president of South Africa's Black Lawyers Association and legal adviser to the Ntsebeza case, the lawsuits were about holding the South African state to its commitment to social change. In an interview, he told me, 'A government which is populated by people who were themselves the victims of the vicious regime of apartheid should now seek to deny a legitimate pursuit in legal courts by victims of the same system? This is the clearest statement that has been made by this government: where the interests of big business are at stake, they decide against their people.' Unlike their South African counterparts, for the U.S. legal teams, as much as they sympathized with the plight of apartheid victims, the apartheid litigations were primarily an opportunity to receive legal clarifications on the applicability of the ATS.

On a few occasions the U.S. and South African teams of lawyers and the named plaintiffs met. In 2009, when the legal teams were presented with the opportunity to amend the lawsuits after Judge Scheindlin's positive but limiting decision, the U.S. teams came to South Africa to directly interact with the plaintiffs and their South African counterparts. It was a fact-finding mission to strengthen the link between the defendants' companies and the injuries. In a two-day meeting with the named plaintiffs, Khulumani, and other concerned individuals, the lawyers presented their ideas of how to make the cases stronger. But what might have looked like a good move for the U.S. lawyers was not necessarily good in the South African political environment. For instance, the U.S. lawyers wanted to bring Desmond Tutu back in more prominently, given that Judge Scheindlin had quoted him in her decision. For South Africans, this was not a good idea; Tutu had just called on South Africans to boycott the 2009 general elections, and he had fallen from grace with the ruling ANC party. The question of how to more sharply delineate the proposed classes of injury was another issue where opinions diverged. From the U.S. perspective, the two lawsuits should propose the same classes of injury and define them as narrowly as possible; from the perspective of the Ntsebeza legal team, keeping its broad and numerous classes was a point of principle.

While these are technical and strategic discussions that are partly dictated by legal procedures, they have an effect on plaintiffs. Eventually, the classes of plaintiffs were narrowed in the Khulumani case, which also reduced the number of named plaintiffs. But being a named plaintiff comes with considerable risk in a society that is marred by social inequalities and unaddressed suspicions (Kesselring 2017: 65–70). Simple changes in a complaint can have dramatic consequences for individual plaintiffs' standing in their communities.

While lawyers were often mediators and mobilizers, they also unintentionally contributed to divisions. Even if the two litigations were consolidated by the U.S. courts, the two South Africa teams never recovered from tensions that go back to the beginning of the lawsuits, and tensions remain. As a result, there was no rapprochement between the plaintiffs of the two lawsuits. The histories of the cases prevented solidarity among victims.

Lawyers have strong motivations to be involved in human rights cases. They hope to alleviate inequality, with the ultimate aim of doing away with it entirely. While they weigh societal and juridical realities, they leave a legal mark on the matter.

Plaintiffs

Plaintiffs also contribute—often unwittingly—to inclusionary and exclusionary practices and thus help to create new inequalities. The office where potential new Khulumani members approach a provincial executive member or an administrator is a crucial place where conceptions and misconceptions about who qualifies to be a victim are formed. Since the apartheid lawsuits were filed in 2001, the stakes have increased for some potential members, since in their eyes becoming a Khulumani member automatically means that one will be considered a plaintiff in the lawsuits. This assumption, however, has never been confirmed in court, as the classes were never bindingly defined and Khulumani as an organization was removed as a plaintiff. Depending on the final definition of the classes, all South Africans were potential beneficiaries of a settlement or damages paid by the defendant companies. Khulumani was simply the organization that held the largest and most detailed database on apartheid victims, which was roughly five times the size of the TRC's.

I was present during hours and days of testimonies by community members who wanted to become Khulumani members. To a certain extent, the Khulumani officers copied the practice of the TRC from two decades earlier and engaged people to record victims' testimonies. In doing so, they not only applied Khulumani's constitution, but also their own perception of a 'good victim'. Most applicants were referred to Khulumani by friends or acquaintances, which allows for both inclusionary and exclusionary practices in the context of localized political histories of the struggle against apartheid. For instance, for many years, there was a conception in the communities that only the residents of certain townships qualified for membership. This distinction went back to events in the 1980s that divided certain neighbourhoods along the lines of displaced people, on the one hand, and those who had to host the displaced in already overcrowded, informal residential areas on the other. As a result, some townships dominated Khulumani's meetings and the membership base for many years; it took considerable effort to work against this divisive practice.

There were further cleavages cutting across victims. The fact that the TRC only acknowledged a particular kind of justice that denied feelings and practices of vengeance (Wilson 2001) and recognized a fraction of victims still comes into play twenty years later, fuelled by the new legal challenges in the United States and the possibility of payout. Ironically, people who received reparations through the TRC process were generally worse off than those who did not qualify or did not even try. In the expectation of soon receiving the reparations, people accumulated debt and often never fully recovered from this situation. People who received reparations were sometimes also eyed suspiciously. People know each other still today by their role in the resistance against apartheid. These histories are very localized and violent. People, especially women, were often caught between gang leaders and their fierce fights for domination (Cole 1987; 2012). In some ways, the lawsuit is reawakening those lingering divisions that were produced by what for many was a nontransparent TRC process.

Victimhood is once again at stake and a potential card to gain entry into processes of redress. In order to qualify as a victim or a Khulumani member, one has to be accepted by the officer taking the statement. It is thus not surprising that Khulumani has experienced a number of challenges from within. In some cases, powerful members in a community set up their own branch, vilified the 'official' Khulumani, distributed alternative membership forms, and made false announcements of a payout. For these and many other challenges to the group, it required considerable effort for Khulumani not to break apart, at both the regional and national levels. Moments of success in the U.S. courts served both to unify and divide. Legal and quasi-legal categories (going back to the TRC) thus have consequences for societal discourses and can jeopardize the chances for solidarity.

I often saw the notion of victimhood perpetuated in simplistic and almost grotesque forms, especially when outsiders and media were involved. Here, I relate an instance where two documentary filmmakers received permission to speak to the members assembled at one of the monthly general meetings to talk with them about 'forgiveness'. The filmmakers had been to other post-transitional countries such as Northern Ireland and Rwanda, and had come to South Africa presumably for its comparative value. South Africa enjoys a reputation of successful transition based on an approach of reconciliation and forgiveness. Few people know what has followed from the truth commission or how dissatisfied and unrecognized the majority of victims feel. Hence, when asked whether any of the roughly hundred members wanted to say something about 'forgiveness', the filmmakers received the expected response. One woman promptly says, 'We can't forgive!' A man in the audience supports her: 'It's a two-way street: action must be done in order to reconcile.' Another man follows suit: 'Look at us, we have nothing. I am on medication. So what is the point of forgiving or reconciling?' Getting straight to the heart of the matter, another person explains: 'No one came to ask [us] for forgiveness.' And then Khulumani members trail off to what concerns them most: 'Our children don't respect us; we have nothing to put on the plate', and 'I have been trying to qualify for a special pension [from the state], but the system is so corrupt. I still don't receive it.'

To the attentive listener, it became quite obvious that forgiveness was not the main concern here. It was even unclear whom to forgive; no one had approached them with this request. The more mundane things were much more important: How will I feed my family tomorrow? How can I get some state support for my disability? To the inattentive listener, the picture emerging from this situation was a notion of the 'unreconciled victim' (as opposed to a person who has been reconciled and has forgiven). While this perspective is probably valid to a certain extent, it misses many important points.

As mentioned in the introduction to this contribution, there is often a gap between the experience of victimhood and the (legal) discourses afforded to talk about it. As I will show below, victimhood is embodied, held close, and difficult to articulate in words. If prompted to put it in words, people can only draw on the dominant discourses, such as the 'unforgiving' and the 'victim'. But this stock vocabulary is limiting; it cannot not capture the experience nor the complexity of victimhood, and tends to perpetuate standard binaries of good and evil, perpetrator and victim, reconciled and unreconciled.

Lived victimhood

While being at the centre of all these concerns, victims somehow have to continue to live their lives. They do so in a realm that is rather removed from legal discourses, but is nevertheless affected by them.

Ethel Khali is one of the older women with whom I regularly passed my afternoons in Philippi. For her, there is no clear break between apartheid and post-apartheid times. She became widowed in the 1980s and was left on her own with three sons, one of them disabled. Like so many of my acquaintances and friends in the township of Cape Town, she still has close ties to the rural area formally known as Transkei, but is somewhat trapped in the urban space, which is unwelcoming and dangerous at times. Employment opportunities are slightly better than in the rural area, although her health is too poor to work and she is beyond retirement age in any case. She rents out the shacks in her backyard for a small fee.

Ms Khali is a dedicated churchgoer and an enthusiastic Khulumani member. She is part of a group of elderly women who live in the vicinity and meet regularly. In these meetings, which I participated in, the women share their daily struggles, their diabetes, high blood pressure and arthritis, and try to help each other out as much as they can. They are all Khulumani members and see themselves as victims of apartheid. This victimhood clearly relates to past experiences such as torture, the killings of their husbands, ongoing loss of property due to raids and fires, 'deportations' to the rural areas, and everyday structural discrimination. Their victimhood is entangled, however, with their position today, which does not look much different from the apartheid days, although the excessive violence has stopped. Their bodies grow older; and with age, their injuries resurface and the pain, both emotional and physical, grows stronger. Many of the women have flashbacks and cannot shake off their memories, which sit uncomfortably in their bodies and prevent them from leading ordinary lives.

During one of my first visits to Ms Khali in 2009, I could sense the pressure she felt to 'tell me her story', and I did my best to change the subject. I was cautious not to evoke strong emotions, and I never asked the women to speak about their pain. Not asking, however, often felt inadequate, not least because researchers before me had created the expectation that life stories are what researchers want. I instead asked her to show me around her house, a crumbling structure in dire need of repair. Years of the humidity of the Cape were absorbed in the bricks and wood, and the strong wind seeped through every corner of the house. She pointed out to me the shacks in the backyard, the leaking roof, but also some items that she treasures: photographs of her mother and sons, and a Singer sewing machine. Then she halted abruptly and said, 'But once reparations from the lawsuit come through ... God willing, I will also pay for the education of my son and the school fees for my grandchild.'

This small exchange describes an effect of the law that could easily be overlooked. The law is not only a piece of legislation that changes the lives of thousands, nor merely the enshrinement of a legal category assigning life chances to broad categories of people. For Ms Khali, the law has a much subtler, but very important effect. She situates herself in a political and social field in relation to a lawsuit. The fact that they feel part of a lawsuit against companies has boosted people's hopes. Ms Khali and her female friends take pride in being part of Khulumani and the classes of plaintiffs, and it has become a point of reference in parts of their lives. The hopes and the connection on which they rely create solidarity and give new meaning to a common social space. There now exists a space in which they can foreground their victimhood freely if they wish, part of which is that they do not have to hide or even explain their pain and their fits of recurring memories. This space is not created by the law, but it is reinforced by shared hopes in a legal solution.

Like any other person, these women of course live multiple subjectivities that partly exclude and partly overlap with their victim personhood. For instance, Ms Khali is still a staunch member of the African National Congress, the ruling party that condemned apartheid victims for being selfish when they turned to U.S. courts. In church, her victimhood can much more easily dissolve into notions of prayer, hope, and community work. In her ordinary life, the apartheid litigations have given her and others a point of action. They produce the potential for emancipation, however fragile and contingent this potential is.

Inequality, Victimhood, and Redress

Broader societal inequality cannot be alleviated by filing suit against multinational companies. In the course of my research, two women from the small group who looked after one another have passed away. These two women died poor and unrecognized in their victimhood by the broader society. However, they were at least part of a shared sociality—the women's group and Khulumani more broadly—which drew on the energy triggered by the legal challenges. This sociality has not yet reached beyond victims, and maybe it never will. Nevertheless, I see this as a first step towards the possibility of levelling inequalities. These attempts are intimate and are probably only successful if they catch on in broader society and ignite institutional change. As outlined above, victims were confronted with a hostile post-apartheid government, which deemed the legal challenges not only unnecessary but also unpatriotic. Victims thus face a number of discursive hurdles, the most daunting of which are the narrow societal notion of apartheid victimhood as produced by the truth commission and the state's resistance against a re-engagement with the apartheid question both in courts and in domestic political processes. Against this background, non-predicated practices of solidarity and tacit recognition among victims must be seen as a seed for social change (Kesselring 2017).

Monetary redress through the law is but one specific way to address inequality, and both scholars and practitioners are often criticized for focusing exclusively on financial redress, to the neglect of other forms. No one would argue that the loss of life can be redressed with money. However, the distinctive characteristic of monetary redress for loss or injury is, I would argue, that it does hold the potential for emancipation from past experiences. It gives the compensated person or group a means to act upon the world in a self-determined manner; attached to the money is the potential of giving some degree of agency back to that person. Most post-conflict projects across the globe—many of which draw on the South African example—forget the need to offer agency to victims and overemphasize symbolic, national gestures, many of which have little effect in individuals' lives. Needless to say, financial redress does not replace other forms of inviting a person or a group of people back into a changed societal structure, but it does have an important role to play in addressing the inequality that is exacerbated by victimhood.

For the injured, the law, then, offers a promising way to claim damages for harm or loss. It is an ambivalent path because in its logic, the law needs to *valuate* life, and with valuation comes the danger of producing *disparities* in the evaluation of human life (see Fassin 2018: 92ff.). Law, life, and redress therefore stand in a complicated relationship. The law offers the potential to valuate and appreciate (the loss of) life, especially with a fair trial and damages; but as soon as life is valued in technical terms, it also undergoes a process of devaluation—if we understand all life as ethically the same.

In this contribution, I have tried to show that the quest for redress and the hopes to reduce inequality are related on a number of levels. First, going to court is often the result of an entrenched system of inequalities (such as apartheid was and its legacy has been); second, pursuing legal means has the effect of creating disparities (between victims and non-victims, for instance); and third, it can create new cleavages within a group (breaking apart a group of victims).

The reasons for the law's role in alleviating and creating inequalities cannot be found in the nature of the law, though. The law does not automatically produce something or someone. A victim is, first and foremost, someone who feels that she has been harmed, and not because the law ascribes this subject position to her. The law thus does not subject one's personhood to its own logics (something that is often called 'legalization'). For the law to have an effect, the legal logic and societal 'preexisting structures' (Bourdieu 1985) need to coalesce. Hence, recourse to the law is a consequence of the attempt to emancipate oneself from a confining discourse (e.g. a discourse that refuses to recognize the continuing suffering of victims) under conditions in which the legal avenue is more promising than the political avenue. The search for emancipation originates in the lived realities of victimhood.

Along the same line of reasoning, the *limits of the law to achieve equality* emerge from a societal context rather than from the law itself. Certainly, on one level, legislation and jurisdiction take their effectiveness from the legal context itself. Apartheid is a case in point: it was difficult to ignore the efficacy of discriminatory law and segregation policies. Their enforcement was one of the central means of suppressing the black population and depriving it of equal opportunities, legitimating torture, and devaluating the lives of a certain group of people. At the same time the law was, for a small group of people, the means by which they successfully managed to accumulate wealth and prevent economic distribution and social change. Law was equally an important means to fight these practices; it was, in other words, politics by other means (Abel 1995).

In terms of the third way that law can effect structures of inequality—through law's discursive forms—the apartheid litigations show that in order to achieve equality, legible lines of inequality first have to be emphasized, mobilized, or even produced. These inequalities often persist long after the end of a legal action—in the case-study, the effects of law-use have remained with apartheid victims, and inequality has not decreased. The limits of the law are just as much the result of procedural limitations as they are of powerful actors (such as governments and corporations) who are unwilling to institute social change. The study of law and inequality must include societal processes beyond material outcomes and legal decisions.

Notes

1. 28 U.S. Code §1350: Alien's action for tort.
2. In an amended version of the case, more banks and mining companies were added to the suit, and the South African government, former president Nelson Mandela, and then president Thabo Mbeki were mentioned as defendants. Because of serious controversies around Fagan's credentials, the American human rights litigator Paul Hoffmann took over the case. For a timeline of the various apartheid litigations, see Kesselring (2012).
3. Four of the nine justices had to recuse themselves because they owned stock in some of the corporate defendants.

References

Abel, R. L. 1995. *Politics by Other Means: Law in the Struggle Against Apartheid, 1980–1994*. New York: Routledge.

Abrahams, C. 2019. *Class Action: In Pursuit of a Larger Life*. Cape Town: Penguin Books.

Bell, T. and D. B. Ntsebeza. 2003. *Unfinished Business: South Africa, Apartheid and Truth*. London, New York: Verso.

Ben Hounet, Y. 2017. 'Crime, Intentionality and Blood Money in Algeria and Sudan'. In D. Puccio-Den and Y. Ben Hounet, eds. *Truth, Intentionality and Evidence: Anthropological Approaches to Crime*, 78–92. London: Routledge.

Benda-Beckmann, F. von. 2002. 'Who's Afraid of Legal Pluralism?' *Journal of Legal Pluralism* 47: 37–84.

Biolsi, T. 1995. 'Bringing the Law Back In: Legal Rights and the Regulation of Indian-White Relations on Rosebud Reservation'. *Current Anthropology* 36(4): 543–71.

Bourdieu, P. 1986. 'The Force of Law: Toward a Sociology of the Juridical Field'. *The Hastings Law Journal* 38: 814–55.

Bowen, J. R. 2010. *Can Islam Be French? Pluralism and Pragmatism in a Secularist State*. Princeton Studies in Muslim Politics. Princeton: Princeton University Press.

Chapman, A. R. and H. Van der Merwe, eds. 2008. *Truth and Reconciliation in South Africa: Did the TRC Deliver?* Philadelphia: University of Pennsylvania Press.

Clark, P. 2010. *The Gacaca Courts, Post-Genocide Justice and Reconciliation in Rwanda: Justice Without Lawyers*. Cambridge: Cambridge University Press.

Cole, C. M. 2009. *Performing South Africa's Truth Commission: Stages of Transition*. Bloomington: Indiana University Press.

Cole, J. 1987. *Crossroads: The Politics of Reform and Repression 1976–1986*. Johannesburg: Ravan Press.

Cole, J. 2012. *Behind and Beyond the Eiselen Line*. Cape Town: St. George's Cathedral Crypt Memory and Witness Centre.

Comaroff, J. and J. L. Comaroff. 2007. 'Law and Disorder in the Postcolony'. *Social Anthropology* 15(2): 133–52.

Conley, J. M. and W. M. O'Barr. 1990. *Rules versus Relationships: The Ethnography of Legal Discourse*. Chicago: University Of Chicago Press.

Das, V. 1996. 'Language and Body: Transactions in the Construction of Pain'. *Daedalus* 125(1): 67–91.

Fassin, D. 2013. *Enforcing Order: An Ethnography of Urban Policing*. Cambridge: Polity.

Fassin, D. 2018. *Life: A Critical User's Manual*. Cambridge: Polity Press.

Fassin, D. and E. D'Halluin. 2005. 'The Truth from the Body: Medical Certificates as Ultimate Evidence for Asylum Seekers'. *American Anthropologist*, New Series, 107(4): 597–608.

Feldman, A. 2003. 'Strange Fruit: The South African Truth Commission and the Demonic Economies of Violence'. *Social Analysis* 46(3): 234–65.

Friedman, J. S. 2003. 'Paying for Apartheid'. *The Nation*, 2003.

Goffman, A. 2014. *On the Run: Fugitive Life in an American City*. Fieldwork Encounters and Discoveries. London: The University of Chicago Press.

Goodale, M. 2017. *Anthropology and Law: A Critical Introduction*. New York: New York University Press.

Goodale, M. and S. E. Merry, eds. 2007. *The Practice of Human Rights: Tracking Law Between the Global and the Local*. Cambridge: Cambridge University Press.

Griffiths, A., K. von Benda-Beckmann, and F. von Benda-Beckmann, eds. 2005. *Mobile People, Mobile Law: Expanding Legal Relations in a Contracting World*. Burlington: Ashgate Publishing.

Hastrup, K. 2003. 'Representing the Common Good: The Limit of Legal Language'. In R. A. Wilson and J. P. Mitchell, eds. *Human Rights in Global Perspective: Anthropological Studies of Rights, Claims and Entitlements*, 16–32. London, New York: Routledge.

Hayner, P. B. 2001. *Unspeakable Truths: Confronting State Terror and Atrocity*. London: Routledge.

Henner, P. 2009. *Human Rights and the Alien Tort Statute: Law, History, and Analysis*. Chicago: American Bar Association.

Kesselring, R. 2012. 'Corporate Apartheid-Era Human Rights Violations Before U.S. Courts: Political and Legal Controversies Around Victimhood in Today's South Africa'. *Stichproben: Vienna Journal of African Studies*, Human Rights in Africa, 23: 77–105.

Kesselring, R. 2017. *Bodies of Truth: Law, Memory and Emancipation in Post-Apartheid South Africa*. Stanford Series in Human Rights. Stanford: Stanford University Press.

Madlingozi, T. 2007. 'Good Victim, Bad Victim: Apartheid's Beneficiaries, Victims, and the Struggle for Social Justice'. In K. Van Marle, ed. *Law, Memory, and the Legacy of Apartheid: Ten Years after AZAPO v. President of South Africa*, 107–26. Pretoria: PULP.

Maine, H. S. 1861. *Ancient Law: Its Connection to the History of Early Society*.

Malinowski, B. [1926] 2013. *Crime and Custom in Savage Society*. New Brunswick: Transaction Publishers.

Mamdani, M. 2002. 'Amnesty or Impunity? A Preliminary Critique of the Report of the Truth and Reconciliation Commission of South Africa'. *Diacritics*, Ethics, 32(3/4): 33–59.

Mattei, U. 2003. 'A Theory of Imperial Law: A Study on U.S. Hegemony and the Latin Resistance'. *Indiana Journal of Global Legal Studies* 10(1): 383–448.

Meckled-García, S. and B. Çali, eds. 2005. *The Legalization of Human Rights: Multidisciplinary Approaches*. London, New York: Routledge.

Merry, S. E. 1990. *Getting Justice and Getting Even: Legal Consciousness among Working-Class Americans*. Language and Legal Discourse Series. Chicago: University of Chicago Press.

Merry, S. E. 2006. *Human Rights and Gender Violence: Translating International Law into Local Justice*. Chicago Series in Law and Society. Chicago: University of Chicago Press.

Merry, S. E. 2008. 'Transnational Human Rights and Local Activism: Mapping the Middle'. *American Anthropologist* 108(1): 38–51.

Nader, Laura. 2002. *The Life of the Law: Anthropological Projects*. London: University of California Press.

Ramphele, M. 2009. *Laying Ghosts to Rest: Dilemmas of the Transformation in South Africa*. Cape Town: Tafelberg.

Ross, F. C. 2002. *Bearing Witness: Women and the Truth and Reconciliation Commission*. London: Pluto Press.

Ross, F. C. 2003. 'Using Rights to Measure Wrongs: A Case Study of Method and Moral in the Work of the South African Truth and Reconciliation Commission'. In R. A. Wilson and J. P. Mitchell, eds. *Human Rights in Global Perspective: Anthropological Studies of Rights, Claims and Entitlements*, 163–82. London, New York: Routledge.

Sapignoli, M. 2018. *Hunting Justice: Displacement, Law, and Activism in the Kalahari*. Cambridge, New York: Cambridge University Press.

Sarkin-Hughes, J. 2004. *Carrots and Sticks: The TRC and the South African Amnesty Process*. Antwerp, Oxford: Intersentia.

Scarry, E. 1985. *The Body in Pain: The Making and Unmaking of the World*. Oxford: Oxford University Press.

Schapera, I. [1938] 1994. *A Handbook of Tswana Law and Custom: Compiled for the Bechuanaland Protectorate Administration*. Classics in African Anthropology. London: LIT.

Thompson, E. P. 1977. *Whigs and Hunters: The Origin of the Black Act*. London: Penguin Books.

Van Cleve, N. G. 2016. *Crook County: Racism and Injustice in America's Largest Criminal Court*. Stanford: Stanford University Press.

Wilson, R. A. 2001. *The Politics of Truth and Reconciliation in South Africa: Legitimizing the Post-Apartheid State*. Cambridge: Cambridge University Press.

Wilson, R. A. 2011. *Writing History in International Criminal Trials*. Cambridge: Cambridge University Press.

Wilson, R. A. and J. P. Mitchell, eds. 2003. *Human Rights in Global Perspective: Anthropological Studies of Rights, Claims and Entitlements*. London, New York: Routledge.

Zenker, O. 2014. 'New Law against an Old State: Land Restitution as a Transition to Justice in Post-Apartheid South Africa?' In G. Anders and O. Zenker, eds. *Transition and Justice: Negotiating the Terms of New Beginnings in Africa*, 113–34. Hoboken: Wiley-Blackwell.

CHAPTER 36

ANTI-DISCRIMINATION RULES AND RELIGIOUS MINORITIES IN THE WORKPLACE

KATAYOUN ALIDADI

INTRODUCTION

WHEN the field of law and society started to blossom in the 1960s, drawing from a variety of perspectives and disciplines including anthropology, it debunked many myths that doctrinal legal scholars had sworn by (see generally Calavita 2010). However, over time, the new discipline also gave birth to a body of established knowledge and tenets of its own. Of particular interest to many law and society scholars (and law and anthropology scholars, who can be considered to belong to this group) are the functions and dysfunctions of the law in complex societies, with 'law' referring to 'law in action' rather than black-letter law or 'law on the books'. Law has various functions, but the troika of social control, social change, and dispute resolution are routinely the starting points for describing the law's basic functions (Lippman 2017: 23–8). In contrast, the dysfunctions of law are manifold and hard to grasp; indeed, law has been used throughout history—at times quite consciously—to exclude, stigmatize, and dehumanize groups of people, including ethnic and religious minorities.[1]

In this chapter, I am less interested in the conscious misuse or the misguided use of law than in the counterproductive effects of the (supposedly) proper and admirable use of law and norms. Drawing on earlier research on European anti-discrimination law,[2] I focus on a particular area of legal development involving the challenges of religious minorities in Europe. Through an analysis and critique of case law (i.e. adopting a doctrinal legal approach), I consider how the law on the books affects the social (in)equality of religious minorities in the European workplace.

My method consists of close readings of recent judicial decisions of European supranational courts, comparing recent developments over time and across jurisdictions. By integrating insights from legal practitioners and scholars, my goal is to offer a partial answer to the larger question of how law can (or cannot) address social inequality, and whether law can hope to ameliorate one aspect of social and economic inequality, namely discrimination and exclusion based on religious minority affiliation and practices in Western societies.

Before discussing these cases, I offer a working understanding of what 'social inequality' entails and how law and policy can address this challenge. Certainly, though people are equal in their dignity and are all entitled to the same civil, social, and political human rights, there are many ways in which individuals and groups distinguish themselves. The term 'social inequality' here denotes a problem which can entail exclusion, limited opportunities, and poverty.

Macro-economic policies are a tool to address the problem of social and economic inequality, which is a matter of global concern. The 2030 Agenda, adopted by the United Nations (UN) in 2015, has set forth a number of sustainable development goals (SDGs). Goal 8 involves a mandate for countries to '[p]romote sustained, inclusive and sustainable economic growth, full and productive employment and decent work for all'. In turn, this relates to goals 1 and 10, which respectively aim to 'end poverty in all its forms everywhere' and 'reduce inequality within and among countries'.

Legal rules throughout recent history have also been used to fight poverty and to institute more equal social conditions for people from all walks of life. Some may consider using the blunt tool of the law to address such deep-rooted and persistent inequalities to be short-sighted and naive at best. Others may consider this approach disingenuous, in particular since the disparities and underlying problems which these global goals seek to address are often created in part by legal institutions and the enforcement of norms that work to the benefit of the powerful and resourceful.[3]

Yet equality norms have undeniably mushroomed, particularly in Western liberal democracies such as those in Europe (Alidadi 2012). The proliferation of legal norms under the heading of anti-discrimination law testifies to the widespread and pervasive faith in the power of law to effect social engineering in complex and diverse societies. Indeed, policymakers must at least nominally believe in the relevance and effectiveness of law to address social inequalities and inequities; otherwise, adopting law for that purpose and, *a fortiori*, continuing to elaborate on those norms would be futile. We can also assume that judges, legal advocates, and the general public have a level of trust in the workings of human rights and anti-discrimination law; if they did not, these norms would lie dormant (as merely law on the books) instead of being the site of social, political, and legal struggle.

Rather than investigating how legal norms infiltrate the social arena more directly (in the tradition of Sally Falk Moore's [1973] 'semi-autonomous social field', this chapter looks at how legal norms are defined and redefined by actors in legal fora—in particular courts, which are presented with particular time- and place-sensitive disputes in need of resolution. In the process, the abstract language of European directives and national legislation, which ban 'direct' and 'indirect' religious 'discrimination' is given a more concrete and accessible meaning. Consider, for instance, a decision determining that the dismissal of a female employee for donning a headscarf in the workplace amounts to a form of discrimination, or that an employer who refuses to provide prayer space is not discriminating if the costs would be excessive. The ensuing semi-abstract norms derived from case law can then form guidelines for dealing with future tensions, controversies, and disputes. However, because they are rooted in specific facts, they can hardly *dictate* the outcome. Thus, the examples above cannot provide a categorical answer to the question whether an employee can be dismissed for refusing to work on the Sabbath. The abstract European norms found in regulations and directives are made more concrete through case law at the domestic and European level. This occurs irrespective of whether the legal system recognizes a formal system of precedent as in common law jurisdictions (which in Europe constitute the notable minority). To be sure, norms need to be transmitted and adopted on the 'shop floor of social life' (Griffiths 1999), and the content of those norms and our understanding of them as they evolve are shaped by the intermediary role of judicial bodies faced with concrete disputes. The facts of these disputes, which are specific and contextual in nature, have the power to shape our current and future understanding of legal norms, all the more when decisions are reported widely through various media.

I use European anti-discrimination law, in particular the abstract legal rule that prohibits 'discrimination' on the basis of 'religion or belief' in Europe, as a case-study to illustrate how such an abstract rule, divorced from time and space, can be made understandable in current-day situations. But I also use this case to show how rules transform as they travel from law on the books through judicial fora to become 'semi-abstract'. By 'semi-abstract', I mean that the rules become more understandable and accessible in a defined context where disputes similar to the ones subject to the judicial decision could reoccur. Abstract norms seeking to ameliorate social inequality leave room—sometimes substantial room—for alternative understandings; the specific facts and circumstances of disputes offer appropriate and relevant contexts and reasons for constructing meaningful understandings of those general norms. The ensuing understandings of norms are not neutral; they are rather products of policy and ideology, which explains why certain legal actors prefer some understandings over others.

To be sure, this reflects a legal realist perspective, which sees the judge not as an umpire but as a policymaker in his or her own right (Lippman 2017: 6).[4] I argue that the semi-abstract is an appropriate and necessary frame of analysis for law and society and legal anthropology scholars who want to understand how norms travel from their enactment in parliaments down to the shop floor of social life and how law in action is negotiated and shaped by law on the books *as interpreted* by judicial decision-makers. This means that social scientists who engage in the analysis of law as a social institution in society stand to gain much from understanding developments in jurisprudence, which reflect current-day and developing tensions on the ground.

As an illustration, this chapter looks at recent European judicial responses to the wearing of religious dress in the workplace, tracing developments from Brussels (the seat of the European Commission, the only European organ able to initiate EU legislation) to Strasbourg (the European Court of Human Rights) to Luxemburg (the Court of Justice of the European Union) and back again to Brussels (the EU/European Commission). In keeping with the volume's aims, this chapter seeks to be accessible to a broad spectrum of readers, whether or not trained in law (and anthropology). For those not familiar with European anti-discrimination law, the chapter offers a brief introduction. Before looking at this case-study, I consider the archetypical role of judges in the transformation of legal norms from abstract to semi-abstract through judgments and opinions.

Judges and semi-abstract norms

One key challenge presented by Europe's changing demographic landscape involves the management of diversity, in particular ethno-religious diversity. While immigration and (minority) religion should not be conflated, religious diversity is to an important extent the effect of relatively recent immigration, which has brought Islam to the fore of the discussion. In the minds of policymakers, politicians, voters, and other stakeholders, Muslims have become *the* minority in Europe. Since the juridification of diversity challenges, judges (both national and European) are also being confronted with the issue of accommodating religion in areas such as public or private services, education, health, and employment (see generally Alidadi and Foblets 2016).

The judiciary in Europe has repeatedly been confronted with cases involving Muslim female employees who want to wear a headscarf on the job while their employers or co-workers object. Employers may be reticent or downright opposed to allowing a veiled or otherwise 'visibly religious' employee to come into contact with customers (who in turn may infer other affiliations, beliefs, or practices because of the symbolization of the visible religious dress). With regard to the workplace, such 'headscarf cases' have become somewhat of an epitome of misunderstanding and entrenched positioning, with each EU country, the Court of Justice of the European Union (CJEU), and the European Court of Human Rights (ECtHR) chiming in with what they see as the appropriate answer (or rather, the appropriate answer in a given context).

For judges,[5] one of these tools or instruments is (European) anti-discrimination law. The existence of Europe-wide norms in such sensitive areas, which touch on national identity and minority relations, is a testament to the rise and importance of harmonized formal norms across the continent. However, the process of legal-formal harmonization in this area has not necessarily led to a cohesive approach to questions of religious accommodation on the ground in the European workplace. Thus, despite the same (abstract) Europe-wide norms being implemented (often in the same way) into domestic anti-discrimination statutes in the twenty-eight (now twenty-seven) Member States, the application of those norms within the judicial sphere and the societal sphere remain considerably divergent (see Alidadi 2017c). In such cases, the CJEU's role is to provide guidance and a greater level of harmonization. Such harmonization necessitates a clearer understanding of what the abstract norms signify in conflict situations. In other words, more concrete norms are needed to move beyond formal harmonization and towards a more meaningful application of common norms which seek to protect and include people belonging to religious minorities.

Law and social inequality: European judicial responses to the wearing of religious dress in the workplace

European 'Equality Law'

Since the entry into force of the Lisbon Treaty on 1 December 2009, the EU has had a legally binding Charter of Fundamental Rights—one which can be enforced in court. The Lisbon Treaty sought to strengthen respect for fundamental rights across the EU and also anticipated the EU's accession to the European Convention on Human Rights (ECHR) (which would have made decisions of the CJEU subject to ECtHR review), which was seen as 'a major step forward towards a stronger and more coherent system of fundamental rights protection' (see Article 6(2) of the Treaty on European Union (TEU); Polakiewicz 2015).

However, despite lengthy negotiations and general expectations, the EU never acceded to the ECHR, which explains today's complex judicial architecture, characterized in part by the interplay between two 'supranational' courts. There is the ECtHR, with its established (though much criticized) freedom of religion/anti-discrimination jurisprudence,[6] and there is the CJEU, which has entered as a relatively new player in the fundamental rights area. The CJEU (previously called the European Court of Justice) is one of the seven EU institutions[7] and the highest court in the European Union for issues related to European law.

When it comes to law and religion cases, scholars and advocates who have looked to the ECtHR to issue progressive, human rights-bolstering rulings consider many of its past cases to be missed opportunities. Could it be that the CJEU, by insisting on its authority as the final arbiter of human rights cases under European law, may strengthen the protection of fundamental rights, including the right to equal treatment irrespective of one's religion or belief? Could the CJEU be the trailblazing judicial player that human rights advocates in Europe have been hoping for?

Two workplace headscarf disputes became important test cases in 2017. *Achbita v G4S* and *Bougnaoui v Micropole Univers*[8] involved two Muslim female employees who wanted to wear a headscarf in their respective workplaces in Belgium and France. These cases came before the CJEU some seventeen years after the adoption of the EU

Employment Equality Directive (EED),[9] which prohibited discrimination in the area of employment on various grounds, including 'religion or belief'. More particularly, the Directive prohibits direct and indirect forms of discrimination, harassment, and instruction to discriminate in the area of employment and occupation in both public and private sectors.

'Direct discrimination' occurs when one person is treated less favourably than another on the basis of one of the protected characteristics, while 'indirect discrimination' means 'an apparently neutral provision, criterion or practice' which places persons with such a protected characteristic at a particular disadvantage compared with others (Article 2.2(a) and (b) EED). In 2014, the European Commission explicitly acknowledged the difficulties surrounding the concept of indirect discrimination both in terms of implementation and application, stating:

> The concept of indirect discrimination is complex and many Member States had initial difficulties in transposing it correctly. It is now enshrined in law, but its application in practice remains a challenge. To illustrate the problem, some Member States report that concerns have been expressed about the lack of clarity or lack of understanding of the concept of indirect discrimination in national courts. Other Member States point out that they do not yet have any case-law providing interpretation of indirect discrimination.[10]

The distinction would go on to play a key role in the first two test cases involving religious discrimination in the European workplace.

The Directive covers four grounds—religion or belief, disability, age, and sexual orientation—and this 'with a view to putting into effect in the Member States the principle of equal treatment' (Article 1 EED (Purpose)). Of these various grounds, religion or belief has led to a surprisingly modest amount of CJEU case law, and only very recently.[11]

The stretch of time between the adoption of these abstract norms and their remaking into semi-abstract norms at the transnational level has to do with the procedural rules for bringing cases before supranational courts as well as the hesitation of lower domestic courts to refer sensitive questions to the CJEU for a preliminary ruling.[12]

Much anticipation surrounded the twin cases of *Achbita* and *Bougnaoui*,[13] decided by the CJEU on 14 March 2017. The two Advocate General opinions on the *Achbita* and *Bougnaoui* cases revealed the differences in approach to reading the Directive's abstract anti-discrimination norms, presenting the CJEU with a difficult task.[14]

Still, there was a sense of hope among a number of scholars and advocates[15] who anticipated that the CJEU would deliver progressive rulings that incorporated its solid equality law approach into the area of religious diversity in the workplace. A closer look at the Court's approach shows, however, that this expectation did not come to fruition, at least not in these two vanguard cases. Instead, the CJEU[16] adopted a much more modest approach and reading of the abstract norms, one which enabled the percolation of the ECtHR's human rights jurisprudential approaches and their various shortcomings into European equality law.

Achbita *and* Bougnaoui *as Illustrative of a Broader Law-and-Religion Approach in* Europe*'s Overlapping Judicial System*

In *Achbita v G4S*, a female Belgian receptionist of Moroccan descent employed by the company G4S wanted to wear a headscarf to the worksite she was outsourced to.[17] Prior to this, she had been working without a headscarf for some years (she would take off her headscarf when she arrived at work). The company argued there had been an 'unwritten rule' that banned headscarves before it implemented a written policy of neutrality, which the company adopted the *day after* Ms Achbita was dismissed. The 'neutrality policy' prohibited employees from wearing any visible signs of 'political, philosophical or religious affiliation'. In Belgium and elsewhere, such neutrality policies—a spillover from the public sector, where they are now on the decline—have mushroomed in the private sector in recent years. Image-based arguments have been mobilized as arguments for restrictive dress policies, at times in response to the prejudices of employers, customers, or the larger society.

Bougnaoui v Micropole Univers concerned a French design engineer who was dismissed by her employer when she refused to take off her headscarf when visiting corporate clients. In this case, there had been a complaint from a client, similar to the *Achbita* case, where there were also indications that the client to whom she was outsourced was opposed to headscarves being worn on the worksite. In *Bougnaoui*, the employer argued that the wearing of a veil had 'embarrassed a number of its employees' and that its requirement for staff to remove the headscarf should be viewed as a 'genuine occupational requirement' under Article 4(1) of Directive 2000/78.

These cases made their way through the domestic legal systems of Belgium and France and ended up being contested before the highest national courts. The Belgian and French cassation courts asked the CJEU whether a refusal to accommodate constitutes direct discrimination on the basis of religion. In particular, the Belgian *Cour de cassation* posed the question to the CJEU as such:

Can article 2.2.a [of the EED] be interpreted to mean that the prohibition for a Muslim to wear the headscarf at work does not imply any direct discrimination when the rule forbids all workers to wear any visible symbol expressing their political, philosophical or religious beliefs?

The question formulated by the French *Cour de cassation* was even more focused on the issue of a 'genuine and determining occupational' requirement (as this would legitimize any direct discrimination). It asked whether:

Article 4 § 1 of the Directive 2000/78 needs to be interpreted to mean that banning the headscarf because of the wish of a customer of an IT company to not have services performed by a staff member, with an engineering diploma, does not constitute a genuine and determining occupational requirement.

Prior to addressing these requests for preliminary rulings, the CJEU solicited non-binding Advocate General opinions. In the *Achbita* case, the German Advocate General (AG) Juliane Kokott issued the opinion. Her answer to whether there is direct discrimination in the Belgian case was a clear 'no'. In contrast, the British AG Eleanor Sharpston opined that there was direct discrimination in the French case.[18]

In AG Kokott's opinion, company neutrality policies such as the one adopted by the Belgian employer G4S subsequent to the employee headscarf dispute 'cannot properly be classified as constituting direct discrimination' since '[t]here is nothing in the present case to indicate that an individual was "treated less favourably"' (paragraphs 47–48). What's more, AG Kokott went (much) further by arguing that such a ban constitutes 'a genuine and determining occupational requirement' (paragraph 84).[19] This is because, in her opinion, it is clear that religion should be characterized as a personal 'choice'. In this way, religion or belief as discrimination grounds are to be separated from other, immutable discrimination grounds like ethnicity, sexual orientation, and sex. Religion or belief is thus less worthy of protection because people can change their beliefs and religious practices. Kokott's approach advocated a significant erosion of anti-discrimination protection for religious employees and a break from the CJEU's equality rights jurisprudence with regard to the other grounds under the EED, for which a broad understanding of the concept of direct discrimination had previously been applied.[20]

For instance, in the seminal *Feryn* case,[21] the CJEU found direct discrimination on grounds of race or ethnicity. The defendant, NV Firma Feryn, was a Belgian company specializing in the sale and installation of garage gates. The company had vacancies for the employees that installed such gates on customers' properties. During an interview with a Flemish newspaper (titled 'Customers don't want Moroccans'), the CEO explained that these vacancies were not being filled because he would not recruit persons of Moroccan origin (Fransen 2005). He confirmed on Belgian national television that he needed to take into account his customers' attitudes: people who wanted such security gates installed did not want to have Moroccans coming near their homes. According to the Belgian equality body Unia, which took up the case, NV Firma Feryn had clearly discriminated against an ethnic group, even if there was no specific victim; by proclaiming that 'Moroccans would not be hired', it was highly unlikely that job applicants of Moroccan descent would apply for the open posts. The CJEU, responding to a number of prejudicial questions from the Belgian labour tribunal, agreed with this stance, thereby confirming the concept of 'discrimination by declaration' under EU Directive 2000/43. The CJEU thus recognized that employers can *directly* discriminate by declaration and held that (real or implied) discriminatory preferences of customers are no justification for discriminating against (future) employees. Indeed, when an employer declares publicly that it will not recruit employees of a certain ethnic or racial origin, such (directly discriminatory) statements are likely to strongly discourage certain candidates from applying, thereby substantially hindering access to the labour market.

When it comes to the question of legitimacy of religious dress restrictions adopted by employers, this CJEU approach would be highly desirable in creating a more employee-protective and minority-inclusive approach. In particular, this approach could lead to the delegitimization of so-called neutrality policies, which private companies use to signal that visibly religious employees need not apply.[22]

In contrast, in her opinion regarding *Bougnaoui v Micropole SA*, AG Sharpston considered the dismissal of the Muslim design engineer for wearing a headscarf to constitute direct discrimination based on religion. In her opinion, she writes, 'Does the prohibition laid down by Directive 2000/78 extend not only to the religion or belief of an employee but also to manifestations of that religion or belief? In my view, it does' (paragraphs 85–6).

Sharpston reasoned that the protection given by EU law against direct discrimination is stronger than under the ECHR, which does not have the direct-indirect discrimination dichotomy (paragraph 63). In comparison, AG Kokott had argued that any exclusion based on religious dress could not amount to *direct* discrimination because the employee has a 'choice' to alter religious practices. AG Kokott's opinion distinguishes 'modes of conduct based on a subjective decision or conviction' (i.e. the decision to wear a form of religious dress) from 'individuals' immutable physical features or personal characteristics—such as gender, age, or sexual orientation' (paragraphs 44–5, references omitted).

On 14 March 2017, the CJEU rejected the argument that private company neutrality policies constitute *direct* discrimination and held that 'the desire to display, in relations with both public and private sector customers, a policy of political, philosophical or religious neutrality must be considered legitimate'.[23] Here it followed AG Kokott's advice in her *Achbita* opinion. However, the CJEU did require certain conditions to be met before the direct discrimination claim can be dismissed. For instance, a specific ban on headscarves would constitute direct discrimination and so would a ban focused *solely* on religious symbols. Strangely, the Court held that if the ban were to cover political and philosophical symbols as well, the direct discrimination would evaporate.

Further, the Court considered the justification of neutrality policies to be *indirect* distinctions and agreed that under certain conditions (e.g. consistent and systematic application limited to employees who come into contact with customers) policies would pass muster.

It should be noted that the two CJEU decisions are awkwardly inconsistent in some respects, for instance with regard to the question whether it can be legitimate for employers to follow customer preferences.[24] In *Bougnaoui*, the CJEU rejected the argument that upholding customer wishes can be a legitimate aim for restricting religious dress. Rather, domestic courts can only consider requirements to be legitimate based on the *nature* of the occupational activities concerned or the *context* in which they are carried out. Yet in *Achbita*, where the dismissal of the outsourced receptionist was clearly motivated by client preferences, the CJEU held that 'the desire to display, in relations with both public and private sector customers, a policy of political, philosophical or religious neutrality must be considered legitimate' by domestic courts. I have argued elsewhere that so-called neutrality policies, which invoke the criterion of 'neutrality' as grounds for banning all religious, philosophical, and even political expressions in the workplace, form a major cause of concern for equal employment. These policies create formidable obstacles to the socioeconomic integration of religious minorities and should be considered to constitute direct discrimination on the basis of religion or belief, as the widespread exclusionary effect of such policies contradicts the entire rationale underpinning anti-discrimination law.[25] However, national courts in certain Member States have condoned such company policies. Now, the CJEU has provided legitimacy to such policies as well. A silver lining is that the CJEU advanced a limited form of reasonable accommodation (offering alternative, back-office positions instead of dismissal), but this may be considered *obiter dicta* and is bound to disappear from purview. Also, the effect—routing religiously visible employees to back-office positions[26]—can hardly be considered desirable in light of the aim of workplace inclusion and participation.

Lucy Vickers has argued that with the *Achbita* and *Bougnaoui* decisions, the protection of religious diversity in the European workplace took 'two steps back' (Vickers 2017). Vickers notes that while the 'the human rights framework for the protection of religion and belief is well established, the level of protection is weak, with low levels of scrutiny applied by the Court in Strasbourg'. This is particularly the case for the protection of religious diversity in the workplace. Vickers elaborates on various shortcomings of the ECtHR doctrinal framework, the most significant being the use of a wide margin of appreciation, which 'results in limited protection for religious minorities'. With *Achbita* and *Bougnaoui*, these shortcomings have now 'infiltrated' European equality law:

> These shortcomings are particularly significant when religious claims are viewed from the perspective of equality. For example, as noted above, in the context of equality law, the idea that a characteristic is chosen, or that the person discriminated against can chose to avoid the discrimination by choosing to resign would not be accepted. More significantly, in its use of the margin of appreciation doctrine, the human rights approach conflicts most directly with an approach based on equality (ibid.).

Instead of the progressive and inclusive approach towards religious diversity that advocates had hoped for and which could have been achieved by duly incorporating equality law standards into the domain of religion or belief discrimination, the CJEU decisions constitute the solidification of a flawed and ineffective approach towards the challenges of religious diversity in the workplace. As Vickers notes, 'incorporating human rights concepts into the equality framework, can lead to limited protection for religious minorities at work'.[27]

And back to Brussels: from judicial semi-abstract norms to legislative abstract norms?

European equality law has developed through a dynamic interplay of judicial decisions and legislative instruments. From the perspective of the European Commission, the

Employment Equality Directive was meant to be the starting point for the development of non-discrimination law in the EU, not its conclusion.

Following calls for the expansion of EU law protection against discrimination by the European Parliament and various civil society actors as well as an elaborate consultation process,[28] the European Commission submitted a 'Proposal for a Council Directive on Implementing Equal Treatment Between Persons Irrespective of Religion or Belief, Disability, Age or Sexual Orientation' on 2 June 2008.[29] Accordingly, the aim of the proposed 'horizontal directive'—termed as such because it would address discrimination on a number of grounds in various areas of social life—was to 'supplement' and 'complete' the protection against discrimination under EU law beyond the areas of employment and vocational training for the same five grounds covered by the EED of 2000. The scope of the horizontal directive was to be the same as that of the Racial Equality Directive,[30] namely applying to the areas of (a) social protection, including social security and healthcare; (b) social advantages; (c) education; and (d) access to and supply of goods and other services which are available to the public, including housing (Article 3).[31]

Clearly, some Member States already provided for protection in all or some of these areas outside of employment and vocational training, but a 2006 commissioned study showed that there was much divergence and 'a good deal of variety between countries as to the degree and nature of the protection'.[32] The horizontal directive was also seen as one way to apply the 2006 UN Convention on the Rights of Persons with Disabilities, which had been signed by (most) Member States and the European Community itself. There had been some calls for a disability-themed directive, but overall stakeholders and the European Parliament favoured a broader approach.[33] Still, the focus on disability in the proposed horizontal directive was obvious, as most articles addressed this issue in particular, for example, the much-discussed Article 4 regarding anticipatory access to various services such as transportation and housing.

Likewise, most of the debate—which is bound to continue as the proposal was never adopted—has centred around provisions related to disability (and age), even if it is claimed that support for expanding protection on that ground is greatest (Waddington 2011). This is in part because the proposed directive seeks to go furthest, and is most ambitious, in the area of disability. The disability-centred debate has taken place both at the level of EU institutions, i.e. the European Parliament, the European Economic and Social Committee, and the Council of Ministers, as well as in civil society and academia (ibid.). To a lesser extent, the debate has involved age, sexual orientation, and—perhaps least of all—religion or belief. Indeed, the relevant provisions of the proposed horizontal directive remained too modest and limited in purpose with regard to protection on the ground of religion or belief. In particular, the right to reasonable accommodation and the right to appropriate modifications or adjustments to allow for access to goods, services, and facilities were only foreseen for persons with disabilities (Article 4) and not on the ground of religion or belief. Thus, the horizontal directive, by cementing differences between the protection of various grounds, also marked a missed opportunity to adequately address protection on the ground of religion or belief. Furthermore, it was to be expected that the EU enlargement and the various social, economic, and political crises in which the EU finds itself would make the adoption of the horizontal directive under the conditions of Article 19 of the Treaty on the Functioning of the European Union (TFEU) (requiring unanimity in the Council) difficult, if not impossible.[34]

Keeping the political reality in mind, and the fact that the proposed directive will at least in the foreseeable future not be adopted for reasons wholly unrelated to the area of religion or belief in society, not much development can be expected from the European legislation for the protection of religious diversity. Rather, any legal progress for the time being is bound to be jurisprudential as opposed to coming through explicit legislative instruments. The same political factors which prevent legislative advances in the area of equality law, however, also play an—albeit more nuanced—role in judicial considerations and reasoning.

Conclusion

To refer back to the Employment Equality Directive of 2000, it must be acknowledged that its passage came about in a time of political and economic momentum.[35] The implementation of this Directive was a long and arduous process, during which the European Commission launched infringement proceedings against twenty-five Member States.[36] Once all European Member States had satisfactorily implemented the Directive into their national laws and policies, the focus appropriately shifted from norm-setting to the practical implementation of equal protection standards. Yet it is well known that the application of the shared norms in domestic case law has not been enforced in a harmonized manner—far from it.

The emergence of two sets of fundamental rights standards in Europe has not significantly raised the standards for equal treatment or ameliorated social inequality in Europe. The religious discrimination norms in the case law of the CJEU do not significantly diverge from or make progress on the standards already established in ECtHR jurisprudence.[37] But many questions remain and close scrutiny is needed to track the interaction and interplay of the supranational court decisions (see e.g. Davies and Avbelj 2018). This is also what lawyers and advocates do in order to assess which forum holds the most promise at any given time.

Law and society scholars are interested in the law in action. Jurisprudential developments, such as the case-study discussed in this chapter, make abstract norms—the law on the books—more tangible and accessible to the non-legal practitioner. Case law applies general rules to specific fact situations that reflect present-day challenges in the field. Judicial interpretations can bolster progressive human rights protections, but they can also condone undesirable developments—such as the rise of company neutrality policies—or cause confusion, which affects the employment opportunities of religious minorities without the mediation of any legislature.

The case-studies presented in this chapter involved two Muslim women living in Belgium and France, respectively, who faced employment sanctions because they wore headscarves. Perhaps one day the issue of the headscarf will be a non-issue in Europe, but as it stands cases such as *Achbita* and *Bougnaoui* illustrate the challenge that exists on the ground and reveal the possible approaches courts can take based on the law on the books. As the first cases in which the CJEU elaborated on the prohibition of—direct and indirect—discrimination on the basis of religion or belief in the European workplace, *Achbita* and *Bougnaoui* will be the start of more significant development of anti-discrimination law in Europe. It is crucial from a law and society viewpoint to take adequate stock of jurisprudential developments, which apply and guide abstract legal rules in a certain direction. The application of abstract legal rules should (aim to) ameliorate a societal problem such as religious discrimination or social inequality, yet sometimes it falls short. Judicial decisions and social attitudes reveal differing levels of protection for religious minorities in the workplace across Europe, and their respective contradictions and shortcomings merit close attention not only from legal researchers but also from law and society scholars who are interested in the operation of norms on the ground. If law and society scholars undertake such an endeavour in their future research, it will bolster the interdisciplinary nature of the discipline and in turn benefit the advancement of equality law.

Acknowledgements

Many thanks to Professor Marie-Claire Foblets for encouraging me to write this chapter, linking my doctoral research on reasonable accommodation on the basis of religion and belief with the larger question of how law can ameliorate the social inequality of vulnerable minorities. I am very grateful for the comments and suggestions from the editors and reviewers, which greatly benefited the chapter.

Notes

1. Examples abound. Lippman (2017: 26–7) refers to, inter alia, the early history of Native Americans in the United States, which reflects then pervasive biases and prejudices, and the use of courts as 'conscious instruments of repression' in Nazi Germany. Other examples are the use of law to institute apartheid in South Africa and the internment camps for Japanese at the end of the Second World War in the United States.
2. For a more in-depth analysis related to religion in the European workplace, focusing on religious dress and other religious practices such as prayer in the workplace and time off to observe religious holidays, see Alidadi (2017a).
3. See generally the landmark article by Marc Galanter (1974).
4. Referring to Oliver Wendell Holmes's (1897: 457) practical definition that law constitutes '[t]he prophecies of what the courts will do in fact, and nothing more pretentious'.

5. Anti-discrimination statutes obviously also serve as tools for other stakeholders (e.g. advocacy organizations and political parties); however, these applications of norms are embedded in a societal context. Depending on the position of these stakeholders, the rules do not provide the basis for formal legal argument and reasoning but rather for arguments that involve ethical considerations. The same norms thus serve different purposes in legal fora than they do in society at large. Importantly, courts are limited in their scope of action and can only address the disputes that are presented to them, while other stakeholders can also utilize the law proactively and in multifaceted ways.
6. Landmark law and religion cases include *Sahin v Turkey*, *Kokkinakis v Greece*, *Lautsi v Italy*, *Eweida v the UK*, *S.A.S. v France*, etc. The Council of Europe, of which the ECtHR in Strasbourg (hence 'the Strasbourg court') is the flagship institution, is a leading international human rights organization founded in 1949. It currently has forty-seven member states, including all twenty-eight (now twenty-seven) EU Member States, but also Turkey and transcontinental states such as Russia, Armenia, and Georgia. Thus, the 'European' state under Art. 4 of the Council of Europe Statute is interpreted very broadly. The Council of Europe seeks to uphold democracy, human rights, and the rule of law in Europe and is a separate institution from the EU, which has its roots in post-Second World War economic cooperation between the devastated countries in Central Europe but which has grown to become a powerful and encompassing socioeconomic and political entity and a world player.
7. These principal decision-making bodies of the EU are listed in Art. 13 TEU: besides the CJEU, these are the European Parliament, the European Council, the Council of the European Union, the European Commission, the European Central Bank, and the Court of Auditors.
8. *Achbita and Centrum voor Gelijkheid van kansen en voor racismebestrijding v G4S Secure Solutions NV*, (Judgment) [2017] ECLI:EU:C:2017:203 (hereafter *Achbita v G4S*) and *Bougnaoui and Association de défense des droits de l'homme (ADDH) v Micropole SA*, (Judgment) [2017] ECLI:EU:C:2017:204 (hereafter *Bougnaoui v Micropole SA*), both of 14 March 2017.
9. Council Directive 2000/78 establishing a general framework for equal treatment in employment and occupation [2000] OJ L 16/22.
10. Commission, 'Joint Report on the application of Council Directive 2000/43/EC of 29 June 2000 implementing the principle of equal treatment between persons irrespective of racial or ethnic origin (Racial Equality Directive) and of Council Directive 2000/78/EC of 27 November 2000 establishing a general framework for equal treatment in employment and occupation (Employment Equality Directive)' COM (2014) 2 final, 8.
11. CJEU cases on religion in the workplace since *Achbita* and *Bougnaoui* include *IR v JQ* [2018] ECLI:EU:C:2018:696; *Vera Egenberger v Evangelisches Werk für Diakonie und Entwicklung e.V* [2018] ECLI:EU:C:2018:257; and *Cresco Investigation GmbH v Markus Achatzi* [2019] ECLI:EU:C:2019:43. Before 2017, there had been no CJEU cases regarding the ground of religion or belief under the EED. In contrast, the other discrimination grounds, in particular the ground of age, had already been the topic of numerous decisions. Among these, CJEU discrimination cases on the grounds of sexual orientation, disability, and racial or ethnic origin were less recurrent than age-related cases.
12. Lower domestic courts only need refer such questions to the CJEU for preliminary rulings if the court considers it 'necessary to enable it to give judgment'. This is different for 'a court of tribunal of a member State against whose decisions there is not judicial remedy

under national law'; those courts 'shall bring the matter ' before the CJEU. See Art. 267 TFEU. Prior to *Achbita*, the Belgian equal treatment body Unia (formerly called CEOOR/ Interfederal Centre for Equal Opportunities) had on a number of occasions requested Belgian labour tribunals to refer questions of European law to the CJEU on the issue of religious discrimination, but the courts found this to be 'unnecessary' in order to resolve the case at hand. For instance, on the Belgian HEMA case involving a temp worker fired for wearing a headscarf on the job, see Tongeren Labour Court [2013] AR 11/2142/A. Local courts can thus form a barrier which prevents pan-European questions that implicate different interpretations of directives from reaching the CJEU.

13. It is worthwhile to note that since 1 July 2018, as an effect of new European data protection law (the GDPR) and to guarantee anonymity for litigants, the CJEU in general no longer uses the names of natural persons in case names except 'in the event of an express request from a party or if the particular circumstances of the case so justify'. (Going forward, in all requests for preliminary rulings brought after 1 July 2018, the court said it will 'replace, in all its public documents, the name of natural persons involved in the case by initials'. See B. Leonard, 'Top EU Court Embraces Anonymity for Litigants', available at <https://www.courthousenews.com/top-eu-court-embraces-anonymity-for-litigants/> accessed 23 May 2020). The effects of this anonymization are interesting to ponder. They may have the incidental effect of making cases involving individuals less compelling, in contrast to Anglo-American countries, where litigants' names are not anonymized (e.g. in the United States, where litigants' names mark landmark civil rights decisions by the Supreme Court such as *Brown v Board of Education* and *Obergefell v Hodges*).
14. These AG opinions are not binding, but the CJEU gives due weight to them and often engages with the reasoning in depth.
15. This assessment is significant since legal advocates and strategists have some leeway in how they frame and present cases so as to bring them before a particular supranational court. For instance, a conflict over a headscarf in the workplace can be framed as a violation of religious freedom case, but it can just as well be framed as a religious discrimination case. In the *Achbita* and *Bougnaoui* cases, attorneys for the parties saw their chances before the CJEU as more promising.
16. The CJEU had rejected an institutional link between the EU and the ECHR in 2014, see Alidadi and Foblets (2016).
17. This part is adapted from Alidadi (2017a: 88ff.).
18. *Achbita v G4S*, (Opinion of Advocate General J. Kokott) [2016] ECLI:EU:C:2016:382; *Bougnaoui v Micropole SA*, (Opinion of Advocate General E. Sharpston) [2016] ECLI:EU:C:2016:553. For a more elaborate analysis of these opinions, see Alidadi (2017b).
19. See para. 94: 'In such a case, a policy of neutrality is absolutely crucial, not only because of the variety of customers served by G4S, but also because of the special nature of the work which G4S employees do in providing those services, which is characterised by constant face-to-face contact with external individuals and has a defining impact not only on the image of G4S itself but also and primarily on the public image of its customers.' However, AG Kokott also does not support the back-rooming of employees. Together, these views entail very widespread employment exclusion for Muslim women who wear a headscarf and other religiously visible employees.
20. Unsurprisingly, then, AG Kokott argues against the extension of a de facto duty to reasonably accommodate on the basis of religion or belief.

21. *Centrum voor gelijkheid van kansen en voor racismebestrijding v Firma Feryn NV* [2008] ECLI:EU:C:2008:397.
22. For a more elaborate argument, see Alidadi (2017a: 157ff.).
23. *Achbita v G4S* and *Bougnaoui v Micropole SA*, para. 37.
24. In contrast, see the *Feryn* case, where the answer was a clear no in the case of ethnic/racial discrimination.
25. See Alidadi (2017a: 157ff.).
26. In *Achbita*, the CJEU reasoned that the employer (G4S) should have explored alternative employment positions for Ms Achbita which would not have required visual contact with customers before deciding to dismiss her. On the front-office/back-office dilemma, see Alidadi (2013).
27. Ibid. Vickers refers to CJEU fundamental rights cases where a 'margin of discretion' is adopted, but notes that 'the CJEU has been less deferential to national context in respect of other equality grounds such as sex or race discrimination'.
28. Commission, 'Explanatory memorandum' COM (2008) 426 final, 3.
29. Commission, 'Proposal for a Council Directive on Implementing Equal Treatment Between Persons Irrespective of Religion or Belief, Disability, Age or Sexual Orientation and Explanatory Memorandum' COM (2008) 426, available at <http://eur-lex.europa.eu/LexUriServ/LexUriServ.do?uri=COM:2008:0426:FIN:EN:PDF> accessed 11 May 2020; see also Commission of the European Communities, 'Commission Staff Working Document Accompanying the Proposal for a Council Directive on Implementing Equal Treatment Between Persons Irrespective of Religion or Belief, Disability, Age or Sexual Orientation', SEC (2008) 2180, 2181, available at <http://register.consilium.europa.eu/pdf/en/08/st11/st11531-ad01.en08.pdf> accessed 11 May 2020.
30. Council Directive 2000/43/EC of 29 June 2000 implementing the principle of equal treatment between persons irrespective of racial or ethnic origin [2000] OJ L 180, 22; on the other hand, the scope of protection from sex discrimination under Directive 2004/113/EC is less extensive, as it does not cover education.
31. Perhaps surprisingly, this article regarding material scope (identical to that of the Racial Equality Directive) has proven to be controversial. Still, the consultation process preceding the horizontal directive proposal made this controversy predictable: 'The responses to the consultation highlighted concerns about how a new Directive would deal with a number of sensitive areas and also revealed misunderstandings about the limits or extent of Community competence.' See Commission, 'Explanatory memorandum' COM (2008) 426 final, 4.
32. Available at <https://eur-lex.europa.eu/legal-content/EN/ALL/?uri=CELEX:52008DC0225R(01)> accessed 22 May 2020.
33. See ILGA and ENAR position statement, 'Why does the European Commission need to propose a Horizontal Directive on the principle of equal treatment? The Case for a Horizontal Anti-Discrimination Directive', available at <http://www.ilga-europe.gov> accessed 30 March 2020.
34. Lisa Waddington has noted, 'While the proposal has been much debated and amended by the Council in the meantime, there is little sign that the Member States are any nearer to agreeing on a final text and adopting a new directive. Agreement is vital, given that the relevant decision-making procedure requires unanimity in the Council. Indeed, all the signs are that, owing to the lack of enthusiasm among some Member States, and absolute

opposition by others, the proposal will not be adopted' (Waddington 2011: 163–4, 182). Isabelle Rorive (2009: 2696) has similarly noted, 'To be adopted, unanimity within the Council is required [under Art. 19 TFEU], and the current political situation in Europe is much less favorable to strengthening anti-discrimination law than it was in 2000.'

35. One of the push factors was the election of the extreme right party of Jörg Haider in Austria.
36. See COM (2014) 2 final, 8.
37. See *Achbita v G4S* and *Bougnaoui v Micropole SA*.

References

Alidadi, K. 2012. 'Reasonable Accommodations for Religion and Belief: Adding Value to Article 9 ECHR and the European Union's Anti-discrimination Approach to Employment?'. *European Law Review* 37(6): 693–715.

Alidadi, K. 2013. 'Out of Sight, Out of Mind? Implications of Routing Religiously Dressed Employees Away from Front-office Positions in Europe'. *Quaderni di Diritto e Politica Ecclesiastica* 16(1): 87–106.

Alidadi, K. 2017a. *Religion, Equality and Employment in Europe. The Case for Reasonable Accommodation*. Oxford: Hart Publishing/Bloomsbury.

Alidadi, K. 2017b. 'Cultural Diversity in the Workplace: Personal Autonomy as a Pillar for the Accommodation of Employee Religious Practices?'. In M.-C. Foblets et al., eds. *The Paradoxes of Personal Autonomy*, 115–26. Abingdon: Routledge.

Alidadi, K. 2017c. 'Religion and Unemployment Benefits: Comparing Belgium, the Netherlands and Great Britain'. *European Labour Law Journal* 2017(1): 1–29.

Alidadi, K. and M.-C. Foblets. 2016. 'European Supranational Courts and the Fundamental Right to Freedom of Religion or Belief: Convergence or Competition?'. *Oxford Journal of Law & Religion* 5(3): 532–40.

Calavita, K. 2010. *An Introduction to Law and Society*. Chicago: University of Chicago Press.

Davies, G. and M. Avbelj. 2018. *Research Handbook on Legal Pluralism and EU Law*. Cheltenham: Edward Elgar.

Fransen, G. 2005. 'Klanten hoeven geen Marokkanen. Firma Feryn vindt geen valabele werknemers' [trans. 'Customers don't want Moroccans. Feryn Firm not finding viable employees']. *De Standaard* (28 April 2005).

Galanter, M. 1974. 'Why the "Haves" Come out Ahead: Speculations on the Limits of Legal Change'. *Law & Society Review* 9(1): 95–160.

Griffiths, J. 1999. 'The Social Working of Anti-discrimination Law'. In M. L. P. Loenen and P. R. Rodrigues, eds. *Non-Discrimination Law: Comparative Perspectives*, 313–30. Alphen aan den Rijn: Kluwer.

Holmes, O. W. 1897. 'The Path of the Law'. *Harvard Law Review* 10: 457.

Lippman, M. 2017. *Law and Society*, 2nd edn. Thousand Oaks: Sage.

Moore, S. F. 1973. 'Law and Social Change: The Semi-Autonomous Social Field as an Appropriate Subject of Study'. *Law & Society Review* 7(4): 719–46.

Polakiewicz, J. 2015. 'The EU's Accession to the European Convention on Human Rights—A Matter of Coherence and Consistency'. In S. Morano-Foadi and L. Vickers, eds. *Fundamental Rights in the EU: A Matter of Two Courts*, xvii–xxvii. Oxford: Hart Publishing.

Rorive, I. 2009. 'Religious Symbols in the Public Space: In Search of a European Answer'. *Cardozo Law Review* 30: 2669.

Vickers, L. 2017. '*Achbita* and *Bougnaoui*: One Step Forward and Two Steps Back for Religious Diversity in the Workplace'. *European Labour Law Journal* 8(3): 232–57.

Waddington, L. 2011. 'Future Prospects for EU Equality Law: Lessons to be Learnt from the Proposed Equal Treatment Directive'. *European Law Review* 36(2): 163–84.

CHAPTER 37

TRANSNATIONAL AGRARIAN MOVEMENTS, FOOD SOVEREIGNTY, AND LEGAL MOBILIZATION

PRISCILLA CLAEYS AND KARINE PESCHARD

Introduction

In the past two decades, transnational agrarian movements have emerged as new political actors. Composed of networks of organizations representing peasants, fishers, pastoralists, agricultural workers, Indigenous Peoples, women, and youth, these agrarian movements have advanced a radical food sovereignty agenda, one that demands at once the relocalization and repeasantization of our food systems (Desmarais 2007; Rosset and Martínez-Torres 2010). Much has been written about this movement of movements, arguably the largest and most dynamic social movement of our time, and its political struggles against neoliberalism and capitalism in agriculture, including against the World Trade Organization (WTO), genetically modified seeds, industrial modes of agricultural production, and market-based approaches to the governance of land and natural resources (Borras et al. 2008; McMichael 2014; Patel 2009; Wittman 2011).

These struggles increasingly have legal dimensions. In the age of globalization, violence increasingly takes legal forms, as opposed to the open use of force or political violence (Mattei 2003). In this context, resistance is increasingly articulated in the language of law (Randeria 2007), and even social movements that express radical critiques of the law often deploy legal strategies (Bereni et al. 2010). Legal actions are an important part of social movements' struggles, although they are often a secondary or supplementary strategy and are combined with other tactics (McCann 2008).

In this chapter, we analyse a diversity of legal mobilizations by contemporary agrarian movements, with legal mobilization understood as a process by which collective actors invoke legal norms, discourses, or symbols to achieve progressive social change.[1] These include a priori legal strategies, such as the framing of human rights claims, advocacy, and participation in policymaking; a posteriori strategies, such as litigation; and extra-institutional forms of legal activism, such as people's tribunals. Our focus is on how peasants and small-scale farmers' organizations engage with the law, while acknowledging that they often operate through inter-sectoral and transnational alliances, coalitions, and networks involving other rural constituencies, NGOs, lawyers, and academics (Borras and Edelman 2016; Claeys and Duncan 2019).[2] We mostly discuss struggles related to access to and control over land, seeds, and biodiversity, but we also cover issues such as trade liberalization agreements, access to local/territorial markets, and food safety standards.

Our objective is to show the diversity and complementarity of agrarian movements' efforts to reconstruct the 'legal dimensions of inherited social relations' (McCann 2008: 509), and assess the potential and limitations of these attempts. To this end, we build on useful concepts in the field of social movement studies, such as framing, political opportunities, resource mobilization, and collective identities (Benford 2011; Benford and Snow 2000; McAdam 1996; Tarrow 1996). Researchers in this field analyse which legal tactics and practices are empowering or disempowering for social movements, highlighting potential pitfalls for movements engaged in legal struggles, such as professionalization, co-optation, and demobilization.[3] Well aware of these challenges, social movements constantly reassess whether institutional or disruptive tactics are more effective to advance their goals, and they try to find the right balance between the two (Tsutsui et al. 2012). They also assess how to combine litigation and legal or policy reform (Bereni et al. 2010).

We analyse cases of legal mobilizations at the transnational, national, and sub-national levels. The domestic arena remains the most relevant for legal activism (Tsutsui et al. 2012), considering the close interconnection between law and the liberal state. However, agrarian movements are increasingly organized at the transnational level, and they are actively seizing and creating new transnational 'legal opportunities'—the opening of institutional spaces allowing for legal changes.[4] This is either because such opportunities do not exist at the national level (Keck and Sikkink 1998) or because the inclusion of human rights principles in a growing number of international agreements offers new entry points to influence food and agriculture governance (Duncan 2015; Tsutsui et al. 2012). At the same time, the local or municipal level re-emerges as an arena for legal mobilizations (Blank 2006).

Our main argument is that there is a need to expand the scope and methods of research in law and anthropology to account for the diversity of actors and alliances, their innovative legal strategies, the different scales, and the multiplicity of institutional and extra-institutional arenas in which transnational agrarian movements engage with the law in their struggles against capitalism and neoliberalism. To document and analyse social movement innovations, lawyers and anthropologists must engage with transnational, multidisciplinary, and transdisciplinary approaches, and critically reflect on their methods, roles, and positionalities as social actors involved in social justice struggles.

Legal mobilizations take place in different phases of a social movement's life: from when a movement coalesces around shared claims and a collective identity, to when movement building is reinforced by legal opportunities to induce social change, or weakened by legal tactics which end up having demobilizing effects. Legal actions can seek to reimagine shared norms in new transformative ways, enforce official but ignored legal norms against existing practices, or try to import legal norms from another realm (McCann 2008). To reflect this diversity, we cover a wide variety of agrarian legal mobilizations, including: the creation of new human rights such as the right to land and the right to seeds at the UN Human Rights Council (HRC); direct engagement in policy-making at the UN Committee on World Food Security (CFS); domestic legal processes to institutionalize the right to food sovereignty in Bolivia, Ecuador, Venezuela, Central America, Canada, the United States, and elsewhere; litigation around seeds and intellectual property rights in Colombia, Brazil, and India; and, finally, extra-institutional legal strategies such as people's tribunals and civil disobedience.

Most of the examples of legal mobilizations we discuss in this chapter are ongoing, and we are therefore unable to fully assess their legacy. While some legal mobilizations have positive legacies, others can fail to generate social change or even provoke a backlash from reactionary political forces. For this reason, we try to conduct research over long timeframes that enable us to identify short-, mid-, and long-term impacts, both on the policy and legal fronts, and on the movements themselves. Moreover, legal relations and norms tend to be double-edged, upholding status quo and at the same time providing opportunities for episodic transformations (McCann 2008). This calls for systematically considering law as both a strategic resource (that provides legitimization or offers alternative avenues for pursuing change) and a constraint (that excludes certain claims or certain actors, and defines who is or is not entitled to participate) (Jacquot and Vitale 2014). This realization guides the preliminary analysis we provide below.

The creation of new human rights: the UN Declaration on the Rights of Peasants and Other People Working in Rural Areas (UNDROP)

In December 2018, a new international legal instrument for the protection of the rights of peasants and other rural working people was adopted by the UN General Assembly (121 in favour, 8 against, 54 abstentions), following six years of negotiations at the UN Human Rights Council. The UN Declaration on the Rights of Peasants and Other People Working in Rural Areas (hereafter UNDROP) and the process leading to its adoption are innovative is several respects.

First, the UNDROP recognizes new human rights. It grants peasants and other rural constituencies the individual and collective rights to land, seeds, water, and other natural resources, and the right to determine their own food and agricultural systems (recognized by some states as the right to food sovereignty—see next section). The UNDROP marks an important evolution in international human rights law because it grants collective rights to groups that are neither Indigenous Peoples nor minorities, signalling the emergence of local communities as legitimate rights-holders. This evolution contributes to the development of a multicultural, cosmopolitan, postcolonial, and transnational human rights regime from below (Bob 2010; Claeys 2015; Eberhard 2011; Goodale 2009; Rajagopal 2003; Santos and Rodríguez-Garavito 2005).

Second, the process of negotiating the UNDROP was requested and initiated by La Via Campesina. Created in 1993, La Via Campesina is now composed of more than 164 organizations in seventy-three countries, and represents about 200 million farmers. Legal scholars tend to emphasize the roles of legal experts, lawyers, and diplomats in norm-making (Benhabib 2009), at the expense of grassroots conceptions of law and human rights. In contrast, the UNDROP represents an instance of transnational lawmaking by social movements. La Via Campesina internally discussed successive versions of its Declaration on Peasants' Rights between 1999 and 2008. In the midst of the 2007–08 global food crisis, it decided to take the declaration to the UN. The movement secured alliances with other rural constituencies, human rights NGOs and states, and created the legal opportunity needed to push the process forward (Edelman and James 2011; Golay 2015; Vandenbogaerde 2017). In particular, La Via Campesina was able to count on the political leadership and commitment of Bolivia to advance its radical agenda. The negotiation process was participatory, with strong involvement of agrarian movements (but no private sector involvement).

In the anthropology of human rights, vernacularization (also called localization) is understood as the process of appropriation and local adoption of globally generated ideas and strategies about human rights (Feyter et al. 2011; Golan and Orr 2012; Merry 2006). This literature analyses the role of human rights 'translators' or intermediaries, i.e. the networks of international leaders or cosmopolitan elites who know both sides, control information flows, and interpret human rights norms in different cultural contexts (Levitt and Merry 2009). The UNDROP offers a contrasting example because peasant movements did not appropriate a global idea and adapt it to their local contexts, but sought to inject their own conceptions of human rights back at the core of the UN human rights system to radically expand its boundaries (Claeys 2012). They did so in response to new threats associated with the neoliberal transformation of the countryside, such as the commodification of nature and the liberalization of agricultural trade.

As anticipated by Peggy Levitt and Sally E. Merry (2009), the active seizure of human rights by social movements is reshaping human rights themselves. A decade ago, they noted that movements 'make claims that are not necessarily in the law. They expand the domain of human rights by coming up with new rights and defining new issues' (Levitt and Merry 2009: 460). Their research also highlighted the 'advocacy dilemma': human rights are a politically powerful tool because they point to global universals, but this non-local dimension makes it difficult for organizations to establish local support. In contrast, with UNDROP, the 'local'—understood as peasant conceptions of their collective identity, work, relationship to the land, and responsibilities as guardians of biodiversity—is what gave the campaign for peasants' rights its potency.

More needs to be said about the role of translators in the UNDROP process. As we have argued elsewhere, agrarian activists played a protagonist role, while benefiting from the support of specialized NGOs and academic allies (Claeys 2019). This support entailed facilitating access to the Human Rights Council, which is restricted to NGOs with accreditation from the UN Economic and Social Council (ECOSOC) that meet a number of criteria that are difficult for social movements to satisfy. It also entailed supporting the 'framing' of agrarian activists' claims in the technical language of human rights. This second aspect proved particularly important, as two understandings of human rights converged in a complex and contentious process of translation: rights as radical activist claims needed to be translated into rights as documents and doctrines for monitoring governments.[5] This required reframing activists' demands and ideas of rights into 'agreed language' to make them consistent with the existing body of international human rights norms and to get a majority of states to vote in favour.[6] This reframing proved to be particularly difficult and contentious for new claims such as collective rights to land, seeds, and other natural resources. With the negotiation of UNDROP, as with the UN Declaration on the Rights of Indigenous Peoples (UNDRIP), the recognition of collective rights derived not from theoretical discussions but from social and political struggles, and it represented an epistemological inversion in the broader intellectual history of human rights (Goodale 2009).

Global food security governance and direct participation in policymaking: the Civil Society and Indigenous Peoples' Mechanism to the UN Committee on World Food Security

In 2009, in the aftermath of the 2007–08 global food crisis, the UN Committee on World Food Security (CFS) was reformed with a view to becoming the foremost inclusive multi-stakeholder platform for the global governance of food security. Civil society actors were proactively involved in the reform process and in establishing the rules that would govern the Civil Society Mechanism (CSM), a self-organized body that facilitates the participation of a wide diversity of civil society organizations from around the world in the policy processes of the CFS.[7]

Over the past ten years, the CSM has grown into a recognized and legitimate actor within the CFS, and its contributions are valued by a wide range of CFS member states and participants, including international organizations, research institutes, philanthropic foundations, and the private sector. The CSM has developed complex governance mechanisms to organize the internal processes that enable participating organizations to reach common positions. It gives explicit priority to agrarian social movement voices, making a clear distinction between social movement organizations (recognized as ten distinct constituencies including small-scale farmers, pastoralists, fishers, and Indigenous Peoples), and NGOs (recognized as the eleventh constituency). A quota system further ensures that women represent at least 50 per cent of all participants and that an adequate balance is kept between the eleven constituencies and between seventeen sub-regions that make up the CSM (Claeys and Duncan 2019). These elaborate governance mechanisms are designed to manage tensions between organizations that compete over material, discursive, and symbolic resources (Jacquot and Vitale 2014). The priority voice given to social movements within the CSM, together with the right of the CSM to autonomous and independent organization within the CFS arena have helped civil society organizations navigate the risks of co-optation, institutionalization, and demobilization (Claeys and Duncan 2018a).

The fact that food producers are organized in transnational networks and have a say in global policymaking processes has important implications for research in law and anthropology. As we highlighted above, most of the literature places NGOs or experts in a key position of 'norm entrepreneur' or 'translator' at the interface between disempowered local communities and national and international NGOs (Merry 2006). The rise of transnational agrarian movements speaking with their own voices brings about a fundamental shift: it does away with the intermediary and empowers agrarian activists with new forms of agency (Gaarde 2017). NGOs and experts nonetheless continue to play important roles in policymaking arenas such as the CFS. Within the CSM, 'technical facilitators' support social movement activists in framing (or translating) their claims in the technical language suited for policy negotiations, and they also deal with logistics and facilitate dialogue among CSM participants. However, these trusted facilitators are chosen from allied NGOs as a result of political alliances (Claeys and Duncan 2019), and the nature of their work has changed as a result of shifting power relations between social movements and NGOs.

The CSM's active involvement in the CFS has enabled agrarian movements to advance progressive human rights language in CFS outputs and to contribute to the development of new soft law instruments that contain important policy recommendations for agrarian struggles. The most important of these instruments are the Voluntary Guidelines on the Responsible Governance of Tenure of Land, Fisheries and Forests (hereafter the Guidelines), which recognize the legitimate tenure rights of local communities and establish clear principles for their participation in decision-making that may affect their livelihoods. According to the Guidelines, states should recognize and respect these rights, including informal and customary rights, and they should protect land rights-holders in the context of land transfers, large-scale investments in land, and programmes designed to adapt to and mitigate the impacts of climate change. States should also facilitate land reform where necessary (Committee on World Food Security 2012).

Although this instrument is non-binding, the fact that it was adopted by consensus, following a participatory negotiation process, gives it considerable legitimacy. In addition, CSM participating organizations have played an important role in facilitating implementation and monitoring of the Guidelines at the national level, through training sessions and dissemination campaigns (International Planning Committee for Food Sovereignty 2016). This is all the more remarkable in a context increasingly characterized by a total absence of state accountability that can only be compensated by a strong civil society. Stated differently, social movements are key to overcoming the weak enforcement capacity of international human rights instruments (Tsutsui et al. 2012). Research is only starting to analyse the challenges linked to the implementation and monitoring of CFS policies at the domestic level. We need further research on how global norms travel, on how they are translated and appropriated in different local contexts, and on the ways in which transnational participatory governance modifies otherwise well-documented processes of norm diffusion and translation (Zwingel 2012).

Finally, the CSM is noteworthy for having brought to the table contentious issues, such as agroecology, in an effort to politicize a multi-stakeholder platform that would otherwise refrain from challenging the status quo (Duncan and Claeys 2018). However, ten years after the reform, state attacks on human and women's rights, the growing influence of the private sector, and the increased emphasis on public-private partnerships make it increasingly difficult for agrarian movements to advance their agenda in this multi-stakeholder platform. The rapid development of multi-stakeholder platforms in food security governance, while opening opportunities for agrarian movement participation, raises inextricable dilemmas for social movements always at risk of co-optation and of legitimizing hegemonic powers. This points to directions for future research on how dominant actors, such as the state and the private sector, experience, justify, and legitimize policymaking through multi-stakeholder platforms.

Food sovereignty policies at the domestic level: agrarian movements and the state

In the past two decades, a great number of agrarian movements have engaged with the state in an effort to institutionalize the right to food sovereignty. While food sovereignty is primarily about the ability of local communities to determine their own food systems, it also defends rights to food-producing resources without interference from the state. Scholars are only beginning to document social movements' efforts to turn food sovereignty into public policy, a long and contentious process that often brings about mixed results. The biggest challenge that movements face is to engage 'in the radical change that is at the heart of food sovereignty while creating the institutional spaces for deliberation and action to meet food sovereignty objectives' (Trauger et al. 2017: 2). Is it even possible to codify the claims of food sovereignty movements within the institutions of the liberal state?

Most accounts of agrarian movements' efforts to institutionalize food sovereignty highlight their difficulty in initiating a deep transformation of the food system and tackle issues of power, redistribution, and agrarian justice. Yet, several accounts point to the emergence of new inclusive, participatory, people-centred, and counter-hegemonic spaces for policymaking (Levkoe and Sheedy 2019). Ecuador adopted a new constitution in 2008 that declared food sovereignty a strategic goal, reflecting many of the proposals put forward by social movements linked to La Via Campesina. However, the implementation of food sovereignty policies has so far proven elusive (Clark 2016). Giunta (2014) points to the tremendous potential of having food sovereignty as a collective and constitutionalized horizon, but also signals the irresolution of a number of conflicts, notably around land, and the complete incoherence of policies and programmes that encourage agribusiness development, GMOs, and land markets. The execution of food sovereignty as a shared vision was left in the hands of the old structures and bureaucracy, and civil society actors lacked the capacity to take advantage of the political opportunity (McKay et al. 2014). Karla Peña (2017), who analyses the state-led participatory mechanisms that led to the approval of Ecuador's 2016 Land Law, concludes that grassroots participation made a clear impact on the content of the law, inducing a shift towards land redistribution to the landless. At the same time, social movements have criticized the law for not regulating land concentration and foreign land acquisitions. In a context marked by neo-extractivist populism, how the law will be implemented is uncertain, but the participatory lawmaking process clearly created spaces for the inclusion of historically marginalized groups (Peña 2017).

Similar tensions are reported in Bolivia and Venezuela, where 'state-sponsored' food sovereignty has opened up new political spaces, but where redistribution of power is at odds with a strong developmentalist state (McKay et al. 2014). In Bolivia, the new 2009 Constitution includes food sovereignty as a central element. Yet, a decade later, Bolivia has been unable to dismantle unequal agrarian structures and continues to rely heavily on resource extraction to fund its social protection programmes. The state has reasserted control over natural resources and encouraged large-scale agriculture for export, undermining local autonomy (Cockburn 2014). A number of social movement actors voiced critiques of Morales' policies, and an overall assessment of his presidency suggests a high degree of co-optation by the state and a loss of autonomy among social movements (McKay et al. 2014). In Venezuela, a national food sovereignty effort, enshrined in state policy, was launched in 1999. This process has agrarian reform as an important component, a direct outcome of peasant mobilizations. Schiavoni (2015) warns against analysing food sovereignty as a state-led effort, as this would fail to account for competing currents within the state and render invisible civil society actors' efforts to work both through and outside the mechanisms of the state, in collaboration with some and in antagonism with others. Civil society has been influential both in shaping state policies and in constraining politically conservative initiatives (Schiavoni 2015).

In her account of the elaboration of Nicaragua's 2009 Law on Food and Nutritional Sovereignty and Security, Wendy Godek (2015) highlights a number of factors that facilitated and impeded the institutionalization of food sovereignty. She suggests that diverse coalitions, direct grassroots participation, the commitment of a number of legislators, and close ties between movement activists and government officials all played a role in advancing legal change. Obstacles included discursive conflicts about the meaning of food sovereignty, private sector opposition, and tensions between the technical approach to food security advanced by international institutions such as the UN Food and Agriculture Organization (FAO) and the political food sovereignty framework pushed by civil society (Godek 2015).

While Latin America is clearly the region where agrarian movements have been most active in translating food sovereignty into policy (Wittman 2015), efforts are under way in a wide range of contexts, many of which have not yet been covered by academic research.[8] In Switzerland, the peasant organization Uniterre, a member of La Via Campesina, made use of a direct democracy provision that allows citizens to propose or modify a constitutional principle via a popular initiative (Vuilleumier 2017). The initiative was defeated in September 2018 after 60 per cent of voters rejected the proposed amendment in a referendum over concerns about its potential impact on the prices of agricultural products.

In Canada, about 3,500 people across the country participated in a grassroots process to develop a food sovereignty policy, the People's Food Policy (2008–11). The process strengthened food movement networks, weaved a coherent discourse, and politicized those involved. Yet, its potential reach was constrained by its inability to align with other related struggles (e.g. labour, Indigenous Peoples) and by its white and middle-class leadership. Nevertheless, it inspired similar experiences in the United Kingdom and Australia, and demonstrated the potential of democratic alternatives for engaging people in policymaking (Levkoe and Sheedy 2019).

This limited overview would not be complete without acknowledging that legal mobilizations for food sovereignty increasingly target the sub-national level, with a focus on municipal governance. Food policy councils that seek to democratize policymaking around food are blooming in North America and Europe (Moragues Faus 2017). Community land trusts and cooperatives are attempting to support land preservation and facilitate access to farmland for peasant farmers through new commons (Monnier 2013). These initiatives innovate with legal schemes that reinvent 'local and vernacular rights' while contesting the legal frameworks—grounded in state sovereignty and free enterprise—responsible for their undermining (Gutwirth and Stengers 2016). Contestation also takes place in the area of food safety standards, which are increasingly designed for large-scale processing and international trade at the expense of residents' rights to produce and consume their own foods (Trauger 2017). As pointed out by Blank (2010), local governments are increasingly seen as vehicles for the implementation of global environmental or human rights norms because they have a unique, territorially-grounded capacity to assume governance roles. Yet, the potential of local governments can only materialize if multiple jurisdictions coordinate and cooperate, rather than seeing their powers as negating each other (Blank 2010).

This is only a sample of the multitude of initiatives led or joined by agrarian movements that seek to turn protest into policy in many different parts of the world. Further research is needed on how local governments and global norms can be leveraged to build autonomous spaces against market and corporate power (Trauger et al. 2017); on how issues of class, exclusion, and neoliberal constraints can be better tackled by the global food sovereignty movement (Alkon and Mares 2012); and on how actions at various scales reinforce each other to support social change (Iles and Montenegro de Wit 2015; Schiavoni 2016).

Litigation: Court Challenges to Intellectual Property Rights by Agrarian Actors

The global expansion of intellectual property (IP) regimes in the era of the World Trade Organization Agreement on Trade-Related Aspects of Intellectual Property Rights (WTO-TRIPs) has opened up a new arena for legal activism. Indeed, the global imposition of U.S. standards of IP protection in agriculture—or IP imperialism (Mattei 2003)—is increasingly encroaching on the socioeconomic and human rights of peasants and farmers. Seed activists have begun to fight back in the courts, as witnessed by the multiplication of lawsuits around IP and seeds worldwide, especially in the past decade. In this section, we present examples of legal challenges in which agrarian actors and their allies strive to establish the primacy of the public interest, food security, and collective rights to seeds over companies' private property rights.

Colombia offers a notable example of agrarian mobilization against seed enclosures. In 2012, the Congress of the Republic of Columbia passed Law 1518 to accede to UPOV 91, one of the requirements of a bilateral trade agreement it had signed with the United States. UPOV—the International Union for the Protection of New Varieties of Plants—is an inter-governmental organization that enforces IP rights on plant varieties, known as plant breeders' rights. Its 1991 Act, UPOV 91, is the strictest to date: it approximates plant breeders' rights to those of a patent holder and restricts farmers' rights over protected plant varieties. The Colombian Free Seed Network (*Red de Semillas Libres*, RSL)—a network of grassroots and activist organizations committed to seed sovereignty—immediately challenged the law before the Constitutional Court on the grounds that it restricted farmers' rights to freely use, save, and commercialize certified seeds, and that it was enacted without previous consultation with Indigenous and Afro-Colombian communities. The RSL is an example of a social movement that privileges grassroots resistance but sees legal activism as a complementary strategy (Gutiérrez Escobar and Fitting

2016). In an unprecedented legal victory for civil society, the court declared Law 1518 unconstitutional. A majority of the Court found that the law violated the Constitution because Indigenous and Afro-Colombian communities had not been consulted prior to its enactment, in spite of the fact that the law might affect their biodiversity, ecosystems, and agricultural practices and knowledge. It must be noted that the Court's objections were limited to the process by which the law was enacted, and that it did not rule on its substantive compatibility with the Colombian Constitution. This example illustrates well the challenges faced by legal activists who have to negotiate multiscalar governance. On the one hand, the Constitutional Court ruling succeeded in stopping Colombia from joining UPOV 91 in spite of U.S. pressure. On the other hand, the ruling did not extend to other UPOV91-based provisions already present in the domestic legislation (Gutiérrez Escobar 2017).

Another important area of litigation concerns challenges to the patents of biotech corporations over transgenic crop varieties. Litigation in Brazil and India provides two examples. In 2009, a class action was brought against Monsanto by the local rural union of Passo Fundo in Southern Brazil, which represents large soybean farmers. The union asked the court to uphold the rights of farmers, as specified in the Brazilian Plant Variety Protection Act, to save seeds from their crops for replanting and to sell their harvest as food or raw material without paying royalties. A state federation of 350 local unions representing family farmers and rural workers soon joined the class action. In the polarized Brazilian agrarian landscape, this changed the profile of the case: no longer simply a dispute about profits among powerful economic actors, it came to encompass the rights and livelihoods of small farmers. In 2012, a civil court judge ruled in favour of the farmers, accepting their argument that Monsanto exhausted its IP rights when it licensed its technology to seed producers, and therefore, that it was not entitled to collect royalties upon harvest. Monsanto appealed and, in 2014, the appellate court overturned the first decision based on a narrow interpretation of domestic patent law, a decision reaffirmed by the Superior Court of Justice in 2019.

In India, a legal dispute has been building since 2015 over seed prices and royalties for genetically modified Bt cotton. This conflict has been simmering since the mid-2000s in a number of cotton-growing states, where farmers' protests against the high price of Bt cotton seeds led the government to fix the maximum sale price of a packet of Bt cotton seeds under the Essential Commodities Act, hereby triggering a string of lawsuits by Monsanto. The conflict escalated following the election of the ultranationalist Bharatiya Janata Party (BJP) in 2014, with Hindu nationalist grassroots organizations opposed to both GM crops and multinational corporations gaining more leverage with the central government. In December 2015, the central government issued an executive order allowing the government to fix the maximum sale price of Bt cotton seeds and the percentage of royalties, which Monsanto immediately challenged before the Delhi High Court. One lawsuit filed by Monsanto against an Indian seed company for patent infringement led the Delhi High Court to revoke Monsanto's Indian patent on Bt cotton in April 2018 in the first decision to examine the legality of patents on biotech seeds in India.[9]

Legal conflicts over intellectual property have mobilized diverse actors and led to unexpected alliances. In the highly polarized Brazilian countryside, the Passo Fundo class action represents a rare instance of two antagonistic sectors—family farmers and large producers—siding together in an alliance that gave momentum to the class action. In India, farmers' groups were the first to challenge royalties for Bt cotton, but they have since been side-lined as the issue has evolved into a legal dispute between the government and national seed companies, on the one hand, and Monsanto, on the other. The dispute has also led to contradictory alliances, with progressive food sovereignty activists and ultranationalist Hindu organizations both opposing Monsanto's aggressive pursuit of IP rights. However, food sovereignty activists are hesitant to engage in disputes over IP rights, because they fear that this might ultimately contribute to legitimizing proprietary regimes in agriculture. They also consider that proprietary issues surrounding transgenic crops are less urgent than preventing their environmental release. This explains why they have not fully embraced these lawsuits.

These legal challenges are ongoing, and it is too early to assess their long-term impacts. However, they have already had important repercussions. The most relevant, from the perspective of our discussion, is that they have forced the judiciary in Brazil and India to examine the legality of biotech patents in the context of their respective domestic legislation, which in each case differs substantially from that of the United States. This is prompting the development of new legal interpretations regarding the patentability of plants life forms that depart from the pro-patent jurisprudence developed by the U.S. Supreme Court (Peschard and Randeria 2019). The class action lawsuit by Brazilian rural unions represents the use of collective action by subaltern actors to question the practices of hegemonic actors (the state and industry) in the name of trade and technical-scientific soundness. In both Brazil and India, activists have used the courts to bring key legal documents into the public domain and to clarify a patent situation until then shrouded in secrecy. Most importantly, activists have challenged the imposition of U.S. intellectual property standards in violation of constitutional rights and domestic legislation, such as the exclusions to patentability under patent acts, and the rights guaranteed to farmers under plant variety protection legislation. In doing so, they contest the global imposition of hegemonic IP norms and its concomitant erasure of human rights and national laws.

Peoples' tribunals: the International Monsanto Tribunal

Since the 1960s, people's tribunals have been an important extra-institutional legal strategy to document and denounce human rights violations. People's tribunals have been organized on a wide range of issues, from human rights violations in conflict and war zones to living wages, environmental justice, economic crimes, and debt. They are established outside formal state and international structures and challenge the historical state monopoly on lawmaking and interpretation. They also monitor the exercise of power by states, international organizations (the World Bank, the WTO), and private corporations in an effort to hold them accountable for their actions (Byrnes and Simm 2013). Building on this tradition, the International Monsanto Tribunal was held in The Hague in October 2016. The steering committee was composed of prominent public figures, and the initiative garnered widespread support, with over a thousand organizations signing on.

The Monsanto Tribunal was noteworthy in a number of respects. First, the organizers modelled the Tribunal on the procedures of the International Criminal Court (ICC). A team of legal researchers prepared detailed legal briefs on each of the six questions submitted to the tribunal. Second, the victims of Monsanto's activities were invited to testify before the Court, an important innovation of the Rome Statute which established the ICC (Monsanto was also invited but declined). Over two days, the judges heard the testimony of twenty-nine witnesses (both injured parties and experts) from sixteen countries. One of the most important roles of people's tribunals is to provide 'a venue for the articulation and validation of claims and experiences where the official state-sanctioned system fails communities' (Byrnes and Simm 2013: 743). As the presiding judge, Françoise Tulkens, emphasized in her concluding remarks, this was one of the central objectives of the initiative (European Civic Forum and Foundation Monsanto Tribunal 2017). Third, the organizers invited legal professionals—prominent lawyers and former judges—to sit on the tribunal, and they insisted on the importance of ensuring the formality and decorum of a regular tribunal. A people's assembly was held in parallel to the tribunal with strong participation by social movements and civil society, including La Via Campesina member organizations.

The tribunal issued its advisory legal opinion on 18 April 2017. Citing international human rights instruments, the Tribunal concluded that Monsanto had engaged in practices that have negatively impacted the right to a healthy environment, the right to food, the right to health, and the right to freedom indispensable for scientific research. The last question of the terms of reference concerned the crime of ecocide, understood as 'causing serious damage or destroying the environment, so as to significantly and durably alter the global commons or ecosystem services upon which certain human groups rely' (International Monsanto Tribunal 2017: 11). This definition deftly positioned ecocide at the intersection of environmental and human rights law (Rouidi 2017). The tribunal concluded that Monsanto's activities could constitute a crime of ecocide if the latter were recognized in international criminal law. The tribunal recommended amending the Rome Statute to legally recognize ecocide as the fifth international crime against peace. However, the tribunal stated that this amendment would only be effective if the Rome Statute were also amended to recognize the criminal liability of legal persons, foremost corporations.

The International Monsanto Tribunal is an example of how civil society is constantly experimenting with new forms of legal activism. It combined the strong symbolic power of people's tribunals with the moral authority of formal legal procedures, albeit extra-institutional and non-binding. Giovanni Prete and Christel Cournil (2019: 205) point out that there were connections between the Monsanto Tribunal and the civil proceedings against the Monsanto pesticide Roundup that were held around the same period in France and the United States, and therefore they conclude that 'opinion tribunals and "real" tribunals should not be regarded as separate arenas of mobilization'. The Monsanto Tribunal also combined advocacy for the implementation of existing socioeconomic rights and advocacy for the recognition of ecocide as a crime in international law.

Civil disobedience: land occupations and direct actions against GMOs

In different parts of the world, agrarian activists have also engaged in disruptive, direct, and illegal actions to defend their rights, often resulting in prosecution. In Brazil, the Landless Rural Workers' Movement (MST) is known for its use of tactical land occupations to put pressure on the government to expropriate unused private land and create agrarian reform settlements. Since a land occupation almost invariably triggers a repossession lawsuit, the MST has had to develop sophisticated legal strategies to defend rights to the land (Houtzager 2005; Santos and Carlet 2010). In one instance, the MST succeeded in fighting an eviction order by reframing the conflict as one between a company's right to private property and the families' right to a dignified and hunger-free life. In another instance, the MST obtained a high court ruling expanding the breath of direct action accepted as civil disobedience, therefore helping to de-criminalize the movement. The ruling determined that 'the MST land occupations could not be considered a criminal act because there was no criminal intent' and that 'land occupations should be seen as exercising the rights of citizenship, particularly the civil right to pressure government to guarantee constitutional rights' (Houtzager 2005: 230). While this ruling was ground-breaking, the MST continues to be criminalized and to refine its legal strategies. This includes training its own lawyers so as not to depend on the services of external lawyers.

In France and the United Kingdom, anti-GMO movements (including the La Via Campesina member organization *La Confédération paysanne*) have engaged in the voluntary reaping of experimental GM plots as an offensive litigation tactic since the 1990s. Activists readily accepted arrest and tried to publicize court cases in an effort to initiate a public debate that they felt was otherwise lacking, effectively turning the courts into a debating chamber on GMOs (Doherty and Hayes 2014).

While the examples listed above highlight proactive engagement with criminal justice systems, it should be noted that most agrarian activists' encounters with the law are the result of unwanted prosecution. In the last two decades, criminalization of agrarian activists has been on the rise, and a UN report noted that human rights defenders working on land rights and natural resources are particularly at risk of being killed (Forst 2016; OBS 2013).

Concluding remarks

The current period has been described as 'a dark time for human rights' (HRW 2019). Human rights are increasingly under attack, not only in practice (UN 2018), but also in theory (Hopgood 2013; Posner 2014). As human rights violations continue unabated, the ineffectiveness of international human rights law and the limits of state-centric human rights advocacy are more apparent than ever before. As a counter to this bleak assessment, the experiences documented in this chapter point to the continued relevance of legal and human rights mobilizations for progressive social change. Indeed, transnational agrarian movements are not only seizing upon and vernacularizing human rights norms but actively creating new norms to address new attacks and challenges.

In a changing global political environment, it is difficult to anticipate what forms legal mobilization will take in the future. As Ian Scoones et al. (2018) observe in their analysis of contemporary rural politics, a 'new political moment is underway', characterized by the rise of authoritarian populism. Populist politics are likely to influence both the prospects for legal activism and the forms taken by legal mobilizations more broadly. The defining features of authoritarian populism are: the rise of protectionist politics and nationalism; highly contested national elections; growing concern over the 'mobile poor'; appeals for security at the expense of civil liberties; and the use of the state to increase surplus for a minority while abandoning its most vulnerable citizens (Scoones et al. 2018). One could add to this list the crisis of the judiciary. Indeed, in countries where populist politics are on the rise, such as Brazil and India, interference by the executive branch and overt political bias have undermined the legitimacy of judicial institutions in the eyes of the population and raised concerns over the weakening of democratic institutions and the rule of law. In addition, the election of right-wing governments has brought about the nomination of more conservative justices, lessening the chances that supreme courts will contribute to progressive legal change.

Authoritarian populism also has implications for legal activism more broadly. India is a case in point. In the late 1970s, the introduction of public interest litigation expanded the sphere of legal activism (Rajagopal 2007). However, with the rise of ultranationalist politics, the space for legal activism is shrinking. Human rights are being recast as a national security concern and a threat to the country's economic development (and foreign capital); the state has come down on foreign-funded NGOs; new corporate social responsibility regulations restrict the scope of NGO activities (and conspicuously exclude human rights); and, finally, a shift towards venture philanthropy further reduces civil society's independence from the corporate sector (Bornstein and Sharma 2016). These trends are not isolated and echo similar developments in other countries around the globe. The rise of authoritarian populism thus represents an important new avenue for research in law and anthropology.

Another avenue for future research concerns the nature and challenges of politically engaged ethnography (Juris and Khasnabish 2013). A growing number of lawyers and anthropologists are taking active part in agrarian movements' struggles rather than studying or observing these from the sidelines. They develop reflexive, collaborative, and activist approaches to research in an effort to tackle power relations in the research process (Duncan et al. 2019). They recognize that social movements are active and reflexive co-producers of knowledge. In addition, they experiment with new fieldwork configurations, going beyond multisited research (Marcus 1995) to engage in 'networked ethnography', that is, fieldwork that is attuned to the complex and place-based meanings of transnational encounters. Jeffrey S. Juris and Alexander Khasnabish (2013) argue that only by becoming active practitioners can researchers grasp the dynamics, frictions, empirical issues, and theoretical insights that are at play in transnational activism. Militant ethnography is key to producing the critical understandings that may help us produce movement-relevant theory (Bevington and Dixon 2005) or even co-theorize with movement actors (Rappaport 2008). We share this perspective and see research with and *as part of* transnational agrarian movements engaged in legal change as a form of activism in itself.

Acknowledgements

We would like to thank Marie-Claire Foblets, Jennifer Burrell, and Mark Goodale for their supportive feedback on this article, as well as Nadia Lambek and Matthew Canfield for their detailed and thorough comments. Having both lawyers and anthropologists review our chapter enabled us to strengthen it in many enriching ways. We are also grateful to Günter Frankenberg for our insightful exchanges on the issue of legal transfer. Karine Peschard acknowledges the support of the Swiss National Science Foundation (SNF) under Grant N°100017_162398/1 (2015–2019).

Notes

1. Our interest lies in collective forms of mobilizations, as opposed to everyday politics (Kerkvliet 2009).
2. For a discussion of Indigenous Peoples and the law, see Chapters 5 and 6 (Burke and Thom, respectively) in this volume.
3. 'Professionalization' refers to how movements tend to internalize formal rules and forms of participation and rely on insider tactics at the expense of direct-action tactics, possibly giving up on more ambitious goals. 'Co-optation' means that movements risk being neutralized when they participate in formal processes because policymaking tends to follow pre-existing interests. 'Demobilization' is the risk of social struggles being taken off the streets to specialized legal arenas where they are only dealt with by a few (Tsutsui et al. 2012).

4. The concept builds on Tarrow's 'political opportunity structures' (Tarrow 1998) but helps provide a better understanding of the role of legal strategies in protest, notably because movements engaged in legal mobilization are constrained in their interpretive schema as they must articulate their claims within pre-established legal categories (Doherty and Hayes 2014). The term 'judicial opportunity' is used in relation to litigation more specifically.
5. Levitt and Merry (2009) make a distinction between (1) human rights as law and (2) human rights as social project, i.e. as an idea that is mobilized by social movements to build civic awareness of injustice. The two involve actors with distinct trainings. The first group is made largely of lawyers, and the second of social activists.
6. Agreed language is a term commonly used by diplomats to designate 'authoritative previous documents' that participants in the negotiations cite 'to advance their causes' (Ramli and Yahya 2014: 346).
7. The initial name of the Civil Society Mechanism was changed in 2018 to reflect and encourage the active participation of Indigenous Peoples' organizations in the Mechanism. The new name is Civil Society and Indigenous Peoples' Mechanism.
8. Peru, Argentina, Guatemala, the Dominican Republic, El Salvador, Indonesia, and West Africa, for example, have legislation or, in the case of West Africa, regional integration frameworks supportive of food sovereignty efforts. The rights to food and food sovereignty were also included in the 2015 Constitution of Nepal, following advocacy by the All Nepali Peasants' Federation (ANFPa), which is a member organization of La Via Campesina.
9. This decision was subsequently suspended by the Supreme Court, which instructed the Delhi High Court to conduct a full trial. The case was ongoing at the time of writing in February 2020.

References

Alkon, A. H. and T. M. Mares. 2012. 'Food Sovereignty in US Food Movements: Radical Visions and Neoliberal Constraints'. *Agriculture and Human Values* 29(3): 347–59.

Benford, R. 2011. 'Framing Global Governance from Below. Discursive Opportunities and Challenges in the Transnational Social Movement Arena'. In C. Bjola and M. Kornprobst, eds. *Arguing Global Governance*, 67–84. London: Routledge.

Benford, R. D. and D. A. Snow. 2000. 'Framing Processes and Social Movements: An Overview and Assessment'. *Annual Review of Sociology* 26: 611–39.

Benhabib, S. 2009. 'Claiming Rights across Borders: International Human Rights and Democratic Sovereignty'. *American Political Science Review* 103(4): 691–704.

Bereni, L., A. Debauche, E. Latour, and A. Revillard. 2010. 'Entre Contrainte et Ressource: Les Mouvements Féministes Face au Droit'. *Nouvelles Questions Féministes* 29(1): 6–15.

Bevington, D. and C. Dixon. 2005. 'Movement-Relevant Theory: Rethinking Social Movement Scholarship and Activism'. *Social Movement Studies* 4(3): 185–208.

Blank, Y. 2006. 'Localism in the New Global Legal Order'. *Harvard International Law Journal* 47(1): 263–81.

Blank, Y. 2010. 'Federalism, Subsidiarity, and the Role of Local Governments in an Age of Global Multilevel Governance'. *Fordham Urban Law Journal* 37: 509.

Bob, C. 2010. *The International Struggle for New Human Rights*. Philadelphia: University of Pennsylvania Press.

Bornstein, E. and A. Sharma. 2016. 'The Righteous and the Rightful: The Technomoral Politics of NGOs, Social Movements, and the State in India'. *American Ethnologist* 43(1): 76–90.

Borras, S. Jr., and M. Edelman. 2016. *Political Dynamics of Transnational Agrarian Movements.* Black Point, NS: Fernwood.

Borras, S., M. Edelman, and C. Kay. 2008. 'Transnational Agrarian Movements: Origins and Politics, Campaigns and Impact'. In Borras et al., eds. *Transnational Agrarian Movements Confronting Globalization*, 1–36. West Sussex: Wiley-Blackwell.

Byrnes, A. and G. Simm. 2013. 'Peoples' Tribunals, International Law and the Use of Force'. *University of New South Wales Law Journal* 36(2): 711–44.

Claeys, P. 2012. 'The Creation of New Rights by the Food Sovereignty Movement: The Challenge of Institutionalizing Subversion'. *Sociology* 46(5): 844–60.

Claeys, P. 2015. *Human Rights and the Food Sovereignty Movement: Reclaiming Control.* New York: Routledge.

Claeys, P. 2019. 'The Rise of New Rights for Peasants. From Reliance on NGO Intermediaries to Direct Representation'. *Transnational Legal Theory* 9(3–4): 386–99.

Claeys, P. and J. Duncan. 2018a. 'Evaluation of the Civil Society Mechanism (CSM) for Relations with the UN Committee on World Food Security (CFS), Full Report <http://www.csm4cfs.org/wp-content/uploads/2018/02/CSM-Evaluation-Report-2018-ilovepdf-compressed.pdf>.

Claeys, P. and J. Duncan. 2019. 'Do We Need to Categorize It? Reflections on Constituencies and Quotas as Tools for Negotiating Difference in the Global Food Sovereignty Convergence Space'. *The Journal of Peasant Studies* 46(7): 1477–98.

Clark, P. 2016. 'Can the State Foster Food Sovereignty? Insights from the Case of Ecuador'. *Journal of Agrarian Change* 16(2): 183–205.

Cockburn, J. 2014. 'Bolivia's Food Sovereignty and Agrobiodiversity: Undermining the Local to Strengthen the State?'. *Theory in Action* 7(4): 67–89.

Committee on World Food Security (CFS). 2012. 'Voluntary Guidelines on the Responsible Governance of Tenure of Land, Fisheries and Forests in the Context of National Food Security'. Rome: FAO United Nations.

Desmarais, A. A. 2007. *La Vía Campesina: Globalization and the Power of Peasants.* Halifax, London, Ann Arbor, MI: Fernwood Pub.; Pluto Press.

Doherty, B. and G. Hayes. 2014. 'Having Your Day in Court: Judicial Opportunity and Tactical Choice in Anti-GMO Campaigns in France and the United Kingdom'. *Comparative Political Studies* 47(1): 3–29.

Duncan J., P. Claeys, M. G. Rivera-Ferre, E. Oteros-Rozas, B. Van Dyck, C. Plank, and A. A. Desmarais. 2019. 'Scholar-activists in an Expanding European Food Sovereignty Movement', *Journal of Peasant Studies.* Published online 1 December 2019. DOI: 10.1080/03066150.2019.1675646.

Duncan, J. 2015. *Global Food Security Governance: Civil Society Engagement in the Reformed Committee on World Food Security.* London: Routledge.

Duncan, J. and P. Claeys. 2018. 'Politicizing Food Security Governance through Participation: Opportunities and Opposition'. *Food Security* 10(6):1411–24.

Eberhard, C. 2011. *Droits de l'Homme et Dialogue Interculturel.* Paris: Éditions Connaissances et Savoirs.

Edelman, M, and C. James. 2011. 'Peasants' Rights and the UN System: Quixotic Struggle? Or Emancipatory Idea Whose Time Has Come?' *Journal of Peasant Studies* 38(1): 81–108.

European Civic Forum and Foundation Monsanto Tribunal. 2017. 'Ecocide: Corporations on Trial'. <http://www.monsanto-tribunal.org>.

Feyter, K. D., S. Parmentier, C. Timmerman, and G. Ulrich. 2011. *The Local Relevance of Human Rights*. Cambridge: Cambridge University Press.

Forst, M. 2016. 'They Spoke Truth to Power and Were Murdered in Cold Blood. Analysis on the Situation of Environmental Human Rights Defenders and Concrete Recommendations to Better Protect Them'. United Nations Special Rapporteur on the Situation of Human Rights Defenders. <https://www.protecting-defenders.org/sites/protecting-defenders.org/files/environmentaldefenders_o.pdf>.

Gaarde, I. 2017. *Peasants Negotiating a Global Policy Space. La Via Campesina in the Committee on World Food Security*. London: Routledge.

Giunta, I. 2014. 'Food Sovereignty in Ecuador: Peasant Struggles and the Challenge of Institutionalization'. *The Journal of Peasant Studies* 41(6): 1201–24.

Godek, W. 2015. 'Challenges for Food Sovereignty Policy Making: The Case of Nicaragua's Law 693'. *Third World Quarterly* 36(3): 526–43.

Golan, D. and Z. Orr. 2012. 'Translating Human Rights of the "Enemy": The Case of Israeli NGOs Defending Palestinian Rights'. *Law & Society Review* 46(4): 781–814.

Golay, C. 2015. 'Negotiation of a United Nations Declaration on the Rights of Peasants and Other People Working in Rural Areas'. Geneva Academy In-Brief No.5, available at <https://www.ohchr.org/Documents/HRBodies/HRCouncil/WGPleasants/Session2/ChristopheGolay.pdf>.

Goodale, M. 2009. *Human Rights: An Anthropological Reader*. Oxford: Wiley-Blackwell.

Gutiérrez Escobar, L. 2017. 'Seed Sovereignty Struggles in an Emberá-Chamí Community in Colombia'. *Alternautas* 4(2): 27–45.

Gutiérrez Escobar, L. and E. Fitting. 2016. 'The Red de Semillas Libres: Contesting Biohegemony in Colombia: Contesting Biohegemony in Colombia'. *Journal of Agrarian Change* 16(4): 711–19.

Gutwirth, S. and I. Stengers. 2016. 'Théorie du Droit'. *Revue Juridique de l'Environnement* 41(2): 306–43.

Hopgood, S. 2013. *The Endtimes of Human Rights*. Ithaca: Cornell University Press.

Houtzager, P. P. 2005. 'The Movement of the Landless (MST), Juridical Field, and Legal Change in Brazil'. In B. de S. Santos and C. A. Rodrígues-Garavito, eds. *Law and Globalization from Below: Towards a Cosmopolitan Legality*, 218–40. Cambridge: Cambridge University Press.

HRW–Human Rights Watch. 2019. World Report 2019. <https://www.hrw.org/sites/default/files/world_report_download/hrw_world_report_2019.pdf>.

Iles, A. and M. Montenegro de Wit. 2015. 'Sovereignty at What Scale? An Inquiry into Multiple Dimensions of Food Sovereignty'. *Globalizations* 12(4): 481–97.

International Monsanto Tribunal. 2017. 'Advisory Opinion', available at <http://www.monsanto-tribunal.org>.

International Planning Committee for Food Sovereignty. 2016. 'People's Manual on the Guidelines on Governance of Land, Fisheries and Forests. A Guide for Promotion, Implementation, Monitoring and Evaluation', available at <http://www.foodsovereignty.org/wp-content/uploads/2016/06/peoplesmanual.pdf>.

Jacquot, S and T. Vitale. 2014. 'Law as Weapon of the Weak? A Comparative Analysis of Legal Mobilization by Roma and Women's Groups at the European Level'. *Journal of European Public Policy* 21(4): 587–604.

Juris, J. S. and A. Khasnabish. 2013. *Insurgent Encounters: Transnational Activism, Ethnography, and the Political*. Durham: Duke University Press.

Keck, M. and K. Sikkink. 1998. *Activists Beyond Borders: Advocacy Networks in Transnational Politics*. Ithaca: Cornell University Press.

Kerkvliet, B. J. T. 2009. 'Everyday Politics in Peasant Societies (and Ours)'. *Journal of Peasant Studies* 36(1): 227–43.

Levitt, P. and S. E. Merry. 2009. 'Vernacularization on the Ground: Local Uses of Global Women's Rights in Peru, China, India and the United States'. *Global Networks* 9(4): 441–61.

Levkoe, C. Z. and A. Sheedy. 2019. 'A People-Centred Approach to Food Policy Making: Lessons from Canada's People's Food Policy Project'. *Journal of Hunger & Environmental Nutrition* 14(3): 318–38.

Marcus, G. 1995. 'Ethnography in/of the World System: The Emergence of Multi-Sited Ethnography'. *Annual Review of Anthropology* 24: 95–117.

Mattei, U. 2003. 'A Theory of Imperial Law: A Study on U.S. Hegemony and the Latin Resistance'. *Indiana Journal of Global Legal Studies* 10(1): 383–448.

McAdam, D. 1996. 'The Framing Function of Movement Tactics: Strategic Dramaturgy in the American Civil Rights Movements'. In D. McAdam, J. D. McCarthy, and M. N. Zald, eds. *Comparative Perspectives on Social Movements. Political Opportunities, Mobilizing Structures, and Cultural Framings*, 338–57. Cambridge: Cambridge University Press.

McCann, M. 2008. 'Law and Social Movements'. In A. Sarat, ed. *The Blackwell Companion to Law and Society*, 506–22. Oxford: Wiley-Blackwell.

McKay, B., R. Nehring, and M. Walsh-Dilley. 2014. 'The "State" of Food Sovereignty in Latin America: Political Projects and Alternative Pathways in Venezuela, Ecuador and Bolivia'. *The Journal of Peasant Studies* 41(6): 1175–1200.

McMichael, P. 2014. 'Historicizing Food Sovereignty'. *Journal of Peasant Studies* 41(6): 933–57.

Merry, S. E. 2006. 'Transnational Human Rights and Local Activism: Mapping the Middle'. *American Anthropologist* 108(1): 38–51.

Monnier, J. L. 2013. 'Terre de Liens: Histoire de Convergences'. *Pour* 220: 289–96.

Moragues Faus, A. 2017. 'Urban Food Policy Alliances as Paths to Food Sovereignty- Insights from Sustainable Food Cities in the UK'. In A. A. Desmarais, P. Claeys, and A. Trauger, eds. *Public Policies for Food Sovereignty*, 147–63. London: Routledge.

OBS–The Observatory for the Protection of Human Rights Defenders. 2013. 'Land and Environmental Rights Defenders in Danger: An Overview of Recent Cases'. <http://www.ciel.org/wp-content/uploads/2013/12/Compilation_LER_HRD_Dec2013.pdf>.

Patel, R. 2009. Food Sovereignty. *Journal of Peasant Studies* 36(3): 663–706.

Peña, K. 2017. 'State-Led Grassroots Participation and Ecuador's Land Law'. In A. A. Desmarais, P. Claeys, and A. Trauger, eds. *Public Policies for Food Sovereignty*, 19–35. London: Routledge.

Peschard, K. and S. Randeria. 2019. 'Propriedade Industrial Sobre Sementes: Contestação Judicial no Brasil e na Índia'. In S. Sauer, ed. *Desenvolvimento e transformações agrárias: BRICS, competição e cooperação no Sul Global*, 157–86. São Paulo: Outras Expressões.

Posner, E. 2014. *The Twilight of Human Rights Law*. Oxford: Oxford University Press.

Prete, G. and C. Cournil. 2019. 'Staging International Environmental Justice: The International Monsanto Tribunal'. *PoLAR: Political and Legal Anthropology Review* 42(2): 191–209.

Rajagopal, B. 2003. *International Law from Below: Development, Social Movements, and Third World Resistance*. Cambridge: Cambridge University Press.

Rajagopal, B. 2007. 'Pro-Human Rights but Anti-Poor? A Critical Evaluation of the Indian Supreme Court from a Social Movement Perspective'. *Human Rights Review* 8(3): 157–86.

Ramli, R. and Z. Yahya. 2014. 'Language of Negotiation for Agreed Conclusions at the UN 57th Session of the Commission on the Status of Women: A Case Study'. *Procedia—Social and Behavioral Sciences* 118: 389–403.

Randeria, S. 2007. 'The State of Globalization: Legal Plurality, Overlapping Sovereignties and Ambiguous Alliances between Civil Society and the Cunning State in India'. *Theory, Culture & Society* 24: 1–33.

Rappaport, J. 2008. 'Beyond Participant Observation: Collaborative Ethnography as Theoretical Innovation'. *Collaborative Anthropologies* 1(1): 1–31.

Rosset, P. and M. E. Martínez-Torres. 2010. 'La Vía Campesina: The Birth and Evolution of a Transnational Social Movement'. *Journal of Peasant Studies* 37(1): 149–75.

Rouidi, H. 2017. 'La Répression des Atteintes à l'Environnement Entre Droit Positif et Droit Prospectif. À Propos de l'Avis Consultatif du Tribunal International Monsanto du 18 Avril 2017'. *Revue Juridique de l'Environnement* 43(1): 13–26.

Santos, B. de S. and C. A. Rodríguez-Garavito. 2005. *Law and Globalization from Below: Towards a Cosmopolitan Legality*. Cambridge: Cambridge University Press.

Santos, B. de S. and F. Carlet. 2010. 'The Movement of Landless Rural Workers in Brazil and Their Struggles for Access to Law and Justice'. In Y. Ghai and J. Cottrell, eds. *Marginalized Communities and Access to Justice*, 60–82. Abington: Routledge.

Schiavoni, C. M. 2015. 'Competing Sovereignties, Contested Processes: Insights from the Venezuelan Food Sovereignty Experiment'. *Globalizations* 12(4): 466–80.

Schiavoni, C. M. 2016. 'The Contested Terrain of Food Sovereignty Construction: Toward a Historical, Relational and Interactive Approach'. *Journal of Peasant Studies* 44(1): 1–32.

Scoones, I., M. Edelman, S. M. Borras Jr., R. Hall, W. Wolford, and B. White. 2018. 'Emancipatory Rural Politics: Confronting Authoritarian Populism'. *The Journal of Peasant Studies* 45(1): 1–20.

Tarrow, S. 1996. 'States and Opportunities: The Political Structuring of Social Movements'. In D. McAdam, J. D. McCarthy, and M. N. Zald, eds. *Comparative Perspectives on Social Movements. Political Opportunities, Mobilizing Structures, and Cultural Framings*, 41–62. Cambridge: Cambridge University Press.

Tarrow, S. 1998. *Power in Movement*. Cambridge: Cambridge University Press.

Trauger, A. 2017. 'Community-Based Rights to Food Sovereignty: The Case of the Local Food and Community Self-Governance Ordinances in Maine, USA'. In A. A. Desmarais, P. Claeys, and A. Trauger, eds. *Public Policies for Food Sovereignty*, 53–70. London: Routledge.

Trauger, A., P. Claeys, and A. A. Desmarais. 2017. 'Can the Revolution Be Institutionalized?' In A. A. Desmarais, P. Claeys, and A. Trauger, eds. *Public Policies for Food Sovereignty*, 1–16. London: Routledge.

Tsutsui, K., C. Whitlinger, and A. Lim. 2012. 'International Human Rights Law and Social Movements: States' Resistance and Civil Society's Insistence'. *Annual Review of Law and Social Science* 8(1): 367–96.

UN–United Nations. 2018. 'Human Rights Under Attack, "No Longer a Priority; a Pariah"—UN Rights Chief'. <https://news.un.org/en/story/2018/05/1010372>.

Vandenbogaerde, A. 2017. 'Localizing the Human Rights Council: A Case Study of the Declaration on the Rights of Peasants'. *Journal of Human Rights* 16(2): 220–41.

Vuilleumier, J. 2017. 'The Involvement of Community Supported Agriculture Networks in a Swiss Popular Initiative for Food Sovereignty'. In A. A. Desmarais, P. Claeys, and A. Trauger, eds. *Public Policies for Food Sovereignty*, 91–106. London: Routledge.

Wittman, H. 2011. 'Food Sovereignty. A New Rights Framework for Food and Nature?'. *Environment and Society: Advances in Research* 2(1): 87–105.

Wittman, H. 2015. 'From Protest to Policy: The Challenges of Institutionalizing Food Sovereignty'. *Canadian Food Studies/La Revue Canadienne Des Études Sur l'Alimentation* 2(2): 174–82.

Zwingel, S. 2012. 'How Do Norms Travel? Theorizing International Women's Rights in Transnational Perspective'. *International Studies Quarterly* 56(1): 115–29.

CHAPTER 38

THE JURIDIFICATION OF POLITICS

RACHEL SIEDER

INTRODUCTION

THE juridification of politics is now widely recognized as a global phenomenon that is here to stay. Since the 1970s, Jürgen Habermas and others have seen in the creeping forms of regulatory bureaucratization that are typical of advanced capitalist democracies the juridification of 'social life-worlds' (Habermas 1981; Teubner 1987); yet by the twenty-first century the turn to law appeared to be a central feature of politics the world over. Rich and poor alike, from economic and political elites to sectors historically marginalized and abused by those in power, all increasingly look to legal norms, mechanisms, and arguments to defend their interests and stake their claims. Juridification is discernible in the politics of states ranging from established liberal democracies to those where authoritarian rule by law prevails. Presidents and former rulers of countries from Asia to the Americas have been impeached and imprisoned on charges of corruption as the judicialization of elite competition has become increasingly central to political calculus. Simultaneously, slum-dwellers, peasants, Indigenous Peoples, and women resisting patriarchal violence figure amongst the numerous collectives demanding respect for their rights and framing their claims with reference to legal discourses.[1] While processes of judicialization for the most part occur in national courts, the overlapping and multiscalar nature of global legal pluralism is a defining feature of contemporary forms of juridification: the contractual rights and obligations of states and global financial capital are routinely fought out in the courts and arbitration tribunals of London, Geneva, and New York, rather than in state courts, whilst those seeking redress for gross violations of human rights often simultaneously pursue their claims in national, regional, and international forums.

Juridification, then, can involve judicialization—the displacement of political battles to the courts—but in fact signals a much broader phenomenon. The concept of juridification has been understood as a form of legal framing, whereby people come to see themselves as legal subjects through the process of claiming rights (Blichner and Molander 2008). It also refers to processes of legal or law-like ordering, wherein courts or other agents, such as non-governmental organizations (NGOs) or international organizations, demand certain standards of legal and organizational 'legibility' from subjects.[2] The turn to the jural is assumed to transform identities and subjectivities. Broadly, we can identify two main perspectives on the phenomenon, perhaps most usefully envisaged as extremes on a spectrum. At one end of the scale, juridification is seen as a new and insidious form of domination via the jural. Jean and John Comaroff (2006), for example, have analysed the current global turn to law as a hegemonic form of standardization, arguing that law (like money) converts the incommensurable into the commensurable, thereby facilitating capitalist expansion and dispossession. The complex global legal pluralism that characterizes late capitalism is integral to this domination through law. For example, Shalini Randeria (2007: 40–1) has shown how the expansion and superposition of legal and quasi-legal forums such as arbitration, mediation, and inspection at different scales (local, national, and international), which now characterizes 'development', is ultimately disempowering for the subjects of development initiatives. According to this line of interpretation, the turn to law privileges technocratic, elite forms of knowledge, depoliticizing and fragmenting political battles and ultimately narrowing the space for collective action.[3] At the other end of the scale, different authors have explored the counterhegemonic possibilities of what Boaventura de Sousa Santos and César Rodríguez-Garavito (2005b) call legal 'globalization from below', maintaining, simultaneously, a critical perspective on the jural and recognizing the contestations that occur through law and the growing importance of legal struggles and rights frames for political activism. These two readings are not mutually exclusive as the impacts of juridification on politics and collective action ultimately depend on context. As Julia Eckert and her colleagues argue in their important volume, juridification is best understood as a wide range of social processes through which law itself is socially constituted, characterized by dialectics of norm diffusion and adaptation with uncertain and contingent outcomes (Eckert et al. 2012a: 15–16).

Juridified subjectivities

Anthropologists have long explored how engagement with different facets of law shapes individual and collective subjectivities, documenting how juridified battles transform perceptions of self, often forging new group identities where previously these did not exist. Political identities, for example, as survivors of gender violence or as individuals who define themselves as LGBTI, have often coalesced through different processes of norm diffusion and sociolegal mobilization. More pessimistic readings have pointed to the technologies involved in different legal initiatives that initially held out the promise of 'justice'—technologies which can end up marginalizing or ignoring the very voices and opinions of those the measures were supposed to benefit. In this sense, the extensive critical anthropological literature on transitional justice has made important contributions to debates on juridification, showing how the promises and mechanisms of this powerful transnational legal paradigm are often at odds with the ways in which people on the ground who suffered gross violations of human rights conceive of harm and redress (Anders 2012; Crosby and Lykes 2019; Niezen 2013a; Rojas-Pérez 2017; Ross 2002; Shaw and Waldorf 2010; Wilson 2001).

Legal encodification invariably involves the categorization and formalization of certain subjects and the exclusion or invisibilization of others. Yet identities are dynamic rather than fixed, with new demands and articulations constantly emerging in response to ongoing engagements with the jural. Recent contributions to the 'anthropology of justice' remind us that formal law is just one sphere of action in political struggles and that the imaginaries of justice of different individuals and groups rarely coincide entirely with the way justice is framed in legal terms, even when it is framed by the NGOs and activist networks that litigate cases on behalf of the marginalized and dispossessed (Brunnegger and Faulk 2016; Goodale 2017: esp. Chapter 3). Other authors have observed that engagement with formal legality rarely leads to the kind of depoliticization posited by the more pessimistic readings of juridification (Eckert et al. 2012b; Sapignoli 2018). Certainly, legal battles can exhaust and divide social movements, prioritize forms of personhood or redress that are at odds with popular subjectivities or aspirations, subject people and their histories to the violence of bureaucratic techniques, or force plaintiffs back to court again and again, leading them to 'litigate as a way of life' (Sapignoli 2018: 13). However, juridification does not signal the end of politics. Indeed, today politics and law appear to be more intertwined than ever, involving complex transnational circuits and multiple and overlapping instances and temporalities of political and legal action.[4] The idea of a public sphere or political field that is somehow 'outside of law' is illusory. The key empirical questions are, rather, how the intercalation of legal and political terrains and idioms may be used to further emancipatory futures, and precisely what effects processes of juridification have on different subject populations. These questions can only ever be answered in specific contexts, through careful, culturally grounded ethnographies of struggles for justice.

Much of the debate in recent years has focused on the processes and possibilities of 'vernacularization', whereby individuals and groups appropriate, deploy, redefine, and transform dominant legal norms, framings, and instruments within specific settings, thereby 'localizing' them (Merry 2006). Sally Merry's influential work in particular focused on the role played by actors 'in the middle', such as the NGOs that litigate public action cases, in translating the law between formal norms, institutions, and claimants. These processes of translation are anything but straightforward, as different actors on the ground disagree and contest legal definitions and concepts, transforming them in the process. For example, a growing body of work in Latin America has explored how Indigenous women have organized to contest hegemonic definitions of women's human rights that emphasize individual over and above collective rights, but also to challenge discriminatory gendered ideologies underpinning Indigenous community law (Arteaga

Böhrt 2018; Barrera Vivero 2016; Hernández 2016; Sieder 2017; Sierra 2004). Instead of 'vernacularization', Eckert and her colleagues prefer the Derridean concept of 'iteration', arguing that the former suggests pre-ordained normative orders that somehow converge, whereas the latter alludes to the ways in which all situated forms of engagement with legal norms and institutions are necessarily interpretative acts that constitute both self and law (Eckert et al. 2012a: 11–13). Participating in related debates, others have considered the extent to which juridification of specific local struggles can in fact transform international or domestic law by shaping the implementation of court judgments, contributing to the development of new legal principles (Kirsch 2018; Rajagopal 2009), and generating 'subaltern cosmopolitan legalities' through specific struggles (Santos and Rodríguez-Garavito 2005a: 5).

Juridification and Indigenous Peoples

In what follows I consider recent contributions that anthropologists have made to understanding the phenomenon of the juridification of politics, centring my discussion specifically on the juridification of Indigenous politics, an area that has elicited a wealth of analysis in recent years (Goodale 2017: Chapter 6; Hernández 2016; Kirsch 2012; Povinelli 2007; Sapignoli 2018; Sieder 2010; Sierra 2004). The late twentieth-century creation of the transnational legal category of indigeneity has afforded new possibilities for political claims for autonomy, sovereignty, difference, and recognition to be played out within and beyond courts. Indigenous Peoples are now defined as collective subjects of rights in both international law and numerous state constitutions; and they have resorted to national and international judicial arenas to fight legal and illegal encroachments on their lands and ways of life and to oppose the multiple forms of racialized violence and criminalization they increasingly face. While Indigenous mobilization is invariably deeply rooted in specific places and ontologies—what Arturo Escobar (2008) has termed 'place-based struggles'—entanglements with law have generated a broader epistemic community which has cemented a transnational identity of 'Indigenous Peoples'. Engagement in legal battles and strategic litigation is today a central part of Indigenous Peoples' politics the world over, and disputing issues on the legal terrain within and also outside the courts is a key element of shared struggles. As Maria Sapignoli (2018: 247) observes in her work on the San people in Botswana, 'litigation has become one of the strategic anchorages of the global indigenous movement'. While the encoding of vastly different subjects as 'Indigenous Peoples' may have encouraged certain kinds of 'strategic essentializing' or demanded the performance of established scripts of indigeneity (Povinelli 2007; Sieder and Witchell 2001),[5] prevailing international norms of self-determination emphasize self-identification and the right to self-definition, elements that Indigenous People have mobilized against the arguments of states and other actors who seek to dismiss them on the grounds of 'inauthenticity'. Towards the end of the twentieth century, Indigenous People, who, historically, had suffered racial discrimination and been excluded from dominant politics, found in juridification a means to amplify their voices and demands and project them onto a broader political stage.

As stated above, much of the broader debate about the juridification of politics tends to refer to the diffusion and vernacularization of state and international law and to the identities, discourses, and forms of collective action generated by engagements with dominant norms and institutions. I argue here that processes of juridification involving indigeneity and Indigenous Peoples are empirically and conceptually different from the juridification of political or moral claims per se. Although the vernacularization of hegemonic law and the associated transformation of identities and subjectivities, which are key elements of all processes of juridification, are certainly in evidence in the very construction of a transnational category of indigeneity (Niezen 2013b), what is at stake ultimately is *a battle for the existence and legibility of different legal orders*, rather than simply greater recognition within state law or international law. In the initial stages of colonial expansion in certain regions of the world Indigenous Peoples were legally recognized as sovereign, with their own forms of organization, law, and jurisdiction. In founding treaties, governments in Canada, Chile, and New Zealand recognized the inherent sovereignty of Native peoples, although their recognition was always partial and they sometimes reneged on the treaties entirely. Importantly, juridification involving Indigenous Peoples is in one sense about disputes between different forms of legal rationality—native peoples' law existed *as law* before it came into contact with colonial legal epistemologies grounded in the racialization and inferiorization of subject peoples. These foundational inequalities of power and ongoing histories of colonization distinguish the juridification of Indigenous politics from juridified battles where plaintiffs implicitly submit to the law's authority to adjudicate, recognizing state sovereignty. For example, contestations over sexual and reproductive rights have become increasingly juridified in recent decades, with both those in favour of expanding or defending women's rights to autonomy over their bodies and those opposing such policies resorting to legal framings and litigation (Bergallo et al. 2018; Cook et al. 2014). A marked feature in the juridification of sexual and reproductive rights has been the gradual replacement of moral and religious discourses and framings with legal ones, with both sides of the political divide resorting to the language of rights (the rights of women, the rights of the unborn child, etc.). By contrast, while contemporary juridification involving Indigenous People certainly hinges on the vernacularization of rights frames (the category of indigeneity itself being rooted in a conception of a collective subject of rights), these human rights frames do not replace the different ontologies underpinning the alternative legal orders that are defended by Indigenous People, nor do they overcome the challenge they pose to hegemonic frames of legality.

Juridification at the interface between hegemonic and subordinated forms of legality was always a feature of colonial contexts, in turn transforming these different bodies of law through multiple processes of contestation, codification, and engagement. Stuart Kirsch (2012) has pointed to the 'looping effect' produced by the juridification of Indigenous political struggles: Indigenous practices and concepts are altered through their engagements with courts, and at the same time legal concepts are reshaped as lawyers, judges, and courts respond to these encounters, sometimes leading to the emergence of hybrid legal precedents.[6] According to Kirsch, even claims made in court that are not taken up and translated into jurisprudential precedents or new legal concepts can still circulate as *political discourse* and concepts, as more horizontal exchanges between Indigenous Peoples are produced as a consequence of juridification. He concludes that 'the juridification of indigenous politics cannot escape the universalizing power of legal language, but can create new political opportunities' (Kirsch 2012: 40). Independently of whether they hold a more or less pessimistic view on the prospects and effects of juridification, most authors point to Indigenous subjects becoming ever more enmeshed in inescapable webs of law, increasingly internalizing dominant legal cultures. For example, Ronald Niezen (2013b: 186) argues that international human rights law has generated 'a body of rights-oriented knowledge, that includes an understanding of the essence of humanity and the legitimate forms and categories of human belonging', something he understands as 'a strategic epistemology that is reinterpreting common understandings of human life and ... redefining human identity'.

Arguably, these readings place too much emphasis on top-down processes of norm diffusion and the vernacularization of hegemonic forms of law. In particular, such perspectives pay insufficient attention to the law of Indigenous Peoples themselves and to the ways ideas about autochthonous norms and practices of governance circulate through more horizontal forms of knowledge transfer and exchange between Indigenous Peoples and their allies, involving complex processes of interpretation that in turn shape collective identities and political futures. Juridification involving Indigenous Peoples is much more than the use of state law or international human rights law against the state in pursuit of greater recognition and distributive justice; it also includes the mobilization and reframing of alternative legal and political orders aimed at ensuring their continuity. The recognition of legal pluralism in Latin America's new constitutional regimes, however limited or ambiguous in normative and practical terms, has meant that lawyers, who defend Indigenous Peoples' collective rights to autonomy, land, and territory, and judges, who adjudicate these cases, have had to engage with alternative cultural conceptions and representations of what 'law' itself is.

The explicit or implicit challenge to hegemonic forms of law contained in Indigenous juridification of politics signals what Audra Simpson (2015) has termed 'indigenous refusal' (see also Richland 2018). Through juridified political engagements, Native people lay bare the racialized juridical frames and categories that have systematically stripped them of their territories in legally sanctioned forms of genocide. The political insistence on Indigenous law, jurisdiction, and sovereignty opposes, then, colonial erasure and challenges the jurisdictional claims, temporalities, and ontologies of state law and international human rights law.[7] Such instances of juridification represent a political claim for epistemologies and ontologies of law grounded in conceptions of time, space, and personhood that may be incommensurable with dominant legal rationalities. As Mark Rifkin (2017: 14) observes, 'the idea of refusing recognition is less about being unimplicated in the choices, affects, policies, imaginaries, and brutalities of non-natives than about insisting that Indigenous people have an existence not a priori tethered to settler norms and frames' (2017: 14).

The juridification of 'Mayan law'

When much of the dominant legal order is seen as alien and illegitimate, and when Indigenous subjects may posit radically different understandings of governance, law, and morality, what processes of subjectivization and politics are generated by juridification? In what follows I explore these issues by analysing different dynamics involved in the juridification of Mayan law in post-war Guatemala. Drawing on my own ethnographic work, I trace the different ways in which Mayan rights activists and their allies have revitalized, analysed, and defended their own forms of law in the context of battles for state recognition of legal pluralism in the post-war period. In the light of my own experience over the years, I also reflect on the responsibilities and challenges for academics engaged in such processes of juridification.

While the social organization and laws of the Mayan peoples date back thousands of years, the self-conscious, political use of the concept of 'Mayan law' emerged in Guatemala in the immediate post-war period, following the final signing of the peace agreements in 1996 that brought an end to thirty-six years of armed conflict. The 1995 Accord on the Rights and Identity of Indigenous Peoples, signed by both the government and the insurgent forces, committed the state to recognize legal pluralism and approve legislative reforms guaranteeing the rights of Indigenous communities to administer their affairs according to their 'customary norms'. A pan-Mayan social movement had emerged in the final years of the armed conflict and participated, albeit indirectly, in the negotiation of the peace accords, subsequently working to secure their implementation (Warren 1999). Different Mayan rights organizations and NGOs across the country allied with academics, NGOs, and international development cooperation agencies in an effort to 'systematize' what came to be termed 'Mayan law'. At the same time, these activists rejected any attempts to have Mayan law codified as part of state law, conscious of the inherently colonial premises of such an undertaking. Instead they lobbied for the constitutional recognition of Indigenous jurisdiction and insisted on their rights to define their own forms of law. Thus, in the 1990s, pan-Mayan Indigenous rights activism found expression in a multifaceted undertaking to enunciate Mayan law and in a conscious positioning of Indigenous law vis-à-vis state legality in a bid to institute a pluricultural legal system. More importantly, it was part of a grassroots movement across the country to reaffirm and revitalize forms of community governance and identity in the wake of the armed conflict which had taken such a tremendous toll on Indigenous lives and culture (Sieder 2011).[8]

'Mayan law' was a form of praxis whereby Indigenous and non-Indigenous intellectuals and communal authorities reflected on and systematized their own governance practices and their underlying moral, philosophical, and historical roots. Guatemala's

Mayan Peoples comprise twenty-one different ethno-linguistic groups, and Indigenous law itself is highly internally diverse, often from one canton to the next. Some groups and regions of the country predominated over others in national efforts to identify or define 'Mayan law', in turn influencing different local processes of revitalization. Intellectuals from the largest ethno-linguistic groups, K'iche' and Kaqchikel, drew on existing studies by non-Indigenous anthropologists and archaeologists at the same time as they critically interrogated them and deployed specific forms of intertextuality that supported the legitimacy of Mayan law, drawing on alternative sources and statements of law, such as the Popol Vuh (the most important Mayan sacred text). For example, the National Conference of Mayan Spiritual Leaders Oxlajuj Ajpop, published a series of books detailing the norms and philosophy of Maya K'iche' legality, emphasizing the links between Mayan spirituality, morality, and law. In describing the principles of Maya K'iche' law, Indigenous intellectuals made a series of epistemological and ontological truth claims. Certainly, their systematizations occurred within the context of claim-making before the state, but they also formed part of a broader process whereby collective identities were reconstituted and the continuity of Indigenous life-worlds was reaffirmed in the wake of the genocidal violence that characterized the armed conflict. The various books, documents, and videos that were produced from the mid-1990s onwards were just one element of a process occurring within a complex field of contestation involving legal and political state authorities and a wide range of international actors engaged in post-war reconstruction. Yet the reorganization of Mayan law in different communities across the country was primarily an inward-looking process responding to conceptions of self and justice stretching far beyond the temporal frames of 'post-conflict reconstruction' or multicultural state reform.

Emblematic contemporary examples of Maya K'iche' law became the subject of study at the same time as communal leaders championed their own forms of law beyond their immediate localities, underlining the political nature of the process. For example, in Santa Cruz del Quiché, the municipal capital of the department of Quiché, a supra-communal Indigenous Mayoralty was reconstituted by local Mayan leaders in 2003 and subsequently gained national prominence—and aroused controversy—for its defence of the application of what it defined as Maya K'iche' law. This included the use of *x'ik'ay*, ritual beatings with the branches of a quince tree, which, as local K'iche' authorities explain, are intended to redirect the energies of those accused of the transgression of community norms. Other practices used to 'recover shame' included *xuklem*, which requires the penitents to go counter-clockwise around a circle on their knees three times in order to ask pardon from the earth. Indigenous authorities in Santa Cruz del Quiché have strongly defended *x'ik'ay* and *xuklem*, refusing to domesticate their local legal practices to cater to the sensibilities of prevailing human rights orthodoxies and thereby inherently challenging the ontological premises of hegemonic law, refusing to re-inscribe its power.[9] What state actors and some elements of the international human rights community perceive as corporal punishment or, in the worst case, as torture, is defended as an alternative frame for justice, redress, and reparations. The continuity and defence of Mayan law thus critically interrogates colonial histories by challenging the very legitimacy of dominant forms of law and instantiating alternative conceptions of sovereignty in a way that is reminiscent of Justin Richland's concept of 'sovereign time'. Richland (2008: 10) developed this concept in his analysis of Hopi narrations of Indigenous norms of law and governance grounded in tradition, which establish juridical authority and function 'as part of the legitimizing backdrop of contemporary [Indigenous] juridical and political action' (Richland 2008: 10).[10]

Engaged ethnography and juridification

The juridification of politics involves multiple processes within and beyond the courts. Diverse research collaborations constituted a central facet of the juridification of Mayan law and were often riven with tensions related to differing understandings of law itself and contrasting perspectives on how its study should be approached, by whom, and to what ends. For example, one collaborative research initiative, eventually published in 2005, documented the application of Maya K'iche' law in the department of Totonicapán in a case of aggravated robbery in the canton of Chiyax. The original plan called for the production of a book and an accompanying video describing the measures adopted by the communal authorities and the specific efforts at interlegal intercultural coordination that ensued following their resolution of the case. Research for the publication and the video was funded by the Danish international development cooperation, IBIS, and undertaken by a Mayan-rights NGO based in the nearby city of Quetzaltenango. However, when the village authorities in Chiyax discovered how much the book and video would cost to produce, they demanded that the NGO and IBIS pay a greater share directly to them to be used in local development projects. Other tensions revolved around how to conceptualize and depict Indigenous law itself: at one forum on intercultural interlegal coordination, hosted by the Soros Foundation in Guatemala in 2011, I was stung by criticism from a Mayan intellectual who was unhappy with the depiction of Maya K'iche' law in our documentary, *K'ixb'al* ('Shame'). Produced in collaboration with the Indigenous Mayoralty of Santa Cruz del Quiché, the film, which analyses the resolution by Indigenous authorities of a case of the theft of a vehicle by three youngsters, includes footage shot by villagers themselves and interviews with key protagonists, who explain the nature and logic of their processes of dispute resolution (Sieder and Flores 2011).[11] Controversially, it includes footage of the application of *x'ik'ay*. The Mayan intellectual at the Soros Foundation meeting argued that the documentary showed Mayan law 'as it is' and not 'as it should be', thus challenging the representational practices that tend to characterize ethnographic approaches and the authoritative accounts that these generate. He argued that state law is normally judged by its declared ideals while Indigenous law is dismissed as a violation of human rights or due process on the basis of its perceived practice. He insisted on the need to counterpose the philosophical and ontological bases of Indigenous legal norms to state law, emphasizing the insufficiency of ethnographic observation as a means of understanding alternative forms of legality. At the time, I read his critique as an appeal to a form of strategic essentializing and atemporal representation that I found to be problematic. Over subsequent years, I have returned to that encounter in order to reflect on the enormous complexities of representing ontologies of Indigenous law and on the role that we as engaged non-Indigenous intellectuals play in its juridification, with all the responsibilities and risks this entails. In my work as an author of special witness reports for key legal cases defending Indigenous Peoples' rights to jurisdictional autonomy in Guatemala, I have engaged in attempts to make Indigenous law legible and credible to judges, prosecutors, and public defenders. Aside from revealing the race and class privilege that structures the terrain of juridification involving Indigenous Peoples, such attempts by anthropologists to mediate between Mayan peoples' theorizations of their own forms of law and dominant legal frames are, however, far from simple. This is because the epistemological bases of both forms of law often differ radically,[12] and the ability of the ethnographer to apprehend and communicate the ontologies of Indigenous law inevitably remains constrained both by hegemonic legal frames and by our own subjectivities.

Conclusions

In this chapter I have argued that the juridification of politics is an inescapable fact of political engagement within the complex global legal pluralism that is characteristic of late capitalism. Law in most places *is* politics, and it is for this reason that minority groups in organized social movements everywhere increasingly take their battles to court. My analysis echoes other authors' findings about the inextricability of law and politics, challenging many of the assumed dichotomies of the critical legal scholarship on juridification (Zenker 2012). Recent anthropologies of justice also complicate these dichotomies and divisions, underlining the fact that ideas of what is just and right are profoundly political and also shaped by different legal imaginaries. I have suggested here that while the inexorable logics of hegemonic forms of law are certainly inescapable, this does not necessarily entail either the weakening of collective action and depoliticization or the colonization of other life-worlds by globally dominant legalities.

In particular I have argued that the juridification of politics engaged in by Indigenous People is different from the juridification of politics per se. This is because, rather than claims for recognition or inclusion that broadly accept the epistemological bases of state law, juridification involving Indigenous Peoples occurs at the intersection between forms of law with often radically different epistemological and ontological bases: on one hand, hegemonic national and international legality and, on the other, the autochthonous forms of law of colonized peoples. Drawing on the experience of the juridification of Mayan law in post-war Guatemala, I have shown how Indigenous Peoples' juridification occurring at the interstices of these different forms of law constitutes a platform on which broader claims for Indigenous autonomy, sovereignty, and jurisdiction are played out. The constant re-elaboration, exercise, and circulation of 'Mayan law' in contemporary Guatemala is simultaneously a form of politics, an enunciation of authoritative norms or legal philosophies, and a guide to ways of being and conducting oneself in the universe. Whilst Mayan peoples use the language of human rights to claim and defend their core interests, their identities are not determined by the epistemologies of human rights law. Mark Goodale (2017: 162) is right to caution that 'the relationship between indigeneity, international law, and political mobilization is riddled with contradictions, overshadowed by the potential for economic exploitation', and clearly law continues to be one of the principal tools of neocolonial dispossession. However, I have pointed here to the potentialities inherent in the juridification of Mayan law, arguing that these different legal engagements can be read as exchanges that also contain and transmit a politics of 'indigenous refusal' (Simpson 2015). It is utopian to expect that these dynamics alone will halt or even slow the onslaught of global capital in the current historical moment, but this does not detract from their importance, which goes beyond the merely symbolic.

Lastly, I have attempted to reflect on the challenges for anthropologists involved in the juridification of Indigenous law, advocating forms of anthropological knowledge production grounded in critical engagement that furthers an intercultural epistemological dialogue aimed at radically transforming racialized structures of dispossession. This demands a high degree of reflexivity about our methods, sources, and forms of representation, along with awareness about the ways in which our representations circulate and are implicated in the juridification of Indigenous politics. As Justin Richland (2008: 24) argues, in contrast to the authority of the standard ethnographic account:

> [S]omething different emerges when anthropologists recognize that the interdiscursivities embedded in notions like tradition and law have been actively taken up by those Others who critics argue were originally marginalized by those notions. There is a difference in the chronotopes generated through ethnography when, like the Hopi legal actors engaging each other in tribal court proceedings, they remain open to the multiplex ways in which the temporalities of tradition, law, norm, and fact, are always being actively remade in the emergent discourses central to everyday indigenous governance practices today. In ethnographic assays of the latter type, the normative discourses of indigenous peoples are treated not as the historical relics of some long-lost past, but as guiding norms that continue to operate in the present.

Acknowledgements

Earlier versions of this chapter were presented at the workshop convened by the editors of this Handbook in December 2018 in Berlin, and at the seminar on empirical studies of law at the Institute of Legal Studies at Mexico's national university (UNAM) in November 2018. My gratitude goes to Julia Eckert, Maria Sapignoli, Maria Paula Saffon, and Francisca Pou for their careful readings and suggestions, which have immeasurably improved this chapter. Any remaining errors are entirely my responsibility.

Notes

1. The judicialization of politics, involving the displacement of executive and congressional decision-making power and public contestation to the courts, is the subject of a significant literature: see Hirschl (2008); Randeria (2007); Sieder et al. (2005), and Tate and Vallinder (1995).
2. NGOs may institute certain kinds of 'audit cultures' or bureaucratic forms and processes among organizations, e.g. the use of statistics in reporting or the privileging of particular kinds of testimony over others (Strathern 2000). The extension of certain cultural patterns through NGOs is part of the broader phenomenon of juridification.
3. Jean and John Comaroff (2006: 30) call this phenomenon 'lawfare', which they define as 'violence rendered legible, legal, and legitimate by its own sovereign word'.
4. Sapignoli (2018: 12) observes how going through a legal process 'involves an almost *hyperpoliticization* of (or through) law, whereby recourse to legal remedies in some ways intensifies political struggles and becomes inseparable from them'.
5. Povinelli (2007) emphasizes the role of anthropological imaginations and tropes in fashioning impossible standards of authenticity for Indigenous peoples in legal battles over land claims in Australia, standards of authenticity which in turn led either to strategic essentializing or misrecognition.
6. e.g. Aida Hernández's (2016) analysis of her own role as special expert witness before the Interamerican Court of Human Rights in the case of Inés Fernández Ortega vs. Mexico, concerning a Me'phaa woman raped by members of the Mexican army, shows how anthropological analysis of community impacts contributed to the court recognizing the rape as a violation of both individual and collective rights, setting an important legal precedent.
7. On the relationship of jurisdiction to sovereignty, see Richland (2011).
8. In thirty-six years of armed conflict, some 200,000 people were killed, the vast majority by members of the armed forces, and a further 50,000 disappeared. Over 90 per cent of victims were Indigenous civilians (Comisión para el Esclarecimiento Histórico en Guatemala 1999).
9. Both International Labor Organization 169 on the Rights of Indigenous and Tribal Peoples (ratified by the Guatemalan state in 1996) and the 1995 Agreement on the Rights and Identity of Indigenous Peoples recognize Indigenous law only if it is in line with international human rights standards.
10. See also the important work of Mark Rifkin (2017) on Indigenous time and settler time.
11. The documentary can be seen at <https://vimeo.com/51473676> (accessed 30 April 2020).
12. Similarly, Stuart Kirsch (2018: 17) writes about the 'overlapping but sometimes incommensurate frames of reference' he has deployed in elaborating anthropological witness reports in defence of Indigenous peoples' rights.

References

Anders, G. 2012. 'Juridification, Transitional Justice and Reaching out to the Public in Sierra Leone'. In J. Eckert, B. Donahoe, C. Strümpell, and Z. Ö. Biner, eds. *Law Against the State: Ethnographic Forays into Law's Transformations*, 94–117. Cambridge and New York: Cambridge University Press.

Arteaga Böhrt, A. C. 2018. *Complementariedad, derechos y despatriarcalización. El debate de los órdenes y las ideologías de género en el marco del proyecto autonómico de Totora Marka (Bolivia).* PhD thesis in Social Anthropology, CIESAS, Mexico City.

Barrera Vivero, A. 2016. *Violence against Women in Legally Plural Settings. Experiences and Lessons from the Andes.* Oxford: Routledge.

Bergallo, P., I. C. Jaramillo Sierra, and J. M. Vaggione, eds. 2018. *El aborto en américa latina: estrategias jurídicas para luchar por su legalización y enfrentar las resistencias conservadoras*, Buenos Aires: Siglo XXI.

Blichner, L. C. and A. Molander. 2008. 'Mapping Juridification'. *European Law Journal Volume* 13(1): 36–54.

Brunnegger, S. and K. A. Faulk, eds. 2016. *A Sense of Justice: Legal Knowledge and Lived Experience in Latin America.* Redwood City, CA: Stanford University Press.

Comaroff, J. and J. Comaroff. 2006. *Law and Violence in the Postcolony.* Chicago: Chicago University Press.

Comisión para el Esclarecimiento Histórico en Guatemala. 1999. *Guatemala Memoria del Silencio.* Guatemala: Oficina de Servicios para Proyectos de las Naciones Unidas.

Cook, R., J. N. Erdman, and B. M. Dickens, eds. 2014. *Abortion Law in Transnational Perspective: Cases and Controversies.* Penn: University of Pennsylvania Press.

Crosby, A. and M. Brinton Lykes. 2019., *Beyond Repair? Mayan Women's Protagonism in the Aftermath of Genocidal Harm.* New York: Rutgers University Press.

Eckert, J., B. Donahoe, C. Strümpell, and Z. Özlem Biner, eds. 2012b. *Law Against the State: Ethnographic Forays into Law's Transformations.* Cambridge and New York: Cambridge University Press.

Eckert, J., Z. O. Biner, B. Donahoe, and C. Strümpell. 2012a. 'Introduction: Law's Travels and Transformations'. In J. Eckert, B. Donahoe, C. Strümpell, and Z. O. Biner, eds. *Law Against the State: Ethnographic Forays into Law's Transformations*, 1–22. Cambridge and New York: Cambridge University Press.

Escobar, A. 2008. *Territories of Difference: Place, Movements, Life, Redes.* Durham NC: Duke University Press.

Goodale, M. 2017. *Anthropology and Law: A Critical Introduction.* New York: New York University Press.

Habermas, J. 1987 [1981]. *The Theory of Communicative Action. vol. 2: Lifeworld and System: A Critique of Functionalist Reason.* Boston: Beacon Press.

Hernández, A. 2016. *Multiple Injustices. Indigenous Women, Law and Political Struggle in Latin America.* Tucson: University of Arizona Press.

Hirschl, R. 2008. 'The Judicialization of Politics'. In G. A. Caldeira, R. D. Kelemen, and K. E. Whittington, eds. *The Oxford Handbook of Law and Politics*, 119–41. Oxford: Oxford University Press.

Kirsch, S. 2012. 'Jurifidication of Indigenous Politics'. In Eckert et al. *Law Against the State: Ethnographic Forays into Law's Transformations*, 23–43. Cambridge: Cambridge University Press:.

Kirsch, S. 2018. 'Dilemmas of an Expert Witness in the Amazon', Working Paper #428, Kellog Institute for International Studies, Notre Dame IN.

Merry, S. E. 2006. 'Transnational Human Rights and Local Activism: Mapping the Middle'. *American Anthropologist* 108(1): 38–51.

Niezen, R. 2013a. *Truth and Indignation. Canada's Truth and Reconciliation Commission on Indian Residential Schools.* Toronto: University of Toronto Press.

Niezen, R. 2013b. 'The Law's Legal Anthropology'. In M. Goodale, ed. *Human Rights at the Crossroads*, 185–97. Oxford and New York: Oxford University Press.

Povinelli, E. A. 2007. *The Cunning of Recognition. Indigenous Alterities and the Making of Australian Multiculturalism*. Durham, NC: Duke University Press.

Rajagopal, B. 2009. *International Law from Below. Development, Social Movements and Third World Resistance*. Cambridge and New York: Cambridge University Press.

Randeria, S. 2007. 'The State of Globalization: Legal Plurality, Overlapping Sovereignties and Ambiguous Alliances between Civil Society and the Cunning State in India'. *Theory, Culture & Society* 24: 1–33.

Richland J. B. 2011. 'Hopi Tradition as Jurisdiction. On the Potentializing Limits of Hopi Sovereignty'. *Law and Social Inquiry* 36(1): 201–34.

Richland, J. B. 2008. 'Sovereign Time, Storied Moments: The Temporalities of Law, Tradition, and Ethnography in Hopi Tribal Court'. *PoLAR: Political and Legal Anthropology Review* 31(1): 8–27.

Richland, J. B. 2018. 'Jurisdictions of Significance: Narrating Time-Space in a Hopi-US Tribal Consultation'. *American Ethnologist* 45(2): 268–80.

Rifkin, M. 2017. *Beyond Settler Time. Temporal Sovereignty and Indigenous Self-Determination*. Durham, NC: Duke University Press.

Rojas-Perez, I. 2017. *Mourning Remains: State Atrocity, Exhumations and Governing the Disappeared in Peru's Postwar Andes*. Stanford: Stanford University Press.

Ross, F. 2002. *Bearing Witness: Women and the Truth and Reconciliation Commission in South Africa*. London: Pluto Press.

Santos, B. de S. and C. Rodríguez-Garavito, eds. 2005b. *Law and Globalization from Below: Towards a Cosmopolitan Legality*. Cambridge and New York: Cambridge University Press.

Santos, B. de S. and C. Rodríguez-Garavito. 2005a. 'Law, Politics, and the Subaltern in Counter-hegemonic Globalization'. In B. de S. Santos and C. Rodríguez-Garavito, eds. *Law and Globalization from Below: Towards a Cosmopolitan Legality*, 1–26. Cambridge and New York: Cambridge University Press.

Sapignoli, M. 2018. *Hunting Justice: Displacement, Law, and Activism in the Kalahari*, Cambridge and New York: Cambridge University Press.

Shaw, R. and L. Waldorf, eds. 2010. *Localizing Transitional Justice: Interventions and Priorities after Mass Violence*. Stanford: Stanford University Press.

Sieder, R. 2010. 'Legal Cultures in the (Un)Rule of Law: Indigenous Rights and Juridification in Guatemala'. In J. Couso, A. Huneeus, and R. Sieder, eds. *Cultures of Legality: Judicialization and Political Activism in Latin America*, 161–81. Cambridge and New York: Cambridge University Press.

Sieder, R. 2011. 'Building Mayan Authority and Autonomy: The "Recovery" of Indigenous Law in Post-peace Guatemala'. *Studies in Law, Politics, and Society* 55: 25–57.

Sieder, R. and C. Y. Flores. 2011. *Autoridad, autonomía y derecho indígena en la Guatemala de posguerra*. Guatemala: F&G Editores-Casa Comal-UAEM.

Sieder, R. and J. Witchell. 2001. 'Advancing Indigenous Claims through the Law: Reflections on the Guatemalan Peace Process'. In J. Cowan, M. Dembour, and R. Wilson, eds. *Culture and Rights*, 201–25. Cambridge and New York: Cambridge University Press.

Sieder, R., ed. 2017. *Demanding Justice and Security: Indigenous Women and Legal Pluralities in Latin America*. New Brunswick: Rutgers University Press.

Sieder, R., L. Schjolden, and A. Angell, eds. 2005. *The Judicialization of Politics in Latin America*. New York: Routledge.

Sierra, M. T., ed. 2004. *Haciendo. Justicia. Interlegalidad, derecho y género en regiones indígenas.* Mexico City: CIESAS.

Simpson, A. 2015. *Mohawk Interruptus: Political Life across the Borders of Settler States.* Durham, NC: Duke University Press.

Strathern, M. ed. 2000. *Audit Cultures. Anthropological Studies in Audit, Ethics and the Academy.* London: Routledge.

Tate, C. N. and T. Vallinder. 1995. *The Global Expansion of Judicial Power.* New York and London: New York University Press.

Teubner, G. 1987. *Juridification of Social Spheres: A Comparative Analysis in the Areas of Labor, Corporate, Antitrust, and Social Welfare Law.* Berlin and New York: De Gruyter.

Warren, K. 1999. *Indigenous Movements and their Critics. Pan-Maya Activism in Guatemala.* Princeton: Princeton University Press.

Wilson, R. A. 2001. *The Politics of Truth and Reconciliation in South Africa.* Cambridge and New York: Cambridge University Press.

Zenker, O. 2012. 'The Juridification of Political Protest and the Politicization of Legalism in South African Land Restitution'. In Eckert et al., eds. *Law Against the State: Ethnographic Forays into Law's Transformations*, 118–46. Cambridge: Cambridge University Press.

CHAPTER 39

THE PERSISTENCE OF CHINESE RIGHTS DEFENDERS

SARA L. M. DAVIS

If you want to go to hell, don't complain of the dark.

—*Liu Xiaobo*

THE current moment is a dark one for human rights practitioners. Authoritarian leaders are on the rise, and space for civil society is closing (CIVICUS 2018). The United States has resigned its membership in the Human Rights Council and now even seeks to remove the word 'gender' from United Nations (UN) policies (Borger 2018; Ford 2019). At the same time, authoritarian states such as China and Russia have launched unprecedented assaults on the UN human rights system (Human Rights Watch 2017a). All of this has sparked criticism of human rights, including by some academics.

Some scholars argue that human rights treaties and mechanisms fail because they represent Eurocentric values rooted in colonialism that have failed to find wider appeal (Mutua 2008). For Stephen Hopgood (2013: 1), rights norms emerged because they 'once served a very specific historical purpose: to inspire a sense of the secular sacred among the new middle classes of a rapidly modernizing Europe'. Now that this purpose is 'defunct', he argues, the movement has reached its logical end. While a lower-case, localized *human rights* movement may persist, in the form of organic local challenges to abuses of power, Hopgood foresees that the international *Human Rights* system of treaties and organizations will crumble away. Eric Posner (2014) similarly argues that it is time to recognize that the treaties 'were not so much an act of idealism as an act of hubris', which should be abandoned in favour of 'a humbler approach'. For Makau Matua (2016), also, human rights overpromised and underdelivered, and their time is now 'over'.

These critics often cite China's rise as evidence. Samuel Moyn (2018: 207) accurately notes China's 'remarkable salvation' of millions from poverty. Posner (2014) notes that China's model of 'political repression and economic liberalism' have made it the envy of other leaders in the developing world. Hopgood (2013: 175) argues that China's imperviousness to human rights pressure has made the Human Rights Council 'a sideshow in Geneva'. More recently, Kathryn Sikkink (2017) counter-argues that the current moment is a vibrant one for rights activism; but the *New York Times* summed up the dominant public cynicism in a 2018 headline: 'An Emboldened China No Longer Cares What Its Critics Think' (Myers and Buckley 2018).

These characterizations, while in line with the public image actively promoted by China's leadership, fail to capture the complexity of this vast and diverse country, its successes or its failings. While China has certainly made historic strides in combating poverty, stark inequalities remain, along with abuses of power that cause frequent protests by impoverished people. Depicting China as uniformly authoritarian also misses the surprising persistence of human rights activism. Activists persist in ways that are sometimes strategic, sometimes recklessly defiant, and usually imperceptible to outside observers; but they persist, nevertheless, in the context of a sweeping, brutal crackdown.

My argument, drawing on the case of China, is that we have reached not the global end times of human rights but something we could call the 'real times'. The world is in a new phase of more intense struggle over whether human beings share common values and, if so, what those values are. Through popular pro-democracy protests and social media—most recently international campaigns such as #metoo—the values of equality and accountability have become popularized. In response, some powerholders have dropped the mask of civility, and brute power is fully engaged. But it would be premature to declare this struggle over. The persistence of human rights advocates, including in the heart of one of the most powerful repressive states in the world, shows that human rights remains an important source of empowerment. Beyond the limits of the law, we encounter a space where law has been adapted and ingrained into everyday practice: what Sally E. Merry (2006) and others call the 'vernacularization' of human rights (see also de Gaay Fortman 2011; Goodale 2003, 2013; Merry and Stern 2005).

In the context of a volume that considers the relationship between law and culture, it may be worth underscoring that all countries, including China, are diverse; they contain multiple vernaculars, both literal and figurative. A country's leaders do not always speak for all the people in that country. As the late UN Secretary-General Kofi Annan observed once, 'It was never the people who complained of the universality of human rights, nor did the people consider human rights a Western or Northern imposition. It was often their leaders who did so' (Annan in Tomuschat 2003: 81).

Here are three examples of this kind of contestation, some from far beyond China:

• Philippines President Rodrigo Duterte, who has engaged in a widespread campaign of extrajudicial execution of accused drug dealers and who has called for police to shoot protestors, has frequently criticized human rights standards as a Western imposition. He specifically told the UN human rights special rapporteur on the independence of judges and lawyers to 'go to hell' (Reuters 2018). But the Republic of the Philippines has also seen numerous public protests affirming human rights standards. For example, in July 2018, Philippines clergy and rights advocates took to the streets to say that 'human rights is dying' under Duterte and to call for justice for 23,000 people killed by police (Catholic News Service 2018).• Kenya's president and deputy president successfully triumphed over criminal charges for election violence, calling the International Criminal Court (ICC) a Western imposition on Africa and suggesting that Kenya withdraw from it (Human Rights Watch 2016; Voice of America 2016). After Kenya's electoral commission declared incumbent Uhuru Kenyatta winner, again, of the 2017 election, the results were nullified by Kenya's Supreme Court. He won the subsequent vote, but efforts to retaliate against some opponents have nonetheless not stifled a vocal civil society, which now demands accountability for 2017 electoral violence (Oloo 2018).• In October 2017, Burundi became the first nation to leave the ICC, saying that the court 'has shown itself to be a political instrument and weapon used by the west to enslave' other states (Agence France-Presse 2017). But the move has been publicly decried by Burundian rights activists: the leadership is the subject of an ICC investigation into violent crimes. In the words of one Burundian law professor, while the court is flawed, 'the people of Burundi, and especially the victims, have made it clear that the only hope for justice rests with the ICC' (CIVICUS 2017).

In these and other countries, leaders have dropped the pretence of endorsing human rights standards and mechanisms. China is certainly leading the charge—all the more reason why its record should be scrutinized.

This chapter summarizes China's recent history of grassroots rights advocacy. In the early 2000s, the country experienced a brief moment of openness, with the growth of civil society, law reforms, and crusading rights lawyers. The past five years has seen a systematic rollback of this progress, with a sweeping crackdown on activists and lawyers. New forms of control have created a 'rule of fear', including ambitious efforts to draw on artificial intelligence and big data in expansive surveillance and policing of social life; the mass detention of hundreds of thousands of Uyghur Muslim minorities in forced labour camps; and the perfection of systems of censorship to exercise ideological control (Blyer 2019; Cook 2019; Gan and Lau 2018). Chinese authorities have also engaged in efforts to disrupt their citizens' participation in international human rights mechanisms, in order to pre-empt criticism.

Yet, as described below, some veteran activists stubbornly persist in objecting, and young activists continue to emerge. While they may no longer be able to actively use international human rights mechanisms and language safely, these Chinese activists show resilience and persistence in finding small pockets of political space to continue their work and in supporting one another—as one puts it, 'huddling together in the cold'. The conclusion of this chapter explores possible implications of their persistence for the broader movement.

AN ERA OF REFORM ENDS IN REPRESSION

2003–2013: The Sun Zhigang Generation

The first decade of the twenty-first century seemed restrictive at the time, but, in hindsight, it now appears to have been a golden age for rights activism and civil society mobilization in China.

In the wake of the Cultural Revolution (1966–76), new leadership emerged to reject the ideological excesses of the Mao era, launching a period of economic growth and stabilization. Presidents Deng Xiaoping and Jiang Zemin, pragmatists who favoured results over ideological purity, promoted the institutionalization, bureaucratization, and rationalization of state governance. The sweeping violence that ended the protests of 1989, largely squashing democratic opposition, was intended in part to shield the state from the unravelling of communist governments underway at that time in the Soviet Union.

Under President Hu Jintao, in the early 2000s, socialist values were largely sidelined in the pursuit of economic growth. In 2002, the Communist Party formally welcomed capitalists as members (Kahn 2002). But while existing power disparities grew in the following decade, citizens were given some limited powers. These included the right to challenge local officials in court, in village elections, and through peaceful labour protests that sometimes ended in negotiated compromise (Minzner 2018). In 2008, China passed Open Government Information Regulations, taking a step towards freedom of information (The China Center n.d.). The growth of media saw the rise of 'a generation of crusading and muckraking journalists' who exposed abuses of power in such relatively independent periodicals as *Nanfang Zhoumo (Southern Weekly)* (Minzner 2018: 23).

At the same time, economic inequality grew rapidly. China's economic boom had benefited some disproportionately, giving elites with Party ties wide leeway to exercise power in the name of economic growth. In response to the resulting emergence of social problems—including the burgeoning HIV crisis, forced evictions, environmental disasters, and more—activists established civil society organizations for the first time. These faced strict limits: no national organizations could be established; public protests were largely forbidden; and most could register only as for-profit enterprises. Nonetheless, hundreds of such organizations did spring up around the country. Some did groundbreaking work in conducting research, litigating, advocating for human rights with government officials, and even mobilizing public protests by impoverished populations.

In 2003, a migrant labourer named Sun Zhigang was detained for lack of a temporary residence permit and beaten to death by police. Thousands of Chinese citizens went online to call for justice. At that time, I was Human Rights Watch's researcher on China. Over a few days, I and other international allies watched memorial web pages and protest messages grow online in number and intensity. The hundreds of posts ranged from wordless images of flickering candles, to outraged all-caps denunciations of police abuse. In particular, online protestors demanded an end to the rigid household registration regime, which had created a vast underclass of desperate rural migrants in China's fast-growing cities. Millions of Chinese citizens seeking employment had in effect been turned into illegal immigrants in their own country, without rights to housing, health care, or education. Those who lacked work permits were vulnerable to police extortion and abusive detention. In response to this national campaign, a group of prominent Chinese experts drafted new legislation, sparking some limited reforms (Yun Xiang n.d.).

For the first time, Chinese activists experienced first-hand the electrifying impact of national rights-based advocacy. 'It was a significant event for the rule of law,' remembered lawyer Teng Biao. 'Then, I was filled with hope, and I decided to devote my life to human rights and NGO work. It was the turning point of my life' (Yu 2013). Subsequently, the first lawyers to explicitly call themselves 'rights defenders' (*weiquan renshi*) emerged in China. Working on the full range of civil rights issues—including religious freedom, due process, housing rights, HIV, and more—they linked informally across the country's vast geographic regions, using the Internet.

This relatively small group of human rights defenders emerged as part of a broader, if more tentative and cautious, effort to proceed with legal reform. New partnerships between Chinese law schools, lawyers, NGOs, journalists, and their overseas counterparts flourished. Seemingly, every week brought a new public interest law meeting or a new training for judges. Some were closed by police. A national meeting on HIV and the law, which I co-organized with a Chinese colleague in 2007, was cancelled just days before participants, including leading international HIV lawyers, were scheduled to arrive. But hundreds of other workshops on less sensitive subjects proceeded successfully. Organizations learned from one another's mistakes and planned more carefully, holding their meetings at universities. New legal aid centres were established around the country.

The mobilization in the early 2000s did not spark optimism in everyone. What Chinese advocates saw as a sign of hope for a more open society, looked to senior officials like the threat of a coming 'colour revolution' (Chen 2010). They were all too aware of what was taking place across the borders in Eastern Europe and Central Asia—and later in the Middle East and North Africa. As Titus C. Chen reports, China's leaders believed 'colour revolutions' were instigated by an explosive mix of domestic grievances, electoral politics, and 'Western ... intervention for geo-strategic interests' (Chen 2010: 5). They feared that 'colour revolutions' would lead to 'chaotic politics, turbulent societies and depressed economies,' warned one official editorial (Ai Jun 2016). This spectre haunts official media even today (Lau 2015).

The state's response was a 'two-steps-forward, one-step-back' incremental approach to reform. Warning signs that this would end with a crackdown began to emerge during the 2008 Beijing Olympics, with the pre-emptive imprisonment of dozens of critics (New York Times 2008). By the end of that year, when 303 Chinese activists signed

'Charter 08', a petition calling for human rights and democratization, the sweeping arrests and abuses that followed were hardly surprising (Hounshell 2010). An anonymous call for a 2011 'Jasmine Revolution' sparked another police crackdown (Branigan 2011). In the months afterwards, defiant NGO activists around the country persisted in humorously serving jasmine tea at office meetings

In 2013, Chinese Communist Party officials circulated 'Document No. 9,' which warned of these threats: 'constitutionalism, civil society, "nihilistic" views of history, "universal values", and the promotion of "the West's view of media" ' (ChinaFile 2013). The writing was on the wall as President Hu stepped down in 2013; the brief golden age of China's almost-open society was at an end.

Post-2013: 'Rule of Fear'

President Xi Jinping and Premier Li Keqiang took office in 2013. Some external analysts hoped that Xi would expand previous reforms. Chinese AIDS activists who remembered the brutal crackdowns during Li Keqiang's reign as Henan Province Party Secretary were less sanguine.

Almost immediately, Xi moved to eliminate political rivals, purging senior Party officials in the name of fighting corruption. A national anti-corruption campaign followed, with dozens of officials either fired or investigated. Senior positions were awarded to Xi loyalists. A national security commission was established that further cemented his leadership role, and the 2017 Communist Party Congress made 'Xi Jinping thought' part of official ideology (Minzner 2018: 28–31). Xi's deployment of slogans and national image-building campaigns has reminded many of Mao's cult of personality (Teng Biao 2015).

At the same time, Minzner notes, China's legal system witnessed 'a steady breakdown of reform-era practices', which consisted in the weakening of previous judicial reforms, the revision of policies in order to grant government forces greater leeway in managing social unrest, the re-emergence of 'ill-defined Party bodies' serving to direct the courts in line with official ideology, and dozens of other moves aimed at eliminating what had been nearly independent governance mechanisms and at centralizing power in the hands of Xi loyalists (Minzner 2018: 100–3). Political campaigns frequently 'remind judges of the supremacy of [Party] rule over the constitution and laws' (Minzner 2018: 24). A 2016 Foreign NGO Management Law has curtailed the support and funding available from overseas allies (OHCHR 2016b). While Taisu Zhang and Tom Ginsburg (2018), conversely, see Chinese legal institutions as increasingly empowered, they also believe this rather serves to entrench Party authority than the reverse.

Sida Liu and Terence C. Halliday's exhaustive ten-year study of criminal defence in China, which drew on interviews with more than 300 lawyers, documents a range of tactics used to undermine lawyers. These include the 'Three Difficulties': obstacles to meeting criminal suspects, accessing case files, and collecting evidence (Liu and

Halliday 2016: 50). Criminal defence lawyers also noted that persuading judges was extremely challenging, given their predisposition to find anyone charged with a crime guilty. Defence lawyers rarely win their cases, due to the 'iron triangle' of 'the police, the procuracy and the courts' (Liu and Halliday 2016: 1). Article 306 of the Criminal Procedure Law, which prohibits lawyers from destroying evidence or inducing witnesses to give false testimony, has been used by procurators to intimidate lawyers (Liu and Halliday 2016: 57). Liu and Halliday (2016: 1) concluded that Chinese criminal defence law had become 'an unhappy story of difficulties and danger'.

On 9 July 2015, with the '709 crackdown', the unhappy story took a turn for the worse. Authorities jailed approximately 300 lawyers, legal assistants, and activists throughout the country (Human Rights Watch 2017a). While some were eventually released, several reported that they had been tortured (Pils 2018). At least one showed signs of mental trauma upon release. In some cases, the lawyers representing these lawyers were effectively disbarred. Lawyer Jiang Tianyong was disbarred, then jailed, and is reportedly in deteriorating health (OHCHR 2018b; Pils 2018). While respected lawyer Xu Zhiyong has been released, Pu Zhiqiang is closely monitored as part of his suspended sentence (Human Rights Watch 2018; Wen and Thomas 2017). Some remain missing or held in prolonged incommunicado detention (Asia News 2018). Most who survived the crackdown have distanced themselves from human rights advocacy, sometimes through staged TV confessions; others have fled into exile.

The retreat from earlier efforts to establish rule of law in China has created what Stein Ringen (2016) calls a 'perfect dictatorship'. This system, says Minxin Pei (2016), relies on a 'rule of fear' in which 'arrests of government officials have become a daily ritual'. Eva Pils (2016) elaborates a list of 'fear techniques' used to intimidate lawyers: tracking and following, soft detention, 'being travelled', being 'asked in for chats' with the police, multiple forms of detention, violent assaults, psychiatric detention, torture, and disappearance. Families and friends of rights defenders are also targeted for persecution with interrogation and detention (Deng Yanhua and O'Brien 2013).

Newer and more expansive forms of control now include piloted forms of social credit, which aim to rank all Chinese citizens by various criteria, including their ideological loyalty (Pils 2018). In ethnic regions, i.e. in regions with large non-Han populations, even more intrusive and sophisticated approaches have been developed (Human Rights Watch 2013).

Expansive Surveillance in Xinjiang

Located on China's borders with Central Asia, Xinjiang is the homeland to numerous ethnic minority peoples. The largest group, the Uyghur, are mostly Muslim. Like Tibet, Xinjiang was an independent self-governing region in the distant past, which gradually came under Chinese control. Today, Xinjiang is the site of an expansive system of social and technological surveillance, drawing on new technologies and artificial intelligence to implement sweeping forms of predictive policing (Sudworth n.d.). This now includes a mass system of abusive re-education camps to which Uyghurs can be sent arbitrarily by order of police or party officials. Approximately 800,000 people have been detained (The Economist 2018).

Related systems of surveillance include expansion of police stations responsible for surveillance of each corner of the province, frequent checkpoints using biometrics, such as facial recognition software; QR codes to track every knife sold in the province; a network of security cameras, and a survey of residents used to rank 'trustworthiness' (frequent prayer is a warning sign). Individual identity cards are linked to 'machine-learning systems, information from cameras, smartphones, financial and family-planning records and even unusual electricity use to generate lists of suspects for detention' (The Economist 2018). More than a million Chinese citizens, most of whom belong to the Han majority, have also been mobilized to occupy the homes of Uyghurs to undertake programmes of indoctrination and surveillance (Byler 2018). The intimidation has reportedly extended to family members overseas (Boscaini 2019).

In response to international criticism of the camps, Xinjiang's regional government issued updated regulations to create a post-facto legal basis for detention.[1] At the same time, China is working in Geneva to pre-empt further international criticism.

Interference with UN human rights mechanisms

In parallel with expanding internal repression, Chinese authorities have also made increasing efforts to curtail external criticism by reigning in UN human rights mechanisms.

As Rana Siu Inboden and Titus C. Chen (2012) show, through their increasingly activist role on the UN Human Rights Council, Chinese delegates have attempted to block criticism of their country's record. Ted Piccone (2018: 1) notes that China promotes 'orthodox interpretations of national sovereignty and non-interference in international affairs that weaken international norms of human rights, transparency, and accountability'. After his official visit to China, the UN Special Rapporteur on Extreme Poverty and Human Rights reported that he was followed by undercover officers and that activists he interviewed may have been intimidated (Hernandez 2016). Human Rights Watch (2017b: 31) also finds that China's active membership of the UN Economic Social and Council Committee (ECOSOC) NGO accreditation process has provided opportunities bureaucratically to stall and derail applications from international organizations that might criticize its record. This approach follows on China's 2014 Fourth Plenum decision: 'Vigorously participate in the formulation of international norms, promote the handling of foreign-related economic and social affairs according to the law, strengthen our country's discourse power and influence in international legal affairs, use legal methods to safeguard our country's sovereignty, security and development interests'.[2]

Direct Chinese civil society participation in the human rights system has been shut down. Domestic rights activists have been forcibly prevented from leaving the country to travel to UN Human Rights Council sessions, and they have experienced harsh retaliation for speaking out internationally (Human Rights Watch 2017a: 14).

Most notoriously, Chinese authorities detained the human rights advocate Cao Shunli at the airport while she was en route to the UN Human Rights Council. The detention ended in her death (Human Rights in China 2014). An attempt by civil society representatives to observe a moment of silence in her memory during the adoption of China's national report to the Universal Periodic Review of the Human Rights Council was prevented by a Chinese point of order (UPR Info 2014). Cases like these have had a chilling effect on the participation of Chinese rights advocates in UN human rights meetings (Human Rights Watch 2017b: 16). Security officials have even harassed Chinese rights advocates on the grounds of the United Nations in Geneva (Human Rights Watch 2017b: 17). At the time of writing this chapter, as China's 2018 Universal Periodic Review approached, it was unlikely that any domestic critics would risk the journey to Geneva.

Chinese officials have also attempted to intimidate other country missions to the United Nations in order to discourage them from even meeting with Chinese rights advocates (Human Rights Watch 2017b: 21). This extended to a UN side-event that was to feature Nobel laureates, including the Dalai Lama (Human Rights Watch 2017b: 28). When imprisoned Chinese dissident Liu Xiaobo received the Nobel Peace Prize, China penalized the Norwegian government for six years (Chan 2016).

While these efforts at stifling criticism are significant, they have not been entirely successful. Domestic rights activists, some UN agencies and some foreign governments may mute their criticism, but transnational allies continue to speak up in Geneva and to submit critical shadow reports to the Universal Periodic Review.

The Office of the High Commissioner for Human Rights has so far resisted pressure: while rights advocates have criticized the UN Secretary-General for tempering his advocacy of visits to China, UN human rights experts have continued to criticize China's rights record (OHCHR 2018a, 2018b, 2018c; Radio Free Asia 2019). In 2016, then-High Commissioner Zeid Ra'ad Al Hussein expressed concerns about the sweeping arrests of Chinese lawyers and intimidation of other government critics (OHCHR 2016a). In her first speech as his successor to the mandate, Michelle Bachelet called on China to allow the UN to investigate the mass detention of Uyghurs (Nebehay 2018). Philip Alston, the UN Special Rapporteur on Extreme Poverty and Human Rights, openly called out efforts by China to silence critics and interfere with his mission to the country in 2016 (Blanchard 2016).

Similarly, in the face of overwhelming state power, some Chinese activists steadily persist in bearing witness.

WEIGUAN, SOLIDARITY, AND SURVIVAL

While the Sun Zhigang generation was decimated by the recent crackdown, Chinese lawyers continue to take on sensitive human rights cases, and a newer generation of civil society activists continues working within the constraints (Teng Biao 2015). In fact, Liu and Halliday (2016: 82) found that some seasoned criminal lawyers persist *because* they perversely relish overcoming the challenges: those who had practised for more than twenty years reported being more motivated than those with less experience.

How do human rights advocates in China survive? By being strategic, flexible, and engaging in solidarity. For some, the solution is to liaise strategically with power-brokers, developing personal connections in the government (Liu and Halliday 2016: 75). Others have been able to engage successfully in advocacy by establishing themselves as someone offering specific expertise, identifying short-term local policy wins, and focusing on those (Davis and Mohamed 2018). Still others focus on showing public support to peers who face ideological persecution.

For practising lawyers handling political cases, finding allies has been critical. Some lawyers taking on sensitive cases work collaboratively in pairs, reducing the risk to either lawyer (Liu and Halliday 2016: 67). Others seek advice from more senior mentors (Liu and Halliday 2016: 68). Lawyers defending persecuted peers have created informal legal teams online to share advice across diverse geographic regions (Pils 2015: 253).

A few activists have defiantly called for accountability: the Tiananmen Mothers, for example, continue publicly to demand justice for family members killed in the June Fourth Massacre in 1989 (Tiananmen Mothers 2019). Similarly, two family members of lawyers detained in the 709 crackdown issued an open letter to representatives of the National People's Congress and the Chinese People's Political Consultative Congress, describing the torture and ill-treatment of detainees and calling on representatives to 'perform your duties' and reign in authoritarian power (Wang Qiaoling and Li Wenzu 2017).

Social media, while heavily monitored and restricted, has remained an important means of generating wider support (Liu and Halliday 2016: 71). For example, in one criminal case in which the defendant had been tortured, defence lawyers who were unable to access their client's files protested outside the courtroom with a sign that read 'CRIMINAL DEFENCE LAWYERS DEMAND ACCESS TO FILES'. Photos of their protest were circulated widely online (Pils 2015: 238).

Activists have sometimes found creative ways to evade online censorship through the use of puns and word play—what feminist folklorists call 'coded messages' (Radner 1993). For example, the propagandistic term 'harmonization' (*hexie*), synonymous with censorship, is also a homonym with 'river crab'. When Chinese authorities announced plans to demolish artist and critic Ai Weiwei's studio, placing him under house arrest, hundreds of his supporters gathered at the studio for a spontaneous crab feast (Shang_Cameron 2018). As Joan N. Radner and Susan S. Lanser (1993: 3) write, 'If the production of coded messages is a sign of oppression and censorship, the deciphering of such messages may be the very process through which liberation becomes possible'.

Activists also use the arts to mock the banality of repression. In 2008, activist couple Hu Jia and Zeng Jinyan created a film, *Prisoners of Freedom City*, about the daily experience of their house arrest by plainclothes police, with footage of officers leaving take-out food cartons on the floor, harassing Zeng on her way to work, and more. This acerbic short documentary was posted online, smuggled out of the country on DVDs, and screened at the Guggenheim Museum and internationally (Guggenheim Museum 2017; Hu Jia and Zeng Jinyan 2007). When film is censored, members of a new generation of activists working on such issues as gender equality and lesbian, gay, bisexual, transgender, and queer (LGBTQ) rights, turn to performance art. For example, one network of lesbian activists wrote an original stage play, inspired by the play *The Vagina Monologues*, to generate income and engage volunteers. Two transgender hosts of a weekly live show on social media use this to educate the public about sexual orientation and gender identity (Hou Ping 2017).

When all else fails, some activists show support in person. *Weiguan* is a term that combines the word for 'surrounding' with the word for 'watching' to mean group observation. Normally, it refers to spontaneous gatherings of bystanders, but *weiguan* has evolved into a Chinese practice of Foucauldian 'counterveillance'—the inverse of the panopticon, in which the powerless surround and watch their abusers (Welch 2011). When sensitive Chinese cases are brought to court, family members, lawyers and activists may gather outside the court house to record the proceedings and bear witness. Other allies follow online, raising the alarm if observers are detained by police (Wang Yi n.d.). Pils (2015: 241) finds that *weiguan* can become a form of public education: 'Lawyers resisting together ... raise legal consciousness and promote the idea of rule of law [in the general population]'. The resulting public discussions sometimes spark small policy changes (Pils 2015: 239).

All these forms of support and resistance help to combat isolation and fear, while nourishing both individuals and the broader network. As one activist tells Pils (2015: 249), 'I think that lawyers are huddling together like people in cold winter. In doing this a lawyer can maximize their own voice while at the same time reducing their own risk'. In turn, their work is amplified by international allies who are less subject to Chinese political pressure.

The following two examples illustrate this point. First, on International Women's Day in March 2015, Chinese police arrested five young women who had planned to protest sexual harassment on public transportation (Fincher 2016). After an international and domestic outcry, the women were released on bail. Second, after the death of Nobel Laureate Liu Xiaobo, authorities placed his wife, Liu Xia, under de facto house arrest. Dozens of international allies, including writers and diplomats, called for her release, attempted to visit her, and lobbied behind the scenes (Hong Kong Free Press 2017, 2018; Lau 2017). In July 2018, she was released and flew to Berlin—a small, but potent victory for rights activists.

Conclusion: The Real Time for Human Rights

> *As Maya Angelou famously quoted: 'A bird does not sing because it has an answer; it sings because it has a song.' We fight for human rights not because we will get the success in our lifetimes, but because we believe in the song in our heart.*
>
> *Hou Ping* (2017)

This chapter has highlighted recent progress and setbacks to human rights in China, as well as the resilience of Chinese rights activists. While China has launched what may be the most sophisticated and overwhelming crackdown on human rights in the world, Chinese activists and their allies persist, taking enormous risks to document abuses and advocate for their rights. The fact that this advocacy transcends linguistic, cultural, and geographic barriers elevates the Chinese practice of *weiguan* into a transnational tactic.

As a Beijing taxi driver I met once said: 'I think that human rights means that a senior official's son should be treated the same as my son.' This idea of fundamental human equality is central to all the human rights treaties, each of which has an article 2 on non-discrimination:

> Everyone is entitled to all the rights and freedoms set forth in this Declaration, without distinction of any kind, such as race, colour, sex, language, religion, political or other opinion, national or social origin, property, birth or other status. (United Nations 1948)

The multivalent historical origins of the principle of human equality begin not with colonialism, but with international resistance to colonialism and racism. Gandhi applied concepts and tactics he learned in resisting racism in South Africa to build a movement that ended colonialism in India (Naidoo 2014). Martin Luther King Jr and American civil rights activists applied Gandhi's thinking and tactics to their fight against segregation in the United States (Kumar 2017). Anti-apartheid activists in South Africa, such as Bishop Desmond Tutu, found inspiration in the U.S. civil rights movement (Greeson 2009). As Merry and others note, activists frequently adopt, or vernacularize, international ideas and practices to suit diverse local contexts (Destrooper and Merry 2018).

Similarly, European colonialism has not been the world's only experience of a hegemonic transnational civilizing project; China also had a long history of conquest and domination of neighbouring peoples, justified through 'the center's claim to a superior degree of civilization' (Harrell 1995). Tibetan and Uyghur resistance to the current form of this 'civilizing' or 're-educating' project, extend to the continuing participation of Tibetan and Uyghur exiles in the Universal Periodic Review process despite the risks to themselves and their family members.

As Margaret E. Keck and Kathryn Sikkink (1998) note, the transnational framework offered by human rights enables a boomerang effect in advocacy. In Myanmar, Lynette Chua (2019) similarly finds local LGBT activists drawing strength and inspiration from a transnational network built through both affection and solidarity. Merry (2018) suggests that framing local arguments in human rights terms gives them added legitimacy by linking them with a global consensus, rendering a local struggle 'legible to a wider audience'. While rights advocate Sharon Hom (2019) rightly warns that China's surveillance technologies are rapidly being adopted elsewhere, the support of international allies constitutes a transnational form of *weiguan* that, even briefly, reverses that lens.

That these global solidarities and mechanisms only rarely work to produce justice should not be surprising at a time when Interpol's chief sits in Chinese detention (Meng Hongwei 2019). Abuses are inherently part of power, and they will recur in every generation. The human rights framework and institutions were created, after the first fall of fascism, to ensure that someone would be around to uphold the principle of equality in every generation also.

Dismantling that human rights system would not put an end to domestic advocacy, what Hopgood (2013) calls lower-case *human rights*, but it would make that work even harder and lonelier than it already is. If Chinese activists can persist while being restricted to what Liu Xiaobo called 'the darkness', scholars should not pre-emptively declare defeat. As long as there is even one activist still filing lawsuits and advocating on behalf of others somewhere in China, the light should stay on in Geneva.

Acknowledgements

The author is grateful for comments on an early draft by Fernanda Pirie, Elizabeth Steyn, and Mark Goodale; and for their suggestions to the following: Susan Finder, Joey Lee, Margaret K. Lewis, Lu Jun, Allan Maleche, Sally Engle Merry, Carl Minzner, Berry Nibogora, Eva Pils, Ed Rekosh, Sophie Richardson, Laurel Sprague, and Elizabeth Wickeri. Any errors are the author's responsibility.

Notes

1. 新疆维吾尔自治区第十三届人民代表大会常务委员会公告 [Statement of the Standing Committee of the 13th People's Congress of the Xinjiang Uyghur Autonomous Region], No. 7, 新疆维吾尔自治区去极端化条例 [Xinjiang Uyghur Autonomous Region De-Extremification Regulations], 9 October 2018. Available at: <http://www.xjpcsc.gov.cn/1009/t4028e49c66534763016658 8b8cf40001001.html?from=singlemessage&isappinstalled=0>
2. 'CCP Central Committee Decision concerning Several Major Issues in Comprehensively Advancing Governance According to Law'. China Law Translate, from Xinhua News Agency, 28 October 2014. Section VII, para. 7. Available at: <https://www.chinalawtranslate.com/fourth-plenum-decision/?lang=en>

References

Agence France-Presse. 2017. 'Burundi Becomes First Nation to Leave International Criminal Court'. *The Guardian*, 28 October. Available at: <https://www.theguardian.com/law/2017/oct/28/burundi-becomes-first-nation-to-leave-international-criminal-court>

Ai Jun. 2016. 'Why hasn't there been a color revolution in China?' *Global Times*, 17 July. Available at: <http://www.globaltimes.cn/content/994793.shtml>

Asia News. 2018. 'After three years of crackdown on 709 lawyers, Wang Quanzhang remains missing', 9 July. Available at: <http://www.asianews.it/news-en/After-three-years-of-crackdown-on-709-lawyers,-Wang-Quanzhang-remains-missing-44385.html>

Blanchard, B. 2016. 'UN Rights Envoy Says Chinese Authorities Interfered with his Work'. *Reuters*, 23 August. Available at: <https://www.reuters.com/article/us-china-un-rights/u-n-rights-envoy-says-chinese-authorities-interfered-with-his-work-idUSKCN10Y192>

Borger, J. 2018. 'Trump Administration Wants to Remove "Gender" from UN Documents'. *The Guardian*, 25 October. Available at: <https://www.theguardian.com/world/2018/oct/24/trump-administration-gender-transgender-united-nations>

Boscaini, J. 2019. 'Chinese Authorities Accused of Intimidating Uyghurs in Australia'. *ABC News*, 30 March. Available at: <https://www.abc.net.au/news/2019-03-31/chinese-government-accused-of-intimidating-australian-uyghurs/10945090>

Branigan, T. 2011. 'China's Jasmine Revolution: Police but No Protesters Line Streets of Beijing'. *The Guardian*, 27 February. Available at: <https://www.theguardian.com/world/2011/feb/27/china-jasmine-revolution-beijing-police>

Byler, D. 2018. 'China's government has ordered a million citizens to occupy Uighur homes. Here's what they think they're doing'. *ChinaFile*, 24 October. Available at: <http://www.chinafile.com/reporting-opinion/postcard/million-citizens-occupy-uighur-homes-xinjiang?fbclid=IwAR2tKCMBz41_NiwWbae3iqsZDSUoXv6yNU2USvwTfoBKTlnpmdFK1xUiyqI>

Byler, D 2019. 'Ghost World'. *Logic: A Magazine about Technology* 6. Available at: <https://logicmag.io/07-ghost-world/>

Catholic News Service. 2018. 'Philippine Clergy, Advocates Say Human Rights Dying under Duterte'. *National Catholic Reporter*, 16 July. Available at: <https://www.ncronline.org/news/world/philippine-clergy-advocates-say-human-rights-dying-under-duterte>

Chan, S. 2016. 'Norway and China restore ties, six years after Nobel dispute'. *The New York Times*, 19 December. Available at: <https://www.nytimes.com/2016/12/19/world/europe/china-norway-nobel-liu-xiaobo.html>

Chen, T. C. 2010. 'China's Reaction to the Color Revolutions: Adaptive Authoritarianism in Full Swing'. *Asian Perspective* 34(2): 5–51.

ChinaFile. 2013. 'Document No. 9: A ChinaFile Translation' 8 November 2013. Available at: <http://www.chinafile.com/document-9-chinafile-translation>

Chua, L. 2019. *The Politics of Love in Myanmar: LGBT Mobilization and Human Rights as a Way of Life*. Stanford: Stanford University Press.

CIVICUS. 2017. 'Burundi Civil Society Sees the International Criminal Court as a Last Resort for Justice', January 2017. Available at: <https://www.civicus.org/index.php/media-resources/news/interviews/2699-burundi-civil-society-sees-the-international-criminal-court-as-a-last-resort-for-justice>

CIVICUS. 2018. *State of Civil Society Report*. Available at: <https://www.civicus.org/index.php/state-of-civil-society-report-2018>

Cook, S. 2019. '"Social Credit" Scoring: How China's Communist Party is Incentivizing Repression'. *Hong Kong Free Press*, 27 February. Available at: <https://www.hongkongfp.com/2019/02/27/social-credit-scoring-chinas-communist-party-incentivising-repression/>

Davis, S. and C. Mohamed. 2018. 'Global Rights, Local Risk: Community Advocacy on Right to Health in China'. In T. DeStrooper and S. E. Merry, eds. *Human Rights Transformation in an Unequal World*, 229–50. Philadelphia: University of Pennsylvania Press.

De Gaay Fortman, B. 2011. *Political Economy of Human Rights: The Quest for Relevance and Realization*. New York: Routledge.

Destrooper, T. and S. E. Merry, eds. 2018. *Human Rights Transformation in Practice*. Philadelphia: University of Pennsylvania Press.

Fincher, L. H. 2016. 'China's Feminist Five'. *Dissent Magazine*, Fall. Available at: <https://www.dissentmagazine.org/article/china-feminist-five>

Ford, L. 2019. 'UN Waters Down Rape Resolution to Appease US's Hardline Abortion Stance'. *The Guardian*, 23 April. Available at: <https://www.theguardian.com/global-development/2019/apr/23/un-resolution-passes-trump-us-veto-threat-abortion-language-removed>

Gan, N. and M. Lau. 2018. 'China Changes Law to Recognize "Re-education Camps" in Xinjiang'. *South China Morning Post*, 10 October. Available at: <https://www.scmp.com/news/china/politics/article/2167893/china-legalises-use-re-education-camps-religious-extremists>

Goodale, M. 2003. 'Introduction: Locating Rights, Envisioning Law between the Global and the Local'. In M. Goodale and S. E. Merry, eds. *The Practice of Human Rights: Tracking Law between the Global and the Local*, 1–38. Cambridge: Cambridge University Press.

Goodale, M., ed. 2013. *Human Rights at the Crossroads*. Oxford: Oxford University Press.

Greeson, M. 2009. 'Fighting for Equality: The Anti-Apartheid Movement and the Legacy of Civil Rights'. *Colgate Academic Review* 5(1): 64–83.

Guggenheim Museum. 2017. 'Guggenheim Museum Presents Documentary Film Series, "Turn it On: China on Film 2000–2017"'. Press statement, 24 August. Available at: <https://www.guggenheim.org/press-release/guggenheim-museum-presents-documentary-film-series-turn-it-on-china-on-film-2000-2017>

Harrell, S. 1995. 'Introduction: Civilizing Projects and the Reaction to Them'. In S. Harrell, ed. *Cultural Encounters on China's Ethnic Frontiers*, 3–36. Seattle and London: University of Washington Press.

Hernandez, J. 2016. 'China's crackdown on dissent could lead to unrest, UN adviser says'. *New York Times*, 23 August. Available at: <https://www.nytimes.com/2016/08/24/world/asia/china-un-human-rights-philip-alston.html>

Hom, S. K. 2019. 'Artificial Intelligence and Affected Communities'. Public presentation, *Democratizing Data: Grassroots Strategies to Advance Human Rights* (conference). New York University Bernstein Institute, 17–18 April. Programme available at: <https://2019.nyubernsteinconference.org>

Hong Kong Free Press. 2017. 'Widow of Nobel Laureate Liu Xiaobo "Should Be Able to Leave China" If She Chooses, Says UN Human Rights Chief', 21 July. Available at: <https://www.hongkongfp.com/2017/07/21/widow-nobel-laureate-liu-xiaobo-able-leave-china-chooses-says-un-human-rights-chief/>

Hong Kong Free Press. 2018. 'Leading Writers and Artists Urge China to Free Liu Xia, Widow of Nobel Dissident', 17 May. Available at: <https://www.hongkongfp.com/2018/05/17/leading-writers-artists-urge-china-free-liu-xia-widow-nobel-dissident/>

Hopgood, S. 2013. *The Endtimes of Human Rights*. Ithaca: Cornell University Press.

Hou Ping. 2017. 'Could volunteer-based CSOs be a model for practicing human rights in China? In China, new laws make fundraising even harder, but the LGBTQ community is getting creative'. *OpenGlobalRights*, 22 February. Available at: <https://www.openglobalrights.org/could-volunteer-based-csos-be-model-for-practicing-human-rights-in-china/>

Hounshell, B. 2010. 'Charter 08'. *Foreign Policy*, 8 October. Available at: <https://foreignpolicy.com/2010/10/08/charter-08/>

Hu Jia and Zeng Jinyan. 2007. *Ziyoucheng de qiutu [Prisoners of Freedom City]*. Documentary film. Mandarin with Chinese and English subtitles, 36 minutes.

Human Rights in China. 2014. 'International Human Rights Award Honors Cao Shunli', 23 April. Available at: <https://www.hrichina.org/en/press-work/international-human-rights-award-honors-cao-shunli>

Human Rights Watch. 2013. 'China: Alarming New Surveillance, Security in Tibet', 20 March. Available at: <https://www.hrw.org/news/2013/03/20/china-alarming-new-surveillance-security-tibet>

Human Rights Watch. 2016. 'ICC: Kenya Deputy President's Case Ends; Witness Interference Undermined Trial', 5 April. Available at: <https://www.hrw.org/news/2016/04/05/icc-kenya-deputy-presidents-case-ends>

Human Rights Watch. 2017a. 'China: On "709" Anniversary, Legal Crackdown Continues'. Press statement, 7 July. Available at: <https://www.hrw.org/news/2017/07/07/china-709-anniversary-legal-crackdown-continues>

Human Rights Watch. 2017b. 'The Costs of International Advocacy: China's Interference in United Nations Human Rights Mechanisms', 5 September. Available at: <https://www.hrw.org/report/2017/09/05/costs-international-advocacy/chinas-interference-united-nations-human-rights>

Human Rights Watch. 2018. 'China: Free Rights Lawyers, Reinstate Law Licenses', 5 July. Available at: <https://www.hrw.org/news/2018/07/05/china-free-rights-lawyers-reinstate-law-licenses>

Inboden, R. S. and T. C. Chen. 2012. 'China's Response to International Normative Pressure: The Case of Human Rights'. *The International Spectator* 47(2): 45–57.

Kahn, J. 2002. 'China's Communist Party, "to Survive", Opens its Doors to Capitalists'. *New York Times*, 4 November. Available at: <https://www.nytimes.com/2002/11/04/world/china-s-communist-party-to-survive-opens-its-doors-to-capitalists.html

Keck, M. E. and K. Sikkink. 1998. *Activists Beyond Borders: Advocacy in International Politics.* Ithaca: Cornell University Press.

Kumar, P. 2017. 'What King Learned from Gandhi'. *LA Review of Books*, 16 January. Available at: <https://lareviewofbooks.org/article/what-king-learned-from-gandhi/>

Lau, M. 2015. 'People's Daily Warns against Colour Revolutions, Blames "Spread of Western Ideology"'. *South China Morning Post*, 14 June. Available at: <https://www.scmp.com/news/china/policies-politics/article/1822063/communist-party-paper-sees-red-over-colour-revolutions>

Lau, M. 2017. 'Foreign Diplomats Blocked by Security Guards at Home of Liu Xiaobo's Widow'. *South China Morning Post*, 4 August. Available at: <https://www.scmp.com/news/china/policies-politics/article/2105513/foreign-diplomats-blocked-security-guards-home-liu>

Liu, S. and T. C. Halliday. 2016. *Criminal Defense in China: The Politics of Lawyers at Work.* Cambridge: Cambridge University Press.

Meng Hongwei. 2019. 'China to Prosecute Former Interpol Chief'. *BBC News*, 27 March. Available at: <https://www.bbc.com/news/world-asia-china-47718827>

Merry, S. E. 2006. *Human Rights and Gender Violence: Translating International Law into Local Justice*. Chicago: University of Chicago Press.

Merry. S. E. 2018. 'Preface'. In T. Destrooper and S. E. Merry, eds. *Human Rights Transformation in Practice*. Philadelphia: University of Pennsylvania Press.

Merry. S. E. and R. E. Stern. 2005. 'The Female Inheritance Movement in Hong Kong: Theorizing the Local/Global Interface'. *Current Anthropology* 46(3): 387–409.

Meyers, S. L. and C. Buckley. 2018. 'An emboldened China no longer cares what its critics think'. *The New York Times*, 14 December. Available at: <https://www.nytimes.com/2018/12/14/world/china-detentions-canadians-human-rights.html>

Minxin Pei. 2016. 'China's Rule of Fear'. *Project Syndicate*, 28 February. Available at: <https://www.project-syndicate.org/commentary/china-fear-bureaucratic-paralysis-by-minxin-pei-2016-02?barrier=accesspaylog>

Minzner, C. 2018. *End of an Era: How China's Authoritarian Revival is Undermining its Rise*. Oxford: Oxford University Press.

Mutua, M. 2008. *Human Rights: A Political and Cultural Critique*. Philadelphia: University of Pennsylvania Press.

Mutua, M. 2016. 'Is the Age of Human Rights Over?' In S. A. McClennen and A. S. Moore, eds. *Routledge Companion to Literature and Human Rights*, 450–8. London and New York: Routledge.

Moyn, S. 2018. *Not Enough: Human Rights in an Unequal World*. Cambridge, MA: Belknap Press of Harvard University Press.

Naidoo, P. 2014. 'Remembering What Gandhi Gave South Africa, a Century Later'. *Daily Maverick*, 17 July. Available at: <https://www.dailymaverick.co.za/article/2014-07-17-op-ed-remembering-what-gandhi-gave-south-africa-a-century-later/>

Nebehay, S. 2018. 'U.N. Rights Chief Bachelet Takes on China, Other Powers in First Speech', 18 September. Available at: <https://cn.reuters.com/article/instant-article/idUSKCN1LQ0QI>

New York Times. 2008. 'Beijing's Bad Faith Olympics', 22 August. Available at: <https://www.nytimes.com/2008/08/23/opinion/23sat1.html>

OHCHR. 2016a. 'UN Human Rights Chief Deeply Concerned by China Clampdown on Lawyers and Activists'. Press release, 16 February. Available at: <https://www.ohchr.org/EN/NewsEvents/Pages/DisplayNews.aspx?NewsID=17050>

OHCHR. 2016b. 'China: Newly adopted Foreign NGO Law Should Be Repealed, Experts Urge', 3 May. Available at: <https://www.ohchr.org/en/NewsEvents/Pages/DisplayNews.aspx?NewsID=19921&LangID=E>

OHCHR. 2018a. 'China: UN Experts Denounce the Criminalization of Linguistic and Cultural Rights Advocacy', 21 February. Available at: <https://www.ohchr.org/EN/NewsEvents/Pages/DisplayNews.aspx?NewsID=22683>

OHCHR. 2018b. 'China: UN Experts Concerned about Health of Jailed Rights Lawyer Jiang Tianyong'. Press release, 23 March. Available at: <https://www.ohchr.org/EN/NewsEvents/Pages/DisplayNews.aspx?NewsID=22890&LangID=E>

OHCHR. 2018c. 'China: UN Human Rights Experts Condemn 5-Year Jail Term for Tibetan Activist'. Press release, 6 June. Available at: <https://www.ohchr.org/EN/NewsEvents/Pages/DisplayNews.aspx?NewsID=23176>

Oloo, A. 2018. 'Kenya's 2017 Election and New Wave of Activism'. *Carnegie Endowment for International Peace*, 12 February. Available at: <https://carnegieendowment.org/2018/02/12/kenya-s-2017-election-and-new-wave-of-activism-pub-75498>

Piccone, T. 2018. *China's Long Game on Human Rights at the United Nations*. Washington: Brookings Institute.

Pils, E. 2015. *China's Human Rights Lawyers: Advocacy and Resistance*. London and New York: Routledge.

Pils, E. 2016. 'Rule by Fear? A ChinaFile Conversation'. *ChinaFile*, 18 February. Available at <http://www.chinafile.com/conversation/rule-fear>

Pils, E. 2018. 'In Whose Service? The Transnational Legal Profession's Interaction with China and Threats to Lawyers' Autonomy and Professional Integrity'. *Fordham International Law Journal* 41(5): 1263–91.

Posner, E. 2014. 'The Case against Human Rights'. *The Guardian*, 4 December. Available at: <https://www.theguardian.com/news/2014/dec/04/-sp-case-against-human-rights>

Radio Free Asia. 2019. 'Activists Say UN Chief's Words in China on Uyghurs Fall Short', 30 April. Available at: <https://www.rfa.org/english/news/uyghur/un-camps-04302019170046.html>

Radner, J. N., ed. 1993. *Feminist Messages: Coding in Women's Folk Culture*. Urbana and Chicago: University of Illinois Press.

Radner, J. N. and S. S. Lanser. 1993. 'Strategies of Coding in Women's Cultures'. In J. N. Radner, ed. *Feminist Messages: Coding in Women's Folk Culture*, 1–30. Urbana and Chicago: University of Illinois Press.

Reuters. 2018. 'Philippines Duterte tells human rights expert: "Go to hell" ', 3 June. Available at: <https://www.reuters.com/article/us-philippines-duterte-un/philippines-duterte-tells-u-n-human-rights-expert-go-to-hell-idUSKCN1IZ063>

Ringen, S. 2016. *The Perfect Dictatorship: China in the 21st Century*. Hong Kong: Hong Kong University Press.

Shang_Cameron. 2018. 'Pictures: Ai Weiwei's River Crab Fest Happens After All'. *Shanghaiist*, 5 May. Available at: <http://shanghaiist.com/2010/11/08/ai_weiweis_crab_fest_happens_after/>

Sikkink, K. 2017. *Evidence for Hope: Making Human Rights Work in the 21st Century*. Princeton: Princeton University Press.

Sudworth, J. n. d. 'China's Hidden Camps'. *BBC News*. Available at: <https://www.bbc.co.uk/news/resources/idt-sh/China_hidden_camps?fbclid=IwAR2KZskzIqEQ5z__A2aPk3PaIut6MDNvTQLw8QidfTXMSk4h7kaUFTK-e5M>

Taisu Zhang and T. Ginsburg. 2018. 'Legality in Contemporary Chinese Politics'. *SSRN*, 9 October (forthcoming in *Virginia Journal of International Law*). Available at: <https://papers.ssrn.com/sol3/papers.cfm?abstract_id=3250948>

Teng Biao. 2015. 'China's Irrepressible Lawyers'. *Washington Post*, July 19. Available at: <https://www.washingtonpost.com/opinions/chinas-irrepressible-lawyers/2015/07/19/81d0a04e-2a7b-11e5-a250-42bd812efc09_story.html?utm_term=.1227e1edb56c>

The China Center. n. d. 'Open Government Information in China' Web site. Available at: <https://law.yale.edu/china-center/resources/open-government-information-china>

The Economist. 2018. 'China has turned Xinjiang into a police state like no other', 31 May.

Tiananmen Mothers. 2019. 'Mourning Our Families and Compatriots Killed in the June Fourth Massacre: A Letter to China's Leaders'. Press release, 15 March. Available at: <https://www.hrichina.org/en/story/press-release>

Tomuschat, C. 2003. *Human Rights: Between Idealism and Realism*. Oxford: Oxford University Press.

United Nations. 1948. *Universal Declaration of Human Rights*. Available at: <https://www.un.org/en/universal-declaration-human-rights/>

UPR Info. 2014. 'China Prevents Moment of Silence in Memory of Human Rights Defender'. Press statement, 26 March. Available at: <https://www.upr-info.org/en/news/china-prevents-moment-silence-memory-human-rights-defender>

Voice of America. 2016. 'Kenya President: International Criminal Court Not Impartial,' 12 December. Available at: <https://www.voanews.com/a/kenya-president-international-criminal-court-not-impartial/3632789.html>

Wang Qiaoling and Li Wenzu. 2017. 'Calling on NPC Deputies and CPPCC Committee Members to Submit Motions, Proposals, or Recommendations on the Prevention of Torture and Ill-treatment'. Open letter, 2 March. Available at: <https://www.hrichina.org/en/citizens-square/calling-npc-deputies-and-cppcc-committee-members-submit-motions-proposals-or>

Wang Yi. n. d. 'Weiguan chuangzao lishi: 4/16 qinli zhe de zishu'. *Zhongguo renquan shuangzhoukan*. Available at: <http://biweeklyarchive.hrichina.org/article/430.html>

Welch, M. 2011. 'Counterveillance: How Foucault and the Groupe d'Information Sur Les Prisons Reversed the Optics'. *Theoretical Criminology* 15(3): 301–13.

Wen, P. and N. Thomas. 2017. 'Prominent Rights Activist Xu Zhiyong Freed from Chinese Jail'. *Reuters*, 15 July. Available at: <https://www.reuters.com/article/us-china-rights-corruption/prominent-rights-activist-xu-zhiyong-freed-from-chinese-jail-idUSKBN1A0066>

Yanhua Deng and K. O'Brien. 2013. 'Relational Repression in China: Using Social Ties to Demobilize Protesters'. *China Quarterly* 215 (September): 533–52.

Yu, V. 2013. 'A Blow for Freedom: The Campaign in Memory of Sun Zhigang, Ten Years on'. *South China Morning Post*, 14 May. Available at: <https://www.scmp.com/news/china/article/1236973/blow-freedom-campaign-memory-sun-zhigang-10-years>

Yun Xiang. n. d. 'Sun Zhigang's Death and Reform of Detention System'. *China Society for Human Rights Studies*. Available at: <http://www.humanrights.cn/zt/magazine/20040200482694708.htm>

PART V

CURRENT DIRECTIONS IN LAW AND ANTHROPOLOGY

CHAPTER 40

THE PROBLEM OF COMPLIANCE AND THE TURN TO QUANTIFICATION

SALLY ENGLE MERRY

A basic tenet of the anthropology of law is the distinction between law on the books and law in action. It is clear from a great deal of research that laws are not necessarily followed and that changing a law will not necessarily change behaviour. When laws are passed that are not supported by parts of a population, achieving compliance often depends on active engagement by civil society and public education. Achieving compliance with the law is a fundamental challenge for any legal system. It is particularly difficult for international law since it lacks the enforcement mechanisms of domestic law—the law of nation-states.

An increasingly popular strategy for promoting compliance with law is the use of numbers to measure performance and to hold violators accountable for their actions. The recent turn to the use of quantification in both domestic and international legal settings is inspired by the hope that numbers can make violations more visible and pressure states and companies to comply with the terms of their legal commitments. The problem of compliance with international law is even more difficult than for domestic law since there are few sanctions beyond exposure, shaming, and blaming. Compliance here requires support from wider social institutions such as non-governmental organizations, international governing bodies, and other states.

Quantification promises to increase accountability and to provide information that is objective. Numbers are appealing to those attempting to hold states accountable for development, corruption, human rights performance, control of human trafficking, and many other concerns. They render the extent of compliance visible. For example, to persuade countries to take a stronger hand in controlling trafficking, it is essential to know the number of victims and how many perpetrators have been arrested and convicted. To enforce human rights, it is helpful to convert broad human rights goals into specific, measurable responsibilities. To pressure states to promote sustainable development, gender equality, and the rule of law, among other goals, it is useful to create indicators for these qualities and score countries by their performance. Similarly, to improve the human rights behaviour of corporations, civil society organizations have developed indicators of corporate compliance with human rights treaties. In each of these examples, the hope is that converting broad normative statements into narrow quantifiable measures will facilitate reporting to international bodies and pressure states to live up to their obligations. Indicators make it possible to rank states, which can damage the reputation of poor performers and encourage them to do better (Davis et al. 2012).

Technologies of audit common in the corporate world now reach into many domains of global governance. Since the mid-1990s, technologies that were developed in the sphere of business regulation have jumped into the domains of human rights and corporate social responsibility, for example. Statistics on income, health, education, and torture are useful to assess compliance with human rights norms and progress in improving human rights conditions. They are increasingly used by the committees charged with monitoring compliance with the major human rights conventions. They make visible forms of violation and inequality that are otherwise obscured.

The world of civil society organizations has also been transformed by the increasing use of statistical measures. There are demands for quantifying the accomplishments of non-governmental organizations (NGOs) and for 'evidence-based' funding. Donors to human rights organizations want indicators of success such as reductions in trafficking in persons or diminished rates of poverty and disease. Donors have increasingly adopted business-based means of accounting for productivity and accomplishments. The concept of 'venture philanthropy' underscores this new perspective. Recipient organizations are tasked to develop measures of what they have accomplished within the period of funding. Given the difficulties of measuring accomplishments such as 'increased awareness of human rights', NGOs tend to count proxies for these accomplishments, such as the number of training sessions or the number of people trained. Thus, the use of quantitative measures and the introduction of ranking systems based on these measures are transforming the way these organizations do their work.

Indicators involve a special use of statistics to develop quantifiable ways of assessing and comparing characteristics among groups, organizations, or nations. They are typically composites of two or more underlying variables that can be compared and ranked. Thus, they require constructing categories of measurement such as ethnicity, gender, income, and more elaborated concepts such as national income. Indicators submerge local particularities and idiosyncrasies into universal categories, generating knowledge that is standardized and comparable across nations and regions. A key dimension of the power of indicators is their capacity to convert complicated, contextually variable phenomena into unambiguous, clear, and impersonal measures (Davis et al. 2012).

Quantification is a promising way of improving compliance, but converting broad ideas such as the rule of law or state failure into numbers is very challenging. To measure human development by creating scores for per capita income, health, and education, as the Human Development Index does, broadens the measurement from a simple income measure but still leaves out many other important dimensions of human flourishing.

Quantification inevitably sacrifices detail, complexity, and context in order to achieve commensurability and objectivity. In order to count phenomena such as gender-based violence or access to justice, for example, it is necessary to produce numbers that are inevitably decontextualized and homogenized. These numbers miss important issues of situation and context (Merry 2016). The distortion of quantification depends in part on what is being measured, of course. Some things are easier to measure, such as weight, height, or income, while others require substantial interpretive work, such as the value of care work for children, a family, or the sick and elderly. Quantifying complex concepts and aspects of social life can be misleading.

This chapter considers two sociological aspects to the expansion of the use of indicators for global governance (Merry 2016). The first is a knowledge effect. Numerical measures produce a world knowable without the detailed particulars of context and history. The constituent units can be compared and ranked according to some criteria. This knowledge is presented as objective and often as scientific. Interpretations lurk behind the numbers but are rarely presented explicitly. These numbers seem to be open to public scrutiny and readily accessible in a way that private opinions are not. As forms of knowledge, indicators rely on the magic of numbers and the appearance of certainty and objectivity that they convey. They represent a technology of producing readily accessible and standardized forms of knowledge. One of the critical ways an indicator produces knowledge is by announcing what it measures, such as 'rule of law' or 'poverty'. Neither of these categories is self-evident. When sponsoring organizations name their indicators, they interpret what the numbers mean. Labelling is essential to produce a measure that is readily understood by the public and simple in its conception. Labels do not necessarily accurately reflect the data that produce the indicators, however. How indicators are named and who decides what they represent are fundamental to the way an indicator produces knowledge.

The second aspect of quantification is a governance effect. Indicators are a technology not only of knowledge production but also of governance. They are widely used for decisions such as where to send foreign aid, where to focus on human rights violators, and which countries offer the best opportunities for business investment. Modern states use statistical information, some of which is bundled into indicators, to decide where to locate highways and railroads, where to build schools and hospitals, how to allocate taxes, and how to deploy police forces to control crime, to give only a few examples. As the modern state came to see its population as its wealth, it put greater emphasis on counting and assessing the nature of that population. Yet, the use of statistical information shifts the power dynamics of decision-making. Indicators replace judgements on the basis of values or politics with apparently more rational decision-making on the basis of statistical information. The massive expansion of quantification in recent times comes from a political culture that demands more openness and seeks to drive out corruption, prejudice, and the arbitrary power of elites even at the cost of subtlety and depth in the analysis of social situations and their variations (Porter 1995: 85–6). This, Porter claims, is the power of numbers.

Theories and values are embedded in statistical measures. They reflect the priorities of those who create them and pay to have them carried out. Measures often incorporate theories of social change as well, such as how to promote development or prevent trafficking. These theories affect whether the measurement system counts income or time use to track development or arrests rather than women freed to chronicle efforts against trafficking. Despite the increase in democratic openness produced by the use of statistics in decision-making, this is a technology that tends to consolidate power in the hands of those with expert knowledge. In some situations, the turn to indicators as a mode of governance does not eliminate the role of private knowledge and elite power in decision-making, but replaces it with technical, statistical expertise. Decisions that were carried out by political or judicial leaders are made by technical experts who construct the measures and develop the processes of classification and counting that produce the numbers. To what extent this occurs depends on how the indicators are created, how much interpretive work they do, and who decides what measures to use and what they claim to measure. Indicators can productively convert unseen violations into visible problems but can also ignore important issues that are very difficult to measure, such as women's unpaid care work in the home.

Statistics may also obscure significant differences among populations by failing to measure variables such as social class or disability. Ideally, numbers are disaggregated by characteristics such as race, gender, and disability, but that may not be done because of cost. Data collection is expensive and requires staff, technology, and planning. There is a widespread absence of data from poorer countries and on problems that do not seem politically or economically important. In addition to the costs of data collection, there is also the possibility of populations and organizations that resist providing information at all, seeing quantification as a mode of surveillance and control. For example, Sara L. M. Davis shows how global public health efforts to count so-called key populations with HIV/AIDS—people who are stigmatized and often criminalized, such as sex workers, men who have sex with men, transgender people, and people who inject drugs—fail to tabulate this population effectively, since these groups resist being counted. Their fear of exposure leads to very limited data on these groups, despite the effort to make them visible (Davis 2017: 1149).

In order to explore these opportunities and challenges of quantification as a mode of enhancing legal compliance, I will discuss four examples of the use of numbers and quantification to increase accountability, all of which operate at the international level: corporate social responsibility, human rights monitoring, trafficking and modern-day slavery, and sustainable development. In each case, the promise of accountability is juxtaposed to the challenges of converting complicated features of social life into simple numbers that can be replicated across cultures, contexts, and countries.

Human rights monitoring

The use of indicators to monitor compliance with human rights is a rapidly growing field. Until the late 1990s, many human rights activists resisted the use of indicators because of concerns about lack of data, oversimplification, and bias (see Alston 2005: 22; Green 2001: 1082–4; Rosga and Satterthwaite 2009). For example, the Freedom House indicator 'Freedom in the World', with its seven-point scale from 'free' to 'not free' based on annual surveys starting in 1972, was widely seen as ideologically biased (Alston 2005: 23). Efforts to develop indicators for social and economic human rights have faced difficulties in making the measures concrete (Rosga and Satterthwaite 2009). Indicators measure aggregates, while human rights are held by individuals (see Green 2001: 1085). Building a composite index of human rights performance promotes quick comparisons of countries along a scale but ignores the specificity of various human rights. Measurement errors are also a major concern. There are significant differences in the quality of data on human rights violations among countries. Countries more concerned about human rights are likely to report a higher proportion of violations than those that resist human rights principles (Alston 2005: 22–5).

Despite these concerns, the use of indicators is growing in the human rights field, migrating from economics through development to human rights compliance. UN agencies such as UNICEF, UNIFEM, the Commission on the Status of Women, the High Commissioner on Human Rights, and the UN Statistical Commission are taking the lead. There are longstanding initiatives to develop statistical indicators among other UN agencies and programmes as well, such as FAO, ILO, UNESCO, UNICEF, WHO, and UNDP (Malhotra and Fasel 2005). Universities and NGOs are also active in collecting and systematizing data. Many economic and social indicators, such as the World Bank Worldwide Governance Indicators and the UNDP Human Development Index, are used to assess compliance with social and economic human rights.

The turn to reliance on numbers marks a shift in the way the administration of human rights law takes place. Instead of pressuring countries to conform to human rights laws upon the basis of ambiguous and contextualized accounts in country reports, some monitoring committees for human rights treaties rely on statistics and indicators as well. Assessment of compliance rests on the agreed-upon standards and means of measurement in the indicator. In one case, the experts developing a set of indicators for monitoring compliance with human rights conventions had to promise that the numbers would not be used to rank or shame countries, but only to assess a country's progress over time. Once an indicator has been created, of course, such rankings are possible (Turku Report 2005). The reliance on numbers, with their apparently simple and straightforward meanings, produces an unambiguous and easily replicated field for judgement. Compliance becomes far more open to inspection and assessment.

Moreover, responsibility for compliance shifts to the monitored organization or country itself, which must seek not only to comply but also to monitor and report the success of its efforts. The enforcement body moves from the role of an authority making judgements to a body that registers performance in terms of already-established indicators. In other words, the process of assessing compliance shifts from the encounter between statements and rules in a quasi-judicial forum, such as a hearing by a treaty committee, to the measure itself. Once the indicator has been established, compliance is simply a matter of recording performance according to the indicator. The UN High

Commission for Human Rights has recently produced a set of indicators covering a wide range of human rights to facilitate assessing compliance (Merry 2016; Rosga and Satterthwaite 2009: 4).

The expansion of the use of indicators in global governance means that political struggles over what human rights mean and what constitutes compliance are increasingly transformed into technical questions of measurement, criteria, and data accessibility. Political debates about compliance shift to arguments about how to form an indicator, what should be measured, and what each measurement should represent. These debates typically rely on experts in the field of measurement and statistics, usually in consultation with experts in the substantive topic. They build on previous research studies and on knowledge generated by scholars. The outcomes appear as knowledge, not as particular representations of a methodology or as political decisions about what to measure and what to call it. An indicator provides a transition from ambiguity to certainty, theory to fact, complex variation and context to truthful, comparable numbers. In other words, the legal process of judging and evaluating is transformed into a technical issue of measurement and counting by the diligent work of experts. Practices of measuring phenomena that are relatively easily counted, such as money or inventories of goods, are transplanted into domains far less amenable to quantification, such as frequency of torture or prevalence of ill health. Technologies of knowledge developed in the economic domain move uneasily into these newer fields. Moreover, many countries lack such quantified information, which is expensive to produce.

Corporate social responsibility

Quantification is increasingly important to corporate social responsibility initiatives. Holding corporations accountable to state legal standards on human rights, environmental protection, and labour rights is particularly challenging, since many companies stretch beyond the legal jurisdiction of nation-states. Companies also have legal obligations under international laws, but efforts to hold them accountable under domestic and international law have not been very effective (Sarfaty 2015: 106). One of the strategies for enhancing compliance is to develop a system of numerical indicators and put pressure on companies to report their performance according to these guidelines. Although the reporting requirements are voluntary, some countries and investors have begun to insist on such reporting as well. The emerging field of corporate social responsibility (CSR) relies on such indicators of corporate performance to promote compliance.

The UN Global Compact and the Global Reporting Initiative (GRI) are two of the most significant and widely used entities promoting corporate social responsibility (UNGC 2006). Both increasingly rely on quantification. There are also NGOs developing toolkits to measure corporate compliance with human rights standards. As is characteristic of audit culture more generally (see Power 1999), these efforts place responsibility for gathering information and assessing it on the organizations themselves.

The GRI also provides for stakeholder discussions of the relevant indicators that they will use. Clearly, this approach to monitoring faces problems of verifying the information it uses, given its reliance on self-reporting and choice of measures. These systems are all monitored only by a corporation's concern for its public respectability and reputation.

The UN's Global Compact is a major corporate citizenship initiative that encourages companies to adopt ten principles of operation in the fields of human rights, labour, environment, and anti-corruption (UNGC 2018a). The ten principles are derived from core UN Declarations and Conventions. The UN launched the programme in the year 2000 and, by 2018, claimed it was the largest corporate sustainability initiative in the world, with more than 9,500 companies and 3,000 non-business signatories based in over 160 countries (UNGC 2018a). The Global Compact uses quantification as its core technique. It asks signatory companies to gather data on their compliance with its ten principles, many of which are based in international law, and to make them publicly available. This is an entirely voluntary process, and there is no effort to check the accuracy of the information provided (UNGC 2018b).

Every signatory company is expected to report on its compliance with the ten Global Compact principles every year. The Global Compact also encourages companies to promote the global development agenda, which is articulated as a set of goals called the Sustainable Development Goals (SDGs), discussed in more detail below. In 2018, 80 per cent reported that they were doing so (UNGC 2018a: 6). Regular reports, called Communications on Progress (COPs), should include a statement of continued support for the Global Compact by the chief executive officer (CEO) or another senior executive. In addition, they should provide descriptions of the company's efforts to implement the Global Compact principles and undertake partnership projects in support of broad UN goals, along with measurements of expected outcomes. The 2012 *Basic Guide to the Communication on Progress* advocates presenting information about commitment, systems in place to ensure compliance (such as policies, programmes, and management systems), activities, and measures of outcomes. A company can withdraw from the Global Compact at any time, but must send a letter from the CEO to that effect, which may be posted on the Global Compact website.[1] If a company fails to file a report after a year, it will be defined as non-communicating. After one year as non-communicating, it will be expelled from the Global Compact (UNGC 2012: 5). Companies that fail to submit reports for two years will be listed on the website. There is no other monitoring of data or enforcement. Thus, this is a system designed to improve compliance with major UN conventions and policy statements through quantification of performance, but it has no coercive force beyond shaming those who fail to participate.

The Global Reporting Index, similarly, has no force and relies on voluntary participation. It has developed guidelines and indicators that have become the global standard for corporate social responsibility accounting (Sarfaty 2015: 107). Established in 1997, the GRI is a private regulatory agency that provides a framework for corporations to report on their environmental, social, and economic performance. This framework incorporates legal standards on corporate governance, human rights, anti-discrimination, labour, corruption, and the environment as well as a variety of international agreements such as International Labour Organization conventions and human rights treaties. As Galit Sarfaty (2015: 107) says, 'The indicators attempt to convert legal norms into quantifiable metrics that are easily compared across corporations and serve as a benchmark for improving performance'. They turn legal norms into terms that are more specific and verifiable.

Yet the approach based on the GRI has drawbacks. Companies may comply only superficially, since the reports are simply graded A, B, or C on the basis of the number of indicators included in the report, rather than on the quality of the performance (Sarfaty 2015: 105). Moreover, the numbers are produced by the companies without mandatory third-party verification, so they may not be accurate. The GRI is interested in maximizing the number of companies that participate and the extent of reporting rather than the quality of reporting in its effort to become the leader in corporate reporting (Sarfaty 2015: 106).

Thus, the monitoring system for the Global Compact and the Global Reporting Index is quite similar to that of UN treaty bodies, in which a governing organization confronts the dilemma of judging compliance based upon information provided by the organization being judged. Like treaty body reports, the information requested for assessing corporate social responsibility focuses on the existence of policies and programmes and on changes in behaviour. In both cases, the process depends on the voluntary provision of data. In both of these domains, quantification seems to offer a solution to the lack of independent information available to those who seek to govern, even though converting broad goals into measurable entities can be problematic.

Human trafficking

In the human trafficking field, numbers have been used widely and wildly, often without firm empirical grounding. The creation of a social movement such as the burgeoning anti-trafficking movement requires quantification in order to show the size and scope of the problem, so national and global leaders have struggled to develop rough estimates of the number of victims and even the costs of trafficking. Yet, providing accurate numbers has proved extremely difficult. Anti-trafficking projects and debates continually confront the difficulty of defining what trafficking is and whether and how much it differs from closely related activities such as labour smuggling, voluntary prostitution, debt bondage, child marriage, child soldiers, and forced labour.

There are several obstacles to accurate quantification of trafficking. First, because the activity itself is illegal, those engaged in it seek to conceal the activity. It is not readily recorded in administrative systems, except when victims are helped by police or criminal justice systems. Moreover, survey techniques are expensive and difficult when the victims are hidden. Consequently, data collection often relies on media reports or small-scale studies by NGOs, states, or international organizations.

Second, although there is some consensus about the meaning of human trafficking based on two major laws, the UN's Palermo Protocol and the U.S.'s Trafficking Victims Protection Act, both written in 2000, the definition of trafficking that they use is quite broad, including an *action* (recruitment), a *means* (use of force, coercion), and a *purpose* (of exploitation). Trafficking generally refers to three activities: child trafficking, trafficking of women for commercial sex, and labour trafficking for exploitation or slavery (Guinn 2008: 123). However, it is particularly difficult to distinguish labour trafficking from migrant smuggling, and activists disagree deeply about whether commercial sex work by adults who have in some fashion consented to sex work is an instance of trafficking.

Third, there are alternative understandings of trafficking at the global, national, and local level developed by international organizations, regional organizations, national statistical systems, and non-governmental organizations. Each of these has developed its own forms of counting based on its definition of trafficking. Moreover, even a single organization may change its understanding of trafficking over time. Many have now adopted the concept of modern-day slavery to describe trafficking, while others focus on labour violations (Kotiswaran 2017). For example, the NGO Walk Free publishes a Global Slavery Index which reports the number of 'modern-day slaves', a new term for trafficking victims, for most of the countries of the world.[2]

Fourth, people themselves change their status over time. Victims of trafficking are coerced into conditions of exploitative labour in a wide variety of ways, and the forms of coercion that control them can change over time. A person may be enticed to move for a better job, only to find that she has been offered work in a brothel, choose to leave the brothel for factory work, subsequently decide she was better off in the brothel, and return there. A person deceived into doing exploitative labour may gradually develop resources to return home and deceive others into joining her, thus becoming a trafficker herself. Because the definitions are broad, the category of trafficking shifting, and the status of victims unstable as they move into and out of various work situations, counting victims is very challenging. Migration under financial coercion blurs with being trafficked, particularly when the trafficker is a relative, neighbour, or friend. Several ethnographic studies of sex work and sex trafficking show this ambiguous and shifting nature of trafficking, as they examine the process of entering into and leaving forms of exploitative sex work. This complexity is clear in studies in India (Kotiswaran 2011), Laos (Molland 2012), Korea (Cheng 2010), and Latin America and Europe (Augustin 2007), for example.

Although the Palermo Protocol, several regional and International Labour Organization protocols, and the U.S. State Department's *Trafficking in Persons Reports* have contributed to developing a clearer definition of trafficking, murkiness remains. Not only is the phenomenon itself multifaceted, but the fierce debates about prostitution and human rights that surround this issue have produced unwieldy definitions. The most widely accepted definition of trafficking is in the Palermo Protocol, an international law developed in 2000 as an optional protocol to the UN Convention against Transnational Organized Crime. It came into force in 2003 and by 2019 was very widely ratified, with 174 state parties. It says: '"Trafficking in persons" shall mean the recruitment, transportation, transfer, harbouring or receipt of persons, by means of the threat or use of force or other forms of coercion, of abduction, of fraud, of deception, of the abuse of power or of a position of vulnerability or of the giving or receiving of payments or benefits to achieve the consent of a person having control over another person, for the purpose of exploitation' (Palermo Protocol 2000). Thus, the victim identity is constructed by both a process and a purpose.

The U.S. State Department sees human trafficking as an umbrella term for a series of activities in which 'one person obtains or holds another person in compelled service. The TVPA [Trafficking Victims Protection Act] describes this compelled service using a number of different terms: involuntary servitude, slavery, debt bondage, and forced labor' (US State Department 2010: 7–8).[3] The U.S. definition states that a person need not be physically transported to be trafficked, and that, even if a person initially consents to prostitution but is maintained in that work through coercion, force, or deception, they are considered a victim of trafficking (US State Department 2013: 29).

The movement into victim status is often a complicated process, in which some steps might be made on the basis of consent, while others are relatively less free. What makes labour exploitative is similarly diverse and hard to specify. To add to the definitional morass, there are currently efforts to frame trafficking victims under new labels such as 'modern-day slavery,' while the U.S. State Department no longer includes the criterion of cross-border mobility in its definition, even though this has long been a core principle of trafficking. Thus, not only are these definitions vague, overlapping, and even contradictory, but they are changing over time. Clearly, all these factors, including the plethora of definitions, make it more difficult to count numbers of victims and of traffickers. Some measures of trafficking victims count forced labourers, some count sex workers, some count cross-border labour migrants, and some count a combination of these and other statuses, such as involuntary domestic servitude and child marriage.

But any system of measurement needs to select some part of this terrain to count. Thus, the act of measurement defines what trafficking is. There are currently a variety of techniques for counting victims that use different conceptions of trafficked victims and different measurement protocols. Each of these systems of counting has an underlying theory about what the problem is and how it should be solved. Under conditions of uncertainty of this kind, a social phenomenon will ultimately come to be defined by whatever system of measurement predominates.

One indication of the difficulty of counting is the wild divergence in estimates of the number of trafficked victims globally. In 2005, estimates ranged from 27 million slaves (Bales 2005) to 12.3 million forced labourers, of whom 20 per cent are trafficked (ILO 2005: 7, 10) to 600,000 to 800,000 victims (men, women, and children) trafficked across international borders annually, of which 14,500 to 17,500 people are trafficked into the United States (US State Department 2005: 6). However, the number of victims actually identified is far smaller than these estimates. For example, according to the U.S. State Department TIP Reports, in 2008, the first year for which this information is provided, there were only 30,961 identified victims, and by 2012 there were 46,570 (US State

Department 2013: 46). It is not clear how many of these are commercial sex workers, although this is the prototype of the trafficking victim. The 2005 TIP Report estimate of 600,000 to 800,000 victims says that approximately 80 per cent are women and girls and up to 50 per cent are minors. Of these, there are 'hundreds of thousands used in prostitution' (US State Department 2005: 6). Despite this diversity in estimated numbers of trafficking victims, a few of these estimates circulate widely, gaining credibility through their use and repetition (Tyldum and Brunovskis 2005). Some are repeated over and over in various documents until they acquire an aura of truth and are commonly cited simply as 'U.S. government' data.

In this situation, as in many other ambiguous situations, the act of measurement creates the object of measurement. As legal and social science scholars and international, national, and non-governmental organizations debate what trafficking is and how to measure it, they implicitly determine what it is and what policies should govern it.

Sustainable Development Goals

One of the major current applications of quantification is in the field of international development. Since the late 1990s, the global UN strategy has been to develop broad policy goals, then convert them into specific, measurable indicators. This strategy was fundamental to the UN's Millennium Development Goals, which shaped development from 2000 to 2015, and also to the more ambitious and social justice-oriented Sustainable Development Goals, in effect from 2015 to 2030. An elaborate set of indicators has been developed by the UN to measure countries' compliance with its goals. The designers hope that quantification will increase the accountability of governments by exposing whether they have complied with the ambitious development agenda articulated in the goals.

The set of targets, goals, and indicators called Millennium Development Goals, or MDGs, was developed in the late 1990s by international experts in the UN and World Bank (Fukuda-Parr 2017). The Sustainable Development Goals (SDGs) are the next generation of global development targets, goals, and indicators. In contrast to the MDGs, the SDGs were the product of two and a half years of discussion among civil society actors, international organizations, and nation-states, with substantial participation by countries of the global South (Fukuda-Parr 2017; Fukuda-Parr and McNeill 2019).

After the widely participatory process through which the SDGs' seventeen goals and 169 targets were created, the task of translating the aspirational goals and targets into numerical indicators was given to the UN Statistical Commission (UNSC), an intergovernmental body. To carry this out, the UNSC formed the Inter-Agency and Expert Group on SDG Indicators (IAEG-SDGs or Expert Group) consisting of representatives of national statistical offices (UN Department of Economic and Social Affairs Statistics Division 2015). The UN Statistical Division (UNSD) is the secretariat—the professional staff—that supports the UN Statistical Commission. By March 2019 there were 232 agreed-upon indicators (UN Statistical Division 2017a, 2017b, 2019).

This indicator framework is built on the MDG approach but has dramatically expanded the scope of issues and type of indicators that are included. The SDG goals and targets were produced by substantial engagement with and advice from civil society as well as the 193 UN member states and UN agencies. The goals are broad, aspirational, and often vague. For example, the SDGs include goals such as 'End hunger, achieve food security and improved nutrition and promote sustainable agriculture (Goal 2)' and 'Promote sustained, inclusive and sustainable economic growth, full and productive employment and decent work for all (Goal 8)' (UN Statistical Commission 2017: 16, 24). Many of the goals and targets had not previously been measured and lacked both specificity and a pre-existing body of data. Many are expensive to measure.

As the statisticians grappled with the question of how to measure the SDGs, they resorted to far narrower conceptions of the goals and targets in order to render them countable. They reduced them to a set of more limited indicators. To illustrate this process, I will look at the indicators for one goal: sustainability and access to justice. As of March 2019, this goal was divided into twelve targets and twenty-three indicators. The following three targets and indicators illustrate how broad goals are converted into measurable things:

Goal 16. Promote peaceful and inclusive societies for sustainable development, provide access to justice for all and build effective, accountable and inclusive institutions at all levels

Target 16.1 Significantly reduce all forms of violence and related death rates everywhere

16.1.1 Number of victims of intentional homicide per 100,000 population, by sex and age

16.1.2 Conflict-related deaths per 100,000 population, by sex, age and cause

16.1.3 Proportion of population subjected to physical, psychological or sexual violence in the previous 12 months

16.1.4 Proportion of population that feel safe walking alone around the area they live

Target 16.2 End abuse, exploitation, trafficking and all forms of violence against and torture of children

16.2.1 Proportion of children aged 1–17 years who experienced any physical punishment and/or psychological aggression by caregivers in the past month

16.2.2 Number of victims of human trafficking per 100,000 population, by sex, age and form of exploitation

16.2.3 Proportion of young women and men aged 18–29 years who experienced sexual violence by age 18

Target 16.3 Promote the rule of law at the national and international levels and ensure equal access to justice for all

16.3.1 Proportion of victims of violence in the previous 12 months who reported their victimization to competent authorities or other officially recognized conflict resolution mechanisms

16.3.2 Unsentenced detainees as a proportion of overall prison population[4]

Clearly the indicators, which specify the measures that will determine if the target has been met, examine a relatively limited slice of the goals and targets. Even with this restriction, however, many of the inspiring SDG social justice goals do not yet have viable indicators and data sources. Many do not yet have a clear methodology for measurement and lack data. The IAEG-SDGs has divided all the indicators into three tiers, depending on whether there is adequate data and an acceptable methodology for measuring each one. Tier I indicators have established methods and available data; Tier II have established methodology but little data available; and Tier III lack established methodology and require further work and development. There has been substantial effort to develop methodologies and data for these indicators. Although in 2017 only a fraction of the goals had a set of indicators, with more than half classified as Tier I (Leong 2017), by May 2019 there were 104 Tier I indicators, eighty-eight Tier II indicators, and thirty-four Tier III—plus six indicators with multiple tiers (different components of the indicator are classified into different tiers). As of May 2019, of the nine indicators listed above for Goal 16, only two were Tier I: 16.1.1, 'Victims of intentional homicide', and 16.3.2, 'Unsentenced detainees in prison', both of which have a custodian agency, the UN Office on Drugs and Crime, that collects the data. The other seven are classified as Tier II. Overall, Goal 16 only had six Tier I indicators out of twenty-three and one Tier III indicator. Many of the more innovative and aspirational indicators remain unmeasured in Tiers II and III.

In sum, the promise that quantification will increase compliance with the SDGs is undermined by the cost and difficulty of counting the aspirational goals of the creators. Unlike previous global measurement efforts, this one was created by a coalition of civil society groups and both global South and global North countries. Yet, the challenges and costs of converting sweeping ideals into measurements—developing methodologies, gathering relevant data, disaggregating the data, and analysing and presenting it—make it likely that only the more conventional indicators will ultimately be measured.

Data collection: the problem of counting

Indicators depend on the collection of comparable data, which means defining phenomena that can be counted. As donors demand evidence-based programming, NGOs must come up with statistical measures for what they have accomplished. Activists jockeying for funding are pressed to engage in activities that can produce measurable outcomes in relatively short time periods. For those with broad social change agendas, bigger accomplishments must be replaced with small, countable activities. For example, a feminist women's centre in which I did research in the 1990s initially sought to transform gender relations and diminish violence through requiring batterers in domestic violence cases to attend eight months of two-hour-per-week training-session meetings. When its funding shifted from community development money to the judiciary, the courts asked the programme to report how many people it had trained. The staff had to shorten the training programme, develop a more therapeutic and less critical way of dealing with violent men in domestic battery cases so that they would drop out less often, and count the number of clients they handled on a monthly basis. Thus, their agenda shifted from transforming the community and gender relations to providing services to battered women and anger management training to those who hit them (Merry 2009: 54–75).

Indicators require converting dimensions of social life into something that can be measured. Some things are more easily measured than others, however, and require less interpretation. Infant mortality is easier to count than the rule of law, for example. However, even phenomena that seem quite countable, such as infant mortality, depend on practices of birth and death registration and reporting mechanisms. Many indicators assess phenomena that are very difficult to quantify, such as justice or the protection of human rights. One solution is to create quantifiable proxies for the phenomenon. For example, if the goal is increasing the consciousness of human rights, this could be assessed by an attitude survey or by a count of the number of training sessions that an organization has carried out. The latter is clearly less expensive.

Those who design an indicator must decide which data-collection methods they can use, depending, in part, on how much they can spend on collecting information. Data collection is expensive, especially when it depends on a designated survey. Cost is often a trade-off against accuracy. Using administrative data already collected by state agencies is less expensive than dedicated surveys, but it is often less accurate. Poorer countries are less likely to gather any data about their populations than rich ones. Problems that are less important, politically, are typically less studied. There has been a recent turn towards the use of so-called big data, collected by companies and other private entities, yet these are often gathered for business purposes rather than social reform or accountability agendas.

Conclusions

The use of statistical information and indicators is an important technique for increasing compliance, particularly with international law. Quantification replaces judgements on the basis of values or politics with more neutral statistical information. In theory, the process is more open, allowing the public access to the basis for decisions. The significant expansion of quantification in recent times comes from a political culture that demands more openness and seeks to drive out corruption, prejudice, and the arbitrary power of elites, even at the cost of subtlety and depth (Porter 1995: 85–6).

Yet, statistical measures have embedded theories and values which shape apparently objective information and influence decisions. Despite the increase in democratic openness produced by the use of statistics in decision-making, this is a technology that tends to consolidate power in the hands of those with expert knowledge. In many situations the turn to numbers as a mode of governance does not eliminate the role of private knowledge and elite power in decision-making, but replaces it with technical, statistical expertise. Decisions that were carried out by political or judicial leaders are made by technical experts who construct the measures and develop the processes of classification and counting that produce the numbers. Increasing reliance on indicators tends to locate decision-making in the global North, where indicators are typically designed and labelled.

As the world becomes ever more measured and tracked through indicators and other forms of quantification, it becomes increasingly important to sort out the technical and political dimensions of this new technology. Indicators produce readily understandable and convenient forms of knowledge about the world that shape the way policymakers as well as the general public understand the world. This form of knowledge production and governance has expanded from its economic origins to national and global governance. The use of these statistical techniques is producing new knowledge of the social world and new opportunities for enhancing compliance with the law at the global level, with all its strengths and weaknesses.

Notes

1. See <http://www.globalcompact.org/> (accessed 30 April 2020).
2. See <http://www.globalslaveryindex.org> (accessed 30 April 2020).
3. 'TIP Report' is the abbreviated name for a Trafficking in Persons Report of the US State Department.
4. UN Statistical Division 2019 A/RES/71/313 E/CN.3/2018/2 E/CN.3/2019/2.

References

Alston, P. 2005. 'Richard Lillich Memorial Lecture: Promoting the Accountability of Members of the New UN Human Rights Council'. *Journal of Transnational Law and Policy* 15: 49–96.

Augustin, L. M. 2007. *Sex at the Margins: Migration, Labour Markets, and the Rescue Industry.* London and New York: Zed Books.

Bales, K. 2005. *Understanding Global Slavery: A Reader.* Berkeley: University of California Press.

Cheng, S. 2010. *On the Move for Love: Migrant Entertainers and the US Military in South Korea.* Philadelphia: University of Penn Press.

Davis, K., B. Kingsbury, and S. E. Merry. 2012. 'Indicators as a Technology of Global Governance'. *Law and Society Review* 46(1): 71–104.

Davis, S. L. M. 2017. 'The Uncounted: Politics of Data and Visibility in Global Health'. *International Journal of Human Rights* 21: DOI: 10.1080/13642987.2017.1348707.

Fukuda-Parr, S. 2017. *The Millennium Development Goals: Ideas, Interests, and Influence.* New York: Routledge.

Fukukda-Parr, S. and D. McNeill. 2019. 'Knowledge and Politics in Setting and Measuring the SDGs: Introduction to Special Issue'. *Global Policy* 10: Supplement 1: 5–15.
Green, M. 2001. 'What We Talk About When We Talk About Indicators: Current Approaches to Human Rights Measurement'. *Human Rights Quarterly* 23: 1062–97.
Guinn, D. E. 2008. 'Defining the Problem of Trafficking: The Interplay of US Law, Donor, and NGO Engagement and the Local Context in Latin America'. *Human Rights Quarterly* 30(1) (February): 119–45.
International Labor Organization. 2005. Report from the Director-General: *A Global Alliance Against Forced Labor: Global Report under the Follow-up to the ILO Declaration on Fundamental Principles and Rights at Work.* International Labor Conference, 93rd session. Geneva, Switzerland. <http://www.ilo.org/declaration>.
Kotiswaran, P. 2011. *Dangerous Sex, Invisible Labor: Sex Work and the Law in India.* Princeton: Princeton University Press.
Kotiswaran, P., ed. 2017. *Revisiting the Law and Governance of Trafficking, Forced Labor, and Modern Slavery.* Cambridge: Cambridge University Press.
Leong, A. K. 4 December 2017. 'Indicators, Indivisibility and the Conceptual Complexity of the SDGs'. *Together 23 Blog.* <https://wp.me/p70hhk-u6>.
Malhotra, R. and N. Fasel. 2005. 'Quantitative Human Rights Indicators: A Survey of Major Initiatives'. Background paper for the UN Expert Meeting on Human Rights Indicators, Turku, Finland., 10–13 March 2005 in Turku/Abo Finland. Document on file with author.
Merry, S. E. 2009. *Human Rights and Gender Violence: Translating International Law into Local Justice.* Chicago: University of Chicago Press.
Merry, S. E. 2016. *The Seductions of Quantification: Measuring Human Rights, Gender Violence, and Sex Trafficking.* Chicago: University of Chicago Press.
Molland, S. 2012. *The Perfect Business? Anti-trafficking and the Sex Trade along the Mekong.* Honolulu: University of Hawai'i Press.
Palermo Protocol. 2000. Protocol to Prevent, Suppress and Punish Trafficking in Persons Especially Women and Children, supplementing the United Nations Convention against Transnational Organized Crime. <http://www.ohchr.org/EN/ProfessionalInterest/Pages/ProtocolTraffickingInPersons.aspx>.
Porter, T. M. 1995. *Trust in Numbers: The Pursuit of Objectivity in Science and Public Life.* Princeton: Princeton University Press.
Power, M. 1999. *The Audit Society: Rituals of Verification.* Oxford: Oxford University Press.
Rosga, A. and M. L. Satterthwaite. 2009. 'The Trust in Indicators: Measuring Human Rights'. *Berkley Journal of International Law* 2(2): 253–315.
Sarfaty, G. 2015. 'Measuring Corporate Accountability through Global Indicators' In S. E. Merry, K. E. Davis, and B. Kingsbury, eds. *The Quiet Power of Indicators: Measuring Governance, Corruption, and Rule of Law*, 103–32. Cambridge: Cambridge University Press.
Turku Report. 2005. *Report of Turku Expert Meeting on Human Rights Indicators.* Institute for Human Rights, Åbo Akademi University, Turku, Finland, 10–13 March. Accessed 17 December 2008. Document on file with author.
Tyldum, G. and A. Brunovskis. 2005. 'Describing the Unobserved: Methodological Challenges in Empirical Studies on Human Trafficking'. *International Migration* 43(1–2): 17–34.
UN Department of Economic and Social Affairs Statistics Division. 2015. First Meeting of the Inter-Agency and Expert Group on the Sustainable Development Goal Indicators New

York, 1–2 June 2015. ESA/ST/AC.300/L3 24 June 2015. <https://unstats.un.org/sdgs/meetings/iaeg-sdgs-meeting-01/>.

UN Statistical Commission. 2017. 'Report of the Inter-Agency and Expert Group on Sustainable Development Goal Indicators'. E/CN.3/2018/2. 19 December 2017. <https://unstats.un.org/unsd/statcom/49th-session/documents/2018-2-SDG-IAEG-E.pdf>.

UN Statistical Division. 2017a. <https://unstats.un.org/sdgs/indicators/indicators-list/>.

UN Statistical Division. 2017b. 'Global Indicator Framework for the Sustainable Development Goals and Targets of the 2030 Agenda for Sustainable Development'. A/RES/71/313. <https://unstats.un.org/sdgs/indicators/Global%20Indicator%20Framework_A.RES.71.313%20Annex.pdf>.

UN Statistical Division. 2019. 'Global Indicator Framework for the Sustainable Development Goals and targets of the 2030 Agenda for Sustainable Development' (A/RES/71/313 E/CN.3/2018/2 E/CN.3/2019/2) <https://unstats.un.org/sdgs/indicators/Global%20Indicator%20Framework%20after%202019%20refinement_Eng.pdf>.

UNGC. 2006. *Making the Connection: The GRI Guidelines and the UNGC Communication on Progress.* UN Global Compact and Global Reporting Initiative. Drafted 2006. <http://www.unglobalcompact.org>.

UNGC. 2008. *The Practical Guide to the United Nations Global Compact Communications on Progress (COPs).* Revised version of 2004 report. Available at <http://www.unglobalcompact.org>.

UNGC. 2012. *UN Global Compact Basic Guide to the Communication on Progress.* <https://www.unglobalcompact.org/library/305>.

UNGC. 2018a. *UN Global Compact Progress Report 2018.* <https://www.unglobalcompact.org/docs/publications/UN-Global-Compact-Progress-Report-2018.pdf>.

UNGC. 2018b. *UN Global Compact*: Frequently Asked Questions. <https://www.unglobalcompact.org/about/faq>.

US State Department. 2005. *Trafficking in Persons Report 2005.* <https://2009-2017.state.gov/j/tip/rls/tiprpt/2005/index.htm>.

US State Department. 2010. *Trafficking in Persons Report 2010.* <https://2009-2017.state.gov/j/tip/rls/tiprpt/2010/index.htm>.

US State Department. 2013. *Trafficking in Persons Report 2013.* <https://2009-2017.state.gov/j/tip/rls/tiprpt/2013/index.htm>.

CHAPTER 41

LAW, SCIENCE, AND TECHNOLOGIES

BERTRAM TURNER AND MELANIE G. WIBER

Introduction

For twenty years, scholars in both anthropology and law (L) have found Science and Technology Studies (STS) useful to understand techno-scientific transformations of the world (Cloatre and Pickersgill 2016; Haack 2014; Jasanoff 1994, 2009; Latour 2002; Riles 2000). Legal scholars recognize that new scientific discoveries and the resulting technologies can create new norms and influence law. In the legal approach to STS, however, the focus has been on the law of the state and/or the law deriving from the production of global governance institutions. A broader look at complex legal configurations has not been part of L-STS.

Anthropology, on the other hand, had long taken into account normative social ordering that was not conventionally identified as law (Vanderlinden 1989:153f.). When adopting an STS perspective, legal anthropology was thus more open to exploring the normative power invested in other domains such as religion, local knowledge, the built environment, and technologies. This work highlighted the plural legal configurations and trans-scalar legal arrangements that affect what Delaney (2010) has called the 'nomosphere'. While law and science and technology are viewed as mutually constitutive of modernity (seeking predictability despite risk and uncertainty), anthropological studies of legal pluralism (LP) have focused on how world-making initiatives create multiple normative orders, including the normative power of technology under the influence of neoliberalism (Benda-Beckmann and Turner 2018, 2020; Robinson and Graham 2018).

In this contribution we bring together L, STS, and LP to explore how normative orders are affected by materiality, technology, and scientific knowledge, resulting in ever more complex heterogeneity. We view law as an assemblage of strategically positioned networks in which human and non-human constituents interact (Cole and Bertenthal

2017: 361) and which extend far beyond institutional boundaries. Such networks connect documents, artefacts, and people to form increasingly complex plural legal configurations (see McGee 2014, 2015). Viewed in this way, (global) law entails networks of normatively active agents, and law itself materializes as practice enacted by people and materiality (see e.g. Robinson and Graham 2018). This approach also recognizes law's fundamental equality (and entanglement) with other domains that make up human societal existence, such as economy, religion, and politics.

We demonstrate how the intersection of these three approaches—L, STS, and LP—can expand our understanding of natural resource management, environmentalism(s), and questions of sustainability. We first discuss the three approaches, then draw on two empirical examples from our respective research to illustrate the core concepts that are useful in linking the three. These concepts include co-production (Jasanoff 2009), translation (Callon 1984; Chrisman 1999), boundary objects (Star 2010), and infrastructure (Bowker et al. 2010; Oswick and Robertson 2009; Star 1999, 2002). We conclude that the integration of these three intersecting fields of study better explains how law, science, and technology together co-construct new worlds.

Three knowledge regimes

In discussing L, STS, and LP, it is important to recognize how they are 'situated knowledge' (Haraway 1988; Valverde 2003), linked but differentiated. While legal practitioners rely on facts to meet the standard of evidence in the production of legal knowledge (Jasanoff 1993), law is not an autonomous subsystem of society, as positivism suggests. The truth claims of law are situated knowledge, meaning that legal world-making may materialize in more than one regime of ordering, and could always have followed different trajectories. Science, despite claims of universality, operates in a similar way. Nevertheless, both law and science are involved in the production of 'truth' and enjoy high epistemic authority. Furthermore, they are mutually constitutive. Scientific facts prefigure ideas about causality, reasoning, and justice in jurisprudence and law (e.g. Reardon 2013). Conversely, looking at legal practice may shed light on the production of knowledge, as law defines the framework conditions of technological research and knowledge production. As co-producing knowledge regimes, their interactions are accessible to social scientific analysis.

Jasanoff (2008) explores the relations between law and science/technology, describing: law lag (legislation lags behind scientific progress), culture clash (resulting from the different aims of law and ST), crisis (incompatibilities between the two), deference (by legal decision-makers towards science), and co-production (simultaneous formation of natural and social order in knowledge societies).[1] With respect to co-production, Jasanoff (2008: 762) emphasizes the effects of legal regulation on science, including freedom of research (see also Barnett and Wiber 2019). But when this lawyer–scientist interaction is viewed from the perspective of LP, we must examine techno-science in its entanglements with the entire nomosphere.

Originally developed in the colonial context, LP theory applies wherever more than one normative order co-exist (Griffith 2015), thereby challenging the law of the state as the only legitimate law. This approach was soon applied to a wide range of legal settings within any and all nation-states, especially once what Moore (1973) called 'semi-autonomous social fields' were recognized to exist virtually everywhere. In the wake of increasing globalization, LP has been taken up by legal scholars such as Paul Schiff Berman (2016), who characterize it as 'global legal pluralism' (GLP). And as techno-science increasingly influences the way normative orders work across multiple scales of space and time, LP has further developed to address multiple ontologies, decolonization, and global citizenship, acknowledging what Davies (2017a, b) has called a 'pluriverse of law'.

In this pluriverse, law materializes as the multiple practices enacted by people as they engage with materiality (Cloatre and Cowan 2019), with the interaction between people and things creating normativity and in turn being regulated by the law. Central concepts such as 'legal assemblages' (see e.g. McGee 2015; Sullivan 2014; de Sutter and McGee 2012), 'law by association' (Levi and Valverde 2008), and 'boundary objects' (De Goede and Sullivan 2016; Foster 2014; Wiber 2015) explicate the emergence and effects of normativity in conjunction with materiality.

The normative power of technologies also corresponds to 'the co-production' of types of political organization. Recent research (Cole and Bertenthal 2017) and pragmatist theory and philosophy (Riles 2003) illustrate the role of law in the most challenging projects of modernity, including those that heighten uncertainty and the unequal distribution of risk. Law assigns power and determines access to justice, but each legal order enables this in its own way, and to different effect.

Rapid scientific and technological change now challenges existing legal orders and legal institutions to an extent never before experienced. Institutions of global governance and epistemic communities are increasingly involved in the transfer of science and technology, as well as in monitoring the effects that technological innovation entails in various settings, including normative processes. Together, LP and STS can investigate how technologies become authoritative such that people no longer have choices—leading to increasingly restrictive nomospheres (Delaney 2010). We will illustrate this in our ethnographic examples.

Recognizing interactions between the three forms of situated knowledge (L, STS, LP) leads us to two very complex regimes: the hybridity of law and the hybridity of knowledge. Fortunately, there are some useful tools that can be borrowed from STS to investigate this complexity. We show how these tools help to address the ways in which various knowledge regimes are reconfigured. We cannot do justice to all the core concepts that are useful in this regard, and those we reference can only be introduced briefly and somewhat unevenly. We place the emphasis on three of these—translation, boundary objects (important links in infrastructure arrangements), and infrastructure. But first a word about our ethnographic illustrations.

Salmon in Canada, argan oil in Morocco

We rely on two very different ethnographic illustrations to explore how unregulated spaces in different parts of the world go through similar technological and legal processes as they are turned into managed extractivism with attendant infrastructures for delivering goods to markets. In the general resource setting of both cases—that is, forests and oceans—there has been much L-STS research into the process of transformation of nature into social products (Eden and Bear 2010; Law and Lien 2012; Lien and Law 2011; Tsing 2005, 2015; Wiber and Turner 2010). However, this transformation is not well understood regarding the normative pluralism that both goes into the new levels of extraction and is itself a product of extractive processes. Our examples come from the rise of salmon aquaculture in Canada (Barnett et al. 2017; Wiber et al. 2012) and of argan oil production in Morocco (Turner 2014, 2016). The two cases have their own unique biographies and trajectories, but nevertheless highlight commonalities. We will turn to the commonalities after using our ethnographic illustrations to explore important core concepts.

Core concepts

While a thorough review of L-STS is impossible here,[2] a few core concepts—co-production, assemblage, and network—are central to understanding L-STS interaction in the world.[3] Such concepts presuppose that law and science and technology are collected together into assemblages of practice that co-produce the future. However, we want to reconsider co-production itself (Jasanoff 2004), which is basic to all STS approaches. We want to make better use of co-production for the analysis of complex scalar, spatial, and temporal arrangements that connect the nomosphere with knowledge production and technology. The concept gains much if made scale-sensitive (see e.g. Valverde 2009) and also if adapted to complex processes of global norm production stimulated by interacting normative repertoires. Existing approaches isolate some sites of knowledge production from others and from sites of knowledge application, which obscures the global interconnectedness of co-production.

Law and science and technology, for example, are increasingly operative within complex plural legal configurations, where they connect the realms of religion, morality, and ethics to the effects of technologies and inventories of knowledge (Latour 2002; Wiber and Turner 2010). The abstract ethics of the legislator often differ from the moralities with which technologies become associated in concrete circumstances. Legitimizing discourses either attach accountability to the options provided by science and technology or they exempt them from accountability. Such processes take place on the level of technologies, of knowledge production, and/or of law production. For example, genetically modified crops (GMCs), reproductive technologies, stem cell research, cloning, organ transplantation, animal experimentation, big data mining, and risk monitoring are all examples of new technologies that have generated critical moral debate (Fischer 2005; Hurlbut 2015; Pálsson and Harðardóttir 2002; Reardon 2013; Sharp 2002; Wiber 2005, 2009). Knowledge transfers between the industrialized world and the Global South are also subject to moral evaluations that affect science and technology and law intersections (Santos 2009), as in the regulation of extraction schemes or value chains (Tsing 2009, 2015; Turner 2014, 2016). Disasters (whether natural or man-made), nuclear power, and climate change also demand responsive legislation and emergency law. Moreover, risk assessment addresses the threats that scientific or technological innovations pose for the society at large (Duckett et al. 2014). Finally, both self-regulation and external legal regulation of science also address risk and security considerations (Healy 2010; Stirling 2012).

One obvious interaction of science and technology and law in a neoliberal world is the making and regulating of markets (Silbey 2008/II). Trade, transfer, and access are all regulated at the transnational scale, often reworking property rights and profit claims through the politics of protection. Pacts such as the Agreement on Trade-Related Aspects of Intellectual Property Rights (TRIPS) involve legal dynamics in other fields such as labour law, and soft governance tools such as corporate social responsibility practices and corporate codes of conduct, fair trade and economies of solidarity, and geographical indicators (GI) (Wheeler 2017). These all require technologies of measurement (see Merry's contribution in this volume). One consequence is the stabilization of imbalances between industrialized and low-income, raw-material-exporting countries (Gonzalez 2017).

Against this background, three core concepts—translation, boundary object, and infrastructure—are key to the analysis of the ways in which legal pluralities are intertwined with technologies and scientific knowledge regimes. All three involve practices and operations within larger assemblages.

Translation

Translation refers to the categorization of things as natural or social and how these can be transferred back and forth across categories through the work of mediators who leave 'traceable associations' (see e.g. Clarke et al. 2015; Gal 2015; Latour 2005: 108). For example, is farmed salmon, with its genetic manipulations, a natural product or a social-technological innovation? Can 'natural' argan oil, a product of a 'wild' forest, be sustainably recreated as a plantation product? Translation processes include the transfer of meaning, significance, interpretation, and agency from science to technology to law to diverse knowledge regimes to practices and applications (see Behrends et al. 2014; Rottenburg 2009; Turner 2016: 391f.). Translation includes the ways that materiality translates into rules (as with ocean spaces turned into salmon farm leases) and normative content translates into technology (when forests become managed eco-reserves). Translation thus connotes the mobility of law-, technology-, and science-based items that can be detached from their contexts and then transformed into something else, with unpredictable effects in both the new environment and the environment of origin.

Law is translated from one context to the next, and law itself translates and transforms the subjects and objects it governs. Translation is therefore our point of departure, as boundary objects and infrastructures constitute what Tsing (2015: x, 217), in reference to supply chains and science, calls 'translation machines'. Such machines organize sequences of translation: from argan forest to forest eco-reserve, and from forest eco-reserve to 'sustainably' managed plantation. In the process, law not only 'mixes' with other law, but also with the normativity of other components such as technology and knowledge regimes. This extends Merry's (2006) model of vernacularization and translation 'from the middle' in two ways. First, this mixing operation always takes place at a number of interstitial spaces (Rottenburg 2009), such as labs where gene splicing creates salmon with faster growth and cold-water tolerance and where the molecular improvement of argan seeds transforms argan into an optimized oil crop. Second, the illusion that the mediator (genetic researcher) has insights into both of the spheres that are connected through translation (fish biology and human fish consumption practices; forest ecosystem and pharmaceutical and cosmetic industries) allows for translational plurality in unpredictable ways. A multiplicity of accepted realities can thus be in play. The first empirical task is to discern how these different realities interact and move on (as when the state sanctions human consumption of genetically modified fish or when a forest is transformed into a plantation); the second task is to determine what ultimately arrives at the grassroots to be translated and vernacularized within another plural legal configuration. Direct translation and intermediary translation (or 'mediated translation' in Merry's terms) thus splits up into an indeterminable number of chains of translation in which each operation generates its own results that, again, are translated into each other.

Translation processes across space and time often comprise techno-normative transfers from the industrial world and their relocation in (post)colonial contexts (see e.g. Merry 2006). Hegemony and power play into such processes. The challenge is to disentangle the normative reading of STS from the hegemonic lawscript of the Global North (Behrends et al. 2014; Best and Walters 2013; Rottenburg 2009).

Boundary Objects

Translation may establish boundary objects (Fujimura 1992), as Wiber (2015) argues has happened to certain legal concepts such as property. Boundary objects allow communication between people who associate different things with the object (Akkerman and Bakker 2011; Star 1993; Star and Griesemer 1989). Susan Leigh Star noted that *boundary* referred to a shared space, where different communities of interest need to collaborate despite lack of consensus, while an *object* is 'something people ... act toward and with' (2010: 603). The materiality or 'thing-ness' derives from action, not from 'a sense of prefabricated stuff' (Star 2010: 603). Boundary objects both inhabit several intersecting social worlds and satisfy the informational requirements of each of them; are plastic enough to adapt to local needs yet robust enough to maintain a common identity across several sites; are weakly structured in common use and become strongly structured in individual site use, and may be abstract or concrete. Star (2010) viewed boundary objects as having three components: 1) interpretive flexibility; 2) the structure of informatics and work process needs and arrangements; and 3) the dynamic between ill-structured and more tailored use of the objects, which requires tacking back and forth between well-structured and ill-structured.

Much of the subsequent literature on boundary objects focused on the first two of these components, and neglected to address the third (see Lee 2007; Oswick and Robertson 2009; Trompette and Vinck 2009). But Star frequently noted that it was attempts to regulate or standardize the structuring of a boundary object that implicated it in power politics (see Bowker and Star 1999; Clarke and Star 2008; Star 1993, 2002). The first and second components are entangled with the third, and all three play an important role in the dynamic processes of engagement at the boundary and in the creation of power in the act of translation.

Bowker and Star (1999: 296–307) traced the trajectory of boundary objects over time and space to explore how they may become 'naturalized' in a particular setting. In the case of argan oil, for example, some international actors are working to develop the argan forest so that it can produce an internationally certified and sustainable product, despite lack of consensus around such normatively loaded concepts as biosphere, ecosystem, nature reserve, conservation, cooperatives, development, traceability, and product purity. Yet despite this lack of consensus, huge networks have emerged to produce and market this valuable commodity. Thus, naturalization requires 'stripping away the contingencies of an object's creation and its situated nature' (ibid.: 299), which 'collapses the difference between an ill-structured, shared object and a locally tailored object' (Star 2010: 614).

Murdoch (1998) notes how well-structured boundary objects come to dominate through standardization, a 'space of prescription' where everyone has to use the same language and categories if they want to be involved in the discussion (as in certification standards). On the other hand, subversive types (with a focus on 'left out' categories) can keep pushing for 'spaces of negotiation', where 'the struggle to reinvent ourselves' is made possible (ibid.: 370) because the power to standardize is resisted or the standardization is negotiated more openly. For example, argan oil can be produced in local cooperatives, empowering local people; alternatively, technological research in mechanization leads to innovations that replace the manual work done in cooperatives. This ultimately results in corporate industrial processing, which further promotes the transformation of the forest into a plantation in order to produce standardized raw material. Such choices imply moral struggles.

Legal formality is often connected to 'concerns about future accountability' (Murdoch 1998: 187). Oswick and Robertson (2009: 188) draw attention to how particular boundary objects sustain or challenge pre-existing power relationships, which in turn affects 'the discursive practices' that control how knowledge is enacted in different contexts (ibid.). Where power relationships are asymmetrical, the goals are often divergent and contested (ibid.: 190).

Infrastructure

Infrastructure results from the linking up of networks around boundary objects (Harvey et al. 2017; Larkin 2013; Pinch 2010; Star 2002; Star and Ruhleder 1996; Turner 2016), and our work particularly explores how the concept links law, technology, place, and time. Infrastructure is commonly understood as a physically reticulated system, like a transport network. In the STS literature, it denotes complex fabrics of interrelated social, technological, and organizational components (see e.g. Bowker et al. 2010; Niewöhner 2015; Star 1999). An infrastructure creates a web of relationships that combines knowledge regimes (marine biologists, engineers, intellectual property lawyers), technologies (open net sea cages; oil-processing technology such as extruding machines, filtration), material elements (pesticides, feed formulas), normative templates (food safety), institutions (universities, labs, corporations, INGOs), bureaucracies (departments of aquaculture, forestry), humans, other-than-human species, resources, and much more into an enabling design (salmon aquaculture; argan oil industry). The composition of components is carefully arranged in such a way that each component, when combined with the others, may have effects other than those it has when acting on its own.

As Star and Ruhleder (1996: 113) put it, the 'configuration of these dimensions forms an infrastructure' which is 'without absolute boundary or a priori definition'. The internal dynamics of infrastructure, then, cannot be kept under control (Tsing 2009), although they may have temporal stability. Depending on its design, an infrastructure's effects may be more or less visible (Bowker et al. 2010). As Larkin (2013: 330) emphasizes, infrastructures are not just 'out there'. They do not provide mere technological solutions to social needs or economic projects. Infrastructures contain embedded narratives on what they are thought to be good for (in the case of salmon aquaculture, providing fish protein without decimating wild fish stocks; in the case of argan oil, combining nature conservation with rural empowerment and creating new edible, pharmaceutical, and cosmetic products). They consist of technological supply structures and, at the same time, fluid embodiments of social, political, and legal decisions (Niewöhner 2015). They rely on flows of inventories of knowledge, material, technologies, regulations, and values. The concept of infrastructure thus explains how a variety of disconnected components can solidify (however briefly) into a larger assemblage.

When analysing infrastructures, it is crucial to determine what components different actors consider to be part of an infrastructure and for what epistemological and political reasons. In other words, one infrastructure (such as that which makes the production and commodification of argan or salmon possible) can inhabit different worlds. This reveals why it is important to factor in law as a constitutive component. Infrastructure as a concept helps to contextualize law (see e.g. Fischer 2005), especially LP, and to address law as part of the underlying invisible structure of the infrastructure. Infrastructures order their constitutive components and develop their own specific legal configurations, combining various legal regimes and normative orders (usufruct rights of local people, intellectual property regimes, development law) with routinized social practices and the normative power of material technologies. The legal architecture of infrastructures offers networked practices and communications that are interwoven with other infrastructural components to stabilize the service provided across spatiotemporal, epistemic, and onto-legal divides (Bowker et al. 2010). Infrastructures emerge out of action. They are not autonomous systems operating independently of individuals (Pinch 2010). Rather, they are trans-scalar networks informed by infrastructural normativities that guide connectivity, flow, communication, participation, authenticity, and flexibility. Infrastructures are amalgamations in which organizations, institutions, and technologies all have normative effects as a result of the way they determine practice and thus interaction with other spatio-temporal layers. Infrastructure deals with making connections throughout, across, and between spaces and places, distances, temporalities, and scales. They combine techno-legal elements with knowledge-based and network-organized components. They embody law as encoded information. The normative tools in use also provide information about values, social concepts, and inclusion in or exclusion from the service provided. Infrastructure thus by definition displays features of legal plurality. Infrastructure, governance, and power as analytical tools (see e.g. Rowland and Passoth 2015) help to discern the production of normativity by routinization of social practices within a given infrastructural design that is itself law producing.

Taken together, these concepts allow us to deal with the central problem that is inherent in techno-scientific-normative assemblages, namely the processing of risk and uncertainty (Beck 2009; Beck et al. 2003; Boholm 2015; Wynne 2002). One cannot discuss the entanglements of law and science without thinking about the risks that they would like to avoid, as our illustrations show. Law and science aim to co-construct a (desired) future.

Commonalities in the Ethnographic Illustrations

Our two ethnographic examples, drawn from widely diverse geographical settings, nevertheless share important commonalities in terms of process. First, there is rich localized biodiversity, with small-scale, local extraction governed by local norms and rules (access via usufruct rights), in some cases linked into international markets (fish) and in other cases providing local needs only (argan oil). Local fishermen catch and sell wild salmon and local villagers produce argan oil from wild trees.

With state governance of such spaces, however, comes increasing demand for information to support industrial-scale managerial approaches. This pulls in science to identify, count, and characterize resources on the basis of their 'value'. In some cases, this generates bioprospecting (argan oil) and in other cases public science is tasked with gaining the greatest public benefit from the resource (maximum sustainable yield from fish stocks). Many (contradictory) state rules follow. Boundary objects proliferate as multiple actors come together to collaborate despite having no consensus around such critical concepts as rights of access and distribution of benefits. As discussions take place about how to actualize these concepts, the boundary objects are often stabilized in unexpected ways. Salmon fishing becomes stabilized as open net pen aquaculture; argan tree forests/plantations are stabilized as a protected biosphere.

Capitalization follows, involving investments from external actors who introduce transnational law (in both our cases utilizing a rhetoric of conservation). Mercantile law and soft law such as ecolabelling often follow. In the case of fish, certification involves the Marine Stewardship Council (MSC) (Parlee and Wiber 2012), while in the case of argan oil many competing organizations provide organic certificates (Turner 2014). As international demand grows and as infrastructures and networks develop to facilitate delivery of the product to global markets, there is a need to secure a continuous and predictable supply of the base product from its source. This is often achieved through both scientific and technological standardization, including transgenic research into farmed salmon (Lien and Law 2011; Shears et al. 1991; Zhu 1992) and selection of genotypes displaying the desired properties for both quality and yield in the case of argan oil. Research is undertaken in places such as laboratories and tree nurseries, which in turn loads new meaning onto legal regulations such as those related to nature conservation or public health.

The objects of translation, however, have agency and may resist. Salmon refuse to transform into standardized fish, and either escape their sea pens or develop unexpected problems with disease or pests (Abolofia et al. 2017). Meanwhile, the argan tree resists its optimization because its differential adaptation to local habitats is further complicated by its symbiosis with fungi that are likewise uniquely adapted to their habitats. This remains an obstacle to standardization. While the local knowledge of traditional users often exceeds scientific knowledge in practical application and efficacy, it is usually either ignored or transformed because the diversity of such knowledge runs contrary to standardized techno-normative production. Despite the resistance of trees and fish (McPhail 2018; Turner 2014), plantation economies begin to emerge and require the transformation of local and state normative regimes using formal legal templates such as ocean leases (aquaculture) and private property (ultimately leading to argan plantations). This gives rise to disenfranchisement and dispossession and, ultimately, to new forms of livelihood insecurity at the local level.

In this process, science and technology is involved in two translations. First, local knowledge is mined for useful content and transformed into 'objective science'. In the case of argan oil, legally unprotected local knowledge about argan is translated into legally protected scientific knowledge on identified and patented molecular and genetic argan properties (generated in laboratories) for the purposes of marketing and capitalization in the pharmaceutical and cosmetic industries. In reaction to patenting, the UNESCO Representative List of the Intangible Cultural Heritage of Humanity (UNESCO 2014) tries to protect local argan practices and know-how. A crucial point of the normative design of intellectual property, however, is that patenting presupposes an invention, with the consequence that something labelled traditional cannot be the subject of a patent (Turner 2014). Such inherent logic forces, on the one hand, the reference to tradition and indigeneity as a strategy to limit outside influences. On the other hand, the same strategy may also impede innovation and creativity in local contexts. However, if the resource is no longer natural but is, rather, designed in a laboratory through scientific research for optimal oil production, then local claims to benefit sharing can be rejected. Natural resources can thus be translated into cultural capital through specialization and the reduction of biodiversity and, in the process, become distinguishable from both natural and alternative cultural landscapes.

Second, science transforms the resource itself, with technological interventions such as genetic manipulation to further standardize the 'natural' resource, as in genetically manipulated salmon that can survive the cold coastal waters of Norway and Canada and grow faster. In the case of argan forests, the scientific optimization of the resource through techno-scientific plant enhancement, in combination with its normative framing as a unique, protected biosphere reserve, results in reforestation measures, resource standardization, and transformation of existing local customary property regimes. Aquaculture and proposed tree plantations replace the original biodiversity in order to standardize the product for global markets. Little research, however, addresses the risks that techno-scientific modifications of nature may entail over the long run.

Through techno-science, the notions of nature and conservation as legal and material enactments are translated into boundary objects. The biological diversity of argan is protected in accordance with the legal template of a UNESCO biosphere reserve in restricted areas, with untouched forest stands that serve as gene pools for further research. 'Reforestation' in the case of argan trees means standardization of the resource and not a return to natural forests. Further, the technical extraction schemes involve new normative templates (developed at the level of global governance) that rule labour standards and modes of production. Regarding salmon aquaculture, new technology is used to monitor fishermen for conservation purposes. This places the burden of responsibility for the sustainability of wild stocks on the fishermen, despite the fact that global forces beyond their control, such as climate change and habitat challenges created by technologies such as aquaculture, are the real threat to wild fish stocks. In this process, co-production also occurs as a result of legal templates for the organization of work and production processes (cooperatives in both the argan oil and salmon cases) (Squires and Wiber 2018; Turner 2014). Argan oil cooperatives transform local resource users into a workforce as an essential component of the normative-technological scheme of resource exploitation. The result is not only a reduction in biodiversity through standardization of nature, but also a reduction in social diversity through normative/technological transformations.

In both cases, normativity constitutes a fundamental and indispensable component in the infrastructural architecture. Such norm construction makes it possible to transform existing economies of solidarity into neoliberal infrastructures. Our research shows how the oil and fish supply chains bring transnational normative blueprints into interaction with a wide variety of pre-existing legal and other non-legal but normatively effective registers. Moreover, the infrastructure model offers insights into the contribution of law to the setup and maintenance of infrastructural designs that are geared towards new or enhanced schemes of extraction. Besides contract law, commercial law, labour law, and voluntary regulations that are subsumed under the heading of 'corporate social responsibility', other *non-legal* links in the network have normative power and thereby increase the legal complexity of schemes of extraction. The resulting legal assemblages we call 'infrastructure legal pluralism', a concept that provides obvious links to attempts at risk management, particularly as it relates to the boundary object of 'sustainability'.

Conclusion

Mercantile law, emerging global environmental standards, and regulation to contain risk all compete and clash with various localized sociocultural and ethical considerations. Such regulation at various scales is contradictory and serves multiple, often competing interests, oscillating between human rights and claims to human dignity, free trade arrangements, and freedom of science. The resulting complexity becomes all the more evident when we look at conditions of legal pluralism. This brief overview of such conditions identifies some basic characteristics of the entanglements of law, materiality, and techno-science. In principle, law and techno-science create distinguishable sets of concepts about facts, truth, and verifiability (Jasanoff 1993). On the one hand, there is evidence to suggest that law determines epistemic spaces, or co-constructs them. The law actively co-constructs the scientific facts that it presumes to 'find' (Jasanoff 2008: 776). Competing accounts of disputed facts are interpreted through the lens of objectifying science, which in turn has been legally defined in its diagnostic significance within specific legal configurations. While science is supposed to produce only one single and coherent result, the admissibility of counter-expertise in various normative orders illustrates the authority of (competing) legal actors over science (Haack 2014). As just one example, rules surrounding expert testimony allow expertise to be restricted to a small community of highly specialized professionals. On the other hand, rapidly developing technological innovations continue to exercise considerable influence on the juridical comprehension of fact and thereby bring about legal change.

Research on techno-scientific-normative entanglements can shed light on how the making of evidence, the processing of uncertainty, the designing of futures, and the attribution of responsibility hinge on one another. We are witnessing processes of change in those interactions. A major challenge to a global regime of ordering upon which one may reach an agreement across ontological differences lies in the circularity that these regulatory regimes generate in the production of evidence and 'truth'. This circularity emerges when the falsification criteria for assessing the validity of evidence excludes the possibility of ontologies other than the one built into the falsification test. As we have suggested, a broad concept of normativity may help in finding ways to escape that circularity.

In terms of the pace of change, technological, scientific, and legal interactions and responses do not occur simultaneously. While the law is often said to be lagging behind, these relationships are in fact more complex than the dominant narrative of the sciences being proactive and the law reactive may suggest (Janasoff 2008: 767; see also Hurlbut 2015). For example, the law anticipates possible developments in science, and in terms of risk prevention, issues legal regulation for science-in-progress. Looking at the social working of law, at the ways law operates and interacts within society, requires sensibility to its complex entanglement with techno-science and materiality in the maintenance of social order.

This chapter explores emergent assemblages in which materiality interacts with legal plurality, and illustrates how infrastructural designs compose specific configurations of such assemblages that display their own specific legal designs. Normative standardizations within infrastructural design, while aimed at predictability, may produce their own unintended consequences. While research on infrastructure is proliferating in anthropology and STS, law as a constitutive component in all its forms and manifestations remains to be put in perspective. Law in infrastructure is in itself inherently plural.

Existing work on the interaction of law and technology tends to be either too legal or too scientific. Our focus, coming out of anthropology, is on the social working of law, and emphasizes how legal pluralism complicates the world-making story. L/STS/LP can learn from each other and can inform each other in terms of future world-making. We argue that there is insufficient knowledge about their important intersections.

Notes

1. Jasanoff (2015) also explores the implications of the law and science relationship for: the authority structures and practices of modernity; the emergence and professionalization of scientific and technical disciplines; shifts in rules of expert testimony; and law as a site for generating new scientific knowledge and technical expertise with implications for individual and social justice.
2. For earlier reviews, see Caudill (2002) and Faulkner et al. (2012).
3. See the work of e.g. Riles (2000), McGee (2014, 2015), Jasanoff (2004, 2008, 2009), Swedlow (2012), and Sarat et al. (2007) for insightful treatments of these concepts.

References

Abolofia, J., J. E. Wilen, and F. Asche. 2017. 'The Cost of Lice: Quantifying the Impacts of Parasitic Sea Lice on Farmed Salmon'. *Marine Resource Economics* 32 (3): 329–49.

Akkerman, S. F. and A. Bakker. 2011. 'Boundary Crossing and Boundary Objects'. *Review of Educational Research* 81: 132–69.

Barnett, A. and M. Wiber. 2019. 'What Scientists Say about the Changing Risk Calculation in the Marine Environment under the Harper Government of Canada (2006–2015)'. *Science, Technology & Human Values* 44 (1): 29–51.

Barnett, A., R. Messenger, and M. Wiber. 2017. 'Enacting and Contesting Neoliberalism in Fisheries: The Tragedy of Commodifying Lobster Access Rights in Southwest Nova Scotia'. *Marine Policy* 80: 60–8. http://dx.doi.org/10.1016/j.marpol.2016.03.002

Beck, U. 2009. *World at Risk*. Cambridge: Polity Press.

Beck, U., W. Bonss, and C. Lau. 2003. 'The Theory of Reflexive Modernization: Problematic, Hypothesis and Research Program'. *Theory, Culture & Society* 20: 1–33.

Behrends, A., S.-J. Park, and R. Rottenburg. 2014. 'Travelling Models. Introducing an Analytical Concept to Globalisation Studies'. In A. Behrends, S.-J. Park, and R. Rottenburg, eds. *Travelling Models in African Conflict Management: Translating Technologies of Social Ordering*, 1–40. Leiden: Brill.

Benda-Beckmann, K. v. and B. Turner. 2018. 'Legal Pluralism, Social Theory, and the State'. *The Journal of Legal Pluralism and Unofficial Law* 50 (3): 255–274.

Benda-Beckmann, K. v. and B. Turner. 2020. 'Anthropological Roots of Legal Pluralism'. In P. Schiff Berman, ed. *The Oxford Handbook of Global Legal Pluralism*, 67–141. Oxford: Oxford University Press.

Berman, P. Schiff. 2016. 'The Evolution of Global Legal Pluralism'. In R. Cotterrell and M. Del Mar, eds. *Authority in Transnational Legal Theory: Theorising Across Disciplines*, 151–88. Cheltenham and Northampton: Elgar.

Best, J. and W. Walters. 2013. '"Actor-Network Theory" and International Relationality: Lost (and Found) in Translation: Introduction'. *International Political Sociology* 7(3): 332–4.

Boholm, Å. 2015. *Anthropology and Risk*. London and New York: Routledge.

Bowker, G. C. and S. L. Star. 1999. *Sorting Things Out. Classification and Its Consequences*. Cambridge, MA: MIT Press.

Bowker, G. C., K. Baker, F. Millerand, and D. Ribes. 2010. 'Toward Information Infrastructure Studies: Ways of Knowing in a Networked Environment'. In J. Hunsinger, L. Klastrup, and M. M. Allen, eds. *International Handbook of Internet Research*, 97–117. Dordrecht: Springer.

Callon, M. 1984. 'Some Elements of a Sociology of Translation: Domestication of the Scallops and the Fishermen of St Brieuc Bay'. *The Sociological Review* 32(1): 196–233.

Caudill, D. S. 2002 'Ethnography and the Idealized Accounts of Science in Law'. *San Diego Law Review* 269: 269–306.

Chrisman, N. 1999. 'Trading Zones or Boundary Objects: Understanding Incomplete Translation of Technical Expertise'. *Proceedings of the Social Studies of Science Annual Meeting 1999*: 28–31, San Diego, California.

Clarke, A. E. and S. L. Star. 2008. 'The Social Worlds Framework: A Theory / Methods Package'. In E. J. Hackett, O. Amsterdamska, M. Lynch, and J. Wajcman, eds. *The Handbook of Science and Technology Studies*, 113–37. Cambridge, MA: MIT Press.

Clarke, J., D. Bainton, N. Lendvai, and P. Stubbs. 2015. *Making Policy Move*. Bristol: Bristol University Press and Chicago: Chicago University Press.

Cloatre, E. and D. Cowan. 2019 'Legalities and Materialities'. In A. Philippopoulos-Mihalopoulos, ed. *Routledge Handbook of Law and Theory*, 433–52. Abingdon and New York: Routledge.

Cloatre, E. and Pickersgill, M. 2016. *Knowledge, Technology and Law*. London and New York: Routledge.

Cole, S. A. and A. Bertenthal. 2017. 'Science, Technology, Society, and Law'. *Annual Review of Law and Social Sciences*. 13: 351–71.

Davies, M. 2017a. *Law Unlimited. Materialism, Pluralism, and Legal Theory*. London: Routledge.

Davies, M. 2017b. 'Plural Pluralities of Law'. In N. Roughan and A. Halpin, eds. *In Pursuit of Pluralist Jurisprudence*, 239–60. Cambridge: Cambridge University Press.

De Goede, M. and G. Sullivan. 2016. 'The Politics of Security Lists.' *Environment and Planning D: Society and Space* 34 (1): 67–88.

Delaney, D. 2010. *The Spatial, the Legal and the Pragmatics of World-Making. Nomospheric Investigations*. Abingdon and New York: Routledge.

Ducket, D., B. Wynne, R. Christley, A. Heathwaite, M. Mort, Z. Austin, J. Wastling, S. Latham, R. Alcock, and P. Haygarth. 2014. 'Can Policy Be Risk-Based? The Cultural Theory of Risk and the Case of Livestock Disease Containment.' *Sociologia Ruralis* 55(4): 379–99.

Eden, S. and C. Bear. 2010. 'Third Sector Global Environmental Governance, Space and Science: Comparing Fishery and Forestry Certification'. *Journal of Environmental Policy & Planning* 12(1): 83–106.

Faulkner, A., B. Lange, and C. Lawless. 2012. 'Introduction: Material Worlds: Intersections of Law, Science, Technology, and Society'. *Journal of Law and Society* 39(1):1–19.

Fischer, M. M. 2005. 'Technoscientific Infrastructures and Emergent Forms of Life: A Commentary'. *American Anthropologist* 107(1): 55–61.

Foster, L. A. 2014. 'Critical Cultural Translation: A Socio-Legal Framework for Regulatory Orders'. *Indiana Journal of Global Legal Studies* 21(1): 79–136.

Fujimura, J. H. 1992. 'Crafting Science: Standardized Packages, Boundary Objects, and "Translations."' In A. Pickering, ed. *Science as Practice and Culture*, 168–211. Chicago and London: University of Chicago Press.

Gal, S. 2015. 'The Politics of Translation'. *Annual Review of Anthropology* 44: 225–40.

Gonzalez, C. 2017. 'Global Justice in the Anthropocene'. In L. J. Kotzé, ed. *Environmental Law and Governance for the Anthropocene*, 219–40. Oxford and Portland Oregon: Hart Publishing.

Griffiths, J. 2015. Legal Pluralism. *International Encyclopedia of Social and Behavioral Sciences—New Edition*. Vol. 13: 757–61.

Haack, S. 2014. *Evidence Matters: Science, Proof, and Truth in the Law*. Cambridge: Cambridge University Press.

Haraway, D. 1988. 'Situated Knowledges: The Science Question in Feminism and the Privilege of Partial Perspective'. *Feminist Studies* 14(3): 575–99.

Harvey, P., C. B. Jensen, and A. Morita, eds. 2017. *Infrastructures and Social Complexity. A Companion*. London and New York: Routledge.

Healy, S. 2010. 'Post-normal Science in Postnormal Times'. *Futures* 43: 202–8.

Hurlbut, B. 2015. 'Remembering the Future: Science, Law, and the Legacy of Asilomar'. In S. Jasanoff and K. Sang-Hyun, eds. *Dreamscapes of Modernity: Sociotechnical Imaginaries and the Fabrication of Power*, 126–51. Chicago: University of Chicago Press.

Jasanoff, S. 1993. 'What Judges Should Know about the Sociology of Science'. *Jurimetrics* 32 (3): 345–59.

Jasanoff, S. 1994. 'Acceptable Evidence in a Pluralistic Society'. In R. Hollander and D. Mayo, eds. *Acceptable Evidence: Science and Values in Risk Management*, 29–47. Oxford: Oxford University Press.

Jasanoff, S. 2004. 'The Idiom of Co-production'. In S. Jasanoff, ed. *States of Knowledge: The Co-production of Science and Social Order*, 1–12. London and New York: Routledge.

Jasanoff, S. 2008. 'Making Order: Law and Science in Action'. In E. J. Hackett, O. Amsterdamska, M. Lynch, and J. Wajcman, eds. *The Handbook of Science and Technology Studies*, 761–86. Cambridge, MA: MIT Press.

Jasanoff, S. 2009. *Science at the Bar: Law, Science and Technology in America*. Cambridge, MA: Harvard University Press.

Jasanoff, S. 2015. 'Science and Law'. In James D. Wright, ed. *International Encyclopedia of Social and Behavioral Sciences*, 2nd edn. Vol. 21: 156–62. Amsterdam: Elsevier.

Larkin, B. 2013. 'The Politics and Poetics of Infrastructure'. *Annual Review of Anthropology* 42: 327–43.

Latour, B. 2002. 'Morality and Technology. The End of the Means'. *Theory, Culture & Society* 19 (5/6): 247–60 (trans. C. Venn).

Latour, B. 2005. *Reassembling the Social. An introduction to Actor-Network Theory*. Oxford: Oxford University Press.

Law, J. and M. E. Lien. 2012. 'Slippery: Field Notes on Empirical Ontology'. *Social Studies of Science* 43(3): 363–78.

Lee, C. P. 2007. 'Boundary Negotiating Artifacts: Unbinding the Routine of Boundary Objects and Embracing Chaos in Collaborative Work'. *Computer Supported Cooperative Work* 16: 307–39.

Levi, R. and M. Valverde. 2008. 'Studying Law by Association: Bruno Latour Goes to the Conseil d'État'. *Law & Social Inquiry* 33(3): 805–25.

Lien, M. W. and J. Law. 2011. '"Emergent Aliens": On Salmon, Nature and Their Enactment'. Ethnos 76 (1): 65–87.

McGee, K. 2014. *Bruno Latour: The Normativity of Networks*. Abingdon and London: Routledge.

McGee, K., ed. 2015. *Latour and the Passage of Law*. Edinburgh: Edinburgh University Press.

McPhail, C. 2018. 'Salmon escape leads Cooke into legal fight with Washington state'. *CBC Online News*, available at <https://www.cbc.ca/news/canada/new-brunswick/cooke-aquaculture-washington-salmon-escape-1.4490171>

Merry, S. E. 2006. 'Transnational Human Rights and Local Activism: Mapping the Middle.' *American Anthropologist* 108(1): 38–51.

Moore, S. F. 1973. 'Law and Social Change: The Semi-Autonomous Social Field as an Appropriate Subject of Study.' *Law & Society Review* 7 (4): 719–46.

Murdoch, J. 1998. 'The Spaces of Actor-Network Theory'. *Geoforum* 29(4): 357–74.

Niewöhner, J. 2015. 'Infrastructures of Society, Anthropology of'. *International Encyclopedia of the Social & Behavioral Sciences*. Vol. 12: 119–25. Amsterdam: Elsevier.

Oswick, C. and M. Robertson. 2009. 'Boundary Objects Reconsidered: From Bridges and Anchors to Barricades and Mazes'. *Journal of Change Management* 9(2): 179–93.

Pálsson, G. and K. Harðardóttir. 2002. 'For Whom the Cell Tolls: Debates about Biomedicine'. *Current Anthropology* 43(3): 271–301.

Parlee, C. and M. G. Wiber. 2012. 'Who is Governing Food Systems? Power and Legal Pluralism in Lobster Traceability'. *The Journal of Legal Pluralism and Unofficial Law* 64: 121–48.

Pinch, T. 2010. 'On Making Infrastructure Visible: Putting the Non-Humans to Rights'. *Cambridge Journal of Economics* 34: 77–89.

Reardon, J. 2013. 'On the Emergence of Science and Justice'. *Science, Technology & Human Values* 38(2): 176–200.

Riles, A. 2000. *The Network Inside Out*. Ann Arbor: University of Michigan Press.

Riles, A. 2003. 'Ethnography in the Realm of the Pragmatic: Studying Pragmatism in Law and Politics'. *PoLAR* 26(2): 1–7.

Robinson, D. F. and N. Graham. 2018. 'Legal Pluralisms, Justice and Spatial Conflicts: New Directions in Legal Geography'. *The Geographical Journal* 184(1): 3–7.

Rottenburg, R. 2009. *Far-Fetched Facts. A Parable of Development Aid*. Cambridge, MA: MIT Press.

Rowland, N. J. and J. Passoth. 2015. 'Infrastructure and the State in Science and Technology Studies'. *Social Studies of Science* 45(1): 137–45.

Santos, B. de Sousa. 2009. 'A Non-Occidentalist West?: Learned Ignorance and Ecology of Knowledge'. *Theory, Culture & Society* 26(7–8): 103–25.

Sarat, A., L. Douglas, and M. M. Umphrey, eds. 2007. *How Law Knows*. Stanford: Stanford University Press.

Sharp, L. A. 2002. 'Bodies, Boundaries, and Territorial Disputes: Investigating the Murky Realm of Scientific Authority.' *Medical Anthropology* 21: 369–79.

Shears, M., G. L. Fletcher, C. L. Hew, S. Gauthier, and P. L. Davies. 1991. 'Transfer, Expression, and Stable Inheritance of Antifreeze Protein Genes in Atlantic Salmon (Salmo Salar)'. *Molecular Marine Biology and Biotechnology* 1 (1): 58–63.

Silbey, S. S., ed. 2008. Law and Science (II): *Regulation of Property, Practices, and Products*. Aldershot: Ashgate.

Squires, K. and M. G. Wiber. 2018. 'Distribution of Fisheries Benefits and Community Well-being: A Review of Increased Access to the Eastern Nova Scotia Snow Crab Fishery'. *Ecology and Society* 23 (2): 25. Available at <https://www.ecologyandsociety.org/vol23/iss2/art25/>

Star, S. L. 1993. 'Cooperation Without Consensus in Scientific Problem Solving: Dynamics of Closure in Open Systems'. In S. Easterbrook, ed. *CSCW: Cooperation or Conflict*, 93–106. London: Springer.

Star, S. L. 1999. 'The Ethnography of Infrastructure'. *American Behavioral Scientist* 43(3): 377–91.

Star, S. L. 2002. 'Infrastructure and Ethnographic Practice: Working on the Fringes'. *Scandinavian Journal of Information Sciences* 14(2): 107–22.

Star, S. L. 2010. 'This is NOT a Boundary Object: Reflections on the Origin of a Concept'. *Science, Technology & Human Values* 35: 601–17.

Star, S. L. and J. R. Griesemer. 1989. 'Institutional Ecology, 'Translations' and Boundary Objects: Amateurs and Professionals in Berkeley's Museum of Vertebrate Zoology, 1907–39'. *Social Studies of Science* 19: 387–420.

Star, S. L. and K. Ruhleder. 1996. 'Steps Toward an Ecology of Infrastructure: Design and Access for Large Information Spaces'. *Information Systems Research* 7(1): 111–34.

Stirling, A. 2012. 'Opening up the Politics of Knowledge and Power in Bioscience.' *PLoS Biology* 10(1): e10011233. https://doi.org/10.1371/journal.pbio.1001233

Sullivan, G. 2014. 'Transnational Legal Assemblages and Global Security Law: Topologies and Temporalities of the List'. *Transnational Legal Theory* 5(1): 81–127.

Sutter, L. de and K. McGee, eds. 2012. *Deleuze and Law*. Edinburgh: Edinburgh University Press.

Swedlow, B. 2012. 'Cultural Co-Production of Four States of Knowledge'. *Science, Technology & Human Values* 37(3): 151–79.

Trompette, P. and D. Vink. 2009. 'Revisiting the Notion of Boundary Object'. *Revue d'anthropologie des connaissances* 3(1): 3–25.

Tsing, A. L. 2005. *Friction: An Ethnography of Global Connection*. Princeton: Princeton University Press.

Tsing, A. L. 2009. 'Supply Chains and the Human Condition'. *Rethinking Marxism: A Journal of Economics, Culture & Society* 21(2): 148–76.

Tsing, A. L. 2015. *The Mushroom at the End of the World: On the Possibility of Life in Capitalist Ruins*. Princeton: Princeton University Press.

Turner, B. 2014. 'Neoliberal Politics of Resource Extraction: Moroccan Argan Oil'. *Forum for Development Studies* 41(2): 207–32.

Turner, B. 2016. 'Supply-chain Legal Pluralism: Normativity as Constitutive of Chain Infrastructure in the Moroccan Argan Oil Supply Chain'. *The Journal of Legal Pluralism and Unofficial Law* 48(3): 378–414.

UNESCO 2014. Argan, practices and know-how concerning the argan tree, Morocco, inscribed in 2014 (9.COM) on the Representative List of the Intangible Cultural Heritage of Humanity, available at <9.COM: https://ich.unesco.org/en/RL/argan-practices-and-know-how-concerning-the-argan-tree-00955>

Valverde, M. 2003. *Law's Dream of a Common Knowledge*. Princeton: Princeton University Press.

Valverde, M. 2009. 'Jurisdiction and Scale: Legal 'Technicalities' as Resources for Theory'. *Social & Legal Studies* 18(2): 139–57.

Vanderlinden, J. 1989. 'Return to Legal Pluralism: Twenty Years Later'. *Journal of Legal Pluralism and Unofficial Law* 28:149–57.

Wheeler, S. 2017. 'The Corporation and the Anthropocene.' In L. J. Kotze, ed. *Environmental Law and Governance for the Anthropocene*, 289–308. Oxford and Portland Oregon: Hart Publishing.

Wiber, M. 2005. The Voracious Appetites of Public versus Private Property: A View of Intellectual Property and Biodiversity from Legal Pluralism. CAPRi Working Paper 40. Available at: <http://www.capri.cgiar.org/pubs.asp#wp>

Wiber, M. 2009. 'What Innocent Bystanders? The Impact of Law and Economics Reasoning on Rural Property Rights'. *Anthropologica* 51 (1): 29–38.

Wiber, M. 2015. 'Property as Boundary Object: Normative Versus Analytical Meanings'. *The Journal of Legal Pluralism and Unofficial Law* 47(3): 438–55.

Wiber, M. and B. Turner. 2010. Moral Talk: The Ontological Politics of Sustainable Development. Max Planck Institute for Social Anthropology Working Paper Series, No. 123.

Wiber, M. G., L. Wilson, and S. Young. 2012. 'Impact of Aquaculture on Commercial Fisheries: Fishermen's Local Ecological Knowledge'. *Human Ecology* 40(1): 29–40.

Wynne, B. 2002. 'Risk and Environment as Legitimatory Discourses of Technology: Reflexivity Inside Out?' *Current Sociology* 50(3): 459–77.

Zhu, Z. 1992. 'Generation of Fast Growing Transgenic Fish: Methods and Mechanisms'. In C. L. Hew and G. L. Fletcher, eds. *Transgenic Fish*, 92–119. Singapore: Singapore World Scientific.

CHAPTER 42

POLITICS OF BELONGING

OLAF ZENKER

Belonging and the Politics of Belonging

According to the seminal work of Nira Yuval-Davis (2011), 'belonging' refers to an emotional attachment to and a feeling 'at home' within specific social collectivities, which are often spatialized in their relation to specific localities or territories. Belonging thereby typically comprises entanglements of three major analytical facets: first, social locations such as citizenship, nationality, ethnicity, gender, class, race, religion, etc. at hierarchically structured intersections within social space; second, narratives of identification and emotional attachment; and third, ethical and political value regimes (Yuval-Davis 2011: 10–18).

While belonging is often naturalized and taken for granted in everyday life, when threatened or not yet fully realized it can also become articulated, formally structured, and politicized within a 'politics of belonging'. Such identity politics, then, comprise specific political projects seeking simultaneously to construct collectivities on the basis of certain characteristics within very specific social and often territorial boundaries and to assign membership to such collectivities for oneself and/or others. This politics of belonging takes place within contested engagements and dynamics in which the differential distribution and use of symbolic power for the continuous production and maintenance of social boundaries between insiders and outsiders is crucial. While based in principle on the interplay between self-ascription and ascription by others, modes of belonging are also frequently imposed on people against their will through acts of epistemic violence. Moreover, these assemblages of entangled political projects of belonging have differential effects on different members of such collectives, who are differentially located in social space, vary in their identifications and emotional attachments, and are committed to different value regimes, thus underlining the need for an intersectional analysis (Yuval-Davis 2011: 3–43). A normative project par excellence, the politics of belonging is imbued with multiple references to existing normative orders, evoking or resisting values, norms, and rules while often also working towards some legal transformation.

Belonging forms part of a broader semantic field that has been analysed in terms of a number of interrelated concepts, including 'identity'. Typically referring to some assumption of sameness with oneself or particular others (which simultaneously establishes differences with other others), the term has been used to study individual identities, the self, and personhood in their cultural variations on the one hand, and various collectivities such as ethnic groups on the other (Finke and Sökefeld 2018). Recent anthropological debates have focused on whether or not the term 'identification' should be used instead to foreground the processual nature of identity (Brubaker and Cooper 2000; Eidson et al. 2017). While studies in the field of identity and identity politics have highlighted the selective and pretentious use of alleged cultural differences in the construction of collectivities (Zenker 2013), works in the key of 'subjectivity' have put the focus on the subjection of individuals to specific discursive orders, which simultaneously—in interpellating them—produce and establish them as the 'subjects' of their own actions (Althusser 2006 [1971]; Foucault 1978).

Acknowledging that there are conceptual alternatives with various advantages of their own, for the purpose of this chapter, 'belonging' has the benefit of emphasizing that individuals not only long to belong to particular others within a shared collectivity, but often also link their collective identity with a particular place where they feel 'at home'—regardless of whether they presently inhabit it. While engaging in multiple 'ways of being' as coexisting networks of social relations and practices, individuals thus selectively point in their 'ways of belonging' to those practices that signal or enact an identity through demonstrating a conscious connection to themselves and others (Levitt and Glick Schiller 2004).

This chapter starts off with a rough sketch of historical engagements in legal anthropology with belonging and its legal implications broadly understood, tracing a massive expansion in the scope and complexity of studied modes of belonging and their various intersections. Such studies have grown from an early focus on law as social order and the special role of kin groups to increasingly include citizenship and alternatively entangled forms of identity politics. The subsequent two sections point towards a few select studies demarcating, on the one hand, the normative import of the arguably still hegemonic mode of belonging of the Westphalian world order (i.e. citizenship), and the multiple projects of belonging alongside, against, and across this form of 'state autochthony' on the other. The next section prepares the ground for analytically apprehending citizenship as 'state autochthony' by proposing the overarching framework of 'contested autochthonies' as a way to consider a family of related territorial modes of belonging—ethnicity, nationhood/nationalism, diaspora, indigeneity, identities conventionally described as 'autochthonous', and citizenship—a framework which allows cross-cutting constructions of individual-territory-group triads, and their mutual interactions, to be studied at shifting scales. Exemplifying this framework with regard to a case study of conflicting autochthonies in postcolonial South Africa, the chapter concludes by highlighting the close interdependencies between the (re)production of distributed senses of *belonging* and the attendant (re)distribution of *belongings*—and thus the need for an integrated analysis of recognition and (re)distribution in any politics of belonging.

From status to contract to multiple modes of belonging

In *Ancient Law*, one of the founding texts of anthropology, Henry Maine (2012 [1861]) characterized the shift from the politico-legal 'status' related to kinship groups to the 'contract' between individuals as a general model for the sociolegal evolution of humankind. Misappropriating this evolutionist argument as a simplifying roadmap for historical developments within anthropology itself,[1] one could say that an early focus on social order within 'traditional' societies or cultures at large and the special politico-legal 'status' of kinship in particular gave way to increasingly broader and more differentiated studies of individuals, also as 'contracting' citizens of modern states, whose political projects of belonging have evidently ventured along multiple other dimensions as well.

Early fieldwork-based legal anthropology in the first half of the twentieth century established a broad focus on law as social order and on the mutual adaptation and dynamics between norms and rules and actual everyday practices within 'traditional' societies (e.g. Malinowski 1926), the boundedness and boundaries of which were largely taken for granted. Moreover, numerous studies emerged in the mould of British structural-functionalist descent theory (Evans-Pritchard 1940, 1951; Fortes 1945, 1949; Radcliffe-Brown 1952; Radcliffe-Brown and Forde 1950) and French structuralist alliance theory (Lévi-Strauss 1969 [1949]), which, despite their differences, both identified kinship and marriage as the backbone of social integration and of a corporatist constitution (without an obvious equivalent in Western state law) transmitting legal rights and duties in 'primitive' societies.

Looking back, this preoccupation with societies and cultures as unproblematic wholes and the special role of kin-based 'status' was seemingly facilitated, among others, by two factors: first, the early division of labour between the newly instituted academic disciplines of sociology, taking charge of 'the modern West', and anthropology, covering 'the traditional rest'; and second, the shared interest of both evolutionist armchair anthropology and early fieldwork-based anthropology in the reconstruction of pre-colonial societies and cultures. Together, these factors allowed awkward questions about the wider incorporation of 'traditional' societies into contemporaneous colonial and capitalist systems of oppression and exploitation, along with all the contested political projects of belonging that came with this imperialist configuration, to be ignored.

Since the 1960s and 1970s, anthropological engagements with the political and legal aspects of belonging have increasingly broadened to include not only individuals as citizens within the global order of formally sovereign states, but also numerous other dimensions of identification. This development has been paralleled by a growing concern with legal pluralism, including 'state law' in its multiple varieties.

If at first the collectivities to which individuals belonged were simply taken as givens, more and more studies problematized such simplistic understandings of collective categories and identities (e.g. Moerman 1965). The shift in the study of ethnicity from an earlier focus on 'tribes' or 'cultures' to 'ethnic groups' illustrates this broader development towards social constructionism: as Fredrik Barth (1969) seminally argued, cultural differences do not produce homologous layers with neat and coextensive boundaries between different collectivities. To the contrary, certain cultural differences have to be singled out and selected situationally as 'ethnic markers' in order to continuously construct and reproduce social boundaries that could also be drawn in quite different ways. Hence it becomes a crucial question as to who has the power to socially construct boundaries that actually stick and to differentially shape the ways in which individuals can engage with each other and their symbolic and material environments.

At the same time, the political and theoretical interventions of second wave feminism also started playing a crucial role both in challenging hitherto unquestioned forms of 'natural' being and belonging and in pointing the way for important social constructionist developments in identity politics with regard to gender, sexuality, and embodied identities in general (Moore 1994). Black feminists such as Kimberlé Crenshaw (1989) further highlighted the need for an intersectional analysis of how different systems of discrimination such as gender, race, class, etc. interlock and thereby produce specific constellations of oppression (Collins and Bilge 2020).

Within the wider context of the civil rights movement in the US, international student revolts, neo-Marxist attacks on the capitalist world-system (Frank 1967; Wallerstein 1974; Wolf 1969), an emerging postcolonial critique of anthropology (Asad 1973; Said 2004 [1978]), and a growing disciplinary reflexivity regarding anthropology's representational conundrums (Clifford and Marcus 1986; Zenker and Kumoll 2010), the multiplicity of potential political projects of belonging thus emerged as an important field of investigation that continues to characterize legal anthropological engagements in the twenty-first century.

The interdependencies between identity politics in its multiple dimensions and the law in its multitude are, of course, crucial. From the legal status of slavery, to full citizenship reserved only for some, to the legal circumscription of 'proper' sexualities and so much more, global history attests to the numerous ways in which modes of belonging have been juridified and legally restricted, and how legal categories have become populated and turned into markers of identity (e.g. Scott 1998). As Ron Niezen puts it, 'conceptions of belonging are necessarily built into or follow from the elaboration and enforcement of any regime of collective rights or recognition' (Niezen 2013: 188), thus creating complex interplays between the politics and laws of belonging.

Citizenship: Hegemonic belonging and its relational others

Yuval-Davis points out that for many people, the formal identification as having a particular nationality or state citizenship is probably still the most consequential construction of belonging, given that 'states are still, in most of the world, the primary source of different kinds of entitlements and rights' (Yuval-Davis 2011: 49).

Although the developments of the past decades, especially related to accelerated economic and cultural globalization, have increasingly called into question the proclaimed politico-legal monopoly and sovereignty of the state, challenging it in its own terms (the topic of this section) and in terms of alternative projects of belonging (the topic of the next section), the identity it conveys—citizenship—still largely remains hegemonic. This was less obvious during the late 1990s, when some presaged the end of the nation-state in the dawning era of globalization (e.g. Hardt and Negri 2000). However, the securitization in international politics and border regimes after 9/11, the so-called refugee crisis and recent upsurge in nationalism and right-wing populisms in various countries of the European Union (EU), and the 'hyperreactionary neoliberalism' of the US under President Trump (Fraser 2019) have demonstrated the continued relevance and hegemony of citizenship as a primary source of entitlements and rights in the late Westphalian global order—as tragically all too visible, at the time of writing, in the ongoing COVID-19 pandemic.

Usually marked with a certain sense of entitlement, citizenship has been characterized as ideally comprising civil and political rights (protecting individuals' freedoms and their entitlement to political participation) as well as socioeconomic and cultural rights (concerned with distributive justice and protecting cultural diversity)—as prominently described by Thomas Marshall (1950, 1981) and echoed in the international and regional human rights instruments and in numerous constitutions. Most basically, citizenship also includes 'spatial security rights', which concern the elementary task of states to keep citizens secure from internal and external enemies and which include the right to enter the territory of a state, to remain there, to learn, study, and work—in short, to more or less securely live one's life (Yuval-Davis 2011: 57).

Citizenship laws typically grant membership by birth or naturalization through variable combinations of elements such as place of birth and/or residence (*jus soli*), descent from citizen parents (*jus sanguinis*), marriage (*jus matrimonii*), adoption, or, especially in the case of naturalization, proof of shared culture (language, values, etc.) and self-identification—elements to which I will return below in the discussion of 'autochthony'.

Although gesturing towards egality, citizenship has always been graded and gradual, legally restricting certain rights—to vote, own property, choose one's work, etc.—in terms of gender, religion, relative wealth, and race. Moreover, as Mahmood Mamdani (1996) shows, late colonialism in Africa brought about the political system of 'indirect rule', which distinguished first between non-native colonial rulers and native majority populations based on race, and second between 'tribes' within the native population, each to be ruled by their supposedly 'traditional leaders' under 'customary law'. With 'natives' in rural areas subordinated as the 'subjects' of tribalized, and thereby fragmented, traditional customary regimes, urban areas emerged as the realm of primarily non-native 'citizens' to be administered according to modern rule-of-law standards. This bifurcated legal system came to pervade the entire colonial state and continues to haunt African postcolonies (Zenker and Hoehne 2018)—as the case study below also demonstrates. Despite its rhetoric of equality, citizenship regimes have thus produced massive inequalities, differentially affecting citizens (and subjects) according to their social locations, identifications, and values.

While often evoking the imagination of a 'national geographic' (Malkki 1992), with each individual ideally having only one citizenship, states have varied in their approach to multiple citizenship, offering diverse incentives for maintaining the long-term long-distance membership of their emigrants in order to continuously benefit economically from their remittances or taxes. While 'methodological nationalism'—the tendency to take the nation-state as the natural frame of reference (Wimmer and Glick Schiller 2002)—for a long time led researchers to assume that migrants either stay loyal to their home country or assimilate and integrate into their host country, transnationalism studies since the 1990s have shown migrants to be often simultaneously engaged in and oriented towards both states (Levitt and Glick Schiller 2004); the transnational flow of people, ideas, and objects across state borders can thus lead to 'flexible citizenship' and the emergence of transnational publics while keeping the respective nation-states intact (Ong 1999).

Formal citizenship, as the prime mechanism for the legal inclusion and exclusion of people within a particular state system, is, of course, subject to an intense politics of belonging. This clearly emanates from studies such as those by Robert Hayden (1992, 1999), which chart the ways in which the law was used in the years before and after the war in the former Yugoslavia to more narrowly define legitimate citizens in terms of ethnicity, a process he labels 'constitutional nationalism' and sees as facilitating civil war and authoritarianism. Conversely, the Tutsi-dominated government in post-genocide Rwanda has introduced various legal measures against 'divisionism' and 'genocide ideology' since 2002, making it a legal offence to refer to 'Hutu' and 'Tutsi', which the new official historiography depicts as merely colonial inventions. Yet, as Simon Turner (2014) shows, the government simultaneously established *ingando* re-education camps for *génocidaires* (effectively Hutu) and *itorero* solidarity camps (networking camps for the Tutsi elite), which—while both ostensibly concerned with the production of common 'good citizenship'—have effectively recreated social divisions within a legal regime that criminalized the articulation of this very division.

Reversing the perspective, anthropological research has also focused on the multiple ways in which formal citizens cope with the fact that they often lack substantive citizenship—that is, the ability to actually claim and benefit from rights they formally possess. In her study of the aftermath of the Chernobyl disaster, Adriana Petryna (2002) traces the development from an initial lack of disclosure to democratizing attempts under postsocialism to compensate affected citizens. Pointing to the massive demand for social welfare, Petryna demonstrates how sufferers mobilize medical, scientific, and legal criteria acknowledging their physical injury—a process she describes as 'biological citizenship'—in order to substantiate and thus benefit from their formal entitlements.

Other research has attempted to come to terms with the seemingly paradoxical demand for substantive citizenship and the vigilante-type provision of state-mimicking security on the one hand, and the often massively violent disregard for the law on the other. Exploring this dynamic under the label of 'insurgent citizenship', James Holston's (2008) study of residents of the urban peripheries of São Paulo explains this phenomenon with regard to the deeply entrenched system of unequal citizenship in Brazil—one that is universally inclusive in formal terms and yet, in substantive terms, massively inegalitarian in its distribution of actual rights and legalization of social differences. Under these conditions, the police and local gangs equally engage in both illegal violence and rights talk, the latter ambiguously serving as a justification for selectively denying citizens' rights through the former.

As these studies show, the formal and substantive realities of citizenship regimes, in all their sociocultural variation, persist as a highly complex politics of belonging, with massively unequal consequences for people who are interpellated in, or excluded from, its terms.

Alternative Political Projects of Belonging

While modern states have aspired, often quite successfully, to turn citizenship into a hegemonic mode of belonging, people have also engaged in numerous alternative political projects of belonging positioned below, alongside, across, and sometimes in opposition to this state-centric affiliation—important political projects in their own right that are shaped by and attempt to transform various normative orders. The following provides a highly selective glimpse into some ongoing engagements of legal anthropology with diverse categories of social location studied individually as well as at their intersections.

One field in which the politics of belonging has recently played out in liberal democracies with much public attention, legal change, and arguably violent repercussions is religion—notably Islam. Focusing on the French veil controversy, John Bowen (2006, 2010) analyses, among other things, the law that was introduced in 2004 prohibiting the public display of signs of organized religions, especially in public schools. While ostensibly neutral with regard to specific religions and directed at the French republican ideology of *laïcité* at large, the law's evident concern was with the public exhibition of the Muslim headscarf, which was portrayed as threatening individual autonomy and freedom of expression as conditions for full civic participation in French public life. Yet, as Bowen emphasizes, this debate around personal autonomy became profoundly infused with the paradox of paternalism, in that the right of Muslim schoolgirls to wear the veil was interfered with against their will for the purpose of advancing their 'true' autonomy and freedom of expression (see also Foblets et al. 2018), thus highlighting the political and legal conundrums following from the various ways in which liberal-democratic states attempt to manage their internal cultural diversity.

Within the anthropology of human rights, Sally Engle Merry (2006, 2009) has prominently tracked the process through which 'gender violence' came to be defined for the first time as a human rights violation in the 1990s. Studying the development and implementation of the monitoring system of the Convention on the Elimination of All Forms of Discrimination Against Women (CEDAW) through observing UN diplomatic negotiations as well as the workings of grassroots feminist organizations in several countries, it becomes evident that seemingly universal human rights have to be translated and 'vernacularized' into local terms in order to become acceptable and potentially effective in changing prevailing cultural understandings and practices of aggression against women. The example of Fiji's country report to the CEDAW committee in 2002 is a case in point: during the UN meeting, CEDAW experts criticized Fiji's representatives for not sufficiently fighting the customary practice of *bulubulu*, which was understood to influence rape cases through reconciliatory gift giving; yet while in Fiji, Merry realized that the political and cultural complexities of *bulubulu* could not be easily translated and parsed into the legal language of the UN, which misleadingly contrasted culture with women's rights. For this, a more nuanced and multidimensional analysis was needed.

In her legal anthropological research of same-sex parenthood in Israel, Sibylle Lustenberger (2013, 2014) offers an intersectional analysis of gender, sexuality, kinship, religion, and nationhood in studying the sociocultural and legal place for children conceived through sperm donation or born to surrogate mothers. Given that personal status in Israel is regulated through religious law, Orthodox rabbis have the state-sanctioned power to define who is Jewish and to enable and recognize marriage. The impediments that religious law poses to same-sex couples and their children are serious, as same-sex couples are excluded from marriage and their children's religious status is at risk. Although lesbian women and gay men reject the rabbinate, Lustenberger shows through male couples' conversions of their children that same-sex couples cannot completely dismiss rabbinic authority over Judaism, as it is important for them to assert their children's Judaism even if they do not define themselves as religious. Accordingly, they carefully carve out strategies and narratives that accommodate both their antipathy towards the rabbinate and the rabbinate's power to define who counts as a Jew. At the same time, using childbirth celebrations and holidays, same-sex couples seek to establish their families' legitimate place in society through social relationships and not the rabbinate, thereby exploring and expanding the social boundaries of what Israeli society may recognize as Judaism.

A final example for a multidimensional analysis of politicized belonging is Seth Holmes's (2013) work *Fresh Fruit, Broken Bodies*, in which racial, ethnic, xenophobic, and class-based oppressions intersect with the harsh realities of citizenship in the lives of indigenous Mexican migrant farmworkers in the US. Holmes followed his informants from indigenous communities in Oaxaca through the locations of the dangerous migration circuit, lived and worked with them on farms in the US, and accompanied them to hospitals and other institutional contexts. He shows how, during encounters with farmers and growers, rural community members, social service providers, medical doctors, and others, the position of indigenous Mexicans at the bottom of the farm labour hierarchy becomes naturalized, normalized, and internalized by the migrant workers themselves as the conjoint expression of their racial, ethnic, class, and citizenship position. In this way, the oppressive conditions of labour migration and farm work in the US—including homelessness, food insecurity, occupational injuries and their expensive medical treatment, exposure to pesticide and harsh working conditions, as well as hate crimes against undocumented immigrants—are maintained and reproduced intergenerationally. The study thus demonstrates the persistent racialization of labour in the global capitalist economy, which seems to care more about the health and well-being of the consumers than of the producers on a farm that is certified for organic agriculture.

Studies like these attest to the multiplicity of coexisting, diversely juridified, and intersecting modes of belonging, which position different people differently within asymmetrical power dynamics of inclusion and exclusion, often with profound consequences for individuals' life chances and trajectories. While not all of these forms of identity politics are necessarily entangled with questions of state membership, several political projects of territorial belonging—as shown in the following—actually do have a lot in common with citizenship, arguably sharing the same underlying logic of 'autochthony'.

Contested autochthonies: Cross-cutting individual–territory–group triads at shifting scales

Over the past two decades, autochthony has emerged as a crucial concern within anthropological research on belonging and its contested politics. Literally meaning 'sprung from the earth' in Greek, autochthony refers to an asserted rightful link between an individual, a territory, and a group, often depicting itself as profoundly 'authentic', 'natural', or 'self-evidently legitimate'. Within anthropological debates, the term has been restricted to a mode of belonging involving first-comer claims to a particular territory, as exemplified among 'original' landowners in Africa or within European right-populist movements (e.g. Bøås and Dunn 2013; Geschiere 2009; Kuba and Lentz 2006). As such, it is often discussed in conjuncture with 'indigeneity', equally referring to allegedly 'original' inhabitants of a territory. In fact, in United Nations circles these concepts are treated as synonymous (Yuval-Davis 2011: 100, fn. 3), whereas in much of the academic literature, 'the term indigenous tends to be used for people who are already marginalised, while autochthonous is generally reserved for people who are dominant in a given area but fear future marginalisation' (Gausset et al. 2011: 139). Moreover, anthropologists have hotly debated whether both terms should be rejected analytically (for their feared essentialism) and/or politically (for propagating exclusion).

As I argue in detail elsewhere (Zenker 2009, 2011, 2013), the value of 'autochthony' extends beyond its application as both an anti-essentialist analytical as well as politically useful term. Indeed, an expanded theoretical framework of 'autochthony' incorporating insights on civic and ethnic nationalism may even provide a helpful analytical lens for a broader and more comprehensive study of where and to whom, how and why, and with what consequences people are seen to rightfully belong. Using this approach for a family of interrelated territorial modes of belonging—ethnicity, nationhood/nationalism, citizenship, diaspora, indigeneity, identities conventionally described in terms of 'autochthony' (see above), but also more regional and kin-based conceptions of localized belonging—this lens thus enables an integrated analysis of coexisting, overlapping, and contested autochthonies at shifting scales.

Two aspects in particular distinguish this framework from related academic discussions: in contrast to the prevailing literature on autochthony, it is argued that 'earlier-coming' is but one mode of rooting individuals and groups in 'their' place, thus requiring two ideal types of autochthony; and in contrast to the established distinction between 'civic' and 'ethnic nationalism', these two autochthonous ideal-types are not seen to differ regarding their constitutive elements (often unduly reduced to *jus soli* vs. *jus sanguinis*), but in terms of the *causal direction* in which individual, territory, and group are imagined as linked through place of birth/residence, group membership with land(ed) rights, and shared culture/descent (see Figures 42.1 and 42.2).

In the mode of 'individualized autochthony', it is the place of birth or residence, or both, which is projected as linking an individual to his or her territory; through this very (f)act, all co-residents are imagined as acquiring land(ed) rights (i.e. both rights in land and rights whose validity is territorially circumscribed) as members of a group that is hereby constituted. Over time, this causal logic might also lead to commonalities of (some) culture and/or (some) descent among these individuals—unless these individuals migrate or are the offspring of migrant parents. This autochthony may be described as 'individualized' since the rightful link asserted to exist between an individual, territory, and group is essentially produced through the co-presence of individuals, that is, through their individual place of birth or residence in their respective presents.

By contrast, in 'collectivized autochthony' it is the alleged commonality of (some) culture or (some) descent, or both, between individuals that is seen as connecting them to a group that, at some point in its proclaimed past, is said to have rooted itself through the establishment of land(ed) rights for its members in 'its' territory, thereby justifying a sense of belonging to that territory in the individual's present as well. Quite often, this imagination results in a constellation in which individuals are born and/or reside within 'their' territory—except in the prototypical case of diasporas. This autochthony can be described as 'collectivized' since the rightful link asserted to exist between an

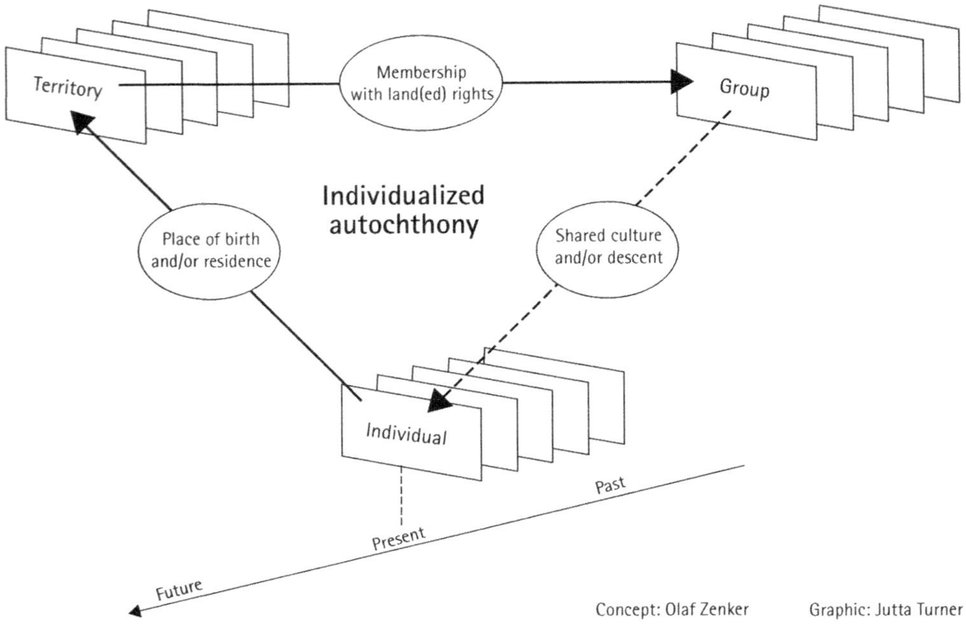

FIGURE 42.1 Individualized autochthony (Zenker 2013: 260)

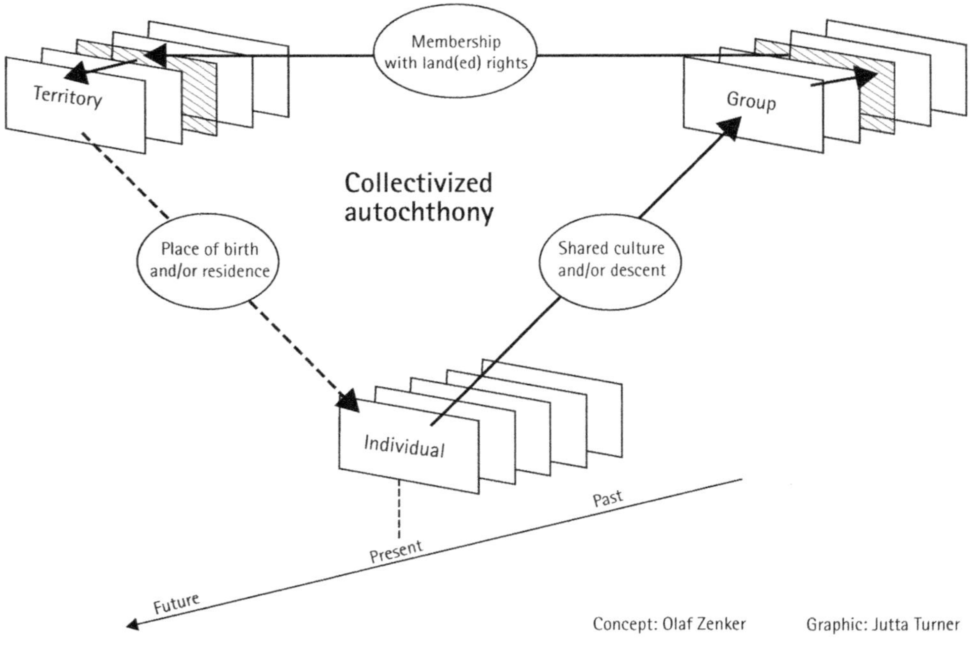

FIGURE 42.2 Collectivized autochthony (Zenker 2013: 262)

individual, territory, and group is essentially established through the alleged collective pasts of various groups, distinguishing between 'earlier-comers' and 'later-comers' to that territory.[2]

These two ideal types of autochthony allow for multiple empirical instantiations, varying in terms of causal direction and scale as well as in the specific meanings and concrete delineations attached to 'place of birth', 'residence', 'territory', 'land(ed) rights', 'group', 'descent', and 'culture'. Given that laws defining citizenship make use of exactly the same elements, this mode of belonging thus reveals itself to be nothing other than a version of autochthony: citizenship is state autochthony, plain and simple. Yet even within a citizenry thus constituted, additional layers of autochthonous contestation live on regarding more specific questions of who rightfully belongs (or should belong) where, to whom, how and why, and with what consequences for his or her landed entitlements.

This last aspect, namely the land rights and landed entitlements following from autochthonous belonging, points towards the crucial but so far neglected issue of the political economy. Put differently: how does the politics of *belonging* link up with the politics of individual and collective *belongings*, and the latter's rightful (re)distribution? A final excursion into a case study of conflicting autochthonies in postcolonial South Africa may point towards the various directions in which this question may be further developed.

Rightful shares: Distributing belongings through distributed belonging

In South African historiography, the year 1652 conventionally marks the beginning of European colonialism, when Jan van Riebeeck established a victualling station on behalf of the Dutch East India Company at what would become Cape Town. The following centuries saw the massive expansion of white settlers—increasingly split between Boer/Afrikaner and British colonialists—into the area of present-day South Africa, thereby subjugating and successively dispossessing pre-existing African populations of their land. The latter, comprising numerous ethno-linguistic groupings, had been living under diverse chieftaincies and kingdoms in which traditional authorities ruled through various forms of customary law (Ross 1999).

These pre-colonial arrangements, including diverse land tenure systems, were subsequently transformed beyond recognition through the colonial in(ter)vention of 'indirect rule', leading to the bifurcated legal system of 'citizens' and 'subjects' so cogently analysed by Mamdani (see the section on 'Citizenship: Hegemonic belonging and its relational others' above): while legally defined as subjects of allegedly 'traditional' (de facto state-defined) authorities ruling over (again state-defined) unviable rural 'homelands', the impoverished Africans were simultaneously forced, out of economic necessity, to participate in the world of citizens as 'modern' cheap labour for white-owned farms and mines (Wolpe 1972).

The complex intermingling of diverse and partly contradictory autochthonous modes of belonging evoking both 'traditionalist' and 'modernist' imaginations and produced by this overall set-up haunts the South African postcolony to this day. This can be illustrated with regard to the land struggles experienced by two communities residing on the farm 'Kalkfontein' just inside 'KwaNdebele'—that is, the former 'homeland' of the ethnic group Ndebele (as defined by the apartheid state), situated to the northeast of Pretoria.[3] These communities consist of descendants of individuals who came together during the 1920s in order to buy farmland previously possessed by the colonial state and granted to white settlers. Kalkfontein fell outside the mere 7 per cent of South African land scheduled in the Natives Land Act of 1913 for acquisition by the black majority, but formed part of those areas to be further released for black occupation. Therefore, the then highest state official—the governor-general—approved exemption, registering the land in the name of the Minister of Native Affairs, who held it in trust on behalf of the co-purchasers.

Both communities originally consisted of ethnically mixed groupings with Ndebele, Pedi, and Tswana origins. However, the situation on the northern portion of the subdivided farm was rather different than on the two southern portions. For southern Kalkfontein, the thirty co-purchasers from different ethno-linguistic backgrounds seemingly agreed to acquire the land unambiguously as private communal landowners organized under an elected committee—an option that was no longer available from the 1930s onwards, when Africans had to buy land as a 'tribe'. By contrast, a considerable majority of the original buyers of northern Kalkfontein were Ndebele (104 out of 126), who apparently wanted to buy land as a 'tribe' under their chief Januarie Mahlangu. But the former white landowner offered to sell the land only as communal land under a committee rather than as tribal land under a chief in order to ensure that his non-Ndebele farm workers could stay on the farm and partake in its management on equal footing. The Ndebele officially agreed; to this day, however, traditionalists have claimed that it had been always clear that the group would accept chiefly rule. Hence, two competing visions of landed belonging existed from the start: either 'modern' land management by an elected committee as officially written into the title deed or a 'traditional' Ndebele chieftaincy.

Numerous conflicts emerged locally over the following decades, all rooted in this basic disagreement. Towards the late 1970s, this root conflict became further entrenched (with the power balance shifting in favour of the traditionalists) when the South African government created the aforementioned homeland for the Ndebele in that very area. Using the powers of the Native Administration Act of 1927, both Kalkfontein communities were constituted as a single 'tribe' under the then chief without their consent and subsequently incorporated into the wider KwaNdebele homeland. Unchecked by the apartheid government, the chiefly excesses that followed—such as 'selling' residential slots to over 1,000 outsider families after they literally paid allegiance, and allocating residential sites on the ploughing lands of the original owners of Kalkfontein and even neighbouring farms—antagonized many local traditionalists as well.

For years, members from both communities used various political and legal means to resist this chiefly despotism. Finally, in 2008, the community of southern Kalkfontein succeeded in getting a court order ensuring the transfer of the land to their elected committee. The descendants on northern Kalkfontein tried the same; yet at the time of my fieldwork, the official title deed had still not been transferred to their committee, and the chieftaincy was still in place.

Until today, two conflicting logics of collectivized autochthony have thus oriented local senses of who belongs to whom, where, and with what kind of rights. One version of collectivized autochthony links today's rights-holders through descent to a group of people united in the past by their intention to buy parts of Kalkfontein as private communal property, albeit managed collectively through male democracy, in order to have a place for both residence and agricultural production. The other version of collectivized autochthony puts forward an ethnicized logic, in which shared (Ndebele) culture and shared (Ndebele) descent are seen as linking individuals to the local 'tribe', which historically established a rightful claim to the land by buying Kalkfontein as future tribal land.

These competing modes of belonging have been cross-cut with additional forms of autochthony, such as the smaller-scale individualized autochthony re-established every generation at the household level: all male descendants of the original buyers have been given residential slots for their own households, each with their own garden for cultivation. While daughters were expected in the past to reside with their husbands, thus ensuring patrilineal land inheritance, this has changed in the postcolonial era, in which women are increasingly given individual slots as well. Yet however such individual-territory-group triads are being construed (whether at the scale of households or communities), the idea of group membership typically entails claims to land(ed) rights—or in James Ferguson's (2015) recent terminology, a 'rightful share' in the group's properties that far exceeds the mere right to use land for agricultural production.

This can be demonstrated with regard to the multiple livelihoods of people belonging to Kalkfontein and their attempts to diversify their senses of autochthonous belonging to different peoples and pieces of land in order to potentially benefit from resource flows within these collectives. To begin with, the actual set of people legitimately belonging to Kalkfontein differed considerably depending on which autochthonous logic was evoked. In the collectivized (non-ethnicized) logic of private property holders on southern Kalkfontein, only their descendants could claim a rightful share of the collective property. Yet under the collectivized logic of ethnicized autochthony on northern Kalkfontein, the numerous outsider families that paid allegiance to the local chief as well as potentially any other Ndebele person, by far outnumbering the descendants of the original buyers, now also legitimately belonged to Kalkfontein.

Against this backdrop, a quite diverse set of land usage strategies could be observed for southern Kalkfontein. All male (recently also female) descendants of the original buyers were entitled to use their overall family share for cultivation as well as the commonly held grazing land for their livestock. Moreover, individual households could also cultivate in their residential gardens (mentioned earlier). While local residents thus had easy access to both cultivating and grazing land, as well as to their own valuable water supply (namely, the local limy fountain from which 'Kalkfontein' gets its name), at the time of fieldwork cultivation land was visibly 'underutilized' in terms of its potential for full-time intensive agriculture. Some locals claimed they lacked seeds and equipment and therefore could not farm. Yet the state did offer help in providing tractors and, to some extent, seeds, and some locals also made use of these provisions. Other reasons may have played a role as well; as one resident put it: 'people, nowadays, don't want to work on the land in the hot sun', but rather prefer an urban lifestyle. In fact, a considerable number of people rightfully belonging to southern Kalkfontein commuted on a daily or weekly basis to nearby Pretoria, where they engaged in wage labour and the informal economy. Echoing South African migrant workers elsewhere, many aspired to build a homestead on Kalkfontein in order to retire there, and many in fact do so. They also periodically returned to Kalkfontein when unemployed or to look after relatives, both young and old. Multiple cash flows connected Kalkfontein with workplaces near and far, resulting from wages and the sale of agricultural products, as well as from social payments such as old age pensions, child care grants, and disability payments.

In this way, descendants of the original buyers of southern Kalkfontein, whether residing on the farm or elsewhere, have evoked their collectivized logic of autochthonous belonging to Kalkfontein in order to maintain and make use of flows of resources and thereby engage in the sharing and distribution of Kalkfontein's 'common wealth'. Belonging to Kalkfontein thereby constitutes only one among several autochthonous modes for joining networks of production, distribution, and consumption, with comparable logics existing, for instance, within migrant communities in Pretoria and elsewhere. Thus, focusing primarily on rights in land—especially for agricultural use, as following from diverse politics of autochthonous belonging—rather than on landed rights risks missing a much broader dynamic in which people distribute their sense of *belonging* in order to partake in different distributive circuits of *belongings*, and thereby mitigate the risk of failing to make ends meet.

Conclusion: Recognition and (re)distribution in the politics of belonging

As this case study illustrates, people partake in multiple political projects of belonging, several of which can be profitably analysed through a unified framework of coexisting, overlapping, and contested autochthonies at shifting scales. Situationally combining elements such as 'place of birth', 'residence', 'territory', 'land(ed) rights', 'group', 'descent', and 'culture', individuals in South Africa and beyond often evoke diverse senses of autochthonous belonging to different collectives and their respective places in order to press for their rightful shares, thus benefitting from the (re)distribution of belongings through their distributed belonging.

Against the backdrop of excursions into some of the specificities of citizenship and other intersecting political projects of belonging, I attempted to show that several political projects of territorial belonging that are usually seen as distinct actually share the same underlying logic of autochthony, with its two ideal-typical variants. This applies not only to 'ethnicity', diasporic or otherwise, but also to 'indigeneity' (as that collectivized autochthony demanding special entitlements from a state in compensation for marginalization by later-comers operating in that state's shadow), to 'nationhood/nationalism' (as that autochthony claiming the very entitlement of the state itself), and to 'autochthony' narrowly understood (as that collectivized autochthony marginalizing later-comers in fear of losing previous privileges) (Zenker 2011).

Most importantly, citizenship was shown to make use of the very same logic of autochthony as ethnicity, nationhood/nationalism, indigeneity, and autochthony (in the narrow sense). This is not an inconsequential observation, as it highlights that 'citizenship' is not a different (or even superior) alternative to, say, 'indigeneity', as for instance polemically claimed by Adam Kuper (2003). Instead, using the very same elements and causal imaginations as any other autochthonous mode of belonging, citizenship is merely 'state autochthony'—the state-sanctioned, often naturalized, and in many contexts still hegemonic version of identity politics with massively differential consequences for people differently interpellated in, or excluded from, its terms.

In a different key, this observation also provides commentary on prominent voices within US-American liberalism that, still shocked by the possibility of Trumpism, propagate the idea that identity politics should be substituted by the allegedly radical we-liberalism of patriotic citizenship (Lilla 2017; Rorty 1998). Yet, as shown, things may not be so simple, given that citizenship cannot escape identity politics but merely instantiates it in yet another variety, with differential effects on differentially located, identified, and normatively committed people (as any other politics of belonging). In other words, the often massive disjuncture between the promises of formal citizenship and the realities of differential substantive citizenship on the ground is precisely the reason why alternative projects of 'identity politics' have often emerged alongside and against 'citizenship' in the first place.

This discussion is helpful for this reason; it brings to the fore once again the need to engage with the multidimensional projects of belonging and their various intersections. While the primary focus in this chapter has been on territorial modes of belonging—and the extent to which these constitute variations within one intersectional category rather than between different ones (McCall 2005)—the South African case study has also pointed towards the crucial interrelations, and intersections, between contested autochthonies and non-territorial modes of belonging such as race, gender, age, and class. The *double entendre* of an overarching *politics of belonging(s)* may thus serve as a reminder to pay close attention to the interdependencies between the reproduction of distributed belonging and the attendant redistribution of belongings—and thus address the need to firmly hold together, analytically and normatively, a combined focus on recognition and (re)distribution (Fraser 1995, 2019; Fraser and Honneth 2003) in any future politics of belonging.

Notes

1. An inspiration shared with Mark Goodale (2017: 1–29), who characterizes the historical development of anthropology of law as a whole in terms of a shift 'from status to contract to cosmopolitanism'.
2. As argued, both autochthonous ideal-types include individualistic and collectivistic elements; hence, referring to the first as 'individualistic' and to the latter as 'collectivistic'—as e.g. Greenfeld (1992) does in her typology of civic and ethnic nationalisms—is misleading. In contrast, speaking of 'individualized' and 'collectivized autochthony' highlights the respective emphasis that each causal imagination ascribes to either the presence of individuals or the past of groups.
3. For a detailed analysis of this particular case, see Zenker 2012, 2018.

References

Althusser, L. 2006 [1971]. 'Ideology and Ideological State Apparatuses'. In A. Sharma and A. Gupta, eds. *The Anthropology of the State: A Reader*, 86–111. Oxford: Blackwell Publishing.

Asad, T., ed. 1973. *Anthropology and the Colonial Encounter*. London: Ithaca Press.

Barth, F. 1969. 'Introduction'. In F. Barth, ed. *Ethnic Groups and Boundaries: The Social Organization of Culture Difference*, 9–38. Oslo/Bergen/London: Universitetsforlaget George Allen and Unwin.

Bøås, M. and K. C. Dunn, eds. 2013. *Politics of Origin in Africa: Autochthony, Citizenship and Conflict*. London: Zed.

Bowen, J. R. 2006. *Why the French Don't Like Headscarves: Islam, the State, and Public Space*. Princeton: Princeton University Press.

Bowen, J. R. 2010. *Can Islam Be French? Pluralism and Pragmatism in a Secularist State*. Princeton: Princeton University Press.

Brubaker, R. and F. Cooper. 2000. 'Beyond "Identity"'. *Theory and Society* 29(1): 1–47.

Clifford, J. and G. E. Marcus, eds. 1986. *Writing Culture: The Poetics and Politics of Ethnography*. Berkeley: University of California Press.

Collins, P. H. and S. Bilge, eds. 2020. *Intersectionality*. Cambridge: Polity Press.

Crenshaw, K. 1989. 'Demarginalizing the Intersection of Race and Sex: A Black Feminist Critique of Antidiscrimination Doctrine, Feminist Theory and Antiracist Politics'. *University of Chicago Legal Forum* 1(8): 139–67.

Eidson, J., D. Feyissa, V. Fuest, M. V. Hoehne, B. Nieswand, G. Schlee, and O. Zenker. 2017. 'From Identification to Framing and Alignment: A New Approach to the Comparative Analysis of Collective Identities'. *Current Anthropology* 58(3): 340–59.

Evans-Pritchard, E. E. 1940. *The Nuer: A Description of the Modes of Livelihood and Political Institutions of a Nilotic People*. Oxford: Clarendon Press.

Evans-Pritchard, E. E. 1951. *Kinship and Marriage among the Nuer*. Oxford: Clarendon Press.

Ferguson, J. 2015. *Give a Man a Fish: Reflections on the New Politics of Distribution*. Durham: Duke University Press.

Finke, P. and M. Sökefeld. 2018. 'Identity in Anthropology'. In H. Callan, ed. *The International Encyclopedia of Anthropology*. Hoboken: John Wiley & Sons. Available at <https://doi.org/10.1002/9781118924396.wbiea2142> accessed 6 October 2020.

Foblets, M.-C., M. Graziadei, and A. D. Renteln, eds. 2018. *Personal Autonomy in Plural Societies: A Principle and Its Paradoxes*. Abingdon: Routledge.

Fortes, M. 1945. *The Dynamics of Clanship among the Tallensi: Being the First Part of an Analysis of the Social Structure of a Trans-Volta Tribe*. Oxford: Oxford University Press.

Fortes, M. 1949. *The Web of Kinship among the Tallensi: The Second Part of an Analysis of the Social Structure of a Trans-Volta Tribe*. Oxford: Oxford University.

Foucault, M. 1978. *The History of Sexuality*. Harmondsworth: Penguin.

Frank, A. G. 1967. *Capitalism and Underdevelopment in Latin America: Historical Studies of Chile and Brazil*. New York: Monthly Review Press.

Fraser, N. 1995. 'From Redistribution to Recognition? Dilemmas of Justice in a "Post-Socialist" Age'. *New Left Review* 212: 68–93.

Fraser, N. 2019. *The Old Is Dying and the New Cannot Be Born: From Progressive Neoliberalism to Trump and Beyond*. London: Verso.

Fraser, N. and A. Honneth, eds. 2003. *Redistribution or Recognition? A Political-Philosophical Exchange*. London: Verso.

Gausset, Q., J. Kenrick, and R. Gibb. 2011. 'Indigeneity and Autochthony: A Couple of False Twins?' *Social Anthropology* 19(2): 135–42.

Geschiere, P. 2009. *The Perils of Belonging: Autochthony, Citizenship, and Exclusion in Africa and Europe*. Chicago: University of Chicago Press.

Goodale, M. 2017. *Anthropology and Law: A Critical Introduction*. New York: New York University Press.

Greenfeld, L. 1992. *Nationalism: Five Roads to Modernity*. Cambridge: Harvard University Press.

Hardt, M. and A. Negri, eds. 2000. *Empire*. Cambridge: Harvard University Press.

Hayden, R. M. 1992. 'Constitutional Nationalism in the Formerly Yugoslav Republics'. *Slavic Review* 51(4): 654–73.

Hayden, R. M. 1999. *Blueprints for a House Divided: The Constitutional Logic of the Yugoslav Conflicts*. Ann Arbor: University of Michigan Press.

Holmes, S. M. 2013. *Fresh Fruit, Broken Bodies: Migrant Farmworkers in the United States*. Berkeley: University of California Press.

Holston, J. 2008. *Insurgent Citizenship: Disjunctions of Democracy and Modernity in Brazil*. Princeton: Princeton University Press.

Kuba, R. and C. Lentz, eds. 2006. *Land and the Politics of Belonging in West Africa*. Leiden: Brill.

Kuper, A. 2003. 'The Return of the Native'. *Current Anthropology* 44(3): 389–402.

Lévi-Strauss, C. 1969 [1949]. *The Elementary Structures of Kinship*. Boston: Beacon Press.

Levitt, P. and N. Glick Schiller. 2004. 'Conceptualizing Simultaneity: A Transnational Social Field Perspective on Society'. *The International Migration Review* 38(3): 1002–39.

Lilla, M. 2017. *The Once and Future Liberal: After Identity Politics*. New York: Harper.

Lustenberger, S. 2013. 'Conceiving Judaism: The Challenges of Same-Sex Parenthood'. *Israel Studies Review* 28(2): 140–56.

Lustenberger, S. 2014. 'Questions of Belonging: Same-Sex Parenthood and Judaism in Transformation'. *Sexualities* 17(5/6): 529–45.

Maine, H. S. 2012 [1861]. *Ancient Law: Its Connections with the Early History of Society and Its Relation to Modern Ideas*. Cambridge: Cambridge University Press.

Malinowski, B. 1926. *Crime and Custom in Savage Society*. London: Kegan Paul & Co.

Malkki, L. H. 1992. 'National Geographic: The Rooting of Peoples and the Territorialization of National Identity Among Scholars and Refugees'. *Cultural Anthropology* 7(1): 24–44.
Mamdani, M. 1996. *Citizen and Subject: Contemporary Africa and the Legacy of Late Colonialism*. Princeton: Princeton University Press.
Marshall, T. H. 1950. *Citizenship and Social Class, and Other Essays*. Cambridge: Cambridge University Press.
Marshall, T. H. 1981. *The Right to Welfare and Other Essays*. London: Heinemann Educational.
McCall, L. 2005. 'The Complexity of Intersectionality'. *Signs: Journal of Women in Culture and Society* 30(3): 1771–1800.
Merry, S. E. 2006. *Human Rights and Gender Violence: Translating International Law into Local Justice*. Chicago: University of Chicago Press.
Merry, S. E. 2009. *Gender Violence: A Cultural Perspective*. Oxford: Blackwell.
Moerman, M. 1965. 'Ethnic Identification in a Complex Civilization: Who Are the Lue?' *American Anthropologist* 67(5): 1215–30.
Moore, H. L. 1994. *A Passion for Difference: Essays in Anthropology and Gender*. Cambridge: Polity.
Niezen, R. 2013. 'The Law's Legal Anthropology'. In M. Goodale, ed. *Human Rights at the Crossroads*, 185–97. Oxford: Oxford University Press.
Ong, A. 1999. *Flexible Citizenship: The Cultural Logics of Transnationality*. Durham: Duke University Press.
Petryna, A. 2002. *Life Exposed: Biological Citizens After Chernobyl*. Princeton: Princeton University Press.
Radcliffe-Brown, A. R. 1952. *Structure and Function in Primitive Society*. London: Routledge & Kegan.
Radcliffe-Brown, A. R. and C. D. Forde, eds. 1950. *African Systems of Kinship and Marriage*. London: Oxford University Press.
Rorty, R. 1998. *Achieving Our Country: Leftist Thought in Twentieth-Century America*. Cambridge: Harvard University Press.
Ross, R. 1999. *A Concise History of South Africa*. Cambridge: Cambridge University Press.
Said, E. W. 2004 [1978]. *Orientalism*. London: Penguin Books.
Scott, J. C. 1998. *Seeing Like a State: How Certain Schemes to Improve the Human Condition Have Failed*. New Haven: Yale University Press.
Turner, S. 2014. 'Making Good Citizens from Bad Life in Post-Genocide Rwanda'. *Development and Change* 45(3): 415–33.
Wallerstein, I. M. 1974. *The Modern World-System*. New York: Academic Press.
Wimmer, A. and N. Glick Schiller. 2002. 'Methodological Nationalism and Beyond: Nation-state Building, Migration and the Social Sciences'. *Global Networks* 2(4): 301–34.
Wolf, E. R. 1969. *Peasant Wars of the Twentieth Century*. New York: Harper & Row.
Wolpe, H. 1972. 'Capitalism and Cheap-Labour Power in South Africa: From Segregation to Apartheid'. *Economy and Society* 1(4): 425–56.
Yuval-Davis, N. 2011. *The Politics of Belonging: Intersectional Contestations*. London: Sage.
Zenker, O. 2009. 'Autochthony and Activism among Contemporary Irish Nationalists in Northern Ireland, or: If "Civic" Nationalists Are "Ethno"-Cultural Revivalists, What Remains of the Civic/Ethnic Divide?' *Nations and Nationalism* 15(4): 696–715.
Zenker, O. 2011. 'Autochthony, Ethnicity, Indigeneity and Nationalism: Time-Honouring and State-Oriented Modes of Rooting Individual-Territory-Group-Triads in a Globalising World'. *Critique of Anthropology* 31(1): 63–81.

Zenker, O. 2012. 'The Juridification of Political Protest and the Politicisation of Legalism in South African Land Restitution'. In J. Eckert, B. Donahoe, C. Strümpell, and Z. Özlem Biner, eds. *Law against the State: Ethnographic Forays into Law's Transformations*, 118–46. Cambridge: Cambridge University Press.

Zenker, O. 2013. *Irish/ness Is All around Us: Language Revivalism and the Culture of Ethnic Identity in Northern Ireland*. New York/Oxford: Berghahn Books.

Zenker, O. 2018. 'Land Restitution (Old and New), Neo-Traditionalism, and the Contested Values of Land Justice in South Africa'. In J. Johnson and G. H. Karekwaivanane, eds. *Pursuing Justice in Africa: Competing Imaginaries and Contested Practices*, 243–63. Athens: Ohio University Press.

Zenker, O. and M. V. Hoehne, eds. 2018. *The State and the Paradox of Customary Law in Africa*. London: Routledge.

Zenker, O. and K. Kumoll, eds. 2010. *Beyond Writing Culture: Current Intersections of Epistemologies and Representational Practices*. New York/Oxford: Berghahn Books.

CHAPTER 43

LEGAL AND ANTHROPOLOGICAL APPROACHES TO INTERNATIONAL REFUGEE LAW

KATIA BIANCHINI

Introduction

The positivist scholarship on international refugee law has been at centre stage in refugee studies for a long time (Lambert 2009: 319). International refugee law was traditionally approached as a 'self-contained regime of international law' (Lambert 2009: 320) historically originating from extradition law, nationality law, and alien law (Weis 1953). Studies on international refugee law only engaged to a limited extent with politics and other social sciences. They mostly viewed international refugee law as a set of abstract rules on a domestic and international level, 'which can be identified, objectively interpreted and enforced' (Chimni 1998: 352; Lambert 2009: 320). Consequently, refugee law was closely linked to the sovereign prerogative of the state to decide on the admission and expulsion of foreigners. In recent years, though, some academics have begun to argue that states and formal rules are unable to fully explain how international refugee law is created and shaped, and they have highlighted the importance of considering processes, networks, and actors (Gowlland-Debbas 1996: x; Lambert 2009: 320).

In light of the foregoing and after reviewing the most significant legal approaches to the study of international refugee law, this chapter discusses the recent unique contributions of anthropology to the field with respect to key legal issues. It identifies gaps and limitations and suggests areas in which future anthropology-oriented work might be developed. This chapter does not claim to be a comprehensive examination of the refugee law literature or associated anthropological debates and theories; it only provides an overview of the main topics and trends in current research. Another limitation is that it adopts a lawyer's perspective, rather than that of an anthropologist. The prime concern is to analyse core legal concepts and debates in the field, and show how anthropology can contribute to a better understanding of them in order to make refugee law more effective. Moreover, it aims to identify areas in which there is potential for collaboration between legal scholars, legal practitioners, and anthropologists.

Dominant legal approaches

Positivist Approach

The centrepiece of the regime for the protection of refugees is the 1951 Convention relating to the Status of Refugees (hereafter 'Refugee Convention') (Lambert 2009: 320).[1] This instrument provides the definition of 'refugee' (Art. 1) and sets forth a number of rights for refugees (Arts. 2–34), including protection against *refoulement*. The non-refoulement principle is the key protection of the Refugee Convention, as it prohibits returning refugees to any country where they are likely to fear for their freedom or life (Art. 33(1)) (Goodwin-Gill and McAdam 2007: 528–30; Lambert 2009: 320). The extent and the content of the protection against refoulement is nevertheless contested in legal arguments, especially regarding states' readmission agreements, internal relocation policies, and return and relocation schemes (Goodwin-Gill 2015: 10). The Refugee Convention also identifies the United Nations High Commissioner for Human Rights (UNHCR) as the United Nations body with supervisory responsibility for its implementation (Art. 33).

The Refugee Convention is not comprehensive, in that it purposefully leaves the concrete modalities of its implementation to states' discretion. In particular, as the Refugee Convention does not provide any guidance on how to make refugee status determinations, states enjoy wide procedural autonomy, and it is debated how this should be regulated and what obligations states have (Lambert 2009: 320). Guy Goodwin-Gill and Jane McAdam argue that states' discretion is limited by the *principle of effectiveness*. Effective implementation involves the adoption of procedures to identify the beneficiaries of protection, as well as measures against laws of general applicability, such as requirements of lawful residence, to make an application. Moreover, it includes facilitating the living conditions of applicants while their cases are pending, as these conditions are closely connected to the ability to pursue their claims. For instance, this may entail prohibiting the systematic use of immigration detention and granting the right to work and receive benefits while a decision is awaited (Goodwin-Gill 2011: 922). Others, such as Stephen Legomsky, stress that some principles of justice are so essential that they should always be respected in asylum procedures (Kneebone 2009: 33; Legomsky 2000). The idea of *essential principles of justice* is often associated with equality, procedural fairness, and independence of the three branches of government, and includes an adequate opportunity for advance preparation of one's case, suitable adjudicators, a fair opportunity to be heard, and fair rules on the burden and standard of proof. These principles are widely discussed in the positivist literature, both on refugee law and administrative law, and some observations will be made in the following sections as far as how they can be enriched by anthropology (Goodwin-Gill and McAdam 2007: 529–37; Legomsky 2000; Verdirame and Harrell-Bond 2005: 80, 92, 94–8). However, in that respect, it is important to highlight that a major research gap exists regarding the refugee status determination conducted by the UNHCR on behalf of states, and whether and how essential procedural elements are guaranteed both in law and practice (Jones 2009: 53; Kagan 2006a: 45).[2] This gap is very serious, considering the UNHCR's responsibility to determine refugee status, which it does alone in over fifty countries and in parallel to or jointly with states in another twenty (UNHCR n.d.). Although the UNHCR's work has already attracted several criticisms in this respect (Alexander 1999: 251; Goodwin-Gill and McAdam 2007: 53; Kagan 2006b: 1), more detailed investigations of this framework and its operation are needed.

Another major area of debate concerns the definition of 'refugee' and how it is applied and interpreted. Article 1A(2) of the Refugee Convention states that the term shall apply to any person who, 'owing to well-founded fear of being persecuted for reasons of race, religion, nationality, membership of a particular social group or political opinion, is outside the country of his nationality and is unable or, owing to such fear, is unwilling to avail himself of the protection of that country'. A person found to meet the definition of Art. 1A(2) can nevertheless be excluded from protection if he or she falls under one of the exclusion clauses (for instance, under Art. 1F, if he or she is a perpetrator of war crimes; crimes against humanity; serious non-political crimes in another country; or actions contrary to UN purposes and principles). The meanings of the words in the definition have been subject to intense scrutiny, both in practice and in scholarly works (Cantor 2016; Goodwin-Gill and McAdam 2007: 63–134; Musalo et al. 2011: 241–820). At present, there is significant divergence on how the definition is interpreted and applied, and even more so on the implementation of the exclusion clauses (Cantor et al. 2017; Li 2017).[3]

Until the 1990s, very few discussions engaged with the relationship between refugee law and human rights law—nowadays, though, scholars agree that *international human rights law* strengthens refugee protection (Hathaway 1991: 113–31; Lambert 2009: 322). Human rights law has become a point of reference when assessing the treatment of refugees in countries of origin (concerning, for example, the identification of ill treatments that constitute persecution and the evaluation of the effectiveness of the internal protection available in a home country)[4] and in countries of refuge (concerning rights granted to asylum seekers and recognized refugees) (Hathaway 2005; Lambert 2009: 322). It is also used to address issues of states' responsibilities towards refugees (Fischer-Lescano et al. 2009; Gil-Bazo 2006: 600; Lambert 2009: 322) and the UNHCR's accountability mechanisms when running refugee camps or handling refugee applications (Pallis 2006). Vincent Chetail even argues that the evolution of human rights law has transformed it into the primary source of refugee protection, 'while the Geneva Convention is bound to play a complementary and secondary role' (Chetail 2014: 22). These views, however, have met with criticism. Goodwin-Gill notes the difficulties concerning a 'system of "universal" human rights', as their protection is linked to states with different capacities, resources, and conflicting views of the world. He adds that 'international lawyers must always beware of theories built on the sands of academic speculation and far removed from the acid test of State practice, let alone the lived lives of people on the move' (Goodwin-Gill 2015: 10).

Limitations of the positivist approach include that the case studies are mostly from developed countries, despite the fact that most refugees are hosted in countries of the Global South. Moreover, state practices are mainly studied through judicial decisions. Some refugee law scholars openly reject approaches that look at the law in action and are mainly interested in what the law says, rather than state practices. In doing so, they overlook social and cultural impacts on the law as it is applied and interpreted. Two recent strands of refugee law, which have their origin in the liberal theory of international law,[5] challenge the focus on state-produced norms and try to understand how refugee law is created and develops in a globalizing world and changing political context (Lambert 2009: 319, 323).

One trend, the *transnational approach*, has expanded the theoretical discussion to include the interaction of several national and international actors (e.g. non-government organizations (NGOs), refugee lawyers, the UNHCR), decision-making processes (e.g. refugee law judges, administrators), networks (e.g. the International Association of Refugee Law Judges), and their impact on refugee law (Canefe 2010: 200; Nah 2016; Szablewska and Karim 2013). According to Hélène Lambert, European Union asylum law can also be studied from this perspective, as it develops through sets of rules, policy networks, and processes aimed at harmonizing domestic legal standards and practices (Guiraudon 2000: 1107; 2001; Lambert 2009: 325).

The other trend, labelled the *participatory approach*, has supported the argument that refugee law should progress through dialogue among participants worldwide, including those from the Global South (Lambert 2009: 326). Crucially, refugees should also be included, especially in the context of refugee status determination, the UNHCR's accountability, refugee transfers to other states, family reunion, and when dealing with long-term solutions such as resettlement and repatriation (Chimni 2001; Simeon 2013). The participatory approach recommends a 'culturally sensitive approach to refugee law' (Lambert 2009: 326; Wilde 2001: 148). Overall, this trend shows a much better appreciation for the refugee experience, although it is unable to capture the complexity of human interpretations and interactions with the law, and further research is required to inform the legal discussions.

In conclusion, while the positivist literature mainly deals with state-produced norms, both the transnational approach and the participatory approach offer a prescriptive view of international law that goes beyond the descriptive approach of legal positivism (Lambert 2009: 320). Their goal is to provide a more dynamic explanation of the development of refugee law, looking at actors and processes in the creation of norms. Besides these approaches, refugee law scholarship has recently become more receptive to an anthropological dimension, as I discuss in the following section.

Anthropological Approach

The emergence of anthropological studies dealing with refugee law is a response to the need for a more comprehensive conception of law, one that goes beyond the idea that law is only found in legislation or judicial decisions. Anthropological studies show that the law also results from the practices of actors who create their own rules of behaviour, as well as from the dominant representations in society. In particular, anthropology has helped in a practical way to assess international refugee law by using traditional methodologies within the field (especially ethnographic fieldwork) and to inform, through data, the main issues of debate (Harrell-Bond and Voutira 1992: 6–7). Importantly, anthropology has given voice to the stakeholders, taking into account sensitive cultural, political, and religious matters, and has put emphasis on 'voices from below'. Furthermore, it has shown that there are no explanations claiming 'to be valid for all groups, cultures and traditions' (Chatty 2014: 74, 80; Chatty and Marfleet 2013: 5–6).

Anthropology is also viewed as being capable of opening new paths of enquiry and providing different frameworks of analysis, allowing for the investigation of broader theoretical questions, such as processes of exclusion and inclusion, borders and the processes of 'bordering', the nature of the modern state and its relationship with forced migrants (Chatty and Marfleet 2013: 10–13), and what justice actually means for refugees.[6]

However, looking at the contributions of anthropology to the field of refugee law, four main observations must be made regarding the limitations of the current state of research. First, in terms of methodology, studies in this area are mostly small-scale and local, consisting of empirical investigations of the micro-level implementation of international refugee law. There exist very few longitudinal and comparative works.

Second, there is a huge geographic gap, especially with regard to Islamic countries, in the investigation of refugee law. Most of the studies focus on Europe, the United States, Australia, and, to a certain extent, Africa, Asia, and South and Central America. The literature is predominantly English-language and authored by Western and Northern academics. As a consequence, the 'sending country' perspective is usually missing (Koser et al. 2004: 59).

Third, there is always one dominant discipline. Genuinely interdisciplinary research combining law and anthropology has not yet become common practice. In part, this is due to difficulties encountered by interdisciplinary scholars that result from different methods, styles of thought, and disciplinary languages. For a better integration and analysis of insights from ethnographic research on refugee law, anthropologists and lawyers should carry out more collaborative work. The few previous attempts have demonstrated the importance of such projects, as they enhance a holistic understanding of refugee law, which, in turn, can promote more efficient and tailored protection (Akram et al. 2015: 287; Chatty 2017).[7] This view is also supported by some legal anthropologists, who more generally argue that law cannot achieve its aims without a grounding in social facts or an appreciation of its implementation. On the other hand, anthropology can reach its objectives, in particular the 'ethnographic capture of lifeways of other peoples in all their subtle permutations' (Donovan and Anderson 2006: 206), only through an appropriate analysis of the law.

Finally, most of the contributions have been in methodological choices and empirical (rather than theoretical) findings regarding aspects of refugee law. Most works are not linked to a wider context, such as human rights, transnationalism, postcolonialism, and so on (Black 2001; Koser et al. 2004: 60). Overall, there is also little elaboration on the impact, pitfalls, and prospects of ethnography in refugee law studies.

In terms of specific input to key debates in international refugee law, anthropological studies can be grouped into three broad areas: (a) procedural frameworks; (b) inclusion and exclusion from protection; and (c) actors. The following subsections analyse this literature and provide insights regarding directions for future research.

Procedural Frameworks

The most significant input to the field concerns investigations of the experiences and treatment of asylum applicants during the procedures. Studies include the analysis of cultural beliefs among caseworkers and the ways judges and lawyers examine applicants' narratives in order to assess truth and credibility. In particular, some anthropologists have looked at unusual and 'unheard narratives'; for example, those that arise as a consequence of rape and gender violence (Baillot et al. 2014) or social change (lesbian, gay, bisexual, transgender, intersex [LGBTI] cases) (Millbank 2002; Sigona 2014: 375). Others explore how decision-makers categorize different claimants according to patterns which indicate whether they deserve protection or not (Jubany 2011: 82). For instance, asylum narratives with 'recurring storylines' are treated suspiciously, as in the case of unaccompanied minors seeking asylum (Sigona 2014: 379, fn. 4). These findings are important because refugee status determination procedures involve some of the most complex adjudication functions (Millbank 2009). Very often, the asylum applicant's account of persecution is one of the main pieces of evidence under scrutiny (Good 2011). Decision-makers must assess the credibility, plausibility, and consistency of such an account against 'objective' evidence, usually consisting of documents on country conditions, expert opinions, and personal documents, when available (Sigona 2014: 375; Sweeney 2009). In many cases, especially when applicants are not represented, the personal account of persecution is the only evidence presented. It is often confusing and unclear, due to a variety of factors, including psychological (such as trauma) and cultural issues, multilingual encounters, and the narrative mode of the interview or hearing. Sometimes, evidence on country conditions consisting of information on history, politics, culture, and human rights in the country of the claimed persecution may not be up-to-date, accurate, or reliable (Thomas 2006: 85). Furthermore, the assessment of asylum cases is challenging both to applicants and decision-makers, due to language gaps, asylum seekers' education level, which is sometimes low, and lack of basic knowledge of principles of law in the host country, as well as different ideas of justice, rights, and procedures (Baillot et al. 2014). On this latter point, Anthony Good draws attention to the idea of studying law not just as a set of rules or formal processes but as a 'system of thought'. Such lenses of analysis on legal pluralism could help to comprehend how different concepts of law coexist within the asylum adjudication context (Good 2007: 18).

Moreover, studies demonstrate a widespread tendency on the part of decision-makers to see asylum applicants as bogus refugees. In the United Kingdom and in France, some commentators frame it as a 'culture of disbelief' (Fassin and D'Halluin 2005; Sigona 2014: 374). To explain such a culture, they point to prejudice and lack of understanding towards people originating from very different backgrounds. For instance, decision-makers lean towards judging the credibility of applications based on their assumptions and cultural logic and what they consider to be 'objective' evidence (Baillot et al. 2014; Good 2009b: 53–4; Rousseau et al. 2002: 62, 64).

Other research highlights structural, organizational, and political issues that may silence refugees' voices (Berg and Millbank 2009; Sigona 2014: 373). They deal with the distortion of language by power relations in the refugee determination process (Blommaert 2001; De Fina et al. 2006; Maryns 2005). In particular, Good argues that the refugees' need to present their cases through lawyers and interpreters constitutes a potential form of disempowerment—applicants may have to give up a certain amount of their autonomy, rely on these people, and become unable to present their accounts of persecution in ways they might have chosen under other circumstances (Good 2007: 21–3; McKinley 1997). According to Melanie Griffiths, trust is another major issue, especially towards government officials and institutions. The lack of trust can cause anxiety during the interviews and push applicants to fabricate some aspects of their accounts in order to please the authorities (Griffiths 2012).

A few studies also address the role of anthropologists as country experts, emphasizing their important function as specialists who can explain local conditions, cultural differences, and misinterpretations (Good 2007: 178, 198–203). In this regard, Good discusses asylum decision-making processes and analyses how the immigration tribunals treat the 'objective evidence' given by country experts as well as medical experts. He criticizes some judges' use of the notion of weight of evidence to avoid the findings of expert reports. At stake are different—and sometimes conflicting—professional standards and attitudes between anthropologists and lawyers relating to the nature of evidence. With this in mind, Good uncovers the difficulty of diverse professionals in appreciating the respective viewpoints, methodologies, and terminologies, and how these problems are exacerbated by the tensions between experts and the judiciary and the desire of the latter to protect their margin of appreciation when deciding on the cases before them in accordance with the law—notwithstanding the duty to take experts' views seriously, which may exist under some legal systems (Good 2004: 129). However, in this regard, Larissa Vetter and Marie-Claire Foblets point to the need to better understand judicial practices and go beyond the belief that they are following a rigid form of legal positivism. According to these scholars, it is essential to identify the discursive practices used to justify the weight given to anthropological expertise in court cases (Vetters and Foblets 2016: 286; see also Barnes 2004: 350).

In light of the foregoing, it can be concluded that despite the acknowledgment of the importance of cultural factors in assessing asylum claims and the practical contribution of anthropologists to legal practice, further research could elucidate the task of decision-making, the practical and organizational pressures under which adjudicators operate, the influence of personal and cultural values and of legal rules on decision-making, and the most appropriate form of procedure (adversarial or inquisitorial). Studies providing insights on the personal, domestic, and international factors which shape the refugees' narratives when they claim protection are also needed (Sigona 2014: 369, 374–5).

Inclusion and Exclusion from Protection

Under the Refugee Convention, an asylum seeker not only has to prove a well-founded fear of persecution but also that such persecution is on account of race, religion, nationality, politics, or membership in a social group. In order to identify the characteristics of the applicant and whether he or she indeed falls within the definition of a Convention refugee, there must be appreciation of his or her cultural and religious circumstances (e.g. religious belief; persecution on account of honour; family disputes; cultural practices, such as female genital mutilation; attitudes towards gays and lesbians, clans, witchcraft). Many refusals of asylum applications can be linked to the legal systems in place, which may fail to recognize certain types of serious discrimination and vulnerabilities as persecution (Türk and Down 2014: 282).

The contribution of anthropology in this area has been to explain the grounds of persecution in context and provide a holistic perspective. For instance, Good explores the legal understandings of 'religion' as grounds for protection, and reveals that there is reliance on ethnocentric stereotypes: given the 'culturally-contextualised, contested character of "religious" beliefs and practices', decision-makers would benefit from an anthropological and sociological approach to religion (Good 2009a: 27, 46). However, he notes one difficulty: the meaning of these terms in case law does not necessarily have any relation to social scientists' understanding, and the two different approaches are difficult to reconcile (Good 2007: 63).

Some studies discuss the particular treatment of certain groups of asylum applicants—women, lesbians, and gays—and most of them take a legal or socio-legal approach (Baillot et al. 2014; Johnson 2011). Sensitivity regarding the assessment of LGBTI asylum applications has been increasing, and most of the attention focuses on experiences in countries of origin, refuge, and resettlement, including criminalization of same-sex relationships, homophobia, and specific forms of persecution, such as mandatory surgery, forced marriage, and forced sterilization (Fiddian-Qasmiyeh 2014: 400; Giametta 2017; Jensen and Spijkerboer 2011). Yet interest regarding the novelty of 'climate change refugees' has remained relatively minimal to date, although this issue is likely to pose serious challenges to debates on protection in the near future.

Against this background, anthropology can further look at the mechanisms apart from the law which shape the inclusion or exclusion of refugees from protection. Questions that may be addressed include which applicants deserve protection; the social meanings of legal concepts, such as 'asylum' and 'refugee' as defined in the international instruments, and the different treatments of categories of refugees (Harrell-Bond and Voutira 1992: 6–7); which applicants should be excluded; and, when a political movement feeds the perception that applicants originating from certain countries are more dangerous than others, the question of which groups should be considered a potential threat to the hosting society. Finally, major debates involve situations where asylum seekers are excluded from protection because they are prevented from reaching a safe place. There remains a lack of studies tackling realities at the border and the treatment of refugees' transit in different countries, as well as whether measures such as pushbacks, interceptions at sea, border controls, readmission agreements, and immigration detention do in fact deter arrivals (Türk and Down 2014: 282).

Actors

A number of actors are involved in the process of implementing refugee law, including NGOs, civil society, and state officials and institutions. Although the anthropological literature rarely engages with an analysis of the law as created and shaped by the practices of these actors, a growing body of work recognizes the importance of their role. In particular, some research focuses on how NGOs have become key players in refugee crises and how they act as 'norm entrepreneurs' by developing and disseminating norms through advocacy and persuasion (Chatty and Marfleet 2013: 7). Other research explains how different social actors act according to various logics—not only moral and political but sometimes also practical agendas. The actors involved have their own mandates and interests and sometimes are in competition with each other to obtain funding. Political and institutional constraints have an impact on their work as well as the functioning of the refugee regime. A few studies reveal the hidden agenda behind the human rights network ideology and suggest models for how to understand these actors from a critical perspective (Goodale 2017: 104; Harrell-Bond 1986; Riles 2000). However, further research could clarify the extent of their action and their capacity to mobilize the law at the national and international levels (Goodale 2017: 103), as well as the way social actors may be paternalistic or unaccountable, the conflicts of interests, and disparities of power that characterize the interactions between them and the refugees.

As far as official actors, such as administrative decision-makers and judges, are concerned, it has been pointed out that their attitudes, legal consciousness, and background have a great impact on how they implement and shape refugee law (Ramji-Nogales et al. 2009). Remarkable examples of recent research demonstrate the relevance of anthropology to understanding human behaviour and decision-making in this context, and point to the consequences of failing to conceptualize how the judiciary and other institutions work inside a wider political field and how they influence refugee law and practices (Campbell 2017; Gilboy 1991). Unfortunately, such examples are few. The UNHCR's mediation role between countries of origin and host countries, as well as its contribution to ensuring refugees' social and cultural rights and long-term solutions, could also be further explored.[8]

Importantly, some anthropological studies have emphasized the views of the refugees themselves and addressed the experience and understanding of the bureaucratic system which they have to navigate to seek protection (Bloch et al. 2011; Griffiths 2012). Whereas these works do not engage with an analysis of the legal frameworks, they complement discussions on the fairness, trust, and implementation of status determination procedures (Jubany 2011; Whyte 2011).

Despite these studies, Nando Sigona calls for a more critical and theoretical notion of the 'refugee voice'; specifically, how it could be heard, what kind of strategies refugees adopt to obtain rights, and how affected people address power relations in the context of asylum procedures, courts, and the international regime (Sigona 2014: v). Furthermore, in this context, several ethical issues continue to be debated, including how to choose data in such a way that the subjects of the study will avoid harm (Koser et al. 2004: 63, 65) and how to balance advocacy and academic work. Moreover, the refugees' point of view on questions of reception, rights, services, and special needs, while asylum cases are pending and after the determination procedures, is rarely taken into account, even though their well-being and ability to pursue claims, integrate, and rebuild their lives are affected by the host country policies in this respect (Dryden-Peterson 2016; Simich 2003). At present, reception and integration services tend to treat asylum seekers as an undifferentiated mass and are often inadequate (Fiddian-Qasmiyeh 2014: 404).[9] Refugees are people who have been forcibly uprooted and must adapt to new social, cultural, political, and economic contexts. Often, such a challenge is highly underestimated—a better outlook could contribute to more effective refugee administration and to the realization of durable solutions (Harrell-Bond and Voutira 1992: 6, 9). Therefore, it is essential for anthropologists to act as cultural meditators to communicate the perspectives, experiences, expectations, and processes of cultural adaptation of refugees (Harrell-Bond and Voutira 1992: 6–7; Howell 1982: 120; Koser et al. 2004: 61).[10] Such involvement may be valuable not only for academic research but also for policy and advocacy purposes.

Overall, it becomes clear that there is a great need to further investigate the human experience, suffering, human agency, and causes of forced migration. Concepts and concerns of anthropology could be extremely valuable to this end.

Conclusion

The positivist scholarship remains dominant in the field of refugee law. As it focuses mainly on state-produced norms and legal sources, it is unable to explain transnational activities and actors and how they affect the way the law is continuously shaped, applied, and interpreted. Addressing these limitations, both the transnational and participatory approaches are helpful for capturing the complexity of the creation and development of the law. Moreover, the recent anthropological influence on the study of refugee law has helped to move the focus away from states, borders, and citizenship, and to underscore a humanitarianism concerned with actual personal experiences. In a way, the shift began with discussions that framed refugee law within the human rights discourse and focused on solutions aimed at guaranteeing effective human rights protection. However, anthropology keeps pushing for a change in paradigms. It considers refugee issues from the bottom up, allowing refugees to participate in the identification and solution of their problems. The anthropological perspective helps one to understand core concepts of refugee law, such as persecution and the grounds of persecution, as well as fundamental issues related to the assessment of evidence during the refugee determination procedures. Its understanding of law goes beyond state-produced norms to include personal behaviours and social perceptions, integrating legal analysis with human interpretations and experiences. For instance, anthropology stresses the importance of gender, victimization, and agency when engaging in a more critical investigation of the law (Chatty 2014). Above all, anthropological methods allow for the empirical exploration of many issues relating to the implementation of refugee law and its future evolution and design. While anthropology clearly has immense potential to shape the development of refugee law, scholars have thus far only scratched the surface of the possible areas of enquiry.

Notes

1. Convention relating to the Status of Refugees (opened for signature 28 July 1951, entered into force 22 April 1954) 189 UNTS 150 (hereafter 'Refugee Convention'). It should be noted that the Refugee Convention was initially applicable only to persons who were fleeing events that occurred before 1951 (essentially in Europe). The 1967 Protocol relating to the Status of Refugees (opened for signature 31 January 1967, entered into force 4 October 1967) 606 UNTS 267 (hereafter 'Refugee Protocol') extended the definition of 'refugee' in the Refugee Convention to all refugees. In addition to the 1951 Convention, there are a number of regional agreements, conventions, and other instruments relating to refugees, particularly in Africa, the Americas, and Europe. These regional instruments deal with such matters as the granting of asylum, travel documents, etc. Some also contain a definition of the term 'refugee' or of persons entitled to protection. The present chapter deals with the 1951 Convention, which is an international instrument of universal scope.
2. The UNHCR must develop international refugee law, try to secure that states faithfully apply it, and apply it in its own operations where states have mandated the UNHCR to determine refugee status on their behalf. In the latter situation, the independence of its interpretation and application of the Refugee Convention cannot be guaranteed.
3. In practice, the exclusion clauses are often applied to deny protection to people with a criminal background or terrorist affiliations.
4. For instance, the assessment of whether a violation of rights amounts to persecution can be made by reference to human rights contained in international treaties (Storey 2014).

5. The liberal theory of international law is associated with Anne-Marie Slaughter, who argued that international law should be based on developments in liberal international relations, where individuals and private associations—not states—are the fundamental actors (Slaughter 1995: 503, 508).
6. The idea of justice is difficult to define because it has both substantive and procedural aspects. While some principles of international law and human rights law attempt to set up universal concepts, questions regarding whether they really create universal standards of justice arise at the national and implementation levels. What justice means, and for whom, must be explored in terms of context.
7. For example, this is the case in Susan Akram's and Dawn Chatty's studies on domestic asylum laws in the Middle East region.
8. For instance, in the context of resettlement, the following issues should be further researched: criteria for the selection, admission, screening, orientation, transfer, and geographical placement of refugees; questions of equity among refugees and between refugees and the local population; identification of priorities for the allocation of resources; coordinating and developing the capabilities of the private and public organizations involved (Howell 1982: 120).
9. Accessing good-quality housing and (re)creating a sense of home represent one of the biggest practical challenges for refugees. Complex regulations, waiting periods, discrimination, and housing crises, among other things, increasingly complicate refugees' housing trajectories in host countries. Scholarly works have highlighted the importance of housing in the settlement of newly arrived refugees as a first step for attaining basic needs.
10. Harrell-Bond and Voutira make a similar observation with regard to humanitarian work.

References

Akram, S. A., S. Bidinger, A. Lang, D. Hites, Y. Kuzmova, and E. Noureddine. 2015. 'Protecting Syrian Refugees: Laws, Policies and Global Responsibility Sharing'. *Middle East Law and Governance* 7(3): 287–318.

Alexander, M. 1999. 'Refugee Status Determination Conducted by UNHCR'. *International Journal of Refugee Law* 11(2): 251–89.

Baillot, H., S. Cowan, and V. E. Munro. 2014. 'Reason to Disbelieve: Evaluating the Rape Claims of Women Seeking Asylum in the UK'. *International Journal of Law in Context* 10(1): 105–39.

Barnes, J. 2004. 'Expert Evidence—The Judicial Perception in Asylum and Human Rights Appeals'. *International Journal of Refugee Law* 16(3): 349–57.

Berg, L. and J. Millbank. 2009. 'Constructing the Personal Narratives of Lesbian, Gay and Bisexual Asylum Claimants'. *Journal of Refugee Studies* 22(2): 195–223.

Black, R. 2001. 'Fifty Years of Refugee Studies: From Theory to Policy'. *The International Migration Review* 35(1): 57–78.

Bloch, A., N. Sigona, and R. Zetter. 2011. 'Migration Routes and Strategies of Young Undocumented Migrants in England: A Qualitative Perspective'. *Ethnic and Racial Studies* 34(8): 1286–302.

Blommaert, J. 2001. 'Investigating Narrative Inequality: African Asylum Seekers' Stories in Belgium'. *Discourse & Society* 12(4): 413–49.

Campbell, J. R. 2017. *Bureaucracy, Law and Dystopia in the United Kingdom's Asylum System*. London/New York: Routledge.

Canefe, N. 2010. 'The Fragmented Nature of the International Refugee Regime and Its Consequences: A Comparative Analysis of the Applications of the 1951 Convention'. In J. C. Simeon, ed. *Critical Issues in International Refugee Law: Strategies Toward Interpretative Harmony*, 174–210. New York: Cambridge University Press.

Cantor, D. J. 2016. 'Defining Refugees: Persecution, Surrogacy and the Human Rights Paradigm'. In D. J. Cantor, ed. *Human Rights and the Refugee Definition: Comparative Legal Practice and Theory*, 349–95. Leiden/Boston: Brill–Nijhoff.

Cantor, D. J., J. van Wijk, S. Singer, and M. P. Bolhuis. 2017. 'The Emperor's New Clothing: National Responses to "Undesirable and Unreturnable" Aliens under Asylum and Immigration Law'. *Refugee Survey Quarterly* 36(1): 1–8.

Chatty, D. 2014. 'Anthropology and Forced Migration'. In E. Fiddian-Qasmiyeh, G. Loescher, K. Long, and N. Sigona, eds. *The Oxford Handbook of Refugee and Forced Migration Studies*, 74–85. Oxford: Oxford University Press.

Chatty, D. 2017. 'The Duty to Be Generous (karam): Alternatives to Rights-Based Asylum in the Middle East'. *Journal of the British Academy* 5: 177–99.

Chatty, D. and P. Marfleet. 2013. 'Conceptual Problems in Forced Migration'. *Refugee Survey Quarterly* 32(2): 1–13.

Chetail, V. 2014. 'Are Refugee Rights Human Rights? An Unorthodox Questioning of the Relations between Refugee Law and Human Rights Law'. In R. Rubio-Marin, ed. *Human Rights and Immigration*, 19–72. Oxford: Oxford University Press.

Chimni, B. S. 1998. 'The Geopolitics of Refugee Studies: A View from the South'. *Journal of Refugee Studies* 11(4): 350–74.

Chimni, B. S. 2001. 'Reforming the International Refugee Regime: A Dialogic Model'. *Journal of Refugee Studies* 14(2): 151–68.

De Fina, A., D. Schiffrin, and M. Bamberg. 2006. 'Introduction'. In A. De Fina, D. Schiffrin, and M. Bamberg, eds. *Discourse and Identity*, 1–26. Cambridge: Cambridge University Press.

Donovan, J. and E. Anderson. 2006. *Anthropology and Law*. New York/Oxford: Berghahn.

Dryden-Peterson, S. 2016. 'Refugee Education in Countries of First Asylum: Breaking Open the Black Box of Pre-Resettlement Experiences'. *Theory and Research in Education* 14(2): 131–48.

Fassin, D. and E. D'Halluin. 2005. 'The Truth from the Body: Medical Certificates as Ultimate Evidence for Asylum Seekers'. *American Anthropologist* 107(4): 597–608.

Fiddian-Qasmiyeh, E. 2014. 'Gendered and Forced Migration'. In E. Fiddian-Qasmiyeh, G. Loescher, K. Long, and N. Sigona, eds. *The Oxford Handbook of Refugee and Forced Migration Studies*, 395–408. Oxford: Oxford University Press.

Fischer-Lescano, A., T. Löhr, and T. Tohidipur. 2009. 'Border Controls at Sea: Requirements under International Human Rights and Refugee Law'. *International Journal of Refugee Law* 21(2): 256–96.

Giametta, C. 2017. *The Sexual Politics of Asylum: Sexual Orientation and Gender Identity in the UK and Asylum System*. London: Routledge.

Gil-Bazo, M. T. 2006. 'The Practice of Mediterranean States in the Context of the European Union's Justice and Home Affairs External Dimension: The Safe Third Country Concept Revisited'. *International Journal of Refugee Law* 18(3–4): 571–600.

Gilboy, J. A. 1991. 'Deciding Who Gets In: Decision-Making by Immigration Inspectors'. *Law and Society Review* 25(3): 571–99.

Good, A. 2004. 'Undoubtedly and Expert? Anthropologists in British Asylum Courts'. *The Journal of the Royal Anthropological Institute* 10(1): 113–33.

Good, A. 2007. *Anthropology and Expertise in the Asylum Courts*. Abingdon/New York: Routledge-Cavendish.

Good, A. 2009a. 'Persecution for Reasons of Religion under the 1951 Refugee Convention'. In T.G. Kirsch and B. Turner, eds. *Permutations of Order. Religion and Law as Contested Sovereignties*, 27–48. Farnham: Ashgate.

Good, A. 2009b. 'Witness Statement and Credibility Assessments in the British Asylum Court'. *Irish Journal of Anthropology* 12(3): 45–57.

Good, A. 2011. 'Tales of Suffering: Asylum Narratives in the Refugee Status Determination Process'. *West Coast Line* 68: 78–98.

Goodale, M. 2017. *Anthropology and Law: A Critical Introduction*. New York: New York University Press.

Goodwin-Gill, G. 2011. 'The Process and Rights of Asylum Seekers'. In K. Musalo, J. Moore, and R. A. Boswell, eds. *Refugee Law and Policy. A Comparative and International Approach*, 921–1095. Durham: Carolina Academic Press.

Goodwin-Gill, G. 2015. 'Introduction'. In J.-P. Gauci, M. Giuffré, and E. L. Tsourdi, eds. *Exploring the Boundaries of Refugee Law: Current Protection Challenges*, 9–28. Leiden: Brill–Nijhoff.

Goodwin-Gill, G. and J. McAdam. 2007. *The Refugee in International Law*. Oxford: Oxford University Press.

Gowlland-Debbas, V., ed. 1996. *The Problem of Refugees in the Light of Contemporary International Law Issues*. The Hague: Martinus Nijhoff Publishers.

Griffiths, M. 2012. 'Vile Liars and Truth Distorters: Truth, Trust and the Asylum System'. *Anthropology Today* 28(4): 8–12.

Guiraudon, V. 2000. 'European Court and Foreigners' Rights: A Comparative Study of Norms Diffusion'. *International Migration Review* 34(4): 1088–125.

Guiraudon, V. 2001. 'Reforming the International Refugee Regime: A Dialogic Model'. *Journal of Refugee Studies* 14(2): 151–68.

Harrell-Bond, B. E. 1986. *Imposing Aid: Emergency Assistance to Refugees*. Oxford: Oxford University Press.

Harrell-Bond, B. E. and E. Voutira. 1992. 'Anthropology and the Study of Refugees'. *Anthropology Today* 8(4): 6–10.

Hathaway, J. C. 1991. 'Reconceiving Refugee Law as Human Rights Protection'. *Journal of Refugee Studies* 4(2): 113–31.

Hathaway, J. C. 2005. *The Rights of Refugees under International Law*. Cambridge: Cambridge University Press.

Howell, D. R. 1982. 'Refugee Resettlement and Public Policy: A Role for Anthropology'. *Anthropological Quarterly* 55(3): 119–25.

Jensen, S. and T. Spijkerboer. 2011. *Fleeing Homophobia: Asylum Claims Related to Sexual Orientation and Gender Identity in Europe*. Amsterdam: Vrije Universiteit Amsterdam.

Johnson, T. A. M. 2011. 'On Silence, Sexuality and Skeletons: Reconceptualizing Narrative in Asylum Hearings'. *Social & Legal Studies* 20(1): 57–78.

Jones, M. 2009. 'Refugee Status Determination: Three Challenges'. *Forced Migration Review* 32: 53–4.

Jubany, O. 2011. 'Constructing Truths in a Culture of Disbelief: Understanding Asylum Screening from Within'. *International Sociology* 26(1): 74–94.

Kagan, M. 2006a. 'Frontier Justice: Legal Aid and UNHCR Refuge Status Determination in Egypt'. *Journal of Refugee Studies* 19(1): 45–68.

Kagan, M. 2006b. 'The Beleaguered Gatekeeper: Protection Challenges Posed by UNHCR Refugee Status Determination'. *International Journal of Refugee Law* 18(1): 1–29.

Kneebone, S., ed. 2009. *Refugees, Asylum Seekers and the Rule of Law. Comparative Perspectives*. Cambridge: Cambridge University Press.

Koser, K., P. Werbner, and I. Ang. 2004. 'Culture Research and Refugee Studies: New Knowledge, Methodologies, and Practical Implications. A Panel Commentary'. *Social Analysis* 48(3): 59–65.

Lambert, H. 2009. 'International Refugee Law: Dominant and Emerging Approaches'. In D. Armstrong, ed. *Routledge Handbook of International Law*, 319–27. Abingdon/New York: Routledge.

Legomsky, S. H. 2000. 'An Asylum-Seeker's Bill of Rights in a Non-Utopian World'. *Georgetown Immigration Law Journal* 14(3): 619–42.

Li, Y. 2017. *Exclusion from Protection as a Refugee: An Approach to a Harmonizing Interpretation in International Law*. Leiden: Brill–Nijhoff.

Maryns, K. 2005. 'Displacement in Asylum Seekers' Narratives'. In M. Baynham and A. De Fina, eds. *Dislocations/Relocations: Narratives of Displacement*, 185–96. Manchester: St Jerome Publishing.

McKinley, M. 1997. 'Life Stories, Disclosure and Law'. *Political and Legal Anthropology Review* 20(2): 70–82.

Millbank, J. 2002. 'Imagining Otherness: Refugee Claims on the Basis of Sexuality in Canada and Australia'. *Melbourne University Law Review* 26(1): 144–77.

Millbank, J. 2009. 'The Ring of Truth: A Case Study of Credibility Assessment in Particular Social Group Refugee Determinations'. *International Journal of Refugee Law* 21(1): 1–33.

Musalo, K., J. Moore, and R. A. Boswell, eds. 2011. *Refugee Law and Policy. A Comparative and International Approach*, 241–820. Durham: Carolina Academic Press.

Nah, A. 2016. 'Networks and Norm Entrepreneurship amongst Local Civil Society Actors: Advancing Refugee Protection in the Asia Pacific Region'. *The International Journal of Human Rights* 20(2): 223–40.

Pallis, M. 2006. 'The Operation of UNHCR's Accountability Mechanisms'. *New York University Journal of International Law and Politics* 37(4): 869–918.

Ramji-Nogales, J., A. I. Schoenholtz, and P. G. Schrag. 2009. *Refugee Roulette. Disparities in Asylum Adjudication and Proposals for Reform*. New York: New York University Press.

Riles, A. 2000. *The Network Inside Out*. Ann Arbor: University of Michigan Press.

Rousseau, C., F. Crepeau, P. Foxen, and F. Houle. 2002. 'The Complexity of Determining Refugeehood: A Multidisciplinary Analysis of the Decision-Making Process of the Canadian Immigration and Refugee Board'. *Journal of Refugee Studies* 15(1): 43–70.

Sigona, N. 2014. 'The Politics of Refugee Voices: Representations, Narratives, and Memories'. In E. Fiddian-Qasmiyeh, G. Loescher, K. Long, and N. Sigona, eds. *The Oxford Handbook of Refugee and Forced Migration Studies*, 369–82. Oxford: Oxford University Press.

Simeon, J. C., ed. 2013. *The UNHCR and the Supervision of International Refugee Law*. New York: Cambridge University Press.

Simich, L. 2003. 'Negotiating Boundaries of Refugee Resettlement: A Study of Settlement Patterns and Social Support'. *Canadian Review of Sociology* 4(5): 575–91.

Slaughter, A.-M. 1995. 'International Law in a World of Liberal States'. *European Journal of International Law* 6(4): 503–38.

Storey, H. 2014. 'What Constitutes Persecution? Towards a Working Definition'. *International Journal of Refugee Law* 26(2): 272–85.

Sweeney, J. A. 2009. 'Credibility, Proof and Refugee Law'. *International Journal of Refugee Law* 21(4): 700–26.

Szablewska, N. and S. Karim. 2013. 'Protection and International Cooperation in the International Refugee Regime'. In M. R. Islam and Md. J. Hossain Bhuiyan, *An Introduction to International Refugee Law*, 189–213. Leiden/Boston: Brill–Nijhoff.

Thomas, R. 2006. 'Assessing the Credibility of Asylum Claims: EU and UK Approaches Examined'. *European Journal of Migration and Law* 8(1): 79–96.

Türk, V. and R. Down. 2014. 'Protection Gaps'. In E. Fiddian-Qasmiyeh, G. Loescher, K. Long, and N. Sigona, eds. *The Oxford Handbook of Refugee and Forced Migration Studies*, 278–89. Oxford: Oxford University Press.

UNHCR. n.d. 'Refugee Status Determination', available at <http://www.unhcr.org/refugee-status-determination.html>.

Verdirame, G. and B. Harrell-Bond. 2005. *Rights in Exile: Janus-Faced Humanitarianism*. New York: Berghahn Books.

Vetters, L. and M.-F. Foblets. 2016. 'Culture All Around? Contextualising Anthropological Expertise in European Courtroom Settings'. *International Journal of Law in Context* 12(3): 272–92.

Weis, P. 1953. 'Legal Aspects of the Convention of 28 July 1951 Relating to the Status of Refugees'. *The British Yearbook of International Law* 30: 478–89.

Whyte, Z. 2011. 'Enter the Myopticon: Uncertain Surveillance in the Danish Asylum System'. *Anthropology Today* 27(3): 18–21.

Wilde, R. 2001. 'The Refugee Convention at 50: Forced Migration Policy at the Turn of the Century'. *Journal of Refugee Studies* 14(2): 135–50.

CHAPTER 44

NORM CREATION BEYOND THE STATE

PHILIPP DANN AND JULIA ECKERT

THE increasing relevance of norms that are created not by states (alone) has been a central feature of globalization since the 1980s. Norms are increasingly made in interaction with actors such as international organizations, corporations, epistemic communities, and social movements; they are made in processes that leave formal locations of lawmaking behind. These norms often emerge in complex and often continuous processes of agenda setting, negotiation, and consensus building that involve a range of actors, while various political, economic, and social factors play a role in determining participants, issues, and normative outcomes. These developments have challenged anthropological and legal scholarship to explore and theorize these novel ways of creating legal norms.

We recount these developments through the lens of the transdisciplinary anthropological and legal discourse on norm creation beyond the state. At the same time, we take this discourse as an example of such a disciplinary interaction and extrapolate from it specific tasks and challenges of legal-anthropological collaboration. In our view, this collaboration has been particularly fruitful in that it has helped to elucidate transnational norm making and normativity in a way that takes into account different processes and aspects of norm creation and the role of and relation between the various agents involved in these processes.

We begin by enquiring into what sensibilities and questions motivated legal and anthropological scholars to engage with questions of norm creation beyond the state. Against this background, we explore which actors and processes have been analysed by anthropologists and legal scholars in relation to norms beyond state institutions in the age of globalization. In particular, we observe that it is the norm-creating activities of international organizations that have triggered the scholarly interest in these processes. Attention has also turned to the new role of experts in these activities and the changing definition of what counts as relevant expertise—topics that raise issues of epistemic power. Lastly, many authors have insisted that we cannot gain a complete picture of the shaping of international and transnational norms without taking into account the role of bottom-up processes of norm generation. The attention to such bottom-up processes leads to the question of the authority of such norms. We distinguish three forms of authority that are addressed in current scholarship: structural dominance, epistemic authority, and authority based on conceptual charisma.

We take a *trans*disciplinary perspective on these questions, attempting to learn from the conversations that have occurred among (rather than only between) legal scholars and anthropologists of various theoretical orientations, conversations that are often hard to disentangle along disciplinary lines, and in which shared concerns, different methodologies, and continuous exchange have produced a vibrant field of enquiry.[1] By way of conclusion we reflect on the particular tasks and challenges of such conversations. We argue that one particular value of transdisciplinary anthropological and legal enquiries lies in the capacity to 'denaturalize' and thereby break open legal categories that constitute, code, and mask realities that must be made visible if we are to understand normative developments, emancipatory politics, and disciplinary self-reflection.

We speak of 'norm creation', not lawmaking, to be able to address the roles of various actors in the creation of rules, and the different processes whereby such norms are developed. The blurring of lines between formal and informal processes is at the core of what our chapter shall cover.

Disciplinary starting points

Legal scholarship has been concerned with forms of norm creation beyond the state since the 1980s, often driven by the question of the normative nature, binding-ness, and legitimacy of such 'norms'. Is it still 'law' if it is not states concluding treaties or creating customary law through practice, but a multiplicity of actors who are producing 'norms'? How do such norms square with the catalogue of sources of public international law as recognized by Article 38 of the Statute of the International Court of Justice?[2] What exactly could this be if it is not law, and is this even a relevant element of normative practice and hence an appropriate object of legal scholarship? The notion of soft law came into use—highlighting more than solving the respective questions and concerns. Such norm creation beyond the state was a highly unsettling development for legal scholarship not least because the characterization of a norm as law in positivist legal theory goes hand in hand with the assumption that such a norm is legitimate (see D'Aspremont 2019; Goldmann 2019; Weil 1983; Weiler 2004).

Questions about the creation of international law were not new, however, at least not for those taking the perspective of the periphery. From the 1950s to the 1970s, the emerging group of 'newly independent states' posed very similar questions. Entering an international legal structure that colonial powers had created before and very much to their own advantage, the new states demanded more participation in and new procedures for the creation of international law, in particular through the General Assembly of the United Nations (Abi-Saab 1962; Bedjaoui 1979). These demands, however, were quickly and vigorously blocked by Northern states and by much of the legal scholarship hailing from there, which insisted on the consensual nature of international lawmaking and the dominant role of states, and rejected this new role for the UN (Bernstorff and Dann 2019; Craven 2007).

For anthropology, the question of the legal nature of norms the source of which is not in 'the state' was conceptually less problematic, since legal anthropology from its very beginnings examined law stemming from other sources, be they of religious, customary, or other communitarian origin. Questions regarding whether that which legal anthropologists observed could or should actually be called 'law' and whether the terms coming out of European legal traditions could be translated so as to make a comparative legal anthropology possible were fiercely debated, famously starting with what became known as the Gluckman–Bohannan debate (Bohannan 1957; Gluckman 1955). While not necessarily agreeing upon one definition of law (Griffiths 1986), anthropologists who did engage in the analysis of normative orders that had legal qualities in the sense of an 'institutionalised doctrine' (Cotterrell 2018: 101) were usually less concerned with the sources and origins of what they observed to be the law of the societies that they wrote about than with the substantive and procedural norms themselves. Questions of how these norms shaped social organization, how they were legitimized and upheld, and what happened when they were breached were at the centre of anthropological concern.

This tradition has relieved anthropologists of some of the conceptual and definitional burdens that, for legal scholars, inhere in examining the role of non-state actors and the processes of norm setting, negotiation, and conflict through which norms are created at the international and transnational levels. In fact, the field of international and transnational law has been one of the most productive sites of knowledge exchange between anthropological and legal scholarship—or perhaps more accurately, of the infusion of anthropological knowledge into legal discourses. As Sally Merry noted in her review article of 2006, analyses of international law have learned much from studies of the law of non-state societies in terms of the creation of norms by negotiation and consensus formation (Merry 2006: 102; see also Riles 2000), sanctions in the form of social pressure and social control (Merry 2006: 101), and the dynamics of legal pluralism (Benda-Beckmann 2002; Griffiths 1986; Zumbansen 2010), all of which entail the question of how different normative systems influence each other and thereby trigger normative change.

Moreover, because legal anthropology developed for the most part in colonial and postcolonial situations and in situations of legal pluralism, it never took for granted that legal norms need to be legitimate or even 'accepted' to be effective. The efficacy of legal norms, that is, their effective regulation of relations and situations, from an anthropological perspective, might be achieved in a number of ways. Anthropologists, therefore, on the one hand, analysed the quotidian operation of 'illegitimate' law (as e.g. in the various case studies related to 'the imposition of law'; see Burman and Harrel-Bond 1979; Mamdani 1996) and the contradictions and tensions in situations of legal pluralism; on the other hand, they examined the diverse processes of the 'legitimation' of norms when they addressed their 'vernacularization' (Merry), their strategic employment (e.g. Eckert 2006; Lazarus-Black and Hirsch 1994), or their shaping of subjectivities.

The insights about how norms are made and legitimated in negotiations, struggles, and conflicts that are gained through the study of non-state law and legal pluralism in 'domestic' settings can be transposed onto international or transnational arenas. In other words, we have available a perspective from which to study how norms are shaped in the process of being adopted and adapted by various actors. Anthropologists have rarely expected an easy identity between law, power, and legitimacy. Rather, they have analysed the dynamic relation among these three elements as momentum for normative change. Consideration of the role of de jure authorities and de facto powers, of interested parties, and of those subjected to laws and regulations, and the holistic perspective characteristic of anthropological enquiries put the confluence of different processes—be they economic, political, or social—at the centre of the understanding of norm creation beyond the state.

Such openness in terms of the processes taken into account and the actors considered appears to be fruitful and perhaps even indispensable for an understanding of norm creation beyond the state. The question that haunts legal studies, namely how such norms acquire authority, thus becomes all the more urgent.

Actors of norm creation

International Organizations

Who makes law when it is not made by states? It was particularly the norm-generating activities of international organizations, especially since the 1980s when the end of the Cold War gave way to new perspectives on world society, that triggered scholarly attention to the generation of international and transnational norms and rules beyond the state in both legal studies and anthropology (Boyle and Chinkin 2007). With the debate on the changing role of the state, its prophesied demise, and its re-emergence with the World Bank's *World Development Report 1997: The State in a Changing World* (World Bank 1997), governance and globalization studies in general captured the expansion of power of international organizations and what has since been called the 'global governance system' (Barnett and Finnemore 2004; Zürn 2018).

At first, much attention was focused on trade law (WTO) and human rights as central fields of legalization and deformalization. Later, the development field, and the role of the World Bank in particular, and became a topic (Benjamin 2007; Li 2007, 2009; Rajagopal 2003). From its early years onwards, the World Bank turned to law as an instrument of agenda setting, control, and justification. Its economic and political mandate of liberal reform and 'development' set in motion a certain dynamic of legalization (Dann 2019; Sinclair 2017). This early turn to law became more pronounced in the 1980s and 1990s. In effect, the World Bank developed its own legal system (including its own 'court', the Inspection Panel), created its own procedures of 'lawmaking', and became a central driver in the diffusion of its agenda through law (Dann 2013; Dann and Riegner 2019). The Bank responded to the growing resistance against its activities with a number of moves to secure its hegemony, for example by paying lip service to some of the criticism and promising reform, but leaving the underlying structures of power, in particular the Northern governments' power to determine World Bank policy, untouched (Benjamin 2007; Dann 2019; Li 2007; Rajagopal 2003).

One central effect of the use of law as a technique of governance is what has been described as deformalization and managerialism (Koskenniemi 2011a, b). As the World Bank not only uses traditional sources of law (such as treaties), but has started to create its own policies and conditionalities, it introduces a new vocabulary of government (see Li 2007).

Non-governmental organizations (NGOs), too, can be seen as contributing to norm creation, as norm multipliers or 'translators' (Boyle and Chinkin 2007; Levitt and Merry 2009; Merry 2006; Rajagopal 2003). NGOs discovered that the law can be used both as an instrument to contest powers and to create entry points. NGOs not only use law, but also very often demand the creation of new law—be it human rights to protect individuals, environmental law (much as consumer law is used in domestic settings), or procedures and institutions (courts, etc.) to pursue their demands. Since the 1970s the globalizing NGO scene has been a central factor in the expansion of law beyond the state.

The turn to law affects not only the law but also its objects. Moreover, governments and civil society have also taken this turn to law. Newly independent states and their elites (government officials, lawyers, etc.) saw international law as a central instrument for emancipation and recognition. They placed high hopes in reformulating world order through the use of law—and therefore promoted the creation of new international law where possible (Bernstorff and Dann 2019; Eslava et al. 2017). States in the Global South are increasingly shaped and educated by these new international regimes. The 'sedimentation' (Bierschenk 2014) of the legal leftovers of subsequent phases of international legal and policy interventions leave countries of the Global South with context-specific assemblages of laws and regulations that continue to structure governmental practices from the local to the national. Some governments point to the binding international regulations in these regimes to eschew responsibility for their policies, a move that Shalini Randeria (2003) has called 'cunning'.

Experts and Epistemic Communities

The activities and efforts of international organizations in the realm of norm creation also point towards a new role for experts and their networks in designing norms and trying to achieve international standardization and global 'harmonization' (Benda-Beckmann et al. 2005; Jasanoff 1994, 2012; Kennedy 2016). Today, the complexity of issues to be regulated and the expertise needed in fields of technology and science necessitates increased participation of technical or scientific 'experts' in regulation. The increasing perception of risk, uncertainty, and global threats has also heightened the demand for (supposedly) rational, objective advice when formulating policy and rules. A shift of rule-making and norm setting into the hands of (non-legal) experts further 'autonomizes' normative developments in individual fields of specialization and heightens differentiation, disconnecting developments in such specialized fields from other fields and their social contexts at large. Experts come from all disciplines, including, of course, lawyers as legal experts themselves (Bouwhuis 2012; Koskenniemi 2011a, b) and anthropologists, particularly in relation to constitutional indigenous rights.[3]

A field in which experts and epistemic communities have played a major role from early on is international environmental law. Taking the example of multilateral agreements on fisheries, Wiber in anthropology and Josephine Toop in law have studied the interplay of regional fishery management organizations, experts, and wider networks of influence (Toop 2017; Wiber 2005; see also Turner and Wiber, this volume). International secretariats, scientific bodies, and compliance commissions interact and cooperate in sharing information and providing capacity to influence norm-creating processes.[4]

In many cases experts enter the fray through the participation of corporations in the negotiation of norm design. Johanna Mugler (2019) explores the role of experts and how they enter into the negotiations around new regulations concerning the taxation of multinational corporations in the OECD's Base Erosion and Profit Shifting (BEPS) project. She describes how '(tax) expertise' in the tax negotiations within the BEPS project consists of specific skills and a degree of specialization that not all countries participating can or do generate, and certainly not many civil society actors. Here, levels of expertise both in issues of tax and in matters of negotiating skills differ widely between the companies involved and the representatives of different countries, and among the countries themselves: countries that can delegate highly specialized tax experts have a different say in the matters under negotiation than those whose representatives who are less specialized and have the BEPS negotiations as one among several tasks.

While experts are staking out a novel role in crafting norms in international relations, epistemic communities that arise around particular fields of practice (Cullen et al. 2017) have also been analysed as generators of norms and regulations for hitherto unregulated or under-regulated fields. Callies and Zumbansen (2010), for example, analyse the creation of norms through consensus building in relatively open forums in private law, and see both the distinction between 'state law' and other norms and regulations, and that between private and public law, as unproductive for the understanding of current regulatory developments.

Bottom-up Processes of Norm Creation

Most challenging, perhaps, is the assessment of what has often been called 'bottom-up' processes of norm creation. While one could count some of the regulatory innovations of epistemic communities among such bottom-up processes in which hitherto unregulated new fields of practice are regulated 'in the doing' (see e.g. Cotterrell 2018), the role of civil society actors and social movements in shaping or even generating transnational and international norms is contested. There is the assumption—possibly going back to Eugen Ehrlich's argument that all legal norms are produced and change in conflictive negotiations between social groups in unequal relations—that forms of 'vernacularization' (Merry 2006), reverse translations (Englund 2012; Kirsch 2012, 2018), the juridification of protest (Eckert et al. 2012) and struggles for legal sovereignty (see Sieder, this volume) can have an impact on the shaping of international and transnational norms.

Ever since the global 'rights discourse' started projecting law as the internationally intelligible and acceptable language of voicing demands, providing categories of global scale and linking local concerns with international forums, it has been common 'to hear the language of jurisprudence in the Amazon or Aboriginal Australia, in the Kalahari or the New Guinea highlands, or among the poor in Mumbai, Mexico City, Cape Town, and Trench Town' (Comaroff and Comaroff 2006: 26). Why is that? The lack of political avenues of participation and partaking in decision-making on the international level might be one reason for this turn to law (and to the courts.) A number of authors have attested to a 'depoliticization' effected through the judicialization that juridification entails (see e.g. Comaroff and Comaroff 2006; Randeria 2007). In his analysis of the Indian social movement Narmada Bachao Andolan, Balakrishnan Rajagopal (2003) came to a pessimistic conclusion regarding the possibilities of social movements actually succeeding in their legal efforts to establish new norms.

Others have explored the normative effects that such mobilizations of law are having. Upendra Baxi argued: 'The rule of law is always and everywhere a terrain of people's struggle to make power accountable, governance just, and state ethical' (Baxi 2004: 327). His intention is to overcome a Eurocentric understanding of the shaping of legal norms and construct 'multicultural ... narratives of the rule of law' (Baxi 2004: 340) by pointing to the ways in which these norms were reformulated and creatively constituted in the interpretations of different historical struggles. Similarly, Boaventura de Sousa Santos and César Rodríguez-Garavito have argued that '[t]hese subaltern actors are a critical part of processes whereby global legal rules are defined' (Santos and Rodríguez-Garavito 2005: 11). Claeys has analysed the contribution of peasant movements, such as La Via Campesina, to the creation and institutionalization of new human rights understandings (Claeys 2015, 2019; see also Rodriguez-Garavito 2005 for the anti-sweatshop movement). We have before us the question of whether and how juridification affects the form and character of such reverse translations, for example by enforcing a canonization or explicit codification of hitherto possibly more fluid and flexible norms, as has been described for colonial situations (see Chanock 1985; Fisch 1992; Mamdani 1996). The struggles for 'legal sovereignty' explored by Rachel Sieder (in this volume) might depend on the fact that indigeneity is also and possibly more than anything else a legal term, raising the question of what limits indigeneity as a (self-)categorization might impose on norm-setting processes. Furthermore, we need to understand what factors are responsible for enabling some bottom-up normative processes and disabling others (see our observations on 'conceptual charisma' below).

Anthropologists have provided methodological and theoretical possibilities to address such processes. In her notion of 'vernacularization', Sally Merry has offered us a model of how to examine the dynamic between the changes effected in social formations in which international law is incorporated and the changes that these norms themselves undergo in those contextual interpretations and usages (Merry 2006). Andrea Behrends, Sung Yong Park, and Richard Rottenburg (2014) offer a methodological avenue in their explorations of 'travelling models', in which models are adopted and differentially adapted as they go through chains of translation. Their employment of the notion of translation potentially incorporates the diverse translations of users, clients, and other subjects of law who make meaning of legal norms.

Often left unexamined in scholarly treatments of such processes, however, are 'reverse translations' (see Englund 2012). Stuart Kirsch, for example, has shown how 'subsistence values' became incorporated into legal decisions and then took on a life of their own, being propagated through precedence in other cases. He has repeatedly demonstrated the law-changing potential of inverse dynamics of travelling models through which indigenous ideas and practices are refashioned through their engagement with the courts (Kirsch 2012, 2018) and policy arenas (Kirsch, n.d.). Similarly, Zenker and Höhne (2018) discuss how state norms have been shaped by their attention to non-state norms. The focus on such translations directs our attention to the structured interaction between different arenas, providing insights into the power relations in which what is translated is determined by fashions and agendas set in arenas different from those from which certain concerns arise. This raises the question of voice and authority in the field of global norm creation.

Interim Conclusion

One way to look at this increasing participation in norm setting is to understand it as pluralization. Norm creation is less and less monopolized by states (i.e. governments), and more and more the shared task of a variety of actors. This opens it up to new voices and constituencies, and creates opportunities to infuse different interests and concerns into transnational normativity. Speaking of pluralization does not indicate merely increased scholarly awareness of the multiplicity of actors active in norm creation, but indeed also a factual increase in participating actors (Boyle and Chinkin 2007: Chapter 7; Scholte 2014).

One can also view this pluralization more sceptically. Such a perspective conceives pluralization as a de-formalization that endangers the protections and avenues of access that formal structures give. De-formalization and the increase of 'relative normativity' weaken formal rules of procedure and formalized limits of competence, and more often than not privileges power over plurality. Critical scholars of international law see increasing managerialism and informal governance that undermine constitutional protections and privilege considerations of efficiency over those of justice (Eckert 2016; Koskenniemi 2011b). Norm creation, one could say, is further relegated to forums in which those concerned have no say, that is, in which not even the minimal communication with democratically elected legislatures is given, because the legislatures of 'weak states' are sidelined by international organizations in which they have little say and by INGOs that are accountable to their donors rather than their recipients. This raises questions about the legitimacy of norms that are generated in this way.

The authority of norms created beyond the state

The question of the authority of international and transnational norms has been explored in various ways.[5] We highlight three different sources of authority that authors have identified: a) structural privilege based on the confluence of legal structures granting powers to specific actors, often also based on or coinciding with factual dominance grounded in unequal economic and political power, resulting in dependencies; b) epistemic authority that resides in expertise; and c) 'conceptual charisma', i.e. the appeal and connectivity of certain normative innovations in a global public sphere. These sources of authority and acceptance are intricately entangled, as 'structural privilege' feeds into the possibilities of calling on expertise and defining what it is, and expertise opens chances to agenda setting, which in turn structures the possibilities of voice and visibility relevant for charisma. However, voice and visibility are not entirely controllable, and therefore often none of these factors can account on their own for the attainment of authority of non-state norms. It appears, therefore, promising for future research to explore the relation between them on an empirical and a theoretical level. We suggest that for this the collaboration of juristic and anthropological studies is particularly fruitful.

Structural Privilege

Realist studies and many critical analyses hold that the authority of specific norms is constituted by superior economic and political power and by the existing legal arrangements of the international field that serve to uphold such structural privileges. Ugo Mattei and Laura Nader, for example, have examined how legal measures related to current conceptualizations of the rule of law enable 'plunder' and the further expansion of Western cultural and economic domination (Mattei and Nader 2008). Authority here enables control over land, access to natural resources, and the determination of terms of trade through law. Analyses of structural adjustment programmes (Anders 2008, 2009), austerity policies (e.g. Koch 2018), and intellectual property law (e.g. Strathern 1999) point to such forms of rather 'brute authority', today observable also in relation to creating environmental norms (on 'green grabbing', see e.g. Fairhead et al. 2012; Bluwstein 2018). Mieville (2005) holds that it is the indeterminacy of law that allows the 'Haves [to] come out ahead' (Galanter 1974) in the international field.

The role of structural privilege, upheld through the legal arrangements of the international field, also moves in subtler ways. 'Conditionalities' in development cooperation are possibly one of the prime avenues for the establishment of such normative authority. Tania Li examined how the World Bank, mandated not to interfere in the political affairs of states receiving its assistance, has developed programmes operating through incentive structures to influence political institutions and reshape domestic norms through 'project law' (Li 2007, 2009). Celine Tan and Philipp Dann describe the legal mechanisms that are used to justify these arrangements (Dann 2013; Tan 2011).

Epistemic Authority

These analyses relate to anthropological concerns with the epistemic power of law. Where formal structures of authority are not well developed, such as in global governance, and where a variety of actors such as private corporations, international organizations, and experts formulate competing claims, other sources of authority have become more relevant, in particular expertise (Barnett and Finnemore 2004; Baumann 2000; Jasanoff 2012; Krisch 2016: 41). Some have argued that the social valuation of knowledge and expertise alone justifies normative acceptance (Zürn 2018: 57); others have pointed to the importance of persuasion (Venzke 2013). Here, the structural conditions for 'expertise'—that is, the relation between 'structural privilege' and the possibility of generating expertise—need to be taken into account. The fact that specialized technological or scientific expertise is highly dependent on resources and infrastructures means that expertise clusters in economically privileged sites, and that alternative knowledge or 'counter expertise' often cannot muster the same degree of specialization or the same quantity of data and is, therefore, not granted the same degree of acceptance or validity. We cannot tell for certain how this affects regulation, but exploring such questions might be an important avenue for future research.

Law here gains epistemic authority by providing the categories through which people, relations, and situations are classified for regulatory purposes, and a language in which people describe themselves and their needs to others. Legal concepts of indigeneity (e.g. Donahoe et al. 2008), gender (e.g. Merry 2003), nature (e.g. Bluwstein 2018), and 'victimhood' (e.g. Mamdani 1996; Wilson and Mitchell 2003) shape how these various phenomena can be represented. International organizations' and governments' increasing reliance on quantitative knowledge for their assessments and interventions in diverse social fields conceals the social theories underlying the counting, turning their specific categories, classifications, and concepts into countable and thus indisputable facts. Indicators employed in all areas of governance are one example of such epistemic authority (see Bogdandy and Goldmann 2012; Merry, Davis, and Kingsbury 2015;

Rottenburg, Merry, Park, and Mugler 2015). They carry a Western notion of the person, with all of its ideological baggage of autonomy, free will, and the primacy of individual and individualistic 'interests' (Collier et al. 1995), and serve to silence (in law) other ways of naming social relations. Santos has called such silencing 'epistemicide' (Santos 2014). Gayatri Spivak's question about whether the subaltern can speak is exacerbated in the field of law, as it is also a knowledge technology through which hegemonies are established.

It is open to debate whether such silencing succeeds or is subverted by the appropriation of these legal terms and categories by those subjected to (and subjectivated by) them. The analyses of bottom-up mobilizations of law (e.g. Santos and Rodriguez-Garavito 2005; Sieder this volume; Eckert et al. 2012; Kirsch 2018) show both the existence of such effective subjugation under the terms inherent in law and their transformation through strategic interpretation. The question is also to what degree legal and anthropological scholarship can (and has the responsibility to) counter such epistemicide, seeing that it often provides the very categories, concepts, and questions that fundamentally contribute to it.

Conceptual Charisma

If the indeterminacy of law privileges those in structurally advantageous positions, and if the weight of epistemic power is exacerbated by the complexities of today's regulatory demands in an entangled world and weighted towards those actors who can actually produce 'expertise', how can we account for the rise of heterodox demands for regulation? Is there reason to assume that some normative ideas are so inherently compelling that they develop a certain form of 'charismatic authority' that propels them to prominence—and possibly even to institutionalization?[6] The question would then be: Under what conditions do norms gain such charismatic authority? We can take a hint from scholars such as Susan Marks (2007: 207), who observed that '[p]ublic opinion is not simply a response to or judge of international legal developments; it partly constitutes those developments'. This gives rise to further questions: Which normative innovations are attributed charisma, and by what publics? Which fail to attain charismatic authority in relevant arenas? What aspects enhance the possibilities of gaining voice and visibility in 'global public opinion'?

Answers to these questions may reside in some of the normative developments initiated or shaped by struggles of social movements, which often employ legal means to further their visions of a just world. One example from constitutional law (rather than international law proper) is the notion of *buen vivir* ('good living', 'the good life'). *Buen vivir* promotes a holistic and harmonious relationship between mankind and nature, and underpins various political agendas such as interculturality, sustainable development, and climate justice. While the concept is considered to have originated in indigenous worldviews in South America, it has been taken up by diverse actors, including indigenous activists, environmental and development agencies, as well as academics (see e.g. Santos 2014) and politicians. It has been included in, among others, the Ecuadorian constitution, has been used to justify legal claims against multinational corporations for violating the 'rights of nature' (Affolter forthcoming), and has been adopted by environmental movements across the globe. Why has the notion of *buen vivir* successfully inspired radical alternative suggestions for the regulation of human–non-human relations, whereas other oppositional norms have remained tangential to this debate? How has this specific notion garnered the necessary charisma to travel in such diverse contexts? Is it because it can serve as a 'container' concept with greater resonance and connectivity than, for example, more diffuse agrarian-animistic cosmologies?

Concepts from international law also come to mind to exemplify authority based on conceptual charisma. One is the notion of self-determination, famously propagated by Lenin as well as Woodrow Wilson at the end of the First World War to strengthen the demands of national movements in Eastern Europe still caged in the Habsburg or Ottoman empires, but quickly taken up by protagonists of anti-colonial liberation movements around the world, such as Ho-Chi Min and Mohandas Gandhi (Manela 2007). Another example from the more recent past is the concept of indigenous rights, which gained enormous traction in the 1980s and became solidified through a variety of norm-creating processes—most notably through ILO Convention 169 on Indigenous and Tribal Peoples, national constitutions in Latin America, World Bank Operational Directive 4.20, and finally the UN Declaration on the Rights of Indigenous Peoples of 2007 (Jampolsky and Carpenter 2015).

These examples point to the complex interactions through which novel norms or interpretations gain authority and are propelled to significance by numerous and diverse translations. This might be less a matter of substantive content than of 'connectivity', that is, a given norm's resonance with or correspondence to other such ideas, and its ability to provide an encompassing expression of the broader web of ideas or concepts. Characteristic of these notions is the connection between an 'idea whose time has come' and its ability to stimulate the imagination of a variety of actors. Such connectivity is probably strengthened by the adoption of existing norms and procedures, as well as by the existence of pre-established networks that already have an agreed-upon, shared language. Thus, connectivity has a cumulative or self-reinforcing effect. It is crucial to study these translations and the selection processes among specific norm-setting networks where some normative suggestions gain traction and others disappear from the debate.

By way of conclusion: some thoughts on transdisciplinary perspectives

The study of norm creation beyond the state needs a broad lens in order to reflect the variety of actors, processes, and forums beyond conventional understandings. We found that observations on norm creation have to be complemented by an understanding of authority in order to understand which norms start to matter and which do not.

Our conversation about norm creation in legal and anthropological scholarship increased our understanding of the possibilities—and limits—of collaboration between our disciplines. One task that could be initiated by anthropologists would be to actively engage in conversation with legal enquiries, and to continuously 'de-naturalize' legal distinctions, be they of the boundaries between different fields of law (such as private and public law, criminal law, or tort law) or of categories of people, things, and issues. At the core of the anthropological endeavour is the attempt not to privilege analytically any one form of social organization, but to enquire into the possibilities and conditions of all. A de-naturalization of legal concepts in this spirit is an ongoing task precisely because legal distinctions do shape the 'social' (Pottage 2004) that they regulate; there is no 'pre-legal' social. The legal 'making (of) persons and things' (Pottage 2004) is often hard to discern, and its effects of constituting the social are often lost from view. We could term this problem 'methodological legalism' (analogous to methodological nationalism; see also Zenker 2016). The question to ask in this regard is what role specific legal institutions play in creating units and conceptions or connections and disconnections, 'links' or 'breaks' in the chains of interrelations, as Marilyn Strathern (2001) has shown, for example, in her analysis of intellectual property rights.

We could go further and ask: To what degree is our scholarly gaze itself shaped by the legal categories we live in? This means not only pointing to the origin of any such categorical distinctions in some law, a fact that all legal scholars will be most aware of, but the productive possibility of blurring these boundaries, of taking perspectives that organize our gaze in a different manner. Hence, ultimately, de-naturalization is not only a task for anthropological studies, but for legal studies too. As Katharina Pistor, for example, has shown with regard to the structures of capitalism, transdisciplinary legal scholarship is superbly positioned to reconstruct the role of legal thought in creating concepts and entities that then take on a life on their own (Pistor 2019). More generally, critical postcolonial scholarship has questioned basic notions of international law and started such a process of 'de-naturalization' or, to put it another way, of de-masking them by describing the historical origins of their creation and function in the (often colonial and imperial) system of international law. Legal notions that have been discussed in this respect are, for example, 'state', 'sovereignty', and 'equality' (Parfitt 2019). The lenses of anthropology, political economy, and law, when activated in concert with one another, seem best placed to look behind the mask of law and decipher structures of power and domination.

Notes

1. Surely, these conversations have taken place not only among anthropologists and lawyers, but also among (legal) sociologists, historians, political scientists, etc. of different stripes and in different contexts (such as the law-and-society movement, the critical legal studies

movement, etc.). Our central observation is that disciplinary boundaries blur and need to be blurred.

2. Art. 38 states: 'The Court, whose function is to decide in accordance with international law such disputes as are submitted to it, shall apply: a) international conventions, whether general or particular, establishing rules expressly recognized by the contesting states; b) international custom, as evidence of a general practice accepted as law; c) the general principles of law recognized by civilized nations; d) subject to the provisions of Article 59, judicial decisions and the teachings of the most highly qualified publicists of the various nations, as subsidiary means for the determination of rules of law.'
3. Anthropologists have served as experts most often in adjudication (rather than lawmaking) in criminal law and asylum law (see e.g. Renteln, this volume; Schiffauer 2000; Riles 2006; Good 2007).
4. The 'Codex Alimentarius' Commission, created by the FAO and the WHO in 1963 to set food standards, has attracted particular attention, not least for its interactions with interested corporations and its role in perpetuating South–North asymmetries (Epstein 2017; Afonso Pereira 2009; Howse 2000).
5. We speak of authority (not of legitimacy or acceptance) to address the whole range of processes by which norms come to effectively regulate social relations. We are aware that such a notion of authority calls for broader discussion, but space does not allow us to engage in it here. For a good overview, see Krisch (2016) and contributions in Raz (1990).
6. We take the term 'charisma' from Cotterrell 2018. For Cotterrell, transnational legal authority today is based on charisma deriving from expertise (2018: 130). Here we make a distinction between the authority of expertise and that of charisma. For Weber, the prototype of charismatic authority was the prophet who breached the teachings of the priests, or of the experts, so to speak. Therefore, it seems productive to apply the notion of charismatic authority to heterodox normative positions. Charisma of (some) expertise is then a specific case of charismatic and expert authority.

References

Abi-Saab, G. 1962. 'The Newly Independent States and the Rules of International Law'. *Howard Law Journal* 8: 95–121.

Affolter, L. forthcoming. *Using the Constitution against the State: Negotiations of (Prospective) Legal Responsibility in the Context of Industrial Mining in Ecuador*. (Manuscript on file with the author).

Afonso Pereira, R. 2009. 'Why Would International Administrative Activity Be Any Less Legitimate? A Study of the Codex Alimentarius Commission'. In A. Bogdandy et al., eds. *The Exercise of Public Authority by International Institutions*, 541–71. Heidelberg: Springer.

Anders, G. 2008. 'The Normativity of Numbers: World Bank and IMF Conditionality'. *Political and Legal Anthropology Review* 31(2): 187–202.

Anders, G. 2009. *In the Shadow of Good Governance*. Leiden: Brill.

Baumann, Z. 2000. *Liquid Modernity*, Cambridge: Polity Press.

Baxi, U. 2004. 'Rule of Law in India, Theory and Practice'. In R. Peerenboom, ed. *Asian Discourses of Rule of Law: Theories and Implementation of Rule of Law in Twelve Asian Countries, France and the U.S.*, 324–45. London: Routledge Curzon.

Barnett, M. and M. Finnemore 2004. *Rules for the World*. Ithaca: Cornell University Press.

Bedjaoui, M.1979. *Towards a New International Economic Order*. Paris: Holmes and Meier.

Benda-Beckmann, F. 2002. 'Who's Afraid of Legal Pluralism?'. *Journal of Legal Pluralism* 38: 37–82.

Benda-Beckmann, F., K. Benda-Beckmann, and A. Griffiths, eds. 2005. *Mobile People, Mobile Law: Expanding Legal Relations in a Contracting World*. Aldershot: Ashgate.

Behrends, A., S.-J. Park, and R. Rottenburg, eds. 2014. *Travelling Models in African Conflict Management. Translating technologies of social ordering*. Leiden and Boston: Brill.

Benjamin, B. 2007. *Invested Interests: Culture and the World Bank*. Minneapolis-St. Paul: University of Minnesota Press.

Bernstorff, J. and P. Dann, eds. 2019. *The Battle for International Law: South-North Perspectives on the Decolonization Era*. Oxford: Oxford University Press.

Bierschenk, T. 2014. 'Sedimentation, Fragmentation and Normative Double-Binds in (West) African Public Services'. In T. Bierschenk and J.-P. Olivier de Sardan, eds. *States at Work. Dynamics of African Bureaucracies*, 221–45. Leiden: Brill.

Bluwstein, J. 2018. 'From Colonial Fortresses to Neoliberal Landscapes in Northern Tanzania: A Biopolitical Ecology of Wildlife Conservation'. *Journal of Political Ecology* 25: 144–68.

Bogdandy, A. and M. Goldman. 2012. 'Taming and Framing Indicators: A Legal Reconstruction of the OECD's Programme for Internationale Student Assessment (PISA)'. In K. E. Davis, A. Fisher, B. Kingsbury, and S. Engle Merry, eds. *Governance by Indicators. Global Power through Quantification and Rankings*, 52–85. Oxford: Oxford University Press.

Bohannan, P. 1957. *Justice and Judgement Among the Tiv*. London: Oxford University Press.

Bouwhuis, S. 2012, 'The Role of an Internatinoal Legal Advisor to Government'. *International and Comparative Law Quarterly* 61: 939–60.

Boyle, A. and C. Chinkin. 2007. *The Making of International Law*. Oxford: Oxford University Press.

Burman, S. and B. Harrel-Bond, eds. 1979. *The Imposition of Law*. Cambridge, MA: Academic Press.

Callies, G.-P. and P. Zumbansen. 2010. *Rough Consensus and Running Code: A Theory of Transnational Private Law*. Oxford: Hart Publishing.

Chanock, M. 1985. 'Law, Custom and Social Order, the Colonial Experience in Malawi and Zambia'. *African Studies Series* 45. Cambridge: Cambridge University Press.

Claeys, P. 2015. *Human Rights and the Food Sovereignty Movement: Reclaiming Control*. Oxford: Routledge.

Claeys, P. 2019. 'The Rise of New Rights for Peasants. From Reliance on NGO Intermediaries to Direct Representation'. *Transnational Legal Theory* 9(3–4): 386–99.

Collier, J., B. Maurer, and L. Suarez-Navaz 1995. 'Sanctioned Identities: Legal Constructions of Modern Personhood'. *Identities* 2(1–2): 1–27.

Comaroff, J. and J. L. Comaroff 2006. 'Law and Disorder in the Postcolony: An Introduction'. In J. Comaroff and J. L. Comaroff, eds. *Law and Disorder in the Postcolony*, 1–56. Chicago: University of Chicago Press.

Cotterrell, R. 2018. *Sociological Jurisprudence; Juristic Thought and Social Inquiry*. London: Routledge.

Craven, M. 2007. *The Decolonization of International Law*. Oxford: Oxford University Press.

Cullen, H., J. Harrington, and C. Renshaw, eds. 2017. *Experts, Networks and International Law*. Cambridge: Cambridge University Press.

Dann, P. 2013. *The Law of Development Cooperation*. Cambridge: Cambridge University Press.

Dann, P. 2019. 'The World Bank in the Battles of the "Decolonization Era"'. In J. Bernstorff and P. Dann, eds. *The Battle for International Law: South-North Perspectives on the Decolonization Era*, 278–293. Oxford: Oxford University Press.

Dann, P. and M. Riegner 2019. 'The World Bank's Environmental and Social Safeguards and the Evolution of Global Order'. *Leiden Journal of International Law* 32(3): 537–59.

D'Aspremont, J. 2019. 'Bindingness'. In J. D'Aspremont and S. Singh, eds. *Concepts for International Law*, 67–82. Cheltenham and Northampton: Edward Elgar.

Donahoe, B., J. O. Habeck, A. Halemba, and I. Sántha. 2008. 'Size and Place in the Construction of Indigeneity in the Russian Federation'. *Current Anthropology* 48(6): 993–1020.

Eckert, J. 2006. 'From Subjects to Citizens: Legalisation from Below and the Homogenisation of the Legal Sphere'. *The Journal of Legal Pluralism and Unofficial Law* 38 (53–4): 45–75.

Eckert, J. 2016. 'Does Evidence Matter?'. *Allegra Lab*, available at <https://allegralaboratory.net/does-evidence-matter/>

Eckert, J., Z. O. Biner, B. Donahoe, and C. Strümpell. 2012. 'Introduction: Laws Travels and Transformations': In J. Eckert, B. Donahoe, C. Strümpell, and Z. Biner, eds. *Law Against the State: Ethnographic Forays into Laws Transformations*, 1–22. Cambridge: Cambridge University Press.

Englund, H. 2012. 'Human Rights and Village Headmen in Malawi'. In J. Eckert, B. Donahoe, C. Strümpell, and Z. Biner, eds. *Law against the State: Ethnographic Forays into Law's Transformations*, 70–93. Cambridge: Cambridge University Press.

Epstein, J. 2017. 'Scientizing Food Safety: Resistance, Acquiescence, and Localization in India'. *Law and Social Science Review* 68: 893–920.

Eslava, L., M. Fakhri, and V. Nesiah, eds. 2017. *Bandung, Global History, and International Law*. Cambridge: Cambridge University Press.

Fairhead, J., M. Leach, and I. Scoones 2012. 'Green Grabbing: A New Appropriation of Nature?'. *The Journal of Peasant Studies* 39(2): 237–61.

Fisch, J. 1992. 'Law as a Means and as an End: Some Remarks on the Function of European and non-European Law in the Process of European Expansion'. In W. J. Mommsen and J. A. de Moor, eds., *European Expansion and Law*, 17–22. Oxford: Berg.

Galanter, M. 1974. 'Why the "Haves" Come Out Ahead: Speculations on the Limits of Legal Change'. *Law & Society Review* 9: 95–160.

Gluckman, M. 1955. *The Juridical Process Among the Barotse of Northern Rhodesia*. Manchester: University Press for the Rhodes Livingston Institute.

Goldmann, M. 2019. 'Relative Normativity'. In J. D'Aspremont and S. Singh, eds. *Fundamental Concepts for International Law*, 740–59. Cheltenham and Northampton: Edward Elgar.

Good, A. 2007. *Anthropology and Expertise in the Asylum Courts*. London: Routledge-Cavendish.

Griffiths, J. 1986. 'What is Legal Pluralism'. *Journal of Legal Pluralism* 24: 1–55.

Howse, R. 2000. 'Democracy, Science and Free Trade'. *Michigan Law Review* 89: 2329–57.

Jampolsky, J. and K. Carpenter. 2015. 'Indigenous Rights'. In J. D. Wright, ed. *International Encyclopedia of the Social and Behaviorial Sciences (2nd Edition)*, 795–803. Amsterdam and New York: Elsevier.

Jasanoff, S. 1994. *The Fifth Branch: Science Advisors as Policymakers*, Cambridge, MA: Harvard University Press.

Jasanoff, S. 2012. *Science and Public Reason*. London and New York: Routledge.

Kennedy, D. 2016. *World of Struggle*. Princeton: Princeton University Press.

Kirsch, S. 2012. 'Juridification of Indigenous Politics'. In J. Eckert, B. Donahoe, C. Strümpell, and Z.O. Biner, eds. *Law against the State: Ethnographic Forays into Laws Transformations*, 23–43. Cambridge: Cambridge University Press.
Kirsch, S. 2018. *Engaged Anthropology*. Berkeley: University of California Press.
Kirsch, S. n.d. 'Why Pacific Islanders Stopped Worrying about the Apocalypse and Started Fighting Climate Change'. Unpublished article m.s. on file with the authors.
Koch, I. 2018. *Personalizing the State: An Anthropology of Law, Politics, and Welfare in Austerity Britain*. Oxford: Oxford University Press.
Koskenniemi, M. 2011a. 'Between Commitment and Cynicism: Outline of a Theory of International Law as Politics'. In M. Koskenniemi, ed. *The Politics of International Law*, 271–92. Oxford: Hart Publishing.
Koskenniemi, M. 2011b. 'The Fate of International Law'. In M. Koskenniemi, ed. *The Politics of International Law*, 331–61. Oxford: Hart Publishing.
Krisch, N. 2016. 'Authority, Solid and Liquid, in Postnational Governance'. In R. Cotterrell and M. Del Mar, eds. *Authority in Transnational Legal Theory*, 25–48. Cheltenham and Northampton: Edward Elgar.
Lazarus-Black, M. and S. F. Hirsch, eds. 1994. *Contested States: Law, Hegemony, and Resistance*. New York: Routledge.
Levitt, P. and S. Merry 2009. 'Vernacularization on the Ground: Local Use of Global Women's Rights in Peru, China, India and the United States'. *Global Networks* 9(4): 441–61.
Li, T. 2007. *The Will to Improve; Governmentality, Development and the Practice of Politics*. Durham, NC: Duke University Press.
Li, T. 2009. 'The Law of the Project: Government and "Good Governance" at the World Bank in Indonesia'. In F. von Benda-Beckmann, K. von Benda-Beckmann, and J. Eckert, eds. *Rules of Law and Laws of Ruling*, 237–56. Aldershot: Ashgate.
Mamdani, M. 1996. *Citizen and Subject: Contemporary Africa and the Legacy of Late Colonialism*. Princeton: Princeton University Press.
Marks, S. 2007. 'International Judicial Activism and the Commodity-Form Theory of International Law'. *The European Journal of International Law* 18(1): 199–211.
Manela, E. 2007. *The Wilsonian Moment: Self-Determination and the International Origins of Anti-Colonial Nationalism*. Oxford: Oxford University Press.
Mattei, U. and L. Nader. 2008. *Plunder: When the Rule of Law is Illegal*. Malden, Oxford: Blackwell Publishing.
Merry, S. 2003. 'Rights Talk and the Experience of Law: Implementing Women's Human Rights to Protection from Violence'. *Human Rights Quarterly* 25(2): 343–81.
Merry, S. 2006. 'Transnational Human Rights and Local Activists: Mapping the Middle'. *American Anthropologist* 108: 38–51.
Merry, S. E., Davis, K., and B. Kingsbury, eds. 2015. *The Quiet Power of Indicators*. Cambridge: Cambridge University Press.
Miéville, C. 2005. *Between Equal Rights: A Marxist Theory of International Law*. Leiden and Boston: Brill.
Mugler, J. 2019. 'Regulatory Capture? Fiscal Anthropological Insights into the Heart of Contemporary Statehood'. *The Journal of Legal Pluralism and Unofficial Law* 50(3): 379–95.
Parfitt, R. 2019. *The Process of International Legal Reproduction: Inequality, Historiography, Resistance*. Cambridge: Cambridge University Press.
Pistor, K. 2019. *The Code of Capital*. Princeton: Princeton University Press.

Pottage, A. 2004. 'Introduction: The Fabrication of Persons and Things'. In A. Pottage and M. Mundy, eds. *Law, Anthropology, and the Constitution of the Social: Making Persons and Things*, 1–39. Cambridge: Cambridge University Press.

Rajagopal, B. 2003. International Law from Below: Development, Social Movements and Third World Resistance. Cambridge: Cambridge University Press.

Randeria, S. 2003. 'Cunning States and Unaccountable International Institutions: Legal Plurality, Social Movements and Rights of Local Communities to Common Property Resources'. *European Journal of Sociology* 44(1): 27–60.

Randeria, S. 2007. 'De-politicization of Democracy and Judicialization of Politics'. *Theory, Culture and Society* 24(4): 39.

Raz, J., ed. 1990. *Authority*. Oxford: Oxford University Press.

Riles, A. 2000. *The Network Inside Out*. Ann Arbor: University of Michigan Press.

Riles, A. 2006. 'Anthropology, Human Rights, and Legal Knowledge: Culture in the Iron Cage', *American Anthropologist* 108(1): 52–65.

Rodriguez-Garavito, A. 2005. 'Nike's Law: The Anti-sweatshop Movement, Transnational Corporations, and the Struggle over International Labor Rights in the Americas'. In B. De Sousa Santos and C. Rodríguez-Garavito, eds., Law and Globalization from Below: Towards a Cosmopolitan Legality, 64–91. Cambridge: Cambridge University Press.

Rottenburg, R., S. Merry, S. Y. Park, and J. Mugler, eds. 2015. *A World of Indicators*. Cambridge: Cambridge University Press.

Santos, B. de S. and C. A. Rodríguez-Garavito, eds. 2005. *Law and Globalisation from Below: Towards a Cosmopolitan Legality*. Cambridge: Cambridge University Press.

Santos, B. de S. 2014. *Epistemologies of the South: Justice Against Epistemicide*. London and New York: Routledge.

Schiffauer, W. 2000. 'Zur Problematik ethnologischer Gutachten'. In G. Wolf, ed. *Kriminalität im Grenzgebiet Band 3: Ausländer vor deutschen Gerichten*, 93–119. Berlin: Springer.

Scholte, J. A. 2014. 'Civil Society and NGOs'. In Weis Wilkinson, eds. *International Organizations and Global Governance*, 322–34. London and New York: Routledge.

Sinclair, G. 2017. *Reforming the World*. Cambridge: Cambridge University Press.

Strathern, M. 1999. *Property, Substance and Effect: Anthropological Essays on Persons and Things*. London: Athlone.

Strathern, M. 2001. 'Cutting the Network'. *Journal of the Royal Anthropological Institute* 2: 517–35.

Tan, C. 2011. *Governance through Development: Poverty Reduction Strategies, International Law and the Disciplining of Third World States*. London and New York: Routledge.

Toop, J. 2017. 'Multilateral Environmental Agreements and Regional Fisheries Management Organisations'. In: H. Cullen, J. Harrington, and C. Renshaw, eds. *Experts, Networks and International Law*, 95–122. Cambridge: Cambridge University Press.

Venzke, I. 2013. '"Between Power and Persuasion: On International Institutions"' Authority in Making Law'. *Transnational Legal Theory* 4: 354.

Weil, P. 1983. 'Towards Relative Normativity in International Law?'. *American Journal of International Law* 77: 413–42.

Weiler, J. 2004. 'Geology of International Law'. *Heidelberg Journal of International Law* 64: 547–62.

Wiber, M. 2005. 'Titek'. In F. Benda-Beckmann, K. Benda-Beckmann, and A. Griffiths, eds. *Mobile People, Mobile Law: Expanding Legal Relations in a Contracting World*, 131–52. Aldershot: Ashgate.

Wilson, R. A. and J. P. Mitchell, eds. 2003. *Human Rights in Global Perspective: Anthropological Perspectives on Rights, Claims and Entitlements*. London: Routledge.
World Bank 1997. *World Development Report 1997: The State in a Changing World* (Washington, DC: The World Bank).
Zenker, O. 2016. 'Anthropology on Trial: Exploring the Laws of Anthropological Expertise'. *International Journal of Law in Context* 12: 293–311.
Zenker, O. and M. Hoehne 2018. *The State and the Paradox of Customary Law in Africa*. London: Routledge.
Zürn, M. 2018. *Theory of Global Governance*. Cambridge: Cambridge University Press.
Zumbansen, P. 2010. 'Transnational Legal Pluralism'. *Transnational Legal Theory* 1(2): 141–89.

CHAPTER 45

CRITIQUE OF PUNITIVE REASON

DIDIER FASSIN

WE live in a punitive age. Speaking of a 'punitive age' means two things. 'Punitive' refers to the fact that we punish more not because there is more crime, which would be logical, but because we have become more severe with crime. 'Age' suggests that this evolution is not a recent phenomenon but one inscribed in a span of several decades. This punitive age is a global fact, which affects almost all countries, although in different ways (Walmsley 2018). Over the past half century, the prison population has multiplied by eight in the United States and by two and a half in France. In the 1990s alone, it has tripled in the Czech Republic, doubled in Italy and the Netherlands, increased by one-half in Britain, Portugal, Greece, Poland, Slovakia, Serbia, and Russia, and expanded by one-third in Germany, Belgium, Spain, Slovenia, and Croatia. Exceptions to this European trend are found mostly in Scandinavian countries. At a global level, a similar tendency is observed. Since 2000, the prison population has almost tripled in South America, more than doubled in Southeast Asia, and almost doubled in Oceania. Only recently has it begun to decline in a few countries, most notably Germany, the Netherlands, Romania, Ukraine, Russia, Japan, and even the United States. But the penal demography is only one indicator, as one should also take into account individuals on parole and probation, whose number is often several times higher than that of prisoners.

Remarkably, this dramatic evolution has not corresponded to an upsurge in crime. With very few exceptions, there is no statistical correlation between crime and punishment. Contemporary societies have not become more severe because more offences were committed. The repressive turn results from two mechanisms: first, the criminalization of offences which were not criminalized in previous periods, for instance traffic violations in France; second, the increase in harshness in sanctions with longer sentences of imprisonment, in particular mandatory sentences such as the 'three strikes and you are out' laws in the United States. How, then, can one understand this global evolution, since it is not due to more criminality but to more severity? It is a complex phenomenon, mostly the conjunction of cultural and political factors. On the cultural side, it is a change in the sensibilities and sensitivities to disorders and deviances, with a growing intolerance of certain offences, especially when they are committed by people belonging to certain ethno-racial and socioeconomic groups. On the political side, there has been penal populism, as it is often designated: a manipulation of people's legitimate anxieties regarding their present and future, turning them into a fear of crime and of others. But underlying these cultural and political factors are concomitant social transformations and increasing economic disparities. Selective toughness towards certain segments of the population has been a common response to inequality, which was precisely affecting them the most, at the same time as welfare policies were becoming less generous. One could argue that the expansive penal state has thus been substituted for a declining social state.

This situation certainly calls for an urgent reconsideration of the way in which crime is punished. However, this urgency should not lead to a hasty analysis. What is needed, on the contrary, is an in-depth inquiry (Fassin 2018). What is punishment? Why do we punish? Who gets punished? Here are the three questions that must be addressed to examine afresh the definition, justification, and distribution of punishment. This requires that we challenge some of the foundational philosophical and legal assumptions regarding punishment. While they are certainly not irrelevant, these valuable theories analyse the world in general and punishment in particular only as they ought to be. Conversely, social scientists try to depict them as they actually are.

Adopting this perspective, I engage philosophers' and jurists' theories on the basis of empirical material that I have gathered between 2005 and 2013 through three ethnographies conducted in France. The first study focused on the largest French police district, where during fifteen months I accompanied police patrols, especially anti-crime squads, in disadvantaged neighbourhoods; the two most important recent urban disorders took place during that period (Fassin 2013). The second study consisted in the observation of a series of French immediate appearance hearings for petty criminals caught red-handed (Fassin et al. 2015). The third study concerned a French short-stay prison, where I was given full access to wards and cells day and night over a period of four years; I could thus meet freely with guards and inmates, directors and chaplains, judges and social workers, attend disciplinary boards, parole commissions, religious celebrations, workshop activities, and military interventions (Fassin 2017). In the following pages, I will successively question the definition, justifications, and distribution of punishment.

A BOUNDING DEFINITION

Let us start with an apparently simple question: what is punishment? The most widely accepted definition, that of the Oxford philosopher and jurist H. L. A. Hart (1959), provides five decisive criteria: (1) the infliction of a pain or of an unpleasant equivalent (2) to an actual or supposed offender (3) in response to an offence against legal rules (4) that is intentionally imposed by a legal authority and (5) administered by human beings with appropriate roles. I want to challenge this definition on two counts: first, it purposely ignores non-legitimate and extra-legal expressions of punishment; second, it questionably takes for granted the centrality of suffering in the administration of punishment. I will develop each of these points; but to be fair to Hart's conception of punishment, it should be added that he himself cautioned his readers not to use these five criteria as a 'definitional stop' that would serve to elude a more radical critique of forms of punishment—a critique that would exceed this determined framework.

Indeed, the definition corresponds to a particular situation: a judge deciding in court the sentence to be given to an offender as a retribution for his offence, which is thus established and punished under the law. It represents the official version of punishment as legally grounded and legitimately imposed. This is certainly a common configuration—although one could argue that, in the United States, the generalization of the guilty plea leads more often to the sentencing without trial of a supposed rather than actual offender. But this configuration is far from being the most frequent.

In particular, there is an institution that does not include punishment among its missions but that punishes routinely and extensively: it is the police. In quantitative terms, their sanctions are much more numerous than those of the justice system. As an example, in France in 2009 there were 135,000 arrests for use of marijuana but only 9,000 prison sentences, twenty times fewer (Obradovic 2012). And to use an even more striking illustration, in the United States, the number of individuals killed by the police is forty times higher than the number of persons executed as a result of a legal process (Karabel 2014). While patrolling with anti-crime brigades in the outskirts of Paris, I realized that policing was the most ordinary mode of punishment experienced by many individuals, especially those from ethno-racial minorities belonging to the working class and living in disadvantaged neighbourhoods. It took multiple forms: harassment through stop and frisk; bullying via insults and threats; humiliation by offensive comments and public handcuffing; gratuitous arrests and being taken into custody; physical brutality and moral violence. Perhaps even more remarkably, it involved presumed offenders as well as mere bystanders, that is, possible culprits as well as obviously innocent people, in good part on the sole basis of who they were rather than what they had done. It was not necessary that the persons punished be guilty of any specific violation of the law: their culpability was assumed on their appearance and residence.

The following scene can serve as an illustration. Three adolescents are messing around joyously in a small square near the hostel of the youth protection service where they stay. Like the other minors residing in the three-floor classic house, they have been placed in this institution by a juvenile judge either because they have committed a misdemeanour or because they are deemed endangered. The three teenagers are of African origin. Two police officers on patrol stop by and ask for their papers. Such a check is banal albeit illegal, since there is no indication of an offence being or having been committed and since it is moreover established that such a stop is often based on racial profiling. The adolescents present their travel passes, normally regarded as sufficient. Not satisfied, the agents demand their identification cards. The adolescents, who do not have the documents with them, explain that they live in the hostel some fifty yards down the street and propose that the officers accompany them to fetch these documents. The police ruthlessly refuse and threaten to take them to the precinct for further verification. Panicked at the prospect of being taken in, one of the teenagers escapes, runs to his lodging, takes the requested card, and swiftly returns to prove his good faith. But the reception is not what he expects. The officers scold him harshly, using racist slurs while slapping him. Alerted by the shouting, one of the social workers in charge of the youth comes out of the hostel, only to hear one of the agents threaten the boy, saying, 'I'm going to kneecap you!', and yell at him, with reference to his being in the youth protection service: 'You, little faggot! You're a failure in your family! You're a failure at school!' Not without difficulty, the social worker interposes herself and finally brings the adolescent back to the hostel. There, with the director, she tries to convince the young man to file a complaint against the agent, telling him that it is important to defend his rights. Still shaken and distressed the teenager keeps repeating in a low voice that it does not matter. Obviously, he knows how little the word of a black minor under the care of a youth protection service would weigh in justice in front of the word of two sworn-in officers, and how easily his complaint could be reversed into a case against him for resisting arrest.

In this scene, the combination of hostility and racism, which is common among the police operating in low-income neighbourhoods, takes a moral resonance: being under the supervision of the judicial institution, the teenagers have already had dealings with the penal system, either as delinquents or as victims or, more often than not, as both. From the viewpoint of the officers, it is legitimate to punish them because of what they think they are. Hence the hassle about the documents, the threat of arrest, the hurtful words, the slaps. More generally, the police justify such acts in two complementary ways. First, they are suspicious of residents of housing projects and more broadly of people belonging to ethno-racial minorities, especially the youth. They view them as delinquents or accomplices, and in their view, even if they are not guilty this time, they have been or will be. Second, they consider judges to be too lenient and constantly repeat that they arrest criminals who are released the next day. Yet statistics show, on the contrary, the increasing severity of the justice system. It is on these purported moral grounds that the police feel entitled to punish in the street those whom they see as potential culprits and who may not get their just deserts in court. These sanctions can take two forms: punitive expeditions, in which the whole group is mishandled, as when officers rush into a neighbourhood in search of a criminal; and random punishments, in which one in the group is arbitrarily spotted, thumped, and arrested, usually the slowest runner or a mere bystander. There is more than retribution in these acts directed, most of the time, at young Arab or black men living in housing projects that police officers designate as a 'jungle' and whose residents they depict as 'savages'. Indeed, these acts also serve to inculcate a social order, as these youths are learning, through the repetition of similar experiences, that they are what John Alan Lee (1981) calls 'police property', by which he means that society delegates to its law enforcement units rather than to its welfare services the management of these populations.

Returning to the initial definition of punishment, it is clear that the police have no legal authority to punish but do punish illegitimately as well as illegally, using ethno-racial profiling for stop and frisk or unjustified and disproportionate physical force for arrests. Moreover, their actions target individuals who are at most suspect and frequently not even that, but who simply belong to stigmatized and dominated categories. They often do not even have the pretext of an offence having been committed. In other words, most of the criteria defining punishment in the philosophical and legal tradition are absent from the actual practices of punishing by law enforcement agents. Although I focused on the police, I could have analysed in the same way other institutions, such as border protection, correction facilities, or the army, and described similar practices, moreover in multiple national contexts. Of the definition, only one criterion seems to pass the empirical test: the infliction of pain as retribution.

The centrality of suffering

That punishment would in the last instance be reduced to the imposition of suffering is probably the least questioned fact about punishment among theorists as well as laypersons. But why would an equivalence be established between committing an offence and inflicting pain? Because we find this equivalence so self-evident, we elude two crucial facts: that far from being universal, this centrality of pain is temporally and spatially circumscribed; and that far from being accidental, it is telling of profound truths rarely acknowledged about our society.

First, punishment has not always and everywhere corresponded to the infliction of pain. In most societies, the commission of a reprehensible action has long called for a collective response in terms of compensation. Etymologically, according to Émile Benveniste (2016), Greek *poinē* and Classical Latin *poena*, from which the word 'punishment' stems, referred to the debt that had to be paid to atone for the crime; only in Late Latin did the connotation of torment appear, which remains explicitly present in the word 'pain'. Similarly, Latin *retribuere*, from which the noun 'retribution' is derived, meant to 'give in exchange' and 'to restitute what is owed', whether this implied recompense or penalty. Interestingly, at the time of the Renaissance, English 'retribution' came to have the negative sense of punishment for a wrong, whereas French '*rétribution*' took the positive meaning of fair salary rewarding work.

Beyond this philological analysis, historical findings from ancient worlds as well as ethnological accounts from pre-colonial societies also attest to the generalized practice of redress in response to an offence. Thus, Georg Simmel (1978) has shown that *wergild* represented the sum required as reparation for a crime in medieval Anglo-Saxon England, with a differentiation of the amount according to the status of the victim, and Leopold Pospisil (1981) has described how the Kapauku of Papua New Guinea practised a form of repayment for the damage done to one of them as compensation. In both cases, it was not the individual who was held responsible but his family or his clan which had to repair the offence. Various similar examples have been reported by historians and ethnologists.

How did this practice come to be replaced by the infliction of pain, according to these authors? In the Western world, it is Christianity at the end of the Middle Ages that substituted Roman law, based on fault and sin, for Germanic law, grounded on repayment. In so-called traditional societies, colonial powers in the Modern Era imposed penal codes and correctional facilities. In both cases, the moral economy of punishment was radically transformed from a dominant logic of exchange into a dominant logic of suffering. In response to the crime committed, the pain inflicted on the offender replaced the debt owed to the offended or his relatives; and, whereas the payment of the debt previously involved a collective obligation for the family or the clan, the infliction of pain henceforth signified the individual liability of the culprit.

Second, the fact that punishment amounts to the imposition of suffering also suggests more troubling truths. Indeed, the act of punishing is always in excess of what it is supposed to be. One can call this excess cruelty, the accursed share of punishment to paraphrase Georges Bataille (1991). But why would that be? Why would police officers purposely put handcuffs incorrectly on a suspect they have arrested so as to painfully twist his arms and risk nerve compressions and paralysis? And why would they make fun of his complaint while taking him into the precinct for questioning? Why should the judge humiliate the defendant with hurtful remarks and embarrassing lectures before sending them to jail, to the point that when I met one of them later in his prison cell, he told me that in court he could not wait for the end of the trial even when he knew this meant his incarceration? Why would a guard refuse a shower to one inmate, while demonstratively letting another inmate take one as they return from the yard where they have played sports? I intentionally use these mundane examples drawn from my observations over the past twelve years, but there are more tragic cases.

In a Florida prison, a fifty-year-old inmate suffering from schizophrenia and sentenced for cocaine possession was punished for having defecated in his cell and refused to clean it. The sanction, called 'the shower treatment' by the guards of the mental health unit, was commonly used with recalcitrant prisoners. The man was locked under a scalding shower and was left shut up screaming for help for more than one hour—until he died. According to witnesses, when his body was carried away, it was so burned that his skin had shrivelled from it. In spite of numerous testimonies by former employees, there was no administrative sanction, no judicial sentence. At some point, an inquiry having demonstrated the banality of such practices, the senior investigators who had made the report were sidelined by their superiors. It took three years for the coroner to publish his conclusions. In his view, the death was accidental: the prisoner had slipped on the floor and hurt himself.

In the assimilation of punishment with suffering and, even more, in the unnecessary torment that is added to it, one cannot not recognize the expression of bare cruelty, what Friedrich Nietzsche (1989) calls the pleasure of inflicting suffering. Such ruthlessness is not, as is often argued, restricted to outliers: pitiless officers, cynical judges, or sadistic guards—although I have encountered such cases in my research. It is not the exception:

it is part and parcel of retribution. In a famous article, Everett Hughes (1962) has argued that society delegates to certain institutions and professions its 'dirty work', in particular that of punishing criminals with the implicit permission to exceed the moral and legal limits of punishment. Thus, during my fieldwork I came to realize that a prison sentence is never only a deprivation of liberty; it is also a deprivation of autonomy, of privacy, of affective and sexual life, of the right to decide about personal things and ordinary events; and ultimately, in most cases, for lack of work, education, and rehabilitation, it is a deprivation of the very meaning of the sentence. The culmination of cruelty is solitary confinement. A punishment within the punishment, solitary confinement is an unbounded torment added to the normal infliction of pain, a form of social and physical death, which affects on any given day in the United States 80,000 inmates, some of them staying there for years and even decades, the record being more than forty years.

Even when it is much more limited, as in Europe, solitary confinement can have dire consequences. At the end of my research in prison, a young man who had been sentenced to a short penalty for a petty crime, and who suffered from mental health issues, was placed in solitary confinement following an altercation with another inmate. According to the account I received from various staff members, shortly after his transfer in the disciplinary unit, in a gesture of despair that resembled many others that I had witnessed or heard of, he set fire to his mattress. His neighbours called to the guard present at the time for help. The officer rushed over, opened the first door, but since he did not have the second key to the grille, he was unable to pull the young man out and save him from the flames. With the inmate crying out in fear and pain, the guard ran back to ask for assistance. When the lieutenant arrived in the disciplinary unit with the key, he found the inmate unconscious, with 80 per cent second- and third-degree burns. The young man was hospitalized in a resuscitation unit. Unfortunately, he did not survive his severe burns. Ironically, a few days before his demise, in light of his circumstances, the judge had formally ordered his release. The young man had died free. His prison sentence had been for a banal misdemeanour.

THE ABUNDANCE OF JUSTIFICATIONS

To have such severe responses to offences committed, society needs justifications. According to John Rawls (1955), there is agreement on the fact that punishment is justified but a disagreement on how it is so. In fact, two theories of justification prevail.

For utilitarians, only the consequences that punishment can have from the point of view of society should be taken into account. In Jeremy Bentham's words (1996: 170), 'all punishment in itself is bad' since it causes suffering, and 'it ought to be allowed only insofar as it promises to exclude some greater evil', namely a decrease in criminality. This can happen as a result of three processes: incapacitation, deterrence, and rehabilitation. Incapacitation can be transitory, or it can be definitive, via executions or life sentences without parole. Deterrence corresponds to the dissuasion of future offences, both by the perpetrator and by others. Rehabilitation concerns the moral reform and the social re-integration of the offender.

For retributivists, only the act that has been committed should be taken into account. The classical argument against utilitarianism was developed by Immanuel Kant (1887: 194): 'Juridical punishment can never be administered merely as means for promoting another good, either with regard to the criminal himself or to civil society, but must in all cases be imposed only because the individual on whom it is inflicted has committed a crime'. A right to retaliation is based on a principle of strict equality between the crime and the punishment.

Much has been written about utilitarianism and retributivism, on theoretical grounds, to refine or criticize these justifications, and on empirical grounds, to analyse their merit. I could myself weigh in on the utilitarian argument with regard to its supposed efficacy. Many studies conducted in several countries show that, far from being a deterrent, incarceration, at least for minor and non-violent crimes, tends to increase recidivism, and that, for lack of rehabilitation programmes in correction facilities, it would be more correct to speak of de-socialization. We are therefore left with incapacitation, which only works in its extreme forms. I could also discuss the retributivist argument with regard to its principle of equality, wondering whether fourteen years or more in prison is a reasonable equivalent to producing or selling marijuana—when these practices are authorized in various states and countries. But rather than assessing these theories on their own terms, I prefer to question the fact that people or institutions that punish actually use these justifications. My point is that, in the real world, punishment is often justified neither by utilitarian arguments nor by retributivist ones. There are many more obscure and largely unacknowledged reasons why one punishes.

Thus, one day, an inmate is brought into the cramped room adjacent to the solitary confinement unit where disciplinary board hearings take place. Behind a small wooden podium, the sinister-looking man faces the three persons who will judge him: a deputy warden, a correctional officer, and a civil society volunteer. He is accused of racial slurs against a black guard as he was returning from the yard several weeks before. Normally, in such a case, the complaint of the officer is detailed and the report of an investigation conducted by a superior is appended. This time, the only evidence is the statement of the correctional officer, whose name is not even revealed to the prisoner. There is no witness, no specifics, no inquiry. Knowing neither his accuser's identity nor the circumstances of the alleged offence, the inmate seems disconcerted: 'Don't even know who the guy is', he mutters. Perhaps by excess of confidence, he has not requested a lawyer. During the deliberation, a trainee correction lieutenant comments to me that, in the facility where he has been working as guard for ten years, they would never have taken a decision on such a vague accusation. Yet, when the prisoner is brought back into the room, he is told that he is sentenced to seven days of solitary confinement. In an irrepressible act of rage, he punches and breaks the podium behind which he stands. Three guards, who were waiting outside rush into the room, pin him against the wall and handcuff him. While he loudly protests against the unfairness of the decision, they take him to his punitive cell. Another warden later explains to me that, even if they do not believe in the veracity of the guards' version, they cannot afford to appear to disown them. 'He who says that we decide on the sole basis of facts and inmate's profile does not tell the truth.' Commenting on the context of recent tensions in the prison, she adds that punishing prisoners, even when it is obvious that they responded to provocations by an officer, serves to satisfy and appease the personnel: 'It avoids the guards taking revenge on the prisoners', she straightforwardly admits.

In this scene, the deputy warden who chairs the hearing knows that, despite the absence of evidence presented to the disciplinary board, the fact that it is an accusation of verbal abuse against a guard renders a sanction necessary. He anticipates that officers and inmates will scrutinize the judgment. An adjournment of the case for lack of established proof and an investigation report or, worse, a clement verdict would be regarded on both sides as an implicit condemnation of the personnel. The prisoners would regard it as a victory and the news would soon be disseminated through the entire facility. The guards would interpret it as an absence of support from their institution and their unions would probably express their anger. Here, the sanction of solitary confinement serves to maintain the order in the prison at the cost of justice. No one is fooled: even the guards tell me in private that it was no surprise to them that this colleague would have been insulted or assaulted, considering how he bullied prisoners, but this would not have prevented them from protesting had the provoked inmate not been punished. One cannot deem the sanction justified on utilitarian grounds, as such decisions generate indignation among inmates and animosity towards the personnel, therefore aggravating the risk of incidents. Nor can one invoke retributivism, since the culpability of the prisoner is not even established. As is often the case, actual justifications do not fit the normative framework, and pragmatic theory seems more adapted. In concrete situations, punishment corresponds to practical considerations rather than theoretical arguments. And these considerations can be of many sorts, such as inspiring fear, imposing order, indulging victims, or pleasing the people.

An unequal distribution

How can we then understand that punishment escapes its official definition and exceeds its determined limits, that extra-legal and non-legitimate retribution is normalized, that suffering is imposed with little restraint, and finally that its actual justifications often differ from what they should be? To answer this question, we have to take into account a dimension that has not received the attention it merits in classical theory: the distribution of punishment. For philosophers and jurists, there is in fact not much to discuss. Punishment should be just, in the sense of adapted to the offence, and fair, in the sense of the same for all in response to a given violation of the law. If it is unjust or unfair, it involves simply a failure to apply these principles satisfactorily. But social scientists acknowledge that such failures are not randomly distributed, and they want to understand the underlying logics. Indeed, it is because certain individuals and groups are more easily targeted that, for them, such exceptions can become the rule, that policing can be an ordinary mode of punishing, that the infliction of excessive pain can seem acceptable, and that retribution can be imposed to maintain a social order rather than simply as a way to decrease crime rates or dispense just deserts.

Convicts are perfectly aware of these logics. One afternoon I had a conversation with a twenty-eight-year old French inmate of Moroccan origin in his cell. Residing in a housing project with his wife and child, he had worked under multiple short-term contracts until he was arrested for possession and resale of marijuana. Although it was his first conviction, he was sentenced to three years in prison. With a disillusioned smile, he told me that he felt 'the injustice of justice'. He admitted that he had committed an offence and accepted being punished for it, but he was indignant about the disparities in the retribution of crime: 'I was dealing pot. I'm not saying it's not wrong, but it's only marijuana. I never hurt anybody. I never stole from anyone. I never even shoplifted. I pay my tax and my fines.' He added with bitterness: 'So, when I see Sarkozy profiting from the riches of a senile old woman or Cahuzac and the millions he owes in taxes ... and they're free!' He was referring to the conservative former French President, who was accused among other crimes of having received clandestine donations from a billionaire suffering from dementia, and to the former Socialist minister of finance, who had to resign following revelations about his secret bank accounts in Switzerland and Singapore. As a result of long procedures and negotiations, the former had managed to avoid prosecution twelve years after the investigation began, and the latter had been given a lenient sentence. Despite the gravity of their crimes and of the damage caused, neither of them had spent one night in prison.

The inmate's observations were validated by official statistics, since in the course of the 2000s, sentences for drug offences have doubled and those for mere use of marijuana more than tripled, whereas sentences for financial crime have decreased by one-fifth (Timbart 2011). Was it due to variations in the frequency of these offences? In the first case, epidemiological studies showed no change in drug consumption: the increase was essentially due to more aggressive repression against users. In the second case, police statistics showed a doubling of the number of offences: the decline was mostly explained by an official policy of de-penalization of the economic world, with cases being negotiated rather than sanctioned. In the end, the man who expressed his bitterness in his cell proved to have a good sociological intuition, rediscovering the famous definition of crime and punishment by Émile Durkheim (1984: 31), according to whom one is not sentenced because one is guilty, but one is guilty because one is sentenced. In fact, this man even went further with this observation, unwittingly adding a touch of Marx's theory, as he compared his fate with that of influential politicians, therefore implying that the penal system was treating individuals differently depending on their social class.

Indeed, in the short-stay prison where I conducted my ethnography, I calculated (conscious that such a survey was illegal in France since it included ethno-racial variables) that black and Arab men, most of them being French citizens, represented two-thirds of the inmates, half of whom were declared to be unemployed. In the United States, these inequalities are even more extreme, as 58 per cent of young black school drop-outs will have been in prison before reaching the age of 35, while this is the case for less than 3 per cent of white youths.

The distribution of punishment across society is, however, obscured by the fact that the differentiation of offenders appears to be a mere differentiation of offences. It is not that black and Arab men are more harshly punished, the champions of law and order policies contend, it is that they commit more crimes deemed punishable. Undoubtedly, the question: Who is punished? is strictly linked to another: What gets punished? Not all offences are sanctioned in the same way. Today, in France, tax evasion is better tolerated socially than shoplifting, and in the United States, financial crime is settled through negotiations leading to fines for the company, whereas petty crime is settled through plea-bargaining leading to prison sentences for the defendant. The explicit differentiation of crime is itself conditioned in large part by an implicit differentiation of populations in terms of their punishability, which has to do not only with the moral evaluation of perpetrators but also with the undesirability of certain social categories. Ethno-racial minorities, immigrants, and the poor are thus definitely more punishable a priori, whereas the powerful and the wealthy are spared, even when their crime has more serious consequences and no mitigating circumstances. In the end, the crucial question is not: What do we want to punish? But: Whom do we want to punish—or spare?

Such differentiation is particularly perceptible in court. In one of the immediate appearance trials I attended, a nineteen-year-old man is charged for 'having violently resisted' three police officers during a stop and frisk and for 'having insulted them via words, gestures and menaces' while in custody at the precinct. A French citizen born from Senegalese parents, he lives in a city where two-thirds of young people are from non-European origin, one-third of households live under the poverty threshold, and one youth in four is unemployed. The accused resides with his mother, who raises her five children alone, in one of the three projects administratively classified as 'sensitive urban zones' due to a combination of unfavourable social indicators. He has dropped out of high school, begun a vocational degree, and unsuccessfully gone on the job market. His criminal record already contains five summonses, including one other accusation of insulting the police and resisting arrest, which makes him the ideal usual suspect. As his mother later explains to me, he is constantly harassed by law enforcement agents, who stop and frisk him without reason, and he has recently been arrested and kept in custody on two occasions for offences that were subsequently discovered to have been committed by others. During the trial, obviously shaken by his stay in the police cell and ill at ease in court, but not wanting to lose face, the young man answers awkwardly and abruptly the questions of the judge, who expresses her exasperation. The earlier encounter with the state-appointed lawyer did not go well, and the speech for the defence lacks conviction. After a brief deliberation, the judge announces that, one of the officers being absent at the trial for not having been summoned on time, the trial is adjourned, but in the interval the accused must be held in remand for lack of guarantee that he will not reiterate his offence and that he will appear in court in due time. As his mother begs for his release until the lawsuit, the judge dismisses her with irritation. The young man is handcuffed and taken to the local jail, while the officers leave the room, visibly satisfied.

To apprehend thoroughly this case, one should take into account the social conditions rendering his criminal history possible. These can be analysed at a dual level: structural (living in a difficult neighbourhood) and circumstantial (interacting with the police), the two being closely linked in his everyday experience. On the one hand, the offences of which the suspect has been guilty in the past, notably the thefts, are offences facilitated by the social environment where he grew up, with its economic precarity, the lack of professional prospects, the existence of unlawful opportunities, and the access to criminal networks. To put it bluntly, depredation is to low-income classes what tax evasion is to the wealthy or fraud and embezzlement to the corporate world. But society is evidently much less tolerant towards the former than towards the latter. On the other hand, the accusation that brings the young man before a judge this time is an alleged offence during a stop and frisk. But as has been established, these are not distributed at random. Law enforcement agents target certain territories and certain populations, and this focus has less to do with the incidence of crime than with logics of control which are not imaginable in other places and with other individuals. Moreover, it is well known among the police themselves that the offence of insulting an officer and resisting arrest is less a sign of their public's aggressiveness than of the agents' confrontational attitude. Thus, in this case, structural factors enlighten past illicit activity as much as circumstantial elements illuminate the present accusation.

Yet, most of the time, the justice system ignores these conditions, and Aaron Cicourel (1967) has shown that the way in which judges perceive them often works against the accused belonging to low-income classes, in particular because the defendants are not in possession of the social codes of the judicial world, as analysed by Marc Galanter (1974). In the present case, both elements—the judge's negative perception and the defendant's ill-adapted attitude—are combined. First, the social representation that the judge has of the young man's milieu increases her suspicion: the image of the housing project so remote from her own world supports the criminal record and the current offence rather than rendering them intelligible. Second, the social competences that the young man is able to mobilize in court are completely at odds with the norms and expectations of the judge: by his attitude he antagonizes her but also lets her think that he probably behaved in the same way with the police when he was arrested. In fact, social factors, far from serving as 'sociological excuses', as politicians tend to argue to discredit social scientists, are, in the justice system, almost systematically unfavourable to the defendants.

This logic becomes even more obvious if we contrast this case with another one, heard on the same day. Minutes later, a student accused of having abused and raped his partner appears before the court. The facts seem to have been easily established as, first, a physician has certified the genital wounds caused by the penetration and which gave the young woman a six-day temporary disability and, second, a previous assault has led her to the emergency room due to the fracture of a finger bone for which she has nevertheless not filed a complaint. The middle-class student, of French origin, lives in a residential town. He expresses himself well, adopts a humble posture, admits having been violent, but denies the sexual abuse, manifests his regrets and promises to mend his ways. The judge, whose son, also a student, attends the hearing with two friends, seems less impatient than in the previous case. The lawyer, who is remunerated by the young man's parents, is unusually verbose in her defence. The hearing lasts twice as long as the average in immediate appearance trials. When the verdict, a six-month suspended prison sentence, is publicly delivered, the student's family loudly celebrates, while the victim, alone on her bench, looks completely overwhelmed.

Thus, whereas the young black man from a disadvantaged environment, accused of having talked back to the police and hindered his arrest as he was once more subjected to an unjustified stop and frisk, is sent to jail, the white middle-class student, accused of repeated physical abuse and rape, goes back home with his parents. Under the French law, individuals convicted of sexual violence incur a five-year prison sentence, extended to fifteen years if a rape has been committed and even more if it has caused wounds, as in the present case. The difference of treatment between the two cases is not so difficult to comprehend when taking into account the distance between the social worlds of the two defendants and the disparity of their social competences in court. Both elements lead the judge to feel animosity against one while showing leniency towards the other, and both weigh in the end on the assessment of the offence as well as the estimation of the risk of recidivism. The objectivation of the decision in legal language allows the judge to elude the subjective aspect of social affinities. For having had various conversations with her, I know that she was sincerely convinced, in this case as in the many others I have attended, that she had ruled with impartiality and for the common good.

But let us make no mistake. This disparity in the treatment of offences occurs not only in court. As is epitomized by the United States, it is the whole chain of the penal system that produces it: the formulation of problems in the public sphere (think of the 'superpredator'); their translation into law (think of the Anti-Drug Abuse Act of 1986 which imposed the same penalty for the possession of an amount of crack cocaine 100 times smaller than that of powder cocaine); their management by the police (think of the selective stop and frisk which, according to one study (ACLU 2013), leads to black people being 3.73 times more likely than white people to be arrested for marijuana possession, despite having the same percentage of users); and finally the judges' decision (think of the 20 per cent longer prison sentences for black offenders compared with white offenders for the same crime, according to an official report [USSC 2017], even when controlling for various factors such as the history of past violence). In other words, the issue of unequal punishment concerns the entire repressive system, and it is widely believed that the current wave of sentencing reforms regarding drugs in the United States is motivated in part by the fact that the current opioid epidemic overwhelmingly affects white people.

To offer a general interpretation of this phenomenon, should we not suppose, then, with Michel Foucault (1979: 272) that 'the prison, and no doubt punishment in general, is not intended to eliminate offenses, but rather to distinguish them, to distribute them, to use them; that it is not so much that they render docile those who are liable to transgress the law, but that they tend to assimilate the transgression of the laws in the general tactics of subjection?' The prime objective of punishment may indeed not be to reduce crime, but to differentiate which legal offences (misdemeanour rather than financial crime) and which social categories (racial minority of low-income class rather than white middle-class) should be punished while others should be spared. In distributing punishment in this unequal manner, society does not only punish offenders. It also punishes their partners and children, and by extension, in disadvantaged neighbourhoods with high rates of incarcerated men, their community. When one therefore considers how the punitive system harshly and unequally affects poor families, it is easy to understand how it plays a major role in the production and reproduction of social disparities.

Conclusion

The critical approach I have developed in this chapter has proceeded in two steps. First, the confrontation of the norm with its implementation revealed the discrepancies between the two: punishment exceeds its definition; its extra-legal use is trivialized; its justifications are problematic; its social distribution is unfair; and its equivalence with the infliction of pain has not always existed. Second, the interpretation of these discrepancies unveils its logics: the determination of punishable populations has as its counterpart the impunity of others, both processes being made opaque via an apparently neutral hierarchy of crime. Punishable populations correspond to undesirable social categories both economically and ethno-racially, whose alleged unworthiness renders possible their mistreatment by the repressive institutions; and punishment is therefore better understood not simply in terms of justice but in terms of unequal allocation of power relations and social resources. In the end, it becomes clear that punishment is not what it is said to be. Both common sense and theoretical discourses tend to represent it in a way that legitimizes it as an institution that is necessary for the common good and the social fabric. Empirical studies, in particular statistics, do not confirm this representation. Punishment, as it is practised in most contemporary societies, contributes to the de-socialization of individuals and destructuring of families in the short term, increases recidivism and illegal activity in the medium term, and generates inequality and insecurity in the long term. Punishment is generally viewed as a response and even a solution to crime. What characterizes the current punitive moment is that it is punishment that has become the problem.

Acknowledgement

The author's 2018 publication *The Will to Punish* served as a theoretical basis for this chapter, and the case studies were drawn from two of the author's other works: *Enforcing Order* (2011) and *Prison Worlds* (2017).

References

ACLU. 2013. *The War on Marijuana in Black and White*. New York: American Civil Liberties Union.

Bataille, G. 1991. *The Accursed Share: An Essay on General Economy* (trans. R. Hurley). New York: Zone Books. 1st French edition 1949.
Bentham, J. 1996. *An Introduction to the Principles of Morals and Legislation*. J. H. Burns and H. L. A. Hart, eds. Oxford: Clarendon Press. 1st English edition 1780.
Benveniste, É. 2016. *Dictionary of Indo-European Concepts and Society*. Chicago: Hau Books. 1st French edition 1969.
Cicourel, A. 1967. *The Social Organization of Juvenile Justice*. New York: Wiley.
Durkheim, É. 1984. *The Division of Labor in Society* (trans. L. Coser). New York: The Free Press, 1st French edition 1893.
Fassin, D. 2013. *Enforcing Order. An Ethnography of Urban Policing* (trans. R. Gomme). Cambridge: Polity Press. 1st French edition 2011.
Fassin, D. 2017. *Prison Worlds. An Ethnography of the Carceral Condition* (trans. R. Gomme). Cambridge: Polity Press. 1st French edition 2015.
Fassin, D. 2018. *The Will to Punish*. Oxford: Oxford University Press, 1st French edition 2016.
Fassin, D. et al. 2015. *At the Heart of the State. The Moral World of Institutions* (trans. P. Brown and D. Fassin). London: Pluto Press. 1st French edition 2013.
Foucault, M. 1979. *Discipline and Punish. The Birth of the Prison* (trans. A. Sheridan). New York: Pantheon Books. 1st French edition 1975.
Galanter, M. 1974. 'Why the "Haves" Come Out Ahead: Speculations on the Limits of Legal Change'. *Law and Society Review* 9(1): 95–160.
Hart, H. L. A. 1959. 'The Presidential Address: Prolegomenon to the Principles of Punishment'. *Proceedings of the Aristotelian Society* 60: 1–26.
Hughes, E. 1962. 'Good People and Dirty Work'. *Social Problems* 10(1): 3–11.
Kant, I. 1887. *The Philosophy of Law. An Exposition of the Fundamental Principles of Jurisprudence and the Science of Right* (trans. W. Hastie). Edinburgh: T. & T. Clark. 1st German edition 1797.
Karabel, J. 2014. 'The Other Capital Punishment'. *Huffpost Politics*, 10 December.
Lee, J. A. 1981. 'Some Structural Aspects of Police Deviance in Relation to Minority Groups'. In C. Shearing, ed, *Organizational Police Deviance. Its Structure and Control*, 49–82. Scarborough: Butterworth.
Nietzsche, F. 1989. *On the Genealogy of Morals* (trans. W. Kaufman). New York: Vintage Books. 1st German edition 1887.
Obradovic, I. 2012. 'La pénalisation de l'usage des stupéfiants en France au miroir des statistiques administratives. Enjeux et controverses'. *Déviance et Société*, 36(4): 441–69.
Pospisil, L. 1981. 'Modern and Traditional Administration of Justice in New Guinea'. *Journal of Legal Pluralism* 19: 93–116.
Rawls, J. 1955. 'Two Concepts of Rules'. *The Philosophical Review* 64(1): 3–32.
Simmel, G. 1978. *The Philosophy of Money* (trans. T. Bottomore and D. Frisby). London: Routledge & Kegan Paul. 1st German edition 1907.
Timbart, O. 2011. 'Vingt ans de condamnations pour crimes et délits', *Infostat Justice*, 114.
USSC. 2017. *Demographic Differences in Sentencing. An Update of the 2012 Booker Report*. Washington, DC: United States Sentencing Commission.
Walmsley, R. 2018. *World Population List*. London: World Prison Brief & Institute for Criminal Policy Research.

CHAPTER 46

GLOBAL LEGAL INSTITUTIONS

MARIA SAPIGNOLI AND RONALD NIEZEN

Global legal institutions in a new world order

It is difficult to have a conversation about institutions like the United Nations (UN), the World Bank, or the International Criminal Court (ICC) without eventually confronting image problems that follow from their structural failings. Critics often see the UN, for example, as a uniform entity and accuse it of being costly and wasteful, its upper echelons occupied by bureaucrats with inflated salaries. Despite its successful interventions in famine, health crises, armed conflict, and world heritage protection, its most significant failures have marked it with indelible stains in public consciousness: UN peacekeepers stood by helplessly during the 1994 genocide in Rwanda, brought cholera to Haiti in 2010, and committed rampant sexual abuse in the Congo. And the civil wars in Iraq, Syria, the former Yugoslavia, and Yemen certainly do not stand out as shining examples of the UN's powers of peace-making. The UN seems unable to give meaningful voice to the world's most marginalized, and the ICC (operating through a Relationship Agreement with the UN) has been largely ineffectual in bringing blatantly criminal—and often state-sanctioned—actors to justice.

Despite such failings and frailties, a key quality of global legal institutions is their ambitions towards the betterment of humanity. Even those organizations commonly characterized as 'regional' share this universal vision. The preamble of the Constitutive Act of the African Union, for example, declares a commitment to human rights and a determination to take up the challenges facing the continent and its peoples 'in the light of the social, economic and political changes taking place in the world',[1] while the Charter of Fundamental Rights of the European Union opens by declaring the body's commitment to 'the indivisible, universal values of human dignity, freedom, equality and solidarity' and the equally universal 'principles of democracy and the rule of law'.[2] This sweeping ambition is at the centre of our understanding of global legal institutions. They are state-centric, bureaucratically hierarchical organizations with legal functions of one kind or another built into their mandates. Even if they are structured as regional bodies in their mandates, their inspiration and moral orientation are universal.

While sharing commitments to universal principles of justice, peace, and the promotion of human rights, global legal organizations vary widely in their structures and powers, above all in the ways that their member states are able (or not) to further their particular interests while adhering to (or flouting with impunity) the rules of the organization. Their widely varying missions have great influence on the extent to which states collaborate or engage in the power struggles that emerge when a great deal is at stake. The Food and Agriculture Organization (FAO) or the United Nations Development Program (UNDP), for example, do not have nearly the same powers as the Security Council (UNSC); nor do they host the same kinds of intrigues and exclusivities (they have their own, to be sure, but without the same gravitas), even though they are all formally part of the UN system.

Global organizations have a penchant towards presenting themselves as stable and grounded in the permanency of their legal mandates, but this is mostly illusory. They are very much subjects of history and have transformed over time. Viewed from the perspective of the post-war era, they have been subjected to pressure to shift from *government* to *governance*, that is, from hierarchical forms of legal ordering organized around the state to more networked and collaborative forms of socioeconomic regulation. Whether or not these pressures have had their desired effects, some critical scholars advocating for 'Third World approaches to international law' (TWAIL) have lambasted the 'predatory system' of international law as one that 'sustains the plunder and subordination of the Third World by the West' (Mutua 2000: 31). Others have pointed out more hopefully that the rise of 'transnational law' is a realistic response to the 'fragility and unattainedness' of international law as it plays host to 'myriad forms of border-crossing relations among state and non-state actors' (Zumbansen 2006). These transformations towards cooperative transnational governance have not gone uncontested, however. The history of global organizations is littered with political and economic struggles over global control, in which hegemonic powers have responded to threats by producing new institutions and legal forms to maintain their dominance. In keeping with this practice, the so-called 'war on terrorism' has gone together with the notion of pre-emptive self-defence, and the exercise of 'extraordinary emergency powers', in a global order that seems increasingly contemptuous of the rule of law on which it is founded (Anghie 2004: Ch 6).

Some anthropologists have taken note of these changes. Mark Goodale, for example, has observed that since 11 September 2001 and the launch of the so-called War on Terror, global governance has been pushed aside in favour of the global security state, marked by the acceptance of torture among well-established Western powers and, in sum, 'the beginning of the end of the "age of human rights"' (Goodale 2018: 9–10). Annelise Riles makes a similar observation from the personal standpoint of a long-term ethnographer.

The contagious faith in dialogue, social progress, and confident universalism through law and institutions that she observed some twenty years ago have dramatically altered in a transformed world: 'Gone is the faith in progress through deliberation in the global public square. Gone is the faith in technocratic expertise that made it possible to imagine that all kinds of knowledge and political points of view might be assembled into a singular document' (2017: 184). The challenge for anthropologists in these circumstances, for Riles, is as much ethnographic as it is institution rebuilding, creating alternative 'anticipatory futures' for anthropological knowledge and global institutions.

There is good reason for drawing attention to the structural failings of global legal institutions. In this chapter, however, we offer a somewhat different perspective by emphasizing that these institutions are moving, for good or ill, in a new direction. For instance, they are capitalizing (quite literally, in collaborations with the private sector, as we shall see) on innovation in ways that involve re-energizing the UN's faith in technology as a source of decision-making. During the last fifteen years or so, new spaces have been created in the UN for private sector involvement in its initiatives, most prominently the UN Forum on Business and Human Rights. The UN, together with its corporate partners, is developing powerful technologies that present both important opportunities and risks in the administration of programmes in which artificial intelligence (AI) and machine learning are essential tools. These developments, as much as the rise of 'authoritarian liberalism' and the structural failure of institutions of global governance to address it, mark an emerging era of human rights and global governance.

We will bring more sustained attention to these developments in the final sections of this chapter. Before arriving at the most recent forms of global institutional power, we will first present a brief outline of the history and methods of ethnography in global legal institutions as well as an account of the main findings of ethnographic work in this context. This will prepare the ground for our discussion of the way that hope has become repositioned onto new digital technologies, going some way towards replacing goal-oriented discussion forums with technical expertise and a greater measure of rule by the non-human.

Redefining the Field

Global legal institutions such as UN agencies (of seemingly infinite variety), the World Bank, and the World Trade Organization (WTO) are not the first thing most people think of when they imagine the work of anthropologists. They are operated and inhabited by the least exotic members of humanity: bureaucratic officials. Their main features are widely understood with reference to a Weberian ideal: efficient, dispassionate, specialized, rule governed, and hierarchical. These qualities, manifested in institutional research settings, would not seem to offer favourable conditions for anthropologists, with their penchant for the informal and accidental. In recent decades, however, global legal institutions have become sites of some of the most innovative research in the social sciences, with implications that carry over into the methods and perspectives of legal scholarship. It is precisely *because* ethnographers pay close attention to the serendipitous and 'ordinary' over the long term that they have been able to offer fresh insight into the essential qualities of global institutions and the systems of international relations that these institutions have developed and embody.

There are two basic approaches that one can take to the history of the ethnography of organizations and its specific extension to global legal institutions. The first involves a direct engagement with globalization and the phenomena sometimes collectively referred to as the 'shrinking world'. Marc Abélès, whose ethnographic field sites have included the Assemblée Nationale in France, the European Parliament, and the WTO, made use of ethnographic methods in these settings because they offered insight into major shifts taking place in the distribution of power. He justified his unorthodox research fields in the following terms: 'The world has shrunk, and the sentiments of strangeness that surrounded populations considered "exotic" has completely disappeared' (Abélès 2011: 18). One of the methods used by anthropologists who gravitate to powerful institutions in this direct way is referred to by George Marcus and his various co-authors as 'para-ethnography', the practice of collaboration with research subjects (often high-ranking officials) in the interpretive work of ethnography. This method makes use of the similarities in education and values between the anthropologist and his or her interlocutors by involving the latter not only in the provision of information, but in the work of analysis, in 'risking interpretations together with the researcher about ideas fundamental to the political organization of their institutional contexts and functions and how these ideas circulate, have effect, and change' (Deeb and Marcus 2011: xx).

Another path towards institutional ethnography in global organizations involves what we might call a process of 'invasion and counter-invasion'. This approach typically began with the more or less sudden appearance of institutional experts, NGOs, advisers, and funds in the field sites traditionally occupied by sociocultural anthropologists, which then prompted them to rethink their ethnography and engage in a kind of 'counter-inquiry' towards institutions (Müller 2013: 4). Several qualities of this oblique approach set it apart from the more direct engagement with global institutions of Abélès and Marcus. First, it began with research 'from below', with its starting point and moral orientation situated in local settings—the people and communities on the margins of states that constitute the 'classic' subject matter of anthropology. It then carried this starting point into the perspectives and priorities of research in the institutional setting. It had a tendency to be collaborative, with team members assigned to different settings in the institution. It also tended to be multisited, with a methodological approach that took into account the differences and miscommunications between 'headquarters' and 'the field'.

Ethnographic innovations in institutions did not necessarily correlate with attention to the research findings of anthropologists, either across disciplines or in the world of policymakers. There is potential in this field of research, however, to contribute more widely to inspiration and influence across disciplines. Legal anthropology is ideally positioned to contribute to a variety of social-scientific engagements with law in a variety of subfields or approaches. Among them, new legal realism and critical legal studies have, each in their own way, taken legal studies away from the mainstream concern with legal doctrines and decisions, towards the insights offered by anthropology.

New legal realists advocated in favour of a new objectivism that turned away from the traditional focus on doctrinal logic and based legal scholarship on the facts of social science (see Erlanger et al. 2005). With its origins in questions concerning the sociopolitical influences on judicial decision-making, it has expanded its scope to include transnational institutions and the flow of people, ideas, and laws across boundaries. The widened scope of new legal realism now includes ethnographic methods and encompasses international law, human rights law, and transitional justice (Merry 2006: 976).

In critical legal studies, this use of social science research was applied towards better understanding the ways that laws maintain the status quo of discrimination and oppression in social power structures. For critical legal theorists, engagement in sustained critiques of mainstream legal thought is above all directed towards demonstrating its incoherence and the oppressive consequences of liberal legalism (Hunt 1986: 32; Williams 1987).

What these two scholarly movements have common is their attention to the everyday experience of those who participate in legal processes and face the consequences of law. New legal realism and critical legal studies are among those approaches to law and society that have opened avenues to the study of institutions outside their formal instruments and procedures, situating them in an interdisciplinary field that came to be called sociolegal studies or the social study of law. This development also created greater room for the influence of anthropology in mainstream legal scholarship. The ethnography of global legal institutions, in other words, is poised to contribute more significantly to legal scholarship through interdisciplinary positions that have already been staked out.

Of course, the method of institutional ethnography is not the same as taking the model advocated by Malinowski in the 1920s—which has had direct or indirect influence on the discipline for nearly a century—and transplanting it to a different setting. There is certainly no dinghy leaving the anthropologist on the beach to figure out a distant setting and its population, not even figuratively. There are basic points of familiarity most people have with bureaucratic structures and officialdom that translate readily to the setting of global organizations. This is not to say, however, that the classic trope of 'culture shock' has no place in this field. Jon Harald Lie recalls that entering the World Bank as a novice researcher was an alienating and terrifying experience: 'Never before had I experienced such a vast, formal and complex bureaucracy as with the Bank's Washington headquarters' (Lie 2013: 217).

One methodological obstacle to the anthropology of institutions has to do with the duration of time, which is a hallmark of the discipline.[3] There are many impediments to remaining in place as an observer over the *longue durée*. These hurdles can involve the institutional curtailment of the researcher's access to the field, either by restricting access or from the simple fact that meetings often only last a week or two at most. Researchers also commonly face circumstances in which everything ends with the working day; and it is usually impossible to conduct a project by entering into the private lives of officials. An entire realm of enquiry, the boundary between private and public lives, which is more naturally overcome in other settings, is all but off limits to institutional ethnographers. Finally, high-ranking officials are usually mobile, based in several offices or flying hither and yon for meetings of various kinds. Under these circumstances, interaction with them often takes the form of a one-on-one 'meeting' and a formal 'interview', which are inimical to the informal nature of ethnographic projects, but which researchers usually accept for want of other pathways to information.

Then there is the question of secrecy, an issue that has always and everywhere been central to ethnography, but that has its own formal configurations in the study of institutions. Global legal organizations have entire realms of official secrecy and invisibility in which the dynamics and agendas of decision-making are hidden from view. There is in these organizations a meticulously cultivated surface appearance of equality and fairness in developing policy and defining the obligations of states, which overlays and conceals a realm of secret diplomacy and public persuasion, to which researchers rarely have access. Diplomacy, more than the etiquette of polite forms of address, depends on providing space for state interests to be articulated away from view. Organizations of global law and governance, in other words, have two sides: their public face, oriented towards the values of transparency and accountability, and a private realm that takes place and exercises influence in the back-room discussions that produce decisions and shape policies. And prying researchers are usually not welcome in this setting.

What, in the middle of all this, is left of ethnographic method? There is of course the practice of nibbling around the edges, getting informal insights into the thinking and activities of diplomats from the serendipitous, accidental occurrences or dropped words that happen simply in the course of participating, to the extent possible, in the work of the organization (Jacob and Riles 2007: 184). Often ethnographers will find that insiders are willing (sometimes for strategic reasons) to share information, often expressed in the form of frustration towards official corruption or unreason. The classic approach of being open to the concerns of the people studied and giving priority to *not* being directive remains key in the context of institutions (Gellner and Hirsch 2001: 7–8).

The great advantage of non-directivity and informality is the debunking effect of ethnography. Researchers using this approach are inevitably—almost platitudinously—able to reveal how bureaucracies fail to function efficiently, undermined by official resistance, by circumvention of the chain of command or its opposite, sticking to the rules with such narrow exactitude that a 'work to rule' effect unravels institutional goals. David Mosse, reporting on the experience of his colleagues in international development, makes the pointed observation that 'expert knowledge [is] the product of semi-clandestine detective work, negotiating gossip, absent data and misinformation, wishful thinking or deliberate lying, not to mention dangerous driving, loneliness, alcohol and sex—a panoply of experiences, quick impressions and hunches stabilized as statistics and rational processes' (Mosse 2011: 10). This debunking effect applies equally to the close-knit communities of experts in the headquarters of global organizations, whose reach, intensity, and centralization is growing through the use of new information and communication technologies, as we discuss further below.

Discovering global legal institutions

The debunking effects of institutional ethnography are on full display when we consider the main findings of the anthropology of global organizations. We presented these findings in the introduction to *Palaces of Hope: The Anthropology of Global Organizations* (Niezen and Sapignoli 2017), which serves as the basis of the outline we now offer in this section. Through the simple exercise of collating this research, it became clear to us that anthropologists have redefined the study of formal institutions through several key areas in which ethnographic methods have brought greater attention to informal structures and processes largely overlooked by other disciplines:

Transparency and invisibility: In their struggles against the rot of corruption at the state level, global legal institutions share as one of their guiding principles the public availability of information on their work, facilitated in good measure by the posting of vast numbers of documents and huge amounts of data on the internet. In some ways, their actual workings are obscured by the sheer mass of information they make public in efforts to be transparent. How could they be anything but accountable and honourable when so much information is there for all to see?

Invisibility is not quite the same as official secrecy. The official secret is explicitly recognized as a secret. It calls attention to itself, including the possibility of breaching the protocol or the law that keeps information under wraps, by illegal acts of 'whistleblowing'. The regime of invisibility, however, is something quite different. It operates more in the everyday. It can involve something as simple as the non-disclosure of motives in diplomatic interaction, in which information discussed as having importance in one context is strategically excluded from the conversation in another.

It has been possible to use ethnographic methods in paying sustained attention to institutional secrecy or what Badaró, a member of a team that undertook a long-term study of the WTO, has termed the *regime of visibility* (or of invisibility). He finds that, even though the role that experts play in the political dynamics of the WTO would almost naturally grant them a certain level of political visibility and exposure, 'the need for neutrality prevents them from leaving explicit traces of their practices' (Badaró 2011: 84).

Sometimes the exercise of institutional secrecy occurs within the complex interconnections between several kinds of interactive space, which interpenetrate and are not so easily defined as might appear from a simple look. Formal space is marked by strict rules of procedure and a complex diplomatic etiquette that can only be acquired by officials through years of experience. Niels Schia, an anthropologist who was given unusual access to the UN Security Council as a member of the Norwegian delegation, finds that this distinction between official formality and back-room politics is arguably more developed in the Security Council than any other agency, for a very simple reason: the principle of non-offence, and hence the rules constituting its diplomatic reinforcement, are particularly important in the forum that handles the threat or actuality of armed conflict between states. Schia (2013) focuses on informal processes—including the place of informal gatherings of diplomats in their favourite bars in Manhattan—to reveal how experienced actors in the Security Council are able to switch between different levels of formality and effectively engage in interrupting the processes of conflict and their internal paradoxes, 'without fragmenting the external continuity and unity of the Council' (2013: 248), that is to say, without coming up against or challenging the formal rules of diplomacy that constitute the basic machinery of the UNSC. Even within the element of indeterminacy pointed to by Koskenniemi (1995) and the informality of its workings brought out by Schia, the Security Council is more or less impervious to reform, with the power interests of the Permanent 5 members making it all but impossible to bring about the kind of sweeping reform necessary to produce a new global order.

Power and fragility: It is important for those conducting research in global legal organizations to recognize that power and fragility are not evenly distributed and do not always take the same forms. Some agencies have mandates that supersede those of others. The Security Council, the International Monetary Fund (IMF), the WTO, and the World Bank all have far-reaching influence on world affairs. Even the most powerful agencies, however, have their points of vulnerability, and only a few organizations have direct influence on the actions of states and transnational corporations. Beyond this, most operate within the limits of structural fragilities, a sense of impermanence, and vulnerability to the collective politics of their constituent states.

The long-term perspective of ethnographic research almost inevitably exposes the falsehood and opportunism behind the myth of organizational power. It is possible through institutional enquiry to show how powerful organizations—including states operating in the UN system—exercise their capacity to conceal the uses (and abuses) of power that take place through the initiatives that they sponsor and the obligations they avoid, downplaying their deeply rooted value judgements as they apply their policies and programmes. Each institution has its own structure of asymmetry between officially proclaimed rules and regulations and their actual enactments, evasions, and renegotiations. These structures often appear most clearly in the informal penumbras of institutional life, making ethnography the best method for bringing them to light. Through attention to this informal realm, technologies of domination are increasingly seen as just that, mechanisms and structures that, through the directed and accidental discoveries of patient and persistent research, can ultimately be identified in their uses and consequences.

Redefining the legal subject: One of the central differences between anthropology and other disciplines that conduct research in and on global organizations is the heightened awareness of social construction that anthropologists cultivate through long-term attention to the everyday. Better than other methods in this sense, ethnography brings out the ways that institutional thinking and bureaucratic action shape loyalties, rivalries, and social forms or categories of belonging.

This happens in a variety of ways, one of which is conceptual, through the construction and recognition of legal subjects. Conceptions of belonging are of necessity built into or follow from the elaboration and enforcement of any regime of collective rights or recognition. The most recent products of human rights standard setting—the Convention on the Rights of Persons with Disabilities (CRPD, 2006); the Yogyakarta Principles on the Application of Human Rights Law in Relation to Sexual Orientation and Gender Identity (2006); the Declaration on the Rights of Indigenous Peoples (UNDRIP, 2007); the International Labour Organization's Convention on Domestic Workers (ILO Convention 189, 2013); and the Declaration on the Rights of Peasants and Other People Working in Rural Areas (2018)—comprise legally formalized categories of collective recognition and belonging. Through the active participation of rights claimants, these ideas constitute a kind of instrumental, rights-oriented, managerial, and, at the same time, publicly engaged and participatory anthropology (Niezen 2017).

Global legal organizations, in other words, engage in the ordering and construction of human life, not through observation and analysis as scholars might, but through the elaboration and application of legal tools. In legal orders, rights are inevitably accompanied by the question, to whom do these rights apply? This question in turn calls for some specificity in conceptualizing the actors who are recognized as legal subjects. Many initiatives have taken place to clarify, redefine, or reposition one or another aspect of human life, sometimes with strategic or instrumental goals expressed clearly, at other times more implicitly; sometimes with input from professional anthropologists, at other times working at a greater remove from academic concerns or standards. The UN's ethnological imagination has applied to Indigenous Peoples, children, women, minorities (of many kinds), 'communities', refugees, states, civilizations, world heritage, and, ultimately, humanity itself.

The constructive powers of quantification: Global organizations also shape social forms through technologies of indicators and quantified measures of almost everything that comes under their purviews. The organizational penchant for numbers not only gives some insight into institutional capacities, they are a central feature of the organizations themselves as a source of policy and identity. Sally Merry, in *The Seductions of Quantification* (Merry 2016) and elsewhere in this volume, points out that numbers have an aura of objective truth and scientific legitimacy that draws attention away from their contingencies and constructive powers. Indicators are outcomes of selection and interpretation of what is to be counted. They rely on the construction of the categories of things to be measured, and hence have a penchant for the conceptual ordering of the world in ways that are simple, hierarchical, and readily understood. One implication of this observation is that we are all being increasingly governed through numbers, using tools of indicators, lists, algorithms, and audits (Shore and Wright 2015: 22). There is a rapidly growing power and reach to this that we will discuss below with reference to the UN's use of digital technologies. There is, at the same time, a socially constitutive element of indicators that corresponds with Marilyn Strathern's (2000) notion of 'audit culture', the idea that creating standards for things to be counted brings particular things into focus and renders others invisible or unsayable. As John and Jean Comaroff put it, 'the statistic is both a figuration and a fact, a medium of communications *and* a unit of knowledge-as-currency, one whose value and veracity accumulate and circulate' (Comaroff and Comaroff 2016: 143, emphasis in original). Numbers are political resources. Those who decide what to count and what not to count are therefore influential in ways that are disproportionate to the limited attention given to the architecture of quantification. The entrenched practices of gathering indicators and emphasizing transparency point to a connection between the two: what is critical and valued in setting policy and practice begins with things that can be measured and compared, data that then also serve the interests of claiming (measurable) transparency.

Utopian visions and hope: One of the consistent findings of ethnographers in the UN is that the further one gets from the content of public relations and the closer one approaches the opinions of those responsible for converting policies into practice, the more we find expressions of frustration, disaffection, and cynicism. Sooner or later, career officials experience first-hand the disconnection between the grand aspirations of institutional endeavour and the day-to-day reality of intervention in the lives of people in seemingly intractable conditions of poverty and crisis.

At the same time—and possibly as an antidote to the inevitable disenchantment of officials—global organizations, more than any other kind of bureaucracy, continually try to push aside the disappointments and limitations of policy in practice and infuse their work with the rhetoric of hope. This is a side to the UN that is not mired in cynicism and disillusionment, and that rarely makes headlines. Despite all of the examples we can find of the dark side of global governance, there continues to be an abiding sense of hope that often attaches to the UN, a hint of growth in the blighted soil of its failures.

Global legal institutions tend to inculcate and publicly present a disproportionate sense of mission that permeates and motivates almost everything they do. They act in accordance with a kind of piecemeal, instrumental, technologically inspired ambition for the betterment of the world, driven by the typically utopian practice of acting on applied visions of prosperity and justice that use only the practical resources of human inventiveness and agency. In the manner of the nineteenth century's socialist visionaries, Fourier and Saint Simon, the UN's intellectual leaders encourage belief in a kind of possibility-beyond-capacity as a source of motivation for the realization of grand designs.

Even in its more extravagant forms, hope still lies hidden behind the sordid reality of humans in conflict, in crisis, in poverty, in sickness, in conditions of injustice—behind all the ills of the world that together make up the UN agenda. Those who inhabit global legal institutions often cultivate hope as a form of defence mechanism: rather than sharing stereotypical notions of unfairness and inefficiency, they participate in the closed intellectual world of the agency's long-term vision of enlightenment-inspired hope for a global rational society and a technologically realized futurity. The hope of global institutions is in one sense unlike other this-worldly ideals in the utopian tradition: it does not intend to bring about a *perfect* world—it is clear to all that this cannot ever exist—but pursues its goals by following an ideal of constantly revised and adjusted perfectibility.[4] In doing so, it is firmly grounded in legalism, scientism, and technologism, in the conviction that crises have a rational solution based in the almost limitless possibilities of human genius. But it is similar to the classic utopias in the sense that the principle of human perfectibility goes beyond interventions in crises; it tries to cultivate and harness new forms of knowledge that have the potential to transform the world.

New technologies, risks, and potentialities

Consistent with the prevalence of utopian imaginings in the context of rampant crises, transformative new technologies are becoming more and more central to the agendas of institutions of global governance. For example, on 13 October 2017, Sophia, a life-size 'social robot', entered the United Nations Headquarters in New York to participate in the event 'The future of everything—sustainable development in the age of rapid technological change' and engaged in a conversation with UN Deputy Secretary-General Amina J. Mohammed about how AI can help to create a better future for humanity (*UN News* 2017). The anthropology of global organizations is being reshaped by changes to its subject matter, with the UN taking on the opportunities inherent in new information and communication technologies.

The future of global legal institutions has been clearly identified as involving efforts to harness the powers of new technologies. Reflecting the kind of utopian visions that go back to its origins, the United Nations Department of Economic and Social Affairs, in a newsletter sent out regularly to email subscribers, offers a Panglossian view of the emergence of what it calls 'frontier technologies':

> Frontier technologies are innovative and often grow fast, with the potential to transform societies, economies and the environment. In recent years, we have seen examples of this in the form of artificial intelligence and machine learning, renewable energy technologies, energy storage technologies, electric and autonomous vehicles and drones, genetic engineering, as well as cryptocurrencies and blockchains. These frontier technologies can help eradicate hunger and epidemics, increase life expectancy, reduce carbon emissions, automate manual and repetitive tasks, create decent jobs, improve quality of life and facilitate complex decision-making processes. In other words, these technologies can make sustainable development a reality, improving people's lives, promoting prosperity and protecting the planet.
>
> (UNDESA 2018)

Miguel Luengo Oroz, Chief Data Scientist for the UN's Global Pulse initiative, has put his own spin on the narrative of a humanity unified by the emerging technologies of Big Data: 'Before 2030, technology should allow us to know everything from everyone to ensure no one is left behind. For example, there will be nanosatellites imaging every corner of the earth allowing us to generate almost immediate insights into humanitarian crises.'[5]

Acting upon these grand aspirations, global organizations are rapidly digitizing the data on which their decisions are based, in part through ambitious programmes of digital archiving and through the creation of new large-scale 'data mining', the extraction of patterns and knowledge from massive and often diverse sources of information. Global organizations, in some ways weakened by state-centric structures of governance, are now turning to the power of big data, that is to say, data sets that are too large for traditional forms of data processing software and that rely on computers with high speeds and storage capacities, complex algorithms, and artificial intelligence as the technological means towards decision-making. The expectation that data processing capacities will continue to increase lies behind much of the hopeful official rhetoric that looks towards an emerging era of techno-legal design and data-driven global governance.

Anthropologists investigating this emerging field will likely find themselves coming to terms with two emergent phenomena: 1) a growing role of data technicians in developing information technologies applied to a myriad of the world's problems; and 2) greater private sector participation in, and responsibility for, human rights and global governance, in ways that are inseparable from corporate goals of image-production and profitability. The agencies and agendas of big data are increasingly imbricated in global governance for the simple reason that the private sector has the resources and proprietary interests involved in the development of new technologies that are being used in a wide range of global governance initiatives.

Tech employees often become human rights practitioners and advocates when they have to predict the form of violence and human rights abuse that a technology they are designing could produce; when they boycott their own company because it does not adhere to its own principles of social good (as was the case of Google employees protesting the involvement of the company in a Pentagon programme that uses artificial intelligence to improve the targeting of drone strikes);[6] and when employees screen violent content in social media platforms and make decisions about what constitutes hate speech that risks inciting violence. Both the capacities and the ethical answerability of global governance have shifted towards technical experts, in particular data technicians who have the requisite training to design and implement programmes involving public, 'for good' use of proprietary software.

Through their development of this technological capacity, major tech corporations—almost exclusively based in the United States—are at the same time burnishing their public image in developing tools oriented towards human rights compliance. Some of these private sector/global governance initiatives are oriented towards human rights compliance and environmental justice, under the banners 'AI for good' and 'AI for Earth'. In 2017–18, several tech corporations developed guidelines on human rights-based approaches to AI and the ethical principles to follow in the development and applications of automated decision-making systems. Microsoft, for example, engaged in developing policies and practices that make use of AI to promote the rule of law and to further human rights compliance.[7] In the summer of 2017, it joined with Facebook, Twitter, and

YouTube to create a Global Internet Forum to Counter Terrorism. It has also formed a partnership with the Office of the UN Commission of Human Rights intended to develop and make use of advanced information technology to 'predict, analyze and respond to critical human rights situations', which are now proliferating and growing in complexity.

At the same time, there are significant human rights challenges arising from new ITs, which have shone a spotlight on the responsibility of social media platforms for human rights violations, such as Facebook's role in spreading hate speech that fuelled the Myanmar crisis (Miles 2018). The impacts of new technologies, in other words, is an emerging field for the development of human rights standards (see Niezen 2020). This field goes beyond the identification of human groups as distinct human rights claimants, and focuses instead on technologies as actors and agents—including digitalization, algorithms, and 'killer robots'—that act in important ways on human lives (see van Veen 2018).

Several authors (e.g. Johns 2016, 2017; Sapignoli 2021; Taylor 2017) whose research makes connections between IT and sociolegal studies have outlined important observations and concerns about some of the UN's initiatives using AI and machine learning, built upon collaboration with the private sector. One of the most prominent of such initiatives to come to critical attention is the Global Pulse sponsored by the UN High Commission For Refugees, which parses data from social media to predict conflict and displacement, and which decision-makers can then use to inform 'programmatic responses and alterations' (UNHCR 2017).[8] The UNHCR has developed a programme for biometric registration of Afghan refugees living in camps in Pakistan, in part to prevent them from duplicating their receipt of humanitarian assistance. The UN refugee agency has also developed the Artificial Intelligence for Disaster Relief (AIDR) platform, 'a free and open source prototype designed to perform automatic classification of crisis-related messages posted to social media during humanitarian crises' (Johns 2017: 3). Considered superficially, such initiatives are performing very much as advertised, identifying conflicts when (or even before) they occur and streamlining the delivery of aid in response. But there is still something disquieting about them, which has to do with their technological positioning outside the reach of the UN's foundational goals of transparency and auditability.

Johns finds that the numerous initiatives that combine lists and algorithms 'seem often to engender a sense of vertigo-inducing unknowability in global policy making' (2016: 138). This relates to the phenomenon that Johns terms 'demotic mismatch': '[t]he problem of laboring to render one form of lawful authority transparent to some delimited demos, only to find it inextricably entangled with authority produced elsewhere' (2016: 141). Algorithms, in other words, are difficult to pin down; their codes are not plain to see and tend to relocate unseen into other algorithms applied to other problems. This means that the legal and bureaucratic requirements of transparency and accountability are impeded by the very structure of the technology. It is not only the inscrutable algorithmic 'black box' that informs decision-making and intervention, but the original data that are used to train machine leaning systems. From these data will depend the prediction, production of knowledge, and ultimately the reality of the intervention. If inputted data have inequalities, biases, or misrepresentations embedded in them, these will be reproduced in the workings of intervention. If data are invisible or absent, they will remain so through the process by which the AI program makes a decision. In other words, new technologically sophisticated practices can reproduce historical inequalities as well as unintentionally create new ones.[9]

Several agencies have produced guidelines on the use of AI in their work, including the office of the UN Secretary-General, which in late 2018 produced its own 'Strategy on New Technologies', a central goal of which is to 'foster inclusion and transparency' in the UN's rapid application of new technologies to many of its projects, including the ambitious 2030 Sustainable Development Agenda (United Nations 2018). The technological obstacles to transparency might go some way towards explaining why the UN still lacks auditability mechanisms for assessing the impacts of AI and the digitization of bureaucracy. The digitally empowered daily operations of UN officers, intervention programmes, and development of international law are occurring largely in the absence of bureaucratic oversight. This highlights the need for research in this area. The development of ITs for use in global legal institutions is arguably *the* most significant challenge for legal anthropologists, with ethnography emerging as one of the most promising methods for considering the applications of AI and its effects. Computational logic, data mining, and algorithmic techniques are a suitable subject for anthropological study because they incorporate complex dynamics of human and other-than-human agency in emerging processes of knowledge formation and power, and because algorithmically mediated knowledge and power are becoming increasingly significant in defining areas of human rights concern and methods for addressing them. Experts' understanding of society, as well as of nature, influences the development and application of machine learning and big data.

Reimagining pluralism in the global order

Focusing on the development of new technologies in global governance offers a way towards understanding how global legal organizations are moving in new directions. Whether a researcher is taking a wide view or engaged in the closer attention of ethnography, these developments offer a guide to what is happening, and what to be attentive to, in a rapidly changing technological and institutional ecosystem. For all the technological innovation behind these developments, however, there remain longstanding questions concerning how law shapes (and is shaped by) its representation of social worlds, the meaning of global 'law', and the people and forms of expertise that bring its authorization into being. In their efforts to bring clarity to these issues, anthropologists and legal scholars have often arrived at shared understandings of the form, operation, and exercise of power within contemporary forms and institutions of global legality.

Sources of expertise are undergoing a shift from the relatively exclusive prerogative of legal and administrative experts towards the informational expertise of engineers, software designers, and digital investigators. The ICC, for example, was initially caught flat-footed with the rise of social media platforms as sources of evidence, and had to seek out experts in the field of open source intelligence to offer ways to assess and enhance the probative value of online videos depicting mass crimes. This example points to another direction that expertise might take, with the near universality of mobile phones as the original sources of data uploaded to social media, contributing an unprecedented informational foundation for global governance initiatives. The usual intermediation of experts sent from 'headquarters' to 'the field' can be bypassed through new channels of communication and information sharing.

Yet technological expertise is emerging as a central source of power, both within UN agencies and through its state members. The private sector has a growing presence in global governance, in part due to the proprietary nature of the technologies being applied to global problems. This involvement of corporations sometimes provides opportunities for global legal institutions to circumvent the worst consequences of state-centrism in international law and governance. If, as ethnographic studies suggest, the UN is often hamstrung by the diplomatic stratagems of states, the rise of voluntary private sector funding and responsibility for international law can only help it in reaching its goals. If the real source of the UN's incapacity comes from the actions of its state members, the growing involvement of corporations extends its reach and potential to intervene successfully in crises, bringing profit motive to intervention in global crises. Private sector involvement in global governance—particularly that emanating from the high-tech world of expert intervention—is bringing to the fore a field where technological, legal, and institutional studies intersect.

Now more than ever, we need global organizations to effectively intervene in what are perhaps the greatest challenges the world has ever faced: environmental catastrophe, displacement, and conflict spurred by climate change, rising economic inequalities, internet-facilitated hate that fuels terrorist recruitment and violent populist movements, and the looming threat of democratic process being hacked and hijacked in a new digital arms race between powerful states. In this troubled and troubling context, anthropology has more to offer than the usual litany of the failings of global institutions. Through their regimes of access and long-term familiarity with their subjects, anthropologists have the tools to take a constructively critical position towards these developments, to go against the grain of institutional self-representation in publicity and the stereotypes of popular knowledge, and point to the consequences, for good and ill, of new uses of emerging technologies of law and governance on people's lives.

Notes

1. Constitutive Act of the African Union, available at https://au.int/sites/default/files/pages/34873-file-constitutiveact_en.pdf accessed 5 August 2020.

2. Charter of Fundamental Rights of the European Union (2000/C 364/01), available at https://www.europarl.europa.eu/charter/pdf/text_en.pdf accessed 5 August 2020.
3. Our outline of the impediments to research in global institutions owes a great deal to articles by Jacob and Riles (2007) and Lie (2013).
4. For an overview of utopianism in international law, see Antonio Cassese's edited volume, *Realizing Utopia: The Future of International Law* (Cassese 2012).
5. Miguel Luengo Oroz, 'From Big Data to Humanitarian in the Loop Algorithms', 22 January 2018, available at https://www.unglobalpulse.org/news/big-data-humanitarian-loop-algorithms accessed 5 August 2020.
6. See https://www.nytimes.com/2018/04/04/technology/google-letter-ceo-pentagon-project.html accessed 5 August 2020.
7. See 'A Digital Geneva Convention to protect cyberspace', available at https://query.prod.cms.rt.microsoft.com/cms/api/am/binary/RW67QH accessed 5 August 2020.
8. For a report on the work of Global Pulse in the area of social media and forced displacement, see http://unglobalpulse.org/sites/default/files/White%20Paper%20Social%20Media%203_0.pdf accessed 5 August 2020.
9. The problem of injustice built into the structure and application of algorithms is central to the work of, for example, Virginia Eubanks (2017), Safiya Umoja Noble (2018), and Cathy O'Neil (2016).

References

Abélès, M. 2011. *Des anthropologues a l'OMC: Scènes de la gouvernance mondiale*. Paris: CNRS Éditions.

Anghie, A. 2004. *Imperialism, Sovereignty and the Making of International Law*. Cambridge: Cambridge University Press.

Badaró, M. 2011. 'Le régime d'invisibilité des experts'. In M. Abélès, ed. *Des anthropologues àl'OMC: Scènes de la gouvernance mondiale*, 81–110. Paris: CNRS Éditions.

Cassese, A., ed. 2012. *Realizing Utopia: The Future of International Law*. Oxford: Oxford University Press.

Comaroff, J. and J. Comaroff. 2016. *The Truth about Crime: Sovereignty, Knowledge, Social Order*. Chicago: University of Chicago Press.

Deeb, H. N. and G. Marcus. 2011. 'In the Green Room: An Experiment in Ethnographic Method at the WTO'. *Political and Legal Anthropology Review (PoLAR)* 34(1): 51–76.

Erlanger, H., B. Garth, J. Larson, E. Mertz, V. Nourse, and D. Watkins. 2005. 'Is It Time for a New Legal Realism?' *Wisconsin Law Review* 2: 335–63.

Eubanks, V. 2017. *Automating Inequality: How High-Tech Tools Profile, Police, and Punish the Poor*. New York: St. Martin's.

Gellner, D. and E. Hirsch, eds. 2001. *Inside Organizations: Anthropologists at Work*. Oxford and New York: Berg.

Goodale, M. 2018. *Letters to the Contrary: A Curated History of the UNESCO Human Rights Survey*. Stanford: Stanford University Press.

Hunt, A. 1986. 'The Theory of Critical Legal Studies'. *Oxford Journal of Legal Studies* 6(1): 1–45.

Jacob, M.-A. and A. Riles. 2007. 'The New Bureaucracies of Virtue: Introduction'. *Political and Legal Anthropology Review (PoLAR)* 30(2): 181–91.

Johns, F. 2016. 'Global Governance through the Pairing of List and Algorithm'. *Environment and Planning D: Society and Space* 34(1): 126–49.

Johns, F. 2017. 'Data Mining as Global Governance'. In R. Brownsword, E. Scotford, and K. Yeung, eds. *The Oxford Handbook of Law, Regulation and Technology*. Oxford Handbooks Online. Oxford: Oxford University Press.

Koskenniemi, M. 1995. 'The Police in the Temple. Order, Justice and the UN: A Dialectical View'. *European Journal of International Law* 3: 325–48.

Lie, J. H. S. 2013. 'Challenging Anthropology: Anthropological Reflections on the Ethnographic Turn in International Relations'. *Millennium: Journal of International Studies* 41(2): 201–20.

Merry, S. E. 2006. 'New Legal Realism and the Ethnography of Transnational Law'. *Law and Social Inquiry* 31(4): 975–95.

Merry, S. E. 2016. *The Seductions of Quantification: Measuring Human Rights, Gender Violence, and Sex Trafficking*. Chicago and London: University of Chicago Press.

Miles, T. 2018. 'U.N. Investigators Cite Facebook Role in Myanmar Crisis'. Reuters, available at https://www.reuters.com/article/us-myanmar-rohingya-facebook/u-n-investigators-cite-facebook-role-in-myanmar-crisis-idUSKCN1GO2PN.

Mosse, D., ed. 2011. *Adventures in Aidland: The Anthropology of Professionals in International Development*. New York and Oxford: Berghahn.

Müller, B. 2013. 'Introduction: Lifting the Veil of Harmony'. In B. Müller, ed. *The Gloss of Harmony: The Politics of Policy-Making in Multilateral Institutions*, 1–22. London: Pluto.

Mutua, M. 2000. 'What is TWAIL?' *Proceedings of the Annual Meeting (American Society of International Law)* 94: 31–40.

Niezen, R. 2017. 'The Anthropology by Organizations'. In R. Niezen and M. Sapignoli, eds. *Palaces of Hope: The Anthropology of Global Organizations*, 294–317. Cambridge: Cambridge University Press.

Niezen, R. 2020. *#HumanRights: The Technologies and Politics of Justice Claims in Practice*. Stanford: Stanford University Press.

Niezen, R. and M. Sapignoli, eds. 2017. *Palaces of Hope: The Anthropology of Global Organizations*. Cambridge: Cambridge University Press.

Noble, S. U. 2018. *Algorithms of Oppression: How Search Engines Reinforce Racism*. New York: New York University Press.

O'Neil, C. 2016. *Weapons of Math Destruction: How Big Data Increases Inequality and Threatens Democracy*. New York: Broadway Books.

Riles, A. 2017. 'Outputs: The Promises and Perils of Ethnographic Engagement After the Loss of Faith in Transnational Dialogue'. *Journal of the Royal Anthropological Institute (N.S.)* 23(S1): 182–97.

Sapignoli, M. 2021. 'The Mismeasure of the Human: Big Data and the AI-turn in Global Governance'. *Anthropology Today*. 37(1): 4–8.

Schia, N. 2013. 'Being Part of the Parade—"Going Native" in the United Nations Security Council'. *Political and Legal Anthropology Review (PoLAR)* 36(1): 138–56.

Shore, C. and S. Wright. 2015. 'Governing by Numbers: Audit Culture, Rankings and the New World Order'. *Social Anthropology* 23(1): 22–8.

Strathern, M., ed. 2000. *Audit Cultures: Anthropological Studies in Accountability, Ethics, and the Academy*. London: Routledge.

Taylor, L. 2017. 'What is Data Justice? The Case for Connecting Digital Rights and Freedoms Globally'. *Big Data & Society* July–December: 1–14.

UN News. 2017. 'At UN, Robot Sophia Joins Meeting on Artificial Intelligence and Sustainable Development', available at https://news.un.org/en/story/2017/10/568292-un-robot-sophia-joins-meeting-artificial-intelligence-and-sustainable.

UNDESA. 2018. 'Frontier Technologies for a Sustainable Future'. *UN DESA Voice* (October 2018), available at https://www.un.org/development/desa/undesavoice/2018/10.

United Nations. 2018. 'Secretary-General's Strategy on New Technologies', available at https://www.un.org/en/newtechnologies/images/pdf/SGs-Strategy-on-New-Technologies.pdf.

van Veen, C. 2018. 'Artificial Intelligence: What's Human Rights Got to Do With It?' *Data & Society: Points*, available at https://points.datasociety.net/artificial-intelligence-whats-human-rights-got-to-do-with-it-4622ec1566d5.

Williams, J. 1987. 'Critical Legal Studies: The Death of Transcendence and the Rise of the New Langdells'. *New York University Law Review* 62(3): 429–96.

Zumbansen, P. 2006. 'Transnational Law'. In J. Smits, ed. *Encyclopedia of Comparative Law*, 738–54. Camberley: Edward Elgar.

CHAPTER 47

LAW AS TECHNIQUE

RALF MICHAELS AND ANNELISE RILES

LAW is a set of knowledge tools—techniques legal experts use to think and work with. Yet the technical quality of law has, for the most part, been curiously ignored in ethnographic studies of law. The anthropology of law has given us excellent accounts of the social effects of law in the world, the cultural meanings of legal texts, the ideological foundations of legal practice, and the rituals of legal institutions. But what of the knowledge practice of law itself—mundane legal technique? Surprisingly little has changed since Richard Abel (1988: 3) delivered his pessimistic verdict on the state of ethnographic studies of law in 1989: 'Except for a handful of very recent ethnographic studies of lawyer-client interaction ... , we know little more about what lawyers do than how they allocate their time among different subject matters'. In this chapter, we argue for imaginative ethnographic analysis of the tools of law. Anthropological theory and methods stand to powerfully elucidate the workings of legal knowledge. Conversely, legal technique offers novel insights into questions of anthropological theory.

What does it mean to understand law as technique? Legal technique is a 'package' that encompasses a variety of things: '(1) certain ideologies—legal instrumentalism and managerialism ... ; (2) certain categories of experts—especially scholars, bureaucrats and practitioners who treat the law as a kind of tool or machine and who see themselves as modest but expertly devoted technicians; (3) a problem-solving paradigm—an orientation toward defining concrete, practical problems and toward crafting solutions; (4) a form of reasoning and argumentation, from eight-part-tests to reasoning by analogy, to the production of stock types of policy to practices of statutory interpretation or citation to case law'; and (5) a set of material artefacts—from boiler-plate collateral agreements to the patent models used in nineteenth-century intellectual property litigation (Riles 2011: 64–5). That technique is used towards myriad projects. Legal technique enables judicial decision in the face of the undecidable, and resolution and closure in the face of ongoing complexity. It enables transfer of entitlements and shaping of interpersonal relations. Legal technique serves as a mechanism of exchange and creator of trust where people lack common cultural understandings—the political, economic, or social means to compel one another's behaviour. Legal technique brings about persons, as in the case of the legal fictions that sustain corporations.

Antipathy towards Legal Technique

When Laura Nader, in 1965, listed 'the main topics that have characterized anthropological work for well over a century', law appeared, in all of these questions, as a body of norms or system of rules, but never as a practice (Nader 1965: 4). Her call to view law as an instrument of social control echoed the legal realist focus on law as a means to an end. But unlike at least some of the legal realists, Nader focused on the ends of law at the expense of the means; she treated legal technique from an external perspective. Indeed, anthropologists have been hesitant to treat law as technique. Most often they have treated legal knowledge practices in one of two other ways. Either they have focused on the context and complexity of law, or they have focused on its critique.

Context and Complexity

A first strand of anthropology insists on the *context* of legal knowledge. This focus on legal context emerges from a tradition in both legal sociology and legal anthropology that seeks to explain law as a function of society at large, not as the actions of its functionaries, to look at law as an element of everyday life instead of official practices, and to focus on 'law in action' as opposed to 'law in the books' (Ehrlich 1936; Pound 1910). To use Lawrence Friedman's distinction, the focus is on external legal culture, the role of law among the general population, not among those performing specialized tasks (Friedman 1975: 223–4).

An important dimension of this anthropological focus on context has been the insistence on complexity—the insistence that the 'real world' beyond the law is more complex than the law makes it appear. For example, the question of whether an employment contract provides for pregnancy leave is not only a matter of legal interpretation but also a question of relations between labour and management, an intervention within human relations that are both professional and personal, an elaboration of gender hierarchies, and so on. Such complexities inspire anthropologists to reject what they take as the simplicity of a lawyer's perspective and to insist on 'telling a more complicated story' (Moore 2001; Pirie 2013: 223).

It is a curious critique, however, to chide the lawyer for not being more anthropological. The lawyer's job, unlike the anthropologist's, is not thick description. To the contrary, recent ethnographies of legal technique demonstrate that in order to be skilled at their craft, lawyers must deeply appreciate that the formal legal story is not the whole story, that there is more to the issue or controversy than the formalities of law allow.

Critique

A second major strand of anthropological work takes the technical character of law as a target of *critique* rather than as a subject in need of contextualization. This work has strong pedigrees in critical theory. Marx (1911) (who had been a law student) famously critiqued law as superstructure derived from underlying economic and political realities. Foucault (2008: 87) later critiqued the form of law, and the specific knowledge that it created, as an exercise of power. The critique of technocratic knowledge seeks to look beneath the veil of the legal and bureaucratic form to reveal its effects (Bourdieu 1987; Chatterjee 2017; Ferguson 1994; Gupta 2012; Merry 2016).

The anthropological critique of legal technique has analogies in critical legal scholarship, where scholars have sought to reveal the hidden exercise of power through legal technique. Scholars endorsing a hard version of the 'indeterminacy thesis' suggest that technique is infinitely malleable towards any wanted result—a smokescreen for underlying politics and ideologies. For critical legal scholars, any attempt to understand the workings of legal technique too closely risks crossing over into unwitting apologism. Legal historian Morton Horwitz critiques Karl Llewellyn's interest in legal technology along these lines, and Duncan Kennedy deploys Weberian ideas of disenchantment against Weber's own (ambivalent) attraction to formal law (Horwitz 1994; Kennedy 2004). Pierre Schlag (1998) likewise has argued that efforts to engage legal technique fall prey to the 'enchantment' of legal reasoning. Yet there are more possible positions than an argument for or against legal technique: an ethnographic understanding should not be confused with a normative defence of legal technique.

Towards an Ethnographic Understanding of Legal Technique

In the contextualizations and critiques, legal technique largely remains a black box—what 'really' goes on is understood through ideologies, context, and outcomes. Curiously absent from such studies are the knowledge practices of lawyers themselves. For lawyers, in contrast, to ignore the nature, experience, aesthetics, and consequences of legal reasoning is to leave out what is most distinctive and significant about the law.

Why has legal knowledge so often evaded anthropological scrutiny? The answer, we believe, lies not in its distance from anthropological knowledge but in its proximity. Contemporary legal technique is distinctively instrumentalist: the lawyer conceptualizes legal technique as a means to an end. This is a foundational tenet of early and mid-twentieth-century legal thought and one that continues to be shared by contemporary schools of legal theory as diverse as critical legal studies and law and economics.

Anthropological engagement with this dimension of legal knowledge is complicated by the fact that anthropology is itself implicated in law's means-ends relationship. When American legal realists sought to frame law as a means to a wider social end, they engaged legal anthropologists from Malinowski to Gluckman and borrowed a key concept from anthropology and cognate fields: social context.

From this point of view, the anthropological urge to contextualize the law appears quite superfluous. An alternative approach, we believe, is to focus ethnographic attention on that aspect of the means-ends relation which most captivates lawyers but is largely ignored by anthropologists: the means. The legal dogma that law is merely a means to social ends entails a commitment to a specific aesthetic: to the law as a tool. Attention to this aesthetic causes the social ends that legal technique is meant to serve to recede into the background as lawyers put their tools to use.

Our own thinking about law begins from a position of ethnographic curiosity about the knowledge practices of lawyers and about the possible deployment of those knowledge practices upon other terrains. An ethnographic understanding of law as technique yields a more sophisticated account of law, but it offers more than that. As we will show, it opens up the possibility of recapturing for anthropology and critical theory the self-reflexivity and recursivity of lawyerly work. That in turn enables its redeployment on new theoretical terrains to revitalize anthropological and legal thought alike. In this respect, the ethnography of legal technique opens up avenues for mutual learning and collaboration across the disciplinary divide between law and anthropology. We suggest, therefore, that engaging ethnographically with legal technique will not only generate new insights about the nature of legal knowledge but also effectuate a transformation of anthropological theory and method.

Sociolegal predecessors: Weber, Llewellyn, Bourdieu

Weber

The systematic theorization of law as technique begins with Max Weber (Friedman 1975: 149). Weber identified and analysed the technical quality of legal knowledge as a subject of sociological inquiry distinct from legal norms, legal processes, legal institutions, actors, or even legal language. He treated legal activity in sociolegal terms as a realm of social and cultural practice in its own right (Riles 2006a).

Weber argued that in the modern world, knowledge becomes increasingly important. From this point of view, legal knowledge deserves an important place in our understanding of modern law. This valuing of knowledge in turn leads to a turning of knowledge on itself: 'Another aspect of intellectualization is the increasing tendency for individuals to act on the basis of conscious reflection about the probable consequences of their action' (Brubaker 2013: 3). It is this self-reflexivity that enables the means-ends calculations of instrumental rationality for which Weber is so well known. Tim Murphy (1997: 50) adds that this self-reflexivity extended to Weber's own highly rational intellectual project: 'For Weber, then, what was, historically, the foundation of critique—rationality—slipped over into being the principal form of closure against which critique had to be directed.'

Weber was in fact deeply ambivalent about the rationality of law—he was both fascinated by what rationality enabled and also highly attentive to its dark sides. As Rogers Brubaker points out, this ambivalence continues to render Weber's work 'challenging and evocative today' (Brubaker 2013: 31). Weber's legacy, therefore, is a sceptical sociological account of legal knowledge that does not reduce legal knowledge to a function of elements outside the law such as society, politics, or culture (Riles 2006a).

Llewellyn

Despite Weber's foundational status in sociolegal studies, his interest in legal experts, their knowledge, and their self-reflexivity gained relatively little traction for many years. An important exception can be found in the work of the American legal scholar Karl Llewellyn, who focused on law as a craft, a set of 'law-jobs' (Scharffs 2001). Llewellyn had studied the work of Max Weber in Germany, but mainly developed his ideas both through his anthropologically informed studies of Native Americans (where he and E. Adamson Hoebel introduced the case method used in professional legal training to legal anthropology) and through his analyses of the American common law (Llewellyn 1960; Llewellyn and Hoebel 1941; Twining 1973). As with Weber, Llewellyn combined a focus on the practices of officials with an interest in the functional implications of these practices. Juristic method is, for Llewellyn, one of 'the ways of handling "legal" tools to law-job ends, and of the ongoing upkeep and improvement of both ways and tools'. Juristic method is performed by tribunals and courts, he argued, but is also found beyond these specific institutions: it 'extends over into reform legislation and especially into the still largely unspoken skills and multiform traditions of the official craftsmen of the Law' (Llewellyn 1940: 1393). For Llewellyn, steeped as he was in the functionalism of the anthropology of his day, this method gave law the coherence of a system, in which errors and abuses in individual cases could be addressed by regularizing processes, such as limiting the erroneous decision to specific concrete cases: 'legal, yes, right, yes, but legal and right only so far, and only when done in such a way' (1394).

Llewellyn's approach to legal technique differs from Weber's in two ways. First, unlike Weber, Llewellyn saw himself first and foremost as a legal practitioner—involved in the training of legal novices, the drafting of laws, and the expert analysis of legal decisions—and hence his analysis begins from an internal perspective on what he called lawyers' craft-skills (Twining 1973). Second, Llewellyn was most of all interested in law as a means to social ends—a way of achieving specific goals. Yet the act of reflecting on legal knowledge from both an internal perspective (a how-to for 'law-jobs') and an external perspective ('functions' of law) at once is, as with Weber, a remarkable exercise in reflexive analysis.

Bourdieu

Weber and Llewellyn were not anthropologists, and their impact on legal anthropology has been limited. One sociologist who has profoundly impacted the direction of legal anthropology is Pierre Bourdieu. In 1987, Bourdieu (1987) applied his field analysis to law. His focus was on the inner workings of law and its practitioners: 'the conceptions that professionals working within the legal world have of their own activity; the mechanisms by which their conceptions of the law, and those of others within their society, are formed, sustained, and propagated; and the objective social effects (both within the field and outside of it) of the professional work of lawyers and the law' (Terdiman 1987). Bourdieu, like Weber, focuses on law's formalities, the artificiality of its practices. His interest is not so much, however, in these practices and formalities themselves but in their effects of legitimation and empowerment, of law and of the lawyers who practise it. This results ultimately in an outside perspective and critique of law as simultaneously concealing and producing power in society.

This focus on the symbolic power of law and its marketability at the expense of a close scrutiny of law's functioning can also be found in scholars working in the tradition of Bourdieu. Sociolegal scholars Dezalay and Garth began to study cultures of legal expertise in settings such as private legal practice, government agencies, and international arbitration courts (Dezalay and Garth 2002). These scholars sought to show how the deleterious effects of projects such as legal pluralism or law and development were the product of something more subtle than simple bad faith on the part of policymakers. Rather than seeing law as the straightforward agent of colonial or capitalist power, Dezalay and Garth drew attention to the inner workings of legal knowledge itself. In this approach, the technicalities of law that so fascinated Weber re-emerge as a legitimate subject of empirical investigation. There is a marked reflexivity in the work of scholars in this tradition: they are aware that legal sociologists are part of the story—that they are not just describing the field of international arbitration they write about, but helping to legitimize it. Nevertheless, for Garth and Dezalay, working in a Bourdieuian framework, legal knowledge is still not particularly interesting for its own sake, as it was for Weber and for Llewellyn (Riles 2006a). Their analysis ultimately renders legal knowledge as a tool of elite social forces—a mechanism of 'palace wars', of competition between individuals and groups, reflecting social hierarchies within legal institutions.

Systems theory and STS approaches to legal technique

Two other social scientific traditions outside of anthropology have more recently impacted anthropologists' engagement with legal technique. Systems theory has brought an understanding and practice of reflexivity and recursivity to the anthropology of legal technique. The impact of science and technology studies (STS) on anthropology writ large over the last three decades has led to an explosion of anthropological work on technical fields of knowledge production such as science and engineering (what Laura Nader (1972) once called 'studying up'). This focus on technical knowledge practices in turn has spurred interest, analogously, in the practice of legal knowledge. Together, these two traditions bring three key concepts to sociolegal studies of legal technique: recursivity, materiality, and the agency of legal technique.

Systems theory: Recursivity

Epitomized by the work of sociologist Niklas Luhmann (2004) and legal scholar Gunther Teubner, systems theory treats law as a form of self-reflexive communication feedback. Luhmann and Teubner share with legal sociologists a view of law as nothing more or less than what legal actors treat as law: law exists whenever the code of legal/illegal is used. However, Luhmann and Teubner treat law as an autopoietic system rather than as an instrument of individual strategy—a realm of communication and description: 'the idiosyncrasies of the profession seem to be a secondary phenomenon. It is the inner logics of the legal discourse itself that build on normative self-reference and recursivity and thus create a preference for internal transfer within the global legal system' (Teubner 1998: 16).

Gunther Teubner's (1998) work brings even greater attention than the sociology of legal experts to the reflexive character of legal systems—to their capacity for building their own autonomy by observing and commenting on themselves (as in legal debates about legal process, e.g.). From Teubner's (1995) point of view, law experts should not be expected to fully take the 'real world' consequences of their decisions into account because their knowledge works otherwise. This is reminiscent of sociologist Santos's claim, informed by the critical projects discussed earlier, 'that laws misread [reality] in order to establish their exclusivity' (De Sousa Santos 1987). Teubner's analysis is, however, different. For him and Paterson, the misreading that law performs 'is not calculated in this way but is rather the *inevitable* result of law's autopoietic nature—reality is constructed on the basis of the selections made by law according to its code (legal/illegal) as it seeks to achieve order from complexity. In other words, it is impossible to avoid a misreading and law can only observe what its code allows it to construct' (Paterson and Teubner 1998: 461; italics in original). Like a learning algorithm, law evolves as a system. Teubner's approach suggests that to understand the law, we must appreciate law's internal autonomy and its disconnection from vernacular social reality as something other than an epistemological failure or an act of bad faith.

Materiality

An increasing number of sociolegal scholars borrow from the 'material semiotics' of STS, and of actor-network theory (ANT) in particular. In a widely cited study of a group of soil scientists in the Amazon, Bruno Latour (1999) challenges conventional sociological understandings of the relationship between reality and scientific representation. Rather than a mere representation of an extant reality, Latour argues that scientific research is a series of material transformations that create the world. He describes this process as: 'circulating reference'. Latour takes us through the various stages through which a group of soil scientists make the Boa Vista forest-savannah transition into a laboratory phenomenon. From the digging of holes to the analysis of soil density and colour, scientists gradually reduce their data into a form that is increasingly mobile. What these practices amount to, Latour argues, is not the creation of a resemblance of the forest in the lab, but the construction of a world internal to the laboratory: 'Knowledge does not reflect a real external world that it resembles via mimesis, but rather a real interior world' (1999: 58).

A number of anthropologists and sociolegal scholars have applied this premise to legal and bureaucratic settings beyond the sciences (Barrera 2018; Davis et al. 2012; Foster 2016; Hull 2012; Mathews 2011; Mathur 2016; Navaro-Yashin 2007). One implication of this approach is that it makes 'impossib[le] the classic distinction between law and society' (Cloatre and Cowan 2018: 438). A basic premise of this approach is that 'materiality and sociality are produced together': materiality and society are both relational effects. Rather than presuming entities like 'society' or 'law'—or 'persons' and 'things'—and then analysing a relationship between them, material semiotic approaches elucidate the assemblages through which such entities are materialized (Law and Mol 1995: 263–4). One instantiation of this approach is the legal scholar Alain Pottage's study of patent law. Pottage approaches law as a 'mode of fabrication' through which inventions and their owners are *constituted* (Pottage 2011).

In this work, legal knowledge and the process by which it comes to frame political, social, and epistemological conflicts becomes a central subject in its own right, one that is not simply reducible to social pressures and forces but that has its own epistemological and material autonomy. Yet in his own ethnography of the French Conseil d'État, although he usefully focuses on all kinds of instruments and technologies around the knowledge practices of law, Latour (2010: 263) ignores legal reasoning itself: 'the Council of State is not made "of law" but consists of walls, corridors, frescoes, files, a body of members, texts, careers, publications, controversies'. The material artefacts of law are not understood in relationship to the knowledge practices that produce them.

It is little surprise, then, that Latour has little appreciation for legal technique. Comparing legal knowledge to the knowledge practices of science and engineering, Latour declares that law is the 'least technical form of enunciation' because it lacks, in his view, an important criterion of technique: it 'never manages to fold space-time, to replace its injunctions by another matter'. Both legal scholars and anthropologists have shown this to be incorrect: the law certainly does fold both space and time (Riles 2011: ch. 4). If we broaden Latour's narrow understanding of technique developed from one very recent historical moment and one kind of expertise, we realize that, contrary to Latour's assertion, the Western legal tradition has always been technical. As Steinhauer (2015: 14–16) puts it, 'There is a technique before the age of technology, and its name is doctrine'.

The Agency of Legal Technique

Another contribution of STS scholarship has been to draw attention to the agency of scientific instruments in the production of facts. The tools that scientists have at hand are more than incidental to the production of scientific facts, in this view. They shape knowledge production in ways that exceed the intentions and control of their users. For example, when a freezer truck carrying samples of Antarctic ice malfunctions, a research project melts along with the ice (O'Reilly 2016). Or again, the microscope guides and limits the ways in which scientists go about their research and the questions that captivate their attention (Latour 1999).

Alongside these analyses of the agency of material instruments—the microscope, the freezer truck, the notebook—STS scholars also draw attention to the agency of scientists' conceptual tools. Andrew Pickering (1995) gives the example of the machine-like way in which one completes '3 + 4 =' by writing '7' or one multiplies out 'a(b + c)' as 'ab + ac'. As Pickering describes it, '[s]uch disciplines—acquired in training and refined in use—carry human conceptual practice along, as it were, independently of individual wishes and intents. The scientist is, in this sense, passive in disciplined conceptual practice' (1995: 115). Here the conceptual techniques of the sciences are agentive, something that Pickering describes as 'disciplinary agency' (1995: ch. 4).

Building on this work, a number of sociolegal scholars understand legal technique as something analogous to scientific conceptual tools, something that not only shapes social, political, or economic phenomena but also constitutes these phenomena. An interesting conversation is emerging in diverse pockets of sociolegal studies around the question of the *agency of legal form*. Law provides a cognitive framework through which social actors, including legal and social scientific observers, not only apprehend but also enact social realities. This work draws attention to the way legal categories function as constraints that shape actors' choices and enable certain kinds of legal subjectivity and objectivity. In this respect, we can speak of the legal categories and techniques—and not just their human authors—as *generative* of certain kinds of social and political realities (Cabot 2012; Grabham 2016; Pottage and Sherman 2010; Riles 2005; Sullivan 2020).

For example, Alain Pottage (2011) demonstrates the distinctive agency of the nineteenth-century patent model in US patent law. He shows that the models that patent lawyers used to demonstrate their clients' inventions in court are themselves agentive. If 'the agency of models', as Pottage puts it, 'preceded, framed, and conditioned lawyers' perceptions and arguments about invention, then there was more to the fabrication of invention than strategy or intentionality' (Pottage 2011: 635). In an analysis co-authored with Brad Sherman, Pottage shows how the 'spectre [of these models] survived into the form of modern patent law' (Pottage and Sherman 2010). Pottage and Sherman do not deny that powerful business interests have shaped modern patent law. But they argue that patent law cannot be understood solely as the product of human interests. By focusing on the technicalities, they show how legal innovations are not simply the product of persons, or even of their social or epistemic contexts. Much like the material tools and disciplinary practices of the sciences, the material and discursive tools of legal technique carry lawyers along in ways that are independent of human wishes and intents.

ANTHROPOLOGY AND THE CONSTRAINTS OF FORM

Recent anthropological work on legal technique intersects with these traditions but begins from a different starting point—the anthropology of gifts and exchange. Anthropologists have drawn attention to the 'constraints of form' inherent in exchange—how people elicit particular effects from one another through the usage of specific aesthetic forms. As Marilyn Strathern puts it in relation to Melanesian aesthetics, '*relations are only recognized if they assume a particular form*' (Strathern 1988: 180; italics in original). The possibilities for interaction are in this respect limiting: one must adhere to the appropriate aesthetic, to the permissible modes of acting. But the same constraints are also the enabling condition for exchange transactions, for producing persons, and for producing relationships. Analogizing from this literature to the production and circulation of legal documents, arguments, and language, anthropologists have considered how legal technique garners efficacy from the constraints of legal form.

This attention to the constraints of form helps us to better understand *how* legal technicalities come to assume the agency noted by sociologists. Legal technique is an aesthetic that calls forth replication. Anthropologists first explored the implications of exchange for legal technique by focusing on the material artefacts of legal knowledge—the production, circulation, and collection of legal documents. More recently, anthropologists have turned ethnographic attention to legal reasoning itself. We consider each of these subjects in turn. We conclude by drawing attention to what in our view is the core aesthetic, or motif, of legal reasoning—the legal fiction.

Documents as Legal Artefacts

The STS scholarship on circulating reference and non-human agency described above first met the anthropology of exchange in a body of anthropological literature on the production and circulation of legal and bureaucratic documents (Barrera 2018; Davis et al. 2012; Foster 2016; Mathews 2011; Navaro-Yashin 2007; Riles 2006b). Mathew Hull (2012), for example, borrows from Latour to describe the document-mediated processes through which a Pakistani bureaucracy constructs a city. In so doing, he draws equally on STS scholarship and on Webb Keane's analysis of how Anakalang people construct corporate authorship during ritual. This helps him to illuminate how the bureaucrats he studied used documents to construct a collective bureaucratic agency that mitigates the potential for individualized responsibility for their policies.

Likewise, Susan Coutin, Bill Maurer, and Barbara Yngvesson (2002) examine the legal documents that construct boundaries and connections between 'legitimate' and 'illegitimate' persons and things. Drawing on fieldwork in the fields of finance, immigration, and intercountry adoption, they show the importance of narratives of origin for legitimizing the global movement and non-movement of people and capital. They demonstrate how '[d]ocuments ... constitute, authorize, and conceal movements' (2002: 824). As Coutin et al. highlight, however, there is always a 'something' beyond the truths that legal documents produce (2002: 824). Drawing on Slavoj Žižek, Coutin et al. argue that such residual 'somethings' reveal the dependence of the conventional legal and bureaucratic order upon the figure of an outside to that order that adoptees—and offshore money and immigrants—embody. By focusing on legal documents, they 'expose the assumptions on which privilege of mobility is based' (2002: 838).

Finally, contributors to the volume *Documents: Artefacts of Modern Knowledge* (Riles 2006b) have drawn attention to the temporality of technocratic documents, the ways in which bureaucratic documents compel creativity, and how anthropologists might respond to mundane technocratic practices by borrowing, extending, and replicating the knowledge practices that produce documentary artefacts (Riles 2006c; Miyazaki 2006; Reed 2006; Strathern 2006). Several of the contributors to the *Documents* volume, including Marilyn Strathern herself, draw explicitly on Strathern's work on exchange to understand legal and bureaucratic documents.

Legal Reasoning

Legal reasoning is a practice of manipulating a closed set of concepts—contract, property, rights—that does not aim to point to anything specific in the material world. This practice translates real-life situations into sets of abstract terms, acting as if a resolution can be found on the basis of those terms. 'The notions and axioms of [legal] science ... are actual beings', says Savigny (1831: 45) about Roman law, and compares it to mathematics, suggesting that the Romans 'calculate with their [legal] notions'.

Indeed, Roman law, with its focus on technical reasoning, could well be called technique *avant la lettre*. Roman litigation required lawyers to follow precise wording in their pleadings or they would lose their case. But used correctly, the words could achieve results otherwise unachievable, like the transfer of property. Social and legal effects could be brought about through the use of form.

Such formalism has long been a point of critique for lawyers and anthropologists alike. Thus legal scholars Jean Stefancic and Richard Delgado (2005) claim that abstract work in the law makes lawyers miserable, and anthropologist David Graeber (2019) includes the job of attorney in his list of 'bullshit jobs'. Such disenchantment undoubtedly exists. However, the opposite is also visible: the pride and pleasure of law students in learning a new language, the aesthetic satisfaction attorneys find in a contract they have drafted, the contentment of a judge who has found a formally convincing answer to a knotty legal problem. Anthropologist Andrea Ballestero (2014: 53) shows how legal reasoning can be a vehicle for 'creat[ing] semiotic, political, and material relations'. In her ethnographic study of water as a human right, Ballestero (2014, 2015) examines Costa Rican water pricing formulas designed to enact the government's legal commitment to water delivery as a not-for-profit service. The controversies surrounding the adjudication of these formulas illuminates the 'technical and ethical labour regulators perform when they mobilize' the 'calculation grammar' governing the human right to water (Ballestero 2015: 274–5). Where anthropologists have often imagined technical work as inherently depoliticizing (Ferguson 1994; Li 2007), Ballestero shows how the 'mathematical expression' of 'technolegal metaphysics' provides a grammar for projects that are both deeply ethical and open to inventive transformation.

Ancient Roman formal law is often thought to rest in magic, which was also a prime interest of anthropologists around 1900. Hubert and Mauss (1902), in their theory of magic, drew a sharp distinction between magic and law: law, unlike magic, had an obligatory effect and had to be distinguished from its ritual acts. That distinction was doubtful. Huvelin (1905) criticized it early on, pointing out that in law, it was the very technicality itself that created the effects. Later, the Scandinavian realists used the connection between law and magic for their version of legal realism (Hägerström 1927, 1941; Olivecrona 1939). For them, that connection provided the basis of a critique of formalism: faith in formalism resembled faith in magic and ignored the social reality of law. One famous example is a 1951 essay by Alf Ross (1957). In the essay, Ross compared modern legal doctrine's faith in legal concepts to an imagined 'primitive' society's faith in the consequences of breaking taboos (Ross calls these 'tû-tû'). Ross cites no actual anthropologists—rather, he confidently invents an exotic distant society and a canon of research about it. His exoticizing imagination of customary practices empowers Ross to set up a problematic juxtaposition of barbaric and irrational customs on the one hand and modern law on the other in order to show the law up as less than modern.

The argument would most likely have found a strong critic in the model for the spoof, Bronisław Malinowski, who, a full twenty years before the publication of Ross's essay, had put forward a far more subtle version of the same analogy of modern legal reasoning to Pacific Islanders' magic towards very different ends. In *Coral Gardens and their Magic*, Malinowski (2013: 231) rejects the dichotomy of realism and magicality and emphasizes instead that 'language in its inception is both magical and pragmatic. It is charged with a mystical effectiveness and is used as a working tool.' Malinowski invokes contemporary legal knowledge as an example of magic, in the technical terms of his thesis, but unlike Ross, he emphasizes the necessity of the sacred to the workings of technique. Against Freud's assertion that magic is a function of the 'omnipotence of thought', Malinowski emphasizes that magic is a tool for overcoming the limits of human thought, for getting over the unknowns. In this sense, it works hand in hand with science and technology rather than against these—it fills in the gaps. Malinowski emphasizes moreover that the magician acts with a knowledge that magic is only 'as if': 'where man knows that his thought is impotent, there and there only does he resort to magic' (2013: 239). Malinowski emphasizes the power of magical incantations—in law as in Trobriand gardening—to facilitate collaboration. In contrast to Ross, Malinowski concludes that in both primitive and modern societies, 'magic has exercised a profound positive function in organizing enterprise, in inspiring hope and confidence in the individual' (2013: 240).

The reason for both the disenchantment and the joy of legal knowledge is one and the same: doctrine operates in an 'as if' modality. Legal problems are discussed *as if* they were solvable, *as if* they could be kept free from politics (Fuller 1967). Legal doctrine relieves the lawyer, for a moment (although crucially, only for one moment (Knop et al. 2012)), from responsibility for outcomes so that it is possible to engage in legal reasoning. This fictionality is the defining modality of legal technique, the underlying orientation of all legal reasoning.

Legal Fictions

All legal reasoning operates on the basis of 'as ifs': lawyers treat corporations as if they really existed, they treat formal legal pronouncements as if they altered kinship relations, they treat irresolvable conflicts as if they were problems that could in fact be resolved. Legal fictions are counterfactual assertions of certain facts understood as such by all involved.

The fiction was a core element of Roman legal reasoning, necessary to achieve certain results even when other legal or social requirements were missing. Some fictions made easier what could have been achieved by other means: ownership in land could be transferred through the fiction that the buyer had always been the owner, for example (Wolff 1958). But other fictions made possible what would otherwise have been impossible: conceiving of a corporation as a (fictitious) person enabled a continuation of life even when all owners had died (Blackstone 1795: 467). Roman lawyers saw nothing wrong with the fiction because in their understanding the reality of the law was itself created in the law. As Yan Thomas (1995: 18) writes, 'the "as if [*comme si*]" of fiction is not an aspect of "legal thought" so much as it is an operationalization of the specific technique of law, its way of doing things'.

To some critics, fictions are signs of the inadequacy of the law. The law finds itself unable to fit a certain socially desirable goal into its current structure, so it resorts to a fiction (Cohen 1923, 1935; Fuller 1967). It seems inadequate, however, to view the fiction as a mere temporary response to a perceived imperfection in the law. Sir Henry Maine (1874), for example, viewed this capacity as the engine of the law's progress. In the same way in which we speak of the mathematical concept of a line even though we understand that no such entity exists as a matter of physical reality, legal reasoning deploys fictions that are known not to be true as starting points for relations of legal ideas. Legal technique translates real-world situations into fact patterns that are counterfactual but as such manageable (Geertz 2008; Scheppele 1990). The fiction is not used to represent an actual reality but is rather a technique to successfully reach certain ends (see Teubner 2001).

Consider, for example, the legal fictions that undergird the swap transactions of global financial institutions (Riles 2011). A swap transaction is an agreement between two parties to exchange one kind of asset for another at a predetermined future point. A risk in such transactions is that one party will go bankrupt before the exchange is scheduled to happen. In most countries, bankruptcy law dictates that in such a circumstance, the non-bankrupt party is still obliged to uphold its end of the swap transaction—they are required to hand over the assets promised, even though the bankrupt swap partner can no longer hold up its end of the bargain. To guard against such a loss, banks require swap partners to post collateral up until the date of the exchange. Posting collateral is, in and of itself, simple enough. But the situation is complicated by the fact that banks often want to be able to rehypothecate the collateral posted with them—to use the collateral they hold for their own purposes in the meantime. The simple solution that lawyers introduce to manage this problem is a legal fiction that the party posting the collateral has already defaulted on the swap transaction. This simple legal fiction gives the party which holds collateral full rights over its disposal.

What anthropological theory helps us to appreciate about this legal fiction is its temporality. Collateral agreements operate within a swap transaction's temporal constraint of form (Riles 2011). The fiction that grants a party complete control over collateral—thereby allowing them to rehypothecate—is a 'placeholder' that allows the parties to the swap transaction to act in the meantime. The fiction does not resolve the ultimate questions of the swap parties' rights and responsibilities to each other's collateral; it simply creates a provisional solution subject to future re-evaluation.

The legal fiction, in this regard, does not entail an epistemological claim: the fiction is in fact *nonrepresentational*. The implication for anthropologists of law is that one cannot expect to uncover the politics of the legal fiction in the gap between worldly reality and legal representation. The politics of the legal fictions contained in collateral agreements are already on the surface: legal fictions are a purposeful, and extremely powerful, tool for governing self and others.

What Can We do with Legal Technique?

What are the possibilities inherent in this practice? What forms of analysis might we engender if we were to adopt, to reorient the intellectual style of legal technique? Extending the anthropology of exchange to the study of legal technique allows not merely a description of the functions of legal technique, but an opportunity to harness the creativity, energy, and power of legal constraints of form for new purposes.

Together with our co-author Karen Knop, we have explored how an understanding and redeployment of the constraints of legal form on novel terrains in the conflict of laws enables us to develop what Michaels (2014) calls a 'post-critical private international law' (Knop et al. 2012; Knop and Riles 2017). Applying this perspective to international legal controversies over claims for compensation for sexual slavery during World War II, for example, Knop and Riles (2017) argue that we might find a novel response to the diffusion of historical injustices in conflict-of-laws techniques. They redescribe conflict-of-laws techniques for dealing with time across space as a matter of 'sequencing' different spatio-temporal horizons. The temporal possibilities of conflict of laws, they argue, offer a more specified and hopeful approach to a feminist future.

Knop and Riles's reworking of conflict of laws to the service of a feminist hope is an iteration of a classic anthropological strategy: one in which anthropologists borrow their analytic strategies from the practices of their ethnographic interlocutors. In this respect, treating legal technique as an ethnographic subject—and not merely an object of critique—opens up possibilities for reorienting legal knowledge towards theoretical innovation.

Conclusion

The anthropology of law has produced important accounts of law in the lives of the general population and insightful critiques of the social effects of law. In taking an external perspective on law, however, anthropologists have historically overlooked the potential to engage lawyers and legal technique as ethnographic subjects. In this respect, anthropologists did not take up Max Weber or Karl Llewellyn's early interest in legal experts and legal knowledge as objects of sociological study. We trace anthropologists' long-standing antipathy to legal technique ironically to the discipline's proximity to modernist legal theory. When, in the early twentieth century, American legal realists began to frame law as a means to a wider social end, they borrowed a key concept from anthropology: social context. It became the job of the anthropologist, from both lawyers' and anthropologists' point of view, to provide the context.

Rather than indulge the urge to contextualize the law, we argue for ethnographic attention to the aspect of law's means-ends relation that captivates lawyers but that is largely ignored by anthropologists: the means. This is the focus of a growing group of sociolegal scholars who draw on systems theory and STS to illuminate the recursivity of legal expertise, the materiality of legal knowledge, and the agency of legal technique. This STS-inflected scholarship intersects with an emerging body of anthropology that examines bureaucratic documents, legal reasoning, and legal doctrine. Taking anthropology's long-standing attention to the constraints of form inherent in exchange as its starting point, this scholarship highlights the potential for anthropological theory and methods to elucidate the workings of legal knowledge. And it demonstrates the possibilities that ethnography of legal technique offers as an engine of theoretical innovation.

References

Abel, R. L. 1988. *The Legal Profession in England and Wales*. Oxford: Blackwell.

Ballestero, A. 2014. 'What Is in a Percentage? Calculation as the Poetic Translation of Human Rights'. *Indiana Journal of Global Legal Studies* 21(1): 27.

Ballestero, A. 2015. 'The Ethics of a Formula: Calculating a Financial–Humanitarian Price for Water'. *American Ethnologist* 42(2): 262–78.

Barrera, L. 2018. 'Gatekeeping: Documents, Legal Knowledge, and Judicial Authority in Contemporary Argentina'. *PoLAR: Political & Legal Anthropology Review* 41(1): 90–107.

Blackstone, W. 1795. *Commentaries on the Laws of England*. Oxford: Clarendon Press.

Bourdieu, P. 1987. 'The Force of Law: Toward a Sociology of the Juridical Field'. *Hastings Law Journal* 38: 814.

Brubaker, R. 2013. *The Limits of Rationality*. London: Taylor & Francis.

Cabot, H. 2012. 'The Governance of Things: Documenting Limbo in the Greek Asylum Procedure'. *PoLAR: Political & Legal Anthropology Review* 35(1): 11–29.

Chatterjee, M. 2017. 'The Impunity Effect: Majoritarian Rule, Everyday Legality, and State Formation in India'. *American Ethnologist* 44(1): 118–30.

Cloatre, E. and D. Cowan. 2018. 'Legalities and Materialities'. In A. Philippopoulos-Mihalopoulos, ed. *Routledge Handbook of Law and Theory Volume 1*, 433–52. New York: Routledge.

Cohen, M. R. 1923. 'On the Logic of Fiction'. *The Journal of Philosophy* 20(18): 477–88.

Cohen, F. S. 1935. 'Transcendental Nonsense and the Functional Approach'. *Columbia Law Review* 35(6): 809–49.

Coutin, S. B., B. Maurer, and B. Yngvesson. 2002. 'In the Mirror: The Legitimation Work of Globalization'. *Law & Social Inquiry* 27(4): 801–43.

Davis, K. E., B. Kingsbury, and S. E. Merry. 2012. 'Indicators as a Technology of Global Governance'. *Law & Society Review* 46(1): 71–104.

De Sousa Santos, B. 1987. 'Law: A Map of Misreading. Toward a Postmodern Conception of Law'. *Journal of Law and Society* 14(3): 279–302.

Dezalay, Y. and B. G. Garth. 2002. *The Internationalization of Palace Wars: Lawyers, Economists, and the Contest to Transform Latin American States*. Chicago: University of Chicago Press.

Ehrlich, E. 1936. *Fundamental Principles of the Sociology of Law*. Cambridge: Harvard University Press.

Ferguson, J. 1994. *The Anti-Politics Machine: 'Development,' Depoliticization, and Bureaucratic Power in Lesotho*. Minneapolis: University of Minnesota Press.

Foster, L. A. 2016. 'The Making and Unmaking of Patent Ownership: Technicalities, Materialities, and Subjectivities'. *PoLAR: Political and Legal Anthropology Review* 39(1): 127–43.

Foucault, M. 2008. *The History of Sexuality: The Will to Knowledge: Vol. 1*. New York: Penguin.

Friedman, L. M. 1975. *The Legal System: A Social Science Perspective*. New York: Russell Sage Foundation.

Fuller, L. L. 1967. *Legal Fictions*. Stanford: Stanford University Press.

Geertz, C. 2008. *Local Knowledge: Further Essays in Interpretive Anthropology*. New York: Basic Books.

Grabham, E. 2016. 'Time and Technique: The Legal Lives of the 26-Week Qualifying Period'. *Economy and Society* 45(3–4): 379–406.

Graeber, D. 2019. *Bullshit Jobs: A Theory*. New York: Simon & Schuster.

Gupta, A. 2012. *Red Tape: Bureaucracy, Structural Violence, and Poverty in India*. Durham: Duke University Press.

Hägerström, A. 1927. *Der römische Obligationsbegriff im Lichte der allgemeinen römischen Rechtsanschauung 1*. Uppsala: Almqvist & Wiksell.

Hägerström, A. 1941. *Der römische Obligationsbegriff im Lichte der allgemeinen römischen Rechtsanschauung* 2. Uppsala: Almqvist & Wiksell.

Horwitz, M. J. 1994. *The Transformation of American Law, 1870–1960: The Crisis of Legal Orthodoxy*. Oxford: Oxford University Press.

Hubert, H. and M. Mauss. 1902. 'Esquisse D'Une Théorie Générale De La Magie'. *L'Année sociologique* 7: 1–146.

Hull, M. S. 2012. *Government of Paper: The Materiality of Bureaucracy in Urban Pakistan*. Berkeley: University of California Press.

Huvelin, P. 1905. 'Magie et le droit individuel'. *L'Année sociologique* 10: 1–47.

Kennedy, D. 2004. 'The Disenchantment of Logically Formal Legal Rationality, or: Max Weber's Sociology in the Genealogy of the Contemporary Mode of Western Legal Thought'. *The Hastings Law Journal* 55: 1031–76.

Knop, K., R. Michaels, and A. Riles. 2012. 'From Multiculturalism to Technique: Feminism, Culture, and the Conflict of Laws Style'. *Stanford Law Review* 64: 589.

Knop, K. and A. Riles. 2017. 'Space, Time, and Historical Injustice: A Feminist Conflict-of-Laws Approach to the "Comfort Women" Agreement'. *Cornell Law Review* 102: 853–1115.

Latour, B. 1999. *Pandora's Hope: Essays on the Reality of Science Studies*. Cambridge, MA: Harvard University Press.

Latour, B. 2010. *The Making of Law: An Ethnography of the Conseil D'Etat*. Cambridge: Polity Press.

Law, J. and A. Mol. 1995. 'Notes on Materiality and Sociality'. *The Sociological Review* 43(2): 274–94.

Li, T. M. 2007. *The Will to Improve: Governmentality, Development, and the Practice of Politics*. Durham: Duke University Press.

Llewellyn, K. N. 1940. 'The Normative, the Legal, and the Law-Jobs: The Problem of Juristic Method'. *The Yale Law Journal* 49(8): 1355.

Llewellyn, K. N. 1960. *The Common Law Tradition: Deciding Appeals*. Boston: Little, Brown & Co.

Llewellyn, K. N. and E. A. Hoebel. 1941. *The Cheyenne Way: Conflict and Case Method in Primitive Jurisprudence*. Norman: University of Oklahoma Press.

Luhmann, N. 2004. *Law as a Social System*. Oxford: Oxford University Press.

Maine, H. S. 1874. *Ancient Law; Its Connection with the Early History of Society, and Its Relation to Modern Ideas*. London: J. Murray.

Malinowski, B. 2013 [1935]. *Coral Gardens and Their Magic: The Description of Gardening*. London: Taylor & Francis.

Marx, K. 1911. *A Contribution to the Critique of Political Economy*. Chicago: C.H. Kerr.

Mathews, A. S. 2011. *Instituting Nature: Authority, Expertise, and Power in Mexican Forests*. Cambridge: MIT Press.

Mathur, N. 2016. *Paper Tiger: Law, Bureaucracy and the Developmental State in Himalayan India*. Delhi: Cambridge University Press.

Merry, S. E. 2016. *The Seductions of Quantification: Measuring Human Rights, Gender Violence, and Sex Trafficking*. Chicago: Chinese University Press.

Michaels, R. 2014. 'Post-Critical Private International Law: From Politics to Technique'. In H. Muir Watt and D.P. Fernández Arroyo, eds., *Private International Law and Global Governance*, 54–67. Oxford: Oxford University Press.

Miyazaki, H. 2006. 'Documenting the Present'. In A. Riles, ed. *Documents: Artefacts of Modern Knowledge*, 206–25. Ann Arbor: University of Michigan Press.

Moore, S. F. 2001. 'Certainties Undone: Fifty Turbulent Years of Legal Anthropology, 1949–1999'. *Journal of the Royal Anthropological Institute* 7: 95–116.

Murphy, T. 1997. *The Oldest Social Science? Configurations of Law and Modernity*. Oxford: Oxford University Press.

Nader, L. 1965. 'The Anthropological Study of Law'. *American Anthropologist* 67(6): 3–32.

Nader, L. 1972. 'Up the Anthropologist: Perspectives Gained from Studying Up'. In D. Hymes, ed. *Reinventing Anthropology*, 284–311. New York: Pantheon Books.

Navaro-Yashin, Y. 2007. 'Make-Believe Papers, Legal Forms and the Counterfeit: Affective Interactions between Documents and People in Britain and Cyprus'. *Anthropological Theory* 7(1): 79–98.

O'Reilly, J. 2016. 'Sensing the Ice: Field Science, Models, and Expert Intimacy with Knowledge'. *Journal of the Royal Anthropological Institute* 22(S1): 27–45.

Olivecrona, K. 1939. *Law as Fact*. London: Oxford University Press.

Paterson, J. and G. Teubner. 1998. 'Changing Maps: Empirical Legal Autopoiesis'. *Social & Legal Studies* 7(4): 451–86.

Pickering, A. 1995. *The Mangle of Practice: Time, Agency, and Science*. Chicago: University of Chicago Press.

Pirie, F. 2013. *The Anthropology of Law*. Oxford: Oxford University Press.

Pottage, A. 2011. 'Law Machines: Scale Models, Forensic Materiality and the Making of Modern Patent Law'. *Social Studies of Science* 41(5): 621–43.

Pottage, A. and B. Sherman. 2010. *Figures of Invention: A History of Modern Patent Law*. Oxford: Oxford University Press.

Pound, R. 1910. 'Law in Books and Law in Action'. *American Law Review* 44: 12–36.

Reed, A. 2006. 'Documents Unfolding'. In A. Riles, ed. *Documents: Artefacts of Modern Knowledge*, 158–80. Ann Arbor: University of Michigan Press.

Riles, A. 2005. 'A New Agenda for the Cultural Study of Law: Taking on the Technicalities'. *Buffalo Law Review* 53: 973.

Riles, A. 2006a. 'Comparative Law and Socio-Legal Studies'. In M. Reimann and R. Z. Zimmerman, eds. *The Oxford Handbook of Comparative Law*, 775–814. Oxford: Oxford University Press.

Riles, A., ed. 2006b. *Documents: Artefacts of Modern Knowledge*. Ann Arbor: University of Michigan Press.

Riles, A. 2006c. '[Deadlines]: Removing the Brackets on Politics in Bureaucratic and Anthropological Analysis'. In A. Riles, ed. *Documents: Artefacts of Modern Knowledge*, 71–94. Ann Arbor: University of Michigan Press.

Riles, A. 2011. *Collateral Knowledge: Legal Reasoning in the Global Financial Markets*. Chicago: University of Chicago Press.

Ross, A. 1957. 'Tû-Tû'. *Harvard Law Review* 70(5): 812–25.

Savigny, C. F. 1831. *The Vocation of Our Age for Legislation and Jurisprudence*. Second edition. London: Littlewood & Co.

Scharffs, B. G. 2001. 'Law as Craft'. *Vanderbilt Law Review* 54(6): 2243–2348.

Scheppele, K. L. 1990. 'Facing Facts in Legal Interpretation'. *Representations* 30(Spring): 42–77.

Schlag, P. 1998. *The Enchantment of Reason*. Durham: Duke University Press.

Stefancic, J. and R. Delgado. 2005. *How Lawyers Lose Their Way: A Profession Fails Its Creative Minds*. Durham: Duke University Press.

Steinhauer, F. 2015. *Vom Scheiden: Geschichte und Theorie einer juristischen Kulturtechnik*. Berlin: Duncker & Humblot.

Strathern, M. 1988. *The Gender of the Gift: Problems with Women and Problems with Society in Melanesia*. Berkeley: University of California Press.

Strathern, M. 2006. 'Bullet Proofing: A Tale from the United Kingdom'. In A. Riles, ed. *Documents: Artefacts of Modern Knowledge*, 181–205. Ann Arbor: University of Michigan Press.

Sullivan, G. 2020. *The Law of the List: UN Counterterrorism Sanctions and the Politics of Global Security Law*. Cambridge: Cambridge University Press.

Teubner, G., ed. 1995. *Entscheidungsfolgen als Rechtsgründe. Folgenorientiertes Argumentieren in rechtsvergleichender Sicht*. Baden-Baden: Nomos.

Teubner, G. 1998. 'Legal Irritants: Good Faith in British Law or How Unifying Law Ends Up in New Divergencies'. *The Modern Law Review* 61(1): 11–32.

Teubner, G. 2001. 'Alienating Justice: on the Surplus Value of the Twelfth Camel'. *Droit et société* 47: 75.

Terdiman, R. 1987. 'Translator's Introduction to Pierre Bourdieu's The Force of Law: Toward a Sociology of the Juridical Field'. *Hastings Law Journal* 38: 805.

Thomas, Y. 1995. *Fictio Legis: l'empire de la fiction Romaine et ses limites médiévales*. Paris: Presses Universitaires de France.

Twining, W. 1973. 'Law and Anthropology: A Case Study in Inter-Disciplinary Collaboration'. *Law & Society Review* 7(4): 561–83.

Wolff, H. J. 1958. 'Constitutive Effect of *In Iure Cessio*'. *Tulane Law Review* 33(3): 525–40.

CHAPTER 48

EMOTION, AFFECT, AND LAW

KAMARI MAXINE CLARKE

ON 6 December 2016, the International Criminal Court (ICC) launched the trial of Dominic Ongwen, a former commander in the Sinia Brigade of the Lord's Resistance Army (LRA). Ongwen was charged with seventy counts of war crimes and crimes against humanity related to attacks against the civilian population in the former internally displaced person camps of Lukodi, Pajule, Odek, and Abok (ICC-CPI-20161206-PR1262). The crimes for which he was eventually convicted happened between October 2003 and June 2004 and included attacks 'against a civilian population; murder and attempted murder; rape; sexual slavery; forced marriage; torture; cruel treatment of civilian and other inhumane acts; enslavement; outrage upon personal dignity; conscription and use of children under the age of fifteen to participate actively in hostilities; pillaging; destruction of property and persecution' (ICC-02/04-01/15). The prosecutor argued that Ongwen and other commanders, including LRA leader Joseph Kony, were part of a common plan to abduct women and girls in northern Uganda and to force them into marriages and sex slavery. The details of how the case against Dominic Ongwen was assembled and adjudicated reveals the actual emotional and affective dimensions of international law. As we will see later in the chapter, this case exemplifies how strategic campaigns are used to mobilize collective emotion towards technocratic ends; in other words, how *affect* shapes the frameworks within which we try to make sense of and ameliorate violence. The Ongwen case is an ideal starting point for reflecting on how theories of emotion, affect, and law have seeded a growing anthropology of law literature, which will continue to make important contributions across disciplinary lines.

Until recently, the study of affect has been dominated by the fields of neuroscience and psychology (see Bower 1981; Bower et al. 1981; Bower and Cohen 1982; Bower and Gilligan 1979; Emde and Shapiro 1992; Fenichel 1945; Fox et al. 2018; Rapaport 1942; Spezzano 1993; Stein 1991; Tangney and Fischer 1995; Tomkins 1962, 1963). This work has focused predominantly on questions relating to the individual's relationship to the past (Kleinman and Good 1985; Lutz 1986; Molino 2004). The prevailing biopsychological literature suggests that affects are pre-social and pre-subjective, existing before human intentions and subjective beliefs form. In this understanding, affects involve noncognitive processes that influence our judgements while dwelling below human consciousness (Leys 2011: 437–43). On the other hand, scholars interested in physiological and cognitive aspects of affect argue that they do relate to the social effects of brain functions and how neurological processes are transformed into social action. Scholars of cognition, such as Brian Massumi (1995; 2002: 29), have characterized affects by examining states of intensity that are nonlinear and unpredictable, and which are seen as being open to creative potential. In this understanding, material brain functions and neurological interactions are viewed as having the potential to shape social meaning.

For more than fifty years, anthropologists have been concerned with understanding the place of emotion within the realm of the social and cultural. The subdisciplines of psychological anthropology (Harkness and Kilbride 1983; Worthman 1992) and medical anthropology (Hollan 2000; Hollan and Throop 2008; Kirmayer 2007; Melzack and Torgerson 1971; Rey 1993; Throop 2010) have been especially influenced by theories on affect. The question of what meaning is produced by what people *do* within the collective of cultural practice (Ahmed 2010), and how this relates to social change, has been the purview of anthropology, but short of the work of a range of phenomenologist and medical anthropologists, the interior psychological world has been largely underexamined (Navaro 2012). Because it has been difficult—and ethically dubious—for social scientists to (presume to) understand the psycho-interior lives of those they study, anthropologists have primarily approached those questions through psychological, psychosocial, and biosocial domains that can be empirically observed through the lens of culture (Arnold 1960; Izmirlian 1977; Harkness and Kilbride 1983; Kirmayer 1984a, 1984b; Rodríguez and Church 2003; Tsai 2007; Worthman 1992; also see Martin 2013). In this regard, anthropology recognizes a gap between biological processes and the psychosocial activities that shape social meaning-making. Within this gap are phenomena that Yael Navaro has referred to as 'interiorities'. In this frame, emotions and sentiments are understood as the exterior manifestation of the subconscious (Navaro 2012). *Affects* include those exterior manifestations that, when practised in the cultural field, contain the potential to drive social and political change. This review prioritizes how the affects that circulate within post-violence contexts may reflect neurological and bodily brain functions while simultaneously manifesting as (and indeed helping to shape) social processes and outcomes. Such an approach to affect allows us to explore the role that introspection and social feeling play in shaping how people come to conceptualize, advocate for, resist, and potentially transform positions around pro-accountability within and outside of legality.

Reflecting the need for a turn to a more systematic methodology in the study of law and anthropology, this chapter explores the nexus of affect, emotion, and the law, particularly in relation to meaning-making. Affects emerge as the bridge that connects interior worlds with collective practices, social regimes, and ultimately hegemonic institutions at the level of governance over the biopolitics of human experience. The domain of affect, generally overlooked in political and legal theory, is in fact a key site of potentiality for social and political change. An anthropology of *affective justice* thus opens up an array of inquiries into how elements of performativity, expertise, memory, aesthetics, and sentimentality underpin larger assemblages of interconnections, which may delimit and subdue or drive and produce social change. This chapter highlights key areas that are critical for understanding how affect is connected to social practice and what that tells us about the study of complexities of law and emotion in the contemporary period.

Towards an Anthropology of Emotion, Affect, and Law

In recent decades anthropology and related disciplines have experienced an 'emotional turn' that has provided an entrance through which to approach how the interior and exterior lives of individuals and collectives relate to each other and to the broader social, cultural, and political norms, institutions, and tensions our field is skilled at examining (Navaro 2012). In legal studies, however, academics have traditionally not viewed the study of emotion as important. At best it is dismissed by mainstream positivists as an interesting luxury or curiosity rather than respected as a key lens through which to understanding complex issues (Abrams 2010; Bandes 1999; Lloyd 2016: 560). For such scholars, law is objective and thus inherently legitimate; the study of emotions is seen as highly personalized, inappropriate, and a distraction from the serious work of rectifying injustice through the progressive evolution of the law (Donnelly 2003; Grossi 2015: 55; Guzzini 1998; Kegley and Wittkopf 1998).[1] In the fields of international law and human rights, questions concerning the role of affect have likewise been dismissed as being highly personalized and not appropriate topics for international politics (Donnelly 2003; Guzzini 1998; Kegley and Wittkopf 1998).

Yet, despite the insistence of those who hold this position, there has been a recent opening of inquiry in legal studies around how the emotions mediate between law and social values in a context of Western jurisprudence (Grossi 2015: 58). Of particular interest has been an examination of how lawyers deploy techniques to elicit or subdue particular emotional responses in order to influence the outcome of a case. An emergent, growing field of study of law and emotion is exploring how emotion interacts with morality and how ensuing practices of individuals and groups are deployed to shape legal actors and their institutions (Bandes and Blumenthal 2012; Barreto 2010; Bertolino 2010; Davies 2010; Ridler 2010). While this development is quite exhaustive, it is also clear that there is much still to be learned about the distribution of sentiment and the production of legal and political subjectivities, especially in relation to understanding the way that affective attachments are held and how they mobilize social action in the international legal domain. In the legal theory literature, affect is at times conjoined with emotions and at others held as distinct, with some scholars arguing that the debate risks being treated as a semantic one rather than a scientific one. The scholarship dealing with the role of affect in the field of law is thus lacking. Political legal approaches, in particular, have been slow to apply the study of complex macro global formations within which emotions circulate. Influential politico-legal anthropologists have explored how people make and remake their social worlds under conditions of conflict and instability, and much of this work examines notions of violence and social reconstruction through the daily texture of meaning-making (Nordstrom 1997; Shaw 2007: 183–207).

Social scientists have begun to add nuance to this debate, locating the place of emotion as central to public policy, democracy, and decision-making (e.g. Barbalet 1998; Calhoun and Solomon 1984; Evans 2001; French and Wettstein 1998; Grossi 2015; Oatley and Jenkins 1996). This new scholarship defies legal positivism by challenging claims related to law's 'value-neutral' and 'rational' features (Grossi 2015: 56). Scholars from across disciplines—with anthropologists lending critical perspectives—are beginning to track the ways in which explicit and implicit expressions of emotion influence legal reasoning and doctrine. Studies of emotion in anthropology can be traced back to Raymond Williams and his conceptualization of 'structure of feeling' (Williams 1977; Williams and Orrom 1954). In *The Autonomy of Affect*, Massumi (2015) offers insights into how affect structures symbolic reality and produces 'expression events', which organize people's expectations and structure what gets seen as suspenseful. Michelle Rosaldo's early work on 'an anthropology of self and feeling' articulated a particular call to the study of embodied thoughts (Rosaldo 1980). And Sherry Ortner also developed a conceptualization of affect by defining subjectivity as the ensemble of 'modes of perception, affect, thought, desire, fear, and so forth that animate acting subjects' (Ortner 2005). It involved the making of cultural and social formations that 'shape, organize, and provoke those modes of affect, thought, etc.' and that are necessary components for making sense of the inner states of acting subjects. This work followed the call for the development of robust ethnographic accounts of how human emotions are socially produced (Martin 2013; also see Mazzarella 2009, 2013).

By the early twenty-first century, scholarly work on 'emotionalization of law' (a term popularized by Karstedt 2002) was used to highlight the emergence of a new public discourse on crime (Bandes 1999; Deigh 2011; Massaro 1997; Mihai 2011: 599; 2016; Minow and Spelman 1988; Nussbaum 2010; Posner 2000, 2001; Sigler 2000). In critical theory, this turn to emotion sought to overcome limitations of post-structuralism in relation to understanding the interplay among bodies, culture, subjectivity, and identity (Clough and Halley 2007: 1, citing Terada 2001). Baruch Spinoza's *Ethics* (1677) is commonly cited as the inaugural text of affect theory, with Henri Bergson's work on perception following behind (Olson 2016: 337). Contemporary approaches to affect have drawn upon queer theory, sociology, history, and narratology, arguing that *affect* is 'an umbrella term that describes assemblages of nodes, waves, materials, and intensities' and might be seen as replacing 'Foucauldian "discourse" as the leading term in current critical commentary' (Olson 2016: 336). Some argue that '[t]he word "emotions" is used from the outset as an umbrella term to capture ideas of affect, feeling and sentiment', and in discussing the many facets of emotions and affects, scholars like Yorke argue that it is this 'perhaps messy and ever-shifting nature of emotions that can deter researchers who seek clarity and neat quantifiable data' (Yorke 2018: 657). The field of law and affect 'utilizes insights from these disciplines to illuminate and assess the implicit and explicit assumptions about emotion that animate legal reasoning, legal doctrine, the behaviour of legal actors, and the structure of legal institutions' (Bandes and Blumenthal 2012). The point of departure involves the conjoining of emotional manifestation with affects to create a way of exploring their interrelationship with a concept that brings together relations between sociality, governance, and psycho-bodily processes.

Over the past two decades, questions about cultural practices in relation to affect have become central to an emerging anthropology of emotion, as seen in work by Richard and Rudnyckyj (2009). In 2010, Ann Stoler examined the relationship between emotional sentiment and affects in order to understand how the historical colonial encounter frames structures of feeling, which order the affective terrain within which people perceive each other and respond (Stoler 2010). She and others have illustrated how subjects are mutually constituted through particular media that relate to how colonial histories, economic hope, and fears of increasing external control affect people's daily responses to political challenges (Lambek and Antze 2004; Povinelli 2006). These contributions have paved the way for theorizing structures of emotion and the particular ways that affects shape new forms of sociality and subjectivity. Legal anthropology has taken this up in examining the role of affect in shaping justice. As scholars develop new approaches to law and anthropology, it is important to explore how law's production of notions of justice are propelled through affective domains that are central to its power (Clarke 2019; also see Grossi 2014; Grossi and Neoh 2016). Legal anthropologists engaged in the study of transitional justice and international court institutions (even those who focus on emotive practices) have generally missed the opportunity to move beyond frames that individualize emotions and embed them in legal solutions. Richard Wilson's *Incitement on Trial: Prosecuting International Speech Crimes* (2017) demonstrates this point. Wilson's analysis centres on the type of speech practices, what he calls *revenge speech*, that can contribute to violent crime. He examines how various armed conflicts are driven by racial, ethnic, national, or religious hatred. By demonstrating the need to address the relationship between speech acts and crimes against humanity, including genocide, the optic of analysis is focused on how particular speech acts contribute to such crimes. It highlights the role of ordering in the perpetration of mass atrocity violence and argues that incitement should be seen as a form of complicity, in turn leading to criminal liability. In advocating a framework for monitoring political speech, the book rethinks criminal liability as a measure for individual culpability without attending to the emotions that fuel hate speech. This omission has resulted in a focus on individualization as well as a misunderstanding of what hate speech does to produce various responses and a detailing of how such speech acts operate within larger domains of power and inequality.

The tension between this focus on culpability-driven individualization and the anthropology of (international human rights) law is growing rapidly. Today's scholarship presents us with an exciting domain for the study of emotion and affect in the realm of practice, and in the context of a rapidly changing and high-stakes world. The work of Jonas Bens and Olaf Zenker has been instructive in this regard. In *Sentiment*, Bens and Zenker explore the Dominic Ongwen case in relation to international criminal law and pinpoint the extent to which affect is relevant to the production of justice in the courtroom (Bens and Zenker 2019; also see Bens 2020). Their contribution is important in showing the workings of affect in the courtroom, particularly in relation to conceptions of justice as mediated through larger regimes of emotional regulation. Yet an outstanding question in relation to such work concerns how those affective embodiments are connected to biopolitical formations and the regimes within which they circulate. By studying how local people in Northern Uganda relate to the ICC proceedings, and by charting different sentiments of justice in the way that people support the ICC proceedings, Bens and Zenker emphasize more effective domestic criminal justice trials through the consideration of 'traditional' forms of reconciliation (including but going beyond *mato oput*), or those favouring religious (mostly Christian) forms of forgiveness. While the tensions between individual liability/moral responsibility and structural colonial legacies of injustice are present in their work, they are not a central organizing tenet, which raises the question of whether legal anthropology, in its attempt to study the processes by which law and anthropology understand culture, power, and social change, ought to be considering relationships between emotion, affect, and law by examining the micro and cultural processes that map people's daily actions—or whether the study of those processes alongside the politics of such affects and emotions and their conditions of possibility ought to be foregrounded. To answer this question involves considering whether it is critical to use a new methodology that presumes a larger span of analysis in order to understand the ways that public discourses are propelled within feeling regimes and, further, how such feelings, themselves embedded in deep histories, organize the range of possible outcomes or resolutions for the future.

In an attempt to clarify the framework through which these practices play out, in *Affective Justice* (2019), I outline three components of a theory of emotional circulation through which legal institutions are constructed, sustained, resisted, and potentially transformed: legal technocratic practices, psychosocial embodied affects, and emotional regimes. The first component—the domain of legal technocratic practice—encompasses the implementation of legal processes as well as associated training of practitioners and has as its main concern the biopolitical management of life and death. Following Michel Foucault, we understand *biopolitics* to index processes by which institutions exert power over bodies (individual people and constituencies) through various techniques of subjugation (Foucault 1981: 140). This term references the economic, political, psychological, and classificatory domains through which bodies and populations are disciplined (Foucault 1976: 252–3). For our purposes we are particularly concerned with the legal bases for biopolitical control as established through relationships among biology, politics, and technocracy. Emergent forms of disciplinary power function across different scales to classify populations juridically as well as to manage life and to classify certain forms of death (and killing) as acceptable and others as illegal. These legal technocracies are structured in relation to various scientific-legal rationalities that are based in Western colonial frameworks and exist at the heart of international justice landscapes. And biopolitical processes have thus produced the social fields in which regimes of international legal knowledge have taken shape and through which they circulate.

If we see this biopolitical process of making international law as being productive of a rationalizing regime in which determinations around 'victims' and 'perpetrators' are popularized, then it follows that the process is also central to shaping the basis upon which international legal morality is being normalized. Narrative emerges as the mechanism through which a biopolitics of sentiment violence (its victims and perpetrators) is established (Schuller 2018). Moreover, in investigating technocratic practices in a legal context, we observe that some justice practices (their ontologies and temporalities) displace other practices through a process of displacement (which I take up further in *Affective Justice*).

The second component important to understanding emotion, affect, and *law* through an affective justice framework is the emergence of a consciousness about the material and psychosocial body within which particular emotions and affects are manifest. Rooted in the philosophical ideas of seventeenth-century philosopher Benedict Spinoza (Spinoza 1951; Spinoza and Curley 2016; Spinoza and Parkinson 1989) and later expanded by French theorists Gilles Deleuze and Félix Guattari (1987), the concept of 'affect' continues to energize social scientists and cultural theorists. Charles Hirschkind describes affect as 'part of the pre-subjective interface of the body with the sensory world it inhabits, a linkage registered at the level of the visceral, the proprioceptive, and other sites where memory lodges itself in the body' (Hirschkind 2006: 85; Massumi 2015). Other definitions emphasize the intense processual forces of affect. Gregg and Seigworth describe it as 'an impingement or extrusion of a momentary or sometimes more sustained state of relation *as well as* the passage (and the duration of the passage) of forces or intensities' (2010: 1; emphasis mine). When we explore affects alongside emotions, we see the dynamic interplay among embodied feeling, sociality, and power. We see the conjuncture of emotional responses with perceived senses of justice that may be materialized through various sensory impressions. Powerful and productive sentiments of anger, pain, and hope percolate around such controversies that emerge when people feel that justice is not delivered as promised, and through the expression of these feelings, constituents may organize forms of refusal or ways of reassigning the effects of displacement. In observing politicized moments of affective responses, it is critical to trace how and why they have emerged as well as how they manifest differently in various domains. The term that I use to describe affective manifestations is *reattribution*.

The concept of reattribution describes a process of attributing guilt through rhetorical strategies that shift the domain on which competing feelings and social positions lie. In law, attribution refers to the determination of whether a particular act can be attributed to another entity, such as a person, corporation, or government. It emerges from the concept of liability and relates to the determination of responsibility for wrongdoing. My use of attribution extends beyond an oversimplified tie to the legal parsing of wrongdoing. It relates to the affective dimension of justice-making *in which sentimentalized responses are both embedded in psychic interiorities and processed within inner responses. These responses shape how people parse meaning and understand legal phenomena such as culpability.* Affective inner worlds can be seen as embodying pre-social responses that are sometimes manifest in emotional expressions, which are often culturally produced and reflective of regimented social worlds. In legal domains, emotions shape how affects are embodied and ultimately drive how people engage with meanings of justice, and especially with concepts around *victimhood* and culpability. Reattribution in both its embodied and discursive forms lies at the core of legal meaning-making, where it is entangled with biopolitical, embodied, and socially regimented configurations that circulate through emotional regimes.

The third component of these legal assemblages involves the emotional regimes themselves, which provide the framework within which all the above negotiations take place. This is the domain of affective responses and associated feeling mobilizations. Interrelations between legal encapsulation and reattribution are negotiated here and take shape through particular discursive tropes. Following William Reddy, an emotional regime is a 'set of normative emotions and the official rituals, practices, and emotions that express and inculcate them', and is a 'necessary underpinning of any stable political regime' (Reddy 2001: 129). I extend this concept to think about the ways that *emotional regimes* underpin popular notions of justice and people's engagement with them. Through certain kinds of representational practices, emotional responses circulate within packages of meaning production indexed by icons, words, utterances, colour deployment, and hashtags, often mobilized by technologically driven campaigns. Through the encoding of bodily meanings and experiences, certain archetypal figures (e.g. 'victims', 'perpetrators', or 'freedom fighters/heroes/heroines') serve to reinforce the discursive appropriateness of images or symbols. For feelings operate through agencies that are embedded in particular historical inscriptions and are part of itinerant responses. These are often collective but never fully predictable; they may or may not align with the emotional climate being produced.

These three interrelated domains—legal technocratic practices, psychosocial embodied affects, and emotional regimes—come together messily through the rule of law movement to constitute *affective justice*. As the enmeshment of these component parts, an alliance between the instrumentalization of the law and expressive embodiments of its regimes propels us to articulate what justice is, and to clarify meanings of justice through its materialization. At the centre of the rule of law movement dwell not only histories of proclamations, treaties, laws, and categories like 'victims' and 'perpetrators', but also discourses and feelings that shape the ethos that inspires the work of international justice. Subjects are inspired to do their part to 'right past wrongs' and 'prevent future atrocities'. By illuminating how complex legal processes relate to private, interior micro processes, the study of affect and emotion gives tremendous insight into how psychosocial and political meanings about justice are forged, and how they also serve to shape historical, contemporary, and future publics.

Taking the products of the international social imaginary as key modalities for understanding the enmeshment of individual sentimental responses and larger entanglements with history and power, a legal anthropology of emotion allows us to foreground the relevance of how affects are embodied, how feeling rules are negotiated, and how they are regulated and resisted in daily life (Hochschild 1979). We contemplate the role of justice aesthetics and techniques, and the emotions they conjure, towards various ends. As anthropologists we insist that one cannot analyse legal processes in a courtroom, do a discursive reading of legal documents, or interpret the reading of a verdict without highlighting the biopolitical regimes that shape the emotional manifestations of meaning-making. The reality is that examining such processes without recognizing the affective labour at the centre of legal representations misses the complexities of cultural formations in the contemporary period. And while extraordinary forms of legal representation might involve spectacular expressions of judicial power, such as opening and closing statements, we also see ordinary forms of meaning-making manifest in the afterlife of judicial performances that are related to the invocation of various aesthetic images or words or concepts through less visible (and certainly less legible) processes.

If contemporary approaches to law, anthropology, emotions, and affects can incorporate a more integrated approach to the micro and macro domains that operate in social life, we can offer a more realistic understanding of the complex assemblages within which emotion and affect circulate. The case of Dominic Ongwen and the biopolitics of individualization provides one site through which to see this assemblage play out. Through the incorporation of a particular legal structuring device, other component parts that shape affects come into relief. Notions such as 'victims' and 'perpetrators' shape the moral economies around which particular emotional regimes are projected.

It is critical to understand that both survivors and perpetrators of violence exist within larger structures of inequality, and therefore that each is integral to sustaining the problem of power in particular ways. Contemporary forms of international legalisms are part of a larger tyranny of violence that does not stop with the individualization of criminal responsibility and the performance of the courtroom trial. They exist within colonial inscriptions of plunder and extraction that structure the forms of violence within which they circulate. They are constitutive of the continuation of empire in the contemporary moment, and their expression through affective registers requires certain expressions of emotional and racialized bodies at the preclusion of other possibilities. Contemporary justice alliances manifest along the fault lines laid by global empire and white supremacy. By moving from the tendency to adopt the individualization of survivors and perpetrators that (neo)colonial imaginaries privilege—and pushing our analysis towards an investigation of how transnational assemblages of power are alternately fabricated and dismantled—we may begin to illuminate features of international justice that have been widely neglected in the anthropology of justice.

The remainder of this chapter returns to the site of Uganda and locating Dominic Ongwen as both victim and perpetrator in order to illustrate how these processes take shape and to what effects. It reflects on this case study to illuminate the need for more intensive analysis on the macro and micro processes through which emotion, affect, and law are played out.

Historical context of conflict in Uganda

Uganda achieved independence on 9 October 1962, with Milton Obote declared the first prime minister of the new republic (Kasozi et al. 1994: 59). In 1966, in the name of unifying Uganda, Obote abolished the Kingdom of Baganda, removing the monarchy (Kiwanuka 1979). Obote became increasingly dictatorial, epitomized by the 1967 Constitution and his use of preventive detention laws and a secret police force (Kasozi et al. 1994: 59; Kiwanuka 1979: 26). Idi Amin came to power in 1971 through a coup staged while Obote was at the Commonwealth Conference in Singapore (Kasozi et al. 1994: 59; Kiwanuka 1979).[2] A war ensued in Uganda and Amin was ousted in 1979 by Yusuf Lule. Through a series of violent coups, power transferred back to Obote in 1980 (Kasozi et al. 1994: 59). He retained power until 1985, when the regime was ended by the Okellos, who in turn were overwhelmed by the National Resistance Movement (NRM) army in 1986 (Allen 2006: 29–30; Kasozi et al. 1994: 59). The NRM's leader, Yoweri Museveni, was made president of Uganda and still holds that position today (Allen 2006: 29).

An important figure in the history of conflict and rebellion in Uganda is Alice Lakwena. In October 1987, Lakwena is said to have marched with 10,000 followers to rebel against the Museveni government. Inspired by Lakwena's movement, groups in the Acholi homeland continued to rebel violently against the government, including groups associated with Sevarino Lukoya and Joseph Kony (Allen 2006: 35–6). Kony even claimed a kinship connection to Alice Lakwena and tried unsuccessfully to create an alliance with her. In 1988, the Museveni government signed a peace agreement with the Uganda People's Democratic Army (UPDA), but many people who refused to surrender instead joined Kony. It was at this point that Odong Latek joined forces with Kony, the former organizing the forces and the latter focusing on healing and divining. In the 1990s, Latek was killed in conflict and, soon after, Kony changed the name of his group from Uganda People's Liberation Army (UPLA) to the Lord's Resistance Army (LRA) (Allen 2006: 37–9). In total, from 1966 to 1985, there were six changes of government, each involving and provoking violence (Kasozi et al. 1994: 59). With each change in authority, anyone in government who could potentially have ties to the preceding regime was removed or killed. The early postcolonial period was thus characterized by cycles of political violence (Allen 2006).

By the mid-1990s, the LRA was fighting the Sudan People's Liberation Army (SPLA) in Sudan (with the support of the Sudanese government) (Allen 2006: 49). The Museveni government had little interest in a diplomatic or negotiated peace with the LRA and favoured military action. This is evidenced by Operation North (1991), which progressed despite the efforts of Betty Bigombe, the State Minister for Northern Buganda, to hold peace talks. While maintaining a presence in Southern Sudan, the LRA remained a terrorizing force in Northern Uganda and in May 1995 massacred 300 people in Atiak (Allen 2006: 48–9). The LRA did announce a ceasefire during the 1995

Ugandan election, indicating it would end conflicts completely if Museveni lost. When Museveni won the election and Bigombe was dropped from cabinet, conflict resumed. Under pressure from the US, the government of Sudan allowed the government of Uganda to attack LRA bases in Sudan in a campaign called the Iron Fist Offensive (Allen 2006: 50–1). The Amnesty Act was passed in Uganda in November 1999 and came into force in January 2000, granting amnesty to all rebels in Uganda other than LRA commanders (Allen 2006: 74; Government of Uganda 2000). A Second Iron Fist Offensive was launched in March 2004 but failed to stamp out the LRA, which continued to operate out of bases in Sudan (Allen 2006: 52).

President Museveni referred the situation in Uganda to the ICC at the end of 2003, as officially announced in January 2004 (Allen 2006: 82). It is within this historical and political context that Dominic Ongwen was thrust into at his birth in 1975 in the Amuru district of Northern Uganda (International Federation for Human Rights 2016). When Ongwen was thirteen or fourteen years old (with some sources indicating he was as young as ten), he is said to have been abducted by the LRA while on his way to school (Justice and Reconciliation Project 2008). An examination of the Ongwen case highlights the workings of affective justice in contemporary international legal domains, but it is critical to also consider the emergence of Ongwen in relation to such histories of control and violence in the Ugandan state. A methodology that combines psychosocial and such geopolitical dimensions of affect and emotion in the study of the case against Ongwen provides a method of understanding the ways that affect, emotion, and the law are fundamentally necessary in contemporary anthropological inquiry.

Biopolitics through legal encapsulation: The case of Dominic Ongwen

In the social media campaigns that paralleled the emotive appeals to capture and arrest Kony, a task which required governmental and non-governmental support, the notion of the 'perpetrator to be stopped' in the name of 'victims to the saved' formed the basis on which international lawmaking gained its moral force (see 'The Kony 2012 Campaign' in Clarke 2019). Various online documentation projects presented Kony as a cruel adult militia leader engaged in committing rape and slavery. As one online presentation showed, 'He only wants to be the chief and you to work for him like a slave, for him and his family. See now, even officers are made to carry his food and luggage so you should take your time and come back home' (Northernews Wire 2015; LRA Crisis Tracker 2018). However, the inability of the international community to capture Kony highlights the relevance of the role Ongwen has played as a proxy for crimes committed by the Kony and the LRA.

Sidiki Kaba, the President of the ICC's Assembly of States Parties (ASP), a representative from Senegal, affirmed, 'I strongly welcome the transfer of Dominic Ongwen to the custody of the Court, which constitutes an important success for the Rome Statute system nearly ten years after the issuance of the warrant of arrest against him. The affected communities will have the opportunity to see international justice address the horrific violence that took place in Uganda' (ICC 2015).

Such articulations feature the individual figure of Ongwen as the perpetrator of violence and the presumption that the work of international criminal justice can have the effect of addressing, through law, the horrific violence that took place in Uganda. Legal encapsulation, seen here through the erasure of Ongwen's more complex identity as both perpetrator and survivor (Ongwen was himself a child soldier who was victimized by violence (Baines 2009; Stauffer 2015)), is reinforced by imagery that portrays him dressed in militia fatigues and donning an M-16 firearm. The imagery is typical of depictions of figures such as Ongwen, who are rendered as ominous villains delinked from any broader or more complex circumstance or context.

Such images compel us to fixate our focus and resources on an individual perpetrator—someone who can be found, apprehended, and brought to justice through the drama of the legal process. When the image of suffering at the hands of a commander is made vivid through a discourse related to a 'victim to be saved', these aesthetic productions of culpability produce illusions (or fetishes) that compel people to engage in the work of justice through the law. This obfuscates alternative solutions that might instead target the structural contributors to violence and ancillary forms of social suffering. What we see is that the 'victim to be saved' operates as a trope that is propelled by emotional regimes and rendered visible through the individualization of criminal responsibility. The aesthetic repackaging of suffering produces it as a condition to be overcome through law. Victimhood is symbolically packaged as *our* suffering, *social* suffering. Through public buy-in accomplished via social action, expressive regimes mobilize

Depicting Dominic Ongwen.

(Image by Cosmos, used with permission.)

affect to produce the conditions of legal action. In technocratic terms, the responsibility to protect those victimized by violence has become a legal duty of the state made actionable through its citizenry. Such action domains operate through the emotional regimes that shape a collective sense of what is appropriate and effective.

However, counter-depictions of Dominic Ongwen do exist, describing a less culpable and more vulnerable person who was himself abducted in childhood by the LRA and subsequently victimized by multiple forms of violence. As the explanation goes, Ongwen was forced to participate within the LRA's killing apparatus. This alternative narrative has been asserted with force and even anger by progressive scholars interested in complicating the domain in which contemporary forms of individual criminal responsibility are playing out (among others, see Baines 2009; Kendall 2011, 2014; Kendall and Nouwen 2013; Koulen 2009; Stauffer 2015). This reconceptualization of culpability, while also driven by emotional practices and feelings, centres on recognizing the impacts of structural inequality. As Kjell Anderson articulated at the Canadian International Council in Saskatoon, Saskatchewan, 'How should we treat perpetrators of horrendous crimes when they themselves started out as victims? And how does participation in violence alter perpetrator memory and self-identity?' (Anderson 2017).

Structures of inequality shape how we see and depict the materiality of suffering, which often obscures the underlying contexts from which violence emerges, ranging from the discovery and extraction of natural resources to the politics of displacement and control of land through the use of tyranny and dominance. In Uganda, as in many places on the continent, the struggle over life in the Northern region has, over the past thirty years, involved a struggle to control resources. As colonial powers shifted, minimal attention was given to developing state institutions. The early postcolonial period saw a highly centralized federal body form in the place of British rule, and a race for political control of resource-rich regions ensued. Within this context, military coups and rebel groups fuelled cycles of extreme violence. The ultimate erosion of state capacities to build viable economies for citizens, to command and regulate access to resources in the domestic economy, and to build innovative mechanisms capable of incorporating indigenous cultural traditions to direct future action all represent a more tragic set of realities that seed inequity and give rise to violence (Mbembe 1992, 2001).

Such postcolonial realities call into question the biopolitical application of legal tools and the moral formations they leverage. In this regard, the strategic modes of mobilization that invigorate emotional strategies in the pursuit of legal processes are critical for making sense of how the process of legal encapsulation (see also Clarke 2019, building on Harding 2000) makes structural inequality unintelligible. The complex conditions that produce the need for legality—such as spheres of colonialism and imperialism—are made to operate within other domains of alliance and representation. We see that globally propelled aesthetics are being deployed centrally in shaping the way that new justice regimes are being framed. Mapping these processes is critical for understanding how particular legal assemblages link emotion to social action in both juridical and non-juridical contexts. It becomes clear that our recognition of an actionable social harm is tied to our senses of particular moral and juridical platforms that are central to the work of the law.

Conclusion: Towards a legal anthropology of emotion and affect

As this chapter has investigated, the Kony 2012 campaign (Invisible Children 2012) prefigured the ICC's case against Dominic Ongwen through the parsing of criminal culpability to the LRA commanders. The aesthetics of the case against Ongwen depicted him as a major militia leader who was criminally responsible for the lives of those victimized by the war in Northern Uganda. Advocates of the mobilization to bring Ongwen to justice deployed both sentimentalized images and legal technocratic knowledge to produce the terms on which his criminal culpability was structured. The prosecution used legal tools to demonstrate beyond reasonable doubt that Ongwen was guilty of the seventy counts against him, which required linking him to the role of directing actions amounting to war crimes and crimes against humanity, including attacks against civilians, murder, rape, sexual slavery, forced marriage, torture, inhumane acts, and so forth. This process involved a particular set of discourses around which the moral force of the court gained its power. In particular, narratives that 'no one is above the law' and that 'victims must be protected' linked to beliefs about how mass atrocity violence can be ended, beliefs that had been mobilized and fanned by campaigns like Kony 2012. By considering the making of 'the victim' and the 'perpetrator' through the construction of various legal actions—and the reattributive affects that are part of people's bodily and social reactions—we see that forms of mediation that shape the way people engage in various international justice projects are central to the expressive management of legal action. Unearthing the technical and biopolitical mechanisms and emotive appeals underlying the responses to Ongwen allows us to reveal the competing structures that constitute the way that affects, emotion, and law co-constitute each other. This perspective urges us to recall that Ongwen was himself a child soldier abducted into a system forged by generations of violence, much of it perpetrated or fabricated by colonial empire.

The scholarship presented here is concerned with the imbrication of the social and the inter-subjective as they relate to histories of coloniality, postcoloniality, and contemporary justice formations. Sentiments about culpability are visible as embodied affects, expressed through speech acts, ritual practices, voting behaviour, and popular campaign icons and articulated through particular cultural lenses such as our senses of judgement, capacities for making distinctions, or our moral sources. As embodied thought, reattributive sentiments animate cognition in ways that make interpretation, thus sociality, visible and meaningful according to various sociocultural rules. The effect of this is a mediated conception of justice facilitated by new domains for understanding law, emotion, affect, and their complex implication in regimes of power. In this regard, the process of legal encapsulation—as forms of reattribution shape internalized senses of culpability that are in turn propelled through particular justice regimes—serves to occlude more radical possibilities for confronting injustice as the root of violence and for indicting the very Western institutions that continue to frame the options for postcolonial governance.

As we have seen, in the contemporary period particular feelings about justice and violence compel actors to participate in various ways. Tapping into these feelings, publics are mobilized both in person, at sites of judicial activity, and online, where humanitarian and legalistic concepts circulate and concretize through the emotional imaginary. Messages become effective because they represent contemporary institutionalized norms through which expressions of emotional convictions are consolidated and regulated. Spectacularized through legal rituals and grassroots mobilizations, campaigns and their afterlives combine to shape the epistemological frameworks of justice and law as modes of power, social ordering, and knowledge production (Foucault 1977, 2002). These formations are visible in the various justice techniques and transnational legal practices around which the categories of the perpetrator and victim are produced. Anthropology is especially well positioned to trace how emotions are connected to affects, and how affects in turn mobilize emotions within the realm of social relations and have an impact on legal processes. Without recognizing dual relationships among embodied affects and their biopolitical emotional regimes, we miss a critical opportunity to relate the micro to the macro processes at play, and to see how histories of subjugation relate to ongoing legacies of extraction, control, and psychosocial expressions of feeling. Ultimately, an anthropology of emotion, affect, and law illuminates how these processes privilege certain fetishes of (neocolonial) justice while delimiting alternative possibilities that would perhaps address more radical (i.e. *root*) causes of generational violence, thus seeding alternative futures.

Notes

1. Some (Hudson 2005; Jervis 1988; Wendt 2004) have presumed that sentiments emerge out of individual spaces of emotion and feeling.
2. Amin announced eighteen points as to why he needed to replace Obote (Kiwanuka 1979: 40–2).

References

Abrams, K. R. 2010. 'Empathy and Experience in the Sotomayor Hearings'. *Ohio Northern University Law Review* 36: 263–86.

Ahmed, S. 2010. *The Promise of Happiness*. Durham: Duke University Press.

Allen, T. 2006. *Trial Justice: The International Criminal Court and the Lord's Resistance Army*. London/New York: Zed Books.

Anderson, K. 2017. 'CIC Saskatoon: The Dilemma of Dominic Ongwen—The Socialisation, Reintegration, and Criminal Culpability of Former Child Soldiers'. Lecture at CIC Saskatoon, 20 September.

Arnold, M. B. 1960. *Emotion and Personality*. New York: Columbia University Press.

Baines, E. K. 2009. 'Complex Political Perpetrators: Reflections on Dominic Ongwen'. *The Journal of Modern African Studies* 47(2): 163–91.

Bandes, S. A. 1999. *The Passions of Law*. New York: New York University Press.

Bandes, S. A. and J. A. Blumenthal. 2012. 'Emotion and Law'. *Annual Review of Law and Social Science* 8(1): 161–81.

Barbalet, J. M. 1998. *Emotion, Social Theory, and Social Structure: A Macrosociological Approach*. Cambridge: Cambridge University Press.

Barreto, J. M. 2010. 'The Turn to Emotions: Law, Geopolitics, Aesthetics'. Paper presented at the Critical Legal Conference Utrecht ('"Great Expectations": Multiple Modernities of Law'), Utrecht University, the Netherlands, 10–12 September.

Bens, J. 2020. 'Transitional Justice Atmospheres: The Role of Space and Affect in the International Criminal Court's Outreach Efforts in Northern Uganda'. In K. Seidel and H. Ellisie, eds. *Normative Spaces and Legal Dynamics in Africa*, 41–60. London: Routledge.

Bens, J. and O. Zenker. 2019. 'Sentiment'. In J. Slaby and C. von Scheve, eds. *Affective Societies—Key Concepts*, 96–106. London: Routledge.

Bertolino, E. 2010. 'Body, Emotions, and Human Rights Justice'. Paper presented at the Critical Legal Conference Utrecht ('"Great Expectations": Multiple Modernities of Law'), Utrecht University, the Netherlands, 10–12 September.

Bower, G. H. 1981. 'Mood and Memory'. *American Psychologist* 36(2): 129.

Bower, G. H. and P. R. Cohen. 1982. 'Emotional Influences on Learning and Cognition'. In M. S. Clark and S. T. Fiske, eds. *Affect and Cognition: The 17th Annual Carnegie Symposium on Cognition*, 291–331. Hillsdale: Erlbaum.

Bower, G. H. and S. G. Gilligan. 1979. 'Remembering Information Related to One's Self'. *Journal of Research in Personality* 13(4): 420–32.

Bower, G. H., S. G. Gilligan, and K. P. Monteiro. 1981. 'Selectivity of Learning Caused by Affective States'. *Journal of Experimental Psychology: General* 110(4): 451.

Calhoun, C. and R. C. Solomon. 1984. *What is an Emotion? Classic Readings in Philosophical Psychology*. New York: Oxford University Press.

Clarke, K. M. 2019. *Affective Justice: The International Criminal Court and the Pan-Africanist Pushback*. Durham: Duke University Press.

Clough, P. T. and J. Halley, eds. 2007. *The Affective Turn: Theorizing the Social*. Durham: Duke University Press.

Davies, G. 2010. 'The Rational Primacy of Emotion in Law and Governance'. Paper presented at the Critical Legal Conference Utrecht ('"Great Expectations": Multiple Modernities of Law'), Utrecht University, the Netherlands, 10–12 September.

Deigh, J. 2011. *Emotions, Values, and the Law*. Oxford: Oxford University Press.

Deleuze, G. and F. Guattari. 1987. *A Thousand Plateaus: Capitalism and Schizophrenia*. Minneapolis: University of Minnesota Press.

Donnelly, J. 2003. 'International Human Rights: Unintended Consequences of the War on Terrorism'. *Contexto Internacional* 25(2): 333–61.

Emde, R. N. and T. Shapiro, eds. 1992. *Affect: Psychoanalytic Perspectives*. Madison: International Universities Press.

Evans, T. 2001. 'If Democracy, Then Human Rights?' *Third World Quarterly* 22(4): 623–42.

Fenichel, O. 1945. *The Psychoanalytic Theory of Neurosis*. New York: W. W. Norton & Co.

Foucault, M. 1976. *Mental Illness and Psychology*. First edition. Alan Sheridan, trans. New York: Harper & Row.

Foucault, M. 1977. *Discipline and Punish: The Birth of the Prison*. New York: Vintage Books.

Foucault, M. 1981. *The History of Sexuality*. Harmondsworth: Penguin.

Foucault, M. 2002. *Archaeology of Knowledge*. London: Routledge.

Fox, A. S., R. Lapate, A. J. Shackman, and R. J. Davidson. 2018. *The Nature of Emotion: Fundamental Questions*. New York: Oxford University Press.

French, P. A. and H. K. Wettstein. 1998. *Philosophy of Emotions*. Notre Dame: University of Notre Dame Press.

Government of Uganda. 2000. 'The Amnesty Act', available at file:///C:/Users/13439/AppData/Local/Temp/ugandan+amnesty+act+2000.pdf accessed 19 June 2021.

Gregg, M. and G. J. Seigworth, eds. 2010. *The Affect Theory Reader*. Durham: Duke University Press.

Grossi, R. 2014. *Looking for Love in the Legal Discourse of Marriage*. Canberra: Australian National University Press.

Grossi, R. 2015. 'Understanding Law and Emotion'. *Emotion Review* 7(1): 55–60.

Grossi, R. and J. Neoh, eds. 2016. *Law and Love: With Michael Kirby on the Future of Law Schools*. Annandale: Federation Press.

Guzzini, S. 1998. *Realism in International Relations and International Political Economy. The Continuing Story of a Death Foretold*. New York: Routledge.

Harding, S. F. 2000. *The Book of Jerry Falwell: Fundamentalist Language and Politics*. Princeton: Princeton University Press.

Harkness, S. and P. L. Kilbride. 1983. 'Introduction: The Socialization of Affect'. *Ethos* 11(4): 215–20.

Hirschkind, C. 2006. *Ethical Soundscape: Cassette Sermons and Islamic Counterpublics*. New York: Columbia University Press.

Hochschild, R. A. 1979. 'Emotion Work, Feeling Rules, and Social Structure'. *American Journal of Sociology* 85(3): 551–75.

Hollan, D. 2000. 'Constructivist Models of Mind, Contemporary Psychoanalysis, and the Development of Culture Theory'. *American Anthropologist* 102(3): 538–50.

Hollan, D. and C. J. Throop. 2008. 'Whatever Happened to Empathy? Introduction'. In C. J. Throop and D. Hollan, eds. 'Whatever Happened to Empathy'. Special issue, *Ethos* 36(4): 381–405.

Hudson, V. M. 2005. 'Foreign Policy Analysis: Actor-Specific Theory and the Ground of International Relations'. *Foreign Policy Analysis* 1(1): 1–30.

ICC. 2015. 'Dominic Ongwen Transferred to The Hague', available at <https://www.icc-cpi.int/pages/item.aspx?name=pr1084> accessed 7 October 2020.

International Federation for Human Rights. 2016. 'Q&A on the Dominic Ongwen Case at the ICC', available at <https://www.fidh.org/en/region/Africa/uganda/q-a-on-the-dominic-ongwen-case-at-the-icc> accessed 17 October 2020.

Invisible Children. 2012. 'Kony 2012', available at https://invisiblechildren.com/kony-2012/ accessed 19 June 2021.

Izmirlian, H., Jr. 1977. 'Anthropology and Affect: A Consideration of the Idiosyncratic Dimension of Human Behaviour'. *International Journal of Social Psychiatry* 23(1): 46–54.

Jervis, R. 1988. 'Realism, Game Theory, and Cooperation'. *World Politics: A Quarterly Journal of International Relations* 40(3): 317–49.

Justice and Reconciliation Project. 2008. 'Annual Report', available at <http://www.justiceandreconciliation.org/publications/reports/2009/2008-annual-report/> accessed 17 October 2020.

Karstedt, S. 2002. 'Emotions and Criminal Justice'. *Theoretical Criminology* 6(3): 299–317.

Kasozi, A. B. K., M. Nakanyike, and J. M. Sejjengo. 1994. *The Social Origins of Violence in Uganda: 1964–1985*. Montreal: McGill–Queen's University Press.

Kegley, C., Jr. and E. R. Wittkopf. 1998. *World Politics: Trend and Transformation*. Seventh edition. New York: St. Martin's Press.

Kendall, S. 2011. 'Donors' Justice: Recasting International Criminal Accountability'. *Leiden Journal of International Law* 24(3): 585–606.

Kendall, S. 2014. '"UhuRuto" and Other Leviathans: The International Criminal Court and the Kenyan Political Order'. *African Journal of Legal Studies* 7(3): 399–427.

Kendall, S. and S. Nouwen. 2013. 'Representational Practices at the International Criminal Court: The Gap Between Juridified and Abstract Victimhood'. *Law and Contemporary Problems* 76(3/4): 1–211.

Kirmayer, L. J. 1984a. 'Culture, Affect and Somatization'. *Transcultural Psychiatric Research Review* 21(4): 237–62.

Kirmayer, L. J. 1984b. 'Culture, Affect and Somatization'. *Transcultural Psychiatric Research Review* 21(3): 159–88.

Kirmayer, L. J. 2007. 'On the Cultural Mediation of Pain'. In S. Coakley and K. K. Shelemay, eds. *Pain and Its Transformations: The Interface of Biology and Culture*, 363–401. Cambridge: Harvard University Press.

Kiwanuka, S. 1979. *Amin and the Tragedy of Uganda*. Munich: Weltforum Verlag.

Kleinman, A. and B. Good, eds. 1985. *Culture and Depression: Studies in the Anthropology of Cross-Cultural Psychiatry of Affect and Disorder*. Berkeley: University of California Press.

Koulen, S. 2009. *The Responsibility to Protect: A Critique of Motherhood and Apple Pie*. Unpublished manuscript.

Lambek, M. and P. Antze. 2004. *Illness and Irony: On the Ambiguity of Suffering in Culture*. New York: Berghahn.

Leys, R. 2011. 'The Turn to Affect: A Critique'. *Critical Inquiry* 37(3): 434–72.

Lloyd, H. A. 2016. 'Cognitive Emotion and the Law'. *Law & Psychology Review* 41: 53.

LRA Crisis Tracker. 2018. 'Invisible Children', available at <https://crisistracker.org/maps?&incident_type=lra_abduction&primary_actors=lra&start_date=2018-01-01&end_date=2018-12-31&start_date_of_reported_location=2018-01-01&end_date_of_reported_location=2018-12-31&date_of_return_start_date=2018-01-01&date_of_return_end_date=2018-12-31&keyword=&search=&record_type=incidents&display_type=incident_type&request_type=paginated&page=1&stream_type=violence> accessed 17 October 2020.

Lutz, C. 1986. 'Emotion, Thought, and Estrangement: Emotion as a Cultural Category'. *Cultural Anthropology* 1(3): 287–309.

Martin. E. 2013. 'The Potentiality of Ethnography and the Limits of Affect Theory'. *Current Anthropology* 54(S7): S149–58.

Massaro, T. M. 1997. 'The Meanings of Shame: Implications for Legal Reform'. *Psychology, Public Policy, and Law* 3(4): 645–704.

Massumi, B. 1995. 'The Autonomy of Affect'. *Cultural Critique* 31: 83–109.

Massumi, B. 2002. *A Shock to Thought: Expression after Deleuze and Guattari*. London/New York: Routledge.

Massumi, B. 2015. *The Politics of Affect*. Malden: Polity Press.

Mazzarella, W. 2009. 'Affect: What is it Good for?' In S. Dube, ed. *Enchantments of Modernity: Empire, Nation, Globalization*, 291–309. London, New Delhi: Routledge.

Mazzarella, W. 2013. *Censorium: Cinema and the Open Edge of Mass Publicity*. Durham: Duke University Press.

Mbembe, A. 1992. 'Provisional Notes on the Postcolony'. *Africa: Journal of the International African Institute* 62(1): 3–37.

Mbembe, A. 2001. *On the Postcolony*. Berkeley: University of California Press.

Melzack, R. and W. Torgerson. 1971. 'On the Language of Pain'. *Anesthesiology* 34: 50–59.

Mihai, M. 2011. 'Emotions and the Criminal Law'. *Philosophy Compass* 6 (9): 599–610.

Mihai, M. 2016. *Negative Emotions and Transitional Justice*. New York: Columbia University Press.

Minow, M. L. and E. V. Spelman. 1988. 'Passion for Justice'. *Cardozo Law Review* 10(1–2): 37–76.

Molino, A., ed. 2004. *Culture, Subject, and Psyche: Dialogues in Psychoanalysis and Anthropology*. Middletown: Wesleyan University Press.

Navaro, Y. 2012. *The Make-Believe Space: Affective Geography in a Postwar Polity*. Durham: Duke University Press.

Nordstrom, C. 1997. *A Different Kind of War Story*. University of Pennsylvania Press.

Northernews Wire. 2015. 'Domnic Ongwen Amplifying Call for All to Return Home', available at <https://www.facebook.com/northernewswire/posts/domnic-ongwen-amplifying-call-for-all-to-return-homeformer-lra-commander-dominic/850097735050988/> accessed 8 October 2020.

Nussbaum, M. C. 2010. *From Disgust to Humanity: Sexual Orientation and Constitutional Law*. Oxford: Oxford University Press.

Oatley, K. and J. M. Jenkins. 1996. *Understanding Emotions*. Cambridge: Blackwell Publishers.

Olson, D. R. 2016. *The Mind on Paper: Reading, Consciousness and Rationality*. Cambridge: Cambridge University Press.

Ortner, S. 2005. 'Subjectivity and Cultural Critique'. *Anthropological Theory* 5(1): 31–52.

Posner, E. A. 2000. *Law and Social Norms*. Cambridge: Harvard University Press.

Posner, E. A. 2001. 'Law and the Emotions'. *Georgetown Law Journal* 89: 1977.

Povinelli, E. 2006. *The Empire of Love: Toward a Theory of Intimacy, Genealogy, and Carnality*. Durham: Duke University Press.

Rapaport, D. 1942. *The Menninger Clinic Monograph Series: Vol. 2. Emotions and Memory*. Second unaltered edition. Madison: International Universities Press.

Reddy, W. M. 2001. *The Navigation of Feeling: A Framework for the History of Emotions*. New York/Cambridge: Cambridge University Press.

Rey, R. 1993. *The History of Pain*. Cambridge: Harvard University Press.

Richard, A, and D. Rudnyckyj. 2009. 'Economies of Affect'. *Journal of the Royal Anthropological Institute* 15(1): 57–77.

Ridler, V. 2010. 'Word and World: The Imperium of Reason and the Possibility of Critique'. *Journal of Critical Globalisation Studies* 1(2): 82–91.

Rodriguez, C. and A. T. Church. 2003. 'The Structure and Personality Correlates of Affect in Mexico: Evidence of Cross-Cultural Comparability Using the Spanish Language'. *Journal of Cross-Cultural Psychology* 34(2): 211–30.

Rosaldo, M. Z. 1980. *Knowledge and Passion: Ilongot Notions of Self and Social Life*. New York: Cambridge University Press.

Schuller, K. 2018. *The Biopolitics of Feeling: Race, Sex, and Science in the Nineteenth Century*. Durham: Duke University Press.

Shaw, M. 2007. 'What Is Genocide?' Cambridge: Polity.

Sigler, M. 2000. 'The Story of Justice: Retribution, Mercy, and the Role of Emotions in the Capital Sentencing Process'. *Law and Philosophy* 19(3): 339–67.

Spezzano, Charles. 1993. 'A Relational Model of Inquiry and Truth: The Place of Psychoanalysis in Human Conversation'. *Psychoanalytic Dialogues* 3(2): 177–208.

Spinoza, B. 1951. *A Theologico-Political Treatise and a Political Treatise*. New York: Dover.

Spinoza, B. and E. M. Curley. 2016. *The Collected Works of Spinoza*, Vol. 2. E. M. Curley, trans. Oxford: Oxford University Press.

Spinoza, B. and G. Parkinson. 1989 [1677]. *Ethics*. A. Boyle, trans. London: Dent.

Stauffer, J. 2015. *Ethical Loneliness: The Injustice of Not Being Heard*. New York: Columbia University Press.

Stein, R. E. K. 1991. *Psychoanalytic Theories of Affect*. Westport: Greenwood Publishing Group.

Stoler, A. L. 2010. *Along the Archival Grain: Epistemic Anxieties and Colonial Common Sense*. First edition. Princeton: Princeton University Press.

Tangney, J. P. and K. W. Fischer. 1995. *Self-Conscious Emotions: The Psychology of Shame, Guilt, Embarrassment, and Pride*. New York: Guilford Press.

Terada, R. 2001. *Feeling in Theory: Emotion after the 'Death of the Subject'*. Cambridge: Harvard University Press.

Throop, C. J. 2010. *Suffering and Sentiment: Exploring the Vicissitudes of Experience and Pain in the Yap*. Berkeley: University of California Press.

Tomkins, S. S. 1962. *Affect Imagery Consciousness, Vol. I. The Positive Affects*. New York: Springer Publishing Company.

Tomkins, S. S. 1963. *Affect Imagery Consciousness, Vol. II. The Negative Affects*. New York: Springer Publishing Company.

Tsai, J. L. 2007. 'Ideal Affect: Cultural Causes and Behavioral Consequences'. *Perspectives on Psychological Science* 2(3): 242–59.

Wendt, A. 2004. 'The State as Person in International Theory'. *Review of International Studies*, 30(2): 289–316.

Williams, R. 1977. *Marxism and Literature*. Oxford: Oxford University Press.

Williams, R. and M. Orrom. 1954. *Preface to Film*. London: Film Drama Limited.

Wilson, R. 2017. *Incitement on Trial: Prosecuting International Speech Crimes*. Cambridge: Cambridge University Press.

Worthman, C. M. 1992. 'Cupid and Psyche: Investigative Syncretism in Biological and Psychosocial Anthropology'. In T. Schwartz, G. M. White, and C. A. Lutz, eds. *New Directions in Psychological Anthropology*, 150–78. Cambridge: Cambridge University Press.

Yorke, C. 2018. 'Researching Emotions in International Relations: Methodological Perspectives on the Emotional Turn'. *International Affairs* 94(3): 657–8.

CHAPTER 49

LEGAL PLURALISM IN POSTCOLONIAL, POSTNATIONAL, AND POSTDEMOCRATIC TIMES

EVE DARIAN-SMITH

Introduction

Legal anthropologists first engaged with *legal pluralism* as a concept in the early twentieth century; in recent decades the concept has been influential in fostering new scholarship both in the discipline and in related sociolegal fields that take seriously the social contexts of law and the inherent plurality of law in everyday social life (see e.g. Adams 2016; Kleinhans and Macdonald 1997). Legal pluralism underscores the fact that there are multiple, contradictory, intersecting, and competing normative frameworks. These frameworks are recognized as having some form of legal authority through which people imaginatively organize their social relations and everyday behaviours. These plural legal frameworks—and their operation across a local/global continuum—shake up modernist assumptions of the centrality of the state as the primary legal entity and conceptual container of social, cultural, political, and economic engagements (Berman 2019; Darian-Smith 2013; Helfand 2015; Zumbansen 2011). As Boaventura da Sousa Santos has long argued, 'Our legal life is constituted by an intersection of different legal orders, that is by *interlegality*' (Santos 1987; Santos 2002: 437, emphasis added; see also Darian-Smith 1998; Twining 2000).

The ever-expanding body of literature on legal pluralism has been enormously helpful in identifying co-existing, conflicting, and often competing visions of legal order that reflect—and give rise to—new forms of legal consciousness (Halliday and Morgan 2013; Ewick and Silbey 1998; Sarat and Kearns 1995). Legal pluralism has also helped in the interrogation of law's relationship to territory and the articulation of non-state processes of legal legitimation and delegitimation, in turn underscoring the dynamic boundaries of legal fields across time and space (Blomley et al. 2001). In this chapter I will not reprise these debates and theoretical contributions, which have been extensively discussed elsewhere (Davies 2010; Michaels 2009; Rajagopal 2005; Tamanaha 2008). Nor do I wish to weigh in on the relative value of legal pluralism in thinking about overlapping and competing non-state and quasi-legal institutions and practices (Berman 2014; Tamanaha et al. 2012). As Sally Merry writes, 'From an anthropological perspective, the question is not whether legal pluralism is a good or a bad thing, but what kind of thing is it?' (Merry 2020).

Typically, scholarship on legal pluralism from an anthropological perspective is informed by colonial and postcolonial histories and settings, often presenting analyses of human rights, Indigenous laws and conflicts, and moments of transitional justice, particularly in the global South. This scholarship is rich and insightful and has enduring relevance given the neocolonial realities of our current era (Benda-Beckmann 2002; Comaroff and Comaroff 2006; Hooker 1975; Moore 1973; Nader 2005; Parma 2015). That being said, a postcolonial lens typically posits marginalized communities—however identified—against the state. This analytical framework arguably restricts scholars from fully engaging with emerging legal pluralities and 'interlegalities' that are challenging a modernist legal landscape built upon the territorial bounding and political authority of an international world order organized along the lines of nation-states.

In this essay, in addition to the enduring implications of postcolonialism, I focus on two legal trends or phenomena that have become more pronounced in recent decades. These trends suggest additional analytical frameworks for understanding legal pluralism. While appearing contradictory, I argue that the trends are in fact mutually constitutive. I refer to the first trend as postnationalism and the second as postdemocracy. As with the concept of postcolonialism, the 'post' does not imply an end to an era of colonialism, but rather a transitional phase in which old forms of colonialism are being phased out even if remnants endure, while new modes of colonialism emerge. Likewise, postnationalism and postdemocracy do not imply that state nationalism or democratic aspirations are no longer important, but rather that taken-for-granted assumptions about the centralized authority and functioning of modern states are being challenged and modified under new legal, economic, political, cultural, and social forces. A significant feature to stress is that postnational and postdemocratic trends should be analysed within global contexts, or more specifically across a local/global continuum (Darian-Smith and McCarty 2017).

The first postnational trend refers to the emergence of new legal identities and subjectivities that bring into question conventional notions of citizenship as it pertains to the nation-state. Postnational processes foster new imaginaries of legal allegiance and the emergence of flexible modes of citizenship within and across state lines. For instance, regional independence movements such as those in Scotland in the United Kingdom and Catalonia in Spain are constant reminders of the destabilizing of state politics and conventional notions of unified national identity. While these independence movements may make claims for their own laws and institutions that mimic modern nation-states, these regional movements are qualitatively different in that they see their future with a united Europe and are willing to compromise exclusive sovereignty and give up certain powers to work collectivity with the rest of the European Union (EU). In addition to these regional movements, an estimated 70 million people are on the move fleeing war, famine, persecution, and environmental disasters. These movements of people break individuals' conventional ties with home countries and underscore the value of global governance institutions such as the United Nations, the European Court of Human Rights, and the International Criminal Court, as well as the need for global humanitarian aid, global climate change regulations, and the importance of international non-governmental organizations (INGOs) and non-governmental organizations (NGOs). While all of these elements of global governance are to some degree flawed, and at times reify an anachronist international order based on interstate relations, they nonetheless point to the need for alternative ways of achieving social justice and legal order in dynamic global contexts. Together mass migrations and regional independence movements challenge the role of the modern nation-state to exclusively rule over certain communities and how people think about and access the law.

The second postdemocratic trend appears to work in opposing directions and affirms a modernist world order based on exclusive sovereignty and the territorialization of law. The increasing political power of radical right-wing parties, populist movements, and authoritarian tendencies urge a re-centring of the nation-state, the bolstering of militarized legal systems, and the securing of borders. Accompanying this ultranationalist trend is the alarming rise of laws and policies that are profoundly anti-democratic in nature and often associated with isolationism, nativism, and discrimination against foreigners and non-nationals in political movements worldwide. Moreover, standard pillars of democracy regarding the separation of powers, independent judiciaries, and an uncensored press are steadily being undermined and chipped away as state leaders seek to consolidate their power and usher in a new political landscape (see Crouch 2004).

In this chapter I ask what legal pluralism is in the context of the EU, focusing on shifts in British legal identity and legal culture in light of Brexit and Britain's referendum vote on 23 June 2016 to leave the EU. This exploration takes into account current legal debates and legal formations revolving around postnationalism as well as heightened support for state nationalism as expressed in radical right-wing populist movements that seek to 'Take Back Control'. These challenges to and affirmations of a modernist nation-state paradigm are materializing in multiple forms and sites and legal practices within the United Kingdom and across Europe, and indeed around the world. Interestingly, these sites of contestation over the meaning and authority of national legal systems are concurrently diminishing and revitalizing the authority of state law and its territorialized jurisdictional boundaries.

In the first section, I describe how the concept of legal pluralism as analysed through a postcolonial framing helps to partially understand the Brexit referendum. In interrogating the limits of this analysis, the second section turns to thinking about legal pluralism in the context of postnationalism. Finally, the third section examines the concept of legal pluralism against a backdrop of right-wing politics and rising authoritarianism. At the outset I want to stress that these sections are artificially divided for analytical purposes, as postcolonial, postnational, and postdemocratic legal formations are simultaneously in play and mutually shaping, impacting, and constituting people's legal consciousness and a range of legal frameworks, overlapping normative systems, and competing systems of legal legitimacy.

Legal pluralism and postcolonialism

Thinking about legal pluralism in the EU returns me to my earlier research on the new configuration of domestic and supranational legal jurisdictions in post-Maastricht Europe. I published this work in a book titled *Bridging Divides: The Channel Tunnel and English Legal Identity in the New Europe* (1999). The book examined how the building of the Tunnel between England and France created a site through which people could project their fears and hopes about connecting the British Isle with mainland continental Europe. Specifically, I was interested in how the 'bridging' of borders was shaping people's understanding of law and order, nationalism and legal identity, and a sense that things were rapidly changing under processes of globalization and aspirations of European unity. In the book's foreword I wrote, 'In a world of increasing talk about unity and transnationalism, what the Tunnel helps articulate is that there are also simultaneously emerging expressions of neonationalism and parochial exclusivity' (Darian-Smith 1999: xiii).

What I then called 'neonationalism and parochial exclusivity' erupted decades later in 2016 when, by a slim margin, the British people voted to leave the EU. I, alongside many others in Britain and around the world, was taken aback by the Brexit vote. I never thought that the optimism of a united Europe—which the building of the Tunnel heralded—could have been rolled back in support of the jingoistic, xenophobic politicking of the U.K. Independence Party (UKIP). However, on reflection, the Brexit vote should probably not have come as such a surprise given that twenty-five years ago Eurosceptics were a loud if somewhat fringe element within the Tory party and have been gaining political traction ever since. As discussed in *Bridging Divides*, it was not just party opposition to the Tunnel that grabbed my attention back in the 1990s. Across the general populace, particularly among those living outside London, I was confronted by people's romantic vision of a proud imperial nation that had compromised its island status and legal sovereignty by joining the EU in 1973 amidst a global oil crisis and fears of the country's economic isolation. Since then Britain has chafed under pressures to abide by a transnational EU legal system and change many of its domestic laws to better conform to the policies of the European Parliament residing in Strasbourg. More importantly perhaps, many British people have resented opening the country's borders to France, Germany, and other member nations despite the obvious economic, political, and social advantages in doing so. There has been a slowly mounting sense that integration with the EU is diluting Britain's unique cultural and social fabric.

Reasserting State Sovereignty and Racial Superiority

At the time of the building of the Channel Tunnel in the 1990s, the themes of war, invasion, racial insularity, and the tunnel undermining a 'naturally' existing English 'civilization' reoccurred often in the popular press (Darian-Smith 1999: 85). Unlike other EU member states with more porous territorial borders, the threat of invasion profoundly challenged essentialized (and racialized) images of what it means to be English and more generally British (MacDougall 1982). For instance, many English people I spoke to in the 1990s expressed concern in terms of the EU 'colonizing' their island nation, and the imposition of EU law diluting their historical legacy as the originators of the common law that has existed since 'time immemorial'. That the great British empire was now being 'colonized' by continental Europe infuriated many people.

Linked to a collective English/British nostalgia for lost empire and island sovereignty is a deeply racialized undercurrent of fear (Gilroy 2005). Back in the 1990s, many people expressed their fear of rabies being transmitted by foxes running through the Tunnel under the sea and 'infecting' the pristine island nation (Darian-Smith 1995). I interpreted the widespread obsession with rabies as a metaphor for racialized fears of dark-skinned postcolonial peoples trying to get into Britain illegally.

Over the decades, popular sentiment based on the fear of Britain's open EU borders ushering in 'invading' darker-skinned Others has not diminished. Many analysts argue that the issues of migration and racial discrimination, particularly against people from the Middle East and Muslim countries, was decisive in the Brexit campaign and the ultimate vote to leave the EU. However, data show that in fact 70 per cent of immigrants to the United Kingdom over the past fifteen years came from non-EU countries and could have been stopped if the British government had wanted to at any point. Moreover, the 30 per cent of migrants coming from EU countries under its open border policies have higher employment rates and draw less on public assistance programmes than native Britons (Kirchick 2017: 168). Yet despite these realities, the Brexit campaigners managed to instil in the minds of voters the idea that the presence of migrants, supposedly all living on welfare, was the fault of EU laws. The slogan 'Take Back Control' suggested that people had little choice but to vote in favour of Britain leaving the European Union. The use of fear stoked by racist rhetoric and imagery was clearly evident in the U.K. Independence Party's campaign to leave the EU (Drainville 2016). The effectiveness of this type of campaigning suggests a hardening and deepening of racist attitudes in recent years among some Britons. The more abstract language of rabies that was prevalent in the 1990s has been replaced by explicit references to terrorist Muslims, marking an increasingly violent and targeted language of public bigotry.

As Wendy Brown dramatically reminds us in her book *Walled States, Waning Sovereignty* (Brown, 2010), in many countries the fear of national identity being diluted by cultural and religious diversity is promoting a frenzied rebuilding of state boundaries and implementation of new strategies aimed to deny legal access and related civil and political rights to various marginalized groups within state territories.

In the early decades of the twenty-first century, perhaps more than in any other era, the spectre of 'invading hordes' of undocumented immigrants and 'illegal aliens' from Latin America, Eastern Europe, Africa, and the Middle East looms large in the Euro-American imaginary. As evidenced by the Brexit vote (and Donald Trump's travel bans), the 'homecoming' of the postcolonial subject is not generally seen by those in Western democracies as an occasion for celebration.

Postnationalism and New Legal Identities

Alongside a perceived threat to English/British identity are the emerging challenges presented by postnationalism that bring into question the assumed legal relationship and social contract between citizen and nation-state (Darian-Smith 2015a; Mitra 2013; Ong 1999; Sassen 2005). As mentioned above, the concept of postnationalism does not mean the end of nation-states and nationalism, but rather new forms of translocal and transnational allegiances working in tension with conventional state nationalism. These processes are reflected in scholarship on the politics of identity, which has expanded in scale and reach as it seeks to analyse the complex relations between individuals and the nation-state in the context of globalization (Ong 2006). This expansion speaks to the ways people conceptualize their legal subjectivity and relations to others in emerging sociopolitical contexts that include the mobilization of global social movements, an expanding international human rights regime, and mass migrations of people that deem some people illegal and stateless and that affect millions of refugees fleeing wars, poverty, and various natural and man-made disasters. This expansion in the literature also reflects new sociopolitical contexts of a less obviously global nature present in subnational regions, global cities, sanctuary cities, borderlands, prisons, immigration offices, hospitals, and tribal reservations (Delgado 2018; Perry and Maurer 2003; see also Constable et al. 2019).

These trans-state and sub-state contexts suggest a diverse range of legal relations occurring across a local/global continuum (Darian-Smith 2013; Darian-Smith and McCarty 2017). Hence, whether we think of ourselves as living in a postnational moment or not, it is clear that the idea of a person's legal subjectivity and identity being constituted solely through the geopolitical boundaries of the nation-state is no longer a given. In other words, those living in the global North can no longer pretend that the modernist concepts of 'the individual' and 'the state' are stable categories and share clearly demarcated relations that up until relatively recently have underscored a person's sense of personal and collective belonging vis-à-vis a national polity. How people conceptualize themselves is now widely acknowledged as not reducible to simplified and essentialized individual and group identities recognized in law through state policies and institutions. Autonomous sovereign states, autonomous sovereign individuals living within those states, and the 'imagined communities' that supposedly bind states to peoples through narratives of a monocultural society are increasingly being recognized among ordinary people as romanticized—albeit at times very powerful—modern secular mythologies (Anderson 1983; Chakrabarty 2000; Hobsbawm 1990). As the international lawyer Thomas Franck wrote back in 1996, we are witnessing new 'possibilities of layered and textured loyalties' such that it is conceivable that many people will 'shed the drab single-hued identities deterministically front-loaded onto their lives by the accidents and myths of birth and blood' (Franck 1996: 359).

Decentring and Recentring London

In Britain, perhaps no group of people has experienced the same degree of 'layered and textured loyalties' as the residents of the city of London. Today London is a global tourist destination as well as a major business and financial centre. London accounts for 13.4 per cent of the United Kingdom's population, but it should be noted that London's residents do not reflect the same demographics as the rest of the country. London, like many so-called global cities, is a huge cosmopolitan and urban centre and home to a culturally diverse population (Roy and Ong 2011; Sassen 1991). The dominant political ideology in London leans to the left. Arguably this is why the residents of London voted overwhelmingly against Brexit, calling loudly for Britain to stay in the European Union. The polarized support for Brexit reflected a country-wide divide between those living in big city metropoles and those who feel left behind in more beleaguered towns and villages where unemployment and poverty have been steadily rising over the past twenty years.

Emblematic of London's cosmopolitan outlook is the Lord Mayor of London, Sadiq Khan, who was voted into office in May 2016. Khan's electoral victory was significant on a number of fronts. He received more votes in one election than any other politician in British history. He is also London's first ethnic minority mayor, the son of a working-class British Pakistani family and practising Muslim. As a former lawyer, Khan has been a long-standing supporter of human rights, anti-discrimination measures, and making law accessible to minority and poor clients. Khan's landslide mayoral election represented a significant turnabout in the national discourse targeting Muslims communities and their supposed association with terrorism. Politically, Khan stands for pluralist ethnic and religious diversity, and his inclusive worldview has come under significant attack from right-wing political groups.

London, of course, is still the capital of the United Kingdom. However, its unquestioned dominance as the locus of power is now challenged by new divides and factions within the nationalist framework that pit young against old, coloured migrants against white nationalists, and cities against smaller towns and village communities. Yet even as London's status as the capital city and locus of national power is buffeted by the contemporary negotiations over Brexit and their aftermath, London has for some years sought to rebrand itself as a postnationalist centre of cosmopolitanism, urbanism, and diversity, and as a home to a broad spectrum of religions, languages, and cultures (Bartlett 2007). In short, London sees itself as a central part of the EU and as such embraces legal, cultural, religious, and ethnic pluralism at the very moment approximately half of Britain is screaming Islamophobic propaganda, denouncing an imagined takeover by sharia law, and demanding to 'make Britain Great Again' (Farrar and Krayem 2017; Jackson 2018).

It appears that while London is decentring itself as the capital of a United Kingdom, it is simultaneously recentring itself as a postnational cosmopolitan city deeply committed to the concept of a united EU. This recentring explicitly engages new forms of politics, legal subjectivities, and hybridized legal systems, and requires submitting to a full range of EU laws and regulations on trade, finance, labour, health, migration, and so on. According to one commentator:

> The fast-moving political terrain of places like London speaks volumes about what politics can be; it brings changes not only to London but also to other nodes worldwide. What we are starting to see is a new kind of informal political architecture which has resonances across many differing groups and countries, but has no necessary connection to the way that politics has been traditionally configured. (Bartlett 2007: 237; see also Butler and Athanasiou 2013)

Scotland and Wales

Furthering the decentring of London as the capital city are growing north/south divides within the United Kingdom that have become more marked in recent decades. When I wrote *Bridging Divides* in the 1990s, in contrast to many people living in suburban and rural England, citizens in Wales, Scotland, and Northern Ireland were supportive of the Tunnel project. This was a period in which the Welsh language was being revitalized and hopes for new kinds of separatist democratic reforms were being openly discussed (Chaney et al. 2001). In particular, Scottish support grew under a strengthening Scottish Nationalist Party in the 1980s and expanding ties to, and financial assistance from, the EU under the principle of subsidiarity as implemented through the European Committee of Regions (Darian-Smith 1999).

In more recent years, Scottish nationalism has grown stronger with expanding job opportunities promoted through the EU and access to EU funding and resources. Many Scots have aggressively argued for freeing the region from British control and increasing its integration into the EU. In 2014, a referendum on Scottish independence was held; while it was ultimately unsuccessful and Scotland remained in the United Kingdom, it did result in considerable legal powers being devolved to the Scottish Parliament, including the right to set income taxes, control drilling and offshore gas extraction, and legislative capacities to amend the Scotland Act (1998) (Bulmer 2016; Lazarowicz and McFadden 2018).

These developments are not unconnected to the politics surrounding Brexit and Scotland's overwhelming vote to stay in the EU. Today there appears to be greater affinity between Londoners and Scots on the issue of EU membership than Londoners and surrounding small-town communities populated by older and whiter generations. What these various cultural and legal divides and political allegiances portend is very difficult to predict. Given the current national crisis as the United Kingdom faces its withdrawal from the EU, there is much uncertainty about Scotland's future direction that may involve an intensification of conversations about Scottish independence from Britain and greater interdependence with EU institutions and laws on such things as trade, labour, health, human rights, and so on.

Legal pluralism and postdemocratic governance

Over three decades ago, Margaret Thatcher negotiated the terms of the Channel Tunnel Treaty with French President François Mitterrand. For Thatcher, the Tunnel was emblematic of free-market economics and fit well with her neoliberal policies and ultimately with the enabling of corporate market logics within government. Thatcher insisted that the Tunnel should not be understood as a state project benefiting the collective good, but a capital venture that must be paid for by corporate funding.

At the time of my research in the early 1990s, I was aware of Thatcher's turbulent term as Prime Minister in the preceding decade, which involved breaking up miners' unions, implementing policies of privatization, deregulation, and 'property-owning democracy', as well as her expedient use of the Falklands War in 1982 to staunch her loss of popular support (Thatcher 1990). But I was not fully aware of the cumulative impact of the free-market policies that Thatcher helped put into practice in Britain and across the EU, and which were concurrently implemented in the United States and spread around the world though organizations such as the IMF, the World Bank, and the WTO. These policies are often referred to as neoliberalism (Harvey 2007). Very simply, neoliberal ideology pushes an economic, social, political, and legal agenda in which profit-seeking capitalists seek to act without restrictions or limitations (Stedman Jones 2012). This agenda includes the dismantling of state responsibilities for citizens by defunding social and health services, public education, and infrastructure. At the same time, neoliberal policies typically seek to lower taxes on the wealthy while allowing corporations to utilize state institutions (e.g. the legal system, health system, penal system) to maximize their profit margins.

Over the past four decades, neoliberal logics have created enormous inequality between the global North and global South. But they have also created enormous inequalities within advanced industrial countries. A small economic elite increasingly controls governments, and these elites have effectively eviscerated the middle classes while expanding the poor and working classes exponentially. Millions and millions of people are suffering as they fall below poverty thresholds (Hickel 2018; Stiglitz 2013). The conventional mythologies of capitalism that hard work and education offer solutions for social advancement have become empty slogans as ordinary people—the precariat—struggle to meet basic needs. In short, a free-market neoliberal agenda now holds sway in various forms across the entire EU and around the world, creating gross socioeconomic inequalities that seem insurmountable to impoverished majorities (Sliwinski 2018).

Legal Pluralism under Neoliberalism

Accompanying growing inequality is the increasing experience by ordinary people that different legal systems exist for different constituencies (Mattei and Nader 2008). For business and financial sectors, the law seemingly operates effectively and efficiently, irrespective of whether a company is based in London, New York, Hong Kong, São Paulo, or Beijing. Global law firms, the 'lubricators of global capitalism', are flourishing despite the economic recession, and special courts facilitating international trade and finance, dispute resolution, and arbitration are a booming global industry (Darian-Smith 2015b; Faulconbridge et al. 2008: 455). In contrast, the legal systems available to ordinary people are often too expensive, confusing, or inaccessible. And when cases are taken to court, these institutions are typically understaffed, slow to process cases, and the outcomes produced often appear to support commercial interests (e.g. insurance companies, privatized health providers, pharmaceutical companies, landlords) over the interests of individuals or communities. Burgeoning working classes feel disenfranchised and disempowered, and the law no longer serves many of their needs, particularly the needs of migrant and minority communities.

A prevailing concern across many societies is a declining trust in the institutions of democracy, which include the institution of a fair and just legal system. One consequence is a broadening sense that national legal systems operate within two quite distinct legal spheres and serve two very different constituencies—the 1 per cent corporate elite and the 99 per cent ordinary people, to borrow language from the global Occupy Movement. So despite the rise of so-called democratic governments around the world since the 1990s, the reality is that across Britain, the EU, and elsewhere a growing global democracy-deficit is the outcome of the undermining of the freedom of the press, judicial independence, regulatory agencies, public education, and political transparency (Abramowitz 2018; Diamond 2016). In the name of greater economic freedom, ultranationalists support new forms of discrimination, racism, and legal inequality. Admittedly, these elements have always existed in so-called democracies, particularly during historical periods associated with laissez-faire capitalism in the late nineteenth and early twentieth centuries. Today, however, these new forms of legal inequality are more insidious and harder to see, in part because they are infused with the neoliberal logics of a global political economy.

The Grenfell Tower Fire

In London the Grenfell Tower fire epitomizes the power of corporate logics over government, and the differences in how people experience various legal systems operating within the national jurisdiction. The twenty-four-storey tower was built in 1967 in Northern Kensington, an inner London neighbourhood with the highest gap between rich and poor anywhere in the country.[1] The tower was built as part of a council project to provide housing to mainly working-class residents. For over a decade the Grenfell Action Group had complained about the lack of maintenance and fire safety practices. Fires had broken out in similar housing towers, leading to council inquiries and the establishment of an All-Party Parliamentary Fire Safety and Rescue Group, which strongly recommended that the government take action and address safety recommendations such as sprinklers, fire doors, and secondary stairwells. After years of complaints being ignored, in 2015 the tower underwent major renovations including new aluminium rainscreen cladding.

The Grenfell Tower fire broke out on 14 June 2017. Fire quickly engulfed the building, racing up the sides of the tower following the highly combustible exterior cladding. It burned for sixty hours, involved 250 firefighters, 70 fire trucks, and over 100 ambulance service crews. It caused seventy-two deaths, many injuries, and was the worst residential fire in Britain since the Second World War. While inquiries continue as to the cause of the fire, there is no doubt that government spending cuts, council neglect, and deregulation of fire safety rules all contributed to the problem. The combustible materials used in the Grenfell Tower renovations were considerably cheaper than non-combustible alternatives. Moreover, inspectors visited the renovation site sixteen times and never tested the substandard materials which the manufacturer later acknowledged would not pass the 'limited combustibility requirements'. Sadiq Khan, Mayor of London, said 'years of neglect' by successive government ministers and the local council were answerable for what had been a 'preventable accident' and called for council members to resign.[2]

The government's ignoring of Grenfell Tower resident complaints, the unregulated outsourcing of the tower's maintenance and renovations, the poor response to the fire by an under-funded fire brigade—all these factors underscore a neoliberal approach to governance. This approach includes the devolving of local power and budgetary responsibility to local councils under the guise that local governments are less corrupt than 'big government'. Democracy, including political representation and adequate accountability, is being corroded from within through neoliberal strategies of governmental organization that deliberately abdicate formal state responsibility.

In horrifying ways, the Grenfell Tower fire echoes other disasters linked to neoliberal policies and a global political economy that foster neglect, deregulation, and blatant disregard for human life in the quest to reduce expenditure and maximize profit. These include the Rana Plaza garment factory collapse in Bangladesh in 2013 that killed 1,135 people and the earlier Bhopal gas tragedy in India in 1984, in which more than 3,500 people were killed and another 500,000 exposed to toxic chemicals. Together such incidents reflect what sociolegal scholar Brenna Bhandar calls 'organized state abandonment'. This term refers to the ways in which state and non-state organizations 'manage their activities in such a way so as to render groups of people irrelevant in their calculations', relying 'on a profound devaluation of human lives, the lives of those without socio-cultural and economic capital'. Bhandar goes on to argue that this leaves us with 'a political ethos of neoliberalism premised on the abandonment of *responsibility* as central to the governing ideals of organizational action' (Bhandar 2018, emphasis in original; see also Brown 2015; Sassen 2014).

Rising Right-Wing Populism and Authoritarianism

Against a backdrop of widening socioeconomic inequality and a sense of disenfranchisement and abandonment, explicit forms of discrimination and racism are on the rise. Across Britain and the EU, hate speech and openly racist attacks upon migrants, ethnic minorities, Jews, and LGBTQ communities have escalated in recent years (Kirchick 2017). Specifically, the Syrian migrant crisis has fuelled fears of non-Europeans taking jobs and depleting health, education, and welfare services, and in the process destabilizing governments and political parties.

The reasons for the current uptick in authoritarianism and anti-democratic legal processes have been decades in the making, coinciding with the global embrace of neoliberalism and for-profit logics that justify legal policies and decision-making. Coinciding with the devaluation of social services, education, health care, unionism, and national ownership of public goods in the 1980s, Michel Wieviorka, a French sociologist, writes that there was also 'growth of renewed and different forms of racism, anti-Semitism, terrorism and nationalism or national-populism … . As long as Europe appears to be undemocratic or insufficiently democratic, possibly non- or post-political or post-democratic … it will be vulnerable to the forces of evil' (Wieviorka 2018: 333). It appears that what we are currently experiencing is a new phase of aggressive neoliberalism that is creating socio-economic conditions prone to racialized violence and despair, as well as fostering the appeal of authoritarianism that is fast becoming an acceptable norm in the global South and the global North (Darian-Smith and McCarty 2020).

Concluding Comments

Britain is facing a dangerous mix of inequality, racism, and popular disillusionment in law and the institutions of democracy. These elements, when coupled with what in effect amounts to the capture of government by corporate interests, creates an extremely volatile and potentially dangerous set of conditions. But Britain is not alone. Countries such as the United States, Hungary, Italy, Brazil, Switzerland, France, Turkey, Australia, Poland, Norway, Denmark, Austria, and the Czech Republic are all experiencing such things as the militarizing of national borders, escalating anti-immigrant legislation, violence against minorities, ultranationalist rhetoric, as well as the violation of multilateral agreements and a turn inwards to tariffs and protectionism. Together these are the hallmarks of our current anti-democratic era.

Severe economic inequalities and the dismantling of the middle classes help us understand the rising support in Britain and around the world for populist radical right-wing parties and emerging policies that increasingly lean towards authoritarianism (Rovira Kaltwasser et al. 2017). But economic determinism does not explain the full story (De Cleen 2016). Here it is important to return to the discussion above of the openly racist Brexit campaign to leave the EU. As I mentioned in the Introduction, postcolonial frameworks overlap with postnationalist frameworks which overlap with postdemocratic/neoliberal frameworks. While these spheres of engagement may involve different histories and genealogies and are not equivalent, they resonate with each other in that they share logics of racism, exploitation, dispossession, and exclusion that are occurring on a global scale. These overlapping spheres of interlegality mutually constitute each other in complex pulls and pushes across economic, social, cultural, political, and legal fields as people constantly reimagine their place in the world. And it is here that we find new forms of legal pluralism that include, and also transcend, postcolonialism as a line of inquiry which often assumes a rather static concept of the nation-state and the territorialization of law.

In thinking about legal pluralism in Britain and the EU, there are similarities between the 1990s and the 2010s that can be analysed through the framework of postcolonialism. However, there are other 'constellations of legal pluralism' in play that are becoming clearer with hindsight and a deeper understanding of the global contexts in which legal pluralism must be analysed (Benda-Beckmann and Benda-Beckmann 2006). My earlier analysis of legal pluralism applied a postcolonial framework to try to better understand English people's concerns with the seeming 'colonization' of their country by mainland Europe as symbolized by the Chanel Tunnel project. However, I did not engage adequately with concurrent legal trends associated with the emerging impacts of postnationalism and the disruption this makes to modernist understandings of citizenship, national allegiance, and people's sense of the legitimacy of state-based law. More fundamentally, I did not engage with Thatcher's neoliberal policies and the cumulative impact of the EU's free-market logics that over time have created an elite system of transnational corporate governance and produced widespread inequalities though the steady erosion of welfare services, dismantling of labour rights, and in some cases crippling austerity policies (Stuckler et al. 2018). Perhaps if I had paid more attention to these sets of legal and political conditions, I may have better anticipated people voting for Brexit and the rise of a racialized and hyper-nationalized rhetoric of nativism in Britain and across the EU. Yet these multiple complexities were simply impossible for me to imagine decades ago amidst the democratic euphoria of the fall of the Berlin Wall (1989), ending of the Cold War (1991), signing of the Maastricht Treaty (1992) enabling the free movement of goods, capital, services, and labour across the EU, and the building of the Channel Tunnel to help make such movement a reality.

What does this discussion suggest with respect to thinking about legal pluralism today? For me, the most important message is that we must not be complacent in how we think about what is going on and constantly interrogate our assumptions and categories of analysis, as well as reflect upon our own cultural and ideological perspectives, subjectivities, and proclivities. Legal pluralism is a dynamic concept that needs to be reframed against the complex, messy, and emerging societies, politics, and legalities of any given historical moment. Moreover, as scholars we must be ever vigilant against allocating greater significance to some legal systems than others in a hierarchal geopolitical fashion, for example, assuming that state legal systems are more important than local or regional legal systems. Rather, productive scholarship about legal pluralism is that which recognizes its value in providing an unrestricted conceptual lens through which to talk about and reflect upon competing and intersecting legal processes that are themselves in constant evolution, adaptation, dissolution, and motion. Specifically, it means recognizing that legal pluralism has always been—and should always be—situated within global contexts in which nation-states are important but not exclusive actors. In short, the world and its complex interlegalities are not standing still, and our concept of legal pluralism as it applies to analysing real-world contexts must try to keep up by expanding and adapting to change as well (Benda-Beckmann and Benda-Beckmann 2006).

This discussion also suggests that anthropology as a discipline in the Euro-American academy should commit to working in unfamiliar conceptual and ethnographic terrain that forces scholars to directly analyse their own societies, as well as to think globally even when analysing the most intimate and mundane of social relations and experiences (Darian-Smith and McCarty 2017). Against a backdrop of enduring postcolonial anxieties, I have argued for a more encompassing line of inquiry that also explores the production of postnational legal identities and impacts of neoliberal postdemocratic modes of governance in the EU. I have attempted to draw attention to spheres of overlapping, emerging, collapsing, and competing interlegality that are markedly absent in the anthropological literature on legal pluralism to date. Given what is at stake, I have high hopes for the discipline rising to the challenge.

Notes

1. See 'Grenfell Tower MP highlights huge social divisions in London', available at: <https://www.theguardian.com/inequality/2017/nov/13/grenfell-tower-mp-highlights-huge-social-divisions-in-london> (accessed 18 March 2020).
2. See <https://www.bbc.com/news/uk-40320459> (accessed 17 March 2020).

References

Abramowitz, M. J. 2018. *Freedom in the World* (annual report 2018). <https://freedomhouse.org/report/freedom-world/freedom-world-2018>.

Adams, W. A. 2016. *Popular Culture and Legal Pluralism: Narrative as Law*. New York: Routledge.

Anderson, B. 1983. *Imagined Communities: Reflections on the Origin and Spread of Nationalism*. London: Verso.

Bartlett, A. 2007. 'The City and the Self: The Emergence of New Political Subjects in London'. In Saskia Sassen, ed. *Deciphering the Global: Its Scales, Spaces and Subjects*, 221–42. New York: Routledge.

Benda-Beckmann, F. von and K. von Benda-Beckmann. 2006. 'The Dynamics of Change and Continuity in Plural Legal Orders'. *Dynamics of Plural Legal Orders* (special issue) *Journal of Legal Pluralism and Unofficial Law* 38 (53–4): 1–44.

Benda-Beckmann, F. von. 2002. 'Who's Afraid of Legal Pluralism?' *Journal of Legal Pluralism* 47: 37–82.

Berman, P. S. 2014. *Global Legal Pluralism: A Jurisprudence of Law Beyond Borders*. Cambridge: Cambridge University Press.

Berman, P. S., ed. 2019. *The Oxford Handbook of Global Legal Pluralism*. Oxford: Oxford University Press.

Bhandar, B. 2018. 'Organised State Abandonment: The Meaning of Grenfell'. <https://criticallegalthinking.com/2018/09/21/organised-state-abandonment-the-meaning-of-grenfell/>.

Blomley, N., D. Delaney, and R. Ford, eds. 2001. *The Legal Geographies Reader: Law, Power and Space*. Oxford: Blackwell.

Brown, W. 2010. *Walled States, Waning Sovereignty*. Brooklyn: Zone Books.

Brown, W. 2015. *Undoing the Demos: Neoliberalism's Stealth Revolution*. New York: Zone.

Bulmer, W. E. 2016. *Constituting Scotland: The Scottish National Movement and the Westminster Model*. Edinburgh: Edinburgh University Press.

Butler, J. and A. Athanasiou. 2013. *Dispossession: The Performative in the Political*. London: Polity Press.

Chakrabarty, D. 2000. *Provincializing Europe: Postcolonial Thought and Historical Difference*. Princeton: Princeton University Press.

Chaney, P., T. Hall, and A. Pithouse. 2001. *New Governance—New Democracy? Post-devolution Wales*. Cardiff: University of Wales Press.

Comaroff, J. and Comaroff, J., eds. 2006. *Law and Disorder in the Postcolony*. Chicago: University of Chicago Press.

Constable, M., L. Volpp, and B. Wagner, eds. 2019. *Looking for Law in all the Wrong Places: Justice Beyond and Between* (Berkeley Forum in the Humanities). New York: Fordham University Press.

Crouch, C. 2004. *Post-Democracy*. London: Polity Press.

Darian-Smith, E. 1995. 'Rabies Rides the Fast Train: Transnational Interactions in Post-Colonial Times'. *Law and Critique* 6(1): 75–94.

Darian-Smith, E. 1998. 'Boaventura de Sousa Santos (1995) *Toward a New Common Sense: Law, Science and Politics in the Paradigmatic Transition* (review essay). *Law and Social Inquiry* 23(1): 81–120.

Darian-Smith, E. 1999. *Bridging Divides: The Channel Tunnel and English Legal Identity in the New Europe*. Berkeley: University of California Press.

Darian-Smith, E. 2013. *Laws and Societies in Global Contexts: Contemporary Approaches*. Cambridge: Cambridge University Press.

Darian-Smith, E. 2015a. 'The Constitution of Identity: New Modalities of Nationality, Citizenship, Belonging and Being'. In A. Sarat and P. Ewick, eds. *The Handbook of Law and Society*, 351–66. Malden, MA and Oxford: Wiley Blackwell.

Darian-Smith, E. 2015b. 'Global Law Firms in Real-World Contexts: Practical Limitations and Ethical Implications'. *Beijing Law Review* 6: 92–101.
Darian-Smith, E. and P. C. McCarty (2020 forthcoming). *The Global Crisis of Democracy and the Rule of Law: Neoliberalism and the Rise of Authoritarianism*. London: Routledge.
Darian-Smith, E. and P. C. McCarty. 2017. *The Global Turn: Theories, Research Designs, and Methods for Global Studies*. Berkeley: University of California Press.
Davies, M. 2010. 'Legal Pluralism'. In P. Cane and H. Kritzer, eds. *Oxford Handbook of Empirical Legal Research*, 805–27. Oxford: Oxford University Press.
De Cleen, B. 2016. 'Populism, Nationalism, and Transnationalism'. *Green European Journal*, 17 November 2016.
Delgado, M. 2018. *Sanctuary Cities, Communities, and Organizations: A Nation at a Crossroads*. Oxford: Oxford University Press.
Diamond, L. 2016. 'Democracy after Trump: Can a Populist Stop Democratic Decline?' *Foreign Affairs*, 14 November 2016. <https://www.foreignaffairs.com/articles/world/2016-11-14/democracy-after-trump>.
Drainville, R. 2016. 'The Visual Propaganda of the Brexit Leave Campaign'. *Hyperallergic* 12 July 2016. <https://hyperallergic.com/310631/the-visual-propaganda-of-the-brexit-leave-campaign/>.
Ewick, P. and S. Silbey. 1998. *The Common Place of Law: Stories from Everyday Life*. Chicago: University of Chicago Press.
Farrar, S. and G. Krayem. 2017. *Accommodating Muslims Under Common Law*. New York: Routledge.
Faulconbridge, J. R., Beaverstock, J. V., Muzio, D., and Taymor, P. J. 2008. 'Global Law Firms: Globalization and Organizational Spaces of Cross-Border Legal Work'. *Northwestern Journal of International Law & Business* 28: 455–88.
Franck, T. M. 1996. 'Clan and Superclan: Loyalty, Identity and Community in Law and Practice'. *American Journal of International Law* 90(3): 359–83.
Gilroy, P. 2005. *Postcolonial Melancholia*. New York: Columbia University Press.
Halliday, S. and B. Morgan. 2013. 'I Fought the Law and the Law Won? Legal Consciousness and the Critical Imagination'. *Current Legal Problems* 66(1): 1–32.
Harvey, D. 2007. *A Brief History of Neoliberalism*. Oxford: Oxford University Press.
Helfand, M. A., ed. 2015. *Negotiating State and Non-State Law: The Challenge of Global and Local Legal Pluralism*. Cambridge: Cambridge University Press.
Hickel, J. 2018. *The Divide: Global Inequality from Conquest to Free Markets*. New York: WW Norton & Company.
Hobsbawm, E. 1990. *Nations and Nationalism since 1780: Programme, Myth, Reality*. Cambridge: Cambridge University Press.
Hooker, M. B. 1975. *Legal Pluralism: An Introduction to Colonial and Neo-Colonial Laws*. Oxford: Oxford University Press.
Jackson, L. B. 2018. *Islamophobia in Britain: The Making of a Muslim Enemy*. London, UK: Palgrave Macmillan.
Kirchick, J. 2017. *The End of Europe: Dictators, Demagogies, and the Coming Dark Age*. New Haven: Yale University Press.
Kleinhans, M.-M. and R. Macdonald. 1997. 'What is a Critical Legal Pluralism?' *Canadian Journal of Law and Society* 12(2): 25–46.
Lazarowicz, M. and J. McFadden. 2018. *The Scottish Parliament: Law and Practice*. Fifth edition. Edinburgh: Edinburgh University Press.

MacDougall, H. A. 1982. *Racial Myth in English History: Trojans, Teutons and Anglo-Saxons*. Montreal: Harvest House.

Mattei, U. and L. Nader. 2008. *Plunder: When the Rule of Law is Illegal*. Malden, MA: Blackwell.

Merry, S. E. 2020 (in press). 'An Anthropological Perspective on Legal Pluralism'. In P. S. Berman, ed. *The Oxford Handbook of Global Legal Pluralism*. Oxford: Oxford University Press.

Michaels, R. 2009. 'Global Legal Pluralism'. *Annual Review of Law and Social Sciences* 5: 243–62.

Mitra, S. K., ed. 2013. *Citizenship as Cultural Flow: Structure, Agency, Power*. New York: Springer.

Moore, S. F. 1973. 'Law and Social Change: The Semi-Autonomous Social Field as an Appropriate Subject of Study'. *Law & Society Review* 7(4): 719–46.

Nader, L. 2005. *The Life of the Law: Anthropological Projects*. Berkeley: University of California Press.

Ong, A. 1999. *Flexible Citizenship: The Cultural Logics of Transnationality*. Durham, NC: Duke University Press.

Ong, A. 2006. *Neoliberalism as Exception: Mutations in Citizenship and Sovereignty*. Durham, NC: Duke University Press.

Parma, P. 2015. *Indigeneity and Legal Pluralism in India: Claims, Histories, Meanings*. Cambridge: Cambridge University Press.

Perry, R. W. and B. Maurer, eds. 2003. *Globalization Under Construction: Governmentality, Law, and Identity*. Minneapolis and London: University of Minnesota Press.

Rajagopal, B. 2005. 'The Role of Law in Counter-hegemonic Globalization and Global Legal Pluralism: Lessons from the Narmada Valley Struggle in India'. *Leiden Journal of International Law* 18: 345–87.

Rovira Kaltwasser, C., P. Taggert, P. Ochoa Espejo, and P. Ostiguy, eds. 2017. *The Oxford Handbook of Populism*. Oxford: Oxford University Press.

Roy, A. and A. Ong, eds. 2011. *Worlding Cities: Asian Experiments and the Art of Being Global*. Chichester: Wiley-Blackwell.

Santos, B. de Sousa. 1987. 'Law: A Map of Misreading. Toward a Postmodern Conception of Law'. *Journal of Law and Society* 14(3): 279–302.

Santos, B. de Sousa. 2002. *Toward a New Legal Common Sense: Law, Globalization, and Emancipation*. Second edition. Cambridge: Cambridge University Press.

Sarat, A. and T. R. Kearns, ed. 1995. *Law in Everyday Life*. Ann Arbor, MI: University of Michigan Press.

Sassen, S. 1991. *The Global City: New York, London, Tokyo*. Princeton: Princeton University Press.

Sassen, S. 2005. 'The Repositioning of Citizenship and Alienage: Emergent Subjects and Spaces for Politics'. *Globalizations* 2(1): 79–94.

Sassen, S. 2014. *Expulsions: Brutality and Complexity in the Global Economy*. Cambridge, MA: Harvard University Press.

Sliwinski, K. 2018. 'European Politics and the Neoliberal Paradigm'. *Australian and New Zealand Journal of European Studies* 10(1): 92–110.

Stedman Jones, D. 2012. *Masters of the Universe: Hayek, Friedman, and the Birth of Neoliberal Politics*. Princeton: Princeton University Press.

Stiglitz, J. E. 2013. *The Price of Inequality: How Today's Divided Society Endangers Our Future*. New York: WW Norton & Company.

Stuckler, D., A. Reeves, R. Loopstra, M. Karanikolos, and M. McKee. 2018. 'Austerity and Health: The Impact of Crisis in the UK and the Rest of Europe'. In M. Castells, O. Bouin, J. Caraça, G. Cardoso, J. Thompson, and M. Wieviorka, eds. *Europe's Crises*, 127–47. Cambridge: Polity Press.

Tamanaha, B. Z. 2008. 'Understanding Legal Pluralism: Past to Present, Local to Global'. *Sydney Law Review* 30: 375–411.

Tamanaha, B. Z., C. Sage, and M. Woodcock, eds. 2012. *Legal Pluralism and Development: Scholars and Practitioners in Dialogue*. Cambridge: Cambridge University Press.

Thatcher, M. 1990. Interview for *Sunday Times*, 18 November 1990. Thatcher Archive. Margaret Thatcher Foundation.

Twining, W. 2000. *Globalisation and Legal Theory*. Cambridge: Cambridge University Press.

Wieviorka, M. 2018. 'Europe Facing Evil: Xenophobia, Racism, Anti-Semitism'. In M. Castells et al., eds. *Europe's Crises*. 205–23. Cambridge: Polity Press.

Zumbansen, P. 2011. *Defining the Space of Transnational Law: Legal Theory, Global Governance, and Legal Pluralism*. Comparative Research in Law & Political Economy Research Paper No. 21/2011.

Index

D

F

G

J

N

S

T